# Financial Assets,
# Markets,
# and
# Institutions

# Financial Assets, Markets, and Institutions

**Gary Smith**

*Pomona College*

**D. C. Heath and Company**
Lexington, Massachusetts    Toronto

*Address editorial correspondence to:*

D. C. Heath
125 Spring Street
Lexington, MA 02173

Acquisitions Editor: George Lobell
Developmental Editor: Patricia Wakeley
Production Editor: Carolyn Ingalls
Designer: Alwyn R. Velásquez
Photo Researcher: Jim Roberts
Production Coordinator: Richard Tonachel
Permissions Editor: Margaret Roll

Cover: Paper currency: Comstock Inc./Stuart Cohen
       Coins, stock certificates, and stock trading room: Comstock Inc.

Published simultaneously in Canada.

Printed in the United States of America.

International Standard Book Number: 0-669-29783-6

Library of Congress Catalog Number: 92-81881

10  9  8  7  6  5  4  3  2  1

For Gabe

*Goodness is the only investment that never fails.*
Henry David Thoreau, *Walden*, 1854

# To the Instructor

Financial institutions can be extraordinarily innovative in adapting to government regulations, responding to new opportunities, and offering additional services to their customers. Financial markets are often quite turbulent—sometimes exhilarating, at other times frightening. In this book, I have tried to convey some of this flux and excitement by emphasizing important financial principles and by illustrating these principles with interesting examples, anecdotes, and historical incidents.

Recent years have seen radical changes in financial assets, markets, and institutions. This continuing innovation and evolution make teaching exciting, but also very challenging. This book responds to that challenge by taking a broad view—looking across a spectrum of financial assets, markets, and institutions, emphasizing general ideas more than soon-outdated numbers. Facts are indispensable for understanding the relevance of financial concepts, and this book does have its share of facts. But facts can be overdone, deluging students with numbers and institutional minutiae. Bewildered and tired, students struggle to memorize these details or quickly skim over them. In either case, students are likely to miss the concepts that the facts were intended to illustrate; and, ironically, in dynamic fields, many of the "facts" in textbooks are inevitably obsolete.

An emphasis instead on broad principles that can be applied to the past, present, and most importantly, the future makes teaching and learning more exciting and rewarding. The enthusiasm of professors and students who have read drafts of this book has been extremely gratifying.

# PEDAGOGY

Several tools are used in this book to focus attention on important principles:

1. **Repetition.** The most important concepts reappear throughout the book for reinforcement. Important terms are boldfaced and reappear in a short list at the end of each chapter and also in a full glossary at the end of the book.

2. **Intuitive verbal explanations.** I have tried mightily to explain everything in simple English. Familiar, even homely, examples are used to involve students in financial reasoning. Financial principles need not use arcane mathematics.

3. **Real-world examples.** Anecdotes and quotations from the financial press are used throughout the book to show the everyday application of financial principles. In addition, there are an average of six highlighted examples per chapter that reinforce the real-world relevance of economic concepts.

4. **Interesting exercises.** There are an average of 30 exercises per chapter that allow students to apply the principles they have learned. Rather than using simple recall, most of these exercises ask students to interpret historical incidents, evaluate institutional changes, and criticize provocative quotations from the newspapers that students are likely to be reading.

    Answers to most of the odd-numbered exercises are given at the end of the text. Because many instructors like to use exercises for homework or examinations, answers to the even-numbered exercises are not included in the text.

# OPTIONAL MATERIAL

Incredible diversity is the hallmark of courses dealing with financial assets, markets, and institutions. Students have a variety of backgrounds and interests, and instructors place widely varying emphases on financial theory, institutional details, policy-making, economic history, microeconomics, macroeconomics, accounting, and mathematics. To accommodate these diverse interests, I have included more material in this book than can reasonably be covered in a single course. Most instructors will consequently omit some sections and even entire chapters.

For example, some instructors may emphasize the financial assets and markets in Part I, while others spend more time on the financial institutions in Part II. I anticipate that many instructors will skim or omit some of the following chapters:

Chapter  3   The Foreign Exchange Market
Chapter 10   Risk and Return
Chapter 11   Using Financial Futures and Options as Insurance
Chapter 12   Using Swaps to Manage Exchange-Rate and Interest-Rate Risk

# TEXT SUPPLEMENTS

**Exercises for Financial Assets, Markets, and Institutions.** This student workbook allows students to apply financial principles to hundreds of interesting real-world exercises. Detailed step-by-step solutions are provided to confirm and assist student reasoning. I wrote this workbook in the spirit of the end-of-chapter problems: learning by doing. The only effective way for students to assimilate the material is by solving problems—using the principles and concepts instead of just reading about them.

**Instructor's Guide.** This helpful manual contains teaching suggestions (including dozens of new examples), detailed solutions to all of the text exercises, 300 additional exercises, and 1000 multiple-choice questions.

**Computerized Testing.** The additional exercises and multiple-choice questions in the Instructor's Guide are also available in computerized versions for IBM and Macintosh. The Quisitor testing program enables the instructor to edit and rearrange questions as desired.

**Financial Decision Making.** This computer software contains two separate modules on one disk. The first does a wide variety of financial calculations; the other allows students to practice managing a financial intermediary:

    **I.** Financial Calculations enables students to make present-value and future-value computations and to analyze loans and bonds. For instance, students can determine the duration of a loan, the unpaid balance on a mortgage, and the realized rate of return when a bond's coupons are reinvested.

    **II.** Clearvalley Banking is a simulation game that allows students to manage a small bank in a town with three banks. Students study a variety of monthly economic data and manage their bank for twelve months. The economic data vary with each simulation, as do the management styles of the competing banks. At the end of the simulation, student performance is evaluated, and advice is offered.

# ACKNOWLEDGMENTS

My largest debts, by far, are to William Brainard and James Tobin, who taught me a great deal of economics and much, much more. I have also learned all sorts of things from Tahir Andrabi, Dave Backus, Eleanor Brown, Willem Buiter, Jack Ciccolo, Kristin Fix, Ed Leamer, Ray Fair, Ben Friedman, Steve Goldfeld, Michael Kuehlwein, Peter Mieszkowski, Bill Nordhaus, Doug Purvis, Roy Ruffin, John Shoven, Joe Stiglitz, Steve Taylor, and Ed Yardeni. This book was immensely improved by many conscientious, knowledgeable reviewers:

James C. Baker
*Kent State University*

Carol J. Billingham
*Central Michigan University*

Dwight M. Blood
*Brigham Young University*

Paul J. Bolster
*Northeastern University*

Burkhard Drees
*The George Washington University*

Michael Fabritius
*University of Mary Hardin–Baylor*

Charles M. Gray
*University of St. Thomas*

Beverly Hadaway
*University of Texas at Austin*

Walter L. Johnson
*University of Missouri*

Raman Kumar
*Virginia Polytechnic Institute and State University*

James Marchand
*Westminster College of Salt Lake City*

Mya Maung
*Boston College*

Elliott Middleton, III
*University of St. Thomas*

John Olienyk
*Colorado State University*

Coleen Pantalone
*Northeastern University*

Kelly Price
*Wayne State University*

Richard C. Schiming
*Mankato State University*

Howard Whitney
*Franklin University*

Arthur Wilson
*University of Connecticut*

Mark E. Wohar
*University of Nebraska at Omaha*

David Zalewski
*Providence College*

I am very grateful to my students at Yale University, Rice University, the University of Houston, and Pomona College, who have been patient and careful readers of various drafts and who have taught me how to teach.

G. S.

# To the Student

Financial institutions are a channel by which the savings of some are loaned to others. This channel between borrowers and lenders is a very important service; but to appreciate its importance fully, we must examine why people borrow and lend, what financial assets are available for borrowing and lending, and why financial institutions are needed to bring borrowers and lenders together. It is the answers to these very questions that you will learn in this book.

Your goal is not to memorize 1000 trivial facts about financial assets, markets, and institutions. If you focus your attention on these details, you may miss the main theme, which is the overall role of financial assets and institutions in an economy. Even worse, with the rapid evolution of financial markets, many of these "facts" you may memorize will be obsolete even before the course is over!

In this textbook, I have tried to emphasize general principles that you will find useful after the final exam. I have included some recent numbers, institutional details, historical graphs, and many anecdotes that I think you will find interesting. These should be viewed as opportunities to apply and test general principles. It is these principles, not the examples, that you should learn.

One of the very best ways to master the principles is to apply them to the exercises at the end of each chapter. You can't become a good soccer player just by watching the World Cup, and you can't learn financial principles just by passively reading about them. You have to dribble the ball and apply the principles yourself. You will make mistakes at first, but soon you will acquire the necessary skills and experience. The surest way to strengthen your economic reasoning is to practice on the exercises in this textbook and in the student workbook.

Financial assets, markets, and institutions encompass many important and wonderfully interesting topics. I envy the pleasure that you will experience learning about this fascinating subject. And I hope that you enjoy reading this book as much as I enjoyed writing it.

G. S.

# Brief Contents

xiii

## Part III Government Regulation and Monetary Policy     645

# Contents

# Part I    Financial Assets and Markets    27

## 16.  **Thrifts**        482

## 23. Monetary Policy Instruments        681

### The Fed's Balance Sheet        682

### The Monetary Base, Money Supply, and Intermediation        689

### Open-Market Operations        690

### Reserve Requirements        695

### The Discount Window        703

# 1

# The Role of Financial Assets, Markets, and Institutions in the Economy

*The master-economist must possess a rare combination of gifts. He must be a mathematician, historian, statesman, philosopher — in some degree. He must understand symbols and speak in words. He must contemplate the particular in terms of the general, and touch abstract and concrete in the same flight of thought.*

*He must study the present in light of the past for the purposes of the future. No part of man's nature or his institutions must lie entirely outside his regard. He must be purposeful and disinterested in a simultaneous mood; as aloof and incorruptible as an artist, yet sometimes as near the earth as a politician.*

**John Maynard Keynes**

A few years from now you may graduate from college and enter the job market, looking forward to a rewarding and satisfying career. Will jobs be plentiful, as in 1967, when the unemployment rate was 3.5 percent and firms had bidding wars, offering new graduates ever more attractive salaries and signing bonuses? Or will it be more like 1982, when the unemployment rate averaged 9.7 percent, and many college graduates ended up flipping burgers while they waited for the job market to improve?

After a few more years, you may want to buy a house. You will save some money from your job, and your relatives may contribute a bit more to help you make a downpayment. You find a wonderful house, make an offer that is accepted, and go to a bank to apply for a loan. Will mortgage rates be a livable 9 percent, as in 1991, or a crushing 15 percent, as in 1982?

We study financial assets, markets, and institutions to learn how financial events affect the overall economy and how they affect us personally, too. Every section of every chapter of this book is intended to help you understand financial

1

events — the reasons behind their occurrence and the economic consequences. If you keep asking *How?* and *Why?* financial events occur the way they do, this book will help answer your questions.

The economic climate is constantly changing, and financial markets and institutions are often central to these changes. Low interest rates and a strong economy make it easier for businesses to expand and hire more college graduates. High interest rates and a weak economy can wreck the job market and the housing market. This text focuses on why and how financial markets and institutions affect the economy and, in turn, are affected by the economy.

Economists, investors, and policymakers have long been interested in the effects of financial events on economic activity, and with good reason. Accessible, reliable financial markets are crucial to a nation's economic development. Financial booms and busts can cause economic expansion and recession. Data on the money supply and financial activity provide clues to the future direction of output, inflation, interest rates, and the stock market. Financial events will affect your job opportunities, the availability of the credit that you need to buy a car or a house, and the purchasing power of your life savings. This is why financial markets and institutions are so often in newspaper headlines:

> "Fed Boss Banking on Housing Slump to Nail Down Inflation" (*Chicago Tribune*, April 20, 1980)
>
> "While Congress Fiddles, More Thrifts Burn" (*The Economist*, February 27, 1982)
>
> "Closing of Ohio S&Ls After Run on Deposits" (*The Wall Street Journal*, March 18, 1985)
>
> "Monetary Policy Caused the Crash" (*The Wall Street Journal*, October 22, 1987)
>
> "Mortgage Market Goes From Feverish to Sick" (*The Wall Street Journal*, March 18, 1989)
>
> "Life Insurers' Real Estate Loans Cause Ever-Rising Worries" (*The Wall Street Journal*, January 31, 1992)

Financial markets and institutions play crucial roles in our economic life — roles that are ever evolving because of the competitiveness of financial markets and the innovativeness of financial institutions. To help explain the strategy this book uses to describe the evolving roles of financial markets and institutions, this book's chapter titles are shown in Figure 1.1.

This first chapter provides an overview of the book and introduces two important principles. The first is that financial assets and liabilities facilitate productive saving and investment; the second is that financial markets and institutions bring savers and investors together.

In the eleven chapters comprising Part I we will look more closely at money, bonds, stocks, and other financial assets, and at the markets in which these are traded. We begin with money because one of the keys to understanding financial markets and events is an understanding of why modern societies use paper money instead of barter or commodity money. Chapter 3 explains some of the consequences of the fact that the world does not use a single universal currency.

## Figure 1.1  Chapter Titles Reveal Our Strategy

1. The Role of Financial Assets, Markets, and Institutions in the Economy

**Part I   FINANCIAL ASSETS AND MARKETS**

2. Money
3. The Foreign Exchange Market
4. Interest Rates and Present Value
5. The Term Structure of Interest Rates
6. The Money Market
7. The Bond Market
8. The Mortgage Market
9. The Stock Market
10. Risk and Return
11. Using Financial Futures and Options as Insurance
12. Using Swaps to Manage Exchange-Rate and Interest-Rate Risk

**Part II   FINANCIAL INSTITUTIONS**

13. Deposit Intermediation and the Money Supply
14. The Benefits and Historical Pitfalls of Banking
15. The Modern Practice of Banking
16. Thrifts
17. Finance Companies
18. Insurance Companies
19. Pension Funds
20. Investment Banks and Security Brokers
21. Investment Companies

**Part III   GOVERNMENT REGULATION AND MONETARY POLICY**

22. Government Regulation of Banks
23. Monetary Policy Instruments
24. Monetary Rules and Discretionary Policies
25. Targeting Monetary Aggregates
26. The Effects of U.S. Monetary Policy on Financial Markets Since World War II

Chapter 4 introduces interest rates and the time value of money. Chapter 5 explains why short- and long-term securities have different interest rates and discusses the consequences of unforeseen changes in interest rates — a risk that has important implications for the behavior of financial institutions. Chapters 6 through 9 then apply some of the principles in the preceding chapters to specific financial markets — including Treasury bills, municipal bonds, mortgages, and corporate stock. Chapter 10 discusses how rational investors should behave in a risky world and some implications of the fact that most investors are risk averse. Chapters 11 and 12 conclude Part I by showing how some special financial instruments can be used to reduce risk.

In Part II we use many of the ideas introduced in Part I to explain the behavior of specific financial institutions — the kinds of assets and liabilities they choose and how they cope with various risks. The first three chapters are devoted to banks, which are the largest and, in some ways, the most important financial intermediaries. Chapters 16 through 21 then consider how six different kinds of financial institutions operate and how their behavior affects their customers and the economy.

Part III describes how government regulation and monetary policies affect the nation's financial markets and institutions. Many of the distinctions among financial institutions are due to laws that restrict and constrain their behavior; for example, insurance companies do not offer checking accounts because the federal government does not allow them to do so. In addition, government monetary policies can have enormous effects on interest rates, asset prices, and the solvency of financial institutions. As individual investors or as managers of financial institutions, we need to know how monetary policies work and anticipate how they will be employed. Chapters 23 through 26 are intended to aid this understanding.

In the remainder of this chapter we will introduce some of the assets traded in financial markets — including stocks and bonds — and some of the savers and borrowers who use financial markets — including households, businesses, banks, and the government. We will discuss, in very general terms, why people save and borrow and why they use financial assets and financial institutions to do so. This overview is intended to lay the groundwork for the detailed discussion provided by later chapters.

## SAVERS AND BORROWERS

To the casual observer, financial institutions may seem little more than imposing buildings where well-dressed people shuffle papers. After all, banks don't really produce anything tangible like wheat, steel, or tennis shoes, do they? With this attitude, financial institutions can be dismissed as little more than harmless curiosities.

This attitude is grievously incorrect. Financial assets and institutions are central to modern economies. They give households and businesses opportunities to protect themselves from a variety of economic risks. They allow workers to be capitalists, sharing in the profits of industrial giants. They transform the meager savings of cautious families into large investments by bold entrepreneurs. Although you can't touch any of these things, they are just as real and important as wheat, steel, and tennis shoes.

Financial markets and institutions play very important roles in our economy, but it is difficult to understand these roles unless we think about the people who buy and sell stocks, bonds, and other financial assets. To appreciate fully the services that financial institutions provide to their customers, both lenders and borrowers, we need to look at why people lend and borrow and how they do so — we will begin doing this in this chapter.

### *Jam Today Versus Jam Tomorrow*

In 1991, U.S. households had $22 trillion in assets and $4 trillion in liabilities. Net worth (the difference between assets and liabilities) was nearly $70,000 per capita, or $280,000 for a family of four. Figure 1.2 shows aggregate household assets, liabilities, and net worth relative to gross national product (GNP) since

**Figure 1.2** **U.S. Household Assets, Liabilities, and Net Worth Relative to GNP**

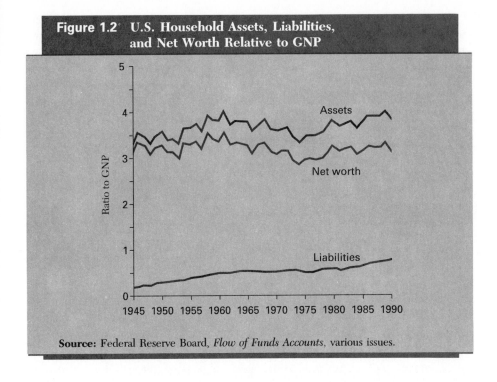

**Source:** Federal Reserve Board, *Flow of Funds Accounts,* various issues.

1945. Over this 45-year period, aggregate household assets and liabilities both increased gradually relative to GNP, while net worth stayed in a relatively narrow range of 3.0 to 3.5 times GNP. Thus household net worth has grown with the economy and, generally, at about the same rate as the economy.

There may be some misers who accumulate wealth for the simple pleasures of counting and admiring it. For most of us, however, wealth is a means to an end rather than the end itself. When we save, we give up some current consumption — food, clothing, and entertainment — in order to enjoy more future consumption. You may save to purchase a car, buy a house, take a trip, pay for your children's education, support your retirement, or provide your heirs with the pleasures that you denied yourself. In each case, you are saving — forgoing current consumption — in order to provide for future consumption. You are trading jam today for jam tomorrow.

If our lifetime income were perfectly synchronized with our spending, there would be little need for saving. Because our spending does not coincide with our income, we save for future expenditures or borrow against future income. For instance, most people hope to live many years after they stop working and try to save during their working years in order to maintain their accustomed standard of living during retirement. We save for vacations, to buy houses, and to provide for our children's educations. We also save a little to bequeath to our children and save some more to protect ourselves against future uncertainties.

EXAMPLE 1.1 *GNP Versus GDP*

Until December 1991, the U.S. government used the gross national product (GNP) to monitor the ebb and flow of economic activity in the United States. GNP is a measure of the market value of the aggregate production of new goods and services — houses, automobiles, haircuts, and financial advice — during a specified period of time, usually three months or a year. GNP excludes the purchase of items that were produced in earlier periods, such as a used car, old house, or work of art, because GNP is intended to measure current productive activity in order to gauge the extent to which workers and businesses are utilized or idle.

GNP data exclude almost all activities that do not involve a financial transaction, since otherwise it is difficult to estimate the size and value of such activities. Thus, do-it-yourself projects and volunteer work are not included in GNP, nor are prostitution, illegal drugs, and other covert activities. A plumber or waitress may hide perfectly legal activities from tax authorities and GNP statisticians. This unreported underground economy makes the gross national product an incomplete tabulation of national output. Nonetheless, GNP is still useful for measuring when an economy is expanding and when it is contracting.

The presence of foreign workers and firms in a country creates another ambiguity. Does the U.S. government want to measure the production of U.S. citizens and firms, no matter where they are employed, or do they want to measure production within U.S. borders, regardless of citizenship? These alternatives lead to two different measures of economic activity. U.S. GNP measures the output of U.S. workers and U.S. owned firms, regardless of their location. U.S. gross domestic product (GDP) measures output within the United States, regardless of the citizenship of the workers and the ownership of the firms. The value of goods produced in Germany by U.S. citizens and U.S. firms is included in U.S. GNP, but it is excluded from U.S. GDP. Goods produced in the United States by Mexican citizens and Japanese machines are included in U.S. GDP but not in U.S. GNP.

In practice, for most countries, including the United States, the difference between GNP and GDP is relatively small because the value of goods produced by U.S. citizens and firms abroad is a small fraction of GNP and is largely offset by the value of goods produced in the United States by foreign citizens and firms. In 1990, for example, U.S. GNP was $5,465.1 billion. The subtraction of $137.4 billion produced by U.S. citizens and firms abroad and the addition of $95.7 billion produced in the United States by foreign citizens and firms gives a GDP of $5,423.4 billion, a difference of 0.8%.

The difference between GNP and GDP is more important in Egypt, Turkey, and other nations where a large number of citizens work in other countries. When there is a substantial difference between GNP and GDP, which should be emphasized by government policy makers? If the government wants to measure the income of its citizens and businesses, GNP is appropriate; if the government is more interested in production within its borders, GDP is preferable. Almost all countries focus on GDP in order to monitor domestic economic activity. After 50 years of using GNP to measure output, the U.S. government joined the rest of the world by switching to GDP in December 1991.

## Financial and Real Assets

**Real assets** are tangible physical assets such as houses, automobiles, and televisions; **financial assets** are paper claims including bank deposits, bonds, and stocks. Figure 1.3 shows the division of total U.S. household assets between real assets and financial assets since 1945. There was a noticeable shift from financial to real assets in the immediate aftermath of World War II; since 1950, real assets have comprised between 30 and 40 percent of total household assets, and financial assets have comprised between 60 and 70 percent.

Most financial assets are the financial liabilities of others. Suppose that Joshua has $4000 and Joanna needs a car to get to her job each day. If Joshua loans Joanna $4000 to buy a used car, he receives an IOU from Joanna, promising to repay the loan plus interest. This IOU is an asset for Joshua, but it is a liability for Joanna, in that part of her paycheck will go to Joshua, allowing him to buy food with her wages.

This financial arrangement appeals to both: it allows Joshua to invest without stockpiling cars and other real assets, and it allows Joanna to buy a car so that she

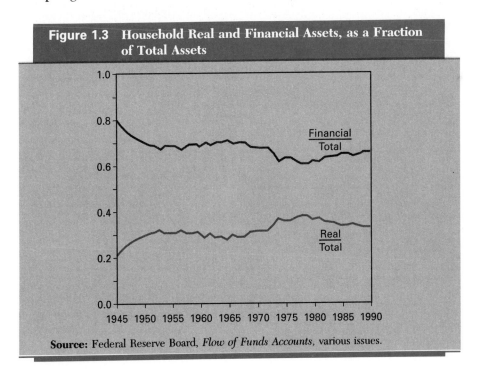

**Figure 1.3    Household Real and Financial Assets, as a Fraction of Total Assets**

**Source:** Federal Reserve Board, *Flow of Funds Accounts,* various issues.

can get to work. If we consolidate their accounts, Joshua's financial asset and Joanna's liability cancel, and their aggregate net worth is the car. Example 1.2 shows how, in the very same way, a nation's aggregate wealth is its tangible assets. The crucial role of financial assets — here Joanna's IOU — is to allow people to borrow money to buy cars, houses, land, and other real assets, and to let other people invest in financial rather than real assets.

Instead of buying a farm, we can deposit money in a bank, which loans money to a farmer who buys land and equipment. The farmer hopes to produce a profitable crop, repay the bank loan plus interest, and keep some reward for hard work. The bank, in turn, uses the money it receives from the farmer to repay our deposit plus interest, and it keeps a little to pay its bills and earn a profit. Implicitly, we and the bank have invested in the farm, in that we have a claim to part of the profits that it will make.

**EXAMPLE** 1.2   *U.S. Net Worth*

In estimating a nation's net worth, we have to take into account the fact that most financial assets are someone else's financial liability. For example, a corporate bond is an asset for the investor who owns it but a liability for the firm that issued it. A home mortgage is an asset for a bank and a liability for a homeowner. In calculating the nation's aggregate net worth, such offsetting financial assets and liabilities cancel each other out.

For the nation as a whole, the net worth that remains after financial assets and liabilities are canceled consists of real assets: houses, automobiles, office buildings, and computers. The table below shows the federal government's estimate of U.S. net worth on December 31, 1990. The $3.7 trillion figure for privately owned land is an estimate of the current market value of this land. (Government-owned land is not included in these data.) The other items in the table are valued at replacement cost — the government's estimates of what it would cost to build these houses, offices, and televisions today.

The largest single category is residential structures — the houses that we live in. Together, residential structures and consumer durables (including furniture, motor vehicles, televisions, and books) are 10 percent larger than aggregate business structures, equipment, and inventories, which are, in turn, 20 percent larger than aggregate government structures and equipment. The final two entries add in foreign assets that are owned by U.S. residents and net out U.S. assets owned by foreigners. The bottom line, $20.5 trillion, averages out to $82,000 per U.S. citizen.

These data do not take into account the nation's most important asset — the citizens themselves. With brawn and brains, or what economists call *human capital*, people grow food, build roads, and heal the sick. Both kinds of capital are important, since people could produce little without machines and machines could do little without people. The value of human capital cannot be measured by market prices, since people — unlike land, buildings, and machines — are not bought and sold. However, we can get a very rough idea of the relative importance of human capital by observing that roughly three-fourths of U.S. aggregate income are paid to labor and one-fourth is paid to the owners of machines and other nonhuman capital. If we infer that human capital is three times the $20.5 trillion in nonhuman capital recorded in the table, then the value of human capital in 1990 was $61.5 trillion — nearly $250,000 per person. If this seems like a lot, you may be underestimating the value of your human capital. In a later chapter you will learn how to estimate your own human capital in another way and probably come up with a comparable figure.

| U.S. Domestic Net Worth (Trillions of Dollars), December 31, 1990 | |
| --- | --- |
| Privately owned land | $3.7 |
| Residential structures | 4.6 |
| Consumer durables | 2.0 |
| Business structures | 2.5 |
| Business equipment | 2.4 |
| Business inventories | 1.1 |
| Federal government structures and equipment | 1.6 |
| State and local government structures and equipment | 3.3 |
| Foreign assets owned by U.S. residents | 0.9 |
| U.S. assets owned by foreigners | −1.6 |
| U.S. net worth | $20.5 |

**Source:** Federal Reserve, "Balance Sheets for the U.S. Economy, 1945–1990," September 1991.

Figure 1.4 is a simplified sketch showing three different routes by which the savings of investors are channeled into the acquisition of tangible assets. Savers can buy houses and other real assets directly; they can buy stocks and bonds issued by others who acquire real assets; or they can deposit funds in banks and

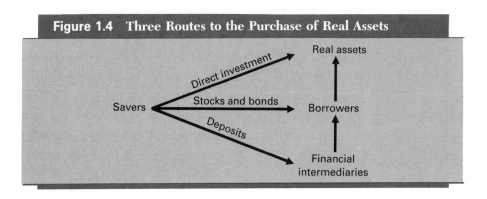

**Figure 1.4  Three Routes to the Purchase of Real Assets**

other **financial intermediaries**, which borrow from savers and lend to those acquiring tangible assets. This sketch is actually oversimplified because people, businesses, and governments are both borrowers and savers. A household that borrows money from a bank to buy a house also may buy corporate bonds, lending money to businesses. A business that borrows money by issuing corporate bonds also may lend money to the federal government by buying Treasury bonds. The federal government issues bonds and also buys household mortgage notes. Nonetheless, Figure 1.4 is useful because it helps us remember that what ultimately lies behind financial claims — the assets of some and the liabilities of others — are real, tangible assets and that the reason financial claims exist is to allow investors to own tangible assets indirectly.

## Rates of Return

The return from an investment consists of **income**, the benefits you receive while owning the asset, and **capital gains**, the profits made when the asset is sold. Income includes the cash flow from the investment — the interest from bonds, dividends from stock, and rent from apartment buildings — and any services provided by the asset — shelter from a house, transportation from an automobile, and entertainment from a television. Rental data can sometimes be used to estimate the value of such services; for example, the value of the services provided by a home can be estimated by the cost of renting a similar home.

## Household Borrowing

Financial markets affect our investment in physical assets in two ways. First, those looking for attractive investments compare the anticipated returns on financial and real assets: when bank deposits, bonds, and other financial assets offer high interest rates, many choose to invest in financial rather than real assets. Second, those considering borrowing money to buy real assets may be dissuaded by high loan rates. Monthly house payments are much higher when mortgage rates are above 15 percent, as they were in 1981 and 1982, than when mortgage rates are below 10 percent, as they were in 1978 and 1991.

The interest rates on bonds and loans generally move together. When bond yields are high, thereby luring savers away from real assets, loan rates are also high, further discouraging physical investment. However, consumer loan rates are often sticky and the loans are rationed; in these cases, the observed increase in loan rates understates the difficulty in obtaining credit. In 1981, although many savings and loan associations listed their mortgage rates at 16 to 18 percent, they wouldn't even accept loan applications. Those that did routinely rejected virtually every loan request. They had no money to lend and didn't lend any.

Banks and other financial institutions make most of the loans that enable households to purchase houses, cars, and other physical assets. People expect their incomes to rise throughout their working years, and early in their careers they want to borrow in order to buy a house or a car and to enjoy a standard of living that is consistent with their anticipated lifetime income, intending to repay these debts with the higher income that they will earn when they are middle-aged. It is difficult, however, for people with few tangible assets to borrow substantial amounts of money because of the risk that they will declare bankruptcy and default on these loans.

Usually, individuals can borrow large amounts only if they have tangible assets, such as real estate, jewelry, and consumer durables, that they can use as collateral. To borrow money, you must first prove that you don't need it! Individuals are said to be **liquidity-constrained** if they would like to spend more but cannot because their future labor income is illiquid in that it cannot be easily converted into spendable cash.

Liquidity constraints provide another channel by which financial markets affect consumer spending. When money is "easy," not only are interest rates low, but also it is easier for weaker credit risks to obtain loans. When money is "tight," interest rates increase, and people who are liquidity-constrained, with only their future income as collateral, are unable to borrow and are forced to curtail spending.

## The Financing of Business Investment

The economic output of a nation is critically dependent on its capital stock — its buildings, machines, tools, trucks, roads, telephone wires, and so on. A nation's physical capital allows citizens to be more productive and to enjoy more leisure. If there is inadequate capital, people will work harder and produce less.

Governments bankroll some investment projects, such as the construction of highways and airports. In a mostly capitalist nation like the United States, though, investment decisions are made primarily by private firms. Individual entrepreneurs start businesses, small businesses expand, and giant corporations erect billion-dollar plants. Financial market events influence all these decisions.

There are more than 15 million businesses in the United States, of which some 3 million are corporations. A corporation is a legal entity that can borrow money from a bank, as you or I would borrow money to buy a car or a house; or a corporation can issue bonds, as the U.S. Treasury does. Most corporations are more creditworthy than you or I, but none is as secure as the U.S. Treasury.

A corporation is said to be publicly owned when it issues shares that can be purchased by any member of the public. The shareholders are the legal owners of the corporation, and they elect a board of directors that supervises the company's operations. Some privately owned companies are very large (for example, Levi Strauss, Mars, and United Parcel Service), but most are small "mom and pop" businesses.

Because the shareholders own the corporation as a group — that is, in common — their shares are called **common stock**. (Some firms also issue preferred stock, which pays fixed dividends and has no voting privileges.) Common stock is very different from loans, bonds, and other **fixed-income securities**

**EXAMPLE** 1.3  *Freddie Laker Bets His Airline on Exchange Rates*

In the 5 years between 1977 and 1982, Freddie Laker transformed Laker Airways from a small charter operation into the world's fifth largest transatlantic airline and became a folk hero for his brash, innovative management. His no-frills Skytrain flights (dubbed "cheap and cheerful") charged passengers extra for food and encouraged them to bring their own sandwiches in brown paper bags.

In 1978, Laker decided to offer flights among 35 European cities and ordered 10 additional airplanes. When 3 of these planes were delivered in 1981, Laker Airways borrowed $131 million from 13 European banks to pay for them. Unfortunately, this loan and the associated interest was denominated in U.S. dollars, and most of Laker Airways' revenue was in British pounds, creating a currency mismatch between its expenses and income. In 1981 the U.S. dollar appreciated 15 percent against the pound, substantially increasing Laker Airways' debt and expenses without a corresponding increase in its assets and income. In January of 1982, Laker Airways was forced into bankruptcy.

In later chapters we will see how Laker Airways might have used foreign-exchange futures, currency swaps, and other financial instruments to protect itself from exchange rate fluctuations.

that specify the amount of money to be paid to the noteholder. A person who buys common stock acquires partial ownership of the company and is said to own **equity**, a claim on the company's profits after interest and other fixed expenses have been paid and, in the event of liquidation, a claim on the company's assets after its debts have been settled.

Imagine that you own a small business that has assets worth $100,000 but owes $20,000 to a bank. Your claim is equity, and its value is equal to the value of the business in excess of its debts, here $80,000. In the same way, if this business were a corporation, the shareholders would be the legal owners of the business, and their stock would be equity, not debt.

Just as a small business owner spends some of the profits and uses the remainder to expand, so a corporation disburses some of its profits to shareholders as dividends and reinvests the remainder. The size of dividend is determined by the corporation's directors, who are elected by the shareholders and who decide how to split the company's profits between dividends and reinvestment.

As with households, there are two ways in which financial markets affect business investment in real assets. Firms choose between investing in real and financial assets, and this choice is influenced by the interest rates available on financial assets. In addition, about half of all business investment is financed by borrowing, and this too is influenced by the cost and availability of credit.

Corporations can sell additional shares of stock to raise cash, but few do, because the dividends they pay shareholders are not a tax-deductible expense and the interest that they pay banks and bondholders is. In most years, corporate stock repurchases actually exceed sales. During the 7 years 1984–1990, U.S. corporations sold $340 billion in new stock and repurchased $980 billion, a net retirement of $640 billion.

In 1990, for example, U.S. nonfinancial corporations spent $380 billion on plant and equipment, of which $330 billion was replacement and repair of existing capital and $50 billion was new investment. These expenditures were not financed by selling stock. On balance, in 1990 businesses repurchased $60 billion more stock than they sold. Their total spending, $380 billion on capital plus $60 billion to retire stock, was financed by $350 billion in retained profits and $90 billion in bond sales, bank loans, and other debts.

Bonds are an important source of funds for large, well-known businesses. Small and medium-sized firms find it difficult and expensive to issue bonds. Denied access to the bond market, many such firms rely on local banks and other financial institutions for loans. Large corporations also borrow from banks, but because they have direct access to financial markets, they demand and get very favorable loan rates. Small and medium-sized firms, without this bargaining power, depend on banks.

Like households, some firms perceive themselves as liquidity-constrained. Their managers are enthusiastic about the firm's future or are willing to take substantial gambles. They want to borrow heavily, expand greatly, and repay their loans out of future profits. Because lenders are wary of enthusiastic profit projections, the amount they are willing to lend may fall far short of the firm's hopes. Young, unproven companies with high hopes and few assets are the most likely to be liquidity-constrained. During credit crunches, funds simply dry up for smaller, less established firms, forcing many to abandon investment projects and even curtail current operations.

## EXAMPLE 1.4 *Leveraged Buyouts*

A takeover wave hit the United States in the 1980s as a dizzying succession of companies was acquired by corporate raiders. Sometimes the takeovers were approved by the target company's board of directors. Often the offer was unfriendly, with the raider buying enough stock from shareholders to elect its own slate of directors and replace existing management.

Takeovers are motivated by a belief that the potential value of a company is substantially larger than its current market value. One reason might be that the current management is incompetent. Another reason, illustrated in the table on the next page, is that a company that has more debt and less equity may be able to use the tax-deductible interest on its debt as a tax shield to protect profits from taxation.

**Annual Corporate Cash Flow with and Without Debt (in Millions)**

|  | (a) Financed by $1 billion in stock, no debt | (b) Financed by $500 million stock, $500 million debt |
|---|---|---|
| Gross income | $100 | $100 |
| Interest | 0 | 50 |
| Taxable income | 100 | 50 |
| Taxes (34% rate) | 34 | 17 |
| Dividends | 66 | 33 |
| After-tax cash flow (interest plus dividends) | 66 | 83 |

The company in the table can be financed by (a) selling $1 billion in stock or (b) selling $500 million in stock and $500 million in bonds to the very same investors. A person who would have bought $10,000 in stock in case (a) buys $5000 in stock and $5000 in bonds in case (b). Either way, the firm's annual before-tax income is $100 million. The after-tax cash flow is very different, though. In case (a), all the firm's annual payments to investors are dividends and cannot be deducted from its taxable income. In case (b), some of the payments to investors are tax-deductible interest. In the example, $17 million additional annual cash flow is created by avoiding $17 million in taxes yearly.

The tax advantage of debt is a primary motivation for the leveraged buyout (LBO) where, using the target firm's assets as collateral, the takeover group uses borrowed money to purchase the target firm's stock. Once the takeover group has control of the firm, there is less equity, more debt, and a larger tax shield. Recognizing that this debt–equity restructuring is the ultimate objective of many takeovers, some target firms have borrowed heavily for self-protection, using the proceeds to repurchase their own stock. Once such firms have created a sufficient tax shield, there is little to be gained from a takeover.

Between 1984 and 1990, U.S. nonfinancial corporations issued $580 billion in corporate bonds and repurchased $640 billion in stock, thereby effectively swapping about $600 billion of debt for equity. The danger is that, because of either a recession or overly optimistic profit projections, heavily indebted companies won't make enough money to pay the interest on their massive debts. A wave of corporate bankruptcies could cause a financial crisis in the United States. One legal remedy is to treat dividends and interest similarly, either allowing firms to deduct both, or neither, from their taxable income.

## Government Spending and Borrowing

The president and Congress determine federal expenditures and tax rates. When the government's outlays exceed its revenue, its budget is in deficit, and the U.S.

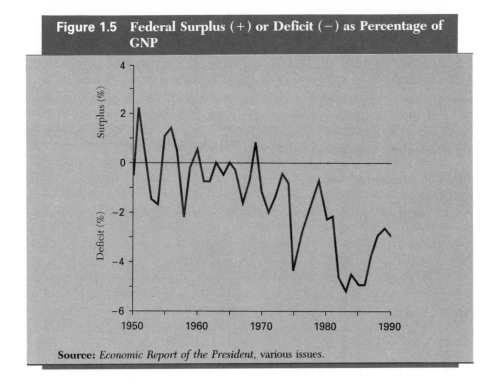

**Figure 1.5    Federal Surplus (+) or Deficit (−) as Percentage of GNP**

Source: *Economic Report of the President*, various issues.

Treasury must sell securities to raise the money needed to pay the government's bills. The Treasury also sells securities regularly to replace old bonds that are maturing. If the government's budget is balanced, so that tax revenue covers government expenses (including interest on maturing debt), then the new securities sold will just offset the old ones maturing, and the government debt, the total amount of Treasury securities outstanding, will be constant. If the government's budget is in deficit, the amount of new securities sold exceeds the amount maturing, and the government debt increases. When there is a budget surplus, the outstanding debt declines.

The distinction between the government's current budget deficit and the level of its outstanding debt is an example of the difference between a **flow**, measuring the volume of transactions during a specified period of time, and a **stock**, which measures the level at a specific time. On December 31, 1990, the outstanding federal debt (a stock), was $2537 billion. The federal deficit (a flow) during 1991 was $275 billion, which increased the federal debt to $2537 + $275 = $2812 billion on December 31, 1991. Similarly, the amount of income you earn during the year is a flow; the amount of money you currently have in your checking account is a stock.

The federal government is the nation's biggest borrower. Figure 1.5 shows the annual federal budget deficits as a percentage of gross national product since 1950. The deficit generally increases during wartime, as military spending expands dramatically, and during economic recessions, when tax revenue declines. The years from 1985 onward were unprecedented in that there were persistently large deficits during peacetime and prosperity. Many observers lament such deficit spending, believing that federal borrowing "crowds out" private borrowers. In their view, the U.S. Treasury is a 300-pound gorilla that sits where it wants and borrows as much as it pleases — leaving others without chairs or loans. We will examine this argument in later chapters.

## *The Federal Reserve*

There is virtually no chance that the U.S. Treasury will default on its debts, because the federal government has the power to raise taxes and to issue currency to meet its obligations. The **Federal Reserve Board (Fed)** controls the supply of U.S. currency. The Fed can increase the amount of currency outstanding by using newly printed paper money — Federal Reserve notes — to buy Treasury bonds. The Fed can, if it wants, reduce the amount of currency outstanding by selling some of the Treasury bonds it holds and retiring the Federal Reserve notes it receives. The Fed makes its own decisions, but there is no doubt that if the Treasury ever had trouble selling bonds, the Fed would step in and buy as many as needed.

The Federal Reserve's monetary policies affect the availability of credit to household and business borrowers. When the Fed buys Treasury bonds and issues new Federal Reserve notes, there is more money available for borrowing and spending: credit markets ease. When the Fed sells some of its bond holdings and retires Federal Reserve notes, credit markets tighten because there is less money to lend and borrow.

The Fed uses monetary policy to stabilize the economy, tightening credit when it perceives excessive speculation and easing credit when it wants to avoid a recession or financial panic. In later chapters we will look at the various policies at the Fed's disposal and at how the Fed implements these policies.

# FINANCIAL MARKETS

A market is a means of bringing together buyers and sellers to make transactions. **Financial markets**, for trading bonds, stocks, and other financial assets, come in many different forms and involve a variety of agents. Here, in this introductory chapter, we need to make two distinctions that are important for understanding all financial markets.

## *Primary Versus Secondary Markets*

The **primary market** is a label used to describe the initial issuance of a security and includes such transactions as these: an individual deposits $1000 in his or her checking account; a bank loans someone $100,000 to buy a house; the U.S. Treasury raises money by selling a $10,000 bond; a company becomes a public corporation by issuing stock. In each case, a financial record of the transaction is created, showing the existence of debt or equity.

If these debt or equity certificates are then resold to others, this subsequent trade is said to occur in the **secondary market**. Examples abound. When a business acquires a certificate of deposit (CD) by depositing $100,000 in a bank (a primary-market transaction), this CD can then be sold to someone else (a secondary-market transaction), who can either trade it again or hold it until it matures. After a bank loans someone money to buy a house (a primary-market transaction), it can sell the mortgage note to a government agency (a secondary-market transaction) that packages it with other mortgages and resells it to a pension fund (another secondary-market transaction). Investors who own Treasury bonds or corporate stock can sell these securities to other investors in the secondary market. In each case the security may pass from hand to hand as one person after another invests for a while and then sells when that person needs some money or decides that this is no longer an attractive investment.

## *Organized Exchanges and the Over-the-Counter Market*

Some trading in the secondary market takes place on organized exchanges, such as the New York Stock Exchange (NYSE), where brokers meet to trade listed securities. Securities that aren't listed on organized exchanges are said to be traded **over the counter (OTC)**, a reference to the practice long ago of dealers literally trading securities over the counters of their shops. Because this trading is now conducted by telephone, telex, and computer links, a more appropriate label might be the "over-the-phone" market. We can distinguish between two different agents who are central to secondary-market trading: brokers who earn commissions for bringing together buyers and sellers, and dealers who use their own inventory of securities to accommodate buyers and sellers.

A commonplace fiction, sometimes promoted by the exchanges themselves, is that the stock exchanges are used to raise capital to finance business investment. In fact, the exchanges are not used by corporations to raise funds. The exchanges are a secondary market where investors trade securities among themselves. When you buy 100 shares of IBM stock, IBM is not involved in the transaction. You buy shares from Jill, who bought from Jack, and so on through endless trades back to the time when IBM first issued the stock. And so it is with virtually all stock transactions. When a new corporation, or an occasional mature one, sells stock to raise money, this is done through investment bankers rather than on the exchanges.

The stock exchanges are unquestionably useful. The hundreds of millions of shares traded daily (and the accompanying fees paid to brokers) are ample proof that people value this marketplace. Buyers use the market to find sellers, while sellers use the market to find buyers. Investors would undoubtedly be reluctant to acquire shares if they could not count on using the stock exchanges to find buyers when they are ready to sell. The exchanges, though, are not the place where businesses raise money to finance expansion.

## *Financial Markets and the Economy*

Financial markets affect the economy and are also affected by the economy. The Federal Reserve's tight-credit policies during the years 1979–1982 are a clear example of how financial markets can affect the economy. In 1979 the rate of inflation was above 13 percent, and in October of that year the Fed decided that its top priority was to reduce the rate of inflation substantially. Over the next three years the Fed tightened credit severely, and interest rates rose to unprecedented levels.

When Paul Volcker, chairman of the Fed, was asked in 1980 if the Fed's stringent monetary policies would cause an economic recession, he replied, "Yes, and the sooner the better."[1] In another 1980 conversation, Volcker remarked that he wouldn't be satisfied "until the last buzz saw is silenced."[2] In 1981 interest rates reached 18 percent on home mortgages and were even higher for most other bank loans. As interest rates rose, households and businesses cut back on their borrowing and on their purchases of automobiles, houses, and office buildings. As purchases slumped, so did the production of automobiles and the construction of houses and offices. Workers who lost their jobs or were laid off were soon spending less on food, clothing, and entertainment, sending ripples through the economy. The unemployment rate rose from 5.8 percent in 1979 to 7.1 percent in 1980, 7.6 percent in 1981, and peaked above 10 percent in 1982, the highest level since the Great Depression in the 1930s. However, the Fed achieved its single-minded objective as the annual rate of inflation fell from 13.3 percent in 1979 to 3.8 percent in 1982.

In the fall of 1982, the Fed decided that the war on inflation had been won and that there were ominous signs of a possible financial and economic collapse. The Fed switched to easy-money policies, supplying funds as needed to bring interest rates down, encourage borrowing and spending, and fuel the economic expansion that lasted for the remainder of the decade. This historical episode dramatically illustrates how financial conditions affect production and employment.

It is equally clear that the economy influences financial markets. When a tax cut, export boom, or other economic event persuades households and businesses to borrow money and build houses, offices, and factories, these increased credit demands put upward pressure on loan rates and on other interest rates. Just as the availability of credit can affect borrowing, so can borrowing affect the availability of credit.

Another familiar example involves the effects of the economy on the stock market. When the economy is booming and businesses are very profitable, corporations are worth more and stock prices increase. When the economy is in a recession and profits are low or nonexistent, stock prices slump. In fact, stock prices usually fall a few months before a recession begins and rise shortly before a recession ends, perhaps because investors anticipate the good or bad times ahead. In later chapters we will look more closely at the interrelationships among the economy, interest rates, and stock prices.

# FINANCIAL INSTITUTIONS

Financial intermediaries borrow from some and lend to others, thereby channeling funds from savers to borrowers. When you deposit money in a savings account paying 5 percent interest, the bank is borrowing this money from you, which it then loans to someone else to buy a car, a house, or a factory. When you buy a life insurance policy, the insurance company is implicitly borrowing your insurance premiums, which it then lends to land developers, the federal government (by purchasing Treasury bonds), or others.

As illustrated by these two very different examples, financial intermediation involves a variety of functions performed by many different institutions. Figure 1.6 gives a stylized overview of some of the more important roles and players. Nine distinct functions have been identified, ranging from checking to insurance. The types of financial intermediaries have been divided into these three broad groups: deposit institutions, investment intermediaries, and contractual saving plans, with the filled-in boxes indicating the primary services of specific institutions.

**Figure 1.6  Functions of Financial Intermediaries**

| Functions | Depository institutions | | Investment intermediaries | | | Contractual saving plans | |
|---|---|---|---|---|---|---|---|
| | Commercial banks | Thrift institutions | Investment banks | Security brokers | Mutual funds | Pension funds | Insurance companies |
| Checking | ■ | ■ | | ■ | ■ | | |
| Saving | ■ | ■ | | | ■ | ■ | ■ |
| Consumer lending | ■ | ■ | | | | | |
| Business lending | ■ | | | | | | |
| Mortgage lending | ■ | ■ | | | | | |
| Security issuance | | | ■ | ■ | | | |
| Security trading | | | ■ | ■ | | | |
| Money management | ■ | | ■ | ■ | ■ | ■ | |
| Insurance | | ■ | | | | | ■ |

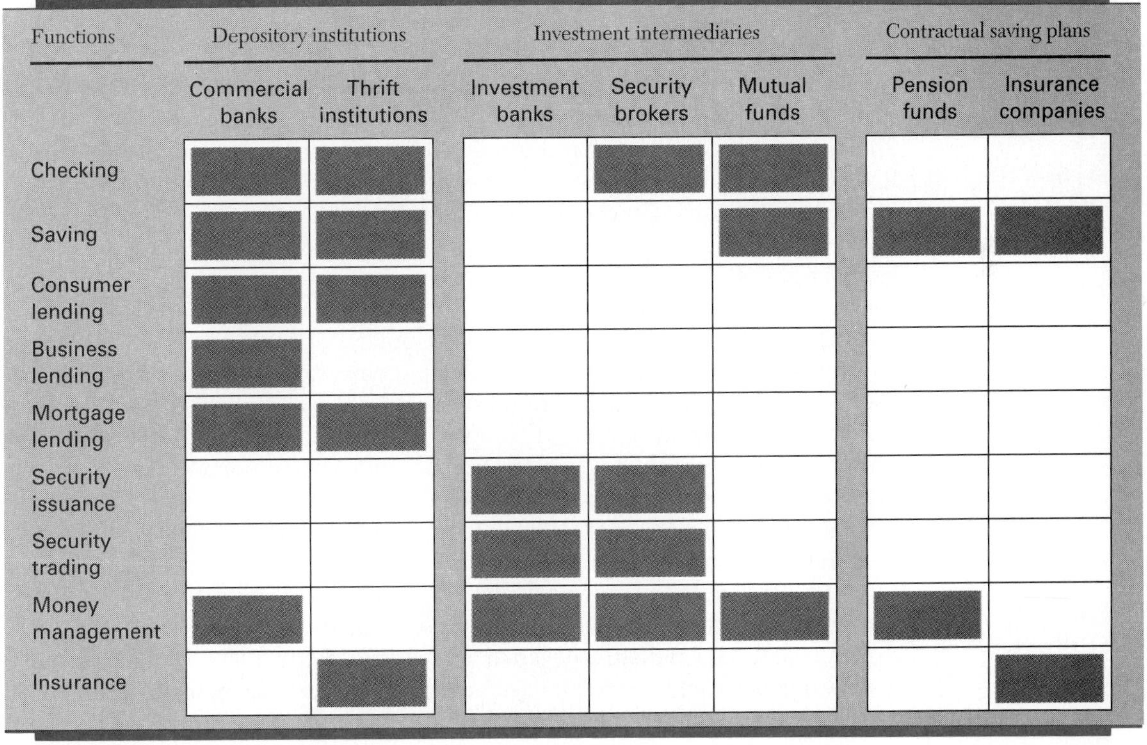

## Deposit Institutions

Deposit institutions offer checking accounts, savings accounts, and other types of deposits that pay specified rates of interest. Savers find these deposits appealing because their money can usually be withdrawn immediately, often by writing a check; the rate of return is known in advance; and the safety of these accounts is generally insured by the federal government. Deposit institutions lend most of the money they borrow from their depositors, making a profit on the spread between the interest rates charged on these loans and the interest rates paid on their deposits.

The Glass-Steagall Act of 1933 prohibited firms from acting as both a **commercial bank** (accepting deposits and making loans) and an **investment bank** (helping businesses and state and local governments issue stocks and bonds). Thus J. P. Morgan, the nation's most prominent bank, was forced to split into two separate companies: J. P. Morgan (commercial banking) and Morgan Stanley (investment banking). Every bank in the United States had to decide whether it would be a commercial bank or an investment bank.

Those that became commercial banks could accept deposits — checking accounts, savings accounts, and so on — and make loans to households and businesses. For nearly 50 years, from 1933 to 1980, commercial banks were the

EXAMPLE **1.5**  *The Thrift Debacle*

In the 1960s and early 1970s, savings and loans and other thrifts paid their depositors interest rates ranging from 2 to 5 percent and loaned their depositors' money out in 30-year mortgages at 4 to 8 percent. When interest rates rose sharply in the 1970s, these thrifts were squeezed. They had to pay double-digit interest rates to hold onto their depositors, but they earned only single-digit interest rates on the mortgages they held. In 1980 the savings and loan industry was technically bankrupted when its aggregate net worth became negative.

Eighty-five percent of all thrifts lost money in the second half of 1981. During the 2-year period 1981–1982, the industry lost $9 billion and more than 800 thrifts disappeared — mostly through absorption by stronger institutions. In response to this crisis, Congress moved to deregulate the industry, allowing thrifts to move away from their traditional emphasis on home mortgages and make more business and commercial real estate loans.

Interest rates fell after 1982, but the industry's losses continued. The problem was no longer an interest-rate squeeze, but mounting loan defaults — caused too often by excessive risk-taking or outright fraud: depositor money squandered on desert land and lavish bonuses. In 1990 it was widely estimated that the thrift industry had a negative net worth of at least $200 billion and that there would inevitably be a financial meltdown in which as many as 70 percent of the existing thrifts would disappear. In later chapters we will look more closely at this thrift debacle.

only institutions allowed to offer checking accounts, and they were prohibited from paying interest on these deposits. Commercial banks were thus protected from competition from other financial institutions and from deposit-rate wars among themselves. In return, they were prohibited from purchasing stocks and from acting as investment banks. Many of these legal restrictions have now been removed, and more will soon disappear.

The thrift institutions identified in Figure 1.6 include savings and loan associations, mutual savings banks, and credit unions. Historically, they borrowed money, mostly by offering savings accounts to small savers, and loaned this money primarily to individuals to buy houses, automobiles, and small appliances. Before 1980 these institutions were prohibited from offering checking accounts, and their share of this market is still quite small.

## Investment Intermediaries

Investment banks, security brokers, and mutual funds are primarily investment intermediaries involved, as shown in Figure 1.6, in the purchase and sale of bonds, stocks, and other securities. One of the functions of investment banks is to underwrite and market new security issues by purchasing securities from the issuer and reselling them to investors. A new issue can be underwritten by a single firm or by a group, called a *syndicate*, with one firm acting as the lead dealer. The underwriters study a firm's financial soundness, agree to purchase the stocks or bonds that will be issued, resell the securities to financial institutions and individuals, and monitor the firm's ability and willingness to fulfill the terms of the securities after they have been issued.

Investment intermediaries also can act as security brokers and dealers, helping individual and institutional investors to buy and sell stocks and bonds in the secondary market. In this capacity, the intermediaries help arrange private trades among borrowers and lenders or execute trades on the organized exchanges or in the over-the-counter market.

Investment banks (such as Morgan Stanley, Salomon Brothers, and Goldman Sachs) have historically emphasized investment banking, whereas brokerage firms (such as Merrill Lynch, Shearson Lehman Hutton, and Charles Schwab) have focused on securities brokerage. Today, however, there is considerable overlap. Merrill Lynch is now one of the nation's largest underwriters of new stocks and bonds; Kidder, Peabody began as an investment bank and is now one of the largest brokerage firms.

The third function of investment intermediaries is to help others manage their money. Such intermediaries may advise investors in the selection of stocks and bonds, advise borrowers about their financing alternatives, or take over the money-management task — actually making decisions rather than merely offering advice.

Mutual funds and other investment companies specialize in managing investors' money for them. Fidelity and Vanguard are two of the largest investment companies, offering dozens of mutual funds with varying objectives. Money-market funds buy Treasury bills and other very short-term securities; most of these funds allow limited checking privileges. Other mutual funds specialize in tax-exempt municipal bonds, growth stocks, or stocks of small savings and loan associations. In each case, these funds pool investor savings and purchase a diversified portfolio of securities. Mutual funds appeal mostly to small investors who don't have enough wealth to amass a diversified portfolio on their own and feel that they don't have enough time or expertise to select securities wisely.

## Contractual Saving

Pension funds and insurance companies offer yet another type of financial intermediation, in which contractual savings — insurance premiums or retirement contributions — are invested on behalf of savers. In the case of insurance, the timing of the payoff generally depends on an accidental event, such as fire or death, and the size of the payoff is determined by the contract. The premium charged by the insurance company reflects its estimate of how much it can earn by investing the customer's money in bonds, stocks, and shopping malls. Some pension plans base their payoff on the size of the worker's wages shortly before retirement so that the retirement benefits will be adequate to maintain an accustomed standard of living. In this case, as with the insurance company, the size of the worker's annual contributions depend on the pension fund's estimate of the rate of return it can earn by investing these contributions. Other pension plans base their payoff directly on worker contributions, crediting the worker with whatever rate of return it earns, less expenses; in this case the pension fund is really acting as a money manager, investing the workers' savings on their behalf.

## Full-Service Intermediaries

Not too long ago, financial intermediaries were pretty specialized. You would go to one for a checking account, to another for a mortgage, to another for a car loan, to another for insurance, and to yet another to buy shares of corporate stock. No more! These artificial distinctions have been permanently breached and are rapidly fading from view. Many of the cells in Figure 1.6 that were left blank really have partly filled-in boxes, as intermediaries have spread beyond their traditional roles.

Specialized financial "boutiques" are being replaced by financial "supermarkets" that can handle all your financial needs: checking accounts, mortgages, car loans, insurance, and stocks. The banking giant Citicorp owns a savings and loan, an insurance company, and a credit card company. So does Sears, Roebuck. Different financial institutions now can compete with each other for your business. Credit unions vie with commercial banks for your checking account. Savings and loan associations try to sell you insurance. Money-market funds go after your savings account.

Historically, the differences between banks, credit unions, mutual funds, and other financial intermediaries were due largely to legal restrictions on their operations. They were all financial intermediaries, but they differed in what was permitted and not permitted for each. The dissolution of the barriers between financial institutions has been going on for some time, with fits and starts, corresponding to various victories and setbacks in legislation, regulatory rulings, and court decisions. Many gains were consolidated and broadened in the historic 1980 Depository Institutions Deregulation and Monetary Control Act. It is hoped that these changes will enable financial institutions to serve their customers better, strengthen them by broadening and diversifying their operations, and promote competition among intermediaries. We will discuss all this and more in the chapters to come.

## SUMMARY

Real assets are tangible physical assets such as houses, factories, and automobiles; financial assets are paper claims, including bank deposits, bonds, and stocks. What ultimately lies behind financial claims — the assets of some and liabilities of others — are real, tangible assets.

The return from an investment — financial or real — consists of income (the cash flow and services received while owning the asset) and capital gains (the profits made when the asset is sold). Those considering investing in real assets compare the prospective return with the returns offered on financial assets and with the interest rates charged on loans to finance their purchase. Financial markets affect investment in physical assets through changes in the yields on financial investments and in the interest rates on mortgages and loans. An easing or tightening of financial markets also affects the availability of credit to liquidity-constrained households and businesses.

While corporate bonds are debt, common stock is equity — a claim on the corporation's profits after interest and other fixed expenses have been paid. The fact that interest is a tax-deductible expense for corporations but dividends are not encourages firms to finance their spending with debt rather than equity.

The U.S. Treasury sells bonds to finance the federal budget deficit. The Federal Reserve can increase or reduce the amount of currency outstanding by buying or selling Treasury bonds. The Fed eases credit when it wants to avoid a recession or financial panic and tightens credit when it perceives excessive inflation and speculation.

The primary market involves the sale of newly created securities. The secondary market is a resale market where existing securities are traded. Financial intermediaries are a channel through which the savings of some are loaned to others. There are a variety of intermediaries — deposit institutions, investment intermediaries, and contractual saving plans — that perform a variety of functions, including checking, saving, lending, issuing and trading securities, money management, and insurance. Competitive, innovative financial institutions have expanded into nontraditional activities and blurred the distinctions among formerly specialized financial institutions.

# IMPORTANT TERMS

capital gains
commercial bank
common stock
equity
Federal Reserve Board (Fed)
financial assets
financial intermediaries
financial markets
fixed-income securities
flow

income
investment bank
liquidity-constrained
over the counter (OTC)
primary market
rates of return
real assets
secondary market
stock

# EXERCISES

1. Which of the following are financial assets and which are real assets?
   a. 100 shares of Apple stock
   b. Money in your checking account
   c. A home mortgage
   d. A Macintosh computer

2. A financial asset is someone else's liability. For each of the following, indicate for which of the identified parties it is an asset and for which it is a liability.
   a. Checking account: depositor, bank
   b. Car loan: car buyer, bank
   c. Treasury bonds: investor, U.S. government
   d. Corporate pension: worker, business

3. Which of the following are income and which are capital gains?
   a. The price of Apple stock goes up $1.
   b. Apple pays a $1 a share dividend.
   c. You save rent by buying a house.
   d. Housing prices collapse.

4. Which of the following transactions take place in a primary market and which occur in a secondary market?
   a. You sell 100 shares of Apple stock.
   b. You deposit money in a bank.
   c. The bank loans money to a home buyer.
   d. The bank sells the home buyer's mortgage note to a federal agency.

5. Young people and old people tend to spend more than they earn, whereas middle-aged people tend to spend less than they earn. How do they do this, and why?

6. Answer this student's question: "I don't understand the significance of liquidity constraints. Everyone, myself included, wishes to have more money. Why do we need the special label 'liquidity constraint' for this universal wish?"

7. One way to gauge the degree of liquidity that is provided by a secondary market is to divide (a) the price you would receive today for an asset if you started looking for a buyer today, by (b) the price you would receive for this asset today if you had started looking for a buyer 6 months ago. Does a low ratio of (a) to (b) indicate that the asset is liquid or illiquid? Using this criterion, identify two relatively illiquid assets.

8. Explain why you either agree or disagree with the claim that "the main function of the stock exchanges is . . . to generate funds to be employed in private businesses."[3]

9. Which of the following financial intermediaries would you use to help incorporate your small business? Open a checking account? Invest in a diversified portfolio of stocks?

a. Commercial bank
b. Investment bank
c. Mutual fund

10. Which of these financial intermediaries would you use to buy 100 shares of IBM stock? Apply for a home mortgage? Issue bonds to finance the expansion of your business?
    a. Investment bank
    b. Savings and loan
    c. Securities broker

11. Which of the following are stocks and which are flows?
    a. General Motors car sales this year
    b. The population of the United States
    c. The number of births in the United States this year
    d. U.S. GDP

12. Explain how the federal debt can increase even while the federal deficit is decreasing.

13. Between 1929 and 1933, output in the United States fell by a third, and the unemployment rate rose from 3 to 25 percent. What do you suppose happened to stock prices? Housing construction? Corporate profits?

14. What did Paul Volcker mean in 1980 when he remarked that he wouldn't be satisfied "until the last buzz saw is silenced"?

15. Look in the most recent monthly issue of the *Federal Reserve Bulletin* and determine the name of the current chairperson of the Federal Reserve Board.

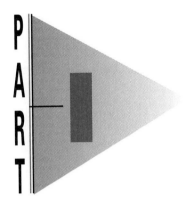

P
A
R
T

# Financial Assets and Markets

# 2 Money

*Money is not, properly speaking, one of the subjects of commerce; but only the instrument which men have agreed upon to facilitate the exchange of one commodity for another. It is none of the wheels of trade: it is the oil which renders the motion of the wheels more smooth and easy.*

**David Hume**

Money is such a familiar and pervasive part of our lives that we seldom stop to consider its nature and importance. As children, we quickly learn that dollar bills are not merely pretty green pieces of paper to be painted, shredded, eaten, or left out in the mud. Dollar bills are special. Dollars are important and valuable because dollars are "money" that can be used to buy things. Stores will trade food, clothing, and toys for dollars. Knowing this, we, too, are quite willing to work or sell things for dollars, because we can use this special green paper to buy useful things.

It has not always been this way. Not too long ago useful things were used as money. In the United States, tobacco, rice, and cattle have been money. In other times and places, people made do without money of any sort. In this chapter you will learn why societies have found money — paper or otherwise — to be a very useful contrivance.

## BARTER IS INEFFICIENT

A logical place to begin is by imagining an economy without money of any sort. This might be a primitive economy in which little economic trading takes place. Perhaps the citizens are self-sufficient and a bit isolated from one another. When their paths do cross and they make trades, it is a simple exchange of goods — corn for potatoes, wood for leather, knives for arrows. This kind of economic activity is called **barter**, the trading of goods and services for other goods and services.

Barter can work tolerably well when people are virtually self-sufficient and only make occasional trades. However, a vital element of economic progress has been the replacement of self-sufficiency with specialization. I teach, consult, do research, and write textbooks on economics. With the fruits of this labor, I can acquire pizza, clothing, a computer, an automobile, and the other necessities of a good life. Other people specialize in making the pizzas that I enjoy. Still others sell the flour for the pizza dough, or turn wheat into flour, or grow the wheat. Through a division of labor, each person can become highly skilled at very specialized tasks. In the aggregate, much more is produced and enjoyed than would be the case if all individuals were self-sufficient — growing their own wheat, making their own flour, concocting their own pizza, and teaching themselves economics. How long would it take you to make a personal computer and write your own word-processing software?

A necessary accompaniment to specialization is the opportunity to trade one's specialized product for the products of other specialists. It is here that barter becomes burdensome, however. In a barter economy, if there is not what W. S. Jevons called a "double coincidence" of wants,[1] each person must make a multiplicity of trades before the desired bundle of goods can be obtained. Too much time and energy are spent swapping goods, and too little time is spent producing and enjoying them.

Suppose that I want a pizza for dinner and my specialization is teaching economics. When I go to the pizza maker, hoping for a trade, I may find that he is interested in a transistor radio but not economics lectures. (For a double coincidence of wants to exist, I would want to trade lectures for pizza and he would want to trade pizza for lectures.) So I trudge off, looking for someone with a transistor radio who would rather listen to an economics lecture. With considerable effort, I locate a woman with 100 radios who wants a red boat and knows a man with a boat who is interested in studying economics. Unfortunately, the boat is yellow and worth more than a one-term economics course (it's a very nice boat). Therefore, I have to find someone who will trade a red boat for a yellow one, and then I have to work out another series of deals to acquire something extra to throw in with my lectures. It will be a very late dinner by the time I have it all straightened out.

Some barter is admittedly useful and even enjoyable. Throughout history, the swapping of goods for goods has gone on even where money existed. In a simple economy with substantial inventories of tradable goods, intimate knowledge of the possessions and desires of others, and some zest for the sport, people have bartered successfully. Often, trading is simplified by the use of customary price ratios (one fish for two bananas) that are fixed for years or even generations. In addition, the use of delayed payments lubricates barter by making it unnecessary to find just the right combination of goods at a specific moment. (For example, if I were friends with the pizza maker, I could eat my pizza now and pay for it later when I come across a radio.) However, in a large, complex, highly specialized society that is neither entirely communal nor entirely totalitarian, some form of money is a virtual necessity.

EXAMPLE 2.1 *Living Without Money*

Money facilitates trade, but it is not absolutely necessary. Within a family, tasks may be highly specialized even without monetary trades. Perhaps the father takes care of the yard and balances the checkbook, the mother buys food and repairs the plumbing, and the son keeps his room clean. Instead of monetary payments, such exchanges can be based on either a communal or a totalitarian organization of the family. Similarly, there have been feudal estates and even entire societies whose communal or totalitarian organization made money unnecessary.

On many Polynesian islands, goods are freely provided to poorer inhabitants and even to strangers. It is considered improper to refuse someone's request for goods. In some communities, even the request is unnecessary: it is customary simply to take whatever is desired. There is little need for money in such circumstances. Many small religious groups in North America have attempted to establish similar moneyless communal societies.

In the Inca Empire, money was unnecessary because the citizens' economic lives were thoroughly regulated by a central administration. Each citizen was told what to produce and what fraction of his or her output to give to the central authorities, who then allocated it among all citizens. There was a limited amount of barter in food, but trades of clothing, housing, or land were forbidden. Money was unneeded and unknown before the Spanish conquest.

After the conquest, the Jesuit Republic of Paraguay was a moneyless totalitarian state established and run by the Jesuits with the intention of protecting the Indians from exploitation. Even after the Jesuits lost their absolute authority, barter continued as the predominant form of exchange in Paraguay. As late as the end of the eighteenth century, taxes and the salaries of religious and government leaders were paid in goods. Although of smaller scale, economic lives within European monasteries and feudal estates during the Middle Ages also were authoritarian and moneyless.

Moneyless societies are generally comprised of self-sufficient citizens, or else they have a communal or totalitarian organization that regulates exchanges of goods and services. In societies with an extensive division of labor, private ownership, and voluntary exchange, barter is unworkably cumbersome and inefficient. In most modern nations, specialization and the use of money are so tightly linked that, like the chicken or the egg, it is impossible to say which came first.

# COMMODITY MONEY

Effective barter is easier if everyone maintains an inventory of easily traded goods. If I, the hungry economics lecturer, have accumulated a collection of desirable trinkets, I can give some of these to the pizza maker, and he can trade them to someone else for a radio. Unlike a pure-barter economy, in which trades are made solely for direct consumption, in a mixed-barter economy, some items are accepted in trade not for consumption but so that they can later be traded for consumables. These traded items that pass from hand to hand are typically goods that are widely recognized and used so that those who accept them can be confident that these goods can be traded to someone else. It is also helpful if these items are portable, divisible, and durable — spices, metals, and wood, for example.

This process is self-reinforcing. The more a certain item is used for trades, the more confidence people have in accepting it. The more confidence people have in accepting a certain item, the more it will be used for trades. At some point we can say that this intermediate item has become so popular that it has assumed the status of a **medium of exchange** — something commonly exchanged that the recipients intend to trade for other items. A commodity that becomes a medium of exchange is called a **commodity money**.

There are several characteristics that a desirable commodity money should possess:

1. It should be easily *verifiable*. It is inefficient to use a commodity money that must be continually inspected for its size, weight, or purity. One of the subtle inefficiencies of barter is that both the items traded must be closely evaluated.
2. It should be intrinsically *useful*. There is something to be said for using a commodity money that can be consumed if worst comes to worst. A citizenry's readiness to accept an item as a medium of exchange is enhanced somewhat by the perception that the item is intrinsically useful.
3. It should be conveniently *transportable*. If trades take place over a wide geographic area, it is helpful to have a commodity money that can be easily and safely carried about.
4. It should be *divisible*. Trades are simplified when the medium of exchange can be divided easily to purchase exactly the desired amount. Commodity moneys that are difficult to divide or that lose their value when split are cumbersome, although the provision for delayed payment eases this problem.
5. It should be *durable*. If you keep an inventory of some medium of exchange that you are always prepared to trade, it is best if the medium does not spoil or rot while you are holding it.

In practice over the past 4000 years, the predominant commodity moneys have been precious metals — mostly silver, to a lesser extent gold, and even less frequently copper. However, in generally small, rural communities, the peoples of the world have used an enormous variety of other commodity moneys. *Wampum* (a string of shells) was used by Native Americans and for a while by American colonists from New England to Virginia. In 1641, *wampum* was made legal tender in Massachusetts (at the rate of six shells to the penny). In Virginia, tobacco was made legal tender in 1642, and contracts payable in gold and silver were outlawed. Tobacco was used widely as a commodity money in Virginia for almost 200 years, in Maryland for about 150 years, and in neighboring states for lesser periods. In various other parts of the United States, rice, cattle, and whiskey have been declared legal tender. Although they lacked legal sanction, musket balls, peas, hemp, furs, and woodpecker scalps also were used as commodity money. Other selected moneys from around the world are listed below to give you some flavor of the great variety:

Whale teeth — Fiji
Sandalwood — Hawaii
Fish hooks — Gilbert Islands
Tortoise shells — Marianas
Red parrot feathers — Santa Cruz Islands as late as 1961
Rice — Philippines
Salt — many places
Pepper — Sumatra
Sugar — Barbados
Tea bricks — many places in inner Asia
Slaves — Equatorial Africa, Nigeria, and Ireland
Reindeer — parts of Russia
Copper — Egypt
Silk — China
Butter — Norway
Leather — France and Italy
Rum — Australia

These examples come from an interesting book, *Primitive Money,* written by Paul Einzig. In 1966, he wrote that there were still "many communities, especially in the Pacific area but also in some parts of Africa and to a less extent in Asia, in which primitive monetary systems are still in operation."[2]

# FIAT MONEY

The stone money of Yap that is described in Example 2.2 is superficially a commodity money. However, it has no real value as a commodity. A Yap stone is accepted in exchange for useful goods and services solely because its recipients are confident that they will also be able to exchange the stone for goods and services. Its acceptance as a medium of exchange rests on this confidence, nothing more. This is an example of **fiat money**, something that has little value as a commodity but, because of law or tradition, is accepted as a medium of exchange.

The dollar bills used in the United States are fiat money. The paper they are printed on has almost no value, but our government says that these dollars are legal tender, suitable for paying its bills and our taxes. We accept these dollars in trades, confident that they have value because we can exchange them for useful goods and services.

**EXAMPLE** 2.2   *The Stone Money of Yap*

The island of Yap in Micronesia is renowned among economists for using stone money for nearly 2000 years. The stones are round like a wheel with a hole in the center, and often they are as tall as a person. Some are twice this size. The stones were obtained by treacherous expeditions to Palau or, for finer and rarer stones, to Guam some 400 miles away through frequently stormy seas. Often only 1 of 20 canoes bound for Guam returned.

In the 1870s, David Dean O'Keffe, an American with a sturdy boat, brought enormous stones into Yap in exchange for coconuts, fish, women, and whatever else he wanted. The largest stone he brought in, said to be 20 feet wide, is at the bottom of the Yap harbor, where it fell while being unloaded from his schooner to a raft. Even though the stone disappeared from view, it was still considered to be part of the possessions of the original owners and then of generation after generation of heirs.

The stones have absolutely no value other than the fact that they are accepted as a medium of exchange. Simple direct barter traditionally was used for most everyday transactions, with debts allowed to accumulate until payment could be made with a large stone. Today the islanders use stone beads, sea shells, beer, and U.S. dollars for small transactions. The large stones are a store of value used to pay for land, permission to marry, and other large debts. When a large stone changes ownership, a tree can be put through its hole and up to a hundred men can roll the stone from its old owner to its new one. Because a broken stone is considered worthless, they are often left in one spot, with the ownership common knowledge. The largest stones are so well known that they even have names. The people pass on, but the stones remain.

In 1944, Willard Price* reported that a waist-high stone was valued at 4000 coconuts, that a 5-foot stone was worth many villages, and that the very largest stones were considered priceless. The largest stones are owned by entire communities and are displayed proudly outside community buildings. The smaller, 2-foot to 5-foot stones are owned by individuals and are displayed outside their homes. In 1984 *The Wall Street Journal* reported that a builder sold a house for $8700 and a 4-foot stone and that another islander bought a building lot with a 30-inch stone, explaining, "We don't know the value of the U.S. dollar."† The value of a stone is determined not only by its size but also by the difficulty in bringing it to Yap. The stones acquired before the arrival of O'Keffe are the most valuable, those brought in by O'Keffe are worth half as much, and more recent stones are virtually worthless.

*Willard Price, Japan's Islands of Mystery (*New York: John Day, 1944*).
†Art Pine, "Fixed Assets, Or: Why a Loan in Yap Is Hard to Roll Over," *Wall Street Journal, *March 29, 1984.*

To each individual, fiat money has value solely because of laws or tradition, conditioned by many years of successful exchanges. To a society, fiat money has value because it successfully serves as a medium of exchange, thereby allowing society to avoid the inefficiencies of barter. For thousands of years, commodity money was preeminent. Today, fiat money reigns. Let's take a quick look at this gradual but now thorough upheaval.

## From Hard Money to Soft Money

Precious metals have many of the desired characteristics of a good commodity money: they are useful, conveniently transportable, divisible, and durable. The one drawback is that metals are not easily verified. Every trade requires trusted scales and a reliable assessment of the purity of the precious metal. To avoid this considerable inconvenience, metals can be made into coins of known weight and purity. Thus the British pound was originally a silver coin stamped with a star, with a weight of 240 coins to the pound. Because the Old English word for star is "sterling," these coins came to be called "pounds sterling"; the symbol £ comes from the Medieval Latin word for a pound: *libra*.

Herodotus noted the use of coins in the ancient kingdom of Lydia around the seventh century B.C. Modern historians believe that coins were independently introduced in China at about the same time, in India a few hundred years earlier, and in Persia a few hundred years later. Coinage flourished in the Greek and Roman empires and then throughout Europe. John Kenneth Galbraith has observed wryly that "after Alexander the Great the custom was established of depicting the head of the sovereign on the coin, less, it has been suggested, as a guarantee of the weight and fineness of the metal than as a thoughtful personal gesture by the ruler to himself."[3]

A recurring difficulty with coins made of precious metal is that people are tempted to make a small profit as the coins pass through their hands by clipping, shaving, or filing bits of metal from the coins. For governments, the temptation is currency **debasement**: degrading the coins by mixing in less expensive metals — for example, the use of one part base metal and four parts gold allows five gold coins to be made for the price of four so that more coins can be made and spent on wars, monuments, and other governmental pursuits. Roman silver coins were reportedly debased until they became 98 percent copper and only 2 percent silver.

With coins of varying quality in existence, those who can tell the difference will keep the authentic coins and spend the debased ones. This is **Gresham's law**: bad money drives out good. That is, bad money will circulate while good money is hoarded. (This observation was made by Sir Thomas Gresham in 1558 but was stated earlier by Copernicus and undoubtedly others.)

Gresham's law implies that money that is more valuable as a commodity than as money will be withdrawn from circulation. For example, in colonial Virginia, fine tobacco was consumed while debts payable in tobacco leaves were paid with the scruffiest and foulest tobacco. Similarly, the American Coinage Act of 1792 provided that the $10 gold eagle would contain 247.5 grains of pure gold and the silver dollar would contain 371.25 grains of pure silver. This act meant that as a medium of exchange ten silver dollars, containing 3712.5 grains of silver were as valuable as the 247.5 grains of gold in an eagle. Implicitly, the 1792 Coinage Act gave a grain of gold the same value as $3712.5/247.5 = 15$ grains of silver. However, as a commodity, the free-market price of gold was about 15.5 grains of silver. In accordance with Gresham's law, this disparity between the value of gold as a commodity and its value as a medium of exchange provided an inducement to use silver dollars as a medium of exchange and to hoard the $10 gold eagles — or to melt them and trade the gold as a commodity for $247.5(15.5) = 3836.25$ grains of silver, worth $3836.25/371.25 = \$10.33$.

In 1834, the mint ratio was changed so that 1 grain of gold had the same value as 16 grains of silver as a medium of exchange. As a commodity, however, the value was still about 15.5 to 1, and consequently, gold eagles circulated while silver dollars were hoarded. More recently, in the 1960s high silver prices drove silver dimes, quarters, half-dollars, and dollars out of circulation in the United States. In the 1970s copper prices soared, and copper pennies were hoarded. The U.S. Mint offered a carrot: an Exceptional Public Service Certificate to persons bringing $25 in pennies to a bank. The Treasury Department tried a stick: a $10,000 fine and 5 years in prison for melting or exporting copper pennies. Neither the carrot nor the stick repealed Gresham's law.

Thus adulteration or hoarding often makes it difficult to keep full-bodied, or hard-money, coins in circulation. One way around this problem is to use a difficult-to-counterfeit piece of paper as a substitute for a full-bodied coin. For each 371.25 grains of silver, instead of coining a silver dollar that can be shaved or melted, the government (or a private bank) can simply hold onto the silver and issue a distinctive piece of paper identified as a "paper dollar," redeemable at any time for 371.25 grains of silver. This is just like a warehouse receipt and, except for the effort of redemption, just as valuable as a full-bodied silver dollar.

The early paper notes issued by banks and governments were warehouse receipts of this type, and except for the counterfeiting danger, they alleviated some of the problems of full-bodied coins. In addition, paper is usually less expensive to mint than coins and often easier to transport. Convenience is especially important in the substitution of paper for not-so-precious commodity moneys; this is why warehouse receipts for tobacco circulated in the American colonies.

The use of paper money presents another opportunity, or danger, that has been exploited repeatedly by both governments and banks: to issue notes for which there is only partial commodity backing or none at all. This was true of the first government paper money (China, starting in the eighth century) and of the first major public bank (the Bank of Amsterdam, established in 1609), and such practices have tempted governments and banks ever since.

Paper that is fully backed by commodities and coins that are made of precious metal are often called *hard money*. *Soft money* refers to unbacked paper and token coins that are used as a medium of exchange but have little value as a commodity. Since 1853, the U.S. Mint has been authorized to produce token coins using metal that is less expensive than the face value of the coins. Congress controls the minting of U.S. coins, and currently, all newly minted U.S. coins are inexpensive alloys made of copper, nickel, aluminum, and the like.

One big advantage of soft money is that, by Gresham's law, it is kept in circulation and fulfills its destiny as a medium of exchange. Governments generally prefer soft money because it can be produced at a profit, called **seigniorage**, that is equal to the difference between the money's value in exchange and its value as a commodity. The word "seigniorage" comes from the Old French word for the lord, or sovereign, of a manor, who made a profit minting coins from precious metals. Today, seigniorage is used to encompass all profits made from issuing money.

In 1974, for instance, it was estimated that switching from copper to aluminum pennies in the United States would save the federal government $40 million a year, thereby boosting its seigniorage by this amount. The seigniorage on token coins and unbacked paper money is nearly 100 percent. The amount of seigniorage varies from country to country depending on whether the government pays its bills by collecting taxes, selling bonds, or printing money. In the United States, less than 3 percent of government revenue comes from seigniorage. In Italy and Greece, seigniorage has often provided more than 10 percent of government revenue. In other countries, the figure has been even higher.

All paper currency now issued in the United States has no metal backing. If you have a $10 bill, the government will not redeem it for gold, silver, or tobacco. It can be exchanged for two $5 bills, ten $1 bills, or a pocketful of token coins. Nonetheless, like any ordinary commodity, it has a value that can be measured by what can be obtained in exchange.

Suppose, for instance, that bread trades at $1 a loaf, milk at $2 a bottle, and steak at $5 a pound. What is the value of a pound of steak? It is worth what can be obtained in exchange: 5 dollars, 5 loaves of bread, or 2.5 bottles of milk. Similarly, what is the value of ten dollars? Ten dollars is worth 10 loaves of bread, 5 bottles of milk, or 2 pounds of steak. In a monetary economy like that of the United States, prices of goods and services are usually expressed in terms of the medium of exchange, and other relative prices must be calculated. The price label on a bottle of milk will say "$2," not "two loaves of bread," because dollars are the medium of exchange.

Thus a dollar has many prices, all of which are relative prices, and all are the inverses of the usual price quotations seen in stores. If the price of milk is $P = 2$ dollars/bottle, then the price of a dollar measured in milk is

$$\frac{1}{P} = \frac{1}{2 \text{ dollars/bottle}} = 0.5 \text{ bottles/dollar}$$

In a market economy, these prices of a dollar (along with all relative prices) are simultaneously influenced by the demands and supplies of all traded items, including bread, milk, steak, and dollars.

Dollars are supplied by the government and are demanded by private citizens because dollars are useful as a medium of exchange. As with other goods, an increased supply of dollars tends to reduce the price of a dollar, just as the price of peaches falls in the summer when peaches are more plentiful. A fall in the price of a dollar is an increase in conventionally measured prices. If there were an unlimited supply of dollars (like clean air in the good old days), they would be free. If the price of money is zero, then conventionally quoted prices are astronomical. In more familiar terminology, an unlimited expansion of the money supply creates hyperinflation. Conversely, inexpensively produced paper money has value because it is useful as a medium of exchange and is in limited supply.

## MONEY'S ROLES

So far we have used the term *money* to describe things that are used as a medium of exchange. Any money that serves as a medium of exchange also will normally serve in at least two other roles — as a unit of accounting and as a store of value.

Because money is used to buy and sell things, prices are normally quoted in monetary units, thereby making money a unit of accounting. In the United States our money is denominated in dollars, and most prices are stated in dollars, as are most laws, regulations, and contracts that require a payment from one party to

---

**EXAMPLE 2.3** *What Is Worn-Out Money Good For?*

Paper money doesn't last forever. The average $1 bill wears out in about a year and a half.* Larger denominations last a bit longer, perhaps because people take better care of more valuable currency. Bank tellers identify some money that is torn, dirty, or mangled, but most worn-out bills are selected electronically by the machines used by Federal Reserve banks to sort and count currency. Bills that are ready for retirement are either shredded into strips an eighth of an inch wide or pulverized into confetti.

Each year the Federal Reserve retires about 3 billion bills, worth $20 billion and weighing more than 3000 tons. Most of the shredded or confettied currency is buried in landfills, some is destroyed in special incinerators designed to reduce pollution when paper is burnt, and some is recycled. One firm makes an oil-drilling lubricant using confettied currency. A few businesses make novelty items such as pillow stuffings, papier-mâché figures, and drinking glasses using readily identified shredded currency. A Salt Lake City entrepreneur buys shredded bills from his local Federal Reserve bank and makes artificial fireplace logs that retail for $2.50 each — a small price to see money burn.

*Peter W. Barnes, "Treasury Officials Have Money to Burn But Generally Don't," Wall Street Journal, *August 20, 1980.*

another. Our economic calculations are simplified by having all prices quoted in dollars, rather than having some prices stated in terms of loaves of bread and other prices in gallons of milk.

Money is also a convenient store of value. Wealth can be held in many forms, including dollars, bonds, and real estate. It is inconvenient and expensive to have to sell some of your bonds and real estate every time you need dollars to buy something. Dollars can be held as a short-term store of value, between the receipt of your paycheck and your purchases of food and other regular purchases, or as a long-term store of value, burying $100 bills in your backyard in anticipation of your retirement. The better money stores value, the more it will be held as a store of value. If money earns no interest and prices are rising rapidly, it won't even be worth your effort to dig up those $100 bills when you retire.

## Nominal Versus Real

Economic numbers that are recorded in a nation's unit of accounting, such as dollars, are called **nominal** magnitudes. If you are paid $5 an hour for a part-time job, that is your nominal hourly wage rate. If you work full time and earn $20,000 a year, that is your nominal annual income. Your nominal net worth is the market value, in dollars, of the difference between your total assets and liabilities.

A fundamental tenet in economics is that people do not work and save solely for the simple pleasures of counting and recounting money. We work and accumulate dollars in order to purchase and enjoy goods and services, and we therefore care about what our dollars will buy. Economic numbers measured in terms of purchasing power are called **real** magnitudes. Suppose, for instance, that you are interested only in purchasing hamburgers. Your real income can then be measured in hamburgers, calculated by dividing your nominal income by the price of hamburgers:

$$\text{Real income (hamburgers/year)} = \frac{\text{nominal income (dollars/year)}}{\text{price of hamburgers (dollars/burger)}}$$

If you earn $20,000 a year and hamburgers cost $2, then your real income is 10,000 hamburgers per year. Similarly, at $5 an hour, your real wage rate is 2.5 hamburgers per hour. Your real wealth is your nominal wealth divided by the price of hamburgers.

The underlying economic principle behind the calculation of real data is that it is these real rather than nominal magnitudes that affect people's behavior. For example, 50 years ago, when a dollar would buy a lot, most people would have been eager to work for $2 an hour. Now, when a dollar buys little, some people would rather watch television than work for $4 an hour. Similarly, in deciding whether to live like a prince or a pauper, you implicitly think about your real income and real wealth. Someone who behaves differently, who thinks in nominal rather than real terms, suffers from an economic myopia that economists call **money illusion**. Anyone who is pleased with a 3 percent increase in nominal income when prices increase by 10 percent is showing definite symptoms of money illusion.

## Inflation

The real value of our income and wealth depends critically on the price level. One reason that we study money and financial markets is that large increases in a nation's money supply often cause an increase in its prices. Figure 2.1 shows some evidence of this relationship using a scatter diagram of money and price data for 10 countries during the 1980s. The horizontal axis gives the annual rate of change of $M1$, a measure of a nation's money supply that includes cash and checking account balances. The vertical axis is the annual rate of change of consumer prices — the annual rate of inflation — in each of the 10 countries in the figure.

There is a rough positive correlation between money and inflation in that those countries with relatively slow money growth (Switzerland, Japan, and France) had relatively low inflation, while those countries with the fastest money growth (Britain, South Korea, and Spain) had relatively high rates of inflation. The correlation is by no means perfect, however. The money supply grew much faster in Britain than in Italy (16.54 percent annually versus 9.67 percent), yet the annual rate of inflation averaged 11.34 percent in Italy and 7.55 percent in Britain. In later chapters we will look more closely at how money affects prices and why other factors matter too.

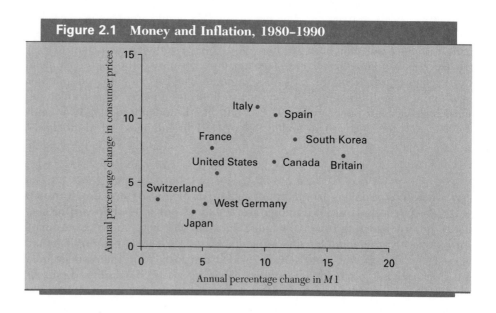

**Figure 2.1    Money and Inflation, 1980–1990**

## EXAMPLE 2.4   *Calculating the Consumer Price Index*

The example in the text used a single price, the price of hamburgers, but we do not live by hamburgers alone. We also buy milk, bananas, clothing, shelter, medical care, haircuts, and football tickets. The purchasing power of our dollars depends on the prices of a vast array of goods and services. Individuals with different tastes attach varying importance to different prices. The well-dressed person keeps a close eye on clothing prices, whereas a traveler notices the cost of airline tickets. People who don't smoke ignore cigarette prices; those who dislike football games ignore the price of football tickets.

To get a general, representative picture of real income, real wealth, and real interest rates, the federal government monitors the prices of thousands of goods and services and calculates several price indexes that measure the cost of representative commodity bundles. The best known is the **consumer price index (CPI)**, which measures the cost of living for typical U.S. households — the cost of food, clothing, shelter, VCRs, and the other necessities and luxuries we consume.

Every 10 years or so, the Department of Labor's Bureau of Labor Statistics (BLS) surveys thousands of households to learn the details of their buying habits — most recently in 1982–1984, when they interviewed more than 140,000 households nationwide. Half were interviewed every 3 months for five consecutive quarters about their major purchases (cars, televisions, and VCRs). The other half recorded their daily expenses in diaries for 2 weeks. Based on this survey, the BLS constructed a market basket of 2000 goods and services. Each month 250 agents call or visit stores in 56 cities to collect current price data on about 400 of these goods and services.

The resulting price data are used to calculate a price index, which measures the current cost of the market basket relative to the cost in a base period, that is,

$$P = 100 \frac{\text{current cost of market basket}}{\text{cost of market basket in base period}}$$

Here, for example, are some selected CPI data using a base period of 1982–1984:

| Year | CPI (100 in 1982–1984) |
|------|------------------------|
| 1970 | 38.8 |
| 1980 | 82.4 |
| 1990 | 130.7 |

These data allow us to compare consumer prices in the given years with the base year and with each other. For instance, consumer prices more than doubled between 1980 and 1970:

$$\frac{1980 \text{ CPI}}{1970 \text{ CPI}} = \frac{82.4}{38.8} = 2.124$$

and increased by nearly 60 percent between 1980 and 1990:

$$\frac{1990 \text{ CPI}}{1980 \text{ CPI}} = \frac{130.7}{82.4} = 1.586$$

One of the most difficult tasks in constructing price indexes is accounting for changes in the quality of goods and services. When the price goes up 10 percent but the box says "new and improved," should we believe it? If the quality has in fact improved 10 percent, then there hasn't really been any inflation. It's like buying a 10 percent larger size; you simply paid more to get more. However, how do you measure quality? Apple's Macintosh computers are very different from earlier Apple II computers and cost a lot more too. What is the percentage change in their quality? Medical doctors have drugs and equipment that didn't exist 20 years ago; their fees are also much higher, and they don't make house calls. What is the percentage change in the quality of medical services? On the other hand, many products have experienced what economists call "candy bar inflation." For years, candy bar prices were constant while the bars gradually became smaller and smaller. Other products and services have deteriorated similarly. Their quality has gone down rather than up. Statisticians try to make quality adjustments in the price indexes, but this task is difficult and subjective.

**EXAMPLE 2.5** *Zero Stroke*

The relationship between money and inflation is clearest in countries with extremely high rates of inflation or **hyperinflation**, where prices increase at double-digit rates weekly or even daily. In Argentina in the 1980s the money supply grew at a rate of nearly 200 percent a year; it is no surprise that Argentina also experienced extremely rapid inflation — with prices rising by nearly 300 percent a year. Even more extraordinary increases in the money supply fueled the German hyperinflation of 1922–1923, in which prices increased at a rate of 322 percent a month, and the Hungarian 1945–1946 hyperinflation, in which prices increased by 19,800 percent a month!

To foreign observers, these hyperinflations were a source of amusing anecdotes. The Hungarian government issued a 1,000,000,000,000,000,000,000,000-pengo note, which bought less than one U.S. penny. The *New York Times* told of an American in a Berlin restaurant who asked for all the dinner that a dollar bill would buy. He received a satisfying meal, but as he was about to leave, the waiter appeared with another soup and entrée, explaining, "The dollar has gone up again."* Others told of buying beer and receiving more for returning the empty bottle than they had paid for it full. The Associated Press sent out this satirical report:

> "Zero stroke" or "cipher stroke" is the name created by German physicians for a prevalent nervous malady brought about by the present fantastic currency figures.
>
> Scores of cases of the "stroke" are reported among men and women of all classes, who have been prostrated by their efforts to figure in thousands of billions. Many of these persons apparently are normal, except for a desire to write endless rows of [zeros].†

On January 1, 1992, Argentina made its fifth currency switch in 21 years, when the austral was replaced by the peso, with 10,000 australs worth 1 peso. A spokesperson for Argentina's central bank explained that the conversion was necessary because of all the digits required to do calculations with australs: "The calculators and computers we import do not have the capacity to do such large sums."‡ The conversion of 10,000 australs to 1 peso eliminated 4 digits; in all, the five currency changes made in Argentina between 1971 and 1992 eliminated 13 digits. Without these changes, the menu price of a 1-peso cup of coffee would read 10,000,000,000,000.

*New York Times, October 30, 1923.
†New York Times, December 7, 1923.
‡National C. Nash, "Argentina Returns to Peso, Saving Numerous Zeros," New York Times, February 10, 1992.

# IS HARD MONEY BETTER THAN SOFT?

With hard money, the denomination of the coin fixes the price of the underlying commodity. For example, when the U.S. $10 gold eagle contained 247.5 grains of gold, the implicit price of gold was $10/247.5 grains = $.040404/grain. The quoted dollar price for a commodity reflects the price of the commodity in gold: if the price of a bottle of wine is $10, this bottle of wine is worth 247.5 grains of gold. It follows that when gold is money, a gold discovery causes inflation: as gold becomes more plentiful, its value declines and it consequently takes more gold to buy other goods and services.

A hard money such as gold serves two purposes, as a commodity and as a medium of exchange. It is sometimes believed that the value of hard money relative to other commodities is determined solely by the value of the hard money as a commodity. This belief is false. It is true that the demand and supply for a commodity money as a commodity affect its price. It is equally and inescapably true, however, that the commodity's price is influenced by its

**Figure 2.2   Month-End Gold Prices**

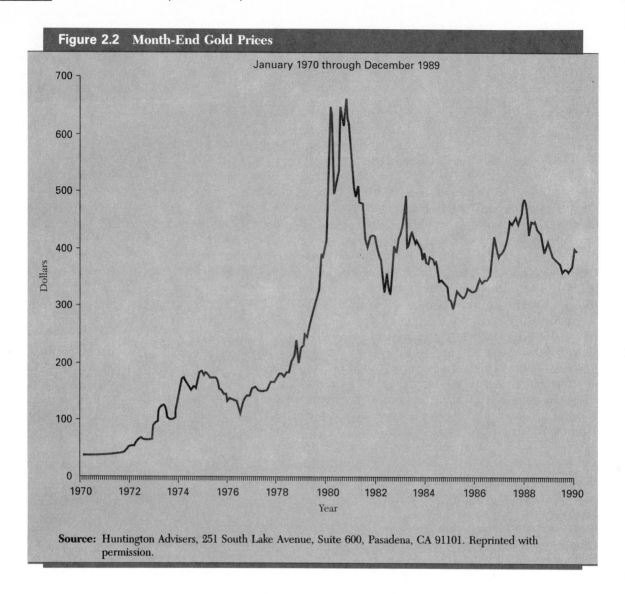

**Source:** Huntington Advisers, 251 South Lake Avenue, Suite 600, Pasadena, CA 91101. Reprinted with
permission.

demand and supply as a medium of exchange — by private citizens using the
commodity money to conduct business and by governments withholding the
commodity for current and future monetary use. Surely, if some commodity
were to fall out of fashion as a medium of exchange, thereby freeing large
quantities for use as a commodity, its value would drop precipitously.

It follows that the use of a commodity as a medium of exchange artificially
raises its price. Less of the commodity is available for use as a commodity, and
more time and effort are spent stockpiling it for monetary uses. The people of

Yap spent boats and lives bringing in worthless stones to use as a medium of exchange. The fact that it costs the United States more to make copper pennies than aluminum ones accurately reflects the fact that copper can be more usefully employed in things other than pennies. This is why Keynes called the use of gold as money a "barbarous relic" that wastes valuable resources. People and equipment are squandered digging holes in the ground, a pointless endeavor known as gold mining. Tongue in cheek, he suggested an easier expedient for increasing the money supply: to put paper currency in empty wine bottles and bury the bottles in existing, easily accessible mine shafts.

Turning this argument around, a prime virtue of a commodity money such as gold is that its limited availability prevents governments from arbitrarily expanding the money supply. With hard money, it is exceedingly difficult to create a hyperinflation. Thus hard money is traditionally advocated by those who favor stable prices. Creditors, of course, are first in line. For sound personal reasons, they object to debts being repaid with cheapened currency. Established merchants are also generally supporters of hard currency. Trade is easier and less worrisome when you can be confident of what the dollars you accept today will buy tomorrow.

The prices of precious metals, the historically predominant hard moneys, do fluctuate. The extraction of precious metals from the Americas quintupled prices in Spain during the sixteenth century. The California gold discoveries caused inflation in the 1850s, as did increased gold supplies at the turn of the century. The incentive to melt silver coins in the United States in the 1960s arose because sluggish supplies and rapidly increasing commodity demands (for such uses as electronic components and photographic film) pushed silver prices sharply higher. The wild gyrations in gold and silver prices in the 1970s and 1980s were front-page news.

Figure 2.2 shows gold prices since the early 1970s. Figure 2.3 shows that prices in the United States were hardly stable between 1793 and 1915, when its currency was backed by precious metal (usually gold). In fact, short-run price fluctuations in the United States were actually greater under the gold standard than under the fiat money system used since World War II.[4] On the other hand, there was no long-run upward trend in prices under the gold standard: the price level in 1915 was actually lower than in 1793. With fiat money, the trend in prices has been relentlessly upward, with the level of consumer prices in the United States in 1990 five times that in 1950.

The fact that three-quarters of the world's gold is produced in a few neighboring mines in South Africa is reason for concern about the future stability of gold production and prices. Silver supplies are more certain, because production is scattered throughout the United States, the Soviet Union, Mexico, Peru, and Canada, but there is considerable uncertainty about the industrial demand for silver. On the criterion of stable supply and demand (and excepting the fling by the American with a good boat), useless Yap stones were a better commodity money than gold or silver.

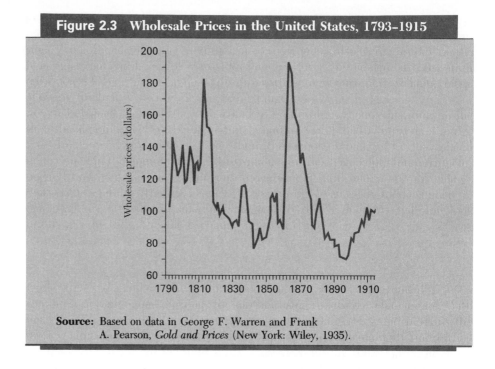

**Figure 2.3   Wholesale Prices in the United States, 1793–1915**

**Source:** Based on data in George F. Warren and Frank
A. Pearson, *Gold and Prices* (New York: Wiley, 1935).

While admitting that precious metal prices do fluctuate in unpredictable ways, hard-money supporters argue that this is a lesser evil than trusting governments to produce soft money. In the famous 1811 British debate on the gold standard, David Ricardo conceded that precious metals "are themselves subject to greater variations than it is desirable a standard should be subject to. They are, however, the best with which we are acquainted. . . . [Without a precious-metal standard, money] would be exposed to all the fluctuations to which the ignorance or the interests of the issuers might subject it."[5]

This debate reflects a deep philosophical disagreement over whether governments do things for citizens or to them. On the one side, with Ricardo in the nineteenth century and with the hard-money enthusiasts today, are those who believe that government officials exploit the citizenry or bungle well-meaning attempts at economic stabilization. On the other side are those who believe that governments can do things for the common good, including an intelligent and beneficial management of the nation's money supply. It is not necessary to divert precious metals from precious uses. It is not necessary to abandon a nation's money supply to the vagaries of commercial demand and discovery. Soft money can be reliably and steadily provided to accommodate commerce and serve dutifully as a medium of exchange.

Hard-money advocates point to the hyperinflations of history as evidence of government irresponsibility. Soft-money advocates look at the same history and argue that these episodes were infrequent and usually financed wars, including the American and French Revolutions.

# A SHORT HISTORY
# OF U.S. GOVERNMENT MONEY

In 1690, Massachusetts paid some of its soldiers with paper money that was redeemable in gold or silver. The colony did not have enough metal on hand to pay off these notes, but it hoped that future taxes would raise sufficient revenue. The notes multiplied faster than taxes and were eventually redeemed for a fraction of their face value. Rhode Island and South Carolina also issued large amounts of unbacked paper money that eventually had little, if any, value. In contrast, the Middle Colonies — Delaware, Maryland, New Jersey, New York, and Pennsylvania — all successfully introduced moderate amounts of unbacked paper money to stabilize prices and stimulate commerce. Unbacked paper money typically was used to finance government spending. However, Maryland conducted a successful experimental monetary policy by declaring a one-time dividend of 30 shillings to every citizen.

England disapproved of the colonists' soft money. New issues of paper money were prohibited in New England in 1751 and in the rest of the colonies in 1764. Many colonists agreed with this prohibition and worried that independence from England would bring irresponsible and destructive printings of unbacked paper money. As it turned out, the Revolutionary War was itself financed by nearly a half-billion dollars of paper money issued by the states and the Continental Congress. Hyperinflation followed. According to Galbraith,[6] a common saying was that "a wagon-load of money would scarcely purchase a wagon-load of provisions." In Virginia, shoes were $5000 a pair, and a full suit cost more than a million dollars. Although eventually redeemed at the rather generous rate of 1 cent of hard money to the dollar, the saying "not worth a Continental" became part of our national vocabulary.

Despite the indispensable role of paper money in financing the Revolution, the disruption caused by the ensuing hyperinflation led to the inclusion of strict monetary regulations in the U.S. Constitution. Only the federal government was permitted to mint coins, and both the state and federal governments were apparently prohibited from issuing paper money. Until the beginning of the Civil War in 1861, the only paper money in the United States was issued by private banks. During the Civil War, military expenditures were financed by the printing of unbacked "greenbacks" (paper money printed with green ink) in the North and unbacked Confederate notes in the South. With the collapse of the Confederacy, Confederate notes became worthless, except as collectors' items.

The constitutionality of the Northern greenbacks was debated in prolonged court battles. Ironically, Salmon P. Chase, who as Lincoln's Treasury Secretary asked Congress to authorize the issuance of greenbacks, later as Supreme Court Chief Justice spoke for the majority in 1870 in declaring them unconstitutional and vigorously dissented in 1871 when a changed court decided that they were constitutional after all.

The fate of the greenbacks also was a political issue, with various congresses voting to retire them or to issue more. In 1878, the Greenback Party, organized to promote the issuance of greenbacks, received more than a million votes and had 14 members elected to Congress. By 1879, commodity prices had fallen to prewar levels, and Congress made greenbacks redeemable in gold at a fixed price of $20.67 per ounce (a price that reflected the quantity of gold in U.S. gold coins since 1834). In addition, gold certificates were issued, and these were fully backed and redeemable in gold.

Earlier, in 1873, Congress had formally stopped the coinage of silver dollars. Because silver prices had been high relative to gold, silver had (by Gresham's law) been used commercially rather than coined for many years. The cessation of silver coinage in 1873 also was consistent with the universal gold standard favored by the leading European countries. Silver prices slumped subsequently, and silver miners in the western states pressed for the resumed coinage of silver dollars at the old rate of 371.25 grains per dollar. Such an action would have given them far more dollars for their silver than could be obtained in commodity markets. Debtors also saw unlimited silver coinage as a way to reverse the post–Civil War deflation. With more dollars being minted than being spent to acquire silver, the nation's money supply and prices would expand.

The unlimited-silver advocates founded the Populist Party and sent supporters, Populists and Democrats, to Congress. Congress swung toward soft money, resuming silver coinage in 1878, and then swung back, stopping it in 1893. In the 1896 election, silver coinage was the main campaign issue. The Republican candidate, William McKinley, supported a firm gold standard, arguing that "we cannot gamble with anything as sacred as money." His Democratic opponent, William Jennings Bryan, made an even stronger religious allusion in arguing for the free coinage of silver. He concluded his emotional speech to the Democratic convention with the memorable battle cry:

> We will answer their demand for a gold standard by saying to them:
> "You shall not press down upon the brow of labor this crown of thorns,
> you shall not crucify mankind upon a cross of gold."

Despite his stirring oratory, Bryan and silver coinage were soundly defeated in the 1896 election. The Gold Standard Act of 1900 ended the bimetallic standard, affirming what had, in practice, been the case for decades.

During the Great Depression in the 1930s, the gold backing for U.S. money effectively stopped. In 1933, all citizens were required to surrender their gold (other than rare coins and jewelry) to the government at the price of $20.67 an ounce. Gold certificates also were called in and exchanged for unbacked money. The official price of gold was raised to $35 an ounce, but, except for legitimate commercial uses, the Treasury sold gold only to foreign central banks and official institutions. From 1933 until 1975 it was illegal for citizens of the United States to own gold.

United States silver certificates had been issued since 1878, and they were redeemable for silver dollars (or silver stored at West Point). These silver dollars were usually token coins in that the silver the coins contained was worth less than a dollar. However, when silver prices rose in the 1960s, silver certificates stopped circulating and were instead either hoarded or redeemed (Gresham's law again).

Today, almost all the currency in circulation is in the form of Federal Reserve notes, unbacked paper issued by the Federal Reserve. Some $300 million, less than 1 percent of the circulating currency, are U.S. Treasury notes. These are the old greenbacks, first issued during the Civil War, and these, too, are now fiat money.

On July 15, 1980, the U.S. Treasury began marketing 1-ounce and 0.5-ounce gold medallions through the U.S. Postal Service. These medallions are emphatically not legal tender. No fixed dollar value is stamped on them. Instead, they are pieces of gold initially issued at a price about 2 percent above the prevailing price of gold on the commodity exchanges. As the price of gold fluctuates, so does the market value of these gold medallions. These medallions are intended to compete with the gold coins sold by more than 80 governments, including the South African Krugerrand and the Canadian Maple Leaf. The 2 percent premium covers minting costs and gives the government a small profit. In addition, it is hoped that the original buyer's filing of an application form with the government will encourage the payment of taxes on any realized capital gains. Gold enthusiasts hoped that these medallions would be the first step toward the return to a gold standard. In later chapters we will see that the future is more likely to bring the softest money of all — invisible electronic money.

## SUMMARY

Barter, the trading of goods and services for other goods and services, may be satisfactory in a small, closely knit community of largely self-sufficient people or in a communal or totalitarian society. In a large community, however, with specialized labor, private property, and voluntary exchange, barter is very inefficient, and trading instead involves a medium of exchange — a commonly exchanged item that people accept not to consume but to trade for other items. A money that serves as a medium of exchange also normally serves at least two other roles — as a unit of accounting and as a store of value.

A commodity — such as silver, gold, or tobacco — that is used as a medium of exchange is called a commodity money. An effective commodity money should be easily verifiable, intrinsically useful, conveniently transportable, divisible, and durable. Paper that is fully backed by commodities and coins that are made of precious metal are often called hard money. Gresham's law (bad money drives out good) implies that money that is more valuable as a commodity than as money will be withdrawn from circulation. An important cost to society of using a commodity money or hard money is that valuable resources are tied up in the medium of exchange. When commodities are used as money, shifts in demand for or supply of the commodity cause inflation or deflation.

Fiat money is something — such as Yap stones or unbacked paper dollars — that has little value as a commodity but, because of law or tradition, is accepted as a medium of exchange. Sellers accept fiat money in trades because they are confident that they can exchange it for useful goods and services. Fiat money, if its supply is limited, has value because it is useful as a medium of exchange. The danger with fiat money is that the government will not manage its supply responsibly.

To get a representative picture of real income, real wealth, and real interest rates, the federal government monitors the prices of goods and services and calculates several price indexes. The best known is the consumer price index (CPI), which attempts to measure changes in the cost of living for typical U.S. households.

# IMPORTANT TERMS

barter
commodity money
consumer price index (CPI)
debasement
fiat money
Gresham's law

hyperinflation
medium of exchange
money illusion
nominal
real
seigniorage

# EXERCISES

1. Which of the following would you classify as a commodity money and which as fiat money?

   a. Gold
   b. Woodpecker scalps
   c. Yap stones
   d. Rice
   e. Federal Reserve notes

2. Explain why each of the following would make a poor commodity money: oysters, diamonds, wine, sand, 1956 Corvettes.

3. Would you rather be paid your monthly salary in gold, old baseball cards, or paper dollars? Explain your reasoning.

4. Why does barter become less workable as people become more specialized?

5. Why is barter simplified when there is a "double coincidence" of wants? Provide an example.

6. Here is a simple four-person economy where each person produces a single item and now wants to trade some of that commodity for another commodity:

| Person | Produces | Wants |
|--------|----------|-------|
| Arlene | Apples | Bananas |
| Bill | Bananas | Donuts |
| Carol | Coffee | Apples |
| Dave | Donuts | Coffee |

If they use pure barter with no medium of exchange, no one can find another person who has what he or she wants and wants what he or she has. What is the minimum number of trades needed for everybody to get what they want if they use apples as a medium of exchange?

7. Is the trading of stones by the people of Yap an example of barter or a medium of exchange? Explain your reasoning.

8. For a hundred years, from 1834 to 1933, the official U.S. price of gold was $20.67 an ounce. If a horse sold for $10, what would have been its price in terms of gold (that is, ounces/horse)? If gold is $1000 an ounce, how much gold is needed to buy a 25-cent package of chewing gum?

9. Explain why the hoarding of rare coins by collectors is an example of Gresham's law.

10. Doesn't Gresham's law imply that fiat money will be driven out of circulation?

11. U.S. Silver Certificates were paper dollars redeemable in silver dollars, which generally contained less than a dollar's worth of silver. What does Gresham's law predict will happen if the price of silver increases so that the silver in a silver dollar is worth more than a dollar?

12. If, while the United States is on a gold standard, the growth of the economy causes the demand for gold to grow faster than its supply, will prices in general tend to rise or fall?

13. Between 1873 and 1896, while the United States was on a gold standard, wholesale prices fell by approximately 50 percent in the United States. What happened to the price of gold relative to the price of commodities during this period?

14. In 1834, the price of gold was set at $20.67 an ounce. Overall, consumer prices increased between 1834 and 1992 by a factor of about 12. If the relative price ratio of gold to consumer goods had been the same in 1992 as in 1834, what would have been the 1992 dollar price of gold?

15. Find the recent prices of gold and silver by looking in the "Money & Investing" section of the most recent Monday edition of *The Wall Street Journal* and locate a box entitled "Cash Prices." In the precious metals group, there are several gold and silver prices. Use the U.S. dollar spot prices determined in the London Friday P.M. fixings. How do these current gold and silver prices compare with the hypothetical prices calculated in the preceding exercise? How does the current gold–silver price ratio compare with the 16:1 ratio set in 1834? If the United States were on a bimetallic standard now with a gold–silver price ratio of 16:1, which metal would, by Gresham's law, be driven out of circulation?

16. Exercise 15 explains how to find some recent commodity prices in *The Wall Street Journal*'s "Cash Prices" box. Look up the prices of gold, corn, and butter for the last trading day for each of the last 12 months. Graph these price series. Which seems the most stable?

17. Gauge the stability of the three price series in Exercise 16 by calculating the standard deviation of each. Also calculate the standard deviation of the consumer price index during these 12 months, obtaining your data from a source such as the *Federal Reserve Bulletin* or the *Survey of Current Business*.

18. In the Mint Act of 1792, the U.S. Congress established a bimetallic standard with the price of gold fixed at $19.39 per troy ounce and the price of silver fixed at $1.292 per ounce — a gold–silver price ratio of 15:1. In 1796, France established a bimetallic standard with a gold–silver price ratio of 15.5:1. Which country do you suppose exported gold and used silver as currency?

19. Name an event that will cause inflation and one that will cause deflation if the United States changes to a monetary system in which all its money is backed by

   a. Gold.
   b. Buffalo.
   c. Postage stamps produced in 1945.

20. U.S. pennies that are made of copper contain 2/3 of a hundredth of a pound of copper. At what copper price (dollars per pound) can a profit be made by melting pennies?

21. In the 1970s, the price of gold increased much faster than the price of most goods and services. If we had been on a gold standard, would there have been inflation or deflation during these years?

22. In the 1960s, the industrial demand for silver grew much faster than silver supplies, sharply increasing the price of silver. If we had been using silver as a commodity money, would there have been an inflation or deflation in the 1960s?

23. An increase in the supply of a commodity generally reduces its price, yet an increase in the money supply usually increases prices. Explain why these two observations are either consistent or inconsistent with each other.

24. When the United States defined a dollar in terms of both gold and silver, the nation was legally on a bimetallic standard. In practice, however, the United States was on either a gold or a silver standard in that only one of these metals circulated as money. Will a legal two-metal standard always turn into a one-metal standard in practice?

25. Will a farmer with large debts benefit more financially from inflation or deflation? Explain your reasoning.

26. The consumer price index was 38.8 in 1970 and 130.7 in 1990. What was the percentage increase during this period?

27. What happens to real income if nominal income increases by 5 percent and if prices increase by 10 percent? What happens if prices fall by 5 percent? Assuming that only the price of hamburgers matters, use some illustrative calculations to confirm your reasoning.

28. The Bureau of Labor Statistics maintains consumer price indexes for several cities and metropolitan areas. Here are the values of some of these price indexes in July of 1986 (all indexes were set equal to 100 in 1967):

| | |
|---|---|
| San Diego | 383.1 |
| Denver | 358.4 |
| Milwaukee | 331.3 |
| Overall average | 328.0 |
| Philadelphia | 323.0 |
| Detroit | 318.4 |
| Chicago | 311.1 |

Do these data show that it is more expensive to live in Milwaukee than in Chicago? Why or why not?

29. It has been alleged that government statisticians underestimate quality improvements in what we buy. If so, will their estimates of inflation and real income be too high or too low?

30. Critically evaluate the following economic commentary:

*When it comes to measuring inflation, the average consumer can do a far better job than the economics experts. . . . Over the years I have been using a system which is infallible. . . . The Phindex [short for the Phillips index] merely requires you to divide the total dollar cost of a biweekly shopping trip by the number of brown paper bags into which the purchases are crammed. You thus arrive at the average cost per bagful.*

*When I started this system some 10 years ago, we would walk out of the store with about six bags of groceries costing approximately $30 — or an average of $5 per bag. . . .*

*On our most recent shopping trip, we emerged with nine bagsful of stuff and* *nonsense, totaling the staggering sum of $114. . . . the Phindex shows a rise from the initial $5 to almost $13, a whopping 153 percent.* [7]

31. Explain the error in this interpretation of inflation data:

    *In the 12-month period ending in December of 1980, consumer prices rose by 12.4 percent after a 13.3 percent increase the year before. Similar measures of inflation over the next three years were 8.9 percent, 3.9 percent, and 3.8 percent. . . . We are certainly paying less for what we buy than we were at the end of the Carter years.* [8]

32. Here are some Sotheby index data, based on auctions affiliated with Sotheby Parke Bernet: [9]

| | 1975 | 1982 | 1983 |
|---|---|---|---|
| Old master paintings | 100 | 199 | 217 |
| Chinese ceramics | 100 | 460 | 445 |
| Continental silver | 100 | 134 | 156 |

    a. Do Chinese ceramics cost more than continental silver?

    b. Which of these three would have been the best investment between 1975 and 1982? Between 1982 and 1983?

33. United States per capita gross national product (GNP) was $205 in 1885 and $16,704 in 1985. Prices in 1985 were, on average, 14.17 times 1885 prices. Calculate real per capita 1885 GNP in terms of 1985 prices; that is, how many dollars in 1985 did it take to buy what $205 bought in 1885?

34. When a child loses a baby tooth, an old tradition is for the tooth to be put under the child's pillow so that the tooth fairy can leave money for it. A survey by a Northwestern University professor indicates that the tooth fairy paid an average of 12 cents for a tooth in 1900 and $1 for a tooth in 1987. [10] The consumer price index was 25 in 1900 and 340 in 1987. Did the real value of tooth fairy payments rise or fall over this period? If tooth fairy payments had kept up with inflation, how large should the 1987 payment have been?

35. During the 1922–1923 German hyperinflation, people reported receiving more for returning their empty beer bottles than they had originally paid to buy full bottles. Could they have made a living buying beer, emptying the bottles, and returning them?

# CHAPTER 3

# The Foreign Exchange Market

*The Bank of England was the instrument of a ruling class. Among the powers the Bank derived from that ruling class was that of inflicting hardship. It could lower prices and wages, increasing unemployment. These were the correctives when gold was being lost; euphoria was excessive. Few or none foresaw that farmers and workers would one day have the power that would make governments unwilling to impose these hardships even in so righteous a cause as defense of the currency.*

**John Kenneth Galbraith**

Many financial transactions crisscross national borders. Countries with large trade surpluses, such as Japan and the oil-exporting nations, recycle their excess revenues by investing in the United States, Europe, and elsewhere. Individuals, businesses, banks, and governments borrow and invest worldwide. Japanese investors buy U.S. stocks, U.S. banks lend money to Brazil, and the Saudi Arabian government buys U.S. Treasury bills. Every day hundreds of billions of dollars worth of foreign currencies are traded worldwide by individuals, businesses, banks, and governments. The twin centers of this international foreign exchange market are New York and London, where currency traders are electronically linked to each other and to other trading areas.

Currency prices have real economic effects. A French company that plants grapevines, expecting to export wine to the United States, may find that by the time the vines mature, the value of the French franc has risen so much relative to the U.S. dollar that the wine cannot be exported profitably. Multinational companies that produce and market products in many countries are continually buffeted by currency revaluations. For example, the 1974 collapse of Franklin National Bank in the United States was due partly to losses incurred in its foreign exchange transactions. Another consequence of the linkage of world financial markets is that economic events in one nation have worldwide repercussions. When credit is scarce and interest rates are high in the United States, U.S. banks borrow in Europe, thereby raising interest rates abroad. When Latin American economies stumble, U.S. banks fail. When the Japanese stock market sneezes, Wall Street shudders.

In this chapter we will acknowledge that there are many national currencies and introduce an idea explored more fully later — that the interrelationships among currencies have important implications for the consequences of financial events and for the conduct of monetary policies. We will see how the gold standard once made national currencies commodity moneys and fixed the exchange rates among them. We will see why the gold standard collapsed and how exchange rates are determined today in the absence of a gold standard.

# THE BALANCE OF PAYMENTS

International transactions take many different forms. Americans buy French wine, and Russians buy American grain. Americans visit China, and the English tour the United States. Americans invest in the Japanese stock market, and Saudi Arabians buy Treasury bills. The U.S. government gives aid to Ecuador, and Japanese firms pay dividends to U.S. stockholders. Americans buy Swiss francs, and Brazilians buy dollars.

When an exhaustive compilation of all such transactions is made, the totals must balance. Every use of funds (such as spending, buying, investing) is someone else's source of funds. Sources equal uses, assets equal liabilities, and balance sheets always balance. Statisticians, economists, and politicians, however, traditionally focus on selected subsets of all transactions.

## *The Current Account*

Table 3.1 shows selected data for U.S. international transactions in 1991. It is a simplified version of the balance-of-payments accounts. One account in particular has long been of considerable interest: a nation's **merchandise-trade balance** (or, more simply, the **trade balance**), which is its exports of commodities minus imports. In 1991 the United States had a trade deficit of $60 billion; that is, it imported $60 billion more in merchandise than it exported. A nation's trade balance is often interpreted as a rough barometer of the competitiveness of its industries. By this standard, U.S. businesses are having difficulties competing with foreign businesses.

Long ago, when trade surpluses and deficits were financed by precious metals, the so-called mercantilists watched trade data because they believed that a nation's wealth was its holdings of gold and silver. Adam Smith, in his book appropriately named *The Wealth of Nations*, argued that this was a very incomplete accounting. Gold and silver may have value, but the sale of commodities for gold does not increase a nation's wealth. It merely substitutes one item for another — food for gold, clothing for silver. The true wealth of a nation

**Table 3.1**   **U.S. International Transactions, 1991 (billions of dollars)**

|  | Receipts | Payments | Cumulative Net |
|---|---|---|---|
| Merchandise |  |  |  |
| Exports | +430 |  |  |
| Imports |  | −490 | −60 = trade balance |
| Net services | +30 |  | −30 = goods-and-services balance |
| Net transfers | +20 |  | −10 = current-account balance |
| **Capital Account** |  |  |  |
| Foreign assets in U.S. |  |  |  |
| Foreign official assets | +10 |  |  |
| Other foreign assets | +40 |  |  |
| U.S. assets abroad |  |  |  |
| U.S. official reserve assets |  | 0 |  |
| Other U.S. gov't assets |  | 0 |  |
| U.S. private assets |  | −50 |  |
| Statistical discrepancy | +10 |  | +10 = capital-account balance |

is the quantity and productivity of its resources: its people, its land, and its capital. Only a miserly nation could be happy perpetually forgoing consumption in order to hoard metal.

By the same logic, spending U.S. dollars on German cars, Japanese televisions, and French wine is not a complete loss. Instead of buying U.S. goods, we buy foreign goods. The foreigners who accept these dollars will presumably eventually use them to buy the U.S. goods that we don't consume ourselves. If they don't, that is even better. Wouldn't you rather drive a Mercedes-Benz than count pieces of paper?

The **goods-and-services balance** is similar to the trade balance but includes services as well as goods. These services include interest and dividend payments, tourist expenditures, purchases and sales of military equipment, and foreign expenses of operating U.S. military bases. The **current-account balance** adds net transfer payments (including foreign aid and private gifts) to the goods-and-services balance; thus the current account includes all international purchases of currently produced goods and services and international transfer payments. Figure 3.1 shows some historical data on the U.S. merchandise-trade and current-account balances.

The current-account balance is important because any deficit or surplus must be financed by the sale or acquisition of financial assets — an increase or decrease in foreign claims against the United States, either U.S. dollars or assets that can be converted into dollars. In 1991 the United States had a current-account deficit of $10 billion that was financed by a $10 billion increase in foreign holdings of U.S. currency, bonds, stock, and other claims.

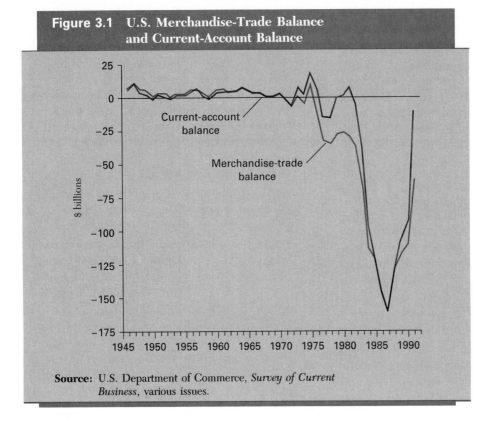

**Figure 3.1**  **U.S. Merchandise-Trade Balance and Current-Account Balance**

**Source:** U.S. Department of Commerce, *Survey of Current Business*, various issues.

## *The Capital Account*

The international purchases and sales of assets are collected in a nation's **capital account**. These transactions are labeled *capital outflows* and *inflows*, terms that can be confusing because they convey an image of something unilaterally leaking out of a country or pouring in. These data describe transactions, the exchange of one item for another. A capital outflow is a U.S. purchase of foreign assets; for example, U.S. dollars might flow out to purchase German bonds or Japanese stock. A capital inflow is a foreign purchase of U.S. assets, such as Germans buying Treasury bills and Japanese buying IBM stock.

A current-account deficit must be financed by a capital-account surplus (and vice versa). Table 3.1 shows a 1991 current-account deficit for the United States of $10 billion. U.S. expenditures on goods and services and transfer payments exceeded revenue by $10 billion, necessitating a $10 billion increase in foreign claims against the United States — a capital-account surplus of $10 billion.

Table 3.1 shows the composition of the capital-account surplus. Foreign assets in the United States increased by $50 billion; these transactions are entered in the capital account with a positive sign because they represent a capital inflow — money is paid to U.S. citizens to acquire these assets. U.S.

assets held abroad increased by $50 billion, which is entered with a negative sign because the money paid to foreigners to acquire these assets is a capital outflow. A statistical discrepancy, shown in the table, is inevitable because many international financial transactions escape the notice of government record keepers. Taking into account the 1991 statistical discrepancy of $10 billion, the capital account showed a surplus of + $50 billion − $50 billion + $10 billion = $10 billion.

It is natural to think of the current-account imbalance as causing an offsetting capital-account imbalance. If we want Taiwanese shoes, Japanese televisions, and German cars, then we must pay for them with U.S. dollars and Treasury bills. However, because of the unique position of the U.S. dollar as "world money," some observers use the capital-account imbalance to explain the current account. If the rest of the world wants U.S. dollars and Treasury bills, they must pay for them with shoes, televisions, and automobiles.

## *Financing Balance-of-Payments Deficits*

From World War II until 1975, the United States routinely exported more goods and services than it imported, with much of this export surplus financed by gifts to foreign individuals, organizations, and governments. Taking these gifts into account, the current-account balance fluctuated between surplus and deficit, approximately balancing over the years. Although the current account was in rough balance, the United States acquired long-term investments while supplying gold and dollars to carry out international trade. The U.S. dollar, in many ways, became "world money," the international medium of exchange.

A nation's **central bank** is the institution responsible for managing its money supply; the U.S. central bank is the Federal Reserve. Central banks hold **international reserves**, consisting of gold and foreign financial assets, that can be used, if needed, to make international transactions. Of the aggregate foreign assets held by central banks worldwide, roughly two-thirds are denominated in U.S. dollars. Central banks in large industrial countries hold almost entirely dollars, whereas developing countries have about half their reserves in dollars. In addition, 25 nations peg the value of their currencies to the dollar, including Afghanistan, Iraq, and Sudan.

Since 1975, the United States has run persistent current-account deficits, mostly the result of large trade deficits. The United States has financed its current-account deficit by selling U.S. currency, bonds, and stocks to foreign citizens, businesses, and governments. Before 1975, the United States traded liquid assets for illiquid ones; since 1975, the United States has traded liquid and illiquid assets for merchandise.

The fact that the United States has supplied dollars and other assets to the rest of the world does not imply that it is about to collapse. If anything, it is a healthy sign that U.S. balance-of-payments deficits allow the supply of world money to grow with international commerce. The international accumulation of

## EXAMPLE 3.1 *The Dollar as World Money*

If Coca Cola is the international soft drink and Big Mac the international hamburger, then the U.S. dollar is the international money. Foreigners own more than a trillion dollars in U.S. financial assets. At the end of 1991, U.S. banks alone held more than $700 billion in foreign deposits, denominated in dollars. Foreign banks hold hundreds of billions in Eurodollar deposits denominated in dollars. The worldwide preference for assets denominated in dollars rather than francs, yen, or rubles reflects a faith in the value of the dollar and its near-universal acceptability in international transactions — ranging from oil to grain to foreign exchange — where prices are quoted in dollars and trades are settled in dollars.

More than $150 billion in U.S. currency is held outside the United States, including 40 percent of the $100 bills. The U.S. dollar is the official currency in Liberia and Panama and is freely used alongside the shekel in Israel. The dollar is an unofficial medium of exchange in many countries, often accepted at a premium above the official exchange rate. In Brazil, Mexico, and other countries with rapid inflation, the dollar is said to be the poor person's Swiss bank — the easiest way to keep one's savings in a sound currency. In Russia, the dollar is used for black-market trades — those outside government-approved stores — because the dollar can be converted into other currencies and the domestic currency cannot. Hardly anyone outside Russia wants rubles; everyone wants dollars.

U.S. dollars reflects the international appeal of the dollar. When small countries have deficits, they must use their foreign-currency holdings — their international reserves — to pay their bills, because their domestic currencies are of little use to other nations. When their foreign-currency holdings are exhausted, such small countries are unable to run further deficits. With the United States, the situation is different. Foreign nations are willing to hold U.S. dollars because, as a world money, these dollars can be used to pay bills.

## EXCHANGE RATES

Almost every nation has its own domestic currency that is used for transactions within its borders — the U.S. dollar, German mark, Swiss franc, Japanese yen, British pound, and so forth. When transactions cross national boundaries, a currency conversion is usually necessary. For example, consumers in the United States have dollars to spend on wine, but French wine producers want francs to spend at their local McDonald's. Thus, when U.S. citizens buy French wine, their dollars will at some point be exchanged for French francs.

As is true of tomatoes, haircuts, and other goods and services, foreign currencies have prices at which they are bought and sold. The **exchange rate** is

**Table 3.2**   Selected Exchange Rates, November 6, 1991

| Country | U.S. Dollars per Currency | Currency per U.S. Dollar |
|---|---|---|
| Britain (pound) | 1.7725 | 0.5642 |
| France (franc) | 0.17835 | 5.6070 |
| Japan (yen) | 0.007692 | 130.00 |
| Germany (mark) | 0.6109 | 1.6370 |

**Source:** *Wall Street Journal*, November 7, 1991.

the price of one currency in terms of another — for example, the price of a French franc in U.S. dollars or German marks. The exchange rates for currency trades among banks (in amounts of $1 million or more) are reported each day in *The Wall Street Journal*. Table 3.2. shows some of these data for trades made on November 6, 1991. Two prices are given: the amount of U.S. dollars needed to buy one unit of the foreign currency and the amount of foreign currency needed to buy one U.S. dollar. The second price is, of course, just the inverse of the first. For example, a German mark costs 0.6109 U.S. dollars and conversely, a dollar costs $1/0.6109 = 1.6370$ marks.

*The Wall Street Journal* understandably reports most exchange rates relative to the dollar, the currency used by most of its readers. However, from these data we can calculate *cross-rates*, such as the price of the British pound in terms of marks:

$$\frac{1.7725 \text{ U.S. dollars/pound}}{0.6109 \text{ U.S. dollars/mark}} = 2.9032 \frac{\text{marks}}{\text{pound}}$$

Because it takes about $1.80 to buy a pound and $0.60 to buy a mark, $1.80 will buy either 1 pound or 3 marks, so it takes about 3 marks to buy a pound.

A nation's currency undergoes **depreciation** when foreign currency becomes more expensive; a currency **appreciates** as foreign currency becomes less expensive. Before World War I, a British pound cost $4.76; in 1991, it cost about $1.80. Over this period U.S. dollars appreciated relative to the pound, and the pound depreciated relative to the dollar.

Figure 3.2 shows the changes since 1970 in the value of the U.S. dollar relative to the Japanese yen, German mark, French franc, and British pound. Because these exchanges rates are stated in terms of U.S. dollars per unit of foreign currency, an increase in the value of the exchange rate reflects a depreciation of the dollar. (For ease of comparison, all four exchange rates have been scaled to equal 100 in March 1973.) There have been many zigs and zags, but overall, since the early 1970s the U.S. dollar has depreciated relative to the Japanese yen and German mark and appreciated relative to the French franc and British pound.

## Figure 3.2   Exchange Rates of Four Currencies Against the Dollar

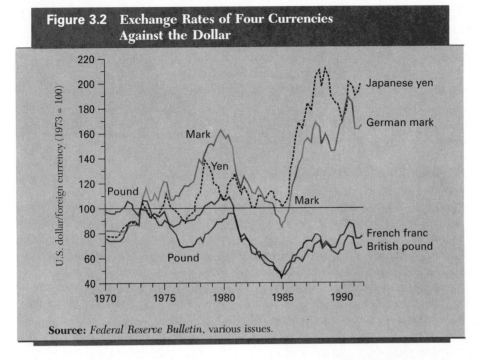

**Source:** *Federal Reserve Bulletin*, various issues.

## The Law of One Price

Exchange rates are important because they determine the domestic price of foreign goods. Suppose that a certain French wine costs 50 francs. What is the price of the wine in U.S. dollars? If a franc costs 20 cents, then the wine implicitly costs $10:

$$P = \left(0.20 \, \frac{\text{dollars}}{\text{franc}}\right)\left(50 \, \frac{\text{francs}}{\text{bottle}}\right) = 10 \, \frac{\text{dollars}}{\text{bottle}}$$

At an exchange rate of $0.20 to the franc, 50 francs cost $0.20(50) = \$10$. Alternatively, we can say that the exchange rate is $1/0.20 = 5$ francs to the dollar, and therefore, $10 costs $5(\$10) = 50$ francs.

In general, ignoring transportation costs, taxes, and other export and import expenses, the domestic price of a foreign item is equal to the exchange rate multiplied by the foreign price:

$$\left(\begin{matrix}\text{domestic price} \\ \text{of foreign item}\end{matrix}\right) = \left(\frac{\text{domestic currency}}{\text{foreign currency}}\right)\left(\begin{matrix}\text{foreign price} \\ \text{of foreign item}\end{matrix}\right)$$

These factors — domestic prices, foreign prices, and exchange rates — are roughly linked through what is called the **law of one price**: the domestic price of a foreign item should equal the domestic price of a comparable domestic item. If the U.S. price of the French wine is $10, then the U.S. price of a comparable

U.S. wine should also be $10. Otherwise, people will buy only the wine that is less expensive.

In general, the law of one price requires that

$$P_d = eP_f \qquad\qquad (3.1)$$

where

$P_d$ = domestic price of domestic item
$P_f$ = foreign price of foreign item
$e$ = exchange rate, domestic currency/foreign currency

In our example, $e = 0.20$ dollars/franc, $P_f = 50$ francs, and the law of one price implies a domestic price of

$$P_d = eP_f = \left(0.20 \,\frac{\text{dollars}}{\text{franc}}\right)(50 \text{ francs}) = 10 \text{ dollars}$$

In Equation 3.1, the law of one price equates the domestic price — dollars in our numerical example — of domestic and foreign products. The exchange rate $e$ is consequently defined as the amount of domestic currency needed to purchase one unit of foreign currency. We could equally well equate the foreign price — francs in our example — by rearranging Equation 3.1 and defining the exchange rate as $1/e$, the amount of foreign currency needed to buy one unit of domestic currency:

$$P_f = \frac{1}{e}P_d \qquad\qquad (3.2)$$

In our example, if the U.S. wine costs $P_d = 10$ dollars and the franc/dollar exchange rate is $1/e = 1/0.20 = 5$ francs/dollar, then the law of one price implies a foreign price of

$$P_f = \frac{1}{e}P_d = \left(5\,\frac{\text{francs}}{\text{dollar}}\right)(10 \text{ dollars}) = 50 \text{ francs}$$

It does not matter whether we convert the prices of comparable domestic and foreign products into domestic currency or into foreign currency. The law of one price states that, either way, comparable products should have the same price. Otherwise, people in both countries will shun the more expensive product.

The law of one price does not hold precisely, at least in the short run. For example, when the U.S. dollar depreciated in 1986 and 1987, the dollar prices of imported BMWs, Hondas, and Toyotas rose by more than 10 percent relative to the dollar prices of U.S. cars.[1] According to the law of one price, this should not have happened. The dollar prices of German, Japanese, and U.S. cars should have stayed aligned. As the dollar/mark and dollar/yen exchange rates $e$ increased, the dollar prices of U.S. cars $P_d$ should have risen or the mark prices of German cars and the yen prices of Japanese cars $P_f$ should have fallen, in accordance with Equation 3.1.

**EXAMPLE 3.2** *German Reunification*

In the spring of 1990, historic negotiations began for the reunification of East and West Germany. An essential part of German reunification was the adoption of a single currency, and the logical choice was the West German deutschemark, anchor of the European Monetary System. To accomplish this, East Germans would have to trade their ostmarks for deutschemarks. But at what exchange rate?

Before reunification, West Germans could buy ostmarks at the official exchange rate of 3 ostmarks for 1 deutschemark, but few of them wanted ostmarks. In East Germany, the black-market rate ranged from 5 to 7 ostmarks for 1 deutschemark. Before negotiations began, West German Chancellor Helmut Kohl suggested, at least for small savings accounts, a generous 1-to-1 exchange of ostmarks for deutschemarks.

However, in April of 1990, West Germany's central bank, the Bundesbank, prepared a confidential report recommending an exchange rate of 2 ostmarks for 1 deutschemark. This report was leaked to the press and set off a storm of protests among East Germans, who were hoping for a 1-to-1 exchange. Much of the ensuing debate was very emotional, with the East Germans arguing that a 2-to-1 exchange rate made them second-class citizens. Understandably, self-interest lay behind the protests of East Germans holding ostmarks.

Several persuasive economic arguments were put forward against a 1-to-1 exchange rate. Those holding ostmarks or savings accounts, bonds, and other assets denominated in ostmarks would surely benefit by receiving more deutschemarks for their ostmarks. Those with debts denominated in ostmarks, however, would be hurt by having to repay these debts 1-to-1 with deutschemarks. The Bundesbank estimated that East Germany's internal debts amounted to 400 billion ostmarks, the equivalent of $125 billion at a 2-to-1 exchange rate and $250 billion at a 1-to-1 exchange rate. In comparison with a 2-to-1 exchange rate, a 1-to-1 exchange rate would effectively transfer $125 billion from debtors to creditors.

The final negotiated agreement required all ostmarks to be deposited in bank accounts by June 30, 1990. On July 1, 1990, depositors were credited with deutschemarks — the first 4000 ostmarks at a 1-to-1 exchange rate, the rest at 2-to-1. For children under 14, the first 2000 were 1-to-1; for people over 59, the first 6000. Other financial assets and debts were converted at a 2-to-1 exchange rate.

A more fundamental problem was that East German products would not be competitive if wage rates and prices were converted 1-to-1 from ostmarks to deutschemarks. The accompanying table compares several preunification West German and East German prices. The East German government's subsidies of basic foods, apartments, and electricity made these bargains at a 1-to-1 exchange rate, but they didn't intend to subsidize the sale of these products to West Germans. In fact, their intention was the opposite — to eliminate these subsidies and move toward market-determined prices. For unsubsidized products, such as coffee and color televisions, the law of one price between East and West Germany required an exchange rate of at least 3-to-1.

Unsubsidized East German color televisions could not be priced at 4900 deutschemarks and compete with West German televisions priced at 1539 deutschemarks. If the East German television were comparable to the West German television, then it needed to have a similar price. No matter what the negotiated ostmark/deutschemark exchange rate, the makers of East German televisions inevitably had to price their product at approximately 1500 deutschemarks.

The underlying problem was that East German wages were too high relative to their productivity for their products to be competitive on world markets at a 1-to-1 exchange rate. To be competitive, East German workers either had to become more productive or be paid far fewer deutschemarks than ostmarks.

### Comparison of West German and East German Prices Before Unification

|  | West German Deutschemarks | East German Ostmarks | Law of One Price, Ostmarks/ Deutschemarks |
|---|---|---|---|
| Loaf of rye bread | 3.17 | 0.52 | 0.16 |
| 11 pounds of potatoes | 4.94 | 0.85 | 0.17 |
| Monthly apartment rent | 411 | 75 | 0.18 |
| Electricity (per kilowatt hour) | 0.42 | 0.08 | 0.19 |
| Color television | 1,539 | 4,900 | 3.18 |
| 2.2 pounds of coffee | 17.86 | 70 | 3.92 |

**Source:** Terence Roth, "East German Winners in Election Now Seek Fast Monetary Union," *Wall Street Journal*, March 20, 1990.

One reason for the nonadjustment of prices is that many items, like automobiles, are traded in imperfect markets with sluggish prices. As the dollar prices of BMWs, Hondas, and Toyotas rose relative to the dollar prices of Chevys and Fords, there was some shift in demand toward U.S. cars. This demand shift didn't translate into price adjustments, however. As the demand for U.S. cars rose, it was met by production rather than price increases.

The law of one price applies to domestic and foreign items that prospective purchasers consider to be comparable; it works best for products that are relatively homogeneous, such as wheat and steel. When consumers perceive unique qualities in different brands of aspirin, shoes, automobiles, and other products, these brand loyalties give firms some degree of monopolistic control over prices. Even though the dollar prices of BMWs and Toyotas rose relative to the dollar prices of U.S. cars, there was no mass exodus, because most BMW and Toyota buyers didn't consider U.S. cars to be good substitutes.

Another barrier to the law of one price is transaction and transportation costs, including tariffs, fees, quotas, and other trade barriers. To the extent that these barriers protect domestic industry, they promote price rigidities and disparities. Wine and automobiles can be relatively expensive in France if the French prohibit foreign alternatives or levy high import taxes. When import and export costs are prohibitively expensive, the affected goods and services are said to be **nontraded goods**. U.S. workers may be paid considerably more than British workers as long as commuting from England is not feasible. A haircut and a round of golf in Japan can cost much more than in the United States because it is impractical for the Japanese to have their hair cut in Iowa and play golf in Georgia.

The law of one price is most appropriate for raw commodities and for financial assets. Indeed, because international financial assets are good substitutes and can be traded relatively inexpensively, hectic international financial markets have developed. The law of one price for financial assets means that changes in U.S. interest rates quickly affect the financial markets of other nations, and vice versa.

For example, the **London interbank offered rate (LIBOR)** is a measure of what the large international banks charge each other for large Eurodollar loans — loans denominated in U.S. dollars. LIBOR is commonly used as an international benchmark to fix the minimum interest rate charged on Eurodollar loans by bank syndicates, often to foreign governments. In April of 1980, LIBOR and the U.S. prime rate (for loans from U.S. banks to the most financially sound U.S. businesses) were both around 20 percent. In June of 1980, LIBOR dropped to 9 percent, but the reported U.S. prime rate fell to only 12 percent. Big U.S. corporations, however, demanded and got loans from U.S. banks based on LIBOR rather than on the reported U.S. prime rate. They were able to do this because of their very real threat to borrow from foreign banks.

Most international transactions today are not imports and exports of wheat, steel, and automobiles but instead are financial transactions. Savers look worldwide, and so do borrowers. Ordinary households may not buy German bonds or British real estate, but banks, insurance companies, and pension funds do so on their behalf. The profits on such transactions depend not only on foreign interest rates but also on the appreciation or depreciation of foreign currencies. A German bond paying 20 percent won't be profitable for U.S. investors if the value of the mark falls by 30 percent relative to the dollar. We will look at such rate-of-return calculations in more detail in Chapters 6 through 8, after financial assets and interest rates have been discussed more fully.

## Purchasing Power Parity

The law of one price is sometimes applied to the overall price levels in two countries to determine the implied value of the exchange rate. We can rewrite Equation 3.1 as

$$e = \frac{P_d}{P_f} \tag{3.3}$$

where now

$P_d$ = domestic price index
$P_f$ = foreign price index
$e$ = exchange rate, domestic currency/foreign currency

Equation 3.3 implies the theory of **purchasing power parity**: the percentage change in the exchange rate between two currencies is approximately equal to the difference in their rates of inflation. We can express this relationship more simply as

$$\%\Delta e = \%\Delta P_d - \%\Delta P_f \tag{3.4}$$

If, for example, U.S. prices increase faster than Japanese prices, then the dollar must depreciate relative to the yen for U.S. products to remain competitive. Specifically, a 10 percent increase in U.S. prices and a 3 percent increase in

---

**EXAMPLE 3.3** *Hamburger Parity*

In September of 1986, *The Economist*, an influential British periodical, tested the theory of purchasing power parity by surveying the prices of McDonald's Big Mac hamburgers around the world. Some of their data are shown in the accompanying table. For customers, the Big Mac is a nontraded good, because an Australian won't go to Brazil or Canada to buy a hamburger and fries. Nonetheless, the implications of purchasing power parity are interesting.

According to purchasing power parity, the exchange rate in each country should be determined by $e = P_d/P_f$, where $P_d$ is the U.S. price of a Big Mac, $P_f$ is the foreign price, and $e$ is the U.S. dollar price of the foreign currency. For instance, the price of a Big Mac in 1986 was 12.50 cruzados in Brazil and $1.60 in the United States. The exchange rate required for hamburger purchasing power parity was

$$e = \frac{P_d}{P_f} = \frac{1.60 \text{ dollars}}{12.50 \text{ cruzados}} = 0.13 \frac{\text{dollar}}{\text{cruzado}}$$

At the actual exchange rate of 0.07 dollar/cruzado, the price of a Brazilian Big Mac was only $0.875, about half the cost in the United States:

$$(12.5 \text{ cruzados})\left(0.07 \frac{\text{dollar}}{\text{cruzado}}\right) = 0.875 \text{ dollar}$$

Even though Americans weren't about to fly to Brazil for Big Macs, *The Economist* concluded that by the hamburger standard, the dollar was overvalued against the cruzado, suggesting that the dollar/cruzado exchange rate should increase. As the accompanying table shows, this did in fact happen over the succeeding 3 years, though by more than predicted by hamburger parity. For the first four countries in the table, the U.S. dollar seemed substantially overvalued. In three cases, the exchange rate did move in the right direction; in the fourth, Hong Kong, there was no change. The U.S. dollar seemed significantly undervalued relative to the currencies of the last four countries in the table. In three of these cases there was virtually no change in the exchange rate; in the fourth, Japan, the dollar became even more undervalued.

Although hamburger parity did not predict the exact movements in these eight exchange rates, it did succeed in separating the countries into two groups, one of which experienced substantially more appreciation relative to the U.S. dollar.

### The Implications of Hamburger Parity

| | Local Price, $P_f$ | Exchange Rate | | | Percentage Change |
|---|---|---|---|---|---|
| | | Implied, $P_d/P_f$ | Actual in Sept. 1986 | Actual in Sept. 1989 | |
| **Dollar overvalued:** | | | | | |
| Australia (dollar) | 1.75 | 0.91 | 0.61 | 0.76 | 24.6 |
| Brazil (cruzado) | 12.50 | 0.13 | 0.07 | 0.36 | 414.3 |
| Canada (dollar) | 1.89 | 0.85 | 0.72 | 0.85 | 18.1 |
| Hong Kong (dollar) | 7.60 | 0.21 | 0.13 | 0.13 | 0.0 |
| **Dollar undervalued:** | | | | | |
| France (franc) | 16.40 | 0.10 | 0.15 | 0.15 | 0.0 |
| Japan (yen) | 370 | 0.0043 | 0.0065 | 0.0070 | 7.7 |
| Sweden (krona) | 16.50 | 0.10 | 0.15 | 0.15 | 0.0 |
| West Germany (mark) | 4.25 | 0.38 | 0.50 | 0.51 | 2.0 |
| United States (dollar) | 1.60 | | | | |

**Source:** "On the Hamburger Standard," *The Economist*, September 6, 1986.
Copyright © 1986 The Economist Newspaper. Reprinted with permission.

Japanese prices implies a 7 percent depreciation of the dollar relative to the yen (a 7 percent increase in the number of dollars needed to buy yen):

$$\%\Delta e = 10\% - 3\% = 7\%$$

Because purchasing power parity is derived from the law of one price, it is subject to the same limitations, including transaction and transportation costs — the extreme case being nontraded goods. Nonetheless, Equations 3.1 and 3.4 help us remember the approximate relationship among domestic prices, foreign prices, and exchange rates. If, for example, the dollar depreciates relative to the mark, what pressures will be exerted on German and U.S. prices? If $e$ is the dollar price of a mark, then a dollar depreciation raises $e$. According to Equation 3.1, an increase in $e$ should put upward pressure on U.S. prices while restraining German prices. This makes good sense. When the dollar depreciates, the dollar prices of imports rise (and the foreign prices of U.S. goods decline), making U.S. goods more attractive and foreign goods less so. This shift in demand from foreign to U.S. goods tends to increase U.S. prices relative to foreign prices. These price adjustments may be slow and imperfect, but Equation 3.1 helps us remember the direction in which prices are pushed and pulled.

Let's try another example. If some economic event causes prices to increase in the United States, how will these higher domestic prices affect foreign prices and exchange rates? According to Equation 3.1, as $P_d$ increases, $e$ or $P_f$ also should increase. Thus U.S. inflation should cause foreign inflation or depreciation of the dollar. Again, this makes good sense. As U.S. prices increase, demand will shift to foreign goods, and people will exchange dollars for foreign currencies to carry out these transactions — putting upward pressure on the foreign prices of foreign goods and on the dollar prices of foreign currencies.

In addition to purchasing power parity, exchange rates are also influenced by investors who buy and sell currencies, looking for high rates of return, including anticipated changes in exchange rates. We will consider this influence in detail in later chapters.

# THE GOLD STANDARD

Because exchange rates have important effects on the relative prices of domestic and foreign goods, let's consider how exchange rates are determined. As explained in Chapter 2, the United States adopted a **bimetallic standard** in 1792 with fixed prices for gold and silver. In 1834 the official price of gold was adjusted from $19.39 to $20.67 an ounce, making silver, in comparison with gold, too valuable as a commodity to be used as a medium of exchange.

After 1834, with the exception of the Civil War and an occasional financial panic, the United States was effectively on a **gold standard**, in which the government bought and sold gold at the fixed price of $20.67 per ounce. Consistent with this commitment, the U.S. $20 gold piece contained a little less than an ounce of gold, and the U.S. $10 golden eagle contained slightly less than a half-ounce of gold.

Most other countries were on a bimetallic standard until the late 1870s, when an international gold standard was established. The British government bought and sold gold at the fixed price of 4.34 British pounds per ounce of gold. If an ounce of gold could be freely traded for 20.67 U.S. dollars or 4.34 British pounds, then 20.67 U.S. dollars had the same value as 4.34 British pounds. Thus one British pound was worth 20.67/4.34 = 4.76 U.S. dollars, and this was the fixed exchange rate at which dollars and pounds were traded. There were similar fixed exchange rates between all gold-standard currencies: *an international gold standard fixes the currency exchange rates for all participating nations.*

Importers, exporters, and banks that deal in foreign exchange generally favor fixed exchange rates because they eliminate the risk of losses caused by unexpected changes in exchange rates. There are invariably delays between when a deal is struck and when final payment is received. Exchange-rate fluctuations during such a delay can turn a good deal into a bad one — a risk that most merchants would rather not worry about. Just as it is widely believed that price instability impedes domestic commerce, so it is thought that exchange-rate instability hinders international commerce. In later chapters we will discuss many financial contracts that have been developed to help businesses deal with fluctuating exchange rates.

## Automatic Balance-of-Trade Equilibrium

Economists in the 1800s (whom we now call *classical economists*) generally favored fixed exchange rates because they seemingly made chronic balance-of-trade deficits impossible. Recall the law of one price:

$$P_d = eP_f$$

Let $P_d$ be the U.S. price level and $P_f$ the British price level. The exchange rate $e$ is fixed by the international gold standard.

Now suppose that U.S. prices double, perhaps because of a gold discovery and consequent increase in the U.S. money supply. Then, temporarily, $P_d > eP_f$ and U.S. items are more expensive than their English counterparts. Both English and U.S. consumers will shift to English goods, and U.S. dollars will flow to the English, who will redeem these dollars for gold at the U.S. Treasury. As the United States loses gold, its money supply will shrink (because, under a pure gold standard, money consists solely of gold and notes backed by gold), and U.S. prices will presumably fall. Similarly, the increased gold in England will expand the English money supply, thereby increasing English prices. In this way, $P_d$ falls and $P_f$ rises until $P_d = eP_f$ is restored and the balance-of-trade deficit is eliminated. Only when this trade deficit ceases does the flow of gold stop exerting its pressure on prices.

altered the two nations' money supplies, inducing these equilibrating price adjustments. In the late 1920s, however, the inclination was to stabilize the money supplies — in one nation to avoid deflation and in the other to avoid inflation. As a result, $P_d$ remained below $eP_f$, and the balance-of-trade disequilibria persisted.

As long as the nations resisted a realignment of prices, the only way out of this impasse was for the exchange rate to adjust: here, $e$ must decline, making the second nation's currency less expensive. If the governments delay adjusting the exchange rate, the situation becomes exacerbated by speculators who anticipate a future adjustment. Expecting the value of the second currency to decline, speculators trade the second currency for the first. To maintain the fixed exchange rate, the two governments must accommodate these speculative demands by using their holdings of the first currency to buy up the second. The dam breaks when the governments decide that an unrealistic fixed exchange rate is no longer worth saving.

During the Great Depression, the shaky international gold standard of the 1920s came crashing down like everything else. Two dozen countries, including England, suspended gold payments in 1930 and 1931. Another dozen followed in the first few months of 1932. The United States held out until Franklin Roosevelt's inauguration in March of 1933. By 1936, virtually every country had greatly modified or completely abandoned the gold standard.

The Gold Reserve Act of January 1934 nationalized all U.S. gold, requiring citizens to turn in their gold and gold coins at the government's new (higher) price of $35 an ounce. Gold could be held privately only for "legitimate" nonmonetary uses. The U.S. government no longer sold gold to private citizens, but it did trade gold at the new price with foreign governments and central banks.

During the remainder of the 1930s, gold poured into the United States, much of it due to the export stimulus provided by devaluation of the dollar. In addition, both people and gold immigrated to the United States, refugees from the political and economic turmoil in Europe. The increase in gold prices also stimulated gold production. In all, the U.S. Treasury's gold stock swelled from $4 billion in the beginning of 1934 to $23 billion in 1941.

# BRETTON WOODS

Before World War II came to an end, an international monetary conference was held in July of 1944 at the Mount Washington Hotel in Bretton Woods, New Hampshire. More than 700 persons from 44 countries came to this small mountain resort to construct a workable international monetary system. As with most such conferences, a plan had been drafted by a few experts and largely accepted beforehand by the principal nations. In this case, England and the United States were the most important participants, and the primary architects were the English economist John Maynard Keynes and Assistant Secretary of the U.S. Treasury Harry D. White.

**EXAMPLE 3.4**  *Who Can Devalue the Most?*

One reason for the collapse of the gold standard in the 1930s was that international lending dried up in the Great Depression. Many governments had borrowed heavily to prop up their overvalued currencies. When these loans were not renewed and new funds could not be found, these governments had no choice but to suspend gold payments at the old prices. In addition, many nations saw their inflated exchange rates as a restraint on foreign sales. With their economies sinking fast, they tried to boost export demand by leaving the gold standard and devaluing their currency. Such actions accomplish little, however, when all nations are devaluing their currencies. For example, by the spring of 1933, the British pound had been devalued by 30 percent against the U.S. dollar (its price had been reduced to $3.40). However, most other currencies also had been devalued against the U.S. dollar by 30 percent or more. Thus the British had only gained ground against the Americans in their efforts to stimulate export demand.

Roosevelt's decision to devalue the dollar was largely intended to offset these earlier devaluations by other nations. He raised the dollar price of gold from $20.67 to $35 an ounce on January 31, 1934, offsetting most of the foreign devaluations and more than offsetting some of them; for example, the dollar price of the British pound was raised from $3.40 to slightly over $5, compared with $4.76 under the old gold standard.

In essence, each nation was trying to stimulate its economy by selling its goods to foreigners at bargain prices and found it easier to devalue the currency than to endure a domestic deflation. Even today, many governments have the peculiar idea that instead of encouraging domestic consumption, it is better to stimulate output and employment by depreciating their currency.

Similarly, some countries sell products to foreigners for less than their own citizens pay. At the request of U.S. businesses, the U.S. and Japanese governments sampled the prices of 124 Japanese and U.S. products in 1989. They found that 60 percent of the Japanese products could be purchased for less in the United States than in Japan and that 10 percent of the U.S. products cost less in Japan than in the United States.* For example, a car made in Japan that sold for the equivalent of $16,880 in Tokyo sold for $13,507 in Chicago. A car made in the United States that sold for $13,507 in Chicago sold for $25,613 in Japan. A Japanese-made laser printer sold for $2903 in Tokyo and $1878 in Chicago.

Another variation on this logic is the argument that foreign aid benefits the donor country economically: foreigners will buy more imported products if given the money to do so. Such subsidized purchases do increase domestic production, but producing goods for others is not an economic gain. Foreign aid should be justified only as a gift, which is what it is.

*Art Pine, "Japanese Pay More When the Label Reads 'Made in Japan,'" Los Angeles Times, November 8, 1989.

The **Bretton Woods agreement** attempted to restore fixed exchange rates without the domestic disruption caused by the pure gold standard. Exchange rates were fixed by specifying currency prices in terms of gold, although governments sold gold only to each other (and not to their citizens) at these official prices. For example, the U.S. gold price was $35 an ounce and the initial English gold price was 8.75 British pounds per ounce, so the fixed exchange rate was $4 per British pound:

$$\frac{35.00 \text{ dollars/ounce}}{8.75 \text{ pounds/ounce}} = 4 \frac{\text{dollars}}{\text{pound}}$$

The participating nations agreed to make whatever currency transactions (using dollars to buy pounds, for example) were necessary to keep exchange rates within 1 percent of the initial fixing. In exceptional circumstances, a nation would be permitted a one-time devaluation of up to 10 percent.

A central reserve fund, the **International Monetary Fund (IMF)**, was established to loan money to nations that needed to purchase their currency in order to support its value. Instead of the deflationary shock inflicted by the pure gold standard, these loans would give a nation time to take gradual steps to strengthen its currency; an escalation of the fees on these loans was intended to discourage procrastination.

The central reserve fund — $6.8 billion in gold, U.S. dollars, and other strong currencies — was financed by contributions from the members, principally the United States and Britain. The IMF was given a home in Washington, D.C., and a staff to administer the reserve fund and to advise and prod nations with weak currencies. In 1970 the IMF expanded its reserve base even further by creating "paper gold," **special drawing rights (SDRs)**, which are credited to members and can be used within the IMF to purchase hard currency. For example, the Bank of England can sell SDRs to the U.S. Treasury in order to obtain dollars that can be used to pay for imports or to buy British pounds and thereby support the value of the pound in the foreign exchange market. Several countries, including Burundi, Iran, and Libya, peg the value of their currencies to SDRs.

The SDR was initially valued at one U.S. dollar. Since 1974, the value of SDRs relative to the dollar has been determined by a weighted average of the exchange rates of major industrial countries, using their exports and currency holdings as weights. Currently, the value of an SDR is based on the value of the British pound, French franc, German mark, and Japanese yen, relative to the dollar. The value of the SDR rose to $1.30 in 1980 (as the dollar weakened), fell to $0.96 in 1985 (as the dollar strengthened), and then rose to $1.40 in 1991.

A small number of international securities have been issued with values indexed to SDRs, and several private banks have offered SDR-denominated deposits and loans which, because the value of the SDR is a weighted average of major currencies, are intended to reduce exchange-rate risks for international banks and businesses. However, SDR-denominated securities and contracts have not turned out to be especially popular, and their aggregate value is minuscule compared to those denominated in a single currency, such as the dollar.

Two other large international institutions are the World Bank and the Bank for International Settlements (BIS). The World Bank was established at the same time as the IMF in 1944. It is legally owned by 135 governments and supported by contributions from these nations. The World Bank borrows in world financial markets and makes long-term loans to develop agriculture and industry in the world's poorest countries, many of which cannot borrow from the IMF or private banks. Mixing metaphors, Alden Clausen, former World Bank president, said that World Bank loans are needed when "a country is really behind the goal posts and needs to borrow for a very long time at a marginal interest rate in order to keep the patient alive and effect the cure."[2]

The Bank for International Settlements was established after World War I to handle Germany's war reparations payments. These payments ended in 1980, but the BIS had by then been thoroughly transformed into a $50 billion central bank for central banks. The BIS invests about 10 percent of the world's official central bank reserves, transfers funds from one central bank to another, and makes short-term loans to central banks.

## Fatal Weaknesses

As noted earlier, the intention of the Bretton Woods agreement was to re-establish the stable exchange rates that everyone seemed to favor without the booms and busts that accompanied the international gold standard. This separa-tion was to be made possible by the central reserve fund, which would allow a nation time to choose the best way to strengthen its currency. It sounded plausible on paper and worked reasonably well for nearly 30 years, but it was undone by two eventually fatal flaws.

The first was that internationally mobile capital stalked overvalued curren-cies like vultures circling a wounded animal. Suppose, for instance, that at the official exchange rate of $4 per British pound, British goods are too expensive to compete with U.S. goods. Perhaps a sweater made in the United States costs $25 and a comparable sweater made in Britain costs 10 pounds. Neglecting transpor-tation costs, the dollar cost of the British sweater is

$$\left(4 \, \frac{\text{dollars}}{\text{pound}}\right)(10 \text{ pounds}) = 40 \text{ dollars}$$

The pound is overvalued at $4 in that British goods are too expensive to compete on world markets.

Speculators who expect the pound to be devalued will borrow pounds and sell them for $4, betting that they will be able to buy pounds back at a lower price. From the speculators' viewpoint, this is a one-sided bet. The overvalued pound is surely not going to be revalued upward. The worst that can happen is that the exchange rate won't change, with no loss to the speculator other than interest and transaction costs. If a devaluation is forced, then the speculator will enjoy a large gain on a brief investment.

To preserve the $4 exchange rate, England has to buy pounds from speculators at $4. When England's dollar reserves are exhausted and it is forced to devalue the pound, speculators make profits and the British government absorbs losses. Persistent, massive speculative selling of overvalued currencies during the Bretton Woods years meant that nations did not, in fact, have much time to take the fundamental economic steps necessary to correct the problem.

The second flaw in the Bretton Woods agreement was that nations were too often unwilling to take these necessary steps. In our example, the British pound is overvalued at $4, British products are too expensive on world markets, and the country runs persistent balance-of-trade deficits. If the $4 exchange rate is to be preserved and the balance-of-trade deficit eliminated, then only two options are available. Either Great Britain must have deflation to make its products cheaper, or other countries must have inflation to make their products more expensive.

In practice, governments had little enthusiasm for engineering either inflation or deflation to correct balance-of-trade problems. Eventually, they decided that the benefits of maintaining fixed exchange rates were not worth the costs.

## *The Fall of Bretton Woods*

Under the Bretton Woods agreement, currency prices were specified in terms of gold. One benefit of this arrangement was that a nation confronted with a trade deficit could simultaneously devalue its currency against all other currencies. In 1949 the English gold price was increased 30 percent, from 8.75 to 12.50 British pounds per ounce, reducing the pound's exchange rate with respect to all other fixed currencies by 30 percent. For example, the dollar–pound exchange rate fell 30 percent, from $4 per British pound to

$$\frac{35.00 \text{ dollars/ounce}}{12.50 \text{ pounds/ounce}} = 2.80 \frac{\text{dollars}}{\text{pound}}$$

The United States played a crucial role in this arrangement because it had the strongest economy and owned three-fourths of the Western world's monetary gold. U.S. dollars served as the world's money. Dollars were used for many transactions and held as reserves by most central banks. The U.S. dollar took its place alongside gold as an internationally accepted medium of exchange and as evidence that a central bank had something solid behind its currency.

One aspect of this special role was that nations used dollars to support their exchange rates. If the British pound was weak, the Bank of England would use some of its U.S. dollar reserves to buy British pounds and thereby support the price of the pound, relative to other currencies. Whereas nations had before redeemed their paper currencies with gold, they now redeemed them with U.S. dollars. The United States did not have to use foreign reserves to stabilize dollar exchange rates because other nations stabilized their currencies relative to the dollar. The second aspect of the privileged role of the United States was that all nations were keenly interested in the soundness of the U.S. dollar. Because they were holding dollars to serve like gold in backing up their currencies, central bankers wanted the dollar to be, in fact, as good as gold.

The Bretton Woods system worked tolerably well through the 1950s. The British pound and several other currencies had been initially overvalued, but this problem was corrected by devaluations in 1949. Through the 1950s, Britain, Italy, and several smaller countries seemed to have chronic difficulties, but at least the system held together. In the 1960s, however, people began to wonder aloud if the U.S. dollar really was as good as gold, at least at $35 an ounce.

The United States had been steadily supplying dollars to the world and exchanging gold for some of these dollars. By 1960 the foreign liquid short-term claims against the United States exceeded the value of the U.S. gold stock (at $35 an ounce). Because the United States no longer had enough gold to meet these foreign claims, many expected the U.S. dollar to be devalued against gold.

After the price of privately traded gold reached $40 an ounce on the London and Zurich gold markets, the United States and the leading Western European nations formed a "gold pool" to peg the free market price of gold at $35 an ounce by committing their resources to buy or sell gold at that price. They managed to hold the market price at $35 an ounce until 1968, largely because the private gold market was very thin, with light trading, while governments held enormous gold reserves.

In 1968 the levels of wholesale and consumer prices in the United States were about twice what they had been when the Bretton Woods agreement was signed and three times their levels when Franklin Roosevelt set the price of gold at $35 an ounce in 1934. It would have been pretty surprising if the free-market price of gold also hadn't increased by 1968. In March of 1968, U.S. inflation and the flow of dollars abroad to pay for the Vietnam War finally burst the $35 lid. In the preceding 6 months, the gold pool had been forced to sell $4 billion in gold; with a 60 percent share in the pool, the United States furnished $2.5 billion of this gold.

There seemed to be only three options: the central banks could sell the rest of their gold, the United States could have domestic deflation, or the market price of gold could be allowed to rise. The central banks chose the third option. An emergency two-tier system was established. One tier was the private gold market; the second was the monetary gold market in which governments traded gold with each other at the official fixed price. The United States continued to sell gold for "legitimate monetary uses" at $35 an ounce and continued to lose gold reserves.

The free-market price of gold unexpectedly fell below $35 an ounce in 1969 and then abruptly shot upward in the fall of 1971. The U.S. Treasury suspended gold sales to foreign governments in August of 1971 and temporarily allowed the dollar to float in foreign exchange markets. It was expected that the dollar would be devalued and that the Bretton Woods agreement could then be revived at new, more realistic exchange rates.

An emergency conference was held at the Smithsonian Institution in Washington, D.C., in December of 1971, with President Richard Nixon hailing the resulting agreements as the greatest monetary reform in the history of humanity.

This was somewhat of an overstatement. The official U.S. price of gold was raised to $38 an ounce, although the United States would not sell gold at this price. The official gold prices of other major currencies also were raised, with the net effect that the U.S. dollar was devalued about 12 percent relative to other currencies. Governments agreed to support these new currency exchange rates, allowing fluctuations within a 5 percent range.

In February of 1973, the dollar had to be devalued again, this time raising the official gold price to $42.22 an ounce, and in March of 1973, fixed exchange rates finally were abandoned. Since then, the major exchange rates have been determined in the open market. (Most small countries have kept their currencies pegged to major currencies.) Because governments still intervene in exchange markets to stabilize their currency, to support its value, or to devalue it to encourage exports, this is called a *managed*, or "dirty," *float*. We will now look briefly at how these flexible exchange rates work.

# FLEXIBLE EXCHANGE RATES

Under the gold standard, the trading of currencies was fairly uneventful — just a routine swapping of one currency for another using the fixed exchange rate. With flexible exchange rates, the currency market is the largest — and perhaps the most volatile — market in the world, with prices often changing by more than 5 percent in a single day.

## The Foreign Exchange Market

Unlike the New York Stock Exchange, the foreign exchange market is not a single physical location where traders meet face to face. Instead, traders are scattered throughout the world and trade currencies using telephones and computer terminals. Among the participants are importers who need foreign currency to pay for products, exporters who want to convert a foreign currency they receive into domestic currency, hedgers who do business internationally and want to protect themselves against unforeseen fluctuations in the prices of foreign goods and services, and speculators who want to bet on the movements of currency prices.

Worldwide, total currency trading exceeded $400 billion a day in 1989, more than 50 times the daily volume of exports of goods and services, with the largest trading centers in London, New York, Tokyo, Frankfurt, and Singapore. Foreign exchange trading in New York averaged $130 billion a day in 1989. The traded currencies are not, however, carried from one country to another. Instead, bank accounts are debited and credited.

Suppose, for instance, that a U.S. importer owes 1 million francs to a French exporter and that the current exchange rate is 0.20 dollar/franc so that the cost of 1 million francs is $200,000. The U.S. bank used by the importer buys 1 million francs from the French bank used by the exporter. Table 3.4 shows that this $200,000 does not leave the United States; the U.S. bank simply debits $200,000 from the importer's account and credits it to the French bank, and the French bank then credits 1 million francs to the exporter's account. The French bank now has a $200,000 deposit in the U.S. bank that it can use to earn interest or to

**Table 3.4  Transactions Between U.S. Importer and French Exporter***

| U.S. Bank Deposits | | French Bank Deposits | |
|---|---|---|---|
| U.S. importer | − $200,000 | French exporter | + 1 million francs |
| French bank | + $200,000 | | |

*U.S. importers do not mail dollars to French exporters. Instead, a French bank receives dollar deposits in a U.S. bank and credits the exporter with a deposit of francs.

fulfill obligations from French importers. The two banks might even be international branches of the same bank.

If the French bank does not want to hold a deposit of U.S. dollars because it fears they will depreciate, it can sell these dollars for francs or for another currency that it hopes will appreciate in value. This transaction will involve a debiting of its dollar account at the U.S. bank and a crediting to the account of the party that buys these dollars, either at this bank or another one. Major banks continually make these portfolio adjustments, reducing their holdings of some currencies and increasing their holdings of others. Less than 10 percent of their trades are for corporate accounts; 90 percent are trades among banks.

**Spot prices** for currency are for trades requiring immediate delivery (within the next 2 days). **Forward prices** for currency are agreed to today but not paid until the specified future delivery date, usually within a year; these might be used by an importer who has agreed to pay a certain amount of foreign currency for a product and wants to guarantee the cost in terms of domestic currency. Chapter 11 includes a detailed discussion of the relationship between forward prices and spot prices.

For simplicity, currency prices are almost always quoted in terms of the U.S. dollar — for example, 0.50 dollar/mark or 2.00 marks/dollars — and trades generally involve dollars. A bank that wants to trade marks for yen will sell marks for dollars and simultaneously buy yen with these dollars, because this is easier than trying to find someone who wants to trade yen for marks. Just as each nation's currency is a domestic medium of exchange that avoids the inefficiencies of barter, so U.S. dollars are an international medium of exchange. The prices in many international contracts, such as European imports of oil from Saudi Arabia and Japanese imports of beef from Australia, are also specified in terms of U.S. dollars.

## Foreign Exchange Demand and Supply

In addition to purchasing power parity, analysts use demand-and-supply reasoning to understand exchange-rate movements, as illustrated by the market for British pounds relative to U.S. dollars shown in Figure 3.3. The exchange rate $e$ is the price of foreign currency in U.S. dollars — here U.S. dollars per British pound. The U.S. demand curve describes the willingness of U.S. citizens to exchange dollars for pounds; it slopes downward because pounds are less attractive as they become more expensive. The supply curve in the figure describes the willingness of foreigners, primarily the British, to sell pounds for dollars. The supply curve slopes upward because the more dollars they can get for their pounds, the more pounds they are willing to sell.

Figure 3.4 shows that an increase in the U.S. demand for British pounds causes an increase in the equilibrium exchange rate — which can be described either as an appreciation of the pound relative to the dollar or as a depreciation of the dollar relative to the pound. An increase in the foreign supply of British pounds causes a drop in the equilibrium exchange rate — a depreciation of the

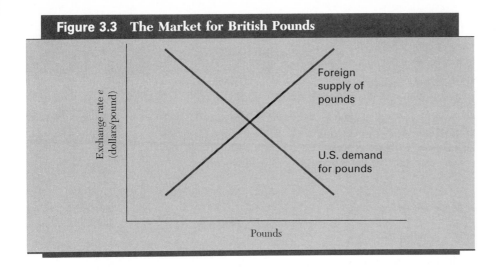

Figure 3.3    The Market for British Pounds

pound and an appreciation of the dollar. With this demand–supply graph in mind, we turn now to Table 3.5, which lists the anticipated exchange-rate effects of several economic events. This table shows the shift in demand relative to supply because most events that cause U.S. citizens to demand more British pounds also persuade foreigners to supply more British pounds.

For instance, an increase in the U.S. price level makes U.S. products more expensive relative to British products. U.S. citizens now demand more British pounds to buy British goods, while the British want fewer U.S. dollars to buy U.S. goods and consequently supply fewer pounds to acquire dollars. The demand for pounds goes up and the supply of pounds goes down; more briefly,

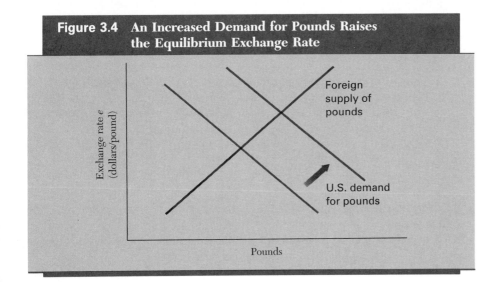

Figure 3.4    An Increased Demand for Pounds Raises
             the Equilibrium Exchange Rate

**Table 3.5   Predicted Demand–Supply Effects on the Value of the British Pound Relative to the U.S. Dollar**

| Economic Event | Demand for Pounds Relative to Dollar | Value of Pound Relative to Dollar |
|---|---|---|
| Increase in U.S. price level | Increases | Appreciates |
| Increase in U.K. price level | Decreases | Depreciates |
| Increase in U.S. income | Increases | Appreciates |
| Increase in U.K. income | Decreases | Depreciates |
| Increase in U.S. interest rates | Decreases | Depreciates |
| Increase in U.K. interest rates | Increases | Appreciates |
| Increase in expected U.S. inflation | Increases | Appreciates |
| Increase in expected U.K. inflation | Decreases | Depreciates |
| Federal Reserve buys pounds | Increases | Appreciates |
| Bank of England buys dollars | Decreases | Depreciates |

we can say that the demand for pounds increases relative to the supply. An inspection of Figure 3.3 or 3.4 confirms that an increase in demand relative to supply increases the value of the British pound, as noted in Table 3.5.

Similarly, the demand for British pounds increases — causing the value of the pound to appreciate — when U.S. income increases (and U.S. citizens buy more of everything, including British goods), U.K. interest rates increase (and people buy more U.K. financial assets), the expected U.S. rate of inflation increases (again, people buy more U.K. financial assets), or the Federal Reserve buys pounds. As an exercise, look at each of the events in Table 3.5 and reason out the consequences listed there.

## The Effects of Exchange Rates on Economic Activity

The primary advantage of floating exchange rates is that they break the impasse created by inconsistent domestic economic policies. If two countries have differing rates of inflation, the discrepancy can be offset by a simple depreciation of the currency of the nation with the more rapid inflation.

Recall again the purchasing power parity equation, which can be written as

$$\frac{1}{e} = \frac{P_f}{P_d}$$

If we consider the United States as the domestic country, then movements in its exchange rate with another currency (measured in terms of the amount of foreign currency needed to purchase a dollar) depend on whether the second country has more rapid inflation than the United States. If, for example, the second country is Germany and its prices increase faster than those in the United

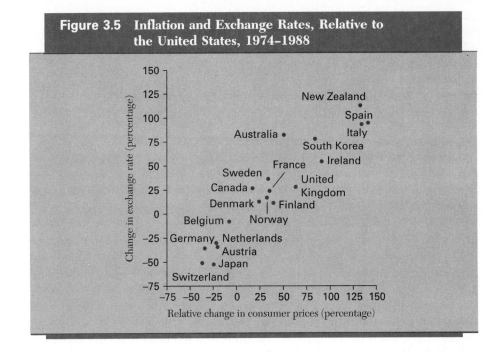

**Figure 3.5  Inflation and Exchange Rates, Relative to the United States, 1974–1988**

States, purchasing power parity can be maintained by an increase in $1/e$ — a depreciation of the German currency, in that it will take more marks to buy a dollar.

Figure 3.5 compares the changes in exchange rates and consumer prices for 20 Western industrial nations over the period 1974–1988 using the United States as the benchmark domestic nation. The horizontal axis is the percentage change in $P_f/P_d$ (or relative change in consumer prices), with a positive value showing that there was a larger increase in consumer prices in the country listed than in the United States. The vertical axis is the percentage change in $1/e$, with a positive value showing a devaluation of the currency of the country listed relative to the U.S. dollar. We shouldn't expect this correlation between exchange rates and inflation rates to be perfect, because it is impractical to trade many items included in the index of consumer prices and because central banks intervene in exchange markets. Nonetheless, the correlation is striking.

Although purchasing power parity may be approximated in the long run, it does not hold in the short run. Exchange rates rise and fall daily, not only to equalize international commodity prices but because investors think that one currency is a more attractive investment than another. Changes in exchange rates consequently have real economic effects: the depreciation of a country's currency reduces the price of its exports and raises the price of its imports; currency appreciation has the opposite effects. For example, Figure 3.2 earlier in this chapter showed that the value of the U.S. dollar rose relative to the Japanese yen and European currencies by about 40 percent between 1980 and 1985, making U.S. products very expensive, and then fell by more than 30 percent between 1985 and 1987, making U.S. products inexpensive. Such swings buffet exporters, importers, and makers of competing products for reasons beyond their control.

Suppose a Japanese automaker needs to sell a certain car for 2 million yen in order to cover its production costs. If, as in 1975, the exchange rate is 300 yen/dollar, the automaker must price the car at

$$\frac{2 \text{ million yen}}{300 \text{ yen/dollar}} = \$6667$$

to break even. If, on the other hand, the exchange rate is 200 yen/dollar (as in 1980), then the break-even price is

$$\frac{2 \text{ million yen}}{200 \text{ yen/dollar}} = \$10,000$$

At a 250-yen/dollar exchange rate (as in 1982), the break-even price is $8000; at 133 yen/dollar (as in 1992), the break-even price is $15,000. The Japanese automaker will make large, unexpected profits or losses — simply because of changes in the value of the yen relative to the U.S. dollar.

Similarly, when the value of the British pound fell from $2.45 in October of 1980 to $1.12 in January of 1985, Americans flocked to England looking for bargains. Harrods, a famous London department store, advertised its post-Christmas sale in the *New York Times* and reported a 21 percent increase in sales. One American couple flew to London for a single whirlwind day of shopping, explaining that they saved more than enough to pay for their plane tickets on the Concorde.[3]

Nonetheless, flexible exchange rates have worked tolerably well during two decades of enormous financial upheaval with large trade imbalances and lightning capital mobility. The petrodollar disruptions were particularly challenging. Unprecedented increases in oil prices in 1973–1974 and 1979–1980 created hundreds of billions of dollars of balance-of-trade surpluses and deficits. The economies of many poorer nations might easily have been crushed by an inability to pay for oil and oil-related imports. The IMF, World Bank, and private banks have so far averted such national collapses by loaning funds from trade-surplus nations to trade-deficit nations.

The IMF did this directly, borrowing heavily from Arab oil-exporting nations and lending to oil-importing nations. The OPEC nations also deposited large amounts in Western banks, and these banks simultaneously lent hundreds of billions of dollars to oil-importing nations. It remains to be seen whether these loans can be repaid. If they cannot, the potential financial default will surely rock the entire world.

The other lingering international finance nightmare is that wild fluctuations in exchange rates will have adverse effects on real economic activity. Tens of

**EXAMPLE 3.6** *Bargain Hunting for California Real Estate*

In 1987, the manager of McKinsey & Company's Tokyo office argued that changes in the dollar–yen exchange rate had made the United States a bargain basement for Japanese investors.* As an example, he related how a 1500-square-foot apartment in Tokyo purchased for $500,000 in 1982 was worth $8 million in 1987; using this property as collateral, the owner of the apartment borrowed $1 million and bought a five-bedroom waterfront house in southern California.

The exchange rate was around 250 yen/dollar in 1982 and below 125 yen/dollar at the end of 1987. This Japanese apartment was worth 1 billion yen in 1987, which converts to $4 million at an exchange rate of 250 yen/dollar but $8 million at the 1987 exchange rate of 125 yen/dollar.

The vast difference in home prices in Japan and the United States reflects the fact that the law of one price does not apply to real estate, because shelter is not a good that can be traded across national borders. Even though Japanese can purchase U.S. real estate and Americans can buy Japanese property, these are hardly perfect substitutes, because it is impractical for a Tokyo businessman to sell his cramped Tokyo apartment and commute to work from southern California.

*Kenichi Ohmae, "Low Dollar Means U.S. Has Become Bargain Basement," Wall Street Journal, November 30, 1987.*

trillions of dollars' worth of foreign exchange trades are now made annually, far more than needed to carry out international transactions. Most of these trades are for speculative purposes — buying currencies that are expected to appreciate and selling those that are expected to depreciate. Does international trade need to be protected from currency booms and crashes?

# SUMMARY

Data on international transactions measure exports versus imports and borrowing and lending among nations. A current-account deficit (which includes purchases of currently produced goods and services and international transfer payments) must be offset by a capital-account surplus (which includes international purchases and sales of assets). Between 1950 and 1975, the United States acquired long-term claims against the rest of the world and sold gold and short-term liquid claims against the United States. Since 1975, the United States has run current-account deficits, supplying dollars and dollar-denominated assets as the world's money.

The exchange rate is the price of one currency in terms of another. The theoretical law of one price states that the domestic price of a domestic item $P_d$ should equal the domestic price of a comparable foreign item. That is, $P_d$ is equal to the exchange rate $e$ (domestic currency per unit of foreign currency) multiplied by the foreign price of the foreign item $P_f$:

$$P_d = eP_f$$

Domestic prices, foreign prices, and exchange rates are roughly linked through purchasing power parity, an application of the law of one price:

$$\%\Delta e = \%\Delta P_d - \%\Delta P_f$$

Although the law of one price and purchasing power parity do not hold exactly, at least in the short run, these concepts are helpful in remembering the direction in which prices and exchange rates move. For example, if one country has substantially more rapid inflation than another country, its currency is likely to depreciate relative to the second country's. Another way to understand and anticipate exchange-rate movements is to consider the demand and supply of a currency. Events that cause an increased demand relative to supply cause the equilibrium value of a currency to appreciate.

The international gold standard pegged exchange rates. This system and the subsequent Bretton Woods plan broke down because nations were unwilling to forgo domestic economic stabilization policies in order to hold exchange rates constant. Since March of 1973, the major exchange rates have been determined in the foreign exchange market — a large, volatile international market in which currencies are traded, usually among banks, using telephones and computer terminals.

Floating exchange rates can help maintain the law of one price when one country's prices increase faster than another's. However, because the law of one price does not hold in the short run, foreign exchange prices have real economic effects. Currency depreciation reduces the price of a country's exports and raises the price of its imports; currency appreciation has the opposite effects. Flexible exchange rates have worked reasonably well since 1973, although there is some concern that speculative activity in the foreign exchange market disrupts international trade.

# IMPORTANT TERMS

appreciation
bimetallic standard
Bretton Woods agreement
central bank
capital account
current-account balance
depreciation
exchange rate
forward prices
gold standard
goods-and-services balance

International Monetary Fund (IMF)
international reserves
law of one price
London interbank offered rate
  (LIBOR)
merchandise-trade balance
nontraded goods
purchasing power parity
special drawing rights (SDRs)
spot prices
trade balance

# EXERCISES

1. Use the data in Table 3.2 to determine these November 6, 1991 exchange rates:
   a. Yen per mark
   b. Francs per pound
   c. Pounds per franc

2. Look in the most recent Friday edition of *The Wall Street Journal* and report the current exchange rates (U.S. dollars per currency) for the British pound, French franc, Japanese yen, and German mark. In comparison with the November 1991 prices in Table 3.2, which of these four currencies have appreciated relative to the U.S. dollar and which have depreciated?

3. Look in the most recent Friday edition of *The Wall Street Journal* and report the current exchange rates (U.S. dollars per currency) for the Israeli shekel, South Korean won, and Swiss franc. What is the price of the shekel in terms of won (wons/shekel)? Of the franc in terms of shekels (shekels/franc)?

4. On October 20, 1989, the Canada–U.S. and Mexico–U.S. exchange rates were 0.8515 U.S. dollars per Canadian dollar and 0.0003846 U.S. dollars per Mexican peso. How many pesos did it take to buy a U.S. dollar? To buy a Canadian dollar?

5. Look in the most recent edition of *The Wall Street Journal* and report the current exchange rates (U.S. dollars per currency) for the Canadian dollar and Mexican peso. In comparison with the October 20, 1989 prices given in Exercise 4, which of these three currencies have appreciated and which have depreciated relative to each other?

6. If the value of the dollar is fixed relative to other currencies by a gold standard, what happens if there is rapid inflation in the United States?

7. If exchange rates are flexible, why does rapid inflation in the United States cause the value of the dollar to fall?

8. The Reagan administration tried to reduce the U.S. trade deficit by encouraging U.S. exports to Japan and discouraging U.S. imports from Japan. Did it try to raise or lower the value of the dollar relative to the yen?

9. How would you explain the following observation?
   *Today, almost anything made in France can be profitably sold in the United States. Four years ago, almost nothing made in France could be sold profitably in the United States.*[4]

10. A September 1986 survey by *The Economist* of the worldwide prices of Big Mac hamburgers found that the price was $1.60 in the United States and 90 francs in Belgium.[5] At the time, the exchange rate was 0.0238 dollar/franc. What was the implied price of a Big Mac in the United States in Belgian francs and the price in Belgium in U.S. dollars? To enforce the law of one price for Big Macs, should the U.S. dollar have appreciated or depreciated relative to the Belgian franc? Use the most recent Monday issue of *The Wall Street Journal* to determine if the dollar has appreciated or depreciated relative to the Belgian franc since 1986.

11. Use the 1986 local prices of Big Macs and the actual exchange rates (dollars/local currency) in Example 3.3 (Hamburger Parity) to calculate the dollar price of a Big Mac in 1986 in each of the countries listed there. In which of these countries was the 1986 dollar price of a Big Mac more than the $1.60 U.S. price? Comparable prices of Big Macs in April of 1988 (no Brazilian data were available) are as follows:[6]

| | Local Price | Exchange Rate (dollars/local currency) |
|---|---|---|
| Australia (dollar) | 1.95 | 1.36 |
| Canada (dollar) | 2.05 | 0.80 |
| Hong Kong (dollar) | 7.60 | 0.13 |
| France (franc) | 17.30 | 0.18 |
| Japan (yen) | 370 | 0.0081 |
| Sweden (krona) | 18.50 | 0.17 |
| West Germany (mark) | 4.10 | 0.60 |
| United States (dollar) | 2.39 | |

In which of these countries was the 1988 dollar price of the Big Mac more than the $2.39 U.S. price? Were these the same countries as in 1986?

12. Between 1873 and 1896, wholesale prices fell by approximately 50 percent in the United States, United Kingdom, Germany, and France — four countries on the gold standard. How would you explain the fact that prices in each of these four countries changed by roughly the same amount in this period? What do you predict would have happened if, instead, prices in the United States had been unchanged while prices in the other three countries fell by 50 percent?

13. Here are some data comparing three nations' exchange rates in terms of the U.S. dollar in 1974 and 1988 (that is, foreign currency/dollar):

| | 1974 | 1988 |
|---|---|---|
| Iceland (krona) | 0.99 | 43.03 |
| Taiwan (dollar) | 38.0 | 28.5 |
| Turkey (lira) | 14 | 1419 |

If purchasing power parity held in 1974 and 1988, which of these countries had more rapid inflation than the United States between 1974 and 1988?

14. During the 10-year period 1976–1985, the average rate of inflation was 13.0 percent in New Zealand, 4.7 percent in the Netherlands, and 7.3 percent in the United States. For purchasing power parity to hold from 1976 to 1985, should the New Zealand dollar and the Netherlands guilder have appreciated or depreciated relative to the U.S. dollar during this period?

15. Table 3.2 shows an exchange rate of 130 Japanese yen for 1 U.S. dollar in November of 1991. Were those speculators who bought dollars and sold yen betting that this exchange rate would rise above 130 or fall below 130?

16. In 1985, many economists argued that the U.S. dollar was too strong, in that foreign goods were too cheap and U.S. goods too expensive. How could they have used foreign exchange markets to bet this belief?

17. Between 1976 and 1988, consumer prices increased at an average annual rate of 8.60 percent in the United Kingdom and 6.28 percent in the United States. If the law of one price held in 1976, should the U.S. dollar have strengthened or weakened relative to the British pound during this 12-year period? The exchange rate was virtually constant, at 1.80 dollars/pound in 1976 and 1.78 dollars/pound in 1988. Do these data suggest that the U.S. dollar was overvalued or undervalued relative to the British pound in 1988?

18. The Canadian consumer price index increased from 41.5 in 1974 to 113.1 in 1988; the United States consumer price index increased from 45.8 to 109.9 over this same period. If the law of one price held in 1974, what percentage change in the exchange rate (U.S. dollars/Canadian dollars) should

have occurred between 1974 and 1988? In fact, the exchange rate was 1.0224 in 1974 and 0.8125 in 1988. If the law of one price held in 1974, do these data suggest that the Canadian dollar was overvalued or undervalued relative to the U.S. dollar in 1988? Should a speculator who wanted to act on the basis of these calculations have bought U.S. dollars and sold Canadian dollars or the other way around?

19. Why do some central banks dislike seeing the value of their currency appreciate? Does a country receive any benefits from currency appreciation?

20. Use demand and supply analysis to determine whether a reduction in government spending should improve or worsen a nation's balance of payments.

21. Use demand and supply analysis to predict the effect on the value of the yen relative to the dollar if quotas are imposed that severely restrict imports of Japanese goods into the United States.

22. Why do you suppose nations don't simply use barter transactions, such as directly trading American Coca-Cola for French wine?

23. Explain the logic behind this argument in a 1990 *Wall Street Journal* editorial:

*The Japanese deserve credit for being canny enough to understand that a strong currency, allowing you to buy more, is better than a weak currency, allowing you to sell more.*[7]

24. Comment on the following quotation:

*International currency stabilization will, however, only be possible when national economies are stable — when the industrial countries have succeeded in combining reasonably high employment with tolerably stable prices. Until then all talk of international currency reform will be in a vacuum and can safely be ignored except by those whose employment depends on the discussion.*[8]

25. Critically evaluate the following analysis:

*Their leaders do not talk about it much, but a strong dollar carries some important benefits to the Europeans. While their imports cost more, their exports carry lower prices on foreign markets. That makes their goods more competitive around the world, and many economists believe Europe will gain in the end because increasing exports just as surely produces jobs as increasing domestic consumption.*[9]

26. After the United States suspended gold sales in 1971 and allowed the dollar to float, many nations bought U.S. dollars to keep the values of their currencies low. Why do you suppose they wanted their currency to be inexpensive?

27. Does the following news story describe a 3-year period in which the value of the British pound rose or fell relative to other currencies?

*British exporters find their products much more competitive in the international marketplace. . . . Three years ago . . . some companies . . . went out of business because they were unable to match foreign prices.*[10]

28. Fuji Bank's chief currency trader lost $48 million during a 4-month period in 1984 when he sold forward contracts agreeing to trade dollars for yen at a specified exchange rate on a given future date. Was this currency trader betting that the value of the dollar would rise or fall relative to the yen during this period?

29. In March of 1987 a real estate columnist wrote that

*Everybody in the business was struck by the prices the Japanese paid for some trophy properties last year — $610 million for the Exxon Building. . . . [F]ew have remembered the plunge of the dollar against the yen. That decline of 55 percent in value in 16 months has made U.S. property look es-*

*pecially cheap in Japanese eyes; applying that arithmetic to the prices paid means that Shuwa really laid out $274.5 million for the Exxon Building — less than what the seller would have gotten from an American institution.*[11]

Did the Japanese pay $670 million or $274.5 million for the Exxon Building?

30. Explain how this divergence is possible:

*The dollar value of such imports [of Japanese goods into the United States] during February equaled $7.1 billion versus $6.1 billion a year ago and $5.1 billion two years ago. In yen terms, our imports from Japan are down 3.9 percent from a year ago and 17.3 percent from two years ago.*[12]

# 4 Interest Rates and Present Value

*The greatest of all gifts is the power to estimate things at their true worth.*
**La Rochefoucauld**

A financial debt is a legally binding IOU that is issued when one person or institution borrows money from another and promises to pay back the amount borrowed plus interest. You issue debt (the mortgage document you sign) when you borrow money from a bank in order to buy a house. The U.S. Treasury issues debt when it sells securities to raise money to pay the federal government's bills. Debts are liabilities for the people who issue them and assets for those who hold the IOUs. A mortgage note is a liability for the borrower and an asset for the bank. A Treasury security is a liability for the federal government and an asset for the investor who owns the security.

Every debt has an interest rate associated with it that reflects the cost of borrowing money. A person or institution that borrows money promises to pay back the amount borrowed plus something extra — interest — for temporarily having the use of the borrowed money. Interest can therefore be thought of as the cost of "renting" money. After they have been issued, debt instruments can be traded among investors. The bank that lends you money to buy a house can sell your mortgage note to a pension fund. The pension fund that buys a Treasury security can sell it to an individual.

The next several chapters describe different kinds of debt and explain some of the factors that influence interest rates and the prices that investors are willing to pay for debt instruments. We will look at household, business, and government debt; at short- and long-term debt; and at collateralized and noncollateralized debt. By using some general principles (such as risk, taxes, and maturity) to distinguish certain types of debts from others, we will be able to see why some debts have higher interest rates than others and why some debts sell for higher prices than others.

This chapter begins the consideration of debts by examining the important mathematical relationship between the amount borrowed, the amount paid back, and the interest rate. We can use this relationship to determine the requisite future payments one must make in order to borrow money at a stated interest rate. We will also be able to determine how much investors are willing to pay for an IOU with specified future payments if market interest rates change after the debt has been issued. We begin by examining the time value of money.

# PRESENT VALUE AND REQUIRED RETURNS

A dollar that you have today is worth more than a dollar that you will receive a year from now because the dollar you have today can be invested for a year. This important principle — the *time value of money* — explains why lenders ask for interest and why borrowers are willing to pay interest. It also can be used to explain how interest rates affect the market prices of IOUs. To make the time value of money more concrete, let's see how interest rates affect the future value of an investment.

## Future Value

The **future value** of an investment is its value after it has earned a given rate of return for a specified period of time. If, for example, you invest $1000 and earn a 10 percent annual rate of return, at the end of 1 year you will have

$$\text{First year:} \quad \text{Principal + interest} = \$1000 + 0.10(\$1000)$$
$$= \$1000(1 + 0.10)$$
$$= \$1100$$

If you reinvest this $1100 for a second year at 10 percent, you earn interest not only on your original $1000 but also on the $100 interest you earned the first year:

$$\text{Second year:} \quad \text{Principal + interest} = \$1100 + 0.10(\$1100)$$
$$= \$1100(1.10)$$
$$= \$1000(1.10)^2$$
$$= \$1210$$

This is called **compound interest**, in that you earn interest on interest.

More generally, if you invest an amount $P$, earning an annual rate of return $R$ for $n$ years, your investment grows to

$$F = P(1 + R)^n \tag{4.1}$$

If the rate of return varies year by year, say $R_1$ the first year, $R_2$ the second, and so on, then your investment grows to

$$F = P(1 + R_1)(1 + R_2) \cdots (1 + R_n) \tag{4.2}$$

after $n$ years. For instance, $1000 invested for 3 years at 10 percent has a future value of

$$F = \$1000(1.10)^3 = \$1331$$

---

**EXAMPLE 4.1**  ***Did Peter Minuit Pay Too Much for Manhattan?***

In 1626 Peter Minuit purchased Manhattan Island from some Algonquian Indians for cloth, beads, and trinkets worth about $24 at the time, an apparent bargain compared with the price of Manhattan real estate today. However, $24 in 1626 is not the same as $24 today, because $24 in 1626 could have earned nearly 400 years of interest. If it had been invested at 6 percent, then in 1993, 367 years later, it would have increased to

$$\$24(1.06)^{367} = \$46.5 \text{ billion}$$

Because the area of Manhattan is 31.2 square miles, this is approximately $53 a square foot.

The so-called miracle of compound interest is that a seemingly modest rate of return compounded over many years turns a small investment into a fortune. The accompanying table shows the corollary that slightly different rates of return compound to vastly different future values. While the difference between 6 and 7 percent interest may seem small, the farther ahead we look, the more the power of compounding separates the results. Thus the answer to our question — Did Peter Minuit pay too much for Manhattan? — depends critically on the rate of return that he and his heirs could have earned.

| Annual Rate of Return | Future Value (1993) | Future Value per Square Foot |
|:---:|:---:|:---:|
| 4% | $42.8 million | $0.05 |
| 5% | $1.4 billion | $1.65 |
| 6% | $46.5 billion | $53.46 |
| 7% | $1,459 billion | $1,677.39 |
| 8% | $44,333 billion | $50,969.11 |

whereas $1000 invested for 3 years at 10 percent, 11 percent, and then 12 percent has a future value of

$$F = \$1,000(1.10)(1.11)(1.12) = \$1367.52$$

## Compound Interest

The sale of Manhattan in 1626 is a dramatic example of the power of compound interest — that earning interest on interest causes wealth to grow geometrically. In the 1960s, banks and other financial institutions began compounding interest more frequently than once a year in order to raise the effective rates of interest on their deposits above the ceiling rates set by the federal government's Regulation Q.

Suppose that the quoted annual deposit rate is 6 percent. If there is no compounding during the year, then $1 grows to $1.06 by year's end. With semiannual compounding, the deposit is credited with 6 percent/2 = 3 percent interest halfway through the year and then, during the next 6 months, the deposit is credited with another 3 percent interest on both the initial deposit and the first 6 month's interest, giving an effective rate of return for the year of 6.09 percent:

$$\$1(1.03)^2 = \$1.0609$$

This is a 6.09 percent effective rate of return in the sense that 6 percent compounded semiannually earns as much as 6.09 percent compounded annually.

With quarterly compounding, 6 percent/4 = 1.5 percent interest is credited every 3 months:

$$\$1(1.015)^4 = \$1.0614$$

raising the effective rate to 6.14 percent. Monthly compounding, paying 6 percent/12 = 0.5 percent each month, raises the effective return up to 6.17 percent. The general formula is that an amount $P$ invested at an annual rate of return $R$ compounded $m$ times a year grows to $P(1 + R/m)^m$ after 1 year and to

$$F = P(1 + R/m)^{mn} \tag{4.3}$$

after $n$ years.

The effective return is increased by more frequent compounding, up to the limit of continuous compounding, where the frequency of compounding is infinitely large and the time between compounding is infinitesimally small. Mathematically,

$$F = \lim_{m \to \infty} (1 + R/m)^m = e^R$$

where $e = 2.718 \ldots$ is the base of natural logarithms.

In practice, of course, banks don't continuously update their account balances. At some specified interval, perhaps quarterly or annually, they use this mathematical formula to determine the amount of interest their depositors have earned. In our example, with $R = 6$ percent, continuous compounding pushes the effective annual rate up to 6.18 percent, only a slight improvement over monthly compounding — even though advertisements proclaiming "continuous compounding" imply that the bank is doing something marvelous to our money.

## Present Value

A future-value calculation answers the question, If you invest $P$ at a rate of return $R$, how much money will you have after $n$ years? Often, we are interested in the reverse question: How much money do you have to invest now in order to have $100,000 after 10 years, perhaps to pay for a daughter's college education? This can be determined by solving Equation 4.1 for $P$ using $F = \$100,000$ and $n = 10$:

$$\$100,000 = P(1 + 0.10)^{10}$$

Rearranging,

$$P = \frac{\$100{,}000}{(1 + 0.10)^{10}}$$

$$= \$38{,}554.33$$

The future-value formula also can be used to answer another important but somewhat different question. Suppose you have been offered an IOU for $100,000 to be paid 10 years from today. How much is this promise of a future payment worth to you *now*? The price you are willing to pay for this IOU depends on the return you require on such an investment. If you are willing to pay $38,554.33 now in order to receive $100,000 in 10 years, then you evidently require a 10 percent return on your investment, because $38,554.33 invested for 10 years at 10 percent will grow to $100,000. If you require a 20 percent return on this investment, then the price $P$ that you are willing to pay is given by

$$P = \frac{\$100{,}000}{(1 + 0.20)^{10}} = \$16{,}150.56$$

An IOU for $100,000 to be paid 10 years from now — even if issued by the U.S. Treasury — is not the same as $100,000 now, because $100,000 now can be invested for 10 years. A payment of $100,000 ten years from now is worth much less than $100,000. The price that you are willing to pay today to receive a specified future amount $F$ after $n$ years is called the **present value** of this future payment and can be calculated from a rearrangement of Equation 4.1:

$$P = \frac{F}{(1 + R)^n} \qquad (4.4)$$

The rate of return $R$ that you use to determine this present value is called your **required rate of return**. If the required rate of return varies from year to year, a rearrangement of Equation 4.2 is appropriate:

$$P = \frac{F}{(1 + R_1)(1 + R_2) \cdots (1 + R_n)} \qquad (4.5)$$

If there is more than one future payment, the present value of this **cash flow** is equal to the sum of the present values of the individual payments. If $X_1$ is received 1 year from now, $X_2$ is received 2 years from now, and so on, the present value using a constant required return $R$ is

$$P = \frac{X_1}{(1 + R)} + \frac{X_2}{(1 + R)^2} + \cdots + \frac{X_n}{(1 + R)^n} \qquad (4.6)$$

Suppose, for instance, that an IOU promises to pay $1000 a year from now and another $1000 the year after that. At a 10 percent required return, the present value is

$$P = \frac{\$1000}{(1 + 0.10)} + \frac{\$1000}{(1 + 0.10)^2}$$

$$= \$909.09 + \$826.45$$

$$= \$1735.54$$

EXAMPLE 4.2 *Creative Accounting by the Federal Home Loan Bank Board*

In 1988 Congress accused the Federal Home Loan Bank Board of making inconsistent and misleading estimates of the resources needed to clean up the savings and loan industry over the next 10 years. In congressional testimony that summer, Board Chairman M. Danny Wall estimated that the present value (in 1988) of closing or merging 500 sick S&Ls was $30.9 billion and that the board expected to collect $42 billion in revenue during the 10 years 1988–1998, giving it $12 billion more than it needed.* Congressional aides and industry analysts soon pointed out that by comparing a present value to a cash flow, the board was, in the words of one senator, "comparing apples and oranges."

The present value of a $42 billion cash flow spread over 10 years may be substantially less than $30 billion. For instance, if the $42 billion cash flow is divided evenly, $4.2 billion a year for 10 years, its present value at a 10 percent interest rate is only $25.8 billion, $5.1 billion less than the $30.9 billion present value of expenses. If the $42 billion cash flow begins at $3.34 billion and grows by 5 percent a year, the present value is $24.9 billion — $6 billion less than the present value of expenses.

It is especially puzzling that a federal bank board would make such an obvious present-value mistake. After aides to the House Banking Committee uncovered this inconsistency in the way revenue and expenses were reported, the committee chairman said, "The miscalculations are serious. They are the result of either gross incompetence or deliberate attempts to mislead and minimize the problem to Congress and the public."

*"*Bank Board Accused of Misleading*," Washington Post, *October 3, 1988.*

If instead of a 10 percent return you require $R = 20$ percent, then

$$P = \frac{\$1000}{(1 + 0.20)} + \frac{\$1000}{(1 + 0.20)^2}$$
$$= \$833.33 + \$694.44$$
$$= \$1527.77$$

## The Appropriate Required Return

The present value of an investment depends critically on your required return. Our previous calculations showed that to receive $1000 for each of the next 2 years, you are willing to pay $1735.54 if you require a 10 percent return but only $1527.77 if you require a 20 percent return: the higher the required return, the lower is the present value of a given cash flow. Put somewhat differently, a lower price for a given cash flow increases the prospective return. This important inverse relationship between required return and present value is illustrated in Figure 4.1, which shows the present values in this numerical example for required returns ranging from 0 to 50 percent.

## Figure 4.1 The Inverse Relationship Between Required Return and Present Value

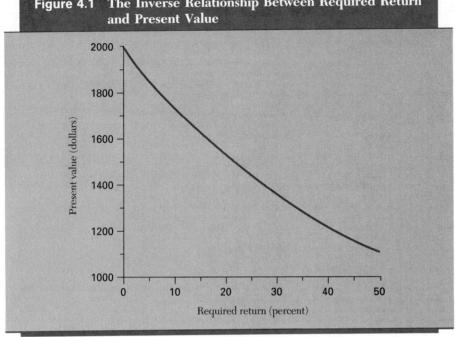

What determines the required return and, implicitly, the price investors are willing to pay for future cash flows? One obvious influence is the rates of return available on other investments. You won't settle for a 10 percent return on an IOU when bank deposits pay 15 percent, but you might when banks offer only 5 percent. Thus required returns rise and fall with the rates of return available on alternative investments.

Many commodities are very close substitutes — brown eggs and white eggs, butter by the pound and butter by the quarter-pound, California orange juice and Florida orange juice. The prices of such close substitutes are tightly linked. The price of brown eggs cannot double while the price of white eggs remains constant, because everyone will buy white eggs. Other commodities are weak substitutes — eggs and geraniums, butter and ketchup, orange juice and beer. The prices of poor substitutes are only weakly related.

The same is true of financial instruments. If two investments are identical in those characteristics that matter to investors, then they are **perfect substitutes** and will be priced using the same required return. Some assets are perfect substitutes (for example, checking accounts with different names); some assets are very close, but imperfect substitutes (for example, 30-day and 60-day Treasury bills); and some assets are not good substitutes at all (for example, a checking account and an apartment building). The more two assets are considered substitutes, the more their required returns move in unison.

If two assets are not perfect substitutes, the one that is less attractive will be priced to have the higher required return. For instance, many people care about an investment's **risk**, how certain or uncertain the promised cash flow is. If you can invest your money safely in a bank at 10 percent and the IOU is just a shaky promise from a disreputable stranger, then you may well require 20 percent, 30 percent, or an even higher return. Similarly, if investors are reluctant to buy securities issued by South African companies, such securities will have relatively high required returns. The less attractive the investment, the higher is the required return and the lower is its present value.

Think about this conclusion carefully, because it implies what many find to be counterintuitive, that the least attractive investments have the highest potential returns. It is the requisite low prices and high potential returns that compensate for the otherwise undesirable features of these investments. This is why, as you will see in later chapters, the "junk" bonds issued by shaky companies have lower prices and higher potential returns than the secure bonds issued by strong companies.

## Constant Cash Flows

In many cases the cash flow is the same, period after period — for example, constant monthly mortgage payments, constant semiannual income from a bond, and constant quarterly dividends from a stock. If this is so, the present value is

$$P = \frac{X}{(1 + R)} + \frac{X}{(1 + R)^2} + \cdots + \frac{X}{(1 + R)^n}$$

where

$X$ = constant cash flow each period
$R$ = required return per period
$n$ = number of periods

In this special case, the present-value formula simplifies to

$$P = \frac{X}{R}\left[1 - \frac{1}{(1 + R)^n}\right] \tag{4.7}$$

This simplified formula can be used to determine the present value $P$ of any investment that yields a constant cash flow. For example, a bond, stock, or machine that pays $1000 a year for 10 years has, at a 10 percent required return, a present value of

$$P = \frac{\$1000}{(1 + 0.10)} + \frac{\$1000}{(1 + 0.10)^2} + \cdots + \frac{\$1000}{(1 + 0.10)^{10}}$$
$$= \frac{\$1000}{0.10}\left[1 - \frac{1}{(1 + 0.10)^{10}}\right]$$
$$= \$10,000(1 - 0.386)$$
$$= \$6140$$

---

**EXAMPLE 4.3** *The Value of a Lottery Jackpot*

In May of 1984 the headlines said "Thousands Seek Millions as Jackpot Fever Grips New York," a fever that has broken out several times since.* The May 1984 story concerned a New York Lotto drawing with a $22.1 million jackpot that lured people into hour-long lines, beginning at 5 A.M., betting more than a million dollars an hour — a total of $24.1 million.

In the New York Lotto game, a machine randomly chooses 6 of 44 Ping-Pong balls that are numbered 1 to 44. The jackpot is divided among those who correctly predicted all 6 numbers (not necesssarily in order). The probability of doing so is about 1 in 7 million. The size of the jackpot depends on the amount wagered, with New York, like most states, keeping about 60 percent of the amount wagered and paying out 40 percent in prizes. For the May 12, 1984 drawing, there had been no winner for three straight games, and the state accumulated the prize money, expanding the jackpot to $22.1 million.

There turned out to be four winning tickets, with each winner receiving $22,100,000/4 = $5,525,000, not all at once, but in 21 annual installments of $5,525,000/21 = $263,095. What is the present value of these annual payments? That is, how much would someone pay for a winning ticket? Alternatively, how much would the State of New York have to deposit in a bank account in 1984 in order to pay a winner $263,095 a year for 21 years? The present value is

$$P = \$263,095 + \frac{\$263,095}{(1 + R)} + \frac{\$263,095}{(1 + R)^2} + \cdots + \frac{\$263,095}{(1 + R)^{20}}$$

which works out to be $1.9 million at a 15 percent interest rate and $2.5 million at a 10 percent interest rate — only 35 to 45 percent of the reported value of $5.5 million! State lotteries not only keep 60 percent of the amount wagered, but they spread the jackpots out so that the present value of the payoff is less than half its reported value. No wonder governments like lotteries.

* *John J. Goldman, "Thousands Seek Millions as Jackpot Fever Grips New York,"* Los Angeles Times, *May 12, 1984.*

---

Another application of Equation 4.7 is to a perpetual, never-ending cash flow, such as the bonds paying a constant annual amount forever that were issued by Great Britain in 1750 to consolidate its debts. Such a bond is generically labeled a **consol**, or a **perpetuity**. To value a perpetuity, observe that the term $1/(1 + R)^n$ in Equation 4.7 approaches zero as $n$ becomes infinitely large (as long as the required return is positive); therefore, the present value of a perpetuity is

$$P = \frac{X}{R} \tag{4.8}$$

If the cash flow is \$100 a year forever and the required return is 10 percent, then the present value is

$$P = \frac{\$100}{0.10}$$
$$= \$1000$$

This makes sense, in that a \$100 annual return on a \$1000 investment does provide the requisite 10 percent return.

## ZERO-COUPON BONDS

Most bonds pay periodic (usually semiannual) interest and a final maturation value (also called its *par value* or *face value*) when the bond matures. The interest payments are called **coupons** because, traditionally, they were literally part of the bond certificate, to be clipped with scissors and redeemed through a local bank or security dealer. **Zero-coupon bonds (zeros)** differ from ordinary bonds in that, as the name implies, they pay no coupons. U.S. Treasury bills, which mature in less than a year, are zero-coupon securities that pay a specified amount, such as \$10,000, at maturity.

Pepsico and J. C. Penney issued corporate zeros in 1981, and a year later, a number of brokerage firms began marketing zeros created from coupon-paying Treasury bonds. Merrill Lynch introduced its version of zeros, called Treasury Investment Growth Receipts ("Tigers," for short) in 1982 by purchasing a pool of \$500 million in long-term Treasury bonds. Merrill Lynch put these Treasury bonds in a trust and created a series of zeros maturing at 6-month intervals by "stripping" away the coupons. For example, a 20-year bond paying \$5000 semiannual coupons and \$100,000 at maturity can be separated into forty \$5000 zeros, with maturities ranging from 6 months to 20 years, and one 20-year \$100,000 zero. These can be split into smaller denominations or combined with pieces of other bonds to give larger zeros. Salomon Brothers sells similar zeros, labeled Certificates of Accrual on Treasury Securities ("Cats"), and other firms use other labels. Encouraged by these successes, the U.S. Treasury now strips its own bonds and sells zeros too; their name is less colorful but accurate: Separate Trading of Registered Interest and Principal of Securities (STRIPS).

The implicit annual rate of return on a zero that costs $P$ and pays an amount $F$ in $n$ years is given by the compound interest formula

$$P(1 + R)^n = F$$

For instance, a \$10,000 Tiger purchased in 1984 will pay \$300,000 in 2014. The implicit interest rate is 12 percent:

$$\$10,000(1 + R)^{30} = \$300,000$$
$$(1 + R)^{30} = 30$$
$$1 + R = 30^{1/30} = 1.12$$
$$R = 0.12 \quad \text{(or 12 percent)}$$

## EXAMPLE 4.4 *Prepaid Tuition Plans*

In 1985 Duquesne University introduced a novel way to prepay college expenses, an idea that has since been imitated by dozens of other colleges and universities. By making a single $5700 payment in 1985, parents could buy 4 year's of tuition for a child enrolling at Duquesne 14 years later, in 1999.

Prepaid tuition is very similar to a zero-coupon bond, but the maturation value, Duquesne's tuition in 1999, is uncertain. In 1985, tuition was $5850, and Duquesne officials assumed that it would increase by 6 percent a year, to

$$\$5850(1.06^{14}) = \$13,226$$

in 1999. They multiplied by 4 to estimate the cost of 4 years of tuition: $4(\$13,226) = \$52,905$.

How much should they charge for this future value? Duquesne treated the $52,905 payoff as a zero-coupon bond with a 17.25 percent annual return and calculated the cost $X$ from

$$X(1 + 0.1725)^{14} = \$52,905$$

implying that

$$X = \$5700$$

which is what they charged parents.

Duquesne invested each $5700 payment that it received in 11 percent zero-coupon bonds maturing in 1999 with a payoff of

$$\$5700(1.11^{14}) = \$24,570$$

Thus Duquesne's future receipt was only about half its own estimated future cost of tuition.

The parents were implicitly credited with a 17.25 percent annual return on their investment, when market interest rates were only 11 percent. The table on the next page shows how their implicit rate of return varies with the rate of growth of tuition. Another risk is whether the child, 3 years old in 1985, will be accepted and want to attend Duquesne 14 years later. Under Duquesne's plan, if the child does not attend, the parents get only their $5700 investment back, with no interest at all. Thus the parents' alternatives are to invest $5700 at 11 percent on their own, giving $24,570 in cash to spend as they wish, or to invest $5700 in Duquesne's prepayment plan, giving $5700 if the child does not attend or free tuition, worth some $40,000 to $90,000, if the child does attend for 4 years.

The plan was initially marketed only to Duquesne alumni, and about 500 signed up. During the subsequent 3 years, interest rates declined and Duquesne raised its estimated tuition growth rate to 8 percent. Together, these events boosted the parents' prepayment to $25,300 in 1988, prompting the school to suspend the plan until the cost declined significantly.

| Rate of Growth of Tuition (%) | Total 4-Year Tuition in 1999 | Implicit Return if Pay $5700 in 1985 (%) |
|---|---|---|
| 4 | $40,521 | 15.04 |
| 6 | 52,905 | 17.25 |
| 8 | 68,730 | 19.46 |
| 10 | 88,861 | 21.68 |

Many investors appreciate the simplicity of zero-coupon bonds and the fact that they don't have to worry about reinvesting future coupons at uncertain interest rates. As we will see in the next chapter, however, zero-coupon bonds are hardly worry-free.

Although zero-coupon bonds don't pay any interest until maturity, the investor pays taxes each year as if interest had been paid. For tax purposes, the value of the investment is assumed to increase each year at a rate $R$, and taxes are levied on this implicit increase. With this tax accounting, the implicit after-tax return is equal to $(1 - t)R$, where $t$ is the investor's marginal tax rate. For example, in a 28 percent tax bracket, the implicit after-tax yield on a 12 percent zero is $(1 - 0.28)12$ percent $= 8.64$ percent.

## COUPON BONDS

To finance the federal deficit, the U.S. Treasury sells not only short-term T-bills but also longer-term, coupon-bearing Treasury notes and bonds. Most bonds issued by businesses and by state and local governments also pay periodic coupons — usually semiannually — before maturity. Let's look at how the interest rates on coupon bonds are calculated.

### Yield to Maturity

The rate of return on a zero-coupon bond held to maturity depends on a relatively straightforward comparison of the purchase price with the maturation value. Coupon bonds are more complex because they involve a sequence of periodic payments. To illustrate the logic, we'll use these May 17, 1986 data for four corporate bonds, as reported in *The Wall Street Journal*:

| Bonds | Current Yield | Close | Net Change |
|---|---|---|---|
| AT&T 3 7/8s90 | 4.4 | 89 | $-\frac{1}{4}$ |
| IBM 9⅜ 04 | 9.1 | 102 1/2 | $-\frac{3}{8}$ |
| IBM 10¼ 95 | 9.3 | 110 | $-2$ |
| Navstr 9s04 | 11.0 | 81 7/8 | $+\frac{7}{8}$ |

These bonds were issued by AT&T, IBM, and Navistar. The first number after the company's name gives the **coupon rate**, the annual coupon as a percentage of the bond's face value. For a $1000 AT&T bond, the annual coupon is $(3\frac{7}{8}$ percent)($1000$) $=$ $38.75$, paid in two semiannual installments of $38.75/2 =$ $19.38$. Similarly, the $1000 Navistar bond pays $45 every 6 months. The next number in the table is the year the bond matures, 1990 for AT&T, 2004 and 1995 for the two IBM bonds, and 2004 for the Navistar bond. You must consult a dealer or a bond fact book to find the exact payment dates for the coupons and maturation value. (The small "s" that sometimes appears between the coupon rate and maturation date is just for style, to help separate the two numbers or because the natural pronunciation of the coupon rate includes an "s.")

The closing prices are the last price at which the bond traded that day, quoted as a percentage of the face value. (The buyer of a bond also must pay the seller a proportionate share of the next coupon payment; for example, if a bond is bought 5 months after the last coupon and 1 month before the next, the buyer must pay the seller an amount equal to $\frac{5}{6}$ of that next coupon.) The last trade in the AT&T bond was at 89, down $\frac{1}{4}$ from the closing price the day before. For an AT&T bond with a $1000 face value, this translates to a price of (89 percent)($1000$) $=$ $890$, down from $892.50. The two IBM bonds also closed lower, while the Navistar bond closed at a higher price than the day before.

It is striking that the price of the Navistar bond was 20 percent less than the price of the first IBM bond, even though both mature in the same year and pay virtually the same coupon. Similarly, we might wonder why the AT&T bond was relatively inexpensive and why one IBM bond sold for less than the other. We will answer these questions in future chapters.

The *current yield* shown in the table is the annual coupon as a percentage of the current price. Thus $3\frac{7}{8}$ is 4.4 percent of 89,

$$\frac{3\frac{7}{8}}{89} = 0.044 \quad \text{(or 4.4 percent)}$$

The 4.4 percent current yield is not a very informative statistic. It is true that if you purchase a $1000 AT&T bond for $890, the annual $38.75 coupon represents a 4.4 percent return on your $890 investment. However, this calculation ignores the fact that you will make another $110 profit when the bond matures in 1990 and pays you $1000. A calculation of your total return must take into account both the coupons and the maturation value.

Logically, the price that investors are willing to pay for a bond is the present value of the cash flow, that is, the coupons and maturation value discounted by a required rate of return. The **yield to maturity** on a bond is the discount rate such that the present value of the coupons and the maturation value is equal to the price. If we use this notation (and assume annual coupons for simplicity),

$P$ = bond price
$C$ = annual coupon
$n$ = number of years until maturity
$M$ = maturation value, or face value
$y$ = annual yield to maturity

**Table 4.1 Prices and Yields of Four Bonds on May 17, 1986**

| Bonds | Current Yield | Close | Yield to Maturity (%) |
|---|---|---|---|
| AT&T 3⅞s90 | 4.4 | 89 | 7.1 |
| IBM 9¾ 04 | 9.1 | 102½ | 9.1 |
| IBM 10¼ 95 | 9.3 | 110 | 8.6 |
| Navstr 9s04 | 11.0 | 81⅞ | 11.4 |

then the yield to maturity $y$ is given by

$$P = \frac{C}{(1 + y)} + \frac{C}{(1 + y)^2} + \cdots + \frac{C}{(1 + y)^n} + \frac{M}{(1 + y)^n} \qquad (4.9)$$

With semiannual coupons $C/2$, the appropriate formula is

$$P = \frac{C/2}{(1 + y/2)} + \frac{C/2}{(1 + y/2)^2} + \cdots + \frac{C/2}{(1 + y/2)^{2n}} + \frac{M}{(1 + y/2)^{2n}} \qquad (4.10)$$

Because we know $P$, $C$, and $M$, we can solve Equation 4.9 or 4.10, whichever is appropriate, for the yield to maturity $y$ using a financial calculator or computer program that, by trial and error, tries different tentative values of $y$ until the present value is approximately equal to the price.

For the AT&T bond discussed earlier,

$$P = \$890$$
$$C = \$38.75$$
$$n = 4$$
$$M = \$1000$$

Because the coupons are paid semiannually, Equation 4.10 is appropriate:

$$\$890 = \frac{\$38.75/2}{(1 + y/2)} + \frac{\$38.75/2}{(1 + y/2)^2} + \cdots + \frac{\$38.75/2}{(1 + y/2)^8} + \frac{\$1000}{(1 + y/2)^8}$$

The solution is $y/2 = 0.0354$, or $y = 2(0.0354) = 0.0708$, rounded off to 7.1 percent. Table 4.1 shows the yields to maturity for all four of the bonds discussed earlier. The puzzles to be explained in later chapters are why the Navistar bond was priced to have such a high yield to maturity and why there were variations among the other three bonds, two of which were issued by the same company.

## Yield to Maturity Versus Price and Coupon Rate

When the financial press speaks of "interest rates," they are generally referring to bond yields to maturity, and we will use the same language. Because interest rates usually change by only a fraction of a percent each day, financial market participants use the term **basis points** to describe hundredths of a percentage point. For example, if an interest rate rises from 5.80 to 5.87 percent, this is said to be an increase of 7 basis points.

Because the yield to maturity is that discount rate for which the present value of the coupons and maturation value are equal to the price of the bond, bond prices fall when interest rates increase and rise when interest rates decline. Thus, whenever the front page of the daily newspaper reports that interest rates have increased, the financial pages report a drop in bond prices.

Equations 4.9 and 4.10 show mathematically the inherent inverse relationship between a bond's yield and its price. Bonds have a fixed cash flow (that's why they're called fixed-income securities), and the higher the required return used to discount this cash flow, the lower is the present value. Put somewhat differently, because the cash flow is fixed, the only way investors can get a higher return, if they require it, is if the price is lower.

Suppose, for instance, that you pay $1000 for an IBM bond with 8 percent coupons ($80 a year). Interest rates now increase; for IBM to sell new bonds for $1000, the company must offer bonds with 10 percent coupons ($100 a year). Will investors pay $1000 in the secondary market for your bond with $80 coupons when they can buy new bonds for $1000 in the primary market with $100 coupons? No. No one will buy your bond unless the price falls enough to make the yield competitive.

People are sometimes puzzled by the fact that a drop in the price raises the yield. Don't investors lose money when the price falls? The explanation is that we must distinguish between the past rate of return on a bond and its current yield to maturity. The price falls so that the future cash flow for those who buy at the new price provides the requisite higher yield to maturity. Investors who bought before the price declined experience a capital loss — a negative rate of return that was no doubt unexpected, because they would have sold yesterday had they known the price would be lower today.

The inverse relationship between a bond's price and its yield to maturity has an important corollary. Notice that the first IBM bond in Table 4.1 has a price ($102\frac{1}{2}$) that is close to its face value (100) and a yield to maturity (9.1 percent) that is close to its coupon rate ($9\frac{3}{8}$). The second IBM bond, on the other hand, has a price above its face value and a yield to maturity below its coupon rate, whereas the AT&T and Navistar bonds have prices below their face values and yields to maturity above their coupon rates. This is no accident. When the yield to maturity is equal to the coupon rate, the price of a bond is equal to its face value. A bond sells for a premium above face value when the yield is below the coupon rate and at a discount when the yield is above the coupon rate.

When a bond is first issued, the coupon rate is usually set close to the prevailing yield to maturity on similar bonds so that the bond will sell for close to its face value. If, after issuance, interest rates fall, the bond's price will rise above its face value so that its coupons are not overly generous. If interest rates rise, the bond's price will fall to a discount from its face value so that its coupons provide an adequate rate of return. For example, the AT&T bond in Table 4.1 was issued in 1956, when interest rates were around 4 percent, and it sold for a discount in 1986 in order to provide a yield of 7 percent.

## *Realized Rate of Return*

It is tempting to interpret a bond's yield to maturity as the investor's rate of return if the bond is held until maturity. However, the investor's overall return depends critically on the rate of interest the investor is able to earn on the coupons received and reinvested before maturity. To illustrate this point, consider a 2-year $1000 bond selling for par that pays 10 percent coupons annually. Because it sells for par, it has a yield to maturity equal to its coupon rate, 10 percent. The investor buys the bond for $1000 and receives one coupon of $100 after 1 year and a second coupon of $100 plus the $1000 maturation value after 2 years. If the investor is able to reinvest the first coupon at 10 percent for a year, then this will grow to $110 by the end of the second year, and the total value of the investment at maturity will be

| | |
|---|---:|
| Reinvested first-year coupon | $ 110 |
| Second-year coupon | 100 |
| Maturation value | 1000 |
| Total value at maturity | $1210 |

The investor's overall rate of return requires a comparison of this total future value with the initial cost of the bond. In particular, the **realized rate of return** on an investment is the rate of return that, applied to the initial cost, gives a future value that is just equal to the actual future value of the investment including the proceeds from the reinvestment of the cash flow, if any. If $P$ is the initial cost of the investment and $F$ is the future value after $n$ years, then the realized rate of return $R$ is given by

$$P(1 + R)^n = F$$

Here, the initial $1000 investment has grown to $1210 after 2 years, and the realized rate of return $R$ is determined by

$$\$1000(1 + R)^2 = \$1210 \quad \text{implies} \quad R = 0.10 \quad \text{(or 10 percent)}$$

In this case, the realized return $R$ is 10 percent, exactly equal to the bond's yield to maturity. It immediately follows, though, that if the reinvested coupon earns more (or less) than 10 percent, then the total future value will be more (or less) than $1210 and the investor's realized rate of return will be larger (or smaller) than 10 percent. This numerical example illustrates the following general point: the realized rate of return on a bond held until maturity is larger or smaller than its calculated yield to maturity depending on whether the coupons are reinvested to earn a rate of return that is larger or smaller than its yield to maturity.

This general conclusion can be proven by reexamining Equation 4.9, which determines a bond's yield to maturity $y$:

$$P = \frac{C}{(1 + y)} + \frac{C}{(1 + y)^2} + \cdots + \frac{C}{(1 + y)^n} + \frac{M}{(1 + y)^n}$$

If we multiply both sides of this equation by $(1 + y)^n$, we obtain

$$P(1 + y)^n = C(1 + y)^{n-1} + C(1 + y)^{n-2} + \cdots + C + M \qquad (4.11)$$

The first term on the right-hand side of Equation 4.11, $C(1 + y)^{n-1}$, is the future value of the first coupon, which is received after one period, if it is invested for $n - 1$ periods at a rate of return that is equal to the yield to maturity $y$. Similarly, the second term, $C(1 + y)^{n-2}$, is the future value of the second coupon, received after two periods, if it is invested for $n - 2$ periods at a rate of return that is equal to the yield to maturity $y$. Thus the right-hand side of Equation 4.11 gives the total future value $F$ from the coupons and maturation value when all the coupons are reinvested to earn a rate of return that is equal to the yield to maturity $y$:

$$F = C(1 + y)^{n-1} + C(1 + y)^{n-2} + \cdots + C + M$$

Equation 4.11 can therefore be rewritten as

$$P(1 + y)^n = F$$

Because the realized rate of return $R$ is defined by

$$P(1 + R)^n = F$$

it follows that the realized rate of return $R$ is equal to the yield to maturity $y$ in this special case where the reinvested coupons earn a rate of return that is equal to the yield to maturity. If the reinvested coupons earn a rate of return that is larger than the yield to maturity, this will increase the future value, and the realized rate of return will be larger than the yield to maturity. If the rate of return on the reinvested coupons is smaller than the yield to maturity, the realized rate of return will be smaller than the yield to maturity.

For example, consider a 20-year bond selling for par with 8 percent coupons paid semiannually. The realized rate of return on this bond will not be equal to its 8 percent yield to maturity unless the coupons can be reinvested to earn an 8 percent rate of return. Figure 4.2 shows the future values of the semiannual coupons when they are reinvested at various interest rates. The following table shows how the reinvestment rate pulls the investor's realized return above or below the reported 8 percent yield to maturity.

| Interest Rate on Reinvested Coupons (%) | Realized Rate of Return on Bond (%) |
|---|---|
| 12 | 10.11 |
| 10 | 9.01 |
| 8 | 8.00 |
| 6 | 7.07 |
| 4 | 6.24 |

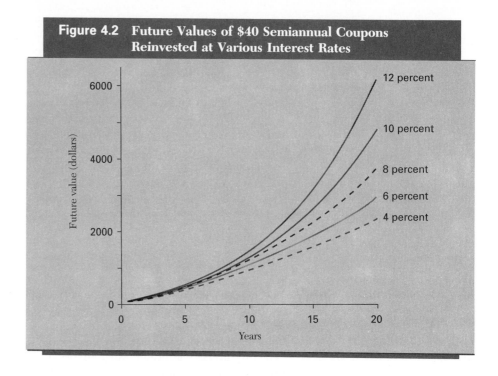

**Figure 4.2    Future Values of $40 Semiannual Coupons Reinvested at Various Interest Rates**

# THE DETERMINATION OF INTEREST RATES

Why do interest rates rise and fall? To understand the various factors that influence interest rates, it is helpful to think of interest rates as the cost of renting money. If you borrow $1000 for a year at a 10 percent interest rate, at the end of the year you will repay the $1000 and also pay $100 in interest, 10 percent of the amount borrowed, in return for being able to use $1000 for a year. That is, you pay $100 to rent $1000 for a year.

In a free-market economy, interest rates are determined by the eagerness of borrowers to obtain funds and the willingness of lenders to supply funds. The **loanable funds theory** states that interest rates are determined by the supply of loanable funds and the demand for loanable funds. Savers, whose income exceeds their spending, supply funds by making loans and buying securities issued by borrowers. Borrowers, whose spending exceeds their income, demand funds by taking out loans and issuing bonds, stocks, and other securities.

Savers and borrowers include households, businesses, and governments, and they can be domestic or foreign residents. A German company demands funds from U.S. financial markets when it sells bonds to U.S. households. A Japanese firm supplies funds to U.S. financial markets when it purchases U.S. Treasury securities.

The demand for and supply of loanable funds depend on several factors, including investment opportunities, money demand and supply, and household time preference for consumption.

## Investment Opportunities

Interest rates on financial assets are influenced by the rates of return available on real assets. One reason that people borrow money is to finance investments in physical assets. Individuals borrow to buy houses, farmers borrow to plant crops, corporations borrow to build factories. The higher the prospective returns on these investments, the higher are the interest rates that borrowers are willing to pay to obtain funds. Similarly, savers who supply funds take into account their alternative investment opportunities. If they can earn high rates of return on physical assets, they will shun lending — investing in financial assets — unless interest rates are high, too.

## Money Demand and Supply

As just explained, one alternative to lending funds is to invest in real assets. Another is to hold money. Just as interest rates affect the choice between making loans and acquiring real assets, so interest rates affect the choice between making loans and holding money. If interest rates are high, savers will hold less money and make more loans; if interest rates are low, they will hold more money and supply less loanable funds. Similarly, if interest rates are low, households and businesses will be more willing to borrow funds in order to obtain the money they need to carry out transactions. Thus the demand for and supply of loanable funds depend on money demand and supply, which in turn are influenced by interest rates and other factors.

For example, money demand depends on the volume of transactions in an economy and on the means available for carrying out these transactions. The widespread use of credit cards reduces the need for money and makes more funds available for lending — increasing the supply of loanable funds. A nation's banking system and monetary authorities — in the United States, the Federal Reserve — can also affect the supply of money and hence the supply of loanable funds.

## Time Preference for Consumption

Some people borrow money in order to consume more goods and services — to buy food, clothing, and entertainment. The money that they use to repay these loans reduces the funds they have available for future consumption. Thus these borrowers give up some consumption tomorrow in order to have more consumption today. Similarly, households who lend money are refraining from buying goods and services today in order to consume more in the future. Lenders give up some consumption today in order to have more consumption tomorrow. The willingness to trade present consumption for future consumption (and vice versa) depends on interest rates and time preferences.

## Using the Loanable Funds Theory

The loanable funds theory is widely used by financial analysts to predict changes in interest rates. Figure 4.3 shows that, for the reasons just discussed, the demand for loanable funds by borrowers is negatively related to interest rates and the supply of loanable funds is positively related to interest rates. The equilibrium interest rate is determined by the intersection of demand and supply.

Events that increase the demand for loanable funds, shifting the demand curve in Figure 4.3 rightward, increase interest rates. Those events that increase the supply of loanable funds, shifting the supply curve rightward, reduce interest rates. More generally, when the demand for loanable funds increases faster than supply, interest rates increase — credit is scarce and expensive. When the supply of loanable funds increases faster than demand, interest rates decline — credit is plentiful and inexpensive.

For example, a tax cut or a strong economy encourages private spending and increases household and business demand for loanable funds to finance this spending, putting upward pressure on interest rates. Similar pressures are exerted when government spending exceeds revenue and government borrowing increases. Decreases in private or government spending and borrowing reduces the demand for loanable funds and causes interest rates to decrease.

The Federal Reserve can increase the supply of loanable funds and ease credit conditions by pumping money into the banking system, thereby lowering interest rates. The Fed can reduce the supply of loanable funds and tighten

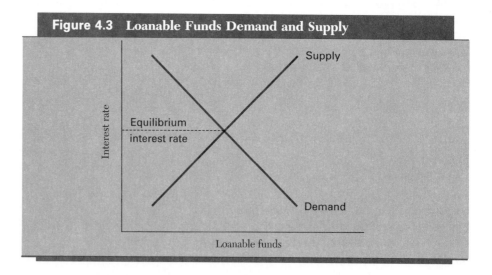

**Figure 4.3   Loanable Funds Demand and Supply**

EXAMPLE 4.5 *Will the Aging of Baby Boomers Reduce Interest Rates?*

In 1988, Edward Yardeni authored a study for Prudential-Bache Securities with the provocative title "The Coming Shortage of Bonds."* He used a loanable funds framework to argue that the aging of the baby boom generation (the 76 million Americans born between 1946 and 1964) should reduce Treasury bond rates from near 10 percent to below 5 percent by the year 2000.

The median age of the baby boom generation was 32 in 1988 and will be 44 in the year 2000. In the 1970s and early 1980s, the baby boom generation overwhelmed the housing market, causing residential mortgages to increase by a factor of 6 (from $348 billion to $2071 billion) between 1970 and 1987. The median age of first-time home buyers was 32 years in 1988, the same as the median age of the baby boom generation, suggesting that housing demand will slacken as the median age of baby boomers increases in the 1990s.

Yardeni argues that as baby boomers age, they will borrow less to buy cars and houses (reducing the demand for loanable funds) and save more to provide for their retirement (increasing the supply of loanable funds). He consequently predicts that the reduced demand for loanable funds and the increased supply will exert downward pressure on interest rates throughout the 1990s.

* Edward Yardeni, "The Coming Shortage of Bonds," Topical Study #13, Prudential-Bache Securities, June 20, 1988; also see Edward Yardeni, "How the Baby Boomers Are Changing the Economy," Topical Study #12, Prudential-Bache Securities, April 6, 1988.

credit by draining money from the banking system. In later chapters we will look more closely at how the Fed alters the supply of loanable funds, trying to keep credit not so tight as to risk recession and not so easy as to risk excessive inflation.

# TAKING ACCOUNT OF INFLATION IN PRESENT-VALUE CALCULATIONS

Many people make the mistake of thinking that present-value logic — that a dollar today is worth more than a dollar tomorrow — hinges on inflation: "A dollar today is worth more than a dollar tomorrow because prices tomorrow will be higher than they are today." It is true that dollars lose purchasing power as prices rise, but present-value logic hinges on something else, that a dollar today can be *invested* to grow to more than a dollar tomorrow.

Imagine a not-so-hypothetical experiment. It is 1982, and safe Treasury bills yield a 14.9 percent rate of return, while the rate of inflation is 3.9 percent — or to make the conclusion even more obvious, let's assume the rate of inflation is zero. In such a situation, how much would you pay today for $1000 a year from now? Would you pay $1000 because there is no inflation? Or would you pay closer to $1000/1.149 = $870 because you could otherwise invest $870 in Treasury bills for a year and have it grow to $1000? It is rates of return that make current dollars valuable, and it is rates of return, not inflation, that should be used to discount future cash flows.

## *Real Rates of Return*

The **nominal rate of return** $R$ on an investment is the dollar profit as a percentage of the dollars invested:

$$\text{Nominal return } R = \frac{\text{dollars earned}}{\text{dollars invested}}$$

If a $100 investment yields a $10 profit 1 year from now, then the nominal rate of return is

$$R = \frac{\text{dollars earned}}{\text{dollars invested}} = \frac{\$10}{\$100} = 0.10 \quad \text{(that is, 10 percent)}$$

The **real rate of return** $r$ measures the profit in commodities as a percentage of the commodities invested:

$$\text{Real return } r = \frac{\text{commodities earned}}{\text{commodities invested}}$$

Normally, you don't actually invest or receive commodities. You invest and receive dollars. The logic of a real-yield calculation is that you take into account the purchasing power of the dollars invested and received.

Suppose that you only buy hamburgers and that the hamburgers you like currently cost $2 each. Investing $100 is therefore equivalent to giving up 50 hamburgers. When you are paid $110 a year later (a 10 percent nominal return), you should deflate these dollars by the prevailing price of hamburgers. If the price of hamburgers has gone up 10 percent to $2.20, then your $110 buys 50 hamburgers. You have given up 50 hamburgers now for 50 hamburgers later, and your real rate of return is 0 percent. You have run fast but stayed in the same place.

In general, the real rate of return on an investment is approximately equal to the nominal rate of return minus the percentage increase $\pi$ in the price level:

$$r = R - \pi \tag{4.12}$$

If, as in the example, you earn a 10 percent nominal return when the price of hamburgers increases 10 percent, then your real return is zero. If the price of hamburgers rises by only 3 percent, your real return is 10 percent − 3 percent = 7 percent. If the price of hamburgers increases by 20 percent, your real return is negative, a disappointing − 10 percent; you give up 50 hamburgers now for 45 hamburgers a year from now.

## The Effect of Inflation Expectations on Nominal Interest Rates

Because the nominal rate of return and the rate of inflation may not be known in advance, we need to distinguish the anticipated and actual rates of return. The anticipated real rate of return $r^*$ depends on the anticipated nominal rate of return $R^*$ and the predicted rate of inflation $\pi^*$:

$$r^* = R^* - \pi^*$$

The actual realized real rate of return $r = R - \pi$ depends on what the nominal rate of return $R$ and the inflation rate $\pi$ turn out to be — and these may differ considerably from the anticipated values.

Nominal interest rates tend to increase during inflationary periods. Suppose that the nominal return on a bank savings account is 5 percent and that the inflation rate is expected to be 2 percent. The anticipated real rate of return is 5 percent − 2 percent = 3 percent. If the anticipated rate of inflation rises to 12 percent, people won't be enthusiastic about investing at a 5 percent nominal return because their anticipated real return will be a disheartening −7 percent. Instead, they may try to stockpile some of the commodities whose prices are rising by 12 percent a year. Neglecting storage and other expenses, stockpiling will give a 12 percent nominal return, for a 0 percent real return — not much, but better than −7 percent. For savings accounts to be competitive with commodities when a 12 percent rate of inflation is expected, they must offer more than a 5 percent nominal return.

Real interest rates are not invariably positive. Throughout the 1970s, many people kept funds in savings accounts paying about 5 percent interest while consumer prices relentlessly increased by more than 5 percent a year. They accepted negative real returns because they believed that these savings accounts were the best of their alternatives. Stocks, bonds, and other assets that might have earned higher yields were too risky or had high brokerage fees for small investors. Some had stiff minimum-investment requirements. It took $10,000 to buy a Treasury bill. It takes millions to buy a shopping center. And it is not possible to guarantee a zero real rate of return by investing in the consumer price index. Some people may have stocked up on wine and soup, but it is difficult to stockpile flammable gasoline, perishable food, fashionable clothing, advanced computers, medical services, sales taxes, and other components of the CPI.

Investor reluctance to invest in savings accounts, bonds, and other financial assets whose anticipated returns are less than the expected rate of inflation does tend to increase interest rates during inflationary periods. However, an increase in the expected rate of inflation does not mechanically raise nominal interest rates by an equal amount, leaving real interest rates constant.

Before-tax realized real interest rates were relatively stable and generally positive in the 1950s and 1960s in the United States, lending credence to the idea that anticipated real interest rates are approximately constant and always

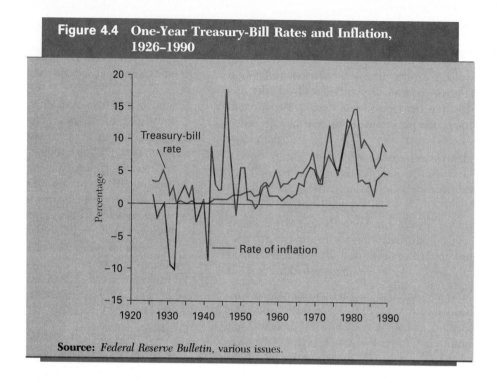

**Figure 4.4**   **One-Year Treasury-Bill Rates and Inflation, 1926–1990**

**Source:** *Federal Reserve Bulletin,* various issues.

positive. These assumptions were treated roughly in the 1970s and 1980s, however, when realized real interest rates turned first persistently negative and then substantially positive, as shown in Figures 4.4 and 4.5. A look in the other direction reveals that realized real interest rates were not very stable before the 1950s either.

A very specific example of volatile anticipated real interest rates occurred in 1985. In January, the average inflation forecast of 462 financial professionals was 5.2 percent inflation over the next decade, whereas the yield on 10-year Treasury bonds was 11.4 percent. A year later, in February of 1986, the consensus inflation forecast was still above 5 percent, whereas the 10-year yield on Treasury bonds had dropped nearly 3 percentage points to 8.7 percent.[1]

Careful empirical studies seem to confirm these informal observations. A study of the realized real returns on corporate bonds all the way back to 1971 found that real interest rates tend to fall during inflation (averaging − 7 percent during 17 years when prices rose by 7.5 percent or more) and to rise during deflations (averaging more than 12 percent during 11 years when prices fell by 6 percent or more).[2] A more mathematical study by Lawrence Summers found that during the years 1860–1940 there was "no tendency for interest rates to increase with movements in expected inflation."[3] In the years since World War II, Summers found a slight positive relationship, but that "in almost every

**Figure 4.5   Realized Real One-Year Treasury-Bill Rates, 1926–1990**

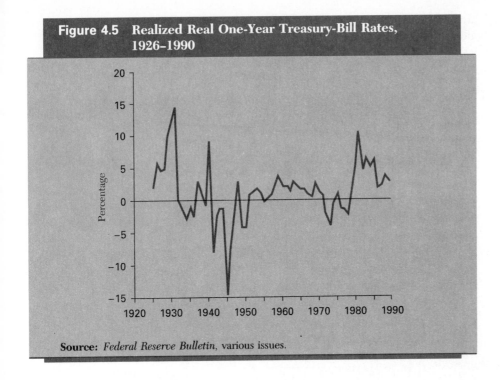

**Source:** *Federal Reserve Bulletin*, various issues.

case the data reject quite decisively the hypothesis" that real interest rates are constant.

A more subtle question is whether nominal or real required returns should be used in present-value calculations. The answer is that either will do, as long as we are consistent with the way the cash flows are measured. If we use nominal cash flows, then we should discount by nominal required rates of return; if we use real cash flows, then real rates of return are appropriate.

## SUMMARY

The future value of an investment $P$ is the value $F$ it will grow to after $n$ years if it earns a specified rate of return $R$:

$$F = P(1 + R)^n$$

Compound interest describes the earning of interest on interest, a powerful arithmetic that causes seemingly slight differences in annual returns to grow to large differences in wealth after many years. Compounding interest more frequently — crediting interest monthly, daily, or even continuously — boosts the effective return on a bank deposit or other investment. An amount $P$ invested at an annual rate of return $R$ compounded $m$ times a year grows to $P(1 + R/m)^m$ after 1 year and to

$$F = P(1 + R/m)^{mn}$$

after $n$ years.

The present value of a cash flow $X_1, X_2, \ldots, X_n$ is the amount $P$ that you are willing to pay for it and is determined by discounting the cash flow by your required rate of return:

$$P = \frac{X_1}{(1 + R)} + \frac{X_2}{(1 + R)^2} + \cdots + \frac{X_n}{(1 + R)^n}$$

The higher the required return, the lower is the present value. This required rate of return depends on the returns available on alternative investments and other characteristics, such as the riskiness of the cash flow, that make this investment relatively attractive or unattractive. An investment that is risky or otherwise undesirable has a low present value; risk-averse investors will not acquire risky investments unless the price is low and the potential return is high.

The yield to maturity $y$ on a bond, coupon-paying or not, is that interest rate for which the present value of the cash flow, coupons $C$ and principal $M$, is equal to its current price $P$:

$$P = \frac{C}{(1 + y)} + \frac{C}{(1 + y)^2} + \cdots + \frac{C}{(1 + y)^n} + \frac{M}{(1 + y)^n}$$

Bond prices and interest rates (that is, yields to maturity) are inversely related. When interest rates rise, bond prices fall; when interest rates fall, bond prices rise. A bond's yield to maturity is equal to its coupon rate (the ratio of its annual coupon to face value) if the bond's price is equal to its face value. Because the price and yield to maturity are inversely related, a bond sells at a discount from face value when its yield is larger than its coupon rate and at a premium when the yield is below the coupon rate.

The nominal return from an investment compares the dollars received with the dollars invested. The real return $r$, measuring the percentage increase in purchasing power, is equal to the nominal return $R$ minus the rate of inflation $\pi$:

$$r = R - \pi$$

Present-value logic, that a dollar today is worth more than a dollar tomorrow, is based not on the observation that inflation reduces the purchasing power of dollars, but on the fact that money invested today will earn additional dollars. Thus the required return used to discount nominal cash flows depends on the rates of return available on alternative investments, not on the rate of inflation. Nominal interest rates do tend to increase during inflations, but not invariably by an amount equal to the rate of inflation, so real interest rates do vary from year to year.

# IMPORTANT TERMS

basis points
cash flow
compound interest
consol
coupon rate
coupons
future value
loanable funds
nominal rate of return

perfect substitutes
perpetuity
present value
real rate of return
realized rate of return
required rate of return
risk
yield to maturity
zero-coupon bonds (zeros)

# EXERCISES

1. Which grows to a larger future value, $1000 invested for 2 years at
   a. 10 percent each year,
   b. 5 percent the first year and 15 percent the second year, or
   c. 15 percent the first year and 5 percent the second year?

2. Which grows to a larger future value,
   a. $2000 invested for 20 years at 10 percent, or
   b. $1000 invested for 20 years at 20 percent?

3. A 1987 advertisement in the *New Yorker* solicited offers on a 1967 Mercury Cougar XR7 (*Motor Trend*'s 1967 car of the year) that had been stored undriven in a climate-controlled environment for 20 years.[4] If the original owner paid $4000 for this car in 1967, what price would he have to receive in 1987 to obtain a 10 percent annual return on his investment?

4. Vincent Van Gogh sold only one painting during his lifetime, for about $30. A sunflower still life he painted in 1888 sold for $39.85 million in 1987, more than three times the highest price paid previously for any work of art. If this sunflower painting had been purchased for $30 in 1888 and sold in 1987 for $39.85 million, what would have been the annual rate of return?

5. In 1987 a small company estimated that someone who invested $6600 in the company might have $106,500 after $5\frac{1}{3}$ years, a "total percentage return" of 1614 percent and a 303 percent "average percentage return." Show the errors in these percentage-return calculations.

6. In 1940 your grandmother put $1000 into a special trust to be paid to a future grandchild (you) 60 years later, in the year 2000. How much will this trust be worth then if it has been earning 8 percent per year?

7. "The United States made the Louisiana Purchase in 1808 for $15 million — a bargain at only $2\frac{1}{2}$ cents an acre." What is the future value of $2\frac{1}{2}$ cents invested for 182 years, until 1990, at 4 percent per year? At 6 percent? At 8 percent?

8. What interest rate was used to determine the following settlement?

   *The Treasury, after 775 years, has settled a debt for death and damage caused by Oxford people in 1209.*

   *The Government has been paying £3.08 a year compensation to Oxford University after people in the city hanged the students for helping a student to murder his mistress. Now the University has accepted a [once-and-for-all] payment of £33.08 in settlement.*[5]

9. A college is considering establishing a publishing house. It can borrow at 10 percent or use endowment funds currently invested in bonds earning an average return of 12 percent. One trustee says that the appropriate required return is 10 percent, while another says it is 12 percent. What do you say?

10. The *annualized* return is calculated by ignoring compounding; for example, the annualized interest rate for a credit card company that charges 1.5 percent a month on unpaid balances is 12(1.5 percent) = 18 percent. What is the effective interest rate, taking monthly compounding into account?

11. A million-dollar state lottery pays $25,000 a year for 40 years. At a 10 percent required return, what is the present value of this payoff?

12. Explain why you either agree or disagree with this argument:

*Your great-grandfather has just died and left you $120,000, which you will invest in a small winery; because this inheritance cost you nothing, your required rate of return is 0%.*

13. In 1987 the College Savings Bank introduced the CollegeSure CD, what its president called "the single most important financial product of the century, and that's an understatement."[6] By paying $14,570 in 1987, the parent of a 5-year-old buys 1 year of private college education 13 years later — when its estimated cost will be $28,580. If the cost does turn out to be $28,580, what is the implicit rate of return on such an investment? If the cost of a comparable year of college education was $11,500 in 1987, what annual rate of increase in college prices is asssumed in the $28,580 estimated future cost?

14. In January of 1990, Mexico agreed to buy 30-year zero-coupon bonds from the U.S. Treasury to use as collateral for a restructuring of its bank loans. The Treasury priced these zeros using an interest rate of 7.925 percent, one-eighth of a percentage point below the average market interest rate on 30-year Treasury bonds at that time. Did this extra one-eighth of a point benefit Mexico or the U.S. Treasury?

15. Below are four bonds and their yields to maturity on November 8, 1988. Which bonds were selling for a premium over face value and which were selling at a discount?
   a. Texaco 13s91, yield to maturity = 11.9 percent
   b. Texaco $13\frac{5}{8}$ 94, yield to maturity = 11.5 percent
   c. Texaco $5\frac{3}{4}$ 97, yield to maturity = 10.0 percent
   d. Texaco $7\frac{3}{4}$ 01, yield to maturity = 10.3 percent

16. Explain why these two 1984 statements by the same author are either consistent or inconsistent:[7]

*Daily price fluctuations of government securities are minimal [p. 44].*

*Since the late seventies, interest rates have fluctuated widely and wildly, with significant changes occurring not only week to week, but even daily [p. 45].*

17. Critically evaluate the following:

*Investors flee from bonds when interest rates rise — or when they think they're going to rise — because bond prices move in the opposite direction from interest rates. Thus bonds — which are interest-bearing debt securities issued by governments and corporations to raise money — are a good investment during periods of low interest rates.*[8]

18. A bond paying a 10 percent annual coupon for 20 years is selling for its maturation value, $1000. What is the annual yield to maturity?

19. A firm that markets time-share condominiums offers prizes to those who endure a tour and sales talk. One prize is a $1000 savings account maturing in 45 years, in return for a $55 fee for "handling, processing, and insurance."[9] What is the implicit annual rate of return to someone who accepts this prize?

20. A home seller was offered $290,000—$140,000 cash plus zero-coupon bonds paying $150,000 after 20 years.[10] If the annual interest rate on these bonds is 10 percent, what is the buyer's actual cost for the seller's property?

21. In 1986 Duquesne University offered these prepaid tuition options:

| Number of Years Until Enrollment | Cost if Prepaid Today | Estimated Cost When Enrolled |
|---|---|---|
| 10 | $13,061 | $54,675 |
| 15 | 8,837 | 76,685 |

What are the implicit rates of return if we consider each of these plans to be a zero-coupon bond paying the estimated enrollment cost in a single lump sum at enrollment?

22. In 1979, Treasury bills yielded a 10.7 percent nominal return and the inflation rate was 13.3 percent. In 1982, Treasury bills yielded 14.9 percent and the inflation rate was 3.9 percent. What were the real after-tax returns during these 2 years for someone in a 30 percent tax bracket?

23. An entrepreneur is considering building a facility for recreational indoor soccer. Because she anticipates a 4 percent inflation over the next several years, she argues that the projected cash flow should be discounted by a 4 percent required return. A financial adviser says that she should use a 10 percent required rate return because she can earn 10 percent by investing in U.S. Treasury bonds. What do you advise?

24. It has been argued that nominal interest rates move up and down with inflation so as to hold real interest rates constant at, say, 2 percent. If a 5 percent *fall* in prices is anticipated, what nominal rate of return will give a 2 percent real return? (Ignore taxes.) How much does a $100 investment have to pay a year from now to give this nominal return? Why won't people willingly make such an investment?

25. In 1984 a Harvard Business School professor observed that from 1926 to 1976 the average real rate of return on long-term Treasury bonds was 1.1 percent and reasoned that, "With long-term Treasury bonds yielding a nominal return of 11 percent [in 1984], this suggests that investors harbor long-term inflation expectations close to 10 percent."[11] What do you think is the implicit assumption?

26. Explain why the following explanation of a bond's yield to maturity, or interest rate, is incorrect.

*The rise and fall of a bond's price has a direct inverse relationship to its yield, or interest rate. As prices go up, the yield declines, and vice versa. For example, a $1,000 bond might carry a stated annual yield, known as the coupon, of 8 percent, meaning that it pays $80 a year to the bondholder. If that bond was bought at 87, the actual yield would be 9.2 percent ($80 annual interest on $870 of principal).*[12]

27. In 1988 a bank offered selected individuals a $35,000 line of credit, allowing them to borrow up to $35,000 whenever they wanted at a monthly interest rate of 2.0 percent (2.5 percent on amounts less than $5000), compounded daily. What is the effective annual interest rate for these two monthly interest rates? (Assume 12 months of 30 days each.)

28. A spring 1992 publication by Rensselaer Polytechnic Institute showed a "smart option" in which the family of a student enrolling in fall 1992 could save $4931 by prepaying 4 years of tuition with an amount equal to four times the current $15,900 tuition:[13]

| Year | Annual Tuition (5% Annual Increase) | Prepayment Tuition |
|---|---|---|
| 1993–1994 | 16,695 | 0 |
| 1994–1995 | 17,530 | 0 |
| 1995–1996 | 18,406 | 0 |
|  | $68,531 | $63,600 |

Explain why this "smart option" may not be so smart.

29. During the 1800s, there were often years of deflation in which consumer prices fell. Do you suppose that nominal interest rates were unusually low or high during these deflations? What about real interest rates?

30. In 1984, after paying $60 million for the Dallas Cowboys and $20 million for the Texas Stadium Corporation (which runs the stadium for the city of Irving, Texas), the new owner H. R. (Bum) Bright itemized the cost of replacing the top two or three rows of seats on the upper deck with 90 luxury boxes that could then be sold to the public for a total of $35 million. Bright's conclusion: "It's a wash deal. Everybody understands that."[14]

| | |
|---|---|
| Fee to Irving, Texas (8% of $35 million) | $2,800,000 |
| Cost of constructing the luxury boxes | $8,000,000 |
| Annual lost ticket sales from removed seats | $400,000 |
| Annual interest payments on money borrowed to buy the Cowboys | $3,000,000 |
| Cost of buying Texas Stadium Corporation | $20,000,000 |

Do these data show that the luxury boxes are a wash, with expenses approximately offsetting income? If you were Bright's financial adviser, what would you advise?

# 5

# The Term Structure of Interest Rates

*The adviser's strategy was long and wrong.*

**Wall Street trader**

Investors who bought 20-year bonds in the 1960s that yielded 4 percent lost money when interest rates rose to 9 percent in 1970. Corporations that sold 30-year bonds in 1982 at 15 percent were dismayed when rates fell below 10 percent in 1986. Banks that bought Treasury bills yielding 8 percent in 1985 were frustrated when they reinvested their money at 6 percent in 1986. Many savings and loans that borrowed short term and lent long term in the 1960s and 1970s went bankrupt in the 1980s.

These are all examples of interest-rate risk, gambles on the future course of interest rates. The cases cited are all gambles lost; there are an equal number of gambles won. The objective of this chapter is to understand the interest-rate wagers that are implicit in all investments. Later chapters will discuss other risks, including default risk and exchange-rate risk. Although we will focus on bonds for concreteness, the general principles that will be discussed apply to all assets.

First, we will look at why bonds of different maturities usually have different interest rates — why long-term rates are often higher than the interest rates on short-term bonds and why the reverse is sometimes true. Then we will compare the risks borne by those who buy long-term assets with the risks inherent in buying short-term securities. Finally, we will look at some tools that have been developed to measure interest-rate risk and, if possible, reduce it.

## THE TERM STRUCTURE OF INTEREST RATES

In May of 1985, short-term Treasury bills were priced to yield less than 8 percent, but long-term Treasury bonds yielded more than 11 percent. Why did some investors willingly settle for an 8 percent yield on one Treasury security

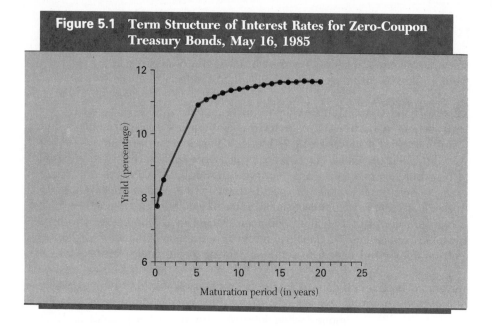

**Figure 5.1**   **Term Structure of Interest Rates for Zero-Coupon Treasury Bonds, May 16, 1985**

when another offered 11 percent? Was this an overlooked bargain, or is there some rational explanation?

Figure 5.1 shows the yields on several zero-coupon Treasury bonds in May 1985, with maturities ranging from 1 to 20 years. There is a whole spectrum of interest rates in this figure, with yields that are relatively low for short-term bonds and then rise with maturity. This is an example of the **term structure of interest rates**, describing the yields to maturity on zero-coupon bonds that have different maturities but are otherwise identical.

With some securities there is considerable risk that the issuer will default by failing to make the promised payments. All the securities considered in a term structure have a similar chance of default; if we compare the yields on a short-term Treasury bond that has no chance of default and a long-term "junk" bond that has a substantial probability of default, we don't know if the difference in yields reflects the term structure or the difference in default risk.

Notice also that the term structure compares the yields on zero-coupon bonds, which, for reasons that will be explained shortly, are not necessarily equal to the yields on coupon-paying bonds. It is easier to work with zero-coupon bonds because then we can associate a single future payment with a single interest rate. A comparison of the yields to maturity on coupon-paying bonds with different maturities is called a **yield curve**.

## THE EXPECTATIONS HYPOTHESIS

Figure 5.1 shows that the term structure in May of 1985 sloped upward, with long-term bonds yielding more than bonds with shorter maturities. Sometimes the term structure is flat, with short- and long-term bonds having the same yields, and sometimes it is inverted, with short-term bonds having the higher yields.

The most important explanation for these variations in the term structure is interest-rate expectations. Consider a choice between two default-free zero-coupon securities, the first maturing in 1 year and paying an annual return $R_1$ and the second maturing in 2 years and paying an annual rate of return $R_2$.

A prospective purchaser of the 2-year zero should consider the alternative of "rolling over" 1-year zeros by purchasing a 1-year zero and, when it matures, purchasing a new 1-year zero. Every dollar invested in 2-year zeros will grow to $(1 + R_2)^2$, whereas every dollar invested in a sequence of 1-year zeros grows to $(1 + R_1)(1 + R_1^{+1})$, where $R_1^{+1}$ is the interest rate on 1-year zeros 1 year from now. Ignoring transaction costs, such investments are perfect substitutes, and the **expectations hypothesis** says that the securities must be priced so that both strategies do equally well:

$$(1 + R_2)^2 = (1 + R_1)(1 + R_1^{+1}) \tag{5.1}$$

Otherwise, investors will shun the inferior bond, reducing its price and raising its return until it is competitive.

Similar logic applied to longer-term securities gives the following extrapolation of Equation 5.1:

$$(1 + R_n)^n = (1 + R_1)(1 + R_1^{+1})(1 + R_1^{+2}) \cdots (1 + R_1^{+n-1}) \tag{5.2}$$

where $R_n$ is the annual yield on an $n$-year zero-coupon security and the returns on the right-hand side are 1-year rates over the next $n$ years. For doing calculations mentally rather than on a computer, we can use this approximation:

$$R_n = \frac{R_1 + R_1^{+1} + R_1^{+2} + \cdots + R_1^{+n-1}}{n} \tag{5.3}$$

Equation 5.2, sometimes called the **Hicks equation** in recognition of the work of John Hicks, a Nobel Prize–winning British economist, is the fundamental equation of the expectations hypothesis. According to the expectations hypothesis, the relationship between short- and long-term interest rates reflects the anticipated future course of interest rates. If, for example, the 1-year rate is 10 percent now and will be 10 percent next year, then 2-year zeros must yield 10 percent, too, to be competitive:

$$\begin{aligned}
(1 + R_2)^2 &= (1 + R_1)(1 + R_1^{+1}) \\
&= (1 + 0.10)(1 + 0.10) \\
&= 1.21
\end{aligned}$$

implies

$$\begin{aligned}
1 + R_2 &= \sqrt{1.21} \\
R_2 &= 0.10 \quad \text{(or 10 percent)}
\end{aligned}$$

If, however, the 1-year rate is now 10 percent and will be 12 percent next year, then comparable 2-year assets must yield approximately 11 percent a year:

$$(1 + R_2)^2 = (1 + R_1)(1 + R_1^{+1})$$
$$= (1 + 0.10)(1 + 0.12)$$
$$= 1.232$$

implies

$$1 + R_2 = \sqrt{1.232}$$
$$R_2 = 0.10995 \quad \text{(or 10.995 percent)}$$

If, instead, the 1-year rate is expected to decline from 10 percent this year to 8 percent next year, then 2-year assets must yield about 9 percent a year:

$$(1 + R_2)^2 = (1 + R_1)(1 + R_1^{+1})$$
$$= (1 + 0.10)(1 + 0.08)$$
$$= 1.188$$

implies

$$1 + R_2 = \sqrt{1.188}$$
$$R_2 = 0.08995 \quad \text{(or 8.995 percent)}$$

The general rule is short and easy: the 2-year rate will be above or below the 1-year rate depending on whether the 1-year rate is expected to rise or fall.

Extending the lesson to longer-term assets, we conclude that if no change in 1-year rates is anticipated, comparable assets of differing maturities will be priced to have the same yield. Longer-term rates will be above the current 1-year rate if rates are expected to rise in the future and below if rates are expected to decline.

Three simple term structures are shown in Figure 5.2. More complex

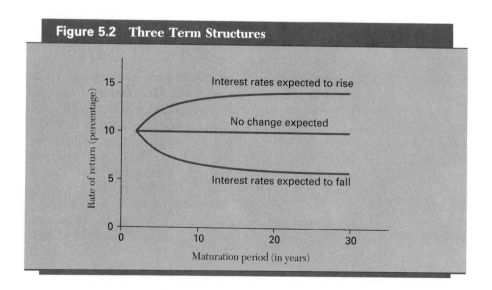

**Figure 5.2   Three Term Structures**

interest-rate expectations (for example, rates that are expected to rise for a few years and then decline) imply more complicated term structures. An upward-sloping term structure often is observed when the economy is expanding and investors anticipate that the rate of inflation and interest rates will increase in the future. A downward-sloping (or "inverted") term structure often occurs when the Federal Reserve uses tight-money policies to cool off the economy. The temporary credit squeeze raises current short-term interest rates, but investors

---

**EXAMPLE 5.1** *Are Some Treasury Bonds Overlooked Bargains?*

The pure term structure of interest rates reflected in the Hicks equation applies to zero-coupon bonds, but most bonds pay semiannual coupons. A yield curve showing the yields to maturity for coupon-paying bonds of differing maturities is not identical to the term structure of returns on zero-coupon bonds, except in the special case of a flat term structure. To illustrate this situation, we assume annual coupons for simplicity. The present value $P$ of an $n$-year bond with annual coupons $C$ and maturation value $M$ is obtained by summing the present values of the payments using the appropriate required returns as follows:

$$P = \frac{C}{(1 + R_1)} + \frac{C}{(1 + R_2)^2} + \cdots + \frac{C}{(1 + R_n)^n} + \frac{M}{(1 + R_n)^n}$$

The yield to maturity $y$ is the constant required return that solves the present-value equation:

$$P = \frac{C}{(1 + y)} + \frac{C}{(1 + y)^2} + \cdots + \frac{C}{(1 + y)^n} + \frac{M}{(1 + y)^n}$$

If the term structure is flat ($R_1 = R_2 = \cdots = R_n$), then the calculated yield to maturity $y$ equals $R_n$, and the yield curve and term structure coincide. If, on the other hand, the term structure slopes upward, then the yield to maturity $y$ is an average of the required returns and will be somewhat less than $R_n$, depending on the size of the coupons. For a zero-coupon bond, $y$ equals $R_n$; the figure on the next page shows that as the coupon rate increases, the calculated yield to maturity falls below the return on a zero-coupon bond. Similarly, when the term structure slopes downward, the yield to maturity is above $R_n$, the more so the larger the coupon is.

The most important implication is that the term structure provides a logical explanation for why bonds from the very same issuer with the same maturity may have different yields to maturity. If you look in the newspaper now, you might find two 10-year U.S. Treasury bonds, one with, say, an 8 percent yield to maturity and the other with 8.5 percent. The latter is not necessarily an overlooked bargain. Perhaps the term structure slopes upward and the second bond has lower coupons than the first.

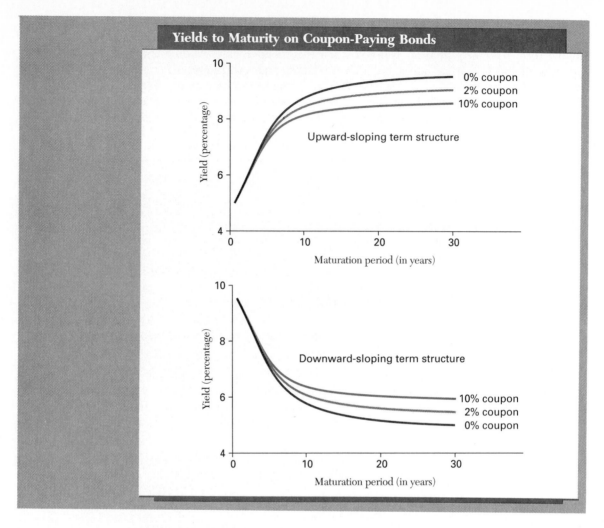

anticipate a future decline in interest rates as private borrowing slackens, inflation declines, and the Fed relaxes credit again.

## Is the Term Structure Always/Ever Right?

The expectations hypothesis is a straightforward yet elegant theory. Because
rolling over short-term assets ("shorts") is an alternative to holding long-term
assets ("longs"), the yields on short- and long-term assets are linked together by
interest-rate expectations. Anticipated movements in short-term rates determine
whether long rates will be above or below short rates, and conversely, we can use

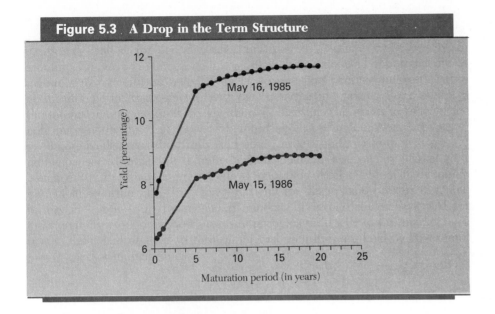

**Figure 5.3  A Drop in the Term Structure**

the observed relationship between short and long rates to infer the interest-rate expectations of financial experts. For instance, the expectations hypothesis interpretation of Figure 5.1, in which long rates are above short rates, is that in May of 1985 investors expected interest rates to increase.

Figure 5.3 shows that interest rates actually fell by several percentage points during the next 12 months, causing investors, in retrospect, to regret that they had not bought long-term securities and locked in high rates of return. Those who passed up long-term bonds yielding more than 11 percent in the spring of 1985 and bought 1-year Treasury bills yielding less than 8 percent, counting on a rise in interest rates, ended up rolling over their money in the spring of 1986 at lower interest rates.

This was not the first time that the interest-rate forecasts implicit in the term structure turned out to be wrong. Interest rates are notoriously difficult to forecast, and investors have made many costly errors. In 1982 and 1983, as in 1985, long-term Treasury bond rates were some 2 percentage points above the yields on short-term Treasury bonds, indicating (according to the expectations hypothesis) that interest rates were expected to increase sharply — yet interest rates tumbled. In 1979 and 1980, long rates were below short rates, and interest rates rose.

Empirical studies suggest that the term structure mispredicts the direction of interest rates as often as not.[1] The safest conclusion is that the term structure may well reflect investors' best guesses about the future course of interest rates, but these guesses are far from guarantees.

---

## EXAMPLE 5.2 *Mexico Profits from the Term Structure*

In January of 1990 the Mexican government bought 30-year zero-coupon U.S. Treasury bonds paying $33 billion in 2020 to collateralize the principal on new bonds that it was issuing. To price these 30-year zeros, the U.S. Treasury agreed to use the interest rate on 30-year Treasury coupon bonds rather than the rate on 30-year Treasury zeros. Because the term structure was downward sloping at the time, the interest rate on coupon bonds was somewhat higher than the rate on zeros, causing the Treasury to use an interest rate of 7.925 percent instead of 7.625 percent.

How much difference did this make in the price Mexico paid for the zeros? Nearly $300 million:

$$\frac{\$33 \text{ billion}}{1.07625^{30}} - \frac{\$33 \text{ billion}}{1.07925^{30}} = \$3.640 \text{ billion} - \$3.349 \text{ billion} = \$291 \text{ million}$$

Mexico saved $291 million because the term structure was downward sloping and the U.S. Treasury agreed to use the wrong interest rate.

*The Wall Street Journal* was one of the first to report the financial consequences of this decision. Initially, the paper suggested that the U.S. Treasury made this decision deliberately in order to give Mexico a hidden $300 million subsidy. After further investigation, the paper concluded that it was an inadvertent giveaway by inept Treasury officials: "The Treasury didn't have the financial acumen to recognize what was going on until after the essential bargain was reached."*

*"Weakening the Treasury," Wall Street Journal, *August 15, 1990.*

---

The expectations hypothesis was derived by assuming that future interest rates are known with certainty. When the future is certain, short- and long-term bonds are priced so that all strategies are guaranteed to do equally well. In reality, the future course of interest rates is unknown, and investors gamble, whichever strategy they follow. If they roll over shorts, they can be hurt by an unexpected drop in interest rates; if they buy longs, an unexpected increase in interest rates is their downfall. Let's now look at how investors can choose a strategy that reflects their opinions about the future course of interest rates.

---

## EXAMPLE 5.3 *Expert Forecasts Aren't Reliable*

In December of 1986, *The Wall Street Journal* asked 35 top forecasters to predict the interest rates on 3-month Treasury bills and 30-year Treasury bonds 6 months later, in June of 1987. In June of 1987, the paper asked for predictions for December of 1987. The results are shown in the accompanying table. In December of 1986, the average prediction for the T-bill rate in June of 1987 was 4.98 percent, with the individual forecasts ranging from as low as 4.1 percent to as high as 6 percent, a span of nearly 2 percentage points. The actual value turned out to be 5.73 percent, 75 basis points above the average prediction. The June 1987 30-year bond rate was 8.5 percent, a full 1.5 percent above the average prediction and, indeed, outside the range spanned by the predictions. Not one of these 35 experts was within 50 basis points of the actual value. There was even more disagreement in the predictions for December of 1987, with the average T-bill forecast turning out to be slightly too high and the long-term bond forecast much too low.

Nine of these forecasters had been surveyed by *The Wall Street Journal* over all 10 of the preceding 6-month periods (from December of 1981 through June of 1986). On 6 of these 10 occasions, the actual Treasury bill rate was outside the range of the 9 forecasts made 6 months earlier. Of the 90 individual forecasts of the T-bill rate, there were 38 correct and 52 incorrect predictions of the direction of change of the T-bill rate. The average error was 1.6 percentage points.*

The problem is not that these forecasters are uninformed, but that interest rates are notoriously difficult to forecast. Interest rates fluctuate considerably, causing large changes in bond prices and substantial capital gains and losses for bond traders. Each gain or loss is largely unexpected. If it were clear that bond prices were about to fall, there would be no buyers at current prices. If a sharp increase were certain, there would be no sellers. Instead, there is always, at the current price, a balance between buyers expecting prices to rise and sellers expecting prices to fall.

## Interest-Rate Forecasts by 35 Experts

|  | December 1986 Predictions of June 1987 Interest Rates (%) | | June 1987 Predictions of December 1987 Interest Rates (%) | |
| --- | --- | --- | --- | --- |
|  | 3-Month T-Bill | 30-Year Bond | 3-Month T-Bill | 30-Year Bond |
| Average | 4.98 | 7.05 | 5.91 | 6.19 |
| Range | 4.10–6.00 | 6.10–8.00 | 4.25–6.63 | 5.88–9.40 |
| Actual | 5.73 | 8.50 | 5.77 | 9.12 |

**Source:** Tom Herman and Mathew Winkler, "Economic Expansion Will Keep Going for at Least Another Year and Interest Rates Won't Change Much, Say Analysts in Survey," *Wall Street Journal*, July 6, 1987.

*Michael T. Belongia, "Predicting Interest Rates: A Comparison of Professional and Market-Based Forecasts," Federal Reserve Bank of St. Louis Review, March 1987, pp. 9–15.*

## *Betting Against the Term Structure*

For any given term structure we can infer the future interest-rate values for which the strategies of buying longs and rolling over shorts do equally well. If we disagree with these projections, we have a reason for choosing between shorts and longs. Suppose, for example, that 1-year bonds are priced to yield 8 percent and 2-year bonds 9 percent a year; that is, $R_1 = 0.08$ and $R_2 = 0.09$. The Hicks equation (either Equation 5.1 or 5.2) implies that shorts and longs will, in retrospect, do equally well if the 1-year rate a year from now, $R_1^{+1}$, turns out to be about 10 percent:

$$(1 + R_2)^2 = (1 + R_1)(1 + R_1^{+1})$$
$$(1.09)^2 = (1.08)(1 + R_1^{+1})$$

implies

$$1 + R_1^{+1} = \frac{(1.09)^2}{1.08} = 1.1000925$$
$$R_1^{+1} = 0.1000925 \quad \text{(or 10.00925 percent)}$$

The logic is as follows: The 2-year bond pays 9 percent a year. To do as well buying a 1-year bond at 8 percent, the investor has to be able to reinvest the second year at 10 percent. For ease of comparison, we can say that a 2-year bond at 9 percent implicitly pays 8 percent the first year, like the 1-year bond, and then 10 percent the second. The implicit future rates of return embedded in the term structure are called **forward rates**. The relevant question is whether the investor expects the 1-year rate next year to be above or below the 10 percent forward rate implicit in the term structure.

If you personally predict a 10 percent rate next year (or have no basis for making an informed prediction), then you have no reason for believing that shorts will do better or worse than longs. If, however, you disagree with the term structure's 10 percent forward rate, then you have cause for betting against the term structure. You would prefer the 2-year bond if you don't think the 1-year rate will reach 10 percent; you would favor the 1-year bond if you believe that it will go above 10 percent.

Notice that a belief in rising interest rates is not sufficient reason for buying short-term bonds. If you think interest rates will rise from 8 to 9 percent, a 2-year bond at 9 percent still does better. You must believe that interest rates will rise above the 10 percent forward rate that is already embedded in the term structure.

Whether or not your decision is an informed bet, there is risk in whichever strategy you choose. If you buy a 2-year bond yielding 9 percent when 1-year bonds yield 8 percent, you are betting implicitly that next year's rate will be below 10 percent. If it is, you earn more than you would have rolling over shorts. If it isn't, you are long and wrong, as was the financial advisor mentioned in the quotation prefacing this chapter.

Either way you go, buying shorts or longs, there is the possibility of disappointment — with longs if interest rates rise unexpectedly; with shorts if rates drop unexpectedly. Economists label the first danger capital risk and the second income risk, as will now be explained.

## CAPITAL RISK

The short-term purchase of a long-term asset creates the **capital risk** that an unexpected change in interest rates will cause an unanticipated change in the asset's price. To illustrate, consider an investor with $10,000 when interest rates on default-free 1-year Treasury zeros are 10 percent and are widely expected to stay at 10 percent for the foreseeable future. In accord with the expectations hypothesis, 1- , 2- , and 30-year Treasury zeros are all priced to yield 10 percent a year, as shown in the second column of Table 5.1. The future values of these three assets have been set so that the present value of each at a 10 percent required return is $10,000. The next column in the table shows that if interest rates stay at 10 percent, as anticipated, the present value of each asset a year from now will be $11,000 — thus providing the requisite 10 percent return.

What if interest rates rise unexpectedly to 20 percent? The fourth column of Table 5.1 shows that the 1-year asset will be worth $11,000 in a year, because it matures then, but that the present value of the 2-year asset is $900 less than expected. This asset now has 1 year left until maturity, and investors will not pay $11,000 to get $12,100 a year later, a mere 10 percent return, when interest rates on other 1-year assets have risen to 20 percent. They will only pay an amount such that $12,100 provides the requisite 20 percent return, and that amount is $12,100/1.20 = $10,083. An increase in the required return reduces the present value of a given future cash flow, and this price variability is labeled capital risk. Capital risk is two-sided, of course; just as an unexpected rise in interest rates reduces the present value, so an unexpected drop in interest rates raises the present value.

The decline in the value of the 2-year asset here is disappointing, but not nearly as crushing as the collapse of the value of the 30-year asset if interest rates rise to 20 percent. One year later there are still 29 years until maturity, and the present value at a 20 percent required return is $882, some 92 percent less than

**Table 5.1   Three Strategies**

| | | Price Next Year | |
| --- | --- | --- | --- |
| Strategy | Current Price | Rates Stay at 10% | Rates Rise to 20% |
| Buy 1-year asset | $10,000 = $\dfrac{\$11,000}{1.10}$ | $11,000 | $11,000 |
| Buy 2-year asset | $10,000 = $\dfrac{\$12,100}{1.10^2}$ | $11,000 = $\dfrac{\$12,100}{1.10}$ | $10,083 = $\dfrac{\$12,100}{1.20}$ |
| Buy 30-year asset | $10,000 = $\dfrac{\$174,494}{1.10^{30}}$ | $11,000 = $\dfrac{\$174,494}{1.10^{29}}$ | $882 = $\dfrac{\$174,494}{1.20^{29}}$ |

the $11,000 that had been anticipated. The startling magnitude of this price decline is a dramatic example of a general principle that we will explore in more depth later in this chapter: the longer the term of the asset, the more sensitive its price is to interest-rate fluctuations and the larger is the capital risk.

## INCOME RISK

Should nervous investors forgo long-term assets to avoid the terrors of capital risk? Not necessarily, because rolling over short-term assets is risky too. If you invest in a perfectly safe 1-year Treasury zero, then you are guaranteed $11,000 when the bill matures 1 year hence (and the price won't stray far from $11,000 in the meantime). However, what rate of return will you earn when you reinvest your $11,000 a year from now, and the year after that? This uncertainty about the rates of return prevailing when you reinvest your money is called **income risk** (or **reinvestment risk**). Income risk refers to the fact that the future value of an investment depends on the rates of return prevailing when the cash flow is reinvested.

Consider the three assets in Table 5.1 again. If the 30-year Treasury zero is purchased, the investor is assured of $174,494 thirty years from now, representing a 10 percent annual rate of return. If, instead of locking in this 10 percent return, the investor rolls over 1-year zeros, year after year, $11,000 is assured at the end of the first year, but there are no guarantees beyond that. If, as is currently anticipated, interest rates stay at 10 percent, wealth will grow to

$$\$10,000(1.10^{30}) = \$174,494$$

the same as with the 30-year asset. However, if interest rates drop unexpectedly to 5 percent and stay there, the future value will be only

$$\$10,000(1.10)(1.05^{29}) = \$45,277$$

some 75 percent less than with the 30-year asset.

The purchase of a 30-year zero guarantees a specified payment in 30 years, when the asset matures, but not its present value in the intervening years. Rolling over 1-year zeros guarantees a payment next year, but not beyond that. With capital risk, you may experience a sudden large loss; with income risk, you may suffer slowly.

Taking into account opportunity losses, no strategy is safe. You could always do better if you had an accurate crystal ball. Lacking one, remember this general principle: the purchase of long-term assets is profitable if interest rates fall unexpectedly; rolling over short-term assets does well if interest rates rise unexpectedly. For borrowers, the reverse is true. Borrowing long term at a fixed interest rate will turn out to be profitable if interest rates rise unexpectedly; rolling over a sequence of short-term loans turns out well if interest rates decline unexpectedly.

# INFLATION RISK

Although a 30-year asset locks in a fixed dollar amount at the end of 30 years, there is still **inflation risk**, in that the purchasing power of these dollars depends on what happens to prices during the intervening 30 years. Let's set the price level today at $1. If, miraculously, there is no inflation for the next 30 years, the price level will still be $1, and $174,494 will still buy as much then as it does now. If there is instead 5 percent inflation each year, the price level will more than quadruple

$$\$1(1.05^{30}) = \$4.322$$

and $174,494 will only buy then what $40,374 buys now,

$$\frac{\$174,494}{4.322} = \$40,374$$

A 10 percent inflation, year after year, will just offset the 10 percent nominal return, giving a 0 percent real return. Wealth goes up by a factor of 17, but so do prices, so the real value of the investment stays at $10,000. And for a final scare, if prices rise by 20 percent a year, the investor with $10,000 who locks in a guaranteed 10 percent nominal return a year winds up with only enough money to buy what $735 buys today.

A long-term asset with a guaranteed nominal payoff does not protect investors from unanticipated inflation. An unexpected increase in the rate of inflation erodes, while an unexpected decrease swells, the purchasing power of fixed nominal cash flows. We saw in Chapter 4 that while inflation and interest rates do not move in locked step, an increase in the rate of inflation does tend to increase nominal interest rates. If this is so, a strategy of rolling over short-term bonds offers some protection against unexpected inflation. Remember, however, that it is only unanticipated changes in inflation that are risky. Anticipated inflation is presumably already built into interest-rate expectations and, hence, the term structure.

# RISK AND THE SHAPE OF THE TERM STRUCTURE

The expectations hypothesis must be modified to account for risk preferences. The expectations hypothesis predicts that short- and long-term securities will all be priced to have the same anticipated return, taking into account investor expectations of future interest rates. Uncertainty regarding interest rates, however, creates income and capital risk, causing risk-averse investors to prefer shorts to longs, or vice versa. If this is so, the expected returns need not be equal: the inferior asset will have to offer a higher expected return — a risk premium — to attract investors.

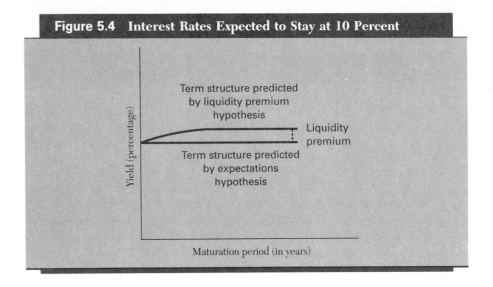

**Figure 5.4   Interest Rates Expected to Stay at 10 Percent**

The **liquidity-premium hypothesis** holds that investors are more concerned with capital risk than income risk and so have a natural preference for short-term assets and require relatively high returns on long-term bonds — higher than predicted by the expectations hypothesis. According to this theory, the term structure normally slopes upward, as illustrated in Figure 5.4.

The **market-segmentation hypothesis**, in contrast, holds that investors have diverse preferences and specialize in different maturities (their "preferred habitats"). Some investors, such as life insurance companies and pension funds, have long horizons. To the extent that such institutions have promised to pay relatively fixed nominal amounts many years from now, based on assumed rates of return, there is considerable danger for them in a strategy of rolling over short-term investments. Insurance companies and pension funds are, in fact, the largest holders of long-term bonds. Other investors, particularly those most concerned with real rates of return, consider long-term bonds very risky and prefer to roll over short-term investments.

If the market is sharply segmented, then the interest rates on different maturities may depend solely on demand and supply within that segment of the market — allowing very different interest rates on bonds with only slightly different maturities. While some investors do have preferred habitats, the evidence is that there are no discontinuities in the term structure; maturities are linked by the willingness of many investors to seek out the highest returns.

On balance, capital risk seems to be the predominant concern of investors in that rigorous studies indicate that long-term interest rates have, on average, been somewhat higher (roughly half a percentage point) than short-term interest rates, evidence that investors need some extra return — a *liquidity premium* — to overcome their aversion to capital risk and persuade them to hold long-term bonds.[2] Similarly, comparisons of the term structure with actual surveys of interest-rate expectations indicate that the interest rates on longer-term securities are slightly higher than implied by the expectations hypothesis, again evidence in support of the liquidity-premium hypothesis.[3]

Interest-rate expectations are the primary determinant of the shape of the term structure and exert a decisive influence on shifts in the term structure. In addition, investor distaste for capital risk requires long-term bonds to be priced to yield a bit more than implied by the expectations hypothesis.

# DURATION

So far we have focused on zero-coupon securities, which pay a lump sum at maturity. Most investments provide a regular cash flow: the monthly payments from an amortized loan, the semiannual coupons from a bond, and the quarterly dividends from corporate stock. A 30-year zero-coupon bond has much more capital risk than a 2-year zero. However, does a 10-year bond with large coupons have more capital risk than a 5-year bond with no coupons? You have to wait longer to receive the face value of the 10-year bond, but you also receive some coupons before the 5-year bond matures. The overall sensitivity of an asset's present value to changes in its required return, taking into account all the cash flow, is gauged by the asset's **duration**. Duration is a very important concept that will be used repeatedly in later chapters to analyze assets, investment strategies, and the behavior of different financial institutions. In this chapter we will see how duration is measured and how it can be used to gauge capital risk.

## *The Duration Formula*

The present value $P$ of an $n$-year investment with cash flow $X_t$ in year $t$ and a constant required return $R$ is

$$P = \frac{X_1}{(1 + R)} + \frac{X_2}{(1 + R)^2} + \cdots + \frac{X_n}{(1 + R)^n} \qquad (5.4)$$

The value of an asset's duration $D$ is determined by this equation:

$$D = (1)\left[\frac{X_1/(1 + R)}{P}\right] + (2)\left[\frac{X_2/(1 + R)^2}{P}\right] + \cdots + (n)\left[\frac{X_n/(1 + R)^n}{P}\right] \qquad (5.5)$$

An understanding of this formula may be helped by analogy to a course grade that depends on the scores on two midterms and a final examination, with 50 percent of the grade determined by the final examination score and 25 percent by each midterm. A student who gets 82 on the first midterm, 75 on the second midterm, and 93 on the final has a course score of

$$X = 84(0.25) + 78(0.25) + 93(0.50) = 87$$

The course score is a weighted average in that the individual scores are multiplied by weights of 0.25, 0.25, and 0.50 to reflect the relative importance of each.

Duration is also a weighted average. The numbers in parentheses in Equation 5.5, that is, 1, 2, . . ., $n$, are the numbers of years the investor must wait to receive the cash flow; $X_1$ is received after 1 year, $X_2$ after 2 years, and so on. An asset's duration is a weighted average of these years, using weights that reflect the fraction of the total present value received at that time; for example, $[X_2/(1 + R)^2]/P$ is the fraction of the present value received in the second year.

To illustrate the calculation of duration, consider a 2-year asset paying $100 one year from today and $100 the year after. At a 10 percent required return, the present value is

$$P = \frac{X_1}{(1 + R)} + \frac{X_2}{(1 + R)^2}$$
$$= \frac{\$100}{(1.10)} + \frac{\$100}{(1.10)^2}$$
$$= \$90.91 + \$82.64$$
$$= \$173.55$$

The second $100 payment has a lower present value than the first because it is a year later. Of the total $173.55 present value, the first $100 payment represents $90.91/\$173.55 = 0.524$, slightly more than 52 percent, and the second $82.64/\$173.55 = 0.476$, the remaining 48 percent. The duration is

$$D = (1)\left[\frac{X_1/(1 + R)}{P}\right] + (2)\left[\frac{X_2/(1 + R)^2}{P}\right]$$
$$= (1)\left[\frac{\$100/(1.10)}{\$173.55}\right] + (2)\left[\frac{\$100/(1.10)^2}{\$173.55}\right]$$
$$= (1)(0.524) + (2)(0.476)$$
$$= 1.476$$

slightly less than $1\frac{1}{2}$ years. Thus the average wait until receiving this asset's present value is $1\frac{1}{2}$ years.

Table 5.2 shows a detailed calculation of the duration of an 8-year $1000 bond with a 10 percent annual coupon rate and a 9 percent yield to maturity. Because the 9 percent yield to maturity is less than the 10 percent coupon rate, this bond sells for a premium over its $1000 face value:

$$P = \frac{\$100}{(1 + 0.09)} + \frac{\$100}{(1 + 0.09)^2} + \cdots + \frac{\$100}{(1 + 0.09)^8} + \frac{\$1000}{(1 + 0.09)^8}$$
$$= \$1055.35$$

Table 5.2 shows that the duration — that is, the average wait until receiving the eight annual $100 coupons and the $1000 maturity value after 8 years — works out to be 5.93 years. In practice, durations are not calculated by hand but are part of the standard output from many financial computer programs.

**Table 5.2  The Duration of an 8-Year Bond with $100 Annual Coupons, a $1000 Maturation Value, and a 9 Percent Yield to Maturity**

| Wait (years) | Cash Flow | Present Value of Cash Flow | Weight for Calculating Duration | Duration Calculation |
|---|---|---|---|---|
| 1 | $100 | $\frac{\$100}{1.09} = \$91.74$ | $\frac{\$91.74}{\$1055.35} = 0.0869$ | $1(0.0869) = 0.087$ |
| 2 | $100 | $\frac{\$100}{1.09^2} = \$84.17$ | $\frac{\$84.17}{\$1055.35} = 0.0798$ | $2(0.0798) = 0.160$ |
| 3 | $100 | $\frac{\$100}{1.09^3} = \$77.22$ | $\frac{\$77.22}{\$1055.35} = 0.0732$ | $3(0.0732) = 0.220$ |
| 4 | $100 | $\frac{\$100}{1.09^4} = \$70.84$ | $\frac{\$70.84}{\$1055.35} = 0.0671$ | $4(0.0671) = 0.268$ |
| 5 | $100 | $\frac{\$100}{1.09^5} = \$64.99$ | $\frac{\$64.99}{\$1055.35} = 0.0616$ | $5(0.0616) = 0.308$ |
| 6 | $100 | $\frac{\$100}{1.09^6} = \$59.63$ | $\frac{\$59.63}{\$1055.35} = 0.0565$ | $6(0.0565) = 0.339$ |
| 7 | $100 | $\frac{\$100}{1.09^7} = \$54.70$ | $\frac{\$54.70}{\$1055.35} = 0.0518$ | $7(0.0518) = 0.363$ |
| 8 | $1100 | $\frac{\$1100}{1.09^8} = \$552.05$ | $\frac{\$552.05}{\$1055.35} = 0.5231$ | $8(0.5231) = 4.185$ |
| | | $1055.35 | 1.0000 | 5.93 |

## The Effect of Maturity, Cash Flow, and Required Return on Duration

For a zero-coupon bond that matures in $n$ years, all the present value is received in year $n$; the duration — or average wait — is consequently $n$ years. The duration of a 5-year zero is 5 years; the duration of a 30-year zero is 30 years. For bonds with coupons, the cash flow before maturity makes the average wait until receiving the cash flow — that is, the duration — less than the number of years until maturity. The larger the coupons relative to the maturation value, the shorter is the duration relative to the bond's maturity. Figure 5.5 illustrates this important point for bonds of various coupon rates that are selling for par. For instance, for 20-year bonds selling for par, the duration is 20 years with no coupons, 16.58 years with 2 percent coupons, 12.87 years with 5 percent coupons, and 9.01 years with 10 percent coupons.

Equation 5.5 shows that an asset's duration also depends on the required return. In particular, it can be shown mathematically that an increase in a bond's yield to maturity reduces its duration (the size of this effect is called the bond's *convexity*). Figure 5.6 illustrates this point by comparing the duration of 10 percent coupon bonds with maturities up to 30 years for 8, 10, and 12 percent yields

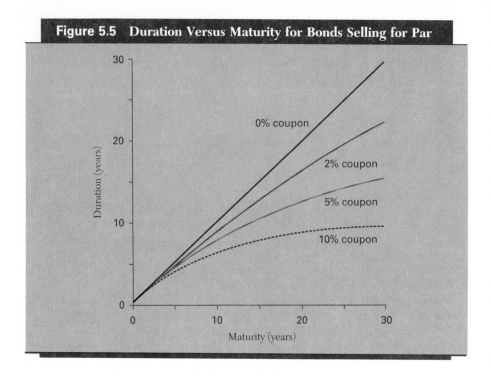

**Figure 5.5    Duration Versus Maturity for Bonds Selling for Par**

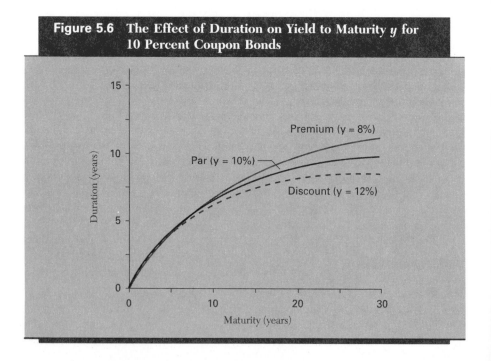

**Figure 5.6    The Effect of Duration on Yield to Maturity $y$ for 10 Percent Coupon Bonds**

to maturity. As shown, the effects of yield to maturity on duration are slight for short-term bonds. For a 20-year bond with a 10 percent coupon, the duration is 9.87 years if the yield to maturity is 8 percent, 9.01 years if the yield to maturity is 10 percent, and 8.20 years if the yield to maturity is 12 percent.

## Using Duration to Gauge Capital Risk

Duration is useful because it gauges the sensitivity of present value to a change in the required return. In particular, the application of calculus to Equation 5.4 shows that the percentage change in an asset's present value, written as $\%\Delta P$, resulting from a small change $\Delta R$ in the percentage required return is given by

$$\%\Delta P = -\frac{D}{1 + R}\Delta R \qquad (5.6)$$

or, approximately,

$$\%\Delta P = -D\Delta R \qquad (5.7)$$

In the preceding example, the 2-year asset has a duration of 1.5 years, and Equation 5.7 says that a 1 percentage point increase in the required return ($\Delta R = 1$) will reduce the present value by about 1.5 percent. Let's see if this is correct. If $R$ rises by 1 percentage point, to 11 percent,

$$
\begin{aligned}
P &= \frac{X_1}{(1 + R)} + \frac{X_2}{(1 + R)^2} \\
&= \frac{\$100}{(1.11)} + \frac{\$100}{(1.11)^2} \\
&= \$90.09 + \$81.16 \\
&= \$171.25
\end{aligned}
$$

about a $1\frac{1}{2}$ percent decline: ($171.25 - $173.55)/$173.55 = 0.013. Thus an asset's duration, the present-value weighted-average number of years until the cash flow is received, is about equal to the percentage change in the asset's present value resulting from a 1 percentage point change in the required return.

Equation 5.6 shows that a more accurate estimate of the percentage change in present value is given by what is called the **modified duration**, obtained by dividing the conventional duration by $1 + R$:

$$\text{Modified duration} = \frac{D}{1 + R}$$

In our example, the value of the modified duration is $D/(1 + R) = 1.476/(1 + 0.10) = 1.34$, which is indeed closer to the actual 1.3 percent change in present value.

The preceding section noted that the duration of a zero-coupon bond is equal to the number of years until maturity. It immediately follows that long-term zero-coupon bonds have a great deal of capital risk. The duration of a 30-year zero is 30 years, implying that a 1 percentage point rise in interest rates

| Table 5.3 | Annual Standard Deviations of Treasury Zeros, 1984–1987 | |
|---|---|---|
| Maturity (years) | | Standard Deviation (%) |
| 5 | | 10.8 |
| 10 | | 20.7 |
| 15 | | 28.8 |
| 20 | | 38.1 |

**Source:** Gary Smith, "Coping with the Term Structure," in William C. Brainard, William D. Nordhaus, and Harold W. Watts (eds.), *Money, Macroeconomics, and Economic Policy: Essays in Honor of James Tobin* (Cambridge, Mass.: MIT Press, 1991), pp. 205–232.

reduces its present value by roughly 30 percent. Conversely, a 1 percentage point drop in interest rates raises the present value by about 30 percent.

Empirical confirmation of the usefulness of duration for gauging risk is provided by the data in Table 5.3, which show the annual standard deviations of the prices of zero-coupon Treasury bonds during the years 1984–1987. Because the duration of a zero is equal to its maturity, we might expect 10-year, 15-year, and 20-year zeros to have, respectively, about two, three, and four times as much capital risk as a 5-year zero. During this period, judging by the relative standard deviations, they did.[4]

A bond with coupons has a duration that is less than its maturity and is shorter the larger are the coupons. For instance, a 20-year bond selling at par with a 10 percent coupon and a 10 percent yield to maturity has a duration of 9.01 years, less than half that of a 20-year zero-coupon bond. It follows that the price of a longer-term bond with high coupons may be less affected by interest rates than is the price of a shorter-term bond with low coupons — for instance, the 20-year bond with 10 percent coupons just mentioned has a duration of 9.01 years, less than that of a 10-year zero. A bond's maturity is an inaccurate measure of capital risk; its duration is the appropriate gauge.

## Asset and Liability Duration

So far we have focused on the risks borne by investors who buy assets. Those who issue bonds also gamble on interest rates. If you take out a 30-year fixed-rate mortgage, you will be glad that you did so if interest rates rise, but you will regret your choice if interest rates decline. If you take out a loan with an adjustable interest rate, you will pay more if interest rates go up and less if they go down.

Individuals and businesses have both assets and liabilities, each with associated future cash flows. Households take out mortgages and buy bonds; businesses sell bonds and buy plant and equipment. Each side of a balance sheet has some interest-rate risk, and to the extent that the durations of the assets and liabilities are not matched, there is an implicit wager on the future course of interest rates. Anxiety over such wagers during interest-rate turbulence in the late 1970s and early 1980s led to the creation of financial futures contracts and other hedging instruments that we will discuss in later chapters.

Banks, savings and loan associations (S&Ls), and other financial intermediaries provide an especially interesting example in that by borrowing from some to lend to others, there is a clear and controllable link between their financial assets and liabilities. In Britain, the actuaries who certify the financial soundness of an insurance company or pension fund are required to compare the maturities of assets and liabilities. There is no such requirement in the United States, and the interest-rate gambles that S&Ls have won and lost have not only shaken the S&Ls but also have scared depositors and policymakers, too.

## EXAMPLE 5.4 *Borrowing Short and Lending Long*

In the 1970s the balance sheets of a small, traditional savings and loan might look like this:

| Assets (millions of dollars) | | Liabilities (millions of dollars) | |
|---|---|---|---|
| Cash reserves | 5 | Deposits | 96 |
| Loans | 95 | Net worth | 4 |
| | 100 | | 100 |

Let's assume that the interest rates paid on the deposits change daily, giving deposits a duration of virtually zero, and that the loans are conventional 30-year mortgages. At a 10 percent interest rate, the duration of a 30-year mortgage works out to be 8.5 years. In practice, not all the S&L's mortgages were made today, so let's assume that the average duration of the loan portfolio is roughly 4 years. If this is so, an unanticipated 1 percentage point increase in interest rates will reduce the present value of this portfolio by 4 percent (about $4 million), enough to wipe out the S&L's net worth:

| Assets (millions of dollars) | | Liabilities (millions of dollars) | |
|---|---|---|---|
| Cash reserves | 5 | Deposits | 96 |
| Loans | 91 | Net worth | 0 |
| | 96 | | 96 |

(The present values of the deposits and reserves do not change because these have a duration of zero.)

Duration provides a dramatic way of seeing how the traditional S&L strategy of borrowing short and lending long is a very dangerous bet on the future course of interest rates. In the stylized example given here, an unexpected 1 percentage point reduction in interest rates doubles the net worth, but a 1 percentage point increase in interest rates reduces the S&L's net worth to zero so that if it were to sell its loans, it would barely have enough cash to pay off its depositors.

As interest rates rose during 1979–1982 (and, to make matters worse, there were significant defaults on farm, oil, and foreign loans), financial institutions with balance sheets comparable with those shown here were devastated. So widespread and severe was the damage that one influential analyst, Edward Yardeni of Prudential-Bache, based his 1984 and 1985 predictions of lower interest rates largely on his belief that the Federal Reserve would have to lower interest rates to bail out financial intermediaries who had borrowed short and lent long.

Duration also helps us understand why banks that have substantial amounts of short-term consumer and commercial loans are less susceptible to interest-rate fluctuations than thrifts that rely on long-term mortgages as well as how thrifts can adjust their portfolios to stabilize their net worth. A move to shorter-term loans (consumer loans and 15-year mortgages in place of 30-year mortgages) reduces asset duration. Even more effective are adjustable-rate mortgages, which can have a duration of 1 year or less depending on the adjustment provisions of the contract. On the liability side, longer-term deposits "with substantial penalties for premature withdrawal" can push duration upward. If these steps roughly match the duration of the assets to the duration of the liabilities, then the net worth of the financial intermediary is insulated from unanticipated interest-rate fluctuations. If the asset duration exceeds its liability duration, then the institution is implicitly betting that interest rates will fall. A liability duration in excess of asset duration is a wager that interest rates will rise.

Duration is a useful measure of interest-rate risk that can be used by both individual and institutional investors. In Part II of this book we will see how financial institutions can use asset and liability durations to measure and manage their exposure to interest-rate risk.

## SUMMARY

The term structure of interest rates describes the relationship between interest rates on zero-coupon bonds (with similar default risks) of varying maturities; the yield curve describes a similar relationship for coupon bonds. The expectations hypothesis says that the shape of the term structure depends on interest-rate expectations:

$$(1 + R_n)^n = (1 + R_1)(1 + R_1^{+1})(1 + R_1^{+2}) \cdots (1 + R_1^{+n-1})$$

where $R_n$ is the annual yield on an $n$-year zero-coupon security and the returns on the right-hand side are 1-year rates over the next $n$ years. A useful approximation is

$$R_n = \frac{R_1 + R_1^{+1} + R_1^{+2} + \cdots + R_1^{+n-1}}{n}$$

According to the expectations hypothesis, long rates are above, equal to, or below short rates depending on whether interest rates are expected to rise, stay the same, or decline. Therefore, we can infer from the shape of the current term structure the direction that investors expect interest rates to move.

Interest rates are very difficult to predict. Those who buy long-term bonds, locking in a rate of return, are betting that future interest rates will be lower than the forward rates implied by the term structure. Those who roll over short-term bonds implicitly wager that future interest rates will be higher than the term structure's forward rates. Short-term bonds have income risk because the interest rates at which the funds can be reinvested are uncertain. Long-term bonds have capital risk because changes in interest rates affect their market value. Fixed-income securities, especially long-term ones, also have inflation risk because the purchasing power of the cash flow depends on uncertain rates of inflation.

The liquidity-premium hypothesis holds that investors fearful of capital risk prefer short-term securities, and therefore, long-term securities must have relatively high expected returns (higher than predicted by the expectations hypothesis) to compensate for their capital risk. The market-segmentation hypothesis says that some investors have short horizons and prefer short-term securities, but others, such as pension funds and life insurance companies, have long horizons and a natural preference for long-term bonds.

An asset's duration $D$ is the present-value weighted-average length of time until the cash flow $X_t$ is received:

$$D = (1)\left[\frac{X_1/(1 + R)}{P}\right] + (2)\left[\frac{X_2/(1 + R)^2}{P}\right] + \cdots + (n)\left[\frac{X_n/(1 + R)^n}{P}\right]$$

The percentage change in an asset's present value $P$ resulting from a 1 percentage point change in the required return $R$ is approximately equal to its duration:

$$\%\Delta P = -D\Delta R$$

A complete picture of exposure to interest-rate risk must consider both assets and liabilities. A savings and loan association, for example, that borrows short and lends long has an asset duration that significantly exceeds the duration of its liabilities: its net worth will be increased by an unexpected decline in interest rates and reduced by an unanticipated increase in interest rates.

# IMPORTANT TERMS

capital risk
duration
expectations hypothesis
forward rates
Hicks equation
income risk (or reinvestment risk)

inflation risk
liquidity-premium hypothesis
market-segmentation hypothesis
modified duration
term structure of interest rates
yield curve

# EXERCISES

1. If the future is certain and the Hicks equation holds, which of the following strategies will be more profitable: buying a 7-year note followed by a 3-year note or buying a 6-year note followed by a 4-year note?

2. The rate of return on 1-year zero-coupon bonds is now 10 percent and is expected to be 15 percent next year and for at least 2 years after that. According to the expectations hypothesis, what should be the current annual yields on 2- , 3- , and 4-year zero-coupon bonds?

3. The annual rates of return on 1- , 2- , and 3-year zero-coupon bonds are 8, 10, and 12 percent, respectively. According to the expectations hypothesis, what is the expected return on a 1-year zero issued 1 year from now? Two years from now?

4. Look in the most recent Monday issue of *The Wall Street Journal* for the bond prices and yields reported in the section "Treasury Bonds, Notes & Bills." Find the subsection titled "Stripped Treasuries," and report the maturity dates and yields for Treasury zeros that mature in approximately 1, 5, 10, and 20 years. Does the expectations hypothesis interpretation of these data imply that investors expect interest rates to rise or fall in the coming years?

5. Look up the prices and yields of "Stripped Treasuries" in the "Treasury Bonds, Notes & Bills" section of the most recent Monday issue of *The Wall Street Journal*, and report the maturity dates and yields for Treasury

zeros that mature in approximately 1, 2, and 3 years. Calculate the anticipated yields implied by the expectations hypothesis on 1-year Treasury zeros issued 1 and 2 years from now.

6. Will Rogers once said, "I am not so much concerned with the return on my money as with the return of my money." Would you say that he was more concerned with income or capital risk?

7. Here is some advice offered in *Woman's Day* to bond investors:

*Many conservative investors are attracted to "income funds" — mutual funds invested mostly in [long-term] bonds — but they are not always as safe as they sound. Bond funds do well when long-term interest rates fall. . . . But bond funds do poorly when long-term interest rates rise. . . .*

*Michael Lipper of Lipper Analytical Services, which specializes in mutual-fund analysis, urges investors to think of bond funds as* speculative *securities: investments to buy and sell according to market conditions, rather than to hold for the long term. . . . if rates rise again, he says, it will pay to sell income funds and switch to the greater security of short-term money-market mutual funds.*[5]

a. Why do bond funds do well when long-term rates fall and poorly when they rise?

b. What does the expectations hypothesis imply about the profitability of shifting to short-term securities after interest rates rise?

c. In what sense do short-term money-market funds offer greater security than do long-term income funds?

8. In November of 1988, 2-year Treasury notes had 8½ percent yields to maturity and 30-year Treasury bonds had 9 percent yields. An article in *The Wall Street Journal* began

*Why would anyone buy 30-year Treasury bonds right now when they can earn nearly the same returns on short-term issues that aren't as susceptible to price decline?*

*Investors are confronting that dilemma because of an unusual development in the bond market — a "flat yield curve."* [6]

a. Why are long-term bonds more susceptible to price decline?

b. Why is a flat yield curve unusual? What is the usual shape?

c. Why would anyone (and someone must) buy 30-year bonds when the yield curve is flat?

9. In a May 1985 *New York Times* interview, John T. Haggerty, national director of personal financial planning for Prudential-Bache Securities, advised

*I wouldn't buy any bond, except maybe a Treasury, that was 30 years in maturity. I don't know if the world is going to be around 30 years from now. . . . If I had to buy, or if I wanted to buy, I'd probably be looking at discount bonds. There you have the maturities working in your favor. You know the bond's going to be going up in price, because it's getting closer to maturity with the passage of time.* [7]

a. Why is the existence of the world 30 years from now of little relevance to an investor's choice between short- and long-term bonds?

b. Evaluate Haggerty's apparent claim that the returns from bonds selling at a dis-

count are inherently more certain than the returns from bonds selling at par or for a premium.

c. Interest rates dropped substantially in 1985. Why, in retrospect, would Haggerty have made especially large profits from the purchase of 30-year bonds early in 1985?

10. A vice president at E. F. Hutton says of zero-coupon bonds backed by U.S. Treasury notes, "The beauty of it is that the investor knows exactly how many dollars go in, and how many dollars will come out." A Merrill Lynch vice president says, "This suits the little old lady in tennis shoes who's watching her nickels, and it's ideal for your kids." [8] Can you think of any reason why conservative investors might be nervous about zeros? Do you think there is any risk in such an investment?

11. In 1985, Ed Yardeni, Prudential-Bache's chief economist, forecast "lower-than-expected interest rates." [9] Why was he careful to say "lower-than-expected interest rates" rather than just "lower interest rates"? Should those who agreed with Yardeni have

a. Bought Treasury bills or long-term bonds?

b. Borrowed at a fixed or variable interest rate?

c. Sold 15-year or 30-year bonds?

12. An investments textbook states that "bond investors will prefer to buy short-term bonds whenever they expect interest rates to rise." [10] What is the logic behind this assertion? Why is it incorrect?

13. Explain this observation: "A bond's duration will always be shorter than its maturity — much shorter for higher coupon bonds." [11]

14. Critically explain and evaluate these excerpts from a *Wall Street Journal* article:

*With inflation abated and interest rates down sharply on money-market funds and bank accounts, consumers are turning to bond products for higher yields. Many investors have shifted dollars out of money funds paying around 7% and into [long-term] Treasury securities paying more than 10%. . . .*

*A California real estate attorney admits that he was "dumbfounded" to find that $192,000 in Treasury zeros he bought in January 1984 were valued at $156,000 when he went to sell them four months later. . . .*

*Nelson Chase, a West Bloomfield, Mich., attorney is representing a group of zero-coupon bond investors that is suing New York–based Merrill Lynch & Co. "All the literature talks about how safe these investments are," he says. "Unless you can be absolutely sure you will hold to maturity, these aren't safe investments."*[12]

In particular, explain

a. What circumstances, if any, would dissuade you from shifting out of a bank paying 7 percent into Treasury securities paying 10 percent.

b. How Treasury zeros could lose nearly 20 percent of their value in 4 months.

c. Why zeros held to maturity may not be safe.

15. In 1990 the Resolution Funding Corporation, a U.S. government agency established to finance the bailout of the thrift industry, sold 40-year zero-coupon bonds. A *Wall Street Journal* article asked

*So who would want to buy a 40-year bond? One group of buyers is expected to be pension funds and insurance companies who need bonds with extra-long maturities. . . . Another likely group of buyers is professional traders eager for yet another vehicle to bet on swings in interest rates.*[13]

Explain why pension funds and insurance companies "need bonds with extra-long maturities" and why 40-year zeros are especially attractive for traders who want to bet on interest rates.

16. Frederick Macaulay's pioneering studies of duration were instigated by his observation that investors seem to prefer high-coupon bonds to otherwise identical bonds with low coupons.[14] Does this preference suggest that investors are more concerned with income or with capital risk? Explain your reasoning.

17. Many lending institutions have been pushing 15-year mortgages in place of the traditional 30-year mortgage. Why do they prefer the 15-year mortgage?

18. In the spring of 1986, David Marks, senior vice president of Cigna Investments, explained how he used duration to implement his fixed-income strategy:

*To look at maturity alone, you are generally not taking into account interest income and reinvestment income. . . . If you're bullish, expecting interest rates to go down and prices up, then your duration should be slightly longer than the [Shearson Lehman bond] index. If you're bearish, your duration should be slightly shorter or the same.*[15]

Explain the advantages of a long-duration portfolio when you are bullish and a short-duration portfolio when you're not. Are there any circumstances in which, confident that interest rates will fall, you would nonetheless choose a short-duration portfolio?

19. Write a paragraph criticizing this advice:

*With a growing sense of gloom hanging over the bond market, many investment analysts said they're urging clients to switch away from long-term securities into the shortest possible maturities. "You can get almost as good yields at the short ends without the worry," says Data Resources' Mr. Eckstein.*[16]

20. In 1986, *The Wall Street Journal* reported that

*Falling interest rates prompt corporations to refinance short-term, high-cost debt with* bonds with lower rates and longer maturities, reducing costs and making them less vulnerable to interest-rate moves. . . . Still, many corporations delay refinancing, expecting interest rates to drop further.[17]

Why might long-term debt have lower interest rates than short-term debt? In what way are those who borrow long term still vulnerable to interest-rate moves?

21. Pacific Investment Management Company (PIMCO) always keeps the duration of its bond portfolio between $2\frac{1}{2}$ and 6 years. It held the duration below 3 years from 1977 to 1980 and increased the duration to almost 5 years in 1985. Why do you suppose PIMCO avoids extreme durations? Why does PIMCO sometimes maintain a relatively short duration and sometimes a relatively long one?

22. In the summer of 1981, Merrill Lynch planned to help Manufacturers Hanover issue money-market notes in $1000 denominations with interest rates adjusted weekly based on the prevailing average rate of return on 30-day commercial paper issued by businesses.[18] At the time, Merrill Lynch was running advertisements predicting a decline in interest rates. The Manufacturers Hanover issue collapsed because of a lack of buyers. If buyers were reluctant to buy these notes, was it because they were concerned about a possible increase or decline in interest rates?

23. Explain why you agree or disagree with this advice: "In an inflationary era, when depreciation of the currency is the order of the day, a fixed, long-term obligation is not the thing to own."[19]

24. Evaluate this argument by a prominent economics professor:

We should curb the political influence that the banking community has achieved through its formal alliance with the Fed. It is not surprising, of course, that creditors are more interested in relatively tight money and high interest rates than debtors and consumers.[20]

25. A commonplace bank procedure to control for interest-rate risk is *gap management*, where gap = (rate-sensitive assets − rate-sensitive liabilities)/total assets.

Interest-sensitive assets are those that mature, or are repriced, within a designated time-frame. For example, a loan may have a stated maturity of one year, but can be subject to rate changes tied to the prime rate and is, therefore, immediately sensitive to interest-rate changes. Similarly, rates paid on money market accounts generally can change daily and are, therefore, immediately sensitive to interest-rate movements.

. . . When the gap is zero, net interest income is fully insulated from interest-rate risk because the maturity of rate-sensitive assets and liabilities should cause them to offset each other and to leave the net interest margin unchanged.[21]

For example, if 10 percent of assets and 12 percent of liabilities have their rates change with market rates, then the gap is −2 percent.

   a. If a bank has a negative gap, will its net interest income rise or fall if interest rates increase?
   b. If a bank wanted to bet that interest rates were headed downward, should it have a positive or negative gap?
   c. Explain how a bank with a gap of zero could nonetheless find itself bankrupted (with its market value driven to zero) by an unexpected decline in interest rates.

26. Here are some excerpts from a 1986 *New York Times* article:

"In my view, making long-term fixed-rate mortgages is simply not a viable strategy any longer," said Dennis Jacobe, director of research at the United States League of Savings Associations.

*The widespread issuance of fixed-rate mortgages in the 1970's led to the collapse or merger of nearly a quarter of the nation's 4,000 savings associations then existing. . . . Of those that survived, some remain in extremely poor shape. . . .*

*Adjustable-rate mortgages reached their height of popularity in late 1984, when 70 percent of the mortgages issued by savings and loan associations were adjustable-rate, according to the savings league.*

*. . . Fixed-rate loans, [however], were the only type Washington Federal [a Seattle S&L] was making. . . .*

*"You can't be reckless, but right now we're in a deflationary cycle . . . ," Mr. Knutson [the company's president and chief executive] said. Referring to 1981, he added that "you can't operate based on one devastating period; otherwise you leave too much profitability on the table."* [22]

a. What is the economic event that caused trouble for S&Ls with fixed-rate mortgages? How do adjustable-rate mortgages provide protection?

b. Some S&Ls have moved to shorter-term mortgages and longer-term deposits. If the duration of their liabilities is greater than is the duration of their assets, are these S&Ls protected from interest-rate fluctuations?

c. Why do you suppose many S&Ls now wish they had issued fixed-rate mortgages during 1981–1984?

27. The Student Loan Marketing Association (Sallie Mae) is a private corporation that uses borrowed money to buy government-guaranteed student loans from banks. The interest rates on all its assets and liabilities adjust up or down with changes in T-bill rates. What is the duration of its assets? Of

its liabilities? How is its net worth affected by interest rates?

28. Explain the logic behind the following assertion and then explain why it is misleading.

*The essential difference between fixed- and adjustable-rate mortgages is the party at risk. In fixed mortgages, the lender takes all the risk, profiting or suffering from changes in the interest rate. . . . With an ARM, the borrower, not the lender, is at the mercy of fluctuating interest rates.* [23]

29. In contrast to producers, retailers have traditionally used mostly short-term debt to finance their inventories and consumer credit. However, volatile financial markets have persuaded some retailers to use long-term debt. For instance, J. C. Penney converted almost all its debt from short to long term in 1980. *The Wall Street Journal* reported that this strategy "reduces the danger of a potential cash shortage, should the nation's financial markets run into a crisis. . . . A company with a large amount of short-term debt must constantly refinance its borrowings as they come due. . . . For some companies, in the worst possible case, failure to refinance their debt could force them into bankruptcy court." [24] What risk is inherent in a strategy of financing inventories with long-term debt?

30. A money manager recommends buying long-term bonds when the yield on such bonds is more than 3.0 percentage points higher than the yield on 3-month Treasury bills and buying Treasury bills when this yield differential is less than 1.5 percentage points. [25] Why is this yield differential normally positive? What logical explanation is there (other than mispriced bonds) for a differential of more than 3.0 points? Of less than 1.5 points?

# 6 The Money Market

*Let us all be happy, and live within our means, even if we have to borrow the money to do it.*

**Artemus Ward**

Financial market participants commonly distinguish between short-term securities — those which mature in less than a year — and longer-term securities. The issuance and trading of short-term securities is said to take place in the **money market**; long-term securities are issued and traded in the **capital market**.

There are a number of reasons for this colloquial separation. As cash continually flows into and out of businesses and financial institutions, they routinely borrow and lend funds for very short periods of time — even just overnight — in order to cover temporary cash deficits or earn interest on temporary surpluses. This short-term cash management is very different from the issuance of long-term securities to finance long-lived construction projects. Thus the money and capital markets are generally used for different purposes.

For financial analysts, the difference between money-market and capital-market interest rates reveals the term structure of interest rates and provides information about interest-rate expectations. For investors, money-market and capital-market securities involve very different wagers on the course of interest rates and involve quite different risks. Money-market securities have very little capital risk: their prices cannot deviate much from maturation value because they will mature so soon. They do have considerable income (or reinvestment) risk because it is uncertain what interest rates will prevail when money-market securities mature and the proceeds are reinvested.

Money-market securities will turn out to be the more profitable investment if future interest rates turn out to be above the forward rates embedded in the term structure; otherwise, capital-market securities will turn out to have been the more profitable investment. For issuers, the implicit wagers are reversed, in that short-term financing is more expensive if future interest rates are surprisingly high.

This chapter discusses the money market, and the capital market will be discussed in the next three chapters — Chapter 7 covering bonds, Chapter 8 covering mortgages, Chapter 9 covering stocks. We begin with one of the most important money-market securities.

# TREASURY BILLS

Just as households borrow money to buy cars and houses and businesses borrow money to buy plants and equipment, so the federal government borrows money to buy missiles and paper clips. When the federal government's expenditures exceed its tax revenues, the U.S. Treasury sells securities to raise cash. Treasury bonds have maturities of more than 10 years. Treasury notes have maturities of 2 to 10 years. **Treasury bills (T-bills)** mature within 1 year and are consequently considered money-market securities.

The minimum face value for a T-bill is $10,000, with multiples of $5000 above this minimum. Treasury bills are short-term zeros in that they mature within a year and pay no interest before maturity. Interest is earned on a T-bill by purchasing it at a discount from its maturation value. For example, if you buy a 1-year $10,000 T-bill for $9400, you receive $10,000 after a year, so the return on your investment is the $600 difference between the purchase price and the redemption value of the bill. The Internal Revenue Service considers this $600 return interest, not a capital gain, and taxes it as such, the same as interest from a bank account.

Many individual investors buy Treasury bills because the $10,000 minimum denomination is lower than the $100,000 or $1 million minimum needed for most other money-market securities. Treasury bills have lower interest rates than most other money-market instruments of comparable maturity because of two desirable characteristics: they have no default risk and the interest on Treasury securities is exempt from state and local income taxes.

## Why Reported T-Bill Rates Are Misleading

Unlike virtually all other securities, the financial press traditionally calculates the returns on T-bills on a **discount basis** relative to the face value rather than the purchase price. If you buy a 52-week $10,000 T-bill for $9400, this $600 discount is a 6 percent discount from the $10,000 face value, and the T-bill rate is conventionally reported as 6 percent. From the standpoint of the investor, however, this is a $600 return on an investment of $9400, not $10,000, and the actual rate of return is $600/$9400 = 0.0638 (6.38 percent). Because T-bill rates traditionally are calculated on a discount basis (relative to the maturation value rather than the purchase price), they understate the investor's actual rate of return.

The federal government does not allow banks to calculate consumer loan rates on a discount basis but uses this misleading arithmetic on its own borrowing — thereby understating the interest rate it pays investors. Perhaps the calculation of T-bill rates on a discount basis made sense long ago when computations were done by hand and it was easier to divide by $10,000 than by a price such as $9423.19, but today we have computers to do our arithmetic for us and this anachronism either misleads investors or forces them to do the computations themselves.

Another quaint practice left over from the days of hand calculations is to pretend that the year has 360 days. Consider, for instance, a T-bill with 30 days until maturity purchased for $9934.38. The discount is

$$\$10,000 - \$9934.38 = \$65.62$$

which, relative to $10,000, is

$$\frac{\$65.62}{\$10,000} = 0.006562 \quad \text{(or 0.6562 percent)}$$

Using a 360-day year, the annual T-bill rate is reported as

$$\frac{360}{30} (0.6562 \text{ percent}) = 7.87 \text{ percent}$$

More generally, if there are $n$ days until maturity and $P$ is the bill's price, the reported T-bill rate is calculated as

$$d = \left(\frac{360}{n}\right)\left(\frac{\$10,000 - P}{\$10,000}\right) \tag{6.1}$$

It makes more sense to calculate what is called the *bond-equivalent yield*:

$$R = \left(\frac{365}{n}\right)\left(\frac{\$10,000 - P}{P}\right) \tag{6.2}$$

For Treasury bills with more than 182 days until maturity, the bond-equivalent yield $R$ is calculated from this equation, which takes into account the fact that most bonds pay interest semiannually:

$$\$10,000 = P\left(1 + \tfrac{1}{2}R\right)\left(1 + \frac{n - 182.5}{365}R\right) \tag{6.3}$$

We will restrict our discussion to T-bills with fewer than 182 days until maturity. In our example using a 30-day T-bill, Equation 6.2 gives a yield of

$$R = \left(\frac{365}{30}\right)\left(\frac{\$10,000 - \$9934.38}{\$9934.38}\right)$$
$$= 0.0804 \quad \text{(or 8.04 percent)}$$

The discount rate $d$ understates the correct yield $R$ — in this example by 17 basis points. Some algebraic manipulation of Equations 6.1 and 6.2 yields the following relationship between $R$ and $d$:

$$R = \frac{365d}{360 - nd} \tag{6.4}$$

The difference between $R$ and $d$ increases with the maturity of the T-bill and with the level of interest rates.

Many newspapers report the T-bill **bid prices** (at which dealers are willing to buy) and **ask prices** (at which they are willing to sell) as rates of return calculated on a discount basis using Equation 6.1; they also often report a *yield* (or *bond-equivalent yield*) calculated with Equation 6.2. For instance, the May 17, 1986, *Los Angeles Times* reported the following data on a T-bill traded the previous day:

| Maturity | Bid | Asked | Yield | Bid Change |
|---|---|---|---|---|
| Nov. 13, 1986 | 6.27 | 6.25 | 6.54 | +0.11 |

This T-bill matures on November 13, 1986, which is 180 days beyond the May 17 trading date. The bid and ask numbers are percentage rates of return calculated on a discount basis, assuming a 360-day year. By manipulating Equation 6.1,

$$P = \$10,000\left(1 - \frac{n}{360}d\right)$$

we can determine the following prices:

$$\text{Bid } P = \$10,000\left(1 - \frac{180}{360}\,0.0627\right) = \$9686.50$$

$$\text{Ask } P = \$10,000\left(1 - \frac{180}{360}\,0.0625\right) = \$9687.50$$

(Notice how small the bid–ask spread is in the T-bill market.)

The reported 6.54 percent yield was calculated using Equation 6.2 with the ask price, which is what you would have to pay to buy this T-bill:

$$R = \frac{365}{180}\frac{\$10,000 - \$9687.50}{\$9687.50} = 0.0654 \quad \text{(or 6.54 percent)}$$

The bid change shows the change in the bid discount rate, because bid prices apply if you want to sell your T-bill. Here the T-bill rate was up 11 basis points, from 6.16 to 6.27 percent.

The yield data reported by some newspapers are logical and useful for investors who want to compare the returns from T-bills with bank deposits and other investments. Bid and ask *prices* also would be useful. However, it is confusing and potentially misleading to have the bid and ask returns calculated on a discount basis, as are the T-bill rates reported in most newspapers, the *Federal Reserve Bulletin*, the *Economic Report of the President*, the *Statistical Abstract*, and virtually all other sources of historical data.

## The T-Bill Market

Treasury bills comprise the largest and most actively traded category of money-market securities. Thirteen-week (91 days) and 26-week (182 days) T-bills are sold by auction every Monday; 52-week (364 days) T-bills are auctioned every fourth Thursday. Other auctions are conducted as needed to meet the Treasury's cash-management requirements.

The Federal Reserve (Fed) acts as the Treasury's agent in collecting and processing auction bids. Before 1992, only some 40 securities dealers, who are known as **primary dealers**, were allowed to submit competitive bids at these auctions. (Similarly, when the Fed buys and sells securities to implement its monetary policies, it only trades with these primary dealers.) To be on the Fed's primary dealer list, a firm must demonstrate adequate financial strength and a willingness to make markets in a full range of government securities in both good and bad market conditions. About a third of the primary dealers are departments of commercial banks; the remaining two-thirds are nonbank securities dealers such as Salomon Brothers and Goldman Sachs.

Since 1992 all Treasury securities brokers and dealers registered with the Securities and Exchange Commission (SEC) have been allowed to participate in Treasury auctions. However, these auctions continue to be dominated by primary dealers, who have a comprehensive, detailed knowledge of the government securities market.

Dealers must submit their bids, stating the quantity of securities they want and the prices they are willing to pay, by 1:00 P.M. New York time on the day of a Treasury auction. Each dealer can make multiple bids, indicating a willingness to buy different amounts at various prices. For example, a dealer could offer to buy $200 million at a discount rate of 6.05 percent and an additional $800 million at a discount rate of 6.00 percent.

Individual and institutional investors can buy T-bills from the Fed at the average auction price by entering a noncompetitive order beforehand. An individual investor can, for example, mail a certified check for the desired face value (perhaps $10,000) and receive a refund once the price is determined. A noncompetitive bidder cannot buy more than $5 million in T-bills. The noncompetitive bids usually comprise 10 to 30 percent of the total volume of securities sold.

After netting out the volume of noncompetitive orders, the competitive bids are filled, starting with the lowest interest rate (and hence the highest price), until the supply is exhausted. At the highest interest rate at which offers are accepted, the remaining supply is apportioned as needed. Suppose, for example, that the Treasury auctions $8 billion in 13-week T-bills and receives $1 billion in noncompetitive bids, plus low bids of 6.00 percent (a price of $98.483 per $100 of face value) for $4 billion in T-bills and 6.04 percent ($98.473) for $6 billion. Subtracting the $1 billion in noncompetitive bids, $7 billion in T-bills are to be allocated to the competitive bids. The low bidders at 6.00 percent purchase $4 billion at a price of $98.483 per $100 of face value. The next lowest bidders at 6.04 percent pay $98.473, but because there are $6 billion in bids and only $3 billion in T-bills remaining, each bidder at 6.04 percent receives only half the amount ordered. The $1 billion in T-bills sold to the noncompetitive bidders use a weighted-average interest rate:

$$\frac{6.00\%(\$4\text{ billion}) + 6.04\%(\$3\text{ billion})}{\$7\text{ billion}} = 6.02\%$$

There is no formal T-bill certificate of title, but purchasers receive a receipt, and ownership is recorded at the Treasury in a book-entry account. Investors who intend to hold their securities until maturity can use the Treasury Direct Program, in which the proceeds from maturing T-bills are automatically reinvested or electronically credited to the investor's account at a bank or other financial institution.

After issuance, T-bills, like all government securities, are traded over the counter. The primary dealers are the cornerstone of this secondary market, since they are committed to maintaining a list of bid prices at which they stand ready to buy Treasury bills and ask prices at which they are willing to sell T-bills. On actively traded T-bills, the difference between the prices charged and paid by dealers averages less than 0.01 percent ($1 per $10,000 of face value).

In addition to making markets for retail customers, dealers in Treasury securities trade among themselves to maintain their desired inventories and to try to profit from anticipated interest-rate movements. When dealers trade with each other, they usually use a special Treasury broker in order to keep their identities confidential.

The auction bids from primary dealers are strongly influenced by current prices in the secondary market for Treasury securities. Suppose, for example, that an auction of new 3-month Treasury bills is imminent. Six-month T-bills that were issued 3 months ago have 3 months remaining until maturity and are now, in effect, 3-month T-bills. The auction prices of new 3-month Treasury bills are consequently very close to the secondary-market prices of what are now effectively 3-month T-bills.

In addition, dealers trade new Treasury securities before the auction date on a "when issued" basis, with settlement on the date the Treasury delivers the securities. Primary dealers can thereby guarantee the resale of securities they hope to acquire at the auction. Because the purchase of securities at the auction is a close substitute for purchase in the when-issued market, auction prices should be very close to the when-issued prices shortly before the actual auction. The next chapter will explain how bond markets were rocked in 1991 by the revelation that Salomon Brothers was able to dominate several auctions of Treasury notes and bonds, thereby squeezing dealers who were unable to deliver securities they had sold in the when-issued market.

# COMMERCIAL PAPER

After Treasury bills, the next largest category of money-market securities is **commercial paper** — short-term unsecured securities issued by financial and nonfinancial businesses. Because commercial paper is unsecured, it is generally issued only by large, established businesses that are thought to be in no financial danger. Although these businesses could borrow from banks, it may be less expensive for them to sell securities directly to investors rather than paying for the services of a financial intermediary.

Commercial paper must mature in 270 or fewer days to be exempt from registration with the Securities and Exchange Commission (SEC). Nonfinancial businesses generally issue commercial paper to meet seasonal or other special needs. In contrast, many banks, finance companies, insurance companies, and other financial institutions sell commercial paper on a regular basis to raise funds for relending. Large finance companies or banks that issue large amounts of commercial paper on a virtually continual basis use their own sales forces to find buyers; other issuers use the services of commercial paper dealers.

Almost all commercial paper is purchased by money-market funds, pension funds, insurance companies, bank trust departments, and other institutional investors. Because of its heterogeneous nature, relatively little commercial paper is traded in the secondary market after issuance.

## EXAMPLE 6.1 *Money-Market Mutual Funds Meet a Need*

The minimum denomination is $10,000 for a Treasury bill and $100,000 or $1 million for most other money-market securities — effectively precluding their acquisition by many small institutions and most individual investors. However, investors can participate in the money market indirectly through short-term investment intermediaries that use pooled funds to acquire a portfolio of money-market securities. Some (*local government investment pools*) are created by state governments for use by cities, counties, and other local government entities; others (*short-term investment funds*) pool money that is managed by bank trust departments. For individual investors, the best-known example is *money-market mutual funds*.

Beginning in the mid-1960s, there were several credit crunches in which the Federal Reserve attempted to fight inflation by using a tight monetary policy to increase money-market interest rates while using deposit-rate ceilings to keep banks and savings and loan associations from engaging in mutually destructive deposit-rate wars. Some depositors withdrew their money and purchased Treasury bills that paid higher interest than allowed on bank deposits. Others were ill-informed about the alternatives to checking and savings accounts or dissuaded by the brokerage fees and minimum amounts needed to buy money-market securities. In 1970 the federal government abetted these barriers by raising the minimum Treasury-bill purchase from $1000 to $10,000.

 Money-market funds were first introduced in 1972 to help small investors earn high market interest rates, and these funds grew explosively in the late 1970s. Aggregate assets increased from $4 billion in 1977 to $75 billion in 1980 and to $235 billion by 1982. In response to pressure from banks, in 1980 Congress mandated the phasing out of deposit-rate ceilings by 1985. In 1982 banks and thrifts were authorized to offer special money-market deposit accounts (MMDAs) that would compete with money-market funds. Depositors can make an unlimited number of MMDA withdrawals in person or by mail and are allowed a maximum of three checks a month or a total of six monthly withdrawals by check, telephone, or automatic bill paying. These accounts have no reserve requirements and, unlike money-market funds, are insured. Nonetheless, money-market funds continue to be popular.

Unlike a bank account, a money-market fund is technically a mutual fund in which the investor buys shares rather than depositing money. Because the money-market fund's portfolio consists of very short-term securities, the market value of the shares fluctuates very little. The vast majority of money-market funds maintain a constant share value of $1 by using *amortized cost* accounting, in which securities are valued at acquisition cost. The Securities and Exchange Commission (SEC) allows this accounting procedure if the fund holds only high-quality securities that mature in 1 year or less, with an average maturity of 120 days or less.

The interest that the fund earns on its securities is apportioned uniformly over the life of the security and, after deducting operating expenses, is recorded as a daily dividend to the fund's shareholders — which is used to purchase additional shares at the fixed $1 price. For the industry as a whole, annual expenses average about 0.6 percent of assets, thereby reducing shareholders' annual rate of return by 0.6 percent.

A shareholder can invest or withdraw funds, without a sales charge, by using written or telephoned instructions to transfer money between the money-market fund and the shareholder's bank account or by writing a check payable to a third party, typically with a $250 or $500 minimum. Because investors generally buy and sell money-market fund shares by telephone, the development of 800 numbers and computerized switchboards was crucial to the success of money-market mutual funds.

Many investors use a money-market fund as a cash-management account in conjunction with their other investments, moving money in and out of the money-market account as they receive interest and dividend income and buy and sell stocks and bonds. In addition to individual investors, money-market funds are also used for short-term investment and cash management by some bank trust departments, pension funds, and other institutional investors.

The most common denomination is $1 million, and very little paper is sold in less than $100,000 units. Commercial paper, like a Treasury bill, is usually a zero-coupon security sold at a discount from face value. The interest rates on commercial paper are higher than on Treasury bills because commercial paper has default risk and Treasury bills are exempt from state and local income taxes. Monthly T-bill and commercial paper interest rates are shown in Figure 6.1. Because investors consider these assets to be close substitutes, their yields move up and down in tandem.

Although commercial paper issuers generally have little risk of default, there are nonetheless perceived differences in their financial strengths. Several independent firms rate the safety of commercial paper, including Standard & Poor's

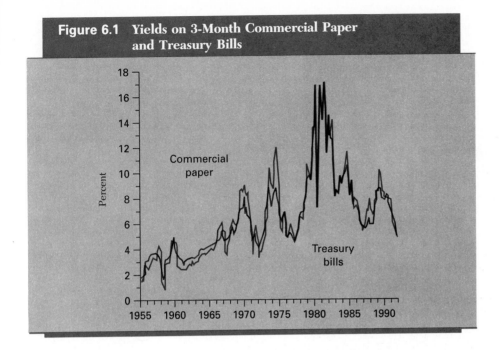

**Figure 6.1  Yields on 3-Month Commercial Paper and Treasury Bills**

(A-1, A-2, or A-3) and Moody's (Prime-1, Prime-2, or Prime-3). More than 75 percent of the issuers are in the top category (A-1 or Prime-1); less than 1 percent are in the lowest category (A-3 or Prime-3).

A commercial paper issuer will often buttress its rating by obtaining a bank line of credit ensuring that the issuer can, if necessary, borrow enough money from the bank to redeem all its commercial paper. Alternatively, a less secure company can obtain a letter of credit from a bank guaranteeing that the bank will redeem the commercial paper if the issuer cannot; in this case, rating agencies evaluate the commercial paper based on the financial strength of the bank rather than the issuer.

## SHORT-TERM MUNICIPAL SECURITIES

Securities that are issued by state and local governments and related agencies are known as **municipal securities (munis)** and have the special characteristic that their interest income is generally exempt from federal income taxes. In addition, states and cities that levy income taxes exempt interest on their own municipal securities, making them double or triple tax exempt. (Capital gains on municipal securities are considered taxable income by cities, states, and the federal government, however.)

The term *short-term municipal securities* is sometimes used to describe municipal securities that mature in less than 3 years and, at other times, it

## EXAMPLE 6.2  *Liquidity Enhancement Agreements*

Traditional short-term municipal anticipation securities are backed by the revenue that will come from taxes, grants, bond sales, or other sources. The redemption of commercial paper, on the other hand, hinges on the issuer's ability to continue selling paper. In a crisis — either for the issuer or for financial markets as a whole — a municipality might not be able to sell enough new paper to raise the funds needed to pay off its maturing paper. Variable-rate municipal securities have a similar risk in that if a great many investors exercise their demand option and attempt to redeem their notes, the municipality might not be able to raise enough money on short notice to satisfy these claims.

In order to reassure investors, municipal issuers often secure their notes with some type of credit enhancement or liquidity enhancement agreement. For example, in a *liquidity-substitution agreement*, a bank promises that, if needed, it will either loan sufficient funds to the municipality or else purchase the securities itself. In a *credit-substitution agreement*, the bank promises that it will use its own funds to make the requisite bond payments if the issuer is unable or unwilling to do so. A nonfinancial business that benefits from a municipal project might secure the notes by making similar promises. A municipality also can protect investors by purchasing municipal bond insurance from an insurance company.

In these ways the issuer pays a fee to an institution that is presumably familiar with the municipality's financial situation so that the municipality can offer reassured investors lower interest rates on its securities. This arrangement is apparently more efficient than letting individual investors purchase their own insurance or rely on rating agencies that have no financial stake in the outcome.

is used to describe those that mature in less than 1 year. We will consider municipal securities that mature in less than 1 year to be *money-market municipal securities.*

Short-term municipal securities traditionally have been used for the temporary financing of expenditures that occur shortly in advance of more permanent revenue. Thus short-term tax-anticipation notes are used to pay for expenditures made before the receipt of quarterly, semiannual, or annual tax revenue. Grant-anticipation notes precede the receipt of a grant, perhaps from the federal government. Short-term bond-anticipation notes are issued before the sale of long-term bonds; for example, a city might use a series of bond-anticipation notes to finance the construction of a sewage treatment plant and, once the final cost is known, issue long-term bonds to pay off the short-term notes.

In addition to traditional anticipation notes, some municipalities now issue short-term commercial paper, with maturities as short as 1 day, to finance both short- and long-term projects. This paper is redeemed as needed by issuing new commercial paper. This is analogous to a homebuyer choosing a variable-rate mortgage in place of a fixed-rate mortgage. Instead of locking in a long-term borrowing rate, the loan rate fluctuates with the financial market conditions.

Similarly, many state and local governments now issue variable-rate securities that allow for periodic rate adjustments — usually daily, weekly, or monthly. These variable-rate securities usually have a demand option that allows investors to redeem the note for its face value plus accrued interest, with a notification period that coincides with the rate-adjustment dates. For example, if the interest rate is adjusted weekly, then an investor who wants to redeem the note must notify the issuer 1 week before the desired redemption date.

Large banks, securities firms, and other dealers underwrite the issuance of municipal securities and, to a limited extent, maintain a secondary market after issuance. Because there are hundreds of thousands of relatively small, dissimilar municipal securities, it is in practice difficult for dealers and brokers to match buyers and sellers in the secondary market. It is particularly awkward for individual investors of modest means to participate directly in this market; as a result, about half of all short-term municipal securities are held by tax-exempt money-market mutual funds.

## Taxable Equivalent Yield

Because the interest on municipal securities is tax exempt and the interest on corporate securities is not, interest rates on municipal securities are generally 1 to 2 percentage points lower than on corporate securities with comparable maturities and default risk. To compare the interest rate $R_M$ on a tax-exempt municipal security with the interest rate $R_C$ on a taxable corporate security for an investor with a tax rate $t$, we note that the respective after-tax interest rates are $R_M$ and $(1 - t)R_C$. These securities have the same after-tax return if

$$(1 - t)R_C = R_M$$

Rearranging,

$$R_C = \frac{R_M}{1 - t}$$

Thus the **taxable equivalent yield** on a municipal security is defined as

$$\text{Taxable equivalent yield} = \frac{R_M}{1 - t} \tag{6.5}$$

The taxable equivalent yield is the interest rate that would have to be earned on a taxable corporate security for it to have the same after-tax return as a tax-exempt muni.

Suppose, for example, that the interest rate on a particular municipal security is 7 percent. For an investor in a 30 percent tax bracket, the taxable equivalent yield is

$$\text{Taxable equivalent yield} = \frac{R_M}{1 - t} = \frac{7\%}{1 - 0.3} = 10.0\%$$

For an investor in a 15 percent tax bracket,

$$\text{Taxable equivalent yield} = \frac{R_M}{1 - t} = \frac{7\%}{1 - 0.15} = 8.24\%$$

If a comparable corporate security has a 9 percent interest rate, investors in a 30 percent tax bracket prefer the muni, whereas those in a 15 percent tax bracket choose the corporate security.

Alternatively, we can compare securities by calculating the break-even tax rate $t^*$ that would make an investor indifferent between a taxable and tax-exempt security. A little algebra reveals that the after-tax returns are equal

$$(1 - t^*)R_C = R_M$$

for a

$$\text{Break-even tax rate } t^* = \frac{R_C - R_M}{R_C} \qquad (6.6)$$

For our example of 7 percent muni and 9 percent corporate yields, the break-even tax rate is

$$t^* = \frac{9\% - 7\%}{9\%} = 0.22 \quad (\text{or } 22\%)$$

Munis are preferred by those paying more than a 22 percent tax rate, and corporate securities are preferred by those paying a lower tax rate. Either approach — taxable equivalent yield or break-even tax rate — leads to the same conclusion.

# NEGOTIABLE CERTIFICATES OF DEPOSIT (CDs)

**Negotiable certificates of deposit (CDs)** are zero-coupon securities that are issued by banks in denominations of at least $100,000 — usually more than $1 million. These large CDs generally mature in 1 to 6 months and cannot be redeemed at the issuing bank until maturity. However, there is an active secondary market where CDs pass from hand to hand before maturity. These CDs are often described as "large CDs" because of their size or "negotiable CDs" because there is a secondary market for them. More detailed labels are used to distinguish various CD issuers: domestic CDs (issued by U.S. banks), Eurodollar CDs (dollar-denominated CDs issued by banks outside the United States), Yankee CDs (issued by U.S. branches of foreign banks), and thrift CDs (issued by savings and loan associations).

Unlike traditional checking and savings accounts, negotiable CDs give banks considerable flexibility in fine-tuning their deposits. When a bank's customers want to borrow more money, the bank can raise its CD rates to attract funds for relending and raise its loan rates to make a profit on this relending. When loan demand slackens, the bank lowers its CD and loan rates. Because of the $100,000 minimum size, only a few individual investors purchase large CDs. Most CDs are acquired by nonfinancial businesses, state and local governments, and a variety of financial institutions — including mutual funds, pension funds, credit unions, and other banks. When small banks purchase CDs from large banks, the small banks are indirectly lending their depositors' money to the large banks' customers. Thus a depositor lends money to a small bank, which lends money to a large bank, which lends money to a large corporation or to other customers.

A CD is technically a bank deposit and, as such, is insured by the Federal Deposit Insurance Corporation (FDIC). Because there is a $100,000 maximum on FDIC insurance, $1 million CDs are issued only by very large and secure deposit institutions — currently about two dozen U.S. banks, one dozen U.S. thrifts, and three dozen foreign banks. There are a dozen or so active dealers in the secondary market, and the average spread between their buying and selling prices is a thin 5 basis points.

# BANKER'S ACCEPTANCES

A **banker's acceptance** is a promissory note that a bank stamps "accepted" to show that the bank has accepted a responsibility to repay the note if the issuing party does not. Banker's acceptances are commonly used in international trade and are often resold in secondary markets.

Suppose that an American wine dealer wants to import some French wine. The American dealer would like to have physical possession of the wine before paying for it, but the French wine maker is reluctant to ship the wine before receiving payment for it. A banker's acceptance can be used to reassure both the wine dealer and the wine maker.

The French wine maker will prepare shipping documents and an invoice for the wine — perhaps $1 million, payable 90 days after the wine is shipped. The American wine dealer's bank then issues a letter of credit guaranteeing that the agreed-upon payment will be made and stating that the wine maker's invoice (called a *time draft*) is eligible for acceptance.

As soon as the wine is shipped, the wine maker can sell the shipping documents, time draft, and letter of credit to a French bank for a discounted price that takes into account the fact that the present value of $1 million payable in 90 days is less than $1 million. The French bank, in turn, will present the documents to the American bank to show that the wine has indeed been shipped. When the American bank stamps the time draft "accepted," it becomes a banker's acceptance — a promissory note that can be redeemed for $1 million on the specified date. The French bank can hold onto this banker's acceptance, sell it to the American bank, or sell it to someone else in the secondary market. In this way, the wine dealer has financed the wine purchase with a short-term loan from the person who is holding the banker's acceptance, using the wine as collateral for the loan. After the U.S. wine dealer pays the American bank $1

| **Table 6.1**   **Money-Market Interest Rates** | 1980 | 1985 | 1990 |
|---|---|---|---|
| Overnight federal funds | 13.36% | 8.10% | 8.10% |
| Discount window borrowing | 11.77% | 7.69% | 6.98% |
| 3-month Eurodollar deposits | 14.00% | 8.28% | 8.16% |
| 3-month commercial paper | 12.97% | 8.11% | 8.23% |
| 3-month banker's acceptances | 13.11% | 8.08% | 8.09% |
| 3-month certificates of deposit (CDs) | 13.07% | 8.05% | 8.15% |
| 3-month Treasury bills | 11.70% | 7.63% | 7.65% |

**Source:** *Federal Reserve Bulletin*, various issues.

million, the wine dealer is given the shipping documents and can then claim the wine.

Banker's acceptances are very similar to negotiable certificates of deposit (CDs) in that both are short-term bank promises to pay a specified amount on a specified date. Banker's acceptances usually have slightly lower interest rates because the borrower — the wine dealer in our example — is also legally liable if the bank should fail. Table 6.1 compares several money-market interest rates in 1980, 1985, and 1990.

# FEDERAL FUNDS

Commercial banks and other depository institutions are required to hold a specified fraction of their deposits as non-interest-earning reserves — either cash in their vaults or deposits in Federal Reserve banks. Bank reserves are monitored every 2 weeks using data on average daily deposits and reserves. Banks with more funds than they need to satisfy their reserve requirement can lend the surplus in the money market; those banks that have reserve deficiencies can borrow in the money market.

**Federal funds** are large overnight loans among banks and other depository institutions of reserves deposited at Federal Reserve banks. (Federal agencies and some nonbank securities dealers are also authorized to lend, but not borrow, in the federal funds market.) Although these are overwhelmingly loans among banks, they are called federal funds because the funds involved are held at Federal Reserve banks. Federal funds should not be confused with money borrowed from the Federal Reserve itself through its discount window.

Federal funds loans are typically unsecured verbal agreements, without a formal written contract. Institutions deal directly with each other or else use the services of a federal funds broker who receives a commission for matching borrowers and lenders. After receiving authorization from the lending institution, the Federal Reserve electronically debits that institution's reserve account and credits the borrower's account. The interest rate on these loans is called the **federal funds rate**.

The federal funds market allows the aggregate reserves in the banking system to be allocated, as needed, to satisfy the reserve requirements of individual banks. In addition, many large banks use the federal funds market as a semipermanent source of funds. Big-city banks now borrow more or less continuously from other banks in order to relend to large corporations and other clients. In this way banks that lend in the federal funds market are indirectly lending money to large corporations.

The federal funds rate is a key money-market statistic because it is the interest rate on overnight loans that are virtually risk free and have very low transaction costs. Because other overnight loans are alternatives for borrowers and lenders in the federal funds market, their interest rates move up and down with the federal funds rate, differing from the federal funds rate because of risk and transaction costs. In addition, in accordance with the expectations hypothesis, interest rates on other money-market securities reflect anticipated future changes in the federal funds rate. If, for example, the federal funds rate is expected to increase during the coming month, the interest rate on 30-day commercial paper will be above the current federal funds rate.

# REPURCHASE AGREEMENTS

In a security **repurchase agreement (RP** or **repo)**, an investor buys securities and the seller agrees to repurchase the securities at an agreed-upon price and date, often the next day. The seller (often a bank) thereby borrows funds for a short period of time using some of the securities it owns as collateral. The buyer (often a corporation) makes a short-term interest-bearing loan. Suppose, for example, that a bank sells Treasury bills with a face value of $50 million for $48,550,100 with a promise to repurchase them the next day for $48,556,600. The $6500 difference between the repurchase price and the selling price is interest: $48,556,600 - $48,550,100 = $6500. Using a repurchase agreement, the bank pays $6500 interest to borrow $48,550,100 for 1 day. Compounded daily with a 365-day year, this is an effective annual interest rate of about 5 percent:

$$\left(1 + \frac{\$6500}{\$48,550,100}\right)^{365} = 1.0501$$

The terminology that participants use to describe the transaction can be confusing to outsiders. Sometimes the buyer and seller are distinguished by saying that the seller of securities does a repo by agreeing to repurchase the securities and the buyer does a reverse repo by agreeing to sell them back. Thus an institution acquires funds with a *repo*, using some of its securities to collateralize a short-term loan; an institution makes a collateralized short-term loan with a *reverse repo* by buying securities with a commitment to resell. In practice, the terminology is further complicated by the fact that a transaction involving a dealer or repo broker is usually characterized from the dealer's viewpoint. For example, if a bank acquires funds by selling securities to a dealer with a commitment to repurchase, this is usually called a *reverse repo agreement* because this is what it is from the dealer's perspective.

Most repurchase agreements involve U.S. Treasury securities, but certificates of deposit, commercial paper, and other securities are also used. Repos with Treasury securities are usually overnight transactions, although other popular maturities range from 1 week to 6 months. Very few repos are for less than $1 million; overnight repos are generally for at least $25 million. It is not economical to trade small amounts of money for very short periods of time. One-day's interest on $10,000 is only a few dollars, which does not cover the time, effort, and other expenses incurred.

Repurchase agreements are arranged by telephone, either directly or using the services of repo dealers and brokers. Repos are commonly used by securities dealers and large banks to finance their inventories of U.S. Treasury securities. If a dealer increases its holdings of Treasury securities (a "long" position), it can finance the purchase with a repo transaction, using these or other securities as collateral. A dealer can use a reverse repo to obtain securities for customers or to establish or cover a "short" position, in which the dealer sells borrowed securities that it does not currently own in anticipation of buying the securities later (at lower prices, it hopes) to cover its short position.

The Federal Reserve (Fed) also uses repurchase transactions lasting up to 15 days to help implement its monetary policies. If the Fed wants to increase the money supply temporarily, it can buy Treasury securities from a primary dealer who agrees to repurchase them in a few days; using the dealer's perspective, this agreement is called a repo. If the Fed wants to reduce the money supply temporarily, it can sell Treasury securities to a dealer who agrees to sell them back; from the dealer's viewpoint, this is a reverse repo.

Interest rates on overnight repos using Treasury securities are generally 25 to 30 basis points below the federal funds rate, because federal funds loans are based on oral agreements and repos are fully collateralized. Repo rates move up and down with federal funds rates, because repos and federal funds are alternative sources and uses of funds for banks, dealers, and other financial institutions that participate in both markets. For instance, the federal funds rate could not rise substantially above the repo rate because banks would then use repos in place of federal funds until the rate gap disappeared.

# EURODOLLARS

The term **Eurodollars** is used to describe U.S. dollars that are deposited in foreign banks or foreign branches of U.S. banks. These banks need not be in Europe. More generally, the term Eurocurrency has come to encompass any bank deposit denominated in a foreign currency. (Sometimes the Eurodollars label is used to describe dollar-denominated deposits in banks that are not subject to U.S. banking regulations; these include not only foreign banks and foreign branches of U.S. banks but also international banking facilities (IBFs) in the United States, which are only allowed to accept deposits from non-U.S. residents.)

The first significant Eurodollar deposits were made by the Soviet Union in 1960. During World War II, Soviet deposits in the United States had been impounded. Remembering this episode and yet still wanting to earn interest on dollar deposits, in 1960 the Soviet Union began depositing dollars that were explicitly redeemable in dollars in British and other European banks. Since 1960, the Eurodollar market has grown dramatically and, net of interbank deposits, now exceeds $1 trillion. Eurodollars are typically fixed-rate time deposits with maturities ranging from overnight to 6 months. Unlike deposits in U.S. banks, Eurodollar deposits generally do not carry deposit insurance.

The U.S. dollar often serves as a medium of exchange outside the United States in that many international transactions are conducted with U.S. dollars. Eurodollar deposits allow those who use U.S. dollars to earn interest on their money without having to convert their dollars into another currency and then back into dollars, with the possibility of an unprofitable change in exchange rates in between. Eurodollar depositors include firms engaged in international trade, investors who want to hold dollars, and speculators betting that the value of the dollar will rise relative to other currencies.

London has long been the center of the Eurodollar market because of its financial expertise and attractive regulatory climate. The **London interbank offered rate (LIBOR)** is an estimate of the interest rate paid on deposits between banks and is widely used as an international benchmark for interest rates on dollar-denominated deposits and loans.

There is also a thriving Eurodollar business in Caribbean branches of most large U.S. banks. These branches receive tax breaks, have no reserve requirements, have few regulations on their foreign currency trading, and are in the same time zone as New York. Overnight deposits in Caribbean branches of U.S. banks are available for spending the next business day. Many of these Caribbean branches are shell banks, little more than small rented offices through which, on paper, billions of dollars pass.

## Exchange-Rate Risk

A key determinant of investor demand for a currency, such as U.S. dollars, German marks, or Japanese yen, is the anticipated rate of return on a deposit or other investment denominated in that currency, taking into account not only the interest rate on the investment but also the anticipated appreciation or depreciation of the currency.

Consider, for instance, a hypothetical case in which the interest rate on a 1-year U.S. Treasury bill is 8 percent and the interest rate on a comparable 1-year French security is 5 percent. The dollar rate of return on a security denominated in a foreign currency, here the French franc, is equal to the interest rate on the foreign security plus the rate of appreciation of its currency relative to the dollar. Suppose that the anticipated exchange rate 1 year hence is $e^* = 0.05$ dollar/franc. If the current exchange rate is also 0.05 dollar/franc, the French security is unappealing because its return — measured in either francs or dollars — is 5 percent, while the U.S. T-bill earns 8 percent. For a French security paying 5 percent to be as attractive as a U.S. T-bill paying 8 percent, investors must anticipate a 3 percent appreciation in the value of the franc relative to the dollar. Therefore, the current value of the franc must be 3 percent lower than its anticipated value a year from now. If the anticipated future exchange rate is 0.05 dollar/franc, the current exchange rate must be $(1 - 0.03)(0.05) = 0.0485$ dollar/franc.

In general, let $R_d$ be the nominal rate of return on a domestic asset (denominated, say, in dollars), and let $R_f$ be the nominal rate of return on a foreign asset (denominated here in francs):

$$1 + R_d = \frac{\text{dollars earned}}{\text{dollars invested}}$$

$$1 + R_f = \frac{\text{francs earned}}{\text{francs invested}}$$

To make these returns comparable, a common currency (either dollars or francs) must be used. Let $e$ be the exchange rate (dollars for francs) at the time of the investment, and let $e^* = e + \Delta e$ be the exchange rate at the end of the investment period. The earnings in dollars divided by the cost in dollars for the French investment is

$$\frac{\text{Dollars earned}}{\text{Dollars invested}} = \frac{(\text{francs earned})(e^*)}{(\text{francs invested})(e)}$$

$$= \left(\frac{\text{francs earned}}{\text{francs invested}}\right)\left(\frac{e^*}{e}\right)$$

$$= (1 + R_f)(1 + \%\Delta e)$$

where $\%\Delta e = (e^* - e)/e$ is the percentage change in the exchange rate. This dollar rate of return on the French investment equals the return on the U.S. investment if the following equation is satisfied:

$$1 + R_d = (1 + R_f)(1 + \%\Delta e)$$

or, approximately,

$$R_d = R_f + \%\Delta e \tag{6.7}$$

The law of one price that was explained in Chapter 3 applies to all traded items: commodities, services, financial assets, and real assets. Assets that are close substitutes — with comparable risk, liquidity, and so forth — should be priced to yield similar percentage rates of return. The law of one price implies that U.S. interest rates should equal French interest rates (on comparable

EXAMPLE 6.3 *A Managed Float by the Group of Five*

The accompanying graph compares the value of the dollar and U.S. prices relative to foreign prices since 1973, when the United States changed from fixed to flexible exchange rates. (The foreign data are weighted by the amount of trade conducted with the United States.) According to purchasing-power parity, movements in exchange rates should match movements in relative prices — but the graph shows substantial disparities.

In 1973 the United States had a small, $1 billion trade surplus. Between 1973 and 1980, U.S. prices increased at a slightly slower rate than the prices of its trading partners, causing the ratio of U.S. prices to foreign prices to decline. Consequently, the dollar should have appreciated slightly relative to these other currencies; instead, it depreciated by 15 percent, making foreign products considerably more expensive in 1980 than in 1973. In 1980, however, the United States ran a $25 billion trade deficit.

Between 1980 and 1985, U.S. prices continued to increase more slowly than the prices of its trading partners. The graph shows that instead of depreciating to eliminate the U.S. trade deficit, the value of the dollar increased by more than 40 percent, making foreign goods increasingly inexpensive. The U.S. trade deficit increased to $122 billion.

One reason for this perverse movement of exchange rates was that while foreign goods became more attractive, so did U.S. financial assets. Real interest rates were very high in the United States during the years 1980–1985. Between 1980 and 1985, the interest rates on U.S. bank deposits averaged 11.5 percent. With an average inflation rate of 6.9 percent, these deposits provided an

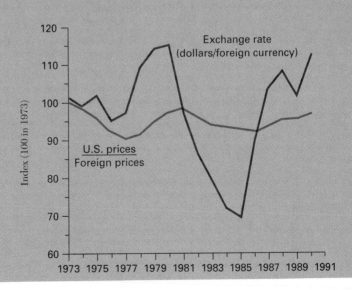

alluring real return of 11.5 percent − 6.9 percent = 4.6 percent. In Germany, in contrast, the average bank deposit rate between 1980 and 1985 was 6.5 percent, the average inflation rate 4.2 percent, and the real interest rate 2.3 percent. In Japan, the average deposit rate was 4.1 percent, the inflation rate was 3.9 percent, and the real rate of return was only 0.2 percent. Because of its high real interest rate, the United States exported financial assets and imported merchandise.

In September of 1985, U.S. government representatives met in New York with counterparts from France, Great Britain, Japan, and West Germany. This "group of five" agreed to take concerted efforts to lower the value of dollar, making U.S. goods less expensive, to help balance the U.S. trade deficit. These nations agreed to pursue monetary and fiscal policies conducive to a devaluation of the dollar and, further, to intervene in foreign exchange markets, selling dollars as needed to drive its value down. In 1986 they met again in Tokyo, along with Canada and Italy, making a "group of seven" pledged to the depreciation of the U.S. dollar. The graph shows that there was indeed a dramatic drop in the value of the U.S. dollar after 1985. However, the U.S. trade deficit continued to increase through 1987, before beginning to decline slowly.

investments) plus the anticipated percentage change in the exchange rate (dollar/ franc).

If the exchange rate is expected to be stable when French securities yield 10 percent, then comparable U.S. securities must yield 10 percent too, or else funds will be invested only in the security with the higher anticipated return. If U.S. securities have higher yields, funds will flow out of French financial markets into U.S. financial markets, thereby driving French security prices down and U.S. security prices up until parity is restored.

When the U.S. dollar is expected to depreciate against the franc, U.S. investments will be unattractive unless they offer relatively high interest rates. If, for example, the dollar/franc exchange rate is expected to rise 5 percent over the next year, then U.S. 1-year interest rates must be 5 percent higher than French 1-year interest rates. Analogous comparisons naturally can be drawn for exchange-rate appreciation and for interest rates in other countries.

As is true of commodities, the law of one price for securities implies that changes in interest rates in one country should cause corresponding changes in other countries or changes in exchange rates. Suppose again that U.S. interest rates are 8 percent, French interest rates are 5 percent, and a 3 percent appreciation of the franc relative to the dollar is anticipated. If economic events in the United States cause interest rates to rise from 8 to 10 percent, then interest rates must rise in France too, or else currency traders will dump francs and buy dollars until the anticipated future appreciation of the franc relative to the dollar is 5 percent rather than 3 percent.

**Table 6.2** Yields to Maturity on Selected International Government Bonds

| Country | Maturity | Yield to Maturity (%) |
|---|---|---|
| Germany | October 1993 | 8.53 |
| Japan | December 1993 | 4.80 |
| United Kingdom | April 1993 | 4.95 |
| United States | June 1993 | 8.22 |

**Source:** *Wall Street Journal*, February 24, 1992.

Every day, *The Wall Street Journal* reports the yields to maturity on selected international securities. Table 6.2 shows some of their data for February 24, 1992, for government bonds that mature in 1 to 2 years. Assuming that these bonds are comparable, the fact that U.S. interest rates were slightly higher than Japanese interest rates and substantially lower than British and German interest rates indicates that investors anticipated a slight depreciation of the dollar relative to the yen and an appreciation of the dollar relative to the pound and the mark over the next 1 to 2 years.

Figure 6.2 shows money-market interest rates for five countries. These data are compiled by the International Monetary Fund (IMF) and are intended to be

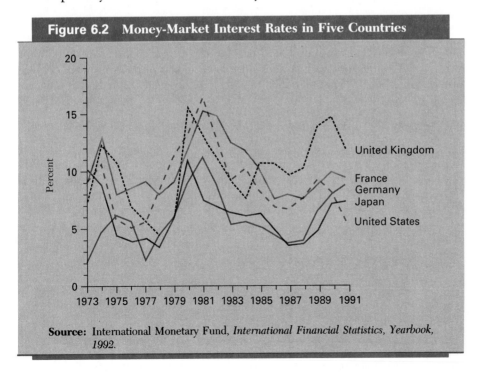

**Figure 6.2** Money-Market Interest Rates in Five Countries

**Source:** International Monetary Fund, *International Financial Statistics, Yearbook, 1992.*

representative of short-term borrowings between financial institutions: the federal funds rate in the United States and comparable interest rates in other countries. The interest rates shown in Figure 6.2 seem roughly to move up and down together, suggesting that international money markets are linked. The relative positions of the interest rates change over time — according to the law of one price, because of anticipated changes in exchange rates. In 1973, U.S. money-market rates were among the highest and U.K. money-market rates were the lowest of these five countries. In 1991 the positions were reversed. According to the law of one price, in 1973 investors expected the dollar to depreciate relative to the pound and in 1991 they expected the reverse.

Because the future course of exchange rates is uncertain, there is **exchange-rate risk** (or **currency risk**) in that investors do not know the terms at which they will be able to convert investments denominated in one currency into another currency. Someone who holds an investment in a foreign currency suffers a capital loss when that currency depreciates unexpectedly. Even for those who invest only in their domestic currency, there still can be an opportunity loss in that they might have been able to earn a higher rate of return by investing in foreign securities. For example, a U.S. investor who only spends dollars and only invests in U.S. securities may have been better off buying foreign securities if the value of the dollar plummets.

## SUMMARY

Securities that mature in less than a year are issued and traded in the money market; long-term securities involve the capital market. The money market is primarily an over-the-counter market of brokers and dealers linked by telephone and is used extensively for short-term borrowing and lending among businesses and financial institutions with temporary cash surpluses and deficits.

Treasury bills are the largest and most actively traded category of money-market securities. T-bills are short-term zero-coupon securities issued (along with longer-term Treasury notes and Treasury bonds) to finance the federal deficit. They are initially sold at auctions at prices determined by competitive bids. T-bill rates are generally reported on a discount basis, which understates the actual rate of interest.

Commercial paper is a short-term unsecured security issued by large, established nonfinancial businesses to meet seasonal or special needs or by a finance company, bank, or other financial institution to raise funds for relending. The interest rates on commercial paper are higher than on Treasury bills because commercial paper has default risk and Treasury bills are exempt from state and local income taxes.

Municipal securities are issued by state and local governments and related agencies, and their interest income is generally exempt from federal (and the appropriate state) income taxes. Short-term munis traditionally have been used for temporary financing in anticipation of taxes, grants, long-term bond sales, and other more permanent revenue. Some municipalities now issue short-term commercial paper and variable-rate securities to finance both short- and long-term projects. The taxable equivalent yield on a municipal security with a tax-exempt return $R_M$ is $R_M/(1 - t)$; this is the interest rate that would have to be earned on a taxable corporate security for it to have the same after-tax return as a tax-exempt muni.

Large certificates of deposit (CDs) are zero-coupon securities issued by banks in denominations of at least $100,000. A banker's acceptance is a promissory note that a bank stamps "accepted" to show that it accepts a responsibility to repay the note if the issuing party does not; these are commonly used in international trade.

Banks that have more funds than they need to satisfy their reserve requirements can use the federal funds market to lend other banks the reserves they have deposited at Federal Reserve banks. The federal funds market allows aggregate bank reserves to be allocated as needed to satisfy the reserve requirements of individual banks and, in addition, allows big-city banks to borrow from other banks for relending. The interest rates on other overnight loans differ from the federal funds rate because of risk and transaction costs. The expectations hypothesis implies that interest rates on money-market securities with maturities longer than 1 day reflect anticipated future changes in overnight loan rates.

In a security repurchase agreement an investor buys securities that the seller agrees to repurchase at an agreed-upon price and date, often the next day. A repo is thus a short-term loan using securities (usually U.S. Treasury securities) as collateral. Repos are commonly used by securities dealers and large banks to finance their inventories of U.S. Treasury securities. A dealer can use a reverse repo to obtain securities for customers or to establish or cover a short position. The Federal Reserve (Fed) also uses repurchase transactions lasting up to 15 days to help implement its monetary policies.

Eurodollars are dollar-denominated deposits that are in foreign banks or in foreign branches of U.S. banks — not necessarily in Europe. Eurodollar depositors include firms engaged in international trade, investors who want to hold dollars, and speculators betting that the value of the dollar will rise relative to other currencies. The law of one price implies that the nominal rate of return $R_d$ on a domestic asset (denominated, say, in dollars) should equal the nominal rate of return $R_f$ on a foreign asset plus the anticipated rate of appreciation of the foreign currency relative to the domestic currency: $R_d = R_f + \%\Delta e$. Exchange-rate risk arises from unexpected fluctuations in the relative values of currencies.

Investors can participate in the money market indirectly through money-market mutual funds that use pooled funds to acquire a portfolio of money-market securities. A money-market fund is technically a mutual fund in which the investor buys shares rather than depositing money; because the money-market fund's portfolio consists of very short-term securities, the market value of the shares fluctuates very little. A shareholder can invest or withdraw funds by using written or telephoned instructions or by writing a check, typically with a $250 or $500 minimum. Many investors use money-market funds as cash-management accounts.

# IMPORTANT TERMS

ask price
banker's acceptance
bid price
capital market
commercial paper
discount basis
Eurodollars
exchange-rate risk (or currency risk)
federal funds

federal funds rate
London interbank offered rate (LIBOR)
money market
municipal securities (munis)
negotiable certificates of deposit (CDs)
primary dealer
repurchase agreement (RP or repo)
taxable equivalent yield
Treasury bills (T-bills)

# EXERCISES

1. Consider a Treasury bill paying $10,000 at maturity that is priced to yield a correctly calculated annual return of 10 percent. (Ignore transaction costs and assume a 365-day year.) What is the price at the following times until maturity?
   a. 365 days
   b. 30 days
   c. 1 day

2. Suppose that a 30-day Treasury bill paying $10,000 at maturity has a price of $9900. Compare the correctly calculated annual return (assuming a 365-day year) with the rate calculated on a discount basis using a 360-day year.

3. Calculate the correct yield on a Treasury bill with a reported 10 percent annual interest rate (calculated on a discount basis) if the number of days until maturity is
   a. 180.
   b. 30.
   c. 1.

4. On May 17, 1986, the *Los Angeles Times* reported the following Treasury-bill data for trading on May 16:

| Maturity | Bid | Asked | Yield | Bid Change |
|----------|-----|-------|-------|------------|
| Jun 12 86 | 5.84 | 5.80 | | +0.09 |

   a. What price did buyers pay on May 16?
   b. What price did sellers receive on May 16?
   c. What is the yield value omitted above?
   d. What was the bid price of this bill on May 15?

5. Explain this newspaper observation: "The discount rate on the new T-bills understates the actual return to investors."[1]

6. In the 1960s, money-market interest rates rose significantly above the interest rates allowed on bank deposits by Regulation Q. Do you suppose that these ceiling rates encouraged or discouraged the issuance of commercial paper by businesses? By banks?

7. What is the interest on a 1-day loan of $10,000 at a 10 percent annual interest rate, assuming a 365-day year?

8. What is the taxable equivalent yield on a municipal security with a 12 percent interest rate for an investor in a 28 percent tax bracket?

9. If the interest rate on a tax-exempt municipal security is 8 percent, what is the taxable equivalent yield for an investor in a 15 percent tax bracket? In a 33 percent tax bracket?

10. What is the break-even tax rate that would make an investor indifferent between a taxable security that is paying 12 percent and

a tax-exempt municipal security paying 10 percent?

11. Suppose that a taxable security has an 8 percent interest rate and that a comparable tax-exempt municipal security has a 6 percent interest rate. How high must an investor's tax bracket be in order for the municipal security to have the higher after-tax return?

12. Is a municipality that issues a series of bond-anticipation notes and then issues long-term bonds to pay off these short-term notes implicitly betting on a rise or decline in interest rates during the time before the long-term bond issue?

13. If a municipality finances a construction project by rolling over short-term commercial paper instead of issuing long-term bonds, is it implicitly betting that future interest rates will be higher or lower than the forward rates embedded in the term structure?

14. If the annual interest rate (correctly calculated) on a 1-year Treasury bill is 10 percent, what annual interest rate on a 1-year CD would give the same after-tax return to an investor subject to a 10 percent state income tax?

15. CD rates are generally reported on the basis of an assumed 360-day year. For example, the interest rate on a 90-day $1 million CD that pays $1,020,000 at maturity is calculated as

$$R = \frac{360}{90} \frac{\$1,020,000 - \$1,000,000}{\$1,000,000}$$

$$= 0.08 \quad \text{(or 8 percent)}$$

Does the use of an assumed 360-day year in place of the actual 365- or 366-day year increase or decrease the reported annual interest rate? Explain why without using any formulas.

16. Exercise 15 shows how reported CD rates are calculated. Does the use of a 360-day year in place of a 365-day year have a bigger

percentage effect on the reported annual interest rate for 30-day CDs or for 180-day CDs?

17. Many CD purchasers believe that the nation's very largest banks are "too big to fail," in that the FDIC will waive the $100,000 insurance limit and fully reimburse all depositors to avoid the financial crisis that might accompany the failure of a very large bank. Does this argument suggest that CD rates at banks that are "too big to fail" will be higher or lower than at somewhat smaller banks?

18. One risk in buying a Yankee CD (issued by a U.S. branch of a foreign bank) is that the foreign government may prevent the bank from redeeming its deposits. If CD purchasers are concerned about this risk, will Yankee CDs tend to have higher or lower interest rates than domestic CDs?

19. After shipping wine to the United States, a French wine maker can sell the shipping documents, time draft, and letter of credit to a French bank for a discounted price that takes into account the fact that the present value of $1 million payable in 90 days is less than $1 million. Why might the wine maker do this rather than wait 90 days for the full $1 million?

20. Interest rates were very low in the 1930s, and aggregate bank reserves far exceeded their required reserves. Do you think that federal funds market loans increased or decreased during this period? Explain your reasoning.

21. In January of 1992, a *Wall Street Journal* columnist wrote, "Was it necessary for the Federal Reserve to cut the federal funds rate and the discount rate in December? To a certain extent, the moves were irrelevant. . . . neither rate is available to businessmen."[2] Explain what the federal funds rate and the discount rate are, and then explain why they are not irrelevant to households and businesses.

22. According to the expectations hypothesis, how is the interest rate on 30-day Treasury bills related to the federal funds rate? (Ignore transaction costs, assume that there is no default risk, and assume that the interest rates are calculated correctly.)

23. On October 4, 1991, the federal funds rate was 5.1 percent and the interest rate on 30-day Treasury bills was 5.0 percent. (Both are correctly calculated annual rates.) How would the expectations hypothesis explain this disparity?

24. The interest earned on an *n*-day repo with a quoted annual interest rate $R$ is calculated on the basis of a 360-day year. For example, on an overnight $10 million repo at a quoted 10 percent interest rate, the interest is

$$\text{Interest} = R\left(\frac{n}{360}\right)\text{investment}$$

$$= 0.10\left(\frac{1}{360}\right)\$10,000,000$$

$$= \$2777.78$$

If the interest rate on an overnight $10 million repo paying $2777.78 in interest were calculated on the basis of a 365-day year, would the reported interest rate be larger or smaller than 10 percent?

25. Does the fact that Eurodollar deposits typically are not government insured suggest that interest rates on Eurodollar deposits will generally be above or below interest rates on insured U.S. deposits?

26. Using the data in Table 6.2, does the law of one price for securities imply that in February of 1992 financial market participants anticipated the mark to appreciate or depreciate relative to the yen over the next 1 to 2 years?

27. If the U.S. dollar is expected to depreciate relative to the Japanese yen, what must be true of interest rates for comparable U.S. and Japanese securities to be equally attractive? What will investors want to do if this does not hold?

28. On October 22, 1991, annualized 3-month money-market interest rates were around 5 percent in the United States and above 10 percent in the United Kingdom. What anticipated annual rate of appreciation or depreciation of the U.S. dollar relative to the British pound would make these alternative investments equally attractive?

29. During October of 1987, the average (dollar) return, interest plus capital gains, on U.S. Treasury bonds was 2.605 percent and the average percentage return (in pounds) on comparable British bonds was 1.165 percent. During this same time period, the pound depreciated by 2.291 percent versus the dollar. Taking into account this depreciation, did U.S. or British bonds give U.S. investors a higher rate of return? What about British investors?

30. Why do you suppose the SEC requires money-market funds that use *amortized cost* accounting, in which securities are valued at acquisition cost, to hold only high-quality, short-term securities?

# 7 The Bond Market

*If there were any guarantees, it wouldn't be called fishing; it would be called catching.*

**Robert L. Nessen**

Traditionally, long-term securities have been used to finance capital construction: long-lived factories, roads, and so on. The issuance and trading of long-term securities — those that mature in more than a year — are consequently said to take place in the **capital market**. We will look at long-term bonds in this chapter and at amortized loans and mortgages and stock in the next two chapters.

All bonds have certain common characteristics, such as the calculation of yields to maturity, that will be explained in this chapter. However, because of differences in tax treatment and default risk, we must distinguish among bonds issued by the U.S. Treasury, private businesses, and state and local government authorities. We begin by describing the various issuers of bonds.

## BOND ISSUERS

The federal government, private businesses, and state and local governments all issue bonds — a distinction that is important because these securities involve different kinds of risks and because the interest income is treated differently by U.S. tax laws. The ability of the U.S. Treasury to repay its debts is unquestioned; the capability of state and local governments to repay their debts depends on their tax base and other revenue sources; and a corporation's financial strength rests on its profitability. The income from federal securities is exempt from state income taxes; interest on state and local bonds is generally exempt from federal income taxes and from income taxes in the issuing city and/or state; but interest on corporate bonds is fully taxable. We will look at each of these issuers, beginning with the U.S. Treasury.

## *Treasury Notes and Bonds*

The U.S. Treasury sells securities to finance the federal government's budget deficit — the difference between federal outlays and revenue. Treasury securities are identified by their maturity when issued: Treasury bills (T-bills) mature in less than 1 year, **Treasury notes** mature in 2 to 10 years, and **Treasury bonds** mature in more than 10 years. The Treasury also sells savings bonds and other nonmarketable debt, so-called because it has no secondary market.

Unlike T-bills, Treasury notes and bonds generally make periodic (usually semiannual) interest payments, called *coupons*, in addition to a final payment when the bond matures. The maturation value of Treasury notes and bonds ranges from $1000 upward. As explained in Chapter 4, the **yield to maturity** on a bond is the discount rate such that the present value of the coupons and the principal is equal to the price. If we assume annual coupons $C$ for simplicity, the yield to maturity $y$ on an $n$-year bond with maturation value $M$ and price $P$ is given by the solution of

$$P = \frac{C}{(1 + y)} + \frac{C}{(1 + y)^2} + \cdots + \frac{C}{(1 + y)^n} + \frac{M}{(1 + y)^n} \qquad (7.1)$$

With semiannual coupons $C/2$,

$$P = \frac{C/2}{(1 + y/2)} + \frac{C/2}{(1 + y/2)^2} + \cdots + \frac{C/2}{(1 + y/2)^{2n}} + \frac{M}{(1 + y/2)^{2n}} \qquad (7.2)$$

A bond sells for a premium above face value ($P > M$) when the yield is below the coupon rate ($y < C/M$) and at a discount when the yield is above the coupon rate. When it issues securities, the Treasury generally sets the coupon rate so that the market price will be slightly below the maturation value.

New 2- and 5-year Treasury notes are auctioned once a month, and 3- and 10-year notes and 30-year bonds are auctioned every 3 months. Auctions for Treasury notes and bonds are very similar to those for Treasury bills, as described in the preceding chapter. Authorized dealers are allowed to submit competitive bids — stated in terms of yield to maturity — and, after netting out the volume of noncompetitive orders, the orders from dealers are filled, starting with the lowest yield to maturity (reflecting the highest price), until the supply is exhausted.

Suppose, for example, that the Treasury auctions $12 billion in 2-year Treasury notes and receives $1 billion in noncompetitive bids plus low yield-to-maturity bids of 7.80 percent for $6 billion in notes and 7.82 percent for $10 billion. Subtracting the $1 billion in noncompetitive bids, there are $11 billion in notes to be allocated to the competitive bids. The low bidders purchase $6 billion at a price that corresponds to a 7.80 percent yield to maturity. The next lowest bidders buy the remaining $5 billion at a 7.82 percent yield, with each bidder

## EXAMPLE 7.1 *U.S. Savings Bonds*

In 1992 there were $140 billion in U.S. savings bonds outstanding. The U.S. Treasury currently sells two types of savings bonds: Series EE and Series HH. Series EE bonds are zero-coupons securities that can be purchased for as little as $25, and are worth twice their issuing price at maturity; for example, a bond that costs $25 is worth $50 at maturity. If these bonds are redeemed before maturity, investors receive a specified redemption value that is increased periodically according to a fixed schedule.

Series EE bonds can be purchased from commercial banks or from many employers through payroll savings plans. In the past, the interest rates were modest. Many people give savings bonds to children for birthdays and other occasions; purchases through payroll savings plans are often motivated by convenience and patriotism.

In recent years, savings bonds have offered reasonably competitive interest rates. In February 1992, the redemption values of Series EE bonds were set to give a 6 percent annual return if the bonds are held at least 5 years. In addition, the redemption value is adjusted upward to give a rate of return equal to 0.85 times the average interest rate on 5-year marketable Treasury notes over the holding period if the adjusted interest rate exceeds 6 percent.

Interest from savings bonds is exempt from state and local income taxes, and, unlike other zero-coupon securities, investors do not have to pay federal income taxes on the implicit interest on Series EE bonds until the bonds are redeemed. The taxes on Series EE interest can be deferred further by exchanging a redeemed Series EE bond for a Series HH savings bond. Series HH bonds are ten-year securities with a 6 percent annual interest rate (paid in semiannual installments) and can be obtained only in exchange for an eligible Series EE bond. The interest from Series EE bonds is completely tax exempt if used for a dependent's college tuition and the owner's income in the redemption year falls below a threshold. In 1992, this tax exemption begins to be phased out for $62,900 of adjusted gross income on a joint tax return.

Because the redemption value of Series EE bonds is adjusted periodically — often semiannually — investors can forfeit a substantial amount of interest if they redeem a savings bond shortly before an adjustment date. For example, a savings bond purchased for $750 in July 1963 could have been redeemed for $4,590 on March 31, 1992, or for $4,727 the next day, a $137 difference. Many investors, banks, and even government officials are unaware of the timing of such adjustments. In April 1992, the executive director of the Treasury Department's Savings Bond Division told *The Wall Street Journal* that interest is credited monthly. He later admitted his mistake, explaining "I'm a political appointee, and I've been here for five months."*

*Karen Slater, "Timing's the Thing With Savings Bonds," Wall Street Journal, *April 25, 1992.*

Another pitfall with savings bonds is that some people put them in a safe place and forget about them. In 1992, $1.76 billion in savings bonds (more than one percent of the total outstanding) had matured and stopped earning interest. No doubt many of these bonds have been tucked away in desks or safe deposit boxes and forgotten. Because all savings bonds are registered, lost bonds can be replaced by contacting the Bureau of the Public Debt.

receiving half the amount ordered. The $1 billion in notes sold to the noncompetitive bidders are priced to give the weighted-average yield to maturity:

$$\frac{7.80 \text{ percent } (\$6 \text{ billion}) + 7.82 \text{ percent } (\$5 \text{ billion})}{\$11 \text{ billion}} = 7.81 \text{ percent}$$

Investors can buy new Treasury securities before the auction date, in what is called the "when issued" market, for delivery on the day that the Treasury issues the securities. Primary dealers and others sell securities in the when-issued market, intending to acquire the promised securities at the auction or shortly afterward. These sellers are said to be "short" in that they do not yet own the securities they have sold. If they do not buy enough securities at the auction to fulfill these commitments, then they will have to deliver borrowed securities and cover their position later by buying securities in the secondary market to replace the ones they have borrowed.

If a single dealer is able to corner the market (or "coup an auction") by acquiring most of the auctioned securities, it can demand artificially high prices from those who need to buy or borrow securities to fill customer orders and cover short positions in the when-issued market. To preclude a corner, the Treasury does not allow a dealer to acquire more than 35 percent of the securities sold at an auction. Example 7.2 explains how Salomon Brothers was discovered to have violated this rule in 1991.

After issuance, Treasury notes and bonds, like Treasury bills, are traded over the counter using telephones to contact dealers who quote bids and ask prices at which they are willing to buy and sell securities. More than $2 trillion in Treasury securities are outstanding, with active trading in a wide range of maturities — making the Treasury market one of the most important and carefully watched financial markets. Treasury prices immediately reflect financial developments and quickly influence the prices of other financial and nonfinancial assets.

Secondary-market bid and ask quotations for Treasury notes and bonds are stated in terms of the price rather than yield to maturity (although the yield can, of course, be calculated from the price). These prices are quoted relative to a par value of 100, in minimum increments of $\frac{1}{32}$. Thus a reported price of 99:8 means $99\frac{8}{32} = 99.25$ and is equal to a fraction 0.9925 of the face value of the security. A $100,000 Treasury bond at a quoted price of 99:8 costs $99,250.

The purchaser of a coupon bond pays not only the quoted price but also accrued interest that represents the seller's share of the next coupon. On

**EXAMPLE 7.2** *Collusion and Price Fixing in the Treasury Market*

Two-year Treasury notes are popular with many individuals and institutions because these notes don't have to be rolled over several times a year and yet don't have the substantial capital risk of longer-term securities. In the 1980s, bond traders began noticing that the prices of 2-year notes often rise in the when-issued market shortly before they are auctioned and then decline after the auction as interest wanes. To exploit this pattern, some dealers started selling 2-year notes in the when-issued market and then covering their position by buying notes at the auction or shortly afterward. These short sales left them vulnerable to a "squeeze," in which other dealers corner the market by buying most of the 2-year notes and charging short sellers exorbitant prices to cover their positions.

The U.S. Treasury tries to prevent such squeezes by prohibiting any dealer from acquiring more than 35 percent of the securities auctioned. There is a loophole, however, in that primary dealers can bid for themselves and as agents for their customers, and their customers' purchases do not count toward the 35 percent limit. A dealer might use an illegal "parking" arrangement in which it submits bids on behalf of clients with an agreement to buy the securities from the clients after the auction. It might even submit unauthorized bids on behalf of its clients and then acquire the securities without the clients' knowledge of the transaction.

In 1991 Salomon Brothers admitted that it had submitted unauthorized customer bids at several auctions in order to circumvent the Treasury's 35 percent rule. The Treasury and Federal Reserve first noticed an irregularity at a February 1991 auction of 5-year notes when Salomon made two bids on behalf of a single customer — one a legitimate bid and the other an unauthorized one. The Treasury inquired about these overlapping bids, not realizing that one was unauthorized. An internal Salomon investigation found that one bid was phony and that Salomon had violated the 35 percent rule. These violations were revealed to Salomon's top management in April of 1991 but were not reported to the government for 4 months. Meanwhile, several other violations occurred. In August of 1991 Salomon reported that it had controlled 46 percent of the 4-year notes auctioned in December of 1990, 57 percent of the 5-year notes auctioned in February of 1991, 41 percent of the 5-year notes auctioned in April of 1991, and an astounding 94 percent of the $12.26 billion in 2-year notes auctioned in May of 1991. Salomon's chairman, the head of its Treasury securities trading department, and a half dozen other top executives resigned or were fired. In May of 1992, Salomon agreed to pay the U.S. Treasury a $290 million fine.

Salomon also revealed that an unauthorized customer bid for $1 billion in 30-year Treasury bonds in February of 1991 had been the accidental outcome of what was intended to be a practical joke on the day before a sales staffer retired. The head of the government securities desk persuaded one of this staffer's clients to place a $1 billion order, which the head trader would secretly cancel. The client would then complain that its order had not been executed, and the head trader would pretend to be angry at the staffer's mistake before revealing the hoax. However, the clerk handling the order did not notice that it had been canceled, and Salomon ended up buying the unwanted securities.

One week after the May 1991 auction, the prices of 2-year Treasury notes jumped by 0.25 percent, from $99\frac{29}{32}$ to $100\frac{5}{32}$ — giving a $30 million profit on the $12.26 billion in notes that were auctioned, almost all of which were purchased by Salomon and its clients. In addition, those dealers who were forced to borrow 2-year notes to cover their short positions were charged abnormally high interest and fees by Salomon. Ironically, Salomon's attempt to squeeze the 2-year market in May may have been prompted by the fact that it lost money in an April squeeze when two investment funds purchased $16 billion in 2-year notes in the when-issued market even though only $12 billion was actually auctioned.*

In the aftermath of the Salomon revelations, *The Wall Street Journal* reported that other primary dealers had occasionally violated the 35 percent rule and, more disturbingly, that several dealers regularly shared confidential information with each other about the bids submitted at Treasury auctions.† The Treasury auction procedure, in which securities are sold at a variety of prices rather than at a single market-clearing price, is intended to maximize Treasury revenue and minimize its cost of borrowing. However, it also encourages collusion, because bidders have a strong incentive to avoid paying more than the minimum successful bid. Perhaps the most serious consequence of the Salomon scandal is that it might undermine the reputation of the Treasury bond market as a fair, competitive, and efficient market.

To reassure investors, in 1992 the Treasury Department and the Federal Reserve announced that they would henceforth allow all government securities brokers and dealers registered with the SEC to participate in Treasury auctions and would check the authenticity of all bids larger than $500 million. In addition, they will combat squeezes by selling or lending billions of dollars of any Treasury security that "is subject to an acute, protracted shortage," and in 1993 the traditional sealed-bid auction of Treasury securities will be replaced by a computerized open-bidding system. The Justice Department also announced that it will investigate whether some dealers had engaged in pre-auction collusion that violated federal antitrust laws.

*Laurie P. Cohen and Michael Siconolfi, "Before May's Squeeze, One in April Wounded Investors in Treasurys," Wall Street Journal, October 7, 1991.

†Michael Siconolfi, Michael R. Sesit, and Constance Mitchell, "Collusion, Price Fixing Have Long Been Rife in the Treasury Market," Wall Street Journal, August 19, 1991.

Treasury securities, the exact number of days between coupons is counted; most other securities assume a 30-day month and 180 days between semiannual coupons. For example, if it has been 3 months and 18 days since the last semiannual coupon and the 30-day month convention is used, this is a fraction

$$\frac{3(30) + 18}{180} = 0.60$$

of the assumed 180-day period between coupons, and the buyer pays the seller the quoted bond price plus an amount equal to 0.60 of the next coupon payment. For Treasury securities, the exact number of days is calculated. If, for example, there are 182 days between coupon payments and it has been 110 days since the last payment, the buyer pays the seller $\frac{110}{182}$ of the coupon.

## Corporate Bonds

**Corporate bonds** are fixed-income securities of various maturities issued by corporations to purchase new plant and equipment, pay current bills, and finance the takeover of other companies. Specific corporate bonds have a number of ever-changing labels, often concocted for marketing purposes. These labels are less important than the general principles.

Most corporate bonds are coupon bonds with minimum par values of $1000 or $5000. *Secured debt* is collateralized by a firm's buildings, equipment, or other tangible assets. *Debenture bonds* are not secured by any specific assets of the issuer; investors instead rely on the issuer's reputation and profitability.

Corporate bonds generally involve a trustee, usually a bank, who handles the payment of interest and principal and represents the bondholders as a group in any dispute with the firm, including bankruptcy. The trustee also ensures that the firm complies with any protective covenants that have been written into the indenture agreement to protect bondholders. These covenants might prohibit the firm from selling its assets and distributing the proceeds as an extraordinary dividend to shareholders, leaving bondholders with worthless certificates. Another covenant might restrict the amount of additional debt that the firm can issue and stipulate that any additional debt must be subordinate (or junior) to the present issue, in that holders of the additional debt cannot receive any payments of either interest or principal if the firm has not satisfied the terms of more senior debt.

A corporate bond issue that is sold to the public must be registered with the Securities and Exchange Commission (SEC) and include an indenture agreement specifying the various terms of the bond issue in precise legal detail that can fill hundreds of pages. Corporations generally use investment bankers to prepare the requisite documents and to predict whether the desired number of bonds can be sold at an acceptable price. The actual marketing of the bonds is done by an underwriting syndicate of dealers, led by the corporation's investment banker, who purchase the bonds from the issuing firm and resell them to the public.

An initial registration statement describing the prospective bond issue is filed with the SEC about 6 weeks before the public offering and is distributed by the underwriting syndicate to prospective buyers. If the syndicate has anticipated the market correctly, its dealers will be able to obtain tentative commitments to purchase virtually all the bonds on the day they are issued. The final coupon rate and offering price for the bonds are set the day before the public offering at a meeting of the underwriting syndicate and the issuing firm. If an agreement is reached, a final prospectus is filed with the SEC and the offering proceeds as scheduled. If a dealer is unable to sell its entire allotment at the offering price, it can hold the residual bonds as an investment or sell them later at the prevailing market price.

After issuance, corporate bonds are traded over the counter or, to a limited extent, on the stock exchanges. Dealers trade large blocks of bonds in the over-the-counter market with other dealers or with institutional investors. Bond transactions on the New York Stock Exchange (NYSE) are handled by designated specialists in a small room off the main trading floor. In comparison with the market for Treasury securities, the corporate bond market is relatively light and sporadic. For many corporate securities there are no transactions for several days or even weeks.

About half of all corporate debt is issued privately, either term loans from banks and insurance companies or **private placements**, in which investment bankers arrange for a small number of investors (typically pension funds and life insurance companies) to purchase the entire bond issue at a negotiated price. Privately placed bonds are exempt from SEC registration requirements. However, bonds acquired through a private placement cannot be resold for at least 2 years. Private placements have lower underwriting and administrative expenses than public offerings have, particularly for small issues, and also tend to have stronger restrictive covenants. In case of financial distress, however, it is easier to renegotiate a bond's terms with a few investors than it is with hundreds or thousands of bondholders. Overall, the interest rates on privately placed bonds average about half a percentage point above the rates on comparable public issues.[1]

SEC Rule 415, adopted in 1982, allows "shelf registration" of securities. Traditionally, businesses issued bonds or stock infrequently and in large amounts, using a familiar investment bank that had been relied on for decades. This trusted investment bank might have a seat on the company's board of directors and would advise the company on its financing options, price new issues, and form a syndicate of investment banks to market the securities at the designated time.

Under Rule 415, publicly traded corporations that report quarterly to the SEC can file a single statement with the SEC describing the company's total potential stock and bond issues over the next 3 years. Instead of relying on a syndicate to market a large issue on a single date, the company has the securities "on the shelf" and can invite competitive bids and issue securities in moderate sizes on numerous dates. It might negotiate to sell the securities to a single investment bank, for the bank to resell, or it can bypass investment banks and sell the securities itself to pension funds, insurance companies, and other investors.

## Municipal Bonds

The interest on bonds issued by state and local governments — often called **municipal bonds** or **munis** — is generally exempt from federal income taxes, whereas interest on U.S. Treasury securities is not subject to state and local taxes. Because federal income taxes are the more substantial, state and local government bonds are said to be **tax-exempt bonds**.

Most states that have income taxes do not tax interest on their own bonds, making them double tax-exempt bonds; for example, Californians who buy bonds issued by the state of California do not have to pay state or federal income taxes on the interest. New York City levies a city income tax, making their bonds triple tax exempt for residents.

There are two primary types of state and local securities. *General-obligation bonds* are backed by the full faith and credit of the issuer and, more important, by its ability to levy taxes. *Revenue bonds,* in contrast, are issued to finance specific projects, such as a road, sports facility, or water project, and will be repaid by the income from the completed project. Usually the agency that issues a revenue bond has no taxing authority, and the bond is not an obligation of the state or local government.

About half the state and local bonds issued in 1985 were private-purpose revenue bonds for such things as hotels, stores, irrigation projects, and industrial parks.[2] Concerned about apparent abuses, Congress put restrictions in the Tax Reform Act of 1986 on the amount and type of munis used to finance essentially private projects. Bonds falling outside these restrictions are not exempt from federal taxes, creating a new class of bond — *taxable munis*. For instance, municipal bonds used to finance sports stadiums or convention facilities owned by private interests are no longer automatically exempt from federal taxes. Congress did include a "grandfather" clause allowing an exemption for existing bonds and even for some private projects that had been planned before the Tax Reform Act but not yet financed.

When first issued, state and local bonds are sold to syndicates of investment bankers by direct negotiation or on the basis of competitive bids and then are marketed to investors. Later, the bonds can be bought and sold in the over-the-counter market, although not always inexpensively. One authority says that "if you have $100,000, you can begin to think about trading, but it's only at close to $500,000 that you can adequately trade municipals."[3] A trade involving less than $100,000 par value is considered an "odd lot" and is subject to larger brokerage fees. Fees on "round lot" trades generally range from 1 to 3 percent; those on odd lots can be 5 percent or even higher. Some 50,000 different authorities have issued more than 2 million different tax-exempt securities; most are traded seldomly or not at all, and significant price concessions may be required to consummate a trade.[4]

Because of the tax advantages, investors in high tax brackets buy state and local bonds even when the before-tax yields to maturity are substantially below

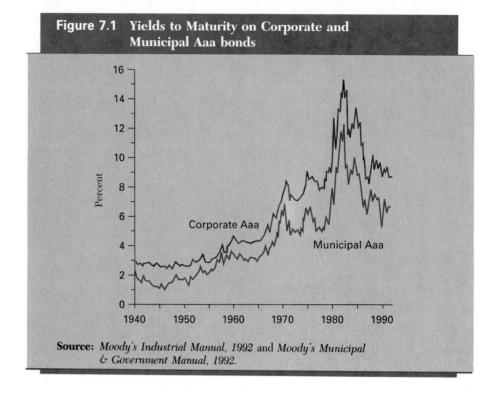

**Figure 7.1** **Yields to Maturity on Corporate and Municipal Aaa bonds**

**Source:** *Moody's Industrial Manual, 1992* and *Moody's Municipal & Government Manual, 1992.*

those on equally safe, but taxable corporate bonds. In recent years, as Figure 7.1 shows, the interest rates on highly rated state and local bonds generally have been roughly 1 to 2 percent below the rates on similarly rated corporate bonds. For instance, during the first week in February 1992, yields to maturity averaged 8.25 percent on Aaa corporate bonds and 6.68 percent on Aaa state and local bonds. College endowments and other investors who don't pay taxes prefer 8.25 percent corporate bonds, whereas those in high tax brackets prefer 6.68 percent tax-exempt bonds. The preceding chapter explained how to calculate the break-even tax rate that would make an investor indifferent between the two bonds. Here, if $t$ is the tax rate, the after-tax yields are $(1 - t)8.25$ percent and 6.68 percent. The break-even tax rate is that value of $t$ such that the after-tax yields are equal:

$$(1 - t)8.25\% = 6.68\%$$

Solving,

$$1 - t = \frac{6.68}{8.25} = 0.81$$

or

$$t = 1 - 0.81 = 0.19$$

Taxable corporate bonds paying 8.25 percent appeal to those with tax rates below 19 percent, whereas tax-exempt munis paying 6.68 percent are preferred by those in higher tax brackets.

## International Bonds

Worldwide, the aggregate value of publicly issued bonds was $9.8 trillion at the end of 1988, of which about two-thirds were issued by governments and government agencies.[5] More than two-thirds of the dollar-denominated and yen-denominated bonds are government issued, but less than a third of the mark-denominated and Swiss franc–denominated bonds are.

Financial markets have become increasingly internationalized, in that many investors who were once reluctant to acquire foreign securities now do so enthusiastically. This willingness — even eagerness — to buy foreign securities means that bond issuers can now market their securities worldwide. The term *international bonds* refers to fixed-income securities that, from the standpoint of the issuer, are sold in a foreign market or denominated in a foreign currency.

Dollar-denominated international bonds are generally identified by the primary trading market. When U.S. corporations, municipalities, and federally sponsored credit agencies sell dollar-denominated securities that are issued and traded outside the United States — primarily in London — these securities are called *Eurodollar bonds*. When foreign governments and businesses issue dollar-denominated securities in the United States, these are called *Yankee Bonds*.

The more general term *Eurobonds* includes not only Eurodollar bonds but also all fixed-income securities that are denominated in the issuer's domestic currency but issued and traded in foreign markets. About a third of all Eurobonds are dollar-denominated — and hence are called Eurodollar bonds. Other popular Eurobond currencies are Japanese yen, Swiss francs, German marks, and British pounds. Bonds that are issued in both foreign currencies and foreign markets have a variety of colorful names. In addition to Yankee bonds, *Samurai bonds* are denominated in yen and issued in Japan by non-Japanese entities; *Bulldog bonds* are denominated in pounds and issued in the United Kingdom by foreigners.

A global perspective gives investors more opportunities to seek high returns and to diversify their portfolios. U.S. investors who restrict their attention to U.S. bonds are ignoring more than half the world's bonds. A global perspective similarly gives bond issuers a broader market for their securities. German corporations can sell bonds to U.S. investors, and the U.S. government can sell Treasury bonds to Japanese investors. Because of government regulations and high fees charged by Japanese underwriters, Japanese firms are heavy issuers of Eurobonds. In 1988, 21 percent of all Eurobonds were issued by Japanese companies.[6]

Between 1980 and 1990, aggregate foreign purchases and sales of U.S. bonds (maturities longer than 1 year) increased at an astounding 41 percent

| Table 7.1 Foreign Transactions in U.S. Bonds and U.S. Transactions in Foreign Bonds | | | | |
|---|---|---|---|---|
| | Foreign Transactions in U.S. Bonds ($ billions) | | U.S. Transactions in Foreign Bonds ($ billions) | |
| | Purchases | Sales | Purchases | Sales |
| **1990** | | | | |
| United Kingdom | 564.62 | 555.67 | 113.95 | 114.16 |
| Japan | 731.08 | 744.96 | 36.71 | 43.50 |
| Canada | 66.81 | 69.46 | 54.48 | 56.91 |
| Germany | 45.31 | 39.87 | 15.91 | 18.23 |
| France | 13.47 | 12.78 | 14.67 | 15.50 |
| Total worldwide | 1,945.19 | 1,906.80 | 313.58 | 335.93 |
| **1980** | | | | |
| United Kingdom | 22.36 | 20.15 | 6.07 | 6.16 |
| Japan | 2.59 | 4.21 | 1.35 | 2.65 |
| Canada | 0.96 | 2.39 | 2.20 | 2.42 |
| Germany | 2.54 | 5.21 | 0.45 | 0.43 |
| France | 0.71 | 0.45 | 0.66 | 0.62 |
| Total worldwide | 66.61 | 56.25 | 17.07 | 17.92 |

**Source:** Peter A. Abken, "Globalization of Stock, Futures, and Options Markets," *Economic Review*, Federal Reserve Bank of Atlanta, July/August 1991, pp. 1–19.

annual rate; U.S. purchases and sales of foreign bonds grew at a 34 percent annual rate. Table 7.1 shows the composition for five countries of foreign transactions in U.S. bonds and U.S. transactions in foreign bonds.

Investors who buy securities that are denominated in a foreign currency expose themselves to exchange-rate risk, as explained in the preceding chapter. The rate of return — calculated in terms of the domestic currency — is enhanced if the foreign currency happens to appreciate relative to the domestic currency and is diminished if it depreciates. Specifically, the rate of return on a foreign security in terms of the domestic currency is approximately equal to the foreign interest rate $R_f$ plus the percentage change in the exchange rate $\%\Delta e$, where $e$ is the quantity of domestic currency required to buy one unit of the foreign currency. Equation 6.7 in Chapter 6 shows that the domestic rate of return on a foreign security will equal the rate of return $R_d$ on a domestic security if

$$R_d = R_f + \%\Delta e \tag{7.3}$$

If a U.S. investor expects the dollar to depreciate by 5 percent annually versus the mark, German bonds will have higher expected returns than comparable U.S. bonds unless U.S. interest rates are 5 percentage points higher than

## EXAMPLE 7.3 *The Market for LDC Debt*

A bank that has loaned money to a foreign country can hold onto its loan note and hope that the loan is repaid or sell the note to someone else who is willing, for the right price, to take this gamble. The prices at which less developed country (LDC) loan notes are traded reflect the participants' views about the probability that the loans will be repaid and the timing of these payments. Loans that are likely to be repaid in full sell for close to face value, whereas those that will probably be repaid in part or not at all sell for a steep discount.

The accompanying table shows the average prices of foreign loans for eight selected countries in 1989.* On March 1 of that year, only Chile's loans sold for more than 50 percent of face value. Argentine debt was the most heavily discounted, trading at 18 cents per dollar of face value. The prices of many of these loans rose sharply on March 10, 1989, after the U.S. government announced that it would provide LDCs with some $30 billion to help them repay their loans.

| Average Price of Foreign Debt (per Dollar of Face Value) | | |
| --- | --- | --- |
| | March 1, 1989 | July 17, 1989 |
| Argentina | $0.18 | $0.19 |
| Brazil | 0.28 | 0.32 |
| Chile | 0.56 | 0.65 |
| Mexico | 0.34 | 0.44 |
| Philippines | 0.38 | 0.54 |
| Poland | 0.32 | 0.39 |
| Venezuela | 0.27 | 0.40 |
| Yugoslavia | 0.44 | 0.54 |

*These data were provided by Salomon Brothers to Peter Truell, "Banks' Credits Buoyed by U.S. Debt Strategy," Wall Street Journal, *July 19, 1989.*

comparable German interest rates. U.S. Treasury bonds paying 11 percent and comparable German government bonds paying 6 percent are equally attractive (to both U.S. and German investors) if the mark appreciates by 5 percent annually relative to the dollar.

The integration of world financial markets also means that financial events in one country quickly affect financial markets in other countries. If interest rates rise in the United States, then interest rates must rise in other countries too, or else there must be a corresponding increase in the anticipated future appreciation of foreign currencies relative to the dollar. Suppose, for example, that U.S. and German government bond rates are both 8 percent and the dollar/mark exchange rate is expected to be stable. If U.S. Treasury bond rates rise to 10 percent and German government bond rates stay at 8 percent, with the dollar/mark exchange rate still expected to be stable, then U.S. bonds have the higher expected return. For these bonds to be equally attractive, U.S. interest rates must fall, German interest rates must rise, or (perhaps because of an immediate appreciation of the dollar) the dollar must be expected to depreciate relative to the mark in the future.

# BOND PROVISIONS

Bonds involve legal contracts containing an enormous variety of detailed provisions. Four general principles apply to a great many bonds: proof of ownership, call provisions, sinking funds, and convertible opportunities.

## *Proof of Ownership*

Bonds are called **bearer bonds** if proof of ownership is demonstrated simply by possession of the bond certificate; owners of bearer bonds can present coupons clipped from the bond at a local bank or brokerage firm, which is then reimbursed by the issuing agency. For a **registered bond**, in contrast, the name of the owner is registered with the trustee, and the payments are sent directly to the owner without the physical presentation of a bond certificate. Registered bonds are safer from theft and reduce the paper shuffling involved with clipped coupons.

Since 1983, all Treasury securities have been in registered form. Similarly, federal law requires all state and local bonds issued since July 1, 1983, to be registered bonds, with the issuing agency maintaining an up-to-date computerized list of the owners and mailing them the semiannual coupon payments. The intent of the federal law is to ensure reporting of any taxable income and to discover suspicious wealth that may have been acquired with unreported income and then tucked into tax-exempt bonds.

## *Call Provisions*

Some Treasury bonds and most corporate bonds have **call provisions** that allow the issuer to redeem the bond before maturity at a specified price. This gives the issuer an opportunity to refinance if interest rates fall, just as a homeowner can benefit by refinancing a home loan if mortgage rates decline. An issuer can choose to call all the bonds issued or a randomly selected subset. Purchasers of callable bonds typically have some call protection specifying that the bond cannot be called in the first few years after issuance and that the issuer must pay a premium over face value (analogous to a mortgage's prepayment penalty) if the bond is called.

Investors understandably prefer noncallable bonds. If interest rates fall, those investors who have their bonds called will have to reinvest their money at low interest rates, whereas those with noncallable bonds have locked-in higher interest rates. Because a callable bond is less attractive to investors, it must be priced to pay a somewhat higher interest rate than a comparable noncallable bond, a rate premium that depends on the amount of call protection and on investor perceptions of the probability that it will be called.

In the early 1980s, virtually all corporate bonds were callable. As interest rates declined after 1982, corporations increasingly issued noncallable bonds. Fewer than 10 percent of the corporate bonds issued between 1990 and 1992 were callable. The U.S. Treasury issues relatively few callable bonds and has not issued any at all since 1985. Callable Treasury bonds can be redeemed at face value, typically during the last 5 to 10 years before maturity; a Treasury bond with a maturity stated as 2012–2017 matures in the year 2017 and is callable after 2012.

In October of 1991 the Treasury announced its first bond call since 1962, when it called $1.8 billion in 20-year bonds with $7\frac{1}{2}$ percent coupons that were due to mature in August of 1993 and could be called at face value after August of 1988. Interest rates had declined sharply in 1991, and noncallable Treasury bonds maturing in August of 1993 with similar coupons were selling for about 103 (per $100 of face value). The call allowed the Treasury to pay the $1.8 billion face value for bonds that would have been worth around $1.03(\$1.8 \text{ billion}) = \$1.854$ billion if they had not been callable. Thus the call was worth about $54 million to the Treasury.

If the market price of a callable bond is above its call price, then it is unrealistic to count on holding the bond until maturity. In place of the yield to maturity, many investors instead calculate the more conservative **yield to call**, which assumes that the bond will be called at the first opportunity. With semiannual coupons, we use Equation 7.2, replacing the number of years until maturity $n$ with the number of years until the first call date and replacing the maturation value $M$ with the call price.

Consider, for example, a 20-year bond with a 12 percent coupon, paid semiannually, and a market price of 115 that is callable in 5 years at a call price of 105. The yield to maturity is given by solving Equation 7.2 with $P = 115$, $C = 12/2 = 6$, $n = 20$, and $M = 100$:

$$115 = \frac{6}{(1 + y/2)} + \frac{6}{(1 + y/2)^2} + \cdots + \frac{6}{(1 + y/2)^{40}} + \frac{100}{(1 + y/2)^{40}}$$

The yield to maturity works out to be 10.22 percent. Because of its generous 12 percent annual coupon, this bond sells for a premium above its face value. However, investors will not receive this 12 percent coupon for the entire 20 years if the bond is called before maturity. To compute the yield to call, we assume that the bond will, in fact, be called after 5 years at a price of 105. Thus we replace $n = 20$ with $n = 5$ and replace $M = 100$ with $M = 105$:

$$115 = \frac{6}{(1 + y/2)} + \frac{6}{(1 + y/2)^2} + \cdots + \frac{6}{(1 + y/2)^{10}} + \frac{105}{(1 + y/2)^{10}}$$

The yield to call turns out to be 9.02 percent, which is 1.20 percentage points lower than the yield to maturity.

## Sinking Funds

Many corporate bonds have **sinking fund** provisions specifying that the issuer will put a certain amount of money into a fund each year to redeem some of its bonds, thereby reducing its indebtedness. These bonds can be called by lottery at a specified premium over face value or repurchased in the secondary market if the market price is lower than the call price. Bond issues that are considered risky often use sinking funds to reassure investors that the firm will repay its debt in an orderly fashion and not have to scramble for funds at maturity. However, investors who buy bonds with sinking funds should be concerned about the possibility that their bonds will be called away if interest rates decline.

## Convertible Bonds

**Convertible bonds** give noteholders the options of exchanging their bonds for other securities, using a specified number of shares of the company's stock — thereby converting debt into equity. The *conversion ratio* is the number of shares received for each bond. The implicit *conversion price* is the value of the bonds (or fraction of a bond) that must be surrendered to obtain one share of stock.

Suppose, for example, that a convertible bond is issued with a 6 percent coupon and a $1,000 par value and that the bond contract allows a bondholder to exchange 1 bond for 10 shares of the company's stock. The conversion ratio is 10:1. If the bond's market price is $1,100, then conversion requires the exchange of an $1,100 bond for 10 shares of stock, an implicit conversion price of $1,100/10 = $110 per share.

If the market price of this stock is greater than $110, investors can make an easy profit by buying the bond for $1,100, converting it into 10 shares of stock, and selling this stock for more than $1,100. Such profits are too easy to be true, in that it is extremely unlikely that such arbitrage activity will ever be possible. Owners of the convertible bonds will not sell them for $1,100 if they themselves can convert the bonds into stock worth more than $1,100.

A convertible bond is a hybrid security. It is a bond plus an option to acquire stock. Its value is consequently equal to the value of a similar nonconvertible bond plus the value of the stock option. Stock options will be discussed more fully in Chapter 11.

# DEFAULT RISK

Why did many investors hold IBM bonds in May of 1986 with a 9.1 percent yield when they could have purchased Navistar bonds with an 11.4 percent yield? These 9.1 and 11.4 percent yield calculations assume that the coupons and principal will be paid as scheduled. If the company doesn't pay or delays the payments, the actual return may be far less than what was promised. In 1986 investors were more confident of IBM's promises than they were of Navistar's.

Those who borrow money are not always able to repay their loans. Individual borrowers may lose jobs, firms may lose customers, and state and local governments may lose their tax base. Only the U.S. Treasury is absolutely certain of always having enough money to repay its debt — because the federal government can literally print money.

In this section we will look at how investors evaluate the creditworthiness of potential borrowers and how interest rates reflect this assessment. You will see how bonds are rated and why bonds with low ratings have high yields to maturity. An extreme example is "junk" bonds — bonds that have the lowest ratings or aren't rated at all.

Borrowers **default** when they don't pay what was promised when it was promised. Holders of defaulted debt may sympathize with the ill fortune of the issuer, but they feel their own personal loss even more keenly, since they may get back nothing or only a few cents out of each dollar they invested. A default is not necessarily a complete loss, in that it may represent merely a temporary suspension of payments or a prelude to a partial payment; in the first month after default, a bond typically trades at about 40 percent of its face value.[7] The price doesn't fall all the way to zero as long as there is still some hope of a resumption of at least partial payments.

Historically, bond defaults have been relatively infrequent because most investors won't buy bonds issued by likely defaulters. The ideal borrower has a good use for the borrowed money — perhaps for the construction of a new factory — but doesn't need cash to stay afloat. In the 1980s, however, investors displayed an increasing willingness to buy high-risk bonds — "junk" debt — issued by businesses and state and local government agencies with acknowledged financial problems.

Even apparently safe loans can be jeopardized by unexpected events. A financially sound firm that issues a 20-year bond may run into unexpected difficulties 10 years later — perhaps the loss of key executives, technological advances by competitors, changes in public tastes, or the imposition of onerous government regulations. Penn Central, Chrysler, Lockheed, New York City, and Texaco were all safe investments — until the unexpected happened.

## Bond Ratings

It is not easy to evaluate the creditworthiness of debt issuers. A lot of information must be gathered, processed, and analyzed carefully. Some large institutional investors have their own internal staffs that specialize in evaluating the merits of bond issuers. Small purchasers usually find it more economical to rely on the evaluations of professional rating agencies such as Moody's and Standard & Poor's. These private organizations provide impartial and up-to-date assessments of thousands of corporate and government bonds using the quality categories

### Table 7.2   Bond Rating Categories

| | Moody's | | Standard & Poor's |
|---|---|---|---|
| Aaa | Best quality | AAA | Highest rating |
| Aa | High quality | AA | Very strong |
| A | Upper medium grade | A | Strong |
| Baa | Medium grade | BBB | Adequate |
| Ba | Speculative elements | BB | Somewhat speculative |
| B | Lack characteristics of desirable investment | B | Speculative |
| Caa | Poor standing; may be in default | CCC-CC | Highly speculative |
| Ca | Speculative in a high degree; may be in default | C | Income bonds with no interest being paid |
| C | Lowest rated class; extremely poor prospects | D | In default |

*Junk*

**Source:** *Moody's Bond Record*, October 1988; *Standard & Poor's Bond Guide*, October 1988.

summarized in Table 7.2. Finer gradations are made within the categories Aa (or AA) to B, Moody's using the numbers 1, 2, and 3 and Standard & Poor's using + or −.

U.S. Treasury securities are not rated because the chances of default are negligible. Corporate and state and local government bonds, as many investors have learned painfully, can and occasionally do default. Unfortunately, many municipalities do not provide enough information to gauge their financial condition accurately. In 1980 the SEC concluded that "the market for municipal securities provides investors with only limited protection compared with corporate, [federal] government or other issuers."[8] A Harvard Business School professor wrote in 1985 that "within wide limits, government accounting rules permit accountants to play games that lead to whatever bottom line the mayor or governor wants,"[9] usually a small surplus so that voters will neither be upset by a deficit nor demand lower taxes.

---

**EXAMPLE 7.4   *The Whoops Default***

Municipal bond defaults have been infrequent and usually involve a postponement of payments because the project financed by the bond takes longer than expected to earn sufficient revenue. For instance, some West Virginia Turnpike bonds issued in 1952 were in default for 20 years before enough toll revenue finally accumulated to pay off the bonds.*

*\*Lynn Asinof, "Possible Effects of a WPSS Bond Failure Are Visible in Past U.S. Municipal Bond Defaults," Wall Street Journal, July 13, 1983.*

In 1975 the municipal bond market was rocked by New York City's financial troubles. With a weak economy and shrinking tax base, the city declared a moratorium on some $2.4 billion in short-term notes. After the courts ruled this action unconstitutional, the city found ways to pay its bondholders, although the principal payments were delayed for up to 2 years and only 6 percent interest was credited during this delay.

In 1983 it was the Washington Public Power Supply System (WPPSS), widely known by the ironic label "Whoops," that disappointed investors. A consortium of nearly 100 public utilities in the Pacific Northwest established WPPSS to sell $8.4 billion in municipal bonds to finance the construction of five nuclear power plants. These public power agencies backed the bonds by signing "take or pay" (also known as "come hell or high water") contracts, agreeing to pay for specified amounts of electricity at set prices regardless of whether or not the power was actually delivered.

Construction costs turned out to be much higher than anticipated and the Northwest's demand for electricity much lower. Two of the plants (nos. 4 and 5) were terminated in January of 1982 after spending almost all the $2.25 billion raised by bond sales to finance their construction. Projects 1 and 3 were later suspended semipermanently, leaving only no. 2 producing any electricity. WPPSS stopped making payments on its no. 4 and 5 bonds in January of 1983 and formally defaulted on them later that year, after the Washington State Supreme Court ruled that the public utilities had no authority to sign take-or-pay contracts and, therefore, had no obligation to fulfill them. Coupons and principal continue to be paid on the bonds for projects 1, 2, and 3 which (unlike nos. 4 and 5) are backed by the Bonneville Power Administration, a federal agency that distributes electricity to public utilities in the Northwest.

WPPSS was the nation's largest issuer of municipal bonds, and the $2.25 billion default on its no. 4 and 5 bonds was, by far, the largest ever. Moody's gave the no. 4 and 5 bonds an A1 rating until June of 1981, and Standard & Poor's rated them A until January of 1982. Investors were shocked and then enraged that these seemingly safe investments were made a shambles by a court-backed default. A collection of lawsuits alleging fraud by WPPSS, the Wall Street firms that marketed the bonds, and other convenient targets (91 defendants in all) is now working its way through the courts.

Despite dire warnings in 1983 of shock waves from this precedent, the municipal bond market recovered quickly, leading some to call WPPSS a "no-fault default." To reassure nervous investors (and reduce interest costs), many local governments and agencies now buy special insurance that guarantees the payment of principal and interest on their bonds. Standard & Poor's automatically gives an AAA rating to bonds that are backed by either of the two major insurers — the Municipal Bond Insurance Association or the American Bond Assurance Corporation. Nonetheless, these insured bonds have been priced to yield up to a $\frac{1}{2}$ percent more than uninsured AAAs because the latter are judged AAA on the strength of the issuing municipality, while there is apparently some fear that a wave of defaults would bankrupt the insurers.

**Table 7.3   Selected Corporate Bond Ratings, 1992**

| | |
|---|---|
| AAA: | Exxon, General Electric, IBM, J. P. Morgan |
| AA : | American Express, Coca-Cola, Dow Jones, Wal-Mart |
| A : | Citicorp, General Motors, Merrill Lynch, Sears |
| BBB: | First Interstate, Hertz, Paine-Webber, Reebok |
| BB : | Georgia Pacific, Home Shopping Network, Inland Steel |
| B : | Chrysler, Embassy Suites, Kroger, Stop & Shop |
| D : | Bally's Grand, Orion Pictures, R.H. Macy, TWA |

**Source:** *Standard & Poor's Bond Guide,* April 1992.

Standard & Poor's estimated that about half the state and local governments issuing bonds in 1980 didn't comply with generally accepted accounting principles. Most only report current expenditures and revenues and ignore anticipated revenue and spending commitments. Many habitually omit important information, and most do not submit to independent audits. Standard & Poor's has even threatened to stop rating the bonds of municipalities that ignore sound accounting practices.

Corporate borrowers provide better information and are rated more confidently by Standard & Poor's and Moody's. Those bonds put in the first four categories (AAA to BBB or Aaa to Baa) are considered investment grade. Historically, about 90 percent of all rated corporate issues have been placed in the first three categories. (This doesn't mean that 90 percent of all corporations are this financially sound, only that less secure companies don't issue many bonds.) Table 7.3 shows some examples of corporate ratings in 1992. (Bonds from the same issuer are sometimes put in different ratings classes because some bonds have senior status, with first claim on the issuer's funds; in the event of financial distress, junior issues do not receive any funds until more senior debt is completely repaid.) Those bonds that are rated outside the first four categories are somewhat speculative and are considered imprudent by many institutional investors.

## Financial Ratios and Bond Ratings

How do Moody's and Standard & Poor's determine the appropriate rating for a company's bonds? They conduct a quantitative evaluation of its current and past financial condition and make a subjective assessment of the firm's future. The relevant question is, "Will this firm have enough profits (and, in particular, enough cash flow) to meet the mandated payments on its debts?" Among the data examined are the four financial ratios in Table 7.4, with the numbers showing average values for seven Standard & Poor's rating categories.

The pretax fixed-charge coverage ratio is the ratio of profits (before taxes and interest payments) to bond payments, lease payments, and other nondiscretion-

**Table 7.4    Four Financial Ratios Used to Judge Financial Condition**

| Rating Category | Pretax Fixed-Charge Coverage | Cash Flow to Total Debt | Pretax Return on Long-Term Capital (%) | Long-Term Debt to Capitalization |
|---|---|---|---|---|
| AAA | 6.05 | 0.48 | 23.8 | 0.12 |
| AA | 4.68 | 0.32 | 21.9 | 0.19 |
| A | 2.97 | 0.13 | 17.9 | 0.28 |
| BBB | 2.32 | 0.07 | 12.4 | 0.34 |
| BB | 1.74 | −0.01 | 11.5 | 0.48 |
| B | 1.45 | −0.06 | 10.6 | 0.57 |
| CCC | 0.12 | −0.02 | −2.2 | 0.73 |

**Source:** Standard & Poor's *CreditWeek*, September 5, 1988.

ary expenses. Pretax profits are used because interest payments are tax deductible; if a firm has $1 million of pretax profits and $1 million of interest to pay, it can do so because it will then owe no taxes. If this pretax fixed-charge ratio is less than 1, the firm is having trouble making ends meet. For the most highly rated firms, profits are many times more than enough to cover mandated expenses.

Of course, the profit calculations of sometimes creative accountants do not ensure that sufficient dollars really are on hand to meet expenses. Cash flow measures the money actually coming into the firm, and the ratio of cash flow to debt (or, more relevantly, a comparison of this ratio with the interest rate on this debt) gauges its adequacy. The most highly rated firms have both high profits and a generous cash flow relative to interest expenses and other fixed charges.

The pretax return on long-term capital is a measure of the firm's basic profitability; an unprofitable firm is financially precarious. Long-term debt to capitalization is the ratio of the firm's long-term debt to the sum of its short-term debt, long-term debt, and stock, essentially the total value of the firm, because those who own its debt and stock receive all the money (interest and dividends) paid out by the firm. If the value of these debt and stock claims is approximately equal to the value of the firm's assets, then the liquidation of an AAA-rated firm with a 0.16 ratio would yield $1/0.16 = 6.25$ times the amount of money needed to retire its long-term debt.

## Risk and Promised Return

Calculated yields to maturity use market prices of bonds and the promised coupons and maturation value, promises that may or may not be kept. The larger the probability that a firm will default, the lower is the market price of its bonds and the higher is the computed yield to maturity. This is why bonds from IBM

| Table 7.5 | Yield to Maturity by Rating Category, May 1986 |
|---|---|
| Rating Category | Yield to Maturity (%) |
| AAA | 9.19 |
| AA | 9.51 |
| A | 9.75 |
| BBB | 10.32 |

**Source:** *Standard & Poor's Bond Guide*, January 1987.

and Navistar with very similar coupons and maturation dates sold for very different prices in May of 1986.

IBM bonds had Standard & Poor's highest rating (AAA), whereas Navistar bonds were rated a speculative B. Under its former name, International Harvester, Navistar had staggering losses for 5 straight years from 1980 through 1985 and by the end of 1985 had a total long-term debt of $888 million as compared with a slender net worth of $42 million (after subtracting its debts from its assets). Its long-term debt-to-capitalization ratio was nearly 1.0, and one more bad year would push its net worth into the red.

Nervous investors paid only $87\frac{7}{8}$ for Navistar's bonds in May of 1986 and $102\frac{1}{2}$ for similar promises from IBM, giving Navistar an 11.4 percent calculated yield to maturity and IBM 9.1 percent. These are consistent with the May 1986 average yields to maturity by the rating category shown in Table 7.5.

Figure 7.2 shows the historical differences between the yields on U.S. government bonds and corporate Baa and Aaa bonds. In recent years, Baa bonds have been priced to yield about 1 percent per year more than Aaa bonds. Bond buyers and sellers price these bonds so that the yields generally move up and down together, keeping the yield spread remarkably stable. If risky bonds were priced to yield only slightly more than safe bonds, many investors would switch from risky bonds to safe ones. If risky bonds yielded substantially more than safe bonds, investors would move in the other direction. To persuade investors to hold both types of bonds, the yields tend to move together.

When a bond's rating changes, so do its prices and promised yield to maturity. For instance, as a company's financial difficulties mount and its chances of bankruptcy grow, Moody's and Standard & Poor's downgrade the bond while its price slips in financial markets. There is some evidence that investors see changes in the financial condition of firms before the rating agencies do. One study found that bond prices reflect changing default conditions a full 6 to 18 months before subsequent rating changes and that the rating changes themselves (being so late) have no perceptible effect on bond prices.[10]

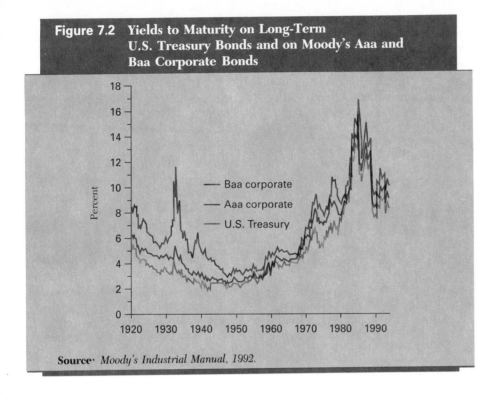

**Figure 7.2   Yields to Maturity on Long-Term U.S. Treasury Bonds and on Moody's Aaa and Baa Corporate Bonds**

— Baa corporate
— Aaa corporate
— U.S. Treasury

**Source·** *Moody's Industrial Manual, 1992.*

## Junk Bonds

**Junk bonds** is the generic label for low-quality debt — unrated bonds or low-rated bonds issued by companies that are either not well known or else known to be risky. Some of these bonds are "new junk," sold to finance risky ventures, and some are "fallen angels," bonds issued by companies that were once financially secure and now are not. Before the 1980s, most investors wouldn't touch junk; this was particularly true of mutual funds, pension funds, and other institutional investors who feared lawsuits if they breached their fiduciary duties with imprudent investments.

Then, according to popular legend, Michael Milken, a student at the University of Pennsylvania, decided that this aversion to junk bonds was excessive. Most companies whose bonds were low rated or unrated were not on the verge of default. Some were experiencing temporary financial difficulty; many were just unknown or didn't have a lot of tangible assets. According to Milken's calculations, the occasional default was more than offset by the fact that the bonds' prices were very low and the promised returns high. Milken joined a small securities firm, Drexel Burnham, and made his argument over and over to anyone who would listen, marketing junk bonds to those he persuaded.

Once Milken found junk buyers, more sellers appeared. A takeover wave hit the United States in the 1980s as corporate raiders acquired companies that appeared to have grown large and lazy and then resold them, often in parts, to those who thought they were better managers. Sometimes a company's own managers borrowed money to buy up the shareholder's stock, converting the firm from a public corporation to a private business. Raiders, external or internal, need financing, but few investors have enough funds to buy billion-dollar companies. Instead, they financed their takeovers by issuing junk bonds, implicitly using the assets of the target company as collateral.

With willing buyers and sellers, there was now a junk bond market, with Drexel Burnham the middleman. Those who wanted to issue junk came to Drexel, which had established a long list of buyers; those who wanted high potential returns knew that Drexel was the place to buy junk bonds. However, there was more to it than this. Drexel didn't just know the names of buyers and sellers, it had their confidence. With traditional investment-grade bonds, the ratings by Moody's and other services give a stamp of approval that facilitates trading. The seller of a triple-A bond knows that there are plenty of buyers; the buyers know from the independent ratings that they are buying quality securities. Not so with junk bonds. By definition, these bonds haven't been certified as safe investments by independent rating services. Junk buyers rely on the knowledge and reputation of the dealer (such as Drexel) to determine that this is an investment well worth making. Issuers count on the dealer's reputation, too, to ensure that all their bonds will be sold quickly and at less than exorbitant interest rates.

Junk buyers may want to sell their bonds eventually, and here, too, a secondary market requires a dealer who knows the players and has their confidence. By 1988 there were $160 billion in actively traded junk bonds, more than half through Drexel. Milken was at the core of this market, with first-hand knowledge of most of the buyers and sellers and a reputed ability to recite the terms of every junk bond in the country. Under him were some 150 traders working 12- to 15-hour days, beginning at 4:30 A.M. Junk turned Drexel into a major securities firm and provided it with $2 billion a year in revenue.

Milken was reportedly paid $550 million in 1987 and became a billionaire in 1988, at age 42. However, in 1988 Drexel was accused of a variety of securities fraud charges and agreed to plead guilty to six felonies, pay $650 million in penalties, and accept Milken's resignation. Milken was separately indicted for 98 counts, including insider trading, stock manipulation, parking of securities with associates to avoid ownership disclosure, the maintenance of false and misleading records, and false disclosures to the Securities and Exchange Commission; he eventually pleaded guilty to a handful of charges. Without Milken's stabilizing skills and with its reputation tarnished, Drexel Burnham was forced into bankruptcy in February of 1990.

Junk bonds are generally priced to yield 4 to 6 percentage points more than less speculative securities, and so far, on average, some 2 percent of all junk bonds have defaulted each year. Table 7.6 compares the average promised yields

**Table 7.6   Junk Bonds and U.S. Treasury Securities, 1978–1986**

|  | Promised Yield (%) | Actual Return (%) |
|---|---|---|
| Treasury bonds | 10.80 | 12.25 |
| Low-rated junk bonds | 14.54 | 13.24 |

**Source:** Edward I. Altman, "The Anatomy of the High-Yield Bond Market," *Financial Analysts Journal*, July/August 1987, pp. 12–25.

to maturity and actual realized returns (coupons plus capital gains) from junk bonds and long-term government securities during the years 1978–1986. However, these calculated default rates are somewhat misleading. Few defaults occur during the first few years after issuance, and because of the rapid growth of the junk bond market, the overwhelming majority of junk bonds have been issued relatively recently. Perhaps only 2 percent of the bonds defaulted this year because 98 percent were issued during the last 6 months. A 1988 study by Paul Asquith, David Mullins, and Eric Wolf calculated cumulative default rates for junk bonds of various ages.[11] They found that 34 percent of the junk bonds issued in 1977 and 1978 and 23 percent of those issued between 1979 and 1983 had defaulted by 1988.

## EXAMPLE 7.5 *RJR Becomes Junk*

Chapter 1 explained how debt provides a tax shield for firms because, unlike dividends, the interest on debt can be deducted from their taxable income. This tax advantage encourages management (or outside raiders) to increase a firm's indebtedness — in the extreme, to the point where its income is exhausted by interest payments and the company pays no taxes at all. The danger is that income may drop below its interest obligations, forcing the firm to default on its debts. As firms increased their indebtedness in the 1980s, the ratings of their bonds deteriorated: the median rating of industrial bonds fell from A in 1981 to BB in 1988, leading the managing director for industrial and utility ratings at Standard & Poor's to comment that "most companies are junk today."*

When a firm increases its indebtedness substantially, those who already own bonds issued by the firm are hurt financially because their bonds are downgraded as the firm's chances of bankruptcy increase. For example, after the 1988 debt-financed buyout of RJR Nabisco was announced, existing RJR bonds were downgraded from A to junk and the prices of these bonds fell by 20 percent. In addition to this immediate loss, the prices of RJR bonds began

*Bill Sing, "Mega-Mergers Leave Bondholders Counting Their Losses," Los Angeles Times, *November 9, 1988.*

fluctuating with the prices of other speculative junk. In 1989 and 1990, investors grew increasingly nervous about the junk bond market; during an especially unsettling 2-day period in January of 1990, the prices of some RJR bonds fell by more than 20 percent.

Investors who purchased RJR bonds when the company was financially strong were understandably upset when their conservative investment became junk. Some pension funds and insurance companies began pushing for take-over-proof bonds that can be redeemed at face value if there is a large increase in a firm's indebtedness. Other investors refused to buy anything but U.S. Treasury bonds, which are presumably safe from a leveraged buyout.

The years 1982 to 1988 were recession-free. Many observers worry that junk bonds were used to finance increasingly dubious ventures, gambles that will collapse during a prolonged recession. In October of 1988, a senior partner of a prominent investment firm that had acquired several corporations without using junk wrote, "Surely, when the history books are written, the reason so many investors bought these bonds will be the financial riddle of our age."[12] In 1989 and 1990, the annual returns from junk bonds averaged $-5.4$ percent, bringing the average annual realized return for the years 1977–1990 down to 8.7 percent, as compared to 9.1 percent for long-term Treasury bonds and 9.4 percent for high-grade corporate bonds.[13]

## Realized Returns

W. B. Hickman did an exhaustive study of every corporate bond issued during the period 1900–1943 and, as shown in Table 7.7, found a striking correlation between a bond's initial quality rating and its chance of eventual default.[14] Only 6 percent of the bonds in the top two rating categories eventually defaulted. Bonds that were lower-rated did, in fact, default more often. Of those few issues outside the first four categories, a stunning 42 percent defaulted. These default fractions are pretty high because so many firms were bankrupted by the Great Depression in the 1930s. No investment-grade bonds defaulted in the 1950s and 1960s.[15] However, several did in the 1970s and 1980s, including Braniff Airlines, W. T. Grant, and Penn Central. Between 1970 and 1984, on average, approximately 0.1 percent of all outstanding corporate bonds and 2.5 percent of the low-rated corporate bonds defaulted each year.[16]

Notice in Table 7.7 that the promised yields to maturity (assuming the coupon and maturation value will be paid as promised) are higher the lower is the bond's rating. The fourth column shows the actual yields, taking into account that defaulting companies did not pay all they had promised. The realized yields are virtually identical for the first three rating categories and rise somewhat for the last two. One complication with these data is that the substantial drop in interest rates in the 1930s made it profitable for many firms to exercise the call provisions in their bonds by paying bondholders a premium over the bond's face value (but a discount to the current market price). Hickman's data include these

| **Table 7.7**  Corporate Defaults by Rating Category, 1900–1943 | | | |
|---|---|---|---|
| Initial Rating (Composite of Rating Agencies) | Promised Yield to Maturity (%) | Fraction Defaulted (% of Par Value) | Actual Yield to Maturity (%) |
| 1 (highest) | 4.5 | 5.9 | 5.1 |
| 2 | 4.6 | 6.0 | 5.0 |
| 3 | 4.9 | 13.4 | 5.0 |
| 4 | 5.4 | 19.1 | 5.7 |
| 5–9 (lowest) | 9.5 | 42.4 | 8.6 |

**Source:** W. Braddock Hickman, *Corporate Bond Quality and Investor Experience* (New York: National Bureau of Economic Research, 1958).

call payments, which push the actual yields above the promised yields for the first four rating categories. Two other researchers redid Hickman's calculations for the first four rating categories, this time assuming that no bonds were called, so as to focus solely on how defaults affected yields. They found that the actual yields, taking into account defaults, were the same, 4.3 percent, in each category — the higher promised yields just offsetting the higher chances of default.[17]

Matters have turned out differently since World War II. There have been so few defaults that lower-rated, higher-yielding bonds have generally outperformed more highly rated bonds. This does not mean that, at present, AA bonds are a better investment than AAA and that junk bonds are better still, only that risky bonds are priced to take into account their susceptibility to default during bad times, and times have, as it turns out, been relatively good since World War II.

# SUMMARY

The capital market encompasses the issuance and trading of long-term securities, including Treasury notes (maturities of 2 to 10 years) and Treasury bonds (more than 10 years), corporate bonds, municipal bonds, mortgage-backed securities, and international bonds. The yield to maturity on a bond is that discount rate $y$ such that the present value of the coupons $C$ and the principal $M$ is equal to the price $P$:

$$P = \frac{C}{(1 + y)} + \frac{C}{(1 + y)^2} + \cdots + \frac{C}{(1 + y)^n} + \frac{M}{(1 + y)^n}$$

A bond sells for a premium above face value $M$ when the yield $y$ is below the coupon rate $C/M$ and at a discount when the yield is above the coupon rate.

Treasury notes and bonds are issued at periodic auctions at prices determined by the competitive bids of authorized primary dealers. Treasury securities can be purchased before the auction date in the when-issued market; after issuance, they are traded over the counter. The Treasury market is one of the world's most important and carefully watched financial markets, with prices and yields that quickly reflect financial developments and influence other financial and nonfinancial markets.

Corporate bonds finance construction, operations, and the takeover of other companies. Those that are sold to the public must be registered with the SEC and are usually marketed by an underwriting syndicate of dealers, led by the corporation's investment banker. After issuance, corporate bonds are traded over the counter or, to a limited extent, on the stock exchanges. About half of all corporate debt is issued privately, either term loans from banks and insurance companies or private placements, in which fewer than 35 investors (typically pension funds and life insurance companies) purchase the bonds at a negotiated price.

Bonds issued by state and local governments are called municipal bonds (munis) or tax-exempts because most are exempt from federal income taxes. If a corporate bond yields 10 percent and a comparably risky tax-exempt bond yields 8 percent, investors with marginal income tax rates higher than 20 percent can earn a higher after-tax return from the tax-exempt bond, whereas the reverse is true of those in lower tax brackets. General-obligation munis are backed by the issuer's ability to levy taxes; revenue bonds, in contrast, finance specific projects and are repaid by the income from the project. State and local bonds are underwritten by syndicates of investment bankers and are traded, to a limited extent, in the over-the-counter market.

Financial markets have become internationalized, in that businesses and governments are able to sell securities denominated in either a domestic or a foreign currency to investors at home and abroad. A global perspective gives investors more opportunities but does expose them to exchange-rate risk. The domestic return on a foreign asset is equal to the foreign rate of return $R_f$ plus the rate of appreciation of the foreign currency relative to the domestic currency: $R_f + \%\Delta e$. The willingness of investors to invest abroad links financial markets so that financial events in one country affect foreign financial markets too.

Proof of ownership of a bearer bond is demonstrated by possession of the bond certificate; the owners of registered bonds, in contrast, are registered with the bond's trustee. Many bonds have call provisions that allow the issuer to redeem the bond before maturity at a specified price — which the issuer will do if interest rates fall sufficiently. Sinking fund provisions require the issuer to redeem some of its bonds each year, thereby reducing its indebtedness. Convertible bonds can be exchanged for other securities, usually a specified number of shares of corporate stock.

Bond issuers with assets, profits, and cash flow that are relatively small in comparison with their debts are given low-quality ratings by Standard & Poor's, Moody's, and other professional rating agencies. Their bonds must have low prices and high (promised) yields to maturity to compensate investors for the risk of default. Low-rated and unrated issues are called junk bonds. Some junk bonds are issued by small, little-known companies; others are known as "fallen angels," once-safe bonds issued by once-strong companies; and some are issued to finance takeovers.

# IMPORTANT TERMS

bearer bonds
call provisions
capital market
convertible bonds
corporate bonds
default
junk bonds
municipal bonds (or munis)

private placements
registered bond
sinking fund
tax-exempt bonds
Treasury bonds
Treasury notes
yield to call
yield to maturity

# EXERCISES

1. Charles D. Ellis, the head of a financial consulting firm, Greenwich Associates, said that "for the average investor, U.S. Treasury securities are the safest investments in the world."[18] In what sense is this true? What risk is there for those who invest in Treasury securities?

2. The U.S. Treasury finances the federal deficit by periodically auctioning Treasury securities ranging from 3-month Treasury bills to 30-year Treasury bonds. If it wanted to minimize the present value of its cumulative interest expense, when should it sell short-term T-bills and when should it sell long-term bonds?

3. One financial observer wrote that a U.S. Treasury bond is "backed by the full faith and credit of the national government. To put it more directly, government paper is backed by the federal government's power to tax."[19] If a balanced-budget amendment or other law restricted the federal government's ability to increase taxes, would there be serious doubts about the U.S. government's ability to pay the interest due on its debt?

4. On October 22, 1991, a Treasury bond with a $15\frac{3}{4}$ percent coupon maturing in November of 2001 closed at a reported price of 155:27. At this reported price, what is the dollar price of $1 million face value of these bonds? Was the yield to maturity on these bonds above or below $15\frac{3}{4}$ percent?

5. On October 22, 1991, a 10-year Treasury zero closed at a reported price of 45:15. At this reported price, what is the dollar price of $1 million face value of these bonds? What was the yield to maturity?

6. On October 22, 1991, a 30-year Treasury bond with an $8\frac{1}{8}$ percent coupon was priced to give an 8.1 percent yield to maturity, whereas a 30-year Treasury zero was priced to give a 9.1 percent yield to maturity. Without doing any calculations, which bond had the higher price (per $100 of face value). Give a rational explanation for why investors would buy a 30-year Treasury bond with an 8.1 percent yield to maturity when one with a 9.1 percent yield was available.

7. Use a computer program to calculate the price that would give a 10-year bond with annual coupons of $600 and a maturation value of $5000 a 10 percent yield to maturity.

8. A 1990 Federal Reserve Bank of New York publication explains how changes in bond prices affect yields to maturity: "As the price falls, the yield rises; the amount of yield increase associated with a $\frac{1}{32}$ drop in price is largest for. . . ."[20] Explain why the omitted end of this quotation is either "long maturities" or "short maturities."

9. What is wrong with the following description of the Treasury securities auction used during the 1991 Salomon Brothers scandal:

*"Assume, for example, that 20 dealers bid on a $10 billion issue, with one bidding 102 for $3 billion and the rest bidding 101 for the same amount. The top bidder would get his $3 billion of securities at 101, because that was the market-clearing price, while the others would each get only one-nineteenth of what was left over."*[21]

10. In the wake of the Treasury bond market scandal, a financial consultant said that "I was always led to believe that the U.S. government securities market was the cleanest, most competitive and most efficient market in the world."[22] If the Treasury bond market's reputation is damaged by scandal, would you expect this damage to put upward or downward pressure on the interest rates on Treasury securities?

11. In congressional testimony on October 30, 1959, Milton Friedman argued that the Treasury securities auctions should allow all successful bidders to pay the same price, the price that clears the market, because the "present method involves payment of different prices by different purchasers, which tends to . . . establish a strong incentive for collusion among bidders."[23] Explain why you either agree or disagree.

12. Milton Friedman observed that for short-term Treasury securities, "there is a large secondary market for a range of maturities, including some very close to the maturity offered. . . . That is not true for long-term securities, for which there is a thinner market, and the securities available in the secondary market may differ more widely in maturity from the new securities offered."[24] Does this observation suggest a greater incentive for colluding on bids at the Treasury auction for short- or long-term securities?

13. When Salomon Brothers cornered the May 1991 auction of 2-year Treasury notes by placing unauthorized bids on behalf of its customers, did this have the effect of in-

creasing or reducing the interest rates that the Treasury paid on these 2-year notes?

14. When a corporate bond is publicly issued, the coupon rate and offering price are finalized at a meeting of the underwriting syndicate and the issuing firm on the day before the public offering. Why do you suppose they leave this crucial decision until the last possible moment?

15. Here is a 1987 analysis of municipal bond prices:

    *Demand for the bonds of states, cities and public authorities, which offer tax-exempt interest payments, has been tremendous. So many have rushed to buy what bond houses advertise as the last tax shelter of the middle class that customary price differentials between tax-exempt and taxable bonds have narrowed. Crowd psychology rather than economics is at work.*[25]

    Consider equally risky tax-exempt and taxable bonds with equal coupons. Which will have the higher price? If the demand for tax-exempts surges, will the price differential narrow?

16. Historically, the yields on tax-free municipal bonds have averaged about 70 percent of the yields on comparable, taxable corporate bonds; for instance, municipals might yield 7 percent when corporates yield 10 percent. If so, investors in which tax brackets receive a higher after-tax return from municipals?

17. A *Wall Street Journal* article began, "Pay $1200 or more for a municipal bond that will return only $1000 [at] maturity? That strikes most investors as a stupid idea."[26] Would it ever be a good idea?

18. The 1986 Tax Reform Act imposed restrictions on municipal bonds used to finance private projects. Why did projects financed by municipal bonds have an "unfair advantage" over projects financed by corporate bonds?

19. Historically, banks have been major purchasers of municipal bonds, but the Tax Reform Act of 1986 changed the tax code so that when banks and other financial institutions calculate their taxable income, they can no longer deduct the interest paid for deposits and other funds that are borrowed to finance the purchase of munis. Can you think of any reason for this change? How do you think it affected bank demand for municipal bonds?

20. What do you predict would happen to the yield spread between equally risky corporate and municipal bonds if municipal bonds lost their tax-exempt status?

21. British consols were generally callable at par after 6 months' notice. All British consols with 3-percent coupons issued before 1880 were called in 1888. Were long-term interest rates at the time above or below 3 percent? Explain your reasoning.

22. In November of 1991, Treasury securities with a 14 percent coupon (paid semiannually) that mature in November of 2011 and are callable at face value after November of 2006 sold for 153:10. Use a computer program to compare the yield to maturity and the yield to call in November of 1991.

23. In November of 1991, Treasury securities with an $8\frac{3}{4}$ percent coupon (paid semiannually) that mature in November of 2008 and are callable at face value after November of 2003 sold for 107:10. Compare the yield to maturity and the yield to call in November of 1991 (just set up). Without doing any calculations, is the yield to maturity larger or smaller than the yield to call?

24. Go to a library and use the most recent issue of *Standard & Poor's Bond Guide* to see if there have been any changes in the ratings of the corporate bonds in Table 7.3.

25. Use a recent publication of Moody's and one from Standard & Poor's to determine if the rating of Navistar bonds has changed from the speculative B assigned in May of 1986. Look in a recent issue of *The Wall Street Journal* and find the prices of the Navistar 9s04 and the IBM $\frac{93}{804}$ bonds discussed in this chapter and in Chapter 4. Does the Navistar bond still sell for 20 percent less than the IBM bond?

26. Explain the following observation by Andrew Tobias:

*Even without checking the ratings, you can tell the quality of a bond just by looking at how its yield compares with the yield of other bonds. . . . If anything, you should shy away from bonds that pay exceptional interest: there is a reason they pay so well.*[27]

27. In explaining its criteria for rating municipal bonds, Standard & Poor's wrote, "It is important for an area to offer economic diversity . . . in employment and income."[28] Why?

28. Standard & Poor's writes that "An S&P rating is not a recommendation to purchase, sell or hold a security."[29] Why not? What else should an investor consider?

29. The text says that "if the company doesn't pay or delays the payments, the actual return may be far less than what was promised." Why does a delayed payment reduce your actual return? For a simple example, consider a bond selling for $1000 that has only one payment left, a $50 coupon, and the $1000 maturation value is scheduled to be paid 6 months from now. What is your (annual) rate of return if the company
    a. makes the payment on time?
    b. delays it 6 months?
    c. delays it 4 years?

30. John Kenneth Galbraith wrote that "anyone who buys a junk bond known as a junk bond deserves on the whole to lose."[30] Why would any rational investor buy a junk bond when it is clearly labeled a junk bond?

# 8 The Mortgage Market

*Lawyer: Look, there's a $100 bill on the sidewalk.*
*Economist: Don't bother. It must be counterfeit, or someone would have picked it up by now.*

People borrow money to finance the purchase of homes, cars, and household appliances. Businesses borrow money to finance the construction of new buildings and equipment and the takeover of existing companies. Financial intermediaries borrow money from some to lend money to others. For each borrower, a loan is a debt, an obligation to repay the borrowed money plus interest. For each lender, a loan is an investment comparable to bonds, stocks, or other assets.

The principles that will be explained in this chapter apply to all loans, but we will focus on home loans — mortgages — to make the discussion more concrete and because mortgages are one of the most important categories of loans. This chapter explains how debt creates leverage, multiplying profits and losses from an investment. You will see how loan payments are determined and how the total-payments criterion used by many to compare loans is flawed. We will look at fixed-rate, variable-rate, and graduated-payment loans and consider the interest-rate gambles that are implicit in these loans for both borrowers and lenders. After discussing these financial details, we will see how the mortgage market has been revolutionized in recent years by the phenomenal growth of mortgage-backed securities. We begin by showing how debt can magnify the profits or losses from an investment.

## THE POWER OF LEVERAGE

We have all seen reports of people, perhaps even relatives or neighbors, who lost their home, farm, or business because they could not repay a loan. This is one reason why many people consider debt to be one of those four-letter words that decent people avoid: if you can't pay cash, then you can't afford it. Yet others swear by, not at, debt. Borrowing allows you to invest other people's money, and many a fortune has been built with other people's money.

Debt has these two faces, like the proverbial two-edged sword, because it creates **leverage**, in that a relatively small investment reaps the benefits or losses from a much larger investment. Suppose that you have $10,000 of your own money and borrow $90,000 of other people's money, giving you $100,000 to invest. We'll look a year into the future and assume that the $90,000 is a simple 1-year loan at 10 percent so that you must pay $99,000 at the end of the year. Your net financial gain depends on the rate of return $R$ that you earn on your $100,000 investment. Table 8.1 shows some possible outcomes.

Look first at $R = 10$ percent. A 10 percent return on $100,000 is $10,000, enough to pay the $9000 interest due on the $90,000 loan with $1000 left over — a 10 percent return on the $10,000 that is your own money. This calculation illustrates the general principle that if you borrow at 10 percent in order to invest at 10 percent, then the borrowing is neither an advantage nor a disadvantage. If the rate of return on the total investment is equal to the rate of interest owed on other people's money, then this also will be the rate of return on your own money.

What if you borrow at 10 percent and the rate of return on the total investment turns out to be 20 percent? Table 8.1 shows that 20 percent of $100,000 is $20,000 and that the payment of $9000 interest leaves an $11,000 gain on your $10,000 — a 110 percent return. You more than double your wealth in a year by borrowing $90,000 at 10 percent and investing at 20 percent!

Because the total $100,000 investment is 10 times the size of your own $10,000, you have 10:1 leverage. The consequence is that every percentage point by which the investment return exceeds the loan rate is multiplied by 10 in determining the return on your own money. A total return of $R = 20$ percent is a 10 percent excess over the 10 percent loan rate, and multiplication by 10:1 leverage pushes the excess return up to 10 percent $+$ 10(20 percent $-$ 10 percent) $=$ 110 percent.

To formalize this logic, a few mathematical symbols are helpful. If a fraction $x$ of an investment is your own money, then your degree of leverage is $L = 1/x$. If

### Table 8.1   Potential Returns with 10:1 Leverage

| Return on $100,000 | | Interest on $90,000 | Return on $10,000 | |
|---|---|---|---|---|
| Percentage | Dollars | Dollars | Dollars | Percentage |
| 0% | $ 0 | $9,000 | − $9,000 | − 90% |
| 10% | 10,000 | 9,000 | 1,000 | 10% |
| 20% | 20,000 | 9,000 | 11,000 | 110% |
| 30% | 30,000 | 9,000 | 21,000 | 210% |

EXAMPLE 8.2 *The Total-Payments Error*

Truth-in-lending laws require lenders to reveal not only a loan's annual percentage rate (*APR*) but also the total amount (principal plus interest) that will be paid over the life of the loan. Unfortunately, the prominent display of this information encourages borrowers to judge loans by the total payments, which is a mistake because it doesn't take into account when the payments are made, and a dollar paid today is more burdensome than a dollar paid 30 years from now.

A simple-minded comparison of total payments says that a 1-year loan at a 100 percent interest rate is better than a 150-year loan at a 1 percent interest rate, a conclusion that present-value logic says is nonsense. A total-payments analysis also implies that, for any given loan rate, you are always better off borrowing less money and repaying the loan as soon as possible because this reduces your total payments. The ultimate strategy, according to a total-payments analysis, is to never borrow any money at all — no matter what the loan rate! Present-value analysis reaches a different conclusion: if the loan rate is favorable (for instance, a below-market loan from the government or your employer), you want to borrow as much as you can for as long as you can.

It is not only unwary borrowers who fall into the total-payments trap; so do otherwise sensible financial advisors. For example, *Consumer Reports* once compared the purchase of appliances from a builder for $450, repaid over 27 years at 7.75 percent, with the purchase of the same goods from an appliance store for $675, repaid over 2 years at 15 percent, and came to the conclusion that "the appliances would cost $290 more from the builder."* With the builder, the buyer pays $3.32 a month for $12(27) = 324$ months, a total of $324(\$3.32) = \$1075$, of which $625 is interest. With the store, the buyer pays $32.71 a month for 24 months, a total of $24(\$32.71) = \$785$, of which $110 is interest charges. The difference is indeed $\$1075 - \$785 = \$290$, yet intuition signals that something is amiss. If the builder charges a third less for the appliances and half the interest rate, how can the store's deal be better?

It isn't. *Consumer Reports'* error is that it simply compared the total payments, $1075 versus $785, ignoring the fact that the payments to the store are made during the next 2 years, while the payments to the builder are spread over 27 years. In the eyes of *Consumer Reports*, time isn't money; a dollar paid 2 years from now is the same as a dollar paid 25 years later.

If we accept the argument that time is money, then we should compare the present values of these two cash flows,

$$\text{Store:} \quad P_S = \frac{\$32.71}{(1 + R/12)} + \frac{\$32.71}{(1 + R/12)^2} + \cdots + \frac{\$32.71}{(1 + R/12)^{24}}$$

$$\text{Builder:} \quad P_B = \frac{\$3.32}{(1 + R/12)} + \frac{\$3.32}{(1 + R/12)^2} + \cdots + \frac{\$3.32}{(1 + R/12)^{324}}$$

*"Notes to Home Buyers on Financing Future Schlock," Consumer Reports, *April 1972*, pp. 258–259.

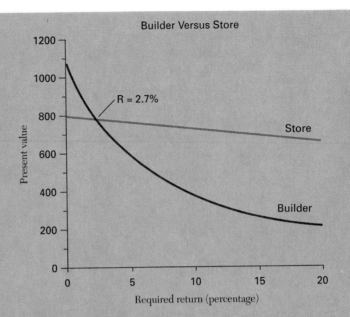

Builder Versus Store

*Consumer Reports* implicitly used $R = 0$ when it added up the undiscounted monthly payments. It makes more sense to use a required rate of return that reflects the reality that a dollar today is worth more than a dollar tomorrow. Instead of buying from the store and paying $32.71 a month for 24 months, the appliance buyer can pay the builder $3.32 a month, and deposit the difference, $32.71 − $3.32 = $29.39, in a bank earning a modest 5 percent return. If so, we can use $R = 5$ percent as the annual required return in the above present-value formulas and obtain these values:

Store:    $P_S = \$745.59$
Builder:  $P_B = \$589.66$

Instead of costing $290 more, the builder's offer actually saves the homebuyer, in present-value terms, $745.59 − $589.66 = $155.93.

Of course, 5 percent is not the only possible value for the required return. For some values (such as 0 percent) the store is more attractive, whereas for others (such as 5 percent) the builder looks better. In general, the higher the interest rate, the more attractive is the builder, because those distant payments are less and less burdensome in present-value terms. The accompanying graph compares the present values of the cash flows for a variety of interest rates. For any required return above 2.7 percent, the builder is the better option.

the third month, and so on until the last month, when only $351.88 is borrowed. The average amount borrowed is only about half of $4000, and therefore, the interest paid is only about half of what would be due if $4000 were borrowed for the entire year.

## EXAMPLE 8.5 *Wrap-Around Mortgages*

*Wrap-around mortgages* are sometimes used when homebuyers are prevented from assuming an existing low-interest mortgage but the seller is not compelled to pay the unpaid balance on the mortgage when the house is sold. Suppose that the seller of a $100,000 house has a conventional 30-year $60,000 mortgage at 7 percent with $399.18 monthly payments, 20 years of payments still remaining, and an unpaid balance of $51,487.71. If the mortgage is assumable, a buyer might pay the seller $20,000 in cash, assume the existing mortgage, and borrow the remaining $100,000 − $20,000 − $51,487.71 = $28,512.29 from the seller at, say, a 12 percent interest rate for 20 years. The monthly payments on the $28,512.29 owner-financed mortgage work out to be $313.94, and the total monthly payment on these two mortgages is $399.18 + $313.94 = $713.12.

| | Principal | Interest Rate | Monthly Payment |
|---|---|---|---|
| Assumable mortgage | $51,487.71 | 7% | $399.18 |
| Owner financing | $28,512.29 | 12% | $313.94 |
| | $80,000.00 | | $713.12 |

Alternatively, the homebuyer could borrow $80,000 from the seller, with the seller retaining the existing mortgage and continuing to make the $399.18 monthly payments. This arrangement "wraps around" the existing mortgage, in that the buyer's monthly payments to the seller include the amount that the seller must pay each month to the original lending institution. The interest rate on a 20-year $80,000 wrap-around mortgage that gives exactly the same $713.12 monthly payments as assuming the existing mortgage and borrowing $28,512.29 for 20 years at 12 percent can be determined by finding the annual percentage rate *APR* such that the present value of the $713.12 monthly payments is equal to $80,000:

$$\$80,000 = \frac{\$713.12}{(1 + APR/12)} + \frac{\$713.12}{(1 + APR/12)^2} + \cdots + \frac{\$713.12}{(1 + APR/12)^{240}}$$

The appropriate annual interest rate works out to be 8.87 percent.

the seller is relieved to have sold the house. Many owner-financing deals have balloon payments due after 3 to 5 years, with borrowers hoping that loan rates will fall by then so that they can refinance inexpensively through a conventional lending institution. Observers called the balloons launched in 1980 and 1981 "the ticking time bomb" in the residential real estate market. Fortunately, mortgage rates finally did drop in 1986, a bit late for some, but just in time for others.

## EXAMPLE 8.6 *Buying a House with Creative Financing*

The following is a fairly typical real estate transaction that was made in 1980 in Cape Cod, Massachusetts. At the time, Cape Cod mortgage institutions were charging interest rates of 18 percent and higher and rejecting most loan applications. The seller of this home was eager to move and agreed to sell for $66,000 with the buyer putting $30,000 down and borrowing $36,000 from the seller at 10.5 percent "amortized over 10 years, with a balloon after 5 years." This language means that the buyer makes monthly payments as if it is a 10-year amortized loan but makes a balloon payment to cover the unpaid balance after 5 years.

Equation 8.2 with

$$P = \$36,000$$
$$APR = 0.105$$
$$n = 120$$

gives the appropriate monthly payments as $485.78. Calculations such as those in Table 8.3 show the unpaid balance after 5 years to be $22,599.08. Alternatively, the unpaid balance $B$ can be determined by equating the present value of the monthly payments and the unpaid balance to the amount borrowed:

$$\$36,000 = \frac{\$485.78}{(1 + .105/12)} + \cdots + \frac{\$485.78}{(1 + .105/12)^{60}} + \frac{B}{(1 + .105/12)^{60}}$$

The solution of this equation gives $B = \$22,599.08$.

What is the value of this below-market loan to the buyer? The seller's 10.5 percent rate is substantially below the 18 percent plus charged by lending institutions, but it is only a 5-year loan. Is this deal worth hundreds or thousands of dollars? To answer this question, we can calculate the present value of the payments using an 18 percent annual interest rate:

$$P = \frac{\$485.78}{(1 + 0.18/12)} + \cdots + \frac{\$485.78}{(1 + 0.18/12)^{60}} + \frac{\$22,599.08}{(1 + 0.18/12)^{60}}$$

which is about $7600 less than the $36,000 borrowed. The buyer's monthly payments with this creative financing deal are the same as if the seller had reduced the price by $7600 and the buyer had borrowed from a bank at 18 percent.

# POINTS

During the 1960s and most of the 1970s, mortgage rates averaged some $1\frac{1}{2}$ to 2 percentage points above the interest rates on long-term U.S. government bonds. However, government bond rates jumped to 10.8 percent in 1980 and then to 12.9 percent in 1981, while many lending institutions were prohibited by state usury laws from charging more than 10 percent on mortgage loans. Unable to charge mortgage rates comparable with the rates of return they could earn on bonds and other investments not subject to usury ceilings, some lending institutions stopped making mortgages. Others discovered that they could circumvent usury ceilings, which restrict stated rather than effective interest rates, by charging **points** (sometimes called an *origination fee* or *buy down*), a fee equal to a specified percentage of the loan paid at the time the loan is made. For example, if you borrow $100,000 via a conventional 30-year mortgage at "12 percent plus 5 points," you only receive $95,000 ($100,000 less the 5 points) but pay 12 percent interest on the full $100,000. Interest rates have fallen from their 1981 peaks, and most usury ceilings have been abolished, but points continue to be added to mortgage loans.

## *The Impact of Points on the Effective Loan Rate*

Because you pay 12 percent interest on $100,000, the implicit interest rate on the $95,000 you actually receive is somewhat more than 12 percent, the exact value depending on the length of the loan and whether it is repaid early. With a 30-year amortized mortgage, Equation 8.2 shows that the requisite monthly payments on a $100,000 loan at a 12 percent annual percentage rate are $1028.61. The effective annual interest rate $R$ can be determined from Equation 8.1, setting the present value of these monthly payments equal to the amount actually borrowed, that is,

$$\$95,000 = \frac{\$1028.61}{(1 + R/12)} + \frac{\$1028.61}{(1 + R/12)^2} + \cdots + \frac{\$1028.61}{(1 + R/12)^{360}}$$

and then solving, by trial and error, for the effective interest rate. (Financial calculators can do this very quickly.) The solution turns out to be $R = 0.1270$, or 12.70 percent. Thus the monthly payments are the same on a 30-year 12 percent mortgage with 5 points and a 12.7 percent mortgage with no points.

The average U.S. family moves every 6 years. What if our borrower changes jobs, marries, divorces, has children, or for some other reason decides to pay off the mortgage before 30 years passes? This effectively shortens the loan and raises the implicit interest rate. Suppose that the loan is paid off after 10 years. The unpaid balance at this point is shown in Table 8.3 to be $93,418. Setting the present value of the borrower's payments equal to the $95,000 actually received, that is,

$$\$95,000 = \frac{\$1028.61}{(1 + R/12)} + \cdots + \frac{\$1028.61}{(1 + R/12)^{120}} + \frac{\$93,418}{(1 + R/12)^{120}}$$

and solving by trial and error gives an effective annual interest rate of $R = 0.1291$, or 12.91 percent, somewhat higher than when the mortgage is kept until the very end. If the mortgage is paid off before 10 years passes, the implicit interest rate rises very quickly, as shown in Table 8.7.

**Table 8.7  Effective Interest Rate on a 30-Year Mortgage at 12 Percent plus 5 Points**

| Year Repaid | Effective Interest Rate (%) |
|---|---|
| 1 year | 17.5 |
| 2 years | 14.9 |
| 5 years | 13.4 |
| 10 years | 12.9 |
| 20 years | 12.7 |
| 30 years | 12.7 |

## The Plight of S&Ls

In the 1960s and early 1970s, S&Ls paid their depositors interest rates ranging from 2 to 5 percent and loaned the money out in mortgages at 4 to 8 percent, enough to pay depositors, cover expenses, and make a profit too. Mortgage rates topped 8 percent in 1971 and hit an unprecedented 10 percent in 1978. Most observers thought that interest rates would soon fall to more normal levels. They were wrong. Interest rates went higher still, to above 16 percent in 1981, and those who borrowed at 8 to 10 percent were lucky to have what, in retrospect, were low-interest loans. The S&Ls they had borrowed from were not so lucky.

Having loaned virtually all their depositors' money out in long-term mortgages, S&Ls literally could not afford substantial withdrawals. While compelled to raise deposit rates to double-digit levels to hold onto depositors who would otherwise invest their money elsewhere, these S&Ls were receiving fixed, single-digit interest rates on mortgages written in the 1960s and 1970s. In 1982, the U.S. League of Savings Associations estimated that the average cost of funds (mainly deposit rates) for S&Ls was $11\frac{1}{2}$ percent and that a mortgage would have to yield 13 to $13\frac{1}{2}$ percent to cover these costs and other expenses. Yet 87 percent of the outstanding mortgages at that time had rates below 13 percent, and 58 percent had rates below 10 percent.[2] This is why the aggregate net worth of S&Ls fell from $23 billion at the end of 1977 to a frightening − $44 billion at the end of 1981[3] and the primary reason why nearly a quarter of the S&Ls operating in the 1970s collapsed or merged in the early 1980s.[4] Collecting single-digit rates on their mortgages while paying double-digit rates to depositors, they suffered alarming losses — simply because interest rates had risen unexpectedly.

What if interest rates had instead fallen unexpectedly? S&Ls would have made enormous profits if they could have reduced their deposit rates to 1 percent while still collecting 4 to 8 percent on mortgages. In reality, however, they would not have been able to keep these high-interest mortgages, because borrowers would have refinanced their loans by taking out mortgages at the new low interest rates and using the proceeds to pay off their old loans. S&Ls made a very asymmetrical bet in the 1950s, 1960s, and early 1970s. Depositors could refinance if interest rates fell, but S&Ls could not renegotiate if rates rose. Heads, depositors win; tails, S&Ls lose.

When S&Ls realized how expensive this asymmetrical bet could be, they changed the rules of the game by revising their standard mortgage contracts in two important ways. First, they inserted *due-on-sale clauses* to make mortgages nonassumable: if the borrower sells the house, the old, possibly low-interest mortgage must be repaid and cannot be passed on to the buyer. Second, to discourage or at least penalize borrowers who refinance when interest rates go down, they inserted **prepayment penalties**, additional charges that the borrower must pay the S&L if the loan is repaid early. Borrowers are, of course, not thrilled with prepayment penalties, and 14 state legislatures have outlawed them. Points can serve as a rough substitute, however, because 5 points on a new loan is about as discouraging as a 5 percent prepayment penalty on the old.

## *The Effect of Prepayment Penalties*

To analyze the consequences of prepayment penalties, consider a 30-year $100,000 mortgage at 12 percent with a $5000 prepayment penalty (penalties can be specified as a dollar amount, as a percentage of the unpaid balance, or by other rules). How does this penalty change the effective interest rate? The analysis is very similar to the case of points, the main difference being that points are tacked on at the beginning and prepayment penalties at the end. For instance, if the loan is paid off after 10 years, we've seen that the unpaid balance at that time is $93,418; a $5000 prepayment penalty forces the borrower to pay $98,418, and the effective annual interest rate is the value of $R$ that solves the present-value equation:

$$\$100,000 = \frac{\$1028.61}{(1 + R/12)} + \cdots + \frac{\$1028.61}{(1 + R/12)^{120}} + \frac{\$98,418}{(1 + R/12)^{120}}$$

Trial and error gives $R = 0.123$, or 12.3 percent. As with points, the effect is larger the sooner the loan is repaid, as shown in Table 8.8. A $5000 prepayment penalty doesn't raise the effective interest rate as much as $5000 in points, because the points are paid right away and the prepayment penalty is paid later (and can be avoided entirely by not prepaying the loan).

| Table 8.8   The Effect of a $5000 Prepayment Penalty on a 30-Year, 12 Percent Mortgage | |
| --- | --- |
| Year Repaid | Effective Interest Rate (%) |
| 1 year | 16.6 |
| 2 years | 14.2 |
| 5 years | 12.7 |
| 10 years | 12.3 |
| 20 years | 12.1 |
| 30 years | 12.0 |

## Does Refinancing Pay?

We also can answer a somewhat different question: How low do interest rates have to fall to make refinancing financially attractive despite the prepayment penalty? To keep the analysis straightforward, let's assume that when a 30-year mortgage is refinanced after $n$ years, the borrower takes out a new loan for $30 - n$ years and borrows just enough money to keep the monthly payments constant. Refinancing is then financially attractive if the amount that can be borrowed is large enough to pay off the old loan plus the prepayment penalty (and any other fees), with something left over. If homeowners voluntarily choose to borrow a different amount for a different period of time, then presumably they are even better off.

(This analysis ignores two messy complications. First, the borrower may decide at some future date to pay off the new loan; if so, the unpaid balance is not the same as with the old loan. Second, even if refinancing is profitable today, it may be even better to wait for still lower interest rates. These possibilities can be explored by comparing present values under a variety of plausible scenarios.)

We will continue to use the $100,000 30-year mortgage with a $5000 prepayment penalty as an example. If the loan is repaid after 10 years, the homeowner pays the bank $98,418. How low must the annual interest rate on the refinanced loan be so that the 20 years of $1028.61 monthly payments will allow the homeowner to borrow $98,418? This is the value of the $APR$ that solves this present-value equation,

$$\$98,418 = \frac{\$1028.61}{(1 + APR/12)} + \frac{\$1028.61}{(1 + APR/12)^2} + \cdots + \frac{\$1028.61}{(1 + APR/12)^{240}}$$

and the solution is $APR = 0.112$, or 11.2 percent. Similar calculations for other prepayment dates yield the values shown in Table 8.9.

Even with a seemingly expensive $5000 prepayment penalty, a 1 percent drop in interest rates makes refinancing attractive in the first 10 years of the loan.

**Table 8.9  Maximum Profitable Interest Rate for Refinancing a 30-Year, 12 Percent Mortgage with a $5000 Prepayment Penalty**

| Year Refinanced | Maximum Profitable Interest Rate (%) |
|---|---|
| 1 year | 11.4 |
| 2 years | 11.3 |
| 5 years | 11.3 |
| 10 years | 11.2 |
| 20 years | 10.4 |
| 25 years | 7.6 |

As time passes and the number of years remaining at the old high interest rate dwindle, it takes a bigger and bigger drop in interest rates to make refinancing profitable.

# ADJUSTABLE-RATE LOANS

In addition to imposing prepayment penalties, many S&Ls responded to the losses sustained in the early 1980s by shifting from fixed-rate mortgages to **adjustable-rate loans**, in which the loan rate rises and falls with market interest rates. If the problem is that the interest rates on old mortgages are fixed while deposit rates increase, then the solution is either to fix deposit rates or adjust mortgage rates. S&Ls tried both — encouraging time deposits with rates that are fixed for 2, 5, or even 10 years and encouraging mortgages with interest rates that vary with market interest rates. Similarly, most bank loans to businesses today have variable rates — for example, the current prime rate plus 2 percent.

These flexible-rate loans go by a variety of names: *adjustable-rate, variable-rate, renegotiable-rate, rollover,* and so on. In each case, the lender adjusts the interest rate to reflect current financial conditions, typically by using a specified formula that ties the loan rate to current market interest rates — approximating the rates paid depositors, with some additional percentage points tacked on to cover expenses. A specific example might be the interest rate on 1-year Treasury bills plus $2\frac{3}{4}$ percentage points. Many S&Ls use the yield on 1-year Treasury bills; others use explicit industry estimates of the average cost of funds. Many variable-rate mortgages have caps that limit the rate adjustment (in either direction) — for instance, no more than 2 percentage points in 1 year and no more than 5 percentage points during the life of the mortgage. The widespread use of variable-rate mortgages was first permitted in April of 1981, and during 1982–1985, roughly half of all new mortgages had variable rates.

There are a number of ways to adjust the payment stream as the loan rate varies. The essential rule is that the present value of the payments equals the amount borrowed or, equivalently, that the amount by which the monthly payment exceeds the interest due on the unpaid balance reduces the unpaid balance each month until it hits zero.

## Variable Payments

A benchmark payment structure is provided by amortizing a loan at a specified interest rate to obtain a planned constant stream of payments. For instance, a 30-year $100,000 mortgage at 12 percent implies monthly payments of $1028.61, some of which is interest on the unpaid balance and the remainder of which reduces that balance. As interest rates fluctuate, each month's payment could rise or fall with changes in the interest charged on the unpaid balance, keeping the planned reduction of principal on course. The borrower pays somewhat more than $1028.61 if the interest rate rises above 12 percent and somewhat less if it falls below 12 percent. In practice, the monthly payments are adjusted once a year rather than every month, but to simplify the arithmetic, we assume a monthly adjustment.

As an example, look again at Table 8.3. After the first month's payment, the unpaid balance declines to $99,971.39. If the interest rate charged in the second month rises to 12.2 percent, then the interest owed increases by $16.67, to $(0.122/12)\$99{,}971.39 = \$1016.38$, and the monthly payment also must increase by $16.67 in order to reduce the unpaid balance by $28.90 as planned:

| Planned | | Actual | |
|---|---|---|---|
| Interest | $ 999.71 | Interest | $1,016.38 |
| Principal | 28.90 | Principal | 28.90 |
| Total payment | $1,028.61 | Total payment | $1,045.28 |

By adjusting the monthly payment, the unpaid balance declines as scheduled and reaches zero after 30 years.

## Negative Amortization

Another possibility is to hold the monthly payments constant (at least temporarily) by varying the division of the monthly payment between interest and principal. Instead of increasing the monthly payment by $16.67 to cover the extra interest due, the repayment of principal can be reduced by $16.67:

| Planned | | Actual | |
|---|---|---|---|
| Interest | $ 999.71 | Interest | $1,016.38 |
| Principal | 28.90 | Principal | 12.23 |
| Total payment | $1,028.61 | Total payment | $1,028.61 |

If the interest rate rises so much that the fixed $1028.61 monthly payment is insufficient to cover the interest charge, there is **negative amortization**, in that the unpaid balance actually increases.

If the monthly payments are held constant and the interest rate stays above 12 percent, the unpaid balance will continue to decline more slowly than originally planned and will not hit zero after 30 years. A balloon payment can be made at that time, or the loan can be lengthened. If, on the other hand, the interest rate averages less than the planned 12 percent, the loan will be paid off before the end of 30 years.

A common variation is a temporarily fixed payment. Here the borrower selects a period of time, usually 1 to 5 years, during which the monthly payments are constant even while the interest rate being charged varies. After the specified period of fixed monthly payments is over, a new payment plan is established to get the unpaid balance back on schedule.

There is nothing inherently wrong with negative amortization, which just reflects the fact that if the loan payments are inadequate, the homeowner must borrow more money to cover the interest that is due. In many business and personal loans (for example, a line of credit from a bank, loans from a stock broker, or credit card balances), there is no set repayment schedule. Each month, interest is charged at a fixed or variable rate on the unpaid balance, and the borrower chooses how much to repay. The unpaid balance grows if the payment does not cover the interest charge and declines if it does.

# GRADUATED-PAYMENT LOANS

A conventional mortgage has constant monthly payments for the length of the loan, typically 30 years. During inflationary periods, the real value of these monthly payments declines steadily. For example, if prices rise by 5 percent a year, the price level at the end of a 30-year mortgage will be 4.3 times the price level at the beginning of the mortgage; therefore, the real value of the monthly payments at the beginning of the mortgage will be 4.3 times the real value at the end of the mortgage. If prices rise by 10 percent a year, the real value of the monthly payments at the beginning of the mortgage will be nearly 18 times the real value at the end of the mortgage.

In place of constant nominal monthly payments, it is more reasonable to have monthly payments that are constant in real terms. Imagine, for example, that you are just beginning a career at a $2000 monthly salary and expect your income to increase by 5 percent each year (perhaps the same rate as prices in general). If you borrow $100,000 at a 10 percent mortgage rate, your constant monthly payments are $877.57 — which is 44 percent of your current income but will be only 10 percent of your $8935 monthly income 30 years from now. Isn't it more sensible to have monthly mortgage payments that grow with your income, keeping the ratio of housing expenses to income roughly constant?

## *Unaffordable Housing*

As a practical matter, constant monthly mortgage payments may be such a large fraction of income in the early years that a young household cannot qualify for a mortgage, even though they will have plenty of income later. Fannie Mae requires a 20 percent down payment and recommends that housing expenses (including mortgage payments, homeowner's insurance, and taxes) not exceed 28 percent of household income. In 1990 the average price of a new home was $153,200 and the average conventional mortgage was for $112,400 for 27.3 years at a 9.68 percent interest rate, plus 1.93 percent in points and other fees. The average buyer put $40,800 down (plus $2000 in points) and obtained a mortgage with monthly payments of $977, which, by Fannie Mae's guidelines and ignoring insurance and taxes, required an annual income of about $42,000. Needless to say, few young households had $42,800 in cash and an annual income of $42,000.

## Mortgage Payments That Increase with Income

To ease the financial burden on young households who expect their nominal income to grow steadily (as is particularly true during inflationary periods), there are **graduated-payment mortgages (GPMs)**, in which the monthly payments are initially low and then grow over time with income. Consider a household whose monthly income is now $2000 and is expected to grow by about 5 percent a year and who wants to borrow $100,000 for 30 years at the prevailing 10 percent mortgage rate. With a conventional loan, the requisite monthly payment is $877.57, 44 percent of the household's current income (which, no doubt, would cause the loan application to be rejected).

We can create an alternative, graduated-payment plan with mortgage payments growing by 5 percent a year. (The exact formula, which equates the present value of the payments with the amount borrowed, is not important here.) The first monthly payment works out to be $537.79 and the last $2402.69, each 27 percent of monthly income. A graduated-payment mortgage attempts to keep housing expenses at a relatively constant share of household income, making mortgages more accessible for people who expect their income to rise as time passes.

Figure 8.3 compares the monthly payments for a 30-year $100,000 mortgage at a 10 percent annual interest rate when the mortgage is structured so that the monthly payments are constant, grow by 3 percent annually, and grow by 5

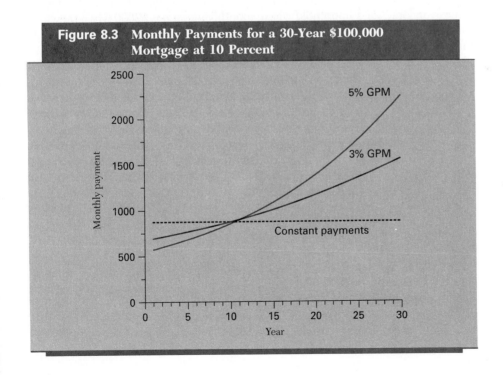

**Figure 8.3  Monthly Payments for a 30-Year $100,000 Mortgage at 10 Percent**

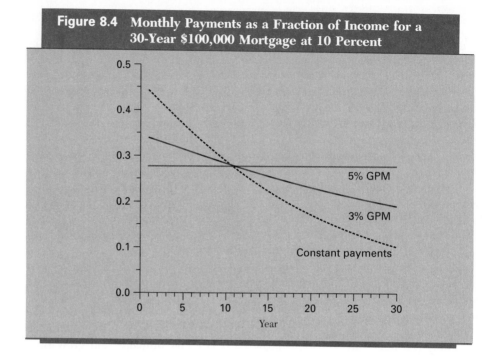

**Figure 8.4**   **Monthly Payments as a Fraction of Income for a 30-Year $100,000 Mortgage at 10 Percent**

percent annually. Figure 8.4 shows these monthly payments as a fraction of monthly income for a household whose monthly income is $2000 when they take out the mortgage and will increase by 5 percent annually. With constant monthly payments, the ratio of payments to income steadily declines; with the 5 percent graduated-payment mortgage, the payments steadily increase in nominal terms but are a constant fraction of income.

In practice, the monthly payments in a typical GPM contract begin low, rise gradually for 5 to 10 years, and then level off. If the early payments are not enough to cover the interest due on the loan, then there is negative amortization for several years until the rising monthly payments overtake the monthly interest. In our 5 percent GPM example, the first month's $537.79 payment does not cover the interest that is due: $(0.10/12)\$100,000 = \$833.33$. Figure 8.5 shows the unpaid balances for a 30-year $100,000 mortgage at a 10 percent annual interest rate with monthly payments that are constant and that grow by 3 or 5 percent annually. With the 3 percent GPM, the unpaid balance peaks at $116,446 after 13 years; with the 5 percent GPM, it peaks at $142,034 after 16 years.

Franco Modigliani, a Nobel Prize–winning economist and enthusiastic advocate of GPMs, attributes their lukewarm acceptance by lenders and borrowers to an irrational distaste for negative amortization.[5] Even some otherwise informed observers are put off by this characteristic. In a 1983 article on mortgage

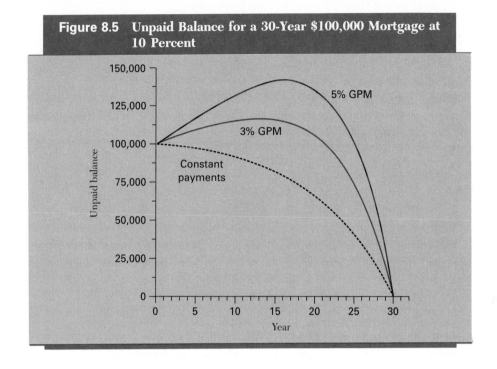

**Figure 8.5  Unpaid Balance for a 30-Year $100,000 Mortgage at 10 Percent**

alternatives, *Business Week* treats negative amortization as a drawback and goes on to state that

> *in the long run it's more expensive than other mortgages. In fact, a $67,000 GPM at a fixed 15 percent rate would start out with monthly payments that are $120 cheaper than the conventional mortgage but would end up costing about $16,000 more over 30 years.*[6]

The total-payments error again! The borrower pays more total interest with a GPM because the unpaid balance grows at first instead of declining, and you pay more interest whenever you borrow more money for a longer period of time. Here your monthly payments are lower at the beginning and higher at the end, and *Business Week* obtains its $16,000 difference simply by adding up the total payments regardless of when they are made. Discounted at the mortgage rate, the present values of a GPM and a conventional mortgage are exactly the same, the amount borrrowed.

## MORTGAGE-BACKED SECURITIES

Traditionally, most individuals financed the purchase of a home with a mortgage from a commercial bank or savings and loan association (S&L) that acted as a financial intermediary by borrowing from its depositors in order to lend money to the homebuyer. Until the 1970s, there was almost no secondary market for mortgages because, unlike bonds, the terms can vary considerably from one mortgage contract to another and because it is difficult for third parties to assess the chances that a particular homeowner might default and to value the property that is collateral for the mortgage. New York pension fund managers are right-fully nervous about loaning money to Bill Myers to finance a three-bedroom, two-bathroom house in Cucamonga, California. In addition, many investors are wary of mortgages because the fact that mortgages can be refinanced at any time creates considerable uncertainty about the cash flow in comparison with bonds, which generally have substantial restrictions on when they can be called.

In the absence of a secondary market for mortgage notes, the bank or S&L held onto the mortgage, using the interest payments from the homeowner to pay interest to its depositors. The only significant exception were mortgage-banking institutions, which originate a mortgage by lending to a homebuyer and then sell the mortgage note to an insurance company or pension fund. The homeowner makes monthly payments to the mortgage banker, which passes these payments along to the note owner, less a servicing fee.

The mortgage market has now been revolutionized by three federally estab-lished agencies that issue **mortgage-backed securities** that are collateralized by mortgages these agencies buy from banks, S&Ls, mortgage bankers, and other financial institutions. The first agency is the **Federal National Mortgage Association** (**FNMA**, or **Fannie Mae**), which was established in 1938 to funnel funds to mortgage borrowers. In 1968 it was split into two separate organizations: a private corporation that retained the name Fannie Mae and a government corporation, the **Government National Mortgage Association** (**GNMA**, or **Ginnie Mae**).

Fannie Mae sells short- and medium-term bonds, using the proceeds to buy mortgages from mortgage bankers and other mortgage originators. Fannie Mae was relatively inactive until the 1960s, when its debt issues jumped from $2.5 billion in 1960 to $15 billion in 1970 and then to $65 billion by 1980. During the 1966 and 1969–1970 credit crunches, thrift institutions sold mortgages to Fannie Mae in order to obtain cash to satisfy withdrawals and to make new mortgage loans.

In the 1968 separation, Fannie Mae became a privately owned corporation, subject to government supervision. Five of the 15 board directors are appointed by the President, and the Department of Housing and Urban Development (HUD) must formally approve all Fannie Mae borrowing. In addition, HUD sets the rate of return paid to stockholders and requires Fannie Mae to channel some mortgage money to low-income homebuyers. In return, Fannie Mae borrows some money directly from the federal government and is able to borrow privately at relatively low rates because it is a quasi-governmental agency. Since 1968, Fannie Mae has mostly bought mortgages from private mortgage bankers.

When Fannie Mae became a private corporation in 1968, Wall Street was enthusiastic. By borrowing short and lending long, with some government protection, Fannie Mae offers investors another way to bet on the course of interest rates — an unanticipated decline in interest rates is good for Fannie

Mae; an increase is bad. On the fourth day after issuance, Fannie Mae was the most actively traded stock on the New York Stock Exchange. The price of FNMA stock went from $5 a share in 1968 to $15 in 1969, down to $8 in 1970, and up to $27 in 1972.

The Government National Mortgage Association (GNMA, or Ginnie Mae) is part of the Department of Housing and Urban Development and was created in 1968 to administer government mortgage-subsidy programs that had previously been handled by Fannie Mae, for example, using Treasury money to make HUD-subsidized housing mortgages. In 1970 Ginnie Mae created the revolutionary idea of selling Ginnie Mae certificates to finance the purchase of FHA and VA mortgages from private institutions. The issuing institutions send the mortgage interest and principal payments to GNMA, which passes them through to those who own Ginnie Mae certificates — hence the label **pass-through securities**. GNMA guarantees the payment of interest and principal and, in return, levies a fee on each mortgage pool it creates. The minimum Ginnie Mae denomination is $25,000, but several brokerage houses offer GNMA investment trusts with units priced at around $1000.

In 1970 the Federal Home Loan Board established the **Federal Home Loan Mortgage Corporation** (or **Freddie Mac**), which is owned by the 12 federal home loan banks and individual thrift institutions. Freddie Mac is similar to both Fannie Mae and Ginnie Mae in that it puts together pools of mortgages, financing its purchases by the sale of pass-through mortgage participation certificates and bondlike instruments called *guaranteed mortgage certificates (GMCs)* and **collateralized mortgage obligations (CMOs)**. CMOs have fixed interest rates and are divided into multiple payoff pools, called *tranches*. If a simple CMO has are five tranches, the first four classes receive regular interest, usually semiannually, with all mortgage principal payments and prepayments initially given to the first-tranch CMOs. After the first-tranch CMOs are retired, all mortgage payments and prepayments go to the second-tranch CMOs, until these are retired, and then to the third and fourth tranches. The last securities, called the *accrual class*, or *Z class*, are like zero-coupon bonds in that the payment of interest and principal does not begin until the prior tranches are repaid. More complex CMOs have complicated rules for determining which tranches receive interest and principal payments.

The total value of mortgage-backed securities issued by Fannie Mae, Ginnie Mae, and Freddie Mac was more than $1 trillion in 1992. There are also a number of private firms that provide a secondary market in mortgages, including MGIC Mortgage Corporation (Maggie Mae), a subsidiary of MGIC Investment Corporation ("MAGIC"), which insures private conventional mortgages.

These institutions with the funny names have revolutionized deposit intermediaries and the mortgage market. More than half of all residential mortgages are now resold in the secondary mortgage market — a process called **securitization** because illiquid mortgages are converted into marketable mortgage-backed securities. The securitization of mortgages means that anyone can invest in mortgages. In addition, some deposit institutions sell their mortgages to GNMA and then purchase Ginnie Mae securities, which are federally insured

EXAMPLE 8.7  *Heads You Win, Tails I Lose*

Those who invest in mortgage pools take the same interest-rate gambles that unsettle thrift institutions. An increase in interest rates is clearly bad news: it reduces the present value of the cash flow from fixed-rate mortgages, the same as it reduces the prices of bonds. Paradoxically, a drop in interest rates also can be bad news — heads you win, tails I lose. Suppose that pass-through certificates are issued for a pool of 30-year mortgages with 10 percent interest rates. If interest rates drop to 8 percent, some borrowers will repay their mortgages ahead of schedule and refinance at lower interest rates. The pass-through owners receive these prepayments and now must reinvest their money at lower interest rates.

Because the timing of the repayment of mortgage loans is uncertain, it is difficult to estimate the rate of return on mortgage pools. The GNMA yields that are typically reported in the financial press assume that the average mortgage in the pool will be paid off after 12 years, which is the approximate historical average. The future is unlikely to replicate the past, however. As a mortgage trader at Salomon Brothers complained, "They get longer [in maturity] when rates go up, and shorter when rates go down."*

For example, in the early 1980s, when interest rates were very high, GNMA certificates issued during the 1970s sold at substantial discounts from their initial issuing prices because high interest rates had reduced the present value of the low-interest mortgages in the pool. At these low market prices, and assuming that the mortgages in the pool would be repaid 12 years after their issuance, these Ginnie Mae certificates were calculated to have very high yields. However, those homeowners fortunate enough to have old low-interest mortgages were understandably reluctant to prepay. The longer they held onto their mortgages, the lower was the actual return to Ginnie Mae investors.

*Quoted in Michael Lewis, Liar's Poker (New York: W. W. Norton, 1989), p. 101.*

against default, geographically diversified, and can be sold quickly if cash is needed. Other deposit institutions use the secondary market to avoid holding mortgages. Burned too often by borrowing short and lending long, they routinely sell their mortgages to mortgage pools, profiting on the points they charge homebuyers.

The development of a secondary mortgage market weakens the separation between mortgages and other securities, making more money available for mortgages from such nontraditional sources as individuals and pension funds. Mortgages have to compete with Treasury bonds, corporate securities, and municipal bonds. Mortgage availability and housing construction now depend on the overall level of interest rates and national saving, not merely on how much money is deposited in banks and S&Ls.

# SUMMARY

Borrowed money is often used to finance the purchase of real and financial assets. This use of other people's money creates leverage in that the return on your relatively small investment depends on the profitability of a much larger investment. If the total investment earns a rate of return larger than the interest rate paid on the borrowed money, this differential is multiplied by the degree of leverage. Leverage is a double-edged sword in that any shortfall between the investment's return and the loan rate is magnified too.

Loan payments are calculated so that the present value of the payments, discounted at the stated annual percentage rate *APR*, is equal to the amount borrowed. In an amortized loan, the constant periodic payments cover the interest due and also reduce the principal — slowly at first, rapidly at the end — so that the last payment reduces the unpaid balance to zero. In a balloon loan, the payments do not reduce the principal sufficiently (often not at all), and a large balloon payment must be made at maturity to cover the still substantial unpaid balance.

Loans are often evaluated and compared on the basis of the total (undiscounted) payments made during the life of the loan — a flawed procedure that favors borrowing as little as possible for as brief a period as possible. A present-value analysis is more appropriate, discounting the loan payments by a required rate of return that depends on market interest rates. Because mortgages are a reasonable substitute for other long-term financial assets, mortgage rates rise and fall with other long-term interest rates.

Points, a percentage fee paid when a loan is made, raise the effective interest rate on the loan — especially if it is a short-term loan or a loan that is repaid early. Prepayment penalties are fees charged when a loan is repaid early; these raise the effective loan rate more the sooner the loan is repaid. Nonetheless, it is often profitable to refinance a long-term fixed-rate loan at a lower interest rate, thereby avoiding many years of high interest payments.

On an adjustable-rate loan, the interest rate is periodically adjusted to reflect current market rates or the lender's cost of funds. These adjustments must either alter the size of the payments or the amount of time it takes to repay the loan. When the loan rate increases and monthly payments don't, there can be negative amortization, in that if the loan payments don't cover the interest due, the unpaid balance increases.

In a conventional constant-payment mortgage, the fraction of household income devoted to mortgage payments is high when the household is young and declines as its income grows over time. Graduated-payment mortgages were developed so that monthly payments would rise with income and thus be a relatively constant fraction of household income. In either case, the present value of the payments, at the quoted loan rate, is equal to the amount borrowed.

The mortgage market has been revolutionized by three federally established agencies — Fannie Mae, Ginnie Mae, and Freddie Mac; these three agencies securitize mortgages by converting them into mortgage-backed securities that are traded in a secondary mortgage market. This securitization of mortgages allows anyone — not just banks and S&Ls — to invest in mortgages and allows investors to buy and sell mortgages just as they trade bonds and other securities.

# IMPORTANT TERMS

adjustable-rate loans

amortized loan

balloon loan

collateralized mortgage obligations (CMOs)

creative financing

Federal Home Loan Mortgage Corporation (or Freddie Mac)

Federal National Mortgage Association (FNMA, or Fannie Mae)

Government National Mortgage Association (GNMA, or Ginnie Mae)

graduated-payment mortgages (GPMs)

leverage

mortgage-backed securities

negative amortization

pass-through securities

points

prepayment penalties

securitization

# EXERCISES

1. You want to invest $80,000 for 1 year but have only $20,000. You borrow an additional $60,000 at 10 percent and owe $66,000 one year from now. What is the percentage return on your $20,000 if the rate of return earned on the entire $80,000 is 10 percent? 50 percent? − 10 percent?

2. You have inherited $50,000 and hope to multiply your new wealth by buying undeveloped land in a resort area. You are considering borrowing $50,000 and buying a $100,000 parcel or else borrowing $450,000 and buying a $500,000 property. Assume that either way you will have to pay back your loan plus 12 percent interest after a year and that the value of each property will increase by an equal percentage. If, for instance, property in this area appreciates by 20 percent, you will either make $20,000 − $6000 = $14,000 or $100,000 − $54,000 = $46,000, depending on which property you buy. Fill in the rest of the table below, showing the net gain on your $50,000 wealth. For what rate of property appreciation do these two strategies do equally well? How much leverage do you have with each strategy?

| Property Appreciation | Borrow $50,000 | | Borrow $450,000 | |
|---|---|---|---|---|
|  | Dollars | Percent | Dollars | Percent |
| − 10% |  |  |  |  |
| 0% |  |  |  |  |
| 10% |  |  |  |  |
| 20% | $14,000 | 28% | $46,000 | 92% |
| 30% |  |  |  |  |
| 40% |  |  |  |  |

3. Banks make profits with other people's money, investing what they have borrowed from their depositors. For a typical bank, out of every $100 that it invests, $95 is borrowed and $5 is net worth. The rate of interest that it pays its depositors is generally specified ahead of time, whereas the rate of return it earns on its investments depends on loan defaults and other economic conditions. What is the annual rate of return on a bank's net worth if it borrows at 7 percent and invests at 7 percent? If it borrows at 7 percent and invests at 9 percent? If it borrows at 7 percent, what rate of return on its investments will bankrupt the bank (a − 100 percent return on net worth)?

4. A house, a car, and many other real assets provide services that are implicitly untaxed income. Imagine that at your college graduation an anonymous benefactor gives you $100,000 — enough to allow you to buy a house near your new job. You can either use this $100,000 gift to buy a house or else buy Treasury bonds and rent a comparable house for $12,000 a year. If you have to pay a 28 percent tax on the income from your Treasury bonds, how much income (in percentage terms) must these bonds yield each year to provide enough after-tax income to pay your rent?

5. You plan to borrow $10,000 for 10 years at a 10 percent interest rate. What is the size of your payments if you make constant

   a. Annual payments?

   b. Monthly payments?

   Why are the annual payments less than 12 times the monthly payments?

6. The owner of a Washington, D.C. real estate firm says that a basic loan equation is[7]

   Principal × interest rate per period × interest periods (time) = total interest paid

   Explain why the total interest on a $2000 two-year monthly amortized loan at a 12 percent APR is *not* $2000 × 12 percent/year × 2 years = $480.

7. At age 82, Fred Benson won a $50,000 state lottery prize that pays $100 a month for 500 months. He sold his claim to a local bank for $13,500 and threw the biggest party in the history of Block Island. What is the bank's implicit rate of return on its investment? (*Hint*: If this were a $13,500 mortgage to be repaid in 500 monthly $100 installments, what would the implicit mortgage rate be?)

8. Mr. I. M. Gone moved to Houston in 1978 and had to sell his home in Philadelphia. He asked $100,000, but mortgage rates were a staggering 18 percent and many banks weren't approving any new mortgage loans. Mr. Gone finally agreed to owner financing by lending the buyer $80,000 for 30 years at 12 percent. The buyer came up with the remaining $20,000. Considering the monthly payments from the buyer's standpoint, how large a price cut was this owner financing equivalent to?

9. Mr. Gone discovers that he has an assumable 30-year $60,000 mortgage at 9 percent with 25 years left on it. He offers to let the buyer assume this mortgage and to lend the buyer an additional $20,000 over 25 years at 20 percent. What is the buyer's effective interest rate?

10. Ms. Yup must sell her Houston home in order to take a job in California. She has two offers on her house. The first is $160,000 cash. The second is $180,000, of which $30,000 is cash and the remaining $150,000 is an owner-financed 30-year mortgage at 8 percent. Assuming that the buyer does not default, which offer is the more financially attractive?

11. Pomona College has agreed to lend Professor Smith $85,000 at 7 percent and an additional $40,000 at 12 percent. Both these loans will be conventional 30-year mortgages with constant monthly payments. For

simplicity, the Pomona College business office wants to combine these two loans into one 30-year mortgage with a single interest rate. What is the appropriate interest rate?

12. You need $100,000 to start your new business. One lender requires 60 monthly payments of $2150 due at the end of each month (beginning a month from the signing of the loan papers). A second lender requires 20 quarterly payments of $6450 due at the beginning of each quarter (starting on the day the loan is signed). Which charges the higher effective loan rate? How much higher?

13. In 1985 a Los Angeles mortgage company was charging 15 percent plus 10 points on second mortgages. What is the effective interest rate on an amortized 20-year $100,000 loan with constant monthly payments if the loan is not repaid early?

14. Calculate the effective annual interest rate on the following loan:

A *study in the city of Bridgeport, Connecticut turned up a $17,000 [30-year conventional amortized] second mortgage that carried an interest rate of 18% plus $5,440 in points (32 points) to the lender and $1,020 (six points) in loan-brokerage fees. In other words, out of the $17,000 second mortgage, the homeowner/borrower ended up with only $10,540 [$17,000 − $5,440 (points) − $1,020 (fees)] in his or her pocket.*[8]

15. Consider a conventional 30-year $100,000 mortgage at 10 percent with payments made monthly. If it costs 5 points to get this mortgage and there is a $5000 prepayment penalty, what is the bank's effective rate of return if the loan is paid off after 5 years?

16. On May 1, 1986, Imperial Savings in California offered conventional 15-year fixed-rate mortgages for either 9.875 percent with 1 point or 9 percent with 4.5 points. Without doing the necessary calculations, explain

how you, the homebuyer, would choose between these two alternatives.

17. In 1986 a former *Wall Street Journal* reporter told how he had been tempted to refinance his 25-year 13.25 percent $55,000 mortgage at 9 to 10 percent but had become discouraged by the $3500 to $4000 he would have to pay in points and other closing costs. Without checking his calculations, critically evaluate his logic:

*But with, say, a saving of $100 a month in principal and interest payments, I still would pocket $36,000 over 30 years, I thought at first. Not so. Since I have only $22\frac{1}{2}$ years left on my existing contract and if I convert it to 25 or 30 years to keep the payments low, I discovered that I could end up paying more total dollars in the long run. And I can't afford the monthly payments for a shorter loan term of 15 or 20 years, which would make the deal work.*[9]

18. Explain why, from the standpoint of the issuer, a zero-coupon bond implicitly involves negative amortization.

19. Explain why there may be negative amortization if interest rates increase and homeowners with adjustable-rate mortgages do not increase their monthly payments.

20. A real estate broker argued that Mike, after buying a $100 raffle ticket, might walk away from the prize, a $150,000 house, because (a) he will have to pay the IRS $75,000 (in a 50 percent tax bracket); (b) "Mike does not have $75,000 in cash to pay the tax; he hardly had the $100 for the raffle ticket"; and (c) if he borrows this $75,000 from a bank at 18 percent for 20 years, he will have to pay $1157 a month × 12 months/year × 20 years = $333,120 total mortgage payments on the house.[10] Would you walk away from this prize?

21. A letter to *The Wall Street Journal* argued that a steady inflation would impose real burdens on homebuyers:

*While all prices, wages, and debt contracts might be indexed to a steady inflation rate, the increase in nominal interest rates . . . increases the cash-flow requirements of borrowers on level-payment continuously amortizing loans. This significantly increases the portion of income [households] must pay for home ownership. . . .*

*At a zero expected inflation rate, home mortgages would cost about 4% per annum with a 2% real return and another 2% for risk premium and administrative costs. At 4% inflation, the nominal interest goes to 8% and monthly payments rise 50%.*[11]

Check the letter writer's assertion that monthly payments increase by 50 percent. How might graduated-payment mortgages help homebuyers adjust to the steady inflation this writer envisions?

22. In 1985 the *Los Angeles Times* described the "sudden, almost explosive, acceptance of the 15-year fixed-rate mortgage" in place of the traditional 30-year mortgage, citing a Mortgage Bankers Association estimate that from "minimal acceptance" just a year ago, they now account for one-seventh of all new mortgages. In explanation, the *Times* cites "common sense" economics[12]:

*At the end of 30 years, that $100,000 mortgage [at 13%, with $1,106.20 monthly payments] has cost the home buyer a grand total of $398,232 — a mind boggling $298,232 in interest. . . . by cutting the same mortgage down to 15 from 30 years (and raising the monthly payments from $1,106.20 to $1,265.25), the total cost to the home buyer is $227,745 for a net saving in interest of $170,487.*

*"While you certainly can't quarrel with the arithmetic of the 15-year mortgage — and the sudden popularity of it . . . there are limits on how far the trend can go," according to Fred E. Case of UCLA's Graduate School of Management. "Not everyone who sees the sense of the 15-year mortgage is in a position to qualify for one."*

The *Times* also quotes an anonymous "cynical" midwestern lender:

*I'd like to think that home buyers have suddenly gotten smart — that they've looked at those figures and realized how much interest they're paying over 30 years. God knows they've been dumb about it long enough.*

Why, by their reckoning, is a 30-year mortgage so expensive? Is there any interest rate at which you would choose a 30-year rather than 15-year mortgage at the same interest rate?

23. Critically evaluate this advice:

*Want to build equity in your home fast, slash 60 percent off the total interest you pay on a mortgage held to maturity, retire the major debt of your lifetime — your home loan — before the kids' college bills come steamrolling in?*

*The 15-year fixed- or adjustable-rate mortgage (ARM) can help you accomplish all that for a relatively low price. For $105 more per month, a 15-year fixed-rate mortgage saves you $115,000 in interest charges (compared to a 30-year fixed-rate mortgage) over the life of the mortgage. A 15-year ARM saves you $95,400 in interest charges (compared to a 30-year fixed-rate mortgage) in this example [$75,000 borrowed for 30 years at 12% or for 15 years at 9.25% the first year and 15% thereafter] provided by Carteret Savings and Loan Association of Morristown, New Jersey. Even though monthly ARM payments may increase each year (if interest rates rise), you come out ahead, thanks to a maximum 15 percent interest-rate ceiling built into this loan agreement. . . .*

*If you can afford modestly higher payments and meet stricter borrowing requirements, there's no denying the advantages of a 15-year versus a 30-year mortgage.*[13]

24. In 1981 the Federal Home Loan Bank Board approved the reverse annuity mortgage (RAM) as a means of allowing homeowners, especially elderly homeowners with valuable houses but little cash, to convert the equity in their homes into monthly income without having to sell their homes. Consider a 66-year-old widow living in a $300,000 home with no outstanding mortgage. With a 10 percent RAM, she could receive $1000 a month for, say, 10 years until she dies, at which time her estate would have to pay the lending institution the amount that the widow had borrowed, including the interest charged each month (at a 10 percent annual percentage rate) on the outstanding balance. How much would this be? (*Hint*: You can convert this future value into a present value by using Equation 4.7 from Chapter 4, and then convert back to a future value.)

25. The owner of a Washington, D.C., real estate firm warns that elderly homeowners can get "RAMed" by reverse annuity mortgages:

    *An $80,000 RAM at 13% interest paid monthly to the homeowner over 15 years would give the homeowner monthly payments of approximately $145/month.*
    *But wait a minute.*

    $145/month × 12 months/year
                    × 15 years = $26,100

    *Yes, the homeowner gets $26,100 (much less if inflation is figured in) and owes $80,000 in 15 years!*[14]

    Explain why the homeowner pays $80,000 while getting only $26,100. Explain why inflation shouldn't be figured in.

26. In a biweekly mortgage, monthly payments are calculated as if the mortgage were a conventional 30-year mortgage amortized monthly, but then half this calculated monthly amount is paid every other week. The result is that

*At 9.25% interest, a biweekly $100,000 mortgage pays off in slightly more than 21 years, instead of 30, and saves $63,819 in interest. On a $200,000 mortgage, the interest saved is $126,637.*

*"And," as G. Randall Kinst, director of secondary marketing for Mortgage Loans America, a large wholesale mortgage banking firm located in Campbell, Calif., says, "a 30-year conventional loan would need an unheard of 6.7% interest rate to achieve the same savings realized on a biweekly."*[15]

How do biweekly payments reduce the interest paid and the length of the mortgage? Would you choose a 9.25 percent biweekly or a 6.7 percent monthly mortgage?

27. One California mortgage banker set up a "simulated" biweekly plan:

*It simply sets itself up as a trust, collects biweekly mortgage payments from its clients and then turns around and pays their lender the regular monthly payment. . . . What it amounts to is simply one extra payment a year being made on the mortgage.*[16]

Why would a mortgage banker do this for his or her clients?

28. In July of 1986 an elderly couple received a letter from their savings bank that began as follows:

*We are very pleased to offer you the opportunity to save a minimum of $1,370.91 in future interest on your mortgage loan. Yes, you can save $1,370.91 in future interest by increasing your monthly payment by only $25.00 per month beginning in August. This extra $25.00 per month will also pay off your mortgage 3 years and 7 months early.*[17]

An enclosed analysis showed this couple had an unpaid balance of $8479.53 on a 7.25 percent loan, with 11 years and 11 months of $89 monthly payments remaining, and that

*With your present monthly payment of $89.00, your future interest paid over the next 11 years 11 months will be*                    $4185.04

*By increasing your monthly payment by $25.00 per month, your future interest over the next 8 years 4 months will be*                    2814.13

*Interest savings (will also pay off your mortgage 3 years 7 months early)*                    $1370.91

a. If we look at the total payments, principal plus interest, how much does the couple save?

b. Why does an extra $25 a month reduce the length of the mortgage?

c. Why do you think the bank offered this opportunity?

29. The Federal Home Loan Bank System says that one of the advantages of Freddie Mac to thrift institutions is

*Higher yields. When interest rates are rising, lenders can sell off their older, low-interest loans and reinvest in mortgages at higher interest rates.*[18]

What is the implicit assumption?

30. Explain this observation regarding pass-through mortgage securities:

*"These securities pose minimal credit risk; however, they still expose investors to interest-rate and early repayment risk."*[19]

# 9 The Stock Market

*If you don't know who you are, the stock market is an expensive place to find out.*

**George Goodman**

Loans, bonds, and other fixed-income securities are legally binding agreements to pay specified amounts of money. Corporate stock, in contrast, represents equity — ownership of a company — and the return, dividends plus capital gains, depends on the profitability of the company. This chapter examines the nature of corporate stock and the markets in which it is traded. We will discuss the reasons why firms choose to incorporate and how stock is traded after issuance on the stock exchanges and over the counter. We will also discuss why the value of a stock depends on its cash flow and on interest rates. This chapter also presents some examples of the madness of crowds, instances where investors as a group pushed stock prices to levels that, in retrospect, were unjustified. Finally, we will consider the important provocative assertion that because financial markets are efficient, changes in stock prices are unpredictable.

## STOCK ISSUANCE AND TRADING

The owners of a corporation's **common stock** are the legal owners of the firm, the name indicating that the shareholders own the firm "in common." Although they do not make production, pricing, and personnel decisions, shareholders elect (normally with one vote per share) a board of directors that hires the top executives and supervises their management of the firm. Some firms have two or more classes of common stock with different voting privileges; for example, Ford Motor Company's class B common stock, owned by the Ford family and related trusts, is not publicly traded and has 40 percent of the total stockholder vote even though it constitutes only 15 percent of the total outstanding shares.

**Preferred stock** pays specified dividends, like a bond's coupons, and generally has no voting privileges. Such stock is "preferred" because its promised dividends must be paid before common stockholders can be paid anything. *Cumulative preferred stock* specifies that all current and past obligated dividends must be paid before common stockholders can receive a dividend. If the firm is liquidated, the claims of preferred stockholders are settled ahead of those of common stockholders but behind those of bondholders. *Convertible preferred stock* offers investors the opportunity to exchange their preferred stock for common stock at a specified ratio, for example, two shares of preferred for one share of common.

## Debt and Equity

The loans, bonds, and other fixed-income securities issued by a corporation are legal debts, whereas common stock is equity, a claim to the residual value of the firm after its debts have been paid. An extremely condensed balance sheet of a hypothetical firm is shown in Table 9.1. This firm has $100 million in assets, mostly plant, equipment, and other real assets. Because it has $40 million in debts outstanding, shareholders' equity (what would be left if the firm were liquidated and the debts repaid) comes to $60 million. If there are 5 million shares outstanding, this works out to $12 a share. This estimate of the firm's value per share is called the **book value** of the firm's stock because it is derived from the firm's books, that is, the accountants' balance sheets.

The market value of the firm's stock may be above or below the book value, because investors don't value a firm the same way that accountants do. Assets are generally carried on the books at original cost and, in the case of buildings and equipment, are depreciated over time to indicate wear and tear. However, if land prices and construction costs increase, the replacement cost of a firm's real assets may be far larger than the original cost, let alone the depreciated cost. If this is so, the firm's stock may be worth far more than its book value of $12 a share. On the other hand, a firm may have very expensive assets that are not profitable, and shareholders won't pay $12 a share for a company that doesn't make profits and can't afford to pay dividends.

Bondholders hold legally binding promissory notes. If the firm does not earn enough profits to pay these debts in full, then it may be forced into bankruptcy, with its assets sold and the proceeds paid to the bondholders and other creditors. The stockholders get nothing but their worthless stock certificates and, we are

**Table 9.1   A Small Firm**

| Assets | | Liabilities | |
|---|---|---|---|
| Real | $ 90 | Debt | $ 40 |
| Financial | 10 | Equity | 60 |
| | $100 | | $100 |

told, an expensive lesson. On the other hand, if the firm grows and prospers, the bondholders receive only the fixed income they have been promised, nothing more, while the stockholders, as owners of the firm, share the growing profits. The firm's directors, acting on behalf of the shareholders, decide how much of the profits to distribute as dividends and how much to retain for buying more plant and equipment to expand the firm.

## Limited Liability

The legal concept of a corporation began in England in the early stages of the industrial revolution with the intention of dividing ownership among many investors and protecting them if the firm were mismanaged. Most investors are "outside" shareholders in the sense that they have nothing to do with the day-to-day operations of the company in which they have shares, leaving that to the firm's management. While stockholders are the legal owners of a corporation, they have **limited liability** in that they are not personally responsible for its debts. Their potential loss is limited to their investment in the firm's stock. Limited liability is the reason many British and Canadian firms have "Limited" or the abbreviation "Ltd." as part of the company's name.

If a corporation cannot pay its debts, then its bankruptcy leaves the shareholders with worthless stock certificates — a disappointing outcome, but still better than having to come up with additional money to satisfy the firm's creditors. Presumably, this limited liability encourages people to invest in stock, thereby becoming part owners of large businesses.

There are disadvantages to being a public corporation, one of the most important being the double taxation of earnings. Suppose that a company earns $10 a share and wants to distribute this to the owners. If the company is not a corporation, the owners receive $10 and pay perhaps a 28 percent personal income tax, keeping $7.20. If the business is a corporation, though, it must pay a 34 percent corporation income tax, leaving $6.60 to be distributed as dividends, on which shareholders then pay a 28 percent tax — leaving only $0.72(\$6.60) = \$4.75$. The double taxation amounts to an effective 52.5 percent tax rate!

## Going Public

Businesses typically begin as small, privately held companies. Imagine that you have an idea for the proverbial better mousetrap and want to produce and market these wonders. After exhausting your own savings, you may be able to borrow some additional funds at, say, a 10 percent interest rate from relatives, a bank, or sympathetic investors. However, their enthusiasm is dampened by your inexperience and lack of tangible assets. If sales happen to be disappointing, as they usually are with new businesses, you won't be able to repay your debts, and their hoped-for 10 percent interest will turn into a 100 percent loss.

If you can't find willing lenders, you may have to settle for partners, investors willing to bankroll your expansion in return for a share of the profits. While the possibility of a 100 percent loss is still there, your investors now have the chance of large profits too. You can form a partnership or, instead, a corporation to obtain limited liability. Businesses can incorporate without selling shares to the public: individuals can form sole-owner corporations and small groups (35 or fewer investors) can form a privately held corporation. If your small business proves successful, however, there may come a point where your ambitious plans for expansion require a great deal of money and you decide to sell shares to the public at large.

The public offering will have to meet the disclosure requirements of the Securities and Exchange Commission (SEC). An investment banker (such as Morgan Stanley, Salomon Brothers, or Goldman Sachs) will prepare a prospectus for potential investors that reveals relevant data regarding your past performance, lays out your plans, and gives boldface warnings that "These shares are very risky." An advertisement may appear in *The Wall Street Journal* announcing the planned incorporation and stating, "This announcement is neither an offer to sell nor a solicitation of offers to buy any of these securities. The offering is made only by the Prospectus." Listed will be several underwriters, including your investment banker and others that have agreed to distribute the stock to their regular customers — insurance companies, pension funds, and individual investors — and to others who can be persuaded to buy shares.

You and your investment banker will agree on the price at which the shares are offered. Experienced financial analysts will scrutinize your books and come up with an estimate of what the company is worth — how much you could sell it for. Suppose that the number they come up with is $20 million. (If we're dreaming, let's make it a good one.) Now you don't intend to sell your company and walk away. You want funds to expand, and in return, you are willing to share your company with others. If you were to raise, say, another $20 million, then you would have $40 million in assets — your company, which is worth $20 million by itself, plus $20 million in cash. In addition, this cash will not sit idle, but rather will be used to enlarge your business. With this new money and your patented mousetrap, you can make enough profits that the company will be worth at least $50 million.

Armed with these conservative estimates, you issue 10 million shares of stock priced at $5 a share. Six million you keep for yourself and your original partners, and your investment banker agrees to buy 4 million at $5 a share (less commission) to raise the intended $20 million. With each share, the buyers are getting one ten-millionth of a $50 million company. You and your initial partners get shares worth $30 million — $20 million for the company as it is today plus $10 million for the profits you can make with this new money. If things work out as planned, everyone will be happy.

Notice that incorporation apparently creates instant millionaires. You were plugging along, building mousetrap after mousetrap, working long hours, and plowing every penny back into the firm. You lived a frugal, "workaholic" lifestyle and didn't look at all like the rich and famous seen on television. Then comes incorporation, and all of a sudden you (and your initial partners, if any) have stock worth $30 million. George Goodman calls these instant riches "super-money" and wrote a book with that title. What might be overlooked is that as owner of a profitable firm, you were really a millionaire all along. Your mousetrap business was worth millions, and incorporation disclosed this fact by transforming your illiquid business into liquid securities.

## The Stock Exchanges

Once issued, shares of stock trade in the secondary market, either on an organized stock exchange or by other means. The most important stock exchange is the New York Stock Exchange (NYSE), followed by the American Stock Exchange (AMEX) and various regional exchanges (Boston, Cincinnati, Midwest, Pacific, and Philadelphia). Securities that aren't listed on organized exchanges are said to be traded **over the counter (OTC)**. The prices of many, but by no means all, OTC securities are reported on the National Association of Securities Dealers (NASDAQ) system.

The exchanges are closed on weekends and some holidays. On a typical trading day on the NYSE about 200 million shares are traded with an aggregate market value of around $8 billion. Table 9.2 compares the NYSE, AMEX, regional exchanges, and NASDAQ at the end of 1987. The average NYSE company had a market value of $1.3 billion, 12 times the size of the average AMEX firm and 19 times the size of the average NASDAQ company. The NYSE is called the "big board" not only because of the number of companies listed and the volume of trading but also because the NYSE companies are mostly the biggest and the best.

To be listed on the NYSE, a corporation must have $16 million in tangible assets, before-tax profits of $2.5 million, at least 1 million publicly held shares with an aggregate market value of at least $16 million, and at least 2000 stockholders owning 100 shares or more. Some large companies have chosen not

| Table 9.2   Stock Trading, 1987 | | | | |
|---|---|---|---|---|
| | NYSE | AMEX | Regionals | NASDAQ |
| Number of companies listed | 1,647 | 869 | 250 | 4,706 |
| Value of shares listed ($ billions) | $2,216 | $95 | na | $326 |
| Number of shares traded (billions) | 48 | 4 | 7 | 38 |
| Value of shares traded ($ billions) | $1,874 | $53 | $248 | $500 |

**Source:** National Association of Securities Dealers, *1988 Fact Book*.

## EXAMPLE 9.1  *The Reporting of Stock Trading*

Daily newspapers record summaries of stock trading for the previous business day. Here is an example of the trading in one stock on November 8, 1989, as reported in *The Wall Street Journal* on November 9 of that year:

| 52 Weeks | | Stock | Sym | Div | Yld % | PE | Vol (100s) | Hi | Lo | Close | Net Chg |
|---|---|---|---|---|---|---|---|---|---|---|---|
| Hi | Lo | | | | | | | | | | |
| 70⅜ | 42⅞ | FstInterste | I | 3.00 | 5.4 | 8 | 1061 | 56⅜ | 55½ | 56 | + ⅝ |

Many company names are abbreviated to save space. Here, "FstInterste" is an abbreviation of First Interstate, one of the nation's largest banks; the symbol I is used by the exchange for recording transactions. After finding the company in the financial pages, investors invariably look first at the last two columns on the right, showing the closing price and the change from the day before. The last trade of First Interstate stock on November 8 was at a price of $56 a share, up ⅝ from the closing price the day before. Moving leftward, we see the high and low prices for the day and the volume of trading (in 100s). On this particular day, 106,100 shares of First Interstate were traded at various prices ranging from $55½ per share to $56⅜ per share.

Right after the company's name and symbol is the latest declared annual dividend, here $3 a share. The "Yld %" is the dividend yield, calculated by dividing the dividend by the closing price of the stock ($3/$56 = 0.054; that is, 5.4 percent). A 5.4 percent dividend yield may seem like a modest return, but shareholders were undoubtedly expecting dividends to increase in the future and to earn capital gains, too.

The reported "PE" (price–earnings ratio) is the ratio of the firm's closing price to the latest annual earnings per share; growth stocks tend to have relatively high price–earnings ratios because investors are willing to pay more for a firm whose future profits are expected to be much higher than current earnings. For comparison, in November of 1989, Apple Computer traded at 13 times earnings and Genentech, a biotechnology company, traded at 139 times earnings. On the far left, *The Wall Street Journal* provides some historical perspective by showing the highest and lowest prices during the previous 52 weeks.

U.S. stock exchanges quote prices in ½, ¼, ⅛, 1/16, and even 1/32, an anachronistic remnant of earlier days when arithmetic was done by hand. The calculations are done by computers now, and most foreign exchanges quote prices in decimals, a logical practice still resisted by U.S. exchanges.

to be listed; for example, Apple Computer is not, and (to avoid the NYSE's disclosure requirements) many financial institutions are not. However, most companies believe that a listing on the NYSE makes their stock more attractive to investors; about half of all investors own only NYSE stocks.

The NYSE and other organized exchanges are physical locations, trading floors, where securities are bought and sold by exchange members, who have seats on the exchange (a terminology dating back to when members had armchairs to rest in). There are 1366 seats on the New York Stock Exchange, and these seats are bought, sold, or leased at negotiated prices that reflect supply and demand. The price of a seat began at $1000 in 1850; reached $625,000 in 1929, before the stock market crash; and has fluctuated considerably since, trading for $250,000 in 1965, $40,000 in 1976, and $1 million in 1987.

Each stock traded on the NYSE is assigned to a **specialist** who acts as both a broker (an agent trading for others) and a dealer (trading for the specialist's own account). As a broker, the specialist collects orders from other members of the exchange and executes a transaction when someone is willing to buy at a price at which another member is willing to sell. Specialists have an obligation to maintain a fair and orderly market and, in this capacity, act as dealers by buying or selling, as needed, for their own account. At any moment a specialist will quote a bid price at which he or she will buy and an ask price at which he or she will sell. The bid price is, of course, somewhat lower than the ask price.

When an investor places an order with a brokerage firm, it contacts a broker on the floor of the exchange who forwards the order to the appropriate specialist for execution. When the trade is completed, the brokerage firm charges the customer a commission, and the customer then generally has 5 working days to settle the trade by paying for the purchased securities or delivering the securities that were sold.

All the organized exchanges restrict members from trading listed stocks outside the exchanges. Because most major brokerage firms are exchange members, these restrictions hamper the trading of listed stocks off the exchanges. Critics have long accused the exchanges of operating monopolies that enrich specialists. Prodded by perceived abuses, Congress passed the Securities Acts Amendments of 1975, instructing the SEC to develop a national market system that will be more competitive and efficient than the exchanges. Many economists envision a national auction market, linked by computers, with the specialist nowhere to be seen. By and large, however, the NYSE has resisted this vision successfully.

Trading is very different off the exchanges, in the over-the-counter market. Dealers voluntarily maintain a market in a security by quoting bid and ask prices at which they are willing to buy or sell securities. Market makers must register with the Securities and Exchange Commission, but there is no limit to their number or their geographic location. At present, the average OTC stock has about eight active market makers. All the market makers' bid and ask prices are public knowledge, to each other and to interested investors. When you place an order to buy an OTC stock, your broker will use a computer to survey current bid–ask prices and determine the most advantageous offer, and then he or she

**EXAMPLE 9.2** *London's Big Bang*

On October 1, 1986, London's financial markets were transformed by extensive deregulation, changes so significant that they were labeled the "Big Bang." Before, the London Stock Exchange was much like a private club, where well-bred gentlemen in bowler hats showed up at 10 A.M. and went home at 4 P.M., with a leisurely 2-hour lunch in between. In this relaxed, noncompetitive atmosphere, the brokers made a fixed 1.65 percent commission on each trade, and all trades passed through jobbers on the floor who, like the New York Stock Exchange's specialists, quoted bid and ask prices and made their profits on the spread.

Foreign banks and securities firms were allowed to join the London Stock Exchange in 1986, and within a year, one-third of the members were foreign. Fixed commissions were abolished, as was the distinction between brokers and jobbers. In its place, authorized members act as market makers, quoting prices at which they are willing to buy or sell securities. To keep track of competing prices, the exchange spent millions of dollars on a massive computer system, and once computerized prices defined the market, there was no real need for the floor of the exchange at all. Now transactions are made from securities houses by traders watching computer screens.

The gentlemen in bowler hats have been replaced by American-style whiz kids driving Porsches, who show up at 7 A.M. and work until the New York Stock Exchange closes, at 10 P.M. London time. Seven top London financiers profiled in *The Economist* on September 20, 1986, right before the "Big Bang," all said that they hoped to have the same jobs 5 years later. In 1991, none did.*

Wide-ranging trades for worldwide clients now make London the International Stock Exchange, the center of trading in currencies, Eurobonds (bonds that are denominated in the issuer's domestic currency but issued and traded in foreign markets), and some commodities, such as gold, tin, and rubber. In addition, hundreds of U.S. stocks are traded on the London exchange, as are the stocks of a dozen other countries. In 1987 some 15 percent of the trading in French stocks took place on the London exchange; for some Dutch companies, the figure was closer to 40 percent.

*"*After the Earthquake*," The Economist, *October 26, 1991, p. 26.*

will make a transaction with that market maker, via either the computer or a phone call.

## Stock Market Indexes

More than 200 million shares of more than 1700 different stocks are traded daily on the New York Stock Exchange alone, providing a mountain of statistical data, more than anyone could absorb or appreciate. Stock market indexes are statistical averages that are intended to summarize changes in stock prices as time passes.

**Table 9.3  The Dow Jones Industrial Average, November 14, 1991**

| Stock | Price per Share | Number of Shares (millions) | Total Market Value ($ billions) |
|---|---|---|---|
| Allied-Signal | 43 | 135.7 | $ 5.8 |
| Alcoa | 61⅞ | 84.8 | 5.2 |
| American Express | 19⅞ | 464.5 | 9.2 |
| AT&T | 38½ | 1,096.6 | 42.2 |
| Bethlehem Steel | 14¼ | 75.9 | 1.1 |
| Boeing | 48⅞ | 343.8 | 16.8 |
| Caterpillar | 44⅞ | 100.9 | 4.5 |
| Chevron | 71¼ | 350.9 | 25.0 |
| Coca Cola | 68⅜ | 667.5 | 45.6 |
| Disney | 111⅞ | 129.9 | 14.5 |
| DuPont | 46⅞ | 670.5 | 31.4 |
| Eastman Kodak | 49¼ | 342.7 | 16.9 |
| Exxon | 59¾ | 1,245.0 | 74.4 |
| General Electric | 70⅜ | 873.1 | 61.4 |
| General Motors | 33¾ | 612.2 | 20.7 |
| Goodyear | 49⅜ | 58.5 | 2.9 |
| IBM | 100 | 572.6 | 57.3 |
| International Paper | 74 | 109.9 | 8.1 |
| McDonald's | 35⅝ | 359.2 | 12.8 |
| Merck | 144⅝ | 386.6 | 55.9 |
| MMM | 91¾ | 219.8 | 20.2 |
| Morgan J.P. | 66 | 186.9 | 12.3 |
| Philip Morris | 70⅜ | 925.4 | 65.1 |
| Procter & Gamble | 84½ | 344.8 | 29.1 |
| Sears Roebuck | 37⅝ | 343.6 | 12.9 |
| Texaco | 63½ | 258.2 | 16.4 |
| Union Carbide | 19⅝ | 125.7 | 2.5 |
| United Technologies | 49⅞ | 121.3 | 6.0 |
| Westinghouse | 16½ | 290.9 | 4.8 |
| Woolworth | 26½ | 129.8 | $ 3.4 |

**Source:** *The Wall Street Journal*, November 15, 1991. Reprinted by permission of *The Wall Street Journal*, 1991. Dow Jones & Company, Inc. All Rights Reserved Worldwide.

The most widely reported index is the **Dow Jones Industrial Average**, an average of the prices of the 30 prominent "blue chip" companies shown in Table 9.3, calculated by adding up these 30 prices and dividing by the divisor $k$, which was equal to 0.559 in November of 1991:

$$DJ = \frac{P_1 + P_2 + \cdots + P_{30}}{k}$$

## EXAMPLE 9.3 *Adjusting the Dow Divisor*

The value of the Dow Jones Industrial Average is calculated by adding up the prices of the 30 stocks included in the average and dividing by the divisor $k$:

$$DJ = \frac{P_1 + P_2 + \cdots + P_{30}}{k}$$

In order to avoid discontinuities in the index, the divisor $k$ is changed when one of the 30 stocks in the index is replaced with another stock or when a stock is split — for example, doubling the number of shares and halving the price of each share.

Using the prices in Table 9.3 and $k = 0.559$ on November 14, 1991, the value of the Dow that day was

$$DJ = \frac{43 + 61\frac{7}{8} + \cdots + 100 + \cdots + 26\frac{1}{2}}{0.559} = \frac{1712.625}{0.559} = 3063.73$$

Suppose that IBM, which closed at $100 a share on November 14, 1991, had been replaced by Ford Motor Company, which closed at $25 a share. This substitution would have reduced the numerator by $75 and reduced the value of the Dow by 134 points, suggesting a dramatic stock market decline when all that had really happened was that a $100 stock happened to be replaced by a $25 stock:

$$DJ = \frac{43 + 61\frac{7}{8} + \cdots + 25 + \cdots + 26\frac{1}{2}}{0.559} = \frac{1637.625}{0.559} = 2929.56$$

To avoid such false signals, the value of the Dow divisor would have been recalculated so that the substitution of Ford for IBM had no effect on the Dow that day. The equation

$$DJ = \frac{43 + 61\frac{7}{8} + \cdots + 25 + \cdots + 26\frac{1}{2}}{k} = \frac{1637.625}{k} = 3063.73$$

implies that

$$k = \frac{1637.625}{3063.73} = 0.535$$

To offset the substitution of a lower-priced stock for a higher-priced one, the Dow divisor is reduced from 0.559 to 0.535.

Similarly, suppose that IBM had declared a four-for-one stock split, in which each old share is replaced by four new shares, each of which is worth one-fourth what an old share was worth. An investor who owned, say, 0.001 percent of the total amount of old shares outstanding would own 0.001 percent of the total amount of new shares outstanding and should be made no better or worse off by the split. Therefore, the market value of four new shares should be the same as the market value of one old share, implying that each new share is worth one-fourth the value of an old share.

In our example, if IBM had declared a four-for-one split, effective after the close of trading on November 14, 1991, then each new share should be worth $25. Using this reasoning, the value of the Dow Jones divisor is adjusted so that the stock split has no effect on the value of the Dow Jones Industrial Average. As in the previous calculation, the replacement of a $100 stock by a $25 stock necessitates reducing the divisor from 0.559 to 0.535, and this is exactly what would have been done. Stock splits are the primary reason that the value of the Dow divisor has declined over time and now has a value less than 1.0.

The current value of the divisor is printed each day in *The Wall Street Journal*; its calculation is explained in Example 9.3.

Unlike the Dow, most other stock indexes multiply the per-share prices by the number of shares outstanding, giving an index of the total market value of the stocks monitored. The Standard & Poor's 500 (S&P 500) index contains 500 important stocks, almost all from the New York Stock Exchange and comprising about three-fourths of the market value of all NYSE stocks; the NYSE composite index includes all NYSE stocks. The AMEX index covers the American Stock Exchange; the NASDAQ index has over-the-counter stocks; and the Wilshire 5000 has 5000 stocks from all these sources. Because these indexes represent a broader selection of stocks and reflect the market value of the stocks in the index, they are a more accurate gauge of what is really happening to the value of investor portfolios. The Dow Jones index, however, has its long tradition and an entrenched spot in the newspaper headlines. When the Dow is up 50 points, people can interpret that statistic readily as very good news about the stock market simply because they remember that the Dow seldom goes up by as much as 50 points in a single day. If they were to read that the NYSE composite was up 5 points, they wouldn't know what to make of that statistic, even though it is describing the same events and probably describing them more accurately.

## Foreign Stocks

If we add together the market values of all U.S. stocks, Japanese stocks, and other stocks worldwide, the aggregate value of the world stock market was $9.6 trillion in 1988. In 1980, U.S. stocks comprised 55 percent of the aggregate world stock market and Japanese stocks comprised 20 percent. In 1988, the U.S. percentage had fallen to below 30 percent and the Japanese percentage had risen to 45 percent. Table 9.4 shows the 1990 volume of trading on nine worldwide stock exchanges and the over-the-counter trading reported on NASDAQ. The annual trading volume on the New York and Tokyo stock exchanges was nearly equal, and it was substantially larger than on the other exchanges.

There has been a dramatically increased globalization of stock markets, in that investors increasingly buy stock in foreign companies. Between 1980 and 1990, aggregate foreign purchases and sales of U.S. stocks increased at a 17 percent annual rate. Because they began from a much smaller base, U.S.

**Table 9.4    1990 Dollar Volume of Trading in World Stock Markets**

| Stock Exchange | $ Billions |
|---|---|
| New York | 1325.3 |
| Tokyo | 1313.2 |
| London | 544.3 |
| Frankfurt | 539.4 |
| NASDAQ | 452.4 |
| Osaka | 249.3 |
| Zurich | 187.5 |
| Paris | 129.0 |
| Toronto | 54.9 |
| AMEX | 37.7 |

**Source:** NASDAQ, *Fact Book 1991.*

purchases and sales of foreign stocks grew at an even more remarkable 30 percent annual rate. Table 9.5 shows the composition for five countries of foreign transactions in U.S. stocks and of U.S. transactions in foreign stocks.

**Table 9.5    Foreign Transactions in U.S. Stocks and U.S. Transactions in Foreign Stocks**

| | Foreign Transactions in U.S. Stock ($ billions) | | U.S. Transactions in Foreign Stock ($ billions) | |
|---|---|---|---|---|
| | Purchases | Sales | Purchases | Sales |
| **1990** | | | | |
| United Kingdom | 44.94 | 48.07 | 44.80 | 45.52 |
| Japan | 27.47 | 30.38 | 30.89 | 31.52 |
| Canada | 19.52 | 18.63 | 4.78 | 4.92 |
| Germany | 5.90 | 6.27 | 6.69 | 7.45 |
| France | 5.82 | 7.01 | 6.05 | 5.90 |
| Total worldwide | 173.04 | 188.34 | 122.49 | 130.89 |
| **1980** | | | | |
| United Kingdom | 7.44 | 4.94 | 1.38 | 1.36 |
| Japan | 0.87 | 1.03 | 0.93 | 1.77 |
| Canada | 6.35 | 5.48 | 3.02 | 3.66 |
| Germany | 2.75 | 2.56 | 0.24 | 0.22 |
| France | 2.73 | 2.24 | 0.47 | 0.67 |
| Total worldwide | 40.32 | 34.96 | 7.89 | 9.97 |

**Source:** Peter A. Abken, "Globalization of Stock, Futures, and Options Markets," *Economic Review*, Federal Reserve Bank of Atlanta, July/August 1991, pp. 1–19.

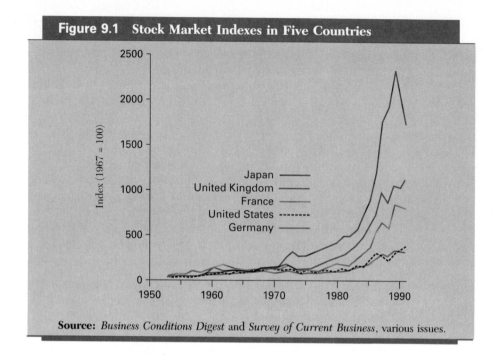

**Figure 9.1   Stock Market Indexes in Five Countries**

**Source:** *Business Conditions Digest* and *Survey of Current Business*, various issues.

Figure 9.1 compares stock market indexes for France, Germany, Japan, the United Kingdom, and the United States since 1953. (All indexes have been scaled to equal 100 in 1967.) The most striking features are how much the German and U.S. stock markets have lagged behind those of the other three countries and the 1989–1991 decline in the Japanese stock market. From a peak that occurred on December 30, 1989, the Nikkei index of 225 leading stocks listed on the Tokyo Stock Exchange fell by more than 40 percent over the next 2 years.

Figure 9.2 compares four countries whose stock market indexes have increased by roughly the same percentage since 1953: Canada, Germany, Italy, and the United States. While some similarities are apparent, there are also obvious differences — years in which one stock market went up much more than another did and years in which one stock market went up and another went down.

Stock prices everywhere are influenced by interest rates and by corporate profits, and to the extent that world interest rates are linked and different national economies go through similar patterns of boom and recession, stock markets throughout the world share similar influences. It is apparent from examination of Figures 9.1 and 9.2, however, that national stock markets are only loosely correlated. While economies may go through similar cycles of boom and

## Figure 9.2  Stock Market Indexes in Four Countries

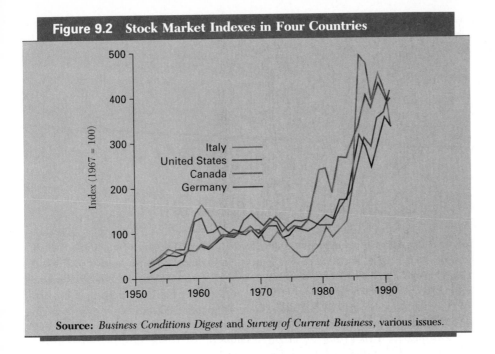

**Source:** *Business Conditions Digest* and *Survey of Current Business*, various issues.

recession, stock prices depend on the anticipated long-run growth of profits, and these anticipated growth rates can go up in one country and simultaneously go down in another. Also, even if interest rates move similarly in different countries, perceptions of risk need not. Other factors, such as changes in capital gains tax rates, also can exert an influence on one country's stock market that is largely independent of other countries.

Statistically, the two most closely correlated stock markets since 1953 were those of Germany and the United States, and the correlation coefficient was only 0.50. In the next chapter we will explain how this imperfect correlation among world stock markets offers investors an opportunity to diversify their portfolios.

## STOCK VALUATION

What is the value of a share of First Interstate or another stock? According to what is called **fundamental analysis**, the **intrinsic value** of a stock is the present value of its prospective cash flow, discounted by the shareholders' required return, taking into account the returns available on alternative investments, its risk, and other salient considerations.[1] True investors consider stocks a long-run investment with a cash flow consisting of an endless stream of dividends. A used postage stamp has no intrinsic value. Neither does a stock that will never pay dividends. John Burr Williams, a Harvard economics professor temporarily turned poet, wrote:

> *A cow for her milk*
> *A hen for her eggs*
> *and a stock, by heck*
> *For her dividends.*
>
> *An orchard for fruit*
> *Bees, for their honey*
> *and stock, besides*
> *For their dividends.*[2]

In contrast to investors who are willing to hold an asset for keeps, **speculators** buy not for the long-run cash flow, but to sell a short while later for a profit. To speculators, a stock (or a used postage stamp) is worth what someone else will pay for it, and the game is to guess what others will pay tomorrow for what you buy today. John Maynard Keynes, an economist and successful speculator, put it this way:

> *It is not sensible to pay 25 for an investment of which you believe the prospective [cash flow] to justify a value of 30, if you also believe that the market will value it at 20 three months hence.*[3]

Those people who believe in fundamental analysis consider such guessing games the "greater fool theory": that is, you buy shares at an inflated price, hoping to find an even bigger fool who will buy the shares from you at a still higher price.

Fundamental analysts readily admit that many who buy and sell stock are speculators, hoping for quick profits, and that speculative binges can cause prices to depart from intrinsic values. Speculators are like the wind that blows a boat about its anchor — present value. We will use fundamental analysis to provide a rational explanation of stock prices.

## Present Value Again

If $D_t$ is the dividend $t$ periods from now and $R$ is the shareholder's required return, then the present value of this cash flow is

$$P = \frac{D_1}{(1 + R)} + \frac{D_2}{(1 + R)^2} + \frac{D_3}{(1 + R)^3} + \cdots \qquad (9.1)$$

(Companies usually pay dividends quarterly and, hence, a quarterly required return is in order, but for simplicity we use annual dividends and annual required rates of return.)

| Table 9.6 | Present Value of a $5 Dividend, $R = 10$ Percent |
|---|---|
| Growth Rate g (%) | Present Value P |
| 0 | $ 50.00 |
| 2 | 62.50 |
| 4 | 83.33 |
| 6 | 125.00 |
| 8 | 250.00 |

A special case is the **constant-dividend-growth model**, in which the dividend grows at a steady rate $g$ each period: $D_{t+1} = (1 + g)D_t$. If $g < R$, then the present value given by Equation 9.1 reduces to this remarkably simple equation:

$$P = \frac{D_1}{R - g} \qquad (9.2)$$

Equation 9.2 gives the present value of a stock whose dividends grow at a constant rate $g$. Dividends never grow at an absolutely constant rate. The appeal of Equation 9.2 is that it is a reasonable and manageable approximation that has some very logical implications.

Notice, particularly, how important the growth rate is to the value of a stock. At a 10 percent required return, a stock paying a $5 dividend is worth $P = $5/(0.10 − 0.00) = $50$ if no growth is expected, and it is worth twice as much if the dividend is expected to grow by 5 percent a year: $P = $5/(0.10 − 0.05) = $100$. The present values for other growth rates are shown in Table 9.6.

Growth makes a big difference because of the power of compounding. The difference between 0 percent and 5 percent growth may not sound like much (and it really isn't for the first few years), but 50 years down the road, the first company will still be paying a $5 dividend while the second will be paying $5(1.05^{50}) = $57.34$. A present-value calculation whittles down the difference somewhat, but still, when all is said and done, taking into account the small difference in near dividends and the big difference in distant dividends, the second stock is worth twice the first.

## The Stock Market and the Economy

The National Bureau of Economic Research has long considered stock prices to be one of the best leading indicators of changes in economic activity. Stock prices usually decline shortly (on average, $4\frac{1}{2}$ months) before a recession begins

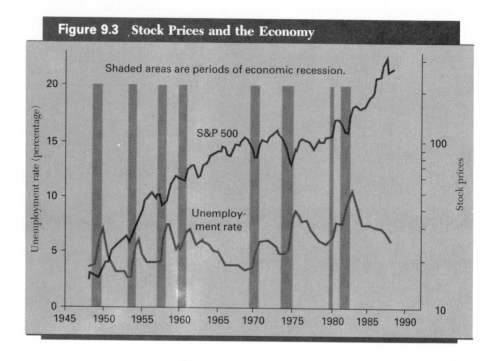

**Figure 9.3**   **Stock Prices and the Economy**

and rise shortly before a recession ends. Figure 9.3 compares the U.S. unemployment rate and the S&P 500 index, with the shaded time periods identifying economic recessions. Each of the eight recessions since 1948 has, in fact, been preceded by a noticeable decline in stock prices. However, stock prices also fell sharply in 1962, 1966, 1977, and 1984 without a recession. To paraphrase Paul Samuelson, the market has predicted 12 of the last 8 recessions.

Nonetheless, there does seem to be a striking correlation between the stock market and the economy. Why? There are three possible explanations that are consistent with fundamental analysis: the stock market may influence the economy, the economy may influence the stock market, or some third factor may influence both. Most likely, all three explanations are correct. As is so often true in economics, everything does depend on everything else, although in varying degrees.

Let's look first at how the stock market influences the economy. When stock prices are high, those who own stock feel richer (with good reason; they are richer). They tend to spend more and live in a manner befitting their new wealth. When stock prices decline, households are likely to retrench, increasing their saving and trying to rebuild their lost wealth. One of the Federal Reserve Board's economic models estimates that each dollar change in the market value of stocks tends to change consumer spending by about 5 cents. With the substantial fluctuations in stock prices in recent years, those nickels add up. In 1973–1974, the aggregate market of stocks dropped by about $500 billion, implying a $25 billion depressant for consumer spending that helps explain the 1974–1975 recession. The 1985–1986 "bull" market increased stock values by nearly a trillion dollars, and the implied $50 billion spending stimulus helps explain why household spending as a fraction of income reached record levels. The $500 billion crash on October 19, 1987, made many, including the Federal Reserve, fearful of recession; the Fed immediately responded by increasing the nation's money supply to support financial markets and the economy.

The economy, in turn, undoubtedly affects the stock market. Stock prices are influenced by anticipated dividends, and when the economy is strong, profits surge and dividends follow close behind. When recession hits, profits slump and dividends grow slowly or even decline. Why does the market go up or down $4\frac{1}{2}$ months *before* the economy does likewise? Perhaps stock analysts can see booms and recessions coming in advance of their actual arrival (at least in 12 out of 8 instances).

Another explanation for the observed correlation is that some third factor influences both the stock market and the economy. The possibilities are endless, ranging from skirt lengths to the heights of the Great Lakes. The most plausible factor is interest rates. As Andrew Tobias, a popular financial writer, put it, "The key to everything financial, and to nearly everything economic, is interest rates."[4]

## The Stock Market and Interest Rates

When investors' required rate of return increases, there is a decline in the present value of any given cash flow. Earlier chapters discussed this inverse price–yield relationship for bonds; the very same logic applies to stocks. For a given dividend stream, a high required return requires a low price, whereas a low required rate of return necessitates a high price.

Because so much of their cash flow is in the distant future, stocks, especially growth stocks, are similar to very long-term bonds in that they have long durations and substantial capital risk. A 20-year bond with a 10 percent coupon selling for par has a duration of 9 years; a stock with a 12 percent required return and 5 percent anticipated growth rate has a duration of 16 years.

To illustrate the effect of required return on present value, consider again the example of a stock with a current $5 dividend and a variety of possible growth rates, this time comparing 11 percent with 10 percent required returns, as in Table 9.7. Notice, first, that stock prices are very sensitive to required returns and, second, that this is especially true for growth stocks. Because a large part of the present value consists of distant dividends, stocks are long-term assets with substantial capital risk.

It is often thought, wrongly, that the only reason high interest rates depress the stock market is that higher interest rates may mean increased costs for businesses or a weaker economy and depressed sales. Even if costs are constant and the economy is stable, higher interest rates depress stock prices for the same reason they depress bond prices. Assets are, to varying degrees, substitutes in investor eyes, and the required rates of return that investors use to discount the cash flow from assets depend on the yields available on alternative investments.

**Table 9.7   The Effect of the Required Return on a Stock's Present Value**

| Growth Rate g (%) | Present Value | | Percentage Change (%) |
| --- | --- | --- | --- |
| | R = 10% | R = 11% | |
| 0 | $ 50.00 | $ 45.45 | −9.1 |
| 2 | 62.50 | 55.55 | −11.1 |
| 4 | 83.33 | 71.43 | −14.3 |
| 6 | 125.00 | 100.00 | −20.0 |
| 8 | 250.00 | 166.67 | −33.3 |

When the returns available on Treasury securities rise, so do the required returns on corporate bonds and stocks, pushing these asset prices downward. Otherwise, investors would forsake corporate stocks and bonds for the higher yields available on Treasury securities.

To the extent financial markets are competitive and efficient, these ripples are felt almost immediately. Because of the dissatisfaction that would otherwise occur, prices fall across a broad spectrum of assets virtually simultaneously. Stock market analysts pay close attention to other financial markets and to news of government financial policies. Stock prices jump right after (and sometimes before) the Fed announces an easing of monetary policy or Citibank announces a drop in their prime lending rate. Daily reports on the stock market routinely refer to interest-rate developments and to perceived changes in financial policies. To cite just one example, a *New York Times* story began, "Stock prices tumbled yesterday, with the Dow Jones Industrial Average dropping more than 11 points, following apparent confirmation that the Federal Reserve was permitting short-term interest rates to move higher."[5] More dramatically, the 1973–1974 stock market crash ended just when interest rates peaked, and the 1985–1986 surge coincided with a 3 percentage point drop in long-term bond rates. The October 1987 crash began after interest rates rose, and the market recovered when the Federal Reserve pushed interest rates back down.

The fact that low interest rates increase both bond and stock prices (and higher interest rates reduce both) does not mean that bond and stock prices always move in the same direction. While bonds have a fixed cash flow (except in defaults), stocks have a variable cash flow, with dividends that go up and down with the economy. Because the economy and interest rates can move in the same or opposite directions, sometimes bond and stock prices move together and other times they diverge.

If the economic outlook is unchanged while interest rates fluctuate, stock and bond prices will move together. If the economic outlook changes, then the relative movements of bond and stock prices depend on whether the economy and interest rates move in the same or opposite directions. When interest rates rise, bad economic news reinforces the drop in stock prices, whereas good economic news cushions the drop, perhaps even propelling stock prices upward at the same time that bond prices are falling. When interest rates decline, good economic news reinforces rising stock prices, whereas a weak economy restrains stock prices.

## Tobin's q

A strong economy encourages businesses to expand and also increases stock prices. Low interest rates also encourage business expansion and raise stock prices. James Tobin of Yale University argues that the net effect of the current state of the economy and interest rates on business investment can be gauged by the level of stock prices, specifically by the value of **Tobin's q**, the ratio of the value placed on a firm by financial markets to the replacement cost of its assets:

$$q = \frac{\text{market value of firm}}{\text{replacement cost of firm's assets}} \qquad (9.3)$$

If a corporation has bonds and other debts, these can be added to the market value in Equation 9.3 or subtracted from asset replacement cost.

The logic behind Tobin's $q$ can be illustrated by a simple example. Consider a restaurant chain that is thinking of building another restaurant that will cost $1 million to construct and is expected to earn a constant $200,000 annual profit (a 20 percent return on its cost), which will be paid out each year to the chain's shareholders. The value that financial markets place on this restaurant depends not on its $1 million cost of construction, but on the value of its $200,000 annual cash flow.

If Treasury bonds yield 5 percent, then perhaps stock in a risky restaurant is priced to yield 10 percent. If so, then Equation 9.2 with a zero growth rate gives a market value of

$$P = \frac{\$200,000}{0.10 - 0.00} = \frac{\$200,000}{0.10} = \$2 \text{ million}$$

Valued at $2 million, the $200,000 cash flow gives shareholders their requisite 10 percent return. The market value of this restaurant is twice its cost of construction,

$$q = \frac{\text{market value of firm}}{\text{replacement cost of firm's assets}} = \frac{\$2 \text{ million}}{\$1 \text{ million}} = 2$$

The value of Tobin's $q$ is larger than 1 because the restaurant's 20 percent profit rate is larger than the shareholders' 10 percent required return.

If, on the other hand, Treasury bonds pay 20 percent and restaurant shareholders price their stock to give a 25 percent return, then the value of a $200,000 annual cash flow is only $800,000:

$$P = \frac{\$200,000}{0.25 - 0.00} = \frac{\$200,000}{0.25} = \$800,000$$

**Table 9.8**   **The 20 Largest Firms in the Computer and Office Equipment Industry, 1989**

| Company | Market Value ($ millions) | Book Value ($ millions) | Tobin's q | Profit Rate (%) |
|---|---|---|---|---|
| IBM | $94,644 | $66,299 | 1.43 | 14.7 |
| Xerox | 20,122 | 18,787 | 1.07 | 11.2 |
| Hewlett-Packard | 14,865 | 6,335 | 2.35 | 18.0 |
| Digital Equipment | 14,853 | 10,553 | 1.41 | 17.4 |
| Unisys | 11,394 | 12,203 | 0.93 | 9.0 |
| Apple | 6,692 | 1,764 | 3.79 | 39.9 |
| Pitney-Bowes | 6,016 | 3,925 | 1.53 | 18.7 |
| Tandy | 5,521 | 3,211 | 1.72 | 19.7 |
| NCR | 5,412 | 3,204 | 1.69 | 19.6 |
| Automatic Data Processing | 3,687 | 1,868 | 1.97 | 17.3 |
| Compaq | 3,453 | 1,248 | 2.77 | 30.5 |
| Wang Laboratories | 3,410 | 3,769 | 0.90 | 5.8 |
| Control Data | 2,633 | 2,872 | 0.93 | 3.5 |
| Amdahl | 2,397 | 1,388 | 1.73 | 21.2 |
| Prime Computer | 2,293 | 1,892 | 1.21 | 10.2 |
| Tandem Computers | 2,256 | 1,466 | 1.54 | 11.7 |
| Sun | 1,907 | 912 | 2.09 | 18.0 |
| Cray Research | 1,756 | 906 | 1.94 | 23.1 |
| Intergraph | 1,133 | 925 | 1.22 | 12.5 |
| Seagate Technology | 1,053 | 798 | 1.32 | 17.7 |

**Source:** *Value Line Investment Survey*, May 5, 1989, pp. 1076–1118. Copyright © 1989 by Value Line Publishing, Inc.; used by permission. For Subscription information to the *Value Line Investment Survey* please call (800) 634–3585.

Because the restaurant's 20 percent profit rate is less than shareholders' 25 percent required return, the value of Tobin's $q$ is less than 1:

$$q = \frac{\text{market value of firm}}{\text{replacement cost of firm's assets}} = \frac{\$800,000}{\$1 \text{ million}} = 0.8$$

Table 9.8 shows some estimates of Tobin's $q$ using market-value and book-value data for the 20 largest firms in the computer and office equipment industry. The ratio of market value to book value is a crude estimate of Tobin's $q$ because book values reflect historical cost, which may be very different from current replacement cost. Nonetheless, as shown in this table and in Figure 9.4, those firms with high profit rates tend to have high values of Tobin's $q$, whereas firms with low profits rates have low values of Tobin's $q$.

The link between Tobin's $q$ and business investment is provided by the observation that business expansion only benefits shareholders if the rate of return that the firm can earn on its investments is larger than shareholders' required rate of return — such as when the restaurant can earn a 20 percent return and the shareholders require only 10 percent. This is one of the primary

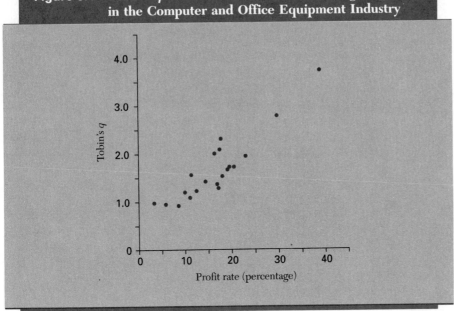

**Figure 9.4  Tobin's *q* and Profit Rate for the 20 Largest Firms in the Computer and Office Equipment Industry**

ways in which financial markets affect real economic activity. When interest rates are low, so are shareholder required returns, making it more likely that prospective investments are sufficiently profitable to justify making them on behalf of shareholders. If, as in the second case, shareholders require a 25 percent return, construction of the restaurant does not benefit shareholders; they would be better off if the firm paid out the $1 million as a dividend and let shareholders invest it themselves.

Equivalently, the firm can ask whether, if it were to sell shares in its new restaurant venture, it could raise enough money to cover the cost of constructing the restaurant. It can do so if the value of Tobin's *q* is larger than 1, but not otherwise. Thus Tobin's *q* provides a barometer of the incentives for business expansion.

## MASS PSYCHOLOGY

Investment decisions are more than arithmetic calculations and mechanical rules. Our information is usually incomplete and often contradictory, and there is always considerable uncertainty about the future. Inevitably, we make subjective decisions that are influenced by our all-too-human emotions. It is natural to hope that a clever investment will yield quick and easy wealth. This hope sometimes turns into a greed that blurs our vision and dulls common sense.

We will use the term **speculative bubble** to describe a situation in which the market price of an asset is determined primarily by speculators hoping to profit from a short-run increase in the asset's price rather than by investors who

**EXAMPLE 9.4**  *The South Sea Bubble*

In 1720 the British government gave the South Sea Company exclusive trading privileges with Spain's American colonies in return for extinguishing much of the national debt by giving debtholders shares of stock in the South Sea Company. None of the company's directors had ever been to America, nor had they any concrete trading plans. Encouraged by the company's inventive bookkeeping, however, English citizens rushed to invest in this exotic venture. As the price of the South Sea Company's stock soared from £120 on January 28 to £400 on May 19, to £800 on June 4, and to £1000 on June 22, some became rich, and thousands rushed to join their ranks. It was said that you could buy stock as you entered Garraway's coffeehouse and sell it for a profit on the way out.

Soon other entrepreneurs were offering stock in ever more grandiose schemes and were deluged by frantic investors not wanting to be left out. It scarcely mattered what the scheme was. One proposed making a machine gun that would fire round or square bullets depending on whether the enemy was Christian. One promised to build a wheel for perpetual motion. Another was formed "for carrying on an undertaking of great advantage, but nobody is to know what it is." These shares were priced at £100 each, with a promised annual return of £100; after selling all the stock within 5 hours, the promoter immediately left England and never returned. Yet another stock offer was for the "nitvender," or selling of nothing.* When the bubble burst, most of the stock became worthless, and fortunes and dreams were lost.

As with all speculative bubbles, there were many believers in the "greater fool theory." While some suspected that prices were unreasonable, the market was dominated by people believing that prices would continue to rise, at least until they could sell to the next fool in line. In the spring of 1720 Sir Isaac Newton said, "I can calculate the motions of the heavenly bodies, but not the madness of people" and sold his South Sea shares for a £7000 profit. Later that year, however, he brought shares again, just before the bubble burst, and lost £20,000. Similarly, when a banker invested £500 in the third offer of South Sea stock (in August of 1720), he explained that "when the rest of the world are mad, we must imitate them in some measure."† After James Milner, a member of the British Parliament, was bankrupted by the South Sea bubble, he explained, "I said, indeed, that ruin must soon come upon us but I own it came two months sooner than I expected."‡

*John Carswell, The South Sea Bubble (*London: Cresset Press, 1960*), p. 142.
†Ibid., p. 161.
‡Virginia Cowles, The Great Swindle (*New York: Harper, 1960*), p. 143.

would be content to hold the asset forever and receive its cash flow. From time to time, investors are gripped by what, in retrospect, seems to have been mass hysteria. The price of some commodity or security climbs higher and higher, beyond all reason — a speculative bubble in that nothing justifies the rise in price except the hope that it will go higher still. Then, suddenly, the bubble pops, and the price collapses. With hindsight, it is hard to see how people could have been so foolish. Paradoxically, however, at the time of the bubble it seems foolish to sit on the sidelines while others become rich.

Speculative bubbles generally begin with important events of real economic significance, such as the building of railroads, the discovery of gold, or the outbreak of war.[6] Seeing the profits made by some, others rush to participate, pushing prices higher. Soon greed displaces common sense, and swindlers emerge to fleece the gullible. The upward rush of prices becomes a speculative bubble in the sense that most of the participants are buying not for the cash flow that their investment might produce, but rather in anticipation that prices will keep rising — a self-fulfilling prophecy as long as there are more buyers than sellers.

When everyone has been convinced that something is a good investment, there is no one left to buy and push the price still higher. The bubble bursts when buyers no longer outnumber sellers. There is a selling stampede, and prices collapse. In the frantic rush for the exit, very few make it through the door.

There have been several dramatic historical episodes when the stock market was seized by a collective euphoria, as investors seemed to put aside common sense, and, instead, were willing to believe whatever was necessary to justify ever-higher stock prices. The subsequent, terrifying collapse of prices not only evaporated fortunes but persuaded many that they would never again buy stock. We'll look first at the stock market crash that accompanied the Great Depression and then at a more recent 1-day crash of unprecedented magnitude.

## The Great Crash

The 1920s were an exciting and turbulent decade — for the economy, for social mores, and for the stock market.[7] In 1924 the Dow Jones Industrial Average hit 100. In December of 1927 it roared past 200, hitting 250 in October of 1928 and 300 in December. Nine months later, in September of 1929, it reached a peak of 386. It seemed that investors could get rich effortlessly by buying stock in rock-solid companies. Between March of 1928 and September of 1929, American Can went from 77 to 181⅞, American Telephone went from 179½ to 335⅝, General Electric went from 128¾ to 396¼, and U.S. Steel went from 138⅛ to 279⅛.

Predicting the future is always treacherous, and history is full of well-informed people making what, with hindsight, are foolish statements. At breakfast before Waterloo, Napoleon remarked, "Wellington is a bad general, the English are bad soldiers; we will settle the matter by lunch time." In 1899, the Director of the U.S. Patent Office said, "Everything that can be invented has been invented." Thomas Edison believed that "the phonograph is not of any commercial value," and President Hayes said of the telephone, "That's an amazing invention, but who would ever want to use one?" Lord Kelvin, a scientist and president of Britain's Royal Society, proclaimed that "heavier than air flying machines are impossible" and "radio has no future." Harry Warner, the president of Warner Brothers, said, "Who the hell wants to hear actors talk?"

and Thomas Watson, the CEO of IBM, said, "I think there is a world market for about five computers."

The stock market and the economy are never easy to predict, and the crash and the Great Depression were no exception. In his final message to Congress on December 4, 1928, Calvin Coolidge boasted, "No Congress of the United States ever assembled, on surveying the state of the Union, has met with a more pleasing prospect than that which appears at the present time." Herbert Hoover took office and in July of 1929 predicted that "the outlook of the world today is for the greatest era of commercial expansion in history." On October 17, 1929, Irving Fisher, the greatest American economist of his day, asserted that stocks had reached "what looks like a permanently high plateau."

However, the 5-year "bull" market was over. After a number of bad days, panic selling hit the stock market on Thursday, October 24, 1929. Terrified investors tried to sell at any price, and market prices plunged, with the panic heightened by the fact that the ticker tape reporting transactions ran hours late so that investors had no information about current prices. The market finally steadied in the afternoon when six prominent New York bankers put up $40 million apiece to buy stocks. The market dropped again the following Monday, however, and was hit by panic selling the next day, Black Tuesday, October 29. Again there was an avalanche of sell orders, more than the brokers and the ticker tape could process and, more important, dwarfing the scattered buy orders. White Sewing Machine had recently traded for $48; on Monday it closed at 11⅛. On Black Tuesday, in the complete absence of buy orders, a messenger boy bought shares for $1.[8]

With fits and starts, the market decline continued. By November 13, the Dow had fallen an incredible 48 percent as the prices of America's premier companies collapsed: American Can was down 53 percent, American Telephone was down 41 percent, General Electric was down 58 percent, and U.S. Steel was down 46 percent. The Dow recovered to nearly 300 in the spring of 1930 but then began a long, tortuous slide, punctuated by brief, but inadequate rallies before finally touching bottom at 42.84 in June of 1932 — down 89 percent from September of 1929. It wasn't until 1956, 27 years later, that the stock market regained its 1929 peak.

Economic historians continue to debate the effect of the 1930s stock market decline on the economy. What is certain is that the Great Depression was more than a stock market crash. Between 1929 and 1933, output fell a third, while the unemployment rate rose from 3 to 25 percent. More than a third of the nation's banks failed, and household net worth dropped by 30 percent. Behind these aggregate numbers were millions of private tragedies. One hundred thousand businesses failed, and 12 million people lost their jobs — and with them, their income and, in many cases, their self-respect. Many lost their life savings in the stock market crash and the tidal wave of bank failures. Without income or savings, people could not buy food, clothing, or proper medical care. Those who could not pay their rents lost their shelter; those who couldn't make mortgage payments lost their homes. Farm income fell by two-thirds, and many farms were lost to foreclosure. Desperate people moved into shanty settlements (called

**EXAMPLE 9.5** *Ponzi Schemes*

In 1920 Charles Ponzi promised to pay Massachusetts investors 50 percent interest every 45 days — compounded eight times a year, $1 would grow to $1.50^8 = \$25.63$, an effective annual rate of return of 2463 percent! His stated plan was to arbitrage the difference between the official and open-market price of Spanish pesos. He would buy Spanish pesos cheap in the open market, use these pesos to buy International Postage Union coupons, and then trade these coupons for U.S. postage stamps at the higher official exchange rate.* If everything worked as planned, he could buy 10 cents worth of U.S. postage stamps for a penny, although it was unclear how he would convert these stamps back into cash. In practice, he received $15 million from investors and appears to have bought only $61 in stamps.

If he didn't invest the money he received, how could he possibly afford to pay a 50 percent return every 45 days? He couldn't. He could, however, create a temporary illusion of doing so. Suppose that one person invests $100, which Ponzi promptly spends for himself. If Ponzi now finds another two people to invest $100 apiece, then he can pay the first person $150 and keep another $50 for himself. Now he has 45 days to find four more people willing to invest $100 so that he can pay each of the previous two investors $150 and spend $100 on himself. These four investors can be paid off with the money from eight new ones, and these eight from sixteen more.

In a **Ponzi scheme**, money from new investors is used to pay off earlier ones, and it works as long as there are enough new investors. The problem is that the pool of fish is exhausted surprisingly soon. The twenty-first round requires a million new people, and the thirtieth round requires a billion more. At some point the scheme runs out of new people, and those in the last round (the majority of the investors) are left with nothing. A Ponzi scheme merely transfers wealth from late entrants to early entrants.

Ponzi's scam collapsed after 8 months when a Boston newspaper discovered that during the time that he supposedly bought $15 million in postage coupons, the total amount sold worldwide came to only $1 million. Despite his protestations that he could pay off his investors by incorporating and selling shares of stock to other investors, the state of Massachusetts froze his accounts and sent Ponzi to jail for 10 years.

*A fictionalized account is given in Donald H. Dunn, Ponzi: The Boston Swindler (New York: McGraw-Hill, 1975).*

"Hoovervilles"), slept under newspapers ("Hoover blankets"), and scavenged for food where they could. Edmund Wilson reported:

> There is not a garbage-dump in Chicago which is not haunted by the hungry. Last summer in the hot weather when the smell was sickening and the flies were thick, there were a hundred people a day coming to one of the dumps.[9]

The unemployment rate averaged 19 percent during the 1930s and never fell below 14 percent. The Great Depression didn't end until the federal government began spending nearly $100 billion a year during World War II.

## October 19, 1987

On October 19, 1987, there was a stock market crash that exceeded any single day's decline during the Great Depression. Fortunately, the 1987 collapse was temporary, and there were no long-lasting effects on the economy — although the same cannot be said for investors who experienced it first hand. We'll look at the events leading up to October 19 and then at the collapse.

The **Federal Reserve Board (Fed)** controls monetary policy in the United States. Alarmed by inflation, in late 1979 the Fed began a tight money policy that pushed interest rates up and discouraged spending, particularly for houses, factories, and other investment projects. By 1982 the economy had been brought to its knees with long-term Treasury bond rates above 12 percent and the unemployment rate above 10 percent for the first time since the Great Depression. Satisfied that inflation had been brought under control — down to a livable 3.9 percent — and fearing the complete collapse of the economy, the Fed gradually eased up. The subsequent decline in unemployment and interest rates fueled a 5-year "bull" market in stocks.

In August of 1982 the Dow Jones Industrial Average was at 777. Five years later it had more than tripled, to 2722. Of course, no one bought at exactly 777 and sold at exactly 2722. Along the way, however, a lot of people noticed the run up in stock prices and wanted to hop on for at least part of the ride.

When the Dow surged past 2000 in January of 1987, stocks were widely perceived to be overvalued by conventional criteria, yet players stayed in the market, hoping for more profits and believing that they could get out before the bubble burst. *The Wall Street Journal* ran a front-page story titled "Stock Market's Surge Is Puzzling Investors; When Will It End?"[10] The story began with the exclamation "Wheee!" and went on to say that "the market madness is as puzzling as it is exhilarating." For a typical view, they quoted Steven Leuthold, the head of a financial advisory service: "You have to realize we're in Looney Tunes land and you should stay fairly close to the exits. . . . [But] It's a lot of fun, and you could make a lot of money here."

When the Dow topped 2700 in August, stocks were selling for 23 times earnings, and dividend yields were a mere 2.2 percent, compared with 10 percent interest rates on Treasury bonds. Fundamental analysis models showed intrinsic values to be some 20 to 40 percent below market prices.[11] However, buyers weren't planning on holding for keeps. There was a lot of wishful thinking, including wildly optimistic forecasts of future earnings and interest rates, and a big dose of the greater fool theory, with hopes that the Japanese were the ultimate bigger fools, with unlimited cash and an eagerness to pay 20 times earnings for U.S. stocks because Japanese stocks were selling for 60 times earnings. *The Wall Street Journal* used this story to illustrate the market's predisposition to believe:

> On June 23, an obscure investment advisor, P. David Herrlinger, announced a $6.8 billion offer for Dayton Hudson Corp. Mr. Herrlinger appeared on his front lawn to tell the Dow Jones News Service that he didn't know whether his bid was a hoax. "It's no more of a hoax than anything else," he said. Later, he was taken to a hospital.
> Yet the news sent the giant retailer's stock soaring, with 5.5 million shares changing hands in frantic trading.[12]

After topping 2700 in late August, the Dow Jones Industrial Average slipped back to 2500 in October. Then the Dow fell by a record 95 points on Wednesday October 14, dropped by another 58 points on Thursday, and fell an unprecedented 108 points on Friday, to close at 2246.74. The volume of trading on Friday was also the highest ever, with 338 million shares traded and falling prices outnumbering gainers by a staggering 17 to 1.

Monday's "Abreast of the Market" column in *The Wall Street Journal* suggested that Friday's bloodletting might have been the "selling climax" that many technical analysts believe precedes a "bull" market. One said that "the peak of intensity of selling pressure has exhausted itself," and another said that "if we haven't seen the bottom, we're probably very close."[13]

The very day this article appeared was "Black Monday," a frightening market convulsion that participants will never forget. When the market opened, the excess of sell orders was so large that trading was suspended in 8 of the 30 Dow stocks for an hour. For the day, an astounding 604 million shares were traded, and the Dow dropped 508 points (23 percent). Losers outnumbered gainers by 40 to 1, and the aggregate market value of stocks fell by roughly $500 billion.

On the next day, "Terrible Tuesday," markets came close to a total collapse. At the opening, many specialists and other market makers quoted prices far above Monday's close and sold heavily. The Dow opened with an extraordinary 200 point gain but by noon had fallen back below Monday's close. During the day, trading was temporarily suspended in many of the best-known stocks, including IBM for 2 hours and Merck for 4 hours. Several major financial institutions were rumored to be bankrupt, and some banks cut off credit to securities firms. Several specialists had difficulty raising cash to buy securities, and some of the largest of the securities firms urged the NYSE to shut down completely.

The day was saved when the Federal Reserve promised to supply much-needed cash and pressured banks to lend money. In addition, with vigorous encouragement from investment bankers, several major corporations announced plans to repurchase their stock, and the system held together — if just barely. (For the week, the 10 largest New York banks ended up lending an extra $5.5 billion to securities firms.) One market participant said that "Tuesday was the most dangerous day we had in 50 years. I think we came within an hour [of the disintegration of the stock market]."[14] The Dow closed Tuesday up 102 points on 608 million shares and rose another 187 points the next day — ending the short-run crisis.

Tidbits of bad economic news preceded the October 19th crash — congressional discussion of restrictions on corporate takeovers, a larger-than-expected trade deficit, and slightly higher interest rates — but nothing that seems substantial enough to explain the magnitude of the crash. A mail survey of individual and institutional investors found little reason for the collapse in prices other than a widespread belief that prices had been too high and that once prices started declining, people tried to sell all at once, swamping the will and financial ability of specialists to maintain orderly markets.[15] The role of an institutionalized compulsion to sell — called *program trading* — will be explained in Chapter 11. Recalling the January advice in *The Wall Street Journal* that "we're in Looney Tunes land, and you should stay fairly close to the exits," it appears that on October 19 too many people tried to squeeze through the exit door at the same time.

# THE EFFICIENT-MARKET HYPOTHESIS

In an **efficient market** there are no obviously mispriced securities and, therefore, no transactions that can be counted on to make abnormally large profits. An efficient stock market does not require zero profits. Stockholders receive dividends and, as time passes, can expect stock prices to increase along with corporate assets, profits, and dividends. Because safe bank accounts and Treasury securities pay positive returns, stocks are priced to have a positive anticipated return too — indeed, a relatively high return to the extent that stocks are risky. The efficient-market hypothesis says that in comparison with other investments, and taking into account risk and other characteristics thought relevant by investors, stocks will not be priced to give a return that is clearly inadequate or excessive.

The stock market would be inefficient if some investors could take advantage of others' ignorance — for example, if some investors knew that a company had discovered an extremely profitable cure for baldness and could buy stock in this company at an unreasonably low price from other investors who were unaware of the discovery. If information is disseminated quickly, market prices will reflect this information, and there is no advantage to "trading on information" — buying or selling on the basis of information about a company or the market as a whole. An efficient market is a fair game in the sense that no investor can beat the market (except by luck).

The efficient-market hypothesis implies an important distinction between events that have been anticipated in advance and those that haven't. For instance, if a toy store's sales increase each December, will the price of its stock also rise in December? When the stock trades in June, the price that buyers are willing to pay and sellers are willing to accept reflects the common knowledge

## EXAMPLE 9.6  *The Super Bowl System*

On Super Bowl Sunday in January of 1983, both the business and sports sections of the *Los Angeles Times* carried articles on the "Super Bowl Stock Market Predictor."* The theory is that the stock market goes up if the National Football Conference (or a former NFL team now in the American Football Conference) wins the Super Bowl. The market goes down if the AFC wins. This theory had proven correct for 15 of 16 Super Bowls — the one exception was 1970, when Kansas City beat Minnesota and the market went up 0.1 percent. In 1983 an NFC team, the Washington Redskins, won, the market went up, and the Super Bowl system was back in the newspapers the next year, stronger than ever. From its discovery through 1991, the Super Bowl system has been right seven of nine times.

The accuracy of the Super Bowl system is obviously just an amusing coincidence, since the stock market has nothing to do with the outcome of a football game. Over these 25 years, the stock market has generally gone up and the NFL has usually won the Super Bowl. The correlation is made more startling by the gimmick of including the Pittsburgh Steelers, an AFC team, in with the NFL. The excuse is that Pittsburgh once was in the NFL; the real reason is that Pittsburgh won the Super Bowl four times in years when the stock market went up.

Inspired by the success of the Super Bowl indicator, a *Los Angeles Times* staff writer uncovered several other entertaining but worthless coincidences.† The "Yo, Adrian Theory" holds that if a Rocky or Rambo movie is released, the stock market will go up that year. On average, the Dow increased by 173 points in the 4 years in which a Rocky movie appeared and 245 points in the years in which a Rambo movie was released. The "Geraldo Rivera indicator" notes that the Dow has fallen an average of 13 points on the day after seven major Geraldo Rivera specials. The "George Steinbrenner indicator" monitors his firing of Yankee managers. On the five occasions that he fired Billy Martin, the Dow rose an average of 5 points the following day; the eight times Steinbrenner fired someone else, the Dow fell an average of 3 points the next day.

*Sue Avery, "Market Investors Will Be High on Redskins Today," and "Morning Briefing: Wall Street 'Skinish on Big Game,'" Los Angeles Times, *January 30, 1983.*

†*James Bates, "Reality Wears Loser's Jersey in Super Bowl Stock Theory,"* Los Angeles Times, *January 22, 1989.*

that toy sales increase during the holiday season. Based on the information available in June, buyers and sellers can estimate these sales and value the stock accordingly. If the actual December increase in sales turns out to be equal to these forecasts, there is no cause for a revision in the value of the stock. The price will change, however, if sales are unexpectedly brisk or disappointing. Future events that are anticipated by investors are already embedded in today's stock prices. Unexpected returns are caused by the occurrence of unexpected events.

It is not enough to know that IBM will make more profits next year than Sears, that ice cream sales increase in the summer, or that automobile sales increase when the economy gets stronger. The benchmark to gauge your investment ideas is not "How will tomorrow differ from today?" but "How does my perception of tomorrow differ from what others believe?" Do you really know something that the experts don't know? If you do, then you may be guilty of using inside information, which is illegal for reasons discussed later in this chapter. If you don't, then your information is probably already embedded in market prices.

Investment decisions are influenced by many different bits and pieces of information, such as recent price movements, measures of investor sentiment, unemployment forecasts, perceptions of Federal Reserve policy, and takeover rumors. It is useful to group such disparate information into three general categories: past prices, other public data, and private information. The corresponding efficient-market hypotheses have been labeled weak, semistrong, and strong, and we discuss each in turn.

## The Weak Form

The **weak form** of the efficient-market hypothesis holds that past data on stock prices are of no use in predicting future price changes. Past price data are widely available, and there is no logical reason for investors to revise their opinions of a stock based on old price data. The immediate implication is that technical analysts who scrutinize historical charts of stock prices are wasting their time. This is often called the *random-walk hypothesis* because it says that each change in a stock's price is unrelated to previous changes, much as each flip of a coin is unrelated to previous tosses and each step by a drunkard is unrelated to previous steps. Academics overwhelmingly believe that technical analysis is worthless and that whatever patterns are discovered in historical data are coincidences that cannot be counted on to persist in the future.[16]

## The Semistrong Form

The **semistrong form** of the efficient-market hypothesis says that abnormal returns cannot be earned consistently using any publicly available information, not only past prices but also such data as interest rates, inflation, and corporate earnings. For instance, most of the data printed in a company's annual report may be known months in advance by analysts who follow the company and are certainly known by investors in general once the report appears. It is hard to see how one could consistently beat the market by trading on the basis of the information in annual reports, and no surprise, academic studies indicate that such information is already embedded in market prices in the sense that it is of little use in predicting prices *after* the report appears.[17]

✓One way of testing the efficient-market hypothesis is to identify an event, such as the publication of a company's annual report, and then see if there is any

**Figure 9.5    Daily Price Changes Before and After a Large
Stock Price Increase**

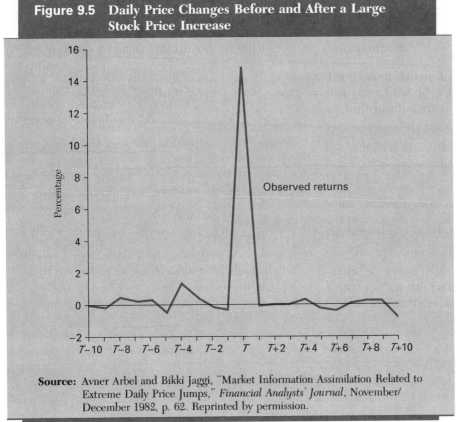

**Source:** Avner Arbel and Bikki Jaggi, "Market Information Assimilation Related to
Extreme Daily Price Jumps," *Financial Analysts' Journal*, November/
December 1982, p. 62. Reprinted by permission.

evidence of a later effect on prices. Another approach is to look at significant
price changes themselves. For instance, every day *The Wall Street Journal* lists
those stocks that experienced the largest percentage price change on the preceding trading day. Two researchers randomly selected 36 days in 1977 and then
examined the behavior of the five stocks that experienced the largest percentage
price increases on each of these days.[18] Their intent was to see if these price
increases, apparently the consequence of a change in the companies' fortunes,
were either preceded or followed by similar price increases. If so, this would
indicate that information spreads gradually through financial markets. If not, this
would indicate that whatever event triggered the price increase was truly a
surprise, whose full price effect was felt on a single trading day. Figure 9.5
summarizes the results of this analysis. The price changes were small and
seemingly random both before and after the large increase, indicating that,
without warning, some event caused a sudden jump in prices, followed by
random fluctuations.

✓Another way of testing the semistrong form of the efficient-market hypothesis is to look at the records of professional investors, who presumably base their

decisions on publicly available information. If they consistently beat the market, then public information is apparently of some value.

The record of professional investors as a group has been mediocre at best. A compilation of 52 surveys of the stocks or stock portfolios recommended by professional investors during the years 1929–1980 found that 77 percent of the professional recommendations underperformed the market.[19] Similarly, a tracking of 44 prominent investment advisory services from 1980 to 1985 found that only 14 outperformed the S&P 500, while 30 underperformed.[20]

In addition, there is little or no consistency in which particular investors do relatively well and which do poorly. For example, there is no correlation between a mutual fund's performance one year and its performance the next year; those funds in the top 10 percent this year and those in the bottom 10 percent are equally likely to be in the bottom 10 percent next year.[21] Similarly, a study of 200 institutional stock portfolios found that of those who ranked in the top 25 percent in the period 1972–1977, 26 percent ranked in the top 25 percent during 1977–1982, 48 percent ranked in the middle 50 percent, and 26 percent were in the bottom 25 percent.[22] A similar scrutiny of 32 bond managers found no correlation at all between the performance rankings for 1972–1976 and 1976–1981.[23]

Many institutions have themselves been persuaded by such evidence and have switched at least part of their portfolios to *indexing* — trying merely to replicate the market rather than outperform it — reasoning that matching a stock market index will beat most of their competitors. The three largest stock managers — Wells Fargo Investment Advisors, Bankers Trust, and the College Retirement Equities Fund — are all index enthusiasts.

It is tempting to think that, as in any profession, good training, hard work, and a skilled mind will yield superior results. And it is especially tempting to think that you possess these very characteristics. The market is not all luck, but it is more luck than nervous investors want to hear or successful investors want to admit.

## The Strong Form

The **strong form** of the efficient-market hypothesis holds that there is no information, public or private, that allows some investors to beat the market consistently. This hypothesis is contradicted by evidence that a few do profit by using information not available to other investors — often in violation of federal laws. Historically, these market beaters were usually corporate insiders who bought or sold stock in the company they worked for based on advance knowledge of new products, sales data, and so on. More recently, the feverish takeover activity of the 1980s provided valuable privileged information to accountants, lawyers, and investment bankers — a few of whom profited by purchasing stock in advance of the public announcement of the takeover bid.

Indirect evidence of the value of inside information is provided by the behavior of market prices shortly before important announcements, such as a takeover offer. According to an SEC study released in 1987, trading volume usually increases noticeably 10 days before a takeover announcement. On average, trading volume is 3 times normal 3 days before the announcement, 5 times normal the following day, and 20 times normal on the day of the announcement. The stock's price increases, on average, by 38.5 percent before the takeover attempt is formally announced. Much of this trading is an educated guess based on public information (both fact and rumor) that is widely reported in newspapers and on the Dow Jones ticker service, for instance, the filing of Form 13D with the SEC when a raider has accumulated 5 percent of a company's stock. Other investors are lured into purchases by the scent of a rising price and surging volume. Some purchases are less innocent.

Section 10(b)5 of the 1934 Securities and Exchange Act makes it

> *Unlawful for any person to employ any device, scheme or artifice to defraud or to engage in any act, practice or course of business which operates as a fraud or deceit upon any person.*

Insider information is not even mentioned, let alone defined, in this law, but over the years, the SEC has successfully applied this law to insider trading cases. The SEC is empowered to seek a penalty equal to three times illegal profits and has also sought prison terms not only for securities violations but also for such related crimes as mail or wire fraud, obstructing justice, and income tax evasion.

The SEC interprets illegal insider trading as that based on material information not yet made public if the information was obtained wrongfully (such as by theft or bribery) or if the person has a fiduciary responsibility to keep the information confidential. Nor can investors trade on the basis of information that they know or have reason to know was obtained wrongfully. For example, the SEC charged that W. Paul Thayer violated Section 10(b)5 when, as chairman of LTV, he tipped his stockbroker about two takeover bids. Both men were eventually convicted of obstructing justice and sentenced to 4 years in prison. The SEC is unlikely to press charges if it is convinced that a leak of confidential information was inadvertent, for example, a conversation overheard on an airplane. Many stock purchases and sales are made on the basis of tips and rumors from unknown sources and sources of questionable accuracy. The boundaries of insider trading are still a gray area that the courts are shaping.

The SEC frequently has taken the position that any trading in securities while in possession of material nonpublic information is illegal. By this definition, the SEC is trying to enforce a level playing field on which all traders have access to the same information — the economists' definition of an efficient market. The SEC worries that insider trading, playing with marked cards, will undermine the integrity of financial markets and drive away honest players.

The SEC has had more success winning cases based on a different principle — that insider trading is robbery, the theft of information. A recent example involved *The Wall Street Journal*'s daily column "Heard on the Street," which reports financial rumors and gossip. In 1983, R. Foster Winans was $18,000 in debt and earning $28,000 a year writing this column when Peter Brant, a leading

**EXAMPLE 9.7**   *The King of the Arbitragers*

Ivan Boesky was a high-profile trader who bet millions of dollars on takeover candidates, usually in advance of any public offer, often winning big and occasionally losing big. In 1985 he had a very hot hand, consistently buying target stocks shortly before a takeover was publicly announced. He boasted of his success and attributed it to superior judgment and sleeping only 3 hours a night:

> *We get up earlier and tend to go to bed later at night. Like all disciplines, when you apply a great deal of energy and work effort and careful judgment, then you have a greater chance of success.**

Another time he claimed,

> *What I am is the best odds-maker in the world. . . . I calculate risk better than anybody else, and that is why our firm has had the success it has. I take pride in that.†*

As it turned out, there was little or no risk because Boesky was cheating, playing poker with marked cards.

In 1986 the SEC accused Dennis Levine, the 33-year-old codirector of Drexel Burnham's mergers and acquisitions department, of trading on the basis of inside information as far back as 1980, while holding jobs at a variety of firms, and, later, of supplying Ivan Boesky with advance notice of mergers and takeovers. In return, Boesky was to pay Levine $2.4 million.

Levine agreed to pay the SEC $11.6 million in civil penalties and pleaded guilty to four felony charges, for which he was fined $362,000 and sentenced to 2 years in prison. He also revealed a network of investment bankers and lawyers who supplied him with inside information. More than a dozen men, almost all under the age of 40, pleaded guilty to felony charges and, perhaps worse, had their reputations and careers ruined.

The SEC accused Boesky of making at least $50 million in illegal profits based on inside information obtained from Levine on seven major takeovers from April of 1985 to April of 1986. Boesky agreed to pay an astonishing $100 million — $50 million in illegal profits (to reimburse investors who sold their shares to Boesky) plus a $50 million fine (to the U.S. Treasury). (Shortly before his arrest, *Fortune* estimated Boesky's wealth at about $200 million.) Boesky also pleaded guilty to a felony (for which he was sentenced to 3 years in prison), agreed to withdraw permanently from the U.S. securities industry (except as an individual investor), and cooperated with the authorities (including the secret recording of all his conversations for more than a month, until this eavesdropping was discovered).

*Quoted in Michael A. Hiltzik, "Ivan Boesky: Prominence Led to Scrutiny, Charges," Los Angeles Times, November 16, 1986.*
†*Quoted in James Srodes, "We Have All Been Robbed by Deceit of 3 'Geniuses,'" Los Angeles Times, March 1, 1987.*

broker at Kidder, Peabody, convinced Winans to give him the columns a day in advance of their publication, on the presumption that a stock's price is influenced by the appearance of a favorable or unfavorable story.[24] Some of the trades worked, and some didn't; the SEC claims that, on balance, the profits came to $690,000, of which Winans received $31,000.

Computers at the SEC and the stock exchanges monitor trading continuously, looking for unusually heavy volume and sudden price changes (announcing any unusual patterns with a computer-generated voice or whistle). Investigators then ask the company about impending announcements and look at brokerage records for suspicious connections. Even if there is no computer alert, after important news is released about a company, employees of the SEC and the exchanges both go back and look at the numbers again for suspicious prior trading activity. Considerable detective work may be needed to penetrate covers created by trades through friends, dummy corporations, and foreign banks. This search is aided by a computerized databank that lists the personal and professional associations of a half million corporate executives and members of the securities industry.

In the Winans case, the stock exchanges were alerted almost immediately by an unusually heavy volume of trading and noticed that the stocks were subsequently mentioned in the "Heard on the Street" column. Soon the SEC learned that the broker was the common denominator in the trades and established his ties to Winans, who admitted his actions. Winans was immediately fired by the *Journal* and eventually was fined and sentenced to federal prison for 18 months. The broker pleaded guilty to two counts of fraud and testified against Winans.

Winans' lawyers appealed the case to the Supreme Court, arguing that Winans had no inside information and was merely passing along gossip. His information was literally heard on the street. Interestingly, the Securities Industry Association, which represents stockbrokers, was worried that stockbrokers might be prosecuted for doing the same thing and filed a brief in support of the appeal. The SEC argued that Winans had violated a fiduciary duty, not to the companies he wrote about, but to his employer, *The Wall Street Journal*, by misappropriating confidential information about the content and timing of columns that the *Journal* planned to publish. The Supreme Court accepted the SEC's arguments and upheld Winans's conviction.

## SUMMARY

Common stock is equity, representing ownership of the company, and stockholders' dividends depend on the company's profitability. Shareholders have limited liability in that they are not personally responsible for the firm's debts. Because dividends are not a tax-deductible expense for the corporation, they are taxed twice, once as corporate profits and again as shareholder income.

Stock is initially offered through investment bankers and then traded on a stock exchange or over the counter. The largest and most prominent companies are generally listed on the New York Stock Exchange. Here, brokerage firms bring investor orders to a specialist who keeps a book of orders, executing trades when possible and buying or selling for his or her own account if this is necessary to fulfill an obligation to maintain a fair and orderly market. Off the exchanges, trades are made by consulting the bid and ask prices quoted by competing market makers.

The Dow Jones Industrial Average is calculated by adding up the per-share prices of 30 large, established companies and dividing by the current value of the divisor. The S&P 500, NYSE composite, and most other stock indexes are market-value indexes, in which each stock's price is multiplied by the number of shares outstanding, thereby reflecting what is happening to the market value of investor portfolios.

Fundamental analysis advises investors to compare a stock's market price with its intrinsic value, the present value $P$ of the prospective dividends $D_t$ (or other cash flow) using a required return $R$ that depends on the returns available on other investments and on the relative riskiness of these investments:

$$P = \frac{D_1}{(1 + R)} + \frac{D_2}{(1 + R)^2} + \frac{D_3}{(1 + R)^3} + \cdots$$

In the constant-dividend-growth model, dividends grow at a steady rate $g$, and the present value simplifies to

$$P = \frac{D_1}{R - g}$$

The intrinsic-value model can be used to explain why stock prices are buoyed by a strong economy and low interest rates. Stock prices tend to change direction a few months before the economy, suggesting that investors anticipate economic developments before such developments are reflected in unemployment and output data or that changes in the stock market influence the economy. Because stocks are long-duration assets with substantial capital risk, stock prices, like the prices of long-term bonds, are very sensitive to interest rates.

A firm should expand if the rate of return that it can earn on its investments is larger than shareholders' required rate of return. When interest rates are low, so are shareholder required returns, making it more likely that prospective investments are sufficiently profitable to justify making them on behalf of shareholders. The value of Tobin's $q$, the ratio of the market value of a firm to the replacement cost of its assets, provides a barometer of the incentives for business expansion:

$$q = \frac{\text{market value of firm}}{\text{replacement cost of firm's assets}}$$

A Ponzi scheme is a zero-sum game that transfers wealth from late entrants to early ones. The promoters, pretending to be financial wizards, send investors fraudulent financial statements and spend most of the money raised on themselves. At times, investors are overcome by what, in retrospect, seems a collective euphoria. In a speculative bubble, asset prices lose touch with intrinsic values as people hope to profit not from the asset's cash flow but from selling the asset at ever-higher prices. When buyers cannot be found, the bubble collapses and prices fall precipitously.

The efficient-market hypothesis says that there are no clearly mispriced securities whose purchase or sale will yield an abnormally large return because there are a sufficient number of well-financed investors to eliminate any obvious mispricings. One implication is that to the extent anticipated future events are already embedded in today's stock prices, price revisions are surprises caused by the occurrence of unexpected events. The weak, semistrong, and strong forms of the efficient-market hypothesis say that abnormal profits cannot be made using information about past stock prices, all public information, and all information.

# IMPORTANT TERMS

book value
constant-dividend-growth model
common stock
Dow Jones Industrial Average
efficient market
Federal Reserve Board (Fed)
fundamental analysis
intrinsic value
limited liability
over the counter (OTC)

Ponzi scheme
preferred stock
semistrong form
specialist
speculative bubble
speculators
strong form
Tobin's $q$
weak form

# EXERCISES

1. Before the 1986 Tax Reform Act, the corporate tax rate was 46 percent and the top individual tax rate was 50 percent. Taking into account the double taxation of dividends, what was the effective tax rate on a dollar of corporate profits paid out as dividends to someone in a 50 percent tax bracket?

2. *The Wall Street Journal* awarded its tongue-in-cheek 1986 "Charity Begins at Home Award"

   *To Merrill Lynch Capital Markets, for its underwriting of Home Shopping Network. Merrill priced the stock at $18 a share. The day it began trading, the stock more than doubled to $42.625. . . . By June the stock had more than doubled again to $100.*[25]

   Why is the price given to three decimal places at $42.625? The creators of Home Shopping Network sold 2 million shares to the public and kept 10 million shares for themselves. What was the total market value of the company at a price of $18? At $42.625? At $100? At $5, the price 1 year later? Did it really make any difference to anyone whether the 2 million shares were initially sold at $18 or $42 a share?

3. The investment banking firm of Morgan Stanley went public on March 21, 1986, by selling 4.5 million shares at 56½. In the secondary market, the stock closed at 71¼ that day on the NYSE. Who gained and lost from this mispricing?

4. Look in the most recent Friday newspaper to see what happened to IBM on the NYSE the previous day.
   a. What is IBM's current annual dividend?
   b. How many shares were traded on Thursday?
   c. What was the price of the last trade Thursday?

d. What was the closing price on Wednesday?

5. Look in the most recent Friday newspaper to see what happened to Apple Computer in the OTC market the previous day.
   a. What is Apple's current annual dividend?
   b. How many shares were traded on Thursday?
   c. What was the price of the last trade Thursday?
   d. What was the closing price on Wednesday?

6. Below are the closing prices on Friday, October 16, 1987, and on Monday, October 19, 1987. Do these data indicate that stock prices fell more on this "Black Monday" for large, established companies or for smaller, more speculative firms?

|  | Friday | Monday |
|---|---|---|
| Dow Industrials | 2,246.74 | 1,738.74 |
| NYSE Composite | 159.13 | 128.62 |
| AMEX Composite | 323.55 | 282.50 |
| NASDAQ | 406.33 | 360.21 |

7. The Dow Jones Industrial Average closed at 144.13 on December 31, 1935, and at 1546.67 on December 31, 1985. The Standard & Poor's 500 index closed on these same dates at 10.60 and 211.28. Which index increased more in percentage terms? Did blue-chip stocks do better or worse than average during these 50 years?

8. In 1981 a New York retailer paid $24,000 for the first case of wine (using 1979 grapes) produced in a joint venture by Robert Mondavi and Baron Philippe de Rothschild from Cabernet Sauvignon and Cabernet Franc grapes. A commentator wrote, "With such a beginning, one wonders if any bottles of the 1979 will ever be enjoyed at a meal. Would you drink up part of your investment portfolio?"[26] Would a fundamental analyst classify the purchaser of this wine as an investor or a speculator?

9. You have decided to endow an economics chair at your college named, coincidentally, in your honor. Assuming that salaries are paid once a year, at the end of each year, and that the college can earn 10 percent per year on your gift, how much must you donate in order to provide $100,000 a year forever? A trustee points out that salaries may rise each year. If this is so, how large an endowment is needed to provide $100,000 at the end of the first year and 5 percent more each succeeding year forever?

10. A certain stock is expected to pay an end-of-year dividend of $10 a share. What is its present value if
    a. The dividend is not expected to increase and the shareholders' required return is 10 percent?
    b. The dividend is expected to grow by 5 percent per year and the shareholders' required return is 10 percent?
    c. The dividend is expected to grow by 10 percent per year and the shareholders' required return is 15 percent?

11. A famous stock advisor once suggested that a conspiracy between stock specialists and bankers is suggested by the fact that

    *when you're having a decline in stock prices you can always anticipate an increase in interest rates.*[27]

    The idea is apparently that when specialists lower stock prices so that insiders can accumulate stocks cheaply, banks raise interest rates so that the public cannot borrow money to purchase stocks at these bargain prices. Is there any nonconspiratorial explanation for the observation that a drop in stock prices is often accompanied by an increase in interest rates?

12. On July 19, 1984, Chrysler sold all the stocks in its pension fund and bought bonds with the proceeds. In January of 1987, rumors that Chrysler was going back into stocks

    *prompted some guffaws on Wall Street because, on the surface, it might appear that Chrysler has missed an enormous stock rally and now wants to get back in at the top.*

    *But it isn't quite that simple, because the bond market did nearly as well as the stock market in the 2½ years between July 1984 and December 1986.*

    *In that period . . . the S&P 500-stock index returned 25% annually, counting dividends . . . [while] the Shearson Lehman aggregate bond index returned 22.4% annually. . . . In fact, the bonds held by Chrysler equaled the stock market's performance because they were slightly longer in maturity than the Shearson index.*[28]

    What economic event would explain simultaneous bond and stock market rallies? What do you think maturity has to do with performance?

13. An article in the *American Banker's Association Journal* discusses the estimation of commercial damages when one company's violation of a contract forces another to go out of business.[29] Instead of trying to estimate the liquidation value, the author argues that a company with current net earnings of $50,000 growing at 5 percent a year would, at a 25 percent discount rate, have a "capitalization rate" of 5, giving it a value of 5($50,000) = $250,000. Where did the value 5 for the capitalization rate come from?

14. In 1986 Michael Sherman, who heads Shearson Lehman's investment policy committee, recommended a portfolio of 70 percent stocks, 30 percent long-term bonds, and no short-term bonds. "If you have cash [short-term bonds] in your account, it means you don't trust what you're doing. . . . More stocks than bonds generally indicates a positive outlook both in Treasury rates and the economy."[30] (The opposite occurred in early 1982, when more bonds than stocks in portfolios said that investors liked interest rates but not the economy.) Explain why forecasts of interest rates and the economy should influence the portfolio allocation between stocks and bonds. Are there any circumstances in which you would recommend holding a substantial amount of "cash"?

15. Peter L. Bernstein found that stock and bond prices generally moved in opposite directions during most of the 1960s but in the same direction in the 1970s.[31] Is there any logical explanation?

16. Here are excerpts from a 1986 newspaper article:

    *The underlying U.S. economy today is not strong enough to support the market's enthusiasm, and it is not gaining. The force driving stock prices up is declining interest rates (and oil prices). Well, interest rates decline when lenders have lots of money but borrowers don't have lots of need for it; that is, when business is slow. Like now.*

    *Every new statistic — retail sales off a bit, unemployment up a bit — indicates that the economy is only so-so. Which wouldn't be so bad if the outlook for the economy were better. But it's not.*

    *Despite lower interest rates, business doesn't seem in a hurry to invest in new plant and equipment. . . .*

    *What does it all mean? Only that the economy will putter along — no disaster but no great glory either — and the stock market will probably take a sharp decline.*[32]

    Is there any rational explanation for why the stock market might be strong even while the economy is not?

17. In 1948 a distinguished economist proclaimed, "Never in the lifetime of anyone in this room will government two-and-a-halves [$2\frac{1}{2}$ percent coupon bonds] sell below par."[33] Was he right?

18. The International Bank of Roseau made this offer: for $300, you can receive a short course on international banking and earn the right to sign others up for this course. If you sign up six people, you receive a $1000 "loan" from the bank that does not have to be repaid. Suppose that you sign up six people, and each of these signs up six people, and so on eight more times. How many people will have taken this course? How much money will the bank have taken in and paid out? Why do you think the Florida attorney general shut down this bank?

19. In late 1983, the J. David Investment Company sent a memo to a bank stating that J. David's cash-flow problems were temporary, because its investor requests for withdrawals could soon be satisfied by the arrival of funds from new investors. Why might such a memo suggest fraud? Why might a legitimate business do the same thing with no fraud whatsoever? If you were a bank officer, how would you tell the difference?

20. A newspaper columnist wrote:

    *More than $500 billion was wiped off stock prices on Oct. 19. . . . Yet there is hope, even a growing belief, that somehow that $500-billion loss doesn't touch the real American economy.*

    *Unfortunately, the hope is false — as you'll see if you think about it. The $500 billion was real enough when it increased corporate cash flow; real enough when investors paid it out for stocks at high prices. Stocks do not rise on air, but on somebody paying real money to buy them.*

    *Where is that real money now? It is gone. It is as if that $500 billion had built 10,000 factories and office buildings and*

    *homes and shopping centers and they had all burned down in a single day.*[34]

    a. Do investors buying stock increase a corporation's cash flow?
    b. If the market value of a company's stock rises by $1 million, must investors have purchased $1 million worth of stock?
    c. Where does the money that investors spend on stock go?
    d. If you were the President of the United States, would you rather have the stock market fall by $500 billion or have $500 billion worth of factories destroyed by fire?

21. The fifth edition of Graham and Dodd's classic *Security Analysis* was published in late 1987, updated by three long-time associates.[35] In it they use the following economic projections from financial institutions to estimate the fundamental value of the S&P 400 industrial stock index:

    Dividend = $9

    Growth rate = 7.5 percent

    Required return = 11.25 percent (8.5 percent Aaa industrial bond rate + 2.75 percent risk premium)

    On October 13, 1987, the actual value of the S&P 400 index was 364. What was their estimate of fundamental value?

22. Explain why this advice is not very helpful:

    *Since we know stocks are going to fall as well as rise, we might as well get a little traffic out of them. A man who buys a stock at 10 and sells it at 20 makes 100 percent. But a man who buys it at 10, sells it at 14½, buys it back at 12 and sells it at 18, buys it back at 15 and sells it at 20, makes 188 percent.*[36]

23. A man gives inspirational lectures on how to make a fortune in real estate by buying "bargain properties"; for example, "if you buy a $100,000 house for $80,000, you've got a

$20,000 profit right off the bat." If this is so, is the real estate market efficient? If the real estate market is reasonably efficient, what is the flaw in this man's advice?

24. Briefly explain why the following allegations, if true, either would or would not provide evidence against the efficient-market hypothesis.

   a. A well-known investment strategy consistently earns a return greater than zero.

   b. When the stock market goes down in January, it usually goes down during the next 11 months.

   c. The stock market almost always goes up at least 20 percent in the 9 months preceding presidential elections and goes down 20 percent during the 12 months following elections.

   d. Corporate bonds consistently give higher returns than municipal bonds.

25. Explain why you won't get rich following this advice in Consumer Digest's *Get Rich Investment Guide*:

   *The ability to track interest rates as they pertain to bonds is made easier by following the path of the Prime Rate (the rate of interest charged by banks to their top clients). If the consensus shown in top business journals indicates that rates are going up, this means that bonds will go down in price. Therefore, when it seems that rates are moving up, an investor should wait until some "peaking" of rates is foreseen.* [37]

26. An advertisement for a penny stock report was headlined "5500% Profit" and said:

   *EXAMPLE: On Sept. 1983 if you had purchased 25,000 shares of MAX AXAM at .25 a share ($6250), you could have sold on Feb. 1986 at $14.00 per share and pocketed $350,000. Imagine a gain of 5500%!* [38]

   Why is this example unpersuasive?

27. In November of 1985, Edward Yardeni, of Prudential-Bache, said, "We still like stocks not so much because we foresee better-than-expected profits, but because we foresee lower-than-expected interest rates." [39] Why was he careful to say "lower-than-expected" interest rates rather than just "lower interest rates"?

28. In 1987 a brokerage firm observed that "since 1965, the Dow Jones Industrial Average declined 16 out of 21 times during the month of May. As of this writing, it appears as if another down May is in the offing. We offer no rational explanation for this 'May phenomenon.' We only observe that it often sets up attractive trading opportunities." [40] Does the evidence in this quotation persuade you to buy lots of stock next April? Why or why not?

29. R. Foster Winans, who leaked stories to be published in *The Wall Street Journal*, wrote, "The only reason to invest in the market is because you think you know something others don't." [41] Is there any other reason to buy stock? If everyone had exactly the same information, do you think anyone would buy stock?

30. In 1983 the SEC enforcement chief said, "Anyone who engages in insider trading is clearly a thief." [42] Explain what the following insiders are stealing and from whom they are stealing it.

   a. A chemist discovers a cure for baldness and buys stock in the company he works for before revealing his discovery.

   b. A company's chief executive officer sells half of her stock in the company before she releases a disappointing earnings report.

   c. A merger and acquisitions lawyer working for a corporate raider buys stock in the target company before a tender offer is announced.

# 10 Risk and Return

*The safest way to double your money is to fold it over once and put it in your pocket.*

**Frank McKinney Hubbard**

Our lives are filled with uncertainties, ranging from tomorrow's weather to the success of a marriage to war and peace. Should you invite someone to a movie? Should you accept a job offer? Should you buy a house or rent an apartment? Financial market participants, too, must confront the unknown. What interest rates should banks offer on deposits? Should a borrower choose an adjustable-rate or fixed-rate loan? Will short- or long-term bonds be a more profitable investment?

Uncertainty, with all the attendant excitement and frustration, is unavoidable. However, in both our personal and business decisions, we can use probabilities to make rational choices. There will still be surprises, pleasant and unpleasant, but we can anticipate, on average, faring better if we think about our alternatives and the likely consequences before we act.

A number of techniques have been developed to help people make rational decisions in an uncertain world, and these tools can be applied to a wide variety of choices. This chapter discusses how uncertainty often can be quantified by specifying probabilities and calculating two statistical measures — the mean and the standard deviation. You will see that these two measures are useful for describing opportunities, but that our choices ultimately depend on our attitude toward risk. Two asset pricing models will then be used to explain why some assets must offer relatively high expected returns to appeal to risk-averse investors. We begin by looking at how probabilities can be used to gauge uncertainty.

## USING PROBABILITIES

Whenever there is uncertainty, more than one outcome is possible. *Probabilities* can be used to quantify our uncertainty by describing which outcomes are likely and which are unlikely. When a coin is fairly flipped, the two possible outcomes, heads and tails, are equally likely, so we assign a probability of $\frac{1}{2}$ to each outcome. What about an investment with two possible outcomes, a $100 loss and a $200 gain? If a financial analyst considers these outcomes equally likely, then each has a probability of $\frac{1}{2}$. If the $100 loss is twice as likely as the $200 gain, then there is a $\frac{2}{3}$ probability of a $100 loss and a $\frac{1}{3}$ probability of a $200 gain.

## Subjective Probabilities

With coins, dice, and cards, we may be able to calculate probabilities by analyzing the physical objects involved and counting the number of equally likely outcomes. In other situations, historical data may be useful: the 0.51 probability that an unborn baby is male and the 0.53 probability that a 20-year-old female will live to be 80 can be estimated from the observed frequencies with which babies are male and females live to be 80. In most personal and business decisions we must use subjective probabilities to assess the likelihood of various outcomes.

Consider, for instance, the probability that the next president of the United States will be a Republican. Unlike a coin flip, the chances are not invariably 50 percent. In 1946, the "Wizard of Odds" used historical data:

> *Miss Deanne Skinner of Monrovia, California, asks: Can the Wizard tell me what the odds are of the next President of the United States being a Democrat? . . . Without considering the candidates, the odds would be 2 to 1 in favor of a Republican because since 1861 when that party was founded, there have been 12 Republican Presidents and only 7 Democrats.*[1]

The probability that the next president will be Republican need not equal the historical frequency with which presidents have been Republican. The electorate, the parties, the candidates, and the nation all evolve as time passes, making the outcome of an election 100 years ago of little relevance today.

In 1936 Democrat Franklin Roosevelt ran for reelection against Republican Alf Landon. Should the forecasters have assumed that Landon had a 70 percent chance of winning because Republicans had won 70 percent of the previous contests? Or should they have taken into account that Roosevelt was a popular president running for reelection against the unexciting governor of Kansas, the standard bearer of the party that many voters blamed for the Great Depression? Were the odds the same in 1972 when Republican Richard Nixon ran against liberal Democrat George McGovern as in 1964 when conservative Republican Barry Goldwater battled incumbent Democrat Lyndon Johnson? Were George Bush's chances in 1988 identical to Landon's in 1936? The odds change from election to election, along with the candidates and the state of the nation.

So it is with many situations. If you buy a certain computer program, what is the probability that 6 months from now you will regret having done so? It is not a 50–50 coin flip, and you surely shouldn't estimate the probability simply by calculating the historical frequency with which people regret their purchases. Your chances of being dissatisfied depend on your needs and the details of this particular program.

EXAMPLE
10.1

## *Probabilities Clarify Our Views*

In some situations, such as a severe sunburn or a broken bone, the doctor is certain about the patient's medical condition. Other conditions, such as heart disease, are uncertain, and a diagnosis may be clarified with probabilities. Consider a patient who takes an electrocardiographic stress test and shows some inconclusive symptoms of coronary heart disease. When the patient asks, "Do I have heart disease?" a definite answer of "yes" or "no" is unwarranted because the test is imperfect. The patient should be told that the results suggest disease, but words alone can be misunderstood.

When 16 doctors were asked to assign a numerical probability to the diagnosis "cannot be excluded," the answers ranged from 5 percent probability to 95 percent, with an average of 47 percent.* When they were asked to interpret "likely," the probabilities ranged from 20 to 95 percent, with an average of 75 percent. Even the phrase "low probability" elicited answers ranging from 0 to 80 percent, with an average of 18 percent. If, by "low probability," one doctor means an 80 percent chance and another means no chance at all, then it is better to state the probability that one has in mind than to risk an unfortunate misinterpretation of ambiguous words.

The same lesson applies to a diagnosis of economic conditions. Instead of saying that the possibility of higher interest rates "cannot be excluded" or that a recession "is likely," financial analysts should use probabilities to clarify their forecasts and ensure that their views are understood.

*George A. Diamond and James S. Forrester, "Metadiagnosis," The American Journal of Medicine, July 1983, pp. 129–137.

A decision to buy long-term bonds also depends on subjective probabilities. Information on past interest-rate fluctuations may be useful, but the present situation is always unique. An assessment of the chances of interest rates rising or falling must be a subjective blending of information about such matters as the state of the economy, government monetary policy, and the volatility of bond prices.

The best alternative to a shrug of the shoulders and a sheepish "Who knows?" is to list the possible outcomes and use whatever information is at our disposal to assign probabilities as best we can. Unlike a coin flip, financial probabilities no doubt vary from person to person, leading some to believe that one investment is very attractive, while others think the opposite. This disagreement is one reason why there are financial markets — so that the "bulls" can buy from the "bears."

## Probability Distributions

Outcomes are seldom as simple as the heads/tails possibilities for a coin flip. The infinite variety of possible returns precludes an exhaustive enumeration, and so, instead, we specify a **probability distribution**, giving the probabilities for ranges of outcomes. Table 10.1 shows a probability distribution for a hypothetical investment. There is a 0.10 probability that the return will turn out to be between 20 and 30 percent, a 0.30 probability that it will be between 10 and 20 percent, and so on. Figure 10.1 is a graphic representation of this probability distribution in which the area of each block shows the probability for that range of outcomes. With a graph we can tell at a glance which outcomes are considered likely and which are thought unlikely. Example 10.2 tells how Morgan Guaranty uses probability distributions to help make its investment decisions.

| Table 10.1 | A Probability Distribution for an Investment Return |
| --- | --- |
| **Return** | **Probability** |
| 20 to 30% | 0.10 |
| 10 to 20% | 0.30 |
| 0 to 10% | 0.30 |
| −10 to 0% | 0.20 |
| −20 to −10% | 0.10 |
| | 1.00 |

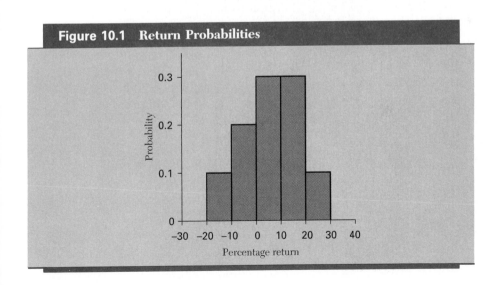

**Figure 10.1    Return Probabilities**

**EXAMPLE
10.2**

## *Interest-Rate Uncertainty at Morgan Guaranty*

The success of asset/liability decisions made by financial institutions depends critically on future interest rates. When interest rates rise unexpectedly, those who invested long term at a fixed interest rate and those who borrowed short term at a variable interest rate find that they made an expensive mistake. An unexpected drop in interest rates is costly for those who invested short term or borrowed long term. Yet interest rates are notoriously difficult to forecast.

Until 1971, the top managers at Morgan Guaranty Trust met regularly to determine the interest-rate forecasts to use in all asset/liability decisions. For each interest-rate prediction, they would come up with a single number, such as "our best estimate of the Treasury-bill (T-bill) rate 3 months from now is 6 percent." Yet, as the senior operations research officer explained,

> *Considerable discussion normally preceded the managers' arrival at the single-valued expectation, but there was no formal procedure for quantifying the collective expectations of the participants, and the uncertainty surrounding these expectations.**

How confident were they in their 6 percent forecast? Did they mean $5\frac{3}{4}$ percent to $6\frac{1}{4}$ percent or 4 percent to 8 percent? If the T-bill rate isn't 6 percent, is it more likely to be somewhat higher or a bit lower? The answers to such questions require probabilities, and so, in 1971, they began reporting probabilities in place of a single interest-rate forecast.

Twice a month, specialists write down interest-rate probabilities individually and then meet as a group to compare notes. Instead of thinking of the most likely value for the interest rate, perhaps 6 percent, each member thinks of the possible values — 5 percent, $5\frac{1}{2}$ percent, 6 percent, and so on — and assigns probabilities to each possibility.

The probability distribution in panel (a) of the accompanying figure reflects a committee member who is pretty confident that the T-bill rate will be 6 percent; the distribution in panel (b) shows considerable uncertainty. In panels (c) and (d), 6 percent is the most likely value, but in one case the person feels that there is a good chance that the T-bill rate will be less than 6 percent and in the other the opposite is true. None of these subtleties is revealed in a 6 percent forecast that is unaccompanied by probabilities. With probabilities, we can see not only the most likely value but also the likely range, and we can see whether the individual believes that the rate is more likely to be above or below 6 percent.

*This quotation and the accompanying discussion are based on Irwin Kabus, "You Can Bank on Uncertainty," Harvard Business Review, May/June 1976, pp. 95–105.

**Four Interest-Rate Forecasts**

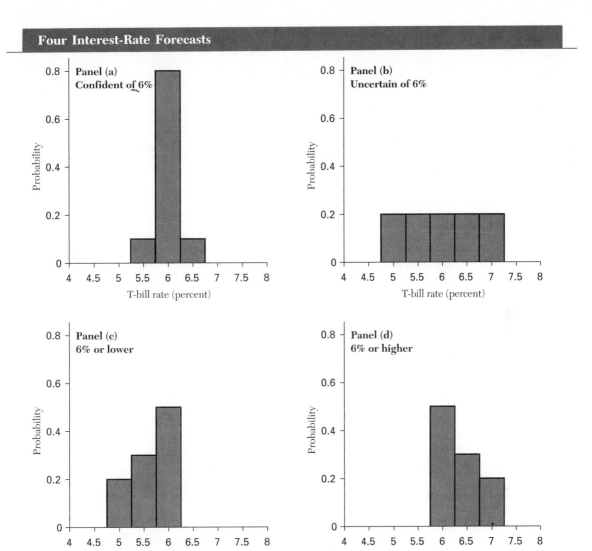

The senior research officer described the value of these probability graphs at a November 13, 1972 group meeting:

*It was useful to know why both Griffin and Riefler felt the rate would stay essentially the same, whereas the others felt it would rise; and to find out why Engle felt that there was no chance the rate would drop below $5\frac{1}{8}$% and felt so strongly that it would rise over $5\frac{5}{8}$ percent, when nobody else in the group felt that way.*

After such discussion, the committee constructs a consensus probability distribution, which is then presented to top management.

The probabilities used by Morgan Guaranty are necessarily subjective, but they accomplish their task of describing the beliefs of committee members:

*The only "incorrect" [distribution] is one which does not correctly reflect its creators' expectations. While there is no guarantee that [probability distributions] will give an accurate picture of the future, they will give an accurate picture of an individual's view of the future.*

# EXPECTED RETURN

Probabilities can be used to help us make informed decisions. Probability theory was originally developed in the 1600s by Blaise Pascal, Pierre de Fermet, and other mathematicians interested in games of chance. One of the questions that Pascal sought to answer was posed by a French nobleman, the Chevalier de Mere. The nobleman asked why, on average, he made money betting that he could roll at least one 6 in 4 throws of a single dice but lost money betting that he could roll at least one double-6 in 24 throws of a pair of dice. Pascal showed that de Mere, in fact, had a 0.518 probability of winning the first bet but only a 0.491 probability of winning the second. With these probabilities, Pascal could calculate de Mere's expected profits.

## *Calculation of the Expected Return*

The **expected value**, usually denoted by the Greek lowercase letter $\mu$ (pronounced "mew"), is a weighted average of the possible returns that uses probabilities as weights to reflect the likelihood of each outcome. Suppose, for instance, that there are two outcomes, winning or losing $100, and each is equally likely:

| Return $x_i$ | Probability $P[x_i]$ |
|:---:|:---:|
| + $100 | 0.5 |
| − $100 | 0.5 |

The expected value uses the probabilities to average these two possibilities:

$$\mu = (+\$100)(0.5) + (-\$100)(0.5) = 0$$

The general formula for the expected value is

$$\mu = x_1 P[x_1] + x_2 P[x_2] + \cdots + x_n P[x_n] \qquad (10.1)$$

The expected value is a statistical average, not, as in everyday English, the outcome that we expect or consider most likely. Indeed, in the example there is no chance that you will win \$0 — you will either win \$100 or lose \$100. The expected value is the long-run average return if the frequency with which each outcome occurs is equal to its probability. If you do win \$100 half the time and lose \$100 the other half, your average winnings will be zero.

The expected value can be used to measure the amount, on average, that de Mere could expect to win or lose in his gambles. If he bet the equivalent of \$100 that he could roll one 6 in 4 throws of a single dice, then his expected value is

$$(+\$100)(0.518) + (-\$100)(0.482) = \$3.60$$

On a single wager, de Mere will win or lose \$100. However, in the long run, if, as expected, he wins 51.8 percent of these bets, he will win an average of \$3.60 per wager. On his second game, betting that he could roll at least one double-6 in 24 throws of a pair of dice, the 0.491 chance of winning gives an expected value of

$$(+\$100)(0.491) + (-\$100)(0.509) = -\$1.80$$

showing that he could expect his losses to average \$1.80 per wager.

## Should You Maximize the Expected Return?

Pascal and other early probability theorists used probabilities to calculate the expected value of various games of chance and determine which were the most profitable. They assumed that a rational person would choose the course of action with the highest expected value. This expected-value criterion is appealing for gambles that are repeated over and over. It makes good sense to look at the long-run average when there is a long run to average over. Casinos, state lotteries, and insurance companies are very interested in the expected returns on the repetitive gambles they offer, because anything with a negative expected return will almost certainly be unprofitable in the long run.

However, an expected-return criterion is often inappropriate. State lotteries have a positive expected return for the state and, because their gain is your loss, a negative expected return for people who buy lottery tickets. Those who buy lottery tickets are not maximizing expected return. Insurance policies give insurance companies a positive expected return and insurance buyers a negative expected return. People who buy insurance are not maximizing expected return either. Diversified investments provide yet another example. An expected-return maximizer should invest everything in the single asset with the highest expected return. Individuals and financial institutions that hold dozens or thousands of assets must not be maximizing expected return.

We also can construct hypothetical situations to show that expected-return maximization is not always appealing. Suppose that a messenger from a rich recluse were to burst into class and announce that you have been chosen to receive a gift of \$1 million. She opens a briefcase filled with \$100 bills to show you that she is serious, but as you reach for them, she closes her briefcase and asks if you would like something a bit more sporting. You can either take the \$1 million, or you can flip a coin five times. If you get heads on every flip, you get $40 million; any tails and you get nothing but a good story. Think about it. If, like most people, you would take the sure million, then you are not maximizing expected return.

# RISK AVERSION

The primary inadequacy of expected-return maximization is that it neglects risk — how certain or uncertain a situation is. An expected return maximizer considers a sure $1 million, a 50 percent chance at $2 million, and a 1 percent chance at $100 million all equally attractive because each has an expected value of $1 million. If these alternatives were offered over and over, there would be little difference in the long run because the payoffs from each would almost certainly average close to $1 million per play. However, if you only get one chance at this game, the possible payoffs are very different, a difference ignored by an expected-value calculation. In an expected-return computation it doesn't matter that in the first option there is a 100 percent chance of receiving $1 million and in the third option there is a 99 percent chance of receiving nothing. This difference does matter to many people, however.

Much of the uncertainty that we face is unique, not repetitive, and it does matter that the actual outcome may differ from its expected value. This possible divergence is called **risk**; the way in which people react reflects their risk preferences.

Risk preferences can be gauged by whether a person prefers to take a gamble or, instead, to receive the expected value of the gamble. Consider, for example, a gamble with a 50 percent chance of receiving $100 and a 50 percent chance of receiving nothing. Would you rather take this gamble or, instead, receive $50, which is the gamble's expected value? There is no right or wrong answer, but how you answer reveals your attitude toward risk.

There are three broad categories of risk preference:

A person who is **risk neutral** chooses the alternative with the highest expected return and, thus, is indifferent between a safe $50 and a 50 percent chance at $100.

A person who is **risk seeking** would rather take the gamble than receive its expected value.

A person who is **risk averse** prefers the expected value to the gamble and takes the $50.

While the risk-neutral person maximizes expected return, a risk-seeking person is willing to give up some expected return to get more risk, and a risk-averse person is willing to give up expected return to avoid risk. A risk-neutral person does not like insurance or lottery tickets because both have negative expected returns. A risk-seeking person may buy lottery tickets even if the expected return is negative. A risk-averse person may purchase insurance with a negative expected return.

## Risk Bearing

This acknowledged variety in risk preferences explains why some people accept gambles that others shun and why some buy insurance that others avoid. A person's response to risk also may depend on the size of the gamble. It is not unreasonable to be risk neutral about a wager involving a few dollars but risk averse about a gamble involving all one's wealth. You might flip a coin to see who buys coffee — and still buy fire insurance.

One implication of this argument is that wealthy citizens may take gambles that others shun because these gambles have a relatively small effect on their wealth. People who own little more than the house they live in buy fire and life insurance, even though the expected return is negative, to avoid the possibility of a catastrophic loss. For the very wealthy, the loss of a house or wages has little effect on family wealth, and a decision not to purchase insurance is a relatively small gamble with a positive expected return.

---

**EXAMPLE**
**10.3**

### Risk Has Its Rewards

If investors are risk averse, they will shun risky investments unless the price is right — that is, unless they are compensated for bearing that risk with a relatively high expected return. A high return cannot, of course, be guaranteed for a risky investment because then it wouldn't be risky. However, a risky investment can be priced low enough to have a high expected value. Therefore, if investors are predominantly risk averse, investments with high standard deviations should have high expected returns.

The annual data shown in the table below confirm this intuition. These are the average and standard deviation of annual realized returns, how well investments did rather than how well investors thought they would do. Nonetheless, the calculations are an intriguing confirmation of our common sense. The safest asset, short-term Treasury bills, also has been the least rewarding, whereas the riskiest investment, common stock, has done the best on average. Stocks went up 54 percent one year and down 43 percent another year. They have been a risky, but also a rewarding, investment.

| Annual Returns, 1926–1990 | | |
|---|---|---|
| | Average Return (%) | Standard Deviation (%) |
| Common stock | 12.2 | 20.8 |
| Long-term corporate bonds | 5.5 | 8.5 |
| Long-term Treasury bonds | 4.9 | 8.5 |
| Short-term Treasury bills | 3.7 | 3.4 |

**Source:** Based on Roger G. Ibbotson and Rex A. Sinquefield, *Stocks, Bonds, Bills, and Inflation: 1991 Yearbook* (Chicago: Ibbotson Associates, Inc., 1992).

In fact, a wealthy person might be willing to sell insurance to a person of more modest means. Consider an individual, named Joe, who owns a $50,000 house and little else. This house is near an earthquake fault, and Joe is afraid that he will lose his house in a quake. Jane, on the other hand, is very rich, and winning or losing $50,000 is, for her, like Joe flipping a coin to see who pays for beer. If both believe that the probability that the house will be destroyed by an earthquake is 0.001 and Jane is risk neutral about a $50,000 gamble, she may offer to insure Joe against an earthquake for a $100 fee. The expected value of the insurance payoff is

$$0.001(\$50,000) + 0.999(\$0) = \$'$$

only half the $100 cost of the policy. A risk-neutral pe·    'ike Jane, is willing to take this gamble, selling for $100 something with an ex,     ed value of $50. Joe, on the other hand, may be sufficiently risk averse that he ᵣays $100 to avoid a gamble with an expected loss of $50. If so, there is room for a deal, in that Joe is willing to buy what Jane is willing to sell.

An earthquake is a real physical danger, a natural risk that has to be borne by someone. Those who are the least risk averse are the most willing to bear such risks. Those who are more risk averse can, for a price, use financial contracts to pass such risks on to others. In the same way, stocks and bonds reflect real economic risks — including the chances of recession or high interest rates — and their prices are set so that, considering the risk and the expected return, some investors are willing to hold such assets.

## The Standard Deviation as a Measure of Risk

Drawing on their statistical backgrounds, in the 1950s Harry Markowitz and James Tobin proposed measuring risk by the standard deviation of the probability distribution — a procedure that is widely used today by financial analysts.[2] If the possible returns are denoted by $x$ and the expected value of $x$ by $\mu$, then the **variance** $\sigma^2$ of a probability distribution is the expected value of $(x - \mu)^2$, that is, the probability-weighted, average squared deviation of the possible outcomes about their mean:

$$\sigma^2 = (x_1 - \mu)^2 P[x_1] + (x_2 - \mu)^2 P[x_2] + \cdots + (x_n - \mu)^2 P[x_n] \qquad (10.2)$$

The square root of the variance is the **standard deviation** $\sigma$ (pronounced "sigma").

For each possible outcome $x_i$ we calculate how far $x_i$ is from its expected value $\mu$ and then square this deviation. By squaring, we do two things. First, we eliminate the distinction between positive and negative deviations. What matters to a variance calculation is how far the outcome is from $\mu$, not whether it is above or below $\mu$. Second, squaring gives primary importance to large deviations. One deviation of 10 squared will increase the variance by as much as four deviations of 5 squared.

After calculating the squared deviations for each possible outcome, we calculate the average squared deviation using the outcome probabilities as

| Table 10.2 | Gauging Three Investments | | |
|---|---|---|---|
| Investment | Expected Return | Variance | Standard Deviation |
| 1-year Treasury bills $P[8\%] = 1$ | 8% | 0 | 0% |
| 10-year Treasury zeros $P[18\%] = 0.5$ $P[-2\%] = 0.5$ | 8% | 100 | 10% |
| 20-year Treasury zeros $P[30\%] = 0.5$ $P[-10\%] = 0.5$ | 10% | 400 | 20% |

weights. This weighted average of the squared deviations from $\mu$ is the variance, and its square root is the standard deviation. Either can be used, but the standard deviation is usually easier to interpret because it has the same units (percent or dollars) as $x$ and $\mu$, whereas the units for the variance are percent squared or dollars squared.

The standard deviation measures uncertainty by considering the probability of returns far from the expected value. Table 10.2 illustrates this principle by showing the means, variances, and standard deviations of the returns after 1 year for three alternative investments. This investor's calculations assume, unrealistically, that there are only two possible outcomes: interest rates will rise or fall by 1 percentage point.

The return on 1-year Treasury bills has an expected value of 8 percent and a standard deviation of 0 percent because the return is certain. For the 10-year Treasury zeros, the return will be either 18 percent or $-2$ percent. The mean is

$$\mu = (18\%)(0.5) + (-2\%)(0.5) = 8\%$$

and the variance is

$$\sigma^2 = (18\% - 8\%)^2(0.5) + (-2\% - 8\%)^2(0.5) = 100$$

which implies a standard deviation of

$$\sigma = \sqrt{100} = 10\%$$

For the 20-year Treasury zeros, the return will be either 30 percent or $-10$ percent. The mean, variance, and standard deviation are

$$\mu = (30\%)(0.5) + (-10\%)(0.5) = 10\%$$
$$\sigma^2 = (30\% - 10\%)^2(0.5) + (-10\% - 10\%)^2(0.5) = 400$$
$$\sigma = \sqrt{400} = 20\%$$

The Treasury bills and 10-year Treasury zeros both have an 8 percent expected return but different degrees of uncertainty or risk. Treasury bills have a 0 percent standard deviation because the return is certain to be 8 percent. The

10-year Treasury zeros have a large standard deviation and the 20-year Treasury zeros have an even larger standard deviation because there is a substantial chance that the return will be far from its expected value.

If the standard deviation is an appropriate measure of risk, then a risk-averse investor prefers Treasury bills to these 10-year zeros and, depending on the degree of risk aversion, also may prefer them to the 20-year zeros. A risk-neutral or risk-seeking investor prefers the 20-year zeros.

## The Normal Distribution

Often it is useful to assume that the possible returns in an uncertain situation can be approximated by a standard probability distribution, such as the bell-shaped Gaussian distribution, or **normal distribution**, shown in Figure 10.2.

Many outcomes are the cumulative consequence of a large number of random events. The central-limit theorem, the most important discovery in the long history of probability and statistics, says that outcomes that are the cumulation of independent, identically distributed random events are approximately normally distributed. In nature, the number of ridges on scallop shells, the number of kernels on ears of corn, the number of leaves on trees, the number of hairs on dogs, the breadths of human skulls, heights, weights, IQ scores, and the positions of molecules and planets all conform to an approximate normal distribution.

In financial markets, asset returns may be the cumulative consequence of independent random events and so may be approximately normally distributed. For example, Figure 10.3 shows that the distribution of the daily returns from

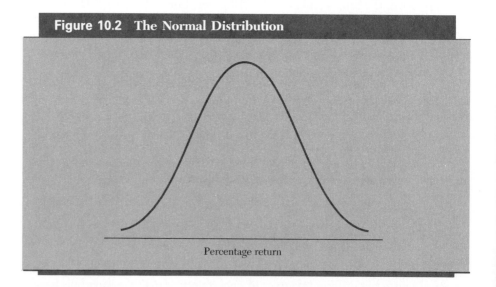

**Figure 10.2   The Normal Distribution**

Percentage return

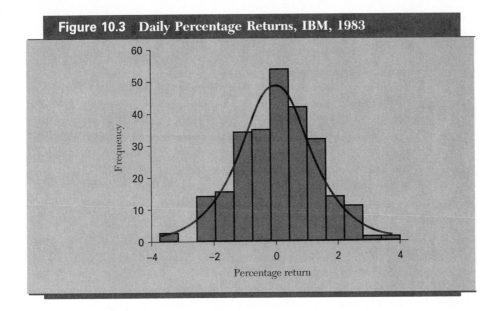

**Figure 10.3   Daily Percentage Returns, IBM, 1983**

IBM stock in 1983 is roughly normal, with a mean of 0.12 percent and a standard deviation of 1.28 percent. The actual distribution is not exactly normal, but it is close enough so that the normal distribution can be used as a simplifying approximation.

Two convenient rules of thumb can help us interpret the standard deviation of a normally distributed random variable. There is about a $\frac{2}{3}$ probability (more precisely, 0.683) that the value of a normally distributed variable will be within 1 standard deviation of its mean and a 0.95 probability that it will be within 2 standard deviations. For the IBM data in Figure 10.3, the 1 standard deviation rule of thumb tells us that approximately 68 percent of the daily returns should be in the interval $0.12 \pm 1.28$ percent, that is $-1.16$ percent to 1.40 percent. In fact, 69 percent fall in this range. With a normal distribution, there is a 95 percent probability of being within 2 standard deviations of the mean; 96 percent of the IBM daily returns are in this range.

## Long Shots and Skewness

The standard deviation is a satisfactory measure of risk if the returns are, like the daily IBM returns, approximately normally distributed. Some asset returns, however, are very asymmetrical, and the standard deviation is not an adequate explanation of why investors find these assets appealing or unattractive. For example, why do otherwise risk-averse people, who buy insurance and own diversified portfolios, buy lottery tickets — a risky long shot with a negative expected return? Similarly, the relatively low average return and high standard

**Table 10.3**   **Two Asymmetrical Investments**

| Investment | Expected Return | Standard Deviation |
|---|---|---|
| 1. $P[-\$100] = 0.999$<br>$P[\$99,900] = 0.001$ | $0 | $3,160.70 |
| 2. $P[-\$99,900] = 0.001$<br>$P[\$100] = 0.999$ | $0 | $3,160.70 |

deviation cannot explain why risk-averse people buy stock in young, unproven companies, hoping to catch the start of an eventual spectacular success such as IBM or McDonald's.

Because the squaring of deviations about the mean treats gains and losses symmetrically, the standard deviation cannot distinguish between the two investments in Table 10.3. These investments have the same expected value and the same standard deviation, yet many people prefer the first asset to the second. Unlike the normal distribution, these investments have very asymmetrical, skewed returns. The first is a positively skewed long shot with a small chance of a large gain; the second is a negatively skewed long shot with a small chance of a large loss. Figure 10.4 shows continuous probability distributions with similar positive and negative skewness.

The purchase of a lottery ticket is a positively skewed gamble, like the first investment in Table 10.3, but with a negative expected return. A decision not to purchase fire insurance is a negatively skewed gamble, similar to asset 2, but with a positive expected return. The use of the standard deviation to measure risk explains why a risk-averse person might buy insurance and spurn lottery tickets,

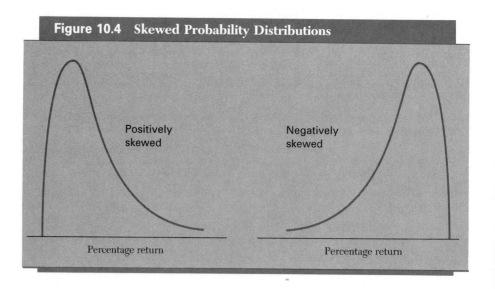

**Figure 10.4**   **Skewed Probability Distributions**

Positively skewed

Negatively skewed

Percentage return

Percentage return

whereas a risk seeker does the opposite. However, the standard deviation offers no easy explanation for the simultaneous purchase of both lottery tickets and insurance.

Perhaps some otherwise risk-averse people enjoy the mild suspense provided by lottery tickets and consider the purchase inexpensive, if brief, entertainment. Or they may have a very mistaken assessment of their chances of winning (what Adam Smith called "absurd presumptions in their own good fortune"[3]). Another explanation is that people care not only about the uncertainty, as gauged by the standard deviation, but also about the skewness. Long shots offer them the slim chance of changing their lives completely, or as one Pennsylvania woman put it, "My chances of winning a million are better than my chances of earning a million."[4]

The popularity of lottery tickets suggests that people like positively skewed returns, a conclusion that is supported by the overbetting on long shots at horse races and by a number of empirical studies.[5] Consequently, we should be cautious in using the standard deviation alone to gauge risk if the probability distribution for the returns is highly skewed, such as with lottery tickets and stock in new companies. In other situations, where the probability distribution is reasonably symmetrical (or, even better, approximately normal), the standard deviation is a very simple and powerful way to measure risk.

# THE GAINS FROM DIVERSIFICATION

We will now use an investment decision faced by banks to illustrate an important principle that applies to all investors. A risk-neutral investor maximizes expected return by investing all funds in the single asset with the highest expected return. A risk-averse person, in contrast, builds a **diversified portfolio** by investing in several dissimilar assets. The prevalence of diversified portfolios suggests that most investors are, in fact, risk averse.

Diversification reduces the chances of an extreme outcome, either good or bad. If you invest all your money in one stock, then your return hinges entirely on the performance of that stock: if the company goes bankrupt, you will too. Similarly, a bank that loans all its money to a single borrower is literally betting the bank on the ability of that borrower to repay the loan. If the bank instead spreads its loans among hundreds or thousands of different borrowers, it will take an incredible string of bad luck for it to lose everything. With thousands of loans, it is unlikely that no one will default, but it is also extremely unlikely that everyone will.

## Asset Correlations

The degree of risk reduction provided by diversification depends on the correlations among the returns on the individual assets. A large number of independent investments provides very effective diversification. If you flip a coin 10,000

**EXAMPLE**
**10.4**

## Continental Illinois Bets the Bank on Oil Prices

In 1981 it was estimated that Continental Illinois Bank had $4 billion (more than 15 percent of its loan portfolio) in energy loans, mostly to independent oil and gas companies. The bank was confident that these energy loans would be profitable, the senior vice president responsible for oil and gas lending explaining that the 1981 drop in oil prices was "just a little blip."* Even though it consisted of a large number of loans to independent producers, this $4 billion energy-loan portfolio was not well diversified because the ability to repay the loans depended critically on oil and gas prices. When the 1981 blip in prices turned into a long-term collapse, Continental Illinois had serious financial problems.

In 1983 the federal government bailed out Continental Illinois with a $4.5 billion subsidy and became an 80 percent owner of the bank. The bank's top management was removed in 1984. Continental Illinois had a number of problems, and an undiversified portfolio of energy loans was one of its biggest.

*Laurel Sorenson, "In the High Flying Field of Energy Finance, Continental Bank Is Striking It Rich," Wall Street Journal, *September 18, 1981.*

times, you don't know which flips will be heads and which tails, but you can be confident of the average result — roughly half heads and half tails. (There is only a 0.02 probability of more than 51 percent heads in 10,000 coin flips and a 0.0003 probability of more than 52 percent heads.) In the same way, a bank doesn't know which loans will default, but if it has estimated the default probability accurately, it can be confident of the average default rate for 10,000 independent loans.

If the outcomes are not independent, then they may be either positively or negatively correlated. If the returns from two assets are negatively correlated, then when one does poorly, the other is likely to do well. Because the losses tend to be offset by gains and the gains offset by losses, a portfolio of negatively correlated assets has very little risk of large losses or gains. The extreme is returns that are perfectly negatively correlated so that the outcome from one investment is certain to be the opposite of the other. In gambling, bookmakers strive for a perfectly hedged portfolio, with an equal volume of wagers on each side of a bet, so that they are guaranteed a profit no matter which side wins. Among loans, bonds, and stocks, there are few negatively correlated returns, because most are affected similarly (although to varying degrees) by interest rates and the economy.

If asset returns are positively correlated, there is less potential for risk reduction through diversification. The extreme case is perfect positive correla-

## Stock Market Indexes in the United States and Germany

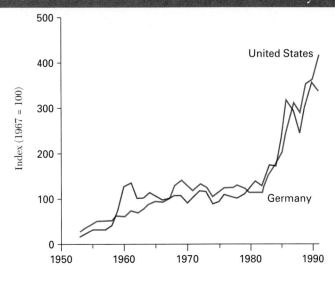

**Source:** *Business Conditions Digest* and *Survey of Current Business*, various issues.

## Annual Percentage Price Changes in U.S. and German Stocks, 1954–1991

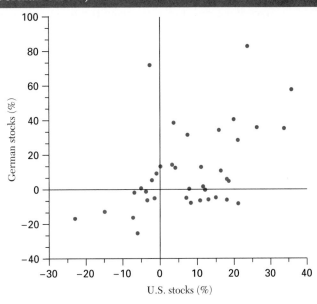

**Source:** *Business Conditions Digest* and *Survey of Current Business*, various issues.

The portfolio managers at Huntington Advisers have made a number of empirical studies buttressing their arguments. Using quarterly data from June 1972 through 1987, they managed hypothetical portfolios using, each quarter, data from the preceding 5 years to estimate the means, standard deviations, and correlation coefficients among the real rates of returns on the assets described above. While the S&P 500 stock index had an average real return of 2.6 percent with a standard deviation of 60.1 percent, this international diversified portfolio had an average real return of 11.4 percent with a standard deviation of 43.5 percent — a higher expected return with less risk. Persuaded by this evidence, Huntington Advisers now uses global diversification in the portfolios that it advises and manages.

## ASSET PRICING MODELS

Which assets are relatively risky and consequently must offer above-average expected returns — risk premiums — to persuade risk-averse investors to hold them? We have seen that the riskiness of an asset that is part of a portfolio depends on how correlated its return is with those of other assets in the portfolio. An asset that invariably does poorly when other assets do poorly is risky because it offers no diversification potential. An asset that is independent of other assets or, even better, does well when others do poorly reduces portfolio risk. Thus the proper gauge of risk for portfolio managers is a measure of how an asset's return is related to the returns on other assets.

In the final section of this chapter we will look briefly at two models that have been developed to make these general principles more specific. The first, the capital asset pricing model, focuses on the correlation between each asset and the overall market bundle of assets. The second, arbitrage pricing theory, looks at how asset returns are affected by underlying factors, such as interest rates and the unemployment rate. We begin with the single-index model, which aids our understanding of both the capital asset pricing model and arbitrage pricing theory.

### *The Single-Index Model*

The single-index model, which was first developed by William Sharpe, assumes that there is a linear relationship between an asset's percentage return $R_i$ and the overall "market" return on all assets $R_M$:

$$R_i = \alpha_i + \beta_i R_M + \epsilon_i \qquad (10.3)$$

Figure 10.6 graphs this relationship. The parameter $\alpha_i$ (pronounced "alpha") is the intercept of the line $\alpha_i + \beta_i R_M$. The parameter $\beta_i$, the **beta coefficient**, measures the extent to which the return on this particular asset moves with the return on all assets. If the market return increases by 10 percent, the return on

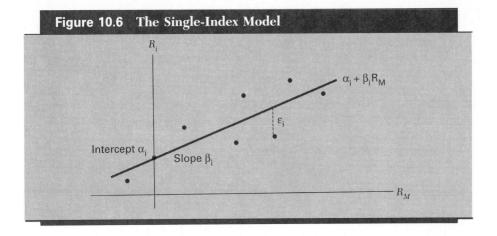

**Figure 10.6   The Single-Index Model**

this asset tends to increase by more or less than 10 percent depending on whether its beta coefficient is larger or smaller than 1.

The error term $\epsilon_i$ (pronounced "epsilon") is a random variable reflecting the fact that no matter what happens to the market, the return on this particular asset may be pushed up or down by unexpected events, such as technological breakthroughs, the loss of key executives, favorable tax changes, or legal setbacks. The $i$ subscripts indicate that alpha, beta, and the error term vary from asset to asset. The asset error terms are assumed to be independent of the market return and of the economy, interest rates, and other macroeconomic factors, although in varying degrees, and that each asset return is also affected by idiosyncratic events. The variance of $R_i$ can be separated into the following two components,

$$\text{var}[R_i] \; = \; \beta_i^2 \, \text{var}[R_M] \; + \; \text{var}[\epsilon_i] \qquad (10.4)$$
$$\text{Total risk} \; = \; \text{macro risk} \; + \; \text{micro risk}$$

The **macro risk**, also called **systematic risk**, market risk, or nondiversifiable risk, concerns macroeconomic events such as unanticipated changes in interest rates, inflation, and the unemployment rate that affect all securities. With macro risk, there is no safety in numbers, in that mere diversification cannot protect investors from recession or high interest rates. The **micro risk**, also called **unsystematic risk**, idiosyncratic risk, or diversifiable risk, arises from events specific to individual companies and can be diversified away.

To see this, consider a portfolio of $n$ assets with a fraction $\lambda_i$ of wealth invested in asset $i$. The overall return on the portfolio is

$$
\begin{aligned}
R &= \lambda_1 R_1 + \lambda_2 R_2 + \cdots + \lambda_n R_n \\
&= (\lambda_1 \alpha_1 + \cdots + \lambda_1 \alpha_1) + (\lambda_1 \beta_1 + \cdots + \lambda_n \beta_n) R_M + (\lambda_1 \epsilon_1 + \cdots + \lambda_n \epsilon_n) \\
&= \alpha + \beta R_M + \epsilon
\end{aligned}
$$

EXAMPLE
**10.6**

## *Farmer Mac*

Farm income is much more volatile than nonfarm wage income, causing a relatively high and volatile default rate on farm mortgages. Throughout the 1980s, for example, the default rate on nonfarm mortgages held by life insurance companies was consistently less than 1 percent. The default rate on farm mortgages, in contrast, was 1 percent in 1980, 3 percent in 1983, 8 percent in 1986, and 6 percent in 1987.*

The volatility of farm income has inhibited the private securitization of farm mortgages. Investors are understandably wary of holding mortgages that have unpredictable default rates and are collateralized by unfamiliar property. In addition, unlike conventional home mortgages, farm mortgages commonly include a revolving credit line that allows farmers to vary the amount borrowed with seasonal needs — which makes it difficult for investors to estimate the cash flow from a farm mortgage and, consequently, to put a price on such mortgages.

The Agricultural Credit Act of 1987 created the Federal Agricultural Mortgage Corporation ("Farmer Mac") to encourage the securitization of farm mortgages. Farmer Mac is a private corporation that guarantees the repayment of principal and interest on privately issued securities that are backed by farm mortgages. To obtain Farmer Mac's guarantee, the institution that issues the farm mortgage must pay initial and annual fees and cover at least 10 percent of any losses due to defaults.

Farmer Mac's solvency is guaranteed by the U.S. government. There is little reason to think that Farmer Mac will be able to estimate default rates and the timing of payments with great accuracy. Because of its size, Farmer Mac may be able to diversify away some idiosyncratic default risk, but it is still vulnerable to interest rates, farm prices, and other macroeconomic risks.

*\*James R. Booth, "Farmer Mac and the Secondary Market," Federal Reserve Bank of San Francisco Weekly Letter, January 5, 1990, pp. 1–3.*

The portfolio intercept $\alpha$ and slope $\beta$ are weighted averages of the intercepts and slopes of the assets in the portfolio. The portfolio error term, too, is a weighted average of the underlying error terms. However, to the extent that these individual errors are independent, their weighted sum will almost certainly be close to zero.

Intuitively, we can visualize each $\epsilon_i$ as the flip of a coin — heads is a pleasant surprise and tails an unpleasant one. With a large number of flips, the average outcome should be close to zero — no surprise at all. In a large, reasonably diversified portfolio, the value of the portfolio $\epsilon$ is virtually certain to be small, and its variance is approximately zero. Thus micro risk can be diversified away, leaving only macro risk,

$$\text{var}[R_i] = \beta_i^2 \text{var}[R_M]$$

The return on a diversified portfolio depends on the portfolio's alpha and beta values and on how well the market does. The critical uncertainty is macro risk, what will happen to the overall market (the value of $R_M$). A portfolio manager can't do anything about $R_M$, but he or she can do something about the portfolio's beta value, which is what determines how sensitive the portfolio is to market fluctuations. A portfolio with a beta value of 1.0 is about as risky as the overall market; if the market return turns out to be 10 percent higher or 10 percent lower than expected, then this portfolio should do about 10 percent better or 10 percent worse than expected. A portfolio with a beta value larger than 1.0, in contrast, is aggressive, with above-average risk; when the market swings 10 percentage points, a portfolio with a beta value of 2.0 can be expected to swing 20 percentage points. Finally, a portfolio with a beta value of less than 1.0 is conservative; when the market fluctuates up or down 10 percent, a portfolio with a beta value of 0.5 can be expected to fluctuate by only 5 percent.

Thus the beta coefficient is an appropriate measure of risk for portfolio managers. High-beta securities are risky because they result in high-beta portfolios; low-beta securities are safer because they create low-beta portfolios. It is not surprising, then, that portfolio managers routinely calculate the beta values of their portfolios and also look at the beta values of individual securities that they consider including in their portfolios.

---

**EXAMPLE**
**10.7**      *The Value Line Investment Contest*

A portfolio's beta coefficient is a convenient and useful way of gauging its aggressiveness. A portfolio with a high beta value can be expected to do well if the market rises rapidly but to do poorly if the market declines. A portfolio with a low beta value is more protected from a market collapse but can expect only modest gains if the market soars. Beta coefficients can thus be used to measure the amount of risk that the portfolio manager is willing to tolerate. Many institutions specify an overall target portfolio beta value that must be maintained by those who select the individual securities in the portfolio. If the fund has a target beta value of 0.8, then any securities with beta values above 0.8 must be balanced by ones with lower beta values.

From a more aggressive viewpoint, the beta coefficient can be used by market timers who wish to bet on the direction of the market. Someone who believes that the market is likely to rise can act on this belief by increasing the portfolio's beta value — for example, by shifting funds from low-beta securities to high-beta ones. Someone who fears a market decline can shift to low-beta assets.

Two finance professors once used these principles to place opposite bets in a nationwide stock market contest organized by Value Line, a large investment advisory service. In the 1972 contest, each entrant picked a hypothetical portfolio of 25 stocks. After 6 months, those entrants with the best-performing portfolios won prizes, while the losers were encouraged to subscribe to Value Line.

The finance professors decided to collaborate on their entries. One picked the 25 stocks with the highest beta values and the other selected the 25 stocks with the lowest beta values (some negative, many near zero) — reasoning that the first portfolio would do well if the market went up and the second would do well if it went down.

As it turned out, the stock market declined and their low-beta portfolio was among the top 2.3 percent of the entries, while the high-beta portfolio was among the bottom 0.6 percent. (The winning entry was a very nondiversified portfolio of 25 oil stocks that profited from OPEC's oil embargo.) For its 1985 contest, Value Line changed the rules, using beta coefficients to separate the 1650 eligible stocks into 10 categories, each containing 165 stocks, and asked contestants to select a portfolio of 10 stocks, one from each category. By forcing contestants to choose some stocks with high beta values and some with low beta values, Value Line ensured that all portfolios would have beta values near 1 so that the contest would reflect stock selection and not just a bet on the direction of the market.

## The Capital Asset Pricing Model (CAPM)

If the beta coefficient is the appropriate measure of an asset's contribution to the riskiness of a portfolio, then risk-averse investors won't hold high-beta securities unless the expected returns are high too. The implications of this insight can be made very precise by assuming that investors choose portfolios based on the expected value and variance and that they all agree about the means, variances, and correlations of asset returns. William Sharpe and John Lintner have shown that risk premiums then have this very simple structure:

$$E_i - R_0 = \beta_i(E_M - R_0) \qquad (10.5)$$

where $E_i$ is the expected return on an individual asset, $E_M$ is the expected return on the market as a whole, and $R_0$ is the return on a risk-free asset.[7]

Although Equation 10.5 is phrased in terms of an asset's expected return, we know from earlier chapters that it is asset prices that adjust so that the anticipated cash flow gives investors their requisite return. Thus Equation 10.5 is really a statement about asset prices, and this model is called the **capital asset pricing model** (**CAPM**): investors who choose portfolios on the basis of the mean and variance, and agree on the opportunities, will price assets so that the expected returns conform to Equation 10.5.

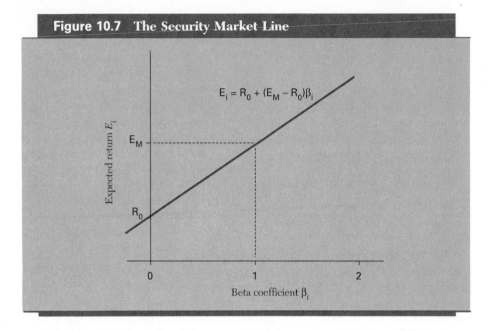

**Figure 10.7   The Security Market Line**

$$E_i = R_0 + (E_M - R_0)\beta_i$$

Expected return $E_i$

$E_M$

$R_0$

Beta coefficient $\beta_i$

0          1          2

The beta coefficient in Equation 10.5 is the very same beta coefficient as in the single-index model, although CAPM makes assumptions about investor preferences and the single-index model makes assumptions about the error term $\epsilon$. The formal definition of the beta coefficient in CAPM is the ratio of the covariance between the asset's return and the market return divided by the variance of the market return:

$$\beta_i = \frac{\text{cov}[R_i, R_M]}{\text{var}[R_M]} \tag{10.6}$$

This is the statistical definition of the beta coefficient in the single-index model and, empirically, is the formula used to estimate the beta value. Thus we can interpret the beta coefficient in Equation 10.5 as the slope of a linear relationship between $R_i$ and $R_M$.

According to Equation 10.5, the risk premium on an asset $(E_i - R_0)$ is proportional to the risk premium on the market as a whole $(E_M - R_0)$, with the asset's beta coefficient the proportionality factor. This relationship, sometimes called the *security market line*, is graphed in Figure 10.7 and gives a structure to expected returns that is shown in Table 10.4.

Notice, particularly, that a zero-beta security, which might be very risky in isolation, adds nothing to portfolio risk (all its risk is idiosyncratic, nonmarket risk that can be diversified away) and consequently requires no risk premium. A negative-beta asset, which reduces portfolio risk because it tends to do well when other investments do poorly, will be held by risk-averse investors even if the expected return is less than the return on a completely safe security. (In practice, very few stocks have negative beta values; one study estimated beta coefficients for 4357 stocks and found that only 7 had negative beta values.[8])

| Table 10.4 | The Relationship Between an Asset's Beta Coefficient and Expected Return | |
|---|---|---|
| Asset | Beta Coefficient | Expected Return |
| Aggressive | $\beta_i > 1$ | $E_i > E_M$ |
| Typical | $\beta_i = 1$ | $E_i = E_M$ |
| Defensive | $0 < \beta_i < 1$ | $R_0 < E_i < E_M$ |
| Uncorrelated | $\beta_i = 0$ | $E_i = R_0$ |
| Hedge | $\beta_i < 0$ | $E_i < R_0$ |

Earlier chapters emphasized the principle that the required rate of return that is used to discount cash flows should take into account the riskiness of the cash flow but were vague about the size of the appropriate risk premium. CAPM gives a very specific answer: The risk premium depends on an asset's beta coefficient. If, for example, an investor is calculating the present value of a certain stock, the required rate of return used to discount the prospective dividends can use Equation 10.5 together with an estimate of the stock's beta coefficient, the rate of return on the safe asset, and a risk premium for the market as a whole. If safe Treasury bills yield 6 percent, the stock's beta value is 1.5, and we will settle for a 5 percent risk premium on the market, then the required return is

$$E_i = R_0 + \beta_i(E_m - R_0)$$
$$= 6\% + 1.5(5\%)$$
$$= 13.5\%$$

These required returns determine the prices investors are willing to pay for securities and, hence, market prices. This is why CAPM is called a pricing model, even though Equation 10.5 is stated in terms of rates of return.

Another application of Equation 10.5 is in corporate finance, where firms are advised to use Equation 10.5 to estimate their shareholders' required rate of return and then use this required return to value investment projects.

## Arbitrage Pricing Theory (APT)

CAPM is appealing because it expresses some subtle, yet plausible ideas in a very simple manner. In some ways, however, the model is too simple. Think of the two primary macroeconomic influences on the stock market: output and interest rates. A booming economy is good for the stock market, and so is low interest rates. Some stocks, such as automobiles and other "cyclicals," are very sensitive to the economy, whereas other stocks, such as savings and loan associations, are more sensitive to interest rates. When the overall stock market rises, will S&Ls go up a lot or a little — how large is their beta coefficient? If the market is booming because of falling interest rates, S&Ls have a high beta coefficient. If the market is being propelled by a strong economy, their beta coefficient is small. And if, as in the 1960s, output and interest rates are rising together, the overall stock market may be rising while S&Ls are falling, giving a negative beta coefficient.

This is a specific example of the more general point that there are a variety of reasons for stock market fluctuations, and the correlation of a particular stock with the market (its beta coefficient) may depend on the cause of the market movement. A single beta coefficient cannot capture this variety. Instead, we need a beta coefficient for output, another for interest rates, and possibly more for other macroeconomic events.

The single-index model

$$R = \alpha + \beta R_M + \epsilon$$

can be extended to include several explanatory factors, thereby becoming a multiple-factor model. The general principle can be illustrated with just two factors, $F_1$ and $F_2$,

$$R = \alpha + \beta_1 F_1 + \beta_2 F_2 + \epsilon \qquad (10.7)$$

(The parameters vary from security to security, as with the single-index model, but the $i$ subscripts have been omitted here for simplicity.) The first factor $F_1$ might be output, the unemployment rate, or some other measure of the strength of the economy; $\beta_1$ tells the effect of this factor on this particular security's return. The second factor might be a long-term interest rate, with $\beta_2$ giving the effect of the interest rate on this security. Most S&Ls have a relatively large $\beta_2$ and modest $\beta_1$, whereas the reverse is true of automobile companies.

Researchers can include as many factors as they think important — output, interest rates, inflation, oil prices, taxes, and so on. The single-index model is the special case of one factor, the stock market itself. With more than one factor, the beta coefficients cannot be visualized in a scatter diagram but can be estimated by statistical multiple-regression procedures.

Stephen Ross has shown that just as the single-index model provides an intuitive explanation for the capital asset pricing model, so a multiple-factor model leads to an asset pricing model — which he called **arbitrage pricing theory** (**APT**).[9] The essential argument is analogous to the single-index model, and so is the conclusion. Equation 10.7 states that the return on any asset depends on some macro (systematic) factors $F_1$ and $F_2$ and on the micro (unsystematic) influences in $\epsilon$. In a large, well-diversified portfolio, the idiosyncratic events in $\epsilon$ balance each other out, leaving only macro (systematic) risk. Risk-averse investors do not need above-average expected returns to persuade them to hold assets with idiosyncratic risk, because such risk can be diversified away. Risk premiums are required for macro risks because these cannot be avoided by diversification.

The crucial divergence from CAPM's conclusion is that APT allows for the possibility that different macro risks may require different risk premiums. For example, in a historical period where there is little chance of interest rates changing, investors do not need to be compensated much for holding assets that are sensitive to interest rates. In general, each asset must be priced to give an expected return that depends on its sensitivity to each factor and on the risk premium for each factor:

$$E - R_0 = (E_1 - R_0)\beta_1 + (E_2 - R_0)\beta_2 \qquad (10.8)$$

where $(E_1 - R_0)$ is the risk premium for the first factor, and $(E_2 - R_0)$ is the risk premium for the second.

The APT Equation 10.8 is very similar to the CAPM Equation 10.5, and in fact, if we were to use the APT model with a single factor, the market return, we would obtain Equation 10.5. However, CAPM and APT are actually derived from two very different sets of assumptions — one regarding investor preferences and the other regarding investment opportunities. CAPM assumes that investors focus on a portfolio's expected return and variance and agree about the available opportunities, whereas APT assumes that the returns can be described by factors and an idiosyncratic term that is independent not only of the factors but also of the idiosyncratic influences on other assets. Empirical tests seem to show that the CAPM and APT models are both generally consistent with available data but that neither is clearly superior to the other.[10]

Factor beta values are inherently useful because it is worth knowing the sensitivity of assets and portfolios to individual factors — for example, to know that a particular asset mix is especially sensitive to interest rates or to the economy and, hence, represents an implicit bet on these factors.

Investors should also be aware of the factor beta values that result from some strategies. After the stock market crash on October 19, 1987, many portfolio managers shifted to stocks with high dividend yields. At the time, many savings and loan associations fell into this category, so a high dividend yield strategy was really an S&L strategy — a bet that interest rates would fall and/or that some suspect loans would be repaid.

Similarly, a portfolio manager who emphasizes small companies may buy a lot of growth stocks, which are very sensitive to interest rates. A manager who looks for low price–earnings ratios may buy energy stocks when oil prices are depressed (implicitly betting on a strengthening of oil prices), or automobile stocks when a recession is anticipated (implicitly betting that the recession won't materialize), or exporting firms when the dollar is strong (implicitly betting that the dollar will weaken). The explicit estimation of factor beta values can help portfolio managers recognize the macro risks they are taking.

Factor beta values gauge the exposure of a portfolio to interest-rate risk, to output risk, or to other risks. There is no presumption that portfolios should try to minimize these risks; presumably, risk bearing is compensated by above-average expected returns. Before you can rationally decide which risks to bear, however, you need to know what the risks are.

Some money managers also may want to structure their portfolios to meet the needs of their clients. For example, a corporate pension fund may be particularly concerned about output risk, because reduced profits will impair its ability to fund retirement benefits, whereas a life insurance company may be more concerned with interest-rate risk and a university endowment may be interested in inflation risk. Other portfolio managers may want to know factor beta values in order to place bets on interest rates, output, and so on. If the market expects a recession and you don't, your portfolio can be tilted toward assets with a high output beta value. To bet that interest rates will fall or at least not rise as much as others expect, shift into assets with large interest-rate beta values. APT is more complicated than CAPM, but this is why some find it appealing — it facilitates richer, more subtle portfolio decisions.

# SUMMARY

The uncertainty of asset returns can be quantified by specifying probabilities, describing the relative likelihood of the possible outcomes. These probabilities are influenced by historical data but are necessarily subjective. The expected value $\mu$ is the long-run average return if the frequency with which each outcome $x_i$ occurs is equal to its probability $P[x_i]$:

$$\mu = x_1 P[x_1] + x_2 P[x_2] + \cdots + x_n P[x_n]$$

The variance $\sigma^2$ is the average squared deviation of the possible returns about the expected value:

$$\sigma^2 = (x_1 - \mu)^2 P[x_1] + (x_2 - \mu)^2 P[x_2] + \cdots + (x_n - \mu)^2 P[x_n]$$

The standard deviation $\sigma$ is the square root of the variance. The standard deviation (or variance) gauges risk by measuring how certain we are that the return will be close to its expected value.

For many assets, the normal distribution is a reasonable approximation that is useful for describing our uncertainty about the return. Two convenient rules of thumb are that there is about a $\frac{2}{3}$ probability that a normally distributed variable will be within 1 standard deviation of its mean and about a 95 percent probability that it will be within 2 standard deviations. Some asset returns are very asymmetrical and cannot be approximated by a normal distribution — for instance, lottery tickets, stock in new companies, and other long shots. Investors who like positive skewness buy such assets, even though the expected returns are low and the standard deviations are high.

A risk-neutral person chooses the alternative with the highest expected return, leading to the placement of "all eggs in one basket." A risk-seeking person accepts fair bets and will even sacrifice expected return to increase risk. A risk-averting person sacrifices expected return to reduce risk and selects a diversified portfolio that contains dissimilar assets. Diversification reduces risk most effectively if the asset returns are uncorrelated or, even better, negatively correlated.

In the capital asset pricing model, an asset's beta coefficient gauges the macro, or systematic, risk that cannot be diversified away; micro, or unsystematic, risk, which arises from events specific to individual companies, can be diversified away in a large portfolio. Beta coefficients are estimated from the slope of a line fit to a scatter diagram of returns on the asset and on a market index. A portfolio's beta is a weighted average of the betas of the securities in the portfolio, using as weights the fraction of wealth invested in each security. According to CAPM, risk-averse investors will not hold assets with high beta coefficients unless they are compensated with large risk premiums:

$$E_i - R_0 = \beta_i(E_M - R_0)$$

Arbitrage pricing theory allows us to take into account the observation that asset returns are affected by a variety of diverse factors and, therefore, have a variety of beta coefficients. Assuming that asset returns can be modeled as dependent on factors and on an idiosyncratic error term that is independent of the factors and of the idiosyncratic influences on other asset returns, assets will be priced in a manner analogous to CAPM, with risk premiums for macro factor risks that cannot be diversified away.

Factor beta values can be used not only to value assets, but also to gauge the sensitivity of a portfolio to various factors, such as unemployment, interest rates, and inflation. A portfolio manager may want to structure the portfolio to reflect his or her beliefs about the future course of these macro factors or, at least, to recognize the risks to which the portfolio is exposed.

# IMPORTANT TERMS

arbitrage pricing theory (APT)
beta coefficient
capital asset pricing model (CAPM)
diversified portfolio
expected value
macro risk
micro risk
normal distribution

probability distribution
risk averse
risk neutral
risk seeking
standard deviation
systematic risk
unsystematic risk
variance

# EXERCISES

1. A pension fund thinks that the average annual rate of inflation during the next 4 years is twice as likely to be below 5 percent as to be 5 percent or higher. What is its subjective probability that the rate of inflation will be below 5 percent?

2. An insurance company is considering investing $1 million in either Treasury bills, with a guaranteed 5 percent return, or in Raider junk bonds, which have a high prospective return if there is no default:

|  | Raider Return |
| --- | --- |
| No default | + 20% |
| Partial default | − 10% |
| Total default | −100% |

Historical data for bonds issued by similar companies suggest that 5 percent have a total default and that another 20 percent have a partial default. If the insurance company applies these probabilities to the Raider bonds, does the expected value of their return exceed that of Treasury bills? If the insurance company buys the Raider bonds, what can we conclude about its risk preferences?

3. A bank has assigned the probabilities below to three economic scenarios over the next 2 years. They have also estimated the fraction of their loans that will default and the return on their loan portfolio in each scenario.

| Economy | Prob-ability | Loan Defaults (%) | Return (%) |
|---|---|---|---|
| Boom | 0.30 | 1 | 12 |
| Muddle | 0.40 | 3 | 10 |
| Recession | 0.30 | 8 | 5 |

Calculate the expected values of (a) the percentage of loans that will default and (b) the portfolio return.

4. A bank estimates that during the coming year a Treasury bond has a 0.5 probability of yielding a 15 percent return and a 0.5 probability of yielding a 5 percent return, whereas a Brazilian bond has a 0.9 probability of yielding a 20 percent return and a 0.1 probability of yielding $-60$ percent. Calculate the expected return and standard deviation for each bond. Which is riskier? Which bond is preferred by a risk-neutral investor? By a risk seeker? By a risk-averse investor? Are the returns from these bonds positively skewed, negatively skewed, or symmetrical?

5. The following table illustrates a firm's anticipated revenues in each of four inflation–unemployment scenarios and the probabilities that it assigns to these scenarios. What is the expected value of revenue?

Is the expected value also the most likely value?

| Scenario | In-flation | Unem-ploy-ment | Prob-ability | Rev-enue ($ millions) |
|---|---|---|---|---|
| 1 | High | High | 0.16 | $2.0 |
| 2 | High | Low | 0.24 | 4.0 |
| 3 | Low | High | 0.36 | 1.0 |
| 4 | Low | Low | 0.24 | 3.0 |

6. Major league baseball players can file for salary arbitration. In arbitration, the player submits a contract, the owner submits a contract, and a three-person panel chooses one of the two contracts. Neither side knows the details of the other side's contract until both contracts have been submitted. In February of 1990, California Angels pitcher Chuck Finley filed for arbitration, asking for a 1-year contract for $810,000; the Angels filed a 1-year contract for $600,000. After learning of each other's contract, Finley and the Angels canceled the arbitration hearing by agreeing to a 1-year contract for $725,000. If $P$ is the probability that the arbitration panel would have chosen Finley's $810,000 contract, for what value of $P$ is the expected value of the arbitration ruling equal to the agreed-upon $725,000 contract?

7. The text tells of a hypothetical choice between a sure $1 million and a chance to win $40 million by having 5 coin flips turn out to be all heads. What is the probability of 5 heads in 5 flips? What is the expected value of this $40 million gamble? Would you take the sure $1 million or go for $40 million?

8. In 1987, with gold selling for $460 an ounce, a mining company offered investors a chance to buy gold at $250 an ounce — but the investors would have to pay the money immediately and not receive their gold for 15 months. The company would purportedly use the investors' money to obtain the gold

from a mine with uncertain reserves.[11] Suppose that there is a probability $P$ that you will get the gold and a probability $1 - P$ that you won't. If you are risk neutral and determined to buy gold (and to hold it for at least 15 months), what is the lowest value of $P$ that persuades you to accept the offer?

9. Limited Liability is considering insuring Howard Hardsell's voice for $1 million. It figures that there is only a 0.001 probability that it will have to pay off. If Limited Liability charges $2000 for this policy, will it have a positive expected value for the company? What is the expected value of the policy to Howard? If Howard's expected value is negative, why would he consider buying such a policy?

10. *Donoghue's Moneyletter* developed a test to differentiate speculators from the risk averse.[12] One of the questions is

   *You are on a TV game show and can choose one of the following. Which would you take?*
   *a. $1,000 cash*
   *b. A 50 percent chance at winning $4,000*
   *c. A 20 percent chance at winning $10,000*
   *d. A 5 percent chance at winning $100,000*

   Which of the answers indicates risk-averse behavior? Risk-neutral behavior? Risk-seeking behavior?

11. Which would you prefer: (a) $200,000 or (b) a lottery with a 20 percent chance of winning $1,200,000 and an 80 percent chance of losing $50,000? How would you characterize a person who prefers (a) to (b)? Prefers (b) to (a)? Is indifferent between (a) and (b)?

12. A computer company must decide whether its new computer, Granny Smith, will have a closed architecture or an open one, allowing users to add enhancements. The estimated profits, in millions of dollars, depend on whether potential customers prefer an open or closed architecture, events considered to be equally likely:

|        | Customer Preferences | |
| Design | Open | Closed |
| --- | --- | --- |
| Open   | 500 | 300 |
| Closed | 100 | 900 |

(For example, if the company uses an open design, there is a 0.5 probability that their profits will be $500 million and a 0.5 probability that profits will be $300 million.) Which action maximizes expected return? If the company chooses a closed architecture, how would you characterize its risk preferences?

13. You have been offered $2 for a raffle ticket with a 1 percent chance of winning $100. What can we say about your risk preferences if you decline this offer?

14. A pension fund estimates that the return from a portfolio of Mexican bonds has an expected value of 18 percent and a standard deviation of 20 percent and that the return from a portfolio of U.S. corporate bonds has an expected return of 8 percent and a standard deviation of 10 percent. A senior executive argues that because the fund is risk averse, it should invest in both. Is this argument more persuasive if the returns on the U.S. and Mexican bonds are positively correlated or negatively correlated? Why?

15. Jill owns stock in company NEW, which may be taken over by company GLOM. If so, Jill's stock will be worth $40 a share; if not, it will be worth $20. Jill considers the two possible outcomes to be equally likely.
   a. What is the expected value of Jill's stock?
   b. If Jill accepts $27 a share for her stock, is she acting risk averse or risk seeking?
   c. Would anyone pay Jill more than $30 a share for her stock?

16. Four thousand years ago Chinese shipowners, worried about pirates and natural disasters, put part of their cargo on each

other's ships. How would you explain this behavior?

17. A stock analyst has found the probability distribution shown in the following table "to be very useful":[13]

| Stock Price Change Over the Next 6 Months (%) | Probability |
|---|---|
| +40 | 0.1 |
| +20 | 0.2 |
| 0 | 0.4 |
| −20 | 0.2 |
| −40 | 0.1 |

What is the expected value and standard deviation?

18. A corporation is going to construct either a 20-story or a 30-story office complex. The market value of the completed building will depend on the strength of the rental market when construction is finished. The firm's chief executive officer (CEO) has assigned the subjective probabilities shown below for the net profit with each option. Use the mean and standard deviation to compare these two alternatives.

| Rental Market | Prob-ability | Profit ($ millions) 20-Story | Profit ($ millions) 30-Story |
|---|---|---|---|
| Strong | 0.2 | 100 | 150 |
| Medium | 0.5 | 50 | 50 |
| Weak | 0.3 | −50 | −100 |

19. Program traders simultaneously buy and sell stocks, stock options, and/or stock futures. When the options or futures expire, these traders unwind their position by liquidating their stock holdings. One study looked at the volume of trading on the New York Stock Exchange during the last hour on Friday afternoon, comparing those days when stock market index options and futures both expired with those days when neither of them expired.[14]

| | Expiration Day | No Expiration |
|---|---|---|
| Mean volume | 31,156 | 15,959 |
| Standard deviation | 11,612 | 5,011 |

Based on these data, write a brief paragraph comparing the last hour of trading on expiration and nonexpiration Fridays.

20. A certified financial planner wrote:

*Allow me one of Cohen's Laws: It is far better to be very aggressive with your investments and hedge them by diversification than to be conservative and put all your eggs in one supposedly safe basket. You're going to do much better if you buy six or seven aggressive stocks than if you buy one conservative stock. How do you limit your risk? By buying different kinds of stocks, say a mix of electronics, drugs, retailing, computers.*[15]

How can a basket of aggressive stocks be safer than a conservative stock? Why would you want to mix a variety of stocks? Isn't it better to find a very profitable investment and stick with it?

21. Identify each of these probability distributions as positively skewed, negatively skewed, or symmetrical:
   a. The normal distribution
   b. A Superfecta bet, where correctly picking the first four finishers in a horse race wins a large amount of money
   c. The purchase of a junk bond whose return has a 0.90 probability of being 18 percent and a 0.10 probability of being −100 percent

22. Why might an insurance company limit the number of homes it would insure against loss by fire or flood in a given area while remaining willing to write such policies in different areas?

23. Figure 10.3 shows that the daily returns on IBM stock were approximately normally distributed with a mean of 0.12 percent and a standard deviation of 1.28 percent. According to the normal distribution rules of thumb, what range encompasses about 95 percent of the returns?

24. An examination of the annual return on stocks and corporate bonds for the period 1926–1988 yielded these estimates:[16]

|                    | Stocks | Bonds |
|--------------------|--------|-------|
| Average return     | 12.1%  | 4.8%  |
| Standard deviation | 21.0%  | 8.5%  |

Assuming these numbers to be the expected return and standard deviation for the coming year, would a risk-neutral investor prefer stocks to bonds, or vice versa? Why might a risk-averse investor prefer to hold both bonds and stocks?

25. A unit bond trust pools money from thousands of investors and buys a package of bonds. Which of these two opinions do you agree with?

*Many trust sponsors argue that because a trust is diversified, investors can accept the higher risk — and higher income — of lower-rated bonds. "A trust is stronger than any of its parts in the same way that a bundle of pencils is stronger than one pencil," insists Norman Schvey, a Merrill Lynch Vice President. "Not so," says Diana Munder, a New York CPA whose clients often ask her for advice about their investments. "If you would not feel comfortable*

*buying individual issues of obscure revenue bonds or lower-grade utilities," she believes, "there is no reason why you should feel more comfortable buying a whole package of them."[17]*

26. A researcher has estimated these equations for two different stocks:

$$R_1 = -6.0 + 1.5R_M$$
$$R_2 = 3.0 + 0.5R_M$$

What are the alpha and beta coefficients for these two stocks? Sketch these equations, identifying the intercept and slope of each line. Which stock has the higher predicted return if $R_M = 10$ percent? If $R_M = -5$ percent? What are the alpha and beta coefficients for a portfolio that is invested one-third in stock 1 and two-thirds in stock 2?

27. Over the coming year, the return on safe Treasury bills is 11 percent and your expected return for the stock market as a whole is 15 percent. What does the CAPM predict about the expected return for a stock with a beta of 1.0? With a beta of 0.5?

28. Many investors look at the beta coefficients provided by investment advisors. Explain why this advice is misleading: "A stock with a low beta is safer than a high-beta stock, because the lower beta is, the less the stock's price fluctuates."

29. Explain why you either agree or disagree with this assertion: "According to the capital asset pricing model, zero-beta stocks have a zero expected return."

30. One researcher calculated the annual returns from 1954 through 1978 on an investment in 15 representative modern prints and found that these returns were negatively correlated with annual returns from corporate stocks.[18] What does this tell us about the beta coefficient for modern prints? Why might someone invest in modern prints even if the expected return were very modest?

31. Value Line, a large private investment advisory service, recommends that investors who own fewer than 15 stocks gauge the riskiness of their portfolio by looking at Value Line's "safety ratings" for these stocks and that investors who own more than 15 stocks instead calculate the portfolio's beta coefficient. Why are the safety ratings not identical to the beta coefficients, and why does the appropriate risk measure depend on the number of stocks in the portfolio?

32. In 1988 *The Wall Street Journal* began a monthly "Investment Dartboard" series in which four experts each select a favorite stock and *The Wall Street Journal* picks four stocks by tossing darts at the financial pages. After the expert portfolio beat the dartboard portfolio 3 months in a row, a letter to the editor objected that,

    *The "random walk" theory suggests that individual investors cannot outperform a randomly selected portfolio. Your procedure pits the random portfolio against the single best choices of different investors, which is an entirely different hypothesis. Since individual stock picks are riskier than diversified portfolios, it is not surprising that the (average) pro's return exceeds that of the dartboard.* [19]

    Do you agree? Write a letter to the editor supporting or refuting the preceding letter.

33. In a two-factor model, which of these assets do you think have relatively high or low output beta values and which have high or low interest rate beta values, in each case in comparison with the output and interest rate beta values of the S&P 500?
    a. Short-term Treasury bills
    b. 30-year Treasury zero
    c. Stock in a regulated water company
    d. Stock in a machine tool compai y
    e. Stock in a breakfast food company

34. Stephen Ross has often used a factor model that includes these three factors:

    $$F_1 = \text{output}$$
    $$F_2 = \text{long-term bond rate}$$
    $$\text{minus short-term rate}$$
    $$F_3 = \text{rate of inflation}$$

    What signs would you expect for the three respective beta coefficients of a typical stock? Explain your reasoning.

35. Annual data for 1972 through 1980 were used to estimate a two-factor model for AT&T stock and for IBM stock:

    AT&T:  $R_{AT\&T} = 18.9 - 4.8F_1 - 1.0F_2$

    IBM:   $R_{IBM} = 13.8 - 11.1F_1 - 0.6F_2$

    where the first factor is the percentage change in the unemployment rate and the second factor is the percentage change in the interest rate on long-term Treasury bonds. Do the signs of the factor coefficients make sense? According to these estimates, which stock is affected more by changes in the unemployment rate? By changes in interest rates?

# 11 Using Financial Futures and Options as Insurance

*If you bet on a horse, that's gambling. If you bet you can make three spades, that's entertainment. If you bet cotton will go up three points, that's business. See the difference?*

**Blackie Sherrod**

Earlier chapters explained how changes in interest rates affect the market prices of bonds, mortgages, and other financial assets. You saw how the net worth of a financial intermediary is vulnerable to unanticipated interest-rate fluctuations if the duration of its assets does not match the duration of its liabilities. Many savings and loan associations have learned this lesson the hard way: with long-term assets and short-term liabilities, their net worth disappeared when interest rates increased unexpectedly, as in 1979–1982.

Financial intermediaries have tried to protect themselves from interest-rate fluctuations by using shorter-term or adjustable-rate loans to reduce the duration of their assets and using longer-term, fixed-rate deposits to lengthen the duration of their liabilities. Many customers resist such changes, however, preferring long-term loans and short-term deposits. One way out of this impasse is provided by financial futures and options — the subject of this chapter — which allow financial intermediaries and others to cope with interest-rate risk by compensating for mismatched asset and liability durations.

This chapter explains the general nature of futures and options contracts, emphasizing the financial contracts used by banks and other financial intermediaries. You will see how these contracts can be used for hedging, speculation, and arbitrage and learn what factors influence their prices. We will also look at stock index futures, which have been blamed by some for the October 19, 1987 crash, in which stock prices fell by more than 20 percent in a single day. We begin by explaining the difference between futures and options.

# FUTURES VERSUS OPTIONS

**Futures** and **forward contracts** are agreements to deliver an item at a specified future date at a price agreed to today but not paid until delivery; for example, a mill might agree to pay a farmer $3 a bushel for 100,000 bushels of wheat delivered 6 months from now. This futures contract insures both the mill and the farmer against fluctuations in the market price, or **spot price**, of wheat for immediate delivery by eliminating the mill's uncertainty about the cost of wheat and the farmer's uncertainty about revenue.

Futures contracts are standardized, homogeneous agreements that are traded in auction markets on organized exchanges. Because of their standardized terms, futures contracts have a large number of potential buyers and sellers and are actively traded. Forward contracts, in contrast, are private agreements with idiosyncratic details designed for specific buyers and sellers. For example, in place of a standard 6-month futures contract, a forward contract can be designed for delivery in 134 days. Forward contracts can be negotiated directly between buyers and sellers, but generally they involve established dealers in the over-the-counter market.

An **option contract** is an agreement conveying the right, but not the obligation, to buy or sell an item in the future at a price that is specified now. A mill might pay a farmer $20,000 for an option giving it the right to buy 100,000 bushels of wheat 6 months from now at $3 a bushel. If the market price of wheat drops below $3, the mill will not exercise its option but will instead buy wheat at the lower market price. The option provides insurance against an increase in the price of wheat by guaranteeing that the mill does not have to pay more than $3 a bushel.

# THE DEVELOPMENT OF FUTURES AND OPTIONS TRADING

One of the earliest references to futures and options is in the Old Testament, where Laban agreed to let Jacob marry his youngest daughter, Rachel, in return for 7 years of labor. It is not clear whether Jacob could change his mind (that is, whether this was an option or futures contract), but in any case, after Jacob had worked for 7 years, Laban broke the contract and gave Jacob his older daughter, Leah. Jacob persisted, working another 7 years so that he could marry Rachel too.

Another early reference is in Aristotle's *Politics*, which recounts how Thales became wealthy through an astute use of options. Based on his study of the stars, Thales believed that the next olive crop would be enormous and, for a small fee, purchased options from the local olive press owners. When the crop did turn out to be large, Thales exercised his options and leased the olive presses at a considerable profit.

Options and futures began trading in the United States shortly after the Revolutionary War and were used widely for both commodities and stock during and after the Civil War. Then, as now, the overwhelming majority of trades were made not by millers, farmers, or other businesses seeking to guarantee the price of a future business transaction, but by speculators hoping to profit from short-term fluctuations in the value of these contracts. In the late 1800s the progressive movement succeeded in having commodity options classified as gambling rather than an investment, making them illegal under antigambling statutes. Stock options continued to flourish, particularly in the 1920s, and in the aftermath of the Great Crash they attracted the attention of Congress, which considered but did not pass a bill outlawing stock options entirely.

Contributing to the speculative and somewhat unsavory reputation of stock options was the fact that such options were not traded on organized exchanges. A loose collection of dealers brought together buyers and sellers through newspaper advertisements, mimeographed sheets, and telephone calls. Each option was virtually unique in its terms — the number of shares, the exercise price, and the date of expiration. Without standardization, there could be no organized secondary market and little basis for comparing prices.

In 1969, with commodity trading at very low levels, the Chicago Board of Trade decided to experiment with stock options trading. After considerable planning, they received SEC approval and in 1973 opened the Chicago Board Options Exchange. One of the five SEC commissioners voted against approval, arguing that this "was essentially a gambling operation. There are enough of those in Las Vegas." While it is true that speculators hope to profit from price changes, hedgers use options and futures to protect themselves from unpredictable price changes.

The organized trading of stock options proved to be very popular and has since been augmented by financial options and futures contracts traded on a variety of exchanges for Treasury bonds, Eurodollars, foreign currency, and even stock indexes. Options and futures are used not only by speculators looking for easy riches but also by arbitragers trying to exploit price differentials among similar securities for a virtually risk-free profit and by financial institutions trying to insure their portfolios against losses. We will first consider how futures can be used for these purposes and then examine options.

## FUTURES

Futures contracts are traded on several exchanges, with the largest the Chicago Board of Trade and the Chicago Mercantile Exchange. Table 11.1 shows the types of futures contracts traded on all exchanges in 1987, and Table 11.2 shows the most actively traded contracts. While agricultural products are still important, they have been joined in recent years by a wide variety of other real and financial assets. The daily pages of *The Wall Street Journal* and other major newspapers list the specific items and the current prices. There is also extensive trading of currency forward contracts among banks, and these can be analyzed using the same principles that we will apply to futures contracts.

**Table 11.1  Contracts Traded on Futures Markets in 1987**

| Group | Contracts (millions) | Percent of Total |
|---|---|---|
| Bonds | 88.0 | 41.2 |
| Agricultural | 39.6 | 18.6 |
| Stock indexes | 26.3 | 12.0 |
| Energy | 20.3 | 9.5 |
| Currencies | 19.9 | 9.3 |
| Metals | 19.4 | 9.1 |
| Total | 213.5 | 100.0 |

**Source:** Paula A. Tosini, "Stock Index Futures and Stock Market Activity in October 1987," *Financial Analysts Journal*, January/February 1988, pp. 28–38.

**Table 11.2  Most Actively Traded Futures Contracts in 1987**

| Contract | Contracts Traded (millions) | Exchange |
|---|---|---|
| U.S. Treasury bonds | 61.1 | Chicago Board of Trade (CBT) |
| S&P 500 stock index | 19.9 | Chicago Mercantile Exchange (CME) |
| Eurodollars | 17.8 | Chicago Mercantile Exchange (CME) |
| Crude oil | 12.8 | New York Mercantile Exchange (NYMEX) |
| Gold | 9.8 | Commodities Exchange, Inc. (COMEX) |
| Corn | 7.2 | Chicago Board of Trade (CBT) |

**Source:** See Table 11.1.

## The Advantages of Standardized Contracts

Organized exchanges standardize the terms of futures contracts and enforce their terms. For example, the corn futures contracts traded on the Chicago Board of Trade specify the delivery of 5000 bushels of no. 2 yellow corn to an approved warehouse on a specified date. The processor who takes delivery is sent a receipt from the warehouse certifying that a sufficient quantity of the appropriate corn has been stored there. An International Monetary Market futures contract for German marks calls for the delivery of 125,000 deutschemarks on a specified date; a Chicago Board of Trade Treasury bond futures contract is for the delivery of $100,000 face value U.S. Treasury bonds with at least 15 years until maturity.

The trading of standardized contracts on organized exchanges allows traders to cancel contracts before the delivery date. Each exchange has a clearinghouse that is an intermediary between buyers and sellers of futures contracts. Because individual buyers are not tied to specific sellers, either party can cancel its position by selling contracts that it previously purchased, or vice versa. A bank that sells Treasury bond futures but does not want to deliver the number of Treasury bonds required by its futures contracts can repurchase futures contracts; a pension fund that buys Treasury bond futures and later decides that it wants fewer Treasury bonds can sell some of its futures contracts.

Participants also can use the futures market to protect themselves against fluctuations in the prices of securities that are similar, but not identical, to those specified in the futures contracts; for example, a bank may own mortgages rather than Treasury bonds or a pension fund may want to buy AA corporate bonds rather than Treasury bonds. Suppose that a pension fund intends to buy $10 million worth of AA corporate bonds 6 months from now and wants protection against a decline in interest rates and an increase in bond prices. This pension fund can buy 100 Treasury bond futures contracts on the Chicago Board of Trade. If interest rates decline and the prices of Treasury and AA corporate bonds rise by comparable amounts, the pension fund can use the profits on its Treasury bond futures to cover the increase in the cost of the corporate bonds.

With a futures market, the pension fund also can make daily adjustments, buying more contracts to lock in the price of additional anticipated bond purchases or, at times, becoming a net seller to protect the value of a large bond inventory. Pension funds, banks, and other investors also can speculate, buying or selling futures contracts to bet on the future course of interest rates.

## Futures Trading

Transactions in the futures market are made through traders who own seats on the exchange. Each item has a trading pit — an oval area with steps leading down to a central floor — where traders buy and sell, either for their own accounts or on behalf of orders from outside the exchange. All offers to buy and sell are by "open outcry" so that, in theory, all traders in the pit have an opportunity to accept the offer. In practice, the pits are often crowded with people pushing and shoving as they use arcane hand signals and loud shouts to try to communicate with each other. At particularly anxious moments, fights break out or someone on the steps will fall, toppling everyone in front.

Futures are created by the willingness of people to buy and sell contracts. Those who buy contracts are said to be "long," and those who have sold contracts are "short." The total amount of outstanding contracts, called the **open interest**, fluctuates daily. Table 11.3 shows some data from *The Wall Street Journal's* report on futures trading on Friday, April 10, 1992.

The first line identifies the item, the exchange, the size of a contract, and the units in which prices are quoted — thus the reported May $253\frac{1}{4}$ price for corn is $2.5325 per bushel. The June Treasury bond price of 100-06 is $100\frac{6}{32}$ percent of face value, that is, $100,187.50 for Treasury bonds with a $100,000 face value.

The left-hand column identifies the delivery dates of the available contracts, and the next three columns show the opening price and the high and low prices

**Table 11.3    Selected Futures Prices, Friday, April 10, 1992**

### CORN (CBT) 5,000 bu.; cents per bu.

| | Open | High | Low | Settle | Change | Lifetime High | Lifetime Low | Open Interest |
|---|---|---|---|---|---|---|---|---|
| May | 253¼ | 254½ | 252¾ | 253½ | | 279¾ | 234¾ | 69,326 |
| July | 259 | 259¾ | 258¼ | 259 | + ¼ | 285 | 239½ | 104,355 |
| Sept | 254¾ | 256 | 254¾ | 255½ | + 1 | 279½ | 236½ | 17,961 |
| Dec | 253 | 254½ | 252¾ | 254 | + 1½ | 275¾ | 236½ | 66,646 |
| Mr93 | 261 | 262 | 260¼ | 261½ | + 1¼ | 281¼ | 258 | 6,242 |
| May | 265¼ | 266½ | 265 | 265½ | + 1¼ | 284¾ | 263 | 1,238 |
| July | 268½ | 268¾ | 268½ | 268¾ | + ¾ | 280 | 266½ | 134 |

Estimated volume 32,000; volume Thur 40,154; open interest 265,907, −4,490

### TREASURY BONDS (CBT) $100,000; pts. 32nds of 100%

| | Open | High | Low | Settle | Change | Yield Settle | Yield Change | Open Interest |
|---|---|---|---|---|---|---|---|---|
| June | 100-06 | 100-08 | 99-07 | 99-27 | −12 | 8.016 | +0.038 | 289,687 |
| Sept | 99-03 | 99-05 | 98-05 | 98-24 | −11 | 8.128 | +0.036 | 18,059 |
| Dec | 98-01 | 98-01 | 97-08 | 97-22 | −11 | 8.238 | +0.036 | 6,025 |
| Mr93 | 97-03 | 97-03 | 96-10 | 96-24 | −10 | 8.337 | +0.033 | 1,899 |
| June | 95-12 | 95-31 | 95-12 | 95-27 | −10 | 8.434 | +0.034 | 804 |
| Sp94 | | | | 92-16 | −10 | 8.804 | +0.036 | 100 |

Estimated volume 425,000; volume Thur 423,860; open interest 316,755, −4,459

### DEUTSCHEMARK (IMM) 125,000 marks; $ per mark

| | Open | High | Low | Settle | Change | Lifetime High | Lifetime Low | Open Interest |
|---|---|---|---|---|---|---|---|---|
| June | 0.6095 | 0.6105 | 0.6041 | 0.6045 | −0.0085 | 0.6490 | 0.5322 | 73,406 |
| Sept | 0.6018 | 0.6022 | 0.5960 | 0.5965 | −0.0084 | 0.6400 | 0.5685 | 2,785 |
| Dec | 0.5908 | 0.5908 | 0.5900 | 0.5896 | −0.0084 | 0.6106 | 0.5645 | 3,977 |
| Mr93 | | | | 0.5841 | −0.0084 | 0.6100 | 0.5750 | 506 |

Estimated volume 56,665; volume Thur 68,469; open interest 80,674, +6,283

### S&P 500 INDEX (CME) 500 times index

| | Open | High | Low | Settle | Change | Lifetime High | Lifetime Low | Open Interest |
|---|---|---|---|---|---|---|---|---|
| June | 0.404.50 | 405.70 | 403.30 | 405.50 | + 2.30 | 424.40 | 374.50 | 133,329 |
| Sept | 0.405.55 | 407.00 | 404.40 | 406.65 | + 2.40 | 425.50 | 376.25 | 3,939 |
| Dec | 0.407.35 | 408.05 | 405.80 | 408.05 | + 2.45 | 427.25 | 391.40 | 1,093 |

Estimated volume 47,862; volume Thur 70,794; open interest 138,361, −1,513

**EXAMPLE**
**11.1**

## *The Chicago Sting*

In January of 1989 the federal government revealed a 2-year undercover investigation of trading at the Chicago Mercantile Exchange and the Chicago Board of Trade (using the code names Operation Hedgeclipper and Operation Sour Mash). With the cooperation of some colleges and businesses, the Justice Department manufactured phony academic and professional records for several undercover FBI agents (moles). Archer-Daniels-Midland, the world's largest soybean processor, trained the agents in commodities trading. The federal government spent over a million dollars buying seats on the exchanges; spent thousands more for offices, high-rent apartments, luxury automobiles, health club memberships, and other accessories to create an illusion of success for its agents; and spent hundreds of thousands of dollars covering their trading losses.*

Some of the moles' conversations, on and off the trading floors, were recorded with hidden video cameras or microphones. In addition, at least one trader was persuaded to join the government investigation and wear a hidden microphone. Several alleged misdeeds were uncovered. Some traders "front ran" large orders, buying or selling for their own accounts before executing large customer orders. Some executed customer orders by making reciprocal trades with each other at noncompetitive prices. Some skimmed money by trading at one price and reporting a different price to their customers, somewhat higher for a buy order and lower for a sell order. One of the government moles told other traders that a private company he owned had large tax losses that could be used to shelter profitable trades. These traders were reportedly persuaded to give some of their profitable trades to the government informant in return for cash passed in plain envelopes. Despite the widespread negative publicity generated by this sting operation, the exchanges have so far largely resisted reform proposals, including a ban on dual trading — the practice of trading for both the trader's own account and for customer accounts. (The Chicago Mercantile Exchange has ended dual trading on contracts with a daily volume of more than 10,000 contracts.)

Of the 48 traders indicted by the government, 16 pleaded guilty to fraud charges and agreed to cooperate with the government. The first trial ended in July of 1990, with two Swiss franc traders found guilty of eight charges of stealing a total of $200; on more than 100 other charges, the jury found the defendants innocent or could not reach a verdict. Also in 1990 a Commodity Futures Trading Commission judge dismissed charges of noncompetitive trading that had been brought against 19 Chicago Board of Trade members, concluding that "the trading which occurred is the best that could be expected in light of the archaic trading methodologies still prevalent in the pits today."

*Scott McMurray and John Koten, "Probe of 2 Exchanges Shows Wild Fraternity Of Traders in Yen Pit," Wall Street Journal, January 26, 1989.*

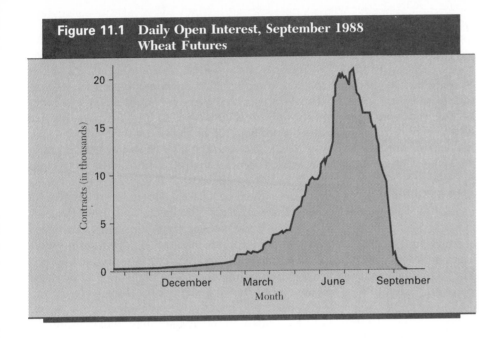

**Figure 11.1   Daily Open Interest, September 1988 Wheat Futures**

for trades made that day. The settlement price is like a closing price and will be discussed shortly. The next column shows the change in the settlement price from the day before. (For Treasury bonds, these changes are in thirty-seconds, ranging here from $\frac{10}{32}$ to $\frac{12}{32}$.) The lifetime highs and lows are the highest and lowest prices at which the contract has traded. In place of the lifetime high and low prices, the Treasury bond data show the yield to maturity corresponding to the settlement price and the change in this yield.

The exchanges try to control short-run price fluctuations by imposing **daily limits** on the price changes of many futures contracts. For instance, the daily settlement price cannot rise or fall by more than $0.10 ($500/contract) for corn, 3 points ($3000/contract) for Treasury bonds, and $0.01 ($1250/contract) for deutschemarks.

The last column shows the open interest, the number of outstanding contracts. As Figure 11.1 illustrates, the open interest is zero when a contract is first introduced, rises as trading increases, typically reaches a peak a few months before expiration, and then declines to zero on the delivery date. The last row for each item in Table 11.3 shows the total trading that day and the day before, the total open interest, and the net change in the open interest.

## Covering Positions

The buyer of a futures contract agrees to pay the seller an agreed price $F$ when the item is delivered. In about 97 percent of the cases, however, there turns out to be no delivery, because the shorts repurchase contracts from the longs before the delivery date. On the delivery date, the price of a futures contract equals the spot price $P$ because both now call for immediate delivery. Suppose that a trader has purchased corn futures at $F = 240$ cents per bushel and that the spot price on the delivery date is $P = 250$ cents per bushel. By taking delivery, the trader can buy for 240 and sell for 250, a profit of 10 cents per bushel (neglecting various transaction costs). This gain can be realized without an actual delivery because the futures price on the delivery date is equal to the spot price. In what is called **covering** or **reversing** a position, the holder of a futures contract sells the contract for the current price of 250, realizing a 10 cents per bushel profit, while the contract writer purchases a contract for 250, taking a loss of 10 cents per bushel.

Virtually all futures traders are either speculators, who have no intention of making or taking delivery, or hedgers, who as producers and users (like the pension fund planning to buy corporate bonds) trade through accustomed channels in the spot market and use the futures market to hedge their position. Tales of tons of sugar dropped on someone's front lawn are amusing but untrue. The worst that can happen is that the commodity will be put in a warehouse and the buyer will be billed for the cost of the commodity plus storage charges.

Because the reckoning of profits and losses does not depend on an actual delivery, futures contracts can be written on intangible things, which cannot be delivered, such as the S&P 500 index of stock prices, using a specified rule for determining the spot price $P$ on the delivery date so that the profit $P - F$ can be calculated. For the S&P 500 index, $P$ is the value of this index on the delivery date; a futures contract at a price of, say, $F = 250$ is a wager on whether the value of the index will turn out to be above or below 250.

## Marking to Market

To help ensure the financial integrity of the market, the exchange's clearinghouse requires a daily settlement of all unrealized profits and losses using, for each contract, a **settlement price** that is set by the exchange at the end of each trading day. For actively traded contracts, the settlement price is the closing price, the price of the last transaction. For inactive contracts, the exchange estimates what the price would have been had there been transactions at the close. These settlement prices are used to calculate the change in the value of each trader's position; those traders with losses that day must make cash payments to the brokerage accounts of those with profits before the beginning of the next trading day. This daily transfer of funds from losers to winners is called a **daily settlement** or **marking to market**.

Suppose that you buy two June Treasury bond futures contracts this coming Monday for 99. Because each contract is for bonds with a $100,000 face value, the total value of your position is $198,000. We'll assume that the Monday settlement price is $99 and that your broker requires a $10,000 deposit, called **margin**, to ensure your ability to cover your possible losses. Table 11.4 shows what might happen to your account during the next three days.

## Table 11.4  Four Days in the Treasury Bond Futures Market

| Day | Settlement Price | Value of Two Contracts | Daily Profit | Cumulative Profit |
|---|---|---|---|---|
| Monday | 99 | $198,000 | | |
| Tuesday | $97\frac{16}{32}$ | $195,000 | − $3,000 | − $3,000 |
| Wednesday | 98 | $196,000 | $1,000 | − $2,000 |
| Thursday | 97 | $194,000 | − $2,000 | − $4,000 |

On Tuesday the settlement price drops to $97\frac{16}{32}$, and your two contracts are worth $195,000 — a $3000 loss for the day. This $3000 is deducted from your account and credited to the account of someone who is short Treasury bonds (has sold Treasury bond futures); your broker will most likely now demand that you either put up an additional margin deposit or sell your contracts. The price rises to 98 on Wednesday, and you receive $1000 from those who are short Treasury bonds. On Thursday the price dips to 97, and you pay $2000.

If you sell on Thursday at 97, your position is closed with a cumulative loss of $4000. Unlike other stocks and bonds, where you don't realize your capital gains and losses until you actually sell the securities, the daily settlement of futures contracts gives you a profit or loss each day. These daily settlements make it very clear that except for brokerage costs, futures contracts are a zero-sum game — any profits for some must be losses for others.

## Speculation

Futures have a well-deserved reputation for offering speculators a way to make or, more likely, lose a lot of money in a hurry. David Dreman, a portfolio manager and *Forbes* columnist, wrote that "futures have no place in the portfolio of a conservative investor and should be looked at only by masochists or the wildest of dice players."[1] Example 11.2 tells how one family wagered billions of dollars on silver futures.

Futures are risky for several reasons. There are no dividends, interest, or other cash flow. A futures contract is just a bet on the price of the underlying item. The prices of futures contracts are volatile, and margin requirements are very low, 15 percent or less, and can typically be met by leaving interest-earning Treasury bills with the broker. In the hypothetical example in Table 11.4, 40 percent of the initial $10,000 margin was lost in 4 days.

Individuals are sometimes lured into futures by firms that make phone calls peddling hot tips ("Our computer says that silver is going to double within a month") or that advertise exaggerated claims in newspapers and magazines ("Spectacular new system. $374,566.47 profit in two days"). These are the same kind of people who auction Oriental rugs in motels, push multilevel distribution plans, and sell books on how to profit from the end of the world. A financial

EXAMPLE
11.2

## The Hunt Brothers Buy Silver

The great East Texas oil fields made H. L. Hunt one of the richest men in America, what a reporter for the *London Sunday Times* called "the archetype of a Texas oil billionaire — arrogant, prejudiced, mean, eccentric, and secretive."* Two of his sons, Bunker and Herbert, stayed in the oil business, and Bunker found oil in Libya in the 1960s, enough to give him control over more oil than any single individual in the world. When Colonel Qadhafi nationalized his Libyan fields in 1973, Bunker Hunt lost $15 billion in oil reserves.

Bunker and Herbert turned to the silver market in late 1973, acquiring futures contracts for 35 million ounces of silver and creating suspicion that they were trying to corner the market. Normally, almost all futures contracts are liquidated before expiration. However, what happens if the Hunts, or others, decide not to liquidate a large block of futures contracts? The shorts, betting against a rise in the price of silver, are squeezed, or cornered, because if they can't find millions of ounces of silver on short notice, they will be forced to buy the Hunts' futures contracts at whatever price the Hunts demand.

A growing fear of a silver squeeze pushed the price of March 1974 futures from $2.90 in December of 1973 to $4 in January and $6.60 in late February. At this point the Bank of Mexico sold 50 million ounces of silver that it had acquired at less than $2 an ounce, thereby providing the spot market with more than enough silver to meet the Hunts' futures contracts. Even though the Hunts ended up buying much of this silver themselves (billionaires can do that), the squeeze fizzled, and futures prices fell back to $4 an ounce.

Convinced that silver was still underpriced, the Hunts continued to roll over a sequence of futures contracts. By the end of 1976, they had accumulated 100 million ounces of silver, and some analysts anticipated an eventual attempt to squeeze the market. In January of 1980 the price of March silver futures hit $37.10, with the Hunts and associates controlling nearly 300 million ounces of silver and silver futures, 80 percent of the total amount mined worldwide in 1979. Some 20 to 50 million ounces of silver came onto the market, melted down from coins, jewelry, teapots, and so on, but this was not nearly enough to satisfy the Hunts' buying power.

On January 9, 1980, the Commodity Futures Trading Commission (CFTC) abruptly increased the margin requirements to $75,000 per contract ($15 an ounce) during the delivery month. Still, on January 14 the price of March futures reached an unprecedented $42.50. At this point the Hunts made a private deal with Engelhard, the world's largest bullion dealer, agreeing to buy 19 million ounces of silver at $35 an ounce on March 31, 1980 (the day that the March futures would expire), thereby canceling 3800 of the Hunts' long and Engelhard's short contracts and relieving the margin pressure on both. Two

*Stephen Fay, Beyond Greed (New York: Viking Press, 1982). Much of this example is based on this book.

days later they agreed to cancel another 2200 contracts by trading 11 million ounces on July 1; as collateral, the Hunts put up 8.5 million ounces of silver. The Hunts bought time in that margin calls were replaced with a 2-month deadline for finding a billion dollars in cash. It was a billion-dollar gamble that the price of silver would stay above $35 an ounce.

Bunker Hunt still held 8580 March contracts (42.9 million ounces), and his associates held more, enough to squeeze the remaining shorts who, unlike Engelhard, didn't own any silver. On January 18 the price of silver topped $50, giving a total market value for the 300 million ounces of silver and silver futures contracts held by the Hunt group of almost $15 billion, ironically the same amount lost to Colonel Qadhafi.

On January 21 the COMEX board changed the rules again, raising margin requirements once more and, in an unprecedented move, henceforth allowing trades only for liquidation — the longs could sell to the shorts but could not buy any more contracts. The price of March futures promptly dropped to $44, and the price dropped another $10 the next day, after the Chicago Board of Trade adopted similar rules. Now it was the Hunts who were squeezed. As their profits evaporated, their brokers made urgent margin calls. Every dollar drop in the futures price cost Bunker Hunt $42.9 million in equity; the 2-day $16 decline cost a staggering $686 million. In all, during January and February, the Hunts had to borrow $1 billion, and an associated company put up another $500 million, secured by land, oil leases, and 70 million ounces of silver.

On March 14 the rules changed once again on the Hunts. As part of the Fed's anti-inflation policies, Federal Reserve Chairman Volcker announced a special credit restraint program, telling banks to stop lending money to finance speculation in commodities and precious metals. Bunker Hunt hurried to Europe and then to Saudi Arabia to borrow money, without success. The Hunts were due to pay Engelhard $665 million on March 31, and the margin calls provoked by sagging silver prices were increasingly difficult to meet. On March 25 the price of silver hit $20.20, and the Bache brokerage firm, which had lent the Hunts $233 million, informed the brothers that they would begin selling silver, silver futures, and other stocks in their accounts to meet margin calls. On March 26, March futures slumped to $15.80, and not only the Hunts were worried.

At 8:00 A.M. on March 27, Herbert Hunt told the CFTC that the Hunts would not sell any of their uncollateralized silver to repay their borrowings and advised the CFTC to close the market and settle all contracts at the previous day's price of $15.80. The CFTC let the exchange open. Fear of the unknown and Bache's liquidation of the Hunts' futures contracts knocked the price as low as $10.40 that day, dubbed "Silver Thursday." On Friday the price rallied to $12, and Bache sold the remaining March futures.

The Hunts' outstanding loans still topped a billion dollars. With Fed Chairman Volcker's blessing, a consortium of 13 banks agreed to make a 10-year $1.1 billion loan (at the prime rate plus 1 percent) to the Placid Oil Company, a Hunt family trust, which Placid then lent the Hunts so that they could pay off their short-term loans. Among the conditions was a requirement that the Hunts not speculate in commodities or futures markets for 10 years, until 1990.

Unfortunately, a worldwide drop in oil prices reduced the market value of Placid Oil's assets, and it filed for bankruptcy in 1986 to protect itself from increasingly worried bankers. It has been estimated that the Hunts lost $1.5 billion in the silver market and that, overall, the total market value of their assets had fallen from $8 billion in 1980 to zero, plus or minus a billion dollars, in 1987. In 1988, in the first of several civil suits, a federal jury ruled that the Hunt brothers had conspired to corner the silver market and awarded $130 million to a Peruvian company that had shorted silver in 1979. Personal bankruptcy proceedings for the Hunt brothers began in September of 1988. One of the more unusual twists in this unique story was a lawsuit filed by the Hunts charging that the banks had engaged in fraudulent practices by lending $1.1 billion to such poor credit risks.

reporter for *Barron's* told how she was bombarded by high-pressure phone calls: "Most of my clients have doubled their money in gold options in the last 6 or 8 weeks, and that's just the beginning. I want to get your $5000 up to $10,000. I feel the worst we should do is 100 percent in a year. . . . but the timing is critical. We really have to make a move by Friday."[2] A 1981 survey found that 40 percent of the readers of *The Wall Street Journal* had similar experiences.[3]

Even if there were no brokerage commissions, futures trading would be, at best, a zero-sum game. The only way one person can make a dollar is if another loses a dollar. The commissions make trading considerably worse than a zero-sum game — much like a high-stakes poker game in which the house confiscates part of every pot. Very few people can bet on cocoa prices against Hershey, orange juice prices against Sunkist, or Treasury bond prices against Salomon Brothers and go home a winner.

A more reasonable use of futures contracts is as insurance, to hedge one's position against adverse changes in spot prices. A chocolate manufacturer can buy cocoa futures to protect itself against an unforeseen increase in cocoa prices. An orange grower can sell orange juice futures to protect against an unexpected decline in orange juice prices. An insurance company that is worried about a possible increase in interest rates but, because of transaction costs and capital gains taxes, doesn't want to liquidate its portfolio can sell Treasury bond futures instead.

## Futures Prices

The most obvious interpretation of a futures price $F$ is as a bet on the price $P$ of the item on the delivery date. Speculators can buy futures contracts if they believe that $P$ will be larger than $F$ and sell futures if they believe the opposite to be true. The market price provides a market consensus on the anticipated price, in the sense that there is a balance between buyers who expect $P$ to be higher than $F$ and sellers who expect $P$ to be less than $F$.

By this interpretation, the corn futures prices in Table 11.3 imply that in April of 1992 traders anticipated that corn prices would increase until July of 1992, decline in September and December, and then begin rising again — a seasonal pattern that is consistent with the spring planting and fall harvest of corn. Even nonparticipants consequently find it useful to look to futures markets for expert opinions on the course of prices. Farmers who do not buy futures nonetheless look at corn, wheat, and soybean futures prices before making their crop plans. Building contractors look at lumber futures before submitting bids, and cattle breeders follow cattle futures.

## The Cost of Carry

For some contracts, the futures price is determined not by the anticipated price of the item in the future but by the cost of buying the item now and holding it until the delivery date. The cost of buying the commodity now and holding it until the futures' delivery date is called the **cost of carry** and includes the cost of storage, spoilage, insurance, and forgone interest minus any cash flow from the item while it is being held. The forgone interest arises because buying the item now ties up your money, money that could be earning interest if you instead buy a futures contract and pay for the item later.

Because buying now (for the spot price plus the cost of carry) and buying later (for the futures price) are alternative ways to acquire the same commodity, the net cost should be the same:

$$\text{Futures price} = \text{spot price} + \text{cost of carry} \qquad (11.1)$$

Equation 11.1 has the very strong and perhaps counterintuitive implication that the price of a futures contract depends on the current spot price, not the anticipated future spot price.

Equation 11.1 can be rewritten to show that the difference between the futures and spot prices (what is called the **basis**) should equal the cost of carry:

$$\text{Futures price} - \text{spot price} = \text{cost of carry} \qquad (11.2)$$

If the cost of carry is positive and increases as time passes, the futures price will exceed the spot price and increase with the length of the contract. If the cost of carry is negative, the futures price will be less than the spot price. No matter which is the case, the cost of carry declines as the time horizon shrinks until, on the delivery date itself, the cost of carry is zero and the futures price equals the spot price.

## Arbitrage Between the Spot and Futures Markets

Someone who believes futures are mispriced according to Equations 11.1 and 11.2 — that the cost of carry differs significantly from the basis — can **arbitrage**, trying to profit from this mispricing by buying the item and selling a futures contract, or vice versa. Consider, for instance, a 1-year futures contract on a generic commodity with a current spot price of $10. At a 10 percent interest

EXAMPLE
11.3

## Baseball Futures

There is an unofficial, unsanctioned market in baseball futures involving some 200 investment professionals who otherwise spend their time trading wheat, silver, and the S&P 500.* Like other intangible futures, there is no actual commodity to be delivered. Instead, the value of the contract at expiration (the end of the baseball season) is determined by the number of games that the specified team wins.

For example, at the start of the 1988 season, the price of New York Yankees's futures was 93. If the Yankees ended up winning 103 games in the season, those who bought contracts at 93 would receive an amount equal to $103 - 93 = 10$ times the agreed value of a game, anywhere from $5 to $500. At $100 a game, there would be a $1000 payment from those who were short Yankees to those who were long. If the Yankees won fewer than 93 games, the longs would pay the shorts.

As with other futures contracts, there is daily trading at prices reflecting current market conditions. Dedicated participants are short dozens of teams and long dozens of others, making hundreds of trades during the course of the season. One participant reportedly lost $60,000 in 1987. Yankee futures dipped into the low 80s in September of 1988 and finished at 85 when the Yankees won 85 games. The Los Angeles Dodgers, in contrast, opened the season at 81 and finished at 94. Those who were long Dodgers and short Yankees made profits in 1988.

*John Crudele, "Baseball Futures Latest Way to Score on the Street," Los Angeles Times, September 18, 1988.

rate, the forgone interest from buying the commodity instead of a futures contract is 10 percent ($10) = $1. If the annual cost of storage, insurance, and so on is $0.50, then the total cost of carry is $1.50, and the price of a futures contract should be $11.50:

$$\text{Futures price} = \text{spot price} + \text{cost of carry}$$
$$= \$10 + \$1.50$$
$$= \$11.50$$

If the futures price exceeds this — at say $12 — then an arbitrager can buy the item for $10 and sell a futures contract for $12. On the delivery date, the arbitrager delivers the item for a profit of $2, which, by assumption, exceeds the $1.50 cost of carrying the item.

If the futures price is too low — say $11 — then an arbitrager who already owns the item can sell it for $10, thereby avoiding the $1.50 carrying costs, and buy a futures contract for $11 so as to recover the item in a year's time with a $0.50 profit. An arbitrager who does not own the item may be able to borrow it and sell it short for $10, hedging the position with an $11 futures contract; if the $10 proceeds can be invested to earn $1 interest and the person who lent the item can be persuaded to pay for the storage costs that would otherwise be incurred, then a $0.50 profit can be realized.

Many commodities, such as butter, potatoes, hogs, and live cattle, are expensive to store and difficult to sell short. The practical impossibility of arbitrage undermines Equation 11.1, and the futures price is not determined by the current spot price and the cost of carry but, instead, largely reflects the anticipated spot price on the delivery date.

Other items, particularly financial assets, are relatively easy to store and to sell short; or, even simpler, such items can be sold by investors who already have these assets in their portfolios. Thus the price of financial futures is determined not by the expected future spot price, but by the current spot price and the cost of carry. For financial assets, insurance, storage, and spoilage are negligible, making lost interest the biggest expense of buying now. This lost interest may be offset to some extent, though, by the fact that many financial assets also yield a cash flow: stocks pay dividends, and bonds pay interest. Thus for financial assets,

$$\text{Cost of carry} = \text{lost interest from buying now} - \text{dividends or interest from holding the asset} \qquad (11.3)$$

We will now apply this logic to three specific futures contracts: foreign currency, Treasury bonds, and stock indexes.

## Foreign Currencies

Chapters 6 and 7 discussed how investors can be hurt by unanticipated changes in currency prices. This exchange-rate risk can be reduced now that there are futures markets for several foreign currencies, including British pounds, German marks, Japanese yen, and Swiss francs. (There are also, as noted earlier, very similar forward currency agreements among banks.) Because foreign currency can be invested to earn the interest rate prevailing in that country, the cost of carry is (approximately) equal to the difference between domestic and foreign interest rates:

$$\text{Cost of carry} = \text{U.S. interest rate} - \text{foreign interest rate}$$

And thus, according to Equation 11.1,

$$\text{Future price of foreign currency} - \text{spot price of foreign currency} = \text{U.S. interest rate} - \text{foreign interest rate} \qquad (11.4)$$

The exact relationship, called the **interest-rate parity equation**, is

$$\frac{F}{1 + R_{US}} = \frac{P}{1 + R_{for}}$$

where $F$ is the futures price, $P$ the spot price, $R_{US}$ the U.S. interest rate, and $R_{for}$ the foreign rate. Each side of this equation is the cost of obtaining one unit of the foreign currency on the delivery day. This equation can be written as $F/P = (1 + R_{US})/(1 + R_{for})$, with Equation 11.4 an approximation.

For example, on August 16, 1988, the German deutschemark cost $0.530 U.S. dollars, U.S. Treasury-bill rates were about 8 percent, German risk-free rates were about 5 percent, and the price of 6-month mark futures was $0.538. It cost more dollars to buy mark futures than to buy current deutschemarks because those who bought marks earned low German interest rates, while those who bought mark futures could temporarily invest their dollars at high U.S. interest rates. Specifically, consider someone who wants 1000 deutschemarks in 6 months. Because these marks can be invested for 6 months to earn 5 percent/2 = 2.5 percent interest, only 1000/1.025 = 975.6 marks need to be purchased, at a cost of 975.6($0.53) = $517. Alternatively, this person can buy a futures contract for 1000 marks at a cost of 1000($0.538) = $538 after 6 months. With U.S. interest rates at 8 percent, the amount of dollars needed today to provide $538 in 6 months is $538/1.04 = $517 — the same as with the first method.

Thus, in August of 1988, 6-month deutschemark futures were 1.5 percent above the current spot price for marks because German 6-month interest rates were about 1.5 percent lower than U.S. interest rates. Futures for the British pound, in contrast, were below the current exchange rate because British short-term interest rates were around 10 percent, 2 percent higher than U.S. rates; carrying costs were negative because dollars invested at U.S. interest rates while waiting for a futures delivery earned less than British pounds invested at British interest rates.

Foreign currency futures can be used for arbitrage if Equation 11.4 is not satisfied or for speculation by those wanting low-money-down bets on the direction of exchange rates (definitely not a recommended gamble). Currency futures also can be used by importers, exporters, and their banks as insurance — to hedge against exchange-rate fluctuations.

Suppose, for instance, that it is April 10, 1992, so that the prices in Table 11.3 apply and a U.S. bank expects to receive 125 million German marks in March of 1993. The U.S. bank can protect itself against a decline in the value of those marks relative to the dollar by selling 1000 March 1993 futures contracts at $0.5841. The possession of these contracts guarantees that the bank will be able to sell the marks when it receives them in March of 1993 at a fixed dollar price of $0.5841. Equivalently, a decline in the value of the mark will be offset by a profit on the futures contracts that the bank has sold.

Similarly, suppose that in April of 1992 a U.S. bank anticipated making a payment of 250 million deutschemarks in March of 1993. The bank can protect itself, hedging its exposure to exchange-rate risk, by buying 2000 March 1993

**EXAMPLE**

**11.4**

## Caterpillar Is Hurt by a Strong Dollar and by a Weak Dollar

Caterpillar is a major U.S. company and the world's largest producer of heavy construction and earthmoving machinery that is used in mining and building projects. In 1991 Caterpillar sold $10 billion in equipment, 55 percent of it overseas. The second largest producer of construction machinery is a Japanese company, Komatsu, with $5.5 billion in sales in 1991.

During the early 1980s, Caterpillar frequently complained to U.S. government officials and to the press that the strong U.S. dollar made it very difficult to compete against Komatsu. With a high value for the dollar, Caterpillar had to charge a relatively high foreign price in order to cover the cost of producing machines in the United States. For example, if it costs Caterpillar $200,000 to produce a certain machine, this represents 42 million yen at a 1980 exchange rate of 210 yen per dollar and 14 percent more, 48 million yen, at a 1985 exchange rate of 240 yen per dollar. In its 1982 annual report to its stockholders, Caterpillar said, "The strong dollar is a prime factor in Caterpillar's reduced sales and earnings." In its 1984 report it warned, "The strength of the U.S. dollar is undermining manufacturing industries in the United States."

To compete with Komatsu and other foreign manufacturers, Caterpillar opened new plants in Britain, Western Europe, Canada, and Japan. Then, in 1986, the value of the U.S. dollar fell by 30 percent against the yen, to below 170 yen per dollar, and by comparable amounts against other currencies. This decline did not help Caterpillar much because the lower value of the dollar increased the cost of the machines that Caterpillar was now making abroad relative to those Caterpillar made in the United States. A machine that costs 40 million yen translates to $166,667 at the 1985 exchange rate of 240 yen per dollar and to $235,294 at the 1986 exchange rate of 170 yen per dollar. In 1986 a writer for *Fortune* magazine concluded, "After years of loudly advertising the need for a weaker dollar, the company finally got one — and got clobbered anyway."*

Caterpillar might have used foreign currency futures to hedge its exposure to exchange-rate risk. In the early 1980s, when it was most concerned that an increase in the value of dollars relative to yen would undermine the profitability of machines produced in the United States, Caterpillar could have sold yen futures. If the dollar strengthened relative to yen, Caterpillar would profit from a decline in the dollar price of yen futures. Similarly, if Caterpillar wanted to hedge against a declining value of the dollar in 1986, it could have bought foreign-exchange futures. It is easier to manage exchange-rate risk by using financial markets than by moving plants from country to country, trying to exploit temporarily weak currencies.

*D. Hutchins, "Caterpillar's Triple Whammy," Fortune, *October 27, 1986, pp. 91–92.*

futures contracts at $0.5841, thereby ensuring that it will be able to buy marks in March of 1993 at this fixed dollar price.

## *Treasury Securities*

Futures contracts are traded for a number of Treasury securities. The cost of carry is the difference between the interest lost by purchasing the bonds now instead of somewhat later and the coupons that can be earned by owning the bonds now. The cost of carry is close to zero if the term structure is flat and Treasury bond coupon rates are approximately equal to current interest rates. (For Treasury bills, which have no coupons, the cost of carry is simply equal to the lost interest between the futures purchase and delivery.) An upward-sloping term structure, with short-term rates lower than long-term rates, reduces the cost of carry and pulls futures prices down relative to spot prices; futures prices have to be low because those who buy bonds earn more interest than those who hold Treasury bills and wait.

As with currency futures, bond futures are used by arbitragers (who try to wring profits out of mispriced futures), speculators (who want to bet on interest-rate movements), and individuals or institutions who want to hedge interest-rate risk. When interest rates rise, bond prices decline, and so do the prices of bond futures, which call for the delivery of now less valuable bonds. Those who buy bond futures are wagering that interest rates will fall (relative to the expectations already embedded in the term structure); those who sell futures are implicitly betting on rising interest rates.

Banks and other risk-averse investors can use bond futures to offset implicit interest-rate wagers elsewhere in their portfolios. For instance, a corporation that has borrowed a large amount at a long-term fixed interest rate can hedge against a fall in interest rates by buying bond futures. If interest rates do fall, making the corporation's long-term loan more burdensome, this loss is offset by the profits it makes on its bond futures contracts, because the prices of bond futures increase as interest rates decline and bond prices rise.

Similarly, consider a savings and loan association that holds long-term, fixed-rate mortgages. These fixed-rate mortgages are an implicit wager that interest rates will decline, making the mortgages more valuable. The risk is that interest rates will rise unexpectedly, reducing the value of these mortgages. This risk of rising interest rates can be hedged by selling bond futures. If interest rates increase, bond prices will decline, and so will the value of bond futures. A savings and loan that has sold bond futures at a price $F$ reaps a profit $F - P$ as bond prices slump. If an appropriate number of futures are sold, any losses on the mortgage portfolio as interest rates rise will be offset by profits on the futures.

This savings and loan with long-term assets and short-term liabilities can use bond futures to insulate its net worth from interest-rate fluctuations, just as if it had short-term assets and short-term liabilities. Bond futures can, in essence, be used to transform fixed-rate mortgages into synthetic adjustable-rate loans. In this way, customers can have the long-term, fixed-rate loans they want, while the financial intermediary gets the protection from interest-rate risk that it wants.

**EXAMPLE**
**11.5**

## Salomon Brothers Hedges $300 Million in IBM Bonds

Investment banks underwrite new security issues by purchasing the securities from the issuer and reselling them to investors. In October of 1979, Salomon Brothers and Merrill Lynch were comanagers of a syndicate of 227 securities firms that underwrote a $1 billion bond offering by IBM, consisting of $500 million in 7-year bonds with $9\frac{1}{2}$ percent coupons and $500 million in 25-year bonds with $9\frac{3}{8}$ percent coupons. This was IBM's first public bond sale, and the largest ever, and it is a good illustration of how bond futures can be used to hedge interest-rate risk.

The bonds were scheduled to be offered in the middle of October, but amid rumors that the Federal Reserve was going to tighten credit, the offering was moved up to Thursday, October 4. The IBM issuing prices were set on October 3, taking into account the closing 9.50 percent yield on 7-year Treasury bonds that day and the closing 9.29 percent yield on 25-year Treasury bonds. With a triple-A rating, IBM's bonds were priced to yield 12 basis points more than Treasury bonds. Specifically, IBM's 7-year bonds were priced at 99.40, to yield 9.62 percent, and IBM's 25-year bonds were priced at 99.625, to yield 9.41 percent.

Treasury bond yields increased by 3 basis points on Thursday, October 4, and only about 60 percent of the IBM bonds were sold that day. On Friday, Treasury bond yields increased another 3 basis points. On Saturday, October 6, Federal Reserve Chairman Paul Volcker announced that the Fed would tighten credit to slow the rate of inflation. Treasury securities markets were closed Saturday and Sunday, and the following Monday as well, in observance of Columbus Day.

In trading on Tuesday, October 9, the price of 7-year Treasury bonds fell by an astonishing 2.6 percent (compared with the Friday close), increasing the yields by 60 basis points to 10.11 percent; the price of 25-year Treasury bond yields fell by 2.4 percent, increasing the yields by 25 basis points to 9.60 percent. A veteran trader said, "I haven't seen anything this bad during my 22 years in the bond business."* With Treasury yields at 10.11 and 9.60 percent, it was clearly no longer possible to sell the remaining IBM bonds at prices corresponding to 9.62 and 9.41 percent yields.

On Wednesday, October 10, the underwriting syndicate still had not placed $250 million to $300 million of the IBM securities and decided to sell them in the secondary market for about a 5 percent loss. The 7-year IBM bonds traded at $94\frac{3}{4}$ (a 10.55 percent yield), and the 25-year bonds traded at $94\frac{3}{8}$ (a 9.92 percent yield). This 5 percent loss amounted to $12 million to $15 million, which swamped the $5 million underwriting profit that the syndicate made on

*Phil Hawkins and Lindley B. Richert, "Drastically Lower Prices, Higher Yields Are Posted in Response to Fed Restraint," Wall Street Journal, October 10, 1979.

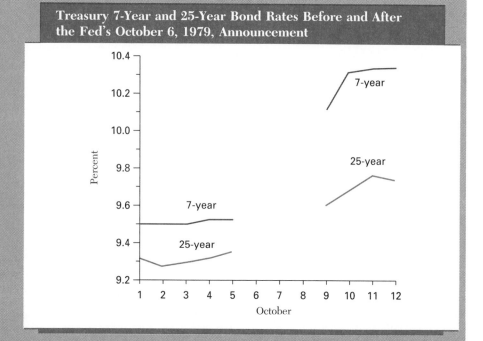

**Treasury 7-Year and 25-Year Bond Rates Before and After the Fed's October 6, 1979, Announcement**

the $700 million in securities that it had been able to sell. *The Wall Street Journal* called this "the greatest loss to Wall Street underwriters in any single marketing venture in the modern era."† The graph above shows the increase in interest rates during the week before and the week after the Fed's October 6 announcement. (Treasury bond markets were closed October 6, 7, and 8.)

When they were unable to place the IBM bonds on October 4, Salomon Brothers and Merrill Lynch both hedged their exposure to interest-rate risk by selling bond futures contracts. Although neither firm would discuss the details publicly, *Business Week* reported that Salomon Brothers apparently took short positions on approximately $100 million in bond futures, on which it realized a profit of roughly $3.5 million, almost exactly offsetting its share of the underwriting losses.‡

An increase in interest rates reduces the prices of bonds and bond futures. The figure at the top of page 343 shows the sharp drop in Treasury bond futures prices after the Fed's October 6 announcement. (Futures markets were closed on October 6 and 7.) If Salomon Brothers sold $100 million in Treasury

†*Phil Hawkins and Lindley B. Richert, "Debt Securities' Prices Continue to Drop, Causing Major Price Concessions on IBM Issue,"* Wall Street Journal, *October 11, 1979.*
‡*"How Salomon Bros. Hedged the IBM Deal,"* Business Week, *October 29, 1979.*

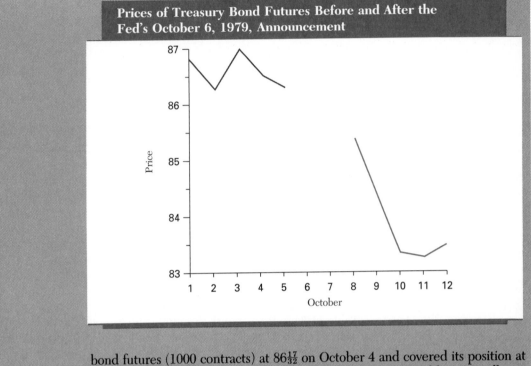

**Prices of Treasury Bond Futures Before and After the Fed's October 6, 1979, Announcement**

bond futures (1000 contracts) at $86\frac{17}{32}$ on October 4 and covered its position at $83\frac{11}{32}$ on October 10, its profit would indeed have been roughly $3.5 million:

$$\text{Sell 1000 contracts on October 5 at } 86\frac{17}{32} = \$86{,}531{,}250$$
$$\text{Buy 1000 contracts on October 10 at } 83\frac{11}{32} = \underline{\$83{,}343{,}750}$$
$$\text{Net profit} = \$\ 3{,}187{,}500$$

## Stock Indexes

Many institutional investors use stock index futures as a fast and inexpensive way to adjust the exposure of their portfolios to the stock market. In 1987 the daily volume of trading in futures contracts for the S&P 500 stock index routinely topped 100,000 contracts, with an aggregate market value of $15 billion — more than the total value of all the stock traded daily on the New York Stock Exchange.

The S&P 500 can be stored by purchasing the 500 stocks included in the index and can be sold by an institution that holds a large diversified portfolio of stocks. Because it is easy to arbitrage S&P futures, their price is determined not by the expected performance of the stock market, but by the cost of carry — the lost interest net of dividends from the S&P 500 stocks. Investors can either buy the stocks in the S&P 500 today for $P$ or buy later for $F$, the futures price agreed to today. The first strategy has the advantage of receiving dividends $D$ between now and delivery; the second strategy earns interest $RP$ by postponing payment. For both strategies to be equally attractive, $P - D = F - RP$. Rearranging,

$$F = P + RP - D$$
$$= P(1 + R - d) \tag{11.5}$$

where $d = D/P$ is the dividend yield on the S&P 500 stocks.

For example, in April of 1992, the annual dividend yield on the S&P 500 stock index was about 2.5 percent and the annual rate of return on 1-year Treasury bills was about 4 percent. Substitution of these values into Equation 11.5 implies that the price of a 1-year S&P 500 futures contract should have been about 1.5 percent higher than the value of the S&P 500:

$$F = P(1 + R - d)$$
$$= P(1 + 0.04 - 0.025)$$
$$= P(1.015)$$

Postponing the purchase of the S&P 500 for 1 year by buying futures contracts allows one to earn 4 percent interest but causes one to miss the opportunity to earn 2.5 percent dividends. Therefore, a 1-year futures contract should cost about 1.5 percent more than the S&P 500 — and in fact it did in April of 1992.

On April 10, 1992, the S&P 500 closed at 404.29. The S&P 500 futures prices in Table 11.3 are for 2-month, 5-month, and 8-month contracts. Applying a 1.5 percent annual return to these fractions of a year gives predicted futures prices that are very close to the actual prices reported in Table 11.3:

$$\text{June: } 404.29\left(1 + .015\frac{2}{12}\right) = 405.3$$

$$\text{Sept: } 404.29\left(1 + .015\frac{5}{12}\right) = 406.8$$

$$\text{Dec: } 404.29\left(1 + .015\frac{8}{12}\right) = 408.3$$

## Program Trading

Stock index futures are used for a variety of purposes. **Program trading** is a loosely used term that originally meant buying or selling a diversified portfolio of stocks. Although program trading existed before stock index futures were introduced in 1982, it has been associated with futures ever since because futures are the easiest way to trade baskets of stock. It is helpful to distinguish two very different kinds of program trading — index arbitrage and portfolio insurance — and we will do so.

An institutional investor holding a diversified portfolio of stocks practices **portfolio insurance** by automatically selling stock futures contracts whenever stock prices fall, an action equivalent to selling stock but with lower transaction costs. If stock prices continue to fall, even more futures are sold, until at some

**EXAMPLE**
**11.6**          *Stock-Index Arbitrage*

When stock market index futures were introduced in 1982, the annual dividend yield on the S&P 500 stock index was about 6 percent and the annual rate of return on Treasury bills was 10 percent, leading many to predict that the price of an S&P futures contract should be larger than the value of the S&P index. Specifically, the no-arbitrage pricing relationship in Equation 11.5 implies that the 1-year futures price should have been about 4 percent higher than the value of the stock index:

$$
\begin{aligned}
F &= P(1 + R - d) \\
&= P(1 + 0.10 - 0.06) \\
&= P(1.04)
\end{aligned}
$$

Futures prices in 1982 were, in fact, typically below the value of the S&P 500, and arbitragers exploited this difference by buying index futures and selling the stocks in the S&P 500.

Suppose, for simplicity, that the value of the S&P 500 is $P = 100$ and that a 1-year futures contract sells at a 1 percent discount to the S&P 500, $F = 99$. A pension fund holding the stocks in the S&P 500 valued at 100 is anticipating a dividend of 6 and capital gains of $P^* - 100$, where $P^*$ is the value of the S&P 500 index on the delivery date. Its total percentage return is $6 + (P^* - 100)$. This pension fund can increase its return by 5 percentage points by selling its stocks for 100, investing the proceeds in Treasury bills paying 10 percent, and buying S&P futures at 99. The value of the futures contracts on the delivery date will be $P^*$, and the pension fund's percentage return is now $10 + (P^* - 99)$, a risk-free 5 percentage point increase:

| | |
|---|---|
| Percentage profit on T-bills and futures: | $10 + (P^* - 99)$ |
| Percentage profit on stock portfolio: | $6 + (P^* - 100)$ |
| Increase in percentage profit: | 5 |

Early index arbitragers made large profits with little effort. Their actions have subsequently eliminated such obvious mispricing. Today arbitragers have to work hard to make small profits.

preset floor (say 10 percent losses) the portfolio is fully hedged, in that the value of the outstanding futures is equal to the value of the portfolio.

**Index arbitrage** is a very different type of program trading, with the objective of earning risk-free profits whenever the spread between the index futures price and the index itself differs from the no-arbitrage equilibrium in Equation 11.5 by more than the transaction costs that arbitrage entails. Arbitragers buy stocks and sell futures if the futures price is too high and do the reverse if it is too low.

The price differences are so slight and the transactions costs on small trades so large that a portfolio of at least $25 million is needed for index arbitrage to be profitable. The practice is dominated by a few dozen brokers and institutional investors who try to earn a few cents per share that will add up to thousands of dollars when millions of shares are traded. A risk-free extra 1 to 2 percent annual return gives them around $150 million in annual profits.

Index arbitragers do not inherently push stock prices up or down. They buy in one market and sell in another so as to keep the price of index futures close to the index itself. Buying or selling pressure that shows up in one market but not the other will be transmitted to the second market by arbitragers. For example, when the stock market rises, portfolio insurers need less protection and buy futures. If futures prices subsequently rise more than stock prices, index arbitragers sell futures and buy stock until equilibrium is reestablished. However, it is not the arbitragers who push up stock prices; it is the portfolio insurers who buy stocks indirectly through futures, a buying power that arbitragers transmit to the stock market itself. If there were no futures market, or if futures prices were allowed to rise significantly above stock prices, portfolio insurers would presumably buy stocks instead of futures and have the very same effect on stock prices. Arbitragers are just the messengers who bring the news to the stock market that portfolio insurers are buying.

The same logic applies to the more worrisome case where portfolio insurers react to a drop in stock prices by selling index futures. If futures prices drop more than stock prices, arbitragers buy futures and sell stock, transmitting the portfolio insurers' sales to the stock market. Again, the cause of the pressure on stock prices is not the arbitragers, but the portfolio insurers who follow the seemingly destabilizing rule of buying stock after prices rise and selling after they fall.

The Brady commission, a presidential task force, concluded that portfolio insurance was the catalyst for the collapse of stock prices on October 19, 1987, when the Dow Jones Industrial Average fell by 508 points (22 percent) and the S&P 500 index dropped 57.6 points (21 percent). The Commodity Futures Trading Commission estimated that portfolio insurers accounted for between 12 and 24 percent of the trading in S&P 500 index futures on October 19 and that about 9 percent of the NYSE trading that day was associated with index arbitrage. The rest of the year, index arbitrage accounted for as little as 1 percent and as much as 19 percent of NYSE trading.

Portfolio insurance assumes that index futures can be sold continuously at the equilibrium values given by Equation 11.5. In the market collapse on October 19, the sellers of index futures far outnumbered buyers, and what trades did take place were at prices at least 10 percent below the no-arbitrage equilibrium price. An astonishing 608 million shares of stock were traded on the New York Stock Exchange, and even then, sales could not be completed because buyers could not be found. Trading stopped in many stocks, and the reporting of prices lagged far behind recent trades, let alone the prices at which new trades could be made. Even though futures prices were much too low, arbitrage couldn't make risk-free profits because they did not know current stock prices and couldn't execute offsetting orders simultaneously. Portfolio insurers were reluctant to sell at these sharp discounts, and those who tried to sell had difficulty finding buyers.[4] Portfolio insurance is supposed to provide protection during a market collapse, but, ironically, this is when it is least effective.

Many clients became disenchanted with portfolio insurance, and some institutions reacted to the public distrust of all program trading by voluntarily stopping their index arbitrage. Trading in S&P futures fell by half after the October crash, and two legendary money managers, Warren Buffett and Peter Lynch, recommended outlawing stock futures and options.[5]

# OPTIONS

An option contract conveys the right, but not the obligation, to buy or sell something in the future at a price that is specified now. The reporting of daily stock option trading takes up a full page in *The Wall Street Journal* and other newspapers. Options for commodities, currencies, bonds, and other financial instruments are scattered throughout the financial pages. We'll use Treasury bonds in most of our examples because these are appealing contracts for many financial institutions.

Because the option seller makes a commitment that may be exercised at the buyer's discretion, the seller is said to have "written" the option. Before 1973, each option agreement was between two specific parties, and the buyer who exercised an option went to the option writer for fulfillment of its terms. With the trading of standardized contracts on the Chicago Board Options Exchange (CBOE) and other exchanges, there is no need to associate a particular writer with a specific contract or to hold a contract until expiration. When buyers exercise options, payment is made to the exchange, which then collects the promised bonds, shares of stock, or other items from the option writers without ever identifying a particular option writer with a particular option holder.

In practice, options are seldom exercised. Instead, on the expiration date, any outstanding options are sold back to the option writers, thereby extinguishing the contract, at a price reflecting the value of the contract as if it were exercised. Option writers also can close out (or "cover") their position by repurchasing options before expiration. The number of outstanding options (called, as with futures, the *open interest*) fluctuates daily, as some write new options and others close their positions.

There are two types of option contracts, puts and calls, which can be combined to create a variety of leveraged and hedged portfolios. We'll look first at calls, then at puts, and then at a few portfolio strategies.

## Call Options

A **call option** gives the holder of the option the right, but not the obligation, to buy an asset at a fixed price on or before a specified date. For instance, a call option could give the purchaser the right to buy a Treasury bond with an 8 percent coupon maturing in the year 2010 at a price of 100 (100 percent of its face value) any time within the next 3 months. The standard Treasury bond option contract traded on the Chicago Board Options Exchange is for $100,000 of face value; a quoted price of 100 signifies $100,000, and a price of 99 means $99,000. The fixed price of 100 that is specified in the option contract is called the **exercise price** or the **striking price**, and the date on which the contract expires is called the **exercise date**.

The value of a call option depends on the exercise price and the value of the underlying asset. The right to buy Treasury bonds for 100 is worth little if they are selling for 80 (80 percent of face value) but is worth a lot if they are trading for 130. The minimum value of a call option is its **exercise value**, the amount you could save if you purchase the bond by exercising the option. If the bond is selling for 100 or less, an option to buy at 100 saves you nothing; if the bond is selling for 130, the option saves you 30. Thus the exercise value is equal to the difference between the market value of the bond $P$ and the option's exercise price $E$ if the bond's price is higher than the exercise price:

$$
\begin{aligned}
\text{Exercise value} &= P - E &\quad &\text{if } P > E \\
&= 0 &\quad &\text{if } P \leq E
\end{aligned}
\tag{11.6}
$$

This relationship is graphed in Figure 11.2. The value of an option is never negative, because you are not compelled to exercise it. An option that has a positive exercise value is said to be "in the money"; one with no exercise value is "out of the money."

If we neglect transaction costs, an option should always sell for at least its exercise value, because the option is worth at least this much to investors who want to buy the bond. If an option sells for less than its exercise value, arbitragers can buy the option, exercise it, and then sell the bond for an immediate easy

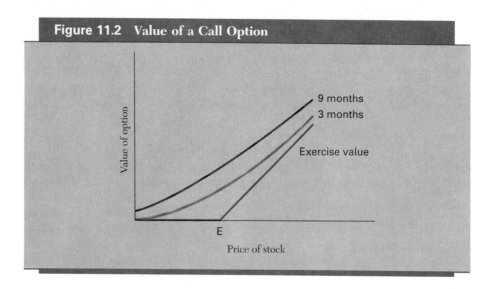

**Figure 11.2   Value of a Call Option**

profit. Suppose, for instance, that the Treasury bond is selling for 108 and that an option to buy at 100 is selling for only 2. An arbitrager can pay 2 for the option, exercise it by paying another 100, and then sell the bond for 108 — making a quick profit of 6 ($6000 per $100,000 of face value). The eagerness of arbitragers to exploit such opportunities keeps option prices from falling below their exercise value.

On the expiration date, the value of an option is equal to its exercise value, because then it must be exercised or discarded. Before expiration, option prices are invariably above their exercise value, because those who buy options do so in the hope that the price of the underlying asset will rise and make their option more valuable. As Figure 11.2 shows, options are more valuable when there is more time until expiration.

## The Lure of Leveraged Profits

Options provide leverage because for the price of the option, you earn profits on an asset that is worth much more than the option. Consider again a 3-month call option on a Treasury bond with an exercise price of 100, and suppose that the price of the option is 1 while the price of the bond is 100. Table 11.5 shows the percentage profits for someone who buys the bond and for someone who instead purchases an option to buy the bond.

If you buy the bond for 100 and its market value rises to 101 after 3 months, you make a 1 percent profit. If you instead buy a call option on the bond, its value at expiration is its exercise value of 1, just what you paid for it, and your profit is 0 percent. Not very attractive so far! However, consider what happens if the price of the bond rises to 102, giving a 2 percent profit to the person who bought the bond. The person who bought the option finds its value rising from 1 to 2, a 100 percent profit. If the price of the bond rises to 103, the option will be worth 3, a 200 percent profit. Because the bond is initially worth 100 times as much as the option, there is 100:1 leverage: each 1 percentage point increase in

**Table 11.5  Options Provide Leverage**

| Price at Expiration | | Percentage Gain (%) | |
| --- | --- | --- | --- |
| Bond | Option | Bond | Option |
| 98 | 0 | −2 | −100 |
| 99 | 0 | −1 | −100 |
| 100 | 0 | 0 | −100 |
| 101 | 1 | 1 | 0 |
| 102 | 2 | 2 | 100 |
| 103 | 3 | 3 | 200 |

the value of the stock brings a 100 percentage point increase in the value of the option. It is this chance for enormous leveraged profits that has historically lured investors to options. This leverage is not symmetrical, because the value of the option cannot be negative. As the option advisory services say, "The most you can lose is the cost of your option" — a peculiarly cheerful way of noting that if the price of the bond doesn't go up, your option will be worthless and you will have a 100 percent loss.

## Put Options

A **put option** is similar to a call option except that the owner has the right to *sell* an asset at a fixed price on or before a specified date. For instance, a put option could give the owner the right to sell an 8 percent coupon Treasury bond maturing in 2010 for 100 any time within the next 3 months. If the price of the bond declines, this put option becomes increasingly valuable. Specifically, the exercise value of a put is equal to

$$\text{Exercise value} = E - P \quad \text{if } P < E$$
$$= 0 \quad \text{if } P \geq E \qquad (11.7)$$

Figure 11.3 graphs this relationship.

As with a call, the exercise value of a put is the minimum value that it can sell for without attracting profitable arbitrage. On the exercise date, the market price of a put is equal to its exercise value; before this date, the price is somewhat higher, as bearish investors buy puts in anticipation of profiting from a drop in the price of the underlying asset.

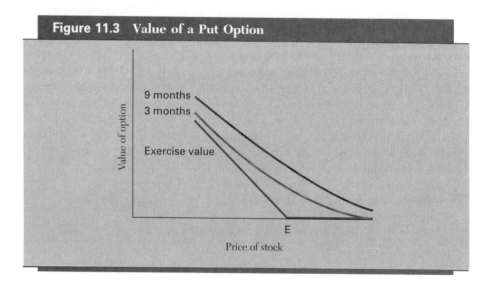

**Figure 11.3   Value of a Put Option**

Value of option

9 months
3 months

Exercise value

E

Price of stock

## Option Strategies

A put is a bet that the price of the underlying asset will fall; a call is a bet that it will rise. Because interest rates and bond prices are inversely related, a call option on Treasury bonds is a bet that interest rates will fall (raising bond prices), while a put is a wager that interest rates will increase. Puts and calls need not be purchased in isolation, as all-out bets on the direction of the asset's price. A variety of positions can be created by buying or selling various combinations of put, call, and the asset itself.

A bank may have a portfolio of long-term bonds, mortgages, and other assets whose value is very sensitive to interest rates. The bank can purchase insurance against a rise in interest rates and a corresponding decline in the value of these assets by purchasing Treasury bond put options. Suppose, for instance, that the bank has $500 million in Treasury bonds that it wishes to insure. If the bank buys 5000 Treasury bond puts, then it has the right to sell $500 million in Treasury bonds at a fixed price, insuring that the value of its portfolio won't drop below this fixed price. The price of this insurance is the cost of the put options.

What if the traded option contracts are for 20-year Treasury bonds with 8 percent coupons and the bank owns bonds and mortgages of various maturities? By comparing the duration of its portfolio with the duration of the 20-year Treasury bonds, the bank can estimate the relative sensitivity to interest rates. If, for instance, the bank estimates that a 2 percentage point decline in the market

**EXAMPLE 11.7** *Betting on Volatility*

A *straddle* is the simultaneous purchase of put and call options. A *Treasury straddle* is the purchase of a Treasury bond call option (a bet that the bond's price will rise) and a Treasury bond put option (a bet that bond prices will fall). Someone who creates a straddle makes a profit if Treasury bond prices either rise or fall, it doesn't matter which, above or below the exercise price by an amount equal to the price of the call plus the price of the put. Thus a Treasury bond straddle is an implicit bet that there will be a large change in interest rates.

Someone who writes a Treasury bond straddle, simultaneously selling a call and a put, is betting that interest rates will not change much, in either direction, during the life of the options. In the 1980s, one investor who routinely wrote stock straddles, betting that stock prices wouldn't change much, built his account up to $120,000 in October of 1987. Then the market fell by more than 20 percent on October 19, 1987, and this investor lost $450,000 in a single day, leaving his account $330,000 in the hole.*

*Tim Metz and James A. White, "A Year After Its Peak, Stock Market Battles a Pervasive Malaise," Wall Street Journal, *August 25, 1988.*

value of Treasury bonds will typically be accompanied by a 1 percentage point decline in the market value of its $500 million portfolio, the bank can buy 5000 Treasury bond puts, anticipating that any losses on its portfolio will be offset by profits on these put contracts.

A bank also might consider writing call options against its bond portfolio. These *covered calls* are a fairly conservative strategy, suitable for those who expect no more than a modest increase in bond prices. If bond prices hold steady or decline, the proceeds from selling now-worthless call options provide extra income; the cost is that the bonds will be called away if prices increase, putting a ceiling on profits. The writer of covered calls trades away the chance for large profits in return for extra income. Many college endowments and pension funds follow this conservative strategy for a portion of their stock and, to a lesser extent, bond portfolios.

## Index Options

In addition to the Treasury bond options used in these examples, financial institutions can trade options on futures contracts for a variety of bonds and for currency. As with futures, because a delivery is not needed to realize profits, options can be written on intangible things that cannot be delivered. An **index option** is an option contract based on the value of an index of asset prices such as the S&P 500 index of stock prices, an index of the prices of oil stocks, or an index of the prices of municipal bonds.

In each case we can use the same principles applied to Treasury bond options. For instance, consider options on the S&P 500 stock index. Those who don't wish to select individual stocks but think they can predict the overall direction of the stock market can buy stock index calls if they are bullish and puts if they are bearish. A pension fund that is willing to trade a chance at large profits for some extra income can write covered calls by buying a diversified portfolio of stocks and writing stock index calls. A fund that wants to protect itself against a market collapse can buy insurance by purchasing stock index puts. An arbitrager who thinks that index options are mispriced can create hedges.

## Option Valuation

Option values depend on the price of the underlying asset relative to the option's exercise price, the length of time until expiration, the volatility of the price of the underlying asset, and interest rates. The first two factors are straightforward. The third reflects the asymmetrical nature of an option. If the price of the asset rises, the price of a call option rises too, without bound, but if the asset's price falls below the exercise price, a call option has no exercise value, no matter how low the asset's price. Similarly, put options become increasingly valuable the lower the asset's price, but the exercise value is zero, no matter how much the price of the asset exceeds the exercise price. Thus an asset whose price will go up or down a lot is attractive to both put and call option holders.

EXAMPLE
11.8

## The Choice Between Callable and Noncallable Bonds

In analyzing callable bonds, it is helpful to split the security into two parts — a noncallable bond and a call option. An investor who buys a callable bond has implicitly bought a noncallable bond and also has sold a call option to the issuer with an exercise price equal to the bond's call price. If the value of the noncallable bond is $P$ and the value of the call option is $C$, then the value of the callable bond is $V = P - C$. It follows that the difference between the price of a noncallable and otherwise identical callable bond, $P - V = C$, is not constant, but rather varies with the value of the implicit call option.

As with any call option, the value of the call increases as the price of the underlying asset increases. For bonds, this means that a drop in interest rates and an accompanying increase in bond prices increases $C$ and widens the gap between the values of noncallable and callable bonds. Further, call options are more valuable if the volatility of the price of the underlying asset increases. Therefore, an increase in interest-rate volatility also increases the prices of noncallable bonds relative to callable bonds. Overall, noncallable bonds do relatively well when interest rates are falling and volatility is increasing, and callable bonds do relatively well when the reverse is true.

Corporate bonds are normally considered riskier than Treasury bonds and should, on average, have somewhat higher returns. However, Treasury bonds are generally not callable and most corporate bonds are. Over the period 1976 to 1986, interest rates declined slightly and volatility increased substantially, causing noncallable bonds to outperform otherwise equivalent callable bonds.* Thus, as it turned out, bond-portfolio managers who bought Treasury bonds did better than their competitors who bought corporate bonds.

An important aspect of bond-portfolio management is the choice between callable and noncallable bonds — an implicit bet on the level and volatility of interest rates. Those who want to make this bet even more explicit can construct hedged portfolios by buying callable bonds and selling noncallable ones, or vice versa.

*Chris P. Dialynas, "The Active Decisions in the Selection of Passive Management and Performance Bogeys," Pacific Investment Management Company, mimeo, 1988.

The fourth factor, high interest rates, is also subtle. Consider a 1-year call option that is likely to be exercised. You can either buy the asset now for its current price or buy an option and then pay the exercise price in 1 year. If interest rates are high, the advantage of paying for the asset later makes the call option more valuable.

To the extent that option and asset prices are related, riskless hedges can, in theory, be constructed by continuously maintaining an appropriate hedge ratio between assets and options. The observation that the return on a riskless hedge should equal the return on safe Treasury bills led Fischer Black and Myron Scholes, using some strong assumptions and advanced mathematics, to drive what is now called the Black–Scholes option pricing formula, a complex equation that is beyond the scope of this book.[6] Many investors now use these theoretical formulas, looking for mispriced options, an arbitrage activity that eliminates significant mispricing.

# SUMMARY

A futures contract is an agreement to deliver an item on a specified date at a price agreed to today but not paid until delivery. Futures can be used to hedge a position (a farmer selling corn futures), to speculate (a wager on the value of the deutschemark), or for arbitrage (between bonds and bond futures). Except for transaction costs, futures contracts are a zero-sum game, and contracts are marked to market each trading day by transferring funds between shorts and longs, depending on whether futures prices went up or down.

Shorts and longs can cover their positions before the delivery date, and almost all do. On the delivery date, the futures price is approximately equal to the spot price. Before the delivery date, the futures price may be influenced by investor expectations of the spot price on the delivery date. For precious metals, financial assets, and other items that can be stored and sold short, the spread between the futures price and the current spot price is determined by the cost of carry — the cost, including forgone interest, of buying the item now and holding it until the delivery date. If the cost of carry is positive, futures prices will be above spot prices and increase with the time until delivery.

For example, with stock index futures, the futures price $F$ should equal the spot price $P$ plus the interest $RP$ earned by postponing payment minus the dividends $D$ earned if the stock is purchased now:

$$P = P + RP - D = P(1 + R - D/P)$$

If the interest rate $R$ is above the dividend yield $D/P$, then the futures price will be above the spot price. If this pricing relationship is violated, then arbitragers can earn excessive risk-free profits by purchasing stocks and selling futures, or vice versa.

A call option gives a person the right, but not the obligation, to buy an asset at a fixed price on or before a specified date. A put option gives the holder the right to sell at a specified price. Option agreements are between private parties and, except for transaction costs, are a zero-sum game in that one's gain is the other's loss.

Options are seldom exercised. Instead, on the expiration date, any outstanding options are sold back to the option writers at a price approximately equal to the option's exercise value — the amount an option holder could save by exercising the option instead of buying or selling the underlying asset at its market price.

Traditionally, many have been lured to options and futures contracts for speculation — high-stakes wagers on whether asset prices will rise or fall. However, the combination of futures, puts, calls, and the underlying asset offers financial institutions and other investors a wide variety of hedging strategies — for instance, insuring a mortgage portfolio by selling Treasury bond futures or buying Treasury bond puts.

## IMPORTANT TERMS

arbitrage
basis
call option
cost of carry
covering
daily limits
daily settlement
exercise date
exercise price
exercise value
forward contracts
futures
index arbitrage

index option
interest-rate parity equation
margin
marking to market
open interest
option contract
portfolio insurance
program trading
put option
reversing
settlement price
spot price
striking price

## EXERCISES

1. Use the data on December 1992 Treasury bond contracts in Table 11.3 to answer the following questions.
   a. What was the opening price on April 10?
   b. How many contracts were in existence?
   c. If a bank bought 1000 contracts at the April 10 settlement price and took delivery, how much would it have to pay at delivery? (Ignore transaction costs.)
   d. What was the change between the opening and settlement prices on April 10?
   e. What was the change between the settlement price on April 9 and the settlement price on April 10?

2. Find Chicago Board of Trade corn futures in the most recent Monday issue of *The Wall Street Journal*. Report the settlement prices, and compare these current prices with those shown in Table 11.3, both in their level and in the existence of a seasonal pattern.

3. Look up COMEX silver futures in the most recent Monday issue of *The Wall Street Journal*. How does the current level of silver futures prices compare with silver prices when the Hunt brothers had billions of dollars invested in silver? Does the pattern of silver futures settlement prices for different delivery dates suggest that silver futures prices are determined by anticipated prices on the delivery dates or by the current spot price and cost of carry?

4. Why might a wheat farmer sell wheat futures contracts even though he doesn't plan

on selling his wheat until 2 weeks after the delivery date?

5. Why might a wheat farmer buy a wheat futures contract even if the farmer doesn't plan on buying the wheat on the delivery date?

6. The text explains how a U.S. bank that expects to receive 125 million German marks in March of 1993 can, on April 10, 1992, sell 1000 March 1993 futures contracts at $0.5841 to protect itself from exchange-rate fluctuations. If the dollar price of deutschemarks on the March 1993 delivery date turns out to be $0.5952, does this hypothetical bank make a profit or loss on its futures contracts?

7. Example 11.3 tells of a baseball futures market. When the Yankees opened the 1988 season at 93, did this price reflect expectations or the cost of carry?

8. Rebut this argument by a Kansas congressman in 1890:

*Those who deal in "options" and "futures" contracts, which is mere gambling, no matter by what less offensive name such transactions be designated, neither add to the supply nor increase the demand for consumption, nor do they accomplish any useful purpose by their calling; on the contrary, they speculate in fictitious products [which are never actually delivered]. The wheat they buy and sell is known as "wind wheat" and doubtless for the reason that it is invisible, intangible, and felt or realized only in the terrible force it exerts in destroying the farming industry of the country.[7]*

9. The cost of storing platinum is $2 per 50 troy ounces per month. If the interest rate is 6 percent, what pattern would you expect to find in 3-, 6-, and 9-month platinum futures prices?

10. Carefully explain why someone who expects the price of gold to rise from $400 an ounce now to $450 an ounce a year from now would prefer paying $420 an ounce for a 1-year gold futures contract to paying $400 an ounce for gold today.

11. On April 10, 1992, the spot price of the German deutschemark was 0.6107 dollars. Do the prices of deutschemark futures in Table 11.3 suggest that German interest rates were higher than U.S. interest rates, lower than U.S. interest rates, or about the same?

12. On August 16, 1988, the exchange rate for Japanese yen was $0.007488, while the prices of yen futures contracts were $0.007589 for December delivery, $0.007660 for March 1989 delivery, and $0.007741 for June 1989 delivery. Were Japanese interest rates higher or lower than U.S. interest rates? Explain your reasoning.

13. Investment banks hold inventories of bonds that they have purchased from some clients and that they intend to sell to other clients. To hedge their exposure to interest-rate risk, should the banks buy or sell bond futures? Explain.

14. A bank has made a commitment to loan a real estate developer $10 million at a 10 percent interest rate 3 months from now. Will this bank suffer a financial loss on this commitment if interest rates move up or move down during the next 3 months? To hedge this risk, should it buy or sell Treasury bond futures?

15. Many savings and loan associations have short-term deposits and long-term mortgages. Will they experience a loss if interest rates go up or go down? To protect themselves, explain which of the following actions are appropriate and which actions are inappropriate.

a. Lengthen the maturity of their assets
b. Issue more variable-rate mortgages
c. Buy 30-year zero-coupon bonds
d. Buy Treasury bond futures
e. Buy call options on Treasury bonds
f. Buy put options on Treasury bonds

16. In 1987 many pension funds grew increasingly nervous about their stock portfolios as price–earnings ratios approached all-time highs. Indicate which of the following they could have purchased and which they could have sold to protect themselves from a collapse in stock prices.
   a. Stock index call options
   b. Stock index put options
   c. Stock index futures

17. The Chicago Board of Trade requires that the purchaser of a U.S. Treasury bond futures contract put up an initial margin of $5000 per contract and at all times maintain a margin of at least $4000 per contract. What criteria do you suppose the board used to choose these particular numbers?

18. In November of 1984, Professor Stephen Figlewski was quoted in the *New York Times* as saying that stock index futures are so new and so complex that the market is not yet dominated by arbitragers and other professionals and is consequently not yet efficient.

*According to Professor Figlewski, a simple formula tells what the stock index future's price should be, if the market were efficient. Take whatever the index is, say 100, and add the interest rate that an investor would make on his money if it were invested in a money market fund or Treasury bills, say 10 percent. Then subtract the dividend rate, for example 4 percent. In this case the answer is 106, so if index futures were selling above or below that, then clearly the market is inefficient, Professor Figlewski said.*[8]

Clearly explain the logic behind the professor's formula. If, in this example, the index future were selling for less than 106, how could you make a safe profit larger than that available on Treasury bills?

19. The interest rates on Eurodollars are typically a percentage point above Treasury bill rates. An investment advisory service recommends a TED spread under certain circumstances, buying Treasury bill futures and selling Eurodollar futures.[9] For this to be profitable, is the service counting on the interest-rate differential between Eurodollars and T-bills to widen or to narrow? Explain.

20. An investment advisory service wrote the following:

*The relationship between the price of gold and the price of silver has changed considerably since the days when Menes I [an Egyptian Pharaoh in around 2850 B.C.] could trade three ounces of silver for one ounce of gold. In 1932, for example, in the midst of The Great Depression, it took 20 ounces of silver to buy one ounce of gold. By 1960, the Ratio was 16-to-1. In recent years, however, it has stabilized in the range of 34 to 38 ounces of silver for every ounce of gold. . . .*

*The Ratio has fluctuated widely just in the past seven or eight years, dipping as low as 19-to-1 in 1980 and soaring as high as 52-to-1 in 1982 and 55-to-1 in 1985.*

*But, as you can also clearly see, it has always — ALWAYS — returned to the range between 34-to-1 and 38-to-1.*[10]

The service recommends acting when the ratio is above 45:1 or below 15:1. In which case should you buy gold futures and sell silver futures, and in which case should you do the reverse? Is there any risk in this strategy?

21. Investors who had been following a stock options strategy touted by brokers as a sure thing lost hundreds of millions of dollars when the Dow dropped 508 points on October 19, 1987. Were they buying calls, selling calls, buying puts, or selling puts? Explain your reasoning.

22. A financial columnist offered several tips to stockholders who want protection from a decline in stock prices, while "allowing yourself room to make money if the bull is still alive."[11] One of his tips was to buy put options. Explain how this action accomplishes the stated objective, and explain the drawbacks (if any).

23. On October 6, 1989, March 1990 Treasury-bill call options with an exercise price of 92.75 traded for 0.86 and March 1990 Treasury-bill put options with an exercise price of 92.75 traded for 0.41. All these prices are as a percent of the $1 million face value of a contract; thus the price of one call option is $8600. Graph the dollar gain from each of the following strategies as a function of the price of Treasury bills on the exercise date: (a) buy one call option; (b) buy one put option. Which strategy is a bet that interest rates will rise?

24. Using the data in Exercise 23, graph the dollar gain from a strategy of buying both one call option and one put option as a function of the price of Treasury bills on the exercise date.

25. In the table below are selected prices from November 15, 1989, for options for Japanese yen futures to be delivered in December of 1989, January of 1990, and March of 1990:

All these prices are in U.S. cents per 100 yen; at the time, the spot price was 69.56 cents for 100 yen.

a. Why do these call prices decline as the striking prices increase, while put prices increase?

b. Why are the March calls worth more than the December calls, and why are the March puts worth more than the December puts?

26. Use the data in Exercise 25 to graph the dollar gain from each of the following strategies as a function of the price of Japanese yen futures on the exercise date: (a) buy one call option; (b) buy one put option. Should a speculator who believes that the value of the dollar will rise relative to the yen buy yen put or call options? Why might a bank that is not interested in speculating on the value of the yen nonetheless buy yen put options?

27. When Professor Smith came to Pomona College, he encountered the Econ Club's annual investment contest. Each contestant is given $10,000 in play money to manage over a 3-month period; the winner is given a real cash prize. Smith managed the portfolios of two contestants, his secretary and a student. All the secretary's money was invested in a put option for a certain company's stock; all the student's money was invested in a call option for the same stock. At the end of 3 months, the student's portfolio had grown to nearly $50,000 — easily winning the contest. Explain Smith's strategy. What do you think happened to the secretary's portfolio?

28. E. G. Capital Management, an investment management company, buys high-dividend

| Exercise Price | Call Options | | | Put Options | | |
|---|---|---|---|---|---|---|
| | Dec | Jan | Mar | Dec | Jan | Mar |
| 69 | 1.07 | 1.55 | 2.04 | 0.40 | 0.63 | 1.13 |
| 70 | 0.51 | 0.98 | 1.50 | 0.83 | 1.06 | 1.58 |
| 71 | 0.21 | 0.58 | 1.09 | 1.52 | 1.66 | 2.14 |

stocks and writes call options against these stocks. The *New York Times* says that this fund has done very well in sluggish markets, but "in surging markets . . . will almost always underperform market indexes."[12] Explain why this is so.

29. A *New York Times* reporter wrote, "Professional stock market traders like [options] because it affords them an opportunity to lose money profitably."[13] Give a specific example of how a trader might lose money in options while making an overall profit.

30. A *married put* is the simultaneous purchase of a stock and a put on that stock. For example, on October 22, 1991, Apple Computer common stock sold for 54½ per share and a January 1992 put with an exercise price of 55 sold for 3¾. Graph the dollar profit on a married put as a function of the price of Apple stock on the date the put expires. What kind of strategy is a married put?

# 12 Using Swaps to Manage Exchange-Rate and Interest-Rate Risk

*The idea is there, locked inside. All you have to do is remove the excess stone.*
**Michelangelo**

The term **swap** is commonly used in financial markets to describe contracts in which two parties agree to make one or more exchanges of specified assets. In this chapter we focus on two kinds of swaps — currency swaps and interest-rate swaps — that are used to transform the currency in which assets or liabilities are denominated and whether their interest rates are fixed or variable. These two types of swaps are now used by many financial institutions, nonfinancial businesses, and government agencies to manage exchange-rate risk and interest-rate risk. Since the first currency swap in 1979 and the first interest-rate swap in 1981, these arrangements have grown remarkably, and at the end of 1992, there were more than $5 trillion in swap agreements in place.

Some swaps are very simple "plain vanilla" agreements. Others require long, complex contracts that spell out a variety of technical details and contingencies designed to meet very specific needs of the participants. We will use no-frills, "plain vanilla" swaps to focus our attention on a few general principles that will help us understand how swaps work and why they have become so popular. We begin with currency swaps.

## CURRENCY SWAPS

In a **currency swap** (sometimes called a *cross-currency swap*), two parties effectively trade assets or liabilities denominated in different currencies. The simplest currency swap is an agreement to sell a currency now at a given price and then repurchase it at a stated price on a specified future date, with the difference between the sale and repurchase price called the *swap rate*. For instance, a German bank might swap deutschemarks for dollars with a New York bank by agreeing to sell 1 million deutschemarks at a price of 0.60 dollars/mark and to repurchase 1 million deutschemarks a year later at a price of 0.61 dollars/mark. This kind of currency swap allows the German bank to borrow dollars and the New York bank to borrow marks.

Often a currency swap is tied to debt issues: two parties issue bonds denominated in different currencies and then agree to swap the proceeds of the debt issues and to repay each other's debts — effectively transforming each debt into the other currency. For example, a U.S. company might want to borrow 10 million deutschemarks. The company may believe, however, that it can get more attractive terms if it issues dollar-denominated bonds in the United States, where it is well known, and then arrange a dollar/mark currency swap with a German company that wants dollars but finds it easier to sell mark-denominated bonds in Germany.

If the exchange rate is 0.60 dollars/mark, the U.S. company issues dollar-denominated bonds worth $6 million in the United States, the German company issues mark-denominated bonds worth 10 million marks in Germany, and they exchange the proceeds. The U.S. company thereby obtains the 10 million marks that it wants and the German company gets $6 million that it wants.

Further, as illustrated in Figure 12.1, the U.S. company agrees to pay the German company (in marks) the coupons and principal that the German firm owes on its German debt, and the German firm pays the U.S. company (in dollars) the coupons and principal that the U.S. firm owes on the American debt. The U.S. company is still legally obligated to pay its bondholders dollars, but these are covered by the dollars that it receives from the German company; its

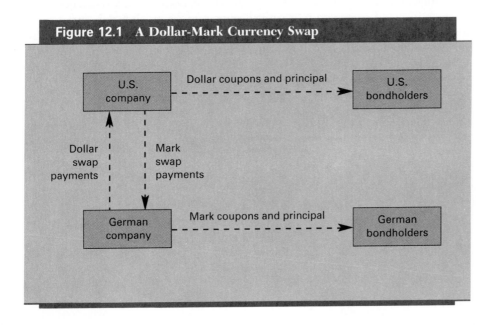

**Figure 12.1   A Dollar-Mark Currency Swap**

effective liability is the marks that it must come up with to pay the German company each year. Similarly, the German company's mark obligations to its bondholders are covered by the marks it receives from the U.S. firm; its effective liability is the dollars it must pay the American firm. The two companies have effectively swapped debts, in that the U.S. company obtains 10 million marks and repays marks while the German company gets $6 million and repays dollars. Because this currency swap allows each firm to transform its debt issue from one currency into another, it is often called an "exchange of borrowings."

In this example, each firm borrows in its domestic market, where it is presumably well known and able to borrow at relatively low interest rates. In other cases, businesses and government agencies that have worldwide reputations issue bonds denominated in foreign currencies and then use currency swaps to convert their debts into domestic currency or into other foreign currencies. By making these conversions easy and inexpensive, currency swaps help link international financial markets. In fact, the development of the swap market in the late 1970s and early 1980s was central to the development of worldwide financial markets in which securities are not necessarily denominated in the domestic currency of the issuer or the purchaser.

## Managing Exchange-Rate Risk

Changes in exchange rates can cause capital gains or losses for multinational firms that have assets and liabilities denominated in a variety of currencies. For example, a firm that has assets denominated in dollars and liabilities denominated in marks suffers a capital loss if the mark appreciates relative to the dollar. A firm does not have to convert all its assets and liabilities into a single currency in order to avoid exchange-rate capital gains and losses, but it is exposed to exchange-rate risk if it has some assets in one currency that are not matched by corresponding liabilities in the same currency.

Consider the firm with the hypothetical balance sheet shown in Table 12.1. All assets and liabilities are calculated in dollars using the exchange rates shown.

**Table 12.1   A Firm with Assets and Liabilities Denominated in Different Currencies**

| Assets | | Liabilities | |
|---|---|---|---|
| Dollar-denominated | $180,000,000 | Dollar-denominated | $50,000,000 |
| Mark-denominated | 12,000,000 | Mark-denominated | 30,000,000 |
| (20 million marks | | (50 million marks | |
| @ $0.60/mark) | | @ $0.60/mark) | |
| Yen-denominated | 8,000,000 | Net worth | $120,000,000 |
| (1 billion yen | | | |
| @ $0.008/yen) | | | |
| | $200,000,000 | | $200,000,000 |

**Table 12.2   Depreciation of the Dollar Relative to the Mark Reduces This Firm's Net Worth**

| Assets | | Liabilities | |
|---|---|---|---|
| Dollar-denominated | $180,000,000 | Dollar-denominated | $50,000,000 |
| Mark-denominated | 14,000,000 | Mark-denominated | 35,000,000 |
| (20 million marks | | (50 million marks | |
| @ $0.70/mark) | | @ $0.70/mark) | |
| Yen-denominated | 8,000,000 | Net worth | $117,000,000 |
| (1 billion yen | | | |
| @ $0.008/yen) | | | |
| | $202,000,000 | | $202,000,000 |

If the dollar depreciates relative to the mark, it will take more dollars to buy marks, making mark-denominated assets and liabilities worth more dollars. Because this firm has more mark-denominated liabilities than assets, it will experience capital losses if the dollar depreciates relative to the mark. Specifically, Table 12.2 shows that this firm (with 30 million more deutschemark liabilities than deutschemark assets) will have a $3 million capital loss if the exchange rate changes from 0.60 dollars per mark to 0.70 dollars per mark.

To reduce its exposure to dollar/mark exchange-rate risk, this firm could swap $18 million (30 million marks) of its mark-denominated liabilities for dollar-denominated liabilities. This would leave it with $12 million in mark-denominated liabilities, which matches its $12 million in mark-denominated assets. With its deutschemark assets and liabilities matched, a change in the dollar/mark exchange rate does not alter the dollar (or mark) value of its net worth. This specific example illustrates the general point that currency swaps can be used to manage exchange-rate risk by matching the currencies in which assets and liabilities are denominated.

**EXAMPLE 12.1**

## The IBM–World Bank Currency Swap

The first substantial currency swap was arranged by Salomon Brothers in August of 1981 and involved IBM and the World Bank. In March of 1980, IBM issued a large number of bonds denominated in a variety of currencies, including the deutschemark and Swiss franc. The funds raised from these bond issues were converted into dollars in the foreign exchange market and used for IBM's operations. Because the coupons and principal on these bonds were denominated in foreign currencies and IBM did not have matching assets in these currencies, IBM was exposed to exchange-rate risk. If the dollar declined relative to the mark, for example, the mark-denominated bonds would be increasingly burdensome for IBM.

## IBM's Currency Swap with the World Bank

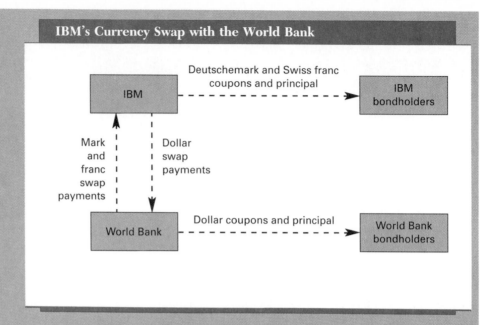

As it turned out, shortly after IBM had issued these bonds, the dollar appreciated substantially relative to the deutschemark and the Swiss franc, and IBM was very interested in locking in these capital gains by effectively converting these bonds into dollar-denominated liabilities. Coincidentally, the World Bank had a formal policy of raising funds in currencies with low interest rates, which at that time included the deutschemark as well as the Swiss franc. Salomon Brothers worked out a currency swap that accommodated both IBM and the World Bank.

The World Bank issued dollar-denominated bonds with maturities that coincided with IBM's deutschemark and Swiss franc bonds and agreed to pay IBM the deutschemarks and Swiss francs that IBM needed to pay the coupons and principal on its bonds. In return, IBM agreed to pay the World Bank the dollars that the World Bank needed to pay the dollar coupons and principal on its bonds. The World Bank's liability was now the marks and francs that it was obligated to pay IBM, and IBM's liability was the dollars it was obligated to pay the World Bank. Thus this currency swap converted the World Bank's liability from dollars into deutschemarks and Swiss francs and transformed IBM's liability from deutschemarks and Swiss francs into dollars (see accompanying figure).

This was the first large currency swap, and it attracted worldwide attention. The international reputations of IBM and the World Bank helped establish currency swaps as legitimate, useful financial tools and launched what was to become a trillion dollar market in less than 10 years.

# INTEREST-RATE SWAPS

Some debts have fixed interest rates; for example, a 10-year corporate bond with 8 percent coupons or a 30-year mortgage at 12 percent. Other debts have variable (or floating) interest rates; for example, a 7-year loan with an interest rate adjusted every 6 months to be 2 percentage points above the current 6-month **London interbank offered rate** (**LIBOR**), the interest rate that large international banks charge each other for Eurodollar loans. In an **interest-rate swap**, two unrelated borrowers in effect exchange fixed-rate and floating-rate loans by agreeing to make each other's interest payments. The two parties do not trade their debts or lend each other money, but they agree to make each other's interest payments as if they had swapped debts.

This kind of agreement is illustrated by the hypothetical example illustrated in Figure 12.2. International Electric has borrowed $10 million from Third National Bank at a floating interest rate equal to the 1-year LIBOR plus 80 basis points. For simplicity, we are assuming that International Electric pays interest annually for 10 years and then the company makes a $10 million balloon payment. Meanwhile, Discount Stores has privately placed $10 million in bonds with 8.60 percent annual coupons with General Insurance, thereby borrowing $10 million at a fixed interest rate of 8.60 percent. In the swap agreement depicted in Figure 12.2, International Electric receives annual floating-rate swap payments that cover its interest obligations; in return, the company makes annual fixed-rate swap payments to Discount Stores. International Electric's floating-

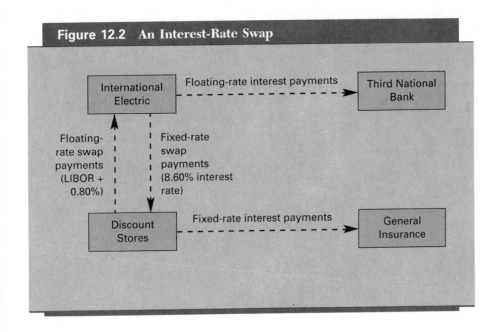

**Figure 12.2   An Interest-Rate Swap**

rate debt is thereby effectively converted into a fixed-rate obligation, and Discount Stores simultaneously transforms its fixed-rate debt into a floating-rate obligation.

As shown in Figure 12.2, International Electric continues to make its floating-rate interest payments to Third National Bank, and Discount Stores continues to pay 8.60 percent annual coupons to General Insurance. However, the swap has reversed their exposure to interest-rate risk. Before the swap, an increase in LIBOR is expensive for International Electric because it must pay more interest to Third National Bank. After the swap, International Electric's increased payments to Third National Bank are offset by the increased interest that it receives from Discount Stores. No matter whether LIBOR goes up or down, International Electric's interest outlay is fixed at 8.60 percent. Similarly, before the swap, Discount Stores did not benefit from declining interest rates because it had fixed 8.60 percent coupons. After the swap, if LIBOR declines, Discount Stores pays less to International Electric but receives enough money from International Electric to cover the 8.60 percent coupons.

In practice, only the net difference in interest payments changes hands. If the 12-month LIBOR happens to be 7.25 percent, then the floating-rate interest rate is LIBOR plus 80 basis points = 7.25 percent + 0.80 percent = 8.05 percent. The net difference in interest payments requires International Electric to pay Discount Stores $55,000:

International Electric owes Discount Stores 8.60%($10,000,000) = $860,000
Discount Stores owes International Electric 8.05%($10,000,000) = $805,000
International Electric pays Discount Stores                        $55,000

Instead of International Electric sending Discount Stores a check for $860,000 and Discount Stores sending International Electric a check for $805,000, International Electric simply sends a check for the difference, $55,000.

One advantage of interest-rate swaps is that someone who wants to borrow at a fixed interest rate may find it easier to borrow at a floating rate through accustomed channels (such as a local bank), while someone else who wants to borrow at a variable interest rate finds it easier to borrow at a fixed rate from familiar investors (perhaps a private placement with an insurance company). These borrowers can then use an interest-rate swap to obtain the fixed or floating rates they prefer.

In addition, interest-rate swaps give firms flexibility in switching between fixed-rate and floating-rate debt. For example, Discount Stores may have wanted a fixed-interest-rate loan when it issued $10 million in 10-year bonds with 8.6 percent coupons. If it subsequently decides that it wants to bet on falling interest rates, it can use a swap to convert its fixed-rate debt into a variable-rate debt. Later, perhaps after interest rates have declined, Discount Stores can use a swap to convert its floating-rate debt back into a fixed-rate debt.

## Managing Interest-Rate Risk

Chapter 5 explained how the net worth of a firm with mismatched asset and liability durations is vulnerable to unexpected interest-rate fluctuations. Swaps can be used to manage this interest-rate risk. For example, if a savings and loan association uses short-term deposits to finance long-term fixed-rate loans, the interest expense on its deposits fluctuates with market interest rates, but the interest income on its assets does not fluctuate. It will consequently experience losses if interest rates rise unexpectedly. An international bank might have the opposite problem: if it has issued long-term fixed-rate bonds to finance the purchase of variable-rate assets (for example, loans tied to Treasury-bill rates), it will suffer losses if interest rates fall unexpectedly. These financial institutions can use the interest-rate swap described in Example 12.2 to reduce their interest-rate risk.

**EXAMPLE**

**12.2**    *Matching Assets and Liabilities*

The figure below depicts an interest-rate swap between an S&L that is using floating-rate deposits to finance fixed-rate mortgages and an international bank that is using fixed-rate bonds to finance variable-rate business loans. The thrift, in essence, takes over some of the fixed-rate interest payments on the bank's long-term bonds, while the bank takes over some of the variable-rate interest

### A Swap Between an S&L and an International Bank

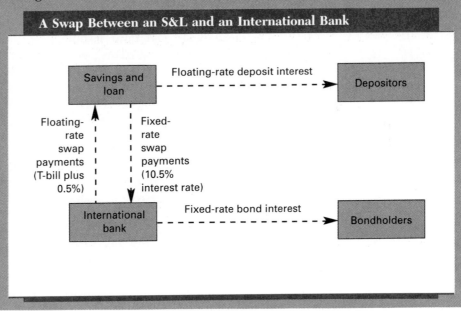

payments on the thrift's deposits — allowing each to adjust its liabilities to match its assets better.

Specifically, suppose that the term structure is flat with Treasury securities paying 10 percent and that the bank has issued $50 million in 10-year debt with a fixed interest rate of 10.5 percent. The bank and thrift might agree to a $50 million 10-year swap, with the thrift paying the bank a fixed annual interest rate of 10.5 percent on $50 million and the bank paying the thrift the 1-year Treasury-bill rate plus 50 basis points on $50 million. If the 1-year Treasury-bill rate stays at 10 percent, their payments cancel and no transfer of funds is necessary. The thrift will make a payment to the bank if the Treasury-bill rate rises and receive a payment from the bank if the Treasury-bill rate declines. If, for example, the Treasury-bill rate rises by 2 percentage points, to 12 percent, the thrift must pay the bank

$$(12.5\% - 10.5\%)(\$50 \text{ million}) = \$1 \text{ million}$$

If the Treasury-bill rate falls by 2 percentage points, to 8 percent, the bank pays the thrift $1 million.

By making fixed-rate payments instead of variable-rate payments, the thrift can hedge part of its fixed-rate mortgage portfolio. By making variable-rate payments instead of fixed-rate payments, the bank's liabilities correspond more closely to its variable-rate business loans. The thrift effectively swaps some of its variable-rate debt for some of the bank's fixed-rate debt — allowing each institution to adjust the duration of its liabilities to match more closely the duration of its assets.

Many commercial banks and thrift institutions use swaps to transform money-market deposit accounts (MMDAs), certificates of deposit (CDs), and other short-term floating-rate liabilities into long-term fixed-rate debt that better matches the durations of their assets. Swaps can accomplish the same thing for a financial institution that has floating-rate assets (for example, short-term assets and variable-rate loans) and fixed-rate liabilities (for example, long-term bonds and fixed-rate deposits).

Similarly, a corporation might pay for a construction project by issuing commercial paper and then use an interest-rate swap in which it makes fixed-rate payments and receives variable-rate payments tied to the commercial paper rate. In this way it finances a long-term asset by issuing short-term commercial paper but paying a long-term fixed-rate of interest.

Another variation is a floating-to-floating swap, in which an asset or debt that is tied to one interest-rate index is swapped for one tied to another index. For example, many floating-rate loans worldwide are indexed to LIBOR. A corporation that has a bank loan tied to LIBOR can use a LIBOR/T-bill swap to link its loan rate to the Treasury-bill rate instead. Similarly, the interest on a U.S. bank's deposits might be linked to the Treasury-bill rate while some of its loans are tied to the **prime rate**, a publicized measure of the interest rate that it charges its most creditworthy borrowers. It can use a prime/T-bill swap to transform these

EXAMPLE
12.3

## A Renault Swap Goes Awry

In 1983, Beverly Hills Savings and Loan (an American savings and loan) and Renault Acceptance (a Netherlands financing subsidiary of the French auto-maker) agreed to an interest-rate swap. Like most S&Ls, Beverly Hills was financing fixed-rate mortgages with variable-rate deposits. In order to reduce its exposure to interest-rate risk, it agreed to pay Renault a fixed rate of interest on $12 million of Renault's long-term debts; in return, Renault agreed to pay Beverly Hills a variable interest rate on $12 million in deposits. The accompanying figure summarizes this swap.

Because of its suspect financial status, Beverly Hills secured the swap by putting $2 million of collateral into an escrow account. Beverly Hills' financial condition worsened, and in April of 1985 the Federal Savings & Loan Insurance Corporation (FSLIC), which had insured Beverly Hills' deposits, seized the S&L in order to limit its losses. A reorganized company reopened as Beverly Hills Savings.

Renault argued that because its swap agreement was explicitly nonassignable, the contract had been breached when Beverly Hills Savings and Loan was declared insolvent and the swap agreement was reassigned to Beverly Hills Savings. Renault prepared to stop its swap payments and asked for half the $2 million collateral as compensation. In response, Beverly Hills Savings obtained a preliminary injunction from the California Superior Court freezing the $2 million collateral and preventing Renault from canceling the swap agreement. This incident understandably made other swap participants nervous about their exposure to default risk, particularly if they had swap arrangements with U.S. savings and loan associations.

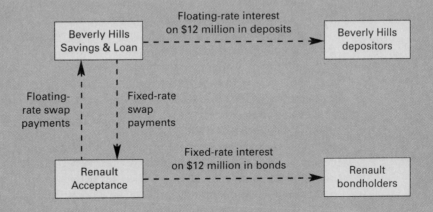

loans so that their interest rates are, like the bank's deposits, based on Treasury-bill rates — thereby eliminating the risk that the spread between the prime rate and Treasury-bill rate will narrow.

The preceding chapter explained how interest-rate futures also can be used to reduce interest-rate risk. One advantage of swaps over futures is that futures do not have maturities longer than $2\frac{1}{2}$ years, but swaps can last decades. Swaps also offer more flexibility in negotiating specific details and do not need to be monitored constantly with daily settlements as futures prices fluctuate. On the other hand, it is easier and less expensive to reverse a futures contract than to cancel a swap agreement.

## Market Imperfections

Swaps can be thought of as a convenient financial instrument that gives people more flexibility in structuring their assets and liabilities. Many swap participants feel that the popularity of swaps is due to something more — that swaps are financially advantageous because they overcome market imperfections that allow some borrowers to obtain more favorable terms in some financial markets than in others, perhaps because the borrower is better known to some investors than to others. For example, a savings and loan may want long-duration liabilities to match its long-duration assets, but it may have a hard time persuading its depositors to make long-term fixed-rate deposits. It could raise money by issuing long-term bonds, but this would require time-consuming registration with the SEC and incur advertising costs, legal expenses, and underwriting fees. The savings and loan could avoid SEC registration by issuing dollar-denominated bonds in the Eurodollar bond market, but because of the absence of registration and disclosure requirements, Eurodollar bond rates are substantially higher than domestic bond rates unless the issuing firm is very well known.

There is seemingly a market imperfection here in that the savings and loan can obtain funds less expensively from local depositors than by selling Eurodollar bonds. Interest-rate swaps may help overcome this imperfection by making it relatively easy and inexpensive for a well-known international bank to borrow in the Eurodollar bond market and swap interest payments with a savings and loan that can attract relatively low-interest deposits.

Similarly, large, well-known corporations are able to issue long-term fixed-rate bonds at reasonable interest rates. Smaller and less creditworthy businesses are usually unable to do so (except at extraordinarily high interest rates) and are therefore compelled to borrow from a local bank. While the small firm may prefer financing its construction project with a long-term fixed-rate loan, banks generally prefer floating-rate loans that match their floating-rate deposits. An interest-rate swap may allow both to have the terms they prefer. The small company can borrow from a local bank at a floating rate and then swap payments with a well-known corporation that is able to issue inexpensive fixed-rate bonds, perhaps in the Eurobond market. Again, the financial advantages of this arrangement may be the consequence of market imperfections.

# CROSS-CURRENCY INTEREST-RATE SWAPS

A cross-currency interest-rate swap involves a fixed-rate loan denominated in one currency and a variable-rate loan denominated in another currency — for example, swapping a dollar floating-rate loan for a deutschemark fixed-rate loan. A relatively small import company might borrow domestic currency from a local bank at a floating rate and then use a cross-currency interest-rate swap to swap payments with a large corporation that has issued fixed-rate bonds denominated in a foreign currency.

One of the first cross-currency interest-rate swaps was arranged by Bankers Trust between Renault, the French car company, and Yamaichi Securities, acting on behalf of Japanese institutional investors. Renault was not permitted to issue fixed-rate yen debt, but it effectively did so by borrowing with a floating-rate dollar loan and then entering into a swap in which it made fixed-rate yen payments to Yamaichi in return for floating-rate dollar payments. Yamaichi passed the fixed-rate yen payments along to Japanese investors. This cross-currency floating-to-fixed swap is depicted in Figure 12.3.

In a cross-currency floating-to-floating swap, a debt that is denominated in one currency and tied to one interest-rate index is swapped for one denominated in another currency and tied to another index. For example, a multinational corporation with a deutschemark loan based on a short-term German interest-rate index can use a cross-currency floating-to-floating swap to transform its loan

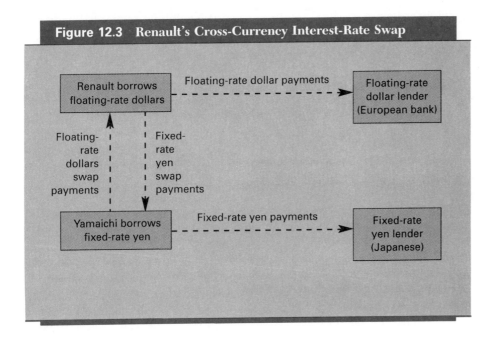

**Figure 12.3   Renault's Cross-Currency Interest-Rate Swap**

EXAMPLE
12.4

## Sallie Mae Shops and Swaps

The **Student Loan Marketing Association** (**Sallie Mae**) was created in 1972 to provide a secondary market for federally guaranteed student loans. Sallie Mae issues unsecured short-term and long-term debts, using the proceeds to purchase student loans from banks, educational institutions, and government agencies. Most of the student loans it purchases are federally guaranteed under the Guaranteed Student Loan Program, and the interest rate the lender receives is set at 3.5 percentage points above the 3-month Treasury-bill rate. The federal government makes the interest payment while the student is in school; the student begins repaying the loan after graduation.

Sallie Mae also lends institutions money — called *warehousing advances* — that must be used to maintain or expand the lender's student loans. In addition, Sallie Mae has developed loan programs for law and medical students and has issued letters of credit to support state and local bond issues to finance student loans.

Most of Sallie Mae's assets are variable-rate loans and advances. To insulate its profits from interest-rate fluctuations, it would prefer to finance its lending with variable-rate liabilities. However, it has often found it less expensive to raise funds by selling fixed-rate bonds. In 1982 Sallie Mae pioneered interest-rate swaps in the United States. By issuing fixed-rate debt and swapping it for variable-rate debt, Sallie Mae found that it could reduce its borrowing costs and restructure its liabilities to match its rate-sensitive assets. Savings and loan associations are a natural partner for such a swap because they can better match their assets and liabilities by swapping variable-rate debt (their deposits) for Sallie Mae's fixed-rate debt.

Sallie Mae also has used currency swaps, issuing bonds abroad that are denominated in foreign currencies and swapping them for dollar-denominated debts that match its dollar-denominated assets. For example, Sallie Mae issued yen-denominated securities and then exchanged its yen obligations with a Japanese firm that had issued a comparable amount of debt denominated in dollars.

Sallie Mae has been a very innovative financial institution, borrowing worldwide by issuing fixed-rate and floating-rate securities denominated in a variety of currencies and then using swaps, as needed, to convert this debt into dollar-denominated floating-rate liabilities. By carefully matching its assets and liabilities, Sallie Mae has largely insulated itself from interest-rate risks and has been consistently profitable — whether interest rates have moved up or down.

into a dollar liability based on the Treasury-bill rate. Similarly, the interest on some of an international bank's deposits may be in dollars and rise or fall with the Treasury-bill rate, while some of its loans may be in French francs and fluctuate with LIBOR. A cross-currency floating-to-floating swap can transform these loans so that the bank's interest income, like its interest expenses, is in dollars and fluctuates with Treasury-bill rates, protecting its profits from changes in the franc/dollar exchange rate and from changes in the spread between LIBOR and the Treasury-bill rate.

# THE SWAP MARKET

It has been estimated that U.S. commercial banks had $857 billion in swaps on their books in 1988.[1] Variable-rate swap obligations are usually tied to the Treasury-bill rate or LIBOR, and the fixed-rate debt used in interest-rate swaps typically matures in 3 to 10 years. However, swaps are extremely flexible, privately negotiated agreements that can take an unlimited variety of forms. In addition to standard "plain vanilla" swaps, many swaps include amortized payments, call or put options, and other frills.

"Plain vanilla" swaps can be put together in a few minutes or even seconds. Swap agreements are normally arranged by telephone and can begin immediately, with the appropriate legal documents signed later. Swaps are generally not collateralized and do not relieve either party's obligation to pay the principal and interest on its own borrowing; indeed, those who have lent money to the swap participants generally do not know that a swap has taken place. Each borrower is responsible for its own debts, regardless of whether the swap contract is breached. If one party does not make its swap payments, the other party will stop its payments too, losing only the net difference.

Commercial and investment banks are both actively involved in arranging swaps. In fact, swaps have become so widely used and such an integral part of many debt issues that many banks feel that they must offer attractive swaps in order to retain customers and be allowed to underwrite security issues. A bank can act as a broker, bringing together two parties that want to swap, or as a dealer, taking one side of the swap. Swap participants may feel more comfortable dealing with a well-known bank because they are then more confident of receiving the swap payment. When a bank acts as a dealer, it has some flexibility in its timing in that it can sell one leg of the swap before selling the other leg.

**EXAMPLE
12.5**     *Dealing in Swaps*

It would be a surprising coincidence to find two parties that wanted exactly offsetting swaps — for example, for one party that wanted to swap a 4-year $30 million fixed-rate debt for a 4-year obligation tied to 6-month LIBOR to find someone who was looking to make a trade of precisely this size, timing, and terms. Individualized, custom-made swaps have become commonplace because of the willingness of swap dealers to become counterparties to trades — a willingness made possible by their ability to use a variety of financial instruments to protect their own portfolios from exchange-rate and interest-rate risk.

In our example, suppose that a swap dealer is approached by a client, International Farms, that wants to swap a 4-year $30 million fixed-rate debt

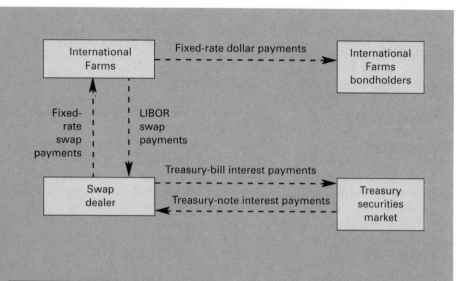

with semiannual coupons for a $30 million obligation with semiannual payments tied to the 6-month LIBOR. As depicted in the accompanying figure, the swap dealer agrees to pay International Farms every 6 months using a fixed interest rate and in return will receive an amount determined by LIBOR. The swap dealer has assumed interest-rate risk in that it is paying a fixed interest rate and earning a variable interest rate. It will suffer losses if interest rates decline unexpectedly.

To hedge its interest-rate risk, the swap dealer buys $30 million in 4-year Treasury notes and sells $30 million in 6-month Treasury bills (and will do so every 6 months for the next 4 years). The dealer's interest-rate risk has been effectively hedged because, if interest rates decline, the reduced payments it receives from International Farms will be offset by the higher prices it receives for selling Treasury bills. This is not a perfect hedge because LIBOR and the Treasury-bill rate are not perfectly correlated; the swap dealer still has some *basis risk* because the spread between LIBOR and the Treasury-bill rate may widen or narrow.

In practice, a swap dealer evaluates the risk exposure of its entire portfolio and usually finds that many transactions hedge each other. As part of another swap, this dealer may agree to a 3-year exchange of floating-rate payments for fixed-rate payments. If so, this 3-year floating-rate for fixed-rate swap partly hedges (in quantity and timing) the 4-year fixed-rate for floating-rate swap. Only the residual risk in the dealer's swap book needs to be hedged.

There is also a limited secondary market in swaps where banks acting as dealers trade legs among themselves. A firm can exit a swap by doing a reverse swap or by selling its leg of the swap in the secondary market.

# SUMMARY

Currency swaps and interest-rate swaps are used to transform assets and liabilities, often to manage exchange-rate risk and interest-rate risk. A currency swap is, in effect, an exchange of assets or liabilities denominated in different currencies. Two parties might issue bonds denominated in different currencies and then agree to swap the proceeds and repay each other's debts — effectively transforming each debt into the other currency. For example, a firm that wants to borrow foreign currency might borrow in its domestic market, where it is well known, and then use a currency swap. A firm that has a worldwide reputation can issue a bond denominated in a foreign currency and then use a currency swap to convert this debt into its domestic currency or into other foreign currencies. Currency swaps can be used to manage exchange-rate risk by matching the currencies in which assets and liabilities are denominated.

An interest-rate swap is, in effect, an exchange of interest-rate obligations, allowing a floating-rate debt to be converted into a fixed-rate debt (and vice versa) or into a floating-rate debt linked to a different interest-rate index. For example, a firm that has borrowed money with a floating interest rate might swap interest payments with a firm that has borrowed money at a fixed interest rate, thereby effectively converting the first firm's liability from floating-rate to fixed-rate debt and transforming the second firm's liability from fixed-rate to floating-rate debt. Interest-rate swaps give firms flexibility in switching between fixed-rate and floating-rate debt and can be used to manage interest-rate risk by adjusting liability durations to match asset durations.

A cross-currency interest-rate swap involves fixed-rate and variable-rate loans denominated in different currencies — for example swapping a dollar floating-rate loan for a yen fixed-rate loan. An import company might obtain a domestic-currency floating-rate loan from a local bank and then use a cross-currency interest-rate swap to transform this loan into a foreign-currency fixed-rate liability.

Many participants feel that swaps overcome market imperfections that make it expensive for some borrowers — perhaps because they are not well known — to obtain funds directly in some financial markets. It may be financially advantageous for a small savings and loan to borrow at low interest rates from its depositors and swap interest payments with a well-known international bank that can sell long-term securities in the Eurodollar bond market. Similarly, a small business might borrow from a local bank at a floating rate and then swap payments with a well-known corporation that is able to issue inexpensive fixed-rate bonds.

Swaps can be arranged quickly by telephone and are seldom collateralized. If one party does not make its swap payments, the other party will stop its payments too, losing only the net difference. Commercial and investment banks often act as swap brokers, bringing together two parties that want to swap, or as swap dealers, participating in swaps themselves. There is also a limited secondary market in swaps where banks acting as dealers trade swaps among themselves.

# IMPORTANT TERMS

currency swap
interest-rate swap
London interbank offered rate (LIBOR)
prime rate

Student Loan Marketing Association
  (Sallie Mae)
swap

# EXERCISES

1. A German bank swapped deutschemarks for dollars with a New York bank by agreeing to sell 10 million deutschemarks at a price of 0.50 dollars/mark and to repurchase 10 million deutschemarks a year later at a price of 0.52 dollars/mark. Did the New York bank get back more or fewer dollars than it paid for the deutschemarks? Did the German bank pay more or fewer dollars to get its deutschemarks back? Why would anyone agree to a deal in which they traded currency today for less of the same currency in the future? Why not just hang on to the currency?

2. Use a diagram similar to Figure 12.1 to depict a dollar/pound currency swap between a U.S. company that issues dollar-denominated bonds and a British company that issues pound-denominated bonds.

3. A German firm has issued a large number of bonds denominated in dollars, with the proceeds from this bond issue converted into marks in the foreign exchange market. Ex-

plain why it will suffer either capital gains or losses on these bonds if the mark appreciates relative to the dollar.

4. A U.S. insurance company issued yen-denominated bonds, converted these yen into dollars, and used the proceeds to buy Treasury bills. Explain why it either gained or lost on this transaction when the yen appreciated relative to the dollar.

5. A Japanese bank issued mark-denominated bonds, converted these marks into yen, and used the proceeds to make yen-denominated loans. To reduce the exchange-rate risk on this transaction, should this bank swap some of its mark-denominated liabilities for yen-denominated liabilities, or vice versa?

6. The simplified balance sheet of a hypothetical international bank is shown below. Will this bank experience capital gains or losses if the dollar depreciates relative to the mark? If the dollar depreciates relative to the pound?

| Assets | | Liabilities | |
|---|---|---|---|
| Dollar-denominated | $58,000,000 | Dollar-denominated | $80,000,000 |
| Mark-denominated | 24,000,000 | Mark-denominated | 12,000,000 |
| (40 million marks | | (20 million marks | |
| @ $0.60/mark) | | @ $0.60/mark) | |
| Pound-denominated | 18,000,000 | Net worth | $8,000,000 |
| (10 million marks | | | |
| @ $1.80/pound) | | | |
| | $100,000,000 | | $100,000,000 |

7. (*continuation*) To protect its net worth from fluctuations in the value of the dollar relative to the mark, should this bank swap some of its dollar-denominated liabilities for mark-denominated liabilities, or vice versa?

8. A U.S. bank has $100 million in loans denominated in French francs, but all its deposits are in dollars. Explain how it can use an *asset swap* to reduce its exchange-rate risk.

9. Suppose that the term structure is flat. If a firm swaps a fixed-rate loan for a floating-rate loan, is this transaction an implicit bet that interest rates will rise or fall in the future?

10. Use a diagram similar to the one in Example 12.2 to depict this transaction: a restaurant borrows from a local bank at a floating rate and then swaps interest payments with a multinational corporation that issues fixed-rate bonds in the Eurodollar bond market.

11. Use a diagram similar to the one in Example 12.2 to depict this transaction: a state agency finances a water treatment plant by selling long-term bonds and then swapping the interest payments with the construction firm, which has issued commercial paper.

12. A bank has financed $20 million in fixed-rate 10-year loans by issuing $20 million in 6-month certificates of deposit (CDs). Explain why a decline in interest rates will either make this transaction more profitable or less profitable. What kind of interest-rate swap for its CDs would eliminate this bank's interest-rate risk?

13. Federally chartered savings and loan associations are allowed to swap variable-rate debts for fixed-rate ones but are not allowed to swap fixed-rate debts for variable-rate ones. Why?

14. A certain finance company's assets have somewhat longer durations than its liabilities. To insulate its net worth from interest rates, should it do a fixed-rate to floating-rate swap, or vice versa? Explain.

15. Explain how a savings and loan association with fixed-rate mortgages and variable-rate deposits could swap some of its mortgages in order to reduce its exposure to interest-rate risk. Who could it swap with?

16. A Japanese firm sells long-term mark-denominated securities and uses the proceeds to purchase short-term yen-denominated securities. What would be an appropriate cross-currency interest-rate swap to reduce its exposure to both exchange-rate risk and interest-rate risk?

17. The prime rate is generally above the Treasury-bill rate. Why is this so? If a U.S. corporation borrows from a bank at a floating interest rate that is linked to the prime rate and then swaps this loan for one indexed to the Treasury-bill rate, is this an implicit wager that the spread between the prime rate and the Treasury-bill rate will widen or narrow?

18. A large U.S. commercial bank issues long-term mark-denominated bonds in Germany and uses the proceeds to make variable-rate dollar-denominated loans in the United States. What kind of liability swap would protect the U.S. bank's profits on this transaction from both exchange-rate and interest-rate risk?

19. In their 1983 interest-rate swap, Beverly Hills Savings and Loan agreed to pay Renault a fixed interest rate on $12 million of Renault's long-term debts, while Renault agreed to pay Beverly Hills a variable-interest rate on $12 million in deposits. Interest rates declined unexpectedly between 1983 and 1985 (when Beverly Hills failed). Did this decline in interest rates make the swap agreement more profitable for Renault or for Beverly Hills? Explain.

20. Sallie Mae issued long-term, fixed-rate bonds abroad denominated in Swiss francs. Explain why it might then do a cross-currency interest-rate swap for floating-rate dollar-denominated liabilities.

# Financial Institutions

# 13 Deposit Intermediation and the Money Supply

*It is a singular and, indeed, a significant fact that, although money was the first economic subject to attract men's thoughtful attention, and has been the focal centre of economic investigation ever since, there is at the present day not even an approximate agreement as to what ought to be designated by the word. The business world makes use of the term in several senses, while among economists there are almost as many different conceptions as there are writers upon money.*

**A. P. Andrew**

You do not need Federal Reserve notes to buy useful goods and services. Most stores accept traveler's checks, personal checks, and credit cards. Which of these, and what else, should be labeled "money"? As the quotation (from 1899!) prefacing this chapter indicates, there has long been disagreement about the proper definition of money. This debate is still unresolved, and data are currently collected on many different measures of a nation's money supply — called *monetary aggregates* — with names like *M*1 and *M*2.

We will look at several monetary aggregates in this chapter, but our focus is on some general principles that should last longer than the current definition of *M*2. We will examine how fractional reserve banking multiplies bank deposits and affects various measures of the money supply and how this deposit multiplication depends on a variety of household, business, and government decisions. Fractional reserve banking also allows banks to be financial intermediaries, borrowing from some in order to lend to others. We will look at the considerable social advantages of this intermediation and at the risks inherent in fractional reserve banking. We begin by looking at the historical roots of modern banking.

# BANK MONEY

Although banking existed as far back as Roman times, the first major public bank was established in Amsterdam in 1609. As a busy trading center, Amsterdam was flooded with domestic and foreign coins of widely varying purity. The Bank of Amsterdam was established to determine the precious metal content of these coins and to store them safely. Coins deposited in the bank did not need to circulate because merchants could conduct business by instructing the bank to transfer funds between accounts.

For many years the bank simply stored coins and kept accurate records. Eventually, the bank loaned some of its coins to the City of Amsterdam and to the prosperous Dutch East India Company. When prosperity faded and these loans were not repaid, anxious merchants tried to withdraw their coins, and the bank folded in 1819. The collapse of the bank and the evaporation of the merchants' deposits reduced both wealth and the money supply, depressing the economy.

This drama has been played out many times in many different places. Another notable episode occurred in eighteenth-century France. A Scotsman, John Law, had greatly impressed the Regent for 7-year-old Louis XV with his gambling prowess. In 1716 he was permitted to establish what was to be known as the Banque Royale. The bank's primary function was to make loans to the hard-pressed government. The bank accepted deposits and printed notes that were declared legal tender and used as a medium of exchange. Law promised that these notes could be redeemed for precious metal and declared that bankers with insufficient metal reserves deserved death.

With time, the bank's size and fame multiplied. The bank was given the tobacco monopoly, the right to coin money and collect the government's taxes, and exclusive trading privileges in China, India, and the South Seas. It planned to extract vast amounts of gold from Louisiana. Money poured into the bank in the form of deposits and stock sales and flowed out as loans to private entrepreneurs and a rapacious government. Those citizens owning deposits and stock counted these as wealth. When their deposits were recycled as bank notes borrowed and spent by the government, these were once again counted as wealth.

A thrifty citizen, Jean, might deposit 1000 livres in the bank. This money would be promptly lent to the government and used to pay some of its tiresome expenses. Jeanne, who receives this payment from the government, can then redeposit the 1000-livres note in the bank. Now two citizens, Jean and Jeanne, each have 1000-livre deposits. As the note is loaned, spent, and redeposited again and again, the citizens' money and wealth seem to expand indefinitely. Such imagined largess was good for spirit and for business. Law was proclaimed a financial genius and became the most respected person in France. He was appointed the Comptroller General of France and ennobled as the first, and only, Duc d'Arkansas.

The problem was that the actual assets of the Banque Royale were far smaller than the presumed value of the deposits and stock. The government had no hope of repaying its vast borrowings with precious metal, and gold had hardly been looked for, let alone discovered, in the Louisiana swamps. In 1720, suspicious, then worried, and ultimately panicky depositors tried to redeem their notes in precious metal. On one frantic day 15 people were reported to have been killed in the crush of anxious note holders. The bank failed. Law fled to Venice, narrowly escaping the Paris mob. With so much apparent wealth evaporated, business and commerce sagged heavily:

> Of all the nations in the world the French are the most renowned for singing over their grievances. . . . When Law, by the utter failure of his best-laid plans, rendered himself obnoxious, . . . the streets resounded with songs. . . . [One] counseled the application of all his notes to the most ignoble use to which paper can be applied.[1]

## A Short History of U.S. Bank Money

At Alexander Hamilton's urging, the Bank of the United States was founded in 1791, with $2 million raised from the federal government and $8 million from private citizens. Modeled after the Bank of England, its eight branches stored private and government funds and made loans to citizens and to the government. The Bank of the United States also issued bank notes that circulated as a medium of exchange and could be redeemed for gold or silver. At the time, fewer than a hundred other banks were in operation, all smaller and located on the East Coast. From its favored position as holder and disburser of government funds, the Bank of the United States made loans to other banks caught short of funds. It also encouraged sound banking practices by refusing to honor bank notes that were not convertible to gold or silver on demand.

Less privileged banks were envious and sometimes hostile to the Bank of the United States. Agrarian interests were suspicious of all banks. Thomas Jefferson wrote in a letter to John Adams that

> I have ever been the enemy of banks; not of those discounting for cash; but of those foisting their own paper into circulation, and thus banishing our cash. My zeal against those institutions was so warm and open at the establishment of the Bank of the U.S. that I was derided as a maniac by the tribe of bank-mongers, who were seeking to filch from the public their swindling, and barren gains. . . . Shall we build an altar to the old paper money of the revolution, which ruined individuals but saved the republic; and burn on that all the bank charters present and future, and their notes with them? For these are to ruin both republic and individuals.[2]

In 1810, on a narrow vote, Congress failed to renew the charter for the Bank of the United States, and it closed. In the succeeding 10 years, state banks and bank notes of varying repute multiplied. One historian wrote that "corporations and tradesmen issued 'currency'. Even barbers and bartenders competed with banks in this respect. . . . nearly every citizen regarded it as his constitutional right to issue money."[3] One successful midwestern banker related his start in the business: "Well, I didn't have much to do and so I rented an empty store and painted 'bank' on the window. The first day a man came in and deposited $100, and a couple of days later, another man deposited another $250 and so along about the fourth day I got confidence enough in the bank to put in $1.00 myself."[4]

Despite his beliefs that banks and paper money were immoral and that a federally chartered bank was unconstitutional, President James Madison proposed a national bank to rein in the reckless banks. In 1816 the Second Bank of the United States was chartered. It was larger than the first but less interested in restraining fellow banks. It actively speculated, particularly in western land, and its Baltimore branch made so many bad loans that it went bankrupt in 1818. In 1819 a new head of the Second Bank reduced its speculative activities by restricting new loans and by forcing some borrowers to pay off old ones, putting a discernible crimp in commerce. As one writer put it, "The Bank was saved and the people ruined."[5] The next president of the Second Bank, Nicholas Biddle, reinstituted the First Bank's policy of refusing to accept bank notes that were not redeemable in gold or silver.

Because of these unpopular policies, the fight to renew the Second Bank's charter in 1832 was bitter. (Biddle's brother, who was director of the St. Louis branch, and an antagonist were shot and killed in a duel — fought at a distance of only 5 feet because of Biddle's nearsightedness.) Populist President Andrew Jackson removed government deposits from the bank and vetoed a bill renewing its charter. Rechartered by the Commonwealth of Pennsylvania, Biddle's bank failed in 1841 after excessive speculation and questionable loans to bank officers.

After the restraining power of the Second Bank of the United States was lifted, there was a surge of new banks and of unbacked bank notes. The older, established banks in the East were typically managed conservatively, with substantial reserves of gold and silver and a readiness to redeem their notes with hard metal. Banks in other parts of the country were more loosely managed and willingly loaned unbacked paper to farmers and businesspeople settling new territories. When the land was fertile and business good, the communities and their banks prospered; when crops and businesses failed, their banks failed with them.

Banks were regulated by the states in which they operated. In 1837 the Supreme Court ruled that the constitutional ban against state-issued money did not prohibit the issuance of notes by state-owned banks. Such banks consequently spread across the country. In addition, thousands of private banks were established by financiers, blacksmiths, trading-post owners, and other banking entrepreneurs. There were state regulations regarding precious metal reserves, but these were unevenly enforced. A bank in conservative Massachusetts with $500,000 in notes outstanding was found to have $86.48 in reserves. In liberal Michigan, a common collection of reserves (including hidden lead, glass, and ten-penny nails) passed from bank to bank, ahead of the state examiners.

By the time of the Civil War, there were some 7000 different types of bank notes in circulation, of which 5000 were counterfeit issues. With the South and the Mississippi Valley not represented in Congress because of the Civil War, the National Bank Act created a system of federally chartered and regulated banks. Congress levied a one-percent, then a two-percent, then in 1865 a ten-percent annual tax on state bank notes. State bank notes consequently declined dramatically, but were replaced by checking accounts. Instead of issuing paper currency that was perhaps backed by precious metal, state-chartered banks issued checks that were backed by deposits (and ultimately by the investments that banks made with these deposits).

Those banks that applied for and received federal charters became known as national banks and, in fact, the word "national" had to be part of the bank's name, as with the Second National Bank of Chicago. National banks were required to hold 25 percent reserves against deposits and were allowed to issue national bank notes that bore the individual bank's name and were uniformly printed in Washington, D.C., by the Comptroller of the Currency. In order to issue national bank notes, a federally chartered bank had to buy U.S. Treasury bonds. The amount of bank notes issued by an individual bank could not exceed 90 percent of the value of the bonds that it had purchased and deposited with the Treasury. This rule ensured that national bank notes had something of value behind them and also ensured buyers for the bonds that the government was selling to finance the Civil War. Ironically, after the Civil War ended, the federal government often had a budget surplus but was unwilling to retire its debt because a diminished supply of Treasury bonds would have forced a decline in the nation's money supply.

After a series of financial panics in 1873, 1884, 1893, and 1907, Congress passed the Federal Reserve Act in 1913, and the Federal Reserve System opened in 1914. We will examine the Federal System in detail in later chapters. Nationally chartered banks were required to join the system, and in 1935 their power to issue national bank notes was revoked. Banks today cannot print money, although they can create deposits that serve as money.

## How Banks Multiply the Money Supply

Governments create money simply by printing it and declaring that it is legal tender. Redemptions can be satisfied by printing more of the same — two $5 bills for every $10 bill. As long as nothing more is promised, governments need never fear a "run," with anxious citizens rushing to redeem their currency. Banks create money a bit more mysteriously and much more dangerously. A run on a bank is a banker's nightmare.

The Bank of Amsterdam began in the seventeenth century by assaying and storing coins, which then sat gathering dust. For such a bank there is no danger of a bank run and bankruptcy so long as there are sufficiently strong safes and personnel to guard the deposits. If banks operated in this fashion — simply keeping records and guarding safe-deposit boxes — depositors would be completely protected and banks would not multiply the money supply. This kind of system is said to have "100 percent reserves."

You could deposit $100 of government currency in such a bank and receive a bank note certifying that you have $100 stored safely. Your $100 bank receipt replaces $100 of currency, and if your bank receipt is accepted as a medium of exchange, there is no change in the total money supply. There is simply $100 of bank money instead of $100 of government money. If your $100 receipt is not accepted as a medium of exchange, then the bank deposit reduces by $100 the total amount of money in circulation outside banks — as if you had buried the $100 in your backyard.

A bank multiplies deposits (and risks) when it does not keep all your $100 deposited in its safe but instead invests some of it, either by making loans or buying securities. As a fictitious Mr. Dooley once said, a banker "takes care of your money by lending it to friends." When only a fraction of deposits is kept on hand, this is called **fractional reserve banking**. The fractional reserve is the fraction $k$ of your $100 that is kept in reserve at the bank; the remaining fraction $1 - k$ is invested. Let's work through the consequences, initially assuming that banks keep 10 percent of each deposit on reserve ($k = 0.1$) and lend the remaining 90 percent.

You deposit $100 in First Bank, and the bank keeps $10 and lends $90. The person who borrows the $90 undoubtedly has some worthwhile purpose in mind and will soon spend this $90. The seller who receives $90 from the borrower deposits this money in Second Bank. She is credited with a $90 deposit, and Second Bank now has $90 to lend.

If Second Bank keeps 10 percent of this $90 and lends the remaining $81, then this $81 can be spent and deposited in Third Bank. A pattern is definitely appearing. On each round, 90 percent of the previous deposit is loaned and then redeposited in a bank. These deposits are $100, $90, $81, and so on. If we look far ahead and use a calculator to add up these deposits, the sum will be found to be $1000. The sum of the reserves in bank vaults is $10 + $9 + $8.1 + \cdots =$ $100. The banking system has converted $100 of government money into $1000 of bank deposits. Is this magic? No, it's banking.

Banks do not print money. They lend money that they have borrowed from their depositors. Their ledgers balance because every dollar deposited is loaned or held as reserves. Table 13.1 demonstrates this formally by using **T-accounts**, which show the changes in a balance sheet caused by some financial event. Each deposit in Table 13.1 increases a bank's assets and liabilities equally.

The banking system ends up with $1000 in deposits, $900 in loans, and $100 in reserves. As for the banks' customers, depositors have a total of $1000 in assets, and borrowers have a total of $900 in debts. For the private economy as a whole, net financial wealth is $100, the initial amount of government money. What banks have done, as illustrated in Figure 13.1, is provide a way for some citizens to borrow $900 from other citizens. In this role as intermediary between borrowers and lenders, banks may well stimulate the economy. To the extent that bank deposits serve as money (either bank notes or checking accounts), banking also facilitates trade.

**Table 13.1  Bank T-Accounts for a Sequence of Deposits and Loans**

First Bank

| | Assets | Liabilities |
|---|---|---|
| First deposit and loan | $10 reserves $90 loan | $100 deposit |

Second Bank

| | Assets | Liabilities |
|---|---|---|
| Second deposit and loan | $ 9 reserves $81 loan | $ 90 deposit |

Third Bank

| | Assets | Liabilities |
|---|---|---|
| Third deposit and loan | $ 8.1 reserves $72.9 loan | $ 81 deposit |

⋮

Banking System

| | Assets | Liabilities |
|---|---|---|
| Total reserves, deposits, and loans | $100 reserves $900 loans | $1,000 deposits |

**Figure 13.1  Financial Intermediaries Channel Funds from Depositors to Borrowers**

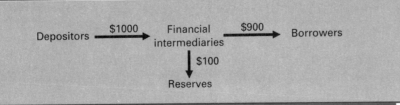

EXAMPLE
**13.1**          ***Bank Runs in Ohio and Maryland***

Most deposits are insured up to $100,000 by agencies of the federal government; but in 1985 there were 10 states in which private companies insured deposits in some savings and loan associations and other thrift institutions. When a privately insured thrift fails, depositors may have to wait months to get their money or, worse, lose their money if the losses are so large that the insurance company itself fails. These risks understandably make depositors nervous when there are rumors of financial difficulties at a privately insured thrift.

E.S.M. Government Securities, a dealer in Treasury securities, was closed in March of 1985 for fraudulent practices, with nine of its officers and an outside auditor eventually pleading guilty to or being convicted of fraud charges. When E.S.M. was closed, it was soon revealed that Home State Savings Bank in Cincinnati had lost more than $140 million in loans to E.S.M. and that Home State was insured by a private firm, Ohio Deposit Guarantee Fund, which had only $136 million in reserves. Anxious depositors camped outside Home State Savings overnight, and when its doors opened in the morning, the line stretched around the block. As the news spread, depositors rushed to 70 other Ohio thrifts insured by the Ohio Deposit Guarantee Fund. Although most of these thrifts were financially sound, none had enough reserves on hand to satisfy nervous depositors. The governor of Ohio was forced to close these 70 thrifts for 6 days while it was determined which could qualify for federal deposit insurance.

Two months later, similar bank runs began in Maryland after the public learned that two savings and loans had sustained losses that exceeded the reserves of the Maryland Savings-Share Insurance Corporation, a private company that insured 102 Maryland S&Ls. The governor stopped the run by limiting withdrawals to $1000 per month and creating a new state-operated insurance fund. A subsequent investigation concluded that some thrifts had been looted by their managers, who used depositor funds to pay for personal expenses and to finance speculative real estate investments by themselves and friends.* The general lesson, though, is that if depositors become nervous, even well-run banks and thrifts are vulnerable to bank runs.

*Steve Swartz, "Investigations Detail How Insiders Wrecked S&Ls in Maryland," Wall Street Journal, March 12, 1986.

If there were no banks or other financial intermediaries, savers would have to loan money directly to borrowers, and both would have to agree to the repayment terms. Borrowers generally spend their borrowed money and plan to pay it back in the future. Perhaps they will use the money to open a store and use the profits from the store to repay the loan. Or they may be a young couple borrowing money to buy a car, a house, or furniture and will repay the loan out of their future wage income. Typically, borrowers need time to repay their loans.

They prefer a fixed and inviolate repayment schedule or, even better, to decide themselves when to pay off the loan. Savers have different preferences. They want the flexibility to call in the loan and demand repayment whenever they need funds. With this fundamental conflict between the preferences of borrowers and savers, there will be few loans and those that are made will require one or both sides to settle for less than they prefer.

One advantage of financial intermediaries is that both borrowers and savers can be accommodated. Borrowers receive loans from banks with fixed repayment schedules that are convenient and consistent with their planned use of the funds. Savers deposit their money in banks and are permitted to withdraw it whenever they please. Both sides are satisfied, and many more loans are made than would occur in the absence of banks. It is because they fulfill this valuable public service that banks throughout history have been so popular and profitable.

The darker side of the coin is that banks succeed only when all depositors do not in fact show up simultaneously to demand their deposits. With a large number of depositors and a reasonable store of reserves, a bank can easily satisfy the occasional depositor who needs funds. As long as depositors believe that their deposits can be claimed at any time, few will actually want to claim them. The danger is that they may lose faith. When depositors think that they may not be able to withdraw their deposits, they will all rush to try. Because it is unable to retrieve the loans it has made with its depositors' money, the bank collapses. This fundamental tension in banking has permitted enormous social benefits and has caused unforgettable panics. In later chapters we will look closely at how modern banks — by and large successfully — cope with this tension.

## Deposit Multipliers

The numerical example summarized in Table 13.1 illustrates how banks bring together borrowers and lenders and multiply deposits. We can easily generalize this principle to cases where the fractional reserve ratio $k$ is not necessarily 0.1. We will then be able to see how household and bank behavior affects aggregate bank deposits and lending and the size of the nation's money supply.

In our simple model, for each $1 of government money deposited in a bank, a fraction $k$ is held as reserves and a fraction $1 - k$ is loaned. For each individual bank, reserves are a fraction $k$ of deposits. The same is true of the banking system as a whole, so total reserves are a fraction $k$ of total deposits. In this simplest deposit-multiplier model, all government money $B$ is held as bank reserves; none is held outside banks. The amount of government money $B$ is consequently equal to the amount of bank reserves $kD$:

$$B = kD \qquad (13.1)$$

If, as before, $k = 0.1$ of every deposit is held as reserves, then $1 in reserves can support $10 in deposits, $100 in reserves can support $1000 in deposits, and $1 billion in reserves can support $10 billion in deposits. (We can think of Equation 13.1 as describing the supply of government money $B$ and the banks' demand for government money to use as reserves $kD$.)

Equation 13.1 can be rearranged to show that the banking system converts every dollar of government money into $1/k$ dollars of deposits:

$$D = \frac{B}{k} \qquad (13.2)$$

The smaller is $k$, the less banks hold in reserves, the more they lend, and the more deposits are created. If only one penny out of every dollar is held as reserves ($k = 0.01$), then bank deposits will be 100 times the initial deposit of government money; that is, $D = 100B$. What if $k = 0$? Then every dollar deposited is loaned, and no reserves are held. If these loans are redeposited and re-lent over and over, there is no limit to the total deposits that can be created.

Early banks that printed their own bank notes could and did expand deposits even faster because your loans can be larger than your deposits when you are just printing paper. You can have one million dollars in deposits, but print two, five, ten, or a hundred million dollars in notes to lend to optimistic entrepreneurs or a thankful government. As long as these notes just pass from hand to hand and borrowers never try to redeem them for precious metal, you can remain in the money-printing business. The wildest successes and most spectacular crashes in banking history accompanied such practices.

Banks today cannot print money and cannot lend all their deposits. In the United States, the Federal Reserve sets **reserve requirements** (within limits set by Congress) that compel banks to hold some fraction of their deposits as reserves, either cash in their vaults or deposits with the Federal Reserve that earn no interest. Any reserves that banks hold beyond those required are **excess reserves**, which allow banks to satisfy normal deposit withdrawals without falling below required reserves. The amount of excess reserves held by banks depends on their perception of withdrawal risks and the availability of attractive investments. Banks hold large excess reserves when withdrawal risks are great or when there are few tempting opportunities to invest these funds. In our deposit-multiplier model, the parameter $k$ describes the fraction of deposits held as total bank reserves, required plus excess:

$$\text{Bank reserves} = kD \qquad (13.3)$$

In practice, banks today hold very few excess reserves, so $k$ is determined primarily by the reserve requirements that are set by the Federal Reserve.

A second bit of realism, so far neglected, is that some of the money loaned by banks does not find its way back into banks. Citizens hold currency outside banks for use as a medium of exchange. We will let the parameter $c$ measure the ratio of currency outside banks to deposits:

$$\text{Currency outside banks} = cD \qquad (13.4)$$

The amount of currency that households and businesses want to hold is influenced by a variety of factors. When deposit rates increase along with other interest rates, deposits become more attractive relative to currency, which earns no interest, and $c$ declines. If depositors become nervous about the solvency of banks, they will withdraw funds — causing $c$, the ratio of currency to deposits, to increase. The demand for currency relative to deposits is also influenced by the size of the so-called underground economy, involving transactions that people want to keep hidden from law enforcement officials and tax collectors.

We are now ready to put the model together. A nation's **monetary base** $B$ is the outstanding amount of government money that is held either as bank reserves or as currency outside banks:

$$B = \text{bank reserves} + \text{currency outside banks} \qquad (13.5)$$

Substituting Equations 13.3 and 13.4 into Equation 13.5, we derive

$$B = (k + c)D$$

We can solve this for $D$, the total level of deposits that can be supported by the monetary base, as follows:

$$D = \left(\frac{1}{k + c}\right) B \qquad (13.6)$$

The parenthetical term in Equation 13.6, $1/(k + c)$, is the **deposit multiplier**, the ratio of bank deposits to the monetary base. Because the monetary base can support a much larger quantity of bank deposits, economists often refer to the monetary base as **high-powered money**. Equation 13.6 is analogous to Equation 13.2, derived earlier for a simpler scenario in which there are no currency holdings outside banks ($c = 0$).

As of January 1992, the approximate values of $k$ and $c$ were

$$k = \frac{\text{reserves}}{\text{deposits}} = \frac{\$60 \text{ billion}}{\$3000 \text{ billion}} = 0.02$$

$$c = \frac{\text{currency outside banks}}{\text{deposits}} = \frac{\$240 \text{ billion}}{\$3000 \text{ billion}} = 0.08$$

The deposit multiplier was

$$\frac{1}{k + c} = \frac{1}{0.02 + 0.08} = 10$$

so deposits were 10 times the monetary base of $300 billion:

$$D = \left(\frac{1}{k + c}\right) B$$
$$= (10)(\$300 \text{ billion})$$
$$= \$3000 \text{ billion}$$

In 1992, every dollar in government money supported about 10 dollars in deposits. This multiplier of 10 is altered if either of the parameters $k$ or $c$ is changed. In particular, an increase in either of these parameters reduces the multiplier and reduces the amount of deposits supported by the monetary base. If the bank reserve-to-deposit ratio $k$ increases, perhaps because of an increase in government reserve requirements, then a larger fraction of the money deposited in banks is held as reserves rather than loaned. With less money recycled to be redeposited and re-lent, fewer bank deposits are created. If the currency-to-deposit ratio $c$ increases, then a larger fraction of the money loaned by banks is held by the public rather than redeposited in banks. With less money returning to be re-lent and redeposited, fewer bank deposits are created.

Seemingly small changes in these parameters can have large effects on deposit creation. If $k$ rose to 0.03 or if $c$ rose to 0.09, the deposit multiplier would fall to 9.09 and deposits would contract by nearly 10 percent, to $2800 billion. If $k$ fell to 0.01 or $c$ fell to 0.07, the multiplier would rise to 11.1 and deposits would expand by more than 10 percent, to $3333 billion.

## Checking Accounts Versus Savings Accounts

Now let's look at another, even more complicated distinction. Some bank deposits are a medium of exchange; others are not. Funds in a checking account are payable on demand, so for most (but admittedly not all) expenses, a check drawn on your checking account is as good as cash. Both government currency and checking account funds qualify as a medium of exchange. Most time and savings deposits do not qualify because you cannot buy something from a store simply by displaying the passbook for your savings account. In practice, this distinction is more complicated and ambiguous, and we will return to it. For now, however, we will draw a sharp distinction between deposits $D_1$ in transaction accounts and deposits $D_2$ in time and savings accounts, with total deposits $D = D_1 + D_2$. As of January 1992, $D_1/D = 0.17$ and $D_2/D = 0.83$.

This distinction, in fact, underlay the pre-1980 monetary aggregates, which we will call Old $M1$ and Old $M2$:

Old $M1$ = currency outside banks plus checking accounts at commercial banks
Old $M2$ = Old $M1$ plus time and savings accounts at commercial banks

Banks are required to hold more reserves against transaction deposits than against other types of deposits. In January of 1992, transaction deposits had essentially a 12 percent reserve requirement (there was only a 3 percent reserve requirement on the first $41.5 million of transaction deposits, a threshold that increases each year), while other deposits had no reserve requirements.

To minimize the mathematical clutter, we will assume that there are no reserve requirements on time and savings accounts and that bank reserves depend solely on transaction accounts; that is,

$$\text{Bank reserves} = kD_1 \qquad (13.7)$$

where $k$ is determined primarily by the Fed's checking account reserve requirements.

If we substitute Equations 13.4 and 13.7 into Equation 13.5, we find that

$$
\begin{aligned}
B &= \text{bank reserves} + \text{currency outside banks} \\
&= kD_1 + cD \\
&= [k(D_1/D) + c]D
\end{aligned}
$$

Solving for total bank deposits, we derive the following deposit-multiplier equation:

$$D = \left[ \frac{1}{k(D_1/D) + c} \right] B \qquad (13.8)$$

This equation is an extension of our previous deposit-multiplier formula, Equation 13.6. The only difference between Equations 13.6 and 13.8 is that the latter recognizes that total bank reserves depend on the fraction of deposits that are checking accounts, because these are subject to reserve requirements.

The substantive difference is that in our expanded model we can track the creation of both types of deposits:

$$D_1 = (D_1/D)D = \left[ \frac{D_1/D}{k(D_1/D) + c} \right] B$$

$$D_2 = (1 - D_1/D)D = \left[ \frac{1 - D_1/D}{k(D_1/D) + c} \right] B$$

Further manipulation yields these equations for the monetary aggregates Old $M1$ and Old $M2$:

$$\text{Old } M1 = \text{currency outside banks} + \text{transaction deposits}$$
$$= cD + D_1$$
$$= \left[ \frac{c + D_1/D}{k(D_1/D) + c} \right] B \qquad (13.9)$$

$$\text{Old } M2 = \text{Old } M1 + \text{time and savings deposits}$$
$$= cD + D_1 + D_2$$
$$= (c + 1)D$$
$$= \left[ \frac{c + 1}{k(D_1/D) + c} \right] B \qquad (13.10)$$

These equations show how banks multiply government money into bank deposits and monetary aggregates. One pitfall to be avoided is the presumption that the various parameters are constant. Reserve requirements can and have been changed by the government, and currency, deposits, and excess reserves depend on the preferences of citizens and banks. Government monetary authorities may try to influence and estimate these parameters, but their values cannot be taken for granted.

Table 13.2 shows illustrative numerical calculations of the effects on Old $M1$ and Old $M2$ of a 10 percent increase in $k$, $c$, or $D_1/D$. An increase in the bank reserve ratio $k$, caused by an increase in either reserve requirements or in excess reserves, reduces Old $M1$ and Old $M2$ by equal percentages. An increase in $c$ (holdings of currency relative to deposits) also reduces Old $M1$ and Old $M2$, although by different percentages. An increase in $D_1/D$ (the fraction of deposits that are transaction accounts) expands Old $M1$ and contracts Old $M2$. Notice that these monetary aggregates do not move in lockstep. Old $M1$ and Old $M2$ can change by identical percentages, by different percentages, or in different directions.

| Table 13.2 | Effect on Old $M1$ and Old $M2$ of a 10 Percent Increase in Parameters | |
| --- | --- | --- |
| Initial parameter values: k = 0.12, $c$ = 0.08, $D_1/D$ = 1/6 with $B$ = \$300 billion implies Old $M1$ = \$740 billion and Old $M2$ = \$3,240 billion | | |
| | Effect on monetary aggregates | |
| Parameter Increased by 10% | Old $M1$ | Old $M2$ |
| k | − \$15 billion (2.0%) | − \$64 billion (2.0%) |
| $c$ | − \$33 billion (4.4%) | − \$218 billion (6.7%) |
| $D_1/D$ | + \$35 billion (4.7%) | − \$64 billion (2.0%) |

Sometimes the changes in deposit multipliers are very large. During the banking panics of the Great Depression, many anxious depositors withdrew what they could from banks, increasing $c$, the ratio of currency outside banks to bank deposits. Bank excess reserves relative to deposits also swelled enormously because of fears of bank runs and a perceived absence of attractive loan opportunities: excess reserves grew from \$48 million in December of 1929 to \$6.6 billion in December of 1940. These increases in $c$ and $k$ exerted enormous contractionary effects on deposit multipliers and monetary aggregates.

In April of 1992 the Federal Reserve attempted to bring the economy out of an economic recession by reducing the reserve requirement on transactions accounts from 12 to 10 percent. This was a very substantial 16.7 percent reduction in reserve requirements ($-0.02/0.12 = -0.167$). At the time, banks held about \$50 billion in required reserves, and a 16.7 percent reduction in reserve requirements freed about 0.167(\$50 billion) = \$8.3 billion for lending. Using the parameter values shown in Table 13.2, Equations 13.9 and 13.10 imply that a 16.7 percent reduction in reserve requirements, holding other factors constant, should increase Old $M1$ and Old $M2$ by about 3.3 percent.

Of course, other factors are seldom constant. Figure 13.2 shows the historical behavior of the Old $M1$ and Old $M2$ money multipliers. Here you can see the monetary collapse in the 1930s. You can also see that money multipliers wiggle around quite a bit in more normal times. Remember, a 10 percent change in a money multiplier corresponds to a 10 percent change in the monetary aggregate, which can be the difference between boom and recession. Notice also that except for the banking collapse in the 1930s, the long-run trend in the $M2$ money multiplier was strongly upward, reflecting the long-run growth of banks. Banks today create far more deposits than in the past. On the other hand, the $M1$ money multiplier was relatively stagnant after World War II because of the increased use of credit cards and other attractive alternatives to bank checking accounts.

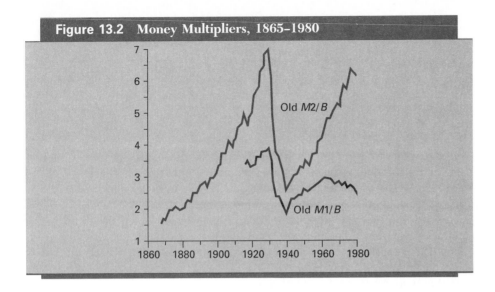

Figure 13.2  Money Multipliers, 1865–1980

The data in Figure 13.2 are annual averages, which smooth out the day-to-day fluctuations in the money multipliers. Figure 13.3 shows the monthly Old $M1$ money multiplier data for 1960–1980. With the annual data in Figure 13.2, the 1960–1980 period looks pretty sedate. The monthly data in Figure 13.3 give

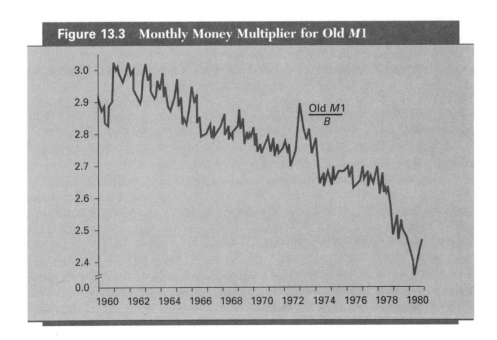

Figure 13.3  Monthly Money Multiplier for Old $M1$

a sharply contrasting picture; weekly or daily money multipliers are even more erratic. In later chapters we will see that the erratic behavior of money multipliers has important implications for Federal Reserve policy. If the money multiplier $M1/B$ is unstable, then when the Fed changes the monetary base $B$, it cannot be confident of the effect on $M1$.

# MONEY TODAY

The quotation prefacing this chapter indicates that there has long been disagreement about the definition of the word "money." For example, Parker Willis of Columbia University, a leading monetary economist in his day, argued as late as 1925 that bank notes were not money, and as late as 1931 he (and many others) contended that Keynes should not have included checking accounts in his definition of money.[6] Today it is difficult to understand such debates. However, changes are now occurring in the means of payment that are just as revolutionary as checking accounts were after the Civil War and that are creating just as much uncertainty about the meaning of money.

Money surely includes anything that is a medium of exchange that is commonly accepted as payment in economic transactions. Government currency, traveler's checks, and checking accounts clearly qualify, although many stores are reluctant to accept checks of uncertain reliability, and some buyers and sellers do not use or accept checks in order to avoid evidence of transactions that they want to keep secret — this is a popular explanation of why there are more than 200 million U.S. $100 bills in circulation.

The $M1$ monetary aggregate includes cash, checking accounts, and traveler's checks but excludes such things as food stamps, discount coupons, and subway tokens that can only be used for certain restricted purchases and not as a generally accepted medium of exchange. However, food is a pretty big category, and in many grocery stores food stamps are accepted more readily than checks. Consider also this question. In some places food stamps can be readily traded for nonfood items and for cash. Does this make food stamps as good as cash? Well, almost. There are some things, such as utility bills, for which food stamps won't be accepted as payment. And selling food stamps for cash is a little less convenient than having cash in the first place.

Is this extra step of having to convert an asset into cash sufficient reason to disqualify it as money? One view is that no matter how fast and easy to accomplish, the additional step means that the asset is not yet money and should not be counted as money. Others argue that if the conversion is fast and easy, then the asset is so close to money that it ought to be called money. Of course, "fast" and "easy" are subjective assessments, and it is impossible to draw a sharp line that persuasively distinguishes fast from slow and easy from difficult. Food stamps may seem like a nuisance item, trivial enough to ignore, but there are many other assets, near-moneys, that are hard to overlook. Because these issues cannot be settled unambiguously, data are collected and reported on many monetary aggregates.

## Checkable Deposits

The $M1$ definition used before 1980 neglected transaction deposits in financial institutions other than commercial banks. In popular usage, the term *banks* encompasses a wide variety of financial institutions: commercial banks, mutual savings banks, savings and loan associations, and credit unions. However, because of regulatory constraints, there have been important differences in the operations of these institutions.

In the aftermath of the 1929–1932 financial collapse in the United States, Congress acted to restrict speculative activities by financial institutions. Persuaded that competitive pressures to pay high interest rates on deposits had led banks to make high-interest, high-risk loans, the Banking Acts of 1933 and 1935 prohibited institutions other than commercial banks from offering checking accounts, prohibited the payment of interest on checking accounts, and under **Regulation Q**, gave the Federal Reserve the power to set the maximum interest rates that banks could pay on other types of deposits.

Mutual savings banks, savings and loan associations, and credit unions were considered thrift institutions, designed for more permanent household savings accounts. As the years passed, these thrift institutions increasingly wanted to share in the lucrative checking account business, which allows banks to borrow funds inexpensively from their depositors and then lend these funds at profitable interest rates. As interest rates rose to double-digit levels in the 1970s, many thrift institutions were eager to offer checking accounts, and many banks wanted to pay interest on their checking accounts in order to attract more deposits.

A favorable 1972 court decision in Massachusetts led to the proliferation of **negotiable order of withdrawal (NOW) accounts** — checking accounts paying $5\frac{1}{4}$ percent interest — throughout the six New England states, New York, and New Jersey. In 1974 credit unions began offering *share drafts* — checking accounts that pay interest on minimum account balances. A scattering of mutual savings banks and savings and loan associations set up non-interest-paying checking accounts. In November of 1978, commercial banks were authorized to offer *automatic-transfer-system (ATS) accounts*, in which funds are automatically transferred from an individual's interest-paying savings account to a checking account as needed. By 1980 the amount of money in these new kinds of checking accounts reached $20 billion, almost one-tenth the size of traditional commercial bank checking accounts.

Many of these and other similar developments had uncertain legal status. The landmark 1980 Depository Institutions Deregulation and Monetary Control Act clarified the situation by explicitly authorizing the financial revolution that was occurring. Deposit institutions other than commercial banks were permitted to offer checking accounts, the prohibition of interest payments on checking accounts was removed, and all interest-rate ceilings on deposits were phased out.

Faced with the growing importance of nonbank checking accounts and increasing criticism of its $M1$ data, the Federal Reserve revised its definition of $M1$ to include all checkable deposits at both banks and thrifts, including NOW accounts, ATS accounts, and credit union share drafts. Recognizing that some of

EXAMPLE
13.2

## *Free Blankets, Toasters, and TVs*

The Banking Act of 1933 prohibited the payment of interest on checking accounts and, through Regulation Q, empowered the Federal Reserve to determine the maximum interest rates that banks could pay on other deposits. On several occasions in the 1960s and 1970s, market interest rates on Treasury and corporate bonds rose far above the ceiling rates on bank deposits, persuading many depositors to withdraw their money from banks and invest elsewhere — a diversion of funds dubbed *disintermediation.*

Banks tried to circumvent these rate ceilings by offering crockery, electrical appliances, and other baubles to depositors. One Colorado bank gave out hunting rifles. Many depositors no doubt would have preferred receiving money instead (in the form of higher interest) so that they could have bought what they wanted, not necessarily a hunting rifle or another toaster oven.

The use of gifts to bypass rate ceilings reached the silly point where 25-inch color televisions were given to depositor "buddies." A *Wall Street Journal* employee wrote a memorable article telling of the difficulties he encountered when he deposited a large sum of money in a bank and discovered that he was entitled to a toaster for himself and a color television for a buddy.* A bank employee kindly explained that most people arrange for a buddy to accept delivery of the television and then give it to the depositor, perhaps in exchange for the toaster. The *Journal* writer dutifully left and returned to the bank with a buddy. His buddy was advised to use the depositor's Social Security Number so that he wouldn't have to pay taxes on the television but was also told that he had to use his own address, which meant that the television would have to be carried across town to the depositor after delivery to the buddy. The *Journal* writer sent this buddy home and found a more convenient one — his babysitter, who could use her business address (his house). The bank officer objected that using the same address for the depositor and the buddy looked suspicious but was persuaded to pretend that this was an apartment house, with the depositor having apartment 1 and the buddy having apartment 2. The *Wall Street Journal* writer finally got his free color TV and a good story.

At the urging of consumer groups (who feel that deposit rate wars are good for consumers) and of banks (who were losing depositors), the 1980 Depository Institutions Deregulation and Monetary Control Act phased out all deposit-rate ceilings.

*\*Jonathan Kwitny, "Finding a Buddy for My Free Color TV," Wall Street Journal, June 17, 1980.*

the money in these versatile checkable accounts is there for saving rather than for checking purposes, in 1981 the Fed introduced another aggregate, $M1$–Shift Adjusted, that subtracted from $M1$ an estimate of the funds that had been deposited in NOW accounts for saving rather than for transaction purposes.

Much of the money in NOW accounts would otherwise be in a checking account, but some would be in a savings account. When the alternatives are a checking account paying no interest and a savings account paying $5\frac{1}{4}$ percent or $5\frac{1}{2}$ percent, depositors will make a serious effort to avoid leaving idle funds in their checking account. However, when the alternatives are a checking account paying $5\frac{1}{4}$ percent and a savings account paying $5\frac{1}{4}$ percent or $5\frac{1}{2}$ percent, there is little cost to leaving extra money in a checking account, funds that can be used if needed for unanticipated expenses. This argument is supported by data on deposit turnover, the ratio of total annual withdrawals (by check or otherwise) to average deposits. The annual turnover rate on ATS and NOW accounts is about 15, as compared with 3 for ordinary savings accounts and 40 for household checking accounts.

Thus some of the funds in the ATS and NOW accounts included in $M1$ are really savings rather than checking assets. These funds can be used to pay bills, but depositors don't plan to and usually won't use these funds for this purpose. The inclusion of such funds in $M1$ forces us to ask this question: If "money" includes funds available for spending, what about other assets that are readily available for bill paying?

## Savings Accounts

Many of the funds in savings accounts at commercial banks, mutual savings banks, savings and loan associations, and credit unions can be easily used to pay bills. For instance, since 1975, banks and savings and loan associations have provided automatic bill-paying services. Regular bills for utilities, rent, mortgage payments, and the like are sent directly to a bank or savings and loan association, where the appropriate amount is withdrawn from the depositor's savings account and credited to the recipient. Since 1975, Federal Reserve member banks and federally chartered savings and loan associations also have been permitted to accept telephone instructions to transfer funds from savings to checking accounts, allowing depositors to leave funds in high-interest-earning savings accounts until a check is written for a purchase. Because these savings account funds substitute for checking account funds, it is reasonable to argue that they too should be counted as money.

## Ready Credit and Easily Liquidated Assets

Many checking accounts have liberal overdraft provisions, often called "ready credit" or "check credit" plans. If you have such an account, you can write a check for more than you have deposited, and the bank will honor the check. The bank uses its own funds to pay your bill and records this transaction as a loan to you. You may be able to repay the loan promptly with a slight service charge or to repay it later with interest. This overdraft privilege means that you have more funds available for spending than are contained in your checking account and than are recorded in $M1$. Overdraft provisions have been popular in Great

Britain for a long time, and Keynes argued that these should be counted as money.[7]

This additional "money" consists of funds that you can spend, up to the overdraft limit set by your bank. In the near future it will become commonplace for financial institutions to transfer funds automatically from savings to checking accounts whenever a checking account is overdrawn. This development will demolish the distinction between checking and savings accounts and put conventional $M1$ aggregates on extremely tenuous ground.

In an unforgettable scene in the 1967 movie *The Graduate*, Dustin Hoffman is advised that the future will be "plastic." We're living in 1967's future, and sure enough, it's plastic. Some 100 million Americans are judged creditworthy by the industry, and 90 percent of these people carry one or more credit cards. The average person owns seven credit cards and charges several hundred dollars a month. As a nation, we have a credit card debt of more than $250 billion. (A Californian is listed in the *Guinness Book of World Records* as Mr. Plastic Fantastic for the dubious achievement of having 1300 different credit cards, giving him a theoretical ability to borrow $1.6 million.)

Credit cards are as widely accepted as checks, and they are used frequently enough to demand inclusion in a realistic definition of money. However, how are

---

**EXAMPLE**

**13.3**    *An Affinity for Credit Cards*

Nearly half of all households promptly pay their credit card balance each month to avoid finance charges; they use credit cards as a convenient way of making transactions and appreciate the delay between when the purchase is made and when the monthly payment is due. Other households use credit cards as a credit line — a way of borrowing money without filling out loan applications or making a commitment to repay the loan according to a fixed schedule.

Credit card issuers generally charge users a fixed annual fee of $20 to $75 plus an interest rate on unpaid balances that is several percentage points higher than interest rates on other types of loans. Merchants deposit the credit card sales receipt in a bank just as they would a check and are given immediate credit for the value of the charge, net of a fee typically set at 2 to 5 percent of the amount charged.

An *affinity card* is a credit card with a tie-in to a designated organization, which may receive part of the annual user fee, a fraction of a percent of the value of each transaction, and part of the monthly interest charges. Users of airline affinity cards are credited with frequent-flier mileage that can be redeemed for ticket upgrades or reduced prices. There are more than 3000 different affinity cards in the United States, ranging from the Sierra Club to the Women's International Bowling Congress, the Society for the Preservation and Encouragement of Barber Shop Singing in America, and the Elvis card.

we to measure the quantity of credit card money? The average volume of purchases is not appropriate. Remember, checking account money is measured by the amount of money in checking accounts at some point in time, not by the volume of checks written during the year.

Another possibility is the available credit limit that is specified by credit card companies. The credit limit is the maximum amount that can be charged, just as checking account balances measure the maximum amount of checks that can be written (neglecting overdrafts). However, credit card limits are unrealistic because few households can prudently charge the credit limits on their seven credit cards. In addition, credit card balances are a debt, and money is generally thought of as an asset. However, this reasoning does suggest a sensible alternative.

The appropriate analogue to the checking account balance is the amount of funds households can obtain easily to pay their credit card charges. Therefore, effective credit card money might be measured by the quantity of readily available funds. Even this yardstick is imperfect, because it neglects the frequently used possibility of paying credit card charges out of future income; however, it seems better than completely neglecting credit cards or simply adding up maximum credit limits.

**EXAMPLE 13.4**

## AT&T's Universal Card

On March 26, 1990, American Telephone & Telegraph (AT&T) introduced its Universal credit card with a nationwide advertising campaign that included numerous full-page newspaper advertisements and a television commercial during that evening's Academy Awards show. AT&T received 75,000 telephone inquiries about its card between midnight and 5 A.M. that night and 250,000 calls during the first 24 hours. Over the next 3 months, AT&T received 10 million inquiries and issued more than 1 million cards.

There were several lures. The Universal card can have either a Visa or a Mastercard format, and hence the card can be used wherever these cards are accepted. While most banks that issue Visa and Mastercard charge an annual fee of $20 to $75, those who signed up for a Universal card in 1990 will never pay an annual fee as long as the card is used at least once a year. The Universal card also can be used to charge long-distance telephone calls at a 10 percent discount.

In addition to its advertising blitz, AT&T recruited cardholders from its list of 70 million AT&T long-distance telephone users. The 46 million people who use AT&T telephone calling cards are a natural audience, although perhaps not a very profitable one — because these people generally pay their bills on time and, with no annual fee on its Universal card, AT&T is hoping to profit from monthly finance charges.

AT&T's credit cards are issued and processed through contractual arrangements with Synovus Financial Corporation, a bank holding company with headquarters in Columbus, Georgia. The cards are issued by a Synovus subsidiary, the Universal Bank of Columbus, a small Georgia bank with $3 million in capital. The receipts are handled by Total Systems Services, another Synovus subsidiary, which is the nation's second largest credit card processor. AT&T puts its name and logo on the card, markets the card, and buys Universal Bank's credit card receivables.

Citicorp, the nation's largest credit card issuer, responded by transferring $30 million of its telecommunications business from AT&T to rival MCI and by offering users of Citicorp credit cards discounts on long-distance phone calls using MCI. Several banking companies, including Citicorp, BankAmerica, and Chase Manhattan, filed regulatory complaints asking the Federal Reserve Board and the Federal Deposit Insurance Corporation to investigate charges that AT&T's arrangement violated federal laws prohibiting industrial and commercial companies from owning commercial banks. Legal briefs filed with the Federal Communications Commission argued that the 10 percent discount on long-distance calls was unsanctioned "predatory pricing" against other telecommunications companies.

From the beginning there was little doubt that AT&T's card is legal and that these complaints from banks were mere harassments, intended to slow AT&T's bold attempt to become one of the industry leaders. In 1992 Citicorp had 30 million cards in the United States and 40 million worldwide. One industry analyst estimated that AT&T would have 35 million cardholders by 1995.* The advantage for all credit card users is that AT&T's aggressive entry will force other issuers to make their cards more attractive.

*John J. Keller and Robert Guenther, "As AT&T Credit Card Charges Ahead, Banks Fight Back," Wall Street Journal, May 18, 1990.*

The reality of credit cards suggests that "money" ought to encompass easily liquidated assets such as large negotiable certificates of deposit (CDs), Eurodollars, and repurchase agreements (repos). **Money-market funds**, which are mutual funds that purchase short-term securities such as bank CDs and Treasury bills, also provide a very liquid investment for small investors. Shareholders can quickly and easily withdraw their money by giving written or telephoned instructions. Most funds allow shareholders to write checks payable to a third party, typically with a $500 minimum. **Money-market deposit accounts** (**MMDAs**) were authorized in 1982 to allow deposit institutions to compete with money-market funds. Depositors can make an unlimited number of withdrawals in person or by mail and are allowed a maximum of three checks a month or a total of six monthly withdrawals by check, telephone, or automatic bill paying.

What about stocks and long-term bonds? Many of these assets are easily sold in well-established markets. Anyone who owns Treasury bonds or IBM stock can sell these in minutes and will receive the proceeds within 5 business days.

EXAMPLE
13.5          *Are Humanities Majors Bad Credit Risks?*

Citibank issued 1 million credit cards in 1987 and 1988 in a nationwide marketing program aimed at college students between the ages of 18 and 25. In March 1988, the campus newspaper at the University of California at Berkeley reported that Citibank was rejecting card applications from older students and from students who majored in some humanities fields. A Citibank spokesman confirmed this policy but refused to identify the majors that were considered to be poor credit risks.

A Wisconsin congressman, Gerald Kleczka, introduced a bill prohibiting the denial of credit cards on the basis of age or major and denounced Citibank's policy as "reprehensible," "narrow-minded," and "capricious discrimination."* Berkeley's student government threatened to organize a boycott of Citibank and to ban Citibank credit card representatives from the Berkeley campus. Embarrassed by the negative publicity, a Citibank representative appeared before Berkeley's student senate to apologize for Citibank's misjudgment and to announce that Citibank would no longer screen applicants on the basis of age or major.

*Robert E. Taylor, "Parents Would Have Appreciated Some Card Burning by Protesters," Wall Street Journal, May 6, 1988.*

However, most economists frown on the counting of such assets as money, because the owner cannot be certain of the market value day to day. This argument applies with more force to less liquid assets such as land, houses, and rare paintings. There is a spectrum, and it is difficult to know where to draw the line.

In practice, monetary aggregates are a conglomeration of various similar and dissimilar assets. Some of the underlying assets are media of exchange, and their owners plan to spend them. Other assets are media of exchange but will probably not be used for transactions. Still others are not media of exchange but can and will be quickly converted and spent. And yet others are not media of exchange, could be quickly converted, but probably won't. Which combination from this monetary smorgasbord best deserves to be called "money"? Because there is no clear answer to this fundamental question, the Federal Reserve collects and studies data on several monetary aggregates.

## Monetary Aggregates in 1992

As financial markets have evolved, new aggregates have been constructed and old aggregates revised. In the 1950s, $M1$ and $M2$ were very popular. Then financial market innovations led observers to concoct $M2'$, $M3$, $M4$, $M5$, and on and on. The list grew and became increasingly bewildering as the years went by. In the 1970s, $M1+$ made a brief appearance. In some circles, double-digit $M$'s

| Table 13.3   Monetary Aggregates, Billions of Dollars, January 1992 | |
|---|---|
| Aggregate and component* | Amount |
| **M1** | 918.3 |
|     Currency | 267.9 |
|     Traveler's checks† | 7.9 |
|     Commercial bank checking accounts | 300.0 |
|     Other transaction accounts‡ | 342.5 |
| **M2** | 3460.1 |
|     M1 | 918.3 |
|     Overnight Eurodollars and repos | 77.8 |
|     Savings deposits and money market deposit accounts | 1055.7 |
|     Money-market mutual fund shares | 360.2 |
|     Small time deposits§ | 1048.1 |
| **M3** | 4185.6 |
|     M2 | 3460.1 |
|     Large time deposits | 424.4 |
|     Term Eurodollars and repos | 128.1 |
|     Institutional money-market funds | 173.0 |
| **L** | 4993.4 |
|     M3 | 4185.6 |
|     Savings bonds | 138.9 |
|     Short-term Treasury securities | 310.9 |
|     Commercial paper | 334.8 |
|     Banker's acceptances | 23.2 |

\* Components generally exclude amounts held by domestic depositary institutions, foreign commercial banks and official institutions, the U.S. government (including the Federal Reserve), and money-market mutual funds.

† Dollar-denominated traveler's checks issued by nonbanks; those issued by deposit institutions are included in transaction accounts.

‡ Includes NOW and ATS accounts, credit union share draft balances, and demand deposits at thrift institutions.

§ Time deposits issued in denominations of less than $100,000.

**Source:** *Federal Reserve Bulletin*, April 1992.

became popular. In 1980, the increasingly apparent ambiguities and the complete neglect of repurchase agreements, overnight Eurodollars, and money-market funds in its monetary aggregates persuaded the Fed to construct a thoroughly revised set, labeled *M*1A, *M*1B, *M*2, *M*3, and *L*. Soon it added *M*1B–Shift Adjusted; then *M*1A dropped from view and *M*1B became *M*1.

    The composition of the most widely reported aggregates in 1992 is shown in Table 13.3. The table shows that the *M*1 aggregate attempts to measure money as a medium of exchange — funds that can be used directly for transactions. The *M*2, *M*3, and *L* (for *liquidity*) series progressively expands to encompass less liquid funds that are a store of wealth and can be converted into a medium of exchange. The items in *M*2 are generally more liquid than those in *M*3, which, in turn, are mostly more liquid than those in *L*. This progression is far from perfect, however. For example, the small time deposits included in *M*2 are generally less liquid than the large time deposits included in *M*3 or the Treasury bills included in *L*.

Our financial markets are too complicated and dynamic for a single collection of assets to be clearly superior to other monetary aggregates. There are too many assets that are almost, but not quite, the same as others, and financial innovations are continually introducing new assets. Analysts of financial markets consequently watch many monetary aggregates.

One way to gauge the stability of the relationship between a nation's monetary base *B* and a monetary aggregate, such as *M*1, is to monitor the money multiplier *M*1/*B*, the ratio of the monetary aggregate to the monetary base. Figure 13.4 on page 406 graphs the annual money multipliers for the revised definitions of *M*1 and *M*2 back to 1970. As shown, *M*2/*B* continues to increase while *M*1/*B* is trendless, but there are substantial year-to-year fluctuations in each multiplier. Earlier in this chapter, the deposit-multiplier model was used to explain how deposit multipliers and money multipliers are affected by bank reserves relative to deposits, the public's holdings of currency relative to deposits, and shifts among different types of deposits.

As a consequence, the historical correlation between changes in government money and changes in monetary aggregates is very tenuous. Two simple scatter diagrams of the historical experience are given in Figures 13.5 and 13.6 on page 407 — ink splotches with no apparent pattern. These figures use annual data; quarterly, monthly, or weekly data are no better. An increase in the monetary base does not cause an immediate, reliable increase in monetary aggregates because other economic events cause the money multipliers to fluctuate.

Some monetary economists, following Milton Friedman, argue that a definition of money should be chosen not for its theoretical coherence but rather for its practical ability to explain fluctuations in output, prices, and other data of interest. The 1980 monetary aggregate revisions were at least partly motivated by a perceived deterioration in the empirical correlations between the old monetary aggregates and output, interest rates, and prices.[8]

For a time, some monetary economists believed that Old *M*1 was reasonably well correlated with gross national product (GNP), although this assumption was disputed by other observers. Figure 13.7 on page 408 shows the annual ratios of GNP to *M*1 and *M*2 since 1970. The ratio of GNP to *M*1 has been increasing ever since the 1950s, because deposit innovations have diminished the attractiveness of checking accounts relative to savings accounts. However, this upward trend was broken by sharp, unexpected declines in GNP/*M*1 in 1982, 1983, 1985, and 1986. The ratio of GNP to *M*2 has been trendless since 1970, with annual fluctuations of 3 to 5 percent commonplace.

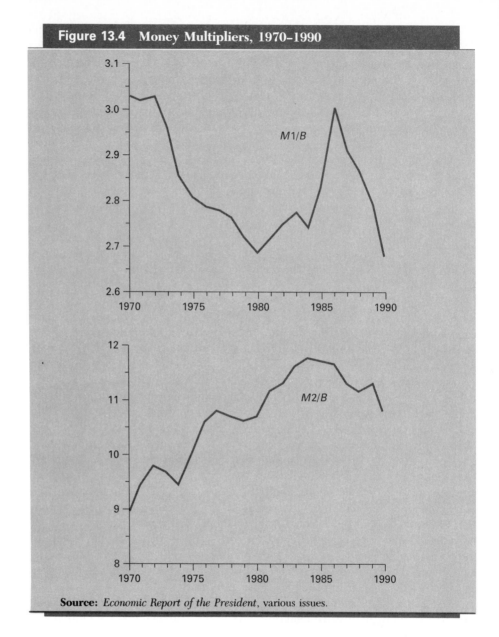

**Figure 13.4   Money Multipliers, 1970–1990**

**Source:** *Economic Report of the President*, various issues.

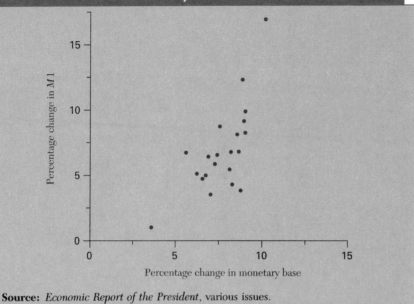

**Figure 13.5  Annual Percentage Changes in *M*1 and the Monetary Base, 1970–1990**

**Source:** *Economic Report of the President*, various issues.

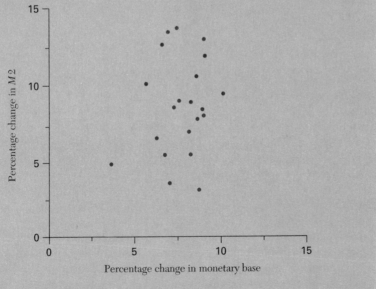

**Figure 13.6  Annual Percentage Changes in *M*2 and the Monetary Base, 1970–1990**

**Source:** *Economic Report of the President*, various issues.

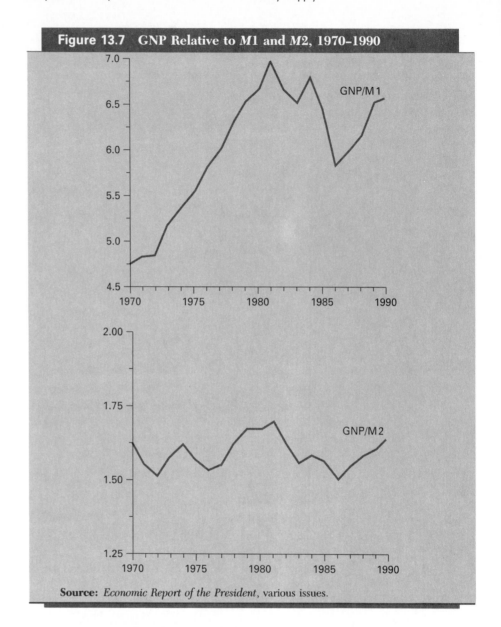

Figure 13.7    GNP Relative to *M*1 and *M*2, 1970–1990

Source: *Economic Report of the President*, various issues.

## MONEY TOMORROW

Currency and paper checks are being replaced by plastic cards and electronic banking. **Debit cards** look like credit cards and are used in stores just like credit cards, but they are really an electronic checking account in that funds are automatically transferred from the customer's checking account to the store's bank account. Some debit cards require the merchant to fill out a paper receipt

EXAMPLE
13.6    *Smart Cards*

Smart cards were introduced in France in 1974, are now used extensively there and in Japan, and seem poised to spread throughout the United States. With simple smart cards, the user pays in advance for 10 movie tickets, 100 pages of photocopying, or 1000 minutes of telephone usage. As the card is used, the outstanding credit is adjusted electronically until it is exhausted. The user can then pay to have it restored. In another variant, used on the Dallas North Tollway, commuters can display a smart card while driving through the toll plaza; the identification number is read with a radio signal, and each month's toll charge is billed to the driver's credit card.

More powerful smart cards can remember the owner's bank balance and keep detailed records of transactions, much like an electronic checkbook. Point-of-sale transactions at participating stores are made by inserting the card into special terminals and punching in a secret identification number, which is verified by the card itself. Some terminals record the transactions on magnetic bands, which store owners periodically take to banks for crediting their accounts and debiting the store's customers. Alternatively, stores can be electronically linked with banks to record transactions immediately. Smart cards also can provide information about customers that businesses may find helpful in understanding sales patterns and in targeting their advertising.

Super smart cards have keypads and displays, which enable the user to store and retrieve information. Travelers using the Thomas Cook Group services are given a super smart card that allows them not only to obtain funds from any Thomas Cook travel agent, much like electronic traveler's checks, but also to record information about their trip's expenses, which can be fed into a personal computer and printed out after the trip is over.

that is sent to the merchant's bank and then to the customer's bank, just as if it were a check. In other cases, the merchant may have a point-of-sale (POS) terminal that is connected to a bank's computer and immediately transfers funds from the customer's account to the merchant's account. Both merchants and banks like the fact that with a POS terminal there is no paper to handle, no credit risk, and no delay in receiving payment. Another variation is a **smart card**, which makes immediate payment for goods and services and has an embedded microprocessor that allows it to keep records of the user's transactions and financial situation.

Within the Federal Reserve System, $200 billion a day is electronically transferred among banks. The New York Clearing House International Payments System transfers a like amount through a computer network linking 80 banking offices. Both these systems are used primarily for large business transactions. The federal government uses the Federal Reserve Clearing House to make nearly 300 million transactions annually. These transactions are mostly direct deposits for the wages of federal employees, Social Security payments, and government pension benefits. In 1987 the Treasury began paying its suppliers electronically through the Vendor Express system. These various government payments are electronically transmitted and directly deposited in the recipients' accounts.

In 1992 it was estimated that two-thirds of government employees, half of Social Security recipients, and 10 percent of private-sector employees are paid electronically.[9] Direct deposits save time, paper, and postage and eliminate stolen checks. In comparison with a check, an electronic payment saves about 75 cents per transaction.[10]

In electronic home banking systems, households can pay their bills, transfer funds among accounts, buy and sell securities, and receive up-to-the-minute information using a personal computer and a modem to send instructions over the telephone wires. This is more convenient than mailing checks or standing in lines at banks, and it allows households to delay payments until the last possible moment.

It is widely believed that these various developments are the initial trial stages of what may someday become a comprehensive electronic funds transfer system in which a nationwide computer network records transactions electronically and instantly transfers funds from the buyers' accounts to the sellers' accounts. Government offices and businesses would have computer terminals connected to this network. Wages, dividends, and interest payments would all be transferred directly between accounts. Individuals with plastic identification cards would be able to pay for most of their purchases by inserting their cards in terminals located in retail stores. Transactions between individuals could be handled by public terminals or by home terminals. The complete elimination of cash will be resisted by participants in the underground economy made up of illegal and untaxed transactions. For the same reason, governments will try to abolish cash.

Funds credited within the electronic network of accounts would earn interest so that funds held in the system would serve both as a medium of exchange and as savings, a store of value. A positive balance would not be necessary to make transactions because of liberal overdraft privileges with interest charged on debits. Despite some loss of privacy, most individuals would benefit from the convenience of making transactions, the improved record keeping, and the savings in resources now spent reading, sorting, and transporting currency and checks.

In a pure currency system, every transaction requires a physical transfer of tangible currency. In this idealized accounting system of the future, there need not be any physical currency. Transactions require only bookkeeping entries of debits and credits. What, then, would we call money? And would we call the system a bank? Both terms would be obsolete.

# SUMMARY

The earliest banks simply stored precious metals and kept accurate records of their customers' deposits. With 100 percent reserves, they did not multiply deposits and the money supply. Before the Civil War, many U.S. banks — especially outside the Northeast — were loosely managed and loaned bank notes that were not fully backed by precious metal reserves. By the time of the Civil War, there were 7000 different types of bank notes in circulation. State bank notes were taxed out of existence after the Civil War, but nationally chartered banks were allowed to issue bank notes until 1935. Now, only the federal government is allowed to issue currency.

Banks multiply deposits and the money supply by holding fractional reserves against deposits, lending the remainder. The amount of deposits $D$ is determined by $D = B/(k + c)$, where $B$ is the monetary base (also called high-powered money), $k$ is the ratio of bank reserves to deposits (determined largely by reserve requirements), and $c$ is the ratio of currency outside banks to deposits. The more reserves held inside banks and the more currency held outside banks, the fewer deposits are created.

During the banking panics in the 1930s, both $k$ and $c$ increased substantially, causing an enormous contraction of deposit multipliers and monetary aggregates. More generally, deposit multipliers fluctuate considerably, and there is only a loose correlation between annual changes in the monetary base and in monetary aggregates.

Banks serve as intermediaries between lenders and borrowers. Lenders are able to withdraw their deposits on demand, while borrowers are given a fixed repayment schedule for their loans. This process creates loans, money, and the risk of bank runs.

Credit cards are widely used as a medium of exchange, but there is no compelling way to measure credit card money. In an idealized electronic funds transfer system, physical currency would be replaced by plastic identification cards and a nationwide electronic record of debits and credits. Interest would be credited on positive balances and charged on negative balances.

There is no firm, fixed definition of "money." There are temporary definitions of alternative monetary aggregates, such as $M1$, $M2$, $M3$, and $L$, because there is a continuum of financial assets and no compelling reason to single out a specific aggregation of these assets as all-important. For any particular definition of money, there are other financial assets, near-moneys, that are not very different from those assets labeled "money." Instead of restricting attention to a single, artificially precise definition of money, the Federal Reserve monitors several different monetary aggregates. Monetary aggregates do not move in lockstep; for example, a shift of funds from savings to checking accounts expands $M1$ and contracts $M2$.

# IMPORTANT TERMS

debit cards
deposit multiplier
excess reserves
fractional reserve banking
high-powered money
monetary base
money-market funds

money-market deposit accounts (MMDAs)
negotiable order of withdrawal (NOW)
  accounts
Regulation Q
reserve requirements
smart card
T-accounts

# EXERCISES

1. Federally chartered banks were initially required to hold 25 percent reserves against deposits. If all banks hold 25 percent reserves against deposits and none of the monetary base is held outside banks, what is the total amount of deposits and loans created by the banking system if the monetary base is $100 million? If it is $150 million?

2. In comparison with the preceding exercise, what happens to bank deposits and loans if the monetary base is $100 million and banks, fearful of bank runs, increase their reserves from 25 percent of deposits to 50 percent?

3. The monetary base is $60 billion and is held as bank reserves or as currency outside banks. What is the size of bank deposits and bank loans if banks hold 10 percent reserves against deposits and the public's ratio of currency outside banks to deposits is 15 percent? What if the public increases the currency/deposit ratio from 15 to 20 percent? Explain why this shift in public preferences expands or contracts bank deposits and loans.

4. In the 1930s, Henry Simons, a University of Chicago economist, and Irving Fisher, a Yale University economist, argued that banks should hold 100 percent reserves against their deposits. How would a 100 percent reserves system affect the ability of banks to multiply the money supply?

How would it affect their ability to withstand bank runs?

5. What is the size of bank deposits and bank loans if the monetary base is $60 billion, banks hold 100 percent reserves against deposits, and the public's ratio of currency outside banks to deposits is 20 percent? What if the public increases the currency/deposit ratio from 20 to 25 percent? Explain why this shift in public preferences expands or contracts bank deposits and loans.

6. Look in the most recent issue of the *Federal Reserve Bulletin* and see if the definitions of *M*1, *M*2, *M*3 and *L* given in Table 13.3 of the text are still used by the Federal Reserve. Report any changes. (These definitions are given in the notes to the *Bulletin's* Table 1.21, "Money Stock, Liquid Assets, and Debt Measures.")

7. Table 1.10 of the *Federal Reserve Bulletin* gives the seasonally adjusted annual rates of changes of the monetary base and of *M*1, *M*2, *M*3, and *L* during four recent quarters. Report these data from the most recent issue of the *Bulletin*. Did all five measures of the money supply increase by approximately the same percentage during each of these four quarters?

8. Give an example of an economic event that would cause *M*1 to increase even while the monetary base is constant.

9. Transaction deposits are about three times as large as currency holdings, but of the payments made by cash or check, more than 90 percent are made by check and less than 10 percent by cash. How is this possible? Use a simple example of a hypothetical economy in which the monetary base is $100 and checking account balances are $300.

10. If depositors transfer funds from checking accounts, subject to a 10 percent reserve requirement, to new tax-free savings accounts, which are included in $M2$ and subject to no reserve requirements, what will be the effect on bank loans, $M1$, and $M2$?

11. When the Federal Reserve reduced the reserve requirement on transaction accounts from 12 to 10 percent in April of 1992, it was widely predicted that this action would increase both $M1$ and bank profits. Explain the logic behind each of these predictions.

12. Why are banks able to pay higher interest rates on deposits that are not subject to reserve requirements than on deposits that have reserve requirements and still make a profit?

13. Here are the percentage changes in the monetary base, $M1$, $M2$, and GNP during 1984 and 1985:

| | B | M1 | M2 | GNP |
|---|---|---|---|---|
| 1984 | 7.3% | 5.2% | 8.4% | 11.0% |
| 1985 | 9.0% | 11.6% | 8.1% | 5.8% |

a. What happened to the money multipliers $M1/B$ and $M2/B$ during these 2 years?

b. What happened to the ratios $GNP/M1$ and $GNP/M2$, during 1984 and 1985?

c. How can the rate of increase of $M2$ diminish while $M1$ is accelerating?

14. The Old $M2$ money multiplier tripled between 1950 and 1980. How could this have happened? Must the government's printing presses have run amok?

15. If there were no legal reserve requirements, how would the government's ability to control $M1$ be altered? Would banks bother to keep reserves? Given total government money of $1 billion, what would be the maximum possible level of deposits?

16. "The latest available data show that $M1$, the basic money supply measure, declined $500 million in the week ended December 19. The broader measure, $M2$, rose $700 million during the week."[11] How could $M1$ have declined while $M2$ rose?

17. The ratio of currency to deposits doubled between 1929 and 1933. What effect do you think this increase had on $M1$?

18. In the 1930s, banks held enormous amounts of excess reserves. What effects, if any, would this behavior have on $M1$? The government, aiming to eliminate these excess reserves, raised reserve requirements in August of 1936, March of 1937, and May of 1937. However, banks continued to hold large excess reserves. What do you think happened to $M1$?

19. Should Federal Reserve notes that are used as a medium of exchange outside the United States be counted as part of $M1$? Defend your position.

20. Money-market deposit accounts were introduced on December 14, 1982, followed by super-NOW accounts on January 5, 1983. Both types of accounts had no interest-rate ceilings as long as the depositor maintained a minimum balance of $2500. Super-NOW accounts allow unlimited checking, while money-market deposit accounts allow a maximum of three checks a month. Which do you suppose was included in $M1$ and which in $M2$? Explain your reasoning.

21. In 1983 the Federal Reserve removed Individual Retirement Accounts (IRAs) at depository institutions or in money-market

funds from *M2* and *M3* because there is a substantial penalty for withdrawal of funds from these accounts before age 59½. What was its reasoning?

22. Some people almost always pay off the outstanding balance on their credit cards each month, while other people almost never do so. Which group would prefer a credit card with a low annual fee and high finance charges, and which would prefer a card with a high annual fee and low finance charges?

23. Banks make substantial profits from some credit card users but would prefer that others use debit cards instead of credit cards. What distinguishes these two groups?

24. Under the national banking system (1864–1914), out-of-town banks were allowed to count their interest-earning deposits in New York City banks as part of their required reserves. Did this provision increase or decrease the money multiplier?

Twice a year, in the spring and fall, farmers drew funds out of their local banks, and these country banks withdrew deposits from New York City banks. What effects do you think this had on the nation's money supply?

25. Charles Ponzi, an enterprising Bostonian, is remembered for his chain-letter approach to investment management in the 1920s. For a while, he was able to pay investors a 50 percent return every 45 days by using the funds of new investors to pay off old investors. For example, John might invest $100. If George and Martha now invest $100 apiece, then John can be repaid $150, with the promoter keeping $50. Hearing of John's success, Bob, Carol, Ted, and Alice then rush to invest $100 each. This chain can be kept up until the pool of fish is exhausted. The net result is simply a transfer of wealth from the late entrants to the earlier investors and the promoter. Is banking a Ponzi scheme?

# 14 The Benefits and Historical Pitfalls of Banking

**The Fairly Intelligent Fly**

*A large spider in an old house built a beautiful web in which to catch flies. Every time a fly landed on the web and was entangled in it the spider devoured him, so that when another fly came along he would think the web was a safe and quiet place in which to rest. One day a fairly intelligent fly buzzed around above the web so long without lighting that the spider appeared and said, "Come on down." But the fly was too clever for him and said, "I never light where I don't see other flies and I don't see any other flies in your house." So he flew away until he came to a place where there were a great many other flies. He was about to settle down among them when a bee buzzed up and said, "Hold it, stupid, that's flypaper. All those flies are trapped." "Don't be silly," said the fly, "they're dancing." So he settled down and became stuck to the flypaper with all the other flies.* **Moral:** *There is no safety in numbers, or in anything else.*

**James Thurber**

Banks and other financial intermediaries borrow money from some in order to lend to others. These institutions are, as their name states, intermediaries. Instead of John lending directly to Mary, John lends to a bank, which then lends to Mary. Why does this happen? Why do John and Mary, and you and I, use financial intermediaries?

This chapter examines some of the economic advantages that have made financial intermediaries such a crucial part of modern economies. We will discuss how financial intermediaries can simultaneously pool the savings of small investors who want safe, liquid financial investments and lend large amounts to borrowers who want to purchase risky, illiquid, real assets. We will also examine how seemingly sound banking practices can exacerbate economic booms and recessions and do not protect banks during financial panics. The economic

415

importance of banks and their historical vulnerability to financial crises — particularly the financial collapse in the 1930s — led to substantial legal constraints on their operations. The next several chapters will then discuss the management of modern banks and other financial intermediaries.

# INTERMEDIATION

The real resource costs to society of financial intermediation are the labor, equipment, buildings, and land used by these institutions. These costs are shouldered by borrowers and lenders in the gap between what borrowers pay and what lenders receive. Instead of John lending to Mary at a 10 percent interest rate, he lends to an intermediary at 9 percent, which then lends to Mary at 11 percent. The 2 percent differential pays for the resources used by the intermediary. Why do we pay higher rates when we borrow and receive lower rates when we lend? What social benefits justify the real resources consumed by intermediaries?

The benefits — both private and social — of intermediaries generally derive from their size. *Economies of scale* are said to occur when the unit cost of providing a service, such as processing a check or evaluating a loan application, declines as the size of the business increases. Economies of scale in banking provide persuasive economic reasons for having intermediaries collect and invest the savings of a large number of individuals and businesses. These economies of scale fall into two broad categories: risk-pooling and specialization.

# RISK-POOLING

Risk-pooling is a fundamental characteristic of financial intermediaries. Funds are taken from many different sources and invested in many different assets. This diversification of funds reduces risk for the intermediary and for the people who have lent it funds. Chapter 10 introduced the idea of risk-pooling in the discussion of risk aversion and diversified portfolios. The practice of risk-pooling can be found in many forms in the operation of various financial intermediaries. Let's look at some of these practices.

## Safety in Numbers

Risk-pooling is based on a statistical principle called the *law of large numbers*, which states that the average outcome is more certain when the number of outcomes is large. There is considerable uncertainty about the results of a few flips of a coin, rolls of dice, or spins of a roulette wheel. With a large number of occurrences, however, the expected statistical regularities appear. In a million flips of a fair coin you can be very confident that the fraction that are heads will be extremely close to 0.5. (Statistically, it is 95 percent certain that the fraction that are heads will be between 0.499 and 0.501.) Similarly, you can be very confident that in a million rolls of a single die the number 4 will come up close to one-sixth of the time and that in a million roulette spins the number 7 will occur about one thirty-eighth of the time. This fundamental statistical principle is what gambling casinos bank on and what banks gamble on.

To make the concept concrete, consider a bank that is concerned about the amount of money that depositors might withdraw on a given day. Withdrawal probabilities vary with the days of the week, of the month, and of the year and with business cycles, credit crunches, or other economic events. Perhaps on this particular day the bank estimates that each dollar that has been deposited with it has a 0.1 probability of being withdrawn. If the bank has only one dollar in deposits, the probability is 0.1 that it will be withdrawn and 0.9 that it won't. If the bank wants to be confident of meeting withdrawal demand, then it doesn't dare lend the dollar. There is too great a chance that the depositor will show up.

What if there are two dollars in deposits? Both dollars will be withdrawn, or only one dollar, or none. The probabilities are

| Dollars Withdrawn | Fraction of Deposits | Probability |
|---|---|---|
| 0 | 0.0 | 0.81 |
| 1 | 0.5 | 0.18 |
| 2 | 1.0 | 0.01 |

Because the probability of both dollars being claimed is only $0.1(0.1) = 0.01$, the bank may be willing to loan out a dollar.

With $10 deposited, the probabilities are

| Dollars Withdrawn | Fraction of Deposits | Probability |
|---|---|---|
| 0 | 0.0 | 0.3486784401 |
| 1 | 0.1 | 0.3874204890 |
| 2 | 0.2 | 0.1937102445 |
| 3 | 0.3 | 0.0573956280 |
| 4 | 0.4 | 0.0111602610 |
| 5 | 0.5 | 0.0014880348 |
| 6 | 0.6 | 0.0001377810 |
| 7 | 0.7 | 0.0000087480 |
| 8 | 0.8 | 0.0000003645 |
| 9 | 0.9 | 0.0000000090 |
| 10 | 1.0 | 0.0000000001 |

The odds of all deposits being withdrawn at once are now minuscule, at 1 in 10 billion. Surely some funds can be loaned safely. Even if half the deposits are loaned and half are kept on reserve, there is only a 1 in 10,000 chance of withdrawals exceeding reserves.

The most likely outcome is that one-tenth of the deposits will be withdrawn. As the quantity of deposits increases, it becomes more and more certain that withdrawals will be extremely close to a tenth of the deposits. With $10,000 deposited, the odds are 1 in 1000 that more than 11 percent of deposits will be

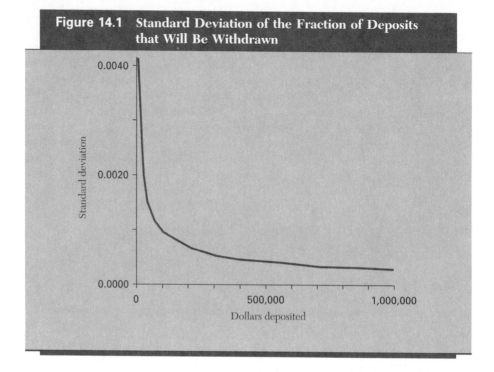

**Figure 14.1   Standard Deviation of the Fraction of Deposits that Will Be Withdrawn**

withdrawn. With $1 million deposited, the odds are 1 in 1000 that more than 10.09 percent will be withdrawn; almost 90 percent can now be lent safely.

Chapter 10 explained how the standard deviation can often be used to gauge risk or uncertainty. Here the standard deviation of the fraction of deposits that will be withdrawn is a simple statistic that quantifies the bank's uncertainty regarding deposit withdrawals. Figure 14.1 shows that this uncertainty declines as deposits increase.

The calculations in this simple, stylized example illustrate the general principle that diversification reduces risk. In a large number of draws, independent risks are diversified away. There will be some bad luck and some good — here some individuals will withdraw money and some won't — but the good and bad luck will roughly balance each other out. This is the same idea we encountered in Chapter 10 in the discussion of risk reduction through the selection of a diversified portfolio. With financial intermediaries, this principle applies to a variety of risks on both the asset and liability sides of the balance sheet.

**EXAMPLE**
**14.1**

## *Bigger Isn't Always Better*

Large banks are generally more profitable than small banks because the unit cost of many financial services declines as the size of the bank increases. It is unclear, however, whether these economies of scale continue indefinitely or whether there is some point at which a further increase in a bank's size does not make it more efficient. For example, a bank that makes only one loan a year cannot afford to hire a specialized, knowledgeable loan officer, but is a bank with 1000 loan officers more efficient than one with 900? Similarly, in Figure 14.1 the standard deviation declines very dramatically for the first $500,000 of deposits, only slightly for the next $500,000, and almost imperceptibly beyond that. In addition, some of the gains from specialization and diversification for very large banks may be offset by the fact that large organizations are often unwieldy and difficult to manage efficiently.

The accompanying table compares the net profits as a percentage of assets for banks in six different size categories. Banks with less than $50 million in assets were consistently less profitable than larger banks. However, profits drop after $500 million in assets. During this particular 5-year period, banks with more than $1 billion in assets were less profitable than banks with $50 to $500 million in assets.

The billion-dollar-plus banks made above-average profits in 1986–1988 but were below average in 1989 and 1990 — due largely to losses on foreign loans and commercial real estate loans. In 1989 and 1990, loan-loss expenses as a percentage of assets averaged 0.61 percent for banks in the $100 to $500 million category, 0.84 percent for banks in the $500 to $1000 million category, and 1.32 percent for billion-dollar-plus banks. Without these loan losses, the very largest banks would have been the most profitable. It is impossible to say whether these large loan losses were just bad luck or somehow systematically related to bank size.

These data are, of course, averages. A small bank can be managed profitably, and a large bank can be bankrupted by poor management. On average, however, large banks tend to be more profitable than small banks — at least up to $500 million in assets and perhaps beyond.

## Percentage Return on Assets, Insured Commercial Banks by Size of Assets

|  | All Banks | $0–$25 Million | $25–$50 Million | $50–$100 Million | $100–$500 Million | $500–$1000 Million | More than $1 Billion |
|---|---|---|---|---|---|---|---|
| **1986** | 0.63 | 0.09 | 0.46 | 0.62 | 0.68 | 0.61 | 0.65 |
| **1987** | 0.99 | 0.26 | 0.46 | 0.66 | 0.75 | 0.51 | 1.15 |
| **1988** | 0.84 | 0.36 | 0.61 | 0.77 | 0.81 | 0.58 | 0.89 |
| **1989** | 0.51 | 0.61 | 0.74 | 0.88 | 0.92 | 0.88 | 0.35 |
| **1990** | 0.51 | 0.61 | 0.72 | 0.82 | 0.81 | 0.77 | 0.39 |
| **Average** | 0.70 | 0.39 | 0.60 | 0.75 | 0.76 | 0.67 | 0.69 |

**Source:** Robert E. Goudreau and B. Frank King, "FYI — Commercial Bank Profitability: Hampered Again by Large Banks' Loan Problems," *Economic Review*, Federal Reserve Bank of Atlanta, July/August 1991, pp. 39–54.

## *Withdrawal Risk*

A fundamental characteristic of banks and other deposit intermediaries is the simultaneous accommodation of the preference of borrowers for illiquid loans that are repaid according to a fixed schedule and the preference of depositors for liquid funds that can be withdrawn at any time. Borrowers seek funds to finance the acquisition of real assets (cars, houses, factories, and equipment) that will yield profits or services over a substantial period of time and generally prefer to repay the loan over a similar period of time. Most households and businesses that borrow money are in no position to repay their loans immediately. If they had such surplus funds lying about, they would not have borrowed in the first place. Instead, borrowers typically have illiquid real assets that cannot be converted quickly into cash.

Those who borrow money to pay for their education would be hard-pressed if repayment were demanded immediately. Those who borrow money to pay for furniture, a car, or a house usually do so because they do not have the funds available to pay cash. If they were suddenly forced to repay their loans, they would have to sell their furniture, car, or house at distress prices. The same is true of businesses. When a firm borrows to pay for labor, materials, equipment, or the construction of a factory, it is normally in no position to pay off its debt at a moment's notice. If this were a provision of the loan, the firm would be reluctant to borrow, and so would you and I.

While borrowers prefer long-term, illiquid loans, lenders prefer short-term and very liquid loans. Unexpected needs always arise, and it is reassuring to know that a loan can be converted quickly and inexpensively into cash. Thus there is a considerable gap between the preferences of borrowers and the preferences of lenders. In the absence of financial intermediaries, both would compromise, and fewer loans would be made.

A primary benefit of deposit intermediaries in that they accommodate the conflicting liquidity preferences of borrowers and lenders by, in essence, manufacturing (and selling) liquidity. Depositors rightfully consider their deposits to be very liquid — redeemable at any time. Simultaneously, the deposit institution has used most of the funds deposited with it to make illiquid loans that it cannot redeem and cannot sell quickly, except at a substantial loss. It can get away with this sleight of hand because withdrawal risks have been pooled. With a large number of depositors, the institution can confidently estimate a prudent level of reserves.

There is an important distinction between the individual **micro**, or **idiosyncratic**, **risk** that can be diversified away and the **macro**, or **systematic**, **risk**, that cannot. In the numerical example, individual withdrawals were assumed to be independent: whether or not someone made a withdrawal had no effect on the likelihood of others making withdrawals. This is the individual micro risk that can be diversified away. It concerns withdrawals that are made for private idiosyncratic reasons that do not matter to others: the purchase of a new television, wedding expenses, a sudden illness.

Macro, or systematic, risk concerns events that may cause many people to withdraw money at once. Some of these events, such as Christmas spending in December and tax payments in April, are easily anticipated. To the extent that they can be predicted, these variations are not risky. The deposit intermediary simply adjusts its estimates of withdrawal probabilities and needed reserves. Other macroeconomic events may be more difficult to predict: recessions, credit crunches, and regulatory changes that allow other institutions to lure away depositors. Macroeconomic risks may be international (a worldwide recession), national (a tight-money policy by the Federal Reserve), or purely local (a drought, a hurricane, or the closing of a factory). The most dangerous and unpredictable macro risk is a panicky run on a bank. If depositors fear that they may not be able to withdraw their deposits, they are all sure to try.

Because such macroeconomic risks affect most depositors, they cannot be diversified away simply by having a large number of depositors. An intermediary's only protection is to keep funds near at hand that can be mobilized in an emergency. A key decision that a deposit intermediary must make is how much funds to keep in precautionary liquid assets and how much to invest in illiquid loans.

The pooling of withdrawal risks appears in other forms besides deposits. Banks commonly extend lines of credit, enabling businesses to borrow money as needed to cover lags between expenses and receipts. Individuals also may have lines of credit or overdraft provisions with their checking accounts that enable them to borrow money from the bank at a moment's notice. From the bank's standpoint, credit lines and overdraft privileges are withdrawal risks, a chance that customers will remove funds from the bank; the danger is that a great many of them may do so at the same time.

Again, much of this risk can be diversified away. With a large number of credit lines, a bank can generally count on those borrowing unusually large amounts to be offset by those borrowing unusually small amounts or repaying earlier loans. In essence, banks are a conduit through which those with excess funds lend to others with temporary deficits. The private and social benefits are that agents can obtain financing to carry out productive activities.

The provision of credit lines requires banks to keep liquid funds near at hand. However, these funds are small relative to the amount of outstanding loans and credit lines because of the pooling of idiosyncratic withdrawal risks. There remain undiversifiable macroeconomic risks. An economic boom or credit crunch may cause many to want to borrow money at the same time, and a bank must be concerned about the danger that it will not be able to fulfill its promises and honor these loan requests.

Another illustration of pooling withdrawal risks is the actuarial risks borne by insurance intermediaries. Insurance companies use the funds of policyholders to acquire financial and real assets. The securities issued to policyholders are special in that the payouts are based on the occurrence of natural events. Insurance companies are nonetheless financial intermediaries, selling financial obligations to some people and buying securities from others. The withdrawal risk is that the specified natural events will occur, causing the insurance benefit to be paid and funds to be withdrawn from the intermediary.

Again, to the extent that these natural events are independent, the withdrawal risk can be diversified away. If the probability of a certain person dying at age 72 is $P$, then, out of a large group of such people, the fraction that die at age 72 will almost certainly be very close to $P$. There remain macro risks that cannot be eliminated by the insurance of a large number of people: a contagious disease that reduces life expectancy, national speed limits that reduce automobile accidents, a revolution that destroys life and property. As with other intermediaries, some macro events are pleasant financial news to insurance companies, and others are expensive surprises.

## Portfolio Risk

In addition to withdrawal risks, financial intermediaries are concerned with portfolio risk. In Chapter 10 we saw how risk-averse investors can use diversified portfolios to reduce risk, or uncertainty, about the return on their investments. The return on a diversified portfolio is more certain than the return on the individual assets in the portfolio because investments that do poorly will be partly balanced by investments that do well.

Transaction expenses and indivisibilities make it impractical for many people to construct well-diversified portfolios on their own. A few thousand dollars cannot be divided economically among dozens of securities. Many poorly divisible assets such as real estate, corporate loans, and $100,000 CDs are inaccessible to a small investor.

A large financial intermediary, in contrast, can easily acquire thousands of assets, including the most poorly divisible, effectively diversifying away idiosyncratic risks. (There remain such macro risks as uncertainty about the future course of interest rates and the economy.) By reducing the risk borne by investors, intermediaries increase the funds available to borrowers.

Diversification is the basic concept underlying mutual funds. An individual investor who does not want to put all his or her savings into a single bond, stock, or other asset feels more secure, and correctly so, in pooling funds with other investors to buy a package of assets. Chapter 21 shows that the historical record indicates that managers of mutual funds are no wiser than other investors or even dart-throwing chimpanzees. However, mutual funds do provide risk-pooling.

Although the organization of other financial intermediaries is more complex, diversified portfolios remain important. Consider bank loans. Uncertainty about the return on any single loan is due mainly to the risk that the borrower will default. Most loans are too large for an individual to construct a diversified portfolio, but a bank with many depositors can effortlessly make even multi-million dollar loans and still diversify away independent default risk; there of course remains macroeconomic risk, such as a stiff recession that causes many borrowers to default. The same principles apply to savings and loan associations making mortgages, credit unions making consumer loans, pension funds buying bonds, and insurance companies acquiring real estate.

# SPECIALIZATION

In addition to pooling risks, financial intermediaries provide specialized services that are impractical for small savers and borrowers to perform on their own. Modern industrial economies rely on specialization: each person does a few tasks very well and trades the product of this specialized labor with other persons. The efficient utilization of large, very productive machinery requires specialized tasks within large firms. Specialization enhances farming, automobile production, and financial intermediation.

Financial intermediaries provide a variety of specialized services. In each case it is more economical to pay the institution for the service than to provide for it on your own. Some of these payments are explicit, such as management fees and checking account service charges. Others are implicit in the gap between the interest rates charged on loans and the rates paid on deposits.

One of these services is deposit and loan brokerage — the bringing together of savers and borrowers. It is expensive for individuals to identify attractive investments or to locate someone who will loan them money at fair terms. Financial intermediaries provide easily located, convenient locations for borrowing and lending. Deposit intermediaries provide facilities — including buildings, telephones, clerks, and automated tellers — for the "loan market" and the "deposit market" that make it easy for borrowers to secure and repay loans and for depositors to invest and withdraw funds.

Intermediaries also provide detailed, accurate records of transactions, safe storage of these records, and written evidence of financial assets and debts. All these services are provided by intermediaries because there are substantial economies of scale in assembling structures, equipment, and skilled employees.

Banking institutions offer a valuable bill-paying service. If you had to pay for all your purchases with cash, in person or by mail, it would be time-consuming, expensive, and risky. Instead, you can pay by check. When the recipient gives the check to his or her bank, your account is debited and the recipient's account is credited — quickly, safely, and efficiently. Banks use a great deal of labor and equipment to provide this service, but it is far less expensive than making cash payments.

Intermediaries also reduce the transaction expenses in buying and selling assets because it is proportionately less expensive to trade large assets. Brokerage fees are typically a fixed minimum amount ($25, $35, or more) plus a declining percentage based on the size of the transaction. Thus brokerage fees are proportionately smaller for large institutions making large transactions.

Large intermediaries also find it economical to acquire expertise that an individual household or nonfinancial business would find prohibitively expensive. Considerable knowledge and experience are required to understand financial dealings. Some of this expertise is mechanical and mundane: how to calculate interest rates, where to call to get a good price, what the tax implications are, what is the appropriate legal wording. Some expertise is very subjective and challenging: which stocks to buy, whether or not to approve a loan, what interest rate to pay or charge. There are considerable economies of scale in acquiring both kinds of expertise.

For example, an accurate estimate of default risk is needed for an informed decision about whether or not to approve a loan and, if the loan is approved, to determine its terms. It would be very inefficient if every household had to evaluate the creditworthiness of loan applicants; instead, specialists collect, process, and assess information relevant to loan requests. More generally, a rational evaluation of any security requires a careful assessment of a great many facts. It is most efficient to have specialized experts and high-speed computers collecting and weighing up-to-date information. Individuals benefit from these economies of scale by lending through intermediaries.

Some of the financial expertise and computer facilities accumulated within financial institutions are also useful for decisions made by households and firms. As a consequence, intermediaries advise customers on such matters as financial strategies, tax laws, and estate planning. This advice is usually part of an overall customer relationship and is paid for implicitly through the high rates charged on loans and the low rates received on deposits. In recent years, some intermediaries have moved to unbundle these services by levying explicit charges so that those who don't use services don't have to pay for them.

All the economies of scale discussed here under the groupings of risk-pooling and specialization argue for intermediaries — large institutions through which households and firms can lend and borrow. These economies of scale explain why John lends to an intermediary at 9 percent, which then lends to Mary at 11 percent. The intermediary is worth even more than the 2 percent it keeps.

Many of these economies of scale are interrelated. A large intermediary can simultaneously pool several types of risk. Structures, machinery, and skilled employees can be used for several purposes. Thus it usually is most sensible to have multifaceted intermediaries that simultaneously exploit several economies of scale and scope. In the past, however, many intermediaries in the United States were specialized, borrowing and lending only for certain restricted purposes — a specialization due more to regulatory constraints than to economic principles. Economic pressures have been eroding these constraints, allowing intermediaries to become financial supermarkets.

Now that we have considered their compelling social benefits, in the remainder of this chapter we will examine some of the pitfalls that intermediaries have fallen into in the past and how these stumblings created a legacy of regulatory constraints. We will then look at the management of modern financial intermediaries in several succeeding chapters.

# PITFALLS IN COMMERCIAL BANKING

The largest, and in many ways the most important, financial intermediaries are those that issue liquid deposits, including commercial banks, savings and loan associations, mutual savings banks, and credit unions. Deposit intermediaries monetize illiquid and poorly divisible assets. If you loan money to a friend or a small business, you have an illiquid asset. You cannot use the IOU to buy anything, and you would have a tough time trying to sell it to raise cash. If you instead deposit your money in a bank, and the bank loans out this money, then you have a very liquid asset. The intermediary monetizes your loan by transforming your illiquid asset into a liquid one.

In the preceding chapter's discussion of how banks multiply deposits and the money supply, you saw that this alchemy is profitable, socially useful, and risky. Now we will look more closely at how banks tried to cope with these opportunities and dangers in the past and how their failures led to a web of government regulations. Although we focus on commercial banks, the historical morals are applicable to other deposit intermediaries as well.

## Commercial Banks and the "Invisible Hand"

The early history of U.S. commercial banks was sketched briefly in the preceding chapter. Throughout this history, the banking system did not seem particularly adept at providing a stable supply of money to the economy or at avoiding financial panics and bank runs. Part of the problem was that the private self-interests of individual banks did not ensure aggregate welfare. The "invisible hand" was a bit clumsy.

When speculative fever was high and it seemed easy to make profits, banks tried to increase profits by issuing more bank notes, which exacerbated the speculative excesses. When the economy was in recession and the outlook gloomy, banks reined in loans and bank notes, intensifying the crisis. When it was in the interest of all to reduce speculation by restraining the money supply, individual banks were imprudent. When it was in the interest of all to be generous, each was frugal. Attempts to maximize private profits do not always serve the public interest.

It is not easy to recognize excessive speculation or gloom. Profits seem certain and easy just before a speculative bubble bursts; in crises, it is difficult to be optimistic when everyone else is so worried. These human emotions affect all participants in these high dramas but are particularly important for banks, given their power to expand and contract the money supply.

This dangerous power wielded by banks is an argument for a public-spirited central monetary authority that is concerned with more than profit maximization. However, the monetary authority's success may be hindered by the difficulty in perceiving whether prudence or aggressiveness is appropriate. This blurred vision is a continuing criticism of monetary authorities that we will look at in Chapter 24 in some detail.

**EXAMPLE**
**14.2**    *A Vietnamese Pyramid*

In 1987 Vietnam implemented a number of economic reforms that were intended to replace central planning with market forces. One reform was the encouragement of private entrepreneurs; another was the introduction of a banking system comprised of government-owned banks that were supposed to accept deposits (encouraging saving) and make loans (financing entrepreneurs). However, these official banks didn't attract many deposits and were reluctant to loan money to small businesses. In their place, small, privately run credit cooperatives sprang up that aggressively sought depositors and borrowers. These cooperatives were unregulated and unsupervised — according to one official, "No legislation, no rules, no nothing."*

The government-owned banks paid depositors 8 percent interest each month; the private cooperatives paid 10 percent, then 12 percent, and then 15 percent monthly. One of the most prominent was Thanh Huong, a combination bank and perfume factory, run by 32-year-old Nguyen Van Muoi Hai. Muoi Hai appeared in newspaper advertisements and television commercials, accompanied by his glamorous wife, hawking Thanh Huong's deposits and perfumes. Sirens blaring, a convoy of limousines and motorcycles carried Muoi Hai about. At each destination, helmeted bodyguards formed two lines for Muoi Hai to walk through, with an aide bowing and announcing, "Welcome, General Director. You have arrived."

Vietnamese lined up by the thousands, waiting hours for a chance to invest their life savings in Thanh Huong and share in Muoi Hai's success. When the bank distributed numbered slips to mark people's places in line, a black market developed for these slips, as people paid for the right to go to the front of the line and guarantee themselves an opportunity to make a deposit.

In 1988 Vietnamese newspapers began questioning Thanh Huong's success, noting that its perfume didn't seem very popular and that Muoi Hai lived very well. Their suspicions increased when Muoi Hai refused to allow reporters to inspect his books or his factory. In the spring of 1990, Muoi Hai was arrested and Thanh Huong was exposed as a Ponzi, or pyramid, scheme that used the money from new depositors to pay interest to old depositors. Government officials found that 140,000 people had invested a total of $27 million in Thanh Huong, but that its only remaining assets were about $7 million in cars, houses, and jewelry. Even the perfume factory was phony. Thanh Huong imported cheap perfume, diluted it with water, and attached labels to make it look like an expensive Western perfume, such as "Charlie." The unraveling of this swindle set off a financial crisis in Vietnam as anxious depositors attempted to withdraw their money from other credit cooperatives.

*Barry Wain, "Big Swindle Throws Vietnam's Experiment in Banking into Chaos," Wall Street Journal, May 14, 1990.

Another noteworthy aspect of the banking system's problems in the nineteenth century was the undisciplined behavior of small, country banks. Opening a bank and issuing bank notes seemed like a pretty easy way literally to make money. Banking was an occupation that attracted the most reputable and public-spirited people and the lowest and most down-and-out scoundrels. Many helped the country prosper, and many simply redistributed its wealth.

In the early crises and panics, bank failures were often regarded as appropriate outcomes for poorly managed banks. Banks that made questionable loans and kept little reserves got what they deserved. Nor were many tears shed for their depositors, who (by some unexplained means) should have exercised better judgment in selecting a bank. As long as the failed banks were small, run by somewhat suspect characters, and outside the eastern banking establishment, little effort was made to regulate banking. With time, the economy grew increasingly interdependent, and the waves of crisis became wider, toppling even scrupulous eastern banks. With these widespread crises came regulation and reform.

It is now apparent that even "sound" banking practices exacerbate business cycles and that with a fractional reserve system no individual bank is immune to bank runs. For both reasons there is a legitimate role for a central monetary authority. In practice, you will see that monetary authorities have been more successful in averting bank runs than in eliminating business cycles.

## Sound Banking Practices

Throughout the nineteenth century, sound banking practices rested on two precepts (or rules):

1. A bank's note issues should be limited by its reserves of precious metals.
2. Banks should make "commercial" loans, which are short-term and self-liquidating.

The first rule put the nation's money supply at the mercy of mining discoveries and foreign trade. Foreign trade had a particularly pronounced roller-coaster effect on the economy. We'll use the United States as a concrete example.

When foreign demand for U.S. goods increased, output increased. In addition, as gold flowed into the United States to pay for these exports, U.S. banks had greater precious metal reserves and so issued more bank notes, as called for by rule 1. As banks increased the money supply, an already stimulated economy was heated further. In theory, the boom would end when U.S. prices had increased sufficiently to choke off foreign demand.

In the opposite case, when there was weak foreign demand for U.S. goods, output declined. As gold left the United States and bank precious metal reserves declined, banks curtailed their loans and note issuance, thereby magnifying the economic recession until prices fell far enough to restore foreign demand for U.S. goods.

A precious metal standard for bank notes was intended to stabilize the balance of trade, but instead it magnified the amplitude of economic booms and busts. These painful roller-coaster episodes eventually led to worldwide abandonment of the principle that a nation's money supply should be rigidly linked to its gold reserves. The first sound banking principle was not a stabilizing influence. Neither was the second.

The second principle is known both as the **commercial loan theory of banking** and the **real bills doctrine**: bank loans should be short-term, self-liquidating, and productive. A classic example is a loan to a business to pay for labor and raw materials, with the revenue from the sale of the finished goods used to repay the loan. Also acceptable are loans to farmers to enable them to plant and harvest crops. Business loans for more than a few months, consumer loans, mortgages, and loans to buy securities were all considered inappropriate for a bank. Some proponents were willing to permit a small amount of these forbidden loans if they were financed out of the bank's capital (the funds invested by the bank's owners) instead of deposits.

In England, where the concept originated, the real bills doctrine was long considered sound banking practice. Early U.S. banks tried to follow the English example, granting only nonrenewable loans for no longer than 30 or, with some banks, 60 days; they soon found that their customers wanted longer-term loans. Until the 1930s, the real bills doctrine was accepted by academics, politicians, and regulatory agencies, but in practice, U.S. banks were directly, or through automatic renewals, making significant long-term loans to buy land, structures, machinery, and securities. By the start of the twentieth century, probably less than half of bank assets were pure commercial loans.[1]

Advocates believed that adherence to the real bills principle ensured bank liquidity. There is merit in the argument that short-term deposit liabilities call for a strategy of holding short-term assets. However, a bank's liquidity is not fully guaranteed unless its loans are entirely safe and liquid. In practice, loans are neither. If, for example, a bank makes only 60-day loans, then each day, on average, $\frac{1}{60}$ of the loans are being repaid. These repayments provide some liquidity, but hardly enough to stave off a bank run.

Commercial loans are not liquid unless the bank can demand repayment at any time. And they are not safe unless it is certain that the loans will be repaid. In a recession, when depositors may want to withdraw their deposits for safety or for food, businesses that are accumulating unsold goods may find it difficult to repay their loans. Self-liquidating loans are then no longer self-liquidating.

It also was believed that the real bills doctrine ensured that a nation's money supply was well behaved. In 1839, a proponent, Condy Raguet, explained the prevailing view:

> [A bank's] loans should not only be for short periods, but should be confined solely to the discounting of what is called "business paper," that is, promissory notes and acceptances received by the holders for merchandise and property sold. If none others were discounted, the expansion of the paper system would only be in proportion to the expansion of business.

*When this was extended, so as to call for more currency, as at particular seasons of the year, more currency would be created; and when business was diminished as at other seasons, so as to require less currency, the excess would be absorbed by the payments made back to the banks. In these operations, the level of the currency would not be disturbed to produce a depreciation [i.e., inflation], for although at times there would be a greater quantity of bank notes in existence than at other times, yet this quantity would be in exact proportion to the increased demand, arising from an increase in transactions.[2]*

Real bills enthusiasts believed that their banking strategy ensured that as business transactions expanded and contracted, the money supply would change proportionately, thereby holding the price level stable. Their analysis was, first of all, incomplete. They considered bank-issued money but ignored fluctuations in the amount of government money available to the public and to banks. For example, nineteenth-century farmers preferred to be paid in cash rather than by check, creating a seasonal withdrawal of government money from banks that restricted the banks' ability to make loans and reduced the nation's total money supply even as transactions increased. Similarly, real bills proponents did not take into account transactions that are not financed by bank loans. A real bills banking strategy does not ensure that an increase in aggregate transactions is matched by a proportionate increase in the aggregate money supply, because such a strategy encompasses neither aggregate transactions nor the aggregate money supply.

A second flaw is that the nominal value of loans requested depends on nominal rather than real transactions. A rise in prices increases the amount of financing desired by firms, and if the real bills doctrine is followed, banks will meet this demand by issuing more money. Thus a rise in prices will increase the money supply, and this increased money supply may increase prices even more, causing businesses to ask for more loans and banks to print more money. Under the real bills doctrine, the money supply and price level may rise (or fall) together indefinitely.

In practice, unlimited inflation or deflation will not occur because there is more to the money supply than bank money and more to transactions than bank-financed loans. However, the essential problem remains that an increase in real economic activity or in prices leads banks to issue more money — an action that further increases economic activity and prices. The real bills doctrine gives a nation a pro-cyclical monetary policy, automatically expanding during booms and contracting during slumps.

Overall, the real bills idea does contain two important insights: (1) liquidity crises are less likely when banks hold short-term liquid assets, and (2) it is advantageous for a nation's money supply to adapt to seasonal, cyclical, and long-run changes in economic activity. However, the real bills principle is not sufficient to avoid liquidity crises or to ensure a well-behaved aggregate money supply. In addition, it prohibits what many view as the principal accomplishment of financial intermediaries: allowing small investors to finance much of a nation's physical capital. Under the real bills theory, banks should provide only short-term financing of production and trade. In practice, banks have successfully financed long-lived plant and equipment.

## *Liquidity Crises and the Creation of the Federal Reserve System*

The inadequacy of "sound banking practices" was exposed in a succession of financial crises that led to the creation of the Federal Reserve System. The end of the nineteenth century and the beginning of the twentieth century were, for the most part, golden times for the U.S. economy. Adventurous and energetic people had spread throughout the country, and many cities were now linked by railroads. Agriculture and industry flourished. Banks gave individuals a place to save and farmers and businesses a place to borrow.

Figure 14.2 shows the number of banks each year between 1840 and 1940. At the time of the Civil War, there were about 1500 banks with aggregate assets of a billion dollars. By the turn of the century, there were 13,000 banks with assets of $11 billion. In 1921, there were 31,000 banks with $50 billion in assets.

Banks seemed to be everywhere — eight separate banks opened in 1886–1887 in Meade, Kansas, a town with a population of 457.[3] Bank failures also were

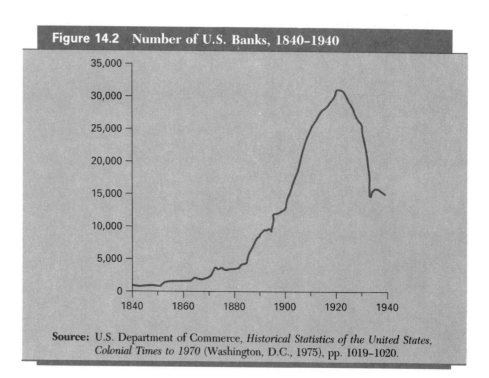

**Figure 14.2   Number of U.S. Banks, 1840–1940**

**Source:** U.S. Department of Commerce, *Historical Statistics of the United States, Colonial Times to 1970* (Washington, D.C., 1975), pp. 1019–1020.

plentiful throughout the nineteenth century and into the twentieth century. By 1860, two-thirds of the banks that had been chartered up to that time had failed. Figure 14.3 shows the number of banks that failed each year between 1864 and 1940. Between the Civil War and 1890, bank failures averaged 30 per year. Twelve hundred banks failed between 1904 and 1920, 5000 between 1921 and 1929, and 9000 between 1930 and 1933. Banks rode a roller coaster of booms and busts, with financial panics in 1819, 1837, 1857, 1873, 1884, 1893, 1907, 1921, and most dramatically, 1929.

In the 1893 panic, 496 banks closed. In the 1907 panic, 246 failed. These painful experiences convinced the public and their elected officials that something had to be done. The 1907 crisis was particularly persuasive because it shook respected New York City banks. In its aftermath, Congress set up commissions, studies, and hearings and in due course (1913) established the Federal Reserve System. There were many sides to this political tug-of-war: country banks versus city banks, states rights versus a central bank, easy money versus hard money, and academics versus bankers versus politicians. The result was a compromise:

1. Twelve regional Federal Reserve banks were established, to be guided by a Federal Reserve Board in Washington, D.C.
2. Federal Reserve banks could issue Federal Reserve notes backed 100 percent by commercial paper and 40 percent by gold or gold certificates.

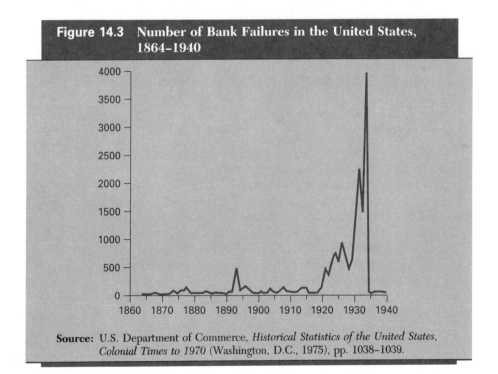

**Figure 14.3    Number of Bank Failures in the United States, 1864–1940**

**Source:** U.S. Department of Commerce, *Historical Statistics of the United States, Colonial Times to 1970* (Washington, D.C., 1975), pp. 1038–1039.

**EXAMPLE**
**14.3**      ***Postal Savings***

After the banking panic of 1907, many frightened people started putting their money in cookie jars, under their mattresses, and beneath their floorboards — anywhere but in banks. In 1910 Congress created the Postal Savings System, hoping to lure some of this cash out of people's houses. For every $1 deposit, a saver had to go to a local post office, purchase a 10-cent card and nine 10-cent stamps, and paste the stamps on the card. At a time when bank accounts paid 5 to 7 percent annual interest, postal savings accounts paid only 2 percent. For many people, however, the inconvenience and modest interest were outweighed by the security of having a deposit with the federal government. Postal savings deposits grew to $1.2 billion in 1933 and, even after the 1933 introduction of federal insurance for bank deposits, to $3.4 billion in 1947. Eventually, as deposit rates increased in the 1960s, even the most skeptical overcame their distrust of private banks, and in 1966, the Post Office stopped accepting postal savings deposits.

3. Nationally chartered banks were required to enter the system; state-chartered banks could join if they wished.
4. Member banks were required to hold reserves against checking and time deposits: 18 percent for banks in reserve cities, 15 percent for banks in other cities, and 12 percent for country banks.
5. Federal Reserve banks could buy and sell government securities as directed by the Federal Reserve Board.
6. Member banks could borrow from Federal Reserve banks, using commercial paper as collateral.
7. Federal Reserve banks were to operate a check-clearing system that was open to all banks.

Even as a compromise, the system was greeted with very mixed reviews, ranging from the American Bankers Association's complaint that "for those who do not believe in socialism, it is very hard to accept" to the comptroller of the currency's argument that it made financial panics "mathematically impossible."[4] The Federal Reserve was neither socialism nor foolproof.

The most important innovation was thought to be number 6 above, the so-called **discount window**, which allows member banks to borrow money in times of distress. The **discount rate** is the interest rate charged on these loans. (For many years these were commonly called the "rediscount window" and "rediscount rate," a reference to the real bills idea that banks discount business IOUs when a commercial loan is made and then rediscount this IOU when it is used as collateral for a loan from the Federal Reserve.)

The discount window was designed to defuse bank runs by making Federal Reserve banks reliable lenders of last resort, a source of emergency cash for banks. The Federal Reserve banks were not intended to use monetary policy to stabilize aggregate output and prices, because the architects were too closely wedded to the gold standard and the real bills doctrine to believe that stabilization policy was necessary.

## Early Federal Reserve Policy

As the Federal Reserve System was being set up, World War I began, and with it both the established order and the gold standard began crumbling. England, France, and the other combatants sent $1.5 billion in gold to the United States to pay for food and weapons. As their gold supplies dwindled, European governments abandoned the gold standard. Private holdings of gold were called in and replaced with paper notes. Citizens were no longer allowed to redeem these paper notes for gold, nor were they permitted to take gold out of their country.

The classical gold-standard scenario would have been for each of these nations to reduce its money supply drastically, thereby reducing domestic prices. As European prices fell, U.S. citizens would buy more European goods, and the balance of trade would balance. Europeans would pay for U.S. wheat and weapons with sweaters and wine instead of gold. In practice, only the British government was willing to inflict deflation and depression on its people, and even the ringing oratory of Winston Churchill, then chancellor of the exchequer, did not completely persuade the English of the rightness of this course.

In the United States, the World War I export boom, the gold inflow, and domestic war spending greatly stimulated the economy and increased prices. Commercial banks and the new Federal Reserve System played a key role in this inflation. Spending by the federal government increased from $0.7 billion in 1916 to $18.5 billion in 1919, mostly financed by the banking system as the Federal Reserve banks made low-interest loans to member banks, which then either bought Treasury securities themselves or loaned the money to customers who bought Treasury obligations. This financing of federal spending was a considerably different use of the discount window than had been intended by the architects of the Federal Reserve System. During World War I, this usage was patriotic and helpful. After the war and through the 1930s, however, Federal Reserve loans through the discount window continued to be misused, with regrettable consequences.

When the war ended, the Federal Reserve kept a low discount rate on loans to member banks, primarily to accommodate the Treasury, which desired low interest rates on its borrowings and, in addition, did not want to see bond prices fall, causing capital losses to those patriotic citizens who had bought low-interest Liberty Bonds to help finance the war. However, a low discount rate also encouraged member banks to borrow freely from the Federal Reserve banks so that they could lend more money to an already strong economy. Much of this money fueled speculation in land, commodities, and securities.

In the spring of 1920, a slackening of exports and government spending began to weaken the U.S. economy. The Federal Reserve banks had by now issued almost as many Federal Reserve notes as permitted by the war influx of gold and, anxious to maintain the convertibility of the nation's money into gold, decided to reduce member bank borrowings by raising the discount rate to an unprecedented 7 percent. The Federal Reserve also hoped that a diminished use of the discount window would force member banks to sell their government securities and return to the commercial loans that were acceptable under the real bills doctrine.

Member bank borrowings did fall sharply, and the economy collapsed. Millions lost jobs, and farm prices fell by 50 percent. The Federal Reserve had helped fuel the speculation and then worsened the recession. Nor did the Fed do anything to cushion the economic collapse, although it was the sharpest yet experienced by the nation. Not until April of 1921 — a full year after the recession began — did the Federal Reserve lower the discount rate (or do anything else to ease the credit crisis). It was not an auspicious beginning for the Federal Reserve System.

The Federal Reserve banks also did little to eliminate bank failures. In 1921, 505 banks failed. And this number turned out to be a below-average failure rate for the 1920s! The Federal Reserve banks provided little supervision of banks and few loans of last resort. They seemed wedded to the view that a bank's failure reflected its poor management and was of little concern: "Each year the Board reported the melancholy figures . . . and confined itself to noting that suspensions were in disproportionate number of nonmember rather than member banks, of banks in small communities . . . of banks in agricultural rather than industrial areas."[5] Two-thirds of the nation's banks, holding one-third of all bank assets, remained outside the system. These nonmember banks were usually managed less conservatively, and they failed disproportionately. However, member banks — many of them large member banks — failed too. Each year throughout the 1920s, from 30 to 50 percent of the deposits in failed banks were in failed member banks.

## The Roaring Twenties

The 1920s was an exciting and turbulent decade, both for the economy and for commercial banks. Banks moved into investment banking, acting as brokers for firms selling securities to the public. They added trust departments, managed individual portfolios, and even opened a few mutual funds. Banks bought speculative securities and loaned money to their customers to do the same. It was a competitive, rough-and-tumble decade. Twenty percent of the banks in existence in 1920 had failed by 1929. There were also almost 4000 bank mergers, and nearly 4000 bank branches opened.

Consistent with the belief of Presidents Coolidge and Harding that government should not interfere with business, the Federal Reserve paid little attention to supervising bank loans. Instead, by and large, the Federal Reserve System financed the aggressive activities of banks by keeping a low discount rate and purchasing large amounts of government securities. By 1922 the Federal Reserve banks had discovered that purchases and sales of securities were powerful monetary actions. When the Federal Reserve printed Federal Reserve notes and purchased government securities from banks, bond prices went up (and interest rates down) while the money supply and bank loans increased.

One reason for the Federal Reserve's easy-money policies during the 1920s was the real bills doctrine — the belief that banks should make commercial loans rather than hold government securities. The Fed bought government bonds from banks in order to encourage commercial lending and, in so doing, increased the money supply and stimulated the economy.

A second reason for the Fed's easy-money policies was a desire to help the world return to the prewar gold standard. The appropriate consequence of the inflow of gold to the United States, which now held nearly half the world's monetary gold, was a large increase in the money supply and price level in the United States. If U.S. prices rose sufficiently, Europeans would stop buying U.S. wheat, U.S. citizens would buy lots of French wine and English sweaters, and gold would flow from the United States back to Europe. The European governments repeatedly urged the Federal Reserve to follow easy-money policies, and this advice from more experienced and respected central bankers was followed. As the speculative boom developed in the 1920s, a final argument for monetary ease was a desire to avoid precipitating a financial collapse.

In December of 1927, the Dow Jones Industrial Average of stock prices topped 200, double its level 3 years earlier. The index reached 250 in October of 1928 and 300 two months later. Some people borrowed heavily to buy stocks and made enviable gains. Many of the envious decided to buy stocks too, and the Dow index reached 386 in September of 1929.

Many historians have criticized the people running the Federal Reserve during this period.[6] For most of the 1920s, the chairman of the Federal Reserve Board was a Warren G. Harding appointee, whose chief qualification seems to have been that he was a friend and neighbor of Harding. President Herbert Hoover described other members of the board as "mediocrities." One exception was Benjamin Strong, who had considerable influence as president of the Federal Reserve Bank of New York and has received generally favorable reviews from historians. His untimely death in 1928 is seen by some as a major factor in bringing on the Great Depression.[7]

## The Crash and the Great Depression

In 1928 the Federal Reserve decided that the time had come when something had to be done to discourage stock market speculation. The new president of the Federal Reserve Bank of New York, George L. Harrison, argued for a "sharp, incisive" increase in discount rates. Others counseled "moral suasion." The Federal Reserve Bank of New York's discount rate was raised from 4 percent in February of 1928 to 5 percent in July and then to 6 percent in August of 1929. The Federal Reserve also sold a half-billion dollars in government securities from the end of 1927 through the summer of 1929, thereby removing that much

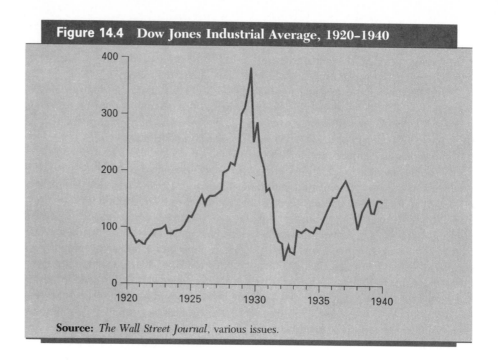

**Figure 14.4   Dow Jones Industrial Average, 1920–1940**

**Source:** *The Wall Street Journal*, various issues.

currency from circulation. The interest rate on loans to stockbrokers fluctuated wildly, reaching 12, 16, and 20 percent.

In October of 1929, the stock market crashed. After a number of bad days, there was panic selling on Thursday, October 24, and then again on Tuesday, October 29. The market was like a drunk stumbling downstairs — a bit of unsteady calm, perhaps a step upward, and then a tumble down a few more steps. When the Dow index finally hit the floor, in July of 1932, it was at 41, a fall of nearly 90 percent from its 1929 peak. Figure 14.4 shows the stock market boom in the 1920s and the subsequent collapse.

Economists still debate the extent to which the stock market crash contributed to the economic depression in the 1930s and the extent to which it was simply a barometer of the economy's collapse. Assuredly, it was both to some degree. The low levels of output, profits, and dividends called for low stock prices. And the collapse of stock prices surely depressed the spending of those who owned stocks — a group that was relatively small in number but large in discretionary spending. The market crash also dealt a stunning blow to the nation's self-confidence.

As financial markets reeled and sordid tales of financial chicanery spread, anxious depositors converged on banks. Many banks suffered losses in the stock market crash, both by their own speculation and by their now-worthless loans to others, and were in no shape to meet the anxious demands of depositors. Bank failures became an epidemic as each failure sent depositors rushing to neighboring banks to withdraw their funds before they, too, collapsed. All told, 1350 banks failed in 1930, 2290 in 1931, 1460 in 1932, and 4000 more in 1933. In desperation, states began declaring banking holidays in late 1932, closing the banks to protect them from their depositors. Looking for an excuse for a bank holiday, the governor of Louisiana, Huey Long, considered honoring Jean Laffite, a pirate; he decided instead to celebrate the breaking of diplomatic relations with Germany in 1916.[8]

By the time of Franklin Roosevelt's inauguration in the spring of 1933, only banks in the Northeast remained open. He soon declared a nationwide holiday and closed all banks. Federal regulatory authorities divided banks into three groups: the good, the bad, and the ugly but salvageable. The good reopened within the next week or so, and the bad were permanently closed. Those in the middle group were opened later, after being given temporary deposit insurance and loans from the newly created Reconstruction Finance Association.

The withdrawal of deposits from banks, the proclivity of frightened banks to hoard funds rather than make loans, and the closing of banks all contracted the nation's money supply and the availability of credit, surely exacerbating the Great Depression. The Federal Reserve System did not perform well in this, its greatest test. Part of the difficulty was the stubborn belief that only the wicked would be bankrupted.

> *The purgative conception of economic policy . . . held that the boom built damaging, though often unspecified, distortions into the economic system.*
>
> *Recovery could only come as these were eliminated. Deflation and bankruptcy were the natural correctives. Joseph Schumpeter, his country's Finance Minister during much of the Austrian inflation, was now emerging as a major figure on the American economic scene. He argued that the economic system had, through depression, to expel its own poisons. Looking at the history of business cycles, he concluded that no recovery was ever permanent until this happened and that any public intervention to speed recovery merely postponed the therapy and therewith the recovery. Lionel Robbins . . . offered essentially the same advice. . . . "Nobody wishes for bankruptcies. Nobody likes liquidation as such. . . . [But] when the extent of malinvestment and over indebtedness has passed a certain limit, measures which postpone liquidation only tend to make matters worse." A rather cruder formulation came from Secretary of the Treasury Andrew Mellon. To promote recovery, he advised, the country needed to "liquidate labor, liquidate stocks, liquidate the farmers, liquidate real estate."[9]*

Few recognized the interdependent nature of modern economies. When workers lose jobs, businesses lose sales. When businesses reduce production, employees are let go. When depositors withdraw funds from banks, loans are reduced, and both spending and production contract. When households, businesses, and banks are liquidated, their neighbors recoil, thereby making matters worse — not better. Reducing spending, withdrawing deposits, cutting production, and curtailing loans are all understandable reactions designed to protect the individual but destined to harm the nation.

EXAMPLE
14.4

## *The Failure of the Bank of the United States*

The preceding chapter discussed two early U.S. experiments with central banking: the Bank of the United States (1791–1810) and the Second Bank of the United States (1816–1835). Each was modeled after the Bank of England and given a 20-year charter; in each case, Congress voted not to renew its charter.

In the 1920s, a private New York bank with the name Bank of the United States grew to become the twenty-third largest bank in the country. Because of its size and name, many people — both in the United States and abroad — apparently believed that it was part of the federal government. In the aftermath of the 1929 stock market crash, the Bank of the United States, like many other banks, was in danger of collapse, yet many government officials were unsympathetic to the plight of these banks and their customers. An officer of the Philadelphia Fed stated:

> *The correction must come about through reduced production, reduced inventories, the gradual reduction of consumer credit, the liquidation of consumer loans and the accumulation of savings through the exercise of thrift. . . . [T]here is no shortcut or panacea for the rectification of existing conditions.* *

Andrew Mellon, the Secretary of the Treasury, argued that bankruptcies "will purge the rottenness out of the system. People will work harder, live a more moral life. Values will be adjusted and enterprising people will pick up the wreck from less-competent people."†

The New York Federal Reserve Bank made a modest effort to persuade some large New York banks to lend money to the Bank of the United States. However, there was some feeling in the banking establishment that this bank had been poorly managed and that it was tied too closely to the garment industry, which some thought was not worth saving because of prejudice against its mainly Jewish owners.‡ The Bank of the United States was allowed to fail in December 1930. With more than $200 million in deposits, this was, at that time, the largest bank failure in U.S. history, and the shock waves were felt across the nation and even overseas.

*William Greider, Secrets of the Temple (*New York: Simon & Schuster, 1987), p. 300.*
†Ibid., p. 300.*
‡J. K. Galbraith, Money (*Boston: Houghton Mifflin, 1975), p. 191. For a more critical view of the bank, see Paul Navazio, "Analyzing the Failure of the Bank of the United States," Working Paper, University of California, Davis, 1984.*

Despite disapproval and censure by the Federal Reserve Board, the Federal Reserve Bank of New York lowered its discount rate in stages down to 1.5 percent in mid-1931, and the other Federal Reserve banks eventually followed suit.

However, the Treasury-bill rate had by then dropped below 1 percent. In addition, member banks could borrow only by putting up short-term commercial paper as collateral, which was by then in short supply, a requirement that reflected the influence of real bills doctrine. It was not until the Emergency Act of 1933 that banks were allowed to use U.S. government securities as collateral. Member bank borrowings from the Fed actually declined significantly in 1930 and 1931.

The Federal Reserve did undertake some modest open-market purchases of government securities. They bought $100 million in 1930 and then, worried that a speculative inflation might be around the corner, sold $40 million back in the first half of 1931. They bought $175 million in the second half of 1931 and, convinced that more than a speculative fever had been broken, bought another $1.1 billion in 1932.

Some economists have been very critical of this lackluster performance, arguing that the Federal Reserve should have flooded the country with currency in an all-out effort to end the economic depression. Others, including the British economist John Maynard Keynes, were skeptical of the monetary authority's ability to turn the tide. Interest rates fell to very low levels and yet households were reluctant to borrow because they feared losing their jobs. Borrowing to invest in physical capital seemed mad when so much of the nation's capital was already idle. Afraid of the future, households, banks, and businesses all hoarded cash. The ratio of currency outside banks to checking accounts rose from 0.17 in 1929 to 0.33 in 1933. Member bank excess reserves rose from $48 million in 1929 to $766 million in 1933 to $6.6 billion in 1940. If more cash had been pumped into the economy it, too, might have been hoarded.

Some argue that in an extreme slump there are limits to the effectiveness of monetary policy. The monetary authorities can stop a boom by tightening credit, but they cannot ensure recovery by easing credit — it is a lot easier to squeeze the toothpaste out than to put it back in the tube. The only sure way to end an economic collapse is an increase in government spending and employment. Critics of the Federal Reserve's inaction admit that aggressively expansionary monetary policies might not have worked, but they argue that at least such policies should have been tried.

The most stinging indictment is that the Federal Reserve banks did not find a way to accomplish what they had been created for, to stop panicky bank runs. Bank runs involve a very delicate but obvious element of mass psychology. When depositors believe that their money can be safely withdrawn, they have no desire to do so. No bank, unless it operates as a mere safe deposit box with 100 percent reserves, can really stand ready to satisfy all depositors at a moment's notice. However, it will not be in jeopardy so long as it maintains confidence by meeting modest tests of its ability to pay depositors. The banks that survived in the 1930s were those that were able to acquire funds promptly to cut short any sign of panic.

Often banks were saved by short-term loans from neighboring banks that realized the contagious nature of bank runs. Too often the Federal Reserve banks would not make similar loans. The Federal Reserve banks were run by the

EXAMPLE
14.5

## Breaking a Bank Run

Banks normally don't need to keep much currency in their vaults, because daily withdrawals are generally offset by daily deposits. As long as depositors believe that they can withdraw their money when they need it, they are content to leave their money in the bank earning interest.

A run on a bank is an abnormal event, instigated by depositor anxiety about the safety of their money. If depositors fear that they may not be able to withdraw their money, they will try to withdraw it. Banks consequently try to stave off bank runs by demonstrating to their depositors' satisfaction that their money is safe. With fractional reserve banking, no bank has enough cash on hand to satisfy all its depositors. Historically, therefore, banks have used a variety of ploys to show that what cash they can muster is sufficient.

In September of 1720, for instance, there was a run on the Bank of England after it failed to honor its promise to buy South Sea Company bonds at a price of £400. The bank successfully defended itself against this run by arranging for allies to be in the front of the line of anxious depositors. These friends were paid slowly in sixpences, which the bank then retrieved and recycled, paying the same money over and over to its allies. The long line melted as depositors grew tired of waiting for their money and became convinced that the bank had the means to pay everyone.*

A similar strategy was employed during the Great Depression by Marriner Eccles, who was to become chairman of the Federal Reserve Board. As manager of a prominent Utah bank, he received word early one morning in the summer of 1931 that a neighboring bank was not going to allow depositors to withdraw their money. Correctly anticipating that this action would cause a run on his own bank, he telephoned the Federal Reserve Bank of Salt Lake City and requested an urgent delivery of currency by armored car.

Before opening his bank, he instructed his bank tellers to smile, talk about the weather, verify all customer signatures very carefully, and double count their money slowly, paying all withdrawals in small bills. Sure enough, when the bank's doors opened, a crowd of anxious depositors surged inside. As instructed, the tellers made small talk and pretended that nothing unusual was happening, while stalling as long as possible.

The armored car from Salt Lake City arrived in time. As the guards brought in sacks of cash, Eccles climbed on top of a table and announced:

> *Instead of closing at the usual hour of three o'clock, we have decided to stay open just as long as there is anyone who desires to withdraw his deposit or make one. . . . As all of you have seen, we have just brought up from Salt*

---

*A. Andreades, History of the Bank of England (London: P.S. King, 1909), p. 137, citing Henry Dunning McLeod, The Theory and Practice of Banking (London: Longmans, Green and Co., 1875), p. 428.

> *Lake City a large amount of currency that will take care of all your requirements. There is plenty more where that came from.*
>
> Later, in his autobiography, he added, "This was true enough — but I didn't say that we could get it."†
>
> Reassured by Eccles' dramatic announcement, the line of depositors melted away. The next day Eccles instructed his tellers to pay out funds as fast as possible to prevent lines from forming and attracting the attention of still-nervous depositors.
>
> †*Marriner S. Eccles*, Beckoning Frontiers *(New York: Alfred A. Knopf, 1951), p. 60.*

most reputable bankers, who had ingrained feelings about loans. To get a loan from a Federal Reserve bank, a member bank seemingly had to prove that it didn't need it. This attitude may have enhanced the profits of the Federal Reserve banks, but it was hardly a strategy for ending bank runs.

## Reform and a Legacy of Regulation

The financial debacle led to the Banking Act of 1935, which gave the seven-member Federal Reserve Board of Governors (the Fed) in Washington, D.C., the dominant role in setting monetary policy. The Board of Governors was given the authority to approve the presidents and first vice-presidents of the 12 Federal Reserve banks, to set reserve requirements within limits fixed by Congress, and to determine Federal Reserve bank discount rates. The board also occupies 7 of the 12 seats on the Open Market Committee, which eases and tightens financial markets by buying and selling Treasury securities. Among the other provisions in this historic legislation are the following:

1. Member banks were allowed to use securities other than commercial paper as collateral for Federal Reserve loans. However, in continued deference to the real bills doctrine, loans backed by government securities could not exceed 15 days, and those backed by other securities were assessed a penalty discount rate. (These restrictions have since been removed.)
2. Member banks were severely restricted from acting as investment bankers (underwriting or trading securities) and from investing in stock.
3. Banks were prohibited from paying interest on checking accounts, and the Board of Governors of the Federal Reserve was given the power (Regulation Q) to limit the interest rates that banks pay on time deposits. (It was thought that fierce deposit-rate competition in the 1920s had pushed banks into making high-yielding but speculative investments.)
4. The Federal Reserve Board of Governors was allowed to establish margin requirements, limiting the use of borrowed money to buy stock. With a 25 percent margin requirement, for example, an investor buying $1000 worth of stock must put up at least $250 and can borrow the remainder from a brokerage firm or other institution. Margin requirements give the Fed a

scalpel for excising stock speculation without precipitating a general credit crunch. When stock prices increased sharply in 1958, the Fed raised margin requirements from 50 to 70 percent and then to 90 percent to wring out what it perceived as excessive speculation.

5. The Federal Deposit Insurance Corporation (FDIC) was established to insure bank deposits.

There are several lessons from this historical legacy of early bank management, early Federal Reserve policies, the excesses of the 1920s, the ensuing financial collapse, and the 1930s reforms. Early banking was a very useful but risky business. Banks exerted a strong influence on the economy and were strongly influenced by the economy. What appeared to be sound banking practices for an individual bank often exacerbated both the nation's economic fluctuations and bank failures. The early Federal Reserve banks were ineffectual or worse, because they, too, tried to follow sound banking practices: automatically adjusting Federal Reserve notes as their gold reserves fluctuated and denying loans to member banks that were most in need of them.

The legislation of the 1930s strongly constrained and shaped the activities of financial intermediaries for the next half-century. In the next several chapters we will look at the recent evolution of these institutions. The legislation of the 1930s also laid the basis for transformation of the Federal Reserve into a powerful, activist, central monetary authority. In later chapters we will look at the present Federal Reserve's powers and their implementation.

# SUMMARY

Financial intermediaries pool funds to provide safe financial investments to small investors while loaning large amounts to those who want to purchase productive real assets. Borrowers prefer long-term, illiquid loans; lenders prefer short-term, liquid loans. Deposit intermediaries bridge this gap by monetizing illiquid and poorly divisible assets.

Intermediaries can diversify away a great deal of idiosyncratic withdrawal and portfolio risk. However, they still must worry about such macro risks as credit crunches, regulatory changes, droughts, and revolutions. There are also important economies of scale in the provision of structures, machinery, and skilled employees for such purposes as bringing together borrowers and lenders, paying bills, maintaining records of transactions, and evaluating loans and other investments.

It was long thought that bank liquidity would be assured and the supply of money would be appropriately regulated if banks made only short-term, self-liquidating loans. In practice, this strategy helps liquidity but does not guarantee it and causes the money supply to exaggerate rather than restrain business cycles. The excesses of the 1920s and the ensuing Great Depression led to regulations and restrictions that shaped financial intermediaries and the Federal Reserve for decades.

# IMPORTANT TERMS

commercial loan theory of banking
discount rate
discount window
idiosyncratic risk

macro risk
micro risk
real bills doctrine
systematic risk

# EXERCISES

1. Write a rebuttal to this argument made by the Locofoco Party in the 1830s:

   *[Bankers are] the greatest knaves, impostors, and paupers of the age who swear they have promised to pay their depositors 30 or 35 millions of dollars on demand, at the same time that they have only 3 or 4 million to do it with. We are opposed to all bank charters because we believe them at war with good morals.*[10]

2. Financial intermediaries earn profits essentially by borrowing at low interest rates and lending out the proceeds at higher rates. Why don't savers simply lend directly to borrowers and earn these higher interest rates themselves?

3. Why do you suppose that banks with more than $100 million in assets tend to be more profitable than banks with less than $100 million in assets?

4. In the 1930s, President Franklin Roosevelt said, "All we have to fear is fear itself." How does this reasoning apply to banks?

5. Provide an explanation for the following observation (*investing* refers to the purchase of long-lived real assets):

   *The key function of a financial system is to offer people opportunities to invest without saving and to save without investing.*[11]

6. In 1920, Federal Reserve banks raised their discount rates, hoping to compel member banks to raise cash by selling some of their government securities. Did this action weaken or strengthen the shaky economy?

7. The last banking panic in England occurred in 1866 when the Bank of England refused to assist a major English bank that had experienced substantial losses. The bank declared its insolvency on the afternoon of May 10, and "the next day, there were runs on all banks. People scrambled for cash because no bank was trusted."[12] On the evening of May 11, the Bank of England announced that it would provide whatever funds were needed to satisfy all depositors of all banks, and the panic ended abruptly. Why did this action end the banking panic of 1866 and make future panics less likely? Did the Federal Reserve Board act similarly in the 1930s in the United States?

8. "Deposit Intermediaries monetize illiquid assets." How do they do this, and who pays them to do it?

9. The single-index model of stock prices assumes that the return on a company's stock depends on both macro (systematic) factors and on micro (idiosyncratic) factors. Which of these two types of risks can investors diversify away by holding a large, diversified portfolio of stocks? Which of the following risks would you classify as macro and which as idiosyncratic?

   a. A company loses an important patent-infringement lawsuit.
   b. A new person is elected president of the United States.
   c. A new person is chosen as the company's chief executive officer.
   d. The value of the dollar declines in foreign exchange markets.

e. An oil embargo causes an economic recession.

10. A bank's assets consist mostly of bonds and loans. Give two examples of macro (systematic) risk and two examples of micro (idiosyncratic) risk.

11. A life insurance company cannot predict with certainty when its policyholders will die. Give two examples of macro (systematic) risk and two examples of micro (idiosyncratic) risk. Which type of risk can be diversified away by writing a large number of policies?

12. Identify which of the following loans were acceptable under the real bills doctrine, and briefly explain why.
    a. To pay for seed and fertilizer
    b. To pay workers' wages
    c. To pay for a house
    d. To restock a grocer's shelves

13. Use the distinction between macro and micro risk to explain why the following observation is misleading.

    *A widely diversified portfolio is not supposed to break downward in value very fast because all its "eggs" won't go bad at once. . . . But this safety mechanism doesn't seem to work particularly well. When steel and motors take a dreadful fall, almost the entire diversified list of securities takes it right along with them.* [13]

14. Irving Fisher, a prominent U.S. economist, compared the 1929 stock market crash to a run on a bank that did not have enough gold in its vaults to redeem all the bank notes that it had issued. [14] In his analogy, U.S. industry was a bank, its stock was the paper money it had issued, and the bank's real assets were the nation's factories and machines. Explain why Fisher's analogy is not apt.

15. In the spring of 1920, with the economy weakening, the Federal Reserve increased discount rates to record levels in order to maintain the convertibility of the nation's currency into gold. Why would an increase in the discount rate affect convertibility? Did this action strengthen the economy, or did it weaken the economy?

16. By 1922, the Federal Reserve banks had discovered that purchases and sales of securities were powerful monetary actions. When the Federal Reserve purchased government securities from banks, what happened to bond prices, interest rates, the money supply, and bank loans?

17. By the 1920s, the U.S. had accumulated nearly half the world's monetary gold. Under the gold standard, what should have happened to the U.S. money supply? How would this required change in the money supply affect U.S. prices, U.S. demand for foreign products, and foreign demand for U.S. products?

18. Between 1924 and 1929, the Dow Jones Industrial Average of stock prices rose from 100 to a peak of 386. What was the annual percentage increase in stock prices during these 5 years?

19. Member bank borrowings from the Fed fell significantly in 1930 and 1931. If the Federal Reserve had wanted to offset the effect of this diminished borrowing on the amount of currency in circulation, should the Fed have purchased government securities or sold them?

20. Interest rates fell to very low levels during the Great Depression, and there was very little borrowing or lending. One imaginative proposal to encourage lending was to tax money holdings: for a dollar to remain legal tender, small stamps would have to be purchased periodically and affixed the dollar. If this proposal had been enacted, what would have happened to the rate of return on currency?

# 15 The Modern Practice of Banking

*Banking is the art of lending money and getting it back.*

**Anonymous**

Historically, the differences among banks, savings and loan associations, credit unions, and other financial intermediaries were due primarily to legal restrictions on their operations. All are financial intermediaries, but different activities were prescribed for each — for instance, only banks could offer checking accounts. High interest rates and new technology made many of these restrictions impractical and unenforceable, and banking is now emerging from the New Deal regulatory web that was provoked by early banking debacles. It is hoped that the changes now occurring will enable financial institutions to serve their customers better, strengthen the institutions by broadening and diversifying their operations, and promote competition among intermediaries.

In this chapter we will examine some important fundamentals of modern-day banking, with the intention that these banking principles are more important than temporary, rapidly disappearing distinctions between intermediaries. As the differences fade, the management issues confronting banks, savings and loans, mutual savings banks, and credit unions will become increasingly similar.

You already know much of the usefulness, pitfalls, and history of banking. Here you will learn more about the operations of modern banks and how they manage their assets and liabilities to cope with opportunities, risks, and regulatory constraints. You will see that banking is a very intense and innovative business. Bankers face tremendous pressures, as well as exciting opportunities, and have responded in flexible and innovative ways. We begin by looking at their overriding goals.

## PROFITS, SAFETY, AND LIQUIDITY

Banks have several, sometimes conflicting, objectives — including profits, safety, and liquidity. A bank's rate of return — its percentage profit — can be calculated in a variety of ways; two of the most common measures are return on assets and

| Table 15.1 | Aggregate Income and Expenses of U.S. Commercial Banks, as a Percentage of Assets | | | | |
|---|---|---|---|---|---|
| | 1985 | 1986 | 1987 | 1988 | 1989 |
| Gross interest income | 9.45 | 8.38 | 8.21 | 8.95 | 9.92 |
| Gross interest expense | −6.06 | −5.10 | −4.94 | −5.42 | −6.41 |
| **Net interest margin** | 3.38 | 3.27 | 3.27 | 3.53 | 3.51 |
| Noninterest income | 1.40 | 1.55 | 1.61 | 1.51 | 1.58 |
| Loss provisions | −0.68 | −0.78 | −1.27 | −0.54 | −0.93 |
| Other noninterest expense | −3.18 | −3.23 | −3.31 | −3.33 | −3.37 |
| **Income before taxes** | 0.91 | 0.81 | 0.30 | 1.17 | 0.81 |
| Taxes | −0.21 | −0.19 | −0.18 | −0.33 | −0.31 |
| **Net income after taxes** | 0.70 | 0.62 | 0.11 | 0.84 | 0.51 |
| Return on assets | 0.70 | 0.62 | 0.11 | 0.84 | 0.51 |
| Return on equity | 11.18 | 9.97 | 1.80 | 13.52 | 7.94 |

**Source:** *Federal Reserve Bulletin*, July 1990.

return on equity. Suppose that a bank with $500 million in assets earns an annual profit of $5 million. Its return on assets is $5 million/$500 million = 0.01 (or 1 percent). If this bank's equity, or net worth, is $30 million, then its return on equity is $5 million/$30 million = 0.167 (or 16.7 percent). As will be explained later in this chapter, bank leverage turns a seemingly modest return on assets into an impressive return on equity.

Table 15.1 shows an annual consolidated income statement for all U.S. commercial banks between 1985 and 1989. All the data in this table (except return on equity) have been divided by aggregate bank assets so that income and expenses are expressed as a percentage of assets. Gross interest income is the interest that banks earn on loans, securities, and other investments; gross interest expense is the interest that banks pay depositors and others to obtain the funds that they invest. The difference, net interest margin, is remarkably stable. Banks don't profit from high or low interest rates; they profit from the spread between the interest they pay to obtain funds and the interest they earn on their investments. Noninterest income includes fees from deposits, credit cards, asset management, and other services. Loss provisions are funds set aside to cover loan defaults; other noninterest expenses include salaries, offices, equipment, and so on. While bank return on assets averaged 0.56 percent over this 5-year period, the leveraged return on equity averaged 8.88 percent.

Profitability is clearly crucial to a bank, but it is also very difficult to predict and control. Will borrowers default on loans? Will households prepay their mortgages? Will businesses exercise lines of credit? Will interest rates rise or fall? Will the Federal Reserve raise reserve requirements? Management decisions made today affect a bank's profits for years to come and depend on future events that cannot be foreseen confidently.

A revolutionary and still evolving aspect of banking is the use of formal computer models to help manage bank assets and liabilities. An important part of this quantification of banking is *management by objectives*, in which bank officers establish numerical goals and are judged by whether or not they meet them. A second part is the use of computer simulation models to project the consequences of various decisions.

Large banks now routinely make sophisticated projections of anticipated inflows and outflows of funds. Some of these projections are very mechanical, though technical, such as interest payments on deposits, loans, and mortgages. Others rely on a blending of computer models and informed assumptions about economic activity, the state of financial markets, and other factors that affect loan defaults, deposit withdrawals, the use of credit lines, and the market value of the bank's portfolio.

These computer models tell bank management how much cash will soon be available to invest or, if a deficit is anticipated, how much cash the bank must raise. Subject to this budget constraint and taking into account a modest margin for error, the bank decides how much to invest or borrow in various specific financial instruments. This is a portfolio-allocation problem — the use of discretionary funds made available by the projected cash flow.

Computer simulation models can be used to trace out the consequences of investment and borrowing decisions. How will profits be affected if the economy weakens and interest rates decline? How will profits be affected by stagflation, a slowdown in the economy with rising inflation and rising interest rates? If the bank's senior management assigns probabilities to the various possible scenarios, the expected value of profits can be calculated. Management also can assess risk, either by calculating the standard deviation of profits across these scenarios or by estimating the probability that profits will fall below some minimum threshold, perhaps a loss that might jeopardize the bank's ability to meet minimum regulatory capital requirements.

In addition to return and risk, banks must maintain an effective balance between illiquid assets and **liquid assets** — either cash or assets that can be readily converted into cash — so that the bank can accommodate withdrawal risks, through deposits and loans. Banks must always have enough funds to meet depositor withdrawals; an inability to do so would destroy depositor confidence and precipitate a run on the bank. Borrowers also need to be accommodated. Many of a bank's customers have established a banking relationship over the years by depositing money, repaying loans in a timely fashion, and compensating the bank for other services. These customers expect, in return, that they will be able to borrow money when they need it. If the bank cannot accommodate their customer's loan requests, then it destroys the incentive for establishing a banking relationship.

Liquidity can be maintained with **primary reserves** — cash, deposits with the Fed, and deposits in other banks — and with **secondary reserves** — Treasury bills and other very safe, short-term assets that can be converted into cash almost immediately. A prudent bank needs enough liquidity to satisfy depositors and borrowers, but it would be foolish to hold 100 percent liquid assets. Some funds can surely be invested in illiquid assets, which usually yield more than liquid ones. The danger is that the bank may become too illiquid. If it exhausts its liquid funds, the bank will be forced to resort to emergency borrowing or distress sales of illiquid assets, or in the worst possible case, the bank may be unable to accommodate withdrawals.

Bank liabilities also influence liquidity; for example, checking accounts are more volatile than passbook savings accounts, and certificates of deposit are more mobile than long-term bonds. How hard should a bank compete for various deposits of differing volatility? Much of the withdrawal risk in individual accounts can be diversified away. There remain macro risks, however. A general increase in interest rates will lure "hot" money out of a bank unless it raises its deposit rates. A slowdown in the economy will squeeze household income and corporate profits and may cause a net outflow from banks. Again, computerized simulation models may help a bank identify the possible effects of today's decisions on future liquidity. Estimates can be made of a deposit floor (the minimum level to which deposits might drop) and a loan ceiling (the maximum level of loans) so that the bank can maintain sufficient liquidity to meet these extremes.

Banks use quantitative models and monitoring to better understand the difficult choices that they must make. The large New York City banks have been playing this technologically sophisticated game for years. Now models are spreading to the hinterlands. Seat-of-the-pants judgments are giving way to numbers-oriented and, it is hoped, scientific management. One of this new breed, Gerald Fronterhouse, president and chief executive officer of the giant First Republicbank of Texas, made the following clever analogy in 1980: "We've begun to fly by instruments rather than by sight."[1] Unfortunately, First Republicbank crashed and burned in 1988 when the Texas economy fell farther than Fronterhouse, or almost anyone else, had anticipated. Fronterhouse resigned in April of 1988, and NCNB took over First Republicbank 4 months later, aided by $4 billion from the federal government. Even flight instruments sometimes fail.

Quantitative models can help a bank to make informed decisions by tracing out the complex consequences of various actions under a variety of economic scenarios. However, a quantitative model is ultimately no better than are its assumptions. If the assumptions are wrong, seemingly reasonable management decisions may then have disastrous consequences. The real virtue of model building is that it helps management to formulate the right questions. A successful strategy still depends on whether the managers, not the computers, have the right answers.

**EXAMPLE**
**15.1**

## The Citi Never Sleeps

New York's Citibank is the nation's largest bank, a position achieved under the aggressively innovative leadership of the legendary Walter Wriston, president and chief executive officer of Citicorp (Citibank's holding company) from 1967 until 1984. Citicorp has aggressively pushed for deregulation and, when legislators dawdled, has found loopholes to expand anyway. In 1991 Citicorp had more than $200 billion in assets.

Citibank tries to span the financial world, offering virtually all financial services to everyone, everywhere. While other banks turn away small depositors, Citibank seeks to be everyone's banker. Under Wriston, Citicorp spent hundreds of millions of dollars on technology, pioneering 24-hour automated teller machines (ATMs) and interactive home computers (prompting the advertising campaign "The Citi never sleeps"). Citibank has nearly 300 New York City branches and thousands of ATMs — that can only be used by its 2 million Citibank cardholders. As early as 1980, two-thirds of Citibank's cash withdrawals in New York City were handled by ATMs. In 1990 it introduced an Enhanced Telephone (E.T.) that, for a $49.95 installation charge and $9.95 monthly leasing fee, works as a sophisticated telephone and also can be used, like a home computer, to obtain bank account information, to transfer funds, and to pay bills.

Citibank's approach to consumer banking has two sides. One is the sleek, easy-to-use ATMs that are to be used by small depositors and for routine transactions. The second side is relationship banking: personal service and financial incentives for depositors with substantial accounts, especially those who do all their banking with Citibank.

Citicorp is the largest issuer of bank credit cards, with 30 million Citibank Mastercard and Visa cardholders, most recruited through nationwide mailings, and another 10 million cardholders outside the United States. In 1979, when New York usury laws prevented Citicorp from charging more than 12 percent on its credit card balances, Wriston persuaded South Dakota to abolish its usury ceiling and, in return, purchased a bank in Sioux Falls, South Dakota, and moved all Citicorp's card processing operations there. In 1989 Citicorp began selling small investors "plastic bonds" — 4-year $1000 bonds backed by its credit card loans.

In 1986 Citicorp introduced its MortgagePower program, a nationwide network of 3000 real estate brokers, lawyers, and mortgage bankers who are connected by computer to Citicorp and can get a home buyer's no-hassle mortgage application approved or rejected within 15 business days. In 1981 Citicorp wasn't among the top 100 companies in the mortgage business; in 1988 it wrote $15 billion in mortgages and was by far the largest mortgage lender in the nation.

Acting as a holding company, Citicorp opened nonbank banks throughout the country. For example, in several states it established "industrial banks" that accept time and savings deposits (but not checking accounts) and make consumer and mortgage loans. Citicorp also acquired footholds in California, Florida, and other states by taking over insolvent S&Ls. In 1989 Citicorp had 600 U.S. subsidiaries and was planning to triple this number. Ultimately, when all barriers to interstate banking are removed, most of these subsidiaries will operate as branches of Citibank. In 1990 it was allowed to change the names of all its S&Ls to Citibank FSB and to offer Citibank credit cards to these customers.

Even now, Citicorp's offices worldwide are linked by satellite and computer. As part of its investment in technology, Citicorp installed its own underground fiberoptic cables at its New York headquarters and produced its own internal telephone system. Robots walk the halls delivering mail.

Citicorp also has been very aggressive in lending to developing countries and establishing foreign subsidiaries, aiming to make Citibank branches and credit cards familiar symbols worldwide, what *The Wall Street Journal* called the "McDonald's and Coke of consumer banking."* In 1991 Citicorp had offices in 90 countries, more than any bank in the world. Citibank's foreign branches are run almost entirely by local citizens and emphasize customer service. As one Citicorp executive observed, "There's enough anxiety associated with financial services that people will pay a premium for comfort and peace of mind. This is a people business, not a money business."† In Spain, Citibank employees seated at desks replaced tellers behind elevated counters; customers who had to wait 2 months to have their mortgage application considered now are told "yes" or "no" within 48 hours. Computerized equipment allows automobile buyers in Spain to contact Citibank from automobile showrooms and have financing approved in a few minutes. In Germany, Citibank executives make evening house calls to their busy customers.

Citicorp was widely criticized when it lost millions of dollars in the 1970s trying to expand its consumer banking business, but in the 1980s its consumer banking became highly profitable. In 1988 Citicorp earned $1.9 billion, of which $500 million came from U.S. consumer banking and $170 million from international consumer banking. In 1990 Citicorp forecast $5 billion in annual profits by the middle to late 1990s, of which 65 percent would come from its worldwide consumer business.

However, many of Citicorp's loans to developing countries turned sour in the late 1980s, contradicting Walter Wriston's adage that "countries don't go bankrupt." In the early 1990s Citicorp was forced to write off billions of dollars

*Robert Guenther, "Citicorp Strives to Be McDonald's and Coke of Consumer Banking," Wall Street Journal, *August 9, 1989.*
†Ibid.

in questionable commercial and real estate loans. In 1991 Moody's lowered Citicorp's commercial paper rating to Prime-3, one level above junk. To reduce its expenses and protect its net worth, Citicorp let 5000 of its 95,000 employees go in 1991 and planned to eliminate another 10,000 jobs by 1993. Stockholders and federal regulators watched nervously to see if consumer banking profits could save the nation's biggest bank.

# LEVERAGE

Chapter 8 explained how someone who borrows and invests other people's money so that the total amount invested is larger than his or her own personal investment creates **leverage,** which magnifies gains and losses because the return on the net worth of the individual or business depends on the return on a much larger investment. For a business, we can restate these principles in terms of the firm's total assets and net worth. A hypothetical balance sheet is shown in Table 15.2. The total amount invested is given by the firm's total assets (here $200 million). These assets are financed in part by the firm's debts (loans plus bonds) and in part by the firm's own money, its net worth (here $100 million). The degree of leverage is measured by the ratio of total assets to net worth:

$$\text{Leverage} = \frac{\text{total assets}}{\text{net worth}} \qquad (15.1)$$

The firm's rate of return on net worth depends on the gap between the gross return on assets (before interest payments) and the interest rate on debt:

$$\binom{\text{Return on}}{\text{net worth}} = \binom{\text{interest rate}}{\text{on debt}} + (\text{leverage}) \left[ \binom{\text{gross return}}{\text{on total assets}} - \binom{\text{interest rate}}{\text{on debt}} \right] \qquad (15.2)$$

**Table 15.2  A Firm's Balance Sheet (Millions of Dollars)**

| Assets | | Liabilities | |
|---|---|---|---|
| Plant | $140 | Bank loans | 50 |
| Equipment | 40 | Bonds | 50 |
| Financial | 20 | Net worth | 100 |
| | $200 | | $200 |

time deposits offered by other institutions were doubly harmful to banks because money was not only lured out of bank time deposits but out of checking accounts too. Households and businesses used credit cards and transferred funds among accounts as needed to economize on holding cash and checking account balances that earned no interest. National income doubled while checking account balances did not increase at all.

In the 1960s, commercial banks decided to play some financial hardball by offering new types of accounts and competitive deposit rates to lure households away from thrifts and to win back business customers who increasingly had been making direct short-term investments in Treasury bills, commercial paper, and other money-market assets.

With a variety of minimum-deposit requirements, expiration dates, and other features, banks tried to attract the mobile "hot" money without making expensive across-the-board rate increases for all depositors. Over the years, other deposit institutions retaliated by introducing competitive accounts and by encroaching on the banks' traditional checking account territory.

## Liability Hunting

This flexibility in seeking funds is now a way of life for banks, particularly large banks. In the three decades from the Great Depression through the 1950s, banks focused on asset management — the allocation of available funds. Checking account rates were fixed by regulation, and time deposit rates were very sticky. For the most part, banks accepted whatever funds depositors made available and then decided how to invest these funds. The classic conflict was between investing in high-yielding illiquid assets or in liquid assets that could accommodate deposit fluctuations. Deposit variations were taken to be a regrettable but uncontrollable fact of nature.

Since the early 1960s, deposit rates have become increasingly variable, and banks have increasingly come to view the garnering of funds as important as their allocation. This aggressive search for attractive funds is called **liability management**. Banks have become more symmetrical intermediaries, voluntarily borrowing from some in order to lend to others. Table 15.7, presented earlier in this section, shows aggregate U.S. commercial bank assets and liabilities.

Figure 15.1 shows that at the conclusion of World War II, nearly 70 percent of all bank funds came from depositor checking accounts. Now 20 percent of the funds come from checking accounts. At large commercial banks, the figure is 15 percent. The declining importance of checking accounts is due partly to the growing importance of small time and savings accounts, for the reasons given earlier. The rest of the story is the dramatic increase in bank money-market borrowing, which is the cornerstone of liability management. Short-term notes are now nearly as important as checking accounts; at most of the very large banks, short-term notes are actually more important than checking accounts.

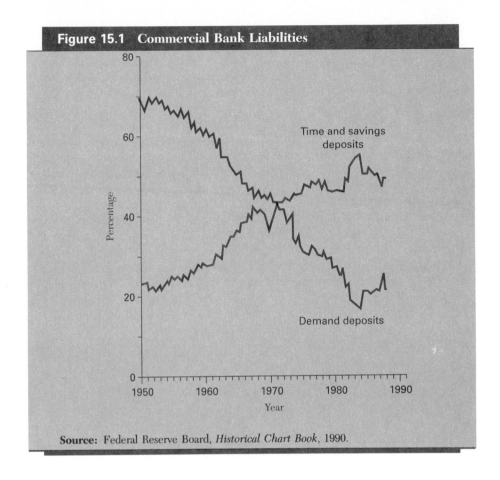

**Figure 15.1   Commercial Bank Liabilities**

**Source:** Federal Reserve Board, *Historical Chart Book*, 1990.

## Certificates of Deposit

One of the most important innovations was large, negotiable **certificates of deposit (CDs)**. Corporate time deposits in banks had been stuck at $1 billion throughout the 1950s. Then, in 1961, Citibank and other large New York City banks began promoting CDs, and in a few years, corporate CD investments swelled to $20 billion. Large CDs have become a prominent form of liability management, and in 1991, commercial banks had $330 billion in large CDs outstanding.

Initially, large CDs were used by aggressive banks to circumvent Regulation Q deposit-rate ceilings. Large CDs remain popular today because administrative expenses are relatively small and CDs can readily be used by banks to attract funds at competitive rates when needed. Businesses, state and local governments, and wealthy individuals find large CDs to be attractive, convenient, liquid, short-term investments. In the late 1970s these big depositors were joined by money-market funds, which, in essence, recycle dollars flowing out of small deposit accounts back into large CDs. Thus large banks gain funds, while small institutions lose deposits.

## Eurodollars

In the late 1960s, severe Regulation Q ceilings were temporarily imposed on bank CDs. Many banks were forced to look elsewhere for funds and discovered **Eurodollars** — deposits of U.S. dollars in foreign banks or foreign branches of U.S. banks. The artificially low interest rates on bank CDs encouraged U.S. banks to borrow dollars from abroad and encouraged potential CD buyers to deposit their dollars abroad. To circumvent CD rate ceilings, dollars were deposited in foreign banks or foreign branches of U.S. banks, which were beyond the control of U.S. regulators, and these dollars were then lent to U.S. banks.

Initially, Eurodollar deposits had the additional advantage that they were not subject to reserve requirements, but since 1969 the Federal Reserve has subjected Eurodollars borrowed from abroad to reserve requirements ranging as high as 20 percent. (There is currently no reserve requirement on Eurodollars.) In addition, Regulation Q ceiling rates on CDs were partly lifted in 1970 and were removed entirely in 1973. Although these developments reduced their competitive advantage, Eurodollars remain an important source of funds for large banks.

Foreign banks multiply Eurodollar deposits in the same way that U.S. banks multiply U.S. deposits. A foreign bank that receives a million-dollar deposit will keep some of these dollars as reserves and lend the remainder. Some of the money that is lent will be deposited in another bank and lent and deposited once again. The deposit-multiplier model developed in Chapter 13 can be used to gauge this process. If, for example, banks hold a fraction $k = 0.02$ of Eurodollar deposits as reserves and the ratio of dollars abroad outside banks to Eurodollar deposits is $c = 0.08$, then every \$1 billion in U.S. dollars abroad $B$ supports \$10 billion dollars in Eurodollar deposits $D$:

$$D = \left(\frac{1}{k + c}\right)B$$
$$= \left(\frac{1}{0.02 + 0.08}\right)B$$
$$= 10B$$

## Federal Funds and Repurchase Agreements

The development of the federal funds market since the mid-1960s has provided another important tool for liability management by large banks. **Federal funds** are large overnight loans of reserves deposited at the Federal Reserve banks. Although these are loans among private banks, the loans are called federal funds

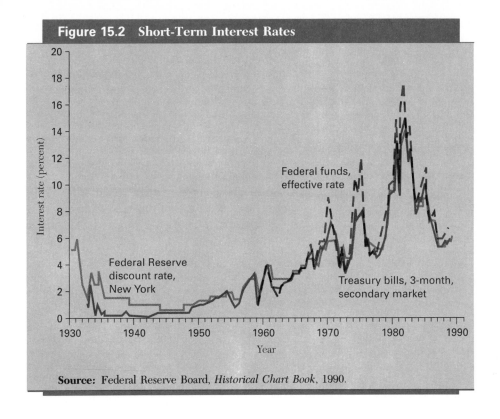

**Figure 15.2  Short-Term Interest Rates**

Federal funds, effective rate

Federal Reserve discount rate, New York

Treasury bills, 3-month, secondary market

Interest rate (percent)

Year

**Source:** Federal Reserve Board, *Historical Chart Book*, 1990.

because it is the Federal Reserve that electronically credits one bank and debits another.

Before the mid-1960s, federal funds loans were temporary arrangements in which banks that happened to end up with excess reserves could lend to banks that happened to be short that day. As shown in Figure 15.2, up until the mid-1960s the interest rate on these interbank loans, called the **federal funds rate**, was generally very close to, but slightly below, the Federal Reserve discount rate (the interest rate charged on member bank borrowing from the Federal Reserve).

Many large banks routinely use the federal funds market to borrow funds from other banks for relending to their clients. Figure 15.2 shows that during credit crunches, when interest rates rise sharply, the federal funds rate jumps as banks scramble to find money for their customers. The federal funds rate can rise far above the discount rate because the Federal Reserve won't tolerate large, continuous borrowing through its discount window. Banks that need funds for their customers will, if necessary, pay a high federal funds rate during credit crunches.

In a security **repurchase agreement (RP** or **repo)**, a bank sells Treasury bills or other securities to a customer, usually a corporation, and agrees to repurchase the securities at a higher price on a given date — often the next day. In this way, the bank borrows money from a corporation, using some of its assets as collateral. Repos are another clever arrangement that banks created to evade restrictions on traditional bank deposits. From their somewhat devious beginnings, repurchase agreements have become established as a commonplace way of making collateralized short-term loans.

## ASSET SELECTION

Bank assets have changed dramatically over the years. Figure 15.3 shows that there has been a very large increase in the fraction of bank assets invested in loans and a corresponding decline in the percentage of bank assets invested in cash and securities. We'll begin our discussion of bank asset choices by looking at the reasons behind this massive portfolio shift.

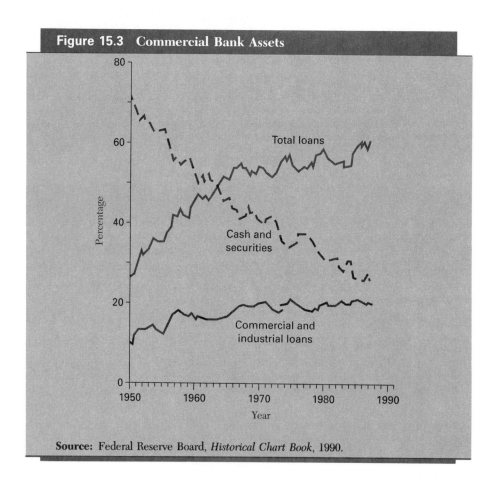

**Figure 15.3   Commercial Bank Assets**

**Source:** Federal Reserve Board, *Historical Chart Book*, 1990.

## Bank Reserves

The Fed's reserve requirements must be satisfied by holding idle, non-interest-bearing reserves — either cash within the bank's own vaults or deposits with the Federal Reserve. Since World War II, bank reserves have fallen dramatically, from 13 percent of bank assets in 1950 to less than 2 percent in 1991.

Bank reserves can be divided into required reserves and excess reserves (reserves in excess of that required by the Federal Reserve):

$$\text{Bank reserves} = \text{required reserves} + \text{excess reserves}$$

Banks hold excess reserves for precautionary purposes to accommodate deficits between customer withdrawals and deposits. The advantage of holding excess reserves is the avoidance of a cash deficiency that compels the bank to incur expenses by raising cash quickly — by calling in loans, selling securities, or borrowing through the federal funds market or the Fed's discount window. In the worst possible case, the bank's illiquidity could force it to close. Banks hold more excess reserves when they anticipate a deficit between withdrawals and deposits and when there is considerable uncertainty about their cash needs. The cost of holding excess reserves is the opportunity cost — the interest that could have been earned by investing this cash in loans or securities. When interest rates increase, banks hold less excess reserves.

Although bank assets and liabilities have increased by a factor of 17 in the last 40 years, from $160 billion to $2,800 billion, excess reserves have been roughly unchanged, averaging slightly less than $1 billion. Interest rates in the 1970s and 1980s were much higher than in the 1950s and 1960s, and banks became very adept at minimizing their idle cash balances — for example, through the federal funds market.

Almost all bank reserves today are required reserves, and these have declined sharply relative to bank assets since World War II. Reserve requirements have been reduced, and in addition, there has been a shift by depositors from checking accounts, which are subject to high reserve requirements, to time and savings deposits, which have no reserve requirements. As banks have come to rely less on checking accounts for funds, there has been an accompanying decline in required and actual reserves.

## Securities

The characteristics of various securities have been discussed earlier, particularly in Chapters 6 through 9. Historically, banks have had an affinity for U.S. Treasury securities, because these are extremely liquid secondary reserves. In 1991, 70 percent of the securities held by banks were marketable Treasury securities. Where permitted by state charters, some banks and thrift institutions ventured into high-yield junk bonds in the 1980s. However, the Financial Institutions Reform, Recovery and Enforcement Act of 1989 prohibits all thrifts, whether state or federally chartered, from investing in low-rated or unrated securities (and forced institutions still holding junk bonds to sell them).

There is no default risk in Treasury securities. The primary management decision for banks is the appropriate maturity or, more precisely, duration. As explained in earlier chapters, short-duration bonds are an implicit wager on rising interest rates (relative to the term structure) and long-duration bonds are an implicit bet on falling interest rates (again relative to the term structure). Banks adjust the duration of their bond portfolios to reflect their interest-rate forecasts and the exposure to interest-rate risk in their other assets and liabilities. We will look at interest-rate risk in depth later in this chapter.

## *Loans*

Figure 15.3 chronicles a massive portfolio shift by banks from cash and securities to loans. Roughly one-third of bank loans are for real estate — 60 percent to households, 40 percent to businesses. Another one-third are commercial and industrial loans. One-sixth are personal loans (for automobiles, education, and so on), and the remaining one-sixth go to farms, finance companies, and foreign banks.

The nation's largest and most prominent corporations do not need to borrow from banks because they have the size and reputation to raise funds by issuing securities directly in the money and capital markets. Yet large corporations like to keep their options open by maintaining access to many sources of funds, including bank loans. In fact, large companies often use established bank credit lines as implicit collateral for the short-term commercial paper they issue. Large, prominent companies are not at the mercy of commercial banks. If banks tried to charge excessive loan rates, large corporations would simply borrow elsewhere. Thus banks are compelled to offer large firms very competitive loan rates.

In December of 1978, short-term business borrowing totaled $276 billion, of which 24 percent was commercial paper and 76 percent was loans from commercial banks. Ten years later, in December of 1988, businesses borrowed $1055 billion short term, of which 43 percent was commercial paper and 57 percent bank loans. This shift from bank loans to commercial paper is a **securitization of borrowing**, the selling of securities directly to investors instead of relying on banks to channel funds from investors to business borrowers.

Many of the businesses that now issue securities instead of taking bank loans were the banks' most creditworthy customers. The loss of these customers has reduced the average quality of the loan portfolios held by banks. In fact, the deterioration of bank loan portfolios has caused the credit ratings of many banks to fall below those of their best customers; in 1991 only one large U.S. bank (J. P. Morgan) was rated triple-A. Highly rated corporations consequently find it cheaper to issue their own securities than to borrow from lower-rated banks that have to pay high interest rates when they issue bonds.

Smaller, lesser-known businesses do not have easy access to money and capital markets and must rely on banks and other intermediaries for funds. These

**EXAMPLE**
**15.4**

## Handshake Loans from Local Banks

Banks are in an advantageous positon for judging the creditworthiness of local businesses and households, particularly if they have maintained a long-standing customer relationship. In comparison with Moody's and the other agencies that rate securities issued by nationally known firms, a local bank may be intimately familiar with a person's competency and integrity and with unique circumstances that affect this person's ability to repay a loan.

With familiar customers, some local banks don't bother with a loan application and a credit check: a handshake and a promise are enough when you're dealing with family. Local banks often feel that they are an integral part of the community, donating money for civic improvements and lending money during hard times to residents who don't satisfy conventional credit standards.

First National Bank of Midland Texas used to be this way, supporting the local community and lending money easily: a superior's signature was required if a loan request was rejected; no signature was required to approve a loan. However, First National collapsed in 1983, along with Texas oil and real estate, and was taken over by another Texas bank, RepublicBank Corporation, which merged with InterFirst Corporation to become First RepublicBank Corporation. In 1988 First RepublicBank was acquired by a regional giant, NCNB Corporation of North Carolina (which was renamed NationsBank in 1991).

Some Midland residents were flabbergasted to find that NCNB insisted on loan applications and credit checks. Many were disappointed at NCNB's reluctance to loan money to those in financial difficulty and claim that most of their deposits are being channeled to loans outside Texas. One local business executive said, "The only way you can get a loan is by putting up an arm or a leg or maybe both." Some Midland residents dubbed NCNB "Nobody Cares, Nobody Bothers" and "No Credit for No Body."*

*Michael Allen, "Out-of-State Bankers Tight with a Dollar Rile Old-Style Texans," Wall Street Journal, *August 10, 1989.*

**EXAMPLE**
**15.5**

## Credit Card Bonds

Credit cards offer users a convenient way of making purchases and an easy way to borrow money — though at interest rates that average close to 20 percent. The banks that issue credit cards raise the funds they lend to credit card borrowers through bank deposits, Eurodollars, and other sources. One relatively recent method of raising funds is to sell bonds, using loans to credit card users ("credit card receivables") as collateral. Bonds backed by credit card debt are called *credit card bonds.*

Citicorp is by far the largest issuer of credit card bonds. As of April 1990, it had $10.5 billion in credit card bonds outstanding, 36 percent of the total issued. The biggest buyers are other banks, looking for relatively secure short-term investments. In this way, banks that issue credit cards and loan money to credit card users share these loans with other banks.

Each credit card bond is backed by a specific, identified package of credit card receivables. If a sufficient number of customers default on their credit card borrowing, then the associated credit card bond defaults too. The issuing bank is not obligated to use other funds to pay off its credit card bonds, and these bonds are not insured by the FDIC.

Credit card receivables are notoriously risky because consumers put up no collateral and defaults average nearly 5 percent. However, credit card bonds are generally given the highest rating, triple-A, because they are insured by a bond insurance company and because the issuing bank builds in a substantial cushion. In the spring of 1990, for example, Citicorp's credit card bonds paid 9.5 percent interest and allowed a 2 percent servicing charge. Because Citicorp was charging consumers close to 20 percent interest on these credit card loans, the annual loan default rate would have to rise to $20\% - (9.5\% + 2\%) = 8.5\%$ before the bonds were endangered.

In comparison to the historical 4.6 percent default rate experienced by Citicorp, these bonds offered about a 4 percent safety margin. If the default rate turns out to be 4.6 percent, the historical average, Citicorp keeps the 4 percent margin. A lower default rate gives Citicorp more profits; a higher default rate cuts into Citicorp's profits — up to an 8.5 percent default rate, at which point Citicorp has no profit and its credit card bonds are on the brink of default.

Investors are apparently not convinced that credit card bonds deserve their triple-A ratings. The 9.5 percent yield on Citicorp's 7-year credit card bonds in the spring of 1990 was about $\frac{1}{2}$ percentage point higher than the market yields on other 7-year triple-A corporate bonds.[*] In April of 1990, one rating service went along with the market, downgrading its rating of Sears, Roebuck's credit card debts from triple-A to double-A.[†]

[*]*Constance Mitchell, "Banks Pour Money into Bonds Backed by Credit-Card Loans,"* Wall Street Journal, *March 26, 1990.*

[†]*Constance Mitchell, "Credit-Card Bonds Are Hot, but May Be Stingy on Yield,"* Wall Street Journal, *April 16, 1990.*

small to medium-sized companies are the cream of the banking loan market. Because of their dependence on banks and their presumed riskiness, they have to pay a substantial price for banking services. This financial market imperfection arises because of the costs of gathering information on the creditworthiness of small to medium-sized businesses. Most investors don't want to buy securities issued by a firm they've never heard of in a town they've never seen. One of the primary virtues of banks is that they bridge this imperfection. As financial intermediaries with specialized knowledge of local firms, banks are able, for a price, to bring together borrowers and lenders.

Not only have bank loans grown since World War II, but their character has changed as well. Short-term commercial loans that are implicitly renewable have been supplanted by loans that are explicitly long term. In part, this development reflects a post-Depression wariness by borrowers. Too many businesses found that their implicitly renewable loans were not, in fact, renewed in the banking panic of the 1930s. Borrowers naturally prefer the security of a formal long-term agreement. For banks, this development reflects a thorough disillusionment with the real bills doctrine. If short-term commercial loans provide little security, then banks may as well give borrowers the long-term loans they want.

Increasingly, banks have come to view themselves as broker intermediaries whose primary function is to find money for their loan clients. In this perception, the difficult part is not deciding to whom they will loan available funds, but rather ensuring that funds will be available when needed. Instead of investing what they have, banks now promise to lend what they think they can raise. In 1985 the nation's 15 largest banks had nearly $1 trillion in contingent liabilities — commitments to make cash available, if needed.[2] These included lines of credit, bond insurance, and letters of credit (guarantees that an importer will pay for goods after they are delivered). The $1 trillion total was 10 percent larger than the total assets of these banks. Clearly, these banks did not anticipate having to make good on all these commitments — and certainly not all at the same time — but they had given many a promise of funds if needed.

Bank liquidity thus has two faces: the capacity to meet deposit withdrawals and the ability to satisfy those who need to borrow money. Depositor withdrawals are seldom a problem. Liquidity crises instead involve a scramble to find funds for borrowers. Liquidity management involves both the selection of a prudent amount of liquid assets and the development of reliably expandable liabilities.

Consider the 1966, 1969, 1973–1974, and 1979–1982 credit crunches. The interest rate spikes in Figure 15.2 chronicle these crunches, and as noted, the federal funds rate shot upward as banks borrowed money for desperate customers. In each of these four episodes, banks sold some of their marketable securities in order to make more loans. In 1973–1974 and 1979–1982, banks also raised funds for their loan customers by issuing large amounts of short-term notes. When the Federal Reserve decides to tighten financial markets, banks are forced to ration credit, and some firms get crunched. During these liquidity crises, banks scramble to find the funds that their loan customers, especially their most valued customers, are begging for.

# MATCHING ASSETS AND LIABILITIES

Many savings and loans managed by honest and competent people were bankrupted in the 1980s by an unexpected increase in interest rates. They invested 80 percent or more of their assets in long-term (typically 30-year) fixed-rate mortgages, while their liabilities were almost entirely short-term flexible-rate deposits that could be withdrawn whenever depositors were dissatisfied with deposit rates.

When interest rates rose, these S&Ls were locked into what, in retrospect, were low-interest-rate mortgages but had to pay high interest rates to hold onto deposits. Their income was negative because they were earning less on their mortgages than they were paying depositors. Another way to look at this is that their net worth was negative because the market value of their mortgages was less than their deposits: they could have not have sold their mortgages for enough money to pay off their depositors.

These S&Ls borrowed short and lent long — and lost. If their assets and liabilities had been mismatched in the other direction — borrowing long and lending short — they might have been bankrupted by an unexpected decline in interest rates. Most deposit intermediaries now try to protect themselves from interest-rate fluctuations by more closely matching the maturities of their assets and liabilities. In some cases, a bank may be able to match a given pool of deposits to a given pool of loans, for example, issuing 5-year fixed-rate CDs to individuals, businesses, or even other banks and using the proceeds for 5-year fixed-rate loans. More often, a bank does not have a perfect match but can estimate, on balance, its exposure to interest-rate risk. There are two primary techniques. One, gap analysis, focuses on how interest rates affect income; the other, duration analysis, considers the effect of interest rates on net worth.

## Gap Analysis

**Gap analysis** estimates the effect of interest rates on income by estimating the fraction of assets and liabilities that are adjustable-rate, with interest rates that move up and down with market interest rates during some target horizon, perhaps 1 year. As illustrated in Table 15.8, all items on both sides of the balance sheet are put into one of two categories: rate-sensitive (interest rates can change during the coming year) and fixed-rate (interest rates cannot change for at least 1 year).

A bank's **gap** is defined as follows:

$$\text{Gap} = \text{rate-sensitive assets} - \text{rate-sensitive liabilities} \qquad (15.3)$$

If there is an equal change in the interest rates on a bank's rate-sensitive assets and liabilities, its annual income will change by the size of its gap multiplied by the size of the change in interest rates.

**Table 15.8   A Bank's Gap Analysis (Millions of Dollars)**

| Assets | | Liabilities | |
|---|---|---|---|
| **Rate-sensitive** (variable-rate loans and short-term securities) | 40 | **Rate-sensitive** (variable-rate deposits and short-term securities | 30 |
| **Fixed-rate** (reserves, fixed-rate loans, and long-term securities) | 60 | **Fixed-rate** (fixed-rate loans, long-term securities, and net worth) | 70 |

The bank in Table 15.8 has a gap of $10 million:

$$\text{Gap} = \$40 \text{ million} - \$30 \text{ million}$$
$$= \$10 \text{ million}$$

If interest rates increase by 2 percentage points (for example, from 7 to 9 percent), its annual income will increase by 2%($10 million) = $200,000.

As this example illustrates, a positive gap is an implicit wager that interest rates will increase; a negative gap is a bet that rates will fall. For some banks, gap management involves adjusting the gap to be consistent with the bank's interest-rate forecasts — increasing the gap when it predicts an increase in interest rates and decreasing the gap when it predicts a decline.

Gap analysis also can be used to gauge the exposure of a bank's profits to interest-rate risk. A bank that wants to protect its income during the next 12 months can adjust its assets and liabilities to obtain a gap of zero; the bank in Table 15.8 could sell $10 million of its short-term assets and use the proceeds to buy long-term assets.

The primary problem with this gap analysis is that it focuses on the effect of interest rates on current income but neglects the effect on the market value of the bank's fixed-rate assets and liabilities. As an extreme example, suppose that a more detailed look at the bank in Table 15.8 reveals the balance sheet shown in the top half of Table 15.9. The fixed-rate assets consist of $10 million in reserves

**Table 15.9  A Peek Behind the Gap (Millions of Dollars)**

*Before interest-rate increase:*

| Assets | | Liabilities | |
|---|---|---|---|
| **Rate-sensitive** | | **Rate-sensitive** | |
| Variable-rate loans | $ 40.00 | Variable-rate deposits | $ 30.00 |
| **Fixed-rate** | | **Fixed-rate** | |
| Reserves | 10.00 | 5-year zeros ($83 @ 6%) | 62.00 |
| 20-year zeros ($233 @ 8%) | 50.00 | Net worth | 8.00 |
| | $100.00 | | $100.00 |

*After interest-rate increase:*

| Assets | | Liabilities | |
|---|---|---|---|
| **Rate-sensitive** | | **Rate-sensitive** | |
| Variable-rate loans | $40.00 | Variable-rate deposits | $30.00 |
| **Fixed-rate** | | **Fixed-rate** | |
| Reserves | 10.00 | 5-year zeros ($83 @ 8%) | 56.46 |
| 20-year zeros ($233 @ 10%) | 34.64 | Net worth | −1.82 |
| | $84.64 | | $84.64 |

and $50 million in 20-year zero-coupon bonds (with an 8 percent interest rate, paying $233 million after 20 years). The fixed-rate liabilities consist of $62 million in 5-year zeros (at 6 percent, paying $83 million after 5 years) and $8 million in net worth.

The bottom half of Table 15.9 shows that a 2 percentage point increase in interest rates reduces the market value of the bank's 20-year assets by $15.36 million and the market value of its 5-year liabilities by only $5.54 million, causing its net worth to fall by $9.82 million. Even though this bank has a positive gap and experiences an increase in its income during the next 12 months, it is made insolvent by the increase in interest rates because the market value of its assets is no longer adequate to pay off its liabilities.

Gap analysis gauges the effect of interest rates on a bank's income during the next year but does not consider whether the market values of the fixed-rate assets and liabilities are equally sensitive to interest rates. To do this, we need to look at duration.

## Duration Analysis

Because the assets and liabilities of a financial intermediary involve future cash flows, the present value of both sides of its balance sheet depend on interest rates. An increase in interest rates reduces the present value of the assets it holds and also reduces the present value of its obligations. Whether an increase in interest rates increases or reduces its net worth depends on whether its assets or liabilities are more sensitive to interest rates.

Chapter 5 explained how duration can be used to measure the sensitivity of present value to interest rates. Here duration can be used to measure the interest-rate sensitivity of the market value of each side of a bank's balance sheet and to determine whether, on balance, an increase in interest rates increases or reduces its net worth.

Equation 5.7, reproduced here, tells us that the percentage change in an asset's price $\%\Delta P$, is approximately equal to the asset's duration $D$ multiplied by the percentage point change in the asset's yield to maturity $\Delta R$:

$$\%\Delta P = -D\Delta R \qquad (15.4)$$

If, for example, a bond has a duration of 5 years, then a 1 percentage point increase in the yield to maturity (for example, from 8 to 9 percent) will reduce its price by approximately 5 percent.

The second rule we need to use is that the duration of a portfolio is a weighted average of the duration of the assets in the portfolio, with weights that reflect each asset's proportionate share of the portfolio. Consider the assets of the bank shown in Table 15.9. The variable-rate loans have a duration of essentially zero, because their market value is virtually unaffected by interest rates. Bank reserves also have a duration of zero. Remembering that an asset's duration is its present-value weighted average number of years until receiving the cash flow, the duration of a 20-year zero-coupon bond is 20 years. Therefore, the duration of this bank's assets is

$$\text{Duration of total assets} = \left(\frac{\text{duration}}{\text{of loans}}\right)\frac{\text{loans}}{\text{total assets}} + \left(\frac{\text{duration}}{\text{of reserves}}\right)\frac{\text{reserves}}{\text{total assets}}$$
$$+ \left(\frac{\text{duration}}{\text{of bonds}}\right)\frac{\text{bonds}}{\text{total assets}}$$
$$= 0(0.40) + 0(0.10) + 20(0.50)$$
$$= 10$$

Similarly, on the liability side, the variable-rate deposits have a duration of essentially zero, and the 5-year zeros have a duration of 5 years. The duration of this bank's liabilities (other than net worth) is

$$\text{Duration of total liabilities} = \left(\frac{\text{duration}}{\text{of loans}}\right)\frac{\text{loans}}{\text{total liabilities}} + \left(\frac{\text{duration}}{\text{of bonds}}\right)\frac{\text{bonds}}{\text{total liabilities}}$$
$$= 0\left(\frac{30}{92}\right) + 5\left(\frac{62}{92}\right)$$
$$= 3.4$$

**EXAMPLE 15.6**

## The Volatility of Bank Stocks

Any business is exposed to interest-rate risk if its asset and liability durations are not offsetting. Financial intermediaries are particularly vulnerable because they are so highly leveraged and because, historically, many thrifts had very long asset durations and relatively short liability durations.

Because shareholder equity is equal to net worth (the difference between the market value of the firm's assets and debts), a vulnerability to interest rates should be reflected in the effects of interest rates on the prices of stock issued by banks and S&Ls. An economist investigated this question using interest-rate and stock-price data for the years 1961–1983, and taking into account statistically the fact that stock prices also depend on the state of the economy.* He estimated that if there were no change in the economy, an increase in long-term bond rates from 10 to 11 percent would reduce the per-share price of industrial stocks by 4 percent, of commercial bank stocks by 9 percent, and of S&L stocks by 24 percent. Thus, compared with industrial companies, banks are twice as sensitive to interest rates, and S&Ls are six times as sensitive.

*G. J. Santoni, "Interest Rate Risk and the Stock Prices of Financial Institutions," Federal Reserve Bank of St. Louis Review, August/September 1984, pp. 12–20.

The change in the bank's net worth depends on its **duration gap**:

$$\text{Duration gap} = \text{duration of assets} - \text{duration of liabilities} \left(\frac{\text{liabilities}}{\text{assets}}\right) \quad (15.5)$$

The duration gap compares asset and liability duration, taking into account the fact that assets are somewhat larger than liabilities other than net worth. The size of the duration gap is an approximate estimate of the change in net worth, as a percentage of total assets, resulting from a 1 percentage point increase in interest rates.

The bank in Table 15.9 has a positive duration gap, that is,

$$\text{Duration gap} = 10 - 3.4 \left(\frac{92}{100}\right)$$

$$= 6.9$$

which means that its assets are more sensitive to interest rates than its liabilities. Therefore, an across-the-board increase in interest rates reduces its net worth; a decline in interest rates increases its net worth.

A positive duration gap is an implicit wager that interest rates will decline; a negative duration gap increases net worth if interest rates rise. A deposit intermediary can adjust its duration gap to reflect its interest-rate forecasts — a positive duration gap when it predicts a decrease in interest rates and a negative duration gap when it predicts an increase. A duration-gap calculation also can be used to estimate a bank's exposure to interest-rate risk. A bank that wants to protect its net worth from interest-rate fluctuations can adjust its assets and liabilities to obtain a duration gap of zero; the bank in Table 15.9 could sell some of its 20-year zeros and use the proceeds to buy shorter-term bonds.

Because the assets and liabilities of financial intermediaries are roughly equal, the duration gap formula in Equation 15.5 can be approximated by

$$\text{Duration gap} = \text{duration of assets} - \text{duration of liabilities}$$

Thus whether the duration gap is positive or negative depends (roughly) on whether the intermediary's assets or liabilities have a longer duration. This approximation explains the following shorthand statement often made by financial analysts: a bank's net worth is protected from across-the-board changes in interest rates if its assets and liabilities have comparable durations; if asset and liability durations are mismatched, a relatively long asset duration is a bet that interest rates will fall, and a relatively short asset duration is a bet that rates will rise.

## Hedging with Financial Futures, Options, and Swaps

A bank may find it undesirable to protect itself from interest-rate risk by restructuring its assets and liabilities. For example, attempts to replace long-term mortgages with short-term mortgages and fixed-rate loans with variable-rate loans may meet with customer resistance. Efforts to encourage depositors to shift to longer-term CDs also may be unsuccessful without substantial interest-rate incentives. A bank may find it more profitable to accommodate customer preferences and then use financial futures, options, and swaps to hedge the interest-rate risk in its portfolio.

Chapter 11 explained a variety of financial futures and options contracts. All hedging strategies rely on the fact that because changes in interest rates affect the values of financial futures and options in predictable ways, these instruments can be used to offset the effects of interest rates on a bank's other assets and liabilities. If a bank has a positive duration gap, an increase in interest rates will reduce its net worth; it can hedge this position by selling Treasury bond futures, selling bond call options, or buying bond put options — all strategies that will make profits if interest rates increase. If this is done in the appropriate amounts, portfolio losses caused by an increase in interest rates will be roughly offset by capital gains on its financial futures and options.

Relatively few banks use financial futures and options to hedge their portfolios against interest-rate risk. Successful hedging requires considerable expertise and regular monitoring, an expense that many small and medium-sized banks don't want to incur. A few banks have made expensive errors, buying or selling inappropriate amounts, and some regulators discourage inexperienced banks from using futures and options.

Chapter 12 explained how interest-rate swaps also can be used to adjust liability durations to match asset durations. By exchanging interest obligations, an interest-rate swap can effectively convert a floating-rate debt into a fixed-rate debt (and vice versa). For example, a bank that has borrowed money from its depositors with a floating interest rate might swap interest payments with another financial institution or with a nonfinancial corporation that has borrowed money at a fixed interest rate by issuing long-term bonds, thereby effectively converting the bank's liability from floating rate to fixed rate — to match its fixed-rate assets.

# FINANCIAL SUPERMARKETS

Bank management is sometimes divided up into functions, such as liquidity management, loan management, investment management, and liability management. These functions should be coordinated, however. For example, if a bank's loans are structured to be very profitable if interest rates increase, whereas its securities are selected on the assumption that interest rates will decline, the bank's assets as a whole may be little affected by interest rates. Such a net position should be made deliberately, and not be the coincidental outcome of independent decisions. Coordination is needed so that the bank's overall portfolio reflects senior management's overall objectives.

In the years ahead, small and medium-sized deposit intermediaries may lose out in their competition with large, experienced, and well-known institutions that can afford expensive expertise and equipment, can borrow in international money and capital markets, and have convenient branches to offer customers. The most attractive feature of small intermediaries may be that they are ready-made branches for the giants. To stay in business, many smaller institutions have welcomed mergers with larger institutions. For the next several years, the big will absorb the weak and get even bigger.

Since the mid-1960s, financial markets have endured great pressures and undergone remarkable changes. The clearing away of regulatory constraints and the aggressive evolution of banks and other financial intermediaries have been central to these changes. One aspect has been the creation and spread of innovative assets and markets to satisfy borrowers and lenders. Eurodollars and money-market mutual funds are good examples.

A second aspect has been the spread of financial institutions outside their traditional roles. Most institutions began with very specific, focused objectives. Often this fine aim was accentuated by regulatory authorities that sharply constricted operations. In recent years, however, most institutions have been acting on the belief that they serve their customers best by offering them many different services — the financial analogue to the supermarket or the shopping center. It is more convenient and practical to use one firm for all your financial services. There is also an element of business diversification. By offering several types of services, the financial intermediary avoids the risk that its specialty will be competed or regulated out of business or adversely affected by other macroeconomic events. Commercial banks are the outstanding example of financial intermediaries that span markets. They are clearly the largest and most successful enthusiasts for this strategy. However, other intermediaries are trying hard to imitate their example, if only for self-preservation.

The fine details of this evolving new world of banking are uncertain. Overall, the distinctions between financial intermediaries are sure to blur further. No longer will we go to one intermediary for checking accounts, to another for a mortgage, to another for a car loan, to another for insurance, and to yet another to buy stock. More and more we will have full-service intermediaries — financial supermarkets, open 24 hours a day, with branches all over the world.

These financial supermarkets may evolve from the largest bank, the humblest credit union, or from outside banking: Merrill Lynch with its vast finance expertise and retail network; Sears, Roebuck & Company, which has far more credit cards than any bank; General Motors or General Electric with their huge finance company affiliates; IBM with its computer expertise; or AT&T with its communications apparatus. We can be pretty confident that there will be a rough-and-tumble scramble for dominant positions. There won't be room for hundreds of giants. Instead, there will be a nasty shakeout of the industry with lots of inefficient or unlucky firms broken or swallowed up by the successful ones.

One concern is that this same type of aggressive diversification, including branch banking and Eurodollars, also was very prevalent in the 1920s. Will the story end the same? From a broader perspective, the innovations are part of a very logical and appealing movement from "mom and pop" banking to financial supermarkets. There were excesses in the 1920s; the Federal Reserve followed less than helpful monetary policies; and the Great Crash led to a web of regulations. As these melt away, financial intermediaries are resuming their longer-run evolution. Distinct types of intermediaries are giving way to general-purpose financial institutions.

**EXAMPLE 15.7**

## *International Banking*

International banks borrow and lend worldwide, either through their domestic offices or through branches in foreign countries. Most obviously, international banks are able to provide financial services to multinational corporations that operate in several countries — including buying and selling foreign exchange, issuing letters of credit and banker's acceptances, and marketing Eurobonds. In addition, a global perspective gives banks a broader source of funds and allows an international diversification of their investments.

Banks in the United Kingdom and Switzerland have a long history of international banking. In England, half of the banks are foreign owned, half of the assets and liabilities are foreign, and 60 percent of bank assets are denominated in foreign currencies. Most Swiss banks target a 50–50 split between domestic and foreign assets, and, in the aggregate, half of their assets and two-thirds of their liabilities are foreign.*

Large U.S. banks invariably have foreign assets and liabilities. The table on page 476 shows the aggregate totals by region of the world. The assets are foreign securities and loans to foreign individuals, financial institutions, nonfinancial businesses, and governments. The liabilities include deposits by foreigners and securities sold abroad. The large Caribbean totals reflect the use of Caribbean banks to evade U.S. regulatory constraints.

Despite substantial increases in recent years, in the United States, Japan, and most other industrialized countries other than the United Kingdom and Switzerland, less than 25 percent of assets and liabilities are foreign; and, on average, 80 percent of these foreign assets and liabilities are interbank claims. Foreign liabilities at Japanese banks are almost exclusively deposits by foreign banks. In Switzerland, in contrast, less than 30 percent of the banks' foreign liabilities are bank claims. One reason that Swiss banks attract so many deposits from foreign individuals and businesses is the long-standing Swiss tradition of

*\*Christine Pavel and John N. McElravey, "Globalization in the Financial Services Industry," Economic Perspectives, Federal Reserve Bank of Chicago, May/June 1990, pp. 3–18.*

complete confidentiality, with substantial penalties imposed on any bank official who discloses information about customers. Many depositors evidently value this confidentiality because they have something to hide from tax authorities, law enforcement officials, or others.

**Foreign Assets and Liabilities of U.S. Banks, December 1991 (Billions of Dollars)**

| Assets | | Liabilities | |
|---|---|---|---|
| Caribbean | 206.7 | Caribbean | 271.3 |
| Latin America | 37.6 | Latin America | 71.6 |
| Asia | 125.2 | Asia | 120.5 |
| Europe | 114.2 | Europe | 249.1 |
| Canada | 15.2 | Canada | 21.7 |
| Africa | 4.9 | Africa | 5.1 |
| Other | 2.4 | Other | 14.2 |
| | 506.2 | | 753.5 |

**Source:** *Federal Reserve Bulletin,* April 1992, pp. A58–A60.

## SUMMARY

Models and computers can be used to assess profits, risk, and liquidity under a variety of plausible scenarios. Asset management is the allocation of funds into reserves, loans, and securities. Liability management is the recognition that funds can be raised by issuing liabilities as well as by selling assets. By aggressively seeking funds, banks have become more symmetrical intermediaries, concerned both with profitably investing the funds of their depositor customers and with finding funds at reasonable interest rates for their loan customers.

Banks can use gap and duration analyses to gauge the exposure of their income and net worth to interest-rate risk. For instance, a positive gap and negative duration gap are an implicit wager on rising interest rates. A bank that wants to insulate its income and net worth from interest-rate surprises can structure its assets and liabilities (possibly using financial futures, options, and swaps) to get a zero gap and zero duration gap.

The simultaneous management of assets and liabilities is a crucial part of the movement of banking toward financial supermarkets — unfettered diversified intermediaries offering customers a wide variety of borrowing and lending options.

# IMPORTANT TERMS

certificates of deposit (CDs)
duration gap
Eurodollars
federal funds
federal funds rate
gap
gap analysis

leverage
liability management
liquid assets
primary reserves
repurchase agreement (RP or repo)
secondary reserves
securitization of borrowing

# EXERCISES

1. Use the data in Table 15.7 to calculate commercial bank net worth as a fraction of total assets and, from this, aggregate commercial bank leverage.

2. Here is the balance sheet of a hypothetical bank:

| Assets | | Liabilities | |
|---|---|---|---|
| Cash | 10 | Deposits | 70 |
| Loans | 70 | Bonds | 20 |
| Securities | 20 | Net worth | 10 |
| | 100 | | 100 |

All data are in millions of dollars. What is this bank's degree of leverage? What will its return on its net worth be if the average interest rate on its deposits and bonds is 8 percent and the gross return on its assets is 8 percent? If the gross return on its assets is instead 10 percent? For what value of the gross return on assets is its return on net worth equal to −100 percent?

3. A thrift institution has a net worth equal to 2 percent of its assets, and the average interest rate on its deposits and bonds is 10 percent. What is its degree of leverage? What is the return on its net worth if the gross return on its assets is 10 percent? 8 percent?

4. The following balance sheet of a hypothetical savings and loan association shows the interest rates on its debts and the gross rates of return on its assets in parentheses. The assets and liabilities are in millions of dollars.

| Assets | | Liabilities | |
|---|---|---|---|
| Cash (0%) | 5 | Deposits (8%) | 70 |
| Mortgages (12%) | 80 | Bonds (10%) | 25 |
| Securities (8%) | 15 | Net worth | 5 |
| | 100 | | 100 |

a. What is its degree of leverage?

b. What is the average interest rate on its deposits and bonds?

c. What is the average gross rate of return on its assets?

d. What is its rate of return on net worth?

5. The following balance sheet of a hypothetical commercial bank shows the interest rates on its debts and the gross rates of return on its assets in parentheses. The assets and liabilities are in millions of dollars.

| Assets | | Liabilities | |
|---|---|---|---|
| Cash (0%) | 5 | Deposits (10%) | 70 |
| Loans (12%) | 60 | Bonds (10%) | 20 |
| Securities (10%) | 35 | Net worth | 10 |
| | 100 | | 100 |

a. What is its degree of leverage?

b. What is the average interest rate on its deposits and bonds?

c. What is the average gross rate of return on its assets?

d. What is its rate of return on net worth?

6. In 1987 Columbia Savings & Loan Association in California had $2.6 billion — 27 percent of its assets — in high-yield junk bonds.[3] During the preceding 5 years, the return on Columbia's net worth had ranged from 44 to 114 percent. If junk bonds pay no more than 18 percent, how could Columbia have such a high profit rate? Use the stylized balance sheet below to calculate the annual rate of return, both in dollars and as a percentage of net worth. (The assets and liabilities are in billions, with interest rates in parentheses.)

| Assets | | Liabilities | |
|---|---|---|---|
| Cash (0%) | $ 0.4 | Deposits (11%) | $ 7.0 |
| Junk (18%) | 2.6 | Bonds (11%) | 2.7 |
| Other (12%) | 7.0 | Net worth | 0.3 |
| | $10.0 | | $10.0 |

7. The U.S. League of Savings Associations estimated the percentage of all outstanding mortgages held by savings and loan associations in 1980 that paid various interest rates:[4]

| Interest Rate (%) | Percentage of Mortgages |
|---|---|
| 5 | 1 |
| 6 | 3 |
| 7 | 8 |
| 8 | 20 |
| 9 | 30 |
| 10 | 24 |
| 11 | 10 |
| 12 | 4 |

Use these data to estimate the average interest rate on the mortgages held by savings and loans. Is this average interest rate higher or lower than the estimated 11 percent average cost of funds for S&Ls in 1980?

8. A newspaper article describing the data used in the preceding exercise said, "The tabulation breaks down 14 million outstanding mortgages, valued at about $5 billion, by the interest rate they carry."[5] What is the error in this statement?

9. Since World War II there has been a dramatic shift in the composition of bank deposits — from checking accounts, which are subject to high reserve requirements, to time and savings deposits, which have virtually no reserve requirements. Why might banks want to encourage this shift? How could they do so?

10. Citibank is sometimes described as a financial supermarket. What advantages do you see, for customers and for the bank, of a financial-supermarket strategy?

11. Seventy percent of the mortgages issued by S&Ls in 1984 were adjustable rate; seventy percent of those issued in March of 1986 were fixed rate. In retrospect, many wished they had issued more fixed-rate mortgages in 1984 and fewer in 1986. Why?

12. In 1982 an economist estimated that the aggregate net worth of U.S. thrifts had fallen from $23 billion at the end of 1977 to −$44 billion at the end of 1981 and that 1000 thrifts would be bankrupt by the end of 1983 if interest rates increased.[6] Why does an increase in interest rates reduce the net worth of thrifts?

13. A French company holding U.S. dollars that will be used to purchase goods at a price stated in terms of U.S. dollars can earn interest in the interim by making a Eurodollar deposit. Alternatively, the company can convert its dollars into francs, make a franc deposit, and convert its francs back into dollars when it is time to pay for the goods. If the company follows the latter course, will it gain or lose if the dollar appreciates relative

to the franc while the company is holding francs?

14. The federal funds market has reduced the amount of reserves held by the banking system as a whole. What has this done to the money multiplier (the ratio of bank deposits to the monetary base)?

15. On October 25, 1979, the Federal Reserve imposed an 8 percent reserve requirement on large CDs, Eurodollar borrowings, federal funds loans, and repurchase agreements. Did this action ease or tighten credit conditions?

16. Walter Wriston, Citicorp's chief executive officer, was confident that the tight-money policies begun by the Federal Reserve in late 1979 would cause interest rates to fall. The bank suffered substantial losses when interest rates rose instead. How might Citibank's management have adjusted the bank's assets and liabilities to bet on falling interest rates?

17. Savings and loan associations borrow short term and lend long term. Why is this a disastrous strategy when interest rates rise unexpectedly? Why did I use the qualification "unexpectedly"?

18. In 1980 the chairman of a Massachusetts mutual savings bank said that matching a $2\frac{1}{2}$-year savings certificate to a $2\frac{1}{2}$-year mortgage note "would be a good trade-off."[7] Why is this strategy appealing to the savings bank? Why might it be unappealing to the savings bank's customers?

19. A bank's assets and liabilities have been divided into those with interest rates that can change within the next 12 months and those that can't:

| Assets | | Liabilities | |
|---|---|---|---|
| Rate-sensitive | $500,000,000 | Rate-sensitive | $200,000,000 |
| Fixed-rate | 300,000,000 | Fixed-rate | 600,000,000 |

Does this bank have a positive or negative gap? Is it implicitly betting that interest rates will increase or decrease? If interest rates increase by 4 percentage points, by how much will the bank's annual income rise or fall?

20. The commercial banks in the Tenth Federal Reserve District (including Wyoming, Colorado, Nebraska, Kansas, and Oklahoma) were separated into small banks (less than $300 million in assets) and large banks (more than $300 million in assets). The aggregate balance sheet for each group on December 31, 1983, was then divided into the rate-sensitive and fixed-rate items:[8]

| | Small Banks | | Large Banks | |
|---|---|---|---|---|
| | Assets | Liabilities | Assets | Liabilities |
| Rate-sensitive | 54.8% | 53.4% | 49.8% | 52.2% |
| Fixed-rate | 45.2% | 46.6% | 50.2% | 47.8% |

Which group of banks had a positive gap, and which had a negative gap? Which group do you think showed an increase in income, and which showed a decrease when interest rates increased during the first 6 months of 1984?

21. Using a 12-month horizon, a small mutual savings bank's assets and liabilities have been divided into rate-sensitive and fixed-rate items:

| Assets | | Liabilities | |
|---|---|---|---|
| Rate-sensitive | $20,000,000 | Rate-sensitive | $40,000,000 |
| Fixed-rate | 30,000,000 | Fixed-rate | 10,000,000 |

Does this mutual savings bank have a positive or negative gap? Will it make more profits during the next 12 months if interest rates increase or decline? If interest rates fall by 2 percentage points, by how much will its annual income change? How could this mutual savings bank obtain a zero gap?

22. Does an S&L that borrows short and lends long have a positive or negative gap? Will its income rise or fall if interest rates decline?

23. In the early 1980s, California Federal Savings and Loan, the nation's fourth largest S&L and the principal subsidiary of CalFed, undertook a massive portfolio restructuring designed to insulate itself from interest-rate fluctuations.[9] For example, 90 percent of the mortgages it issued in 1985 were adjustable rate; overall, its total loan portfolio changed from 17 percent adjustable rate in 1982 to 50 percent in 1984. CalFed also issued a variety of longer-term securities, to lengthen its liabilities at the same time that it was shortening its assets. In 1985, $14.2 billion of its $19.0 billion in assets and $16.7 billion of its liabilities were interest sensitive within 10 years. CalFed divided these interest-sensitive assets and liabilities into subperiods:

| Interest Sensitivity | Assets (Billions) | Liabilities (Billions) |
|---|---|---|
| Within 1 year | $8,766 | $12,980 |
| 1 to 5 years | 2,900 | 3,352 |
| 5 to 10 years | 2,582 | 369 |

Use these data to write a one-paragraph report describing the exposure of CalFed's income to interest-rate risk.

24. A bank wants to bet that interest rates will decline within the next year. Should it increase or decrease its gap? Should it increase or decrease its duration gap?

25. A 1985 study of banks in the Tenth Federal Reserve District (including Wyoming, Colo-

rado, Nebraska, Kansas, and Oklahoma) found that between 1976 and 1983 these banks typically had positive gaps and negative duration gaps.[10] How is this possible? If a bank is in this situation, how will an increase in interest rates affect its current income? Its net worth?

26. A commercial bank has a negative gap and a negative duration gap. What will happen to its income and net worth if interest rates increase?

27. Here is the balance sheet of a hypothetical bank (all data are in millions of dollars):

| Assets | | Liabilities | |
|---|---|---|---|
| Adjustable-rate mortgages | 70 | Money-market accounts | 50 |
| 1-year Treasury bills | 20 | 5-year zero-coupon CDs | 40 |
| Reserves | 10 | Net worth | 10 |
| | 100 | | 100 |

Assume that the interest rates on the adjustable-rate mortgages and money-market accounts adjust continuously with market interest rates. Is this bank's duration gap positive or negative? Will its net worth increase or decrease if market interest rates fall by 1 percentage point?

28. The bank described in Table 15.9 wants to sell some of its 20-year zeros and use the proceeds to buy 5-year zeros so that it will have a duration gap of zero. How much must it sell? What if it uses the proceeds to buy 1-year zeros?

29. At the top of the next page is the balance sheet of an industrial corporation, with durations shown in parentheses:

**Assets**

| | |
|---|---|
| Financial (duration = 1) | $ 10,000,000 |
| Real (duration = 15) | 90,000,000 |
| | $100,000,000 |

**Liabilities**

| | |
|---|---|
| Debt (duration = 10) | $ 50,000,000 |
| Equity | 50,000,000 |
| | $100,000,000 |

Does this firm have a positive or negative duration gap? Will the value of its equity increase or decrease if market interest rates rise? Estimate the effect on the value of this firm's equity of a 5 percentage point increase in interest rates.

30. Some corporations issue bonds instead of borrowing money from a bank. Explain why a corporation may be able to issue bonds at a lower interest rate than the bank can obtain when it issues bonds.

# 16 Thrifts

*Things are seldom what they seem*
*Skim milk masquerades as cream.*

**W. S. Gilbert**

There are three types of thrift institutions ("thrifts"): savings and loan associations, mutual savings banks, and credit unions. These institutions are grouped together because, like commercial banks, they are deposit intermediaries — using deposits to raise funds for lending. Thrifts have differed from commercial banks historically in that for nearly 50 years, from 1935 to 1980, thrifts were not allowed to offer checking accounts and were required to invest mostly in consumer loans and residential mortgages. The term *thrifts* was employed to describe their emphasis on using savings deposits to finance household loans and mortgages and to distinguish them from banks. As government restrictions are being relaxed, thrifts are evolving to become more like banks — offering checking as well as savings accounts and diversifying their portfolios to include a variety of assets.

The deregulation of deposit institutions has allowed what were quite different institutions to become increasingly similar. The preceding chapter's discussion of the modern practice of banking is consequently very relevant to thrifts. For example, all deposit intermediaries must be concerned with interest-rate risk and the consequences of mismatched assets and liabilities. In fact, regulators are increasingly requiring all deposit institutions to report their asset and liability maturities and to estimate the potential effects of changes in interest rates on profits and net worth.

Figure 16.1 compares the aggregate assets of thrifts and commercial banks since 1945. Both grew steadily and by roughly comparable dollar amounts until the late 1980s, when the troubled thrift industry began shrinking. Because thrifts began from a much smaller base, the percentage increase in thrift assets since World War II has been larger than the percentage increase in commercial bank assets. Figure 16.2 shows that the ratio of thrift assets to bank assets rose from less than 0.2 in 1945 to nearly 0.8 in 1988, before declining sharply.

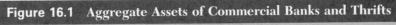

**Figure 16.1    Aggregate Assets of Commercial Banks and Thrifts**

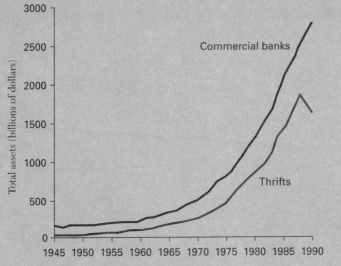

**Source:** Federal Reserve Board, *Balance Sheets of Financial Institutions*, March 1991.

**Figure 16.2    Ratio of Aggregate Thrift Assets to Aggregate Commercial Bank Assets**

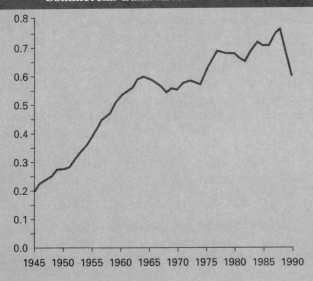

**Source:** Federal Reserve Board, *Balance Sheets of Financial Institutions*, March 1991.

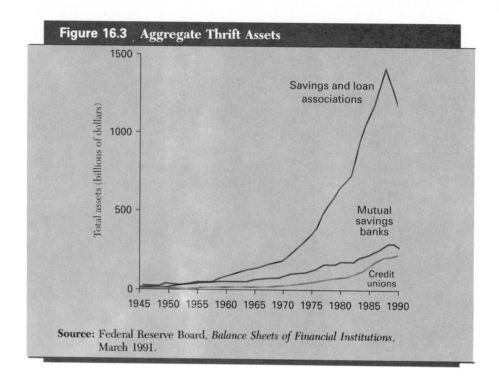

**Figure 16.3**   **Aggregate Thrift Assets**

**Source:** Federal Reserve Board, *Balance Sheets of Financial Institutions*, March 1991.

Figure 16.3 compares the three thrift sectors. Until 1954, mutual savings banks had more assets than savings and loan associations, but S&Ls then grew much more rapidly than mutual savings banks. By the mid-1980s, aggregate S&L assets were nearly five times the size of aggregate mutual savings bank assets. Credit unions have grown even more rapidly in percentage terms, because they began from such a small base — only $400 million in total assets in 1945. Aggregate credit union assets were less than 3 percent of aggregate mutual savings bank assets in 1945; now they are almost equal.

In this chapter we will look at the evolution of these three types of thrift institutions — their origins, the regulations that restricted their operations, their growth after World War II, the challenges they faced in the 1980s, and their future potential. We begin with savings and loan associations.

## SAVINGS AND LOAN ASSOCIATIONS

Until the 1980s, **savings and loan associations** (**S&Ls**) were very specialized deposit intermediaries — either state or federally chartered — that used funds obtained from their depositors' time and savings accounts to make long-term fixed-rate mortgages. Since 1980, deregulation and financial difficulties have given S&Ls opportunities and incentives to change dramatically. Many S&Ls have disappeared, and more will follow. Most of the survivors are trying to become modern, full-service financial intermediaries.

## *Early Building and Loan Associations*

Savings and loan associations were originally known as building and loan associations. The first such association was established in Philadelphia in 1831 to provide mortgages to small homeowners at low interest rates. Initially, these were small, temporary associations designed to use the pooled funds of members to finance each other's mortgages. Each member of the association paid a constant monthly amount into the pool, which, together with interest, was credited toward repayment of an eventual mortgage. Available funds were then auctioned off to members as mortgage loans. After repayment, members left the association.

These associations grew steadily, though slowly, until the Civil War. After the Civil War, their objectives were broadened to include regular savings deposits, and their growth was explosive. By 1893 there were some 5600 associations scattered throughout the country. Some 240 national associations aggressively sold shares door to door on a commission basis. These national associations extracted very stiff fees and imposed harsh penalties for withdrawals or failure to make monthly deposits. In the late 1890s the nationals collapsed, and public confidence in savings and loans sagged.

## *The Great Depression*

The local associations, which were generally well intentioned and well run, soon recovered and resumed their rapid growth. By 1929 the United States had more than 12,000 savings and loan associations with $7.5 billion in assets. These S&Ls held a quarter of the nation's nonfarm home mortgages.

The Great Depression hurt savings and loan associations more than any other type of intermediary. Their assets were almost exclusively illiquid mortgages, and when nervous depositors tried to withdraw their money, a savings and loan's cash was quickly exhausted. When borrowers lost their jobs and could not make their mortgage payments, S&Ls were left with homes that, in the collapsing real estate market, were worth less than the unpaid mortgages. In the aggregate, S&L assets declined by 30 percent and the number of S&Ls fell by 40 percent (15 percent folded and 25 percent were absorbed by others). Those S&Ls that kept afloat were awash with foreclosed homes. By 1935 more than 20 percent of the assets of the surviving savings and loans was real estate, mostly foreclosed properties.

The S&L debacle in the 1930s prompted several actions by the federal government. More than $3 billion in mortgages (nearly $1 billion from S&Ls) was taken over by the government in exchange for liquid bonds. The government also made a small number of direct loans to troubled S&Ls. The **Federal Savings and Loan Insurance Corporation** (**FSLIC**) was established to insure member deposits, just as the Federal Deposit Insurance Corporation (FDIC) was set up for commercial banks. The **Federal Home Loan Bank** (**FHLB**) system was established to regulate the S&L industry and to provide a pool of reserves that could be lent to member institutions.

## *Prosperity*

After World War II, savings and loan associations grew rapidly. Substantial tax incentives led them to invest more than 80 percent of their assets in mortgage loans, and with the postwar housing boom, S&Ls aggressively spread and prospered throughout the American suburbs. High-yielding mortgages allowed them to pay higher interest rates than commercial banks to attract depositors and still make profits. Through the 1950s, S&L deposit rates were about $1\frac{1}{2}$ percent above commercial bank deposit rates. The ratio of aggregate S&L assets to aggregate commercial bank assets rose from 6 percent in 1945 to 32 percent in 1960 and 38 percent in 1965.

## *The S&L Crisis*

The annual rate of inflation averaged 2 percent between 1950 and 1964 and 7 percent between 1965 and 1979. Although inflation and interest rates do not move in locked step, Figure 16.4 shows that this rise in the rate of inflation was accompanied by an upward movement in interest rates. The average interest rate on 1-year Treasury bills rose from 3 percent between 1950 and 1964 to 6 percent between 1965 and 1979.

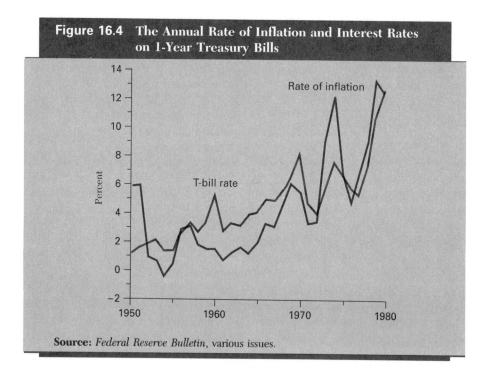

**Figure 16.4    The Annual Rate of Inflation and Interest Rates on 1-Year Treasury Bills**

**Source:** *Federal Reserve Bulletin*, various issues.

As interest rates rose in the late 1960s and into the 1970s and hit double digits in 1979, the S&L strategy of borrowing short term (from their depositors) and lending long term (to homebuyers) made their financial health increasingly precarious. Having used their depositors' funds for long-term mortgages, S&Ls had to persuade their depositors not to withdraw their money. Paying high interest rates to retain depositors whose money had been invested in old, low-interest mortgages, S&L profits and net worth were badly shaken.

During the last 6 months of 1981, 85 percent of all thrifts insured by the FSLIC lost money. During the 2-year period 1981–1982, the industry lost $8.9 billion, and 813 thrift institutions disappeared — mostly through absorption by stronger institutions. The FSLIC provided financial assistance to 92 thrifts and liquidated 2 others. In the Federal Home Loan Bank Board's own words, "so intense was the search for healthy merger partners," that it authorized the FSLIC for the first time to arrange interstate mergers.[1]

The most pressing problem was that because they borrowed short and lent long, S&Ls and other thrifts were vulnerable to rising interest rates. In addition, the erosion of many regulations (such as deposit-rate ceilings and barriers to interstate banking) that protected small thrifts would inevitably lead to a consolidation of the industry. Because of the economies of scale discussed in earlier chapters, small thrifts would have a tough time surviving in an unregulated environment. In 1980 the FHLB board chairman acknowledged the turmoil ahead:

> I think that we must reconcile ourselves to the fact that thrifts will be somewhat fewer in number. There will be, obviously, a number of reasons for the shrinkage, but the basic underlying reason will be that what was once a relatively simple industry has, in a very short span of years, become a very complex industry with all the hazards that accompany complexity.[2]

In response to the S&L crisis, the **Garn–St Germain Depository Institutions Act** of 1982 hastened the deregulation of the banking industry in several ways. Three of the most important provisions were

1. Banks and thrifts were authorized to offer money-market deposit accounts, with no interest-rate ceiling and no reserve requirement, so that they could compete with money-market funds.
2. Federal thrifts were allowed to diversify their assets away from home mortgages by making business loans and by increasing their loans to consumers and loans secured by nonresidential real estate.
3. The act affirmed the power of the FDIC and FSLIC to arrange interstate mergers, if necessary, and to allow banks to make interstate acquisitions of closed banks or thrifts with assets of at least $500 million.

A 1982 Brookings Institution study concluded that "the thrift industry has been rescued," explaining that "the best reason for optimism about the future of thrifts is the expansion of their asset and liability powers."[3] The optimism of Congress and others turned out to be unjustified.

## *An FDIC Barbeque*

Some of the details behind the seizure of a bank or thrift were revealed in 1985 when a *Los Angeles Times* reporter was allowed to accompany FDIC officials when they took control of an insolvent San Diego bank.* Because the target bank was state chartered, the California banking commissioner issued the formal closure order and appointed the FDIC to act as receiver. Fifty FDIC employees were summoned to a secret 4-day meeting at a hotel near the bank to scrutinize the bank's records and make a realistic estimate of its net worth. To avoid frightening depositors, the officials registered as employees of a fictitious company, Mission Bay, Ltd., and referred to the takeover as a barbecue. Only a handful of FDIC employees knew which bank was to be closed before they were sequestered at the hotel.

Two days before the scheduled closure, seven San Diego banks were invited to examine the records and submit bids for the troubled bank. On Friday, the day of the seizure, the head of the operation reminded everyone to be polite, say as little as possible, and accept no money from any bank employee. That evening, minutes before the bank's regular 6 o'clock closing time, two FDIC officials walked into the bank president's office, while two state banking officials locked the bank's doors. After the closure notice was delivered to the bank president, the head of the FDIC team addressed the bank's employees: "I'd like to welcome you aboard. You are all now employees of the FDIC." He explained the situation and asked each employee to stay late that night and work through the weekend, helping the FDIC organize and examine all the bank's records. Each bank employee would be paid time and a half. Since the bank no longer existed, the phone should be answered "FDIC." Dozens of FDIC employees then entered; a locksmith changed all the bank's locks, while armed guards stood outside.

On Saturday morning the FDIC accepted a bid from another bank; that afternoon, the new owners arrived and invited the previous employees to continue working at the bank. Sunday the signs were changed, and plans were made to serve customers coffee and doughnuts Monday morning. Large depositors were telephoned and reassured that their money was safe. When the bank's doors opened Monday at 8 A.M., there were two customers waiting. Both had come to make deposits.

*Bruce Horovitz, "Behind the Scenes of a Bank Takeover by FDIC," Los Angeles Times, January 5, 1986.

Interest rates declined in the second half of 1982, and the losses stopped at many thrifts. However, a third of the FSLIC-insured thrifts continued to lose money in 1983, and even using generous accounting procedures, the ratio of net worth to assets was below the mandated 3 percent level at one-fourth of all FSLIC-insured institutions.[4] Interest rates continued to fall in 1984 and 1985, but losses at weaker S&Ls continued to increase. The problem was no longer an interest-rate squeeze, but mounting loan defaults — caused too often by excessive risk-taking or outright fraud that ultimately reflects inadequate supervision by state regulators and the FSLIC.

## Gambling and Fraud

Most problem loans — to wildcat oil drillers, farmers, real estate developers, and developing countries — can be attributed to unforeseen economic developments and, in retrospect, excessive optimism. Some losses were less innocent: depositor money squandered on executive planes, automobiles, yachts, beach houses, trips to Europe, and lavish bonuses.

Some states, including California and Texas, allowed state-chartered thrifts to invest in almost anything, including restaurants, health clubs, and wind farms. The biggest lure was commercial real estate. In many cases, real estate developers bought S&Ls so that they could, in effect, lend themselves money to finance speculative real estate projects, sometimes paying themselves large fees for finding such attractive borrowers — themselves! One developer acquired an $11 million savings bank in California and increased its deposits to $1 billion in $2\frac{1}{2}$ years, using half the deposits to finance the developer's real estate deals. After the FSLIC forced the developer out, claiming that too much had been invested in overvalued real estate, he defended his actions: "Who would you rather lend to, yourself or to a stranger?"[5]

Some lost money, particularly in Texas, when real estate prices collapsed. Some lost money on dubious developments. If they lost money, they often tried to recoup their losses by investing more money in even riskier ventures. Once the S&L's net worth vanished, there was little personal risk in taking more chances. These insolvent thrifts were literally throwing good money after bad, but it wasn't their money — it was their depositors' money and, because it was federally insured, ultimately the taxpayers' money. If the S&Ls couldn't get enough money from local depositors, they turned to deposit brokers who channeled deposits from investors looking for high rates of return. The ailing S&Ls might have to pay an extra 1 percent for brokered deposits, but this fee won't deter a thrift desperate for one more roll of the dice.

In the infamous I-30 case, officers of Empire Savings and Loan in Texas were accused of making loans based on fraudulent appraisals and falsified financial statements to finance the construction of condominiums along Interstate 30 in Dallas. The FSLIC paid $300 million to Empire's depositors, and 83 individuals were eventually convicted of a variety of charges, including perjury, tax fraud, and racketeering. In 1984 Empire's chief executive officer agreed to pay a $100 million civil penalty to the FSLIC. While the FSLIC did not expect to receive $100 million from the CEO, it was intended that this penalty would result in the forfeiture of virtually all his assets. In 1992 the chairman and two real estate speculators were sentenced to 20 years in prison for federal conspiracy and racketeering charges, and a real estate appraiser was given a 10-year sentence.

EXAMPLE
16.2     *The Worst of the Worst?*

In 1984, American Continental Corporation of Phoenix, a real estate development company controlled by the family of Charles H. Keating, Jr., acquired Lincoln Savings & Loan of Irvine, California. When it was seized by federal regulators 5 years later, it was estimated that Lincoln had lost $2 billion in federally insured deposits plus an additional $200 million raised from the sale of bonds to 22,000 investors, of whom some 15,000 were elderly southern Californians who purchased the bonds at Lincoln branch offices, many incorrectly believing these were federally insured CDs.

Under Keating, Lincoln virtually abandoned traditional single-family mortgages in favor of junk bonds, corporate stock, currency futures, and real estate development. Officials of the California Office of Thrift Supervision, a state regulatory agency, later told Congress that "a thrift was a perfect cash cow for a real estate developer."* According to this congressional testimony, a typical Lincoln acquisition, construction, and development (ADC) loan involved no downpayment and included funds not only for the property and construction, but also for architectural fees, developer fees, points and other loan fees, and the first few years' interest on the loan. No principal payments were required for the first 2 to 5 years of the loan. Lincoln recorded the loan fees and interest as income, although it received no cash from the developer for at least 2 years. According to the regulator, "hundreds of such loans were made with no loan application, no credit checks, with no appraisal or feasibility study." After the Federal Home Loan Board (FHLB) imposed restrictions on direct investments, Lincoln allegedly made loans to straw companies that never intended to repay the loans, leaving Lincoln with ownership of the foreclosed property.

If a thrift is growing fast enough, losses on defaulted loans can be covered by recording ever larger loan fees and interest on new loans, income that isn't received by the thrift but is merely loaned to the developer. To disguise the lack of cash flow, some troubled thrifts swapped loans, paying each other more than the book value of the loans. No money changed hands, but each recorded a profit based on the sham sale. According to the California regulator, a common expression was "I'll trade you my dead cow for your dead horse."

In 1986 FHLB regulators in the San Francisco regional office began a year-long audit that concluded that the federal government should take over Lincoln Savings & Loan and that the Federal Bureau of Investigation should look into possible crimes by Lincoln officials. M. Danny Wall, then head of the FHLB, overruled this recommendation and, a year later, transferred the responsibility for supervising Lincoln from San Francisco to the Washington offices of the FHLB.

*William J. Eaton, "Lincoln Exemplifies How S&Ls Collapse, Official Says," Los Angeles Times, October 28, 1989.

The Washington examiners eventually confirmed the San Francisco investigation and, in addition, suggested that Lincoln had improperly channeled $94 million to its parent company, American Continental, under the guise of a nonexistent tax liability. An accounting firm hired by the FHLB concluded that "seldom in our experience have we encountered a more egregious example of the misapplication of generally accepted accounting principles. . . . Lincoln was manufacturing profits by giving money away."†

Federal authorities finally seized Lincoln in April of 1989. Many wondered if the seizure had been delayed, allowing losses to reach unprecedented levels, because of Keating's political connections — including Alan Cranston and four other U.S. senators who spoke with FHLB officials on Keating's behalf and accepted $1.4 million in contributions from Keating, his family, and business associates. In December of 1989, Wall was forced to step down as head of the FHLB, and an investigation was begun into possible improprieties by those senators — the "Keating five." In November of 1991, Cranston was rebuked by a senate ethics panel for "improper and repugnant" behavior. In December of 1991, Keating was convicted of 17 counts of securities fraud in California, for which he was fined $250,000 and sentenced to 10 years in prison. He was also indicted for federal securities violations.

†*Brooks Jackson, "How Regulatory Error Led to the Disaster at Lincoln Savings,* Wall Street Journal, *November 20, 1989.*

Some frauds escaped detection by the regulators; many were uncovered but ignored because of political pressure from sympathetic congressmen, sympathy seemingly encouraged by large campaign contributions. Vernon Savings and Loan of Texas kept a 112-foot yacht in Washington, D.C. that was used frequently by the Democratic Congressional Campaign Committee. When Vernon was taken over by the FSLIC in 1987, it was discovered that 96 percent of its loans were delinquent and that millions had been spent on Vernon's president, including $2 million for a beach house in California, $200,000 for furnishings, and $36,780 for 1-month's flowers.[6]

## *The Bailout*

In the summer of 1989 it was widely estimated that the federally insured deposits at insolvent S&Ls exceeded the assets of these institutions by at least $100 billion. The FSLIC had the legal power to shut down these insolvent thrifts but didn't have enough money to pay off their depositors or to subsidize their acquisition by stronger institutions. FSLIC officials also were concerned that a wave of public bankruptcies — particularly of large thrifts — would panic depositors at healthy institutions.

A policy of allowing insolvent thrifts to continue to operate is known as *regulatory forbearance.* The government's extreme regulatory forbearance regarding large banks and thrifts convinced many in the industry that government

**Risk-Based Capital Requirements for U.S. Banks and Qualified Thrifts**

| | Risk Weights (%) | Capital requirements (%) | |
|---|---|---|---|
| | | Tier 1 | Tier 1 plus Tier 2 |
| U.S. government and government-guaranteed securities (including Ginnie Mae securities) | 0 | 0.0 | 0.0 |
| U.S. government agencies (including Fannie Mae and Freddy Mac securities) and general-obligation municipal bonds | 20 | 0.8 | 1.6 |
| Nonsecuritized residential mortgages | 50 | 2.0 | 4.0 |
| Commercial loans and other assets | 100 | 4.0 | 8.0 |

requirements. (There are also rules for a variety of off–balance sheet items, including interest-rate swaps and standby letters of credit.)

Under these risk-based guidelines, a bank that held only U.S. Treasury and Ginnie Mae securities would not need any capital at all. U.S. regulators consequently imposed an additional requirement that all banks and thrifts, regardless of the composition of their assets, must hold tier 1 capital equal to at least 3 percent of total unweighted assets. Banks and thrifts that the regulators consider to be risky are required to hold even more capital.

There is considerable arbitrariness in the Basel Agreement's four asset risk classes. Every commercial loan is not equally risky, and every commercial loan is not twice as risky as every home mortgage. The Basel standards also ignore interest-rate risk. The S&L crisis in the late 1970s began with an unexpected increase in interest rates, which sharply reduced the market value of long-term fixed-rate assets. Borrowing short and lending long is a risky strategy, but the Basel risk-based capital standards ignore asset and liability durations. If the FDIC scrutinizes a deposit institution's portfolio and interest-rate risk, this will have to be in addition to the Basel risk-based capital standards. The FDIC is scheduled to implement interest-rate risk standards by summer 1993, and the Basel Committee is currently working on comparable international standards.

Risk-based capital requirements have had a profound effect on bank and thrift portfolios, encouraging deposit institutions to shift their securities holdings from corporate bonds to Treasury bonds and mortgage-backed securities and to shift their lending from commercial loans to residential mortgages. The cumulative effect has been to make it more difficult and expensive for businesses to obtain credit.

EXAMPLE
16.4

## The Value of a Thrift Charter Versus a Bank Charter

The Financial Institutions Reform, Recovery and Enforcement Act (FIRREA) compels a savings and loan association to meet the standards established for a "qualified thrift lender" by holding 70 percent of its assets in residential mortgages and mortgage-backed securities or else to convert to a bank charter (or, what is essentially equivalent, comply with all restrictions on federally chartered commercial banks). This 70 percent requirement severely constrains the asset choices made by thrifts. Are there persuasive offsetting advantages of having a thrift charter rather than a bank charter? The table below summarizes four potentially important factors.*

| Factor | Advantage to Thrifts or Banks in 1991 |
| --- | --- |
| Deposit insurance | No advantage |
| FHLB advances | Slight advantage to thrifts |
| Taxes | Increases thrift after-tax income by up to 2.72 percent |
| Capital requirements | Potential advantage to banks |

Historically, savings and loan associations paid lower deposit-insurance premiums to the FSLIC than banks paid to the FDIC. Now thrifts are insured by the Savings Association Insurance Fund (SAIF) and banks are insured by the Bank Insurance Fund (BIF), with both funds administered by the FDIC. The deposit premiums to these two funds need not be the same, but in 1991 they were both equal to 23 cents on every $100 of insured deposits.

Another historical advantage of a thrift charter was access to loans — called "advances" — from Federal Home Loan Banks at low interest rates. Qualified thrift lenders are still allowed to borrow from Federal Home Loan Banks, but now commercial banks can too if they hold more than 10 percent of their assets in residential mortgages. Although the rules are complex, commercial banks are required to hold somewhat more Federal Home Loan Bank stock in order to obtain advances, thereby conveying a slight advantage to a thrift charter.

Historically, thrifts were allowed to deduct 40 percent of their income from corporate income taxes as a loan-loss reserve to cover potential loan defaults, regardless of the size of actual defaults. Commercial banks, in contrast, were only allowed to deduct actual loan losses each year. The Tax Reform Act of 1986 reduced this 40 percent deduction to 8 percent, and this provision was not

*For more details, see Mark E. Wohar, "The Value of a Thrift Charter: An Economic Comparison of Bank and Thrift Powers," Consumer Finance Law Quarterly Report, Fall 1991, pp. 358–361.

changed by FIRREA. With a 34 percent corporate tax rate, exempting 8 percent of income from taxation raises a thrift's after-tax income by 0.34(8 percent) = 2.72 percent — for example, from $100 million to $102.72 million.

In the past, one of the primary advantages of being a thrift was the relatively lenient capital requirements, which allowed thrifts to become more highly leveraged than commercial banks. FIRREA requires thrift capital requirements to be at least as stringent as bank capital requirements, potentially giving an advantage to bank charters.

Overall, these four factors do not convey a compelling financial advantage to either a thrift charter or a bank charter. For a thrift that, other things being equal, would choose to specialize in residential mortgages, there is little reason to change to a bank charter. For those thrifts that want greater flexibility in choosing their investments, there is little reason to retain a thrift charter.

In the past, regulatory authorities were often reluctant to close insolvent thrifts because of the costs of arranging a merger or paying depositors. However, regulatory forbearance — allowing an insolvent thrift to continue its operations, paying high rates for deposits and making speculative gambles — can be even more expensive. FIRREA gives the FDIC and OTS the authority and some money to enforce capital requirements strictly and to move quickly to contain the financial damage that zombie thrifts impose on themselves and on healthy institutions. In 1991 Congress went even further, mandating that the FDIC restrict the activities of banks that are undercapitalized and allowing the FDIC to close a bank when its ratio of capital to assets falls below 2 percent.

The $50 billion Resolution Trust Corporation liquidation fund was based on incredibly optimistic assumptions — virtually no inflation between 1989 and 1994, growth of S&L deposits by 7 percent a year, and no economic recession between 1989 and 1999. The lowest credible private estimate in 1989 of the cost of liquidating insolvent thrifts was $100 billion. Some government officials were candid about the inadequacy; an assistant Treasury secretary argued, "It's a good start. You shouldn't give anyone more than $50 billion to play with at one time."[8] By December of 1990, the present value of the cost of the bailout was generally estimated to be about $200 billion. Example 16.5 tells where this money went.

Table 16.1 shows the aggregate assets and liabilities of savings and loan associations in June of 1991. (The net worth is exaggerated because mortgages are recorded at face value rather than market value.) You can see that for the industry as a whole, small time and savings deposits are still the most important source of funds and mortgages are still the most important use of funds. While no detailed figures are available, the aggregate asset duration is no doubt still longer than the aggregate liability duration, and the S&L industry is still vulnerable to an unexpected increase in interest rates. On the other hand, many individual S&Ls have drastically reduced their exposure to interest-rate risk by aggressively shortening the duration of their assets (through shorter-term and

**Table 16.1**  **Savings and Loan Association Assets and Liabilities, June 1991 (Billions of Dollars)**

| Assets | | Liabilities | |
|---|---|---|---|
| Cash and reserves | 12.5 | Checkable deposits | 23.5 |
| Time deposits | 5.5 | Small time and savings deposits | 732.8 |
| Federal funds and repos | 0.2 | Large time deposits | 36.8 |
| Bonds | 198.9 | Federal funds and repos | 30.2 |
| Consumer credit | 39.0 | Long-term bonds | 11.8 |
| Business loans | 20.7 | FHLB loans | 79.0 |
| Mortgages | 605.3 | Other liabilities | 103.5 |
| Real assets | 41.9 | | |
| Other assets | 131.5 | Net worth | 37.9 |
| | 1,055.5 | | 1,055.5 |

**Source:** Federal Reserve Board, *Flow of Funds Accounts, Second Quarter 1991.*

EXAMPLE
16.5

## *Where Did the $200 Billion Go?*

The $200 billion bailout of savings and loan associations is one of the biggest wealth transfers in U.S. history — from taxpayers to depositors, homeowners, real estate developers, and others. A December 1990 article in *The Wall Street Journal* attempted to estimate where the money went and came up with the values shown in the accompanying table.* These data include only the losses at S&Ls that were taken over by the federal government; other S&Ls lost money, but have so far survived.

| Losses at Bankrupt S&Ls | |
|---|---|
| Real estate | $40 billion |
| Homeowners | $25 to 30 billion |
| Brokered deposits | $20+ billion |
| Junk bonds | $4 billion |
| Overcapacity and gold-plating | $15 billion |
| Fraud | $10 to 20 billion |
| Deterioration of seized S&Ls | $7 billion |
| 1988 thrift deals | $4 to 6 billion |
| Government administrative costs | $10 to 15 billion |
| Interest cost of delay in resolution | $43 billion |
| Total | $178 to 200+ billion |

*Paulette Thomas and Thomas E. Ricks, "Just What Happened to All That Money Savings & Loans Lost?," Wall Street Journal, December 5, 1990.*

Insolvent savings and loan associations lost some $40 billion on defaulted loans that financed the construction of condominiums, office buildings, and shopping malls that, in a sagging real estate market, turned out to be worth $40 billion less than the loans that financed their construction. Landowners, construction workers, and real estate developers benefited. Bankrupt savings and loan associations lost an additional $25 to $30 billion on their fixed-rate mortgages when interest rates rose in the late 1970s and the early 1980s, while homeowners profited by being able to pay low interest rates on their mortgages.

Financially shaky S&Ls that wanted another roll of the dice paid at least $20 billion above market interest rates to obtain brokered deposits. A study cited by *The Wall Street Journal* found that a third of the deposits in 54 of the largest failed thrifts were larger than $80,000; many of these were no doubt brokered deposits. Large depositors and the brokers who guided their money to S&Ls willing to pay excessive interest rates benefited. Insolvent S&Ls lost another $4 billion on defaulted junk bonds; the beneficiaries were the firms that issued these securities and the investment bankers that marketed them.

Some $15 billion was wasted on overcapacity and gold-plating — lavish expenditures for S&L executives who enjoyed an extravagant lifestyle — and another $10 to $20 billion was lost to fraud, a misappropriation of bank funds for personal profit. Although the occasional trials and jail sentences were widely reported, only about 5 to 10 percent of the $200 billion lost by S&Ls seems to have involved criminal fraud.

When an S&L is seized by the government, the institution is sometimes dismantled and key employees and loyal depositors leave before the S&L is sold to private investors. Losses due to such deterioration were estimated at $7 billion. Money is also lost if the government is too generous in its rush to sell seized S&Ls. It was estimated that when the government sold 196 seized thrifts in 1988, it gave the buyers some $4 to $6 billion in excessive tax breaks and other assistance. The government has also incurred some $10 to $15 billion in legal fees, salaries, and other administrative expenses involved in liquidating failed S&Ls and another $43 billion in interest.

Overall about half of the $200 billion in losses at bankrupt S&Ls is attributable to inadequate investment returns and excessive deposit rates. The remaining half was lost by lavish spending, fraud, and the cost of the government cleanup.

variable-rate loans), lengthening the duration of their liabilities (through long-term bonds and CDs), and hedging their portfolios with interest-rate futures, options, and swaps. In June of 1992, the federal government reported that S&Ls had, overall, made modest profits for five consecutive quarters—a bit of good news for an industry that had suffered through much too much bad news.

# MUTUAL SAVINGS BANKS

**Mutual savings banks** are legally owned by their depositors. Typically, when an account is opened, the depositor signs a proxy statement electing a board of trustees who appoint and supervise the savings bank's managers. Aside from such legal technicalities, mutual savings banks are virtually identical to savings and loan associations.

---

**EXAMPLE
16.6**

## The Appeal of Adjustable-Rate Mortgages

Savings and loan associations that borrowed short term and lent long term in the 1970s suffered losses when interest rates rose sharply in the early 1980s. To reduce the mismatch between their asset and liability durations, many savings and loan associations subsequently shifted their emphasis from fixed-rate mortgages to adjustable-rate mortgages, in which the interest rate on the mortgage rises and falls with market interest rates (and, in particular, with S&L deposit rates).

A mortgage with an adjustable interest rate is, in terms of capital risk, really a short-term loan (unless the rate cap prevents the loan rate from moving with market interest rates). For instance, a 30-year mortgage with an interest rate that is adjusted annually to reflect current market interest rates is essentially a sequence of thirty 1-year loans and has a duration of less than 1 year.

A thrift whose liabilities are entirely variable-rate deposits and whose assets are entirely variable-rate loans has very little interest-rate risk. There may be increased default risk, however, because a substantial increase in interest rates may raise the monthly payments on adjustable-rate mortgages beyond the financial capability of some borrowers. A 5 percentage point increase in interest rates, from 10 to 15 percent, will increase a borrower's monthly mortgage payments by about 50 percent.

In April of 1981, federal regulators authorized the widespread use of variable-rate mortgages, and during the next 4 years, roughly half of all new mortgages had adjustable interest rates. To persuade their customers to take adjustable-rate rather than fixed-rate loans, thrifts often have to make significant rate concessions, setting the initial interest rate on adjustable-rate mortgages a full percentage point or more below the interest rate on fixed-rate mortgages. As markets have developed for financial futures, options, and swaps, some thrifts have found it more profitable to give their customers the fixed-rate mortgages they want and then use futures, options, and swaps to hedge their interest-rate risk.

## *Modern Credit Unions*

Credit unions today are sponsored by a wide variety of businesses, labor unions, religious groups, and other local organizations. Roughly 60 percent of credit unions are work related, and another 15 percent are affiliated with a labor union, religious organization, or other nonprofit group. The sponsoring organization often provides rent-free space, and some of the credit union employees may be volunteers or be paid by the sponsor. Credit unions can be chartered by either the federal government or a state government; currently, about 60 percent are federally chartered.

Federal credit unions are chartered and regulated by the National Credit Union Administration (NCUA), an independent agency of the federal government. The NCUA also administers the National Credit Union Share Insurance Fund (NCUSIF), which insures deposits (to $100,000) at all federal credit unions and at many state-chartered credit unions that meet NCUA's standards.

Credit union depositors are legally considered shareholders — owners of the credit union — with one vote per member, regardless of the size of the account. Their deposits are often called "shares," and their interest payments are called "dividends." In practice, there is little difference between these credit union accounts and deposits in other thrift institutions. Traditionally, the distinguishing characteristic of credit unions has been that they specialize in making short-term consumer loans to their shareholders. Before 1977, federal credit unions were prevented from making mortgages and credit card loans by requirements that loans could not exceed specified sizes, loan maturities could not exceed 5 years for unsecured loans and 10 years for secured loans, loan rates could not exceed 12 percent, and loans had to be approved by a loan committee.

In 1977 credit unions were given the authority to offer 30-year mortgages, 15-year mobile-home and home-improvement loans, 12-year nonresidential loans, and self-replenishing lines of credit (such as credit cards). In 1978 they were given permission to sell mortgages to the Federal National Mortgage Association (Fannie Mae), Government National Mortgage Association (Ginnie Mae), or Federal Home Loan Mortgage Corporation (Freddie Mac). In addition, credit unions are now authorized to offer a wide variety of share accounts, including what are, in essence, checking accounts and money-market deposit accounts. Many now offer insurance, financial planning services, and automated teller machines (ATMs).

Aggregate credit union assets more than doubled between 1980 and 1990, to more than $200 billion. Credit unions are now the third largest source of consumer loans in the United States, behind commercial banks and finance companies. Of all outstanding U.S. consumer loans in June of 1991, 12 percent were held by credit unions.

Table 16.3 shows aggregate credit union assets and liabilities in June of 1991. Like other thrifts, credit union liabilities are overwhelmingly short-term deposits with interest rates that are sensitive to market interest rates. However, in contrast to savings and loan associations and mutual savings banks, credit union assets are predominantly short-term consumer loans rather than long-term

**Table 16.3** Credit Union Assets and Liabilities, June 1991 (Billions of Dollars)

| Assets | | Liabilities | |
|---|---|---|---|
| Cash and reserves | 4.9 | Checkable deposits | 24.7 |
| Time deposits | 32.3 | Small time and savings deposits | 190.0 |
| Federal funds and repos | 14.2 | Large time deposits | 3.1 |
| Securities | 26.3 | Other liabilities | 22.0 |
| Consumer credit | 91.9 | | |
| Mortgages | 51.0 | | |
| Real assets | 9.0 | | |
| Other assets | 10.4 | Net worth | 0.2 |
| | 240.0 | | 240.0 |

**Source:** Federal Reserve Board, *Flow of Funds Accounts, Second Quarter 1991.*

mortgages. Because there is less of a mismatch between their asset and liability durations, the market value of credit unions was not severely damaged when interest rates increased in the 1970s and early 1980s. In addition, with fewer mortgages (and virtually no commercial mortgages), credit unions were little affected by the weak real estate market in the late 1980s and early 1990s.

The industry net worth shown in Table 16.3 seems alarmingly small, but because credit unions are nonprofit organizations, their net worth has always been tiny. Credit union net worth as a fraction of aggregate assets was 0.1 percent in 1960, 0.4 percent in 1970, and 1.1 percent in 1980. The increases in net worth that they have experienced are due mostly to appreciation in the value of their facilities.

## Future Potential

There are a large number of credit unions — some 17,000 — spread throughout the country, although this number is down from a peak of nearly 24,000 in 1969. Individual credit unions are typically very small, because each serves a very limited group of customers, and their aggregate assets are also small, although they have been growing more rapidly than other deposit institutions. The future evolution of credit unions into more diversified intermediaries is enhanced by their favorable tax status, convenient locations, and enviable reputations for serving their customers.

For job-related credit unions, payroll-deduction plans encourage a steady flow of deposits and timely repayment of loans. The common-bond characteristic also encourages customer loyalty, with some members willing to accept slightly lower deposit rates and to pay somewhat higher loan rates. In addition, the vast majority of credit unions are so small that they are exempt from reserve requirements. (The Garn–St Germain Act of 1982 exempts $2 million in reservable liabilities, a figure that is adjusted each year and was equal to $3.4 million in 1990.)

The biggest threat to this bright future is that their small size will be a serious competitive disadvantage against larger and more efficient institutions. The common-bond requirement inherently constrains the size of a credit union and limits the possibilities for diversification, in both its assets and liabilities. For instance, an employment-based credit union is very vulnerable to financial difficulties by the sponsoring firm. If the firm lays off workers, the credit union is certain to lose deposits and experience loan defaults. In recent years, a more flexible interpretation of the common-bond requirement has allowed some credit unions to expand their membership and to merge with other credit unions. For example, credit unions are now allowed to accept as a member anyone who is related by birth or marriage to a current member. As credit unions become more like other thrifts, they may lose their tax-exempt status and some of their customer loyalty.

As nonprofit organizations, credit unions have always had conflicting objectives regarding depositors and borrowers. A credit union can dissipate its potential profit either by charging relatively low loan rates or by paying generous deposit rates. Members are both borrowers and lenders, but not proportionately so: some members have large deposits and small loans, while others have small deposits and large loans. No matter how the credit union allocates its potential profit, it is bound to benefit some members more than others.

The problem for credit unions is not, like other thrifts, mismatched asset and liability durations, but that they are small, relatively unsophisticated institutions in an increasingly competitive and precarious environment. To survive so that they can continue to serve their customers well, credit unions are increasingly using professional managers and focusing their attention on earnings and net worth.

## SUMMARY

Thrift institutions — savings and loan associations, mutual savings banks, and credit unions — are deposit intermediaries that use deposits to raise funds for lending. Government restrictions have long encouraged specialization, but thrifts are now becoming more diversified, full-service financial intermediaries — more like commercial banks.

Until the 1980s, savings and loan associations (S&Ls) raised funds almost exclusively from time and savings accounts, and more than 80 percent of their assets were long-term fixed-rate mortgages. Mutual savings banks are legally owned by their depositors but, in practice, are very similar to savings and loan associations. Credit unions are nonprofit, tax-exempt (generally very small) deposit intermediaries for members who share a common bond. Sponsored by businesses, unions, and other local organizations, they use member deposits to lend money to other members; in contrast to S&Ls and savings banks, credit union assets are predominantly consumer loans rather than mortgages.

During the Great Depression, when aggregate S&L assets declined by 30 percent, the federal government established the Federal Savings and Loan

Insurance Corporation (FSLIC) to insure member deposits and the Federal Home Loan Bank (FHLB) to regulate the industry and lend money to member institutions. S&Ls prospered during the post–World War II housing boom, paying their depositors slightly more than commercial banks and making profitable fixed-rate mortgages. When interest rates increased in the 1970s and early 1980s, the profits and net worth of S&Ls and mutual savings banks were crippled. Deregulation that was intended to allow diversification lured some S&Ls and savings banks into unprofitable speculation and allowed fraudulent practices by some unscrupulous managers.

The 1989 Financial Institutions Reform, Recovery and Enforcement Act (FIRREA) replaced the insolvent FSLIC with the Savings Association Insurance Fund (SAIF), imposed higher risk-based capital requirements and disallowed "goodwill" as capital, prohibited thrifts from investing in junk bonds, established the Office of Thrift Supervision to regulate and supervise all thrifts, authorized the FDIC to terminate deposit insurance and seize any insured bank or thrift, and established the Resolution Trust Corporation to liquidate the assets of insolvent thrifts.

Today the thrift industry is struggling to diversify, equalize asset and liability durations, and take advantage of economies of scale. There will surely be a dramatic consolidation of the industry as weak institutions — large and small — go bankrupt or are absorbed by regional and national giants. Many healthy thrifts will change their charters to become full-service commercial banks with diversified balance sheets that are largely insulated from interest-rate risk. Others will be "qualified thrift lenders," with residential mortgages comprising at least 70 percent of their assets, and use financial futures, options, and swaps to protect their net worth from interest rate fluctuations.

## IMPORTANT TERMS

credit unions
Federal Home Loan Bank (FHLB)
Federal Savings and Loan Insurance Corporation (FSLIC)
Financial Institutions Reform, Recovery and Enforcement Act (FIRREA)

Garn–St Germain Depository Institutions Act
mutual savings banks
savings and loan associations (S&Ls)

## EXERCISES

1. Did commercial banks or thrifts have more checking accounts in the 1950s? Why?

2. Why were S&Ls especially vulnerable to bank runs in the 1930s?

3. In the 1960s, was the ratio of short-term consumer loans to mortgages higher at S&Ls or at credit unions? Why?

4. Explain the error(s) in the following newspaper column:

   *Thomas M. Poor, manager of the Scudder Short-Term Bond Fund in Boston, suggests that you focus on a volatility index known as "duration." This is a calculation in which you determine the present value of a bond's future interest payments and principal repayment. Sound complicated? It is. Suffice it that bond funds with lower duration numbers are less volatile.*

*According to Poor, money market funds have a duration of zero, while a portfolio filled with 30-year Treasury bonds would have a duration of 10.*[9]

5. Why do you suppose some thrifts encourage homebuyers to take out 15-year mortgages rather than 30-year mortgages?

6. The Federal Home Loan Bank Board estimated that during the second half of 1981, thrift institutions had an average return of 10.02 percent on their mortgage portfolio and paid an average of 11.53 percent on their deposits. Yet withdrawals from FSLIC-insured institutions exceeded deposits by $32 billion in 1981–1982.[10] How do you explain the gap between the return on their mortgages and the cost of deposits? Won't thrifts always set their mortgage rates above their deposit rates? How do you explain the large withdrawals when their deposit rates seem so generous?

7. In 1979, Gibraltar Savings & Loan of California made $1.2 billion in new fixed-rate mortgages at an average interest rate of 11.3 percent, increasing its loan portfolio by 29 percent, to $3.69 billion. These new loans were financed by $1.2 billion in short-term money-market certificates and $100,000-plus CDs. In 1980 a financial analyst concluded that "Gibraltar gambled and lost."[11] What was Gibraltar gambling on, and how did it lose?

8. To reduce the mismatch between their asset and liability durations, many S&Ls have shifted from fixed-rate mortgages to adjustable-rate mortgages. If their customers have a choice between fixed-rate and adjustable-rate mortgages and prefer fixed-rate mortgages, how can an S&L shift to adjustable-rate mortgages?

9. Between December of 1990 and December of 1991, the interest rate on 1-year Treasury bills fell by more than 2 percentage points, from 6.6 to 4.5 percent. Was this decline more profitable for thrifts that held mostly fixed-rate mortgages or for those with mostly adjustable-rate mortgages?

10. Explain why the cap rate on a 30-year adjustable-rate mortgage can cause the duration of the mortgage to exceed 1 year. Provide a hypothetical example to explain your reasoning.

11. In July of 1986 an elderly couple that had 12 years remaining on a 7.25 percent mortgage received a letter from their savings bank encouraging them to reduce the total interest they would pay on their mortgage by increasing their monthly payments and paying off the mortgage early. Why would the savings bank encourage this couple to pay less interest by paying off their mortgage early?

12. A *Wall Street Journal* advertisement for a mutual fund that invests in adjustable-rate mortgages claimed that adjustable-rate mortgages have "more price stability than other longer-term investments."[12] Explain why you either agree or disagree with this claim.

13. A thrift institution has a net worth equal to 3 percent of its assets, and the average interest rate on its liabilities (other than net worth) is 8 percent. What is its degree of leverage? What is the percentage return on its net worth if the gross return on its assets is 8 percent? 5 percent?

14. The following balance sheet shows the assets and liabilities (in millions of dollars) of a hypothetical savings and loan association:

| **Assets** | | **Liabilities** | |
|---|---|---|---|
| Cash | 5 | Deposits | 90 |
| Mortgages | 80 | Bonds | 6 |
| Securities | 15 | Net worth | 4 |
| | 100 | | 100 |

What is this S&L's degree of leverage? What is its percentage return on its net worth if the average interest rate on its deposits and bonds is 5 percent and the gross return on its assets is 5 percent? 6 percent? If loan defaults reduce the value of this S&L's mortgages from $80 million to $77 million, what happens to this S&L's net worth? To its leverage?

15. If a thrift with long-term fixed-rate assets and short-term variable-rate liabilities wanted to reduce its exposure to interest-rate risk, should it buy or sell bond futures? Explain. How could it use an interest-rate swap to reduce interest-rate risk?

16. A California S&L used a question-and-answer format to explain the 1989 Financial Institutions Reform, Recovery and Enforcement Act to its customers. Explain why the following answer is misleading:

*Q. Why does the taxpayer have to pay to bail out the S&Ls?*

*The taxpayer is not paying to bail out the S&Ls or anyone else in the industry. Taxpayer funds will be used solely to help uphold the government's promise to protect insured depositors' money. Consumers will pay nothing directly; the legislation does not directly increase taxes at all.*[13]

17. Why were financially sound S&Ls eager to see the 1989 Financial Institutions Reform, Recovery and Enforcement Act passed so that insolvent S&Ls could be closed down?

18. Shortly after the passage of Financial Institutions Reform, Recovery and Enforcement Act, a *Wall Street Journal* article appeared that was entitled "High Yields for Deposits Fall, Thanks to Thrift Rescue."[14] How could this act, which closed some insolvent thrifts and lent money to others, affect interest rates on deposits at healthy thrifts?

19. How was the weak U.S. real estate market in 1990–1991 exacerbated by FIRREA's capital requirements?

20. Why is a credit union not allowed to loan money to someone who has not deposited money in the credit union?

21. Many employees of credit unions are unpaid volunteers. Identify two possible advantages and two possible disadvantages of this situation.

22. Why do you think it is financially advantageous for a small credit union to be exempt from reserve requirements?

23. Were credit unions or S&Ls hurt more by the Fed's 1979–1982 tight-money policies? Why?

24. Why does a 30-year mortgage with an interest rate that is adjusted annually have a duration of less than 1 year?

25. Use the data in Tables 16.1, 16.2, and 16.3 to compare the leverage of savings and loan associations, mutual savings banks, and credit unions.

# 17 Finance Companies

*I'm going to do you a favor. . . .*

Unlike commercial banks and other deposit institutions, there is no precise legal definition of a finance company. When it monitors financial activity, the Federal Reserve defines a **finance company** as a company (other than a deposit intermediary) whose primary assets are loans to households and businesses. Finance companies are thus financial intermediaries that borrow funds (but not through deposits) for relending, making a profit on the difference between the interest rates they pay to borrow money and the interest rates they charge for lending it.

Early finance companies fell into three distinct groups by lending money to three very different types of customers. These distinctions blurred over time as specialized finance companies broadened their asset bases to include all three customer groups. Today, many finance companies are evolving into diversified financial intermediaries offering a wide variety of services, including insurance, safe-deposit boxes, and even automated teller machines (ATMs). We will look at the three traditional clientele and then at the management of modern finance companies.

## THREE ROOTS

Finance companies developed in the United States in the early 1900s from three distinct roots: sales finance companies, consumer finance companies, and commercial finance companies. These distinctions are of little importance today, because finance companies generally perform all three functions. Nonetheless, a description of these three separate origins is useful for understanding the varied roles of modern finance companies.

## Sales Finance Companies

In 1904 a piano manufacturer set up a *sales finance company* to lend money to people who bought the manufacturer's pianos. Automobile and appliance manufacturers soon established similar subsidiaries, and by 1922 there were more than 1000 sales finance companies in the United States. Many sales finance companies (including General Electric Capital and General Motors Acceptance Corporation) are called *captive* finance companies because they are subsidiaries of manufacturers and were established to finance sales of the parent company's product or service. Independent sales finance companies, in contrast, are not manufacturing subsidiaries and finance consumer purchases of competing products and services.

A typical sales finance arrangement involves an installment contract in which the consumer agrees to make specified monthly payments until the purchase price and financing charges are repaid. The finance company implicitly loans money to the consumer, with the piano, automobile, or appliance serving as collateral. Installment lending developed as the United States became an industrial nation because, in contrast to loans to farmers who have seasonal credit needs and seasonal income, installment contracts are well-suited for wage earners who have a steady income and want to buy an automobile or home appliance.

Because of British common law tradition, in the early years of U.S. finance companies, the difference between an item's price and the sum of the installment payments was not considered interest — a distinction that exempted sales finance companies from state usury laws and other lending regulations. Today, the difference between the consumer's cumulative installment payments and the price of the purchased item is considered interest, and installment contracts are subject to state and federal truth-in-lending laws and other loan regulations.

## Consumer Finance Companies

A second type of finance company also originated in the early 1900s. At the time, established businesses were able to borrow money from commercial banks and homebuyers were able to obtain mortgages from thrift institutions, but households without collateral had a difficult time borrowing from legitimate financial institutions. Many were forced to resort to loan sharks who charged annual interest rates of 200 percent or more and considered the borrower's body to be collateral.

The Russell Sage Foundation (a New York philanthropic organization) campaigned nationwide for state laws that would authorize the establishment of regulated *consumer finance companies* to make small personal loans that were not collateralized. The first such law was passed in Massachusetts in 1911; it allowed annual interest rates of up to 42 percent on loans of up to $300. As other states passed similar legislation, consumer finance companies spread throughout the United States.

These companies gave consumers an alternative to loan sharks when they needed to borrow a small amount of money for a short period of time. The relatively high interest rates protected consumer finance companies from defaults on noncollateralized loans. State regulations protected consumers from outrageous interest rates and physical harm.

**EXAMPLE 17.1**

## Pawnshops

Queen Isabella financed Christopher Columbus's first trip to America by pawning her jewelry. Pawnbrokers, then and now, lend money quickly and conveniently based on collateral, not on a customer's credit history. Customers can generally borrow money from a pawnbroker in less than 10 minutes just by showing some identification and turning over sufficient collateral.

Pawnbrokers in the United States are regulated by state and local governments. It has been estimated that at the end of 1988 there were 6900 pawnshops in the United States with $689 million in loans outstanding and that, during 1988, these shops made 35 million loans totaling $1723 million, an average of about $50 per loan. The typical loan is for 1 to 3 months at an annual interest rate of 36 percent to more than 200 percent.*

Pawnbrokers generally lend up to 50 percent of the estimated market value of the collateral — often watches, jewelry, and electronic equipment. Because of the customers and the collateral, pawnshops often have an unsavory reputation as fences for stolen merchandise.

After a loan is overdue for a specified period of time — usually 1 to 3 months — the collateral becomes the property of the pawnbroker, who will try to sell it. Some states require pawnbrokers to auction off the collateral and give the customer any excess over the value of the defaulted loan. Defaults occur on between 10 and 30 percent of all loans, and pawnshops are consequently frequented by people looking to buy bargain merchandise.

Because of their high interest rates, pawnbrokers are lenders of last resort. They report that their customers generally have low incomes and little education and that 70 to 80 percent of their business is with repeat customers. In addition to making loans, most pawnshops also cash checks, sell money orders, and assist in other routine financial transactions.

Cash America Investments of Fort Worth, Texas, operates 150 stores in six states and became a publicly traded corporation in 1987. In its 1989 annual report, Cash America describes its customers as follows:

*Most of the data and quotations in this example are from John P. Caskey, "Pawnbroking in America: The Economics of a Forgotten Credit Market," Journal of Money, Credit, and Banking, February 1991, pp. 85–99.

> *They do not use checking accounts or credit cards, but choose to pay bills and purchase goods and services with cash and money orders. . . . Why do these people need a pawnshop? First, there are times when they need extra cash. Maybe a child is ill and the doctor's bill must be paid. Maybe the car needs a new transmission. There are countless reasons why the customer might have an emergency need for cash, but banks and finance companies will not make this customer a loan.*
>
> Cash America's founder told *The New York Times,* "I could take my customers and put them on a bus and drive them down to a bank and the bank would laugh at them. That's why they're my customers."†

†*N. R. Kleinfield, "Running the Little Man's Bank,"* New York Times, *August 13, 1989.*

## Commercial Finance Companies

A third type of finance company, aimed at small businesses, began at virtually the same time as consumer finance companies. A group of Chicago encyclopedia salesmen had been frustrated by their difficulties in obtaining loans to finance their inventories and the loans that they made to encyclopedia buyers. They stopped selling encyclopedias and in 1905 formed the Mercantile Credit Company to provide salesmen with the credit that they themselves had been denied. This was the first example of a *commercial finance company*, which provides short-term collateralized (or "asset-based") business loans.

Commercial finance companies are similar to consumer finance companies in that they provide loans — at relatively high interest rates — to those who would otherwise have difficulty borrowing money. Few banks were interested in lending to traveling salesmen. And what would they do with cartons of encyclopedias if a salesman defaulted on a loan? Commercial finance companies were willing — for a price — to take such chances.

When finance companies began in the early 1900s, there were these three distinct types, each with its own specialized clientele: installment-contract loans, unsecured consumer loans, and asset-based commercial loans. Before considering how modern finance companies serve all three groups, let's look at how interest is calculated on a typical finance company loan.

## AMORTIZED-LOAN ARITHMETIC

Finance company loans are generally **amortized loans**, in which the periodic payments cover the interest that is due plus part of the principal so that the loan is paid off gradually rather than with a balloon payment at the end. For example, a consumer who buys an automobile, appliance, or other product with an amortized installment contract makes equal periodic payments — usually monthly — until the purchase price and finance charges are repaid.

As explained in Chapter 8, the general rule for all loans is that the present value of the periodic payments, discounted at the stated loan rate, is equal to the amount borrowed. The loan rate is generally stated as an **annual percentage rate (APR)**, which is then divided by the number of payments per year in order to determine the periodic loan rate. For example, a 2-year $2000 loan with monthly payments and a 15 percent APR has a periodic loan rate that is equal to APR/12 = 15 percent/12 = 1.25 percent.

For an amortized loan with constant monthly payments, the present-value formula is

$$P = \frac{X}{(1 + APR/12)} + \frac{X}{(1 + APR/12)^2} + \cdots + \frac{X}{(1 + APR/12)^n}$$

where

$$P = \text{amount borrowed}$$
$$X = \text{monthly payments}$$
$$APR/12 = \text{monthly loan rate}$$
$$n = \text{number of monthly payments}$$

Equation 4.7 shows that this present-value formula simplifies to

$$X = \frac{(APR/12)P}{1 - \dfrac{1}{(1 + APR/12)^n}} \qquad (17.1)$$

For a 2-year $2000 loan with 24 monthly payments and a 15 percent APR, the monthly payments are determined by solving Equation 17.1:

$$X = \frac{(0.15/12)(\$2000)}{1 - \dfrac{1}{(1 + 0.15/12)^{24}}} = \$96.97$$

Thus the borrower's monthly payments are $96.97 for a 2-year $2000 loan with a 15 percent APR.

The total of the 24 monthly payments is 24($96.97) = $2327.28, of which $2000 is repayment of the amount borrowed (the principal) and $327.28 is interest. If, instead of this amortized loan with monthly payments, $2000 had been borrowed at a 15 percent APR, compounded monthly, with no payments for 2 years, the amount owed at the end of 2 years would have been

$$\$2000(1 + 0.15/12)^{48} = \$2694.70$$

of which $2000 is principal and $694.70 is interest.

Notice that the $327.28 total interest with an amortized loan is only about half the size of the $694.70 interest due when no payments are made for 2 years. The reason is that the monthly payments on an amortized loan cover the interest

**Table 17.1    A 2-Year $2000 Installment Loan with a 15 Percent APR**

| Payment Number | Total Payment | Interest Portion of Payment | Principal Portion of Payment | Unpaid Balance after Payment |
|---|---|---|---|---|
| 1 | $  96.97 | $ 25.00 | $  71.97 | $1,928.03 |
| 2 | 96.97 | 24.10 | 72.87 | 1,855.16 |
| 3 | 96.97 | 23.19 | 73.78 | 1,781.38 |
| 4 | 96.97 | 22.27 | 74.70 | 1,706.68 |
| 5 | 96.97 | 21.33 | 75.64 | 1,631.04 |
| 6 | 96.97 | 20.39 | 76.58 | 1,554.46 |
| 7 | 96.97 | 19.43 | 77.54 | 1,476.92 |
| 8 | 96.97 | 18.46 | 78.51 | 1,398.41 |
| 9 | 96.97 | 17.48 | 79.49 | 1,318.92 |
| 10 | 96.97 | 16.49 | 80.48 | 1,238.44 |
| 11 | 96.97 | 15.48 | 81.49 | 1,156.95 |
| 12 | 96.97 | 14.46 | 82.51 | 1,074.44 |
| 13 | 96.97 | 13.43 | 83.54 | 990.90 |
| 14 | 96.97 | 12.39 | 84.58 | 906.32 |
| 15 | 96.97 | 11.33 | 85.64 | 820.68 |
| 16 | 96.97 | 10.26 | 86.71 | 733.96 |
| 17 | 96.97 | 9.17 | 87.80 | 646.17 |
| 18 | 96.97 | 8.08 | 88.89 | 557.28 |
| 19 | 96.97 | 6.97 | 90.00 | 467.27 |
| 20 | 96.97 | 5.84 | 91.13 | 376.14 |
| 21 | 96.97 | 4.70 | 92.27 | 283.87 |
| 22 | 96.97 | 3.55 | 93.42 | 190.45 |
| 23 | 96.97 | 2.38 | 94.59 | 95.86 |
| 24 | 96.97 | 1.20 | 95.77 | 0.09 |
|  | $2327.28 | $327.37 | $1999.91 |  |

due on the loan and also partially repay the loan, reducing the unpaid balance. Table 17.1 shows the details for our example.

After 1 month, the borrower owes 1-month's interest on $2000: (15 percent/12)$2000 = $25. The $96.97 monthly payment covers this $25 in interest and, in addition, reduces the loan's unpaid balance by $96.97 − $25 = $71.97 to $2000 − $71.97 = $1928.03. The amount borrowed during the second month is only $1928.03, and the interest due at the end of the month is (15 percent/12)$1928.03 = $24.10. The $96.97 monthly payment covers this interest and reduces the unpaid balance by the difference, $96.97 − $24.10 = $72.87. Table 17.1 shows that the monthly payments reduce the unpaid balance to zero after 24 months (except for a 9-cent rounding error). In general, as here, the average size of the unpaid balance is about half the amount borrowed, and the

EXAMPLE
17.2
## *How Sweet Is a Sweetheart Loan?*

Employers sometimes loan their employees money at below-market interest rates. For example, Pomona College offers to lend up to $3000 for 3 years interest-free to any faculty member who purchases a personal computer. How financially attractive is this offer? Does an interest-free loan reduce the effective cost of a computer by $5 or by $500?

Each $3000 loan is to be repaid in 36 equal monthly installments of $3000/36 = $83.33. The burden of this loan is the present value of the 36 payments:

$$P = \frac{\$83.33}{(1 + R)} + \frac{\$83.33}{(1 + R)^2} + \cdots + \frac{\$83.33}{(1 + R)^{36}}$$

What monthly required return is appropriate? From the faculty member's standpoint, two possibilities suggest themselves. If the professor would have withdrawn money from a savings account or other investment to buy the computer, then Pomona College's loan allows these funds to stay put earning interest. In this case, use the rate of return on such investments. If, instead, the professor would have borrowed from a bank or computer store to make the purchase, then use the interest rate charged on such loans.

Pomona College's program started in 1983, when many safe investments were paying 10 percent and when loan rates averaged 17 percent on personal bank loans, 19 percent on credit card purchases, and even higher on installment contracts at many computer stores. The present values for annual required returns ranging from 10 to 18 percent are shown in the accompanying table (using Equation 17.1 with the annual rates divided by 12 to give monthly rates). Notice that the present value drops as the required return increases. Here we are considering the present value of an expense ($83.33 a month for 36 months), and so, the lower the present value, the lighter is the burden of these payments.

Notice, also, that we do not use Pomona College's interest rate on the loan— 0 percent—as the required return. If we did that, we would just go around in a circle, showing that 36 monthly payments of $83.33 do indeed add up to $3000:

$$P = \frac{\$83.33}{(1 + 0)} + \frac{\$83.33}{(1 + 0)^2} + \cdots + \frac{\$83.33}{(1 + 0)^{36}} = 36(\$83.33) = \$3000$$

We shouldn't try to measure the present value of the $83.33 monthly payments by discounting them with an artificial, below-market interest rate; rather, we should gauge the burden of these payments by taking into account market interest rates. A present-value calculation should always discount the cash flow, no matter how that cash flow is determined, by a required return that reflects market interest rates, adjusted for risk and other salient characteristics of the cash flow.

The last column in the accompanying table represents the difference between the $3000 the professor receives from Pomona College and the present-value burden of the monthly payments. This difference, the implicit value of the interest-free loan, ranges from $400 to $700, a substantial saving on a $3000 computer. Naturally enough, the saving is smaller for someone who would otherwise buy the computer with $3000 that could be earning 10 percent than for somebody who would otherwise have to borrow the $3000 at 18 percent.

| Required Return (%) | Present Value | Saving ($3000 Minus Present Value) |
|---|---|---|
| 10 | $2583 | $417 |
| 12 | 2509 | 491 |
| 15 | 2404 | 596 |
| 18 | 2305 | 695 |

total interest is consequently about half of what it would be if there were no monthly payments.

This arithmetic does not imply that amortized loans are inherently advantageous because they reduce the total interest paid. As explained in Chapter 8, the burden of a loan should not be measured by the total interest, or the total payments, made over the life of the loan without regard for the timing of the payments. Two dollars paid 30 years from now is twice as burdensome as one dollar paid today. Example 17.2 illustrates the general principle that to avoid the total-payments error, borrowers should look at the present value of the loan payments.

The real issue is whether, at the given loan rate, the borrower wants to repay the loan quickly or slowly. If the loan rate is high, the borrower should pay it off as soon as possible. Suppose, however, that an automobile dealer offers to loan a car buyer $10,000 at a 1 percent interest rate; the consumer should repay this low-interest loan as slowly as possible. Unfortunately, truth-in-lending laws require finance companies to inform borrowers not only of the loan's annual percentage rate (APR) but also of the total amount (principal plus interest) that will be paid over the life of the loan, which encourages borrowers to judge loans by the total payments rather than by the present value of the payments. Example 17.3 illustrates some of the mischief that can be caused by concentrating on total payments.

**EXAMPLE**
**17.3**

## *Should You Borrow at 12 Percent to Invest at 7 Percent?*

Car buyers who try to pay cash are sometimes dissuaded by sales managers who claim that a car buyer can save hundreds of dollars by leaving, say, $12,000 in the bank earning 7 percent and borrowing through the dealer at 12 percent.* Here is their persuasive, but fallacious argument. If the $12,000 is kept in the bank for 4 years, the total interest, compounded monthly, comes to $3864. The monthly payments on the amortized car loan are $316, and the total interest comes to $3168, which is $696 less than the interest earned on the bank account.

How can 7 percent interest come to more than 12 percent interest? The gimmick is that the loan is amortized, so the amount borrowed is $12,000 only for the first month. Each month's $316 payment covers the interest due and also reduces the principal, so each month the unpaid balance declines, until it reaches zero at the end of the last month. Instead of borrowing $12,000 for 4 years, the car buyer borrows $12,000 at the beginning and almost nothing at the end, and the average amount borrowed is about half the initial loan. This is the sales manager's trick: comparing 7 percent interest on $12,000 with 12 percent interest on roughly half of $12,000. It is also the basis for *Sperling's rule*, named after a bank vice-president who advised that borrowers come out ahead if the loan rate is less than twice the interest rate earned on the bank deposit.

This apples-and-oranges comparison is illogical, however, and Sperling's rule is wrong. If the sales manager's advice is followed, the car buyer won't earn interest on the entire $12,000 for 4 years. At the end of the first month, the bank deposit will have earned only $12,000(0.07/12) = $70 in interest and the $316 car payment reduces the amount in the bank account by $316 − $70 = $246. Month after month, the bank account balance declines in order to pay off the car loan. The sales manager uses the fact that, on average, the buyer pays interest on roughly half of $12,000 but also ignores the fact that, on average, the buyer only earns interest on half of $12,000 too. The buyer would break even earning 7 percent and paying 7 percent but must inexorably lose money earning 7 percent and paying 12 percent. In our example, the bank account runs dry midway through the fourth year, and in order to make the last five car payments, the buyer must use other funds. As the table on the next page shows, at the end of 4 years, the buyer is not $696 ahead, but instead is $1581 behind.

---

*\*S. J. Diamond, "Credit or Cash? The Difference Can Add Up," Los Angeles Times, September 23, 1985; S. J. Diamond, "Credit Doesn't Always Rate Better than Cash," Los Angeles Times, September 30, 1985; and Gary Smith, "The Car Financing Fallacy," Sylvia Porter's Personal Finance Magazine, September 1986, pp. 75–76.*

What if the buyer leaves the $12,000 in the bank untouched and makes the car payments out of monthly income? The answer is the same, because each $316 monthly car payment could have been deposited to earn 7 percent interest. At the end of 4 years, the $12,000 will have grown to $15,865, but the buyer will have lost 48 deposits plus interest, a total of $17,446 — on balance, a deficit again of $1581. It really doesn't matter whether each $316 monthly payment comes out of old savings or new. Either way, intuition is right. You cannot make a profit borrowing at 12 percent in order to invest at 7 percent.

| | Car loan at 12 percent | | | | Bank account paying 7 percent | | | |
|---|---|---|---|---|---|---|---|---|
| Month | Unpaid Balance | Interest Due | Monthly Payment | Loan Payoff | Bank Balance | Earned Interest | Car Payment | Net |
| 1 | $12,000.00 | $120.00 | $316.00 | $196.00 | $12,000.00 | $70.00 | −$316.00 | −$246.00 |
| 2 | 11,804.00 | 118.04 | 316.00 | 197.96 | 11,754.00 | 68.56 | −316.00 | −247.44 |
| 3 | 11,606.02 | 116.06 | 316.00 | 199.94 | 11,506.56 | 67.12 | −316.00 | −248.88 |
| . . . | | | | | | | | |
| 43 | 1,831.40 | 18.32 | 316.00 | 297.70 | 330.66 | 1.92 | −316.00 | −314.08 |
| 44 | 1,533.72 | 15.34 | 316.00 | 300.66 | 16.58 | .10 | −316.00 | −315.90 |
| 45 | 1,233.04 | 12.34 | 316.00 | 303.68 | −299.32 | −1.74 | −316.00 | −317.74 |
| 46 | 929.36 | 9.30 | 316.00 | 306.72 | −617.08 | −3.60 | −316.00 | −319.60 |
| 47 | 622.66 | 6.22 | 316.00 | 309.78 | −936.68 | −5.46 | −316.00 | −321.46 |
| 48 | 312.88 | 3.12 | 316.00 | 312.88 | −1,258.14 | −7.34 | −316.00 | −323.34 |
| 49 | .00 | | | | −1,581.48 | | | |
| | | $3,168.00 | $15,168.00 | $12,000.00 | | $1,586.52 | −$15,188.00 | $13,581.48 |

# THE ROLE OF FINANCE COMPANIES

Figure 17.1 on the next page compares the aggregate assets of finance companies and thrift institutions since World War II. As shown, finance companies hold substantially more assets than mutual savings banks and credit unions, but only about half the aggregate assets of savings and loan associations.

Finance companies fill in some of the gaps left by other financial intermediaries. They raise funds by issuing debt (primarily short-term debt) and borrowing from commercial banks, and they use the proceeds mostly to make short-term consumer loans or loans to small businesses that are temporarily strapped for cash. Often the households and businesses that seek personal or commercial loans from finance companies are those that are not judged sufficiently creditworthy to obtain loans from banks. Not surprisingly, interest rates are higher on loans that are not secured by collateral and perceived to be risky. Because the costs of evaluating a loan and other administrative expenses do not rise proportionately with the size or length of the loan, finance company loan rates also tend to be relatively high for loans that are small or of short maturity.

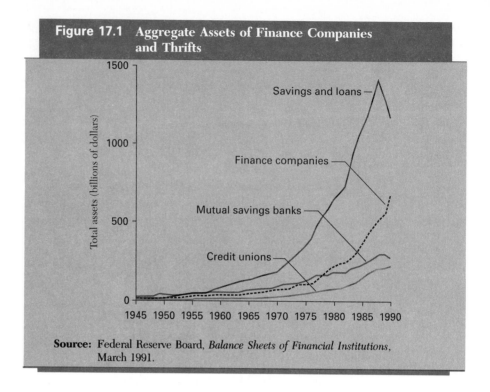

**Figure 17.1    Aggregate Assets of Finance Companies and Thrifts**

**Source:** Federal Reserve Board, *Balance Sheets of Financial Institutions,* March 1991.

A 1983 Federal Reserve survey found that in comparison with those who borrow from commercial banks and thrifts, households who borrow from finance companies have, on average, lower income, smaller checking account balances, and fewer financial assets, and they are less likely to own a home.[1] Similarly, businesses that borrow from finance companies are generally young and small, without an established record of profitability. The finance company takes on these higher-risk personal and business loans and charges relatively high loan rates, often 25 to 35 percent.

Sales finance agreements are somewhat different in that the automobile, refrigerator, or other purchased item provides collateral (though repossession of a car or household appliance is neither easy nor inexpensive). Finance companies and banks actively compete with each other for sales installment contracts and have roughly equal shares of the automobile loan market. In fact, captive finance companies sometimes offer unprofitable loans in order to increase sales of their parent companies' products. For example, in 1986 General Motors' finance subsidiary offered car buyers a 2.9 percent interest rate on 36-month loans for GM's 1986 models; Ford and Chrysler responded with similar offers, and American Motors' finance subsidiary countered with a 0 percent loan rate.

Some finance companies are private, and some are public corporations. Some are subsidiaries of manufacturers, bank holding companies, or insurance companies. Finance companies are regulated almost exclusively at the state level, although they are subject to federal truth-in-lending and consumer protection laws, and a finance company that becomes part of a banking holding company is subject to federal regulation. State regulations may set the maximum interest rate finance companies can charge on loans and the maximum length of loans. Both state and federal laws govern efforts to collect delinquent or defaulted loan payments, including garnishing wages (receiving payments directly from an employer), assessing penalties and legal fees, and seizing collateral. Such *creditor remedy restrictions* are particularly important to finance companies because they make a relatively large number of high-risk loans.

Unlike banks and thrifts, finance companies have never been prohibited from interstate expansion, and a few large finance companies have nationwide branches. Some now offer banking services, and some have acquired insurance companies. Even so, most finance companies are still relatively small. The number of finance companies fell by nearly half, from 3400 to 1800, between 1975 and 1985 because of increased competition and mergers that were intended to take advantage of economies of scale, which occur when an increase in the size of a firm reduces the unit cost of providing a service, such as evaluating a loan application. Despite these mergers, in 1985, three-fourths of the remaining finance companies had less than $5 million in assets.

**EXAMPLE**

**17.4**     *Add-On Interest*

Traditionally, interest on an installment loan is calculated using the *add-on method*, in which the monthly interest is based on the amount initially borrowed rather than the unpaid balance. Suppose that a consumer borrows $10,000 to purchase a car with an add-on interest rate of 12 percent for 4 years (48 months). The monthly interest at 12 percent on a $10,000 loan is (12 percent/12)($10,000) = $100, and a 48-month loan gives a total interest of 48($100) = $4800. This amount would indeed be appropriate if the consumer borrowed the full $10,000 for 48 months, with no compounding of interest, making a single payment of $10,000 + $4800 = $14,800 at the end of 48 months.

However, the installment contract calls for 48 equal monthly payments of $14,800/48 = $308.33, and these payments reduce the unpaid balance month by month. Because the car buyer is paying monthly interest on $10,000 but the unpaid balance is, on average, only about half this amount, the effective interest rate is nearly double the quoted 12 percent add-on rate. The effective annual percentage rate (APR) is that annual interest rate such that the present value of the $308.33 monthly payments is equal to the $10,000 borrowed:

$$\$10,000 = \frac{\$308.33}{(1 + APR/12)} + \frac{\$308.33}{(1 + APR/12)^2} + \cdots + \frac{\$308.33}{(1 + APR/12)^{48}}$$

The solution works out to be APR = 20.753 percent.

The accompanying condensed amortization table confirms that, at a correctly calculated 20.753 percent/12 monthly interest rate, the $308.33 monthly payments reduce the unpaid balance to zero. Although many finance companies and other lenders continue to use the add-on method to compute monthly payments, they are now required by the Federal Reserve Board's Regulation Z (which implements federal truth-in-lending laws) to inform borrowers in writing of the actual APR.

| Payment Number | Total Payment | Interest Portion of Payment | Principal Portion of Payment | Unpaid Balance after Payment |
|---|---|---|---|---|
| 1 | $   308.33 | $   172.94 | $   135.39 | $9,864.61 |
| 2 | 308.33 | 170.60 | 137.73 | 9,726.88 |
| 3 | 308.33 | 168.22 | 140.11 | 9,586.77 |
| . . . | . . . | . . . | . . . | . . . |
| 46 | 308.33 | 15.46 | 292.87 | 601.02 |
| 47 | 308.33 | 10.39 | 297.94 | 303.09 |
| 48 | 308.33 | 5.24 | 303.09 | 0.00 |
| | $14,800 | $4,800 | $10,000 | |

## MANAGING FINANCE COMPANIES

Finance companies are financial intermediaries: they borrow from some in order to lend to others. They differ from banks and other deposit intermediaries primarily in that finance companies cannot offer transaction accounts, do not have federal deposit insurance, and have fewer regulatory constraints on their lending activities. Nonetheless, they face many of the same management issues as deposit intermediaries, including the evaluation of borrowers' default risk, diversification of assets and liabilities, exploitation of economies of scale, and management of interest-rate risk.

Table 17.2 shows the aggregate balance sheet for the finance company industry in June of 1991. Finance company assets are overwhelmingly loans and mortgages — roughly one-half business loans, one-quarter consumer credit, and one-quarter mortgages. Figure 17.2 shows these three asset categories as a fraction of total finance company assets since 1945. In the decade following World War II, finance company loans to businesses stagnated, while consumer credit expanded rapidly. In 1956, consumer credit comprised 56 percent of finance company assets. Since then, finance company assets have steadily shifted away from consumer credit to business loans and mortgages.

**Table 17.2   Finance Company Assets and Liabilities, June 1991 (Billions of Dollars)**

| Assets | | Liabilities | |
|---|---|---|---|
| Cash and reserves | 12.4 | Bank loans | 32.0 |
| Consumer credit | 155.5 | Commercial paper | 323.3 |
| Business loans | 301.8 | Bonds | 191.7 |
| Mortgages | 168.2 | Other liabilities | 71.5 |
| Real assets | 26.0 | Net worth | 45.3 |
| | 663.8 | | 663.8 |

**Source:** Federal Reserve Board, *Flow of Funds Accounts, Second Quarter 1991.*

**Figure 17.2   Finance Company Assets**

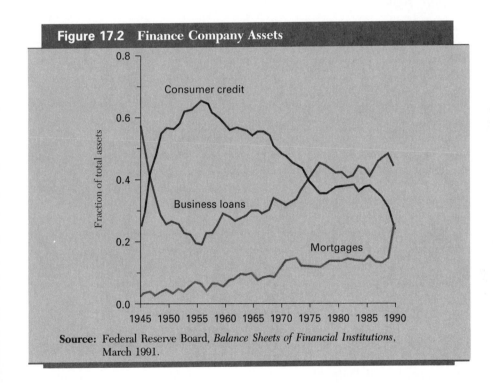

**Source:** Federal Reserve Board, *Balance Sheets of Financial Institutions,* March 1991.

## Home Equity Loans

Some finance companies began making home equity loans in the 1980s, and these are now a substantial part of aggregate finance company assets. A *home equity loan* uses the borrower's home as collateral; the loan is a second mortgage, however, in that the original mortgage that financed the purchase of the house has first claim on the house if the borrower defaults. Home equity loans are attractive to finance companies because the home does provide some collateral;

they are attractive to borrowers because, unlike personal loans, the interest is generally tax deductible.

The Tax Reform Act of 1986 phased out the deductibility of personal interest expenses, including interest on credit card balances and car loans. In 1987, only 65 percent of personal interest was deductible; in 1988, only 40 percent, and after 1990, none at all. Because interest on home mortgages is generally still tax deductible, many people now finance their purchase of a car or a home appliance with a home equity loan. Figure 17.2 shows a dramatic decline in consumer credit after 1986 and an equally dramatic surge in mortgages in 1989 and 1990. Finance company mortgages increased from $68.8 billion in 1988 to $82.3 billion in 1989 and then doubled to $174.8 billion in 1990.

## Default Risk

Commercial loans and large household loans to finance home appliances, automobiles, mobile homes, boats, and private planes are most important for large finance companies because of a variety of economies of scale, including the diversification of default risk. Lending by small finance companies generally consists of relatively small, unsecured personal loans.

Because most of the unsecured personal loans made by finance companies are less than $5000, there is substantial potential for diversification, even at small finance companies. However, such loans are also worrisome because there is no collateral and many of these customers come to finance companies because they are unable to borrow from banks and thrifts — presumably because they are poor credit risks. Finance companies face similar challenges with commercial loans, in that many of their customers are small businesses with little financial history that have difficulty obtaining loans from commercial banks.

Finance companies rarely have the same kind of customer relationships with loan applicants as do banks — where customers may have an extensive financial record and considerable evidence of their income, expenses, and credit history. Finance company loan rates are relatively high because of the default risk and because administrative costs are a relatively large fraction of a small loan. Thus the profit potential is substantial if the finance company can distinguish between those borrowers who are likely to default and those who aren't.

Default risk is particularly important to finance companies because, unlike deposit intermediaries, their liabilities are not insured. If a commercial bank experiences loan defaults, these defaults may have little effect on the interest rates the bank must pay to attract depositors, because these deposits are federally insured. The situation is very different for a finance company. Those who lend money to a finance company are keenly interested in its loan portfolio, because if the finance company experiences loan defaults, it may default on its borrowings. Although finance companies are not subject to explicit capital requirements, their leverage is in practice constrained by the possibility that

EXAMPLE
17.5          *Credit-Scoring Models*

Consumer loans are evaluated by investigating the applicant's past employment and credit history. The loan officer in charge of approving or rejecting the loan application looks for a record of stable employment at a wage adequate to repay the loan and to meet other financial obligations, as well as evidence of the repayment of earlier credit obligations — including a home mortgage, car and education loans, and credit card purchases. Some financial institutions quantify an individual's creditworthiness using a **credit-scoring model** that is based on the economic and demographic characteristics and default frequencies of past borrowers.

Credit-scoring models are constructed by studying past data to identify borrower characteristics that are good statistical predictors of whether or not a loan is repaid on schedule. If persons who change jobs frequently default on loans more often than those who have been at one job for many years, then loan applicants are given points for job stability. If single people default more often than married couples, then those who are married get points. The specific categories and points are determined by an appropriate statistical procedure, such as multiple regression analysis. Once the credit-scoring model has been constructed, each loan applicant is asked to fill out a questionnaire that yields the desired information, and then the applicant's total score is calculated. If the score falls below a specified minimum acceptable score, then the loan request is rejected because the credit-scoring model predicts an unacceptably high probability of default.

In theory, a credit-scoring system uses past experience in an objective way to predict default probabilities. In practice, such systems have been challenged as discriminatory for judging individuals based on the behavior of groups. Very similar issues arise when insurance premiums are based on sociodemographic characteristics. It is discriminatory to charge a careful and responsible teenage male a high automobile insurance premium because, on average, teenage males have more accidents than other groups? Is it discriminatory to charge the elderly high life insurance premiums because historical data indicate that the young, on average, have longer life expectancies?

Standard & Poor's and other rating agencies may downgrade the company's bonds, forcing it to pay higher interest rates.

For example, Chrysler Financial is the captive finance subsidiary of the Chrysler automobile company, and in 1991 Chrysler Financial's debt was downgraded to junk because of the parent company's financial problems. Even though Chrysler Financial was still profitable, it was unable to sell unsecured commercial paper — a relatively inexpensive source of funds for other finance companies — and had to sell some of its best assets to raise cash.

## Matching Liabilities to Assets

Finance company assets are financed mostly by short-term commercial paper and long-term bonds. Figure 17.3 shows the changing composition of finance company liabilities as a fraction of total liabilities (other than miscellaneous liabilities and net worth) since World War II. Over the years, bank loans have become a less important source of funds, and commercial paper has become more important.

Large, established finance companies can issue commercial paper and long-term bonds, which are often privately placed with insurance companies, pension funds, and other institutional investors. Small finance companies generally rely on bank loans for funding, because they are too small and not well enough known to issue commercial paper or long-term bonds at reasonable interest rates. This can create awkwardness, because a finance company that relies on a bank for funds may be competing against this very same bank in making loans. Some small finance companies are wary of loan-rate competition that would aggravate the banks that loan them money.

Table 17.2 on page 521 shows that finance companies have chosen to emphasize short-term assets and liabilities. The long-term mortgages they do hold are roughly balanced by the long-term bonds that they have issued. Because their asset and liability durations are reasonably well matched, finance company

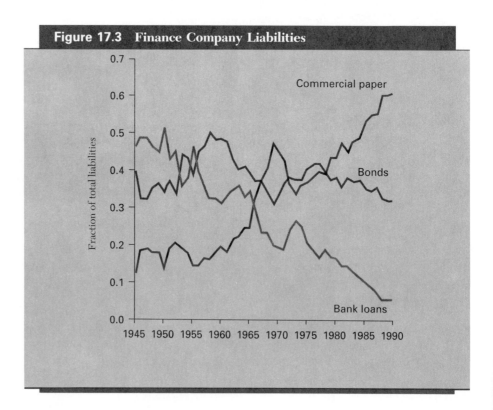

**Figure 17.3   Finance Company Liabilities**

profits and net worth did not disappear when interest rates rose in the 1970s and early 1980s. Aggregate finance company net income as a fraction of total assets stayed in a relatively narrow range of 1.2 to 1.9 percent from 1977 through 1985.[2]

In recent years, large finance companies have been fine-tuning their asset and liability durations by offering consumer loans with interest rates explicitly tied to interest rates on the commercial paper that the finance companies issue to raise funds for these consumer loans. In addition, finance companies can adjust their portfolios to a limited extent by selling automobile loans and second mortgages in secondary markets. Some also use financial futures, options, and swaps to align their asset and liability durations.

## A Diversified Future

Finance companies are no longer specialized. Here is a common example of the mingling of commercial and consumer lending. A finance company may provide *wholesale financing* (also called *floor-plan financing*) to an appliance store to finance the store's purchase of inventory. As long as the appliances are in the store, they serve as collateral for this commercial loan; as the appliances are sold, the store uses the proceeds to repay its loan. The finance company also may have an arrangement with the store to provide *retail financing* for household purchases of the appliances. In this case, when the appliance is sold, the commercial

---

**EXAMPLE**

**17.6**  *GE Capital*

General Electric Contracts was founded in 1932 as a captive sales finance company to issue installment contracts to purchasers of GE products; in 1947 its name was changed to General Electric Credit. In 1987 the name was changed once again, to GE Capital, to reflect the fact that the company has shifted its activities from consumer finance to asset-based commercial lending and a wide array of financial services, ranging from real estate development to issuing and servicing department store credit cards. In 1991 GE Capital was the nation's second-largest finance company (behind General Motors Acceptance Corporation), with $70 billion in assets, but less than 5 percent of its loans involved General Electric products.

GE Capital manages dozens of diversified businesses, including equipment leasing, intermediate-term construction loans, commercial real estate, leveraged buyouts, insurance, car leasing, investment banking, and security brokerage. Many of these products are interrelated. GE Capital can lend money to a company that wants to lease cars, and GE Capital also can sell the company automobile insurance. GE Capital can provide temporary financing to a construction company while GE Capital assists the company in a private placement of equity and long-term debt.

GE Capital offers very competitive loan rates because its AAA credit rating allows it to issue bonds with lower interest rates than virtually all commercial banks. GE Capital has hundreds of offices nationwide, and local managers are given considerable autonomy in designing and approving loans. Using the management-by-objective principle, managers are judged by profitability — what they accomplish rather than how they do it. One example of this flexibility is that some of its business loans are structured so that GE Capital obtains an equity position. In lending money to a real estate developer or a wildcat oil company, GE Capital might receive, in addition to interest on its loan, a share of the profits from a shopping mall or oil well.

GE Capital is a very innovative and profitable financial intermediary, with a management group that a competitor compared to the 1927 Yankees, a baseball team with a "murderer's row" of sluggers, including both Babe Ruth and Lou Gehrig.* During the 1980s, GE Capital's return on net worth averaged 18 percent, and its net income increased at an annual compounded rate of 22 percent.

*Gary Hector, "GE Credit Corp. Braces for the Tax Reformers," Fortune, August 5, 1985, p. 66.

loan is rolled over into a consumer sales loan — with the appliance still providing collateral. Such arrangements are now commonplace for automobile dealers and appliance stores.

In some states, finance companies can obtain charters as industrial banks, allowing them to accept savings deposits and make small installment loans. In addition, finance companies can be subsidiaries of a wide variety of businesses. Ford Motor Company owns not only a captive finance subsidiary but also First Nationwide Savings, an interstate savings and loan operation, and The Associates, one of the nation's 10 largest credit card issuers. Household International owns more than 1000 finance company offices and a nationwide banking operation, Household Bank. In the future, finance companies are likely to become, either directly or as subsidiaries, even more diversified financial intermediaries.

## SUMMARY

Finance companies are a varied collection of nondeposit financial institutions that lend money to households and businesses. Early finance companies fell into three distinct groups — sales finance companies (either captive or independent), consumer finance companies, and commercial finance companies — but finance companies today make all three types of loans: installment sales contracts, unsecured personal loans, and commercial asset-based loans. Finance companies raise money for relending by borrowing from banks and by issuing commercial paper and long-term bonds.

Finance companies are subject to state and federal consumer-protection laws but are regulated almost exclusively at the state level. Loan payments are determined by equating the present value of the payments, discounted at the stated annual percentage rate (APR), to the amount borrowed. In an amortized loan, the constant periodic payments cover the interest that is due and also reduce the principal so that the last payment reduces the unpaid balance to zero.

Finance companies must be especially concerned about default risk, since they make many loans — often unsecured loans or second mortgages — to households and businesses that are not sufficiently creditworthy to borrow from commercial banks and thrifts. Because their asset and liability durations are reasonably well matched, they are not exposed to much interest-rate risk, and unlike thrifts, their profits and net worth did not collapse when interest rates rose in the 1970s and early 1980s.

## IMPORTANT TERMS

amortized loans
annual percentage rate (APR)

credit-scoring models
finance company

## EXERCISES

1. Why might a piano manufacturer be more interested than a bank in lending money to piano buyers?

2. Why might door-to-door salespeople have trouble persuading banks to lend them money to finance their inventory?

3. For many years, Arkansas had a 10 percent usury ceiling on all loans and there were no consumer finance companies in Arkansas. Explain the relationship between these two facts.

4. In 1990 the average length of finance company loans was 54.6 months for the purchase of a new car and 46.1 months for the purchase of a used car.[3] How do you explain this difference?

5. In 1990 the average new home mortgage was for 27.3 years with an interest rate of 9.68 percent, and the average interest rate on a 10-year loan to finance the purchase of a mobile home was 14.02 percent.[4] How do you explain the fact that interest rates on mobile homes are so much higher than those on regular home mortgages?

6. Why might a finance company rationally charge a higher interest rate on a vacation loan than on an automobile loan?

7. There is a 2 to 3 percentage point difference between the interest rate on a loan to buy a new car and that on a loan to buy a used car. Which loan do you suppose has the higher interest rate? Why?

8. Why do you think a credit-scoring model might give points to someone who has a home telephone?

9. Most credit-scoring models look at whether the applicant is a renter or homeowner and how long the applicant has lived at the current address. Why might the probability of the applicant defaulting on a loan be related to these variables?

10. Many credit-scoring models take into account the age of the loan applicant. Why might default rates be related to age?

11. When interest rates reached record levels in 1981, many finance companies stopped making personal loans in states where usury ceilings constrained the interest rates they could charge. Beneficial Finance, for example, closed 400 of its 1900 offices nationwide. Why are finance companies particularly vulnerable to state usury ceilings?

12. A 1983 Federal Reserve survey found that households who borrowed from finance

companies had, on average, less consumer debt than did households who borrowed from commercial banks and thrifts.[5] Explain how the fact that they have relatively little debt could be consistent with the presumption that those who borrow from finance companies are relatively bad credit risks.

13. The assets of small finance companies consist primarily of short-term personal loans. To finance these loans, should they borrow short term or long term if they want to bet on a rise in interest rates? If they want to minimize interest-rate risk?

14. Use the data in Table 17.2 to estimate the leverage of finance companies. Do finance companies, as a whole, have more or less leverage than commercial banks and thrifts?

15. In 1985 GE Credit's managers said that they did not want to increase the company's leverage beyond 12:1, even though they were not prevented from doing so by regulatory constraints. What are some of the disadvantages of increased leverage?

16. Between 1977 and 1985, finance company net income averaged 1.4 percent of total assets. What would be the value of finance company net income as a fraction of net worth if net income averaged 1.4 percent of total assets and net worth was 10 percent of total assets?

17. Traditionally, an asset-based commercial loan, in which some of a company's assets are used as collateral for the loan, has been viewed as risky because the pledging of assets was considered a sign of financial distress. Why might a bank or finance company consider an asset-based loan relatively safe?

18. Do you think that the probability of default on a commercial loan is higher for a 1-year or a 10-year loan? Why?

19. Before the 1968 truth-in-lending law, a finance company using an add-on interest calculation could loan you $1000, charge you $100 interest (with $1100/12 = $91.67 due

each month for 12 months), and say that the interest rate was only 10 percent. What is the true annual percentage rate on such a loan?

20. Example 17.4 shows a condensed amortization table for a 48-month $10,000 loan at a 20.753 percent APR. Explain why the principal portion of the second monthly payment is $137.73.

21. A consumer finance book advises that

*A second method of reducing costs is to make the largest downpayment possible and repay in the shortest period of time.*[6]

How does this strategy reduce costs? Would you recommend this strategy no matter what the loan rate?

22. *Consumer Reports* gave the following advice about automobile loans:

*The nice thing about auto loans is that you can locate the lemons before you sign on the dotted line. Just keep your eye on the APR — the Annual Percentage Rate. . . . Obviously, the lower the APR, the better. Another point to keep in mind: the shorter the loan the better. . . . a one-year loan is much cheaper than a four-year loan. Say you borrow $4000 at 11%. For a one-year loan, the total interest would be $242. The total interest for a four-year loan would be $963 — about four times as much. Of course, the monthly payments for the longer loan would be smaller, but remember that you pay heavily for that convenience.*[7]

a. Why is the $242 total interest on a 1-year loan far less than 11 percent of $4000?

b. Why is the total interest on a 4-year loan more than that on a 1-year loan?

c. Why are the monthly payments smaller on the 4-year loan?

d. What is the present value of each stream of monthly payments, discounted at an 11 percent required return?

e. Assuming the same interest rate on each loan, are there any circumstances in which "the shorter the loan, the better" is not true?

23. In December of 1991, *The Wall Street Journal* reported that a Denver concert promoter had pawned his Cadillac with Autopawn USA, using the car as collateral for a 1-month loan of $1000 at a 10 percent monthly interest rate.[8] If Autopawn USA is able to loan $1000 every month at a 10 percent monthly interest rate, what is the effective annual interest rate?

24. The owner of Dial Auto Pawn in Long Beach, California, says, "We aren't lenders" and "we aren't pawnbrokers." In December of 1991, *The Wall Street Journal* reported that the company will make a $10,000 "cash advance" to a customer who leaves a luxury car with Dial Auto Pawn; the customer can reclaim the car by paying back the $10,000 plus a storage fee of $39 a day.[9] If the cash advance is considered a loan, what is the effective annual interest rate?

25. Rent-A-Center rents televisions and other appliances by the week to customers without a credit check, allowing them to apply the rental payments toward eventual purchase. For example, for a 19-inch portable TV that can be purchased from a discount store for $229, Rent-A-Center charges $9.95 a week for 78 weeks.[10] If a customer does buy the set by paying $9.95 a week for 78 weeks, what is the implicit annual interest rate on this $229 TV?

26. In 1980 Chrysler announced that interest rates (then about 20 percent on car loans) were "7 percent too high" and that it was consequently giving a 7 percent rebate on new cars financed by car loans. Consider a new car costing $10,000 for which you will put $2000 down and pay the remainder over 5 years with a conventional amortized monthly car loan. Would you rather have

the price reduced 7 percent to $9300 or have the loan rate reduced to 13 percent?

27. On August 28, 1986, General Motors announced "The Big One," a 2.9 percent interest rate on 36-month loans for its 1986 models; Ford and Chrysler followed with similar deals. If you are buying a $12,000 car and you have $2000 for a downpayment, would you rather borrow the difference at 2.9 percent or have the price reduced by $1000 and borrow from a finance company at 10 percent?

28. A 1986 *Newsweek* article said of the 2.9 percent loan rate offered by GM and the 0 percent loan rate from American Motors,

*Don't think this is a never-again opportunity. The American auto market is going to be flooded with new cars in the years ahead. . . . there seems no way to avoid a market where there will be too many cars chasing too few passengers. So what will come next — a pitch featuring negative interest rates?*[11]

How would a negative interest rate work? In particular, would the total of the monthly payments be more or less than $10,000?

29. Find the error in the following financial analysis of three auto deals Chrysler (no rebate), Ford (5 percent rebate), and GM (12.8 percent financing):

*Assume, for instance, that you are going to buy a car with a $10,000 sticker price. It would normally be financed for 48 months at 16.5% interest . . . after a 20% or $2000 downpayment. If the manufacturer doesn't provide any assistance in the purchase of the car, the total cost at the end of the four-year financing period would be $12,979.04 according to Detroit Bank & Trust. Monthly payments would amount to $228.73. That is what a buyer would pay under Chrysler's incentive plan, which offers no help on the purchase price.*

*If you bought that same car from Ford, the purchase price plus financing interest would amount to $12,479.04, reflecting a 5% or $500 rebate paid to you by Ford and used as part of your $2000 downpayment. Again monthly payments would be $228.73. You could lower the total cost and the monthly payments slightly if you used the rebate to increase the downpayment to $2500.*

*The same $10,000 car purchased from a GM dealer under the 12.8% financing program, which expires May 31, would cost $12,263.68. Monthly payments would drop to $213.83. Thus, it appears that the GM financing plan saves the customer the most money in the direct purchase of the car, all other things being equal.*[12]

30. Critically evaluate these excerpts from a newspaper column:

*At first, Berkeley psychology professor Geoffrey Keppel rejected out of hand his Toyota dealer's offer of financing. He had saved up the price of a new Corolla and, like many people, didn't want a loan because "that's the way I'd been brought up." The dealer even told him he could earn more on the same $8300 in an 8% certificate of deposit than he'd pay out on a 14.2% car loan, "but you just don't believe it," he says. . . .*

*That night, however, Keppel awoke and went to his computer to "work it out for myself, month by month." Calculating different investment yields and weighing them against the total interest that he'd pay on the 14.2% loan, he saw that he'd break even with only a 7% investment, and, if he could earn 10%, he'd make almost $1500.*[13]

# 18 Insurance Companies

*No one has as much endurance as the person who sells insurance.*

**Anonymous**

Insurance companies provide financial protection against unpredictable hazards. We know that the proverbial lightning does strike and damage people and property, but we don't know when and where it will strike. Insurance can't prevent lightning from striking, but it can lessen the financial hardship for those who are hit by lightning. With insurance, we don't have to worry about how we will rebuild our house if it burns down or how those who are financially dependent on us will manage if we are killed. The financial protection provided by insurance gives individuals and businesses greater financial security (and less mental anxiety).

The cost of insurance — called the *premium* — is accumulated by insurance companies and invested until needed to pay insurance benefits. In addition, life insurance policies often include contractual saving, with the insurance company operating much like a bank — crediting interest to policyholder deposits and allowing policyholder withdrawals or loans. Thus insurance companies are financial intermediaries characterized by a regular contractual inflow of funds from insurance premiums and an outflow of funds for insurance benefits. Figure 18.1 on page 532 shows that the aggregate assets of insurance companies have been roughly the same size as aggregate thrift assets since World War II.

In this chapter we will look at why people find insurance companies to be useful financial intermediaries. We will discuss several different kinds of insurance contracts and some of the underlying economic principles. We will look at how insurance companies are regulated and at how insurance companies manage their assets and liabilities. We begin with some fundamental principles of insurance, including why people buy insurance and how insurance policies are priced.

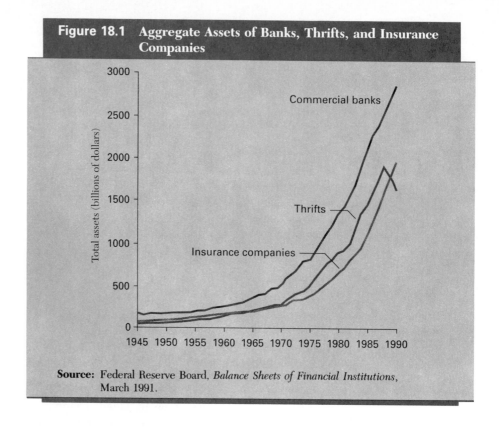

**Figure 18.1    Aggregate Assets of Banks, Thrifts, and Insurance Companies**

**Source:** Federal Reserve Board, *Balance Sheets of Financial Institutions*, March 1991.

# SOME INSURANCE PRINCIPLES

An insurance contract provides protection against financial losses arising from unpredictable events — such as fire or death. Although it is impossible to predict exactly when and where such events will occur, probabilities can be used to quantify their likelihood and to estimate the expected value of the financial loss.

## Expected Value Again

The premium that a company charges for insurance naturally depends on the estimated probability of having to make a payoff. Insurance companies want to charge more to insure the sickly than to insure the healthy. They want to charge more to insure a rundown wooden house than to insure a new brick house. They want to charge accident-prone drivers more than safe drivers.

Interestingly, this wasn't always so. Early life insurance companies largely ignored life-expectancy data collected by statisticians. For example, at least as far back as the 1500s, the British government sold life annuities, which paid a fixed annual amount over the life of the purchaser. Until 1789, however, the price of these annuities did not depend on the age of the purchaser! These life annuities were consequently unattractive to the elderly and a bargain for the young. It is not surprising that life annuities were purchased mainly by the young and that the British government paid dearly for its neglect of life-expectancy probabilities.

Modern insurance companies pay close attention to probabilities. **Actuaries** use statistical data to estimate the probability of losses of various sizes for policyholders with various characteristics (for example, their age or smoking habits, the proximity of a house to the fire department) and calculate the corresponding insurance premiums required for the insurance company to be profitable. Probability estimates are admittedly imperfect, and there are legal and regulatory constraints on insurance premiums. However, insurance companies use probabilities to the extent they are allowed to do so, charging high-risk customers more than low-risk customers and charging everyone enough for the insurance company to expect to make a profit.

Here is a specific example. In 1980 the U.S. Census Bureau calculated that there were 2 million 25-year-old women in the United States and that 1300 died that year. We can use this observed frequency of death as an estimate of the probability $P$ that a 25-year-old woman will die within a year:

$$P = \frac{1300}{2,000,000} = 0.00065$$

How much would an insurance company have to charge for a 1-year $100,000 life insurance policy for a 25-year-old woman so that, on average, it will make a profit? As explained in Chapter 10, this question can be answered by calculating the expected value $\mu$ (pronounced "mew"), which is a probability-weighted average of the possible payoffs:

$$\mu = x_1 P[x_1] + x_2 P[x_2] + \cdots + x_n P[x_n] \qquad (18.1)$$

where the $x_i$ are the possible dollar payoffs and the $P[x_i]$ are the respective probabilities of these payoffs.

For a 1-year $100,000 life insurance policy for a 25-year-old woman, the payoff will be $100,000 if she dies and $0 if she doesn't. Using the estimated probability of death $P = 0.00065$, the expected value of the policy is

$$\mu = \$100,000(0.00065) + \$0(1 - 0.00065) = \$65$$

This life insurance policy has a $65 expected value, meaning that the insurance company can anticipate paying, on average, benefits of $65 per policy if its probability estimate is accurate. If the insurance company wants to make a profit, on average, on such contracts, it will have to charge more than $65 for each one.

In fact, in the early 1980s, the cost (or "premium") for a 1-year $100,000 life insurance policy for a 25-year-old U.S. woman was around $120 — roughly twice the expected value of the policy. On any single policy, the insurance company will receive $120 and pay either nothing or $100,000. If, as anticipated, a fraction 0.00065 of the insured 25-year-old women die, the company will collect $120 per policy and pay out, on average, $65 per policy. Roughly half the money that the insurance company receives will be paid back out to beneficiaries and half will be retained by the company to cover administrative expenses and provide a profit.

| Table 18.1 | Cost of a 1-Year $100,000 Life Insurance Policy | |
| --- | --- | --- |
| Age | Female | Male |
| 25 | $120 | $120 |
| 35 | 120 | 120 |
| 45 | 132 | 165 |
| 55 | 205 | 315 |
| 65 | 475 | 870 |

This 50 percent benefit-to-premium ratio is representative of many insurance policies.

Table 18.1 shows some comparable life insurance premiums in the early 1980s for 1-year $100,000 life insurance policies for men and women of various ages who pass a mandatory medical examination. Notice that men generally pay more than women and that the old pay much more than young — reflecting the differing probabilities of death during a 1-year period. Most insurance companies use even more detailed risk distinctions in setting life insurance premiums, for example, lower premiums for nonsmokers than for smokers.

Some probabilities are admittedly difficult to estimate, for example, when insuring a basketball player's knees or part of a movie star's anatomy. However, it is surely better to use imperfect probabilities than to ignore probabilities altogether. Modern insurance companies use probabilities and expected values to determine their premiums. Interest rates are also an important component of insurance calculations, because invariably time passes between when the policy is sold and when the benefits, if any, are paid; we will explain this point in more detail later in this chapter.

**EXAMPLE 18.1**

## *Insuring Muhammad Ali*

In 1964, a brash 21-year-old boxer named Cassius Marcellus Clay was a 10:1 underdog when he fought Sonny Liston, the intimidating and seemingly invincible heavyweight champion. Liston was a huge, muscular champion who associated with gangsters and, before becoming champion, had been arrested 19 times and convicted twice — serving 2 years for armed robbery and another year for assaulting a police officer with intent to kill.

Cassius Clay was named after a fiery Kentucky abolitionist who was the son of a large slaveholder and yet published pamphlets denouncing slavery and served as a major general for the Union in the Civil War. When the first Cassius Marcellus Clay was 84 years old, he married a 15-year-old girl. On his deathbed, at age 93, he shot flies with a pistol.

The second Cassius Clay was equally colorful. He called Sonny Liston "the chump" and "a big ugly bear" and said, "I don't know whether to whip him or cage him." At almost every opportunity, he proclaimed, "I am the greatest." Clay promised to "float like a butterfly, sting like a bee" and did, outboxing Liston so badly that the embarrassed and beaten fighter refused to continue. A few days after the fight, Liston was carrying a loaded revolver when he was arrested for driving 76 miles per hour in a 30 mile per hour zone.

Clay changed his name to Cassius X and agreed to a 1965 rematch in Lewiston, Maine. Rumors circulated that Cassius would be murdered by Liston's gangster friends. Shortly before the match, the fight's closed-circuit-television promoter paid $1000 for a 3-day $1 million life insurance policy for Cassius.

How did the insurance company price this policy? One way to approach this question is to ask, for what probability $P$ of Cassius' death during this 3-day period is the expected value of this policy less than its $1000 cost? The expected value of the insurance policy is

$$\mu = (\$1,000,000)P + (\$0)(1 - P) = \$1,000,000(P)$$

This will be less than the $1000 cost if

$$\$1,000,000(P) < \$1000$$
$$P < \frac{\$1000}{\$1,000,000} = 0.001$$

Evidently, the insurance company thought that the probability of Cassius being assassinated before the fight was substantially less than 0.001 (1 in 1000).

As it turned out, there was no assassination attempt on Cassius, and he knocked Liston out in the first round. He later changed his name to Muhammad Ali and became, as he said, "the most famous person on earth."

## Risk-Pooling

If the cost of the insurance policy is larger than its expected value, then the insurance company will, on average, make a profit on such policies. It immediately follows that if the insurance company's probability is correct, then people who buy insurance will, on average, lose money on such policies. Why, then, do people buy insurance?

Some people have medical and life insurance because it is automatically provided by their employer. Some have automobile insurance because it is required by the state in which their car is registered; some have homeowner's insurance because they cannot obtain a mortgage without it. In addition to these examples of mandatory insurance, many people voluntarily buy insurance knowing that the cost is larger than the expected value of the benefit because, as explained in Chapter 10, they are risk averse — they are willing to give up expected return to reduce risk.

Specifically, a person might own a house worth $200,000 and estimate that there is a 0.002 probability that it will be destroyed by a fire this year and a 0.998 probability that it will not be damaged at all. (For simplicity, we ignore the possibility that fire will damage the home without destroying it completely.) If this person does not buy fire insurance, she is taking a gamble with an expected value of

$$(-\$200,000)(0.002) + (\$0)(0.998) = -\$400$$

Alternatively, she can buy fire insurance for $750. If she is indifferent toward risk, she prefers not to buy insurance because the cost of the insurance is larger than the expected value of the fire damage. If she is sufficiently risk averse, however, she willingly pays $750 to avoid a gamble with an expected loss of $400 because she wants to avoid the risk of losing $200,000.

When a person buys insurance, the insurance company takes the gamble that the policyholder is avoiding. For example, when a homeowner buys fire insurance because she doesn't want to risk losing a $200,000 home, the insurance company stands to lose $200,000 if the house burns down. Why is the insurance company willing to take a gamble that the homeowner wants to avoid? The insurance company insures a great many houses for many years, and while it does not know which houses will be damaged when, the insurance company is confident that it can predict approximately how many will be damaged by fire in an average year.

When a symmetrical coin is tossed fairly, the probability of a heads is 0.5. We cannot accurately predict the outcome of a specific flip, but if this coin is tossed fairly 1 million times, we can be very confident that heads will come up close to half the time. Specifically, in 1 million flips it can be shown statistically that there is a 0.95 probability that the fraction of the flips that comes up heads will be between 0.499 and 0.501. The **law of large numbers** is a statistical principle that generalizes this conclusion: if an event has a probability $P$ of occurring in a single trial, then in a large number of independent trials, the fraction of these trials in which the event occurs will almost certainly be close to $P$. While an insurance company cannot predict who will experience bad luck (which particular flips will come up heads), it may be able to estimate fairly accurately the fraction of a large number of people who will have bad luck (the fraction of 1 million flips that will be heads).

Consequently, insurance can be thought of as a pooling of risks, in which the contributions of the fortunate majority who do not experience bad luck are used to offset the economic losses of the few who suffer misfortune. For example, suppose that 1 million homeowners in a city buy fire insurance for the coming year and it turns out that 2000 of these homes are damaged by fire during the year. The 1 million homeowners implicitly share the risk that fire will damage homes in their community, in that all pay insurance premiums to repair the damage from fire — without knowing whose particular homes will happen to be damaged.

Insurance not only spreads risk across many individuals but across time too. While there is a substantial probability that a house that we (or our children or our grandchildren) live in will at some point be damaged by fire, we cannot predict when this damage will occur. By purchasing annual insurance, we (and our children and grandchildren) pay a substantial amount in the long run to protect ourselves against a large sudden loss.

The law of large numbers comes into play because if the probability $P$ of fire is estimated accurately, if the incidence of fire at one house is independent of the incidence of fire at other houses, and if a large number of homes are insured, it is unlikely that the fraction of these homes that are damaged by fire will differ significantly from $P$. For example, with 1 million homes and $P = 0.002$, there is a 0.975 probability that the fraction of homes damaged by fire will be between 0.0019 and 0.0021. While we cannot know which particular homes will be damaged by fire, we may be able to predict accurately the percentage of the homes that will be damaged. And most important for the insurance company's solvency, it is unlikely that an unusually large number of insured events will occur simultaneously.

One important qualification, which was discussed in Chapter 14, is that there is an important distinction between the **micro**, or **idiosyncratic**, **risk** that can be diversified away by having a large number of insurance policies and the **macro**, or **systematic**, **risk** that is not reduced merely by increasing the number of policies. In our fire insurance example, we assumed, unrealistically, that fire damage is independent — that the probability of a home suffering fire damage does not depend on whether other homes catch fire. However, fire can spread from house to house, simultaneously damaging many homes in a community — and bankrupting insurance companies. In the terrible 1835 New York City fire, most New York insurance companies went bankrupt. In the 1871 Chicago fire, only a quarter of the insurance companies involved paid their claims fully. Many insurance companies failed after the 1904 Baltimore fire and the 1906 San Francisco earthquake.

Fire risks are not perfectly correlated. If one house catches fire, this will not cause every house in the world to catch fire. The point is that fire risks are not completely independent in that fire can spread from one house to many. An insurance company that sells fire insurance only to neighboring houses is exposed to the risk that they will all catch fire. Modern insurance companies try to diversify away risk by insuring homes in many different communities.

Life insurance is another example involving both micro and macro risks. If the probability of a certain person dying at age 85 is $P$, and if the deaths are caused by independent idiosyncratic factors, then out of a large number of such people, the fraction that die at age 85 will almost certainly be very close to $P$. However, there are also macro risks that cannot be reduced simply by insuring a large number of people, for example, a contagious disease that reduces life expectancy.

All forms of insurance have some idiosyncratic risks that can be diversified away by writing a large number of policies — this is why insurance companies exist! However, there are also macro risks that cannot be diversified away. This is why insurance policies often exclude macro events such as war, plague, or insurrection.

## Adverse Selection

There are other risks that concern insurance companies. Insurance premiums are based on estimated probabilities; however, because insurance companies cannot identify high-risk and low-risk people perfectly, they invariably offer the same premiums to people with differing degrees of risk. The danger for the insurance company is that people who are above-average risks will buy lots of insurance and that low-risk people will buy little or no insurance, thereby invalidating the probabilities on which the premiums are based. Economists call this sorting **adverse selection**: when some people have more information than do other potential parties to a contract, they self-select in ways that are disadvantageous to the less-informed.

With life insurance, for example, potential customers know more than the insurance company about their own health. If the company cannot distinguish those in good health from those in poor health, it must offer the same premium to both. Those in poor health are most attracted to such policies, and consequently they self-select in a way that is financially harmful to the insurance company — adverse selection. Similarly, when the British government sold life annuities that did not depend on the age of the purchaser, there was adverse selection in that the annuities were a bargain for the young and mainly purchased by the young.

For a more concrete example, suppose that all houses are worth $100,000 and that there are two kinds of people, the Careless and the Careful. There is a 0.010 probability that fire will destroy a home inhabited by Careless people but only a 0.001 probability that fire will destroy a Careful home. If 90 percent of the people are Careful and 10 percent are Careless, the overall probability of fire damage is $0.001(0.9) + 0.010(0.1) = 0.0019$.

If insurance companies cannot distinguish the Careful from the Careless, they will price their fire insurance policies using the overall 0.0019 probability of fire damage. For a $100,000 home, the expected loss is $0.0019(\$100,000) = \$190$, and an insurance company might charge $400 to cover the expected loss, its administrative expenses, and a profit.

For the Careful, the expected loss is $0.001(\$100,000) = \$100$, and they may choose not to pay $400 for fire insurance. For the Careless, on the other hand, the expected loss is $0.010(\$100,000) = \$1000$, and $400 fire insurance is a bargain. If the Careless buy fire insurance and the Careful don't, the insurance company will have sold policies for $400 that have an expected payout of $1000, and it might go bankrupt. The insurance company used the overall 0.0019 probability of fire to price its policies, but the Careless people who choose to buy insurance have a 0.010 probability of fire.

Insurance companies try to protect themselves from adverse selection in a variety of ways. For example, fire insurance premiums depend on whether the

EXAMPLE
18.2

## *Unisex Insurance*

A 1983 Supreme Court decision struck down the use of sex-based mortality tables in company-funded insurance and pension plans as unlawful job discrimination. In a 1987 *Wall Street Journal* article on unisex insurance, an economist with the Insurance Information Institute spoke for the industry in arguing that insurance premiums should take into account the statistical fact that the sexes have different claim patterns: "It's a basic issue of fairness. The price should reflect the risks involved. If I'm a maker of fireworks, I should pay more for insurance than a garment maker does."* A spokeswoman for the National Organization for Women countered that "There's no compelling reason to divide the human race in that fashion," and argued that women would, on average, pay less for unisex insurance.

At that time, Hawaii, Michigan, and North Carolina required equal automobile insurance for males and females, and Massachusetts and Montana required equal premiums for males and females on all insurance. In those states where different rates are charged for males and females,

1. Males under 25 pay about twice as much as females under 25 for car insurance; for those over 25, males pay about the same or slightly more than females.
2. Males pay about 10 to 30 percent more than females for life insurance.
3. Females under 55 pay some 30 to 50 percent more than males for health insurance.

An interesting study of 8300 people in Erie County, Pennsylvania, concluded that the overwhelming reason women live longer than men is that they don't smoke as many cigarettes.† When women are compared with men of the same age and social level who do not smoke and are not killed violently, the life expectancy figures are "virtually identical." The authors recommend that insurance premiums be based on cigarette smoking rather than gender.

*John R. Dorfman, "Proposals for Equal Insurance Fees for Men and Women Spark Battle," Wall Street Journal, August 27, 1987.
†G. H. Miller and Dean R. Gerstein, "The Life Expectancy of Nonsmoking Men and Women," Public Health Reports, July/August 1983, pp. 343–349.

people living in the house are owners or renters. Automobile insurance premiums depend on the driver's age, sex, and driving record. Insurance companies increase the premiums of or refuse to insure people who file lots of claims. Life insurance and medical insurance policies generally require a medical examination. Some insurance contracts protect against adverse selection by setting the premiums substantially above the expected value of the contract and then return "dividends" to policyholders if the actual average cost does not exceed the expected value.

## Moral Hazard

Another risk for insurance companies arises from what economists call **moral hazard**: a person who enters into a contractual agreement alters his or her behavior in order to profit from the contract at the other party's expense. For example, a person with theft insurance may be less careful about locking doors, or a person with medical insurance may be less cost conscious about medical expenses.

In extreme cases, unscrupulous people crash insured automobiles and burn down insured buildings, as illustrated by the following joke. Two American friends meet each other unexpectedly at a European resort. The first person explains that he bought a warehouse and it burned down, so he is using the insurance proceeds to pay for his vacation. The second person responds that he bought some property that was destroyed in a flood and that he too is spending the insurance money on a vacation. "Gee," the first person asks, "How do you start a flood?"

Deliberately causing damage to collect insurance is *insurance fraud* and is illegal. However, it is not illegal to be less careful about one's behavior. Insurance companies consequently try to find ways to discourage careless behavior. One way to combat moral hazard is to make the policyholder pay for some of the consequences of being careless. Many insurance policies have a deductible, which requires the policyholder to pay for the damages up to a set limit, after which the insurance company pays. For example, an automobile collision insurance policy might have a $500 deductible, meaning that in an accident the policyholder pays the first $500 in costs. Similarly, insurance policies often have co-insurance, which requires the policyholder to pay a specified fraction of the damage. Under a medical insurance policy with a 20 percent co-insurance rate, the policyholder pays 20 percent of the medical bill and the insurance company pays the remaining 80 percent. Another way to combat moral hazard is for the policy to include explicit provisions that are designed to ensure careful behavior, for example, requiring the installation of burglar alarms or smoke detectors.

# INSURANCE CONTRACTS

There are many different varieties of insurance, and specific types of insurance are often packaged together in various combinations designed for individual customers. Here we will focus on a few general principles, beginning with the distinction between life insurance companies and property and casualty (P&C) insurance companies. (For brevity, property and casualty insurance is often described simply as "property insurance" or "casualty insurance.")

## Life Insurance

Life insurance companies sell three general categories of insurance that reduce financial hardship when death, illness, or retirement reduces or eliminates a person's income:

*Life insurance* provides benefits to beneficiaries — typically a spouse and children — who are financially dependent on the income of a person who suffers an untimely death.

*Medical insurance* and *disability insurance* provide benefits when accident or illness requires large medical expenses and curtails one's income.

*Savings plans* and *annuities* supplement income that has been diminished by retirement.

A life insurance policy may consist of insurance only or may combine insurance with a savings plan. **Term life insurance** is temporary insurance, usually for 1 to 5 years, that provides a death benefit (called the *face value*) while the insurance is in effect but generally has no value unless the insured person dies. It is pure insurance, without contractual saving.

In contrast, *whole life*, *universal life*, and *variable life insurance* are combinations of term insurance with what is, in essence, a savings account. The policyholder's premiums are credited to the savings account, the cost of term insurance plus expenses is deducted from the account, and the savings account is credited with interest that is determined by the details of the insurance policy.

The savings account balance is called the *cash value* or the *gross cash value*. The policyholder can borrow the cash value, paying interest that is deducted from the account. The policyholder also has the option of canceling the insurance contract and receiving a *surrender value* that is equal to the cash value of

---

**EXAMPLE**

**18.3**  *Tontines*

Tontines were the idea of Lorenzo Tonti, an Italian who dreamed up a variety of money-making schemes in France in the late eighteenth century. In a *tontine*, subscribers contribute a pool of money which, together with interest, is paid to the last surviving member. This is essentially a savings lottery that provides an old age pension or, more often, a sizable bequest to heirs. This extreme form of a tontine never caught on in the United States, mostly because it was viewed as providing a substantial financial inducement to murder one's fellow subscribers. Modified tontines, in which the proceeds are distributed after a specified number of years to a handful of survivors, were more popular and financed a number of notable buildings in the United States in the 1790s.

Insurance companies launched their own modified tontines shortly after the Civil War. Their version was more subtle, so subtle in fact that most subscribers probably did not understand that they were in a tontine. Subscribers made regular payments which, together with interest, were much larger than actuarially required to satisfy the face values of their policies. The beneficiaries of those who died were paid only these face values. Those subscribers who were still alive after a specified period (10, 15, or 20 years) received the face values plus the surplus contributions (net of the company's expenses). This innovation proved immensely popular and attracted a considerable amount of household savings.

the savings account minus a surrender charge. If the contract is not surrendered, the beneficiary receives the cash value plus an insurance benefit when the policyholder dies.

While whole life, universal life, and variable life insurance policies all combine term insurance with a savings account, they differ in how interest is credited to the account. In general, whole life policies assume a fixed rate of interest on the savings account for the life of the policyholder, universal life policies allow the interest rate to rise or fall with market interest rates, and variable life policies allow the policyholder to choose to invest the savings account in stocks and other assets besides bonds. However, there are many hybrid combinations with a variety of means of determining the savings account's rate of return. There is also considerable latitude in determining the annual premium (and hence how much is contributed to the savings account).

Universal life and variable life policies were introduced in the 1970s to satisfy increasingly sophisticated customers who were dissatisfied with the low, fixed interest rates used in whole life policies and were increasingly choosing term insurance instead. The introduction of competitively priced universal and variable insurance retained customers but reduced life insurance company profit margins and made their cash flows less predictable.

## Life Annuities

A security that makes periodic payments for a specified period of time (for example, until a person's death) is called an *annuity*. A **life annuity** pays a person (the *annuitant*) a periodic income as long as one or more specified persons are still alive. Life annuities are essentially life insurance in reverse. Life insurance involves a large number of people contributing money to a central fund, with each person's beneficiaries receiving benefits from the fund when the policyholder dies. Life annuities also involve a large number of people paying money to a central fund. In contrast to life insurance, however, life annuities pay benefits *until* people die. The purpose of life insurance is to protect the beneficiaries if the policyholder dies unusually young. The purpose of life annuities is to protect the beneficiaries if they live unusually long lives.

Life insurance and annuities are both risk-pooling arrangements designed to protect people from uncertainty about how long they will live. In each case, the premiums depend on life expectancies and on the rates of return that the insurance company expects to earn on the pooled funds. Life insurance companies provide an important service to their policyholders by organizing and managing such pooled funds. As with banks and other financial intermediaries, life insurance companies are socially useful because of economies of scale — here the law of large numbers implies that risk diminishes with the size of the pooled fund.

Another similarity with banks is that if policyholders get nervous about an insurance company's financial situation, they may cash in their insurance and annuities, which is similar to a bank run. An insurance company invests much of its policyholders' premiums in long-term illiquid assets and may not have enough cash or liquid assets to pay off a large fraction of its policyholders. A run on an insurance company can exhaust its liquid assets and force it to sell its other assets at distress prices.

A more subtle consequence of policyholder anxiety involves adverse selection. When policyholders get nervous about an insurance company's financial viability, the low-risk customers are most likely to cash in their policies for what they can get, while the high-risk customers hang on to their policies because they may have difficulty obtaining insurance elsewhere. Thus the troubled insurance company is left with high-risk policyholders — which worsens its financial outlook.

## Property and Casualty Insurance

Property and casualty insurance companies sell several kinds of insurance that provide funds for unexpected expenses resulting from physical damage to property — damage either to the insured's own property or to other property for which the insured is liable. Here are several examples:

> *Property insurance* protects against loss from property damage caused by fire, theft, or negligence.
>
> *Liability insurance* protects the policyholder in the event of personal injury to others or damages to property owned by others.
>
> *Homeowner's insurance* is a combination of property and liability insurance that covers many of the risks associated with home ownership.
>
> *Automobile insurance* provides comprehensive protection against property damage and personal injury that are related to ownership of an automobile.
>
> *Marine insurance* covers transportation-related losses (both on land and water).
>
> *Surety insurance* guarantees that specified duties will be performed, for example, that a construction project will be completed as scheduled or (with a bail bond) that a person will appear in court at a specified time.
>
> A *fidelity policy* protects an employer against theft or other specified dishonest acts by employees.

Property and casualty insurance is generally for a year, but it can be even shorter term — as brief as an airplane flight, for example. The premiums depend critically on estimated probabilities, and in comparison with life insurance, property and casualty probabilities are notoriously difficult to estimate. Property and casualty insurance claims surge and ebb with changes in technology and in people's behavior.

Property and casualty profits have been eroded in recent years by the growing propensity of Americans to sue each other and the willingness of judges and juries to award large sums to the victors. Property and casualty firms have naturally responded to these trends by raising insurance premiums substantially, in some cases to levels that some customers literally cannot afford, or by discontinuing some kinds of insurance.

For example, vicarious liability laws generally hold an employer responsible for the actions of employees; in the 1980s these laws began to be extended to nonemployees. Between 1988 and 1990, Hertz Corporation spent $45 million settling large ($25,000-plus) insurance claims in New York City, mostly due to New York's vicarious liability laws, which hold that a car rental company is responsible for injuries caused by drivers who rent their cars.[1] In 1991 Hertz began imposing car rental surcharges of up to $56 a day on New York City residents. Budget Rent-A-Car and National Car Rental both stopped renting cars in the New York area.

Many property and casualty companies have tried to reduce their claim risk by becoming more diversified. For example, many have become *multiple-line companies*, which offer a wide range of insurance policies, hoping to protect their solvency if unfavorable events or legal developments cause large losses in a particular line of insurance. Similarly, many property and casualty companies now use *reinsurers* — insurance companies for insurance companies — who receive a share of an insurance company's premium income in return for agreeing to pay a share of its claims.

### Regulation

Because few individuals have the statistical, financial, and legal expertise to evaluate insurance contracts, state government agencies try to protect policyholders by regulating insurance companies. The McCarran-Ferguson Act of 1945 confirmed the long-standing practice that state governments have sole responsibility for regulating insurance companies. State insurance commissioners license insurance companies, monitor their financial condition, approve the language of insurance contracts, and establish rate structures (upper limits or lower limits, or both). State laws, regulations, and court decisions constrain the investments made by insurance companies. Because insurance companies are not confined to a single state, the National Association of Insurance Commissioners was established in 1871 to promote consistent regulations and uniform accounting rules, as well as to avoid unnecessary duplication in the supervision of insurance companies.

## MANAGING INSURANCE COMPANIES

The oldest continuously operated life insurance company in the world was established in Philadelphia in 1759 — the Corporation for Relief of Poor and Distressed Presbyterian Ministers and the Poor and Distressed Widows and Children of the Presbyterian Church, now known more simply as the Presbyterian Ministers' Fund. Insurance companies were the most prominent financial institutions in Colonial America. Although life insurance was then rare, fire and marine insurance were widespread. With time, marine insurance faded with

America's maritime industry, and automobile insurance bloomed. The biggest development, however, was the growth of life insurance.

Around the time of the Civil War, the idea of life insurance took hold and was rapidly spread by aggressive salesmen: "No one has as much endurance as the person who sells insurance." One innovation that fueled this growth was the introduction of small policies (as little as $25) peddled door to door, with payments collected weekly. A second innovation was the incorporation of systematic saving through tontine plans, as described in Example 18.3. By 1929, life insurance companies had $17.5 billion in assets, far more than was held by other types of insurance companies. Overall, insurance company assets in 1929 were larger than those of mutual savings banks and savings and loan associations combined, and about one-third the size of all commercial banks.

Early insurance business was itself risky, with crude statistics and frequent losses from wars, fires, earthquakes, and other disasters. On the asset side of their balance sheets, insurance companies — particularly life insurance companies — have been conservative investors, partly because of watchful regulatory agencies and partly because of a long tradition of not risking the funds upon which orphans will depend.

This conservative investment approach paid off in the 1930s when the insurance industry, and particularly life insurance companies, escaped relatively unscathed by the Great Depression. Because they largely shunned stocks and risky bonds, they avoided the painful collapse of financial markets. There was some increase in policy loans to hard-pressed households, but nothing approaching a liquidity crisis. Indeed, many life insurance companies were reluctant to write new policies in the 1930s because of a surplus of cash and a perceived shortage of attractive investment opportunities.

Figure 18.1, presented earlier in this chapter, compares the combined aggregate assets of life and property and casualty insurance companies with those of banks and thrifts since World War II. There are currently more than 4000 U.S. chartered insurance companies — of which 40 percent are life insurance companies and 60 percent are property and casualty companies. Like the banking industry, the U.S. insurance industry has thousands of very small firms — far more companies than in other countries. Japan has a total of 24 life insurance companies and 23 property and casualty companies.

Figure 18.2 compares the assets of life insurance companies with those of property and casualty companies since 1945. While the assets of life insurance companies are still much larger than those of property and casualty companies, Figure 18.3 shows that there has been a gradual, modest erosion of their relative importance. In 1945, life insurance companies held 88 percent of total industry assets; in 1990, they held 73 percent.

One potentially important change in recent years has been the adoption of a holding-company organizational structure. This arrangement gives insurance companies the opportunity to diversify into other forms of financial intermediation. For example, regulatory agencies traditionally have kept insurance companies from issuing debt. A holding-company structure circumvents this

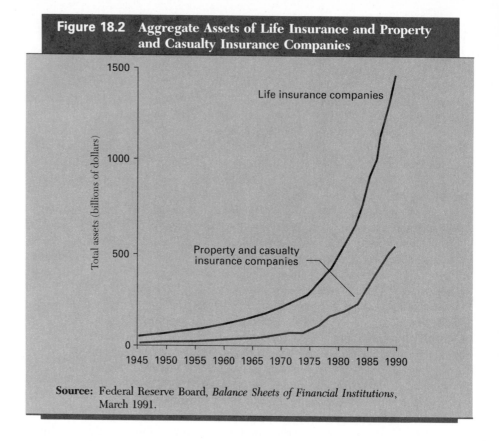

**Figure 18.2   Aggregate Assets of Life Insurance and Property and Casualty Insurance Companies**

**Source:** Federal Reserve Board, *Balance Sheets of Financial Institutions*, March 1991.

restriction by allowing the parent company to issue debt. As another example, a holding-company umbrella can allow the introduction of other financial services such as a mutual fund subsidiary. Similarly, some life insurance companies offer property and casualty insurance through a subsidiary, and some property and casualty companies offer life insurance through a subsidiary. Insurance companies are increasingly trying to straddle financial markets and use their sizable assets to compete for lucrative business.

Insurance companies employ a large number of people with a wide variety of specialized skills. Each insurance company has its own sales department; in addition, independent insurance agents sell insurance offered by several different insurance companies. Marketing is particularly important to insurance companies because they rely on the law of large numbers to reduce their risk exposure. An insurance company's claims department verifies and settles insurance claims. For routine cases, the insurance agent who sold the policy will usually handle the claim. Actuaries quantify risks and specify rate structures that will be profitable. The investments department manages the insurance company's asset portfolio and is of particular interest to our understanding of financial assets and institutions.

## Figure 18.3 Life Insurance and Property and Casualty Insurance Company Assets as a Fraction of Total Insurance Assets

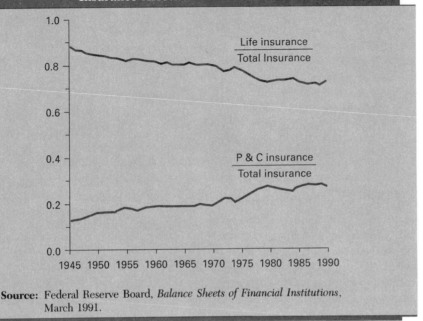

**Source:** Federal Reserve Board, *Balance Sheets of Financial Institutions*, March 1991.

## EXAMPLE 18.4 *Demutualization*

A stock ownership company issues stock and is owned by its stockholders; a mutual insurance company is legally owned by the policyholders — although, in practice, the policyholders have little if any control over the management of the company. Less than 5 percent of life insurance companies are mutually owned, but mutual companies are generally long-established and very large, holding roughly half of all life insurance company assets. Two-thirds of property and casualty insurance companies are stockholder-owned, and they own three-fourths of aggregate property and casualty assets.

For many years, mutual insurance companies had lower state regulatory net-worth requirements and paid lower federal income taxes, in comparison with stockholder-owned insurance companies. Changes in state and federal laws have now largely eliminated these advantages, and insurance companies have been moving away from mutual ownership because of difficulties in generating net worth internally.

State insurance commissions set net-worth requirements as a percentage of a company's assets. These minimum capital requirements consequently can restrict the ability of insurance companies to expand and, in extreme cases, can force liquidation of the company. For example, if there is a 10 percent net-worth requirement and a company has $5 million in net worth, it cannot have more than $50 million in assets.

The only way for a mutual insurance company to increase its net worth is through retained earnings — a slow and unreliable process. However, a mutual insurance company can increase its net worth substantially and quickly by converting from a mutual company to a stock-ownership company and selling shares of stock to raise capital. "Demutualization" is the awkward word used to describe this conversion from a mutual organization to a stockholder-owned organization.

## Insurance Companies as Financial Intermediaries

Insurance companies are financial intermediaries: they sell financial obligations to some people and buy securities from others. Insurance companies are most similar to banks and thrifts on the asset side of their balance sheets, in that they invest in similar financial assets and are concerned with similar questions of risk and return. The primary difference is on the liability side of the balance sheets, where insurance company "withdrawals" depend heavily on the occurrence of insured events, such as fire and death.

Tables 18.2 and 18.3 show the aggregate June 1991 balance sheets of life insurance companies and property and casualty insurance companies. Insurance company funds come primarily from insurance premiums and from insured pension plans that they manage for businesses. For a life insurance company, the "reserves" liability shown in Table 18.2 refers to the estimated present value of

**Table 18.2   Life Insurance Company Assets and Liabilities, June 1991 (Billions of Dollars)**

| Assets | | Liabilities | |
|---|---|---|---|
| Cash | 4.9 | Life insurance reserves | 387.1 |
| Money-market funds | 12.8 | Pension fund reserves | 830.7 |
| Commercial paper | 30.5 | Other liabilities | 128.2 |
| Policy loans | 68.6 | | |
| Bonds | 797.9 | | |
| Mortgages | 259.2 | | |
| Corporate stock | 144.2 | | |
| Real assets | 27.0 | | |
| Other assets | 104.3 | Net worth | 103.4 |
| | 1449.4 | | 1449.4 |

**Source:** Federal Reserve Board, *Flow of Funds Accounts, Second Quarter 1991.*

its insurance obligations — including death benefits, medical expenses, and annuity payments — net of the present value of future premium payments from those who are currently insured. The "loss reserves" shown in Table 18.3 perform a similar function for property and casualty companies; however, their statutory accounting practices generally ignore the time value of money and simply add up the undiscounted estimates of future claims. Because property and casualty insurance is generally short term, the distortion is not as severe as it would be if life insurance companies ignored present values.

Table 18.2 shows that life insurance company assets are heavily concentrated in long-term bonds, mortgages, and corporate stock. Because their insurance premiums and pension contributions provide a steady inflow of funds, life insurance companies hold very little cash (currency and checking account balances). Because their liabilities are long term, life insurance companies hold relatively few short-term assets.

Of the $797.9 billion in bonds shown in Table 18.2, $587.6 billion are corporate bonds. Life insurance companies have long been the largest single holders of corporate bonds, and in 1991 life insurance companies held roughly half of all outstanding U.S. corporate bonds. Most of these bonds were acquired through private placements rather than public offerings. Privately placed bonds are very illiquid, but life insurance companies are more concerned with locking in high rates of return than with liquidity. Life insurance companies are, of course, keenly interested in assessing corporate default risk, because they own so many corporate bonds.

Unlike commercial banks and thrifts, insurance companies are generally allowed to invest freely in corporate stock and real estate. While they do hold substantial amounts of stock, their enthusiasm is restrained by the fact that when calculating an insurance company's capital (or net worth), state insurance commissions generally value corporate stocks at market value and bonds at cost. Insurance companies are consequently wary of investing heavily in stock, fearing that a drop in the stock market will reduce their net worth sharply, leading the

**Table 18.3   Property and Casualty Insurance Company Assets and Liabilities, June 1991 (Billions of Dollars)**

| Assets | | Liabilities | |
|---|---|---|---|
| Cash and reserves | 6.4 | Loss reserves | 400.0 |
| Repos | 26.0 | Other liabilities | 0.3 |
| Bonds | 352.5 | | |
| Mortgages | 6.9 | | |
| Corporate stock | 103.6 | | |
| Real assets | 10.0 | | |
| Other assets | 50.5 | Net worth | 155.6 |
| | 555.9 | | 555.9 |

**Source:** Federal Reserve Board, *Flow of Funds Accounts, Second Quarter 1991.*

state insurance commission to limit the amount of insurance they can write or, in the worst possible case, seizing the company.

In the aggregate, life insurance net worth was equal to 7 percent of total assets in June of 1991, giving the industry 14:1 leverage:

$$\text{Life insurance leverage} = \frac{\text{total assets}}{\text{net worth}} = \frac{\$1449.4 \text{ billion}}{\$103.4 \text{ billion}} = 14.0$$

Table 18.3 shows that property and casualty companies had an aggregate net worth equal to 28 percent of total assets, giving them 3.6:1 leverage:

$$\text{Property and casualty leverage} = \frac{\text{total assets}}{\text{net worth}} = \frac{\$555.9 \text{ billion}}{\$155.6 \text{ billion}} = 3.6$$

State regulators require property and casualty insurance companies to have more net worth (and less leverage) than life insurance companies because their insurance claims are much less predictable.

Because their cash inflow is more volatile and their liabilities are shorter term, property and casualty companies hold somewhat more short-term assets than do life insurance companies. They also have traditionally held proportionately more corporate stock because damage claims tend to rise with inflation and the stock market may be a hedge against inflation.

Property and casualty insurance companies are subject to relatively high income tax rates and consequently are heavy purchasers of tax-exempt municipal securities. The Tax Reform Act of 1986 requires property and casualty companies to pay some taxes on municipal securities (the specific rules are quite complex), but there are still tax advantages to holding municipal bonds, and property and casualty companies continue to be large holders. Life insurance companies hold virtually no municipal bonds, but 40 percent of the bonds held by property and casualty companies are munis. Two-thirds of property and casualty munis mature in more than 10 years.

## Matching Assets and Liabilities

Because the major liabilities of life insurance companies are long-term contractual obligations to pay death benefits and annuities, long-term assets are appropriate for insulating their portfolios from interest-rate risk. It is not surprising then that life insurance company assets are heavily weighted toward long-term bonds and mortgages. Long-term assets that match the long-term liabilities of insurance companies can protect their profits and net worth from fluctuations in interest rates. If the actuarial probabilities are estimated accurately and the insurance company earns a rate of return that is larger than the interest rate used in calculating insurance premiums, it is sure to be profitable.

The liabilities of property and casualty insurance companies are shorter term than those of life insurance companies, and property and casualty companies therefore hold somewhat shorter-term assets. In recent years, property and casualty companies have increasingly used financial futures and options to further reduce their exposure to interest-rate risk.

**Table 18.4  Bond Results When Interest Rates Stay at 10 Percent**

| Year | Future Value of Coupons | Bond Price | Total Future Value | Realized Rate of Return (%) |
|------|------|------|------|------|
| 1 | $ 100.00 | $1,000.00 | $1,100.00 | 10.00 |
| 2 | 210.00 | 1,000.00 | 1,210.00 | 10.00 |
| 3 | 331.00 | 1,000.00 | 1,331.00 | 10.00 |
| 4 | 464.10 | 1,000.00 | 1,464.10 | 10.00 |
| 5 | 610.51 | 1,000.00 | 1,610.51 | 10.00 |
| 6 | 771.56 | 1,000.00 | 1,771.56 | 10.00 |
| 7 | 948.72 | 1,000.00 | 1,948.72 | 10.00 |
| 8 | 1,143.59 | 1,000.00 | 2,143.59 | 10.00 |
| 9 | 1,357.95 | 1,000.00 | 2,357.95 | 10.00 |
| 10 | 1,593.74 | 1,000.00 | 2,593.74 | 10.00 |
| 11 | 1,853.12 | 1,000.00 | 2,853.12 | 10.00 |
| 12 | 2,138.43 | 1,000.00 | 3,138.43 | 10.00 |
| 13 | 2,452.27 | 1,000.00 | 3,452.27 | 10.00 |
| 14 | 2,797.50 | 1,000.00 | 3,797.50 | 10.00 |
| 15 | 3,177.25 | 1,000.00 | 4,177.25 | 10.00 |
| 16 | 3,594.97 | 1,000.00 | 4,594.97 | 10.00 |
| 17 | 4,054.47 | 1,000.00 | 5,054.47 | 10.00 |
| 18 | 4,559.92 | 1,000.00 | 5,559.92 | 10.00 |

Consider, for instance, an 18-year Treasury bond with a maturation value of $1000, paying annual coupons of $100, and selling for par with a 10 percent yield to maturity. The duration is 9.02 years. Table 18.4 traces the future value of the coupons if these are reinvested at 10 percent and the market value of the bond if the yield to maturity stays at 10 percent. At the end of 1 year, the bond pays one $100 coupon and has 17 years yet to run. With the yield to maturity still equal to the coupon rate (10 percent), the bond continues to sell for par, $1000. Thus the value of the investment has grown to $1100, representing a 10 percent realized rate of return. After another year, a second $100 coupon is paid and the reinvestment of the first coupon has earned 1 year's interest at a 10 percent annual rate, giving a future value for the coupons of $210. With the yield to maturity still 10 percent, the price of the bond stays at $1000, and the total $1210 future value (coupons plus bond) represents a 10 percent realized annual rate of return, compounded annually. And so it goes, period after period. The bond continues to sell for par while the reinvested coupons accumulate, providing a realized annual rate of return of 10 percent.

What if interest rates do not stay at 10 percent? We know from Chapter 4 that, at maturity, the realized rate of a return on a bond, including the reinvested coupons, is higher or lower than the quoted yield to maturity depending on

| | | | | |
|:---:|:---:|:---:|:---:|:---:|
| **Table 18.5   Bond Results When Interest Rates Fall to 9 Percent** | | | | |
| Year | Future Value of Coupons | Bond Price | Total Future Value | Realized Rate of Return (%) |
| 1 | $   100.00 | $1,085.44 | $1,185.44 | 18.54 |
| 2 | 209.00 | 1,083.13 | 1,292.13 | 13.67 |
| 3 | 327.81 | 1,080.61 | 1,408.42 | 12.09 |
| 4 | 457.31 | 1,077.86 | 1,535.17 | 11.31 |
| 5 | 598.47 | 1,074.87 | 1,673.34 | 10.85 |
| 6 | 752.33 | 1,071.61 | 1,823.94 | 10.54 |
| 7 | 920.04 | 1,068.05 | 1,988.10 | 10.31 |
| 8 | 1,102.85 | 1,064.18 | 2,167.02 | 10.15 |
| 9 | 1,302.10 | 1,059.95 | 2,362.06 | 10.02 |
| 10 | 1,519.29 | 1,055.35 | 2,574.64 | 9.92 |
| 11 | 1,756.03 | 1,050.33 | 2,806.36 | 9.83 |
| 12 | 2,014.07 | 1,044.86 | 3,058.93 | 9.77 |
| 13 | 2,295.34 | 1,038.90 | 3,334.23 | 9.71 |
| 14 | 2,601.92 | 1,032.40 | 3,634.32 | 9.66 |
| 15 | 2,936.09 | 1,025.31 | 3,961.40 | 9.61 |
| 16 | 3,300.34 | 1,017.59 | 4,317.93 | 9.57 |
| 17 | 3,697.37 | 1,009.17 | 4,706.54 | 9.54 |
| 18 | 4,130.13 | 1,000.00 | 5,130.13 | 9.51 |

whether the rate of return earned on the reinvested coupons is larger or smaller than the yield to maturity.

Table 18.5 shows the case of a general decline in interest rates to 9 percent. The price of the bond initially rises by about 9 percent (as predicted by the 9-year duration), and together with the $100 coupon, the total investment has a realized return of 18.54 percent. As time passes and interest rates stay at 9 percent, the price of the bond falls inexorably toward its $1000 maturation value, and the reinvested coupons continue to earn 9 percent a year. Comparing Tables 18.4 and 18.5, the price of the bond is higher with a 9 percent interest rate every period until maturity (the good news), but the value of the reinvested coupons is lower in every single period (the bad news). Overall, a 9 percent interest rate increases the total future value (bond price plus reinvested coupons) in the early years but decreases it in the later years, when the reinvested coupons become more important. At maturity, the reinvestment of the coupons at 9 percent rather than 10 percent reduces the final future value from $5559.92 to $5130.13, representing a 9.51 percent rather than 10 percent annual rate of return.

Table 18.5 also shows that whether the interest rate is 10 or 9 percent, the future value is approximately the same after 9 years, which is the duration of the bond. That is, remarkably enough, for a horizon equal to the duration, the future value of a bond and its reinvested coupons is not affected by (small) changes in interest rates.

**Table 18.6  Bond Results When Interest Rates Rise to 11 Percent**

| Year | Future Value of Coupons | Bond Price | Total Future Value | Realized Rate of Return (%) |
|------|------------------------|-----------|-------------------|----------------------------|
| 1  | $ 100.00  | $ 924.51  | $1,024.51 | 2.45  |
| 2  | 211.00    | 926.21    | 1,137.21  | 6.64  |
| 3  | 334.21    | 928.09    | 1,262.30  | 8.07  |
| 4  | 470.97    | 930.18    | 1,401.15  | 8.80  |
| 5  | 622.78    | 932.50    | 1,555.28  | 9.23  |
| 6  | 791.29    | 935.08    | 1,726.36  | 9.53  |
| 7  | 978.33    | 937.93    | 1,916.26  | 9.74  |
| 8  | 1,185.94  | 941.11    | 2,127.05  | 9.89  |
| 9  | 1,416.40  | 944.63    | 2,361.03  | 10.02 |
| 10 | 1,672.20  | 948.54    | 2,620.74  | 10.11 |
| 11 | 1,956.14  | 952.88    | 2,909.02  | 10.19 |
| 12 | 2,271.32  | 957.69    | 3,229.01  | 10.26 |
| 13 | 2,621.16  | 963.04    | 3,584.20  | 10.32 |
| 14 | 3,009.49  | 968.98    | 3,978.47  | 10.37 |
| 15 | 3,440.54  | 975.56    | 4,416.10  | 10.41 |
| 16 | 3,918.99  | 982.87    | 4,901.87  | 10.45 |
| 17 | 4,450.08  | 990.99    | 5,441.08  | 10.48 |
| 18 | 5,039.59  | 1,000.00  | 6,039.59  | 10.51 |

To confirm this conclusion, Table 18.6 shows the case of a rise in interest rates to 11 percent, which reduces the bond's price during every period prior to maturation and simultaneously increases the value of the reinvested coupons. The total value and the realized rate of return at maturity are pulled up by the above–10 percent rate of return on the reinvested coupons. The date where the reduced value of the bonds is just offset by the increased value of the coupons is again the duration, 9 years. Figure 18.4 shows this relationship graphically.

If an investor plans to hold an asset for a horizon that is equal to the asset's duration, the investment is said to be **immunized**, in that its realized rate of return is constant regardless of whether interest rates rise or fall. Thus an investor who has a definite horizon can minimize interest-rate risk by holding securities with a duration equal to that horizon. A young couple needing $30,000 for a downpayment on a house 5 years hence can buy bonds with a duration of 5 years. A family needing $100,000 for their child's college education 15 years from now can buy bonds with a 15-year duration. A life insurance company expecting to pay $1 million 30 years from now can hold bonds with a 30-year duration.

Thus insurance companies not only can use asset and liability durations to stabilize their net worth, but to the extent that they can identify the timing of their future obligations, they also can immunize these liabilities by choosing

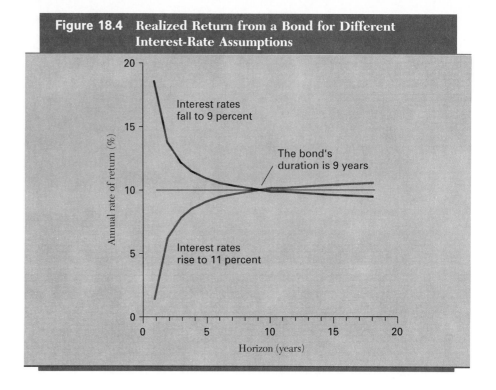

**Figure 18.4    Realized Return from a Bond for Different Interest-Rate Assumptions**

assets with matching durations — thereby locking in their future realized returns. Both these goals argue for a portfolio of long-duration assets, and this is what they have chosen. In sharp contrast to thrifts, who have short-term liabilities and long-term assets, insurance companies — particularly life insurance companies — have long-term liabilities and long-term assets.

## SUMMARY

Life insurance companies and property and casualty insurance companies offer a variety of insurance policies and annuities that are intended to protect households and businesses from unexpected financial hardship. The socially useful risk-pooling that is accomplished by insurance companies is based on the law of large numbers: although we do not know which particular individuals will experience bad luck, we may be able to estimate accurately the fraction of a large group who will be unlucky.

There is, however, an important distinction between the idiosyncratic risk that can be diversified away and the macro risk that is not reduced merely by increasing the number of policies. Even the largest insurance companies are vulnerable to macro risk. Insurance companies also must be concerned with adverse selection (when people self-select in ways that the insurance company cannot identify) and moral hazard (when people become more careless after obtaining insurance).

Insurance premiums are based on probabilities estimated by actuaries and on interest rates, since insurance premiums are invested by insurance companies until needed to pay benefits. Insurance companies are thus financial intermediaries with a regular contractual inflow of premiums and savings and a statistically predictable outflow of funds for insurance benefits.

The percentage change in an asset's present value resulting from a 1 percentage point change in the required return is approximately equal to its duration. Increases in interest rates reduce the present value (and market price) of an asset's future cash flow but also increase the returns that can be earned on the reinvested cash flow. An increase in interest rates is bad news in the short run but good news in the long run. An asset's duration determines the horizon over which the change in an asset's market price is just offset by the change in the value of the reinvested cash flow, leaving the total future value unaffected.

Insurance companies have long-term liabilities and consequently invest in long-term assets to protect their net worth from unexpected increases in interest rates and to protect their future realized returns from unexpected decreases in interest rates.

## IMPORTANT TERMS

| | |
|---|---|
| actuaries | macro risk |
| adverse selection | micro risk |
| idiosyncratic risk | moral hazard |
| immunized | systematic risk |
| law of large numbers | term life insurance |
| life annuity | |

## EXERCISES

1. Use the data in Table 18.1 to estimate the probability of death within a year for a 55-year-old woman if the expected value of a $100,000 life insurance policy is equal to half its cost.

2. Following are some recent Swedish mortality data, showing the percentage of those in the specified age group that died during the year.[2] What prices would an insurance company have to charge for 1-year $100,000 policies so that the expected value of each payout is equal to half the price?

| Age | Male (%) | Female (%) |
|---|---|---|
| 20 | 0.095 | 0.036 |
| 40 | 0.221 | 0.117 |
| 60 | 1.427 | 0.681 |
| 80 | 9.774 | 6.282 |
| 100 | 51.999 | 46.756 |

3. Assume that the probability that a 25-year-old U.S. woman will die within a year is 0.00065. If 20,000 such women each contribute $X$ dollars to an insurance fund that will invest the money for a year at 8 percent and at the end of the year pays $1 million to the beneficiaries of any of these women who died during the year, for what value of $X$ will the insurance fund just have enough money to cover the expected value of the year-end benefits?

4. (*continuation*) Does your answer to the preceding exercise depend on the number of 25-year-old women who participate? What advantage is there to having a large number of women participate?

5. For $100,000, an insurance company purchased a 25 percent stake in a venture that was estimated to have a 0.20 probability of being worth $4 million (giving their 25 percent stake a value of $1 million) and a 0.80 probability of turning out to be worthless. Unexpected difficulties have caused the insurance company's managers to revise these estimates. Now they believe that there is a 0.10 probability that the venture will be worth $3 million and a 0.90 probability that it will be worthless. One of the other partners has offered to buy the insurance company's 25 percent stake for $80,000. If the insurance company is risk neutral, should it accept this offer?

6. Prior to their summer 1990 release, an independent movie industry analyst estimated the projected profit under two scenarios — hit or dud — for the five movies listed in the following table.[3] Assuming, unrealistically, that these are the only two possible outcomes, which of these five movies has the highest required hit probability for the expected value of the projected profit to be zero?

| Movie | Projected profit (millions) | |
| --- | --- | --- |
| | If a Hit | If a Dud |
| *Another 48 Hours* | $100 | − $47 |
| *Days of Thunder* | 101 | − 56 |
| *Dick Tracy* | 111 | − 47 |
| *Die Hard II* | 83 | − 69 |
| *Total Recall* | 102 | − 16 |

7. A promoter has scheduled an outdoor rock concert for April 15 in New Jersey. If the weather turns out to be good, he will make a profit of $600,000; if the weather is bad, he will lose $300,000. What is the expected value of his profit if there is a 0.6 probability of good weather and a 0.4 probability of bad weather? For what probability of good weather is the expected value of his profit equal to zero?

8. (*continuation*) If the probability of good weather is 0.6, what is the expected value of an insurance policy that will pay the promoter $900,000 if there is bad weather, guaranteeing him a $600,000 profit (before deducting the cost of the insurance policy) no matter what the weather?

9. A break in a barrier sandbar is threatening to wash away shorefront property, but federal law requires homeowners to allow the break to close naturally. One of the threatened homes will be worthless if the house and land underneath are washed away or else worth $2 million if the break closes before washing away the property. If an insurance company estimates that there is a 0.2 probability that the property will be washed away and a 0.8 probability that it won't, how much must it charge to insure this property in order for the cost of the policy to be twice its expected value? Why

would a rational homeowner buy such an expensive policy?

10. For each of the following three events, predict whether the event will directly increase, reduce, or have virtually no effect on life insurance premiums.

   a. A cancer treatment increases life expectancies.

   b. The average age of marriage increases.

   c. Interest rates increase.

11. It is less expensive to buy life insurance for a child, naming the parents as beneficiaries, than to buy life insurance for a parent, naming the children as beneficiaries. Why? Why do you suppose that, nonetheless, it is much more common to buy life insurance for a parent than for a child?

12. How can a property and casualty company that specializes in earthquake insurance diversify its earthquake policies to reduce its risk of bankruptcy?

13. Describe the macro and micro risks involved in issuing automobile collision insurance policies.

14. Many professional and social organizations offer group life insurance to their members with no physical examination required, leading some people to join these organizations just to take advantage of the life insurance. Explain why the cost of such insurance is either higher or lower than the cost of insurance when the policyholder must pass a physical examination.

15. With decreasing term life insurance, the annual premiums are constant but the size of the death benefit declines over time. Why would anyone buy such a policy?

16. "Term life insurance is perverse, because you must die in order to get any money back from the insurance company." Pretend that you are an agent for a company that sells only term insurance and explain the advantages of this kind of life insurance policy.

17. Explain the error in this explanation of the law of large numbers:

   *According to this law, one cannot determine the probability that an individual will die (or become disabled, or have an automobile accident, or lose a home in a fire) in a given period. However, the number of persons among a large group who will die or face other losses in a period is more predictable.*[4]

18. Why do banks require people with mortgages to insure their houses?

19. Under legislative and judicial pressures, life insurance companies have been moving toward "unisex" rates, in which males and females pay equal premiums. Explain why men gain and women lose, or vice versa, from unisex life insurance premiums.

20. (*continuation*) Does the adverse-selection principle imply that unisex pricing of life insurance will encourage women to buy more or less life insurance?

21. In 1989 First Executive had $60 billion in life insurance policies and $19 billion in assets. How can an insurance company legitimately issue policies that are worth much more than its assets?

22. Collapsing junk bond prices reduced the market value of First Executive's bond portfolio in 1989 and 1990. After the stock market closed on Friday, January 19, 1990, First Executive announced that it was recording a $515 million loss on its bond portfolio and that it had a further loss of $1.4 billion that had not yet been recorded. The following Monday, the aggregate market value of First Executive stock fell by $250 million. Give a plausible, rational explanation of why the aggregate market value did not fall by $1.9 billion on that Monday.

23. (*continuation*) After First Executive's announcement, people stopped buying life insurance from the company. Why?

24. "Insurance companies tend to be leveraged at between 10 and 20:1 for life companies and 4 and 5:1 for casualty companies."[5] If you were assigned to estimate the leverage ratio for an insurance company, which of these data would you use and how: before-tax profits, after-tax profits, assets, liabilities, net worth, or stock price?

25. The traditional net-cost method of comparing life insurance policies is explained by Consumers Union: "You add up the premium you will pay over some period (say 20 years). Then you subtract the dividends you expect to receive (if any), and the cash value you can get by turning the policy in at the end of the period (if it's a cash-value type policy)."[6] Could a policy that is profitable to an insurance company have a negative net cost? How would you recommend comparing the costs of different life insurance policies?

26. An insurance company needs to price fire insurance for a house worth $200,000. If it wants the cost of the insurance to be twice the size of the expected value of the policy and uses the probabilities shown below, how much should it charge for a policy with no deductible? With a $20,000 deductible?

| Fire Damage | Probability |
| --- | --- |
| $0 | 0.990 |
| $20,000 | 0.008 |
| $200,000 | 0.002 |

27. A household is considering buying fire insurance for a house that is worth $H$. Assuming, unrealistically, that there are only two possible outcomes, there is a probability $P$ that the house will be destroyed by a fire and a probability $1 - P$ that it will not be damaged at all by fire. The household must choose what fraction $k$ ($0 < k < 1$) of the house's value to insure. The insurance costs $kC$ and pays $kH$ in the event of fire. If the household wants to maximize the expected value of its wealth, under what conditions will it fully insure the house (choose $k = 1$)?

28. A best-selling investments book notes that

    *Term-insurance premiums escalate sharply when you reach the age of sixty or seventy or higher. If you still need insurance at that point, you will find that term insurance has become prohibitively expensive. But the major risk at that point is not premature death; it is that you will live too long.*[7]

    How can living too long be a financial risk?

29. Insurance company accountants are allowed to value the company's bonds at cost even if the market value is only 25 percent of cost so long as the company does not plan to sell the bonds and can reasonably expect to receive the coupons and principal. Explain why this accounting practice may give a misleading picture of the company's financial health.

30. Explain this reasoning:

    *A portfolio duration of eight years is about as long as one can obtain on conventional coupon-paying bonds, given double-digit interest rates, but investment horizons of 40 years are not uncommon for pension funds or life insurance companies. . . . such portfolios will surely suffer when interest rates decline, even though the associated temporary increase in market value . . . may create the illusion of investment success.*[8]

31. In most life insurance policies, the policyholder makes a constant monthly payment until he or she dies. How can this payment structure be profitable for an insurance company, since the chances of death increase with age?

32. An insurance company wants to price a $1 million life insurance policy (with no cash value before death) for an individual with a life expectancy of 50 years. Neglecting its administrative expenses and profit, the insurance company can invest at a 7 percent annual return and wants to have $1 million 50 years from now. How much should the insurance company charge if the policyholder makes a single payment today? If the policyholder makes 50 equal annual payments beginning today? (Just set up the appropriate equations, without doing the requisite calculations.)

33. Insurance companies often make a forward commitment to buy corporate bonds several months in advance of the actual transaction at a price to be determined by the level of interest rates at the time of the transaction. If the insurance company wants to protect itself against an unexpected increase in the price of these bonds, should it buy or sell bond futures?

34. You want to lock in a 10 percent return over the next 5 years using one of the three bonds described in Table A, each with a $1000 maturation value. What is the future value of each of these bonds, including reinvested coupons, 5 years from now if, immediately after purchasing the bond, interest rates drop to 9 percent and stay there? Rise to 11 percent and stay there? Which bond does a better job of guaranteeing a 10 percent realized return?

35. An article explaining duration used a graph showing that (a) bond price risk is highest when the bond is held only a short while and declines to a minimum when the holding period is equal to the bond's duration and (b) reinvestment risk is highest when the bond is held until maturity and declines to a minimum when the holding period is equal to the bond's duration. It concludes, "When a bond is held to its duration, the price risk and the reinvestment risk are at a minimum."[9] Explain why you disagree.

### Table A

| Bond | Maturity | Annual Coupon | Current Price | Yield to Maturity (%) |
|------|----------|---------------|---------------|------------------------|
| A | 5 years | $100 | $1,000.00 | 10 |
| B | 7 years | 150 | 1,243.42 | 10 |
| C | 10 years | 50 | 692.77 | 10 |

# C H A P T E R 19 Pension Funds

*Weathervanes and anemometers in the cities do not diminish the value of a wet finger aloft in the wilderness.*

**Robert Luskin**

When a nation's productivity increases, people can choose to produce more or to work less. During the past several decades, Americans have chosen to do both — to enjoy a higher standard of living and yet work fewer hours per day, fewer days per year, and fewer years during their increasingly long lives. People now retire at age 65 or earlier, looking forward to several years of hobbies, traveling, and other entertainment.

While retirement ages have been declining, life expectancies have been increasing, from less than 50 years in 1900 to nearly 80 years in 1990. In addition, the elderly in the United States usually do not live with their children or rely on their children for financial support. Although cause and effect are uncertain, the dissolution of the extended family requires people to provide — by savings or other means — for maintaining their standard of living after they retire and their wage income ceases.

A **pension plan** is a program that provides income for workers who retire or become disabled, usually in the form of an annuity that makes constant monthly payments until the employee dies or the employee's dependents exhaust their legal claims. The organization that administers the pension plan by collecting and disbursing funds as well as managing the plan's portfolio is called a **pension fund**. In actual practice, the terms *pension plan* and *pension fund* are often used interchangeably.

More than 95 percent of all U.S. workers are covered by the Social Security System, the largest and most well-known pension plan. In addition, about half of all workers — both private and public — are covered by pension plans established by their employers.

In this chapter we will look at why pension plans have become so commonplace — not only why people prepare for retirement, but why they use formal pension plans to do so. We will discuss some of the most important features of pension plans and see why the federal government has enacted laws to protect employee rights.

Pension funds are very important institutional investors, comparable in size to the insurance industry and the thrift industry. We will look at the types of assets that pension funds buy and the reasons for doing so, and we will examine their investment performance. We begin with a description of how pension plans operate.

# PROVIDING FOR RETIREMENT OR DISABILITY

Pension plans are either private or governmental. In a private pension plan, the employer makes payments (called *contributions*) on behalf of an employee into a pension fund that invests these funds and provides retirement or disability benefits to the employee. Self-employed individuals can set up private pension plans on their own behalf, to which they contribute money that is invested and will eventually provide income during retirement.

Almost all private pension programs are designed to secure the approval of the Internal Revenue Service (IRS) as a "qualified" plan, because then the employer contributions are a tax-deductible expense in the year they are made but are not taxable income for the employee that year. Pension contributions to a qualified plan are considered deferred wages, and the employee does not have to pay income taxes on them (or on the investment income earned in the plan) until the benefits are received. As explained in Example 19.1, tax deferment has persuasive financial advantages.

Most pension plans for state and local government employees are very similar to private pension plans, in that the government employer makes tax-deferred contributions on behalf of its employees, which are invested in various assets and provide retirement and disability benefits. One important difference is that private pension plans are subject to federal regulation, but state and local plans are supervised by state governments.

Pension plans for federal employees are different from private and state and local plans in that they are generally **pay-as-you-go plans**, in which retirement benefits are paid out of the federal government's current tax revenue rather than out of contributions invested on behalf of employees. The federal government also operates the Social Security program, which covers almost all private and public employees. Social Security is a pay-as-you-go program that provides retirement, death, and disability benefits that are financed almost entirely out of current tax revenue. We will now look at some of the details of accumulated savings plans and the Social Security System.

**EXAMPLE**
**19.1**          *The Financial Advantages of Tax Deferment*

Most retirement plans benefit from the fact that taxes are deferred: the investor avoids current income taxes on money put into the plan but must pay taxes later on money withdrawn from the plan. Many knowledgeable investment advisors claim that this tax-deferral is advantageous because income is shifted to retirement years, when the investor will presumably be in a low tax bracket. Others worry that by putting so much money into tax-deferral plans, they will actually be in the same, or an even higher, tax bracket when they retire.

However, the advantages of tax deferral do not hinge on lower future tax brackets. Even if the investor is in the same tax bracket throughout his or her entire life, tax deferral is still an extraordinarily powerful tax shelter. A simple rule summarizes the power of tax deferral: if the tax rate is the same when tax-deferred income is placed in the plan and when it is withdrawn, then the participant's implicit after-tax return is equal to the before-tax return earned while the money is in the plan.

To keep the arithmetic simple, consider an investor in a 50 percent tax bracket who puts $1000 of wage income into a tax-deferred plan for 1 year, earning a 10 percent (before-tax) rate of return. At the end of the year, she pays a 50 percent tax on the $1100 withdrawn from the plan, leaving $550. If, instead, she does not put $1000 into the tax-deferred plan, she must pay a $500 tax on this wage income immediately, leaving her only $500 left to invest. For this $500 to grow to the $550 provided by the tax-deferral plan, she will have to earn a 10 percent *after-tax* rate of return. Thus tax deferral allows the investor to earn an effective after-tax return that is equal to the retirement plan's 10 percent before-tax return.

If we use 5, 10, or 50 years, the principle is the same. Nor does the value of the before-tax rate of return matter, nor the tax bracket, so long as it is the same at the beginning and end. For a second example, consider a 28 percent tax bracket and $1000 invested in a tax-deferred retirement plan that earns 8 percent a year for 30 years. After 30 years of tax deferral, the initial $1000 grows to

$$\$1000(1.08)^{30} = \$10,062.66$$

and a 28 percent tax leaves $7245.11. If the investor does not put the $1000 in a tax-deferred plan, then she must pay an immediate 28 percent tax and will have only $720 to invest. What after-tax rate of return is needed for this $720 to grow to the $7245.11 provided by tax deferral? No surprise; it's 8 percent:

$$\$720(1.08)^{30} = \$7245.11$$

Again, the effective after-tax yield from tax deferral is equal to the plan's before-tax rate of return.

There are several implications. Any investor who is tempted to invest funds outside a tax-deferred plan should remember that he or she needs to earn an after-tax return outside the plan that is higher than the before-tax return on money inside the plan — no easy feat. A second implication is that tax-deferred plans shouldn't invest in tax-advantaged investments that offer low before-tax returns. It is foolish to invest tax-deferred funds in municipal bonds. The natural candidates are instead heavily taxed corporate and Treasury bonds, especially zero-coupon bonds (which give no cash flow but are taxed anyway).

What if the investor has no current savings to put into a tax-deferred plan? Suppose that our investor in a 50 percent tax bracket was considering putting $1000 of income in a retirement plan but has a $500 car repair bill. She may skip the retirement plan, pay the $500 income tax on her $1000 income, and use the remaining $500 to fix her car. Alternatively, she may be able to borrow $500 to fix her car and put her $1000 of before-tax income in a tax-deferred plan. As before, at a 10 percent interest rate, her tax-deferred plan will give her $550 after taxes at the end of a year. If the interest on her loan is tax deductible, at what loan rate does such borrowing make sense? If she borrows for a year at 20 percent, she will owe $500(1.20) = $600, of which $100 is tax deductible (saving her $50 in taxes), leaving a $550 out-of-pocket cost. The investment of borrowed funds in a tax-deferred plan is profitable if the plan's before-tax return is at least equal to the after-tax interest rate on the loan.

The one serious fly in the tax-deferral ointment is that money invested in such plans may be illiquid, in that it cannot be touched (or touched only with penalty) before retirement. An investor anticipating major preretirement expenses, such as a child's education or a vacation home, may want to keep funds in more liquid investments. However, some tax-deferred plans (for example, some tax-sheltered annuities) can be liquidated before retirement, and others, even though involving penalties for early withdrawal, may still be attractive, so powerful is the tax-deferral arithmetic.

## Accumulated Savings

Private pension plans and most state and local plans involve the accumulation of retirement contributions that are invested on behalf of employees. These contributions can be viewed as deferred wages, with the employee paid later — during retirement — for work that is performed now. Retirement contributions also can be thought of as contractual savings, income that cannot be spent now but must be saved for retirement.

There are two very different ways of determining the size of contributions. In a **defined-contribution plan**, each employee has a personal account to which contributions are credited, and the employee's retirement benefits depend on the size of these contributions and whatever rate of return the pension fund earns on them. In a defined-contribution plan, the pension fund essentially acts as a money manager, investing workers' savings on their behalf.

In a **defined-benefit plan**, in contrast, the employee's retirement benefits are specified, and the plan's sponsors must estimate the contributions that are required to meet these promised benefits. As with life insurance, such estimates depend on projected life expectancies and interest rates. Because the benefits, rather than the contributions, are specified, the employer, rather than the employee, profits if the pension fund's investments do well and suffers if they do poorly.

Of those workers covered by private pension funds, approximately half belong to defined-benefit plans and half to defined-contribution plans. Defined-benefit plans tend to be larger, since roughly two-thirds of all private pension fund assets are in defined-benefit plans and one-third are in defined-contribution plans.[1] Private pension plans can be further separated into **insured pension plans**, which are managed by life insurance companies, and **noninsured pension plans**, which are managed by a trustee, such as the trust department of a commercial bank.

Many defined-benefit pension plans base their retirement benefits on the employee's number of years of employment with the firm and the size of the worker's wages before retirement, intending that the retirement benefits for long-time employees will help them maintain an accustomed standard of living. A *career-average plan* is based on the average wages during the worker's entire employment with the firm; a *final-pay plan* averages wages during the last few years before retirement. If wages have been rising over time (because of inflation or productivity increases), the final-pay salary will be higher than the career-average salary.

Table 19.1 illustrates this point by showing the ratio of final-pay salary to career-average salary, when the final-pay salary is computed over the last 5 years of employment, for various assumptions about the annual rate of increase of wages and the number of years of employment with the firm. These calculations demonstrate that the final-pay salary can be much higher than the career-average salary. While a final-pay formula takes into account inflation while a person is working, neither formula protects the retirement benefits against an unexpected increase in the rate of inflation after retirement.

The ratio of annual retirement benefit to annual average salary is called the *replacement rate*. For instance, a firm might pay an employee at retirement at age 65 an annual benefit equal to 1 percent of the average pay during the final 5 years before retirement multiplied by the number of years of employment with the firm. The replacement rate in this case is equal to the number of years of employment multiplied by 1 percent. Someone who had worked for the firm for 20 years would receive an annual pension equal to 20 percent of the final-pay salary; someone who had worked 40 years would receive 40 percent.

In a defined-contribution plan, the pension fund's assets are always equal to its liabilities. In a defined-benefit plan, however, the value of the accumulated pension contributions may be larger or smaller than the plan's contractual obligations. A plan is said to be *underfunded* if the accumulated funds are inadequate and *overfunded* if they are excessive. Such funding gaps can be caused by misestimates of employee retirement ages and mortality or by unexpectedly low or high rates of return on the pension fund's portfolio. Defined-benefit plans become underfunded when the portfolio's rate of return is smaller than expected and overfunded when the return is surprisingly large.

**Table 19.1  The Ratio of Final-Pay Salary (Averaged Over the Final 5 Years) to Career-Average Salary**

| Annual Rate of Increase of Wages (%) | Number of years of employment | | |
|---|---|---|---|
| | 20 | 30 | 40 |
| 0 | 1.00 | 1.00 | 1.00 |
| 5 | 1.46 | 1.77 | 2.12 |
| 10 | 1.96 | 2.65 | 3.41 |

Another concern is whether the employee has **vested benefits**, meaning that an employee who leaves the firm before retirement is still entitled to retirement benefits based on the pension contributions that were made while the employee worked for the firm. In a *nonvested* plan, an employee who leaves the firm — voluntarily or involuntarily — loses all retirement benefits. As explained in Example 19.2, U.S. Senate hearings in the early 1970s revealed horror stories of long-time employees who were fired before the company's normal retirement age and consequently received no retirement benefits. Federal law now specifies minimum vesting standards that ensure that most employees are fully vested after 15 years.

EXAMPLE
19.2        *Pension Fund Victims*

Most workers rightly consider their pension benefits to be deferred income that belongs to them. Part of their wages has been invested on their behalf and will be returned to them when they retire. In the past, many people were shocked to find that they lost their pension benefits if they quit their jobs or were fired or if their employer went bankrupt, merged with another firm, or signed a contract with a new union. U.S. Senate hearings in the early 1970s revealed that workers often did not understand their pension plans and that many had been victimized by unreasonable rules.*

Dozens of disillusioned workers testified that even though thousands of dollars had been contributed to pension plans on their behalf, they received no pension benefits because their benefits were not vested and their employment was terminated before the company's official retirement age. A man who had worked for the Great Atlantic and Pacific Tea Company for 32 years, from age 19 to age 51, lost his job when the warehouse he worked at closed in 1970; because the company only paid retirement benefits to those who retired at age 55 or older, he received no benefits at all. Because of declining profits,

*U.S. Senate Committee on Labor and Public Welfare, Interim Report of Activities of the Private Welfare and Pension Plan Study, 1971 (Washington, D.C.: U.S. Government Printing Office, 1972).

Anaconda terminated a woman in 1971 who had worked for the company for 30 years, from age 18 to age 48; because she was not 60 years old, she lost all her retirement benefits.

Several cases of underfunded pension plans also were presented. For example, Studebaker closed an automobile plant in South Bend, Indiana, in 1964 and left 8500 employees without a fully funded pension plan. The pension fund had $24 million in assets, and it cost $22 million to purchase annuities for those employees who were currently retired or were eligible for retirement because they were 60 years old and had worked for the company for at least 10 years. Only $2 million was left to be divided among 4000 other employees who, in theory, had accumulated vested pension benefits. A typical employee, 40 years old with 20 years of employment at Studebaker, was given a lump-sum payment of $350.

The pension fund horror stories recounted at these Senate hearings laid the groundwork for the 1974 Employment Retirement Income Security Act (ERISA), which was intended to clarify and establish employee pension rights — including reasonable vesting rules as well as protection against underfunding.

Beyond these minimum standards, vesting details vary from plan to plan. Some plans give full vesting after 10 or 15 years of continuous employment with the firm, with no vesting before this cutoff. Other firms phase in vesting — for example, 25 percent vesting after 5 years, 30 percent after 6 years, and so on.

A pension plan is said to be *portable* if it moves with the employee from job to job, with the retirement benefits from the previous job merged with the benefits from the current job. A pension plan that is vested but not portable typically makes a single lump-sum payment to the employee when he or she changes jobs. From the standpoint of the employee, the most secure pension plan is fully funded, vested, and portable.

## The Social Security System

The formal name for the federal Social Security program is Old Age, Survivors, Disability and Health Insurance (OASDHI). It includes not only retirement pensions, but also medical insurance for the elderly, disability insurance, and benefits for widows, widowers, and the children of deceased parents.

Ninety-five percent of all wage earners belong to the Social Security System, including most government employees and virtually all privately employed and self-employed people. The Social Security System is financed by taxes on member earnings; these deductions show up on pay stubs as FICA (Federal Insurance Contributions Act) or OASDI (Old Age, Survivors and Disability Insurance). In 1991, Social Security taxes consisted of a 6.20 percent tax on wages up to $53,400 plus a 1.45 percent Medicare tax on wages up to $125,000. For those earning less than $53,400, this adds up to a 7.65 percent tax. This wage tax is matched by an equal employer contribution, doubling the effective tax rate to 15.30 percent. In 1991, Social Security taxes totaled $396 billion, as compared

**EXAMPLE**

**19.3**

## Pensions for College Professors

The Teachers Insurance and Annuity Association, College Retirement Equities Fund (TIAA-CREF) is a nationwide private nonprofit pension program for college teachers. In 1991 TIAA-CREF had 1 million active participants, 200,000 retired professors, and $99.6 billion in assets — an average of $80,000 per professor — making it the nation's largest pension fund.

TIAA-CREF is a defined-contribution plan, and its pension contracts are with individual professors, not with the college or university that happens to be employing them. The college or university that currently employs the professor makes tax-deferred contributions to TIAA-CREF on the professor's behalf, but these contributions and the income they earn belong to the professor — making the plan fully vested and portable. The plan is fully funded because it is a defined-contribution plan. A professor's retirement benefits are paid directly from TIAA-CREF, and their size depends on the individual professor's contributions and the income they have earned.

TIAA and CREF are two separate pension funds. TIAA was established in 1918; its premiums are invested in a diversified portfolio of business loans and mortgages, publicly traded bonds, and real estate. CREF premiums are invested in one of five separate accounts:

The *stock account*, established in 1952, is a diversified stock portfolio.

The *money-market account*, introduced in 1988, invests in Treasury bills, large CDs, and other money-market securities.

The *bond-market account*, introduced in 1990, invests in long-term bonds and mortgage-related (or other asset-backed) securities.

The *social-choice account*, introduced in 1990, invests in stocks, bonds, and money-market securities issued by socially responsible companies or governments. Companies are excluded, for example, if they have ties to South Africa, produce nuclear energy, or have a significant portion of their business involved in making or marketing weapons, alcoholic beverages, or tobacco products.

The *global-equities account*, introduced in 1992, invests at least 50 percent of its assets in foreign stocks and at least 25 percent in U.S. stocks, with the remaining 25 percent distributed as deemed appropriate.

Participants decide how to allocate their investments among TIAA and the five CREF accounts.

The stock account is by far the oldest and largest of the five CREF accounts. On December 31, 1991, the stock account had $44.0 billion in assets, of which 53 percent was indexed to the S&P 500, another 14 percent was indexed to U.S. stocks not included in the S&P 500, 18 percent was invested in selected U.S. stocks, 14 percent was invested in foreign securities, and 1 percent was in cash (money-market securities).

It is noteworthy that a large portion (currently almost 70 percent) of CREF's stock portfolio is chosen not by trying to identify undervalued stocks but by passively matching the U.S. stock market. This buy-and-hold philosophy is based on the assumption that the U.S. stock market is reasonably efficient and that it is consequently difficult to beat the market with active portfolio management. Instead, CREF tries to beat actively managed funds by minimizing its own transaction costs, management fees, and other expenses. The annual expenses for CREF's stock account average about 0.3 percent of its assets, which is much lower than for competing actively managed pension funds. During the 10-year period ending on December 31, 1989, the compounded annual rate of return on CREF's stock account was 17.66 percent, as compared with 17.45 percent for the S&P 500 and 15.39 percent for the 270 institutional stock portfolios monitored by Lipper Analytical Services.*

Because TIAA-CREF is a defined-contribution plan, participants bear the risk that the pension fund will be managed well or poorly. To date, it has been managed very well, and many college professors have been pleasantly surprised to find that their annual TIAA-CREF retirement income is substantially larger than the salary they earned when they were working.

*The TIAA-CREF Participant, *March 1, 1990, pp. 1–2.*

with $468 billion in personal income taxes. Most workers pay more Social Security taxes than income taxes, and their prospective Social Security pension is their largest single asset.

In determining eligibility for Social Security benefits, every year is divided into four 3-month periods; in each of these quarters, a worker who pays Social Security taxes on a specified minimum level of wages ($540 in 1991) earns one quarter of credit. Currently, workers with 40 quarters (10 years) of credits are eligible for Social Security benefits at retirement; the size of the benefits depends on a formula that takes into account the amount of Social Security taxes a person has paid and the number of quarters in which taxes have been paid.

Workers born before 1938 can choose a normal retirement after age 65 with full benefits or an early retirement after age 62 with 80 percent benefits. For those born after 1938, the normal retirement age gradually rises until it reaches age 67 for those born after 1959 (with 70 percent benefits for those who choose early retirement).

Although an individual's benefits depend on the amount of Social Security taxes that he or she has paid, the benefits do not rise proportionately with taxes — causing the replacement rate to decline with income. The system's current formula provides annual benefits for the average worker that are equal to 41 percent of annual wages before retirement. For workers who always paid the maximum Social Security tax, benefits are equal to 27 percent of the maximum income subject to Social Security tax.

One big difference between Social Security and private pensions is that Social Security payments are indexed to the rate of inflation. Every January,

**EXAMPLE
19.4**

## Is Social Security a Ponzi Scheme?

Workers save for retirement in a variety of ways: voluntary accumulations of stocks and bonds, employer contributions to private pension plans, and involuntary Social Security taxes. Beneath the financial details, the crucial point is that the value of what workers produce is greater than what they consume. Part of this surplus is purchased and consumed by those who are currently retired, using their private assets, pension benefits, and Social Security checks. The retired consume more than they produce, whereas workers produce more than they consume — anticipating that, when they are retired, they will be able to consume more than they produce. Stocks, bonds, pension plans, and the Social Security System facilitate this intergenerational chain letter. Each generation acquires its claims by providing for earlier generations; in return, they expect to be provided for by future generations.

This intergenerational chain letter sounds suspiciously like the Ponzi schemes described in Example 9.5. A primary difference between Social Security and a Ponzi scheme is that retirement benefits increase slowly over time, with the nation's population and output. The growth of the work force and productivity increase the aggregate amount produced by each generation and allow it to give the retired more than they gave the previous generation — in essence, a positive real rate of return. A slowdown in population growth or productivity growth would obviously strain this intergenerational chain letter.

The sacrifice that workers must make to provide for the retired depends on the number of retired people relative to the number of workers, which depends on the population growth rate: the faster the population is growing, the lower is the fraction of the population that is elderly. For a stylized example, imagine a society in which everyone lives for exactly 80 years. If the number of births each year is constant, say 3 million, then there are 3 million 1-year-olds, 3 million 2-year-olds, and so on up until age 80. There is zero population growth because the 3 million people dying at age 80 each year are matched by 3 million new births. There are $3(80) = 240$ million people in the country, of whom $3(15) = 45$ million are over the age of 65. The ratio of the number of people over 65 to the rest of the population is $45/240 = 0.1875$.

If, instead, the annual number of births increases by 2 percent each year, then there will be 2 percent more 1-year-olds than 2-year-olds, 2 percent more 2-year-olds than 3-year-olds, and so on (and the elderly will be a relatively small fraction of the population). Because every age bracket has 2 percent more people each year, the total population also increases by 2 percent annually. The accompanying figure shows the number of people in each age bracket for societies with 0, 1, and 2 percent population growth rates. (Each society's data have been scaled so that the total population is 240 million.) The ratio of the number of people over 65 to the rest of the population is 0.1875 for 0 percent

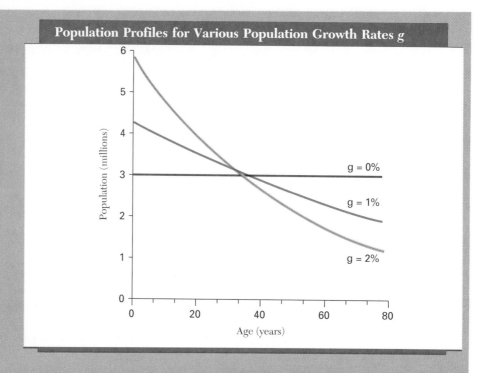

**Population Profiles for Various Population Growth Rates g**

population growth, 0.1323 for 1 percent growth, and 0.0892 for 2 percent growth.

These calculations illustrate how a decrease in the rate of population growth increases the fraction of the population that is elderly and consequently increases the fraction of national output that must be transferred from workers to the elderly to maintain their standard of living. Of course, the ratio of workers to beneficiaries depends not only on the fraction of the population that is elderly, but also on the fraction of the working-age population that is working.

There may be intergenerational strains from such demographic changes as slowing population growth, earlier retirement ages, or longer life expectancies. These demographic changes are, in fact, responsible for the fragility of the U.S. Social Security System. The ratio of workers to beneficiaries in the United States has fallen from 146 in 1940 to 22 in 1947, to 5.8 in 1957, to 3.1 in 1967, and to 2.6 in 1990. It is expected to fall below 2 by the year 2025.

Workers may resist giving up the output necessary to provide the retired with a standard of living comparable with their own. They may express this resistance as political opposition to increased Social Security taxes or through high levels of spending that push up prices and reduce the purchasing power of the retired generation's financial assets. In a 1990 Gallup poll, 53 percent of Americans between the ages 35 and 54 said that they do not think they will receive any Social Security retirement benefits.* This opinion is surely misinformed; nonetheless, it reflects an anxiety that may well have important political consequences.

*Melynda Dovel Wilcox, "The Fortysomething Generation Will Get Bigger Social Security Checks than Today's Retirees," Changing Times, January 1991, p. 22.

Social Security benefits are increased by the percentage increase in the consumer price index (CPI) during the preceding year. In 1990, 43 million Americans received Social Security retirement benefits averaging $566 per month ($6782 a year).

Unlike private pensions, in which contributions are invested and accumulate to provide retirement benefits, Social Security is a pay-as-you-go system in which Social Security taxes are used to pay benefits to the currently retired. The financial solvency of the Social Security System consequently depends on having enough workers paying taxes to finance the benefits of the retired.

# MANAGING PENSION FUNDS

Private pension funds began in the United States with the railroads in the 1870s and spread slowly in the early twentieth century. In 1929, fewer than 4 million workers were covered by pension plans, and the aggregate assets held by these plans were $500 million — only $125 per worker. The Social Security Act of 1935 established an initially modest federal retirement and disability program that was intended to be supplemented by private plans. However, private pension funds did not become significant until after World War II.

During World War II (and again during the 1950–1953 Korean War), wage and price controls and high taxes on corporate profits encouraged firms to pay workers through generous retirement plans. Money that a firm contributed to an employee pension fund was not subject to wage controls, even though employer and employee both realized that it was valuable compensation. Although firms were not allowed to pay high wages to attract good workers, they could lure them with generous pension plans. In addition, a firm's pension fund contributions were considered a tax-deductible expense and therefore were not subject to the large excess profit taxes that were levied during the war.

In 1949 the U.S. Supreme Court let stand a ruling by the National Labor Relations Board that pension benefits are deferred wages and, therefore, firms must bargain in good faith with unions over pension benefits along with other wages and working conditions. Prior to this ruling, many companies considered retirement benefits to be a gift, like a gold watch, for retiring employees and therefore not a binding obligation on the firm.

Another important milestone was the 1962 Self-Employed Individuals' Retirement Act (or Keogh Plan, after its Congressional sponsor, Eugene Keogh), which allows an employee who is not covered by a pension plan to put money in a tax-deferred Keogh account or **individual retirement account** (**IRA**). The specific rules are complicated and change frequently. The 1986 Tax Reform Act allows everyone, self-employed or not, to put up to $2000 of earned income (plus $250 for a nonworking spouse) into an IRA account annually. These contributions are fully tax deductible for employees who are not covered by a pension plan or earn less than $25,000 ($40,000 for married couples) and partially deductible for those earning up to $35,000 ($50,000 for married couples). In all cases, taxes are deferred on the IRA's interest income. Persons with self-employment income can make fully tax-deductible contributions to a Keogh plan of up to the lesser of $30,000 or 20 percent of their self-employment income, regardless of whether they are covered by other pension plans.

Withdrawals from IRA accounts and Keogh plans can begin at $59\frac{1}{2}$ and must begin by age $70\frac{1}{2}$. Any withdrawals before age $59\frac{1}{2}$ are subject to a 15 percent penalty tax in addition to the normal income taxes on retirement benefits.

## ERISA

U.S. Senate hearings in 1971 and 1972 disclosed that many private pension plans were apparently mismanaged and underfunded and had unreasonable vesting and portability requirements. The subsequent 1974 federal **Employment Retirement Income Security Act** (**ERISA**) was intended to ensure that private pension plans are financially sound and that pension fund trustees act solely in the interest of the plan's participants. ERISA also broadens the opportunities for persons who are self-employed or who work for companies that do not have retirement plans to make tax-deferred retirement contributions. ERISA does not apply to government retirement plans.

ERISA encourages trustees to specify formal objectives, guidelines, and management standards and requires plans to file annual audited financial statements with the federal government and to report their operations and financial condition to plan participants, written in language that the average participant can understand.

ERISA establishes actuarial guidelines that are intended to prevent underfunding problems. It also prohibits unreasonable vesting rules; its minimum vesting requirements ensure that most employees are fully vested after 15 years. ERISA increases portability by allowing workers who receive a lump-sum distribution of vested benefits when they change jobs to invest this distribution, without penalty, in a new tax-deferred pension plan, either with their new employer or on their own.

A federal agency, the Pension Benefit Guaranty Corporation (PBGC), was established to insure retirees' pension benefits against the default or termination of a pension fund. Sponsors of private defined-benefit pension plans are required to buy PBGC insurance, and the PBGC is authorized to seize mismanaged pension funds. In addition, if a company turns its pension fund obligations over to PBGC, it also must turn over all the plan's assets, and the PBGC has a claim on the company's own assets to cover the unfunded pension liability. PBGC's claim (up to 30 percent of the company's net worth) along with the Internal Revenue Service's tax claims take precedence over all other unsecured claims on the company's assets. In 1986, PBGC's own net worth had fallen to − $2 billion, and it was forced to triple its insurance premiums to stay afloat.[2] The PBGC now charges underfunded pension plans higher insurance premiums and also does not allow the voluntary termination of an underfunded plan.

Legally, a pension fund is a trust, and the managers of a trust are called *fiduciaries*. Fiduciary duties have traditionally been based on the **prudent man rule,** which requires an investment manager to use the same care and judgment that a prudent person would use with his or her own personal investments. Before ERISA, the fiduciary duties of pension fund managers were unclear, and some funds made seemingly unwise investments. For example, a 1973 book coauthored by Ralph Nader disclosed that the United Mine Workers' retirement fund had $75 million (44 percent of its assets) deposited in a bank checking account that paid no interest.[3]

The Senate hearings that preceded ERISA found that some pension plans invested heavily in securities issued by the employer. For example, the Woolworth Company had 35 percent of its pension plan's assets invested in Woolworth mortgages, real estate, and other property.[4] Such overlapping investments have the advantage of giving employees a stake in the firm, presumably providing an incentive to work hard and efficiently. However, they increase risk for employees. If the company fails, not only do contributions to the pension plan cease, but many of the plan's assets will be worthless. Overlapping investments also create a potential conflict of interest in that such investments may benefit the employer at the expense of the employees.

ERISA prohibits pension plans from investing more than 10 percent of their funds in employer assets and requires each fiduciary to act for the sole benefit of the plan's participants using "care, skill, prudence, and diligence." It encourages pension funds to diversify investments to reduce the risk of large losses. Those who breach these fiduciary duties are personally liable for the plan's losses.

## Assets and Liabilities

The growth of pension funds since World War II has been phenomenal. Figure 19.1 compares the total assets of pension funds, insurance companies, and thrifts since 1945. (These data do not include Social Security or retirement programs for federal workers, because these programs are financed out of current tax revenue and do not accumulate assets to provide for future benefits.) In 1945, aggregate pension fund assets were only one-fourth the size of aggregate thrift assets and were one-eighth the size of insurance company assets. In 1960, 21 million Americans were covered by pension plans with aggregate assets of $58.2

**Figure 19.1**    **Total Assets of Pension Funds, Thrifts, and Insurance Companies**

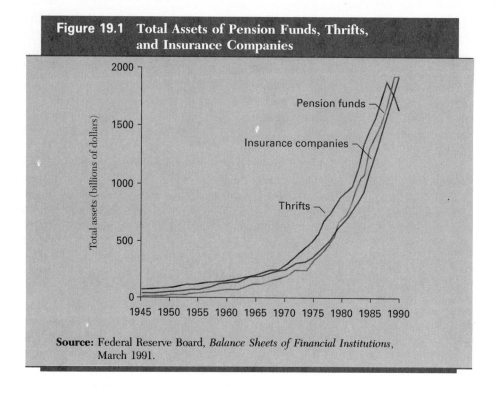

**Source:** Federal Reserve Board, *Balance Sheets of Financial Institutions*, March 1991.

billion — nearly $3000 per worker. In 1991, pension funds had $2 trillion in assets — $300 billion more than thrifts and virtually the same amount as insurance companies. The 20 largest U.S. pension funds on December 31, 1991, are listed in Table 19.2.

Table 19.3 shows the aggregate June 1991 balance sheet of pension funds. As in Figure 19.1, these data include private pension funds and state and local government retirement plans but exclude federal programs. As with insurance companies, the contractual liabilities of pension funds are called *reserves*. The reserves shown in Table 19.3 are, in theory, the estimated present value of pension fund death and disability benefits, net of the present value of future contributions from those who are currently covered. In practice, the Federal Reserve data in Table 19.3 assume that pension liabilities are exactly equal to assets. Pension fund liabilities are estimated by actuaries, and their validity depends on the accuracy of the assumed retirement ages, life expectancies, and portfolio rates of return. Because actuaries tend to make conservative estimates, pension funds are typically overfunded. In 1991 it was estimated that 76 percent of all U.S. single-employer pension funds are overfunded.[5]

On the asset side of their balance sheets, pension funds hold very little cash (currency and checking account deposits) because their outlays are very predictable and are generally smaller than the inflow of new contributions. Pension

**Table 19.2   Twenty Largest U.S. Pension Funds**

| Fund | Assets (billions of dollars) |
|---|---|
| TIAA–CREF | $99.6 |
| California Public Employees | 64.7 |
| New York State & Local | 50.1 |
| New York City | 48.9 |
| AT&T | 45.0 |
| General Motors | 40.8 |
| California State Teachers | 37.4 |
| New York State Teachers | 32.5 |
| New Jersey | 31.3 |
| General Electric | 31.1 |
| Texas Teachers | 29.5 |
| IBM | 29.0 |
| Florida State Board | 25.5 |
| Ohio Public Employees | 24.3 |
| State of Wisconsin | 22.8 |
| Ford Motor | 22.7 |
| E.I. du Pont | 20.5 |
| North Carolina Retirement | 20.3 |
| Ohio State Teachers | 20.2 |
| State of Michigan | 20.1 |

**Source:** "Top 1000 Funds," *Pensions & Investments*, January 20, 1992, p. 20.

**Table 19.3   Pension Fund Assets and Liabilities, June 1991 (Billions of Dollars)**

| Assets | | Liabilities | |
|---|---|---|---|
| Cash | 8.8 | Pension fund reserves | 2,052.1 |
| Time deposits | 68.5 | | |
| Money-market funds | 26.9 | | |
| Commercial paper | 36.0 | | |
| Bonds | 753.0 | | |
| Mortgages | 31.0 | | |
| Corporate stock | 1,122.4 | | |
| Real assets | 0.1 | | |
| Other assets | 5.4 | Net worth | 0.0 |
| | 2,052.1 | | 2,052.1 |

**Source:** Federal Reserve Board, *Flow of Funds Accounts, Second Quarter 1991.*

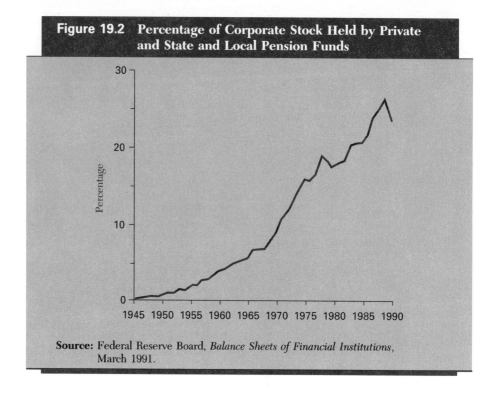

**Figure 19.2   Percentage of Corporate Stock Held by Private and State and Local Pension Funds**

**Source:** Federal Reserve Board, *Balance Sheets of Financial Institutions*, March 1991.

funds do hold some short-term securities that they consider to be desirable investments.

Because of their long-term retirement liabilities, pension funds are heavy purchasers of long-term bonds and corporate stock. At the end of World War II, pension funds held only $200 million in corporate stock, less than 0.2 percent of the total outstanding. Figure 19.2 shows that the fraction of outstanding stock held by pension funds has increased dramatically since then. In June of 1991, pension funds held $1122.4 billion in corporate stock, 27 percent of the total outstanding. The wealth of many middle-income Americans consists largely of their human capital, perhaps a house, and their pension fund. Through their pension funds, workers have become capitalists, owning a large part of corporate America!

Encouraged by ERISA to diversify, some pension funds hold real estate and foreign securities. Because pension funds are exempt from income taxes, they generally do not invest in municipal bonds, which have lower interest rates than comparably risky corporate bonds. The exception is state and local government retirement funds, which sometimes find it politically expedient (or have a legal mandate) to purchase municipal bonds issued by the employees' government agency.

## Portfolio Management

A pension fund is a financial intermediary that invests pension contributions on behalf of the plan's participants. Its assets are the securities and real property that it acquires with these contributions; its liabilities are the pension benefits that will be received by participants. As with other financial intermediaries, a pension fund can use asset and liability durations to gauge the effects of interest-rate changes on its portfolio and net worth.

Pension fund asset–liability decisions differ from those of commercial banks and thrifts in that the present value and duration of a pension fund's liabilities depend not only on interest rates but also on actuarial assumptions about retirement ages, mortality, and the vesting of employee benefits. Pension funds are similar to life insurance companies in their reliance on actuarial assumptions and, also, in their long-term horizons.

A life insurance company wants its assets to be adequate to meet distant death benefits; a pension fund wants its assets to be adequate to meet distant retirement benefits. Because they have long horizons, pension funds and life insurance companies are keenly interested in the potential long-run effects on their portfolios of unexpected changes in interest rates. For example, a decline in interest rates increases the market value of pension fund and life insurance assets, but the long-run decline in reinvestment income will eventually more than offset the short-run increase in market value. If a pension fund has promised to pay fixed nominal amounts many years from now, based on assumed nominal rates of return, there is considerable risk in a strategy of rolling over short-term investments.

To immunize their portfolios against interest-rate risk, pension funds, like life insurance companies, need assets with long durations to match the long durations of their liabilities. In fact, British actuaries who evaluate a pension fund's financial soundness are explicitly required by law to compare the maturities of the fund's assets and liabilities. It is not surprising that pension funds and life insurance companies are both heavy purchasers of long-term securities.

The Securities and Exchange Commission (SEC) requires that business financial statements conform to generally accepted accounting principles, in accordance with guidelines that have been adopted by the Financial Accounting Standard Board (FASB). The FASB is an independent organization, supported by the accounting profession, that was established to encourage consistent and informative reporting procedures. From time to time, the FASB deliberates on an ambiguous accounting issue, circulates a draft proposal among those who prepare and use financial statements, and then publishes a "statement" that specifies accounting practices that the FASB considers acceptable.

Financial Accounting Standards Board Statement Number 87 (FAS 87) defines two ways to calculate a defined-benefit pension fund's liabilities:

*Accumulated benefit obligation (ABO)*: The present value of retirement benefits if the plan is terminated today. This is an estimate of the sponsor's legal liability if the plan were terminated.

*Projected benefit calculation (PBO)*: The present value of projected retirement benefits if the plan continues, taking into account the effects of estimated increases in salary levels on the retirement benefits of active employees.

These calculations include retired employees, vested ex-employees, and currently active employees but exclude prospective future employees. FAS 87 mandates that the discount rate used to calculate these present values reflect market interest rate, but does not specify a particular interest rate.

A comparison of the ABO with the market value of a plan's assets reveals if the plan is underfunded or overfunded. If the plan is underfunded, FAS 87 specifies that the difference be reported as a liability on the sponsoring firm's balance sheet. An overfunded pension fund is not reported as an asset of the sponsoring firm because it is unclear — legally and in practice — who owns this surplus.[6]

The difference between the PBO and the market value of a plan's assets is an estimate of the present value of future contributions that the sponsoring firm will have to make to meet its pension liabilities. If the plan's assets are less than its PBO, FAS 87 requires that the amortized value of this difference be reported on the firm's balance sheet as a plan expense, which reduces its reported profit. If the difference persists, the firm will be compelled to make additional contributions to the pension fund to keep it from being underfunded.

When a pension fund computes its ABO and PBO, it can determine the sensitivity of these calculations to changes in interest rates. These sensitivities are estimates of the duration of the pension fund's liabilities. For example, if the fund's calculations indicate that a 1 percentage point change in the assumed value of interest rates changes the value of the ABO by 20 percent, then its ABO has a duration of 20 years.

The pension fund can immunize itself against interest-rate risk by selecting assets with a duration that matches the duration of its liabilities. For example, if its ABO has a duration of 20 years and the fund chooses an asset portfolio with a duration of 20 years, then (small) changes in interest rates will not affect the difference between its ABO and the market value of its assets and will not affect the underfunding liability on the sponsoring firm's balance sheet.

The ABO calculation is relatively straightforward because the retirement benefits are fixed if the plan is terminated. The pension fund's managers can use interest-rate and life-expectancy data to estimate the present value and duration of these benefits. Suppose, for example, that the benefits include a group of retirees with a life expectancy of 10 years who are receiving a total of $100,000 each month. If interest rates are 10 percent and the fund's managers assume that the retirees in this group will live exactly 10 years, then it can calculate the present value of these benefits to be $756,712 and the duration to be 4.23 years. These benefits can consequently be immunized against interest-rate risk (but not mortality risk) by investing $756,712 in assets with a duration of 4.23 years.

EXAMPLE
19.5     *Citicorp Sells Its Pension Fund*

U.S. stock prices more than tripled during the 5-year period from August of 1982 to August of 1987, a compound annual rate of return of 28.5 percent, not counting the dividends received along the way. This 30 percent plus rate of return far exceeds the rate of return assumed by actuaries when they calculate the annual contributions required to fund defined-benefit pension plans. Because the stock market did so much better than expected, many pension funds became substantially overfunded.

Citicorp decided to cash in some of its pension fund chips in 1987. In May of that year, Citicorp added $3 billion to its loan-loss reserves because of troubled foreign loans, thereby (after taxes) reducing its net worth by roughly $2 billion. Citicorp then took several steps to bolster its net worth in order to meet the capital standards set by bank regulators. In September of 1987, Citicorp obtained $1.4 billion in capital by issuing additional shares of stock. On October 5, Citicorp sold two-thirds of its Citicorp Center in Manhattan and one-third of an adjacent building to Dai-ichi Mutual Life Insurance Company of Japan for $670 million. (The floors that Citicorp sold were not occupied by Citicorp but were rented to Price Waterhouse and other tenants.) This was the largest New York real estate transaction in history and, at $430 a square foot, one of the priciest. The value of these properties had appreciated considerably over time, but this appreciation did not appear on Citicorp's balance sheet. By selling the property, Citicorp was able to realize a pretax capital gain of $450 million and bolster the net worth shown on its books.

Citicorp also used its overfunded pension fund to boost its reported net worth. In September of 1987, Citicorp's principal domestic retirement plan had $1.5 billion in assets and $900 million in obligations — a $600 million overfunding. However, generally accepted accounting principles do not allow a company to report an overfunded pension fund as an asset on its balance sheet. Citicorp got around this accounting convention by paying Metropolitan Life Insurance Company $400 million from Citicorp's pension fund assets to irrevocably take over $400 million of Citicorp's pension fund obligations. This transaction left Citicorp's pension fund with $500 million in obligations. Out of the pension fund's $1.5 billion in assets, $400 million was given to Metropolitan Life, $940 million was retained by the pension fund, and $160 million was added to Citicorp's after-tax income and net worth.

The PBO calculation is more difficult because the pension benefits of those employees who are not yet retired depends on how fast their wages increase, how long they stay with the firm, and the ages at which they retire. The pension fund must make assumptions that may prove to be incorrect. Even if the fund immunizes its liabilities against interest-rate risk, they are still exposed to inflation, vesting, retirement, and mortality risk.[7] (And if its ABO and PBO have different durations, then the fund cannot immunize both against interest-rate risk.)

Defined-contribution plans are very different, in that the pension fund bases its benefit payments directly on each worker's contributions, crediting the worker with whatever rate of return the pension fund earns, less expenses. The pension fund is, in effect, simply managing the worker's pension portfolio; and, barring fraud, the pension fund can never be underfunded or overfunded. Although there are no explicitly defined benefits, the pension fund may reasonably consider the participants to have target retirement benefits that are comparable with those in defined-benefit plans. If so, long-duration assets may again be appropriate.

## Pension Fund Performance

If a pension fund makes unusually profitable investments, the beneficiaries of this superior performance depend on whether it is a defined-contribution or defined-benefit plan. Unexpected profits increase the retirement benefits in a defined-contribution plan but do not affect pension benefits in a defined-benefit plan. In a defined-benefit plan, large profits reward the employer rather than the employee, because the employer does not have to contribute as much money to the plan.

Similarly, lower-than-expected profits reduce retirement benefits in a defined-contribution plan but hurt the employer if it is a defined-benefit plan. Therefore, in a defined-contribution plan, the employee bears the risk that the pension fund will be managed poorly; in a defined-benefit plan, the employer bears this risk.

The federal insurance for defined-benefit plans provided by PBGC has the laudable intention of protecting vulnerable employees from mismanaged pension funds. However, federal insurance creates a moral hazard for an employer-managed pension fund because a company experiencing financial difficulties has an incentive to make high-risk investments. If the investments turn out well, the company's pension fund contributions will be reduced; if the investments do poorly, the insolvent fund will be taken over by the PBGC. As with federal deposit insurance, federal regulators must be vigilant to prevent excessive risk-taking.

Most pension funds are managed by insurance companies or bank trust departments with commissions based on the size of the fund and, in some cases, on the fund's performance. The historical evidence is not flattering to their performance. Although 90 percent of pension fund managers believe that they can beat the market,[8] the empirical evidence is that most do not.[9]

Some, including the nation's three largest pension funds — Wells Fargo Investment Advisors, Bankers Trust, and the College Retirement Equities Fund

(CREF) — now index substantial parts of their portfolios, attempting to reduce expenses, rather than select undervalued securities.

# SUMMARY

Pension plans — private or governmental — provide retirement (or disability) income to workers and their dependents. The Social Security program is a pay-as-you-go system, in which taxes levied on current workers are used to pay benefits to the currently retired. With private and most state and local plans, tax-deferred wages accumulate with interest to provide benefits at retirement. Private and state and local pension funds are financial intermediaries, investing contractual savings to provide benefits at retirement.

In a defined-contribution plan, contributions are credited to each employee's personal account, and the retirement benefits depend on the size of these contributions and the rate of return the pension fund earns on them. In a defined-benefit plan, the employee's retirement benefits are specified — often by a formula that takes into account salary and years of employment — and the plan's sponsor adjusts the contributions as needed to meet these promised benefits. ERISA, passed in 1974, mandates reasonable vesting and portability and protects pensions from mismanagement or underfunding.

Defined-benefit contributions are calculated so that the pension plan will be able to pay the projected annuity if wages increase at the expected rate, the worker retires at the expected time, and the fund is able to earn the anticipated rate of return on its investments. The managers of the fund must make assumptions about employee demographics as well as the fund's investment performance. Pension funds are more like life insurance companies than banks and thrifts in that they have to worry about demographic risk in addition to interest-rate risk.

The aggregate assets of private and state and local pension funds are comparable with those of insurance companies and thrifts. Because their liabilities are long-term retirement benefits, pension funds invest mainly in long-term bonds and corporate stock and now hold more than a quarter of all outstanding U.S. stock. Although most pension fund managers believe that they can earn above-average returns in financial markets, most don't, and some now use indexing to reduce expenses.

# IMPORTANT TERMS

defined-benefit plan
defined-contribution plan
Employment Retirement Income Security Act
  (ERISA)
individual retirement account (IRA)
insured pension plans

noninsured pension plans
pay-as-you-go plans
pension fund
pension plan
prudent man rule
vested benefits

# EXERCISES

1. Is TIAA-CREF, the college professor's retirement fund, a defined-benefit or defined-contribution plan?

2. A small manufacturing company allows early retirement at age 55 with an annual pension benefit equal to 0.5 percent of the average pay during the final 5 years before retirement multiplied by the number of years of employment with the firm. Is this a defined-benefit or defined-contribution plan? What is the replacement rate?

3. A Midwest aircraft manufacturer provided vesting of retirement benefits when an employee's age plus the number of years of employment with the firm reached 60. For example, a 42-year-old who had worked for this firm for 18 years would be vested. Does this formula encourage or discourage the hiring of older workers?

4. The fine print in a recent advertisement for a municipal bond fund said that munis are "not suitable for retirement plans." Why not?

5. Check this calculation:

   *You're 25 years old, but you wait until age 26 to start your IRA. If we assume the interest rate you earn on your funds is 10% annually, and you deposit the maximum $2000 IRA contribution into your account each year, by the time you reach age 65, that one year delay would cost you over $90,000![10]*

6. Did the financial strain on the Social Security System increase or diminish when the normal retirement age of 65 was increased for those workers born after 1938? Explain your reasoning.

7. The Social Security Administration estimated that someone 28 years old earning $16,000 a year in 1985, who works steadily and retires at age 65 in 2022, would begin receiving annual benefits of about $27,500 in 2023.[11] This calculation assumes that something costing $1.00 in 1985 will cost $4.40 in the year 2023. If this is so, how much will this $27,500 buy in terms of 1985 dollars; that is, how many dollars in 1985 will buy as much in 1985 as $27,500 will buy in 2023?

8. Lucille Cooper is 62 years old and can either (a) collect 80 percent of her full Social Security benefits for the rest of her life or (b) wait 3 years and collect her full Social Security benefits ($600 a month) for the rest of her life. Which of these cash flows has the higher present value if her required rate of return is 10 percent and she assumes that she will live 11 more years (the life expectancy for an average 62-year-old U.S. white female)?

9. Why doesn't the federal government allow private pension plans to be funded on a pay-as-you-go basis, as the Social Security System is funded?

10. Explain why you think that the 1982–1987 stock market boom (with a 30 percent average annual rate of return) caused pension funds to be either underfunded or overfunded.

11. Some companies opposed ERISA's minimum vesting rules, arguing that these would increase employee turnover. Explain their reasoning.

12. In January of 1986, *Money* magazine gave this advice:

    *In 1986, as always, you'll likely make fullest use of your IRA's tax advantages by stocking it with such income-producing investments* as CDs, corporate and government bonds, and income mutual funds.[12]

Why did this publication encourage investors to invest their retirement funds in assets that have lots of fully taxable income, as opposed to precious metals, real estate, and other assets that produce capital gains, which at the time were lightly taxed?

13. It has been reported that "roughly half of all zero-coupon bonds are bought with IRA money."[13] Why are zeros attractive for IRAs?

14. Sue Milhone's employer has offered either to give her a $1500 bonus or to put an additional $1500 in her tax-deferred retirement plan. What is the primary advantage of the retirement plan? What is the primary disadvantage?

15. Kinsey Grafton is in a 40 percent tax bracket and is thinking of investing $2000 in a tax-deferred retirement plan paying a fixed annual interest rate of 9 percent. If she instead invested this $2000 outside the retirement plan, what before-tax rate of return would she have to earn to do as well?

16. An investor in a 33 percent tax bracket is considering borrowing $2000 at a tax-deductible fixed interest rate of 8 percent to invest in a tax-deferred retirement plan. What before-tax rate of return must the investor earn on the money invested in this retirement plan for this to be a profitable financial decision?

17. Does an increase in the rate of inflation have more effect on the retirement benefits of a worker who is in a career-average or final-pay defined-benefit plan? Explain.

18. Explain this observation regarding life insurance companies and pension funds:

*Contemporary accounting practice tends to promote the view that increases in bond value are a positive outcome even when the long-run impact of the associated decline in interest rates is negative.*[14]

19. In return for a lump-sum contribution of $X$ dollars today, a pension fund has promised to pay a worker a lump-sum benefit of $1 million 40 years from now. How large must $X$ be if the fund can earn a 10 percent annual rate of return on its investments? (Ignore taxes and the fund's expenses.) Explain why there is considerable risk for the pension fund if it plans on investing the worker's money in a series of forty 1-year Treasury bills. What type of security would guarantee that it can pay the worker the promised $1 million?

20. If a person contributes $2000 a year for 40 years to a defined-contribution plan, beginning today, and is able to earn a 10 percent return on this money, what is the total value at the end of 40 years? (Just set up the appropriate equations, without doing the requisite calculations.)

21. (*continuation*) At retirement, this person will use the accumulated value calculated in the preceding exercise to purchase an annuity that pays a constant annual amount for 20 years. Ignoring taxes and using a 10 percent interest rate, what constant payment for 20 years, beginning a year after retirement, can be purchased at retirement? (Just set up.)

22. Some pension funds buy diversified stock portfolios and then write stock index calls. In comparison with simply buying a stock portfolio, describe the effects of this strategy on a pension fund's profits. Assume that as long as the calls are not worthless, the dollar change in the value of the calls is exactly equal to the dollar change in the value of the stock portfolio.

23. Identify which of the following events would, in the long run, weaken and which would strengthen the financial solvency of the U.S. Social Security System. Briefly explain your reasoning.
    a. An increase in life expectancies
    b. An increase in the age at which people retire
    c. An increase in the birth rate

24. Consider a hypothetical country in which everyone has the same 80-year life cycle: beginning work at age 20, retiring at age 60, and dying at age 80. As shown in the following table, the population has been doubling every 20 years:

| Year | Population by age group (millions) | | | |
|------|------|-------|-------|-------|
|      | 0–20 | 20–40 | 40–60 | 60–80 |
| 1920 | 32   | 16    | 8     | 4     |
| 1940 | 64   | 32    | 16    | 8     |

After a special pill is invented, the population growth rate falls to zero:

| Year | Population by age group (millions) | | | |
|------|------|-------|-------|-------|
|      | 0–20 | 20–40 | 40–60 | 60–80 |
| 1960 | 64   | 64    | 32    | 16    |
| 1980 | 64   | 64    | 64    | 32    |
| 2000 | 64   | 64    | 64    | 64    |

For each of the 5 years shown, calculate the fraction of the population that is ages 0–20, 20–60, and 60–80. In words, summarize the effect of slowing population growth on the fraction of the population that is elderly and the fraction of the population that works. Also compare the worker/elderly ratio in 1920 and in 2000.

25. (*continuation*) Suppose that each worker produces $20,000 worth of goods and services annually and that aggregate output is divided among the population so that everyone over 20 consumes the same amount and persons under the age of 20 consume half this amount. What fraction of their output are workers able to consume themselves in 1940? In 2000?

# 20 Investment Banks and Security Brokers

*Don't gamble; take all your savings and buy some good stock and hold it till it goes up, then sell it. If it don't go up, don't buy it.*

**Will Rogers**

Securities firms perform two important functions: **investment banking** (helping issue new securities in the primary market) and **security brokerage** (helping investors trade securities in the secondary market after they have been issued). Investment banking is not done solely by specialized investment banks, nor is security brokerage done solely by specialized brokerage firms. Until the late 1960s, Merrill Lynch only did security brokerage; now not only is it the largest brokerage firm in the United States, it is also one of the largest investment banks. Kidder, Peabody began as an investment bank and is now one of the largest brokerage firms. Citicorp, the holding company for Citibank, and Sears, best known for its department stores, both have large investment banking and security brokerage subsidiaries. This combination of functions is becoming increasingly common.

Because firms often do investment banking as well as security brokerage, we can use a more general label, such as *securities firms* or (as the Federal Reserve does) *security brokers and dealers*. In this chapter we will look at the varied services — including investment banking and security brokerage — that securities firms provide for their customers and at how these financial intermediaries manage their assets and liabilities. We begin by looking at the origins of investment banking firms in the United States. Although their history may be dimmed by time, it is rarely dull.

# THE ORIGINS OF INVESTMENT BANKS

In the 1800s, U.S. businesses began using investment banks to help find investors who would purchase the stocks and bonds they were issuing. Then, as now, an investment banking house would scrutinize a firm's books, advise an appropriate price for new securities, and then market the securities to individuals and financial institutions. Investment bankers played a key role in financing the Union during the Civil War and in financing industries, particularly railroads, in the post–Civil War industrialization of America. Investment bankers held a dominant position in American finance during the period 1860–1929, and many of the leading firms of that era remain important today: J. P. Morgan, Goldman Sachs, and Kidder, Peabody.

In the 1920s the investment banking industry was flooded with aggressive new firms that brashly competed for new issues to peddle to the public. The old-line houses thought it unethical, and a bit demeaning, to go out and actually compete for business. Issuers should come to them, as they always had, because of the house's impeccable reputation and long-standing, intimate relationship with the issuer. Indeed, the old-line houses turned away issuers and investors who lacked the proper credentials.

These traditional ways were eroded in the first half of the twentieth century by the development of organized stock exchanges and the growth of a broad middle class with savings to invest. To accommodate these changes, many securities firms developed retail capabilities — the ability to sell securities to individual investors of modest wealth. The most successful of these retail security brokerage firms was Merrill Lynch. The dominant position of the old-line banks also was undermined by federal legislation that separated commercial banking from investment banking.

## The Glass-Steagall Act

In the 1920s the most powerful investment banks were often part of large integrated trust firms that handled checking and savings accounts, loans, security brokerage, investment banking, and asset management. During the collapse of the stock market and the economy between 1929 and 1932, thousands of U.S. banks failed, many of which speculated in the stock market. To insulate commercial banks from stock market fluctuations, Congress passed the **Glass-Steagall Act** in 1933, which prohibits firms from acting as both a commercial bank (accepting deposits and making loans) and as an investment bank (helping businesses raise funds through the sale of securities).

To comply with the Glass-Steagall Act, the most prominent bank of the day, J. P. Morgan, chose to become a commercial bank, and several partners left the bank to form a separate investment bank (Morgan Stanley). Other banks were similarly forced to specialize in either commercial banking or investment banking. (Foreign banks can operate both as commercial and investment banks in the United States, unconstrained by Glass-Steagall.)

EXAMPLE
20.1

## The Fall of Banking's Berlin Wall

Much as the Berlin Wall divided Germany into East and West, the Glass-Steagall Act of 1933 forcibly divided banking into two separate activities: commercial banking and investment banking. Thus the banking powerhouse J. P. Morgan was separated into a commercial bank (Morgan Guaranty) and an investment bank (Morgan Stanley). This financial Berlin Wall was intended to protect depositors (and the deposit-insurance system) from losses that might be incurred by security underwriting, trading, and brokerage. Morgan Guaranty, Citibank, and other commercial banks were allowed to accept deposits and make loans, but they could not deal in securities. Morgan Stanley, Merrill Lynch and other investment banks were permitted to deal in securities, but they could not offer insured deposits.

This legal separation is clearly artificial. Many commercial and investment banking activities overlap, and these activities can be done more economically by sharing buildings, equipment, and information. Much of the financial expertise that is crucial to successful commercial banking is also essential to profitable investment banking. For example, a commercial bank's evaluation and pricing of a business loan are not very different from an investment bank's evaluation and pricing of a security issue.

For nearly 60 years Congress resisted banking industry appeals to overturn the Glass-Steagall Act. Commercial banks suffered as individuals and businesses transferred deposits to money-market funds and other securities firms. The banks' most creditworthy corporate borrowers took out fewer loans and increasingly obtained funds by issuing securities through investment banks. Investment banks complained that commercial banks had FDIC insurance and could borrow money from the Fed.

In January of 1989, the Federal Reserve gave J. P. Morgan and three other commercial banks permission to underwrite corporate debt. J. P. Morgan is the holding company for Morgan Guaranty, the giant New York commercial bank created after passage of the Glass-Steagall Act. In September of 1990, the Fed put another large crack in the wall separating commercial and investment banking by giving J. P. Morgan permission to underwrite, trade, and sell corporate stock, a clear sign that commercial and investment banks will soon compete head to head. The Securities Industry Association, which had lobbied long and hard against an expansion of commercial bank activities, called the Fed's momentous decision "astonishing."

The Fed requires J. P. Morgan's investment banking activities to be handled by a subsidiary, J. P. Morgan Securities, with its own capital and management, to ensure that Morgan Guaranty's assets are protected from any losses incurred by Morgan's investment banking activities. In 1991, J. P. Morgan Securities was the twelfth largest underwriter of corporate securities, as it managed 73 issues with a total market value of $9.7 billion. Morgan Stanley was the sixth largest underwriter, managing 278 issues with an aggregate market value of $48.2 billion.

Banking's Berlin Wall is not expected to crumble overnight, since Fed permission will be given only to the very strongest banks. It is fitting that the Fed's initial approval went to J. P. Morgan. Will the House of Morgan, like East and West Germany, someday be reunited?

Countries that make no legal distinction between commercial banks and investment banks are said to have a system of *universal banking.* The United States is now moving toward such a system. In the 1970s and 1980s, investment banks increasingly competed for commercial bank customers by offering money-market funds that lured depositors out of bank accounts and by persuading businesses to raise funds by issuing securities through investment banks instead of taking loans from commercial banks. Commercial banks, in turn, lobbied for the right to underwrite securities and looked for loopholes in the Glass-Steagall Act. The comptroller of the currency now allows national banks to handle private placements, underwrite commercial paper and general-obligation municipal bonds, and help plan, finance, and execute business mergers and acquisitions — activities long restricted to investment bankers. Many large U.S. banks use foreign branches to underwrite and deal in securities outside the United States.

The Federal Reserve Board now permits several commercial bank holding companies to underwrite and deal in money-market securities, municipal revenue bonds, corporate debt, and securities backed either by mortgages or consumer receivables. These various activities must be carried out within a holding-company structure in which the investment banking subsidiary is independent of the commercial banking subsidiary. This arrangement technically conforms to the Glass-Steagall Act and insulates the Federal Deposit Insurance Corporation (FDIC) from responsibility for investment banking losses.

The Glass-Steagall barriers that separated commercial and investment banks have been substantially eroded and will most likely soon disappear entirely, giving the United States a universal banking system. Earlier chapters have described commercial banking services in some detail. Let's now look at some of the important services provided by investment banks.

## SECURITIES ISSUANCE

Investment bankers help private firms and state and local government agencies issue stocks, bonds, and other securities to raise funds for construction, equipment, day-to-day operations, and other purposes. A stock issue could be an **initial public offering** (**IPO**), in which a corporation sells shares to the public for the first time, or it could be a sale of additional shares by a corporation that is already publicly owned. Bond issues can be of any maturity, but public issues that are registered with the Securities and Exchange Commission (SEC) are generally long term because the administrative expenses involved make short-term issues impractical.

When a business or government agency is considering issuing securities, investment bankers study the client's current and prospective financial soundness and offer both general advice (for example, stocks versus bonds) and specific details (such as the price and timing of the issue). One of the crucial questions is whether the securities will be sold publicly or privately.

## Underwriting

If the securities are to be issued publicly, the investment bank will act as an **underwriter** by purchasing the new securities from the business or government agency for an agreed-on price and then selling these securities to the public, profiting on the price difference (the *spread*). In advance of actual issue, the underwriters — either a single firm or a group called a *syndicate* — prepare the necessary legal documents and contact individual and institutional investors, hoping to persuade them to buy the securities. On the issuing date, the underwriters purchase the securities for immediate resale to customers that, if all goes well, have been lined up in advance.

Because the underwriters buy the newly issued securities and resell them, they bear the risk that the securities were initially mispriced or that there will be unforeseen events between the purchase and resale. Underwriters generally try to reduce these risks by lining up purchasers beforehand and by selling the securities quickly. In addition, underwriting syndicates are used to spread the risk among dozens or even hundreds of investment banks. An initial public offering is especially difficult to value because the shares have never been traded and there is no direct information about the prices that investors are willing to pay for this particular company's stock.

After securities have been issued, the lead underwriter continues to monitor the client's ability and willingness to fulfill the terms of the securities, because a banker's ability to place securities depends on its reputation for good information, appropriate pricing, and integrity. If an investment bank underwrites too many securities that turn out to be bad investments, it will lose its customers' confidence and, with that, its ability to underwrite securities.

Occasionally, the issuing firm or government agency is so small, little known, and risky that investment banks may refuse to purchase and resell the securities. Instead, they agree only to market the securities on a "best effort" basis, charging a commission on each sale. If they are unable to sell all the securities by a specified date, the unsold securities are extinguished, and the issuing firm does not raise as much money as intended.

Table 20.1 on page 592 lists the top 20 corporate underwriters in 1991. In contrast to commercial banking, investment banking is highly concentrated, with the top half dozen firms consistently accounting for more than half of all the funds raised through new security issues.

A distinction is often made between *institutional sales* to pension funds, insurance companies, and other financial institutions and *retail sales* to individual investors. Firms such as Merrill Lynch, Prudential-Bache, and Dean Witter that

**Table 20.1** Twenty Largest Underwriters of Corporate Securities

| Securities Firm | Number of Issues | Value (billions of dollars) |
|---|---|---|
| Merrill Lynch | 561 | $100.5 |
| Goldman Sachs | 442 | 69.6 |
| Lehman Brothers | 490 | 68.6 |
| First Boston | 310 | 58.0 |
| Kidder Peabody | 199 | 50.8 |
| Morgan Stanley | 278 | 48.2 |
| Salomon Brothers | 199 | 46.4 |
| Bear Stearns | 98 | 33.8 |
| Prudential-Bache Securities | 68 | 17.1 |
| Donaldson, Lufkin & Jeanrette | 67 | 11.5 |
| PaineWebber | 70 | 10.4 |
| J. P. Morgan Securities | 73 | 9.7 |
| Alex, Brown & Sons | 63 | 7.3 |
| Smith Barney, Harris Upham | 64 | 5.8 |
| Dean Witter | 37 | 5.6 |
| Normura Securities | 15 | 5.3 |
| Citicorp | 24 | 5.0 |
| Greenwich Capital Markets | 15 | 5.0 |
| Daiwa Securities | 13 | 4.8 |
| Chase Securities | 5 | 3.3 |

**Source:** "The 1992 Corporate Sweepstakes," *Institutional Investor,* February 1992, p. 73.

have substantial retail sales usually have strategically located branch offices to encourage walk-in customers. Dean Witter, for example, is a subsidiary of Sears and has offices in high-traffic areas inside Sears department stores. Firms such as Morgan Stanley, First Boston, and Salomon Brothers that largely ignore retail sales have centralized offices that are not open to the general public.

## Rule 415

The sale of new securities to the public involves considerable expense in preparing the requisite legal documents that describe the details of the issue and disclose pertinent financial information. Consequently, firms have found it economical to issue securities infrequently and in large quantities, using underwriters to design and market the securities.

An important change in investment banking was inaugurated with Rule 415, adopted by the SEC in 1982, which allows "shelf registration" of securities. Rule 415 allows publicly traded corporations that report quarterly to the SEC to file a single statement describing the company's total anticipated stock and bond issues during the next 3 years. These potential new securities are said to be "on the shelf" and can be sold in large or small chunks whenever deals can be worked out. Because the securities do not have to be sold on a single date, the firm does not have to rely on underwriters to guarantee that the entire issue will be sold on that day.

Under Rule 415, the issuing firm has the option of selling the entire issue to a single investment bank or to a syndicate, letting them resell the securities as with a traditional underwriting. Alternatively, the firm can choose to sell some of or all the securities itself to pension funds, insurance companies, and other investors. Rule 415 has weakened the traditional close relationship between some firms and investment banks.

## Private Placements

An alternative to a public issue of securities is a private placement, in which an investment bank arranges for a small number of investors (typically pension funds and life insurance companies) to purchase a security issue at a negotiated price. Privately placed securities are exempt from SEC registration requirements and consequently can be done quickly and, particularly for small issues, relatively inexpensively. In addition, a firm may prefer not to make the public disclosures about its operations that are required with public offerings.

The securities firm that constructs and markets a private placement is paid a fee for its services. Investment banks are heavily involved in private placements because this capability allows them to maintain a broad, continuing relationship with customers, underwriting a public offering when this is appropriate and arranging a private placement when this is preferable. Because a private placement does not technically involve underwriting, commercial banks can provide this service without violating the Glass-Steagall Act, and some banks are increasingly doing so.

# MERGERS AND ACQUISITIONS

Large investment banks have mergers and acquisitions (M&A) departments that — as the name implies — help two companies merge or help one company acquire another firm. A small securities firm might specialize solely in mergers and acquisitions. The experts in an M&A department analyze, solicit, and negotiate potential deals — and arrange financing, if needed. The key to M&A success is being able to value a company's assets, as they are currently used and as they might be employed. The investment bank's commission usually depends on the size of the transaction and can be very lucrative — tens of millions of dollars for a large deal. The Glass-Steagall Act does not exclude commercial banks from mergers and acquisitions activity, but the field is largely dominated by investment banks.

When securities firms invest their own money in real estate, new security issues, mergers and acquisitions, and other ventures, this is called **merchant**

**banking**. Traditionally, U.S. investment banks have been extremely reluctant to invest their own money in their customers' businesses or securities because of potential conflicts of interest. If an investment bank advises a price for a new security issue and then buys a substantial part of this issue, not for resale, but as an investment, customers might wonder if the investment bank advised a low price in order to increase its profits. As investment banks became more heavily involved in mergers and acquisitions in the 1980s, many began investing their own money in their clients' bonds and especially stocks. Such investments are not considered to involve a conflict of interest because the investment bank is sharing the risks and potential rewards that it recommends to its clients. The conventional response to financial advisors is, "If this is such a good deal, why don't you invest your own money?" Merchant bankers do.

Mergers and acquisitions activity includes both friendly mergers and hostile takeovers. Some investment banks specialize in acquisitions; others help potential target companies value their assets and advise them how to erect defensive barriers, both before and after a takeover offer is made.

## Hostile Takeovers

Many takeover attempts begin with one company making a "friendly" offer to acquire another company. After some negotiation, the target company's board of directors may approve the offer and submit it to shareholders with their recommendation that it be approved. If the management of the target company does not approve the offer, the bidder may go to the shareholders directly and make an "unfriendly" tender offer to buy enough of their shares to gain effective control of the company.

If the target stock is selling for $30 a share, the bidder might offer shareholders $40. Although the organized exchanges and the over-the-counter market can accommodate normal trading easily, the volume of purchases needed to gain control of a company might, if made on the open market, create a demand–supply imbalance that drives the price well above $40. Takeover attempts often begin with modest purchases on the stock exchanges or over-the-counter market, made surreptitiously until 5 percent of the stock is acquired — at which point a public disclosure must be made by filing Form 13D with the SEC. The initial purchases are done quietly because news of a possible takeover would cause the price to jump upward in anticipation of higher prices yet to come. To acquire most or all of a company's stock, the bidder invariably makes a tender offer, inviting shareholders to sell their shares at a price substantially above the market price at the time the offer is made.

Why does the acquiring firm believe that the target company is worth substantially more than the market price? Takeover battles are struggles over the control of a company's assets. Under current management, the cash flow produced by these assets is valued by investors at $30 a share; the bidder believes that a new management can do better. Perhaps the company as a whole can be better managed, increasing its earnings and dividends, or perhaps parts of the company can be sold to other owners and put to other uses because the company is literally worth more dead than alive. As *Barron's* said of the department store chain Marshall Field, "the dismal management of which makes the company far more valuable as commercial real estate (or possibly a parking lot) than a going concern."[1] Yet Marshall Field's management fiercely resisted repeated takeover attempts, including an offer of $42 a share in 1978, when its stock was selling below $20; finally, in 1982, to avoid a hostile takeover by Carl Icahn, it agreed to a merger for $30 a share.

When a company's stock is selling for $20 a share and an outside group offers shareholders $42 a share to gain control of the company, it is hard to see how shareholders benefit by takeover defenses that cost the company millions of dollars and keep the price at $20 or below as assets are squandered. Yet this is exactly what many managements have done.[2] In most large corporations, the owners and managers are different people, with interests that do not always coincide. Shareholders want to maximize the value of their stock, while a firm's executives may want to maximize their own compensation or the size of the firm. The most public examples of management disregard for shareholder interests are the bitter, expensive campaigns fought by entrenched management to repel takeover attempts and protect their jobs. Example 20.2 describes some of these "shark repellents."

Some managers have protected their jobs by diluting the votes of shareholders. In 1986 (with no takeover attempt in sight), Chase Manhattan's shareholders approved (in some cases, barely) a series of rules giving the board of directors sole authority to accept or reject a takeover bid and made it virtually impossible to remove a member of the board; further, these rules cannot be changed or a decision of the board overruled without a 75 percent majority vote by shareholders. MCI reduced the voting power of those who might acquire more than 10 percent of its outstanding stock with a rule that gives every share beyond 10 percent only 1 percent of a vote. (Thus for a company with 100 million shares outstanding, someone who acquired 20 million shares would have only 10 million + 10 million/100 = 10.1 million votes.) In 1987 the U.S. Supreme Court upheld an Indiana state law that keeps stockholders holding more than 20 percent of an Indiana company's shares from voting at all, unless specifically approved by a majority of the remaining shareholders.

Figgie International used a variety of rules to entrench the conglomerate's founder, Henry E. Figgie, Jr. First, two classes of stock were created, and existing shareholders were offered a dividend of 8 cents per share to choose the second class, which has only a 5 percent of a vote per share. Second, the company's retirement fund bought up much of the full-vote stock. Third, any shareholder owning more than 10 percent of the stock of either class gets only 1 percent of a vote on the additional shares. Fourth, Mr. Figgie is exempted from these restrictions, effectively giving him 80 percent of the votes even though he owns only 10 percent of the outstanding stock.[3]

**EXAMPLE**
**20.2**

## Shark Repellents

On average, takeovers allow the shareholders of target companies to sell their stock for 30 percent more than the market price before the takeover offer.* Yet the managements of target companies often resist takeovers mightily; the defenses, called "shark repellents," they employ in their no-holds-barred maneuvering have come to be labeled by a variety of colorful names.

*Greenmail* is what a company pays a raider to go away; for example, Goodyear paid Sir James Goldsmith nearly $100 million to drop his takeover attempt. A greenmail of sorts occurred in December of 1986 when General Motors made headlines not for designing a better car but for ousting H. Ross Perot from its board of directors. When GM acquired Perot's Electronic Data Systems, it gave him 11.4 million shares of GM class E stock and a seat on its board. A long-time maverick, Perot took the job seriously and began suggesting changes at GM. For instance, when he learned that GM executives get new, specially serviced cars every 3 months, he pointed out that they might get a more accurate impression of GM's product if they spent some time in the same cars the public was supposed to buy. Looking at GM's falling sales and plant closings, he suggested that management didn't deserve large bonuses. The chairman of a pension fund group called Perot "the best thing that happened to General Motors since Frigidaire."† However, GM decided to get rid of Perot by paying him $100 million plus $56.50 a share for his stock, then trading at $31⅜. In return for this $400 million premium, Perot resigned from GM's board of directors and agreed to stop criticizing its management (or pay fines of up to $7.5 million).

*Scorched earth* describes the situation when a company sells its prized assets to make the company less attractive. For instance, Pabst Brewing Company was a company in trouble in 1981. Its market share was shrinking, its earnings had dropped by two-thirds over the previous 5 years, and, in the words of its chief executive officer,

> There was extravagance everywhere, lack of control in the sales area, people didn't have the direction they should, marketing money was being spent on brands that shouldn't have been, . . . there was overcapacity at the plant level and there was a tremendous morale problem.‡

After a year-long fight against a variety of takeover attempts, Pabst finally drove away its suitors by selling its three best plants to another brewery: "We realized

*Michael C. Jensen, "Takeovers: Folklore and Science," Harvard Business Review, November/December 1984, pp. 109–121.

†Oswald Johnston, "Big Holders Grill GM on Perot Buyout," Los Angeles Times, December 18, 1986.

‡Debra Whitefield, "The Ordeal of Takeover Battles," Los Angeles Times, November 11, 1984.

we had to do something really drastic to get the thing over with. So, we sold off the crown jewels." Pabst emerged a beaten company, close to bankruptcy. From a broader perspective, the takeover pressure did succeed in reallocating Pabst's assets to a more successful brewer.

In another scorched-earth example, Whittaker Corporation attempted to acquire Brunswick in 1982, primarily for its very profitable medical products subsidiary, so Brunswick sold the subsidiary to someone else, Whittaker went away, and Brunswick stock dropped from $25 to $14. Interestingly, the failed takeover traumatized Brunswick into promoting a new chief executive officer who quickly laid off redundant executives, tied management pay to performance, sold two of the three company planes, and rented out two-thirds of what he called the "big corporate palace we were in."§ Within 2 years the price of Brunswick stock was up to $70.

*Poison pills* are rules that provide for excessive cash payments if the company is ever taken over. For instance, a company might specify that if any group acquires more than 20 percent of the company's stock, it will sell new shares to others at bargain prices, in effect giving away assets. *Golden parachutes* are similar in that they provide lavish severance pay to displaced executives. For example, when Allied took over Bendix, it had to pay a total of $18 million to 22 top executives. Herman Miller, an office furniture company, created *silver parachutes* specifying that any employee with 2 years' service who is let go after a takeover will receive a full year's pay.

§*Debra Whitefield, "Brunswick Is Stronger than Before It 'Scorched the Earth',"* Los Angeles Times, *November 11, 1984.*

Such measures weren't invented in the 1980s; since 1956 the Ford family has retained control over Ford Motor Company via their ownership of nontrading class B shares. However, the 1980s brought an unsettling explosion of takeover defenses in which shareholders voluntarily relinquished even the appearance of control over management. How do such measures pass? Apparently many shareholders, even supposedly alert and sophisticated institutional investors, are apathetic or easily persuaded by management. In addition, a commercial bank, investment bank, insurance company, or pension fund might understandably be reluctant to antagonize a potential business customer. James E. Heard, of the Investors Responsibility Research Center, is blunt: "Institutional investors are voting for these proposals either on a completely uninformed basis or to preserve their commercial relationships with clients."[4] Interestingly, the College Retirement Equities Fund (CREF) for college professors is one of the few institutions in the country that consistently votes against takeover defense rules.

Takeovers can be a wrenching experience not only for a company's executives, but for its rank-and-file workers and the communities in which they live. Such dislocations are sometimes economically necessary, and takeovers are the catalyst that overpowers management resistance to change. The empirical evidence is that, overall, takeovers have improved corporate performance.[5]

Admittedly, some managers have devoted their lives to their companies, and many firms have long, admirable, even noble traditions that are worth preserving. There is something to be said for continuity and for the plight of companies whose shares are buffeted by economic events or stock market speculation over which they have no control. Some dislodged managements may not deserve their fate, but some do. Shark repellents protect not only the unlucky, but also the incompetent.

Managers who believe that an unreasonably low market price for their company's stock invites an unwarranted takeover have a very persuasive alternative to shark repellents. The company can simply repurchase its own shares. If these repurchases immediately increase the price of the stock, a takeover will be discouraged and shareholders will benefit from the opportunity to sell their shares at a higher price. If the market price is really irrationally low, the repurchased shares will turn out to be a great investment for the company.

# SECURITY BROKERAGE AND TRADING

In addition to underwriting new security issues, investment banks are also active in the secondary market, where securities are bought and sold after they have been issued. There is an important distinction between security brokers and dealers. A **broker** arranges trades between buyers and sellers without risking any of its own capital; it earns income by charging fees for bringing together buyers and sellers. A **dealer**, in contrast, participates in trades, buying and selling for its own account. Dealers generally try to maintain only modest inventories, selling securities shortly after they buy them and vice versa, profiting on the difference between the buying and selling prices. However, a dealer can make a profit if prices move up while it is holding securities, and it can lose money if prices move adversely.

## *Security Brokerage*

Security brokers help individual and institutional investors buy and sell securities in the secondary market. They can arrange private trades among borrowers and lenders or execute trades using the organized exchanges and the computerized over-the-counter market. **Discount brokers** just execute trades; **full-service brokers** not only arrange trades but also advise investors. As explained in Example 20.4 on page 601 and Example 20.5 on page 603, such advice can be tainted by the fact that stockbrokers make profits when investors make trades.

Discount brokerage firms do little more than answer the telephone, give current information about market prices, and record trades. Some transactions can be handled electronically, without the customer even speaking to a clerk. Full-service brokers, in contrast, provide investment advice in person, over the phone, and in periodic newsletters. Full-service brokers compile mountains of data, prepare indepth analyses, make buy/sell recommendations, and hold the hands of timid investors. They are also more expensive, because investors must

**EXAMPLE 20.3**

## *Buying Stock on Margin*

When an investor borrows money from a brokerage firm to buy securities, this transaction is called *buying on margin*, where the margin is the amount of money put up by the investor. If you buy 200 shares of ZYX stock for $50 a share (a total cost of $10,000), a brokerage firm with a 60 percent margin requirement requires you to put up at least $6000 (and loans you the remainder). Since 1934, the Federal Reserve Board has been empowered to set *margin requirements*, the minimum margin that brokerage firms must require of their customers. The Fed's minimum margin requirement has been as low as 40 percent and as high as 100 percent; it has been 50 percent since 1974.

To protect itself, the brokerage firm registers stock purchased on margin in its own name (called the *street name*). Your margin agreement also allows the firm to use your stock as collateral for its borrowing and to lend your stock to short sellers. When a dividend is paid, it is credited to your account, reducing the outstanding loan balance. Annual reports and other correspondence are forwarded to you.

The brokerage firm charges you interest on this loan, but, as with any leveraged investment, you come out ahead if the rate of return on your stock exceeds the interest rate on your loan. Suppose that you put up $5000 of the $10,000 cost of your ZYX purchase and borrow the rest from your broker. Neglecting the commission, your brokerage account will look like part (a) of the table on the next page, with your equity equal to the current market value of the stock minus the loan balance.

The rate charged on your loan fluctuates with the broker's *call rate*, their cost of borrowing from banks the money they lend investors. Active shareholders who borrow large amounts pay the call rate plus (or, in rare cases, minus) a fraction of a percent, while other borrowers pay the call rate plus 2 percent or even more. For simplicity, we'll use a fixed 12 percent annual interest rate and assume that a month has passed since your purchase.

If the stock doesn't pay a dividend this month but its price rises 1 percent, to $50.50, the 1 percent return on the stock and the 1 percent loan rate cancel, leaving a 1 percent profit on your $6000 cash investment, as shown in part (b) of the table. If the stock's price goes up by more than 1 percent this month, then the power of leverage is unleashed. Part (c) of the table shows that if the price goes up by 10 percent, to $55, your equity will increase by $950 — a 19 percent return on your initial $5000 investment. Part (d) of the table shows that if the stock drops 10 percent, your losses are magnified (as with any levered position) because not only do you lose 10 percent on the $5000 of your own money, but there is also an 11 percent shortfall on the borrowed money that is doubled by 2:1 leverage.

If your equity — the market value of your stock minus your current loan balance — falls below a specified *maintenance margin*, you will get a margin call from your broker requesting additional funds to reduce your indebtedness (or more securities to build up your equity). The stock exchanges require a 25 percent maintenance margin, but most brokers use a more conservative 30 percent of market value. Part (e) of the table shows that you will get a margin call if the price falls to $35.75, because $2100/$7150 = 0.294 < 0.30.

If you fail to meet a margin call, your broker will unilaterally sell your stock and pay off your loan for you. In 1929, when 10 percent margin was the norm and leveraged speculation was the rage, every significant drop in stock market prices set off an avalanche of margin calls and forced sales, adding to the downward pressure on stock prices.

## Buying Stock with a 50 Percent margin at a 12 Percent Annual Interest

**(a) Initial purchase**

| | |
|---|---:|
| Market value of stocks (200 shares @ $50) | $10,000 |
| Money balance | −5,000 |
| Equity | 5,000 |

**(b) Price rises 1 percent in a month**

| | |
|---|---:|
| Market value of stocks (200 shares @ $50.50) | $10,100 |
| Money balance | −5,050 |
| Equity (1 percent gain) | 5,050 |

**(c) Price rises 10 percent in a month**

| | |
|---|---:|
| Market value of stocks (200 shares @ $55) | $11,000 |
| Money balance | −5,050 |
| Equity (19 percent gain) | 5,950 |

**(d) Price falls 10 percent in a month**

| | |
|---|---:|
| Market value of stocks (200 shares @ $45) | $9,000 |
| Money balance | −5,050 |
| Equity (21 percent loss) | 3,950 |

**(e) A margin call**

| | |
|---|---:|
| Market value of stocks (200 shares @ $35.75) | $7,150 |
| Money balance | −5,050 |
| Equity (only 30 percent of market value) | 2,100 |

EXAMPLE
20.4

## *Churning Is Dangerous to Your Wealth*

Beginning brokers generally try to build a client base by making "cold calls" to a list of people who have been identified as potential customers, often as a result of newspaper or magazine advertisements offering free financial reports.* Those who respond to the ad receive follow-up phone calls from brokers hoping to find investors who will buy and sell securities and pay commissions. These cold calls are known as "dialing for dollars" because the only way a broker can make a profit is by having clients who make trades.

Once a broker has clients, the broker has a persuasive economic incentive to recommend active portfolio management (*account upgrading* is the euphemism, *churning* the goal) — sell GM to buy Ford; then sell Ford to buy Chrysler; then sell Chrysler to buy GM; and on and on. One cynical observer put it this way: "Movement is [the broker's] breath of life. Like the shark, he will drown if he lies still."†

Transaction costs generally average 2 to 3 percent of the dollar value of a transaction, with these expenses mostly brokerage fees for modest trades and mostly bid–ask spreads and price concessions for larger trades. One detailed empirical study found that the total cost, commission plus price spread, ranged from 1 to 8 percent for large companies (depending on the size of the trade) and from 17 to 44 percent for small companies.‡ Of course, if you sell one asset to buy another, then you have to pay two transaction costs. At, say, 5 percent a round trip, active trading becomes pretty expensive. Trading once a year, the stock you buy has to have a 5 percent higher annual return than the stock you sell to cover the cost of the trade; that is, if the stock you sell has a 10 percent annual return, the stock you buy has to yield 15 percent. The required differential rises to an implausible 20 percentage points if you trade every 3 months.

*For an insider's account, see C. David Chase, Mugged on Wall Street (New York: Simon & Schuster, 1987).

†John Train, Preserving Capital and Making It Grow (New York: C.N. Potter, 1983), p. 71.

‡Thomas F. Loeb, "Trading Cost: The Critical Link Between Investment Information and Results," Financial Analysts Journal, May/June 1983, pp. 41–42.

pay the substantial salaries of investment analysts and advisors. For example, one leading discount broker, Brown & Company, charges $25 plus 3 cents a share for transactions in listed stocks and $25 plus 2 cents a share on NASDAQ. Table 20.2 on page 602 compares its costs for several representative trades with the average costs using full-service brokers.

At full-service firms — such as Dean Witter, Merrill Lynch, and Prudential-Bache — security brokerage is part of a wide range of investment banking

### Table 20.2    Brokerage Commissions at Discount and Full-Service Brokers

| Transaction | Cost of Shares | Brown & Company | | Typical Full-Service Broker | |
|---|---|---|---|---|---|
| | | Commission | Percent | Commission | Percent |
| 1,000 shares @ $5 | $ 5,000 | $55 | 1.1 | $148 | 3.0 |
| 200 shares @ $30 | $ 6,000 | $31 | 0.5 | $151 | 2.5 |
| 300 shares @ $50 | $15,000 | $34 | 0.2 | $284 | 1.9 |

**Source:** Tom Petruno, "Fees of Brokers That Discount Keep Dropping," *Los Angeles Times*, March 23, 1992.

services, including underwriting, mergers and acquisitions, and asset management. Discount brokerage firms — such as Brown & Company, Quick & Reilly, and Charles Schwab — generally focus solely on brokerage; however, many discount brokerage firms are subsidiaries of financial conglomerates that offer a wide range of services.

In 1982 some commercial banks began setting up independent divisions to offer discount brokerage services, arguing that technically they weren't violating the Glass-Steagall prohibition against security dealing because they weren't buying or selling securities, merely handling their customers' orders. As with all discount brokerages, orders to buy and sell securities are placed over the telephone and handled by whichever clerk happens to answer the phone. Unlike Merrill Lynch and other full-service brokerage firms, there are no designated account executives to advise clients, no research reports on securities, and no branch offices where the customer can drop in to read financial reports and chat with brokers. With most bank discount brokerages, customers can pick up and deliver securities through a local bank branch and can use their checking account to settle transactions.

Since World War II, Merrill Lynch has risen to dominate retail security brokerage. Merrill Lynch's strength derives from a vast retail network and innovative efforts to cover all aspects of financial markets. When Donald Regan became president of the company in 1968, Merrill Lynch was a private firm that did security brokerage exclusively; in the 1970s it became a publicly traded financial supermarket. For example, Merrill Lynch became one of the top five securities underwriters, created the country's largest money-market fund, and established a nationwide network for real estate brokerage, financing, and insurance.

In 1977 Merrill Lynch introduced its cash management account, which combines a regular securities account with a money-market fund, from which money can be withdrawn by check, credit card, or debit card. The regular securities account is used for trading stocks and bonds, with funds automatically transferred out of the money-market fund to pay for purchases and automatically transferred into the money-market fund when securities are sold or when dividends and coupons are received.

EXAMPLE
20.5

## Jaws: Stockbroker Horror Stories

Most stockbrokers are hard-working, conscientious professionals who, while realizing that they profit from customer transactions, also recognize that excessive expenses and dismal performance will alienate their customers. As with any profession, though, there are some unscrupulous brokers who, like vicious sharks, churn their clients' accounts mercilessly and then move on to feed elsewhere.

The front page of the June 19, 1985, *Los Angeles Times* carried a story subtitled "Beware, Unwary" that detailed some stockbroker abuses.* In one case, a broker who had earned only $4782 in commissions in 5 months and filed for personal bankruptcy found a divorcee with $400,000 in corporate bonds and, in 10 months' time, churned $143,754 in commissions while losing all of her $400,000 and then some — just like the Woody Allen joke, "A broker is someone who invests other people's money until it is all gone." A federal jury awarded her $175,000 in compensatory losses and $3 million in punitive damages (later reduced to $1.5 million), to be paid by the broker and the firm that employed him. In another case, a 70-year-old retired radio actress saw her $550,000 nest egg shrink to $67,000 while thousands of pointless trades generated $310,000 in commissions. When she asked her broker about the blizzard of trade confirmation slips mailed to her, she says he told her to just "throw them away."

A freshman at Princeton turned his trust account of 20,000 shares of Natomas Corporation over to a stock broker who, during 2 years in which the market rose 40 percent and Natomas 60 percent, allegedly charged $92,000 in commissions while losing $300,000. Other cases cited by the *Times* involved a 73-year-old blind woman and a man who lost a leg in a car crash and most of his legal settlement in stock churning.

In 1986 an even more astounding story came to light. During 2 years at two brokerage firms, a 23-year-old aspiring actor turned stockbroker generated a staggering $5 million in commissions, which, it later turned out, came almost entirely from churning the account of a millionaire great uncle whose $16 million account was allegedly whittled down to $8 million.† (This sad story is eerily like the old joke, "How do you make a small fortune in the stock market? Start with a large fortune.")

According to the *Times* article, brokers at Merrill Lynch, the nation's largest brokerage firm, are paid roughly half their customers' commissions, and those who do not generate $250,000 in annual commissions after 3 years are

*Michael A. Hiltzik, "Churning: Trading in Stock Abuse," Los Angeles Times, *June 19, 1985.*

†Roger Lowenstein, "How a 23-Year-Old Broker Went from Riches to Scandal and Jail," Wall Street Journal, *February, 27, 1986.*

asked to leave the firm. Despite these strong economic incentives to churn accounts, most broker–client relationships are not like the horror stories recounted here. However, these tales warn that the broker's and customer's objectives are not always the same and that investors should understand their transactions and be vigilant that their broker is carrying out their instructions. In explaining why the compensatory damages to the divorcee discussed above were less than her actual losses, the jury said that her "inattention to her own affairs, as well as her incredible gullibility, contributed to her losses." As the *Times* put it, "Beware, Unwary."

When the customer writes checks or uses the account's debit card or credit card, funds are transferred as needed from the money-market fund to a checking account established by Merrill Lynch. Because the customer's money is parked in the money-market fund until a check is written, there are no checking account balances subject to reserve requirements. Merrill Lynch can consequently afford to pay more interest than a commercial bank could pay on a checking account. If the money-market fund's balance drops to zero, Merrill Lynch automatically loans money as needed, using the customer's securities as collateral. Following Merrill Lynch's lead, other brokerage firms soon established similiar asset-management accounts.

Customer accounts at brokerage firms are insured up to $500,000, of which $100,000 can be in cash, by a government corporation, the Securities Investor Protection Corporation (SIPC). All registered security brokers and dealers and all firms that are members of national securities exchanges are required to pay annual fees (in 1991, approximately 1 percent of their gross income) in order to obtain SIPC insurance. Many brokerage firms acquire additional insurance of $1.5 million per account from private companies so that their customers are insured up to $2 million.

SIPC's insurance does not cover commodities accounts, nor some kinds of margin accounts — including margin used to buy futures contracts. SIPC does not protect customers from fraud or from a decline in the market value of their portfolios. Between 1971 (when it was created) and August of 1991, SIPC paid out $171 million dollars to 300,000 customers of 230 liquidated brokerage firms, an average payment of about $570 per customer and $740,000 per firm. In August of 1991, SIPC had a cushion of $600 million in reserves.

## Market Making

In addition to serving as brokers, many investment banking firms also act as dealers — participating in trades — in order to make markets in securities. Market making involves the quotation of a **bid price** at which the dealer is willing to buy a security and an **ask price** at which the dealer is willing to sell the security. A successful market maker must have accurate information about other dealers' prices of similar securities and also must be able to react quickly and accurately to financial events. A market maker will not last long if it raises prices when it should lower them and lowers prices when it should raise them.

All the organized exchanges restrict members from trading listed stocks outside the exchanges. Because most major securities firms are exchange members, these restrictions hamper the trading of listed stocks off the exchanges. One crack in the exchanges' stranglehold on listed stocks is SEC Rule 19c-3, which eliminated off-board restrictions for stocks listed (or delisted) after April 26, 1979. When AT&T split into eight holding companies, the seven spinoffs were newly listed and fell under Rule 19c-3, so they can be traded over the counter as well as on the exchanges; about 10 percent of the trades in these seven spinoffs are made off-exchange.

Trades of large blocks of stock (at least 5000 shares) are generally negotiated in the *upstairs market*, using telephones and linked computers to arrange a private deal among securities firms and institutional clients, before being executed on the exchange floor. Except for Rule 19c-3 stocks, block trades negotiated by member firms must be brought to a stock exchange specialist, where they are subject to the exchange's commission. With these exceptions, market making in stocks by investment banks is confined to over-the-counter securities that are not listed on organized exchanges.

The bond-trading department at an investment bank is generally separate from the stock-trading (or equity) department. Investment banks that make markets in the U.S. Treasury bonds handle a large volume of trades, but the profit margins are generally very slim. The difference between the prices dealers pay and charge on actively traded Treasury bills averages less than $1 per $10,000 of face value. Because the profit margin is so slim, Treasury dealers must trade enormous volumes to make significant profits.

Corporate and municipal bond markets are less active, and bid–ask spreads are considerably wider than in the Treasury market. There are millions of heterogeneous corporate and municipal securities, most of which are traded infrequently. Because considerable time may elapse between trades of a particular security, the relatively large bid–ask spread compensates the market maker for tying up capital and for bearing the risk that market prices may change substantially between transactions.

## Trading Positions

Market makers hold inventories of securities not only to be prepared for buyers but also as a consequence of their willingness to accommodate sellers. For example, a pension fund might want to sell 250,000 shares of a particular stock, which would swamp the specialist's order book on the New York Stock Exchange. Instead of accepting a substantial price concession on the NYSE, the pension fund uses the services of an investment bank. The investment bank may be unwilling to buy so many shares itself (acting as a market maker), but (acting as a broker) it might be able to find another institution (or two) that can be persuaded to acquire most of these shares at a reasonable price.

Perhaps the investment bank quickly locates an insurance company that is willing to buy 200,000 shares at a price that is acceptable to the pension fund. Because speed is important to the pension fund, the investment bank closes the deal by buying 50,000 shares for its own account, with the intention of selling these shares as soon as possible. The investment bank receives a commission for arranging the trade between the pension fund and the insurance company and hopes that this commission will not be eroded by a capital loss on the remaining 50,000 shares. To be a profitable market maker, an investment bank must be able to find customers quickly, have enough capital to absorb residual shares, and be willing to take risks.

For example, in 1983 Allied Corporation acquired Bendix Corporation and, with it, 5.4 million shares of RCA common stock, which it wanted to sell as quickly as possible. At 3:15 P.M. on March 30, 1983, Salomon Brothers agreed to buy all 5.4 million shares at $23.75 a share (a $128 million transaction), even though it apparently had no waiting buyers for the stock. By 3:30, Salomon's sales force had resold all 5.4 million shares at an average price of $24. For being willing and financially able to take a huge risk, Salomon earned $3 million in commissions and capital gains in 15 minutes.[6]

Although market makers accommodate trades, they generally take an active role in soliciting trades too. In the preceding example, the investment bank will try to find buyers for the residual 50,000 shares rather than merely waiting for buyers to appear by coincidence. Similarly, acting as a market maker, a dealer may buy $50 million in 10-year Treasury zeros from a customer; not wanting to hold this many 10-year zeros in its inventory, the firm's sales staff calls up customers and peddles the bonds as quickly as possible. As in this example, a dealer's ability to make markets profitably depends on up-to-date knowledge of its customers — what securities they hold, what securities they would like to hold, and what securities they can be persuaded to hold.

Dealers make active trades for a number of reasons: to rebalance their portfolios (for example, to replenish their Treasury-bill inventory), on behalf of their customer accounts, and for their own proprietary accounts (hoping to profit from temporarily mispriced securities). These reasons can be complementary in that acting as a market maker or on behalf of customers, the securities firm may temporarily deplete its inventory or accumulate a large position.

Dealer inventories are generally financed with repos or bank loans. The composition of their inventories — for example, short-term versus long-term securities — takes into account not only demand but also their own interest-rate predictions. If the term structure is flat but the dealer anticipates a decline in interest rates, it can bet on this decline by using short-term variable-rate financing to increase its holdings of long-term Treasury securities.

Many securities firms run *matched books*, in which they make two offsetting transactions, profiting on the price difference. Figure 20.1 illustrates an example in which a dealer does a $25 million overnight reverse repo with a finance company (lending money to the finance company, with Treasury bonds as collateral) and does an overnight $25 million repo with a pension fund (borrowing money from the pension fund, with the Treasury bonds as collateral). In effect, the securities firm has acted as a market maker by arranging for the

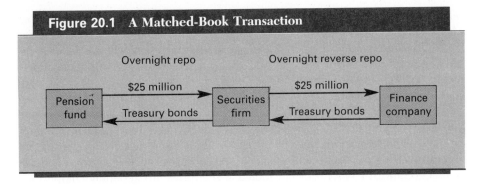

**Figure 20.1  A Matched-Book Transaction**

pension fund to loan money to the finance company, profiting on the interest-rate differential.

In an *unmatched book*, the two sides of the transaction are not identical, and the dealer accepts the risk that the prices may move adversely. If the term structure is upward sloping, the dealer might use overnight repos to finance a 60-day reverse repo — attempting to profit from the fact that the overnight interest rate is less than the 60-day rate. This position can turn out to be an unprofitable wager if the term structure inverts so that overnight interest rates unexpectedly rise relative to longer rates. The dealer will then be paying higher interest rates on its overnight repos than it is earning on its 60-day reverse repo.

# ARBITRAGE

Dealers also engage in arbitrage activities by making offsetting purchases and sales of similar securities. In a **pure arbitrage** transaction, an identical security is simultaneously purchased and sold in two different markets. If, for example, a stock is trading at a higher price on the New York Stock Exchange than on the London Stock Exchange, an investment bank's arbitrage desk can make a risk-free profit by buying the stock in London and selling it in New York. Because arbitragers monitor such opportunities closely and move quickly, large price differentials are rare.

Some securities firms make substantial profits arbitraging slightly mispriced securities that are similar but not identical. For example, Chapter 5 explained why Treasury securities with the same maturity but different coupon rates should have different yields to maturity if the term structure is not flat. If the observed difference in yields is inexplicably wide or narrow, an arbitrager can buy Treasury securities with one coupon rate and sell Treasury securities with another coupon rate, counting on the temporary mispricing to disappear. Similarly, if the yield on 20-year Treasury bonds seems high in comparison with the yields on 19-year and 21-year Treasury bonds, an arbitrager can buy the 20-year bonds and sell the 19-year and 21-year bonds. If corporate bond rates seem unusually high relative to Treasury yields, an arbitrager can buy corporates and sell Treasuries, hoping that the yield differential will return to its normal level. More complex strategies involve bonds with different coupons and maturities from different issuers. By purchasing some bonds and selling others, the arbitrager tries to construct a portfolio that is protected against general movements, up or down, in interest rates while betting that an inexplicable yield spread is only temporary.

It is also possible to construct arbitraged positions by combining stocks and bonds with derivative securities, such as options and futures. For instance, Example 10.4, earlier in the book, described stock-index arbitrage, which involves buying stocks and selling stock-index futures, or vice versa. Arbitrage transactions with similar, but not identical securities are generally complicated and must be done carefully to avoid excessive risk-taking; they are consequently usually handled by arbitrage specialists who are separate from the dealers who make markets.

Another kind of arbitrage — called **risk arbitrage** — involves a corporate merger, acquisition, or restructuring in which an offer has been made to buy most of or all a company's stock from its shareholders, and an arbitrager makes a transaction that will be profitable if the offer is successful. For example, a corporate raider might offer $40 for a stock that had recently been selling for $30, immediately driving the price up to $38. The price does not rise all the way to $40 because there is a chance that the takeover attempt will fail. An arbitrager might buy the stock at $38, betting that the takeover will succeed and, perhaps, that the raider will ultimately offer even more than $40 a share. This transaction is called risk arbitrage because it is not riskless.

Even larger profits can be made if the arbitrager can identify a likely takeover candidate ahead of time and buy shares at $30 before the $40 offer is announced — a strategy likely to be successful if the arbitrager has an inside tip from the corporate raider or the raider's investment banker, as in the Ivan Boesky case recounted in Chapter 9.

The scope of the Boesky scandal was stunning, both in the number of people involved and in the size of the illegal profits, and it unquestionably shook the public's confidence in the integrity and fairness of financial markets. It also tarnished takeovers because of an unfortunate confusion of takeovers with insider trading. Takeovers make insider trading profitable, but the reverse is not true. Insider trading is not the reason raiders want to acquire a company. If anything, insider trading hurts corporate raiders because the runup in the target stock's price prior to the takeover attempt forces the raider to offer an even higher price to persuade stockholders to tender their shares. Raiders try to keep their intentions secret, prefer investment bankers who keep valuable information confidential, and sue people who leak their plans.

The investment bankers, in turn, try to maintain a "Chinese wall" between investment banking and securities trading; if they fear a breach, they put the stock on a restricted list, notifying traders that they cannot buy or sell the stock for the firm's own account. Morgan Stanley's Manhattan offices are monitored by closed-circuit cameras, segregated by computerized access cards, and operated with a fortress mentality. Their general counsel observed that "the preservation of insider information is the backbone of our business."[7] Curbing takeovers to prevent insider trading makes about as much sense as outlawing oil drilling, medical research, and computer-software development to prevent the leak of inside information.

# ASSET MANAGEMENT

Another area of services provided by securities firms involves helping others manage their portfolios. Securities firms advise borrowers about their financing alternatives, advise investors in the selection of stocks and bonds, and, in some cases, take over the money-management task — making decisions rather than merely offering advice.

Research departments at securities firms study the overall state of the economy and financial markets and individual securities as well. They might make predictions about interest rates, inflation, and the unemployment rate that are relevant to both buyers and sellers of securities. They also may identify specific securities that they believe to be underpriced or overpriced — putting the former on a buy list and the latter on a sell list. These research reports, predictions, and opinions are used by the firm's brokers and traders and may be available to customers. Reports that are especially detailed and elaborate may be sold to institutional investors or provided free to customers that do a lot of business with the firm. Securities firms provide these various kinds of financial advice both to encourage trading activity and to fortify customer loyalty.

**EXAMPLE**
**20.6**      *Wrap Accounts*

Many brokerage firms offer wrap accounts, which allow individual investors to use the services of professional money managers who make investment decisions for pension funds, mutual funds, and other institutional investors. Most wrap accounts have a $100,000 minimum. For a $100,000 stock portfolio, brokerage firms generally charge the investor an annual fee equal to 3 percent of the account's assets. The percentage fee is lower for larger accounts and for portfolios that include bonds as well as stocks. This annual fee covers the cost of professional management, trading expenses, custodial fees, and detailed quarterly performance reports.

Brokerage firms usually do not manage wrap accounts themselves, but instead have the investor select an outside money-management company from a list supplied by the firm offering the wrap account. In 1992, an estimated $30 billion was invested in wrap accounts.*

*James A. White, "Insurers and Banks Join 'Wrap' Business," Wall Street Journal, *May 26, 1992.*

Until the 1990s, wrap accounts were offered exclusively by brokerage firms. Now, the Fidelity mutual-fund family offers wrap accounts using its own mutual funds as money managers. Based on responses to questions intended to determine the investor's objectives and degree of risk aversion, each investor's assets are invested in one of 18 portfolios, each of which contains a mixture of Fidelity no-load mutual funds. The minimum Fidelity wrap account is $100,000, and investors are charged an annual 1 percent fee in addition to the management fees and expenses incurred by the mutual funds.

In 1992, Chase Manhattan Bank became the first commercial bank to offer a wrap account through its brokerage subsidiary Chase Manhattan Investment Services; Chase's maximum annual fee is 2.75 percent of assets, slightly less than brokerage firms charge. Equitable Life Insurance was the first insurance company to offer wrap accounts. Equitable Classic Strategies has a $250,000 minimum and a standard 3 percent fee, is sold by Equitable's insurance agents, and, unlike most other programs, does not use outside money managers. Instead, investors choose a money manager from one of Equitable's subsidiaries, including Equitable Capital Corporation and Donaldson, Lufkin & Jenrette.

Because they have expertise in a wide range of financial areas, securities firms often provide financial consulting services to businesses, either for a fee or as part of an ongoing customer relationship. These consultations range from informal discussions to detailed formal reports. Typical financial strategy topics include debt–equity policy, dividend policy, fixed-rate versus variable-rate financing, and managing interest-rate risk.

Going beyond mere advice, securities firms manage investment portfolios, pension plans, and mutual funds for individuals and institutions. The managers of an investment portfolio or pension fund are given specified objectives and discretionary power to make day-to-day decisions, with their performance subject to periodic review. Mutual funds are generally managed through subsidiaries; the different types of mutual funds are discussed in detail in the next chapter.

## MANAGING SECURITIES FIRMS

A securities firm has several sources of profits, including underwriting spreads, private placement fees, mergers and acquisitions fees, brokerage fees, bid–ask spreads in its market making, arbitrage profits, and asset-management fees. In addition, as a financial intermediary, a securities firm can profit from its interest-rate *carry* (the difference between the rate of return on the securities it holds and the cost of financing these securities) because the dealer is able to borrow relatively inexpensively.

Many of these activities are complementary. When a firm acts as a market maker, it gets a feel for the market that is valuable in pricing new security issues.

**Table 20.3  Assets and Liabilities of Securities Firms, June 1991 (Billions of Dollars)**

| Assets | | Liabilities | |
|---|---|---|---|
| Cash | 10.8 | Customer credit balances | 65.0 |
| Commercial paper | 17.4 | Repos | 73.4 |
| Customer loans | 41.7 | Bank loans | 25.7 |
| Treasury securities | 114.9 | Other liabilities | 79.4 |
| Corporate bonds | 25.8 | | |
| Municipal bonds | 7.0 | | |
| Corporate stock | 8.5 | | |
| Real assets | 6.0 | | |
| Other assets | 46.1 | Net worth | 34.7 |
| | 278.2 | | 278.2 |

**Source:** Federal Reserve Board, *Flow of Funds Accounts, Second Quarter 1991.*

Underwriting activities help the firm value potential merger and acquisition targets that might be split up and resold. An arbitrage department can show how to hedge a large position instead of reselling it. Research information aids virtually all of a securities firm's activities, and these activities, in turn, yield valuable information about financial markets. Customer relationships that a firm develops in one activity can create business in other activities: a new security issue might lead to a takeover defense; market making might lead to a private placement; a private placement might lead to an asset-management contract.

Clients often require a wide range of financial services and prefer to use a single securities firm that can provide all these services. For example, in 1985 Monsanto used Goldman Sachs to assist in its acquisition of G.D. Searle & Company, a pharmaceutical firm. Goldman Sachs helped plan and price the acquisition, arranged for the private placement of commercial paper and the public issuance of long-term bonds to finance the acquisition, and then handled the sale of part of Searle. Also in that same year, Goldman Sachs helped Owens-Corning acquire Armco's Aerospace and Strategic Materials Group and used a variety of markets to finance the deal: it issued $150 million in commercial paper, using interest-rate swaps to convert this paper into a longer-term obligation; it issued $100 million in 5-year bonds, using Treasury futures to hedge the interest-rate risk until the notes could be sold; and it issued $100 million in 15-year Swiss franc and German mark Eurobonds, using currency swaps to convert these bonds into dollar obligations. A large, diversified securities firm such as Goldman Sachs can attract and retain customers by putting together an attractive package of services.

Table 20.3 shows the aggregate assets and liabilities of securities firms in June of 1991. Most of the items are familiar by now, but two might require explanation. On the asset side of the balance sheets, customer loans ($41.7 billion in June of 1991) are funds that investors borrow from securities firms to finance their stock and bond purchases; these are explained more fully in Example 20.3. On the liability side, customer credit balances ($65 million in June of 1991) are cash balances that customers hold in their brokerage accounts. Investors earn money-market interest rates on these accounts, which they use to park dividends, coupons, and the proceeds from security sales before they reinvest these funds.

Securities firms are highly leveraged financial intermediaries, borrowing from some in order to lend to others. Table 20.3 shows that, in the aggregate, they held nearly $300 billion in assets in 1991, almost all of which was financial, and that nearly 90 percent of these assets were financed by borrowed money. Much as an individual borrows money to buy a house, securities firms borrow money to buy financial assets — for instance, using repos to finance the underwriting of a new stock issue or to pay for Treasury bonds acquired as a market maker. Their assets, the securities they acquire with borrowed money, serve as collateral for their loans.

The fact that securities firms finance almost all their security purchases with borrowed money has some immediate implications. To make a profit, the rate of return on their investments must be higher than the interest rates they pay on their loans. Such profits might be attainable because, like commercial banks, securities firms serve a valuable role as financial intermediaries and are able to borrow more cheaply than their customers. Or, with considerable expertise and intimate knowledge of financial markets, they may be able to identify securities that are temporarily mispriced.

Because they are highly levered, small differences between the rates of return on their assets and the interest rates on their liabilities can yield a large rate of return on net worth. Changes in this interest differential have a multiplied effect on a securities firm's rate of return on net worth. For the industry as a whole, annual aggregate pretax profits generally range from 1 to 4 percent of assets and from 10 to 40 percent of net worth.[8]

In addition to their effects on current income, changes in interest rates affect the market value of a securities firm's assets and liabilities. As with other financial intermediaries, securities firms are vulnerable to interest-rate risk if their asset and liability durations are mismatched. In practice, securities firms have considerable flexibility in selecting assets and liabilities and are very adept at using sophisticated mathematical models to protect their net worth from interest-rate risk. If their asset and liability durations differ, it is because they want to bet on the direction of interest-rate movements.

The future evolution of securities firms will be exciting and challenging. The Glass-Steagall Act defined separate roles for commercial banks and investment banks. These compartmentalized roles are now disappearing, and securities firms are aggressively diversifying into new areas, focusing on special niches or being absorbed by stronger firms. Innovation will be increasingly necessary if investment banks are to avoid the twin perils on the horizon: competition from powerful commercial banks with large deposit bases and FDIC insurance and the realization by financially secure and sophisticated corporations that they don't need investment bankers to help them issue securities. Some investment banks will no doubt become more like commercial banks — in fact, virtually indistinguishable when universal banking is a reality. Other securities firms will become niche companies that offer specialized services such as discount brokerage, foreign securities, or junk bonds.

# SUMMARY

The 1933 Glass-Steagall Act prohibits firms from acting as both a commercial bank (accepting deposits and making loans) and as an investment bank (helping businesses raise funds through the sale of securities). Investment banks and other securities firms are financial intermediaries that provide a variety of financial services, including securities issuance, mergers and acquisitions assistance, security brokerage, market making, arbitrage, and asset management. Several investment banking firms — including First Boston, Goldman Sachs, Morgan Stanley, and Salomon Brothers — focus on underwriting and large-scale trades rather than on retail brokerage. Other securities firms — such as Merrill Lynch and Prudential-Bache — derive substantial revenue from retail brokerage. Some discount brokerage firms only do retail brokerage.

Securities issuance includes underwriting public offerings and arranging private placements to finance construction projects, equipment leasing, inventories, debt–equity swaps, mergers and acquisitions, and leveraged buyouts. The customer relationship between an investment bank and a client generally extends far beyond a single fund-raising effort to include ongoing financial advice on a wide range of issues. The investment bank may even have a seat on the firm's board of directors. The client purchases not only the investment bank's ability to sell securities but also its financial expertise.

Mergers and acquisitions activities include the analysis, negotiation, and financing of the merger of two companies or the acquisition of one company by another. Some investment banks advise potential targets how to erect defensive barriers to protect the company from an unwanted takeover. Shark repellents installed to discourage takeovers seem a clear case of management putting their own interests above those of their shareholders. An easy alternative for discouraging takeovers that benefits stockholders is for a firm to repurchase its stock when the managers feel the price is too low.

In addition to underwriting new security issues, investment banks are also brokers and dealers in the secondary market. Acting as brokers, they arrange trades between buyers and sellers and charge a commission for doing so. Acting as dealers, they make markets in securities by quoting bid and ask prices at which they will buy or sell, as needed, for their own accounts.

Stockbrokers earn income when investors make trades, giving brokers an economic incentive to encourage trading. Dealers earn income from bid–ask spreads and from the securities they hold. Some securities firms make substantial profits from arbitrage transactions in which they simultaneously buy and sell identical or very similar securities in different markets or from a risk-arbitrage transaction that will be profitable if a proposed merger or takeover succeeds. Securities firms also give individuals, businesses, and financial institutions financial advice or, in some cases, manage their portfolios for them.

Securities firms are highly levered financial intermediaries that borrow money for relending, intending that the rate of return on their investments will be higher than the interest rates on their borrowed funds. Except to the extent that they want to bet on interest-rate movements, securities firms generally insulate their net worth from interest-rate risk by matching their asset and liability durations.

## IMPORTANT TERMS

ask price
bid price
broker
dealer
discount brokers
full-service brokers
Glass-Steagall Act

initial public offering (IPO)
investment banking
merchant banking
pure arbitrage
risk arbitrage
security brokerage
underwriting

## EXERCISES

1. Do you think that it is generally more difficult for an investment bank to determine a price for an IPO or for an issue of additional shares by a corporation that is already publicly owned? Explain your reasoning.

2. Investment banks that underwrite a bond issue often monitor the firm's ability and willingness to pay the interest due on these bonds after they have been issued and, in some cases, even lend the firm money to do so. Why would an investment bank care if a firm defaults if it has invested none of its own money in the firm's securities?

3. Why do you suppose new issues are often underwritten by a syndicate rather than by a single securities firm?

4. One advantage of a private placement is that a firm does not have to make the public disclosures required by the SEC for public issues. Why might a completely honest firm want to avoid such disclosures?

5. Why might a corporation's board of directors enthusiastically recommend shareholder approval of an outside offer to acquire the firm?

6. In 1987 a financial writer argued for more laws governing takeovers:

*Raiders shouldn't be permitted to invest first and disclose later. Investment banking firms shouldn't be permitted to set up the financing for a takeover without disclosing their intention first. And no one should be permitted to buy a publicly owned company without having to pay for it [using their own money, rather than borrowed money].*[9]

How would such laws affect takeover activity? Explain your reasoning.

7. Some people argue that golden parachutes facilitate takeovers by making the top management of the target company less fearful of losing their jobs and salaries. Why might golden parachutes discourage takeovers?

8. Why would an investment bank that is handling a takeover offer not want its traders to buy stock in the target firm in advance of the announcement of the takeover offer?

9. In April of 1987, the bid and ask prices for a seat on the NYSE were $750,000 and $1.5 million. Which price was the bid, and which was the ask? Is this bid–ask spread wide or narrow compared with the Treasury-bond market?

10. If a market maker in Treasury bonds purchases $10 million in 20-year Treasury zeros, what will be the (approximate) size of its capital gain or loss on these zeros if the interest rate on 20-year zeros increases by 10 basis points?

11. In the 1970s, many securities firms found it profitable to broker shopping centers, office buildings, and other commercial real estate. Why might an investment bank prefer to broker a shopping center than to invest in one?

12. Explain this remark: "Since brokers are usually compensated by commissions, it is possible that some brokers may not be completely objective about a client's buy/sell decision."[10]

13. Why do you think an investor who has an asset-management account and who needs cash would borrow money using his or her securities as collateral instead of just selling the securities?

14. An astute market observer wrote that "margin is how brokerage firms make it easy for you to overextend yourself with leverage."[11] Another says, "If you and your broker are nonetheless determined to give margin a try, be prepared for an intense and perilous relationship that may well last till debt do you part."[12] Explain how margin gives you leverage and why it might be a perilous strategy.

15. If the Federal Reserve wants to discourage stock market speculation, should it raise or lower margin requirements?

16. Bonds can be bought on margin — 30 percent for corporate bonds and as little as 5 percent for Treasury bonds. Why would anyone want to buy Treasury bonds on margin, since the loan rate charged by the broker is presumably higher than the interest rate on Treasury bonds?

17. If you buy 400 shares of stock at $25 a share, what is your percentage gain (neglecting taxes and commissions) if the price immediately jumps to $30? Now assume that instead of buying 400 shares, you had used 50 percent margin to buy 800 shares. Show your debt and equity and calculate the percentage return on your investment if the price jumps to $30 and if the price immediately drops to $20.

18. During the 1920s, some investors would pyramid their position by borrowing more money as stock prices went up. For instance, an investor might use $2000 of his money and $8000 in borrowed money to buy 1000 shares of stock at $10. If the price goes up to $16, the total market value is $16,000 — of which $8000 is debt and $8000 is equity. The investor can now borrow an additional $24,000 and buy 1500 more shares, giving $32,000 debt and $8000 equity — still 20 percent margin. Fill in the

| Price per Share | Number of Shares | Debt | Equity | Total Value |
|---|---|---|---|---|
| $10 | 1,000 | $ 8,000 | $2,000 | $10,000 |
| 16 | 1,000 | 8,000 | 8,000 | 16,000 |
| 16 | 2,500 | 32,000 | 8,000 | 40,000 |
| 20 | 2,500 | 32,000 | | |
| 20 | 4,500 | | | |
| 25 | 4,500 | | | |
| 25 | 8,100 | | | |
| 20 | 8,100 | | | |

table above, showing the debt, equity, and total market value when the following events then happen in succession: the price rises to $20; the investor buys another 2000 shares with borrowed money; the price rises to $25; the investor buys an additional 3600 shares with borrowed money; the price falls back to $20.

19. Is the bid price for a security higher or lower than the ask price?

20. Company ABC has proposed merging with company XYZ, giving XYZ's shareholders one share of ABC stock in exchange for each share of XYZ stock that they own. Right after the merger proposal is announced, ABC stock trades for $50 a share and XYZ stock for $47.50. If an investment bank's risk-arbitrage department wants to bet that the merger will be consummated, should it buy ABC stock and sell XYZ stock, or vice versa? Explain your reasoning.

21. Suppose that the term structure is flat and a bond dealer accumulates a very large inventory of 30-year Treasury bonds, financed by a sequence of overnight repos. Is it implicitly betting on an increase or decrease in interest rates? Explain your reasoning.

22. When the term structure is upward sloping, a securities dealer might try to maximize its interest-rate carry (the difference between return on the securities that it holds and the cost of borrowing money to purchase these securities) by using overnight repos to finance the purchase of long-term Treasury bonds. What is the interest-rate risk in this strategy?

23. If the spread between the interest rates on corporate double-A and triple-A bonds seems unusually large and a securities dealer wants to bet that the spread will narrow, should it buy double-A bonds or triple-A bonds? How can it hedge its position so that it is betting just on the spread narrowing and not on a general movement in market interest rates?

24. Suppose that the term structure is upward sloping and there is an inexplicably wide spread between the yields to maturity on 20-year Treasury bonds with 4 percent coupons and 20-year Treasury bonds with 8 percent coupons. If a securities dealer wants to bet that the spread will narrow, regardless of whether the general level of interest rates goes up or down, should it buy the 4 percent bonds and sell the 8 percent bonds, or vice versa?

25. Use the data in Table 20.3 to estimate the aggregate leverage of securities firms.

# 21 Investment Companies

*There are two kinds of investors: those who have made mistakes and those who are liars.*

**Anonymous**

An **investment company** pools the funds of investors to purchase a diversified portfolio of securities. The first investment companies were simple arrangements in which a professional managed the investments of wealthy investors. Each account was kept separate, and different securities were selected to suit individual needs. The advantages of these trust arrangements derived from the professional manager's presumed expertise in selecting securities. In the twentieth century, the growing middle class wanted to buy stocks, and investment companies that pooled funds from many investors became popular.

In the 1920s the public clamored for securities and for investment companies. The number of investors holding stocks and bonds multiplied in a decade from 1 million to almost 20 million. In 1929 there were almost 700 investment companies in operation, with assets in excess of $7 billion. Most were organized by prominent investment banking houses and commercial banks. However, many were local trusts set up by public-spirited entrepreneurs in Columbus, Milwaukee, Boise, and wherever willing investors could be found.

Almost all the investment companies of the 1920s borrowed money; overall, they were financed by roughly 40 percent debt and 60 percent equity. The great stock market crash in the 1930s bankrupted many investment companies and left the rest with damaged reputations. It wasn't until the 1950s that households again began putting substantial sums of money into investment companies — mostly in a new variation popularly known as *mutual funds*.

Mutual funds and other investment companies issue shares, like other corporations, but instead of using the shareholders' money to build factories and office buildings, they buy portfolios of securities. About two-thirds of all investment company shareholders have less than $10,000 invested.[1] By pooling these small amounts, investment companies give many investors access to securities they could otherwise not afford (for example, $10,000 Treasury bills) and diversification that they could otherwise not achieve. Moreover, as investment companies emphasize, people who are busy with other things can have their money managed by professionals.

We begin this chapter by looking at the general characteristics of investment companies and at two important distinctions: between open-end and closed-end companies and between load funds and no-load funds. Then we'll look at performance.

## REGULATED INVESTMENT COMPANIES

Almost all investment companies meet the criteria for **regulated investment companies** established by the Investment Company Act of 1940 — a designation that exempts them from corporate taxes. The most important criteria are

1. The company must register with the SEC and comply with its disclosure requirements.
2. At least 90 percent of its interest and dividend income must be distributed to shareholders as it is received.
3. At least 50 percent of its portfolio must be diversified, in that no more than 5 percent of this diversified part may be invested in any one firm and it may not own more than 25 percent of any firm's outstanding securities.

The interest, dividends, and capital gains that an investment company earns on its portfolio are passed directly to shareholders, usually either monthly or quarterly. While the fund pays no taxes on this income, shareholders must. Most investment companies allow shareholders to reinvest interest, dividends, and capital gains automatically, but this has no effect on the shareholders' tax liability.

There are now more than 2000 regulated investment companies. Most fall into one of three broad categories:

*Money-market funds* buy very short-term securities, including Treasury bills and certificates of deposit.

*Bond funds* buy longer-term bonds, with some funds specializing in Treasury bonds, some in high-yield "junk" bonds, and others in tax-exempt municipal bonds.

*Stock funds* buy corporate stock, with some funds emphasizing dividend income, others potential capital gains.

Many investment companies try to establish an appealing identity by specializing. Some focus on commodity options, convertible bonds, covered calls, and other specific types of securities or strategies. There is a fund open only to employees of General Electric, another for baptized Lutherans, one for airline pilots, and another for cemetery owners. One fund buys only aviation stocks;

another buys stock in small savings and loan associations. One fund invests in Canadian securities; one in Ohio businesses. Another does not invest in liquor, tobacco, or drug stocks.

Many investment companies are part of a family of funds. Fidelity operates more than 100 separate funds, and Vanguard has nearly that many. These fund families offer a smorgasbord of funds and allow investors to switch money from one to another with just a telephone call — although, as some investors learn to their dismay, each switch is technically the sale of one fund and the purchase of another, and the sale may involve the taxable realization of a capital gain.

Our objective here is not to catalog funds or to describe the details of each, but to explore some general principles that apply to all investment companies. To do so, we must make two crucial distinctions: between open-end and closed-end investment companies and, within the open-end category, between load and no-load funds. We begin with the open-end funds.

# OPEN-END FUNDS

The number of shares issued by an **open-end investment company** is not fixed, but instead increases as more money is invested in the fund and declines as money is withdrawn. Open-end investment companies are more commonly known as **mutual funds**. Each day, or several times a day, the fund calculates the total market value of its portfolio and divides this figure by the number of outstanding shares to obtain a **net asset value** (**NAV**) per share, the price at which it will redeem shares or issue new ones.

If a fund has 10 million shares outstanding and a portfolio worth $100 million, then each share in the mutual fund is worth $10. Suppose that people now invest another $20 million in the fund. At $10 a share, $20 million will buy 2 million new shares, bringing the total number of shares to 12 million and increasing the assets of the fund to $120 million — the asset value of each share is still $10. Similarly, if existing shareholders decide to withdraw $20 million, they will redeem 2 million shares, reducing the fund's assets and shares proportionately, so that the asset value per share stays at $10.

**EXAMPLE**

**21.1**    *Money-Market Funds*

Money-market mutual funds give individual and institutional investors a convenient and relatively inexpensive way to invest in Treasury bills, commercial paper, and other short-term low-risk securities. In the late 1970s, short-term interest rates rose substantially above the deposit-rate ceilings permitted by the Federal Reserve's Regulation Q, and money-market funds grew explosively — from $4 billion in assets in 1977 to $75 billion in 1980 and $235 billion by 1982. Responding to pleas from banks and thrifts, Congress allowed them to offer special money-market deposit accounts (MMDAs) and phased out deposit-rate ceilings. Nonetheless, money-market funds continue to attract investors.

## Assets and Liabilities of Money-Market Funds, June 1991 (Billions of Dollars)

| Assets | | Liabilities | |
|---|---|---|---|
| Cash | 2.0 | Shares outstanding | 532.8 |
| Repurchase agreements | 71.6 | | |
| U.S. CDs | 30.4 | | |
| Eurodollar CDs | 27.1 | | |
| Commercial paper | 211.3 | | |
| Treasury securities | 91.4 | | |
| Municipal securities | 87.3 | | |
| Other assets | 11.7 | Net worth | 0.0 |
| | 532.8 | | 532.8 |

**Source:** Federal Reserve Board, *Flow of Funds Accounts, Second Quarter 1991.*

In June of 1991, money-market funds held $532.8 billion in assets, compared with $681.3 billion for all other types of mutual funds combined. The average maturity of money-market fund assets is usually less than 60 days and sometimes less than 14 days. The accompanying table identifies the various securities money-market funds hold. The largest category by far is commercial paper, which comprises 40 percent of aggregate money-market fund assets. Asset holdings are not uniform across funds, since individual money-market funds specialize in particular securities — for example, risk-free Treasury securities or tax-exempt municipal securities.

Because they are a mutual fund, money-market funds have no net worth and their liability to their shareholders is always equal to the value of their assets. Unlike a bank deposit, those who invest in a money-market fund technically buy shares in the fund. Most money-market funds keep the value of each share constant at $1 by using "amortized cost" accounting, in which the fund's assets are valued at acquisition cost and the interest that the fund earns (net of operating expenses) is recorded as a daily dividend to the fund's shareholders and automatically used to purchase additional shares at the fixed $1 price. Thus the number of shares — not their value — increases.

A shareholder can invest or withdraw cash, without a sales charge, by giving written or telephoned authorization to transfer money between the money-market fund and the shareholder's bank account. Most funds also allow shareholders to write checks, with a $250 or $500 minimum, drawn on their account. Many households, businesses, and government agencies use a money-market fund as a formal or informal cash-management account, temporarily investing surplus cash until needed.

Annual expenses for money-market funds average about 0.6 percent of assets; the shareholders' annual rate of return is consequently about 0.6 percentage points below the interest rates on the securities held by money-market funds. For many investors, this slightly lower rate of return is more than offset by the fact that money-market funds allow them to buy and sell shares conveniently and with no charge.

Unlike bank accounts, investments in money-market funds are not protected by deposit insurance. Banks and thrifts are consequently able to attract investors with deposit rates that are slightly below the interest rates paid by comparable money-market funds. When banks and thrifts have offered deposit rates above the interest rates that money-market funds are able to earn on their assets, they have been able to lure many investors away from money-market funds. In 1983, for example, the aggregate amount invested in money-market funds declined by $40 billion (18 percent).

Barring fraud, a money-market fund will never default. The risk for shareholders is that they will experience capital losses if the market value of the fund's portfolio declines. In practice, money-market fund portfolios have very little interest-rate risk and default risk in comparison with the assets held by commercial banks and thrifts. However, in order to increase their rates of return as interest rates fell in the 1980s, some money-market funds invested in commercial paper with low ratings and high yields. In 1989, Integrated Resources defaulted on nearly $1 billion in commercial paper, much of it held by money-market funds. The SEC subsequently limited the exposure of money-market funds to default risk by prohibiting any fund from investing more than 5 percent of its assets in low-rated securities and more than 1 percent in securities issued by a single corporation.

Investors need not buy a round number of shares. If you invest $2356.50 in a fund with a net asset value of $10 per share, you will be credited with $2356.50/$10 = 23.565 shares. As in this example, funds keep track of shares to three decimal places. Fractional shares are necessary because many shareholders automatically reinvest their profits in more shares, and each investor's monthly dividend and interest income will seldom, if ever, buy a round number of shares.

## Load Charges

Mutual funds can be bought through a mutual fund salesperson, insurance agent, or stockbroker or directly from the fund itself. No matter which route is used, the fund may levy a sales charge, called a **load fee**. For a *full-load fund* that is purchased through a stockbroker or other financial advisor, the load is likely to be at least 4 percent, split between the salesperson and the fund itself. Funds, such as those in the Fidelity group, that sell directly to investors are generally *low-load funds*, with a fee of 3 percent or less, all of which goes to the fund. Funds that charge no load fees at all are called **no-load funds**, or **no-loads**.

Load charges are reported in a fund's prospectus but are typically stated, like Treasury-bill yields, on a discount basis. If you invest $10,000 in a fund with an 8.5 percent load, the load charge is 8.5%($10,000) = $850, and you are credited with a $9150 investment in the mutual fund. A more appropriate calculation is that in order to invest $9150 in the fund, you have to pay an additional $850, which is $850/$9150 = 9.3 percent of your investment.

Load fees also can be calculated from the mutual fund prices reported in newspapers. The quotations show two prices, sometimes labeled "Bid" and "Ask," sometimes "NAV" and "Offer." The *bid price*, or *NAV*, is the net asset value of the fund's shares. The *ask*, or *offer*, *price* is the cost of buying a share, including the load charge. If the bid and ask prices are the same, or if there is an entry "NL" in place of the ask price, then there is no load charge for buying the fund's shares. If the bid and ask prices differ, the load can be calculated by comparing the two prices.

Figure 21.1 shows a sampling of price quotations. On this date, John Hancock's Advanced Technology Fund ("AvTech") had a NAV of $10.55 and an offer price of $11.11. To purchase one share, worth $10.55, you must pay $11.11, which is $0.56 more than the net asset value. The load is $0.56/$10.55 = 5.3 percent. (The fund calculates its load fee as $0.56/$11.11 = 5.0 percent.) All the funds in the Janus group have an "NL" in the offer price column, indicating that these are no-load funds, and each fund's offer price is consequently equal to the net asset value.

Because no-loads have no sales force, investors must find the addresses on their own and then mail in their investment. Some no-loads advertise in newspapers; others are described in such books as Wiesenberger's *Investment Companies*, Morningstar's *Mutual Funds*, and the American Association of Individual Investors' *Guide to No-Loads*.

The maximum load charge allowed by the SEC is 9.589 percent. Until recently, a 9.3 percent load was standard. In the 1980s, many funds reduced their load charges in response to the proliferation of funds and the recognition by the public of the advantages of small load fees. Unfortunately, these diminished front-end loads (levied on the initial investment) have been offset by increased annual fees and by the imposition of redemption fees, also called **back-end loads**, that are charged when money is withdrawn from the fund.

## Other Fees

Investment companies charge an annual management fee for their expertise, typically 1 percent of the fund's asset value for stock funds and somewhat less for bond funds. Because the cost of managing a $2 billion portfolio is not twice that of a $1 billion portfolio, many funds have a sliding percentage fee that declines as the fund's assets increase.

The Tax Reform Act of 1986 requires investment companies to report the fund's income and management fees separately, and for most investors these management fees are no longer tax deductible. Consider an investment company shareholder whose $20,000 worth of shares earn $1000, from which a $200 management fee is subtracted. The shareholder receives $800 and, before the 1986 act, paid taxes only on the net income of $800. Now the shareholder must report the full $1000 as income and include the $200 management fee with other

## Figure 21.1  A Sampling of Price Quotations for Open-End Funds

# MUTUAL FUND QUOTATIONS

### Friday, March 27, 1992

Price ranges for investment companies, as quoted by the National Association of Securities Dealers. NAV stands for net asset value per share; the offering includes net asset value plus maximum sales charge, if any.

| | NAV | Offer Price | NAV Chg. |
|---|---|---|---|
| **Ivy Funds:** | | | |
| Gthinc | 9.34 | 9.91 | −.12 |
| Gwth | 16.57 | 17.58 | −.22 |
| Intl | 20.25 | 21.49 | +.11 |
| JP Grth | 17.16 | 18.16 | −.19 |
| JP Inco | 9.35 | 9.89 | +.01 |
| **Janus Fund:** | | | |
| Fixinc | 9.19 | NL | +.01 |
| Fund | 18.08 | NL | −.12 |
| Grinc | 12.80 | NL | −.10 |
| IntGvt | 5.16 | NL | ... |
| Twen | 22.27 | NL | −.24 |
| Ventur | 46.77 | NL | −.36 |
| WrldW | 18.60 | NL | −.01 |
| JapanFd | 9.07 | NL | −.02 |
| **John Hancock:** | | | |
| AstAll p | 12.51 | 13.17 | −.08 |
| AvTech | 10.55 | 11.11 | −.13 |
| Bond p | 15.04 | 15.75 | +.02 |
| CA TE | 11.35 | 11.88 | +.01 |
| Globl p | 18.01 | 18.96 | −.08 |
| GlRx p | 13.80 | 14.53 | −.23 |
| GlTech | 15.62 | 16.44 | −.40 |
| GvSp p | 10.45 | 10.94 | +.01 |
| Grwth p | 16.26 | 17.12 | −.29 |
| MA TE | 11.31 | 11.84 | +.02 |
| NYTE p | 11.39 | 11.93 | +.02 |
| PcBas p | 8.91 | 9.38 | +.02 |
| Sovin p | 14.02 | 14.76 | −.12 |
| SpclE p | 10.56 | 11.12 | −.30 |
| Strinc p | 7.74 | 8.10 | +.01 |
| TxEx p | 10.88 | 11.39 | −.02 |
| USGv p | 8.75 | 9.16 | ... |
| KS Mun | 11.76 | 12.28 | ... |
| Kaufmn r | 2.64 | NL | −.04 |
| **Kemper Funds:** | | | |
| AdjGov | 8.43 | 8.74 | ... |
| BluCh | 12.99 | 13.78 | −.17 |
| CalTx | 7.35 | 7.70 | +.01 |
| DivInc | 7.79 | 8.16 | +.01 |
| EnvSv | 14.55 | 15.44 | −.20 |
| FL Tx | 9.84 | 10.30 | +.02 |
| Glbinc | 9.46 | 9.91 | −.01 |
| Grth | 13.77 | 14.61 | −.24 |
| Hi Yld | 9.58 | 10.03 | +.01 |
| Income | 8.19 | 8.58 | +.01 |
| IntlFd | 9.78 | 9.32 | +.02 |
| Mun B | 9.98 | 10.45 | +.01 |
| NYTF | 10.50 | 10.99 | +.01 |
| Retir1 | 12.31 | 12.96 | −.11 |
| Retir2 | 12.49 | 13.15 | −.06 |
| Retir3 | 9.06 | 9.54 | +.02 |
| ST Glob | 9.37 | 9.71 | −.03 |
| SmCpEq | 5.78 | 6.13 | −.12 |
| Tech | 10.38 | 11.01 | −.29 |
| TX TF | 9.54 | 9.99 | +.02 |
| Tot Rt | 10.25 | 10.88 | −.10 |
| US Gv | 9.21 | 9.64 | +.01 |

e-Ex-distribution. f-Previous day's quotation. s-Stock split or dividend. x-Ex-dividend. NL-No load. p-Distribution costs apply, 12b-1 plan. r-Redemption charge may apply. t-Both p and r footnotes apply.

investment expenses as a miscellaneous itemized deduction. This $200 expense is not tax deductible unless the investor itemizes deductions (in place of a standard deduction) and, in addition, the investor's total miscellaneous deductions exceed 2 percent of adjusted gross income.

Investment companies also incur expenses in buying and selling securities, commissions that might be paid to an affiliated company that handles the transactions. This trading of securities is gauged by a fund's **turnover**, the ratio of the dollar value of its annual sales (or purchases) of securities to its total assets. A fund with a $100 million portfolio that buys and sells $50 million in securities in a year has a turnover of 50 percent; many funds have turnovers of nearly 100 percent or even higher. At a cost of 2 to 3 percent per transaction, including both brokerage fees and bid–ask spreads, this turnover can reduce shareholder profits considerably.

In 1980 the SEC issued Rule 12b-1, which allows mutual funds to charge an additional annual fee to cover marketing expenses (including sales commissions). Many funds subsequently reduced their front-end loads and instituted an annual Rule 12b-1 charge equal to 1 percent of assets, or even more. If you invest in a fund for several years, the Rule 12b-1 fees can be far more expensive than a front-end load fee. The exact amount of the Rule 12b-1 fees is often difficult to find in a prospectus, but it is invariably included in the mandatory disclosure of total annual expenses to assets. Some funds keep their total annual expenses below 1 percent of assets; others charge more than 2 percent. Two percent may not seem like much, but with the stock market up an average of 10 percent a year, a 2 percent annual fee eats up 20 percent of your profits.

To discourage early redemptions, many funds with substantial Rule 12b-1 fees also impose redemption fees (back-end loads). These are typically 4 to 6 percent on withdrawals made during the first year and then decline to zero on withdrawals after 4 to 6 years. This structure ensures that investors either pay several years of Rule 12b-1 fees or else a substantial back-end load.

Since 1988 the SEC has required investment companies to present all charges in a standard table in the prospectus, including estimates of how these fees affect a $1000 investment (assuming 5 percent annual growth) over periods of 1, 3, 5, and 10 years. Unfortunately, the table is not mandatory reading. The director of the SEC's investment management division estimates that fewer than 10 percent of mutual fund investors ever open the prospectus.[2]

## Are More Expensive Funds Worth It?

Numerous studies have found that there is no relationship between a fund's performance (before fees are deducted) and the size of its load charges, management fees, and other expenses. Thus, after such fees are deducted, investors do better with inexpensive funds. For instance, a comparison of investor returns from load and no-load mutual funds over the 5-year period 1979–1984 is given in Table 21.1.[3] Notice that, with one exception, the disadvantage of load funds is approximately equal to the load charge. The one exception is the group of funds

## Table 21.1  Average 5-Year Mutual Fund Returns, 1979–1984

|  | No-Load Funds (%) | Load Funds (Including (%) Load) | Average Load (%) |
|---|---|---|---|
| Maximum capital gains | 152.2 | 128.2 | 8.2 |
| Long-term growth | 114.8 | 105.2 | 7.8 |
| Growth and income | 98.5 | 93.1 | 7.9 |
| Income | 78.0 | 72.2 | 7.5 |
| Corporate bonds | 54.8 | 47.2 | 7.2 |
| Municipal bonds | 19.2 | 14.1 | 5.4 |

**Source:** Gerald W. Perritt, "Is the Load Too Much to Bear?" *American Association of Individual Investors Journal,* June 1984, pp. 18–21.

aiming for maximum capital gains; not only did the load funds charge an 8.5 percent fee, but also, even before subtracting the fee, they did substantially worse than the no-loads.

Despite such evidence, most mutual funds are able to charge investors load fees, and some funds with the highest load charges are among the most popular. The reason is that mutual funds are not bought but are sold, in the sense that most people who invest in mutual funds are talked into doing so by persuasive salespeople. The most effective salespeople are drawn to the most lucrative funds, the ones with the highest load charges. Those who represent a variety of funds have a natural self-interest in recommending the ones with the highest load charges. Salespeople get no commission for persuading someone to invest in a no-load fund and consequently have no interest in doing so.

## CLOSED-END FUNDS

Unlike their open-end relatives, **closed-end funds** have a fixed number of shares outstanding. They do not issue new shares or redeem old ones. If you want to invest in a closed-end fund, you must buy shares from an existing shareholder; those who want to redeem their shares must find someone to buy them. To facilitate these trades, the shares of closed-end funds are traded on the stock exchanges or over the counter, at a market price that need not equal the fund's net asset value.

Closed-end funds have no load fees because they do not issue new shares, but investors do have to pay the usual brokerage fees for trading shares of stock. With no load charges, closed-end funds also have no salespeople, and no doubt as a consequence, the aggregate assets of all closed-end funds are less than 1 percent of the assets of open-end funds.

The market prices of closed-end shares are reported each day along with the prices of other corporate stock. The net asset value can be obtained by a phone call to the fund or, once a week, in most newspapers. Many papers report these

## Figure 21.2 A Sampling of Price Quotations for Closed-End Funds

# PUBLICLY TRADED FUNDS

Friday, March 27, 1992

Following is a weekly listing of unaudited net asset values of publicly traded investment fund shares, reported by the companies as of Friday's close. Also shown is the closing listed market price or a dealer-to-dealer asked price of each fund's shares, with the percentage of difference.

| Fund Name | Stock Exch. | N.A. Value | Stock Price | % Diff. |
|---|---|---|---|---|
| **Diversified Common Stock Funds** | | | | |
| Adams Express | NYSE | 19.63 | 18 7/8 | – 3.85 |
| Allmon Trust | NYSE | 10.40 | 9 3/4 | – 6.25 |
| Baker Fentress | NYSE | 22.05 | 18 1/2 | – 16.10 |
| Blue Chip Value | NYSE | 7.94 | 7 7/8 | – 0.82 |
| Clemente Global Gro | NYSE | b10.53 | 9 1/8 | – 13.34 |
| Gemini II Capital | NYSE | 16.79 | 13 3/8 | – 20.34 |
| Gemini II Income | NYSE | 9.50 | 13 1/2 | + 42.11 |
| General Amer Invest | NYSE | 27.62 | 28 1/2 | + 3.19 |
| Jundt Growth Fund | NYSE | 14.65 | 14 1/4 | – 2.73 |
| Liberty All-Star Eqty | NYSE | 10.58 | 10 1/2 | – 0.76 |
| Niagara Share Corp. | NYSE | 15.01 | 14 5/8 | – 2.56 |
| Quest For Value Cap | NYSE | 24.36 | 19 1/2 | – 19.95 |
| Quest For Value Inco | NYSE | 11.58 | 13 1/4 | + 14.42 |
| Royce Value Trust | NYSE | 12.15 | 11 1/2 | – 5.35 |
| Salomon Fd | NYSE | 15.17 | 13 7/8 | – 8.54 |
| Source Capital | NYSE | 41.47 | 44 1/2 | + 7.31 |
| Tri-Continental Corp. | NYSE | 27.62 | 26 3/4 | – 3.15 |
| Worldwide Value | NYSE | 15.42 | 12 7/8 | – 16.50 |
| Zweig Fund | NYSE | 11.50 | 13 1/4 | + 15.22 |
| **Closed End Bond Funds** | | | | |
| CIM High Yield Secs | AMEX | a7.67 | 7 1/2 | – 2.22 |
| First Commonwealth Fd | NYSE | 13.76 | 15 | + 9.01 |
| Franklin Multi Inc Tr | NYSE | b10.14 | 9 5/8 | – 5.08 |
| Franklin Prin Mat Tr | NYSE | b8.30 | 8 | – 3.61 |
| Franklin Universal Tr | NYSE | b8.42 | 7 5/8 | – 9.44 |
| Muni Yield NY Fd | NYSE | 14.20 | 15 3/8 | + 8.27 |
| **Flexible Portfolio Funds** | | | | |
| America's All Seasn | OTC | 5.87 | 5 5/16 | – 9.50 |
| European Warrant Fd | NYSE | 7.56 | 6 1/4 | – 17.33 |
| Zweig Total Return Fd | NYSE | 9.19 | 10 1/2 | + 14.25 |
| **Loan Participation Funds** | | | | |
| Pilgrim Prime Rate | NYSE | 10.00 | 9 1/8 | – 8.75 |
| **Specialized Equity and Convertible Funds** | | | | |
| Alliance Global Env Fd | NYSE | 12.51 | 10 7/8 | – 13.07 |
| American Capital Conv | NYSE | 21.98 | 19 5/8 | – 10.71 |
| Argentina Fd | NYSE | 11.88 | 13 1/8 | + 10.48 |
| ASA Ltd | NYSE | bc40.91 | 44 3/4 | + 9.39 |
| Asia Pacific | NYSE | 13.41 | 15 1/2 | + 15.59 |
| Austria Fund | NYSE | 9.87 | 9 3/8 | – 5.02 |
| Bancroft Convertible | AMEX | 21.87 | 19 1/8 | – 12.55 |
| Bergstrom Capital | AMEX | 95.91 | 107 1/8 | + 11.69 |
| BGR Precious Metals | TOR | be7.81 | 7 3/8 | – 5.57 |
| Brazil | NYSE | b17.81 | 17 3/8 | – 2.44 |
| CNV Holdings Capital | NYSE | 11.63 | 7 1/2 | – 35.51 |
| CNV Holdings Income | NYSE | 9.65 | 12 1/2 | + 29.53 |
| Castle Convertible | AMEX | a23.89 | 21 1/4 | – 11.05 |
| Central Fund Canada | AMEX | b4.25 | 3 3/4 | – 11.76 |
| Central Securities | AMEX | 12.12 | 10 1/8 | – 16.46 |
| Chile Fund | NYSE | 39.46 | 34 3/8 | – 12.89 |
| Couns Tandem Secs | NYSE | 15.02 | 13 1/2 | – 10.12 |
| Duff&Phelps Utils Inc | NYSE | 8.87 | 9 1/2 | + 7.10 |
| Ellsw Conv Gr&Inc | AMEX | 8.95 | 7 5/8 | – 14.80 |
| Emerging Ger Fd | NYSE | 9.00 | 7 7/8 | – 12.50 |
| Emerging Mexico Fd | NYSE | b24.04 | 23 7/8 | – 0.69 |
| Engex | AMEX | 11.93 | 10 3/16 | – 14.61 |
| Europe Fund | NYSE | 12.17 | 11 1/8 | – 8.59 |
| !st Australia | AMEX | 10.46 | 8 3/4 | – 16.35 |
| First Financial Fund | NYSE | 10.51 | 10 | – 4.85 |
| First Iberian | AMEX | 9.13 | 8 | – 12.38 |
| First Phillipine Fund | NYSE | 11.48 | 9 | – 21.60 |
| France Growth Fund | NYSE | 11.05 | 8 3/4 | – 20.81 |
| Future Germany Fund | NYSE | 14.61 | 12 3/4 | – 12.73 |
| Gabelli Equity Trust | NYSE | 10.80 | 11 | + 1.85 |
| Germany Fund | NYSE | 11.02 | 11 1/4 | + 2.09 |

a-Ex-dividend. b-As of Thursday's close. c-Translated at Commercial Rand exchange rate. e-In Canadian Dollars. f-As of Wednesday's close, using the official exchange rate

**Source:** From *The Wall Street Journal*, March 30, 1992. Reprinted by permission of *The Wall Street Journal*, 1992 Dow Jones & Company, Inc. All Rights Reserved Worldwide.

**Figure 21.3    Average Premium (+) or Discount (−) from Net Asset Value for Closed-End Funds**

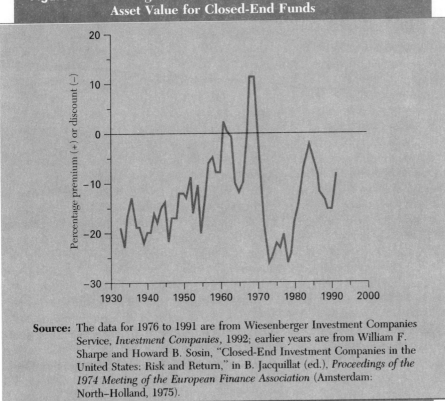

**Source:** The data for 1976 to 1991 are from Wiesenberger Investment Companies Service, *Investment Companies*, 1992; earlier years are from William F. Sharpe and Howard B. Sosin, "Closed-End Investment Companies in the United States: Risk and Return," in B. Jacquillat (ed.), *Proceedings of the 1974 Meeting of the European Finance Association* (Amsterdam: North–Holland, 1975).

net asset values on Saturday or Sunday; *The Wall Street Journal*, which is not published on weekends, reports these figures every Monday. Figure 21.2 shows an example. The first fund, Adams Express, is traded on the New York Stock Exchange and had a net asset value of $19.63 per share. The price of Adams Express shares was 18⅞, a 3.85 percent discount from net asset value.

Until the late 1920s, all investment companies were closed-end. The hundreds that flourished in the 1920s were often very speculative and highly leveraged, and most sold at substantial premiums over net asset value. Many of these funds went bankrupt in the great crash, and those that survived sold at substantial discounts in the 1930s. Today, as Figure 21.2 illustrates, closed-end funds generally trade at a discount from net asset value, although a few special cases trade at premiums. The Gemini II Income fund, for instance, is part of a dual-purpose fund (which we will discuss below) and pays exceptionally high dividends. The discounts on all closed-end funds ebb and flow with time, increasing when small investors leave the stock market and shrinking when they return. Figure 21.3 shows these annual fluctuations. In the 1970s, discounts of 20 to 30 percent were common. Discounts subsequently declined, perhaps because investors became more aware of their existence and advantages.

## A Discount Is an Advantage

Those who consider buying closed-end shares at a discount from net asset value are sometimes discouraged by the possibility that the discount will persist forever. However, the attractiveness of such shares does not hinge on the eventual disappearance of the discount. Even if the discount never narrows, closed-end funds can be financially advantageous simply because investors receive dividends and capital gains on more stock than they actually pay for.

Suppose that a closed-end fund has a net asset value of $10 a share. Each share represents a portfolio of securities that would cost $10 if purchased directly. If a share of the fund can be acquired for $9, then, for a $9 investment, the investor receives the dividends and capital gains on $10 worth of stock. If these annual dividends and capital gains are, say, 10 percent of the $10, the investor receives $1 on a $9 investment — an 11.1 percent return. At a 20 percent discount, a 10 percent return on the fund's portfolio gives the investor a 12.5 percent return; at a 30 percent discount, the return swells to 14.3 percent. Why pay $10 for stock when you can buy it for $9 or $8 or $7?

Funds do have annual expenses that can be avoided by buying stock directly. These expenses are typically, as with open-end funds, 1 percent a year, a figure that is roughly consistent with a 10 percent fund discount. (In the preceding example, investors earn 10 percent if they buy stock directly; a fund that earns a 10 percent return and charges 1 percent for expenses will distribute $0.90, a 10 percent return to investors if its shares sell for $9, a 10 percent discount.) However, these annual fees do not explain why funds sell for 20 or 30 percent discounts. And why do so many people invest in load funds with similar annual fees, paying a premium over net asset value, when they could buy shares in a closed-end fund at a discount from net asset value? Closed-end funds may not beat the market, but they do beat open-end funds.

The explanation that most observers have settled on is, again, that shares in investment companies are not bought but are sold.[4] Large investors prefer to manage their own portfolios, while small investors, the natural audience for investment companies, are not familiar with closed-end funds and are sold open-end funds with load charges by salespeople who profit from the load.

## Share Repurchases

Tobin's $q$ was introduced in Chapter 9 to compare the market value of a firm's stock with the replacement cost of its assets:

$$q = \frac{\text{market value of company}}{\text{replacement cost of assets}}$$

We can apply the same principle to a closed-end investment company. The replacement cost of a fund's assets is equal to the net asset value of its portfolio, and Tobin's $q$ is consequently

$$q = \frac{\text{market value of fund}}{\text{net asset value}}$$

If a closed-end fund sells at a discount from net asset value, then its $q$ is less than 1. Such a fund is worth more dead than alive, in that its shareholders would benefit if the fund sold its assets and distributed the proceeds either through special dividends or by repurchasing its own stock.

To illustrate this point, consider a closed-end fund with 1 million shares outstanding and assets with an aggregate market value of $10 million. The net asset value is $10. If the fund can repurchase 250,000 shares at $8 a share (a 20 percent discount from NAV), this will cost $2 million, reducing its assets to $8 million and reducing the number of outstanding shares to 750,000. Now the net asset value is

$$q = \frac{\$8,000,000}{750,000} = \$10.67$$

If the fund continues to sell at a 20 percent discount from its net asset value, the market price rises to $0.8(\$10.67) = \$8.54$. If, instead, the fund buys half its shares at $8, the net asset value of the remaining shares rises to $12. If it buys all its shares at $8, the net asset value of the last share is $2,000,008.

The repurchase of shares at a price less than net asset value always increases the net asset value of the remaining shares. Those who sell do so voluntarily; those who stay enjoy an increase in the net asset value of their shares. If a fund's repurchase plan increases the price of its shares, narrowing the discount, so much the better.

Why, then, don't all closed-end funds automatically repurchase shares whenever a discount appears? Some are subject to regulatory restrictions that limit the amount of their repurchases. A more general explanation is simply that management fees depend on the size of a fund's assets, so while repurchases are good for shareholders, these are not good for management. Sometimes this understandable reluctance by the fund's management is overcome by aggressive investors who buy enough shares to gain control of the fund and liquidate its assets. In the 1930s, Claude Odell made millions by liquidating closed-end funds. Example 21.2 recounts a more recent case.

EXAMPLE
21.2

## Conversion of the Japan Fund

In 1987, 30-year-old T. Boone Pickens, III, the youngest son of the famous corporate raider, announced that he and several partners had acquired a 5.5 percent stake in the Japan Fund, which was then selling at a 20 percent discount from net asset value. With $700 million in assets, this 20 percent discount implied a $140 million gap between the market value of the Japan Fund's shares and the liquidation value of its assets.

Fearful that Pickens would force a liquidation, the fund's managers recommended that shareholders approve a resolution converting the company into an open-end fund. This move would eliminate the discount, increasing the value of the fund's shares, satisfying Pickens and other shareholders, and preserving the managers' jobs. The resolution was overwhelmingly supported by those shareholders who voted, but not enough voted to give it the necessary approval by 51 percent of all outstanding shares. The fund's managers quickly resubmitted the resolution and lobbied even harder for shareholder approval. This time it did pass, and Pickens and his partners had a $10 million profit for their efforts on behalf of all shareholders.

# DUAL-PURPOSE FUNDS

**Dual-purpose funds** have two classes of shareholders — income and capital. The income shareholders receive all the dividends from the stock in the fund's portfolio; the capital shareholders receive capital gains at the fund's termination date, typically 10 to 15 years after the fund's inception. On the termination date, the income shareholders receive a specified redemption price (usually close to the size of their initial investment) or whatever assets the fund has if it cannot pay the redemption price. The capital shareholders receive any excess of the value of the fund's portfolio over this redemption price.

Consider a fund that starts by selling 1 million income shares at $10 and 1 million capital shares at $10, with a termination in 15 years at a $10 redemption price for the income shareholders. Neglecting any initial sales charges, the fund has $20 million to invest in a portfolio of stocks. Each income share costs $10 and receives the dividends on $20 worth of stock, plus the return of $10 in 15 years, unless the total portfolio has lost more than 50 percent of its market value. If the stocks initially have a 5 percent dividend yield, then the income shareholders get an initial 10 percent dividend yield, which continues to grow over time as dividends increase.

The value of the capital shares at termination depends critically on the value of the portfolio at that time. The net asset value of the capital shares is equal to the total value of the portfolio minus the amount due the income shareholders divided by the number of capital shares. Table 21.2 shows some possible outcomes. (Those who studied Chapter 11 may recognize this profit structure as that of a call option, and indeed, the capital shares have an implicit call option on the fund's portfolio with a striking price of $10 million.)

## *Leverage*

As long as the capital shares' net asset value is positive, the percentage change in the net asset value that accompanies a 1 percent change in the total value of the fund's portfolio depends on the capital shares' leverage, the ratio of the total value of the portfolio to the value of the capital shares:

$$\text{Leverage} = \frac{\text{total value}}{\text{capital value}}$$

**Table 21.2  Net Asset Value of Capital Shares at Termination**

| Total Value of Portfolio (Millions of Dollars) | Aggregate Value of Income Shares (Millions of Dollars) | Aggregate Value of Capital Shares (Millions of Dollars) | NAV of Capital Shares |
|---|---|---|---|
| $ 0 | $ 0 | $ 0 | $ 0 |
| 5 | 5 | 0 | 0 |
| 10 | 10 | 0 | 0 |
| 15 | 10 | 5 | 5 |
| 20 | 10 | 10 | 10 |
| 25 | 10 | 15 | 15 |
| 30 | 10 | 20 | 20 |

For instance, at a total value of $20 million, the capital shares are worth $10 million and the leverage is 2/1, implying that each 1 percent change in the value of the total portfolio causes a 2 percent change in the net asset value of the capital shares. If the portfolio increases 25 percent (to $25 million), the net asset value increases 50 percent (to $15); if the portfolio rises 50 percent (to $30 million), the NAV rises 100 percent (to $20).

## Catering to Preferences

Dual-purpose funds were created to satisfy the differing needs of investors. Corporations that own shares in other corporations are not taxed on 85 percent of the dividends they receive. This tax advantage provides an incentive for buying stocks with high dividends — for example, buying the income shares in a dual-purpose fund. Some tax-exempt institutions also may prefer the large and stable dividend stream from income shares. For many years, individual investors paid lower taxes on capital gains than on dividends, and these investors were consequently drawn to capital shares. Some investors like the leverage inherent in the capital shares.

Furthermore, no one can be made worse off by splitting the fund's shares into two classes, because investors are free to buy equal amounts of both types of shares. If you own 1 percent of the income shares and 1 percent of the capital shares, then you receive 1 percent of the profits, no matter how these are divided, just as if the company were an ordinary closed-end fund. Unlike ordinary closed-end funds, however, a dual-purpose fund gives investors flexibility in varying the proportion of dividends to capital gains.

Like most closed-end funds, dual-purpose funds typically sell at substantial discounts. The intriguing difference is that the discount must go to zero on the termination date. The prices given in Figure 21.2 show Gemini II's income

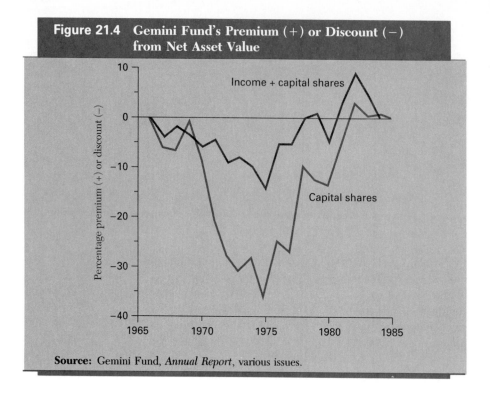

**Figure 21.4**   **Gemini Fund's Premium (+) or Discount (−) from Net Asset Value**

**Source:** Gemini Fund, *Annual Report*, various issues.

shares selling at a 42.11% premium (apparently because of the generous dividend yield), while the capital shares sell at a 20.34% discount. Together, the combined net asset value of one share of each is

$$\$16.79 \ + \ \$9.50 \ = \ \$26.29$$

while the market price of a share of each is

$$\$13\tfrac{3}{8} \ + \ \$13\tfrac{1}{4} \ = \ \$26.875$$

a modest 2.2 percent premium. For the other dual-purpose funds in Figure 21.2, the combined discount is 8.9 percent for Quest for Value and 6.0 percent for CNV holdings.

These dual-purpose funds were started in the period 1985–1987, replacing an earlier group of seven funds that had started in 1967 and since reached their termination dates. Gemini II is a sequel to Gemini, a very successful dual-purpose fund that terminated on December 31, 1984. Figure 21.4 shows the original Gemini Fund's discount during its 17-year history.

# INVESTMENT COMPANY PERFORMANCE

Many people are drawn to investment companies by the advertised expertise, reasoning that just as they pay a doctor for medical services and a lawyer for legal assistance, so they should pay a professional for investment management. They naturally look at past performance and choose a fund with an outstanding record. If this fund's subsequent performance turns out to be disappointing, they switch to a fund that has been more successful.

## *The Quest for Performance*

Because management fees depend on the amount of assets managed, a fund's fees are doubly affected by performance because capital losses not only reduce the fund's market value but also incite shareholders to invest elsewhere. Mutual funds that make large capital gains are swamped by investors looking to share in the success. This investor chase for successful funds encourages funds to trade feverishly, looking for the quick profits that will lure more investors. Funds seeking quick profits become speculators, disdaining patient, long-term investments for guesses about short-term price movements.

In 1967 and 1968, the fastest and quickest fund managers were called "gunslingers": able to spot a concept at 100 paces and pull the trigger (invest heavily) before anyone else. Gerald Tsai's Manhattan Fund was up 40 percent in 1967, while Fred Carr's Enterprise Fund was up 118 percent in 1967 and Fred Mates' Mates Fund was up 158 percent in 1968. Another, John Hartwell, disdained diversification: "If you have more than a half dozen positions in an account of, say, $500,000, it only means you are not sharp enough to pick winners."[5]

Some of their profits were artificial, made in thinly traded stock that could not be sold at the market price used to calculate profits; some shares were *letter stock*, issued at a discount with the proviso that it not be sold for a specified number of years. Some profits were the result of self-fulfilling crowd psychology; others imitated the experts, by buying what the experts bought, pushing the prices upward and confirming the experts' choices. And some profits were due to good fortune, as subsequent losses revealed that many gunslingers had profited more from luck than skill. Between 1968 and 1974, the value of Manhattan Fund shares dropped by 80 percent, Enterprise by 70 percent, and Mates by more than 90 percent.

## *You Cannot See the Future Looking Backward*

Many mutual fund salespeople capitalize on the short-term vagaries of chance by focusing their sales pitch on whichever funds have compiled spectacular records recently, giving the misleading impression that investors are assured of a similarly spectacular performance in the future. Mutual fund families seemingly play this game too, promoting whichever funds have had recent successes while not mentioning disappointments. Fidelity manages more than 100 mutual funds and spends more than $50 million a year marketing its funds. It introduces new mutual funds at a rate of about one a month, and many in the industry suspect that they do this to ensure that they will have some successes, which are then heavily promoted.[6] An extreme, cynical version of this strategy is to start two new funds, one that leverages the market while the other sells stocks short. Or one could buy call options while the other buys puts. Whichever does well is advertised heavily, while the other is forgotten.

Several factors caution against investor hopes of getting rich quickly with a mutual fund. First, a well-diversified fund has little chance of enormous profits or losses, because the gains and losses on individual stocks tend to offset each other. This diversification should, in fact, be the primary attraction of mutual funds. As Paul Samuelson put it, "The prudent way is also the easy way. . . . What you lose is the daydream of that one big killing. What you gain is sleep."[7]

Second, the efficient-market hypothesis warns that it is difficult for any fund manager to beat the market consistently. In any given year, some do well and others poorly, just as some guesses about the outcomes of coin flips turn out to be correct and others incorrect, but past success does not guarantee future success. If anything, the feverish turnover of portfolios by managers trying to beat the market only ensures that transaction costs will drag average investment company performance below the market averages that they are trying to surpass.

## Do Mutual Funds Beat the Market?

In 1940 an astute stockbroker wrote that "in actual practice American invest-ment trusts have varied between the disappointing and the catastrophic. The whole subject makes an interesting study of the generous gap between theoretic promise and practical fulfillment."[8] Matters have changed little since, as study after study has found that investment companies consistently underperform the market averages.

If a fund cannot beat a market index, such as the Dow Jones Industrial Average or the S&P 500, then its efforts to select undervalued securities and to time the market are in vain. Researchers have generally found that before expenses are deducted, about half the funds do better than market indexes and that after expenses have been deducted, about two-thirds do worse than market indexes. For example, a seminal study by William Sharpe found that before management fees were deducted, 19 of 34 mutual funds did better than the Dow Jones Industrial Average but that after management fees were paid, 23 of 34 mutual funds did worse than the Dow Jones Industrial Average.[9] Another seminal study, by Jensen, found that before deducting management fees, 60 of 115 mutual funds did better than the S&P 500; after management fees were deducted, 76 of 115 (about two-thirds) did worse than the market.[10] Overall, the expertise of mutual fund managers is apparently not worth its cost.

EXAMPLE
21.3

## What You See Isn't Necessarily What You Get

Investment companies have considerable latitude in reporting past results, and understandably, many choose the most favorable method. Some tricks are obvious. If the fund has done relatively well during the past 3 years and poorly in the years before that, then just report the record over the past 3 years. If several funds are managed, focus on the ones that have done well. Even if a successful portfolio manager leaves the fund, continue to report the past record as if nothing has changed. Other tricks are more subtle.

If two funds are merged, the manager can choose which of the two performance records to attribute to the combined fund. For instance, if Fund A has earned 10 percent a year and Fund B has lost 10 percent a year, the manager can merge B into A and continue to report the fund's return as 10 percent a year. In this way, embarrassments disappear. The chairman of the Vanguard Group has strongly criticized this practice, observing sarcastically that "we are able to get rid of our poor performing funds by merging them into sister funds with lustrous records, and the record of the 'turkey' simply vanishes into thin air."*

A bond fund can temporarily boost the yield to maturity on its portfolio by buying lots of recently issued junk bonds, because relatively few bonds default in the first year or two after issuance. Another trick is to buy callable bonds that have high yields to maturity — yields that won't last until maturity because the issuers will soon exercise their call rights. Similarly, some funds that hold mortgage portfolios quote attractive yields based on the assumption that none of the borrowers will prepay their mortgages. If interest rates fall (or have already fallen), however, homeowners will refinance, and the fund's high quoted yields will never be realized.

While advertisements may be misleading and salespeople deceptive, the Securities and Exchange Commission requires a more complete and accurate disclosure in an investment company's prospectus. One of the best ways to peek behind the hype is to read the prospectus carefully.

*James A. White, "How a Money Manager Can Pull a Rabbit Out of a Hat," Wall Street Journal, *March 16, 1989.*

## Are Mutual Funds at Least Consistent?

Investors pour money into recently successful mutual funds, paying substantial load fees and other expenses, in the belief that a fund's recent performance ensures future success. While mutual funds, as a whole, do not beat the market, perhaps some consistently do well, and investors need only identify these above-average funds.

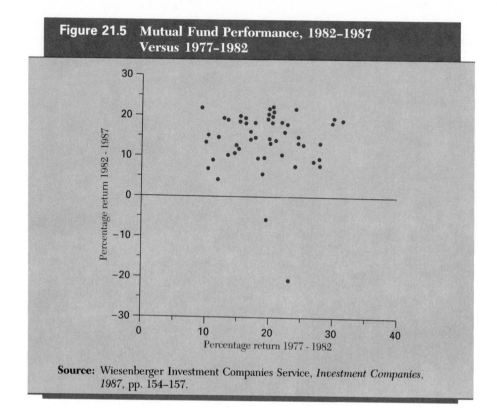

**Figure 21.5   Mutual Fund Performance, 1982–1987 Versus 1977–1982**

**Source:** Wiesenberger Investment Companies Service, *Investment Companies*, *1987*, pp. 154–157.

Unfortunately, performance seems to be random, in the sense that funds with above-average records are no more likely to do well in the future than are funds with below-average records. The discussion in Chapter 9 of the efficient-market hypothesis has already presented some evidence that there is no correlation between fund performance in one period of time and in the next. Here is some more. A study was made of the records of 64 mutual funds that, according to the Wiesenberger Service, seek to maximize capital gains. First, each fund's annual percentage return, dividends plus capital gains, was calculated over the 5-year period January 1, 1977, to January 1, 1982. These returns are the performance record that investors might have used to choose a mutual fund in 1982. Then each fund's annual percentage return was calculated for the subsequent 5-year period, from January 1, 1982, to January 1, 1987, giving the 5-year return for an investor who bought in 1982 on the basis of performance over the preceding 5 years. The resulting scatter diagram in Figure 21.5 shows that there is no correlation between fund performance in one 5-year period and in the next.

Overall, neglecting transaction costs, investors apparently cannot rely on investment companies to beat the market. What mutual funds do offer is inexpensive diversification for the small investor. It is far more economical to invest $20,000 in a mutual fund than to invest $500 in each of 40 stocks, or even

$1000 in each of 20 stocks. For some investors, this advantage may outweigh the annoying load charges and management fees.

## Index Funds

As indicated in earlier chapters, mutual funds are not the only professionally managed portfolios whose performance has been disappointing. Money managers as a whole have found it difficult to beat the market, after paying transaction costs, management fees, and other expenses. As this evidence accumulated in the late 1960s, many realized that if most professionals do worse than the market indexes, then one can compile an above-average record simply by matching these indexes. Instead of trying to pick stocks that will beat the market, an **index fund** buys the stocks in a designated market index, such as the S&P 500, in proportion to the stocks' index weights. For the S&P 500 and other market-value indexes, this strategy implies the purchase of an equal percentage of each company's shares. For the Dow Jones Industrial Average, an equal number of shares in each company is appropriate.

In 1992 stock market index funds managed more than $200 billion in assets. An index fund is deliberately passive, seeking to beat other funds with low transaction costs and management fees. Wells Fargo Investment Advisors started an index fund for pension funds and other institutional investors in 1971 and is now the largest single investor in the stock market. Wells Fargo employs only about 100 people to manage a $100 billion portfolio, and its annual management fees are as low as 0.05 percent.

Vanguard introduced the first index fund open to small investors in 1976 and now manages several index funds, including Index Trust-500 (indexed to the S&P 500), Total Stock Market Portfolio (indexed to the Wilshire 5000, which includes all U.S. securities regularly traded on the New York Stock Exchange, the American Stock Exchange, and the NASDAQ over-the-counter market), the International Equity Index Fund European Portfolio (indexed to the Morgan Stanley Capital Europe Index), and the International Equity Index Fund Pacific Portfolio (indexed to the Morgan Stanley Capital Pacific Index). For the 10 years ending on March 31, 1991, Vanguard's Index Trust-500 had a total return of 300 percent, as compared with 234 percent for the average stock fund.

Index funds routinely beat two-thirds of the managed funds. In addition to their low expenses, another advantage is that they are always virtually 100 percent invested in stocks, which presumably have a higher expected return than Treasury bills and other money-market securities that managed funds buy when they are not fully invested in stocks. In bull markets, such as that of 1982–1987, index funds are bound to look especially good in comparison with managed funds that, fearing a market downturn, keep a significant part of their assets in cash. The longer-run success of index funds hinges on two assumptions: that, because investors are risk averse, stocks will, on average, do better than money-market securities and that, because the stock market is efficient, efforts to select stocks and time the market are not worth the added expense.

EXAMPLE
21.4

## *The Ultimate Buy-and-Hold Fund*

In 1935, in the midst of the Great Depression, the Corporate Leaders Fund was established.* It invested its initial shareholders' money in 30 blue-chip stocks, including American Telephone, Eastman Kodak, Exxon, Sears, and Westinghouse. Fifty-three years later, in 1988, it still held 24 of these 30 stocks. Some of the other six stocks, such as Nabisco, were taken over by other companies. A few, such as International Harvester, were dropped when Corporate Leaders reluctantly decided that these were no longer leading companies.

Although Corporate Leaders is an open-end fund, it accepted no new investors for 17 years, from 1960 to 1987. There is no portfolio manager, because the fund follows a mechanical rule of always owning an equal number of shares in the 24 stocks in its portfolio. Any cash that accumulates is automatically reinvested in these 24 stocks; if a stock splits, the extra shares are sold. With this minimal management role, the fund's ratio of annual expenses to total assets is a minuscule 0.08 percent.

Critics argue that the fund has not changed with the economy; it owns no automobile, airline, or computer stocks. One mutual fund advisor said, "Any fund calling itself corporate leader that does not own stock in IBM makes no sense." In its defense, the fund's managers point out that the portfolio does evolve as large companies adapt to the changing economy — for example, Westinghouse expanded into broadcasting and financial services.

How has Corporate Leaders done? In the 10 years from 1978 to 1988, its total return was 341 percent, compared with a 294 percent total return for general equity mutual funds and a 266 percent total return for all mutual funds.

*The information in this example comes from Constance Mitchell, "Trapped in a Time Warp, or Simply Looking Ahead?," Wall Street Journal, November 4, 1988; and Wiesenberger Investment Companies Service, Investment Companies, 1987.*

## SUMMARY

An investment company pools investor funds and buys a portfolio of securities, providing diversification and, it is hoped, superior management. An open-end company, or mutual fund, has a variable number of shares outstanding, which fluctuates as investors buy more shares or redeem shares, in either case at net asset value. Most open-end funds charge a load fee, part of which may go to the salesperson who signs up the investor. Some funds also levy load charges on withdrawals, in addition to annual fees for management of the fund and other expenses. Fund performance (before fees are deducted) does not seem to be related to the size of the load charges, management fees, and other expenses.

A closed-end fund has a fixed number of shares, which are traded on the stock exchanges or over the counter at prices that may represent a discount or premium from net asset value. Other things being equal, a closed-end fund selling at a discount seems better than an open-end fund selling at a premium (the load charge). Yet the latter are more popular. A closed-end fund selling at a discount has a value of $q$ that is less than one and could benefit its shareholders by selling its assets and repurchasing its own shares. Most don't, no doubt influenced by the fact that management fees depend on the size of the fund.

Many fund managers are keenly interested in short-term performance, aware that an impressive record will attract more investors, increasing the size of the fund and the management fee. The evidence is that most funds do not beat the market and that there is little consistency in performance — knowing which funds have done well in the past is no help in predicting which will do well in the future. Persuaded by this evidence, some have turned to passive index funds, which merely try to match a market index, hoping that they can beat most other funds simply by minimizing expenses.

## IMPORTANT TERMS

back-end loads
closed-end funds
dual-purpose funds
index fund
investment company
load fee

mutual fund
net asset value (NAV)
no-load funds or no-loads
open-end investment company
regulated investment companies
turnover

## EXERCISES

1. Use a recent Monday issue of *The Wall Street Journal* to determine which of the following investment companies are open-end and which are closed-end and, among the open-end funds, which are load funds and which are no-load.

   ASA Limited
   Baker, Fentress
   Fidelity Puritan
   Oppenheimer Target
   Vanguard High Yield Corporate

2. Go to the library and use Wiesenberger's *Investment Companies,* Morningstar's *Mutual Funds,* or a comparable publication on investment companies to research the five companies listed in Exercise 1. Write a 250-word report comparing the objectives of these funds.

3. On March 25, 1992, newspapers reported that Fidelity's Magellan Fund had a NAV of 69.29 and an offer price of 71.43. In order for you to buy one share of this fund, what additional percentage must you pay as a sales commission?

4. Use *The Wall Street Journal* or another newspaper to figure the load charge on these mutual funds. Show your work.
   a. Dreyfus Leveraged
   b. Kemper Environmental Services
   c. Price Rowe New Era
   d. Shearson California Muni
   e. Vanguard Windsor

5. Figure 21.3 shows the average discount on closed-end funds through 1991. Look in the most recent edition of Wiesenberger Service *Investment Companies* to see whether the average discount has widened or diminished since 1991.

6. The text tells how, on March 27, 1992, the market price of one income share and one

capital share of the Gemini II dual-purpose fund was $26.875, a 2.2 percent premium over the combined $26.29 net asset value of these two shares. Redo this calculation using current data from the most recent Monday edition of *The Wall Street Journal.* Has this discount increased or decreased?

7. An advertisement by the Investment Company Institute boasted that $10,000 invested in mutual funds in 1950 would, neglecting load charges and assuming the reinvestment of all dividends, have grown to $113,500 in 1972, 23 years later. A finance professor calculated that, over this same time period, an investment in the NYSE composite index, including the reinvestment of dividends, would have grown by 12.54 percent per year.[11] Did the mutual funds do better or worse than the NYSE composite?

8. In late 1987, Fidelity Brokerage announced that it would waive its brokerage fee on stock sales:

   *Fidelity Brokerage will usher in the year-end stock trading season with commission-free trading.*
   *This limited-time offer will run through January 15, 1988. It will allow investors to sell stocks free when they reinvest the total proceeds of the stock sale in a Fidelity load fund.*[12]

   How can Fidelity Brokerage make a profit on this offer?

9. Why do you suppose that mutual funds strongly encourage their shareholders to reinvest their dividends and capital gains in the fund, even if there is no load charge on this reinvestment?

10. In 1986 the Korea Fund, a closed-end investment company that invests in Korean securities, had 5 million shares outstanding with a net asset value of $18 and a market price of $32, a 78 percent premium over NAV. The Korea Fund then sold 1.2 million new shares at $32, raising $38.4 million. Did this sale hurt or help the NAV of existing shareholders? Explain.

11. A market observer wrote, "Frequently, closed-end shares representing $25 in assets will be selling for $20. Such profits may be largely illusory, however, because when the time comes to sell, the discount may persist."[13] Is there any advantage to buying a closed-end fund at a discount if the discount never changes?

12. Explain the flaw in this advice: "The problem of picking a mutual fund seems to be simplicity itself: The investor should select whichever fund will give him the largest percentage return, year after year."[14]

13. Ginnie Mae mutual funds buy a pool of residential mortgages that are guaranteed by the Government National Mortgage Association. Investors in these funds receive the monthly mortgage payments (interest and principal) made by homeowners. While investors are protected against default, they can be hurt both by a rise in market interest rates and by a decline. Explain how this is possible.

14. In the 1920s, most investment companies leveraged themselves by borrowing money; on average, they were financed by roughly 40 percent debt and 60 percent equity. How much leverage does an investment company have if it is financed by 40 percent debt and 60 percent equity?

15. Write a 250-word essay arguing against this viewpoint:

    *The manager of a fund has a fiduciary obligation to obtain the highest possible return on the money entrusted to his keeping. In an overheated market such as the one that began to build up in the mid-1980s, the fiduciary obligations of the fund managers actually compelled them to speculate — and to speculate massively.*[15]

16. Wiesenberger Investment Companies Service classifies mutual funds by their stated

objectives. Shown below are the annual percentage returns in 1989, 1990, and 1991 for 18 of 90 funds (every fifth fund from an alphabetical list) that seek to maximize capital gains.[16] Make a scatter diagram for these 18 funds, putting the percent return in 1989 on the horizontal axis and the percent return in 1990 on the vertical axis. Does there seem to be a close relationship between a fund's performance in 1989 and 1990?

| | 1989 | 1990 | 1991 |
|---|---|---|---|
| American Capital Comstock | 30.6 | −3.4 | 31.9 |
| American National Growth | 24.3 | −2.9 | 37.0 |
| Delaware Group DelCap — Concept I | 33.9 | −3.5 | 42.3 |
| Dreyfus Strategic Investing | 32.3 | 0.7 | 41.3 |
| Fidelity Special Situation | 33.0 | −6.6 | 23.7 |
| First Eagle Fund of America | 26.6 | −17.6 | 21.1 |
| Fund Trust — Aggressive Growth | 21.9 | −7.4 | 38.0 |
| IDS Strategy — Aggressive | 32.7 | −0.7 | 51.2 |
| Lexington Worldwide Emerging | 28.1 | −14.4 | 24.2 |
| MFS Managed Sectors Trust | 41.8 | −13.4 | 62.1 |
| Oppenheimer Fund | 23.7 | −4.5 | 29.0 |
| Phoenix Stock Fund | 21.6 | −5.6 | 29.6 |
| Putnam Voyager Fund | 34.8 | −2.8 | 50.3 |
| Security Ultra Fund | 11.9 | −27.4 | 59.7 |
| Shearson Aggressive Growth | 41.4 | −6.0 | 42.3 |
| Strong Discovery Fund | 24.0 | −2.7 | 62.8 |
| Twentieth Century Growth | 43.1 | −3.8 | 69.0 |
| WPG Tudor Fund | 25.1 | −5.2 | 45.8 |

17. Make a scatter diagram for the 18 randomly selected mutual funds shown in the preceding exercise, with the percent return in 1990 on the horizontal axis and the percent return in 1991 on the vertical axis. Is there a close relationship between a fund's performance in 1990 and 1991?

18. Explain what is misleading about this analysis of dual-purpose funds:

*Say that Widow A, who has $1,000 and wants all the income she can get from it, and Executive B, who also has $1,000 and wants all the growth he can get, join forces. The result is $2,000, which is duly invested and, in a year's time, has produced a not-unreasonable five percent in dividends and ten percent in capital gains. Five percent of $2,000 is $100, and that would go to the widow, who finds that she has received a ten percent return on her $1,000 investment. The ten percent in capital gains amounts to $200, and that goes to the executive, who discovers he's blessed with a 20% return. Almost miraculously, both are making twice as much as they would if the fund hadn't brought them together.[17]*

19. An investment consultant has telephoned you to report that he has identified the top 0.5 percent of all mutual funds, funds that have averaged a 16 percent return over the past 5 years. Why might you hang up without paying to learn their names?

20. Before the SEC required money-market funds to compute a standard 30-day yield, some funds would, at times, report their shareholders' return over the past year and, at other times, report their shareholders' return over the past week. Which do you suppose they reported when interest rates had fallen during the past year? What about a mutual fund that holds a portfolio of long-term bonds?

21. RJR Nabisco was taken private in a leveraged buyout in 1989, when a private partnership purchased all of RJR's outstanding

shares. At the time, RJR was the eleventh largest company in the S&P 500 index. When RJR was removed from the S&P 500 and replaced by a smaller company, what actions were required of index funds that attempted to match the S&P 500?

22. Dean LeBaron, president of Batterymarch Financial Management, in a February 1986 speech to fellow money managers and corporate financial executives, said:

*In the past, if you [a corporation] thought your stock was too cheap, you held a lunch and told everyone so. Now if you think it's cheap, you buy it. . . .*

*What we are seeing at the moment are individual securities that are selling like closed-end funds — that is, securities that appear to be selling in the aggregate at a discount from some of the marketable components. To realize the value of these components you must go open end. Institutions won't do that. Individual shareholders won't do it. But public companies will.*[18]

a. What is the value of $q$ for such companies?
b. How can corporate stock ever sell at a discount from the liquidation value of its assets?
c. Why might these discounts shrink if the company forgoes expansion to repurchase stock?

23. Comment on the following remark: "A mutual fund has been defined as an outfit which, for a fee, spares investors the trouble of losing their own money. The fund takes over the task for them."[19]

24. In the 1970s a series of unprofitable investments gave one dual-purpose fund, Hemisphere, a net asset value for its capital shares that was often close to zero and sometimes negative. If a dual-purpose fund has 2 million income shares, 2 million capital shares,

a redemption price for the income shares of $10, and a portfolio of $25 million, what is the net asset value of the capital shares? If the portfolio goes up or down by $x$ percent, what will happen to the net asset value of the capital shares?

25. One financial advisor wrote that "for the man who couldn't care less about the intricacies of high finance but still appreciates wealth and all the freedom it implies, mutual funds may be the best investment of all."[20] Acting as an independent financial advisor, what would you advise a recent college graduate who has inherited $20,000 and wants to buy stock?

26. In 1986 the S&P 500 increased by 22 percent, while the average stock mutual fund gained 16 percent. Why do mutual funds tend to underperform the S&P 500, particularly during bull markets?

27. In 1990 Wiesenberger Services identified 90 mutual funds that seek to maximize capital gains. Shown in the following table are the 1990 and 1991 rankings of the 10 best-performing funds in 1990.[21] Is this performance record surprising?

| | 1990 Rank | 1991 Rank |
|---|---|---|
| Twentieth Century Ultra | 1 | 1 |
| Pru–Bache Flexi–Strategy | 2 | 73 |
| Pacific Horizons Aggressive Growth | 3 | 9 |
| Flex Fund — Growth | 4 | 82 |
| Fidelity Contrafund | 5 | 24 |
| Crabbe Huson Growth Fund | 6 | 86 |
| Merriman Timed Capital Appreciation | 7 | 81 |
| Scudder Development Fund | 8 | 6 |
| Tocqueville Fund | 9 | 88 |
| Seligman Capital Fund | 10 | 26 |

28. Some people criticize dual-purpose funds because the funds' managers cannot possibly satisfy both classes of shareholders. For example, the purchase of high-dividend, slow-growth stocks benefits the income shareholders at the expense of the capital shareholders. Explain why this claim is refuted by the argument that dividing the fund's shares into two classes cannot make shareholders worse off.

29. A 1989 *Wall Street Journal* article noted that after a closed-end fund is set up, the market price of its shares usually slips to a discount from net asset value. As a consequence, some investors are reluctant to buy the initial offering (and pay a sales fee to the sponsoring brokerage firm) when they can wait a short while and buy the shares at a discount. To overcome this reluctance, some closed-end funds have open-end provisions guaranteeing that after a specified number of years shareholders will be allowed to redeem their shares at full net asset value. The *Wall Street Journal* article was unenthusiastic about such open-end provisions:

*Big deal, specialists say. So you're assured of getting the portfolio's full net asset value. That's often a far cry from getting your original investment back.*

*What matters is how the markets behave over the years: If stocks or bonds in general slump, so do the values of assets in related portfolios. Open-ending plans "aren't going to insulate you against the marketplace," says Douglas Dent of the Closed-End Fund Digest.* [22]

Write a 250-word essay supporting or opposing the argument that open-end provisions are worthless.

30. An author recommends this superhedge strategy: buying dual-purpose capital shares selling at a discount from net asset value and writing call options on stocks similar to those held by the fund.[23] In what sense is this a hedge?

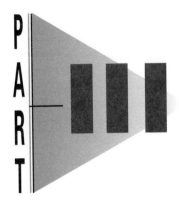

# Government
# Regulation and
# Monetary Policy

# 22 Government Regulation of Banks

*During World War I, Will Rogers sent a telegram to the Secretary of War stating that he had figured out how to sink Germany's submarines. When he met with the Secretary, he suggested filling the German submarines with water. Asked how that could be done, Rogers replied, "I've given you the idea; now you work out the details."*

Earlier chapters have described some of the historical motivation for government regulation of banks and other deposit intermediaries. Banking is too important and crises have been too frequent for society to rely solely on the self-interest of individual banks — what is good for one bank may not be good for all banks. In addition, there have been too many unscrupulous and mismanaged banks, and it is difficult for depositors to identify these villains until it is too late. Finally, even honest, well-managed banks are vulnerable to bank runs. These varied concerns have created a web of regulations designed to protect depositors and banks.

Because of their importance to the nation's money supply, commercial banks and thrifts are subject to considerable federal supervision and regulation. Finance companies, insurance companies, and other nondeposit intermediaries are generally chartered and regulated at the state level, although some of their activities may be constrained by the Securities and Exchange Commission, federal truth-in-lending laws, and ERISA, all of which have been discussed in earlier chapters. In this chapter we will focus on regulation of the banking system, a discussion that leads into several chapters covering the nation's monetary policies.

Policymakers need to understand the powerful tools at their disposal and the consequences of their use. As private citizens, we need to anticipate how the government's financial policies will affect us; as voters, we judge the wisdom with which these tools are employed.

In this chapter we will look at some of the important ways in which government agencies regulate banks — trying to ensure that banks are solvent and well managed by inspecting their books, insuring their deposits, and restricting their activities. We begin by identifying the regulators.

# THE DUAL BANKING SYSTEM

The United States has a diverse and complex governmental structure with origins in the American Revolution and the formation of the Union. As the states banded together, they were quite wary of a centralized, authoritarian government. The founders divided power among three branches of the federal government — executive, legislative, and judicial — and reserved substantial powers for the individual state governments. This complex system of checks and balances was intended to keep any single branch of government from becoming excessively powerful. This philosophy has strongly shaped the development and present regulation of U.S. financial institutions.

Early U.S. money and banking history was described in Chapters 2 and 13. To recap briefly, the U.S. Constitution seemingly prohibited the issuance of paper money by either the federal or state governments. Early banks were state-chartered and issued paper money. At the time of the Civil War, a new system was established, which allowed banks to obtain national charters and issue national bank notes that were liabilities of the private banks that issued them. Bank notes issued by state-chartered banks were taxed out of existence. Private national bank notes were prohibited in 1935 and replaced by Federal Reserve Notes.

Early attempts at a central bank were bitterly opposed and short-lived. The First and Second Banks of the United States each lasted only 20 years (1791–1811 and 1816–1836, respectively), and nearly a century then passed before the Federal Reserve System was established and operated like a central bank. The Federal Reserve was conceived as a decentralized organization that would be independent of the president and Congress and would pay due respect to states' rights. State-chartered banks are not required to join the system, and 90 percent choose not to belong. Power within the system initially resided with the 12 regional Federal Reserve banks, but after the great stock market crash, considerable authority was given to the Federal Reserve Board in Washington, D.C. Yet banks and other intermediaries are still governed by a complex web of state and federal regulations.

## Overlapping Authority

One aspect of this dispersion of authority is a **dual banking system** in which banks can be chartered (and supervised) by either the federal or state government. Presently, about one-third of all banks are federally chartered. These banks tend to be larger banks, and they contain nearly 60 percent of all deposits. Nationally chartered banks are supervised by the comptroller of the currency, an executive of the U.S. Treasury. State-chartered banks are regulated by individual state agencies.

National banks and those state banks that have joined the Federal Reserve System are also regulated by the Federal Reserve. The Federal Deposit Insurance Corporation (FDIC) is yet another regulatory layer. All Federal Reserve

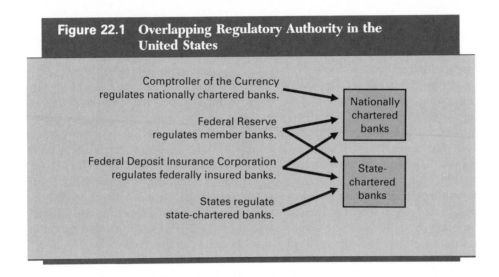

**Figure 22.1    Overlapping Regulatory Authority in the United States**

Comptroller of the Currency regulates nationally chartered banks.

Federal Reserve regulates member banks.

Federal Deposit Insurance Corporation regulates federally insured banks.

States regulate state-chartered banks.

Nationally chartered banks

State-chartered banks

member banks are required to join the FDIC, and almost all nonmember banks have chosen to join. The FDIC has its own set of regulations and bank examiners. Thus a nationally chartered bank is supervised by three separate entities: the comptroller of the currency, the Federal Reserve, and the FDIC. A state-chartered bank is typically regulated by the FDIC and its state agency, and it also may be supervised by the Federal Reserve. Figure 22.1 depicts this system of overlapping authority.

## Coordination and Conflict

In practice, some duplication is avoided. The Federal Reserve and the FDIC accept the comptroller of the currency's examinations of national banks, and the FDIC accepts Federal Reserve examinations of state-chartered member banks. However, neither accepts the reports of state bank examiners. A state bank that belongs to either the Federal Reserve or the FDIC will be examined by one or the other, in addition to the state authorities.

In 1978 the comptroller of the currency, the Federal Reserve, and the FDIC adopted a common framework and guidelines for assessing a bank's soundness. The comptroller's office examines the balance sheet of each national bank four times each year. Two of these examinations occur regularly in June and December, and two are unannounced calls. Bank examiners determine a so-called CAMEL rating of five bank characteristics:

*Capital adequacy*
*Asset quality*
*Management ability*
*Earnings level and quality*
*Liquidity*

Each characteristic is given a rating of 1 (strong) to 5 (unsatisfactory). The bank is also given an overall composite rating of 1 (sound in almost every respect) to 5 (requires immediate aid and corrective action). This common framework is intended to provide uniform supervision of individual banks.

Conflicts can arise, however. In the mid-1960s, the comptroller of the currency fought with the Federal Reserve over which types of bank liabilities should be subject to reserve requirements and over the expansion of bank subsidiaries into nonbank activities. Similarly, in 1974, the comptroller of the currency ruled that remote electronic tellers are not branches of a bank and therefore are not subject to state restrictions on the operation of bank branches. This decision was sharply criticized by other regulatory authorities, and the comptroller amended the ruling to exclude terminals that are more than 50 miles from a bank. A number of state courts subsequently ruled that remote terminals are indeed branches, and the Supreme Court has let these rulings stand. Since then, about a third of the state legislatures have passed laws stating that remote terminals are branches, and another third have passed laws saying that they are not.

In the 1980s several states allowed state-chartered banks to engage in activities that are prohibited for national banks. Some states, including California, permitted banks to invest in real estate. Some allowed securities underwriting and travel agency services. South Dakota openly invited banks to move to South Dakota, where they had permission to sell insurance in all 50 states.

Critics argue that this duplication and triplication of authority is chaotic and wasteful. Despite the recommendations of various study groups, Congress has resisted consolidating power in a single agency. A natural candidate would be the Federal Reserve, but some feel that bank supervision and regulation should be divorced from the conduct of monetary policy.

There is also a continuing sentiment for the checks and balances provided by diffuse power. Proponents of the existing system argue that competing regulatory authorities provide more flexibility and opportunity for innovation: when one agency is moribund, another can authorize imaginative changes. Unsatisfied banks can even change regulators by switching from a national to a state charter, or vice versa. However, some fear that regulations are dangerously weakened by the banks' opportunity to pit one regulator against another. Arthur Burns, a former Federal Reserve chairman, has stated:

> *The present regulatory system fosters what has sometimes been called "competition in laxity." Even viewed in the most favorable light, the present system is conducive to subtle competition among regulatory authorities, sometimes to relax constraints, sometimes to delay constructive measures. I need not explain to bankers the well-understood fact that regulatory agencies are sometimes played off against one another.*[1]

A not so subtle example occurred in 1975 when the FDIC reversed its earlier rejection of a proposed bank merger. FDIC Chairman Frank Wille dissented from this reversal and wrote as follows:

*I suppose it is indelicate to suggest that the real reason for the Board's reversal has something to do with the explicitness of Mr. \_\_\_\_'s reminder that he can recast the proposal so that the resulting bank would be a national bank, thus permitting the Comptroller of the Currency alone to approve the desired transaction under the Bank Merger Act.*[2]

# THE FEDERAL RESERVE SYSTEM

From the beginning, there has been debate about whether or not all banks should be compelled to join the Federal Reserve System. This debate is concerned with the virtues of central control, of focused versus dispersed power. The compromise that was adopted permits state-chartered banks to choose, and as noted earlier, 90 percent of them have chosen not to join the Federal Reserve System.

The initial conception of the Federal Reserve System placed considerable power in the 12 district Federal Reserve banks that are shown in Figure 22.2. Each of the Federal Reserve banks is privately owned by the member banks in its district, although the member banks cannot be paid more than a 6 percent annual return on their compulsory investment in the Federal Reserve banks.

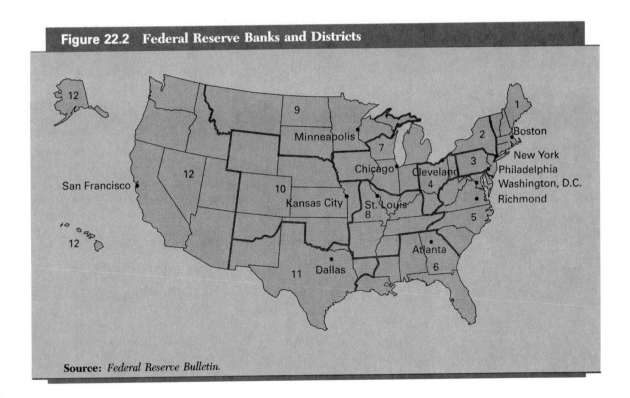

**Figure 22.2  Federal Reserve Banks and Districts**

**Source:** *Federal Reserve Bulletin.*

Part of the extra revenue that is generated by the Federal Reserve banks is used to pay for the operations of the Federal Reserve Board in Washington, D.C.; the remainder is turned over to the U.S. Treasury. In 1990 the Federal Reserve System earned $24 billion, of which $23.6 billion was given to the Treasury.

The perceived failure of the Federal Reserve banks in the great stock market crash led to the centralization of power in Washington, D.C. Today, the primary tasks of the 12 Federal Reserve banks are to clear checks and carry out the federal government's financial transactions.

Historically, only member banks had access to the Federal Reserve's discount window, a privilege offset by the fact they were subject to relatively high reserve requirements and that the reserves required by many states could be met by holding liquid, interest-earning assets. In addition, many state regulatory agencies have been more lenient than the Federal Reserve on such issues as permissible banking activities and asset holdings, loans to bank officers, required disclosures, and interlocking organizations.

In the late 1960s and through much of the 1970s, high interest rates made it expensive to hold idle reserves. A substantial number of state banks dropped their Federal Reserve membership, and some national banks converted to state charters and left the Federal Reserve System. The Federal Reserve was disturbed because these defections lessened its control and even its knowledge of the banking system and the money supply. There were renewed calls for compelling all banks to join the system or giving the Federal Reserve the power to regulate all banks, whether they join or not. The historic 1980 Depository Institutions Deregulation and Monetary Control Act included the following provisions:

1. It authorized interest-bearing checking accounts and phased out all deposit-rate ceilings.
2. It set aside state usury ceilings on residential mortgages and tied state usury ceilings on business and agricultural loans of $25,000 or more to the Fed's discount rate.
3. It broadened lending opportunities for thrift institutions — for example, allowing federally chartered savings and loan associations to offer consumer and commercial loans, credit lines, and credit cards.
4. It authorized the Federal Reserve to set reserve requirements on checking account balances and nonpersonal time deposits in all depository institutions.
5. It gave all depository institutions offering checkable deposits access to the Federal Reserve's discount window.
6. It instructed the Federal Reserve to charge for various services, including check clearing and collection, wire transfer, and securities safekeeping.

The first three provisions were important steps to deregulate deposit intermediaries. In the fourth and fifth provisions, the Federal Reserve Board was given the authority to set reserve requirements at all financial institutions offering checkable deposits; in return, nonmember institutions are now entitled to use the Federal Reserve discount window and other services. The 1980 Monetary Control Act was a landmark centralization of authority, leading the *Financier* to editorialize, "Now, suddenly, the truce is over after all these years. The centralizers have won."[3]

## The Board of Governors

The seven governors of the Federal Reserve Board are appointed by the president to overlapping 14-year terms, one term ending in January of each even-numbered year. Thus, during 4 years in office, the president of the United States normally appoints two of the seven members to the Federal Reserve Board. Deaths or resignations may create additional openings. Governors cannot be appointed to two full terms, but they can serve part of an unexpired term plus one full term. In continuing deference to the dispersion of power, no two board members can be from the same Federal Reserve district.

In the past, Federal Reserve governors have often been successful private businessmen, with backgrounds in business or finance. In recent years, many have been professional economists, including Alan Greenspan, the current chair. The board employs a large staff of professional economists who, at the request of board members, prepare reports on policy issues. Although board members usually have well-formed opinions on most monetary issues, the staff studies and discussions do reshape some of these views. The collaboration between the board and its staff has been enhanced by the fact that several recent governors worked on the staff before their appointment to the board.

## Chairman of the Board

The chairman of the board of governors is appointed by the president of the United States to a 4-year term, which is not coincident with the president's term. A new chairman is normally appointed to a 14-year term on the board and appointed to a 4-year term as chair simultaneously. The 4-year term as chair can be renewed (and often is). The Fed chairman usually is the dominant figure on the board, leading financial market participants to refer to the Burns Federal Reserve board, the Volcker board, and the Greenspan board.

Marriner S. Eccles, the Utah banker in Example 14.5, was appointed Fed chairman by Franklin Roosevelt in 1934 and was the principal architect of the 1935 and 1936 banking laws that consolidated power in Washington under Eccles' board. Eccles was an early and persuasive advocate of the use of monetary, spending, and taxation policies to stabilize the economy. During the Great Depression, he was convinced that monetary policy was ineffectual (you can give people money, but you can't make them spend it), and he argued for increased government spending. Eccles was chairman for 15 years, from 1934 to 1948, and continued to serve on the board until 1951.

EXAMPLE
**22.1**

## *Democracy at the Federal Reserve Board*

The Federal Reserve chair is usually the dominant figure on the board and at FOMC meetings. The Fed chair is seldom outvoted on monetary policy decisions and speaks for the Federal Reserve to the press, the president, and Congress (in part to avoid the confusion that might result if two governors made contradictory statements about monetary policy). Many people know the name of the Federal Reserve chair; most would have difficulty naming one other governor or the president of any of the 12 Federal Reserve banks.

Fed chairmen are chosen because they are proven leaders who have the respect of the worldwide financial and business community. U.S. monetary policy is too important to be in the hands of someone who is not well known or credible. The other Fed governors, in contrast, often have been appointed after consultation with the Fed chair — their primary qualification might be a willingness to go along with the chair.

Like many of his predecessors, Paul Volcker was an aloof and autocratic Fed chairman — more apt to lecture other board members about his decisions than to ask their opinions. Nor did he pay much attention to the president and Congress. Determined to keep the Fed independent of the administration, Volcker once refused to meet with Ronald Reagan at the White House.

Treasury Secretary Donald Regan urged Reagan to choose governors who would be more independent of Volcker, and he did so with his appointments of Martha Seger, Wayne Angell, and Manuel Johnson. In a stunning watershed vote in 1986, the board asserted its independence by outvoting Volcker 4 to 3 on a key decision to cut the discount rate.

Alan Greenspan was appointed to the Fed and became chairman in August of 1987, and the board soon became more open and democratic. Greenspan is more collegial than Volcker and not only listens carefully to other governors but actively solicits their opinions. This independence soon became contagious, and even the district Federal Reserve bank presidents began demanding a larger voice. In August of 1988, on the eve of a presidential election, the presidents took the lead in persuading the reluctant governors to raise the discount rate by half a percentage point. In the spring of 1991, Greenspan responded to complaints from the district presidents by agreeing not to change federal funds rate targets in between FOMC meetings without consulting them.

Greenspan usually, but not always, gets the monetary policy that he wants. However, policy changes are now more cautious and take longer to implement. For example, at the FOMC meeting on October 2, 1990, Greenspan proposed supporting the sagging economy with two separate quarter-point reductions in the federal funds rate. The majority of the committee was more concerned about inflation than recession and voted for a single quarter-point reduction in the federal funds rate and to delay this reduction for 4 weeks until Congress and the president agreed on a new budget package. One Fed governor explained that the Fed is "now a more collegial group, rather than a school-marm lecturing third graders." But another governor warned that "democracy is messier than dictatorship."*

*Alan Murray, "Democracy Comes to the Central Bank, Curbing Chief's Power," Wall Street Journal, April 5, 1991.

Thomas McCabe was appointed chairman by President Truman in 1948, and he served through three stormy years in which the board tangled with both the U.S. Treasury and Truman (the details are in Chapter 26). When McCabe resigned in 1951, he was replaced by William McChesney Martin, who served for 20 years, from 1951 to 1970. After Martin, Arthur Burns was chairman from 1970 to 1978. G. William Miller served briefly, resigned under pressure, and was replaced in August of 1979 by Paul Volcker, who almost immediately began a tight-money policy that, during the next 3 years, slowed inflation from double-digit rates to under 4 percent. Volcker stepped down in 1987 and was replaced by the current chairman, Alan Greenspan.

The chairmen are purposely chosen for their dynamic leadership and the respect that they command in the financial community. In addition, the chair has various duties and powers that can be subtly employed to sway the other governors. Eccles, Martin, Burns, and Volcker all fit the mold of a strong, forceful leader. In contrast, the primary criticism of Miller was that he did not dominate the Federal Reserve Board. The financial community was aghast when it learned that Miller had been outvoted by the other members of the board.

## The Open Market Committee

The **Federal Open Market Committee (FOMC)** meets approximately every 6 weeks to discuss and decide policy matters. Its 12 members are the seven board governors, the president of the Federal Reserve Bank of New York, and four of the other 11 Federal Reserve bank presidents. The other seven Federal Reserve bank presidents attend the FOMC meetings and participate in the discussion but do not vote.

The permanent seat for the Federal Reserve Bank of New York reflects New York's traditional role as the nation's financial capital. The Federal Reserve Bank of New York holds nearly a quarter of the aggregate assets of the 12 Federal Reserve banks, and the salary of its president is nearly double that of the chairman of the Federal Reserve Board. In addition, the FOMC's open-market operations are executed by the Federal Reserve Bank of New York.

The Federal Open Market Committee discusses the state of the economy and financial markets and makes monetary policy decisions. With 7 of 12 votes, the board of governors dominates these meetings. In addition, the board itself has the final say on policy matters. Thus, in essence, the monthly FOMC meetings are where monetary policy is discussed, recommendations are offered by the

Federal Reserve bank presidents, and decisions are made by the board of governors, normally in accordance with the wishes of the board chairman.

The dynamics of decision making are, of course, more subtle and complex than this caricature. Although the chairman and the governors have authority and want that authority to be clearly understood, there is always a risk that arrogance will sufficiently alienate others so that they seek to undermine that power. The board tries to avoid offending the Federal Reserve banks, and the chairman of the board does not bully the other governors. When others feel strongly about an issue, the chairman is likely to be flexible. When opinion is divided, the chairman molds a consensus, giving considerable weight to the chair's own views. This is surely a delicate business, but board chairmen are chosen and respected because they are good at it. A tabulation of the votes at FOMC meetings between 1959 and 1987 found that of 1900 votes cast by individual Fed governors, only 8 percent were dissents from the majority opinion.[4]

Federal Open Market Committee meetings are held in secrecy. Before 1967, the FOMC wouldn't even announce when it was meeting, let alone what was decided. Since the passage of the 1967 freedom-of-information laws, the FOMC has been compelled to report its deliberations. Currently, a summary of FOMC discussion and policy actions is released about a month after each meeting and subsequently is published in the *Federal Reserve Bulletin*. In addition, since 1975, the chairman of the board of governors has met quarterly with Congress to discuss the board's objectives for the coming year, including target rates of growth of key monetary aggregates. The chairman also meets regularly with White House economists to discuss the state of the economy and monetary policy.

# THE FEDERAL HOME LOAN BANK SYSTEM

The **Federal Home Loan Bank (FHLB) system** was created in the 1930s to supervise and assist financial institutions that make residential mortgages — primarily savings and loan associations and mutual savings banks. All federally chartered savings and loans were required to join the FHLB system and qualified state-chartered S&Ls could join if they wish. Insurance companies with substantial mortgage portfolios have been permitted to join the FHLB since the 1930s, and commercial banks have been allowed since 1989. Currently, any financial institution with at least 10 percent of its assets in residential mortgages is eligible, but the FHLB rejects applications from troubled institutions (for example, banks with a CAMEL rating below 3). With the S&L crisis, the number of S&L members fell from 3183 at the beginning of 1990 to 2550 at the end of 1991, a decline that was partly offset by 300 commercial banks that joined the FHLB in 1991.

The FHLB system consists of 12 district Federal Home Loan Banks, which, since 1951, have been privately owned by the member institutions. The Federal

Home Loan Bank Board supervised the FHLB system until 1989, when it was replaced by two new organizations:

1. The Office of Thrift Supervision, which now charters, regulates, and supervises S&Ls.
2. The Federal Housing Finance Board, which now oversees the 12 Federal Home Loan Banks.

The Federal Home Loan Banks raise funds from membership fees and by selling bonds and make loans (called "advances") to member institutions. Although FHLB bonds are not explicitly guaranteed by the federal government, FHLB bonds are rated triple-A, and FHLB banks can borrow at interest rates some 5 to 50 basis points above the rates on Treasury securities. In July 1991, the FHLB had $150 billion in assets, including $90 billion in advances to members and $50 billion in liquid assets.

FHLB loans were particularly helpful to savings and loan associations during credit crunches in 1966, 1969–1970, 1973–1974, and 1978–1980. The important difference between the FHLB banks and the Federal Reserve is that the FHLB banks cannot issue currency and are consequently not an utterly reliable lender of last resort. The 1980 deregulation act filled this gap by permitting all deposit intermediaries to use the Federal Reserve discount window.

# DEPOSIT INSURANCE

The New York Safety Fund was created in 1829 to protect the creditors of New York–chartered banks. This central emergency fund was financed by bank contributions equal to 3 percent of their capital, paid over 6 years, and protected both depositors and holders of bank notes. In 1842, coverage was restricted to noteholders. A few other states set up similar plans, but charter expirations and bank failures largely exhausted these scattered safety funds.

In 1933, with the banking system a shambles, Congress created a nationwide **Federal Deposit Insurance Corporation (FDIC)** to insure deposits in commercial and mutual savings banks. The companion **Federal Savings and Loan Insurance Corporation (FSLIC)** was established at the same time to insure deposits in savings and loan associations. With the rapid growth of credit unions since World War II, the **National Credit Union Administration** was established and initiated nationwide credit union deposit insurance in 1970.

Deposit insurance was opposed by the American Bankers Association, which called the FDIC "inherently fallacious . . . one of those plausible, but deceptive, human plans that in actual application only serve to render worse the very evils they seek to cure."[5] On another occasion, the ABA called it "unsound, unscientific, unjust, and dangerous."[6] President Roosevelt threatened to veto the Banking Act of 1933 if it contained deposit insurance. In retrospect, the FDIC succeeded in eliminating contagious bank runs, immensely benefiting depositors and even the reluctant bankers.

The FDIC is financed by an annual fee, in 1991 equal to 23 cents for every $100 of insured deposits, levied on member banks. Initially, FDIC deposit insurance was limited to $5000 per depositor per bank. With growth of the economy and deposits, this limit has increased over time, and in March of 1980 it was increased to its current limit of $100,000 — which just covers a single $100,000 negotiable CD. Because larger deposits are at risk, rumors of insolvency can precipitate a liquidity crisis at a bank that has a substantial number of large deposits; for example, the Franklin National Bank collapsed when it lost a half billion dollars in unrenewed CDs during 5 anxious months in 1974.

When the FDIC seizes a bank, it has three options: liquidation, purchase and assumption, and socialization. Liquidation is generally used with smaller banks that are in severe trouble. The FDIC closes the bank, pays each depositor up to the limit allowed, and sells the bank's assets, dividing the proceeds among the FDIC, the excess uninsured deposits, and other creditors.

For larger banks, the FDIC generally uses the purchase-and-assumption method, in which the bank is reorganized and sold to a healthy bank — a sale encouraged by the FDIC's willingness to pay a generous price for some of the troubled bank's questionable assets (or to indemnify the purchaser against losses on these assets). In such a merger, no depositor (even those with deposits beyond the insurance limit) loses a penny, although the stockholders of the disappearing bank lose plenty.

For example, Franklin National suffered enormous losses in 1974 in foreign exchange transactions and what turned out to be bad loans. Nevertheless, it had plenty of attractive assets and was quickly taken over by the European-American Bank and Trust Company, a New York bank owned by six large European banks. Another prominent example occurred in 1980 when First Pennsylvania, then the nation's twenty-third largest bank, was bailed out by the FDIC. First Pennsylvania held billions of dollars in long-term bonds and mortgages and sustained large losses when interest rates rose sharply in 1979 and 1980. As fears for its solvency spread, it lost $1.6 billion in deposits — mostly very large CDs. The FDIC and 22 private banks put together a $1.5 billion loan package to avert a liquidity crisis. As part of the bailout plan, First Pennsylvania sold a half billion dollars worth of government bonds, sold its mortgage banking and consumer finance subsidiaries to Manufacturers Hanover, and liquidated a bond-trading subsidiary. In all, 25 percent of its assets were liquidated, but it continued in business as a slimmed-down, more conservative bank.

The FDIC's third option is to take over the failed bank and run it itself, hoping eventually to sell it to private investors. In the 1983 Continental Illinois episode (discussed in Chapter 10), the FDIC pumped $4.5 billion into the bank and, in return, became an 80 percent owner of the bank. At the time, Continental Illinois was the nation's seventh largest bank with $40.7 billion in assets. The FDIC bought its loan portfolio for $3.5 billion, agreed to lend another $1 billion, and forced Continental Illinois's two top managers and the ten senior members of the board of directors to resign. When the FDIC sold the last of its Continental Illinois stock in 1991, the net cost to the government (not taking into account

EXAMPLE
22.2

## Has FDIC Insurance Kept Up with Inflation?

The Federal Deposit Insurance Corporation (FDIC) was chartered in June of 1934 and initially insured accounts at member banks up to a limit of $5000 per account. This maximum limit was increased to $10,000 in 1950, $15,000 in 1966, $20,000 in 1969, $40,000 in 1974, and $100,000 in 1980. Has this limit kept up with inflation?

The accompanying figure shows the real value of the insurance limit in 1991 dollars, using annual values of the consumer price index (CPI) between 1934 and 1991. Because prices increased by a factor of 10 between 1934 and 1991, the real value of the initial $5000 limit is $50,000 in 1991 dollars. The graph shows that, in real terms, the 1991 limit of $100,000 is roughly equivalent to the $40,000 limit in 1975.

The real value of the deposit-insurance limit peaked in 1980, when the limit was increased to $100,000, which was equivalent to $165,000 in 1991 dollars. Stated another way, if the insurance limit had been increased in 1991 to take into account inflation between 1980 and 1991, the 1991 limit would have been set at $165,000. However, because of concern about the moral-hazard problem, the debate in 1991 was not about whether to increase the insurance limit, but whether to reduce it.

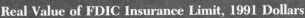

**Real Value of FDIC Insurance Limit, 1991 Dollars**

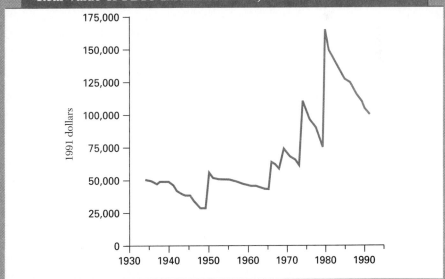

EXAMPLE
22.3

### The FDIC Decides to Run CrossLand Savings

In the 1980s, New York–based CrossLand Savings was the fourteenth largest thrift in the United States. At the end of 1990, however, half of CrossLand's assets were related to relatively risky real estate, and the slumping New York City real estate market was causing massive losses for CrossLand. At the end of the third quarter of 1991, CrossLand's assets were down to $9.2 billion, of which $1.55 billion (17 percent) were nonperforming real estate loans.

The FDIC solicited offers from healthy banks, hoping to sell CrossLand and then indemnify the purchaser against losses from CrossLand's nonperforming loans. The FDIC estimated that this guarantee would cost the government between $500 million and $1 billion. The FDIC received two bids, from Chase Manhattan and Republic National Bank, but rejected both as inadequate. On Friday, January 24, 1992, the FDIC closed CrossLand's 47 New York area branch offices and reopened them 1 hour later as a new federally chartered thrift, CrossLand Federal Savings Bank, owned and operated by the FDIC. The FDIC put $1.2 billion of its own money into CrossLand, hoping that the New York real estate market would recover and that it could sell a rejuvenated CrossLand to private investors by 1994.

the time value of money) was $800 million. Example 22.3 describes another case in which the FDIC decided to socialize a failed bank.

## Why Does It Work?

Overall, nearly $3 trillion in deposits are covered by FDIC insurance, an amount that would dwarf the FDIC's reserves were there a nationwide run on banks and thrifts. However, the FDIC is not intended to have reserves equal to the deposits it is insuring. On the whole, banks have the assets to back up their deposits because the FDIC supervises its insured banks closely and withholds insurance from any that are poorly managed. One of the subtle virtues of the FDIC is that it brought almost all state-chartered banks under the supervision of a hard-nosed federal agency. Both the FDIC and the Federal Reserve Board have the power to remove officers or directors of member banks who have taken reckless actions that threaten a bank's solvency. Bank runs are a danger not because banks have insufficient assets to support their deposits, but because much of their assets are illiquid and cannot be mobilized in a hurry — they are illiquid, not insolvent. Temporary loans from the federal government can stave off bank runs and, if necessary, allow a gradual liquidation of a bank's assets.

The second reason why the FDIC's assets are adequate to forestall bank runs is that it has the complete support of the president, Congress, and the Federal Reserve. If a panic began to develop, these sources would provide as much cash as necessary to abort the panic. When Franklin National, then the nation's twentieth largest bank, was crunched in 1974, the Federal Reserve made $1.7 billion in emergency credit available to keep it afloat until it could be permanently salvaged.

The third reason why the FDIC's modest reserves have stopped bank runs is that when depositors are confident that their funds are safe, there is no need for these funds to be available. Depositor faith in federal deposit insurance has virtually eliminated contagious bank panics in the United States.

Bank runs could be stopped without deposit insurance. England did not adopt deposit insurance until 1979 but has had no major banking panics since 1866, a panic the Bank of England ended in a day by announcing that it would be a reliable lender of last resort, providing cash to any bank that needed funds to satisfy depositors. In the United States, FDIC funds would surely have to be supplemented with Federal Reserve loans in a national banking panic. Nonetheless, U.S. depositors may have become psychologically accustomed to the idea that the liquidity of their deposits is dependent on federal insurance, not on the willingness of the Fed to supply cash in an emergency.

The 1985 Ohio and Maryland bank runs recounted in Chapter 13 are instructive. There were no runs on federally insured institutions. Moreover, Federal Reserve loans to the privately insured institutions did not stop the panic. The panic ended when the governor of each state required the privately insured institutions to either obtain federal deposit insurance or close.

Throughout the 1980s, the public was well aware of the enormous financial losses of the S&L industry and knew that depository institutions were failing in numbers not seen since the Great Depression. Yet there were no runs on federally insured institutions. In theory, the public's confidence could have been maintained by a widely recognized and well-established commitment of the Federal Reserve to supply cash in an emergency. In practice, the public's faith in deposit insurance held the fragile system together.

## Are Banks Overprotected?

A more appropriate measure of the adequacy of FDIC reserves is whether the FDIC has enough funds to protect insured deposits at insolvent banks and thrifts. The FSLIC went bankrupt in 1989. Qualified thrifts are now insured by the Savings Association Insurance Fund (SAIF), and banks are insured by the Bank Insurance Fund (BIF). Both insurance funds are administered by the FDIC, and both were in precarious financial condition in the early 1990s, leading economists and lawmakers to debate the extent to which deposit insurance had encouraged excessive risk-taking in the 1980s and whether the deposit-insurance system should be modified substantially or scrapped altogether.

A **moral hazard** arises when one of the parties to a contract alters his or her behavior so as to profit from the contract at the other party's expense. For example, a homeowner who has fire insurance may become less careful about avoiding a fire; a person with medical insurance may be less frugal about medical expenses. The primary criticism of deposit insurance is that it creates a moral-hazard problem that encourages reckless banking practices. Because the owners of the deposit intermediary keep the profits if their speculation turns out to be profitable and the federal government absorbs the losses if the speculation fails, deposit insurance encourages excessive risk-taking. And, perversely, if the intermediary experiences losses, even less of the institution's own capital is at stake, and the incentive for risk-taking increases.

Critics of deposit insurance often speak as if there were no penalty for failure. The stockholders of a failed bank do lose a lot, and so do the bank's officers, who are likely to become unemployed if the bank flounders. The problem is that these penalties do not increase with the size of the risks taken.

Some critics consequently argue that deposit-insurance premiums should vary with the riskiness of the bank in order to discourage reckless bank management.[7] In 1991 Congress agreed and instructed the FDIC to implement such a system by January 1, 1994. Unfortunately, bank risk is difficult to quantify, and any system is necessarily imperfect. How are government regulators to measure the riskiness of loans to finance a New York apartment building, oil exploration in the Gulf of Mexico, or a shoe manufacturer in Brazil? Not only are such loans difficult to gauge individually, but Chapter 14 teaches us that to judge the overall riskiness of a bank's portfolio, we need to separate the systematic risk from the idiosyncratic risk that can be diversified away.

Even if we could quantify a bank's overall riskiness, much of the clearly excessive risk-taking occurs when the deposit institution is insolvent, or nearly so, and has nothing more to lose. These one-sided bets won't be discouraged by modest increases in deposit-insurance premiums. The only sure cure for a zombie bank is burial.

The FDIC does supervise banks carefully, and if there is a danger of insolvency, it can close the bank or, what is virtually the same thing, terminate its deposit insurance. The real danger to the FDIC is that it will misestimate the risks that the bank is taking and not recognize the insolvency until it is too late. The risk is not that the bank will take chances and experience losses, but that the FDIC will not notice that this is happening. How is the FDIC to price this elusive monitoring risk?

Chapter 16 describes how the capital requirements on banks and thrifts now depend on the type of asset, as shown in Table 22.1. The higher capital requirements for assets that are not securitized is one rough way of penalizing risks that are difficult to detect.

The overall increase in capital requirements mandated by the Financial Institutions Reform, Recovery and Enforcement Act (FIRREA) reduces the incentive for risk-taking by ensuring that it is the bank's capital, rather than the FDIC's, that is at risk. The Federal Deposit Insurance Corporation Improvement Act of 1991 requires the FDIC to take prompt corrective action when an insured institution's capital falls below minimum standards and to increase its scrutiny and restrictions as capital falls. The FDIC's mandate to restrict or seize

**Table 22.1  Risk-Based Capital Requirements for U.S. Banks and Qualified Thrifts**

| | Risk Weights (%) | Capital requirements (%) | |
| --- | --- | --- | --- |
| | | Tier 1 | Tier 1 plus Tier 2 |
| U.S. government and government-guaranteed securities (including Ginnie Mae securities) | 0 | 0.0 | 0.0 |
| U.S. government agencies (including Fannie Mae and Freddy Mac securities) and general-obligation municipal bonds | 20 | 0.8 | 1.6 |
| Nonsecuritized residential mortgages | 50 | 2.0 | 4.0 |
| Commercial loans and other assets | 100 | 4.0 | 8.0 |

any insured bank or thrift that falls below the toughened capital requirements is intended to take away the opportunity to increase risk-taking after a decline in net worth.

In the absence of federal insurance, depositors would have a compelling financial incentive to monitor the solvency and risk-taking of banks, perhaps in the same way that they now use Moody's, Standard & Poor's, and other rating agencies to monitor corporations and municipalities that issue bonds. However, it is unclear whether depositors and rating agencies can make accurate assessments of a bank's financial condition without access to the detailed data that are now available only to bank examiners. A 1991 study of large publicly traded banks that were downgraded by bank examiners found no tendency for stock prices to decline in advance of the downgrading, suggesting that investors have no advantage over regulators in identifying problem banks.[8]

Even bank examiners may not have enough timely information. A 1991 study of 39 failed banks by Congress's General Accounting Office found that, using generally accepted accounting practices, these banks had set aside a total of $2.1 billion for loan losses, but that after seizure by the government, the market value of their loans indicated a loss of $9.4 billion. The General Accounting Office concluded that in order to meet government capital requirements, banks have a strong incentive to underestimate the declining value of their assets and that the banks' quarterly reports to the government consequently "failed to provide regulators with advance warning of the true magnitude of the deterioration of the banks' financial condition and performance."[9]

The strict enforcement of the $100,000 limit on deposit insurance would encourage the very largest (and probably best informed) depositors to scrutinize a bank's financial strength carefully. When Penn Square Bank became insolvent in 1982, the FDIC decided not to arrange an acquisition by another bank, which

EXAMPLE
22.4   ## *Buying Junk with Insured Deposits*

Junk bonds are risky and, because most investors dislike risk, are priced to offer relatively high expected returns. Junk buyers are less risk averse than others or more optimistic about the junk firm's chances of paying its debts. Some savings and loan associations bought junk because they were using other people's money — their federally insured deposits.

These S&L junk purchases are a clear example of the moral-hazard problem. S&Ls were willing to borrow from their depositors at 5 to 10 percent interest to invest in junk bonds promising 15 to 20 percent returns because any profits would go to the S&L and most of the losses would be paid by federal deposit insurance. Depositors played along because their deposits were federally guaranteed. Heads, the S&L wins. Tails, the FSLIC loses.

As it turned out, until the end of 1989, junk bonds were, on average, relatively profitable investments for thrifts. A 1989 General Accounting Office report found that junk had not contributed to the S&L crisis up to that point and that, after credit cards, junk bonds had in fact been the S&L industry's second most profitable category of investments.*

However, the years surveyed in this report had been recession free. Concerned about potential future defaults and recognizing the moral-hazard problem, the 1989 Financial Institutions Reform, Recovery and Enforcement Act (FIRREA) prohibited thrifts from buying additional junk bonds and gave them 5 years to sell their current holdings. As FIRREA neared completion, some thrifts made substantial last-minute junk purchases. One industry analyst said that these thrifts "realized this was their last window of opportunity, so they jumped in. It was a case of speeding up at the yellow light."† During the last 40 days before FIRREA was enacted, 10 of these hot-rod thrifts bought a total of more than $1 billion in junk bonds, increasing their holdings by 19 percent.

In retrospect, their timing couldn't have been worse. With further purchases prohibited and sales mandated, FIRREA created an excess supply of junk. Coupled with Drexel-Burnham's bankruptcy, the junk bond market collapsed, as prices fell some 10 to 15 percent in the first 3 months after FIRREA's prohibition went into effect. The industry analyst quoted above continued the analogy: "After they got to the [yellow] light, the market went over the cliff."

*Glenn Emory, "Reading Between the Lines of High Risk and Reward," Insight, September 4, 1989.

†Roger Lowenstein, "Junk-Buying Thrifts Made Problems Worse with Purchases Made Before Market Plunge," Wall Street Journal, January 15, 1990.

**EXAMPLE**
**22.5**    *The Tobin Plan*

Nobel Prize winner James Tobin of Yale University argues that deposit insurance encourages banks and thrifts to gamble with taxpayer money but that checking account deposits must be insured because the nation's means of payment is too important to be allowed to collapse, as happened in the 1930s. His proposed solution is to make a sharp distinction between checking accounts, which should be fully insured, and other deposits, which should have no insurance.* To protect taxpayers, insured checking accounts can be protected by requiring financial intermediaries to hold 100 percent reserves against these accounts. The reserves must be free of default risk and have very little market-value risk: cash, balances at Federal Reserve banks, and short-term U.S. securities. These reserves would be segregated from other bank assets to ensure that they are always available to cover checking account deposits and never used for any other purpose.

Intermediaries could offer other deposits that cannot be used for checking but, like money-market funds, are backed by the intermediary's investment in Treasury bills, commercial paper, and other short-term liquid assets. Yet other segregated categories of deposits could be invested in commercial loans, mortgages, junk bonds, or stock, with the depositor fully aware of how the funds are invested. The federal government would not implicitly or explicitly guarantee any deposits other than checking accounts. The uninsured deposits would be much like mutual funds are today, to be evaluated by depositors with no guarantee of their market value or their solvency.

*James Tobin, *"Financial Innovation and Deregulation in Perspective,"* Bank of Japan Monetary and Economic Studies, *September 1985, pp. 19–29.*

would have protected all depositors. Instead, the FDIC closed the bank and paid each depositor up to the $100,000 limit, no more, in part to encourage large depositors to monitor the condition of other banks.[10] Because a loss of large deposits and the accompanying damage to the bank's reputation is costly, such monitoring exerts market pressure for prudent behavior by bank management.[11]

However, for nearly 10 years after the Penn Square episode, whenever there were rumors of trouble at any of the nation's largest banks, the FDIC gave assurances of full repayment of all deposits, no matter how large, leading many to conclude that some banks were too big to fail. Apparently the FDIC believed that market discipline was less important than preventing a giant bank run by large depositors. In 1991 Congress ended the Fed's informal "too big to fail" policy by prohibiting the reimbursement of uninsured deposits after December 31, 1994, unless the FDIC, the Federal Reserve Board, and the president all agree that such reimbursement is necessary to protect the financial system. This kind of public declaration will presumably be discouraged by the anticipated reaction of voters.

## *Market-Value Accounting*

The FDIC may have difficulty monitoring the solvency of banks and thrifts because generally accepted accounting principles allow many assets and liabilities to be reported at values that do not accurately reflect current market prices. For example, when interest rates change, so do the market values of all assets with fixed cash flows. A given cash flow is worth more at low interest rates and less at high interest rates. However, the conventional balance sheets of banks and thrift institutions do not reflect the effects of interest-rate changes on the value of their assets. The accounting value of a bond is its cost plus any accrued interest; the accounting value of a loan is its unpaid balance. Changes in market values are recorded only if the institution realizes the profit or loss by selling the bond or loan to someone else.

In 1986, for example, almost all of troubled Bank of America's reported profit came from the sale for $80 million of some Tokyo property acquired in 1946 for $50,000. The property had long been worth millions and was worth $80 million in 1986 whether or not Bank of America decided to sell it. To the accountants, however, it wasn't worth a penny more than $50,000 until the bank did sell it.

These misleading accounting conventions lead some institutions to take actions that are superficially beneficial but actually undesirable. Many banks do not sell assets that have declined in value because these sales will force them to show losses on their balance sheets, even though they might have a better use for the funds and could receive a tax break by using realized losses to offset operating profits. Others sell appreciated assets in order to disclose publicly the profits they have made, even though this disclosure forces them to pay taxes on their profits. A sound investment rule is to realize losses and hold onto gains,[12] but book-value accounting induces many financial institutions to do just the opposite.

The capital requirements in FIRREA are based on book rather than market values. A bank could be book-value solvent but market-value bankrupt, in that the FDIC could not sell its assets for enough to cover the institution's deposits. A bank that realizes that it is market-value bankrupt, even though book-value solvent, may be tempted to take the same kinds of risks that plagued the S&L industry before FIRREA.

Several people have recommended that banks and thrifts change to market-value accounting,[13] and in December of 1991, Congress gave federal regulators 18 months to publish final regulations that "take adequate account" of interest-rate risk, which must necessarily involve some market-value accounting. One difficulty with comprehensive market-value accounting is that assets and liabilities that are not traded in organized markets may be difficult to value. Market-value accounting requires an estimate of loan defaults and early repayments, which can be subject to legitimate debate and intentional fraud.

If financial intermediaries are compelled to take into account the effects of interest-rate fluctuations on their net worth, they will either be extremely

EXAMPLE
22.6

## *The Extraordinary Case of Franklin Savings*

In the 1970s, Franklin Savings Association was a traditional Kansas savings and loan association that borrowed short and lent long, using savings deposits to finance residential mortgages. In 1980, interest rates rose unexpectedly, and Franklin lost $40 to $60 million. Franklin's chairman, Ernest Fleischer, then hired Wayne Angell, professor of economics and finance at Ottawa University (later to become a Federal Reserve Board governor), to find a way to make Franklin Savings Association profitable and less vulnerable to interest-rate fluctuations.

Franklin Savings was subsequently transformed into an $11.4 billion institution that used brokered deposits to buy GNMA and other mortgage-backed securities, hedging the interest-rate risk with financial futures contracts. To implement this strategy, Franklin Savings hired dozens of finance MBAs and PhDs with practical experience, including the head of the research department at Merrill Lynch and the comanager of Goldman Sachs financial strategies group. Using sophisticated computer models, Franklin Savings simultaneously bought mortgage-backed securities and sold financial futures, intending to guarantee a substantial profit whether interest rates went up or down. If interest rates rose unexpectedly, the value of the mortgages would fall and so would the value of the futures Franklin had sold, with the gains on the futures offsetting the mortgage losses. If interest rates fell, the value of Franklin's mortgages would rise, offsetting the futures-contract losses.

When interest rates dropped in 1989, financial-futures prices rose, and, as anticipated, Franklin lost money on the contracts it had sold. For accounting purposes, Franklin deferred these losses, arguing that they would be offset by the high-interest income on its mortgage portfolio. In February 1990, federal regulators forced Franklin Savings to recognize $119 million in losses on its financial futures contracts and then seized Franklin because its revised net worth could no longer satisfy federal capital requirements.

Franklin Savings filed suit, and on September 6, 1990, federal judge Dale Saffels, former chairman of the board of the Federal Home Loan Bank of Topeka, issued an extraordinary ruling. He noted that

*This is not a case involving fraud, corruption, or self-dealing by the management or directors of Franklin. There has been no allegation or even hint of illegal or unethical conduct by Franklin's management or directors. Essentially this case boils down to a dispute over accounting practices.*

The federal regulator who had been assigned to Franklin Savings had read only one form 10K [annual report] in his life and was unaware of the mandatory disclosures required in such reports. He consequently misinterpreted the requisite cautionary warnings as predictions that Franklin would experience financial difficulties. Judge Saffels concluded that this interpretation by the regulator and OTS was

> *arbitrary and capricious and without reasonable basis. Members of the OTS-Topeka staff appeared to lack adequate training and understanding to evaluate the nature of Franklin's operation. The written analyses and memoranda prepared by the Topeka staff . . . contained fundamental factual errors as well as material errors of interpretation and analysis. . . . This court is convinced and finds that the hedge accounting policies . . . are consistent with GAAP [generally accepted accounting principles].*
>
> *The expert opinion evidence presented in this case clearly convinces the court that the challenged provisions of Franklin's correlation policy are safe and sound practices.*

Judge Saffels ruled that OTS had to vacate Franklin's offices by 10 a.m. the next morning. A few hours after federal regulators left Franklin's offices, a Denver appeals court granted an emergency stay and returned Franklin to the control of federal regulators.

In May of 1991, the appeals court overturned Judge Saffel's ruling, finding that

> *Congress has given the Director [of OTS], not the courts, the power to define what is an unsafe and unsound condition. Congress did not mandate a hearing or specific finds of fact be made. . . . Rather, it required only that the [OTS] director be of the opinion statutory grounds for appointment of a conservator exist.*

The court noted that Webster's Dictionary defines opinion as a "belief held with confidence, not substantiated by direct proof or knowledge."

vulnerable to insolvency or else be compelled to hedge away most of their exposure to interest-rate risk. In 1979, for instance, a sudden increase in interest rates gave the 10 largest mutual savings banks in New York $2 billion in unrealized losses on their bond holdings alone, an amount equal to 93 percent of their net worth. Had they been using market-value accounting for their bonds and loans, all would have been bankrupt.[14]

Market-value accounting would give financial intermediaries a compelling reason to match the duration of their assets and liabilities, eliminating interest-rate risk. The social cost is that savers who prefer short-term assets and borrowers who prefer long-term assets might have to compromise and settle for less than they would like. Banks can use pass-through contracts and financial options, futures, and swaps (as discussed in Chapter 15) to shift these risks onto others, but ultimately, if borrowers issue long-term debts, someone must hold these contracts and bear the associated interest-rate risk.

# INTEREST-RATE CEILINGS

The Banking Acts of 1933 and 1935 prohibited the payment of interest on checking accounts and, through Regulation Q, gave the Federal Reserve Board the power to set maximum allowable interest rates on the time and savings deposits offered by member institutions. Beginning in the mid-1960s, the Federal Home Loan Bank (FHLB) system and Federal Deposit Insurance Corporation (FDIC) imposed analogous ceiling rates on their member institutions. Deposit-rate ceilings ended in 1986, but they deserve a brief eulogy.

## Safety by Collusion

The original rationale for deposit-rate ceilings was to protect bank solvency by stifling deposit-rate competition. It was thought that excessive competition for depositors in the 1920s had seduced banks into making risky high-yielding investments in order to pay high deposit rates. H. Parker Willis, a prominent monetary economist, expressed this common view in a 1933 book:

> There is no doubt that payment of higher interest rates (on deposits) has been the cause for the making of speculative loans and the purchase of doubtful securities which have, in turn, contributed so largely to bank failures during the past decade of this century.[15]

Banks in the 1930s generally endorsed rate ceilings because these kept costs low and profits high.

An across-the-board 3 percent ceiling rate was imposed on commercial bank savings and time deposits in 1933. This ceiling was reduced to $2\frac{1}{2}$ percent in 1935, adjusted slightly in 1936, and then held constant for the next 20 years. During this long period, ceiling rates were generally above market interest rates and above the deposit rates paid by commercial banks and consequently of little practical importance. There were two notable exceptions. One was the prohibition of interest payments on checking accounts. The second was that businesses and government units were not allowed to open passbook savings accounts, and the ceiling rates on permissible deposits were often below market interest rates on Treasury bills and other money-market securities.

As market rates rose above $2\frac{1}{2}$ percent in the 1950s, pressure built for a relaxation of ceiling rates. In January of 1957 the Federal Reserve raised ceiling rates a half percentage point and publicly expressed its skepticism of using ceiling rates to control bank lending practices.[16] Through the 1960s and 1970s, the board raised ceiling rates repeatedly and permitted banks to offer an increasing variety of deposits. Banks competed aggressively, keeping deposit rates at the maximum allowable limits and offering innovative instruments, including large CDs without ceiling rates and money-market certificates tied to Treasury-bill rates.

However, throughout this period, the belief lingered that ceiling rates should be used to protect the profits of otherwise uncompetitive (often small) intermediaries from more efficient institutions. Most economists do not think much of wage, price, or interest-rate controls that distort the verdict of the marketplace: if some intermediaries are less efficient, they shouldn't be in business. (It is said that economists are the social scientists with keen minds but no hearts.)

## Disintermediation

Interest-rate controls, like wage and price controls, eventually proved futile as people found ways to circumvent them. Institutions paid implicit interest by distributing gifts, reducing loan rates to depositors, and opening convenient branches. Money-market mutual funds were created to surmount the barriers placed between savers and high market interest rates. Such evasions forced the monetary authorities to relax deposit-rate ceilings.

Figure 22.3 compares the Treasury-bill rate with the ceiling rate on commercial bank savings deposits. There are, of course, other institutions and other types of deposits, but Figure 22.3 gives an adequate picture of the relevant history. The four periods 1966, 1969–1970, 1973–1974, and 1978–1980 are noteworthy in that the monetary authorities kept deposit-rate ceilings significantly below market rates. During each of these periods there was financial **disintermediation** — instead of depositing money in financial intermediaries, savers withdrew money and purchased Treasury bills and other market securities. During periods of disintermediation, when deposits shrink, intermediaries must look elsewhere for funds and cut back on their lending.

Savings and loan associations and mutual savings banks were squeezed the hardest during these credit crunches. Their long-term fixed-rate mortgages made them especially vulnerable to unexpected increases in interest rates, and they had much less flexibility than banks in seeking alternative sources of funds. Deposit-rate ceilings seemed necessary to keep them afloat but caused them to lose depositors.

The regulatory authorities tried compromise policies with, as might be expected, mixed success. The minimum Treasury-bill purchase was raised to $10,000. Temporary reserve requirements were imposed on money-market funds. The FHLB and other organizations pumped money into savings and loan associations and mutual savings banks. Thrifts were allowed to offer special deposits to try to hold onto mobile funds without increasing the cost of immobile deposits. Deposit-rate ceilings were used to protect thrifts from commercial banks — in the 1966 crunch the Fed tried to help beleaguered savings and loan associations by *lowering* the maximum rate that commercial banks could pay on small time deposits.

Profits were hurt but not destroyed; depositors left, but not all of them. During the four credit crunches in Figure 22.3, mortgage rates increased and

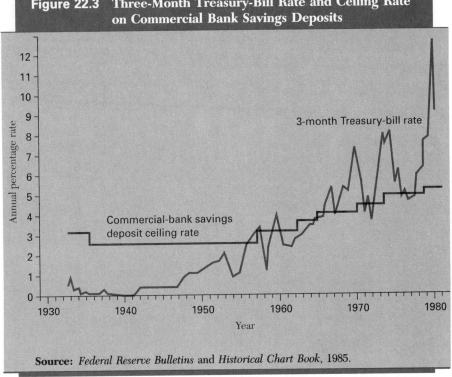

**Figure 22.3**  Three-Month Treasury-Bill Rate and Ceiling Rate on Commercial Bank Savings Deposits

**Source:** *Federal Reserve Bulletins* and *Historical Chart Book,* 1985.

mortgage loans contracted; many S&Ls stopped even taking mortgage applications. When mortgage loans dry up, home purchases and housing construction are never far behind, as documented in Figure 22.4. The four crunches (1966, 1969–1970, 1973–1974, and 1978–1980) were all difficult times for housing construction. Comparing Figures 22.3 and 22.4, we see that the less publicized periods 1951–1953, 1956–1957, and 1959 also fit the pattern. When market rates rose above ceiling rates, mortgages sagged and housing construction slumped.

The Fed deliberately threw these body blows at housing. To cool the economy and thereby restrain inflation, the Fed periodically combined tight monetary policies with deposit-rate ceilings to knock out home building. In the midst of the spring 1980 crunch, Fed Chairman Volcker reportedly said that he wouldn't be satisfied "until the last buzz saw is silenced."[17]

There is another side to disintermediation — the small savers left behind. Deposit-rate ceilings cost them billions of dollars in interest payments. James Tobin has eloquently condemned this inequity:

> *One of the least attractive features of recent policy has been discrimination against the small saver. . . . The small saver cannot easily go into the open market in search of higher yields. He is impeded by the significant minimum denominations and lot sizes of market instruments, by brokerage fees,*

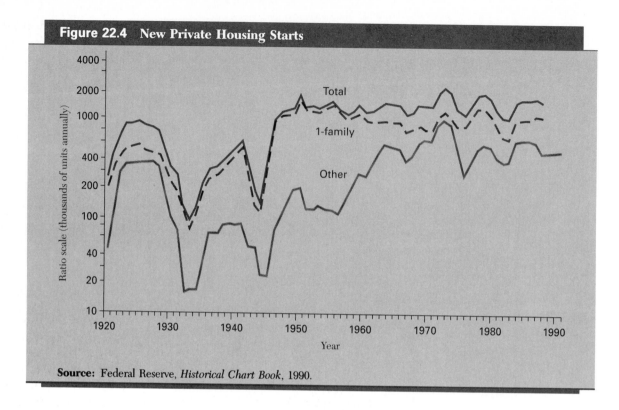

**Figure 22.4**   **New Private Housing Starts**

**Source:** Federal Reserve, *Historical Chart Book*, 1990.

by his own unfamiliarity and ignorance. Of course, the policy makers were counting on precisely this segmentation of the market; without it the ceiling rate policy could not work at all. But from a larger perspective, the reason that financial intermediaries exist and receive government support is to overcome just this kind of segmentation, to make markets more perfect rather than to exploit their imperfections.[18]

Because of ceiling rates and the structure of deposit institutions, tight-money policies were felt most strongly by thrift institutions, small savers, and the housing industry. This uneven pressure is illogical and inequitable. One of the motivations for deregulation in the 1980s was to remove these distortions by eliminating ceiling rates and permitting deposit institutions to become more balanced financial intermediaries.

# BRANCH BANKING

Many surveys have shown that depositors and borrowers are attracted to banks that are convenient, both in location (near one's home or business) and in banking hours. Knowing this, banks compete with one another by offering attractive locations and hours. Figure 22.5 shows that while there has been little

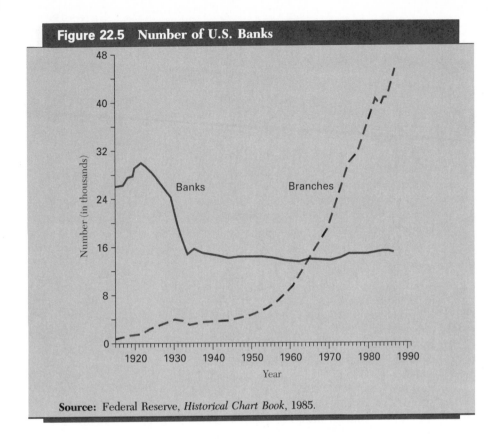

**Figure 22.5  Number of U.S. Banks**

Number (in thousands)

Banks

Branches

Year

**Source:** Federal Reserve, *Historical Chart Book*, 1985.

change in the total number of banks, the number of branches has increased dramatically since World War II. (These data do not include foreign branches of U.S. banks, which also have increased greatly.) The increase in bank branches reflects the provision of convenient locations within large cities, expansion into suburbia to compete with savings and loan associations, and the acquisition of small banks in order to take advantage of some of the economies of scale discussed in Chapter 14.

Branching, however, has long been constrained by state and federal laws designed to protect small banks from competition from the branches of large banks. The United States is unique in having nearly 30,000 deposit intermediaries (roughly half commercial banks and half thrifts), of which 85 percent have assets of less than $100 million and 97 percent less than $500 million. In contrast, Canada has 65 banks, Japan 150, the United Kingdom 550, and Germany 900. Table 22.2 shows that Citicorp is the only U.S. bank that is among the 25 largest banks in the world. (The predominance of Japanese banks in this list reflects the fact that Japanese banks held a lot of extremely valuable Japanese stock and real estate in December of 1989 and that Japanese companies rely on bank loans rather than bond issues to raise funds.)

**Table 22.2**  **The 25 Largest Banks in the World,
December 31, 1989**

| | Country | Total Assets (Billions of U.S. Dollars) |
|---|---|---|
| 1. Dai-ichi Kangyo Bank | Japan | 403.4 |
| 2. Sumitomo Bank | Japan | 368.2 |
| 3. Fuji Bank | Japan | 362.6 |
| 4. Mitsubishi Bank | Japan | 360.0 |
| 5. Sanwa Bank | Japan | 353.7 |
| 6. Industrial Bank of Japan | Japan | 256.9 |
| 7. Credit Agricole Mutuel | France | 242.3 |
| 8. Banque Nationale de Paris | France | 231.8 |
| 9. Tokai Bank | Japan | 227.7 |
| 10. Citicorp | United States | 227.0 |
| 11. Norinchukin Bank | Japan | 220.0 |
| 12. Mitsubishi Trust & Banking Corp. | Japan | 213.5 |
| 13. Credit Lyonnais | France | 211.0 |
| 14. Barclays Bank | United Kingdom | 205.5 |
| 15. Mitsui Bank | Japan | 203.3 |
| 16. Deutsche Bank | Germany | 202.6 |
| 17. Bank of Tokyo | Japan | 200.5 |
| 18. Sumitomo Trust & Banking Co. | Japan | 190.9 |
| 19. National Westminster Bank | United Kingdom | 187.1 |
| 20. Mitsui Trust & Banking Co. | Japan | 182.6 |
| 21. Societe Generale | France | 176.0 |
| 22. Long Term Credit Bank of Japan | Japan | 174.2 |
| 23. Taiyo Kobe Bank | Japan | 173.0 |
| 24. Yasuda Trust & Banking Co. | Japan | 157.8 |
| 25. Daiwa Bank | Japan | 155.5 |

**Source:** American Banker, *Top Numbers: Part Two, 1990 Update*, p. 130.

The **McFadden Act** of 1927, which was largely motivated by a fear that Bank of America would span the nation, prohibits interstate branching and allows branching within a state to be regulated by each individual state. In 1975, 15 states (mostly in the Midwest) still prohibited branching entirely; their **unit banking** laws permit a bank to have only one geographic location. In 1991 only one state (Colorado) still had a unit banking law.

Some banks evaded restrictions on branching and other activities by setting up **holding companies**, which can control a variety of banking and nonbanking subsidiaries. Some holding companies are established to administer several banks; others are conglomerates like C. I. T. Corporation and Hershey Foods, which control a variety of nonfinancial businesses as well as banks. The holding company may be able to engage in nonbanking activities (such as investment banking) or issue commercial paper or corporate bonds, while the bank cannot. Branching barriers also may be breached by a holding company; in a unit banking state, for instance, a holding company may be able to acquire a large number of individual banks — although customers still cannot use the facilities of one bank to make deposits or withdrawals in another bank.

In 1960 there were only 47 bank holding companies, and they controlled less than 10 percent of aggregate bank assets; in 1987 there were more than 6000 bank holding companies, encompassing more than 90 percent of all bank assets. All bank holding companies are regulated by the Federal Reserve.

In many states, electronic banking has, in effect, multiplied bank branches through **automated teller machines (ATMs),** which allow deposits, withdrawals, and account information without entering a traditional "brick and mortar" bank branch. The first ATMs were installed in the outside walls of banks, to allow for after-hours transactions. Much of the subsequent growth has been off-premises, to provide convenient banking locations. Half of all off-premise ATMs are in shopping malls and supermarkets; many others are in office and apartment buildings. ATMs at universities are among the most heavily used, averaging more than 300 transactions a day.[19]

# INTERSTATE BANKING

The Douglas amendment to the McFadden Act prohibits holding companies from crossing state lines unless specifically authorized by state authorities. Banks have nonetheless breached state borders in several ways. For example, the 1919 **Edge Act** allows bank holding companies to establish interstate subsidiaries (known as *Edge Act corporations*) for accepting deposits and making loans related to international business transactions; BankAmerica has a dozen such subsidiaries which, if combined as a separate bank, would be one of the nation's largest banks.

The **Bank Holding Company Act** of 1956, amended in 1970, defines a bank as an institution that accepts deposits that can be withdrawn on demand and also makes commercial loans. A financial institution that did one of these activities, but not both, was technically not a bank — what some call a **nonbank bank** — and hence was not regulated by the Federal Reserve. For example, J. C. Penney's federally chartered J. C. Penney National Bank accepts deposits but is not considered a bank because it does not make commercial loans. The Bank-America and Citicorp holding companies have hundreds of interstate subsidiaries that don't accept deposits but do arrange business and personal loans and engage in mortgage banking, leasing, and pension fund management. The Competitive Banking Equality Act of 1987 closed the nonbank-bank loophole by defining a bank as any FDIC-insured institution, but it exempted nonbank banks established before March 5, 1986.

Bank holding companies also cross state lines when they offer nonbank services such as credit cards. Interstate automated teller machines (ATMs) allow customers to withdraw cash and transfer funds among accounts but not make interstate deposits. Because these systems are not owned by banks but are paid on a per-transaction basis, they are not considered bank branches. The Federal Home Loan Bank Board allowed all S&Ls to put ATMs nationwide. Three of the largest shared banking ATM networks are the New York Cash Exchange, the PLUS SYSTEM, and CIRRUS.

By 1986, 39 state legislatures had approved some form of interstate banking. Three states allow any out-of-state bank to acquire a bank within the state. Three other states require a reciprocal arrangement: banks from state B can operate in state A if banks from A are allowed in B. Twenty-seven other states have approved regional interstate zones that are intended to allow the development of large regional banks that are protected from the nation's giant banks. Regional banking zones were challenged in court by some of the giant banks, but they were upheld in an unanimous 1985 Supreme Court decision.

As noted earlier in this chapter, banks and thrifts have been allowed to cross state lines to acquire financially troubled institutions. The first major acquisition occurred in 1982, when New York's Citicorp acquired Fidelity S&L of Oakland, California. Fidelity S&L was renamed Citicorp Savings and now operates nearly 100 branches in 66 California cities as a subsidiary of the Citicorp holding company.

Citibank lobbied for years for a reciprocal banking bill that would allow New York and California banks to open a limited number of branches in each other's state. Such bills were repeatedly defeated in the California legislature because California banks felt that they were getting the short end of the stick. One California banker said, "I wouldn't trade two blocks of Fresno for the entire city of New York."[20] Nonetheless, large California banks did want to spread eastward, one observing that "someday an earthquake might make California an island. We want to have operations on the mainland."[21] In 1986 the California legislature finally approved a bill allowing reciprocal interstate banking, initially within a nine-state western region, but nationwide after January 1, 1990.

Is it better for a nation to have a handful of giant banks spanning the nation or thousands of local banks? Regulation Q, higher reserve requirements on large banks, and antibranching restrictions were at least in part intended to protect small banks from large banks that are more efficient due to economies of scale. In recent years, the trend has been in the opposite direction — to remove some of the barriers to the formation of giant banks. The hope is that the branches of these giants will be more efficient than small local banks. In addition, nationwide banking allows geographic diversification so that a bank's solvency is not overly dependent on the economic health of a specific region of the country.

Barriers to interstate banking will eventually disappear. Such restrictions are an obvious nuisance for households and businesses that cross state lines. These restrictions are outmoded and discriminatory at a time when credit cards, money-market funds, security brokers, and other financial institutions span the nation. In an electronic age, you don't need bricks and mortar to operate a bank.

**EXAMPLE 22.7**

## *The Largest Bank Merger in U.S. History*

Three megamergers in 1991 provided dramatic evidence of the ongoing consolidation of the banking industry. First, Chemical Bank ($74 billion) and Manufacturers Hanover ($65 billion) combined to create the nation's second largest bank. Then NCNB ($66 billion) and C&S/Sovran ($49 billion) formed NationsBank, the third largest bank. Finally, on August 12, 1991, California-based BankAmerica ($100 billion) and Security Pacific ($90 billion) announced the largest bank merger in U.S. history. BankAmerica acquired Security Pacific by exchanging 0.88 shares of BankAmerica stock for each share of Security Pacific stock. The combined bank retained the name BankAmerica and, with $190 billion in assets, leapfrogged Chemical and NationsBank to become the nation's second largest bank, close behind number one, Citicorp.

These megamergers are intended to take advantage of economies of scale and to marshal the resources needed for nationwide expansion when full interstate banking is authorized. BankAmerica estimated that within three years, the merger with Security Pacific would result in annual savings of $1.2 billion through reduced personnel (the elimination of more than 10,000 jobs) and the closing of several redundant buildings. In preparation for nationwide expansion, BankAmerica has been acquiring insolvent banks to give it footholds in several states. The merger with Security Pacific gives it the resources for national banking competition with Citicorp, NationsBank, Ohio's Banc One, and other powerhouses. Wall Street agreed with this logic as BankAmerica stock rose 7 percent and Security Pacific stock rose 40 percent on the day their merger was announced.

## SUMMARY

Bank runs and insolvencies have inspired a web of regulations designed to protect depositors and banks. The United States has a dual banking system in which banks can be chartered (and supervised) by either the federal or state government, sometimes leading to conflicts among state regulatory officials, the comptroller of the currency (which charters national banks), the FDIC (which insures bank deposits), and the Federal Reserve (which controls the nation's monetary policies).

The Federal Reserve Board is a largely independent branch of government, with the seven board governors appointed to overlapping 14-year terms. The Federal Open Market Committee (FOMC), consisting of the 7 board governors and 5 Federal Reserve bank presidents, meets approximately every 4 weeks to discuss the state of the economy and financial markets and make monetary policy decisions.

Federal deposit insurance has virtually eliminated contagious bank runs but also has encouraged insured institutions to take excessive risks, especially if they are close to or actually insolvent. The Financial Institutions Reform, Recovery and Enforcement Act (FIRREA) imposes higher, asset-based capital requirements, which are to be strictly enforced, with insolvent institutions promptly closed.

Deposit-rate ceilings were created in the 1930s and phased out in the 1980s. These ceilings stifled competition and protected small banks; in the 1960s and 1970s, they repeatedly caused disintermediation. Small banks also have been protected historically by restrictions on bank branches within a state and between states. As these barriers disappear, it is expected that the United States will evolve to a banking system similar to that of other countries, dominated by a small number of giant banks with nationwide branches.

## IMPORTANT TERMS

automated teller machines (ATMs)
Bank Holding Company Act
disintermediation
dual banking system
Edge Act
Federal Deposit Insurance Corporation (FDIC)
Federal Home Loan Bank (FHLB) system
Federal Open Market Committee (FOMC)

Federal Savings and Loan Insurance Corporation (FSLIC)
holding companies
McFadden Act
moral hazard
National Credit Union Administration
nonbank bank
unit banking

## EXERCISES

1. Historically, banks that belonged to the Federal Reserve System had higher reserve requirements than nonmember banks. Why are high reserve requirements expensive, and how does this expense vary with the condition of the economy?

2. In 1986 economist Herbert Stein wrote in a newspaper column that

   *On Monday, March 17, the Evans and Novak column broke the news that the Board of Governors had voted 4–3 against Chairman Paul Volcker and in favor of cutting the discount rate. Wow!*[22]

   What is so newsworthy about a narrow vote to cut the discount rate?

3. The FDIC gives banks a rating of 1 to 5, but it is illegal to divulge these ratings to the public. Why do you suppose this information is kept confidential?

4. Between 1982 and 1985, interest rates fell, yet there were 289 bank failures in the United States, of which 70 percent were in just 10 states: Illinois, Iowa, Kansas, Missouri, Nebraska, Oregon, Oklahoma, and Texas. How do you explain this concentration of bank failures?

5. Why, historically, did 90 percent of the state-chartered banks choose not to join the Federal Reserve System? Why did relatively more nationally chartered banks belong to the Federal Reserve System?

6. Explain this *Wall Street Journal* editorial: "Regulation Q, which has been part of the banking laws for years, has done a fine job of . . . limiting the interest income small savers can earn."[23]

7. Comment on the following quotation:

   *This discriminatory policy (deposit rate ceilings) will gradually be eroded by the ar-*

*bitrage which makes it possible. The gaps between market lending rates and the ceiling rates on small savings will encourage new ways of bringing together small lenders and large borrowers. What mutual funds have done in equities can be done in other markets; the growing popularity of mortgage trusts is indicative. Here again the authorities, by stimulating some irreversible creation of institutions outside their control, may have bought future trouble in return for present expediency.*[24]

8. Why is it that when the Fed steps on the monetary brakes, it is housing construction that comes to a stop?

9. The comptroller of the currency examines the books of each national bank four times a year; two of these examinations are regularly scheduled, and two of them are not announced in advance. Why do you suppose that the comptroller's office makes unannounced examinations?

10. A Texas congressman who frequently criticized the Federal Reserve Board once called it "a wholly owned subsidiary of the ABA [American Bankers Association]."[25] For each of the following actions, explain how the Federal Reserve Board either helps or hurts banks as a whole.

   a. Engineers a credit crunch that increases all interest rates.

   b. Lowers the discount rate.

   c. Imposes tight interest-rate ceiling on deposits.

   d. Imposes reserve requirement on money-market mutual funds.

11. In the 1800s the English banker and economist Walter Bagehot argued that a central bank should plainly and clearly announce that it is a lender of last resort, always willing to lend at high interest rates to any bank in need of cash. Why is it important that a central bank announce this policy to the public? Why do you think Bagehot specified high interest rates?

12. In every major U.S. banking panic during the 1800s, the banks in large cities stopped withdrawals by collectively declaring a moratorium on cash payments. Depositors and noteholders were not allowed to redeem their claims against the banks for gold and silver coins or, after 1860, for national bank notes. They could continue to write checks and make payments to other depositors within the banking system, with the banks making bookkeeping entries of the transfer of funds among accounts. After several months, when the panic had ended, the banks permitted withdrawals again. In comparison with unrestricted withdrawals during a banking panic, how did a moratorium affect the total amount of gold and silver coins in circulation? The total amount of bank deposits?

13. Explain the moral-hazard problem that arises when an automobile owner buys theft insurance. Is this moral-hazard problem exacerbated or alleviated by a $500 deductible, mandating that, in the event of theft, the first $500 of the replacement cost will be paid by the owner?

14. What aspect of deregulation is responsible for the following observation?

   *Deregulation has, for example, clearly diminished the tendency for savings deposits to drain out of banks and savings institutions whenever interest rates rise elsewhere . . . a situation long deemed unfair to depositors and dangerous to the institutions and to the housing industry.*[26]

15. It has been proposed that market-value accounting be implemented for banks with publicly traded stock by using the market value of their stock to measure their net worth, which could then be compared with the bank's liabilities. The FDIC would seize a bank if the ratio of the bank's net worth to

its liabilities fell below a specified percentage, such as 5 percent. As the owner of a publicly traded stock, what objection could you raise to this proposal?

16. An employee of a California bank that had been seized by the FDIC said afterwards, "It was almost a relief when they finally closed us. We could stop looking out the window every Friday to see if they were coming up the walk."[27] Why do you suppose they expected the regulators to come on a Friday?

17. In April of 1986, Center National Bank, a one-branch California bank, was declared insolvent. Independence Bank, a large local bank, paid the FDIC $322,000 for the right to absorb Center National's $36.7 million in deposits and $19.7 million of its assets. In addition, the FDIC paid Independence $16.9 million for the remaining $18.7 million in Center National assets.[28] Why do you suppose Independence agreed not only to sell $18.7 million in Center National assets to the FDIC for $16.9 million but to pay an additional $322,000?

18. In 1989 a *New York Times* writer observed that "because price changes in the securities are reported only when the notes and bonds are sold, analysts say, many banks and other firms tend to sit on paper losses and sell only those issues that show a profit."[29] Ignoring accounting conventions, do such actions increase or decrease the total value of a firm's assets? That is, would an outside firm pay more for a bank that has realized gains and held onto losses or one that has held onto both gains and losses?

19. In 1989 the American Institute of Certified Public Accountants proposed that banks, thrifts, and other financial institutions report the value of their bond holdings at cost or market value, whichever is lower, unless they have the ability and intention to hold the securities until maturity. In what ways is this proposed accounting convention poten-

tially misleading as compared with reporting all assets at market value?

20. The Financial Accounting Standards Board issued Financial Accounting Standard Number 33 in 1979, requiring large, publicly held firms to include supplementary information in their annual reports showing how inflation has affected the firm's balance sheets. Why, for a bank, is this not the same as market-value accounting?

21. In the 1980s, some prominent banks increased the net worth shown on their balance sheets by selling their corporate headquarters and then renting the building back. If the price they receive for the building is its fair market value, why would this sale cause a large, sudden increase in the bank's reported net worth?

22. When the Banking Acts of 1933 and 1935 were passed, some members of Congress argued that Regulation Q was needed to help banks pay their annual FDIC premiums. Explain why Regulation Q might be helpful in this way.

23. "State law in Texas prohibits full-scale branch banking but, paradoxically, allows financial institutions [including the state's 1400 commercial banks] to place ATMs in supermarkets, airports, and shopping centers."[30] What are ATMs, and why could this state law be considered paradoxical?

24. For decades, Canada has had unlimited branching, interest-bearing checking accounts, and no deposit-rate ceilings. Explain what, if any, relationship there is between these regulations and the fact that Canada has only 65 banks.

25. Critically evaluate the following quotation:

    *California is already so competitive, what would more competition do for the public? The smaller banks in the West have strong misgivings about such basic changes [interstate banking]. . . . It wouldn't be the smaller banks that would gain.*[31]

# 23 Monetary Policy Instruments

*There have been three great inventions since the beginning of time: fire, the wheel, and central banking.*

**Will Rogers**

A nation's central bank is responsible for managing the money supply, taking into account the effects of its monetary policies on interest rates, credit availability, output, employment, inflation, and other economic variables. The central bank monitors various measures of the money supply, financial conditions, and economic activity and decides whether it should increase or slow the growth of the money supply. If, for example, the central bank wants to help bring the economy out of a recession, it takes steps that increase the money supply. If it wants to reduce the rate of inflation, it restrains the money supply.

The central bank of the United States is the Federal Reserve Board (the Fed). In 1979 the rate of inflation in the United States was 13.3 percent, and the Fed decided to step on the monetary brakes, slowing the rate of growth of the money supply in the hope that this would slow the rate of inflation. The rate of inflation did decline — to 12.5 percent in 1980, 8.9 percent in 1981, and 3.8 percent in 1982. However, the unemployment rate increased from 5.8 percent in 1979 to 10.8 percent in November of 1982. Persuaded that the rate of inflation had been reduced sufficiently and fearful that the economy might collapse, the Fed switched to an expansionary monetary policy that helped end the recession and fuel the economic boom that lasted the remainder of the decade.

In the next several chapters we will consider how the Fed chooses a monetary policy and how it implements its policies. We begin in this chapter by looking at three of the Fed's most important policy tools: open-market operations, reserve requirements, and the discount rate. We will look at how each of these three policy instruments works and at how these tools affect financial markets. Then, in the subsequent three chapters, we will see how the Fed decides whether it will use these monetary policy tools to ease or tighten financial markets.

To understand how the Federal Reserve's monetary policy tools affect the money supply, we need to distinguish between policies that change the amount of government money that is outstanding and policies that affect the extent to which banks and other financial intermediaries multiply deposits and loans for a given supply of government money. We begin by showing that the amount of government money outstanding depends on several factors, which can be most easily understood by considering the Fed's balance sheet.

# THE FED'S BALANCE SHEET

The Federal Reserve maintains careful records of its financial condition, and each Thursday the Fed releases a summary report of its balance sheet as of that Wednesday. More detailed weekly records are published in the monthly *Federal Reserve Bulletin*. Table 23.1 shows the Fed's balance sheet on September 30, 1991. The Fed's balance sheet is much like any balance sheet, with assets on one side and liabilities on the other. However, some of the entries are unusual and probably a bit puzzling. We will identify each item in turn.

*Gold certificates*: When the U.S. Treasury buys gold, it issues gold certificates to the Fed and is credited with a deposit in its account at the Fed, upon which it can write checks to pay its bills. The gold certificate is an asset for the Fed because it is a claim to the Treasury's gold.

*SDR certificates*: As explained in Chapter 3, special drawing rights (SDRs) are "paper gold" issued by the International Monetary Fund (IMF) to governments for settling international debts. As with gold certificates, the U.S. Treasury gives SDR certificates to the Fed and is credited with a deposit at the Fed.

*Treasury currency*: A constant $300 million in U.S. Treasury notes, which trace back to the Civil War greenbacks, are outstanding, and in 1991 another $20 billion in coins issued by the Treasury was outstanding. Some of this Treasury currency, mostly coins, is held by the Fed. When the Treasury mints coins, it deposits these in its Fed account and can write checks against this balance. The coins come into circulation when depository institutions request coins from their local Federal Reserve banks, which they pay for either with currency or by debiting their account balances at the Fed.

*Loans to depository institutions*: These are borrowings through the Fed's discount window, one of the policy tools discussed later in this chapter. These loans are a liability of the borrowing institution and an asset for the Fed.

*Securities*: The Fed's largest asset category by far is securities, of which some 97 percent are U.S. Treasury securities, and the remainder are securities issued by federal agencies. The Fed's holdings of securities fluctuate with its open-market operations, another of the Fed's primary policy tools.

*Cash items in process of collection*: This category is related to the "deferred availability cash items" listed on the liability side of the Fed's balance sheet, and both relate to Federal Reserve float, which will be explained in some detail later.

*Assets denominated in foreign currencies*: In recent years the Fed has held an increasing amount of foreign currency and securities for facilitating international transactions and as a consequence of its efforts to stabilize exchange rates.

**Table 23.1** **Federal Reserve Balance Sheet, September 30, 1991 (Billions of Dollars)**

| Assets | | Liabilities | |
|---|---|---|---|
| Gold certificates | 11.1 | Federal Reserve notes | 273.8 |
| SDR certificates | 10.0 | Deposits by deposit institutions | 27.4 |
| Treasury currency | 0.6 | U.S. Treasury deposits | 7.9 |
| Loans to depository institutions | 0.3 | Foreign official accounts | 0.4 |
| Securities | 258.6 | Deferred availability cash items | 2.3 |
| Cash items in process of collection | 2.6 | Miscellaneous | 9.8 |
| Assets denominated in foreign currencies | 26.0 | | |
| Miscellaneous | 12.4 | | |
| Total | 321.6 | | 321.6 |

**Source:** *Federal Reserve Bulletin*, November 1991.

*Federal Reserve notes*: This is the currency issued by the Fed.

*Deposits by deposit institutions*: These are the deposits made by banks and other depository institutions with the Federal Reserve in partial fulfillment of their reserve requirements. The Fed's reserve requirements are another policy tool.

*U.S. Treasury deposits*: The Treasury deposits money with the Fed and then pays its bills by writing checks against these deposits. The Treasury has accounts (called *tax and loan accounts*) in commercial banks throughout the country that are used for the deposit of income taxes and Social Security taxes withheld by employers and for the proceeds from the sale of savings bonds. The Treasury withdraws funds from these accounts periodically (every few days from large banks, every few weeks from small banks) by a transfer from the commercial bank's reserve account with the Fed to the Treasury's account at the Fed. The Treasury then pays the government's bills by writing checks drawn on its Federal Reserve account.

*Foreign official accounts*: These are deposits with the Fed by foreign governments, central banks, and international agencies such as the World Bank.

## Currency and the Monetary Base

Table 23.1 shows that the Fed's liabilities consist primarily of Federal Reserve notes and deposits by banks and other deposit institutions. Federal Reserve finances are unique in that when the Fed wants to buy something, it can print money to pay for its purchases. To keep its balance sheets balanced, the Fed records these new Federal Reserve notes as a liability, which offsets the asset it acquires.

These Federal Reserve notes are very different from the liabilities of ordinary citizens and businesses. If you borrow funds to buy a house, the mortgage liability is a real burden in that the requisite monthly payments come out of your income and reduce the funds available to buy food, clothing, and entertainment. The Fed's Federal Reserve note liability is quite different. If you present a $10 Federal Reserve note for redemption, the Fed governors won't have to mine gold, sell furniture, or take second jobs. The Fed will simply have two $5 bills printed up, or ten $1 bills, whichever you prefer. Clearly, the Federal Reserve's notes are a special kind of liability that any of us would enjoy having.

The Fed's balance sheet is closely related to the nation's supply of government money because the Fed's two primary liabilities shown in Table 23.1 — Federal Reserve notes and deposits by deposit institutions — comprise most of the government money supply. The total supply of government money to the economy is called the nation's **monetary base**; in the United States, the monetary base consists of **U.S. currency outstanding** (currency that is held outside of the Federal Reserve and the U.S. Treasury) plus the reserves of depository institutions with the Federal Reserve:

$$\text{Monetary base} = \text{U.S. currency outstanding} + \text{reserve deposits with Fed} \tag{23.1}$$

Federal Reserve notes make up about 90 percent of the nation's currency. The remaining 10 percent consists of $300 million in U.S. Treasury notes and about $20 billion in coins issued by the Treasury. Some Treasury currency is held by the Fed, and some Federal Reserve notes are held by the Treasury. In practice, these holdings are small (about a half-billion dollars apiece), but they complicate our calculations of the amount of currency in private hands. A further difficulty is that an undetermined amount of currency has left the United States or has been tucked into coin collections, hidden in forgotten places, or lost at the beach or inside sofas. Ignoring this missing cash, U.S. currency outstanding consists of Federal Reserve notes and Treasury currency that are not held by the Fed or the Treasury:

$$
\begin{aligned}
\text{U.S. currency outstanding} = &\ \text{Federal Reserve notes} \\
&+ \text{Treasury notes and coin} \\
&- \text{Fed holdings of Treasury currency} \\
&- \text{Treasury holdings of Fed currency}
\end{aligned} \tag{23.2}
$$

Some of this outstanding currency is in private hands outside banks, and some is inside bank vaults:

$$\text{U.S. currency outstanding} = \text{currency outside banks} + \text{vault cash} \tag{23.3}$$

Equation 23.1, which defines the monetary base, can consequently be rewritten as follows:

$$
\begin{aligned}
\text{Monetary base} &= \text{U.S. currency outstanding} + \text{reserve deposits with Fed} \\
&= (\text{currency outside banks} + \text{vault cash}) \\
&\quad + \text{reserve deposits with Fed} \\
&= \text{currency outside banks} + \text{bank reserves}
\end{aligned} \tag{23.4}
$$

## The Role of Bank Reserves

Analysts are often particularly interested in the bank reserve part of the monetary base, because bank reserves support bank deposits, and deposits are a major component of various monetary aggregates, such as $M1$ and $M2$. Deposit institutions can satisfy their reserve requirements either with vault cash or with deposits at the Federal Reserve, and both are consequently included in the monetary base. The advantage of vault cash is that it is near at hand for meeting withdrawals of customers who want cash. The primary advantage of deposits at Federal Reserve banks is that these can be used for interbank transfers within the Federal Reserve.

When a private bank sends $100 million in Federal Reserve notes to its regional Federal Reserve bank, the private bank is credited with a $100 million deposit, and the notes are either shredded or stored for future use. One hundred million dollars of bank reserve deposits replaces $100 million of outstanding Federal Reserve notes, and the monetary base is unchanged. The T-accounts showing the changes in the balance sheets of the private bank and the Fed are as follows:

Private Bank

| Assets | | Liabilities |
|---|---|---|
| Vault cash | – $100 | |
| Deposits at Fed | + $100 | |

Federal Reserve

| Assets | Liabilities | |
|---|---|---|
| | Federal Reserve notes | – $100 |
| | Deposits by banks | + $100 |

## Changes in the Monetary Base

Because the monetary base includes Federal Reserve notes and bank reserve deposits with the Fed, which are both Federal Reserve liabilities, events that affect the asset or liability side of the Fed's balance sheets also affect the monetary base. Figure 23.1 on page 686 separates the Federal Reserve's liabilities into monetary base liabilities and nonbase liabilities. Other things being equal, an increase in a Federal Reserve asset requires a corresponding increase in the Federal Reserve's monetary base liabilities and, consequently, an increase in the monetary base. An increase in a Federal Reserve nonbase liability requires an offsetting decrease in the Federal Reserve's monetary base liabilities and a consequent reduction in the monetary base.

For example, when the Federal Reserve acquires assets denominated in foreign currencies, an item on the asset side of its balance sheet, the Fed can pay for these assets with Federal Reserve notes, thereby expanding its monetary base liabilities and the monetary base. For an example of the liability side of its

**Figure 23.1    The Relationship Between the Federal Reserve's Balance Sheet and the Monetary Base**

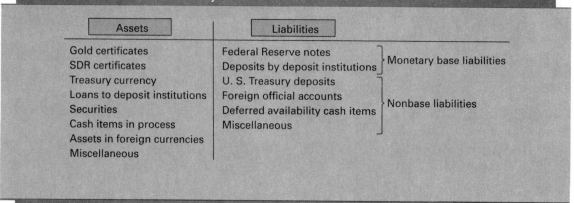

| Assets | Liabilities | |
|---|---|---|
| Gold certificates | Federal Reserve notes | ⎫ |
| SDR certificates | Deposits by deposit institutions | ⎬ Monetary base liabilities |
| Treasury currency | U. S. Treasury deposits | ⎫ |
| Loans to deposit institutions | Foreign official accounts | ⎪ |
| Securities | Deferred availability cash items | ⎬ Nonbase liabilities |
| Cash items in process | Miscellaneous | ⎪ |
| Assets in foreign currencies | | ⎭ |
| Miscellaneous | | |

balance sheet, suppose that the Treasury transfers $100 million from a commercial bank account to its Fed account, thereby increasing U.S. Treasury deposits, a Fed nonbase liability, by $100 million. The T-accounts are shown in Table 23.2. The bank loses $100 million in deposits and reserves, and the Fed transfers $100 million from bank reserves to the Treasury's account, reducing the monetary base by $100 million. This monetary contraction will be reversed when the

**Table 23.2    The Treasury Transfers Funds from a Private Bank to the Fed**

U.S. Treasury

| Assets | | Liabilities | |
|---|---|---|---|
| Deposits at bank | − $100 | | |
| Deposits at Fed | + $100 | | |

Private Bank

| Assets | | Liabilities | |
|---|---|---|---|
| Deposits at Fed | − $100 | Treasury deposits | − $100 |

Federal Reserve

| Assets | | Liabilities | |
|---|---|---|---|
| | | Deposits by banks | − $100 |
| | | Treasury deposits | + $100 |

Treasury writes $100 million in checks on its Fed account. When the recipients cash their checks, Treasury deposits at the Fed will fall by $100 million and bank reserves will increase by $100 million. This example shows how the Treasury's receipts and outlays can have large, though temporary, effects on the monetary base. This is also an example of a change in the monetary base that is not instigated by the Fed.

## Federal Reserve Float

**Float** arises from discrepancies in the dates on which payments and receipts are recorded. For example, bank float arises when a depositor's balances are credited before the bank itself receives credit for the funds. Suppose that Mary deposits a $2000 paycheck in her local bank, and this bank immediately credits her account — allowing her to earn interest on this $2000 and, if she wishes, to write checks against this amount. Because it takes time for Mary's paycheck to clear and her bank to receive $2000 in cash or credit from her employer's bank account, bank float is created. Mary's bank has implicitly loaned $2000 interest free to Mary until her paycheck clears.

If, on the other hand, Mary's bank imposes a waiting period and doesn't give her credit for a $2000 deposit until sometime after the check clears, then Mary is loaning money interest free to her bank. The Federal Reserve now requires (with the exception of new accounts and large or questionable checks) that banks credit depositor accounts within 1 business day for local checks and 4 business days for other checks.

The Federal Reserve's check-clearing procedure creates float for banks. Suppose that you have a checking account in Ohio and go to Daytona Beach, Florida, for a vacation. In Daytona Beach, you pay for a motel room with a $100 check drawn on your Ohio bank, and the motel deposits your check in a Daytona Beach bank. If the check had been drawn on the same bank in which it is deposited, it would have been cleared internally, with the bank simply crediting one account and debiting another. Because the check is drawn on a different bank, the Daytona Beach bank will use a private clearinghouse or the Federal Reserve System to clear the check. To use the Federal Reserve System, the Daytona Beach bank sends your check to the district Federal Reserve Bank of Atlanta. From there, your check is sent to the Federal Reserve Bank of Cleveland and on to your Ohio bank.

The Federal Reserve has a fixed estimate (0, 1, or 2 days) of the time needed to deliver a check from a Federal Reserve bank to each bank in its district. After this time period has passed, the Daytona Beach bank is credited with $100 in reserves at the Federal Reserve Bank of Atlanta. However, $100 is not subtracted from the reserves of your Ohio bank until the bank actually receives your check and verifies that it is valid. Every day the check is delayed past the minimum period, two banks are credited with $100 in reserves. This double-counting is *Federal Reserve float* and implicitly represents an interest-free loan to banks from the Federal Reserve. (In Table 23.1, deferred availability cash items are the checks that the Fed has received but not yet credited as bank

EXAMPLE
**23.1**

## E. F. Hutton's Check Kiting

If someone tries to profit by a coordinated exchange of checks among bank accounts with insufficient funds, it is called *kiting* — and it is illegal. A desperate character might open checking accounts at three different banks. A $50 check drawn on the first bank is used to pay for groceries. After a few days, a check drawn on a second bank is deposited in the first bank before the $50 groceries check shows up. After a few more days, a check drawn on a third bank is deposited in the second bank. Then, a few days later, a check drawn on the first bank is deposited in the third. And so it goes, running from bank to bank to avoid paying for groceries.

In 1983 the U.S. government began an investigation of allegations that the giant brokerage firm of E. F. Hutton (since acquired by Shearson Lehman) had set up an elaborate overdraft system in the mid-1970s that generated millions of dollars in profits in the early 1980s. The government eventually estimated that E. F. Hutton's securities unit had made $4.35 billion in overdrafts at 400 banks around the country between July of 1980 and February of 1982, a period when interest rates topped 20 percent.

The officer of a small Massachusetts bank related the apparently typical procedure.* The local Hutton office would deposit a large check in this Massachusetts bank drawn on a bank in Phoenix or another distant city. Although these checks took several days to clear, "Of course, we would credit the Hutton account right away." Hutton's New York office then wired this money from the Massachusetts bank to a money-market fund, where it could earn 3 or 4 days worth of interest until it had to be wired to Phoenix to cover the original check.

> *I didn't realize they were engaged in such a grand, colossal scheme, or even something illegal. I thought it was aggressive cash management, where they were intentionally increasing the float in their favor. It never occurred to me that a major corporation would be involved in a check kite.*

Government investigators found one case in which Hutton officials wrote a check for $9.7 million on an account with a balance of less than $3500. A Hutton branch manager in Boulder, Colorado, testified that he had been subject to constant pressure from his superiors to overdraft accounts.†

In May of 1985, E. F. Hutton's securities unit pleaded guilty to 2000 felony counts of mail and wire fraud and agreed to pay a $2 million fine, reimburse the

*"Locally, E. F. Hutton Isn't Talking," Cape Cod Business Journal, *August 1985.*
†*Andy Pasztor, "House Panel: Ex-Hutton Chief Told of Overdrafts," Wall Street Journal, *August 3, 1985.*

government for $750,000 in legal expenses, and pay up to $8 million to the banks it had defrauded. The government agreed not to prosecute any individual employees. Hutton also was fined $350,000 by Connecticut regulators and $65,000 by Massachusetts ones and signed an agreement with the New York State attorney general to pay its New York customers in the future with checks drawn on New York banks, instead of California banks.

reserves; cash items in process of collection are the checks that the Fed has not yet delivered and subtracted from bank reserves; and the difference is Federal Reserve float.)

This $100 check will soon clear, but millions of new checks flow through the system every day. In 1979 the daily Federal Reserve float averaged $6.6 billion. With the 11.2 percent average federal funds rate that year, Federal Reserve float saved banks about $740 million in interest. Float also can cause fluctuations in bank reserves and the monetary base; for example, a snowstorm that causes a delay in the Fed's delivery of checks increases float, bank reserves, and the monetary base.

The 1980 Depository Institutions Deregulation and Monetary Control Act directed the Federal Reserve to eliminate Fed float or to begin charging banks interest on it. The Fed has subsequently reduced float by about 80 percent by improving its check-clearing procedures and revising its delivery estimates to reflect the average rather than the minimum time needed to deliver a check. The Fed charges interest on the remaining float by applying the federal funds rate to an annual estimate of the size of the float and adding this cost to the amount it charges banks for its check-clearing services.

In the past, the human handling of paper checks allowed banks to earn interest on Federal Reserve float. The demise of this profitable opportunity will encourage the spread of electronically transferred funds, which have very little float.

# THE MONETARY BASE, MONEY SUPPLY, AND INTERMEDIATION

Chapter 13 explained how banks are able to multiply deposits and multiply the money supply so that it is several times larger than the nation's monetary base. The checkable deposits that can be used to pay for goods, services, and assets are bank liabilities that are matched on the asset side of their balance sheets by bank loans for the purchase of such things as cars, houses, and factories. At the same time that banks and other deposit intermediaries are multiplying deposits that can serve as money, they are also making loans to finance spending.

The Federal Reserve affects financial markets through changes in the monetary base and through policies that affect the utilization of a given monetary base — either way, altering the amount of money available for lending, investing, and spending. For instance, when the Fed loans money through its discount window, the monetary base increases; when the Fed lowers reserve requirements, a given monetary base can support a larger level of deposits and loans.

The Fed's crucial policy question is whether to ease or tighten financial markets. Easy-money policies make funds readily available and at lower interest rates, which encourages borrowing and spending and increases the nation's output and prices. Tight money has the opposite effects: higher interest rates, reduced borrowing, a contraction in spending, and restraint on inflation. Here we will concentrate on three broad-based instruments of monetary policy that can be used to ease or tighten financial markets: open-market operations, reserve requirements, and the discount rate.

# OPEN-MARKET OPERATIONS

Table 23.1 shows that the largest category of Fed assets is U.S. Treasury securities. The Fed's purchases and sales of securities are known as **open-market operations**. These transactions expand or contract the nation's monetary base and are, in practice, the predominant instrument of Fed monetary policy. We will look briefly at how these policies are implemented and at some of their consequences.

## Securities Transactions

The Fed can use open-market operations to offset changes in the monetary base — for example, fluctuations that are caused by changes in U.S. Treasury deposits. The Fed also can use open-market operations to expand or contract the monetary base as part of a deliberate easing or tightening of credit conditions.

When the Fed purchases securities, it increases the monetary base; open-market sales contract the monetary base. Consider the details of an open-market purchase. Table 23.3 shows the T-accounts when the Fed purchases $100 million in Treasury securities from a bank and the bank leaves the sale proceeds deposited with a Federal Reserve bank. Bank reserves and the monetary base both increase by $100 million.

If the Fed buys $100 million in Treasury securities from someone other than a bank, it will pay for the securities with a Federal Reserve check. This check may be cashed, thereby increasing the amount of Federal Reserve notes in circulation, or it may be deposited in a bank and sent on to the Fed to be added to the bank's reserve account. Most likely, some of each will occur. In any case, the monetary base — currency outside banks plus bank reserves — will increase by $100 million.

The policy rule is very simple: the Fed buys securities when it wants to increase the monetary base and sells securities when it wants to reduce the monetary base. Such transactions ease or tighten financial markets. An open-market purchase by the Fed increases bond prices (thus reducing their yields) and expands the monetary base, either through bank reserves or Federal Reserve notes, leading to more bank deposits and loans. An open-market sale of securities

**Table 23.3   The Fed Purchases Securities from a Private Bank**

Private Bank

| Assets | | Liabilities |
|---|---|---|
| Deposits at Fed | + $100 | |
| Treasury securities | − $100 | |

Federal Reserve

| Assets | | Liabilities | |
|---|---|---|---|
| Treasury securities | + $100 | Deposits by banks | + $100 |

has the opposite effects, pushing bond prices down and interest rates up and contracting the monetary base, causing bank deposits and loans to shrink.

To the extent that various financial assets are good substitutes, open-market operations are a broadly based policy instrument with dispersed effects throughout financial markets. When Treasury-bill rates change, ripples are felt in the markets for bonds, loans, stock, and real assets.

## The FOMC Directive

When the Federal Reserve System was established, open-market operations were not well understood or considered to be very important. In the 1920s, open-market purchases were discovered and used, with ultimately ill effects, in an attempt to maintain the gold standard and real bills doctrine. As explained in Chapter 14, the Fed believed that the inflow of European gold called for an expansion of the U.S. money supply, which could be accomplished directly by open-market purchases. In addition, the Fed wanted to buy Liberty Bonds from banks so that banks would hold commercial loans instead. The Fed soon learned that open-market operations are a fast and reliable way to ease or tighten financial markets. Today, open-market operations are the predominant monetary policy tool employed by the Fed.

Before 1935, open-market transactions had been conducted by the individual district Federal Reserve banks with only informal coordination. The Banking Act of 1935 established the **Federal Open Market Committee** (**FOMC**) to plan and supervise open-market operations. In order to coordinate all monetary policy actions, most policy questions are now discussed and decided at the FOMC meetings.

Most policy actions are direct and specific: the discount rate is increased by 1 percentage point; reserve requirements on checking accounts are reduced by 2 percentage points. Open-market operations are, however, considerably fuzzier because, with imperfect foresight, the FOMC cannot spell out a precise daily plan for the coming month.

Instead, the FOMC issues a general directive (that is published in the *Federal Reserve Bulletin* several weeks later) describing its broad objectives. The structure of these directives and even much of the language vary little from month to month. As with State Department statements, a trained eye is needed to ferret out the slight nuances that reveal what it is that the committee is trying to say without actually saying it. Consider the following three paragraphs:

> *In light of the foregoing developments, it is the policy of the Federal Open Market Committee to foster financial conditions conducive to abatement of inflationary pressures, a sustainable rate of advance in economic activity, and continued progress toward equilibrium in the country's balance of payments* [October 1973].

> *In light of the foregoing developments, it is the policy of the Federal Open Market Committee to foster financial conditions conducive to resisting inflationary pressures, supporting a resumption of real economic growth, and achieving equilibrium in the country's balance of payments* [March 1974].

> *In light of the foregoing developments, it is the policy of the Federal Open Market Committee to foster financial conditions conducive to stimulating economic recovery, while resisting inflationary pressures and working towards equilibrium in the country's balance of payments* [March 1975].

Any one of these statements in isolation would seem to be little more than a recitation of the virtues of motherhood, apple pie, and a stable economy. Taken together, they might appear to be only a monthly reaffirmation of these virtues. Experienced analysts, however, correctly deduced a significant policy shift toward easy money.

In October of 1973, on the eve of the 1974–1975 recession, inflation was of foremost concern to the FOMC (and was listed first among the three standard objectives). By March of 1974, the recession was underway, with unemployment up sharply. The subtle shift in the directives from the "abatement" of inflation to "resisting" inflation and from sustaining growth to "supporting a resumption" of growth signaled an easing of monetary policy. The March 1974 paragraph was repeated verbatim through November of 1974. Then, in December of 1974 and January of 1975, the phrase "cushioning recessionary tendencies" was inserted. In March of 1975, economic recovery replaced inflation as the first of the three stated objectives. In late 1974 and early 1975 a credit crunch was eased, and interest rates tumbled sharply downward. The FOMC had indeed made a momentous decision, although it was reluctant to come right out and say it.

Now, admittedly, hindsight is a great help, but even with hindsight, Fed policy is not always easy to interpret. For example, in August of 1980, *The Wall Street Journal* reported that financial markets were still puzzled by the Fed's announcement 10 months earlier that it was going to place "greater emphasis"

**EXAMPLE
23.2**

## *Does the Federal Deficit Increase the Money Supply?*

The president and Congress determine federal expenditures and tax rates. If expenditures exceed tax revenue, then the Treasury sells securities to make up the difference. Except for temporary lags between receipts and outlays, the monetary base is unaffected, because the money that the Treasury receives from its sales of securities is paid out again in its expenditures. The Federal Reserve, not the Treasury, decides whether to increase or decrease the monetary base by purchasing or selling Treasury securities.

Three accounting identities allow us to see the relationship between federal deficits and monetary policy. The Treasury's budget constraint is

$$\text{Federal deficit} = \text{Treasury bond sales}$$

These bonds will be purchased either by the public or, though open-market operations, by the Fed:

$$\text{Treasury bond sales} = \text{increase in Treasury securities held by public} \\ + \text{Treasury securities purchased by Fed}$$

The earlier discussion of the Fed's balance sheets showed that Federal Reserve purchases of securities leads to an equal increase in the monetary base:

$$\text{Treasury securities purchased by Fed} = \frac{\text{increase in monetary}}{\text{base from Fed purchases}}$$

Combining these three equations, we have the government's consolidated budget constraint, which simply states that the financing of the federal deficit must lead to additional Treasury securities held by the public or to an increase in the monetary base caused by the Fed's purchase of some Treasury securities:

$$\text{Federal deficit} = \text{increase in Treasury securities held by public} \\ + \text{increase in monetary base from Fed purchases}$$

The consolidated government budget constraint is useful because it shows that government spending, taxation, bond sales, and monetary-base creation are interrelated. A federal deficit must implicitly be financed either by an increase in publicly held Treasury bonds or in the monetary base. To the extent that the deficit is financed by an increase in the monetary base (what is loosely called *printing money*), the deficit is said to have been **monetized**.

The consolidated government budget constraint can be misleading though, in that it suggests that government policy is centralized when, in fact, the president, Congress, and the Federal Reserve Board each have considerable autonomy. In many countries, the treasury is allowed to print money and consequently decides how much of the government deficit is financed by money creation. In the United States, the Fed is a separate entity that makes its own decisions about purchasing and selling Treasury securities.

The Fed's decisions depend on its policy objectives and the state of the economy. Its decisions are affected by federal deficits only indirectly, to the extent that these deficits affect inflation, interest rates, unemployment, and other factors that matter to the Fed. In practice, during the 1980s, the federal deficit averaged about $150 billion a year and the annual increase in the monetary base was about $10 billion. Thus, on average, the Fed monetized less than 10 percent of the annual federal deficit.

on the supply of bank reserves,[1] a policy change that we will discuss in more detail in Chapter 26.

The Fed's open-market operations are carried out by the system's account manager, who is a vice-president of the Federal Reserve Bank of New York. The account manager trades securities over the counter through electronic links with approximately 40 primary dealers, private firms that are allowed to trade directly with the Fed. When the Fed wants to make a transaction, its Open Market Trading Desk solicits bid and ask prices from all primary dealers and then accepts the best offers, with these securities debited or credited to the 12 Federal Reserve banks, based on their shares of total Federal Reserve assets.

The account manager's general instructions come from a decoding of the most recent FOMC directive. These instructions are coupled with a personal interpretation of financial market conditions and are sifted through a daily telephone conference with two members of the FOMC. If, on a given day, financial markets seem tighter than desired, then the account manager makes open-market purchases, easing interest rates and increasing the monetary base. If financial markets seem excessively loose, the account manager sells securities, firming interest rates and shrinking the monetary base.

## Dynamic and Defensive Transactions

Most open-market operations, perhaps 80 to 90 percent, are defensive, made to offset short-term tremors in financial markets rather than to implement a policy change.[2] With daily fluctuations and aberrations in the economy, the account manager buys on some days and sells on others. Whether the account manager bought or sold on a particular day is consequently not a reliable guide to the overall thrust of monetary policy.

Many of the events that shake financial markets are easily anticipated. Other events surprise even the most knowledgeable market participants. Some events cause only small, almost insignificant blips in asset demands and supplies. Others threaten to become genuine crises.

The account manager often uses repurchase agreements (which were discussed in detail in Chapter 6) to offset temporary financial disturbances. In a

Federal Reserve repurchase agreement, the Fed buys (or sells) securities to a primary dealer, who agrees to sell (or buy) them back at a set price on a certain date, usually within a week or two. Thus the securities are collateral for a short-term loan. The Fed uses repurchase agreements to cause an explicitly temporary expansion or contraction of the monetary base.

The public reliably increases its demand for cash before Christmas, Labor Day, July 4th, and other holidays. Every other Wednesday banks may need to borrow money to meet reserve requirements. Corporations predictably borrow money at the end of each quarter to pay taxes. The U.S. Treasury, large corporations, and foreign governments buy and sell large blocks of securities at irregular intervals. There are important seasonal variations in the cash needs of different parts of the country. Strikes, accidents, and bad weather can create temporary fluctuations in payment schedules and money demand. Rumors, hunches, and tea leaves lead powerful speculators to make huge transactions, flooding markets with funds or leaving them high and dry.

Deposits and withdrawals from the Treasury's tax and loan accounts are another potential source of financial market turbulence. The Treasury tries to synchronize its bill paying and withdrawals from its bank accounts in order to avoid disrupting currency in circulation, bank reserves, and the monetary base. Misestimates and mistimings inevitably disturb financial markets, however. As a consequence, every day the Fed's account manager tries to neutralize any dissynchronization in the Treasury's withdrawals and payments.

Federal Reserve float is another important source of daily fluctuations in the monetary base. Other events that disturb the Fed's balance sheet also cause the monetary base to fluctuate; for example, Treasury gold transactions, changes in outstanding Treasury coins or in Treasury holding of Federal Reserve notes, or changes in discount window loans.

For a given level of the monetary base, a variety of economic events, including a shift between bank reserves and currency outside banks, cause fluctuations in monetary aggregates, interest rates, and other measures of financial market conditions. Through it all, the Fed's account manager buys and sells securities, trying to smooth out the air pockets while keeping financial markets on whatever course the Federal Open Market Committee has charted.

# RESERVE REQUIREMENTS

The second of the Fed's three primary policy tools is reserve requirements. Within limits established by Congress, the Federal Reserve Board sets **reserve requirements** for deposit intermediaries, mandating that they hold non-interest-bearing reserves (either vault cash or deposits in Federal Reserve banks) equal to a specified fraction of their deposits. Ninety percent of all banks use vault cash to meet their reserve requirements, but the 10 percent who maintain deposits at Federal Reserve banks account for 75 percent of all bank deposits.

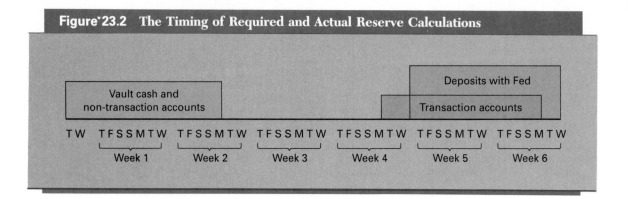

**Figure 23.2**   **The Timing of Required and Actual Reserve Calculations**

Compliance with the Fed's reserve requirements is monitored every 2 weeks, as shown in Figure 23.2. Each maintenance period begins on a Thursday and ends on a Wednesday, using the institution's average daily deposits with Federal Reserve banks over this 2-week period. The average daily balances in transaction accounts (also called checkable accounts) are calculated over a similar 2-week period, ending 2 days earlier, on a Monday. Other reservable liabilities and the bank's vault cash are calculated over a 2-week period ending on a Monday 4 weeks earlier.

Reserve deficiencies or excesses of up to 2 percent of required reserves can be carried over to the next 2-week maintenance period. If, after allowing for these carry-forward provisions, the bank still has a reserve deficiency, it is charged an interest rate equal to the Fed's discount rate plus a 2 percentage point penalty on the amount of the deficiency until it is corrected.

The accounting lags in monitoring reserves allow deposit institutions and the Fed time to compile information on actual and required reserves so that they can better anticipate and meet reserve requirements. Those institutions that turn out to have reserve deficiencies at the end of the maintenance period can borrow funds overnight from surplus institutions through the federal funds market or else from the Federal Reserve through its discount window. Every other Wednesday is consequently a potentially hectic day in financial markets as banks scramble to obtain reserves to meet reserve requirements.

## *Reserve Requirement Levels*

Historically, the Fed's reserve requirements applied only to those banks that chose to be members of the Federal Reserve System. Until 1935, reserve requirements were set by Congress and were seldom changed. The Banking Act of 1935 gave the Federal Reserve Board the authority to vary these requirements within broad limits specified by Congress, and the Fed began using reserve requirements to ease or tighten financial markets. The landmark 1980 Monetary

Control Act ordered the phasing in of the following reserve requirements for all depository institutions:

1. Three percent on the first $25 million of transaction account balances (with that initial $25 million figure indexed to change annually by 80 percent of the percentage change in aggregate transaction balances).
2. Twelve percent on an institution's transaction account balances above $25 million (this can be adjusted within the range 8 to 14 percent).
3. Three percent on nonpersonal time deposits (this can be adjusted within the range 0 to 9 percent). Nonpersonal deposits are those in which a beneficial interest is held by a depositor, such as a corporation, that is not a natural person.
4. Three percent on Eurocurrency liabilities.

In addition, the Fed can require interest-earning supplemental reserves of up to 4 percent of transaction account balances. The interest rate paid on these supplemental reserves can be no higher than the Fed's rate of return on its asset portfolio. The Garn–St. Germain Act of 1982 exempted from reserve requirements the first $2 million of transaction deposits or other reservable liabilities that would otherwise be subject to a 3 percent reserve requirement. (This $2 million exemption is increased annually by 80 percent of the percentage increase in aggregate reservable liabilities.) Money-market deposit accounts (MMDAs) allowing up to six transfers per month by check, telephone, or automatic bill paying, with no more than three by check, are considered savings accounts and are subject to time deposit reserve requirements.

As of April 1992, there was a 10 percent reserve requirement on transaction accounts (with the first $3.4 million exempt and the next $37.7 million subject to only a 3 percent reserve requirement). There were no reserve requirements on any other bank liabilities.

## The Effect on Bank Profits

Reserve requirements reduce bank income by preventing banks from profitably investing these idle reserves. Suppose, for example, that a bank pays 5 percent annual interest on deposits subject to a 10 percent reserve requirement. On $100 in deposits, the bank must hold $10 in reserves and can invest $90. Because it must pay (5 percent)($100) = $5 to obtain $90 in investable funds, it is effectively paying an interest rate of

$$\text{Effective cost of funds} = \frac{\$5}{\$90} = 0.0556 \quad \text{or (5.56 percent)}$$

The 10 percent reserve requirement raises the effective cost of funds from 5 to 5.56 percent, in that the bank must earn at least 5.56 percent interest on the $90 that it is allowed to invest in order to pay 5 percent interest on the $100 deposit.

| Table 23.4 | Effective Cost of Funds, Taking into Account a 10 Percent Reserve Requirement | |
| --- | --- | --- |
| Deposit Rate (%) | | Effective Rate (%) |
| 5.00 | | 5.56 |
| 7.00 | | 7.78 |
| 9.00 | | 10.00 |
| 11.00 | | 12.22 |
| 13.00 | | 14.44 |
| 15.00 | | 16.67 |

In general, if the deposit rate is $R$ and the reserve requirement is $k$, then the effective cost of funds is given by this equation:

$$\text{Effective cost of funds} = \frac{R}{1 - k} \qquad (23.5)$$

Some illustrative examples are shown in Table 23.4.

Before 1980, Federal Reserve member banks were at a competitive disadvantage compared with nonmember banks because their relatively high reserve requirements forced them to hold a sizable fraction of their assets as idle reserves. The 1980 Monetary Control Act retained reserve requirements but applied them equally to all depository institutions.

For about one hundred years, from 1864 to 1966, reserve requirements depended on a bank's geographic location, with banks in large cities subject to higher reserve requirements than country banks. There is considerable arbitrariness in defining and measuring cities in a nation with suburbs, exurbs, and metroplexes, particularly when banking can be done by mail or phone. Between 1966 and 1972, reserve requirements were modified to reflect a bank's size as well as its geographic location. In 1972, geography was eliminated as a criterion. The 1980 Monetary Control Act took the next logical step by erasing the distinctions between member and nonmember banks and between banks and other deposit institutions.

## A Powerful Tool

Reserve requirements are a powerful instrument of monetary policy. In a liquidity crisis, they offer a reservoir of funds that the Fed can tap to maintain bank solvency. In noncrisis situations, they can be used to ease or tighten financial markets. If the Fed reduces reserve requirements, almost all the freed reserves will be invested by banks, easing credit conditions and stimulating the economy. If the Fed raises reserve requirements, banks curtail their lending and the economy contracts.

In April of 1992, required reserves totaled about $50 billion. A 10 percent reduction in reserve requirements (essentially a reduction in reserve requirements on transaction accounts from 10 to 9 percent) would increase the funds available to banks and other deposit intermediaries by $5 billion. Almost all these newly freed reserves would be invested by banks, loaned to borrowers, and recirculated through banks — just as if the Fed had increased the monetary base by $5 billion. (During the years 1986–1992, the monetary base increased by an average of less than $15 billion a year.)

The deposit-multiplier model developed in Chapter 13 can be used to estimate the impact of reserve requirements on aggregate deposits. The basic model was given by Equation 13.6:

$$D = \left(\frac{1}{k + c}\right) B \qquad\qquad (23.6)$$

where $D$ is deposits, $B$ is the monetary base, $k$ is ratio of bank reserves to deposits (determined by reserve requirements and bank decisions to hold excess reserves), and $c$ is the ratio of currency outside banks to deposits.

To illustrate the computations, we'll use the following numbers, which are approximately equal to those prevailing in April of 1992:

$$D = \$3000 \text{ billion}$$
$$B = \$300 \text{ billion}$$
$$k = 0.0167$$
$$c = 0.0833$$

The deposit multiplier is 10:

$$D = \left(\frac{1}{0.0167 + 0.0833}\right) \$300 \text{ billion}$$
$$= 10(\$300 \text{ billion})$$
$$= \$3000 \text{ billion}$$

The $50 billion in reserves held by banks and other deposit institutions in April of 1992 was almost entirely required reserves; to simplify matters, we will assume that there are no excess reserves at all. This $50 billion in required reserves was only 1.67 percent of deposits, because deposit intermediaries had far more time and savings accounts subject to 0 percent reserve requirements than transaction accounts subject to 10 percent reserve requirements.

If reserve requirements are reduced by 10 percent (that is, from 10 to 9 percent on transaction accounts) so that $k$ declines from 0.0167 to 0.0150 and there is no change in $c$, the deposit multiplier will increase from 10 to

$$\frac{1}{0.0150 + 0.0833} = 10.17$$

EXAMPLE

23.3

## The Fed Learns from a Mistake

In the mid-1930s, banks held very large amounts of excess reserves because there were few attractive investment opportunities and they were fearful of bank runs. The Federal Reserve was concerned because these reserves gave banks flexibility, which weakened the Fed's control over the money supply; for example, a sudden perceived improvement in the economy might have persuaded banks to invest their excess reserves, thereby expanding bank deposits and lending as described by the deposit-multiplier model. The Fed thought that it could eliminate bank excess reserves and curtail bank flexibility by raising reserve requirements and consequently doubled requirements between August of 1936 and May of 1937.

Their reasoning was fallacious. The Fed assumed that banks are concerned solely with total reserves relative to deposits and do not care whether these reserves are required or excess. This assumption is wrong because excess reserves can be fully used to meet deposit withdrawals or to meet loan demands, while required reserves cannot. Banks consequently do care about excess reserves relative to available funds. When reserve requirements were increased in 1936 and 1937, banks maintained their large holdings of excess reserves by curtailing investments — a policy that staggered financial markets and precipitated a sharp recession. The Fed was subsequently forced to reduce reserve requirements.

and the level of deposits will increase by $51 billion, to

$$D = \left(\frac{1}{0.0150 + 0.0833}\right) \$300 \text{ billion}$$
$$= \$3051 \text{ billion}$$

Another way to estimate the increase in deposits resulting from a reduction in reserve requirements is to note that a 10 percent reduction in reserve requirements reduces required reserves by (10 percent)($50 billion) = $5 billion, effectively increasing the monetary base that is available for lending and depositing by $5 billion. Applying the initial deposit multiplier of 10, just as if there had been a $5 billion increase in the monetary base, gives a predicted deposit expansion of

Change in deposits = (deposit multiplier)(change in monetary base)
= 10($5 billion)
= $50 billion

which differs slightly from the actual value of $51 billion because the application of the deposit multiplier in this way is a linear approximately to a nonlinear equation.

**Table 23.5  The Effect of a Reduction in Reserve Requirements on Bank Deposits, Reserves, and Investments (Billions of Dollars)**

*Panel a (before decrease in reserve requirements):*

| Assets | | Liabilities | |
|---|---|---|---|
| Required reserves | $50 | Deposits | $3,000 |
| Investments | 2,950 | | |
| Total | $3,000 | | $3,000 |

*Panel b (after decrease in reserve requirements):*

| Assets | | Liabilities | |
|---|---|---|---|
| Required reserves | $46 | Deposits | $3,051 |
| Investments | 3,005 | | |
| Total | $3,051 | | $3,051 |

Table 23.5 shows the effects of this increase in reserve requirements on aggregate deposits, reserves, and bank investments. The only investments shown in this table are those funded by deposits; other assets and liabilities are omitted. The deposit-multiplier model tells us that bank deposits increase from $3000 billion to $3051 billion. Required reserves decline from $50 billion to 0.0150($3051 billion) = $46 billion. Aggregate bank investments funded by deposits consequently increase by $55 billion — of which $4 billion comes from the decline in required reserves and $51 billion comes from the consequent increase in deposits.

The important policy conclusion is that a seemingly slight reduction in reserve requirements can have a substantial effect on bank deposits and on the bank loans and other investments financed by these deposits. An increase in reserve requirements is an equally strong depressant. Raising reserve requirements by 10 percent would immobilize $5 billion in bank funds, almost all of which would come from curtailed bank investments. If there were no change in $c$ (the ratio of currency outside banks to deposits), deposits would shrink by approximately $50 billion and bank loans and other investments would contract by more than $50 billion.

A Fed change in reserve requirements is widely publicized and usually interpreted as dramatic evidence of a change in monetary policy. Reserve requirement changes are so powerful that they must be implemented with extreme caution. Frequent changes would be too disruptive to bank portfolio management. Between 1950 and 1980, reserve requirements were changed

**EXAMPLE**
**23.4**

## Using Liability Management to Evade Reserve Requirements

From a bank's standpoint, the lower are reserve requirements, the better — because more funds can then be invested profitably. Banks consequently have an incentive to raise funds through liabilities with low reserve requirements, and this encouragement inspired many innovations in bank liability management — and responses by the Federal Reserve. For example, Eurodollars (U.S. dollars deposited in foreign banks or foreign branches of U.S. banks) were initially free of reserve requirements, and this feature enhanced their appeal in the mid-1960s. In 1969 the Fed imposed a 10 percent reserve requirement on new Eurodollar borrowing; in 1970 it raised this reserve requirement to 20 percent, successfully dampening the enthusiasm for Eurodollar loans. In subsequent years Eurodollar reserve requirements were substantially reduced, and Eurodollars again became an attractive source of funds.

Similarly, the formation of bank holding companies was encouraged by the absence of reserve requirements on debts issued by holding companies. In 1970 the Fed imposed a 5 percent reserve requirement on commercial paper issued by bank holding companies. In October of 1979 the Fed put 8 percent reserve requirements on federal funds purchases, repurchase agreements, and even asset sales to foreign branches and announced that it would extend reserve requirements to all liability-management innovations by banks. The Fed withdrew this threat after passage of the 1980 Monetary Control Act, and today, only transaction accounts are subject to reserve requirements.

about once a year, usually by small amounts and often accompanied by cushioning changes in other policy instruments. Between 1980 and February of 1992, the only changes in reserve requirements were a reduction between November of 1980 and October of 1983 in the maturity of nonpersonal time deposits subject to a 3 percent reserve requirement (from 4 years to $1\frac{1}{2}$ years), the elimination in December of 1990 of 3 percent reserve requirements on nonpersonal time accounts and Eurocurrency liabilities, and the automatic annual adjustment of the level of transaction accounts subject to a 3 percent reserve requirement and of the level of reservable liabilities exempt from reserve requirements.

In February of 1992 the Fed announced the first significant change in reserve requirements in 12 years. Concerned about the weak economy and the fragile financial condition of banks, the Fed reduced the reserve requirement on transaction deposits to 10 percent from its previous level of 12 percent. This 16.7 percent reduction in reserve requirements was expected to increase bank profits and to expand bank investments and deposits substantially. In order to give banks time to prepare for this important change, the new 10 percent reserve requirement did not become effective until April 2, 1992, six weeks after the Fed's announcement.

# THE DISCOUNT WINDOW

Now we will look at the third of the Fed's three primary policy tools. The Federal Reserve loans money to deposit intermediaries through its **discount window**; the **discount rate** is the interest rate charged on these loans. Before the 1980 Monetary Control Act, with a brief exception in 1966, the discount window was open only to member banks, and bankers generally considered the discount window to be the primary advantage of Federal Reserve membership.[3] The Monetary Control Act of 1980 gave all deposit intermediaries access to the discount window. In 1991 Congress further mandated that brokerage firms can borrow from the Fed during financial crises.

When a bank borrows from the Fed, bank reserves and the monetary base are increased (the T-accounts are left as an exercise). The Fed may be able to anticipate some of this discount window borrowing — for example, to meet reserve requirements every other Wednesday. In other cases, the borrowing may be caused by an unanticipated emergency.

When the Federal Reserve was created in 1913, Congress intended that the Fed would be a reliable lender of last resort, using the discount window to avert bank runs by providing cash to temporarily illiquid banks. Discount lending also might be used to adjust the nation's money supply to meet seasonal needs, particularly those arising from farming. The Federal Reserve banks soon learned that the discount window can be used to manipulate the money supply for other purposes, such as financing government spending during World War I and keeping the money supply proportional to gold holdings. On the other hand, Federal Reserve banks were reluctant to loan money to unsound banks — those banks that needed funds to keep open. Thus the early use of the discount window was primarily to regulate the nation's money supply rather than to avert bank runs.

Banks that are considering using the Fed's discount window can alternatively obtain funds quickly with certificates of deposit, repurchase agreements, and the federal funds market. The willingness of banks to use the discount window consequently depends on how high the discount rate is relative to money-market interest rates.

An increase in the discount rate relative to money-market interest rates discourages borrowing from the Federal Reserve and represents a tightening of monetary policy. When bank borrowing declines, there are fewer funds available for lending and less money in circulation, putting upward pressure on loan rates and on interest rates for substitute assets. To raise cash, banks may sell some of their assets and issue certificates of deposit, repurchase agreements, and federal funds, putting upward pressure on these interest rates too. The repercussions of diminished borrowing from the Fed affect all bank assets and liabilities and virtually all financial markets.

A decrease in the discount rate relative to money-market interest rates is an easy-money policy, which makes funds available for a wide variety of purposes and puts downward pressure on virtually all interest rates. In some extreme situations, such as the Great Depression, a lowering of the discount rate may have little effect on economic activity. The Federal Reserve may make funds more easily available to banks, and yet banks may be reluctant to borrow if they do not see attractive lending opportunities: you can lead a horse to water, but you can't make it drink.

## Short-Term Liquidity

In recent years the discount window has been supplanted by open-market operations as the Fed's primary means of regulating the nation's money supply. The discount window is now used mainly as a safety valve to meet the temporary liquidity needs of individual banks.

Deposit institutions must calculate and satisfy reserve requirements every 2 weeks. If an institution's reserves happen to be inadequate, then it can temporarily borrow through the Fed's discount window to make up the difference, an action that is less disruptive (and expensive) than forcing the deficient bank to sell some of its securities.

The discount window is also made available in emergencies. In June of 1970, Penn Central, a large, seemingly conservatively managed railroad, declared bankruptcy and defaulted on its loans. Many firms subsequently had great difficulty selling commercial paper to nervous investors and turned to their banks for help. The Fed supplied the funds to stop a corporate financial crisis by allowing these banks special discount window loans. (The Fed also suspended Regulation Q rate ceilings on some large certificates of deposit and lowered reserve requirements in August of 1970.)

Similarly, when Franklin National Bank was on the verge of bankruptcy in 1974, it was allowed to borrow through the Fed's discount window until a shotgun merger could be consummated. The Continental Illinois collapse in 1985 (discussed in Chapter 10) and the stock market crash October of 1987 were both mitigated by discount window loans.

Since 1973 the Federal Reserve has allowed seasonal discount window borrowing — for example, letting small banks in farming or resort areas meet their seasonal liquidity needs through the discount window. This seasonal borrowing is less expensive and disruptive than if the bank holds excess cash all year or sells bonds every busy season. Thus the Fed uses the discount window to offset temporary turbulence in financial markets rather than as a tool for implementing a general, longer-lasting easing or tightening of financial markets.

## Misuse of the Discount Window

Populist politicians have often criticized the Federal Reserve and its discount window as a bank subsidy. If the discount rate charged banks is significantly below the rate of return that deposit intermediaries can earn on their investments, then the discount window increases bank profits by allowing them to borrow inexpensively. Another recurring criticism of the discount window is that

EXAMPLE
23.5

## The Day the U.S. Stock Market Almost Disintegrated

Chapter 9 recounted the stock market crash on October 19, 1987, a day dubbed Black Monday, when 604 million shares were traded on the New York Stock Exchange, the Dow Jones Industrial Average fell 508 points (23 percent), and the aggregate market value of stocks fell by about $500 billion.

The next day, Terrible Tuesday, the stock market came close to a complete collapse. Many traders were drained of capital, and several large securities firms were rumored to have been bankrupted by the previous day's drop in stock prices. Banks were understandably wary of lending money to firms that might soon declare bankruptcy. Without cash or credit, potential buyers were far outnumbered by anxious sellers. The stock exchanges temporarily suspended trading on Tuesday in even the best-known stocks, including IBM for 2 hours and Merck for 4 hours.

Some observers blamed the Monday crash on excessively loose monetary policies and urged the Fed to reduce the money supply.* However, Alan Greenspan, recently appointed chairman of the Fed, was fearful of a wave of bankruptcies and of a complete loss of confidence in financial markets. People would be much less likely to invest in securities if they could not be certain of a reasonably efficient market in which securities can be sold quickly at a fair price. Before the stock market opened Tuesday, Greenspan called a press conference and announced the Fed's "readiness to serve as a source of liquidity to support the economic and financial system." During the day, the Fed pressured large banks to lend money to securities firms and promised to finance this lending with virtually unlimited discount window loans. The 10 largest New York banks lent a total of $5.5 billion to securities firms that week. After seesawing wildly, the Dow Jones Industrial Average closed up 102 points on Terrible Tuesday and up another 187 points the next day. A financial collapse was averted, although memories of Black Monday and Terrible Tuesday will linger for years.

Felix Rohatyn, an experienced financier, said later that "Tuesday was the most dangerous day we had in 50 years. I think we came within an hour of the disintegration of the stock market."† Alan Greenspan deserves much of the credit for saving the market.

*Victor A. Canto and Arthur B. Laffer, "Monetary Policy Caused the Crash: Not Tight Enough," Wall Street Journal, October 22, 1987; also see the discussion in Paul R. Krugman, "Can We Avert the Next Financial Crisis," Los Angeles Times, October 29, 1989.

†Felix Rohatyn, a general partner in Lazard Freres & Co., quoted in James B. Stewart and Daniel Hertzberg, "How the Stock Market Almost Disintegrated a Day after the Crash," Wall Street Journal, November 20, 1987.

it encourages banks to be illiquid. If the Federal Reserve can be counted on to bail banks out of liquidity crises, then there is little incentive to avoid such crises. Instead, banks will make excessively illiquid, high-yielding loans and borrow from the Federal Reserve whenever necessary. This is another of those seemingly permanent philosophical debates: does government assistance sap the self-reliance of its citizens? The differing views were illustrated by this joke told during the 1980 presidential election campaign:

> *What's the difference between a conservative and a liberal? If a man is drowning, the conservative will throw a life preserver 10 feet from the man and tell him, 'Swim for it, it will do you good.' The liberal, on the other hand, will throw the drowning man a wad of money and tell him to go buy himself a boat.*

The Federal Reserve employs a number of strategies to discourage excessive reliance on the discount window. When a bank uses the discount window repeatedly, it is reminded that the Fed does not have to lend money to a bank. The discount window is "a privilege, not a right," and this privilege must not be abused. In 1977 the Fed pointedly told some large banks to stop using the discount window unless there really were no good alternatives. In less drastic circumstances, the Fed discourages discount borrowing with fines, public criticism, and frequent, thorough audits (on the presumption that excessive borrowing suggests financial difficulties or mismanagement). Sometimes the Fed adopts a formal rule, for example, that a bank is abusing the discount window if it borrows in 7 weeks of a 13-week period.

Another strategy to discourage excessive reliance on the discount window is to set the discount rate high enough to make borrowing truly a last resort rather than a regular, inexpensive source of funds. Since 1972 the Bank of England has followed a policy of setting the discount rate a half a percentage point above the interest rate on short-term government securities. In recent years the Federal Reserve has followed a similar, though less mechanical policy. When the federal funds rate and other short-term market interest rates rise substantially, the Fed raises its discount rate to discourage banks from borrowing from the Fed at low interest rates for reinvestment at high interest rates. When market interest rates fall, the Fed reduces the discount rate to avoid penalizing banks that have legitimate liquidity needs. With these semiautomatic adjustments, the discount rate has become a largely passive reflection of monetary conditions rather than an active tool for changing the money supply and interest rates.

Since 1986 the Fed has put each bank's discount-window borrowing into one of these three categories:

1. *Adjustment credit:* short-term, temporary loans to help depository institutions meet needs for funds that cannot be met through reasonable alternative sources.

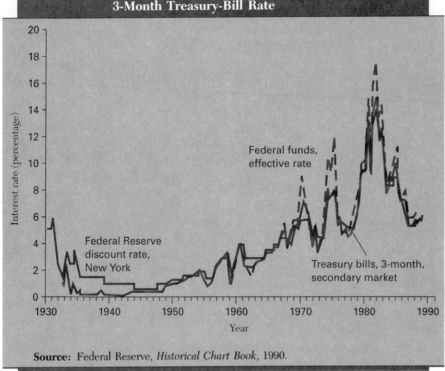

**Figure 23.3   The Discount Rate, Federal Funds Rate, and 3-Month Treasury-Bill Rate**

**Source:** Federal Reserve, *Historical Chart Book*, 1990.

2. *Seasonal credit:* temporary loans to smaller depository institutions to meet regular seasonal needs that cannot be met through special industry lenders.
3. *Extended credit:* loans to an institution in exceptional circumstances or experiencing difficulties adjusting to changing market conditions over a longer period of time.

In 1985, 1986, and 1987, the discount rate on seasonal credit was set at a half percentage point above the rate on adjustment credit; this half-point surcharge was removed in 1988. The discount rate for the first 30 days of extended credit is equal to the discount rate on adjustment credit plus a minimum of half a percentage point after 30 days. In December of 1991, for instance, the discount rate was 5 percent for adjustment credit, seasonal credit, and the first 30 days of extended credit; extended credit beyond 30 days was charged 5.75 percent, a 0.75 percent surcharge over the basic discount rate.

Figure 23.3 compares the Federal Reserve discount rate (before surcharges) with the Treasury bill rate and the federal funds rate. In recent years, changes in market interest rates have typically preceded changes in the discount rate, suggesting that the Fed usually adjusts the discount rate in response to changing

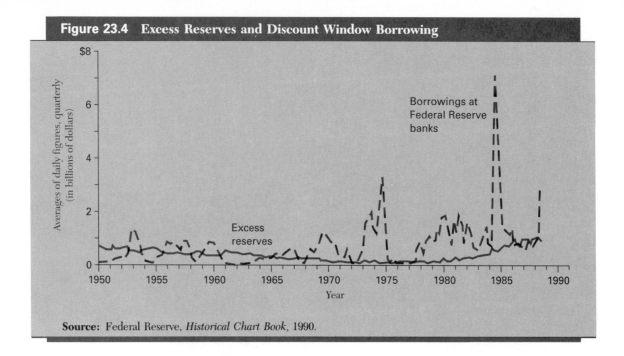

**Figure 23.4    Excess Reserves and Discount Window Borrowing**

**Source:** Federal Reserve, *Historical Chart Book*, 1990.

financial conditions rather than using the discount rate to change financial conditions.

Figure 23.4 shows excess reserves and discount window borrowing. Comparison of these two figures reveals that use of the discount window picks up when market rates rise above the discount rate. Despite administrative reprimands, some profiteering apparently does go on; however, the fact that borrowings are relatively small in the face of substantial interest-rate differentials indicates that the Fed is largely successful in discouraging abuse of the discount window.

## Policy Signals

Market interest rates fluctuate continuously, while the Fed changes the discount rate infrequently, causing the gaps between market rates and the discount rate to widen and narrow. Many financial market participants believe that these fluctuations provide useful information about the Fed's monetary policy objectives. If, for example, market rates rise and the Fed promptly raises the discount rate, this action might be interpreted as a signal that the Fed is committed to a tight-money policy because the increase in the discount rate suggests that the Fed expects interest rates to remain high or to go even higher.

**EXAMPLE
23.6**

## The Bank of Japan Deflates a Stock-Market and Real-Estate Bubble

The Nikkei index of 225 leading stocks on the Tokyo Stock Exchange climbed from 12,000 in January 1985 to an all-time high of 38,915 on December 29, 1989. The Japanese economy was very strong but some observers thought that Japanese stocks were wildly overpriced and that the market was a speculative bubble. In 1989, dividend yields on Japanese stocks averaged a minuscule 0.5 percent, price-earnings ratios averaged an incredible 70, and the aggregate market value of Japanese companies was 5 times their book value.

Many explanations were offered for why the Japanese stock market was different from other stock markets. Foremost was the importance of *keiretsu*: business groups, such as Mitsubishi and Sumitomo, that include large flagship companies and dozens of suppliers and creditors. The *keiretsu* involve extensive cross-shareholding among members of the group. For example, banks own stock in the companies they lend money to, and the companies, in turn, own stock in the banks that lend them money. One consequence of these interlocking relationships is that when a Japanese company encounters financial difficulties, the firm's main bank does not cut off credit and force the company into bankruptcy; instead, it replaces the firm's management.

Because 70 percent of the shares of all listed Japanese stocks are tied up by the *keiretsu* system of cross-shareholding, some argue that high Japanese stock prices are justified by the small supply of stock relative to demand. However, this argument doesn't really answer the question of why investors who are not *keiretsu* members would buy Japanese stocks with 0.5 percent dividend yields when they could buy bonds, at home or abroad, with much higher interest rates.

Rising Japanese stock prices in the late 1980s were also closely linked to soaring Japanese real estate prices. As stock prices rose, many Japanese companies issued stock at inflated prices, using the proceeds to buy real estate and stock in other companies — pushing up these prices too. Inflated real estate, in turn, provided collateral for loans that were used to buy stock, real estate, and stock in companies owning real estate. Japanese banks were at the center of this bubble as they own considerable amounts of prime real estate and stock in companies owning real estate. In 1987, 40 percent of Japanese commercial bank loans were used to finance real-estate purchases; Japanese bank assets consisted of 7 percent real-estate loans and 30 percent Japanese stocks. Bank stocks constituted a third of the market value of all Japanese stocks.* For the

*Patrick J. Regan, "Japan — Land of the Rising Risk," Financial Analysts Journal, July–August 1988, pp. 17, 28.

nation as a whole, aggregate capital gains on stock and real estate totaled $3.4 trillion in 1987, 40 percent more than Japan's GNP.†

In 1990, it was estimated that the market value of Japanese land comprised 60 percent of the world total — 5 times the value of all U.S. land and $1\frac{1}{2}$ times the market value of all land outside Japan.‡ Land in Tokyo's Ginza shopping district sold for $250,000 a square meter at the beginning of 1990. In March of 1990, a front-page story in *The Wall Street Journal* began by quoting a Japanese real-estate agent:

> *The only real question is how quickly you buy property. Land will never come down. Banks are dying to lend money, so you can borrow easily. Don't worry. If they thought prices would come down, they wouldn't lend. Orders are pouring in so fast that we alternate between joy and embarrassment.§*

At the time, small two-bedroom apartments in Tokyo sold for more than $1 million, prefabricated homes an hour away sold for $500,000, and homes two hours from Tokyo sold for $250,000. To help finance these expensive properties, the Nippon Housing Loan Company offered a 100-year mortgage, to be repaid by the borrower, the borrower's children, and the borrower's grandchildren.

Japanese rents in 1990 averaged 2 percent of real-estate prices, compared to 7 percent in the United States, again suggesting a speculative bubble. Sounding very much like the greater fool theory, *The Wall Street Journal* explanation was that there was little relationship between real-estate prices and rents in Japan because "land investors count on capital gains, not rental income, to make a profit."

At the time, the possibility of a decline in land prices seemed remote. The chief economist at Sumitomo Bank said that "The most we can expect is for land prices to level off." The ministry of construction said that land prices should remain firm because there is a limited supply of land in Japan and building heights are limited by the danger of earthquakes. An analyst at the Long-Term Credit Bank argued that the government would not let land prices fall because a majority of the nation's voters would lose money. All of these rationalizations avoid the reality that an investment in real estate with a 2 percent cash flow makes sense only if prices continue to rise rapidly.

In November of 1989, Yasushi Mieno took over as head of Japan's central bank, the Bank of Japan, and the government began deflating the Japanese stock-market and real-estate bubbles. During the next 9 months, the discount rate was increased from 3.75 percent to 6 percent, and the rate of growth of the

†*Robert Cutts, "Power From the Ground Up: Japan's Land Bubble,"* Harvard Business Review, *May–June 1990, pp. 164–172.*

‡*Elaine Kurtenbach, "Japanese Are Facing Up to Land Inflation and Soaring Costs for Real Estate,"* Washington Post, *April 21, 1990.*

§*Marcus W. Brauchli and Masayoshi Kanabayashi, "Land Prices in Japan Are Getting So Steep the Nation Is Jittery,"* Wall Street Journal, *March 23, 1990.*

money supply slowed from 13 percent to 2 percent. Between the third quarter of 1989 and March 1990, long-term government bond yields increased two percentage points, from 5 percent to 7 percent.

The Nikkei 225 average fell by 57 percent over the next $2\frac{1}{2}$ years, to 16,718 on July 3, 1992, bringing stock prices down to a still-high, but not incredible, 30 times earnings. The daily volume of trading on the Tokyo Stock Exchange dropped by 75 percent from 1.2 billion shares in 1989 to 300 million shares in 1992. In April 1992, real estate prices had declined from their peak by 30 percent in downtown Tokyo and by closer to 40 percent in Kyoto and Osaka.

Under the Basel Agreement capital requirements (discussed in Example 16.3), banks can count 45 percent of the unrealized capital gains on their stock portfolios as bank equity. This accounting rule was good for Japanese bank capital ratios when the Japanese stock market was booming, but potentially disastrous as stock prices fell, forcing Japanese banks to cut back on lending at home and abroad.

If, on the other hand, market rates rise and the Fed does not raise its discount rate, this inaction might be interpreted as a signal that the Fed expects the increase in interest rates to be temporary — perhaps because it will use open-market operations to bring interest rates back down. Analogous interpretations can be affixed to a reduction in the discount rate, or a failure to do so, when market rates fall.

Because the announcement of a change in the discount rate conveys information about Federal Reserve objectives, there is said to be an **announcement effect**: the policy change, by itself, is not very important, but its announcement signals intentions that are likely to be carried out in other ways. In recent years, discount rate changes have been more signal than substance. Changes in discount rates are seldom large enough to affect financial markets very much. As a perceived policy signal, however, an unexpected change in the discount rate (or the absence of a change) sometimes sends tremors through financial markets.

# SUMMARY

The Fed can use Federal Reserve notes to buy assets or pay debts, recording these notes on the liability side of its balance sheets. A small amount of Federal Reserve notes is held by the U.S. Treasury, considerably more notes are in bank vaults, and the bulk is held by the public. An open-market purchase of securities by the Fed enlarges the monetary base, either through bank reserves or Federal Reserve notes, easing credit conditions: bond prices rise, interest rates fall, and bank deposits and loans expand. A Fed open-market sale of securities has the opposite effect, reducing the monetary base and tightening financial markets: bond prices fall, interest rates increase, and bank deposits and loans contract.

The Fed uses open-market operations not only to implement policy changes but also to stabilize financial markets, offsetting daily fluctuations in bank reserves and the monetary base caused by U.S. Treasury receipts and outlays, Federal Reserve float, and other economic events.

There is currently a 10 percent reserve requirement on transaction accounts (above a modest threshold), which depository institutions can meet either with vault cash or deposits with the Federal Reserve. Reserve requirements reduce bank income because these idle reserves cannot be invested profitably. An increase in reserve requirements is a very powerful tight-money policy; a reduction in reserve requirements eases credit conditions.

The Federal Reserve loans money to deposit intermediaries for adjustment, seasonal, and extended credit through its discount window. Deposit institutions are discouraged from borrowing what the Fed considers to be excessive amounts by the imposition of discount rate surcharges, the threat of closer regulatory scrutiny, and, in extreme cases, loss of access to the discount window.

An increase in the discount rate tightens financial markets; a reduction makes credit more readily available. In recent years the Fed has not used the discount rate as a primary monetary policy instrument to ease or tighten financial markets but has instead kept the discount rate roughly aligned with market rates of interest, using the discount window to provide temporary liquidity during run-of-the-mill turbulence and extraordinary crises. Thus the Fed does not change the discount rate in order to cause changes in market interest rates, but rather adjusts the discount rate to keep it aligned with market rates.

## IMPORTANT TERMS

announcement effect
discount window
discount rate
Federal Open Market Committee (FOMC)
float

monetary base
monetized
open-market operations
reserve requirements
U.S. currency outstanding

## EXERCISES

1. Explain how the monetary base is affected by each of these economic events.
   a. The payment of taxes to the federal government each April 15
   b. Holiday shopping in December
   c. A snowstorm in Chicago and New York

2. The text discusses the example of a check drawn on an Ohio bank that is deposited in a Daytona Beach bank. Under the rules used by Canada's private check-clearing system, the Ohio bank would retroactively debit the check writer's account as of the date that the check was deposited in the Daytona Beach

bank. Does the Canadian system have a great deal of float or very little?

3. Banks, money-market funds, and corporations transfer some $200 trillion each year using Fedwire, the Federal Reserve's electronic transfer service. The Fed credits the recipients of these wire transfers immediately but does not debit the senders until the end of the day. Does this float create profits for the Fed or for Fedwire users?

4. In 1982 the FBI investigated a firm suspected of a check-kiting scheme involving banks in California, the Caroline Islands,

Guam, Hawaii, Massachusetts, and Ohio. What is check kiting, and why do you suppose these banks were so widely scattered?

5. The Federal Reserve's reserve requirements are reported each month in the *Federal Reserve Bulletin.* Use the most recent issue to determine if there has been any change in reserve requirements from the April 1992 requirements described in the text.

6. Why is there sometimes a substantial increase in federal funds market activity on Wednesdays?

7. The imposition of reserve requirements increases a bank's cost of funds by reducing the amount that it can invest profitably. Use Equation 23.5 in the text to determine the bank's effective cost of funds if
   a. Its deposit rate is 6 percent and there is a 10 percent reserve requirement.
   b. Its deposit rate is 5 percent and there is a 20 percent reserve requirement.

8. What rate of return must a bank earn on its investments to break even if it pays depositors 8 percent interest and these deposits are subject to a 10 percent reserve requirement? A 3 percent reserve requirement? (Assume that the 8 percent figure includes all the bank's administrative expenses.)

9. A bank has $500 million in transaction deposits subject to a 10 percent reserve requirement and $500 million in other deposits subject to a 0 percent reserve requirement. What is its average reserve requirement (the ratio of total required reserves to total deposits)?

10. A savings and loan has $200 million in transaction deposits subject to a 10 percent reserve requirement and $800 million in other deposits subject to a 0 percent reserve requirement. Assuming that the S&L holds no excess reserves, fill in the following balance sheet showing the S&L's reserves and available funds.

**Assets**

| | |
|---|---|
| Reserves | |
| Investments | |
| **Total** | $1,100,000,000 |

**Liabilities**

| | |
|---|---|
| Transaction accounts | $200,000,000 |
| Other deposits | 800,000,000 |
| Net worth | 100,000,000 |
| | $1,100,000,000 |

What is this S&L's average reserve requirement (the ratio of total required reserves to total deposits)? This S&L's annual interest plus other administrative expenses is equal to 10 percent of both transaction and other deposits, a total of (10 percent)($1 billion) = $100 million annually. What rate of return must it earn on its investments to make a profit?

11. What rate of return would the S&L in the preceding exercise need to earn on its investments to earn a 10 percent return on its net worth if the Fed eliminated all reserve requirements? (Assume that the S&L continues to hold no excess reserves.) What if the Fed maintained its reserve requirements but paid 10 percent annual interest on all required reserves?

12. In the 1920s, "in an apparent effort to further reduce the highly visible subsidy that member banks appeared to receive at the [discount] window, the Federal Reserve began actively discouraging continuous discount borrowing by individual banks."[4] Why would discount window borrowing be a subsidy to member banks?

13. The 1980 Monetary Control Act reduced the maximum reserve requirement on transaction accounts from $16\frac{1}{4}$ to 12 percent. How much does this reduction increase the annual income of a bank with $1 billion in transaction accounts subject to these maximum reserve requirements if the bank can

earn a 10 percent annual rate of return on its investments?

14. If a bank can earn a 10 percent annual return on its investments, how many extra dollars does it earn each year from
    a. Having its first $41.5 million of transaction accounts subject to a 3 percent rather than 10 percent reserve requirement?
    b. Having no reserve requirements on its first $3.4 million in deposits that would otherwise be subject to a 3 percent reserve requirement?

15. Do you think that the special reserve requirements described in the preceding exercise primarily benefit large or small banks? Explain your reasoning.

16. Panel (b) of Table 23.5 shows the effects on bank deposits, reserves, and investments of a 10 percent reduction in reserve requirements, from 1.67 to 1.5 percent. Construct a similar panel (b), with data rounded to the nearest billion dollars, showing the consequences of a 10 percent increase in reserve requirements, from 1.67 to 1.84 percent.

17. Many brokerage firms offer cash-management accounts that allow funds to be withdrawn by check or debit card. If it is a *sweep account*, excess funds are automatically swept into a money-market fund at the end of each day, and funds are transferred from the money-market fund to the checking account as needed. If there are insufficient funds in the money-market fund, then the brokerage firm lends money, using the customer's stocks and bonds as collateral — just as with a margin account. Because funds are swept out of the checking account at the end of the day, the brokerage firm avoids reserve requirements. What is the advantage of avoiding reserve requirements? Isn't it prudent to keep reserves on hand to satisfy possible customer withdrawals?

18. James Tobin has proposed that transaction accounts be subject to 100 percent reserve

requirements. How would this affect the interest rate that banks pay on transaction accounts?

19. An empirical study of the effect of reserve requirements on the prices of bank stocks found that the Monetary Control Act of 1980 significantly increased stock prices for Federal Reserve member banks relative to nonmember banks.[5] How would you explain this finding?

20. For the week ending on September 29, 1989, the federal funds rate was 9.02 percent and the Fed's discount rate was 7 percent on adjustment credit, seasonal credit, and the first 30 days of extended credit; extended credit beyond 30 days was charged 9.2 percent. Use a recent issue of the *Federal Reserve Bulletin* to determine the average federal funds and discount rates during the most recently reported week. Is the gap between the federal funds rate and the basic discount rate as large as that prevailing in September of 1989? Is the discount rate on extended credit beyond 30 days above or below the federal funds rate?

21. After the Federal Reserve raised the discount rate from 6.5 to 7 percent on February 24, 1989, a *Wall Street Journal* reporter wrote:

    *Although the discount rate isn't tied directly to the returns individuals get on their investments or what they pay to borrow, it can have a significant effect . . . because the discount rate plays a key role in financial markets as a signal of Fed policy.*[6]

    Explain what the discount rate is and how it might signal Fed policy.

22. It is generally agreed that, other than the announcement effects, most changes in the discount rate would have little impact on the money supply or credit conditions. Why, then, does the announcement of an increase in the discount rate lead people to expect higher future interest rates?

23. In 1980 it was reported that

    *The Federal Reserve Board today increased its bank discount rate by a full percentage point to a record 13 percent, a move local economists said is certain to send interest rates higher. . . . Bond prices plummeted in reaction.*[7]

    Explain why bond prices might fall when an increase in the discount rate is announced. Describe a situation in which an increase in the discount rate would have little or no effect on bond prices.

24. If market interest rates fell and the Fed did not reduce the discount rate, would you interpret this as a signal of easy or tight money? Explain your reasoning.

25. When member banks borrow heavily from Federal Reserve banks, there usually seems to be a credit crunch. Why? Doesn't member bank borrowing expand the money supply, ease credit, and reduce interest rates?

26. Write a paragraph supporting or refuting the conclusion that the discount rate "is an absolute necessity for the sound management of a monetary system, and is a most delicate and beautiful instrument for the purpose."[8]

27. Discount window borrowing is usually large when the discount rate is high and small when the discount rate is low. Shouldn't it be the other way around?

28. In the table below are some data for selected periods on adjustment borrowings through the Fed's discount window and the spread between the federal funds rate and the Fed's discount rate.[9] Do these two variables seem to be positively or negatively related? How would you explain the observed empirical relationship?

29. Show the T-accounts when a bank uses the Fed's discount window to add $100 million to its reserves with the Fed.

30. Suppose that the Fed buys $1 million in securities from private citizens and that, after the complete expansion of bank deposits and loans, there is an extra $500,000 in Federal Reserve notes outside banks and an extra $500,000 in bank reserves at the Fed. Assume that reserve requirements are 10 percent and that banks hold no excess reserves. Show the T-accounts for the Fed, banks, and the nonbank public.

31. The 1980 Monetary Control Act reduced reserve requirements, on average. If the Federal Reserve wanted to offset the expansionary or contractionary effects on financial markets, should they have bought or sold Treasury bills?

32. Has the shift in the composition of bank deposits from transaction to savings accounts increased or diminished aggregate required reserves? If the Fed wanted to offset the effects of this change in required reserves on financial markets, should it have bought T-bills or sold them?

33. Between 1929 to 1933 there was an outflow of gold from the United States, which the Federal Reserve did little to offset. After 1933, gold began flowing back into the

| Period | Adjustment Borrowing ($ millions) | Federal Funds Rate Minus Discount Rate (%) |
|---|---|---|
| May 1981–October 1981 | 1,525 | 3.59 |
| October 1981–November 1981 | 612 | 0.68 |
| November 1981–July 1982 | 1,012 | 1.73 |
| July 1982–October 1982 | 553 | 0.14 |
| October 1982–November 1982 | 352 | −0.06 |

United States, and even though the nation was still in the midst of the Great Depression, the Federal Reserve was concerned about a possible inflation and used monetary policies to offset this inflow. Did they raise or lower reserve requirements? Did they make open-market purchases or sales?

34. Explain the error made by this 1986 investment newsletter:

    *By 1995 those [federal] deficits are expected to top $775 billion. That's the amount of money the government will spend each year — above and beyond the money it collects.*

    *Worse yet, that's the amount the Federal Reserve will have to cover by printing batches of new paper money.*[10]

35. In the 1960s the U.S. government wanted to reduce long-term interest rates to stimulate corporate investment while raising short-term interest rates to improve the balance of payments. The Fed tried "Operation Twist," trading in short- and long-term government securities to twist the term structure. Should the Fed have bought shorts and sold longs, or vice versa? What are the implications, if any, of the expectations hypothesis for Operation Twist?

36. Use the expectations hypothesis to interpret this empirical observation:

    *A good measure of the stance of monetary policy is the yield curve. . . . The yield curve is said to be inverted when short rates are above long rates, a consistently accurate prediction of tight money. During recessions and the early stages of economic recovery the yield curve is positive (i.e., short rates are below long rates), implying easy, or at least cheap, money. During the late stages of the recovery cycle, when inflation is strong and monetary policy has been forced to tighten sharply, short rates rise and the yield curve usually becomes inverted. . . . inverted yield curves have tended to precede downturns in economic activity.*[11]

37. Read this excerpt from a syndicated newspaper column and then be prepared to answer the questions that follow:

    *For all their importance, interest rates remain a subject of immense confusion and mystery. The striking aspect of the current decline is that long-term interest rates have dipped far more than short-term rates. Since January 1985, for example, rates on long-term Treasury bonds have fallen more than 3 percentage points while those on short-term Treasury bills have declined roughly 1 percentage point. . . .*

    *The implication is that the Federal Reserve has so far played a secondary role in lowering rates. Its direct influence is concentrated on short-term rates.*[12]

    According to the expectations hypothesis of the term structure, how can long-term rates fall more than short-term rates? How can the Fed affect long-term interest rates, even if it only buys and sells short-term Treasury bills?

38. Assume that the expectations hypothesis is correct and that the Hicks equation applies. The yield on 1-year Treasury zeros is initially 10 percent and is expected to remain at 10 percent. The Fed now sells a large quantity of 1-year zeros, driving the yield up to 12 percent. However, it is still believed that 1-year yields next year and thereafter will be 10 percent. What is the yield now on 2-year zeros? On 3-year zeros? Which yield changed the most?

39. In October of 1977, *The Wall Street Journal* reported that "the Federal Reserve Bank of New York has reprimanded some large banks in New York for abusing their borrowing privilege at its discount window."[13] Explain why this reprimand to certain New York banks suggests that, at the time, the federal funds rate was either above or below the discount rate.

# 24 Monetary Rules Versus Discretionary Policies

*We do not know enough to be able to achieve stated objectives by delicate, or even fairly coarse, changes in the mix of monetary and fiscal policy. In this area particularly the best is likely to be the enemy of the good. Experience suggests that the path of wisdom is to use monetary policy explicitly to offset other disturbances only when they offer a "clear and present danger."*

**Milton Friedman**

The Federal Reserve was originally intended to be a lender of last resort to banks as financial markets rode a roller coaster over economic booms and busts. The Fed was not supposed to vary the money supply to moderate these booms and busts and, for many years, did not try to do so. Since the Great Depression in the 1930s, the Federal Reserve has generally taken a much more active role in trying to stabilize financial markets and the economy. In this chapter we discuss some of the operating procedures that the Fed uses to monitor the state of the economy and to determine an appropriate monetary policy.

We will consider several general issues, including the distinction between monetary policies and fiscal policies, political pressures on the Fed, and the Fed's ability to implement timely policies. We will pay particular attention to the implications of the observation that the Fed is not able to achieve its objectives with great precision. Some observers, noting the historical instability of financial markets and the economy, endorse the Fed's discretionary use of admittedly imperfect policies. Other observers, worried about imperfections in even well-intentioned policies, propose that monetary policy be turned over to a computer that has been programmed to ignore the economy. We begin our consideration of these controversies with the distinction between monetary and fiscal policies.

# MONETARY VERSUS FISCAL POLICIES

The Federal Reserve has broad control over the nation's **monetary policy**, using open-market operations, reserve requirements, and discount rates to alter the monetary base, interest rates, and $M1$ and other monetary aggregates. Congress and the president determine the federal government's **fiscal policy**, which includes government expenditures and tax rates. When the federal government's outlays exceed its revenue — which is generally the case — this deficit is financed by the sale of Treasury debt. The Federal Reserve could, if it wanted, partly monetize the federal deficit by making open-market purchases of Treasury securities. However, the Fed's monetary policy is generally directed toward stabilizing the economy, not financing the federal deficit.

## *Coordination and Conflict*

Monetary and fiscal policies do not have identical effects on the economy, and monetary and fiscal policy decisions are made by different people, who do not always agree with each other's policies. For the achievement of some objectives, monetary policy is appropriate; for others, fiscal policy is best. Most of the time, a combination of both is needed. For instance, if policymakers want to reduce military spending without depressing the economy, then reduced government spending (a contractionary fiscal policy) can be accompanied by open-market purchases (an expansionary monetary policy).

   In practice, this kind of coordination does not always occur, because the Fed, Congress, and the president do not always have the same objectives and because none is subservient to the others. For instance, the president and Congress may want to stimulate the economy in order to increase output and reduce unemployment, while the Fed may want to cool the economy in order to fight inflation. The president cannot order the Fed to make open-market purchases, and the Fed cannot force Congress to reduce spending or increase taxes.

   The Federal Reserve is independent of both the president and Congress. The Fed governors are appointed by the president (to nonrenewable 14-year terms), and at any point in time most of the governors were chosen by the current president's predecessors. Congress has little direct control over the Fed's day-to-day operations, although it can impose general constraints, such as minimum and maximum levels for reserve requirements. The president and Congress have both tried to influence the Federal Reserve and have sometimes been successful.

## *Political Pressures*

The Fed usually gives the president the kind of monetary policy he wants. In the 1950s the Fed was very cautious and, to avoid inflation, accepted three recessions during Dwight Eisenhower's 8 years in office. John F. Kennedy became president in January of 1961, having promised voters that he would reduce unemployment and get the country moving again. The Fed obligingly swung to a more expansionary monetary policy. In 1969 Richard Nixon took office, promising to stop inflation, and the Fed tightened the screws in a painful credit crunch. In 1977 Jimmy Carter became president, and his expansionary fiscal policies were, for a while, supported by expansionary monetary policies. In 1981 Ronald Reagan became president, promising to reduce inflation, and the Fed continued the tight monetary policy begun in October of 1979.

Paul Samuelson once said that Federal Reserve governors were given two eyes so that they could watch both interest rates and the money supply.[1] The Fed actually appears to have three eyes: one for interest rates, one for the money supply, and one for election returns.

Example 24.1 describes a specific instance in which a president's administration tried to influence monetary policy. Thomas Havrilesky of Duke University has made a more systematic study of the effects of political pressure on the Fed by constructing a signaling index (labeled SAFER) that cumulates the number of articles in *The Wall Street Journal* in which administration members indicate a desire for an easier ( +1) or tighter ( −1) monetary policy. Havrilesky found that each 1-point increase in this index over a 3-week period tended to increase *M1* by $300 million and to reduce the federal funds rate by 90 basis points by the end of the 3-week period.[2]

---

**EXAMPLE**
**24.1**       *Threatening the Fed*

In March of 1990, the *Los Angeles Times* printed a front-page story with the headline "Interest Rates Peril Fed Chief's Job, Sources Say." The story began

> *President Bush is so upset over Federal Reserve Board Chairman Alan Greenspan's refusal to push interest rates down further that he is unlikely to reappoint him as Fed chairman when his term expires in August of 1991, sources said Thursday.**

The primary source for this story — identified only as a "longtime Bush adviser" — said that Bush was "mad as hell" about Greenspan's policies and added that "I can't believe he will reappoint him and I don't know a soul in the White House who thinks he will." Bush's press secretary immediately denied this story and said that Greenspan's reappointment hadn't even been discussed at the White House.

The story behind the story, according to a personal conversation with a *Times* reporter, was that Bush's advisers had criticized Greenspan for months for what they considered excessively high interest rates and now wanted to send

**Jack Nelson, "Interest Rates Peril Fed Chief's Job, Sources Say," Los Angeles Times,* March 9, 1990.*

an even stronger message. A member of the administration contacted a *Times* reporter and, on the usual condition of anonymity, leaked the story. (A reporter who violated the anonymity condition would lose all sources.)

Bush's press secretary routinely denied the story, but there was no doubt that the Fed received and understood the message: Bush and his advisers wanted lower interest rates and would keep pushing for lower interest rates. The *Times* reporters were well aware that they were not merely reporting economic events but, instead, were being used to deliver a message to the Fed. However, the *Times* printed the story anyway because it thought that the message was newsworthy.

The Federal Reserve uses the same media techniques when it wants to send a message to the president, Congress, or financial markets. A staff member or one of the Fed's governors contacts a trusted member of the press and, requiring anonymity, leaks information or expresses an opinion, perhaps about the state of the economy. The subsequent news story attributes these opinions to a "senior Fed official" or a "well-placed source." Often the unidentified well-placed source is the Federal Reserve chairman!

As it turned out, Bush did reappoint Greenspan in August of 1991.

The Fed does not always bend to the wishes of the administration and Congress. Federal Reserve officials are repeatedly cajoled by the president and called before congressional committees, often because monetary and fiscal policies seem to be working at cross-purposes. Since 1965 there have been several occasions when expansionary fiscal policies were pitted against tight-money, contractionary monetary policies.

Because they are not elected officials, the members of the Federal Reserve Board are presumably less likely to manipulate the economy for personal political gain, although there still might be temptations to assist favored politicians. For instance, Federal Reserve Chairman Arthur Burns vehemently denied charges that the Fed pursued an easy-money policy in 1972 to assist Richard Nixon's reelection campaign. Former Fed Governor Sherman Maisel later wrote about the persistent pressure applied by the Nixon administration: "An election was approaching; from their point of view, the faster money grew, the better was monetary policy."[3]

It sometimes seems, particularly before elections, that the Federal Reserve is trying to cool the economy to fight inflation while the president is trying to stimulate the economy to reduce unemployment. For example, when Jimmy Carter ran for reelection in 1980 and lost, his advisors were bitterly critical of the Federal Reserve's tight-money policies, including an increase in the discount rate 6 weeks before the election. To some, these conflicts show that the system is working as intended. When a president, prime minister, or king has controlled a nation's money supply, there has too often been irresponsible and ultimately destructive inflation. The political independence of the Federal Reserve allows it to follow unpopular but necessary policies.

**EXAMPLE
24.2**

## *The Fed's Preference for Secrecy*

The Federal Reserve's policy deliberations take place in secrecy, and so do most of the Fed's actions. For many years, the Fed's Open Market Committee wouldn't announce when it was meeting, let alone disclose what was discussed or decided at the meeting, and it refused even to confirm or deny reports of its open-market operations. Verbatim minutes of Federal Open Market Committee meetings were not published until 5 years after the meeting was held.

Today, the timing of Federal Open Market Committee meetings is public knowledge, but they are still closed meetings and the only public record is a brief summary published several weeks later in the *Federal Reserve Bulletin.* Verbatim minutes are no longer kept, lest they be made public under the Freedom of Information Act, and internal memos remain confidential for 5 years. The Fed continues to conduct its open-market operations in secrecy. Since 1983 it has agreed to confirm outside reports of its operations, but it still refuses to say whether its purchases and sales of Treasury securities are defensive transactions or represent a shift in monetary policy.

A small army of financial analysts — Fed watchers — tries to discern the Fed's actions and intentions by monitoring zigs and zags in financial data and mulling over nuances in speeches by Federal Reserve governors. Often the Fed watchers are wrong. For example, on Wednesday, November 22, 1989, the federal funds rate dropped sharply, leading Fed watchers to conclude that the Fed was easing credit. In fact, the rate decline had been an unintended consequence of the Fed's efforts to make technical adjustments in the money supply; the following Monday the Fed made conspicuous open-market sales, pushing the federal funds rate upward and sending an unambiguous signal that it was not easing credit conditions.*

Fed Chairman Alan Greenspan argues that a public announcement of policy changes "would reduce our flexibility to implement decisions quietly at times to achieve a desired effect, while minimizing possible financial market disruptions."† After a minicrash in the stock market on Friday, October 13, 1989, in which the Dow Jones Industrial Average fell by 190.58 points (6.9 percent), the second largest drop in history, Fed Vice-Chairman Manuel Johnson told reporters from the *New York Times* and *Washington Post* that the Fed would provide funds to prevent a financial crisis. Both newspapers reported these assurances on the front page of their Sunday editions, citing a

*\*Douglas R. Sease, "Bonds Fall on Move by the Fed," Wall Street Journal, November 28, 1989.*

*†David Wessel and Tom Herman, "Should Fed Hide Its Moves, Leaving Markets Confused?" Wall Street Journal, November 29, 1989.*

"senior Fed official." Fed Chairman Greenspan was furious about the publication of these stories. The next day, in a telephone conference call to the members of the Open Market Committee, the president of the Federal Reserve Bank of New York reportedly "delivered a long tirade" about this public discussion of Fed policy.‡

Most economists consider it implausible that a risk-averse public is better off having to guess what the Fed is doing. One observer, William Greider, author of the book *Secrets of the Temple*, a probing look behind the Fed's veil, suggests that its passion for secrecy is intended to create an almost religious aura:

> *The central bank, notwithstanding its claims to rational method, enfolded itself in the same protective trappings that adorned the temple — secrecy, mystique, an awesome authority that was neither visible nor legible to mere mortals. . . . Its decrees were cast in a mysterious language people could not understand, but its voice, they knew, was powerful and important.§*

Another explanation is that if the Fed does not announce its actions and intentions, then it won't be blamed for its mistakes. It was, for example, after Senator William Proxmire criticized Fed Chairman Arthur Burns publicly that the Fed stopped keeping and reporting verbatim minutes of Open Market Committee meetings.‖

A more moderate view is that the Fed might be reluctant to tighten credit, particularly before elections, if it had to publicly announce a policy that irritated the incumbent president. Thus one full-time Fed watcher argues that "if the Fed officially announced every single policy shift, it would attract excessive political attention — and that might intimidate the Fed and cause it to not fight inflation as much as it should."¶ Whether or not it would be able to resist such political pressure, the Fed has so far resisted efforts to make its deliberations and actions public.

‡*Alan Murray, "Oct. 13's Stock Slide Shows Fed Officials' Differences,"* Wall Street Journal, *November 29, 1989.*

§*William Greider, Secrets of the Temple* (New York: Simon & Schuster, 1987), p. 240.

‖*Ibid, p. 345.*

¶*David M. Jones, quoted by Wessel and Herman, op. cit.*

---

**EXAMPLE
24.3**

## *The Political Business Cycle*

An only slightly cynical explanation of the periodic conflict between expansionary fiscal and contractionary monetary policies is that economic events can have a decisive influence on political elections. People think of their pocketbooks when they vote and judge the incumbent political party by the state of the

## The Political Business Cycle

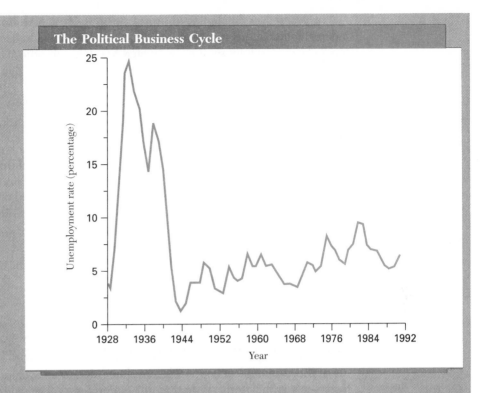

economy. Casual observation and formal empirical studies indicate that high output and low unemployment sway votes to the incumbent party.*

There are two other, more subtle observations. First, changes in the levels of output and employment during the year preceding the election seem to be very important, perhaps more important than the levels themselves. Second, inflation tends to lag behind the economy in that the economy can be stimulated, thereby increasing output and reducing unemployment, with relatively little immediate impact on the rate of inflation.

These apparent phenomena show why an incumbent party may try to stimulate the economy before an election and to cool it off after an election. This preelection stimulus and postelection restraint is called the **political business cycle**. The accompanying figure shows that the unemployment rate seems to decline before presidential elections and to rise afterwards. (1992 is not shown.) In 1932 the unemployment rate rose 7.7 percent, and the incumbent president, Herbert Hoover, was soundly defeated. Since 1932 there has been only one instance in which the unemployment rate in a presidential election year was higher than during the preceding year: 1980, when the unemployment rate rose 1.3 percent and the incumbent, Jimmy Carter, lost decisively.

*See William D. Nordhaus, "The Political Business Cycle," The Review of Economic Studies, April 1975, pp. 169–190; and Ray Fair, "The Effect of Economic Events on Votes for President," Review of Economics and Statistics, May 1978, pp. 159–173.

In the 1970s, many economists and Fed officials believed that $M1$ might be difficult to control (flawed by the first criterion) but that there was reliable relationship beteen $M1$ and many of the Fed's objectives (good by the second criterion). Later in this chapter we will look more closely at the advantages and disadvantages of interest rates and monetary aggregates as intermediate targets.

If the Fed uses an intermediate target, such as $M1$, that it does not control directly, then it may use **operating targets** to help achieve its intermediate targets. For instance, the Fed may want to reduce the rate of inflation and may decide to use a 5 percent rate of growth of $M1$ as an intermediate target. Because $M1$ contains checkable deposits subject to reserve requirements, there may be a close relationship between bank reserves and $M1$. If this is so, the Fed might set an operating target of, say, 5 percent growth in bank reserves. The Fed will then use open-market operations to try to keep bank reserves growing at 5 percent a year, hoping that this will ensure a 5 percent annual growth of $M1$ and that this growth rate for $M1$ will reduce inflation as desired. Other potential operating targets include nonborrowed reserves, borrowed reserves, and the monetary base. A perfect operating target would be easy to control and reliably related to the Fed's intermediate target. Unfortunately, there are no perfect operating or intermediate targets.

# OBSTACLES TO EFFECTIVE POLICY

All operating and intermediate targets are imperfect for two fundamental reasons: uncertainty and policy lags. We will discuss the consequences of uncertainty first and then of policy lags.

## *Uncertainty*

Politicians are often impatient with economists who admit that they are not omniscient. Harry Truman once exclaimed in frustration, "Give me a one-handed economist! All my economists say 'on the one hand, . . . but on the other.'" If economists were certain about how the economy works and what the future holds, policy decisions would be easy. Congress, the president, and the Fed could negotiate target values of unemployment, inflation, and other key variables and select policies that achieve these objectives. The problem is that we have imperfect economic data, cannot accurately anticipate the economic decisions humans make, and do not understand fully the complex consequences of economic events. We don't understand the past completely, cannot see the present clearly, and have only imperfect predictions about what is going to happen in the future.

We frankly do not have enough accurate, timely data to describe the economy's current condition with precision, let alone know what conditions will be like 5 years or even 5 months from now. A policymaker who doesn't know much about the current state of the economy will almost certainly make some memorable policy errors. In June of 1930, for example, in the midst of an

**EXAMPLE**
**24.4**   *A Case of Mysterious Excess Reserves*

When bank reserves are scarce, the federal funds rate increases and the aggregate amount of excess reserves in the banking system declines. When funds are plentiful, the federal funds rate declines and excess reserves swell. During July of 1980, however, the federal funds rate increased and, surprisingly, so did excess reserves. In the first week of August, excess reserves topped $1 billion, the highest level in 20 years, even though the federal funds rate had increased by nearly a percentage point, from an average of 8.68 percent during the week ending on July 25 to an average of 9.60 percent during the week ending on August 8. *The Wall Street Journal* reported that the spokesman for the Federal Reserve Bank of New York who reported the August data "simply shook his head, saying that it was all 'quite mysterious' why banks would want to keep such large idle reserves."*

Finally, on August 25, the Fed announced that the case of the mysterious excess reserves had been solved. Federal Reserve statisticians estimate excess reserves by subtracting an estimate of required reserves from an estimate of total bank reserves, and for 3 consecutive weeks, they had underestimated required reserves by about $300 million — causing them to overestimate excess reserves by a like amount.

Aggregate required reserves is normally one of the Fed's most reliable data series. In this instance, however, the Fed had misinterpreted its own rules for calculating required reserves. In July of 1980 the Fed removed a special 2 percent supplementary reserve requirement on large certificates of deposit (CDs), and the Fed's statisticians simultaneously reduced their estimate of aggregate required reserves on large CDs by 2 percent. However, they forgot that each bank is subject to another rule, mandated by Congress, that fixes the minimum average reserve requirement on all savings and time deposits at 3 percent. Because of this special rule, required reserves must be calculated on a bank-by-bank basis. When the Fed's statisticians did this, they found their $300 million error and solved the excess reserves puzzle. Fortunately, the Fed's governors suspected that the reported sharp increase in excess reserves was misleading and did not overreact to this illusory signal that there was a glut of reserves.

*Edward P. Foldessy, "The Fed Clears Up Mystery of Data on Bank Reserves," Wall Street Journal, August 26, 1980.

economic depression that would continue for 10 years, Herbert Hoover told a group that had come to Washington to urge an expansionary fiscal policy, "Gentlemen, you have come 60 days too late. The depression is over."[5]

Hoover was mistaken because he had very little information about output and employment. Gross national product data were not collected until the mid-1930s, and before 1940 the only regular unemployment figures were collected in the census, once every 10 years. Other economic data were scarce before World War II and often not very reliable.

Today we have much better information about the current state of the economy. However, we still don't have all the data we need, and we probably never will. Some data (including estimates of the gross national product and gross domestic product) are only available quarterly. Some data, like real interest rates, are not officially available at all. Some, like weekly values of $M1$, are not very reliable and are often substantially revised weeks or even months after their initial release. A Fed study found that, between 1968 and 1975, in a third of the cases the final estimate of the growth rate of a monetary aggregate differed from the preliminary estimate by more than 3 percentage points. How can the Fed accurately stabilize real interest rates or monetary aggregates if it barely sees them?

## Forecasting Errors

Even more challenging, the Fed's policies must be aimed at the future, not the present, and economic forecasts are notoriously difficult, as evidenced by the embarrassingly inaccurate predictions that have been made in the past. Because the Great Depression was so calamitous, it is not surprising that it is also the source of many dramatically incorrect forecasts. In his final message to Congress on December 4, 1928, President Calvin Coolidge boasted:

> No Congress of the United States ever assembled, on surveying the state of the Union, has met with a more pleasing prospect than that which appears at the present time. . . . The country can regard the present with satisfaction and anticipate the future with optimism.

Herbert Hoover took office in January of 1929 and in July predicted that "the outlook of the world today is for the greatest era of commercial expansion in history." A few months later the stock market crashed. Herbert Hoover's optimism persisted. In his December 3, 1929 state of the union message, he concluded that "the problems with which we are confronted are the problems of growth and progress." In March of 1930 Hoover predicted that business would be normal by May. In early May he declared that "we have now passed the worst"; in late May he predicted recovery by fall.

As the economy collapsed, politicians, businesspeople, and economists kept predicting a quick return to prosperity. Charles Schwab, chairman of the board of Bethlehem Steel, said, "Never before has American business been as firmly entrenched for prosperity as it is today" (December 10, 1929). Andrew Mellon, Secretary of the Treasury, stated, "I see nothing in the present situation that is either menacing or warrants pessimism" (January 1, 1930). Robert Lamont, Secretary of Commerce, predicted that "business will be normal in 2 months" (March 3, 1930). Even Irving Fisher, perhaps the greatest American economist, joined the chorus of optimists: "I expect to see the stock market a good deal higher than it is today within a few months" (October 15, 1929). Fisher lost his family fortune and a good deal of credibility. The politicians and businesspeople didn't fare much better.

## Unpredictable Behavior

Economic forecasting is much better now than in the 1930s, but it is not perfect and never will be, because the consequences of economic events are difficult to predict and because economic decisions are made by humans — who are emotional, fallible, and unpredictable. An economist can tell you what is rational, what is reasonable, and what usually happens, but in any situation, fickle humans can turn around and do something entirely different. This is how Keynes explained the mayhem in the stock market and why he wrote that "there is nothing so disastrous as a rational investment policy in an irrational world."[6]

Similarly, to predicting the consequences of government policies, we need to take into account how citizens will interpret these policies and how they will react to them. For example, government officials have long believed that the public sometimes overreacts to policy announcements. This is why incumbent presidents often announce potentially popular (but possibly unwise) policies only hours before a primary election or shortly before the presidential election itself. The president hopes to exploit the initial public enthusiasm before sober reflection sets in. With bad news, the best timing is months before the election or right after it. The Fed often announces unsettling financial news late Friday, after U.S. financial markets have closed, to give investors the weekend to calm down.

Citizens can react to policies in unexpected ways. When the government announces an expansionary policy, one possible reaction by the public is: "This policy will stimulate the economy; a boom is on the way." But another plausible response is: "If the government is trying these stimulative policies, the economy must be in really bad shape; we must be sliding into a recession." Sometimes citizens react the first way, sometimes the second way, and sometimes in other ways.

This fickleness can be very frustrating for government officials. In the Great Depression, President Hoover kept trying to buoy the economy with optimistic pronouncements, such as, "Prosperity is just around the corner." This cheerleading was such an embarrassing failure that Simeon Fess, the National Chairman of the Republican Party, finally complained that

> Persons high in Republican circles are beginning to believe that there is some concerted effort on foot to utilize the stock market as a method of discrediting the administration. Every time an administration official gives out an optimistic statement about business conditions, the market immediately drops.[7]

In the spring of 1970 President Nixon stated that, if he "had any money," he would buy stocks. Stock prices promptly fell by more than 10 percent. Investors seemed to feel that the economy must be in even worse shape than they had thought if the president had to tout stocks. In 1981 President Ronald Reagan was similarly disappointed by Wall Street's negative response to his tax program. We have all seen other government officials surprised by public reaction to their policies and predictions.

## Policy Lags

Another reason why policymakers cannot achieve their objectives with precision is that there are significant lags between when an economic problem occurs and when a policy response affects the economy. These delays are of three kinds:

1. *Recognition delays.*   We don't have reliable data on many important economic variables until some time after the fact. For example, gross national product and gross domestic product data are not available until several weeks after each quarter has ended; thus data for January through March are not available until mid-April. In addition, economic data are never final but are always subject to revision. Because the data are inexact and the world is full of surprises, policymakers like to see confirming data before making decisions; this is why a recession is not declared until output has declined for two consecutive quarters. Recognition delays mean policymakers may need some time to be convinced that policy changes are needed. One study estimated that recognition delays average around 5 months.[8]

2. *Action delays.*   It takes time for policies to be formulated and agreed on. Government spending and tax laws are especially time-consuming. Monetary policy has a relatively short action delay because Fed decisions are made by a small committee, strongly influenced by one individual — the Federal Reserve chair.

3. *Transmission delays.*   Most policies have far-reaching effects, and it takes some time for these ripples to work themselves out. Government expenditures and tax changes affect the income of households and businesses and thus their spending, which affects the income and spending of yet other households and businesses. It takes a long time for such ripples to fade away completely, but empirical models generally find that an increase in government spending has most of its effects within 6 months.[9]

Monetary policies have considerable transmission delays between their implementation and their ultimate effects. When the Fed makes an open-market purchase, it takes some time for the increase in the monetary base to complete its repeating cycle of loans, expenditures, and deposits. Milton Friedman concluded that there is a lag of about 12 to 18 months between changes in the rate of growth of the money supply and economic activity. John Kareken and Robert Solow interpret the data as indicating a shorter but still substantial lag:

> *Monetary policy works neither so slowly as Friedman thinks, nor as quickly and surely as the Federal Reserve itself seems to believe. . . . Though the full results of policy changes on the flow of spending may be a long time coming, nevertheless the chain of effects is spread out over a fairly wide interval. This means that some effect comes reasonably quickly, and that the effects build up over time so that some substantial stabilizing power results after a lapse of time of the order of six to nine months.*[10]

Economic statistics are, as here, sometimes susceptible to a wide variety of interpretations. Friedman's lag of 12 to 18 months is based on a comparison of

---

**EXAMPLE 24.5**

## Expectations and the Reporting of Monetary Data

The public's reaction to government policies and pronouncements depends critically on their interpretation of these events. The weekly release of data on monetary aggregates is one example. In theory, an increase in the money supply should stimulate the economy and increase stock market prices. Yet, in the early 1980s, when the Fed reported a large increase in $M1$ and other monetary aggregates, stock prices often fell sharply.

The answer to this puzzle illustrates the critical role of expectations. During the early 1980s the Fed was using $M1$ and other monetary aggregates as intermediate targets, trying to reduce inflation by keeping monetary aggregates within target guidelines. However, the Fed does not directly control these monetary aggregates and does not know how fast they have been growing until data are gathered and analyzed. The Fed's weekly release of monetary data was a reporting of past increases in monetary aggregates, which, when they occurred, may well have reflected economic expansion. By the time of the announcement, however, financial market participants were looking ahead and trying to predict future Fed policy. If $M1$ had increased more than planned, market participants feared that the Fed would now use open-market sales to reduce the growth of monetary aggregates. Stock prices consequently declined, as theory says they should, in anticipation of this tightening of the monetary policy.

---

the rate of change of monetary aggregates with the *level* of economic activity. Kareken and Solow, and others, argue that a more useful comparison is between changes in the money supply and *changes* in economic activity, or between deviations of the money supply and economic activity from their long-run trends. Friedman acknowledges that such comparisons reduce the lag down to about 5 months.[11]

These three virtually inescapable delays — recognition, action, and transmission — mean that there normally is a substantial lag between the time when economic stimulus or sedation is first needed and the time when policy changes actually affect the economy. If the recession or boom is brief, then it may be over by the time the counteractive policy is working. Increased government spending, tax cuts, or open-market purchases intended to cushion a recession may not stimulate the economy until the middle of the next boom. If so, then stabilization policy may be destabilizing!

Policymakers are usually competent and well-intentioned. However, inherent policy lags may require policymakers to be clairvoyant, too. If government officials are mere mortals who cannot see the future clearly, then the wrong policies may be chosen as often as not. Some economists argue that business cycles are very short, while monetary and fiscal policies take a long time to take

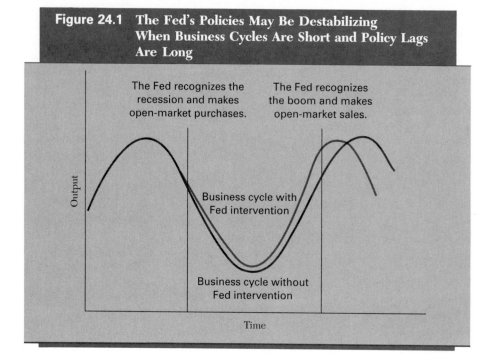

**Figure 24.1** **The Fed's Policies May Be Destabilizing When Business Cycles Are Short and Policy Lags Are Long**

effect. A recession or boom will be over by the time the government has identified it, decided what to do about it, done it, and the stabilization policy has had its effects.

To see how these delays can undermine policies, consider monetary policy during a recession, as depicted in the stylized Figure 24.1. From data that measure the recent performance of the economy, the Fed sees some signs of weakness. Is this a telling sign, a temporary blip, or a statistical quirk? The Fed decides to wait and gather more data. After a few weeks or months, there are some confirming data, but it is still not clear how severe and pronounced the weakness is. Should the Fed make large open-market purchases or wait a while longer?

Time passes, and the Fed decides that the economy really is in a significant recession and should be given some substantial stimulus. Open-market purchases are used to increase the monetary base, reduce interest rates, and encourage spending. With time, the increase in the monetary base is spent, deposited in banks, loaned, spent again, redeposited, and loaned yet again. By the time this monetary tonic is circulating through the economy, however, the recession may have already ended and the economy may be growing briskly. If so, then instead of softening the last recession, the monetary elixir exacerbates the next boom. By the time the Fed recognizes this excessive stimulus and starts draining money from circulation, the next recession may have already begun.

The Fed will then cool off an already cold economy after having heated a hot one; it would have been better had they kept their medicine locked up.

When policies have substantial lagged effects, the monetary authorities may find themselves repeatedly acting to offset the lingering effects of earlier policies. As a consequence, active policy may not be able to stabilize the economy completely. Whether or not this is the case in practice depends on the horizon over which policymakers try to stabilize the economy. For a horizon of hours or days, the lagged effects of monetary and fiscal policies are surely greater than the contemporaneous effects; therefore, policymakers cannot hope to stabilize the economy hour to hour or day to day. For a horizon measured in months, the answer may be reversed. With an annual horizon, the lagged effects of most policies probably are smaller than the contemporaneous effects. Government policymakers may consequently be able to stabilize the economy year to year. Although fine-tuning the economy may be an unrealistic goal, smoothing out year-to-year performance may be possible.

# RULES VERSUS DISCRETION

What kind of government policies should be followed in a very uncertain world? Before the 1930s, many economists and policymakers believed that the government should do very little, except perhaps get out of the way of the private sector; the government should pursue neutral policies that do not upset or distort the private economy. Implicit, and sometimes explicit, in this recommendation was the belief that the economy is inherently stable — that booms and busts are short-lived and self-correcting so that the economy is never far from full employment.

During the Great Depression, the British economist John Maynard Keynes published *The General Theory of Employment, Interest and Money*, arguably one of the most influential books written during this century. In this book he persuaded most economists to reject the economic theories that they had learned — what Keynes called "classical economics." Before Keynes, economists generally assumed that an economy's resources were fully employed. In *The General Theory*, Keynes wrote:

> *Professional economists after Malthus were apparently unmoved by the lack of correspondence between the results of their theory and the facts of observation. . . . which has led to economists being looked upon as Candides, who, having left this world for the cultivation of their gardens, teach that all is for the best in the best of all possible worlds provided that we let well enough alone. . . . It may well be that the classical theory represents the way in which we should like our economy to behave. But to assume that it actually does so is to assume our difficulties away.*[12]

Keynes' arguments and the evidence of the Great Depression convinced most people that there was a legitimate role for a nation's central bank and other government policymakers to cushion economic recessions and moderate spec-ulative booms. In recent years there has been a revival of the classical belief that government stabilization policies are unnecessary and perhaps counterproduc-tive and that the government should consequently adhere to neutral policies that do not distort or disrupt household and business decisions.

## Neutral Policies

It is not easy to design truly neutral monetary and fiscal policies. All government expenditures use resources that could be used for other purposes and thus convey uneven benefits to the citizenry. For instance, expenditures on national defense divert bright scientists, skilled workers, and scarce material from other uses and provide more benefits to the young than to the old, to the healthy than to the ill, to worriers than to the carefree, and to those living in areas most likely to be attacked.

How are government expenditures to be financed? Taxes, bond sales, and money printing are not neutral. In fact, one argument that has received consider-able attention over the years is that it is precisely because monetary policy has important effects on the economy that the government should try to follow a neutral monetary policy. However, even the foremost advocates of a neutral policy (such as Friedrich von Hayek) have been unable to come up with a persuasive definition of a neutral monetary policy. Should the government regulate private money? Should it issue government money? How much? Should it hold this money (or some monetary aggregate) constant, or should it allow money to increase at a constant rate? How is the increased money supply to be put into circulation? These examples are but a sampling of the simple, but apparently unanswerable questions. And the specific answers do make a dif-ference: if money is not neutral, then no monetary policy can really be neutral.

Another conceptual difficulty for advocates of neutral policies is that individ-ual and corporate income taxes increase with output, reducing the government's budget deficit during booms (and increasing it during recessions). The govern-ment's consolidated budget constraint tells us that an increase in tax revenue presents policymakers with three options: the additional tax revenue can be spent on goods and services, used to purchase bonds, or used to reduce the monetary base (the Treasury can purchase bonds while the Fed simultaneously sells bonds so that the bond supply is constant while the monetary base declines).

If the additional tax revenue raised during an economic boom is used to increase government spending or to purchase bonds, increasing bond prices and reducing interest rates, the economy will be further stimulated. If, however, the tax revenue is used to reduce the monetary base, the expansion is moderated. Adjusting government spending or bond sales to variations in tax revenue is a pro-cyclical fiscal policy that magnifies economic booms and busts. Varying the money supply with tax revenue, in contrast, commits the government to an automatically countercyclical monetary policy.[13] None of these responses is neutral.

## Fixed Rules

A variant on the neutral-money recommendation, one that is more operational, is that it really doesn't matter very much what the government does as long as the government is consistent about it. The seminal statement of this view was made by Henry Simons, a University of Chicago economist, in 1936:

> *In a free enterprise system we obviously need highly definite and stable rules of the game, especially as to money. The monetary rules must be compatible with the reasonably smooth functioning of the system. Once established, however, they should work automatically, with the chips falling where they may. . . . The responsibility for carrying out the monetary rules should be lodged in a federal authority . . . closely controlled in their exercise by a sharply defined policy. . . . Political control in this sphere should be confined exclusively to regulation of the quantity of money and near money.*[14]

In Simons' view, monetary authorities should be subservient to monetary rules. In monetary matters, as in other areas, we should be a nation governed by laws rather than by people.

This belief was roughly consistent with the broad antigovernment views then espoused by other members of what came to be called the Chicago School, which strongly extolled the virtues of unfettered markets and sharply criticized government interference. For many years Milton Friedman was the most visible and effective proponent of the Chicago School.

Simons sidestepped the problem of defining a neutral monetary policy by arguing that the most important issue is that discretionary policy be replaced by fixed monetary rules. The actual rules are less important than the private sector's confidence that the rules will not be changed in midgame. Nonetheless, there remains the practical question of making up the rules.

One of Simons' proposals was to fix the quantity of money, but this requires a precise definition of money, a definition that includes some assets and excludes other, very similar assets. In his 1936 essay, Simons expressed his frustration with the "unfortunate character of our financial structure — with the abundance of what we may call 'near-moneys' — with the difficulty of defining money in such a manner as to give practical significance to the conception of quantity."[15]

This dilemma led Simons to urge the abolition of such near-moneys as bank deposits and short-term securities:

> *A liberal program of monetary reform should seek to effect an increasingly sharp differentiation between money and private obligations and, especially, to minimize the opportunities for the creation of effective money substitutes. . . . The abolition of private deposit banking is clearly the appropriate first step in this direction and would bring us in sight of the goal; but such a measure, to be really effective, must be accompanied, or followed closely, by drastic limitation on the formal borrowing powers of all private corporations and especially upon borrowing at short term.*[16]

Simons proposed requiring banks to hold 100 percent reserves against their deposits, restricting short-term business and consumer loans severely, and limiting government debt to cash and very long-term bonds (ideally consols that never mature) An even more extreme proposal was to prohibit debt entirely.[17] Ironically, Simons, a free-market economist, in his quest for a neutral monetary policy, was led to advocate pervasive government regulation of financial markets.

The modern descendants of this Chicago tradition have generally eschewed such radical constraints on financial markets but have continued to recommend passive monetary policy via fixed monetary rules. Milton Friedman, for instance, has long advocated that the Fed choose a monetary aggregate, such as *M*1 or *M*2, and simply keep this measure of the money supply growing at a constant rate, perhaps 3 to 5 percent a year, regardless of the state of the economy.

Such advocates of passive policy are critics of discretionary demand-management policies. Their central criticism of monetary and fiscal stabilization policies is that because of uncertainty and delays, policymakers have done a poor job and will continue to do so. Thus Edward Shaw wrote of the Fed:

> *The antimanagement brief does not deny that monetary policy could perform miracles, promoting stable growth and fending off shocks to growth. But our experience contains no miracles. Management skills are not equal to the job of realizing the potentialities of monetary policy.*[18]

## RATIONAL EXPECTATIONS AND THE NEW CLASSICAL ECONOMISTS

Classical (pre-Keynesian) economists assumed that an unfettered economy is always close to full employment and that full-employment output is unaffected by monetary and fiscal policies. They assumed that economic fluctuations about full employment are so brief and unimportant that they can be ignored. Robert Lucas, a University of Chicago economist, and other **new classical economists** have extended the classical models to allow for voluntary fluctuations in employment and output.

In new classical models, workers sometimes misjudge the price level and consequently miscalculate real wages. For example, if workers overestimate the price level, they underestimate the real value of the wages that firms offer. Some misinformed workers decide (mistakenly) that wage rates are not high enough to make work worth their while. As they leave their jobs, employment and output both decline. This voluntary unemployment is soon corrected, without the need for monetary or fiscal policies, when workers learn that they overestimated prices and underestimated real wages.

Thus, according to the new classical economists, business cycles are caused by misjudgments regarding prices, mistakes that could be minimized if the government directed its attention to stabilizing prices. Robert Lucas states this as follows:

*The policy problem of reducing business cycle risk is a very real and important one, and one which I believe monetary and fiscal policies directed at price stability would go a long way toward achieving.*[19]

## Only Surprise Policies Matter

Why are workers sometimes mistaken about the level of prices? If the economy fluctuated very little, there would be little reason for errors. Mistakes occur because of major events that are unforeseen or whose consequences are not accurately perceived. The new classical macroeconomists focus on government-instigated events, in reaction to the persistent Keynesian advocacy of active government stabilization policies. In this way, the new classical macroeconomists agree with earlier classical economists that government intervention is unneeded and even counterproductive.

Citizens are aware of well-publicized, easily accessible information. If the government were to announce, and the news services dutifully report, that the money supply will be decreased by 10 percent on February 8, people will anticipate this contractionary monetary policy. If a 10 percent decrease in the money supply reliably decreases prices 10 percent, people will be aware of this, too. They will fully anticipate this price deflation, and it will not be a source of error in calculating real wages. These are **rational expectations** based on the efficient utilization of available information.

If, as in the new classical models, all unemployment is voluntary, then with rational expectations, well-anticipated changes in the money supply do not cause mistakes in gauging the price level and consequently have no effect on employment or output. The only way that the Fed can affect employment and output is by using a surprise monetary policy, perhaps reducing the money supply after announcing that the money supply was going to be increased. Even this trick won't work very many times, however. A rational public will soon learn to expect the government to do the opposite of what it says. Policymakers will have to tell the truth every once in a while, just to keep the public guessing. In fact, any simple, consistent rules for conducting monetary policy will soon be learned by the public and rendered ineffective. The only monetary policy that can consistently alter employment and output is a random policy, using a secret coin flip to determine whether the money supply will be increased or decreased.

Of course, by definition, a random policy cannot be used to achieve purposeful objectives. Therefore, in a new classical model with full employment and rational expectations, a passive policy is best because active policies only affect the economy by fooling people into making decisions they later regret.

## Expectations and Government Policy

In new classical models, the best government policy is a passive one: keep the money supply growing at a stable, well-publicized rate, allowing the private sector to make decisions on the basis of good information. While this model has some appealing features, the assumption that business cycles are caused by misinformation about prices is questionable. To obtain reasonably accurate up-to-date price information, all people need to do is listen to news reports or glance at newspaper headlines.

Some households do purchase bundles of goods and services that differ substantially from those included in the consumer price index reported in the news, but it does not seem plausible that their price errors are sufficient to cause the large, lengthy swings in unemployment that occur. For instance, between 1974 and 1975, unemployment increased by 2.8 million, from 5.6 to 8.5 percent of the labor force, while the CPI increased by 9.1 percent. It is hard to believe that this large increase in unemployment was due to a voluntary withdrawal from the labor force caused by widespread overestimates of inflation — to people thinking that prices were increasing much faster than they really were.

The new classical economists are ingenious and provocative, but even they admit that their models tell only a part of the story — that they contain some interesting insights but are an incomplete explanation of business cycles. Robert Lucas has written that these models

> . . . *Do succeed in their twin objectives. They provide examples of mone-tary economies in which money has . . . long-run neutrality . . . , yet re-tains the capacity to induce short-run disruptions of the sort documented by Friedman and Anna J. Schwartz. . . . Now it does not seem to me a critical or an economic insight to observe that one can detect differences between the world described in this paper and the United States, or that it utilizes "questionable ad hoc assumptions," or that it leaves facts unex-plained. If ever there was a model rigged, frankly and unapologetically, to fit a limited set of facts it is this one. Ad hoc? If you only knew how hard it was.*[20]

Lucas and others have shown that price errors can cause voluntary fluctua-tions in employment. Business cycles may be partly instigated and magnified by such errors. However, other factors surely matter too. The Great Depression was not simply a quarter of the labor force deciding to stay home because wages were too low to make work worthwhile. The drop in the unemployment rate to 3.5 percent in 1969 and the increases to 8.5 percent in 1975 and to 9.7 percent in 1982 were not due solely to mistakes about prices.

Keynes emphasized expectations, too, although he stressed largely inexplica-ble "mass psychology" and "animal spirits" rather than rational expectations. Expectations were central to his analysis of production decisions, investment plans, money demand, and the stock market. Yet the early Keynesian models used by his followers largely ignored expectations, partly for lack of a theory explaining expectations and partly for lack of good data measuring them. A major contribution of the rational expectations literature is to reemphasize the point that expectations are important and are influenced by government policies. Policymakers, in turn, need to take into account private reactions to their policies; government policy does not operate in a vacuum. For example, monetary policy may be most effective when policymakers have established their credibility so that the public readily believes the Fed's analysis of the economic situation and the Fed's commitment to its announced policies.

The new classical economists are right that expectation errors can affect the economy, that private expectations are influenced by anticipated government policy, and that expectations should be taken into account in selecting policies. However, monetary and fiscal policies, even when fully anticipated, do have real economic effects.

# THE ECLECTIC VIEW

The question of passive or active policy, of rules versus authority, elicits a good deal of passion. The debate applies to many economic policies and is of deep personal concern to the protagonists as well as to the ordinary citizens whose lives are affected by government policies.

One fundamental disagreement is whether the private economy is inherently stable. Can the "invisible hand" of market forces invoked by Adam Smith keep the economy on course, or should the government put a visible hand on the wheel? Classical economists believed that the economy was never far from full-employment equilibrium. After a rough roller coaster ride through booms and busts, culminating in the Great Depression, a lot of citizens with empty stomachs weren't so sure. Keynes legitimatized the view that the private economy is not inherently stable. The government should and could stabilize the economy, smoothing out or even eliminating business cycles. For 30 years the Keynesian view had the upper hand. However, Keynesian economics, too, did not deliver all that it had promised. In the 1970s there was *stagflation* — high unemployment and rapid inflation simultaneously — and the pendulum swung back toward the classical skepticism of government.

The consensus among economists is that there is merit in both sides of this debate. Because of fundamental, inescapable errors and lags, it is, in fact, very difficult to fine-tune the economy. Very intelligent and well-intentioned experts have tried and have been found wanting. It is also true that in many ways government has become too big and meddlesome. However, it is equally true that the good old days were not all that great, that the economy on occasion went through some fearsome, stressful times when a lot of decent, hard-working people suffered greatly.

Fixed policy rules do ensure less uncertainty about government actions, but they may mean more uncertainty about the economy. A commitment not to let the economy disintegrate may well be more reassuring to households and businesses than an unshakable promise to ignore the economy. The federal government may not be able to eliminate business cycles completely, but when things turn sour — really obviously sour — policymakers need to be ready to step in and push the economy hard in the right direction.

EXAMPLE
24.6

### U.S. Interest Rates Are Affected by Foreign Interest Rates

At its meeting on December 19, 1989, the Federal Reserve's Open Market Committee discussed the state of the U.S. economy and reached a consensus that although a recession did not appear imminent, there were troubling signs of economic weakness. They voted to reassure financial markets and bolster the economy by using open-market operations to lower interest rates somewhat. The following morning the Fed's trading desk bought Treasury bills, reducing interest rates. However, during the next $2\frac{1}{2}$ months, long-term Treasury bond rates rose by three-quarters of a point.

The reason? The dramatic reunification of East and West Germany and the anticipated need for huge amounts of capital to modernize eastern Europe caused large increases in European interest rates. At the same time, concerns about Japan's rising rate of inflation caused Japanese interest rates to rise sharply. U.S. Treasury bond prices consequently fell and Treasury bond rates rose so that these bonds would be competitive with European and Japanese securities.

This incident illustrates how the linkages among world interest rates can constrain and blunt the Federal Reserve's monetary policies and how financial events now have international repercussions. In the past, the Federal Open Market Committee focused almost exclusively on U.S. economic data. Now they study detailed statistics for all its major trading partners.

It is also evident that many government regulatory agencies, such as the Securities and Exchange Commission, have been beneficial in increasing the quantity and accuracy of information available to the public. Market forces do not always protect the needy or restrain corruption and banditry. The fundamental, and perhaps unsolvable, puzzle in economics is when to trust the market and when to trust government.

There are admittedly practical difficulties with implementing both points of view. If policymakers are to use discretionary policies, what signals should guide them? When should they alter government spending and tax rates? When should they tighten financial markets, and when should they ease them? Should they watch an interest rate, some measure of the money supply, some price index, some output level, some unemployment rate, or what? And when they do decide to act, what action should they take? If they want to tighten financial markets, should they raise the discount rate, raise reserve requirements, make open-market sales, or what? And how much of whatever they do should they do?

These are difficult questions, and they apply to passive rules as well as discretionary policymaking. If we are going to encode some rules permanently in the law books and in a computer program to control fiscal and monetary policies automatically, which rules should they be? Human judgment is fallible, but it must be used whether by exercising discretionary authority or by writing rules. Paul Samuelson has argued that when people "set up a definitive mechanism which is to run forever afterward by itself, that involves a single act of discretion which transcends, in both its arrogance and its capacity for potential harm, any repeated acts of foolish discretion that can be imagined."[21]

In the next two chapters we will look at some very specific policies, passive and discretionary, that might be followed by the Fed and at the actual policies employed since World War II. You will see that while fine-tuning may be impossible, the risks inherent in inflexible rules have consistently led the Fed to follow an eclectic approach, applying judgment to diverse measures of the condition of financial markets and the economy.

# SUMMARY

The Federal Reserve Board has considerable autonomy, and its actions do not always please the president and Congress. Broadly speaking, the Fed generally gives each president the kind of monetary policy he wants, but there are sometimes important conflicts, particularly before elections — when economic expansion usually has more appeal for the president than for the Fed.

The Federal Reserve has a variety of objectives, including low unemployment, low inflation, stable financial markets, and stable exchange rates, but the Fed does not directly control any of these. If there were no lags and uncertainties, this would not matter, because the link between open-market operations and the Fed's objectives would be quick and sure. With lags and uncertainties, however, the Fed cannot be sure of the effects of its policies, nor can it instantly revise its policies to fine-tune aggregate demand.

Because uncertainties and delays make the conduct of policy difficult, some observers recommend that the Fed follow simple, mechanical rules instead of actively trying to stabilize the economy. Implicit in this recommendation is the classical belief that the private economy is inherently stable — that booms and recessions are short-lived and self-correcting.

Classical economics assumed that an economy's resources were fully employed and that government stabilization policies are consequently unnecessary. Keynes argued that economies sometimes experience considerable involuntary unemployment and that central banks and other government policymakers should use monetary and fiscal policies to moderate economic recessions and speculative booms. The new classical economists assume, like the classical economists, that the economy is always at full employment but argue that economic fluctuations are due to errors in assessing prices. Employment voluntarily expands when workers temporarily overestimate real wages and contracts when they underestimate real wages. If there is both full employment and rational expectations, then well-anticipated government policies do not cause such mistakes and, consequently, do not affect employment and output.

# IMPORTANT TERMS

fiscal policy
intermediate targets
monetary policy
new classical economists

operating targets
political business cycle
rational expectations

# EXERCISES

1. Identify which of the following choices are monetary policies and which are fiscal policies and which are expansionary and which are contractionary.
   a. Reserve requirements are reduced.
   b. Personal income taxes are reduced.
   c. Military spending is reduced.
   d. The discount rate is reduced.
   e. The Fed buys Treasury bills.

2. The unemployment rate seems to go up at least as often as it goes down. Yet the unemployment rate has risen in only 1 of the 14 presidential election years from 1936 through 1988. Is this just a coincidence? If not, how would you explain this pattern?

3. Early in the 1984 presidential election campaign, a strategist for incumbent Ronald Reagan said that Paul Volcker, rather than the Democratic leader Walter Mondale, "may be our biggest political foe."[22] What did he mean by that?

4. In 1981 two staff writers for the *Los Angeles Times* wrote of government public works projects to reduce unemployment: "Because of ____, such measures have usually not taken effect until after recovery was well under way."[23] What was the explanation omitted from this quotation? Give your own version of the argument that these staff writers may have learned in an economics course.

5. Leonall Anderson, a monetarist, argued that

   *Monetarist theories and empirical studies point to a relatively quick, but short-lived, response of output to a change in money growth, with a longer time period required*

   *for prices to respond fully. Post-Keynesian econometric models, on the other hand, produce an impact of money changes only over a much longer period.*[24]

   If monetary policies do have quick and short-lived effects, does this make them more or less useful for short-run economic stabilization? How would you explain Milton Friedman's recommendation that monetary policy not be used for short-run economic stabilization?

6. Populist politicians have often accused the Fed of being run by bankers for the benefit of bankers — in particular, of deliberately raising interest rates to increase bank profits. What do you think is the critical flaw in this argument?

7. In December of 1983, Milton Friedman showed a graph for 1980–1983 purporting to show a close association between changes in *M*1 and changes in nominal GNP 3 months later.[25] Explain how this evidence either supports or undermines Friedman's recommendation that the Fed not use monetary policies to stabilize the economy.

8. Explain why "Simons advocated a system in which all financial wealth would be held in equity form, with no fixed money contracts, so that no institution that was not a bank could create effective money substitutes."[26]

9. Explain the economic logic behind the following argument:

   *Unemployment would be low when inflation was high only as long as the high rate of inflation was unexpected.*[27]

10. Explain this 1982 remark by Lyle Gramley, a Federal Reserve Board governor, regarding proposals that the Fed target real interest rates: "We observe only nominal interest rates and then infer what real interest rates might be by guessing the price expectations of borrowers."[28] (Be sure to define real interest rates.)

11. How do new classical economists explain the rise in the unemployment rate to 10 percent in 1982?

12. On October 22, 1987, a celebrity economist recommended that monetary policy be gauged by the ratio of $M1$ to the monetary base $B$, with $M1$ a proxy for money demand and $B$ for money supply.[29] When, as in September and October of 1987, $B$ grew faster than $M1$, the ratio $M1/B$ fell, and he recommended that the Fed "tighten up" because money supply was growing faster than demand. Can you think of any circumstance under which $M1/B$ would fall even though the economy was slipping into recession?

13. Explain why in new classical rational expectations models an increase in the money supply is just as likely to reduce output as to increase it.

14. It has been proposed that the Federal Reserve pay member banks interest on their excess reserves, total reserves, or deposits with Federal Reserve banks. How would such a plan affect bank behavior? How would it affect Fed control over monetary aggregates? Suppose that the Fed did pay interest on total bank reserves. If the Fed were to raise that interest rate, would this action ease or tighten financial markets?

15. Explain the logic behind this argument:

    *The short-run view encouraged concentration on the possibilities of raising the level of output, relative to potential, by demand expansion, even though that might be inflationary. Such a policy would not work in the long run. It worked by surprise — by the actual inflation rate exceeding what people had expected, which made employers willing to hire more workers. But people could not be surprised indefinitely; they would catch on and then the inflation would lose its power to lower unemployment.*[30]

# 25 Targeting Monetary Aggregates

*The unexpected decline and greater variability of velocity have made it more difficult for the Federal Reserve to set targets for monetary growth that are consistent with acceptable rates of growth of GNP.*

**Brian Motley, Federal Reserve Bank of San Francisco**

In this chapter we will consider a long-standing proposal that the Fed should focus its attention on a monetary aggregate, such as $M1$, and ignore interest rates, unemployment, inflation, and other economic data. We will discuss the logical underpinnings of this proposal and also examine why the Fed has resisted implementing it. We begin by explaining why the Fed cannot peg both interest rates and monetary aggregates and why a policy of stabilizing interest rates is sometimes counterproductive. Then we will examine a policy of targeting monetary aggregates.

## THE CONFLICT BETWEEN INTEREST-RATE AND MONEY-SUPPLY TARGETS

The Federal Reserve can increase the nation's monetary base by purchasing securities and paying for them with Federal Reserve notes or by crediting banks with additional reserves — putting downward pressure on interest rates. The Fed can reduce the monetary base by selling some of its security holdings and either retiring Federal Reserve notes or debiting bank reserve accounts — putting upward pressure on interest rates.

Through its daily open-market operations, the Fed can set the size of the monetary base or it can set the interest rates on the securities that it is buying and selling. However, the Fed cannot peg both the monetary base and interest rates. If the Fed is committed to pegging the monetary base at a given level, then it cannot buy or sell securities to stabilize interest rates. If interest rates begin to rise, for instance, the Fed cannot buy securities to restrain interest rates, for the monetary base would then rise above its target level.

**Figure 25.1   The Fed Can Hold the Monetary Base Constant or Can Adjust the Monetary Base to Peg Interest Rates**

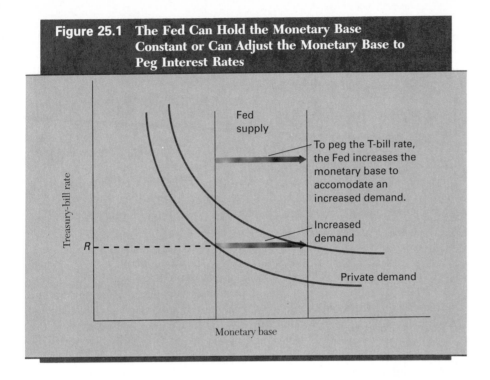

Figure 25.1 uses a demand and supply graph to illustrate this point. The demand curve is downward sloping because the demand for monetary base declines as the Treasury-bill rate increases. The cost of holding idle currency and reserves is the interest that could be earned instead by investing in Treasury bills. When the Treasury-bill rate increases, households, businesses, and banks all try to hold less of the monetary base.

Figure 25.1 shows that if the Fed holds the supply of monetary base constant when there is an increase in demand, the Treasury-bill rate will rise. Instead of pegging the monetary base, the Fed could announce that it is willing to buy or sell unlimited amounts of certain securities, such as Treasury bills, at given prices. The Fed has then pegged the nominal interest rates on these securities at the levels that correspond to these fixed prices. If the demand for monetary base increases, then, as shown in Figure 25.1, the Fed can accommodate this increased demand by using open-market purchases to supply more monetary base. If there is instead a drop in the demand for monetary base, the Fed sells Treasury bills to reduce the monetary base.

These target interest rates are pegged as long as the Fed runs out of neither will power nor securities. However, when the Fed pegs an interest rate, it relinquishes control of the monetary base, because it must adjust the supply to accommodate fluctuations in private demand. Thus the Fed can peg the monetary base or interest rates, but not both.

In practice, the Fed follows neither extreme path. It influences both the monetary base and interest rates but pegs neither. Throughout its history, the Fed has sometimes paid more attention to interest rates and has sometimes emphasized various monetary aggregates. We will now look at the advantages and drawbacks of each of these targets.

# INTEREST-RATE TARGETS

The basic argument for interest-rate targets is that these are the financial market variables that influence fundamental economic decisions: whether to spend or save, whether to invest in financial or real assets. If the Fed wants to cool off the economy by discouraging household and business spending, then it should tighten financial markets by increasing interest rates. Interest rates affect saving and borrowing and are consequently a barometer of the tightness of financial markets.

One criticism of interest-rate targets is that the Fed must deal with nominal interest rates, while private spending decisions depend on real interest rates. Some argue that the Fed has no control over real interest rates, that an expansionary monetary policy may simply increase inflation and nominal interest rates equally, leaving real interest unchanged. In Chapter 4 we saw that real interest rates are by no means constant, but it is uncertain how much control the Fed has over real interest rates.

A second criticism of interest-rate targets is that a policy of stabilizing interest rates may destabilize the economy. Consider the case in which households and businesses save less and borrow more in order to increase their spending. Their increased spending causes an economic expansion; their increased borrowing tightens financial markets and increases interest rates. If the Fed uses open-market purchases to keep interest rates from rising, then it will pump more money into an already strong economy — putting gasoline on a fire so to speak. In contrast, a policy of holding the money supply steady and allowing interest rates to rise stabilizes the economy by encouraging saving and discouraging borrowing.

Similarly, if business and household spending and borrowing decline, causing a recession, interest rates will sag. If the Fed makes no open-market transactions and allows interest rates to fall, these lower interest rates cushion the recession by encouraging borrowing and spending. If the Fed instead makes open-market sales to stabilize interest rates, these bond sales will draw money out of the economy. By withdrawing money and keeping interest rates from falling, the Fed discourages borrowing and spending, exacerbating the recession. Thus stabilizing interest rates may destabilize the economy.

In rejoinder, interest-rate enthusiasts argue that they advocate monitoring interest rates, not mechanically pegging them and ignoring the condition of the economy. Interest rates are both the channel by which monetary policy affects the economy and a barometer by which these effects can be measured. If the economy is in a recession that the Fed wants to end, then easy money and lower interest rates are appropriate.

We have seen that a policy of targeting interest rates may cause the Fed to increase the money supply during economic booms and to reduce the money supply during recessions. Some recommend that the Federal Reserve instead target the money supply. To understand the logic behind this recommendation, we need to consider whether there is a stable, systematic relationship between the money supply and economic activity.

# VELOCITY AND THE QUANTITY THEORY

Classical economists assumed that there is a close link between a nation's money supply and the nominal value of its transactions. In the early 1900s the great U.S. economist Irving Fisher observed that in every transaction the buyer exchanges a quantity of money equal to the price of the purchased item.[1] Applying this accounting identity to the nation as a whole, the **equation of exchange** states that

$$MV_T = P_T T \tag{25.1}$$

where $M$ is the money supply, $T$ is the number of transactions, $P_T$ is the average price of these transactions, and $V_T$ is **velocity**, the average number of times that money is exchanged during a given accounting period.

Suppose, for example, that there are $T = 500$ billion transactions a year, involving items with an average price of $P_T = \$100$. The total dollar value of these transactions is $P_T T = \$50,000$ billion. If the money supply is $M = \$1000$ billion, then velocity is

$$V_T = \frac{P_T T}{M} = \frac{\$50,000 \text{ billion}}{\$1000 \text{ billion}} = 50$$

A velocity of 50 means that, on average, a dollar is used about 50 times a year. Equivalently, a dollar is held, on average, about a week between transactions.

Fisher believed that velocity — the average number of times the money stock is exchanged — is fixed by institutional details concerning society's bill-paying habits — how often people are paid and how frequently they shop. Another prominent U.S. economist, John Burr Williams, argued that

> *Whatever cash most people have in their purses or their checking accounts they are compelled to have there in order to pay their bills when the time comes. In consequence it may be said that the velocity of circulation of most cash balances is habitually kept at the maximum figure that the ingenuity of producers and consumers can devise under the existing customs of the country concerning the frequency of pay days, salary days, rent days, and settlement days for charge accounts, and that nothing could substantially increase the velocity of circulation of such cash and deposits as actually do circulate at all in the proper meaning of the term except to make pay days come daily instead of weekly, salary and rent days weekly instead of monthly, and tax days monthly instead of yearly.[2]*

## *The Quantity Theory*

If $V_T$ is, in fact, constant, then Equation 25.1 implies that the nominal value of transactions is proportional to the money supply. Other economists reached an even stronger conclusion by replacing the dollar value of all transactions $P_T T$ in Equation 25.1 with the dollar value of a nation's gross national product (GNP) or gross domestic product (GDP), the most widely used measure of a nation's production of new goods and services. If $y$ is real gross domestic product and $P$ is an index of gross domestic product prices, their product $Py$ is nominal GDP. Rewriting Equation 25.1 with nominal GDP in place of the nominal value of all transactions, we have

$$MV = Py \qquad (25.2)$$

Velocity $V$ now measures how frequently the money supply is used for gross domestic product transactions — for purchasing newly produced goods and services.

The money supply can be measured by a variety of monetary aggregates — $M1$, $M2$, $M3$, and so on (as defined in Chapter 13). If $M1$ data are used in Equation 25.2, then velocity is usually identified as $M1$ velocity and labeled $V1$. Similarly, the use of $M2$ data yields $M2$ velocity, labeled $V2$.

If we use $M1$ (essentially cash and checkable accounts) to measure the money supply, then in 1990 the average level of the U.S. money supply during the year was approximately \$800 billion and the dollar value of U.S. gross domestic product was about \$5600 billion. $M1$ velocity was

$$V1 = \frac{Py}{M1} = \frac{\$5600 \text{ billion}}{\$800 \text{ billion}} = 7$$

On average, in 1990 the currency and checking account balances in $M1$ were used about 7 times a year for gross domestic product transactions; equivalently, $365/7 = 52$ days passed between gross domestic product transactions.

If velocity is constant, then Equation 25.2 implies that the nominal (or dollar) value of the gross domestic product is proportional to the money supply. If velocity is fixed at 7, for instance, then Equation 25.2 can be rearranged as

$$Py = 7M$$

If the money supply increases by 10 percent, from 800 to 880, then nominal GDP will increase by 10 percent also, from $7(800) = 5600$ to $7(880) = 6160$. This is a very strong assumption, which is known as the **quantity theory**: the quantity theory of money states that because velocity is constant, a change in the money supply causes a proportionate change in nominal gross domestic product.

If we also assume, as some economists do, that the economy is always at full employment, then real gross domestic product $y$ is fixed at any point in time. If both velocity $V$ and real GDP $y$ are constant, then Equation 25.2 tells us a change in the money supply causes a proportionate change in the price level. Suppose that there is a 10 percent increase in the money supply. If velocity is constant, then nominal gross domestic product must increase by 10 percent. If real gross domestic product is constant, then the only way nominal gross domestic product can increase by 10 percent is if prices increase by 10 percent.

## The Imperfect Link Between Transactions and Output

A fundamental difficulty with the quantity theory is that there is an imperfect link between transactions and production. Money is used for many more transactions than for the newly produced goods and services included in a nation's gross domestic product. The purchase of old houses, used automobiles, gold, bonds, stocks, and other existing assets involve a transfer of ownership — not production — and are not included in gross domestic product. This imperfect mesh between production and transactions means that transactions are not necessarily fixed even if there is full employment and that the velocity of asset swaps cannot be considered institutionally determined.

A comparison of U.S. gross domestic product with $M1$ gives an $M1$ velocity of about 7, suggesting that a dollar is used, on average, about once every 2 months. This estimated interval between transactions is much too long because the total value of transactions dwarfs the gross domestic product. The value of stock market transactions alone is equal to a third of GDP; foreign exchange transactions are several times GDP.

In 1989 the total value of checking account transactions was about 800 times the average balance in these accounts: the average interval between transactions was less than half a day. This rapid turnover of checking account deposits reflects the cash management of large corporations and financial institutions, not typical households. In large New York City banks, the annual transactions are more than 3000 times the average balance. For households, annual transactions are, on average, about 50 times their average checking account balances. For both households and businesses, total transactions are much larger than gross domestic product transactions, and velocity is much faster than seven transactions a year.

## Monetarism

In addition to the quantity theory, classical economists assumed that the economy is at full employment, so those people without jobs have voluntarily chosen to be unemployed, and that there is consequently little need for the nation's central bank and other government policymakers to try to stabilize the economy. With the world economy in shambles in the 1930s, the British economist John Maynard Keynes argued persuasively that much unemployment was involuntary and that, during recessions, governments should use monetary and fiscal policies to bolster employment and output.

Early interpreters of Keynes were enthusiastic about the use of fiscal policies but skeptical of the potency of monetary policy. In Keynesian models, open-market purchases by the Fed reduce interest rates, which stimulates spending. During the 1930s these linkages seemed weak. Interest rates were already very low, and entrepreneurs were so worried about sales that lower interest rates might not have made much difference anyway. Early Keynesians looked to fiscal policy (government spending and tax cuts) as the most promising means of stimulating the economy.

An important dissenter was Milton Friedman, who argued that monetary disturbances are the major cause of economic fluctuations. For this argument, he was dubbed a *monetarist*, and his views were labeled **monetarism**. In professional academic circles, he argued that money matters. In the public arena, it sounded more like only money matters.

In Friedman's early years, many economists thought that his views reflected the quantity theory, Equation 25.2, with velocity constant. For if velocity is constant, then money, and only money, causes fluctuations in nominal gross domestic product. This interpretation was enhanced by the publication of a professional paper by Friedman entitled, "The Quantity Theory of Money: A Restatement."[3]

With the passage of time, three important shifts occurred. The first was that Friedman's views became increasingly popular. More and more economists identified themselves as monetarists, and as this happened, the meaning of the term *monetarist* broadened. Monetarism meant so many different things to different people that economists wrote survey articles on "typical monetarist propositions."[4]

The second shift was that Keynesians acknowledged that, outside of deep depressions, monetary policy does affect the economy. For example, James Tobin, a leading Keynesian economist, has done the bulk of his work on monetary theory. In the 1970s and 1980s it was the Keynesians who urged the government to use monetary policy to strengthen the economy.

The third shift reflected the fact that it became increasingly apparent that the simple quantity theory was untenable. Theoretical arguments and dozens of empirical studies indicate that velocity is not constant, but rather depends on interest rates and other factors.[5]

Velocity $V = Py/M$ is the ratio of annual nominal GDP to the amount of money that people hold in those forms emcompassed by $M$. For example, suppose that the money supply is measured by $M1$ so that velocity $V1 = Py/M1$ is the ratio of annual nominal GDP to the amount of money that people hold in cash outside banks and checkable accounts. Velocity increases if, for a given level of GDP, households and businesses hold less cash and lower checking account balances; the same annual volume of transactions can be accomplished with less cash and lower checking account balances if money passes faster from hand to hand. The crucial point, neglected by Irving Fisher, is that people can choose how much money they have in their wallets, purses, cash registers, and checking accounts and can choose how rapidly they transfer money from savings accounts to checking accounts to grocery stores. Velocity is consequently not fixed by society's bill-paying habits but is determined by how much cash and checking account balances people want to hold.

The primary advantage of cash and checking accounts is that these can be used to pay for transactions; the disadvantage is that cash earns no interest and

EXAMPLE
25.1     *Velocity During Hyperinflations*

According to the simple quantity theory, velocity — the ratio of nominal gross domestic product to the money supply — is constant. Keynes argued that velocity is not constant, but rather increases when interest rates rise. Dramatic evidence of this effect occurs during rapid inflations. The nominal return on a physical asset is the income or services it yields plus its price appreciation, net of taxes and transaction costs. In a rapid inflation, physical assets have very high nominal rates of return, while cash pays no interest at all. The essence of a hyperinflation is a flight from currency, an extreme attempt to economize on money balances, which only pushes prices up even faster. During the German hyperinflation in 1922–1923, prices increased at a compounded rate of 322 percent per month. Workers were paid daily, or two or three times a day, and their children would bicycle back and forth between factories and home so that their parents' wages could be spent as soon as possible, before prices increased once again. In the Hungarian hyperinflation between August of 1945 and July of 1946, prices increased at 19,800 percent per month. At one point the government issued a 1,000,000,000,000,000,000,000-pengo note, which bought less than one U.S. penny. As the value of cash fell relative to real assets, the velocity of the Hungarian pengo increased by a factor of 300.

checking account balances earn much less interest than Treasury bills, commercial paper, and money-market funds. When interest rates increase, households and businesses economize on their money holdings because, despite the inconvenience, funds needed for transactions can be invested temporarily to earn high rates of return. As they reduce the amount of time that money is held between investments, velocity increases. In the opposite situation, when interest rates fall, the gains from active money management diminish and households and businesses allow money to sit longer in their purses, cash registers, and checking accounts. Figure 25.2 provides some empirical evidence of this relationship. In the early 1970s, Friedman accepted the evidence that velocity is affected by interest rates.[6] Friedman's subsequent policy recommendations seemed to rely less on the quantity theory and more on the classical assumption that the economy is never far from full employment.

Today there is a great diversity among monetarists. Some believe that fluctuations in velocity are sufficiently small that the quantity theory is a useful approximation. Others acknowledge that velocity does vary and is significantly related to interest rates but that these variations are predictable. While acknowledging that a change in the money supply does not automatically cause a proportionate change in nominal gross domestic product, they argue that the effects are at least predictable.

Some monetarists make the classical assumption that the economy is always at or near full employment — so that changes in the money supply affect prices

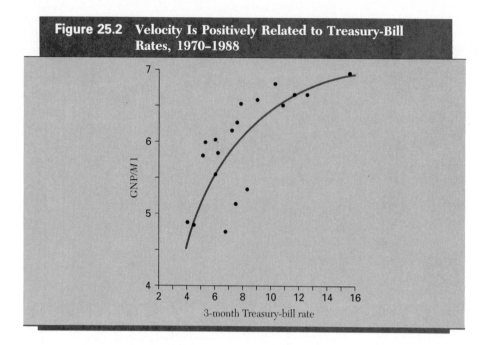

**Figure 25.2**   **Velocity Is Positively Related to Treasury-Bill Rates, 1970–1988**

but not output. Others believe that changes in the money supply affect both output and prices, at least in the short run. Figure 25.3 is a stylized sketch to assist our understanding of these linkages.

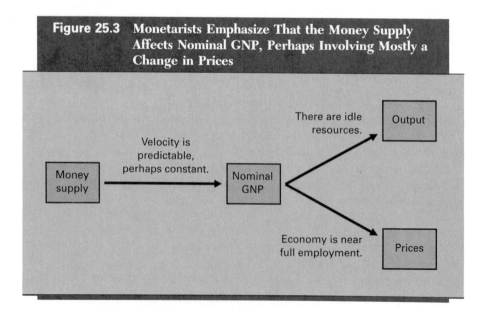

**Figure 25.3**   **Monetarists Emphasize That the Money Supply Affects Nominal GNP, Perhaps Involving Mostly a Change in Prices**

# THE CLASSICAL LINK BETWEEN MONEY AND INFLATION

**Inflation** is a sustained rise in the price level, which is often measured by the annual rate of change in the consumer price index (CPI). Inflation is often associated with rapid increases in the money supply. Nobel Laureate Milton Friedman said, plainly enough, "Inflation is always and everywhere a monetary phenomenon." The economic logic linking money and inflation can be found in classical analysis by assuming full employment and institutionally determined velocity. The simple quantity theory equation (Equation 25.2 on page 748) can be rewritten as

$$P = \left(\frac{V}{y}\right) M \tag{25.3}$$

If, as classical economists assumed, velocity $V$ and output $y$ are fixed in the short run, then the price level $P$ depends solely on the money supply. Government spending, budget deficits, militant unions, and oil embargoes do not affect the price level in the classical model.

Money is said to be "neutral" in the classical model, because the money supply only determines the price level and does not affect the level of output. A 10 percent increase in the money supply raises the level of prices by 10 percent; a 10 percent reduction in the money supply reduces the price level by 10 percent. In either situation, employment and output stay at their full-employment levels.

Classical economists acknowledged that, as time passes, there may be gradual changes in velocity (due to the evolution of society's bill-paying habits) and in full-employment output (due to changes in the nation's work force, capital stock, and technology). The percentage change in prices — the rate of inflation — depends on the rate of increase in the money supply relative to the rate of growth of velocity and the rate of growth of output:

$$\%\Delta P = \%\Delta M + \%\Delta V - \%\Delta y \tag{25.4}$$

If, for example, output grows at 2 percent a year and improvements in society's bill-paying habits increase velocity by 3 percent a year, then a 5 percent rate of money growth implies a 6 percent rate of inflation:

$$\%\Delta P = 5\% + 3\% - 2\% = 6\%$$

and a 10 percent money growth implies an 11 percent rate of inflation:

$$\%\Delta P = 10\% + 3\% - 2\% = 11\%$$

Summarizing, in classical models, with full employment and institutionally determined velocity, the level of the money supply determines the price level, and the rate of growth of the money supply relative to the rates of growth of velocity and output determine the rate of inflation.

## Short-Run Correlations

Figure 25.4 shows some annual data on the rate of inflation and the rate of growth of $M1$. There is not much correlation between the two. In years when $M1$ has increased by 4 to 6 percent, the rate of inflation has been anywhere from 3 to 11 percent. Figure 25.5 shows a similar conspicuous lack of correlation between the rate of increase in the monetary base and the rate of inflation. Evidently, the current rate of inflation depends on more than the current rate of change in the money supply.

## The Long Run

In the classical model, the explanation of inflation is quite simple — too simple, it turns out. The classical link between money and inflation is, like most classical propositions, more appropriate for the long run than for the short run. When Friedman said that inflation is always and everywhere a monetary phenomenon, he did not mean that literally every jog in the consumer price index was due to a corresponding wiggle in the money supply. Instead, he meant that major inflations, involving rapid and sustained price increases, are generally accompanied by rapid and sustained increases in the money supply. This long-run argument is reasonable. If the money supply grows at 20 percent per year for several years, then (apply the quantity theory equation $MV = Py$) either output must grow rapidly, velocity must fall rapidly, or prices must increase rapidly.

In the short run, some or all of these three things may happen — but not in the long run. Output can increase very rapidly as an economy emerges from a recession, but the long-run growth of output is limited by a society's resources. It is difficult to imagine real output growing at 20 percent per year forever. Similarly, velocity does fluctuate considerably in the short run, but it is hard to imagine it falling by 20 percent per year forever. This leaves prices. If the money supply grows by 20 percent per year, year after year, it is almost certain that there will be rapid inflation.

Conversely, if the money supply consistently grows at 2 percent annually, then a rapid, sustained inflation requires a large, continual decline in output or a rapid, continuing increase in velocity (so that money circulates progressively faster). Output can decline substantially in the short run and velocity can increase considerably, but long-run movements sufficient to sustain a triple- or even double-digit inflation are implausible. The higher the rate of inflation and the longer it persists, the more certain it is that the money supply is increasing rapidly.

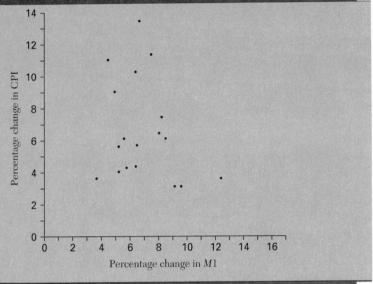

**Figure 25.4    Annual Percentage Changes in *M*1 and the Consumer Price Index, 1970–1988**

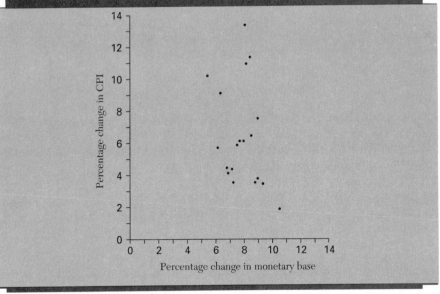

**Figure 25.5    Annual Percentage Changes in the Monetary Base and the Consumer Price Index, 1970–1988**

# MONEY-SUPPLY TARGETS

Milton Friedman has long recommended that the Fed ignore the economy and keep the money supply growing at a steady annual rate — for example, that the Fed focus its efforts on keeping M2 growing at 3 percent to 5 percent per year. Because of his close association with monetarism, such rules — whether advocated by Friedman or by others — are often identified as monetarist policy recommendations.

The specific numbers used in these rules can be rationalized in terms of the quantity theory equation,

$$MV = Py$$

which implies that the percentage increase in nominal gross domestic product $Py$ is equal to the percentage increase in the money supply $M$ plus the percentage increase in velocity $V$:

$$\%\Delta(Py) = \%\Delta M + \%\Delta V \qquad (25.5)$$

If the Fed could accurately predict the percentage change in velocity, then it could use Equation 25.5 to determine the percentage increase in the money supply (its intermediate target) consistent with a desired increase in nominal GDP. For example, a 4 percent increase in the money supply and a 3 percent increase in velocity would give a 7 percent increase in nominal gross domestic product.

If real gross domestic product can be counted on to increase at a given rate, then the Fed will know how much of the target increase in nominal gross domestic product will be real and how much will be inflation. In particular, Equation 25.4 showed that the quantity theory equation implies that the percentage increase in prices is approximately equal to the percentage increase in the money supply plus the percentage increase in velocity minus the percentage increase in real gross domestic product:

$$\%\Delta P = \%\Delta M + \%\Delta V - \%\Delta y$$

Friedman estimated that real gross domestic product grows, on average, by about 2 to 3 percent per year, while M2 velocity falls, on average, by about 1 to 2 percent. Therefore, Equation 25.4 implies that a 3 to 5 percent growth in M2 is consistent with a 0 percent rate of inflation:

$$\begin{aligned}
\%\Delta M2 &= \%\Delta P + \%\Delta y - \%\Delta V2 \\
&= 0\% + (2\% \text{ to } 3\%) - (-1\% \text{ to } -2\%) \\
&= 3\% \text{ to } 5\%
\end{aligned}$$

The underlying assumptions are that velocity and real output deviate little from their long-run trend paths. Neither of these assumptions is strictly true. Velocity varies (for example, as interest rates change) and income fluctuates as the economy departs from full employment.

## The Stability of Velocity

Figure 25.6 shows the velocity of $M1$ and $M2$ up to 1980, when these monetary aggregates were redefined. Figure 25.7 shows $M1$ and $M2$ velocity using the new definitions, with data estimated back to 1970. None of these velocities has been constant, either in the short run or the long run.

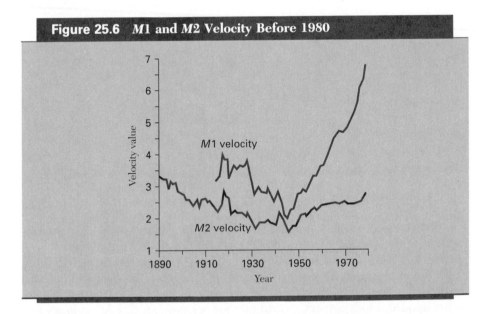

**Figure 25.6   $M1$ and $M2$ Velocity Before 1980**

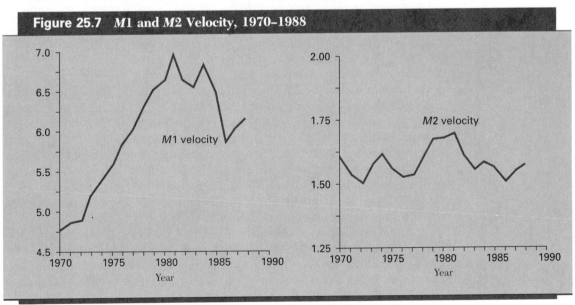

**Figure 25.7   $M1$ and $M2$ Velocity, 1970–1988**

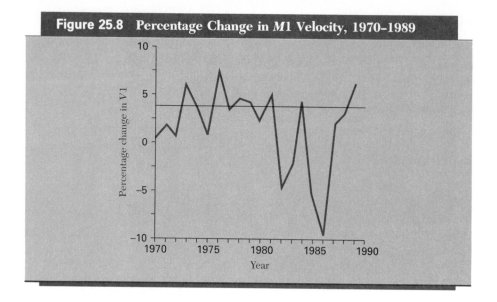

**Figure 25.8   Percentage Change in *M*1 Velocity, 1970–1989**

Milton Friedman favored *M*2 velocity in his monumental *A Monetary History of the United States, 1867–1960*, written with Anna Schwartz and published in 1963. *M*2 velocity declined markedly between 1880 and 1915 (most likely due to the explosive growth of checking accounts). Friedman argued that the long-run trend of *M*2 velocity would continue to be downward, and his recommended 3 to 5 percent growth rate for *M*2 assumes that *M*2 velocity falls by 1 to 2 percent a year. However, Figure 25.6 shows that *M*2 velocity using the pre-1980 definition did not follow a consistent long-run trend. Using the current definition of *M*2, Figure 25.7 shows that *M*2 velocity has been similarly trendless since 1970, although annual fluctuations of 3 to 5 percent have been common.

Many who follow monetary aggregates, including the Federal Reserve, focused their attention on *M*1 rather than on *M*2 in the 1970s. *M*1 velocity has been reasonably stable during some historical periods but erratic at other times. Figure 25.6 shows that *M*1 velocity was very high in the 1920s, when interest rates were high, and fell along with interest rates during the Great Depression. Between 1950 and 1980, rising interest rates lured money out of traditional checking accounts, restraining *M*1 and tripling *M*1 velocity. This 30-year upward trend was broken by sharp, unexpected declines in velocity in 1982, 1983, 1985, and 1986. These sharp breaks are shown in Figure 25.8 by an examination of the annual percentage changes in velocity.

These erratic swings in velocity undermined the credibility of a monetarist strategy. Suppose that the Fed had adopted an unwavering monetarist rule at the beginning of 1986, based on the historical 3 percent average annual increase in *M*1 velocity since 1950. Equation 25.5 implies that the predicted percentage

EXAMPLE
25.2
## The Effects of International Trade on Velocity

The quantity theory equation $MV = Py$ shows that velocity $V$ is the ratio of nominal gross domestic product $Py$ to a measure of the money supply $M$:

$$V = \frac{Py}{M}$$

Velocity is affected by economic events that alter the amount of money that people hold relative to nominal gross domestic product. Events that increase money holdings reduce velocity; events that reduce money holdings increase velocity.

The growing importance of international trade for the United States has implications for money holdings and, therefore, for velocity. Gross domestic product (GDP) is intended to monitor domestic production and consequently includes U.S. exports because these are produced in the United States but excludes imported goods because these are produced elsewhere. However, money holdings in the United States depend on imports rather than exports, because U.S. consumers need dollars to buy German cars and Japanese cameras, but German and Japanese consumers do not need dollars to buy U.S. wheat and blue jeans.

Matters are even more complicated than this because U.S. workers are paid in dollars for blue jeans that the Japanese buy with yen, and Japanese workers are paid in yen for cameras that Americans buy with dollars. The important point is that the amount of money that households and businesses want to hold depends not just on domestic production — GDP — but on the size and relative magnitudes of exports and imports. As a consequence, velocity, the ratio of GDP to money holdings, varies with exports and imports.

In 1969 U.S. imports were equal to 5.6 percent of GDP; in 1989 they were equal to 12.9 percent. In 1985 the difference between U.S. exports and imports was $+\$26.3$ billion ($+0.8$ percent of GDP); in 1987 the difference was $-112.6$ ($-2.5$ percent of GDP). Variations of this magnitude can cause substantial changes in velocity.

increase in nominal gross domestic product is 3 percentage points larger than the percentage increase in $M1$:

$$\%\Delta(Py) = \%\Delta M1 + \%\Delta V1$$
$$= \%\Delta M1 + 3\%$$

Aiming for a 6 percent increase in nominal gross domestic product (perhaps 2 percent real and 4 percent inflation), the Fed might have committed itself to a 3 percent rate of growth of $M1$.

Now what if (as actually happened) $M1$ velocity unexpectedly falls by 9 percent? This 12 percentage point error in predicting velocity means a 12 percentage point error in gross domestic product if the Fed refuses to budge from its 3 percent growth rate for $M1$. Instead of rising by 6 percent, nominal gross domestic product will fall by 6 percent:

$$\%\Delta(Py) = \%\Delta M1 + \%\Delta V1$$
$$= 3\% - 9\%$$
$$= -6\%$$

The Fed will have gotten the magnitude right and the sign wrong! In the unlikely event that this contraction only affects prices, not real output, prices will fall by 8 percent instead of rising by 4 percent — hardly consistent with price stability.

There hasn't been an 8 percent deflation in the United States since the 1930s. If nominal gross domestic product fell by 6 percent, this would no doubt involve a substantial drop in real output. There would surely be an unexpected and unwanted economic recession if the Fed adhered to an $M1$ target and $M1$ velocity dropped unexpectedly, as it did in 1982, 1983, 1985, and 1986. If, on the other hand, $M1$ velocity increases unexpectedly, as it did in 1989, then strict adherence to an $M1$ target will cause an unintentional increase in the rate of inflation. The erratic behavior of velocity is a primary reason why the Fed has resisted monetarist advice to target a monetary aggregate and ignore the economy.

## Is the Money Supply Controllable?

For a monetary aggregate, such as $M1$, to be a useful intermediate target, not only must there be a stable relationship between it and the Fed's objective, such as the rate of inflation, but the Fed must be able to hit its intermediate target with reasonable accuracy. The Fed cannot ensure a constant growth rate of $M1$ merely by maintaining a constant growth rate for the monetary base. During the 1970s, the annual growth rate of the monetary base was never more than 1.5 percent above or below the average growth rate for the decade, yet there were substantial fluctuations in monetary aggregates, output, and inflation.[7] Figures 13.2 through 13.6 show that there has been only the loosest connection between annual changes in the monetary base and in $M1$ and $M2$. If there is a stronger relationship, it involves considerable lags.

Monetary aggregates are influenced not only by the Fed but also by the economic decisions of households, businesses, and financial institutions and not only by current policies but also by past policies and events too. It takes a considerable amount of time for an increase in the monetary base to cycle through the banking system and cause an eventual change in monetary aggregates. There are lots of slippages and external influences, substantial errors and delays, along the way. The very same errors-and-lags argument that was used in the preceding chapter to explain why the Fed may not be able to fine-tune the

**EXAMPLE**
**25.3**

### The Monetary Base and Monetary Aggregates

Chapter 13 used a deposit-multiplier model to explain how, with fractional reserve banking, deposits and monetary aggregates are multiples of the monetary base $B$. Thus

$$M1 = mB$$

where the money multiplier $m$ depends on bank reserves relative to deposits, currency outside banks relative to deposits, and transaction accounts relative to other deposits. The percentage change in $M1$ is approximately equal to the percentage change in the deposit multiplier plus the percentage change in the monetary base:

$$\%\Delta M1 = \%\Delta m + \%\Delta B$$

If the money multiplier $m$ is constant, then a change in the monetary base causes a given proportional change in $M1$. However, the money multiplier is not constant. It changes as banks decide to hold more or less reserves and as households and businesses shift funds among currency, transaction accounts, and other deposits.

For instance, the Federal Reserve Bank of St. Louis (which has a consistently monetarist research group) reported that the monetary base grew at a 7.5 percent annual rate during the first 7 months of 1982 and at a 7.4 percent annual rate during the next 3 months.* If the money multiplier $m$ had been constant, or had grown at a constant rate, during this period, $M1$ would have grown at a constant rate too. In fact, the money multiplier declined at a 4.5 percent annual rate during the first 7 months of the year and increased at a 5.8 percent annual rate during the next 3 months, giving very different growth rates for $M1$ over these two periods:

Jan. 1982–July 1982:   $\%\Delta M1 = \%\Delta m + \%\Delta B = -4.5\% + 7.5\% = 3.0\%$

July 1982–Oct. 1982:   $\%\Delta M1 = \%\Delta m + \%\Delta B = +5.8\% + 7.4\% = 13.2\%$

*Dallas S. Batten, U.S. Financial Data, *Federal Reserve Bank of St. Louis, March 25, 1983, p. 1.*

economy also implies that the Fed may not be able to fine-tune monetary aggregates.[8]

In December of 1981, Anthony Solomon, respected president of the Federal Reserve Bank of New York, speculated that "we may already be nearing the point where the Federal Reserve can influence the growth of these broad measures only indirectly by first influencing the behavior of the economy itself."[9]

A most provocative reversal: the economy may be an intermediate target for monetary aggregates rather than the other way around! Monetarists advise the Fed to stabilize the economy by stabilizing monetary aggregates, and the Fed responds that, as a practical matter, the only way it can get monetary aggregates to grow at a steady rate is somehow to keep the economy growing at a steady pace. It is apparently at least as difficult to stabilize monetary aggregates as it is to stabilize the gross domestic product.

## A Plethora of Monetary Targets

Since 1975, the Fed has regularly announced annual target growth rates for most monetary aggregates. The Full Employment and Balanced Growth Act of 1978 (also called the Humphrey-Hawkins Act) requires the Fed to report semiannually to Congress on its monetary targets. Each February the Fed announces its monetary targets for the current year, using a 1-year period that begins in the fourth quarter of the preceding year and ends in the fourth quarter of the current year. These targets are ranges, such as a rate of growth of $M2$ that is between 6 and 9 percent. In July the Fed informs Congress of its progress in achieving these objectives, its intentions to maintain or alter these targets for the remainder of the year, and its tentative targets for the following year.

The Fed is not required to hit its targets and frequently doesn't. Because the Fed does not directly control monetary aggregates, it uses an empirical model to help predict how its monetary policies will affect monetary aggregates. This model has frequently gone awry, causing the Fed to miss its targets by substantial amounts. In the 11 years from 1976 through 1986 (after which the Fed stopped targeting $M1$), the Fed hit its target range for $M1$ only twice, in 1976 and 1984.

Because of the imperfections of all monetary aggregates as intermediate targets, there is considerable debate among monetarists about which aggregate should be targeted. Edward Shaw, an advocate of a constant-money-growth rule, freely acknowledged in the following statement the difficulties of selecting a money supply target:

> If you suspect that growth in money was under tight restraint, you can tailor a definition to your suspicion. If you prefer to think that restraint was mild, you can be right again — with a different definition. . . .
> The "supply of money" that central banks manipulate, that people hold most of the time and spend once in a while, that economists investigate is not, then, a simple concept. It can be a figure so transformed in the statistical beauty parlor as to be hardly recognizable by its closest friends.[10]

Friedman chose $M2$. Shaw picked $M1$. After Arthur Burns became chairman of the Fed in 1970, he converted from $M1$ to $M5$ (which is closest to today's $M3$). Others prefer the monetary base.[11]

There are several alternative targets, and it does make a difference which target is selected, because forcing one monetary aggregate to grow at a constant

EXAMPLE
25.4

## Interpreting Shifts Among Monetary Aggregates

Portfolio shifts can cause monetary aggregates to move in divergent ways, giving potentially misleading signals about the condition of financial markets and the economy. For instance, because many of the transaction accounts in $M1$ pay interest, some of the money in these accounts is kept there for savings, not for bill paying. On the other hand, money-market funds and cash-management accounts, which are not included in $M1$, can be used to pay bills, and some of the money in these accounts is for bill paying, not savings. This blurring of the distinction between transaction and savings balances makes it difficult to interpret movements in monetary aggregates. Funds may switch from one type of account to another in response to changes in interest rates or the features of these accounts, causing changes in monetary aggregates, without reflecting any change in spending behavior and, thus, in gross domestic product.

Here is another example. As part of their banking relationship, many businesses maintain *compensating balances* in their corporate checking accounts in return for lines of credit and cash-management services. These funds are different from other checking account balances in that they are not normally used to make transactions. In January of 1988, the Fed surveyed 60 major banks to learn why there had been a sharp decline in checking account balances during the preceding month. They found that many corporations had held excessive compensating balances earlier in the year and in December were allowed to reduce their checking account balances.* This shift was of little or no economic significance, but the accompanying drop in $M1$ might have provoked open-market purchases by a more doctrinaire Fed.

Seemingly trivial differences in how business investment is financed also can cause monetary aggregates to diverge. If a business borrows money from a bank that has raised funds by selling repurchase agreements to an insurance company, these repurchase agreements are included in $M2$. If the bank instead raises money to loan the business by selling large certificates of deposit to the insurance company, these CDs are put in $M3$. If the business sells commercial paper directly to the insurance company, the commercial paper is included in $L$. If it sells bonds to the insurance company, the bonds are ignored completely. These very similar transactions have virtually identical macroeconomic consequences for interest rates, employment, and prices but very different effects on monetary aggregates.

*Bondweek, *February 22, 1988.*

rate does not ensure that others will. Example 25.4 explains how unexpected shifts of funds by households, businesses, and banks often cause one monetary aggregate to grow faster than the Fed intends, while another grows slower.

When this happens, the Fed must use subjective judgment in deciding whether it will respond to these changes and in assessing which of these divergent monetary aggregates it will believe.

In dynamic, innovative financial markets, controlling one monetary aggregate almost ensures that new financial assets will develop and expand. When the government tried to restrain bank notes issued by state-chartered banks after the Civil War, checking accounts took their place. The Fed's efforts to restrain traditional checking accounts in the 1970s fueled an explosion of checklike accounts. These kinds of financial market innovations increase the volume of transactions that can be carried out with a given monetary aggregate and, hence, increase velocity. For example, the introduction of NOW accounts reduced the appeal of traditional checking accounts and thereby increased $M1$ velocity, undermining an $M1$ target rule. Charles Goodhart, a senior economist at the Bank of England (which currently watches its $M5$), offered Goodhart's law: "Any definition of money which becomes an official target will lose all relationship with events in the real economy within 2 years."[12]

New near-moneys continue to be developed, and attempts to control some are sure to spawn others. Some new moneys and near-moneys, such as electronic payments systems with overdraft privileges, will be exceedingly difficult to monitor. In a rapidly changing world, an up-to-date monetary rule is akin to the economics professor who gives the same exam year after year but changes the answers each year. In the same spirit, the appropriate monetary rule might be "have the money supply grow at a constant rate year after year but change the definition of the money supply each year." If so, is this really very different from a discretionary policy?

Herbert Stein, an economic advisor to several Republican presidents, has jokingly said that monetarism is "the theory that there is a stable and predictable relation between the price level as effect and the supply of money as cause. This theory has firm empirical support if the definition of the money supply is allowed to vary in an unstable and unpredictable way."[13] The continuing challenge for monetarism is to find a stable definition of the money supply that the Fed can control and that is reliably related to the Fed's ultimate objectives.

## Destabilizing Policies?

We've seen a variety of cases in which the Fed might take regrettable actions if it myopically pegs a particular monetary aggregate. Here is one more example. During an economic boom, inflation reduces the purchasing power of currency, encouraging people to hold less money and buy more commodities before prices go higher still. The excess unwanted currency passes from hand to hand like a hot potato as consumers try to spend it before it depreciates further. We saw in Chapter 4 that an increase in the expected rate of inflation tends to raise nominal interest rates. If market interest rates increase more than the interest rates on checking accounts, funds will flow out of checking accounts, causing $M1$ to decline. If the Fed ignores the inflation and stabilizes $M1$, it will make open-market purchases, expanding the monetary base during an inflation — gasoline on the fire.

A final consideration is that economic events seldom affect all financial markets equally. Thus it is often useful to have specific, detailed policies directed at particular financial markets or institutions. Before becoming Fed chairman, Paul Volcker argued that

> *There have been a number of occasions in the 1970s when the Federal Reserve had to pay the closest possible attention to particular financial problems and to the potential vulnerability of various credit markets. The recurrent concerns . . . about the capacity of thrift institutions to perform their role as intermediaries between savers and the mortgage market is one example. The potential disturbances growing out of the Penn Central Railroad and the Franklin and the Herstatt Bank affairs are another class of examples. The strain on the municipal bond markets and the concerns about the rising level of losses commercial banks were taking on loans a year or so ago are other cases in point. Their problems had to be dealt with — actually or potentially — by techniques that cannot be encompassed by any simple monetary rule.[14]*

The most reasonable conclusion for this chapter is that there is no simple, perfect policy for all times and all places. Doggedly pegging interest rates, $M1$, or some other specific target will, in some circumstances, be a poor policy. Instead of myopically focusing on one bit of data and ignoring everything else, it is more logical to monitor many data.

The Fed is well aware that it is difficult to control monetary aggregates and that these can give an incomplete and possibly misleading description of the state of financial markets and the economy. It instead follows a rather eclectic course, monitoring not only interest rates and monetary aggregates but also output, employment, inflation, the balance of payments, and election returns. If the economy is in a serious recession, which the Fed wants to soften, then easy money is called for. Rather than stubbornly pegging an interest rate or monetary aggregate as the economy falls apart, the Fed makes substantial open-market purchases, increasing the monetary base, reducing interest rates, and stimulating spending.

It tries to keep monetary aggregates and the economy growing at a reasonably steady pace, but it is not slavishly tied to any particular aggregate or to an eternally fixed growth rate. The Fed exercises subjective judgment and has made mistakes. In the next chapter we will review the details of Fed policy since World War II. You will see that it has been tolerably successful in achieving its objectives, although it remains an unsettled issue whether it would have been more successful following other operating procedures.

EXAMPLE
25.5

## The Bank of Japan's Monetary Projections

Since July of 1978, Japan's central bank, the Bank of Japan, has made quarterly announcements of its projected growth rate of a monetary aggregate called $M2$ + CDs. $M2$ is a broad monetary aggregate that includes savings deposits in addition to the checkable deposits included in $M1$. Large CDs are part of $M3$, rather than $M2$, although an active secondary market for large CDs makes them as liquid as many of the funds that are included in $M2$. The Bank of Japan has consequently chosen to include large CDs with $M2$.

Some observers have argued that the Bank of Japan has been more successful than the U.S. Federal Reserve in meeting its monetary aggregate projections. However, such comparisons are misleading. The Bank of Japan projects only a single aggregate, while the Fed projects several aggregates. Because monetary aggregates do not move in locked step, it is necessarily more difficult to meet several projections than it is to meet one projection.

In addition, the Bank of Japan's projected growth rates are stated as annual percentages but only extend one quarter into the future, as they compare $M2$ + CDs in the coming quarter with $M2$ + CDs, three quarters earlier. Thus, three-fourths of the year to which the projection relates has already occurred. Finally, the Bank of Japan has repeatedly emphasized that these monetary projections are predictions, not targets, and that the bank does not automatically react to differences between the actual and predicted values of $M2$ + CDs. The accuracy of the bank's projections may consequently be evidence of their short-run forecasting ability rather than their targeting skill.

The U.S. Federal Reserve, in contrast, makes an annual announcement of ranges for several monetary aggregates for the coming year. The Fed's announcement is made in February and involves a comparison of the fourth quarter of that year to the fourth quarter of the previous year. Thus the Fed's projections are essentially 9 to 10 months into the future, rather than the Bank of Japan's 3 months into the future. During the period October 1979 to October 1982, the Fed's monetary ranges were treated as targets, and the Fed routinely responded to differences between actual and targeted monetary growth rates.

Since early 1983, the Fed's monetary ranges have become projections, rather than firm targets, comparable to the Bank of Japan's projections. In order to equalize the horizons, a 1992 study examined the Fed's one-quarter ahead projections of various monetary aggregates that are published in the *Records of Policy Action of the FOMC* approximately 6 weeks after the FOMC meeting at which the projections are made.* The primary difference between these Fed projections and the Bank of Japan's projections is that the Fed does not make a public announcement until 6 weeks after the projections are made.

*Michael Hutchison and John P. Judd, "Central Bank Secrecy and Money Surprises: International Evidence," Review of Economics and Statistics, February 1992, pp. 135–145.

The 1992 study concluded that the Bank of Japan's one-quarter projections of $M2$ + CDs and the Fed's one-quarter projections of $M2$ were equally accurate. This study also found that the Bank of Japan's monetary projections were of little use to private analysts, in the sense that forecasts of $M2$ + CDs using the Bank of Japan's projections in addition to other economic data available at the time were no better than forecasts that did not take into account the Bank of Japan's projections. In the United States, in contrast, the Fed's projections would have significantly improved money growth forecasts, had these projections been available to the public. Thus we have the ironic conclusion that Japan's central bank announces projections that are of little value, while the U.S. central bank delays announcing useful projections.

## SUMMARY

The quantity theory assumes that velocity, the ratio of nominal gross domestic product to some measure of the money supply, is constant — implying that gross domestic product moves proportionately with the money supply. However, the opportunity cost of holding money is the interest that can be earned on other assets; therefore, increases in interest rates tend to reduce money holdings and increase velocity. Classical economists generally assumed not only that velocity is constant but that the economy is at full employment. Monetarists are a diverse group, with varying degrees of faith in these two classical assumptions.

Inflation is a continuing increase in the price level. In a classical model (with full employment and institutionally determined velocity), the level of the money supply determines the price level, and the rate of growth of the money supply determines the rate of inflation. In particular, the rate of inflation is equal to the rate of growth of the money supply plus the rate of growth of velocity minus the rate of growth of output, and the last two are assumed to be predetermined. Inflation in the long run is a largely monetary phenomenon in that a sustained rapid monetary growth will almost certainly cause inflation. However, there is only a loose relationship between money and inflation in the short run because both output and velocity can vary considerably from year to year.

A policy of stabilizing interest rates may destabilize the economy. If, for example, an increase in business and consumer borrowing and spending causes an economic expansion, interest rates will rise. If the Fed uses open-market purchases to keep interest rates from rising, then this increase in the monetary base will fuel an already strong economy.

Mechanically pegging some measure of the money supply is not an infallible policy either, for a variety of reasons. Velocity is not sufficiently stable. Lags and uncertainties make it difficult to control monetary aggregates. Shifts among assets cause monetary aggregates to move in divergent directions, giving contradictory signals about the state of financial markets and the economy. In practice, the Fed monitors not only interest rates and monetary aggregates but many other economic indicators before deciding whether monetary ease or restraint is appropriate.

# IMPORTANT TERMS

equation of exchange
inflation
monetarism

quantity theory
velocity

# EXERCISES

1. A certain economy has 100 billion transactions a year, involving items with an average price of $120. If the money supply is $M = \$1$ trillion, what is the value of velocity? On average, how long is a dollar held between transactions?

2. An economy has a money supply $M = \$100$ billion and 1 billion transactions a week, involving items with an average price of $100. What is the value of velocity? On average, how long is a dollar held between transactions?

3. What will the rate of inflation be if the real gross domestic product increases by 2 percent, velocity increases by 2 percent, and the money supply increases by 4 percent?

4. The money supply is $1 trillion, and velocity is constant at 6. According to the quantity theory, what will happen to nominal gross domestic product if the money supply increases by 5 percent? If the economy is at full employment, how much of this increase in nominal gross domestic product will reflect an increase in output, and how much will simply be an increase in prices?

5. The money supply is $1 trillion, and nominal gross domestic product is $5 trillion. What is the value of velocity? What will happen to nominal gross domestic product if velocity is constant and the money supply falls by 10 percent? What if both velocity and real gross domestic product are constant?

6. If nominal gross domestic product is $5 trillion and the money supply is $400 billion, what is the value of velocity? How many days, on average, is money held between GDP transactions? If the money supply increases by 4 percent, by what percentage (approximately) will

   a. Nominal gross domestic product increase if velocity is constant?
   b. Prices increase if velocity and real gross domestic product are both constant?

7. For many years Milton Friedman recommended a 3 to 5 percent annual growth of $M2$. Why might this specific range be consistent with a 0 percent rate of inflation? If $M2$ velocity is constant and real gross domestic product increases by 2 percent per year, what will happen to prices if $M2$ increases by 3 to 5 percent per year?

8. Explain the important omission from this statement in a publication by the Federal Reserve Bank of Cleveland: "The quantity theory of money states that over the long run, prices will rise in proportion to the rise in the money supply."[15]

9. During the 1945–1946 Hungarian hyperinflation, prices increased 19,800 percent per month. How fast must prices increase each day, compounded daily, to increase by 19,800 percent in a 30-day month?

10. From 1966 through 1969, the rate of inflation in Israel averaged 4 percent per year. The inflation record for 1970–1981 is shown in the table that follows.

| Year | Inflation Rate (%) |
|------|-------------------|
| 1970 | 8 |
| 1971 | 13 |
| 1972 | 14 |
| 1973 | 21 |
| 1974 | 35 |
| 1975 | 37 |
| 1976 | 27 |
| 1977 | 43 |
| 1978 | 55 |
| 1979 | 82 |
| 1980 | 128 |
| 1981 | 126 |

The real Israeli money supply fell from 4 billion shekels in 1973 to 1.3 billion shekels in 1981. How is it mathematically possible for inflation to increase while the real money supply is decreasing? What do you suppose happened to velocity during this time period?

11. Explain how the price level can increase even while the rate of inflation is decreasing.

12. What will the rate of inflation be if the money supply increases by 5 percent, velocity falls by 2 percent, and real output increases by 3 percent?

13. The quantity theory assumes that velocity is a constant, depending essentially on institutional factors. Explain how each of the following situations would affect velocity, as measured by the monetary base and gross domestic product.

    a. An increase in the use of credit cards
    b. Checkable saving deposits
    c. An increase in interest rates

14. What explanations can you provide for the empirical evidence that $M1$ velocity moves pro-cyclically (increasing in booms, falling in recessions) and also has greatly increased over the past 30 years? In the 1974–1975 recession, $M1$ velocity actually increased. What might explain this unusual event?

15. Between August of 1945 and July of 1946, the number of Hungarian pengos (the unit of Hungarian currency) in circulation increased by a factor of 12,000,000,000,000,000,000,000,000, while the price level increased by a factor of 4,000,000,000,000,000,000,000,000,000,000. Do you think the real money supply increased or decreased? Why do you suppose prices increased either faster or slower than the money supply?

16. In October of 1985, an economist at the Federal Reserve Bank of Cleveland wrote that "the rapid growth of $M1$ typically indicates a strong economy. The recent growth of $M1$, however, has been associated with an unusually weak economy."[16] What happened to $M1$ velocity during this period?

17. If the Fed keeps $M1$ on a steady target, while $M1$ velocity increases unexpectedly, what will happen to nominal gross domestic product?

18. If the Fed follows an eclectic approach, hoping to stabilize nominal gross domestic product, what will it do when $M1$ velocity declines?

19. The quantity theory assumes that velocity is a constant, depending essentially on institutional factors. If there is an increased use of credit cards, what do you predict will happen to velocity, as measured by the monetary base and gross domestic product? Explain your reasoning.

20. Before the Fed's 1980 revisions, $M2$ included savings accounts in commercial banks but excluded saving accounts in savings and loan associations; $M3$ included savings accounts in both institutions. How do you suppose $M2$ velocity was affected by the relatively rapid growth of savings and loan associations in the 1950s and 1960s?

21. Before 1980, $M1$ included traditional checking accounts in commercial banks but excluded NOW accounts and other checklike accounts. These other accounts were included in $M2$ or $M3$, depending on whether they were offered by commercial banks or thrift institutions. How did the shift of funds from commercial bank checking accounts to checklike accounts affect $M1$ velocity?

22. Before 1980, money-market funds were not included in the Fed's monetary aggregates. How did the shift of funds in the 1970s from commercial bank savings accounts (included in $M2$) to money-market funds affect $M2$ velocity?

23. In January of 1986, Prudential-Bache's director of economics and fixed income research predicted that "$M1$ could explode during the first few months of the year as a result of the elimination of minimum deposit requirements for Super NOW accounts."[17] What effect would such an explosion have on $M1$ velocity? What effect would you predict on gross domestic product if the funds going into super NOW accounts come from time and savings accounts?

24. Is it contradictory for Milton Friedman to argue that money matters, but that we shouldn't use monetary policies to stabilize the economy? Why did he recommend that $M2$ grow at 3 to 5 percent a year, rather than 0 percent?

25. Write a one-paragraph essay explaining why you agree or disagree with this analogy:

*[Nonmonetarists argue that] whether monetary growth is excessive and inflationary can be judged only in relation to the behavior of many other indicators, such as interest rates and unemployment.*

*To use an analogy, there is generally a fairly predictable relation between the amount of gas the driver feeds to his car and the speed of the car. But it does not follow that the safest way to drive a car is to use a constant pressure on the accelerator. . . .*[18]

26. Congress authorized nationwide NOW accounts beginning on January 1, 1981. An Associated Press news story reported that funds pouring into these accounts during the first week of that year caused $M1$ to increase by $11.6 billion, to $417.6 billion. The story went on to report that business loans fell by $2 billion that week "in line with analysts' expectations for a slowing in monetary expansion as the central bank's tight-credit policy of recent weeks, aimed at cooling inflation, restrains economic growth."[19] How could a rapid growth in $M1$ possibly be consistent with a tight-credit policy?

27. Tell the reasoning behind the following quotation, and explain why you either agree or disagree.

*Sometimes Friedman and his followers seem to be saying: "We don't know what money is, but whatever it is, its stock should grow steadily at 3 to 4 percent per year."*[20]

28. Give the logic behind this quotation, and explain why you either agree or disagree with it.

*Perhaps we should abolish the Federal Reserve Board. Its functions could be handled by a new bureau of the Treasury, patterned on the Bureau of Alcohol, Tobacco and Firearms. Certainly monetary policy can be as dangerous as booze, butts and guns. . . .*

*[We could] require the Fed to slow money-supply growth steadily until it reached a rate compatible with the economy's ability to grow. If that were the law of the land all we would need would be a few capable clerks.*[21]

29. Explain the quotation from Brian Motley at the beginning of this chapter.

30. In 1982 congressional testimony on a constitutional amendment intended to compel Congress to balance the federal budget each year, Federal Reserve chairman Paul Volcker spoke of "the difficulty of attempting to write a constitutional provision to induce discipline otherwise lacking, a provision that will serve us in fair weather and foul, and in economic circumstances that can be only dimly foreseen."[22] Do you think that he would have supported or opposed a constitutional amendment requiring the Federal Reserve to keep M1 growing at 3 to 5 percent per year? Put yourself in his place, and write a 250-word essay defending your support or opposition to an M1 amendment.

31. In 1986, households and businesses shifted billions of dollars from saving accounts to checking accounts. If you were chairman of the Fed, would you predict that such a development would raise or lower interest rates?

32. The Federal Reserve has been announcing targets for monetary aggregates since 1975 but has generally used judgment rather than precise rules when monetary aggregates deviate from these targets. Between 1979 and 1982, the Fed paid more attention to its monetary targets, as explained by a Federal Reserve economist:

*Before 1979, the FOMC did not react automatically to short-run deviations of M1 from target. After the [1979] change in operating procedure, the FOMC continued to monitor the same set of economic indicators, but its automatic reaction was to resist short-run deviations of M1 from the target.*[23]

Would open-market purchases or sales be in order if M1 began to exceed its target range?

33. "Until 1982, the M1 aggregate was considered to be the primary focus of the Federal Open Market Committee (FOMC), which had relied on the aggregate with an increasing degree of certitude through the 1970s."[24] What is the FOMC? Why might it focus more on M1 than on M2? Look at Figure 25.8 and speculate about why the FMOC paid increasingly less attention to M1 after 1982.

34. Why do you suppose that it is generally easier for the Fed to hit a target for the federal funds rate than for M1?

35. Write a 250-word paragraph explaining and clarifying this argument by a Federal Reserve Board governor:

*If the [FMOC] acted immediately to counter an observed change in money growth, and the change then proved to be temporary, the action could be destabilizing and require a subsequent offsetting adjustment. . . . such attempts at fine tuning could produce perverse results.*[25]

only 1.2 percent. Throughout this period, the postwar economy was very strong. Large wartime incomes and the forced saving caused by rationing had left citizens with considerable financial assets and pent-up demands for houses, automobiles, and household appliances. Businesses also were big spenders as they built the factories and equipment to satisfy these consumer demands.

## An Engine of Inflation

By keeping interest rates very low, the Fed encouraged this economic boom. Most households and businesses did not want to hold securities paying 1 percent interest when the prices of consumer goods, housing, plant, and equipment were rising rapidly. They sold their securities to the Fed, and the money that the Fed used to buy these securities increased the nation's monetary base.

The Fed correctly recognized that pegging low interest rates fueled the economic boom and inflation, and it struggled for the freedom to switch to a more restraining monetary policy. The Fed raised margin requirements on stock purchases to 100 percent, thereby eliminating loans for buying stock. The Fed increased the discount rate three times, but banks weren't using the Fed's discount window very much. When banks wanted cash, it was easier and cheaper to sell Treasury securities to the Federal Reserve. The Fed also kept reserve requirements high, and in 1948 it convinced Congress to give it the authority to raise them even higher. However, banks offset this credit restraint by selling more Treasury securities to the Fed to acquire the needed reserves.

The economy cooled in 1949, but it started overheating again in the spring of 1950. In June, fighting broke out in Korea, and more inflation was clearly on the horizon. The Fed was convinced that its policy of pegging low interest rates had made it an engine of inflation. In August of 1950, as the Treasury was announcing the sale of another $13 billion of low-interest short-term securities, the Federal Open Market Committee announced that it would henceforth do whatever was necessary to fight inflation.

## The Accord

The Fed allowed short-term Treasury-bill rates to rise somewhat and, during the next 6 months, increased both reserve requirements and discount rates. On February 19, 1951, the board of governors publicly contradicted earlier announcements by both the secretary of the Treasury and President Truman that interest rates on Treasury bonds would be held below 2.5 percent. Finally, after some posturing and peacemaking, on March 4, 1951, the Treasury–Fed Accord was announced:

> *The Treasury and the Federal Reserve System have reached full accord with respect to debt-management and monetary policies to be pursued in furthering their common purpose to assure the successful financing of the government's requirements and, at the same time, to minimize monetization of the public debt.*

Beneath this diplomatic language, a landmark precedent had been established. The **1951 Accord** acknowledged the independence of the Federal Reserve to choose the monetary policy it deemed appropriate.

# THE 1950S: WATCHING NET FREE RESERVES AND INTEREST RATES

For the next several years the Fed exercised its new freedom cautiously, perhaps fearing congressional action if there appeared to be too much conflict with the Treasury. The Fed's stated objective now was to maintain "an orderly market" for government securities. The Fed need not peg interest rates, but it dare not let them gyrate wildly. William McChesney Martin was the chairman and spokesman for the Fed for almost 20 years, from 1951 to 1970, and although the Fed's policies did change and evolve over these 20 years, Martin provided a great deal of continuity.

The Fed adopted a **bills-only policy** in 1953, under which it restricted open-market operations to Treasury bills. (Brief exceptions were made in 1955 and 1958 when the Treasury had difficulty finding buyers for its security issues.) Apparently, the Fed followed this bills-only policy because it did not want even to suggest that it would support long-term Treasury bond prices, since such support might have been interpreted as a return to the pre-Accord policy of pegging interest rates.

The Fed's main argument for a bills-only policy was that the Fed had to step back and allow the development of an independent, self-reliant market to allocate capital. However, the expectations hypothesis teaches us that long-term bond yields are affected by both present and future short-term interest rates and, therefore, by the Fed's current and anticipated Treasury-bill transactions. The Federal Reserve's monetary policy affects all interest rates, even if it only buys and sells short-term Treasury bills. The Fed eventually decided that a bills-only policy served no useful purpose and abandoned it in 1961.

Figure 26.1 uses a variety of measures to trace monetary policy in the 1950s. (As explained in Chapter 9, Tobin's $q$ is the ratio of the market value of corporate stock to the replacement cost of their assets.) The shaded areas identify the recessionary periods as designated by the National Bureau of Economic Research. During the 1950s, the Fed watched net free reserves, interest rates, and $M1$ — in that order of importance. Net free reserves are bank excess reserves less borrowed reserves, which is the same as unborrowed reserves less required reserves. Net free reserves, which can be either positive or negative, measure the reserves available for lending after borrowed reserves have been paid back.

Figure 26.1 shows that net free reserves generally behaved in an appropriate countercyclical way during the 1950s, falling during booms and rising during recessions. It is unclear, however, whether it was the economy or the Fed that caused this pattern. Net free reserves automatically decline during economic booms when loan demand is brisk and rise during recessions when loan demand is slack. For example, banks held enormous net free reserves during the Great

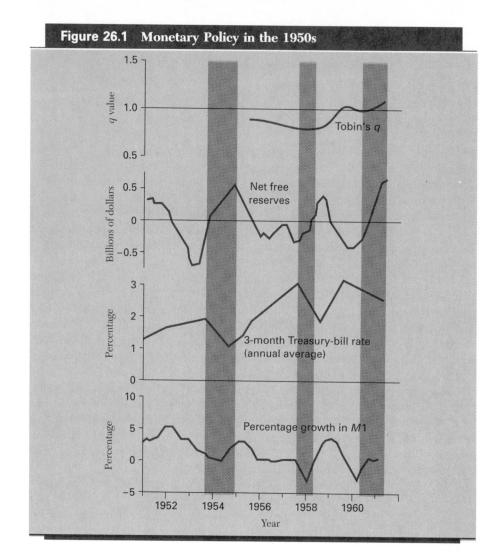

**Figure 26.1  Monetary Policy in the 1950s**

Depression because there were no attractive investment opportunities, not because the Fed pursued an aggressively expansionary monetary policy. Nevertheless, it is true that in the 1950s the Fed did allow bank reserves to drop during booms and rise during recessions. With effort, the Fed could have pumped enough money into the economy during booms and pulled enough out during recessions to have caused a reverse pattern.

The monetary-aggregate data in Figure 26.1 give a different picture. Monetary aggregates seem to have grown faster in booms than in recessions. Again, it is uncertain whether the economy or the Fed was responsible — and for the same reason as with net free reserves. Remember our Chapter 13 discussion of how banks create money. When bank excess reserves are depleted by loans, more funds are put into circulation, and more bank deposits are created. Thus in booms the same strong loan demand that reduces net free reserves also increases monetary aggregates. The conflicting movements in free reserves and monetary aggregates indicate that the Fed played a mostly passive role in the 1950s. Nonetheless, for those who emphasize monetary aggregates as barometers of monetary policy, Figure 26.1 suggests that the Fed's record was mediocre.

The interest-rate data in Figure 26.1 show that the Fed allowed interest rates to rise during booms, thereby exercising restraint, and allowed interest rates to fall during recessions, thereby encouraging recovery. The board did seem a bit more concerned with fighting inflation than recession, and it might have been too cautious. However, those who emphasize interest rates as a barometer of monetary policy gave the Fed generally good marks in the 1950s.

Overall, in the 1950s the Fed's performance was good by the free-reserves and interest-rate criteria and mediocre in terms of monetary aggregates, accurately reflecting the fact that the Fed was cautious and paid more attention to the former than the latter. The major criticisms of Fed policy during the 1950s are that it was not aggressive enough, it permitted three recessions in 10 years because of an excessive fear of inflation, and it paid too little attention to monetary aggregates.

# THE 1960S: ECONOMIC EXPANSION

John F. Kennedy was elected president in 1960, and economic growth was the new administration's major concern. Kennedy and his successor, Lyndon Johnson, were concerned by the nation's high unemployment rate and the resulting lost income and wasted resources. There also was a keen desire to best the Soviet Union by demonstrating that the U.S. economy could grow faster and put a man on the moon sooner. An investment tax credit and liberalized depreciation rules were authorized in 1962. In 1964 a substantial reduction in personal and corporate income taxes took effect.

The Fed generally accommodated these expansionary programs. After an almost obsessive concern about inflation in the 1950s, the Fed changed to easy-money policies to accommodate economic expansion. This switch seemingly reflected the Fed's attention to election returns or at least a sensible intention to avoid a fight with the president.

Figure 26.2 shows the behavior of various monetary barometers. The 1960s were nearly recession-free — reflecting persistently expansionary monetary and fiscal policies. Monetary aggregates grew at a faster clip than they did in the preceding decade. Interest rates rose only moderately, considering the booming economy and the pickup of inflation to 4.7 percent in 1968 and 6.2 percent in 1969. The $q$ data show that financial markets were generally supportive of business investment.

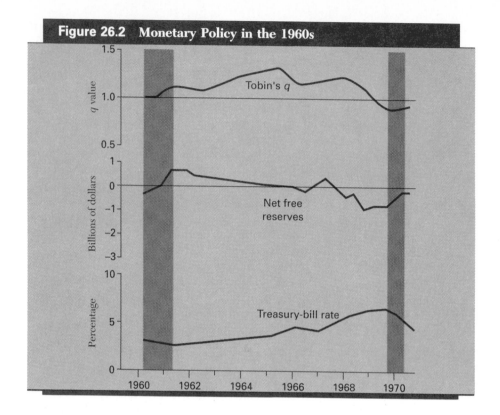

**Figure 26.2   Monetary Policy in the 1960s**

## Credit Crunches

The two exceptions were the 1966 and 1969–1970 credit crunches caused by the Fed's increasing concern about inflation. In 1966, unemployment fell to 3.8 percent, and consumer prices increased by 3.4 percent, the highest rate of inflation since 1951. With the economy booming in 1966, banks were pressed with heavy loan demands, and the Fed decided to cool the economy by not supplying funds to satisfy these demands. Net free reserves fell, interest rates rose, $q$ fell sharply, and the rates of growth of monetary aggregates declined. All these data confirm the painful cries heard in 1966 when the monetary screws were tightened.

The interest-rate data in Figure 26.2 do not tell the complete story of this credit crunch, because the Fed did not raise deposit-rate ceilings in 1966 to keep pace with rising market interest rates. Depositors withdrew their money — disintermediation — leaving banks and thrifts with insufficient funds to satisfy potential borrowers. Rather than increase interest rates to discourage loan applications, deposit institutions rationed credit by scaling down or rejecting applications.

With their greater flexibility and resourcefulness, large banks scrambled for Eurodollars and other alternative sources of funds. Smaller banks and thrift institutions were the hardest hit, and the housing market suffered most. Judged by the aggregate data, the Fed turned in a deft performance. Inflation slowed from 3.4 percent in 1966 to 3.0 percent in 1967 without a recession. The unemployment rate stayed at 3.8 percent. Below the surface, however, the effects were very uneven. The sledgehammer blows to housing made "credit crunch" part of the national vocabulary.

Somewhat alarmed by the disarray in financial markets, the Fed switched to an easy-money policy in 1967. Reserve requirements and discount rates were reduced, and large open-market purchases were made. Bank reserves and monetary aggregates both jumped upward. Interest rates fell, and $q$ increased. Vietnam War spending was by now overheating the economy. The unemployment rate fell to 3.6 percent in 1968 and 3.5 percent in 1969. Consumer prices increased by 4.7 percent in 1968 and by a shocking 6.2 percent in 1969.

In retrospect, the decision to cool the economy in 1966 by crunching a single sector was unwise. Similarly, the Fed can be criticized for trying to rescue that sector by stimulating the entire economy in 1967–1968. The fundamental problem was that distortions had been built into the economy by deposit-rate ceilings and by the unbalanced assets and liabilities of savings and loan associations and other thrift institutions. When these distortions were removed in the 1980s, the Fed was able to pursue more even-handed policies.

In 1969–1970 those regulations were still very much in place, and the monetary screws were again tightened. The 1968 election returns, which put Richard Nixon in the White House, may have influenced this Fed decision. All

---

**EXAMPLE 26.1**

## Guns and Butter in the 1960s

The unemployment rate was 3 percent during the Korean War years (1951–1953) and near 4 percent during the peacetime prosperity of 1955–1957. However, prosperity faded during the last 3 years of the Eisenhower administration. The unemployment rate averaged 6.8 percent in 1958, the highest since the Great Depression, and stayed above 5 percent during the entire period 1958–1960.

John F. Kennedy became president in 1961, with a campaign pledge to get the country moving again — in particular, to reduce the unemployment rate to 4 percent. The cornerstone of his economic program was a substantial reduction in personal and corporate income taxes. However, Kennedy couldn't sell his proposed tax cut to a Congress that was fearful of large budget deficits. The economy stayed in the doldrums with a 6.7 percent unemployment rate in 1961. The 1962 government spending increased by 8 percent, and the unemployment rate fell to 5.5 percent — encouraging, but still far from the administration's 4 percent target.

Lyndon Johnson, succeeding to the presidency after Kennedy's assassination in November of 1963, managed to coax substantial tax legislation out of a still-reluctant Congress — roughly a 20 percent reduction in personal income taxes and a 10 percent cut in corporate taxes. Government spending increased for a variety of health, education, and welfare programs as Johnson waged what he called a War on Poverty to achieve a Great Society. Lower taxes, higher government spending, and an accommodating monetary policy reduced the unemployment rate steadily, until it reached 4.1 percent in the fourth quarter of 1965 — almost exactly on target. These 2 years of economic recovery convinced many skeptics that monetary and fiscal demand management policies could end recessions and maintain full employment.

The Vietnam War was heating up in late 1965, and Lyndon Johnson wanted more guns and butter — guns to fight a war and butter to achieve a Great Society. The Fed, meanwhile, allowed $M1$ to expand faster than prices in 1967 and 1968, as shown in the table below. The unemployment rate fell to 3.5 percent, output strained the economy's full-employment capacity, and inflationary pressures surfaced. The economy was having trouble delivering more guns and more butter, and in 1969 the Fed switched to a contractionary monetary policy in order to fight inflation.

| Year | Change in $M1$ (%) | Unemployment Rate (%) | Rate of Inflation (%) |
|------|------|------|------|
| 1966 | 2.7 | 3.8 | 3.5 |
| 1967 | 6.3 | 3.8 | 3.0 |
| 1968 | 7.4 | 3.6 | 4.7 |
| 1969 | 3.8 | 3.5 | 6.2 |

the data agree that there was another, even tougher credit crunch. This time the monetary authorities stepped on the brakes long and hard enough to cause an unmistakable recession. The unemployment rate jumped to 4.9 percent in 1970 and to 5.9 percent in 1971.

Overall, the 1950s and 1960s were relatively successful decades for the Federal Reserve. The Fed awoke from a long slumber and engaged in active monetary policy. Its objectives were unmistakably influenced by political leaders. The Fed supported caution in the 1950s at the expense of prosperity and risked inflation in the 1960s to support economic growth. As the 1960s ended, the Fed followed the politicians back to an emphasis on fighting inflation.

There were no major errors during these 20 years and no calamities to compare with the monetary debacles before World War II. The Fed pretty much achieved its objectives, and criticism centered more on these objectives than on their implementation. The major imperfection in Fed policy was that, because of banking regulations enacted during the 1930s, its efforts to cool the economy affected some sectors of the economy much more than others.

EXAMPLE
26.2

## Operation Twist

The Fed faced a dilemma during the booming 1960s in that economic growth called for low interest rates to persuade households and businesses to borrow and spend, but low U.S. interest rates encouraged investors to send funds abroad, seeking higher yields. To meet these conflicting objectives, the Fed tried what has become known as **Operation Twist** from 1961 to 1963 — an attempt to twist the term structure by raising short-term interest rates and lowering long-term interest rates. (The use of a code name reflected the high regard in which the military and CIA were then held.)

The idea was that the Fed should sell short-term securities, thereby raising short-term interest rates, and use these funds to buy long-term bonds, thereby reducing their yields. Low long-term interest rates would encourage borrowing and spending, contributing to economic growth, while high short-term rates would keep funds from flowing abroad.

Economists who believed in the expectations hypothesis explanation of the term structure were openly skeptical. How, they asked, could long-term rates fall below short-term rates unless short-term rates were expected to decline greatly in the future? Apparently, the Fed would have to convince financial markets of an entirely unlikely scenario in which short-term rates rise temporarily and then decline drastically. In rebuttal, supporters of Operation Twist noted that when the future is uncertain, buying longs and rolling over shorts are imperfect substitutes and changes in relative supplies can affect relative yields.

As it turned out, Operation Twist fizzled. The Fed made only modest sales of shorts and purchases of longs, which were overwhelmed by the Treasury's sale of long-term bonds to finance its deficit. Over the postwar period as a whole, the average maturity of outstanding government debt steadily declined. However, during 1961-1963 — the years in which Operation Twist was supposed to reduce the supply of long-term government bonds — the average maturity of privately held government debt actually increased. The Fed's Operation Twist was so timid that it allowed bond supplies to twist in the wrong direction.

# THE 1970S: DISAPPOINTMENTS AND A REASSESSMENT

Arthur Burns followed William McChesney Martin as chairman of the Federal Reserve Board in 1970. He was expected to focus on controlling inflation and monetary aggregates, and he did — although some of his supporters were disappointed by his flexibility and pragmatism.

The early 1970s, like much of the rest of the decade, were characterized by high unemployment, rapid inflation, and large balance-of-payments deficits. The

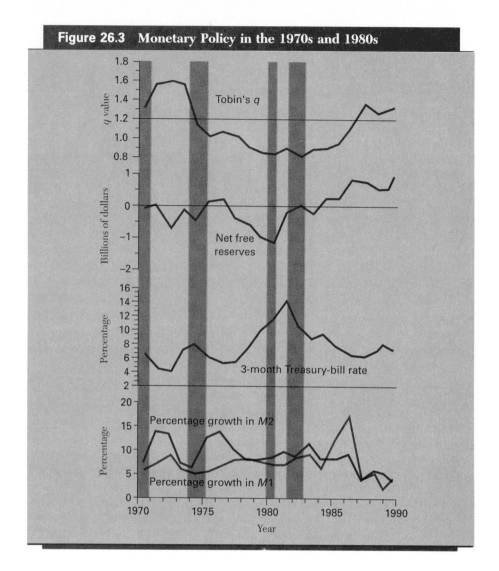

**Figure 26.3    Monetary Policy in the 1970s and 1980s**

decade was spent in a fruitless search for a painless way to solve all three problems.

The Fed and the Nixon administration first tried what one official called "the old-time religion" — a recession to cool the economy and reduce inflation. As the 1972 election grew near, monetary and fiscal policies turned sharply expansionary, and an impatient president tried to have an economic boom without inflation by imposing wage and price controls in late 1971. The Fed reduced reserve requirements and discount rates and made large open-market purchases. Figure 26.3 shows that the now more closely watched monetary aggregate data picked up steam. Interest rates tumbled, and $q$ increased.

After the 1972 elections, monetary and fiscal policies again turned restrictive. The rates of growth of monetary aggregates slowed, interest rates rose, and $q$ plunged. In 1973–1974, there was yet another credit crunch, reflecting a Fed decision to use a recession to cool inflation and slow the decline in the value of the dollar. The unemployment rate averaged 8.5 percent in 1975 — the highest level since the Great Depression — but, with oil and food shortages, consumer prices increased by 12.2 percent in 1974 and 7.0 percent in 1975.

As the 1976 presidential election approached, monetary and fiscal policies again turned expansionary. The growth of monetary aggregates increased, interest rates fell, and $q$ increased. Nonetheless, the Republican party had been tainted by the Watergate scandal and the Democratic candidate, Jimmy Carter, won the presidency. The new president wanted to reduce unemployment, and with help from the Fed, the economy continued strong in 1977 and 1978. The money supply grew at a brisk pace, and interest rates increased only modestly considering the inflation rate of 7 percent in 1977 and 9 percent in 1978. As double-digit inflation loomed ahead, the president (reluctantly) and the Fed (aggressively) swung to contractionary policies. In 1979 there was another credit crunch, and in January of 1980 a recession began.

Overall, the 1970s were similar to the 1950s and the 1960s in that the Fed was reasonably successful in pursuing the easy- or tight-money policies that it chose. The major disappointment was that two substantial recessions had so little effect on inflation. Living standards in the United States were reduced by energy-related shocks to the economy, which could hardly have been offset by monetary policies.

The 1970s also saw the elevation of monetary aggregates as a closely watched barometer of monetary policy and the temporary demise of bank reserves data. The Fed continued to keep its second eye on interest rates and its third eye on election returns.

The Federal Reserve does not seem to have been guilty of clumsily destabilizing the economy, of exacerbating booms and recessions because of poor timing. The Fed pretty much stimulated and cooled the economy when it wanted. The Fed is more open to the criticism that it knowingly helped put the economy on a 4-year business cycle coinciding with presidential elections. The only departure from this pattern was the 1976–1980 reversal during Jimmy Carter's presidency, when the economy expanded after Carter's 1976 election and went into recession before his 1980 defeat.

# THE 1980S: THE TAMING OF INFLATION

As the 1970s came to an end, Paul Volcker took over as Federal Reserve chairman. He faced the same problems that had greeted Arthur Burns at the beginning of the decade: high unemployment, rapid inflation, and large balance-of-payments deficits. The only changes were in degree: each problem was now worse. Volcker brought a fresh determination to stop inflation, but no miracles.

The value of the U.S. dollar fell to new lows in the fall of 1979 as currency traders grew increasingly nervous about inflation in the United States. At an

EXAMPLE
26.3
## Targeting Nonborrowed Reserves

The Federal Reserve used a nonborrowed reserves control procedure between October of 1979 and October of 1982. After each meeting of the Federal Open Market Committee, Fed staff members estimated the level of total bank reserves consistent with the committee's targets for the growth of monetary aggregates, particularly $M1$, because Fed studies had indicated that, of the various monetary aggregates, $M1$ was most closely correlated with nominal gross domestic product and prices.[*]

After determining a target path for total reserves for the 3 to 5 weeks between committee meetings, the staff members subtracted an assumed level of borrowed reserves that had been determined by the committee. The open market desk was then instructed to use open-market operations to achieve a weekly nonborrowed reserves target equal to this difference between targeted total reserves and assumed borrowed reserves. Approximately once a week, the Fed staff adjusted its targets for total reserves and nonborrowed reserves in light of new information about the relationships between bank reserves and monetary aggregates.

Because the nonborrowed reserves target is obtained by subtracting a desired level of borrowed reserves from an estimate of the level of total reserves consistent with desired levels of monetary aggregates, there was some ambiguity, even among Fed governors, about whether the operating procedure could best be described as targeting nonborrowed reserves or using nonborrowed reserves to hit a target for borrowed reserves.[†]

The Fed procedure was based on the belief that its trading desk could hit its nonborrowed reserve target with considerable accuracy and that the maintenance of such a target would control monetary aggregates automatically. The underlying theory was that if $M1$ started to grow faster than intended, banks would need funds to meet their reserve requirements. If the Fed held nonborrowed reserves steady, then banks would have to meet their reserve requirements by borrowing through either the federal funds market or the Fed's discount window. A reluctance to abuse their discount window privileges would lead them to the federal funds market, causing a substantial increase in the federal funds rate and, with it, other short-term interest rates. As interest rates rose, funds would be taken out of transaction accounts and invested at these higher market interest rates, causing $M1$ to decline. Thus it was intended that a policy of targeting nonborrowed reserves would achieve the Fed's targets for $M1$ and other monetary aggregates.

[*]*Lyle Gramley, "Financial Innovation and Monetary Policy,"* Federal Reserve Bulletin, *July 1982, p. 396.*

[†]*See, for example, the speech by Board Governor Henry C. Wallich, "Recent Techniques of Monetary Policy," reprinted in Federal Reserve Bank of Kansas City, Economic Review, May 1984, pp. 21–30.*

International Monetary Fund meeting in Belgrade in late September, European central bankers told Volcker that they were skeptical of the Fed's efforts to reduce inflation and, more ominously, threatened to sell all the U.S. dollars they were holding.[1] Volcker left the conference early, flew back to the United States, and convened an extraordinary Saturday meeting of the Fed's Open Market Commitee on October 6, 1979. Late that afternoon Volcker announced to the press that the Fed would henceforth place

> Greater emphasis in day to day operations on the supply of bank reserves and less emphasis on confining short-term fluctuations in the federal funds rate.[2]

Prior to this announcement, open-market operations were used to keep the average value of the federal funds rate (over a month, a week, or even a day) within 0.5 or 1.0 percent of its target value. After October 6, 1979, the width of the Fed's target range was widened to 5 to 6 percentage points; if the federal funds rate went outside this target band, the Federal Open Market Committee met and, in practice, simply widened the band.

While allowing interest rates to fluctuate more, the Fed targeted bank reserves more closely in order to stabilize monetary aggregates, as explained in a record of the FOMC meetings:

> The principal reason advanced for shifting to an operating procedure aimed at controlling the supply of bank reserves more directly was that it would provide greater assurance that the committee's objectives for monetary growth could be achieved.[3]

The details of these operating procedures are described in Example 26.3.

The Fed's increased attention to monetary aggregates and deemphasis of interest rates was called an "experiment in monetarism." In retrospect, the main objective of the Volcker Fed in 1979 seems to have been to slow the growth of monetary aggregates in order to reduce the rate of inflation. The Fed was less committed to the monetarist idea of maintaining a constant growth rate for monetary aggregates, no matter what the state of the economy. Nonetheless, some interesting lessons can be learned from the Fed's policies during this period.

## Interest-Rate Instability

Without the Fed's steadying support, interest rates went through some truly breathtaking gyrations. In April of 1980, the prime lending rate ran up to 20 percent and then retreated almost as rapidly as it had climbed that uncharted hill. The federal funds rate jumped from less than 13 percent in mid-February to above 19 percent in early April and then fell below 10 percent in late May. On a single day, August 5, 1980, the federal funds rate swung between 8.75 percent in the morning and 2 percent in the afternoon. The Fed meant what it had said about letting interest rates fluctuate.

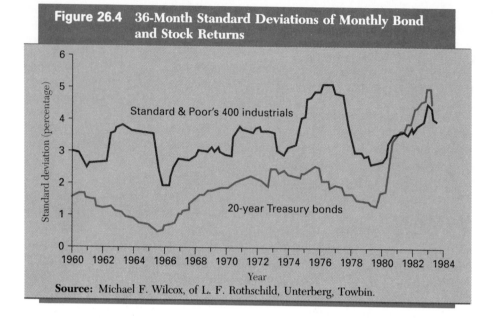

**Figure 26.4**   **36-Month Standard Deviations of Monthly Bond and Stock Returns**

**Source:**  Michael F. Wilcox, of L. F. Rothschild, Unterberg, Towbin.

Such wild interest-rate swings caused disarray, even despair, in financial markets, as both borrowers and lenders came to the historic conclusion that long-term bonds, traditionally a conservative investment, were now riskier than stocks. Figure 26.4, using one measure of risk, the standard deviation of monthly returns, reveals the increase in the riskiness of bonds after October of 1979.

The president of the E. F. Hutton brokerage firm said, "This market has made traders queasy, uneasy, and at times shaken. The greatest problem of all is the volatility. Even in Government securities, prices have sometimes changed in a single day more than they did in an entire year in the past."[4] The chairman of Manufacturers Hanover bank said, "We ask ourselves, where's the roller coaster going in the next 12 months, but you can't even begin to think that far ahead anymore. You can't even think one month ahead."[5] The cautious left the long-term bond market, looking to short-term securities for price stability. The adventurous discovered long-term bonds now to be an exciting speculation, rivaling foreign currency and pork bellies.

## Monetary-Aggregate Instability

And yet, as shown in Figure 26.5, monetary aggregates fluctuated almost as wildly as interest rates in 1980. Monetary aggregates fell at a record clip in April and soared at a record pace in August. For the rest of the year, monetary aggregates seemed to seesaw upward, although the Fed revised its data frequently. Those monetarist economists who had welcomed Volcker's demotion of interest-rate stability were, after 1 year, decrying the instability of monetary

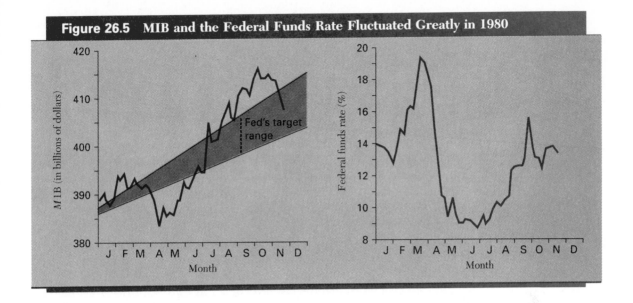

**Figure 26.5    MIB and the Federal Funds Rate Fluctuated Greatly in 1980**

aggregates. Volcker responded that monetary aggregates aren't "something you control from week to week or even month to month. We always knew that, but we learned it in spades this year."[6] Overall, the standard deviation of the quarterly growth rate of $M1$ was 2.6 percent for the 10 quarters preceding October 1979 and 5.2 percent for the 10 quarters afterwards.[7]

One observer, Salomon Brothers' widely respected Henry Kaufman, blamed the instability of interest rates on the instability of monetary aggregates. Investors could no longer count on the Fed to stabilize interest rates, nor could they accurately gauge Fed intentions by movements in the federal funds rate. Instead, they had to guess the future course of interest rates from conjectures about how the Fed would react to wild short-term swings in bank reserves and monetary aggregates.

For the year 1980 as a whole, the Fed did a pretty good job of controlling $M1B$, which is now called $M1$. $M1B$ increased by only 6.3 percent in 1980, as compared with 7.4 percent in 1979 and 8.2 percent in 1978. Yet, at the same time that the rate of growth of $M1B$ was slowing, the rate of inflation accelerated from 7.6 percent in 1978 to 11.3 percent in 1979 and to 13.5 percent in 1980. This reaffirms our earlier observation that there is not a close positive correlation between the money supply and prices.

## Divergent Aggregates

The 1980 experience also confirms that it does make a difference which aggregate is targeted, because monetary aggregates do not all grow at the same rate. In 1980 the government monetary base increased by 4 percent, $M1A$ by 3.9 percent, $M1B$ by 6.3 percent, $M2$ by 9.4 percent, and $M3$ by 10.0 percent. In 1981 it was more of the same. The Fed's target growth rates and actual monetary growth rates in 1981 were as follows:

|  | Target Range (%) | Actual (%) |
|---|---|---|
| M1A | 3.0–5.5 | −6.1 |
| M1B adjusted | 3.5–6.0 | 2.3 |
| M1B unadjusted | 6.0–8.5 | 6.3 |
| M2 | 6.0–9.0 | 10.0 |
| M3 | 6.5–9.5 | 11.4 |

One out of five isn't bad! The disconcerting problem was that M1A and adjusted M1B were substantially *below* their targets, while M2 and M3 were well *above* their targets. What should the Fed do? Some, watching the M1s, argued for monetary ease to avoid a recession. Others, watching M2 and M3, argued for more restraint to fight inflation.

The Fed concluded that the low level of M1 in 1981 was misleading because a lot of transaction money had temporarily gone into M2 in search of high interest rates. In 1982 the situation was reversed: M1 grew rapidly and M1 velocity suddenly dropped 5 percent below its predicted value. The Fed concluded that this increase in M1 was misleading, too, because these additional funds were precautionary savings rather than transaction funds. This flexible interpretation of seemingly arbitrary and ambiguous monetary aggregates led *The Wall Street Journal* to editorialize that "gearing monetary policy to movements in one or another of the Ms is as smooth and steady — and as reasonable — as a Keystone Kops chase."[8] They suggested a new monetary aggregate: M-w for "M-whatever."

## A More Flexible Policy

In the summer of 1982 the unemployment rate hit 10.8 percent. The economy was in the worst recession since the 1930s, and some feared a complete economic collapse. Yet M1 was well above the Fed's target ranges, creating a crucial litmus test of the Fed's dedication to its M1 target.

The Fed was using M1 as an intermediate target to help achieve its goals for nominal gross domestic product. The targeted value of M1 was based on a predicted value of M1 velocity, the ratio of nominal gross domestic product to M1, that is,

$$V1 = \frac{Py}{M1}$$

In 1982 gross domestic product was lower than the Fed wanted, but M1 was well above the Fed's target range, reflecting an unexpected drop in M1 velocity. One option for the Fed was to ignore the decline in velocity and stick to its M1 target, using contractionary monetary policies to restrain $M1$. Another option was to abandon the $M1$ target and react to the low level of gross domestic product, in effect targeting gross domestic product when there is a conflict between gross domestic product and $M1$. The Fed chose to ignore $M1$ and respond to the ailing economy by shifting to an expansionary monetary policy.

The Fed changed its formal operating procedures in October of 1982, ending its 3-year experiment in using nonborrowed reserves to control monetary aggregates. While the open market desk continued to monitor bank reserves on a daily basis after October of 1982, the Fed's reserve targets were no longer automatically adjusted to reflect deviations of monetary aggregates from their targeted paths. Instead, the Federal Open Market Committee's bank reserve targets are now based on the members' policy judgments, reflecting a variety of economic data in addition to monetary aggregates. The open market desk is instructed to use flexible targets for nonborrowed reserves in order to achieve the Open Market Committee's target for borrowed reserves during each 2-week reserve maintenance period.

When the Federal Open Market Committee wants more reserve restraint, the open market desk makes open market sales, compelling banks to increase their borrowing through the Fed's discount window. Because of banker reluctance to abuse their discount window privileges, this discount window borrowing signals a tightening of credit availability and puts upward pressure on the federal funds rate and other short-term interest rates.

The Fed made this change in 1982 because it accepted the argument that changes in monetary aggregates are often the result of financial market developments — for example, shifts among various types of bank accounts — that do not significantly affect gross domestic product and prices and consequently do not need to be offset by open-market purchases or sales. The Fed would use discretion in deciding when to tighten and when to ease.

By the end of 1983, Volcker conceded that the erratic behavior of $M1$ velocity had persuaded the Fed to disregard changes in $M1$ for the foreseeable future. Preston Martin, vice-chairman of the Fed, explained succinctly that short-term movements in $M1$ "are absolutely meaningless."

In 1985, $M1$ grew by 12 percent, while nominal gross domestic product increased by only 6.5 percent (3 percent real and 3.5 percent inflation) — so velocity unexpectedly declined by 5.5 percent. The rapid 12 percent growth of $M1$ signaled to some observers a need for tightening, but Volcker concluded that "all other indicators are currently signaling either that monetary policy should be kept unchanged or even eased further."[9] Again, the Fed chose to let the $M1$ signals be overruled by other indicators.

In 1986, $M1$ velocity declined by an incredible 9.5 percent. While $M1$ increased by more than 15 percent, nominal gross domestic product rose by about 5 percent (half real and half inflation). Again monetarists warned of an imminent rapid increase in the rate of inflation, and again, the Fed chose to abandon its $M1$ targets and let its monetary policy be guided by other economic data. In February of 1987 the Fed stopped targeting $M1$ entirely.

Overall, after increasing at an average rate of about 3.5 percent per year between 1948 and 1981, $M1$ velocity declined, on average, by about 4 percent per year between 1982 and 1987. This change in the behavior of velocity created an enormous gap between the actual value of $M1$ and the value consistent with the historical relationship between $M1$ and gross domestic product.

To demonstrate this break with the past, the Federal Reserve Bank of San Francisco used data through 1980 to estimate how $M1$ is affected by changes in gross domestic product, interest rates, and other relevant factors.[10] This equation was then used to predict $M1$ using the values of these explanatory variables

## EXAMPLE
### 26.4

## *Increases in M1 May Be Contractionary!*

Portfolio shifts among assets can cause changes in monetary aggregates that provide misleading signals about the economy. One particularly striking case occurs when households or businesses transfer funds into transaction accounts (which are subject to 10 percent reserves requirements) from savings accounts, money-market funds, and other assets that are not subject to reserve requirements.*

The deposit-multiplier model analyzed in Chapter 13 showed that such a portfolio shift increases $M1$, signaling monetary expansion. Yet this relocation of funds may reflect no change whatsoever in spending behavior by households and businesses. They have simply decided to hold more funds in their transaction accounts and less elsewhere. Perhaps new features have increased the attractiveness of transaction accounts. Or investors may be nervous about the safety of uninsured money-market funds. Or fearing an increase in interest rates, they have reduced their holdings of longer-term assets. In each case, the portfolio shift is not indicative of a change in spending, output, or employment.

In fact, because transaction accounts are subject to substantial reserve requirements, this portfolio shift actually reduces the amount of funds available for bank lending. Less of the monetary base circulates through financial markets because more is sitting idle in bank vaults. When funds are transferred into transaction accounts from accounts that are exempt from reserve requirements, there is an increase in required reserves for the banking system, which tightens credit — despite the increase in $M1$.

The Fed is well aware of the fact that such a rearrangement of asset portfolios causes $M1$ to give a misleading signal about financial market conditions.† When $M1$ grew rapidly in 1985 and 1986, the Fed believed that this increase was caused by just such a portfolio shift and consequently ignored the misleading signal given by $M1$.

*Iman Anabtawi and Gary Smith, "Money, Credit, and Banking in a Keynesian Macroeconomic Model," Eastern Economic Journal, 1992.

†Bharat Trehan and Carl Walsh, "Examining the Recent Surge in M1," Federal Reserve Bank of San Francisco Weekly Letter, November 15, 1985, pp. 1–3.

after 1980. Early in 1982, actual $M1$ began to rise above predicted $M1$, reflecting the unexpected decline in $M1$ velocity. By the end of 1986, actual $M1$ was nearly 25 percent higher than predicted $M1$, a gap of $125 billion dollars. If the Fed had ignored this cumulative deterioration in the relationship between $M1$ and economic activity and insisted on keeping $M1$ growing at a rate consistent with historical trends, the contractionary effect on the economy might have been devastating.

$M2$ and $M3$ velocity also dropped unexpectedly in 1985 and 1986, but not as dramatically as $M1$ velocity. $M2$ velocity, which had been roughly trendless since

**EXAMPLE**

**26.5**  **Reagan's Supply-Side Economics**

The imposition of taxes provides an incentive to avoid the activity that is being taxed. Gasoline taxes discourage the purchase of fuel-inefficient cars. Tariffs discourage the purchase of imports. Income taxes discourage income earning.

In the late 1970s, some supply-side economists argued that high tax rates in the United States were discouraging work, production, and investment. For instance, high-income taxpayers were in a 70 percent tax bracket, paying 70 cents in taxes on every additional dollar of income. Supply-side economists argued that a reduction in tax rates would encourage people to work more, particularly those who are very productive — as gauged by their high incomes. This increased enthusiasm for work could push wages down, persuading firms to hire more people and reduce prices.

In 1980, supply-side economists told presidential candidate Ronald Reagan that he could promise voters the enticing combination of lower taxes, increased output, and lower prices. The more enthusiastic claimed that output would increase so much that a tax cut would actually increase federal tax revenue, reducing the federal deficit. (This would happen, for instance, if tax rates were reduced by 10 percent and taxable income increased by more than 10 percent.)

Most economists (including many of Reagan's long-time advisers) were skeptical of these supply-side effects and particularly dubious of the claim that lower tax rates would reduce the federal deficit. Lower tax rates do make work more rewarding, encouraging the sacrifice of leisure of work, but lower tax rates also allow workers to keep more of what they are already earning. They consequently may decide that they do not need to work as much in order to provide food and shelter. It is ambiguous whether a cut in tax rates will increase or reduce labor supply.

In addition, very few people have the option of being paid for working a few extra minutes or hours every week. Their realistic alternatives are not to work, work at one job, or work at more than one job. Most people settle into a workstyle and lifestyle that suits them. They become efficient secretaries, plodding bureaucrats, workaholic professors, or whatever. Few will be persuaded by slightly lower tax rates to change their work habits dramatically.

A final difficulty is that the supply-side theory assumes that workers will accept a decline in before-tax wages readily because they want to work more and the tax cut has caused their after-tax wages to increase. In practice, though, most wages never decline. Unions don't like to negotiate wage decreases, and employers do not like to cut the salaries of executives and other nonunion employees. If wages don't fall, employment won't increase, because it is lower wages that are supposed to persuade firms to hire more people.

Income tax rates were substantially reduced during the Reagan years, but whatever supply-side effects occurred were swamped by the demand-side effects of its fiscal policies (low taxes, higher spending) and the Fed's monetary policies (very contractionary until 1982 and then expansionary). The federal deficit didn't disappear; it increased to record levels. So overwhelming were the demand-side effects, that some pundits called Reagan a born-again Keynesian.

1960, fell by 2.25 percent in 1985 and by 4.25 percent in 1986. $M3$ velocity declined by about 0.75 percent between 1960 and 1980 and fell by 1.25 percent in 1985 and 3.25 percent in 1986. The Fed concluded that these velocity surprises reflected unanticipated shifts among assets (both within and outside the monetary aggregate categories) that had little bearing on economic activity.

The Fed consequently followed an increasingly eclectic approach from 1987 onward, monitoring a wide variety of economic indicators. Alan Greenspan replaced Paul Volcker as Fed chairman in 1987 and seems more tolerant of divergent opinions, perhaps because of the accumulated evidence that monetary policy cannot be guided reliably by one or two simple criteria. Individual members of the Federal Open Market Committee have their own favorite indicators, including the unemployment rate, nominal gross domestic product, the consumer price index, exchange rates, term structure of interest rates, and the prices of gold, soybeans, and other commodities. All now use a variety of data to gauge the condition of financial markets and the economy.

## EXAMPLE 26.6

## *Establishing the Fed's Credibility*

Arthur Burns was chairman of the Fed during most of the inflation-filled 1970s. In his public speeches and congressional testimony, he repeatedly talked of the need to reduce the rate of inflation, often with words unusually passionate for a central banker. In a September 1973 speech at the Minneapolis Federal Reserve Bank, he said:

*The time will surely come when monetary policy can again be less restrictive, but that time has not yet arrived. . . .*

*The principal source of my optimism, however, lies not in these general indicators of progress in dealing with economic and financial problems, but in my faith in our Nation and its good people. Our country has been blessed with rich natural resources and our people have been endowed with the vision and energy to strive for a better life.* \*

Burns concluded an August 1974 statement to the Joint Economic Committee of Congress with these words:

*This illustrious Committee has on past occasions provided timely and courageous leadership to the Congress and to the Nation. The opportunity has arisen once again for the Joint Economic Committee to help our country find its way out of the great peril posed by raging inflation. Our people are weary, and they are anxiously awaiting positive and persuasive steps by their government to arrest inflation and to restore general price stability. The Federal Reserve pledges to you its full cooperation in your search for ways to restore a stable and lasting prosperity.* †

Some thought that the Fed was more talk than action. Burns often spoke of the need to maintain or restore prosperity and of the role fiscal policy could play in slowing inflation, suggesting less than an all-out commitment by the Fed to reduce the rate of inflation. There also was evidence that the Fed was susceptible to political pressure, particularly before presidential elections. Workers, businesses, and financial analysts were not convinced of the Fed's willingness to endure a long, severe recession to stop inflation.

In March of 1978, Jimmy Carter appointed G. William Miller, a businessman, to replace Arthur Burns as Fed chairman. By the summer of 1979, the rate of inflation had reached double digits, and the value of the U.S. dollar had fallen to new lows. Miller was perceived by many to be insufficiently independent of the administration and Congress and, perhaps worse, too indecisive.

In August of 1979, with financial markets in disarray, Carter replaced Miller with Paul Volcker, the widely known and respected president of the Federal Reserve Bank of New York. Two months later, Volcker established a "take no prisoners" approach. Over and over he said that the Fed would do whatever was necessary to stop inflation — warning that those who were betting on inflation in their wage agreements and investment strategies would lose their bets. For instance, in a January 1981 statement to the Senate Banking Committee, he said:

*The task is both difficult and painful because patterns of inflationary behavior are by now so deeply ingrained in individual attitudes that the process feeds on itself. That will change only when there is a visible, sustained commitment to policies that will in fact reduce the strong upward*

\**Arthur F. Burns, "Objectives and Responsibilities of the Federal Reserve System," September 8, 1973 speech,* Federal Reserve Bulletin, *September 1973, pp. 655–657.*

†*Arthur F. Burns, statement before the Joint Economic Committee, August 6, 1974; reprinted in* Federal Reserve Bulletin, *August 1974, pp. 561–567.*

*price thrust — and will permit market processes to penalize those speculating on inflation. . . . Credibility in policy commitment will have to be earned by performance maintained through thick and thin.*‡

And he meant what he said. Volcker stuck to his anti-inflation objectives during the 1980 presidential election, despite bitter complaints and severe pressure from the Carter administration. He was unmoved by 3 years of protests, lectures, and scolding by congressional committees. Volcker stayed the course until October of 1982. The rate of inflation finally dropped below 4 percent, while the unemployment rate reached double digits, the highest level since the Great Depression, and there were genuine fears that the economy was on the brink of financial collapse. Only then did the Fed relax its grip.

Tests of Volcker's credibility occurred in 1982, 1983, 1985, and 1986, when M1 grew rapidly. Monetarists warned of imminent inflation. Volcker observed the unanticipated declines in M1 velocity and concluded that inflation was not a threat. Most important, the public had learned from the 1979–1982 experience that Volcker would not hesitate to apply the monetary brakes — as long and as hard as necessary — if the rate of inflation did begin increasing. Financial markets shrugged off the rapid growth of M1 because Volcker had established the credibility of the Fed's commitment to restrain inflation.

Alan Greenspan replaced Volcker as Fed chairman in August of 1987. Any questions about his competence were quickly answered by his deft handling of the October 1987 stock market crash. His reputation grew during the next 2 years as the Fed's eclectic approach guided the economy between the shoals of inflation and recession. When Greenspan appeared before congressional banking committees in 1990, there were mostly empty chairs and perfunctory questions, the chairman of the Senate Banking Committee explaining that "the job is in the best possible hands."§

‡*Paul A. Volcker, statement before the U.S. Senate Committee on Banking, Housing, and Urban Affairs, January 7, 1981;* Federal Reserve Bulletin, *January 1981, pp. 17–21.*

§*Tom Redburn, "How Times Have Changed: Fed Chief Off the Hot Seat,"* Los Angeles Times, *February 23, 1990.*

## THE 1990S: EIGHT YEARS OF EXPANSION COME TO AN END

The economic expansion that began in the fourth quarter of 1982 finally ended in the fourth quarter of 1990, when real GDP fell at an annual rate of 3.9 percent, followed by a 2.5 percent decline during the first quarter of 1991. Real GDP subsequently rose at anemic annual rates of 1.4, 1.8, and 0.8 percent in the second, third, and fourth quarters of 1991. For 1991 as a whole, real GDP

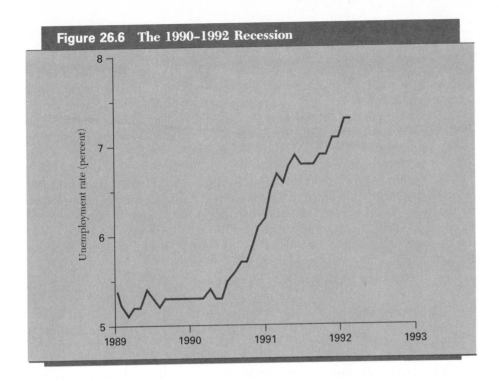

**Figure 26.6   The 1990–1992 Recession**

increased by only 0.4 percent, not nearly enough to provide jobs for a growing labor force.

With productivity and the labor force both increasing, U.S. output needs to grow by about 3 percent a year to keep unemployment from increasing. Figure 26.6 shows that the unemployment rate rose from 5.3 percent in June of 1990 to 7.0 percent in June of 1991, before declining slightly to 6.7 percent in September and then rising to 7.3 percent in February and March of 1992.

Several factors contributed to this economic recession. The meltdown of the savings-and-loan industry made many people anxious about the future, and cautious households and businesses tend to save rather than borrow and spend. These anxieties were heightened by the weak real estate market. After increasing at near double-digit levels during most of the 1970s and 1980s, home prices fell by an average of 2 percent in 1990, with prices in some parts of the country declining by 20 percent to 50 percent. Falling real estate prices and well-publicized foreclosures no doubt caused some homeowners to retrench and persuaded many financial institutions to cut back on lending.

The risk-based capital requirements discussed in Example 16.3 further encouraged financial institutions to buy Treasury securities (which have a 0% risk weight) instead of making loans (which have a 100% risk weight). Commercial bank holdings of Treasury securities increased by $60 billion in 1991, while consumer and business loans declined by $40 billion (the first decline since 1975). Mortgages at thrift institutions plunged by $100 billion.

## Contradictory Signals

Monetary aggregates gave mixed and contradictory signals in 1991. $M1$ velocity unexpectedly fell by 5 percent in 1991, and Table 26.1 shows that $M1$ accelerated in 1991, while $M2$ and $M3$ grew very slowly. During the third quarter, $M2$ actually declined by 0.3 percent, the first quarterly decline in the 32 years of data available on the current definition of $M2$. The 2.9 percent growth rate of $M2$ in 1991 was near the bottom of the Fed's 2.5 to 6.5 percent target range. Similarly, the 1.5 percent growth rate of $M3$ in 1991 scraped the bottom of the Fed's 1.0 to 5.0 percent target range.

The relatively rapid growth of $M1$ reflected a portfolio shift into checkable deposits that clearly did not represent increased spending. In fact, as explained in Example 26.4, because checkable deposits are subject to reserve requirements, this portfolio shift actually tightened financial markets in 1991. Recognizing the misleading behavior of $M1$, the Fed did not specify a target range and virtually ignored the robust growth of $M1$.

The Fed instead watched $M2$ closely, though its behavior was at times puzzling. In July of 1991, Fed Chairman Alan Greenspan told Congress that the link between $M2$ and the economy had been "one of the most enduring in our financial system," and that the Fed was concerned about the recent deterioration of that relationship. The rates of growth of $M2$ and $M3$ between 1989 and 1991 were considerably lower than predicted by the Fed's economic models, which take into account the historical effects of national income and interest rates on $M2$ and $M3$ velocity. $M2$ and $M3$ velocity were substantially higher than predicted, and the levels of $M2$ and $M3$ in 1991 were more than $200 billion below the values predicted by the Fed's model. The primary explanation that was cited by the Fed was the extraordinary contraction of the thrift industry and the accompanying shift of funds out of time and savings accounts (which are included in $M2$ and $M3$) into bonds, stocks, and mutual funds (which are not included in $M2$ or $M3$).

Some economists were alarmed by the slow growth of $M2$ and urged the Fed to follow a more expansionary policy. Others argued that the portfolio shifts underlying the slow growth of $M2$ were inconsequential and that the low level of $M2$ was therefore misleading. The rising unemployment rate persuaded the Fed to follow an expansionary monetary policy.

**Table 26.1   Growth Rates for $M1$, $M2$, and $M3$**

|  | 1987(%) | 1988(%) | 1989(%) | 1990(%) | 1991(%) |
|----|----|----|----|----|----|
| $M1$ | 3.5 | 4.9 | 0.9 | 4.0 | 8.6 |
| $M2$ | 3.5 | 5.5 | 5.0 | 3.2 | 2.9 |
| $M3$ | 5.3 | 6.6 | 3.5 | 1.4 | 1.5 |

**Source:** Federal Reserve Bank of St. Louis, *Monetary Trends*, January 1992, p. 1.

## The Fed Lowers Interest Rates to Help
## Banks and the Economy

In 1990 and 1991, the FOMC's policy directive focused on "the degree of pressure on [bank] reserve positions." Because bank demand for reserves depends on the federal funds rate, the FOMC's target objectives for bank reserves imply corresponding values of the federal funds rate. Thus the Fed used open market operations to alter the federal funds rate and thereby influence total bank reserves, borrowed reserves, and unborrowed reserves.

Figure 26.7 shows that the Fed brought the federal funds rate down slightly in 1990 and dramatically in 1991 as evidence of the deteriorating economy accumulated. The Fed also lowered the discount rate 5 times in 1991 to match the decline in the federal funds rate. In addition, the Fed lowered the reserve requirement on nonpersonal time deposit with an original maturity of less than $1\frac{1}{2}$ years from 3 percent to 1.5 percent on December 13, 1990, and eliminated it entirely on December 27, 1990. In February 1992, the day before Fed Chairman Alan Greenspan presented the Fed's economic forecast and monetary objectives to the House Banking Committee, the Fed announced a reduction in the reserve requirement on checkable deposits from 12 percent to 10 percent, effective April 2, 1992.

Lower interest rates and reserve requirements were not only good for the economy but also a welcome tonic for the fragile banking system. Lower reserve

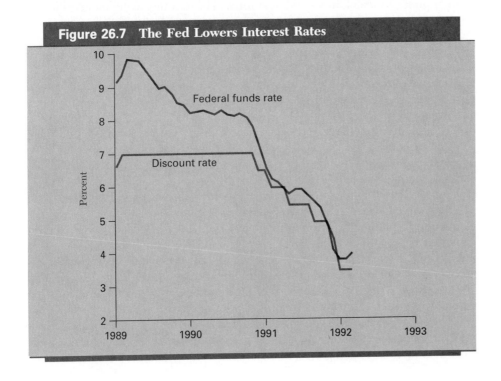

**Figure 26.7   The Fed Lowers Interest Rates**

requirements allow deposit institutions to invest more of their deposits and earn more income. Lower interest rates help institutions — particularly S&Ls — that have borrowed short and lent long. As interest rates fell in 1991, the thrift industry recorded a $1.9 billion profit, its first profitable year since 1985.

As this book went to the printer, output rose at a 2.7 percent annual rate in the first quarter of 1992, not enough to make a dent in the unemployment rate but giving President Bush hope that the recession would be over by the time voters went to the polls in November. However, in June of 1992, the unemployment rate surged to 7.8 percent, the highest level since March of 1984. On the day that this depressing news was announced, the Fed cut the discount rate another one-half percentage point, to 3 percent, the lowest level in 30 years; and it reduced its target for the federal funds rate by a comparable amount, from 3.75 percent to 3.25 percent. That afternoon, a House banking subcommittee announced that it would begin hearings the following week on "the politicization of the Fed in an election year."

# SUMMARY

The U.S. Treasury insisted that the Fed peg interest rates on Treasury securities at low levels during and after World War II. In a booming economy, this policy compelled the Fed to make open-market purchases, buying Treasury securities at high prices to maintain low interest rates. The accompanying increase in the monetary base made the Fed an involuntary engine of inflation. The 1951 Accord between the Fed and the Treasury established the important principle that the Federal Reserve was an independent branch of government, free to follow monetary policies that it deemed appropriate.

After the Accord, the Fed nonetheless continued for many years to "maintain orderly financial markets" by using open-market purchases to keep interest rates from fluctuating wildly. The Fed followed fairly cautious policies in the 1950s, monitoring net free reserves, interest rates, and $M1$ — in that order of importance. Fed policy during this period has been criticized for allowing three recessions in 10 years because of exaggerated fears of inflation and for paying too little attention to monetary aggregates.

In the 1960s the Fed generally accommodated the wishes of Presidents John Kennedy and Lyndon Johnson to reduce unemployment and increase the nation's output, although concern about inflation led to Fed-engineered credit crunches in 1966 and 1969–1970. During the 1970s, the economy was often characterized by high unemployment, rapid inflation, and large balance-of-payments deficits. The Fed watched monetary aggregates more closely and frequently tried to reduce inflation with a recession, although these anti-inflation efforts were often interrupted by presidential elections.

Between October of 1979 and October of 1982, the Fed under Paul Volcker paid less attention to stabilizing interest rates and more attention to reducing the growth of monetary aggregates sufficiently to wring inflation out of the economy.

In this it largely succeeded, although at the cost of the most severe recession since the Great Depression. With the inflation rate below 4 percent and the economy on the verge of collapse in the fall of 1982, the Fed changed to more expansionary policies that accommodated economic growth through the remainder of the decade. The divergent movements in monetary aggregates and erratic behavior of velocity, particularly $M1$ velocity, during the 1980s persuaded the Fed that it should not follow mechanical rules based on the behavior of one or two monetary aggregates. Instead, the Fed has followed an increasingly eclectic approach, using judgment and a variety of economic indicators to guide its policies.

## IMPORTANT TERMS

1951 Accord
bills-only policy
Operation Twist

## EXERCISES

1. The 1951 Accord established the principle that the Fed is not subservient to the Treasury and need not restrict open-market operations to doing whatever is necessary to maintain low interest rates. Explain how such a restriction might make the Fed, in its own words, an "engine of inflation."

2. Explain why net free reserves can be negative and whether this is more likely to happen when credit is easy or tight.

3. Net free reserves are an imperfect indicator of the state of the economy. Identify some circumstances in which net free reserves can increase during an economic boom and some circumstances in which net free reserves can increase during a recession.

4. Interest rates often decline during a recession, as borrowing slackens and inflation diminishes. Explain why interest rates can increase during a recession, making interest rates an imperfect indicator of the strength of the economy.

5. Alan Walter, a monetarist economics professor and personal economic advisor to British Prime Minister Margaret Thatcher, wrote in 1985 that

*Monetarists would normally agree that transaction money — the stuff with which people settle accounts — is the proper target. Financial assets, such as term savings accounts or certificates of deposit (CDs), are not transactions money. Nobody uses CDs to pay bills, so they should not appear in the money target.*[11]

Explain how some monetarists, including Milton Friedman, justify the targeting of monetary aggregates such as $M2$ and $M3$, which include time and savings accounts and certificates of deposit.

6. In the early 1960s the Federal Reserve argued that "the long-run rise in the volume of near money assets . . . has not reduced the effectiveness of monetary policy" and that $M1$ velocity had reached its "practical limit" of 3.0.

   a. Explain clearly what a velocity of 3.0 means.

b. Why might there be a practical limit to velocity?

c. Why would it matter to Fed policy whether or not velocity was at a practical limit?

d. At the end of 1986, M1 velocity was 6.0. Did M1 or gross domestic product grow faster between 1960 and 1986?

7. Since the end of World War II, time deposits have increased much more than transaction accounts have. When there is this kind of shift in public preferences, how does the shift affect required reserves? In the absence of government policy actions, do you think that monetary conditions tighten or ease?

8. When the shift described in the preceding exercise does occur, will the Fed tighten or ease monetary conditions if it acts to stabilize interest rates? M1?

9. In a November 1985 speech, Preston Martin, the vice-chairman of the Federal Reserve Board, said that "the Fed will continue to take a careful look at its M1 aggregate since declines in M1 velocity have 'cast doubt' on M1's reliability. . . . We may continue to deemphasize M1 and rely on the eclectic approach adopted this year."[12] What did he mean by "M1's reliability," and why does a decline in M1 velocity cast doubt on this?

10. What's wrong with the logic of the following argument: "Unless something politically improbable is done about the federal deficit, the deficit will continue to be financed largely with printed money flowing from the government."[13]

11. The text says that "the value of the U.S. dollar fell to new lows in the fall of 1979 as currency traders grew increasingly nervous about inflation in the United States." Explain why the value of the dollar is affected by inflation fears.

12. Compare these two news stories, the first from September of 1980 and the second from May of 1986.

*The nation's money surged upward again in the latest reporting period [M1 up by $1.2 billion in the previous week]. Analysts said that while the figures were not a surprise, fears of rising interest rates will grow unless the money supply declines in the next few weeks.*[14]

*The nation's money supply [M1] rose $4.2 billion in mid-April, the Federal Reserve reported Thursday.*

*Although the increase was larger than expected and pushed the money supply [more than $4 billion] above the Fed's growth target, there was virtually no reaction in the credit markets.*[15]

How do you explain the fact that a $1.2 billion increase that was not unexpected worried financial markets in 1980, while an unexpected $4.2 billion increase was of no concern in 1986?

13. In a 1989 speech in Toronto, the president of the Federal Reserve Bank of Cleveland said:

*A look at recent history reminds us vividly of the economic pain resulting from inflation. Every recession in the recent history of North America has been preceded by an outburst of cost and price pressures. . . . Today, in both Canada and the United States, people seem to be more aware than ever that the proper role of the central bank is to prevent these losses by stabilizing the price level.*[16]

Why do you think inflation so often preceded recession?

14. In 1980, financial analysts voiced the novel opinion that bonds had become riskier than stocks, as indicated by the following quota-

tions from the October 29, 1980 issue of *The Wall Street Journal*. Explain the reason for this remarkable shift in risk perceptions.

*"The long-term markets are in a state of disarray," says Sanford L. Weill, chairman and chief executive officer of Shearson Loeb Rhoades, Inc., a large New York investment firm. "We have a lot of clients completely out of the long-term markets, period, because they've been burned so badly."*

*During the past two weeks alone, bond prices have fallen almost 8%. A decline of the same magnitude in the Dow Jones Industrial Average would represent a drop of 75 points.*

*"Stocks used to be twice as volatile as bonds," says Leon C. Cooperman, chairman of the investment policy committee at Goldman, Sachs & Co. "Now bonds are more volatile."*[17]

15. The news story in the preceding exercise went on to report:

    *With a growing sense of gloom hanging over the bond market, many investment analysts said they're urging clients to switch away from long-term securities into the shortest possible maturities. "You can get almost as good yields at the short ends without the worry," says Data Resources' Mr. Eckstein.*

    Is there any worry in the shortest possible maturities?

16. Professor Robert J. Gordon of Northwestern University asserted that "monetarism has been decimated by the collapse of velocity in 1982."[18] What is velocity, and why would the collapse of velocity undermine monetarism?

17. The Congressional Budget Office argued that $M1$ velocity in 1984 might have been affected by a shift in the use of transaction balances to purchase imported products rather than U.S. products.[19] Explain why such a shift might either increase or decrease $M1$ velocity. (Remember that U.S. gross domestic product includes only goods and services that are produced in the United States.)

18. In a November 6, 1985, letter to Congressman Walter Fauntroy, Fed Chairman Paul Volcker wrote that after an unexpected decline in $M1$ velocity during the first half of 1985, the Fed adjusted its $M1$ targets in July with "the expectation that velocity behavior would be closer to historical patterns in the second half of the year. . . . As a practical matter, however, the velocity of $M1$ continued to decline over the summer, continuing the unusual pattern of the earlier part of the year." A financial analyst commented that "the historic pattern may no longer bind $M1$ and GNP. Disinflation, falling interest rates, and financial deregulation are major structural changes in our economy which undoubtedly have affected $M1$ velocity. In [June 1985] we argued that the Fed should just forget about $M1$."[20] Explain how each of the three changes cited might reduce $M1$ velocity.

19. The record of the Federal Open Market Committee's meeting on May 17, 1988 states that "the members generally agreed that some further tightening of reserve conditions was needed to counter the risks of rising inflationary pressures in the economy."[21] If you were managing the Fed's open-market operations and received this directive, would you interpret it as an instruction to make more open-market purchases or sales? How would these transactions affect borrowed and unborrowed reserves?

20. In 1986, Prudential-Bache's chief economist wrote about "Monetarist Melancholia":

    *The only positive thing we can say about monetarists is that they've been wrong for so long that they're overdue to be right. Last year, M1 monetarists warned that a reaccelerating economy would stimulate reflation. Instead, the economy muddled and the CPI inflation rate fell from 4.0% in 1984 to 3.7% in 1985.*

*Monetarists blame their forecasting error on an unexpected drop in velocity. . . . GNP is supposed to be a good proxy for the transactions which M1 is supposed to be financing. We don't believe that GNP is a good proxy for all transactions in our economy. . . .*

*Even if they could forecast nominal GNP, monetarists have no model for predicting the breakdown between real growth and inflation. Traditionally, monetarists assume that the economy is at or close to full employment. So "excessive" monetary growth always leads (with a long and variable lag) to inflation. But in a world of gluts (in a world where too many goods are chasing too few consumers) the monetarist model is bound to fail. And it has.*[22]

a. How is velocity measured, and how did the Fed know that it had collapsed?
b. If velocity collapses and the Fed targets M1, what will happen to GNP?
c. Why does a collapse in velocity undermine monetarism? Does an increase in velocity bolster monetarism?
d. Why isn't the annual volume of transactions equal to gross domestic product?
e. Explain how a monetarist model with full employment implies that monetary growth leads to inflation.

21. In 1982 an economist at the Federal Reserve Bank of St. Louis presented data indicating that in 1981 and 1982 "rising market interest rates tended to shift funds [from checkable deposits subject to interest rate ceilings] into time deposits [with no interest-rate ceilings], while falling market interest rates tended to shift funds into checkable deposits."[23] Explain why you find this em-

pirical observation to be either plausible or implausible. Do you predict that a shift from checkable deposits to time deposits will ease or tighten financial markets? Imagine that you are working for a Federal Reserve bank, and then write a paragraph justifying your prediction.

22. In 1988 and 1989, one Fed governor, Manuel Johnson, paid particular attention to the shape of the term structure of interest rates, believing that an increase in long-term rates relative to short-term rates signals financial market expectations that inflation will increase in the future. Provide a logical explanation for this belief.

23. In November of 1985, two economists with the Federal Reserve Bank of San Francisco wrote that "the rapid growth of M1 relative to M3 thus appears to be a portfolio shift by the public out of term balances into, among other things, M1 balances. This explanation of the recent rapid M1 growth implies that the surge does not indicate stimulative monetary policy."[24] Why might the increase in M1, in fact, reflect a tightening of credit conditions?

24. On February 20, 1990, bond and stock prices fell after Fed Chairman Alan Greenspan told a House banking subcommittee that the likelihood of recession had faded. Two days later, bond and stock prices rose when Greenspan told the Senate Banking Committee that the sharp January increase in the consumer price index was just an aberration and that inflation might decline during the months to come. How would you explain these reactions by financial markets?

25. In 1986 an investment advisory service reported that stock prices usually decline when the Treasury-bill rate rises above the discount rate.[25] Explain why the success of this indicator depends on whether the Federal Reserve is targeting interest rates or monetary aggregates.

# References

## CHAPTER 1

1. Arthur Schlesinger, Jr., "Inflation Symbolism vs. Reality," *Wall Street Journal,* April 9, 1980.
2. Dan Dorfman, "Fed Banking on Housing Slump to Nail Down Inflation," *Chicago Tribune*, April 20, 1980.
3. Gerald Krefetz, *How to Read and Profit from Financial News* (New York: Ticknor & Fields, 1984), p. 1.

## CHAPTER 2

1. W. S. Jevons, "Barter," in *Money and the Mechanism of Exchange* (New York: D. Appleton, 1892), pp. 1–7.
2. Paul Einzig, *Primitive Money*, 2nd ed. (Oxford: Pergamon Press, 1966), p. xi.
3. John Kenneth Galbraith, *Money* (Boston: Houghton Mifflin, 1975), p. 8.
4. Richard N. Cooper, "The Gold Standard: Historical Facts and Future Prospects," *Brooking Papers on Economic Activity*, I, 1982, pp. 1–45.
5. David Ricardo, *The Works and Correspondence of David Ricardo*, Vol. IV: *Pamphlets 1815–1823*, Piero Sraffa, ed. (Cambridge: Cambridge University Press, 1951), pp. 59, 62.
6. Galbraith, *op. cit.*, p. 59.
7. Lil Phillips, "Phindex Shows Horrific Inflation," *Cape Cod Times*, July 10, 1984.
8. John A. Johnson, "Sharing Some Ideas," *Cape Cod Times*, July 12, 1984.
9. *Barron's*, July 30, 1984.
10. "Inflation to Smile About," *Los Angeles Times*, January 11, 1988.

## CHAPTER 3

1. Jack L. Hervey, "Dollar Drop Helps Those Who Help Themselves," *Chicago Fed Letter*, March 1988, pp. 1–3.
2. *Houston Chronicle*, November 16, 1980.
3. William Tuohy, "The Pound: Pride Goeth Before a Fall," *Los Angeles Times*, January 17, 1985; Paul Lewis, "Weak Pound: An Opportunity," *New York Times*, January 18, 1985.
4. Lester Thurow, *Los Angeles Times*, May 26, 1985.
5. "On the Hamburger Standard," *The Economist*, September 6, 1986.
6. "Junk Currencies," *The Economist*, April 2, 1988, p. 66.

7. Editorial, "A Financial North Star," *Wall Street Journal*, February 26, 1990.
8. John Kenneth Galbraith, *Money* (Boston: Houghton Mifflin, 1975), p. 310.
9. "Why Europeans Care About U.S. Interest Rates," *Boston Globe*, July 14, 1981.
10. William Tuohy, "The Pound: Pride Goeth Before a Fall," *Los Angeles Times*, January 17, 1985.
11. Andrew Reinbach, "Topping Out," *U.S. Real Estate Week*, March 9, 1987, p. 7.
12. Edward Yardeni, *Money & Business Alert*, Prudential-Bache Securities, April 22, 1987.

## CHAPTER 4

1. Robert J. Samuelson, "Interest Rates Are Lower—Does that Equal 'Right'?" *Los Angeles Times*, March 13, 1986.
2. Stephen C. Leuthold, "Interest Rates, Inflation, and Deflation," *Financial Analysts Journal*, January/February 1981, pp. 28–41.
3. Lawrence H. Summers, "The Non-Adjustment of Nominal Interest Rates: A Study of the Fisher Effect," in James Tobin, ed., *Macroeconomics, Prices, and Quantities*, Essays in Memory of Arthur M. Okun (Washington, D.C.: Brookings Institution, 1983), pp. 201–241.
4. *New Yorker*, September 22, 1986, p. 111.
5. *London Times*, quoted in the *New Yorker*, March 11, 1985, p. 138.
6. Jane Bryant Quinn, "A Savings Program for College Tuition," *Cape Cod Times*, September 6, 1987.
7. Gerald Krefetz, *How to Read and Profit from Financial News* (New York: Tichnor & Fields, 1984), pp. 44 and 45.
8. Debra Whitefield, "Money Talk," *Los Angeles Times*, June 4, 1987.
9. Carmella M. Padilla, "It's a . . . a . . . a . . . All-Terrain Vehicle, Yeah, That's It, That's the Ticket," *Wall Street Journal*, July 17, 1987.
10. Family Real Estate advertisement, *Claremont Courier*, November 1, 1986.
11. William E. Fruhan, Jr., "How Fast Should Your Company Grow?" *Harvard Business Review*, January/February 1984, p. 87.
12. Glenn Emory, "Reading Between Lines of High Risk and Reward," *Insight*, September 4, 1989.
13. "The Rensselaer Plan," January 1992.

14. Robert W. Creamer, "Scorecard," *Sports Illustrated*, June 4, 1984, p. 13.

# CHAPTER 5

1. Robert J. Shiller, "Conventional Valuation and the Term Structure of Interest Rates," National Bureau of Economic Research Working Paper No. 1610, 1985 (and several references therein).
2. For example, B. G. Malkiel, *The Term Structure of Interest Rates* (Princeton, N.J.: Princeton University Press, 1966); and C. R. Nelson, *The Term Structure of Interest Rates* (New York: Basic Books, 1972).
3. Gary Smith, *Money and Banking* (Reading, Mass.: Addison-Wesley, 1982), pp. 98–99.
4. Another study found that the standard deviations increased less than proportionately for bonds with durations of 1 to 5 years during the period 1950–1979: Jonathan E. Ingersoll, Jr., "Is Immunization Feasible?" in George G. Kaufman, G. O. Bierwag, and Alden Toevs, eds., *Innovations in Bond Portfolio Management: Duration Analysis and Immunization* (Greenwich, Conn.: JAI Press, 1983), p. 175.
5. Jane Bryant Quinn, "Woman's Day Money Facts," *Woman's Day*, April 27, 1982, p. 29.
6. Tom Herman and Matthew Winkler, "Curve on Yields Poses Dilemma for Bond Buyer," *Wall Street Journal*, November 11, 1988.
7. "Personal Investing," *New York Times Financial Planning Guide*, May 19, 1985.
8. Martin Baron, "'Lions,' 'Tigers,' 'Cats,' Await Small Investor," *Los Angeles Times*, November 21, 1982.
9. Edward Yardeni, *Money & Business Alert*, Prudential-Bache Securities, November 20, 1985, p. 1.
10. Jack Clark Francis, *Management of Investments*, 2nd ed. (New York: McGraw-Hill, 1988), p. 500.
11. Bob Edwards, "Bond Analysis: The Concept of Duration," *American Association of Individual Investors Journal*, March 1984, p. 37.
12. Karen Slater, "Jumping on the Bondwagon," *Wall Street Journal*, December 2, 1985.
13. Constance Mitchell, "U.S. Needs a Few Good Investors as It Tries to Sell 40-Year Bonds," *Wall Street Journal*, April 6, 1990.
14. Frederick R. Macaulay, *Some Theoretical Problems Suggested by the Movement of Interest Rates, Bond Yields, and Stock Prices in the United States Since 1956* (New York: Columbia University Press, 1938).
15. Quoted in Steven Mintz, "Strategies," *Investment Management World*, May/June 1986, p. 22.
16. Tom Herman and Edward P. Foldessy, "Bond Prices Dropping in Market's Upheaval," *Wall Street Journal*, October 29, 1980.
17. "Business Bulletin," *Wall Street Journal*, March 13, 1986.
18. "For Merrill Lynch, An Idea That Fizzled," *New York Times*, August 8, 1982.
19. Gerald Krefetz, *How to Read and Profit from Financial News* (New York: Ticknor & Fields, 1984), p. 27.
20. David M. Gordon, "Reining In on the Federal Reserve," *Los Angeles Times*, September 30, 1986.
21. Paul Watro, "Bank Earnings: Comparing the Extremes," Federal Reserve Bank of Cleveland, 1987.
22. Eric N. Berg, "Fixed-Rate Mortgages Held Threat to Lenders," *New York Times*, March 10, 1986.
23. Alice Priest Shafran, "Streetsmarts for Househunters," *Sylvia Porter's Personal Finance Magazine*, September 1986, p. 37.
24. Jeffrey H. Birnbaum, "J. C. Penney Switches to Long-Term Debt to Fight Burgeoning Interest Expenses," *Wall Street Journal*, October 14, 1980.
25. Barbara Donnelly, " Pros Offer Methods for Sizing Up Bonds," *Wall Street Journal*, May 11, 1989.

# CHAPTER 6

1. *Progress Bulletin*, October 6, 1982.
2. Lindley H. Clark Jr., "Do We Really Need Lower Interest Rates?" *Wall Street Journal*, January 22, 1992.

# CHAPTER 7

1. P. A. Hays, M. D. Joehnk, and R. W. Melicher, "Determinants of Risk Premiums in the Public and Private Bond Market," *Journal of Financial Research*, Fall 1979.
2. James A. Wilcox, "Tax-Free Bonds," *Federal Reserve Bank of San Francisco Weekly Letter*, March 14, 1986.
3. Robert Lamb, professor at New York University, quoted in Elaine Johnson, "To Have and To Hold," *Wall Street Journal*, December 2, 1985, p. 16D.
4. Wilcox, *op. cit.*
5. Rosario Benvides, "How Big Is the World Bond Market?—1989 Update," *International Bond Market*, Salomon Brothers, June 24, 1989.
6. "Look East, Young Eurobond," *The Economist*, September 16, 1989, pp. 83–84.
7. Edward I. Altman and Scott A. Nammacher, "The Default Rate Experience on High-Yield Corporate Debt," Morgan Stanley & Co., March 1985.
8. Securities and Exchange Commission, "Report to Congress on the Accounting Professions and the Commission's Oversight Role," 1980.
9. Robert N. Anthony, "Games Government Accountants Play," *Harvard Business Review*, September/October 1985, p. 161.

10. M. Weinstein, "The Effect of a Rating Change Announcement on Bond Prices," *Journal of Financial Economics*, December 1977, pp. 329–350; and G. Hettenhouse and W. Satoris, "An Analysis of the Information Value of Bond-Rating Changes," *Quarterly Review of Economics and Business*, Summer 1976, pp. 65–78 agree, but Louis H. Ederington, Jess B. Yawitz, and Brian E. Roberts, "The Information Content of Bond Ratings," NBER Working Paper No. 1323, April 1984 disagree.

11. Paul Asquith, David W. Mullins, and Eric D. Wolff, "Original Issue High Yield Bonds: Aging Analysis of Defaults, Exchanges, and Calls," *Journal of Finance*, September 1989, pp. 923–952.

12. Theodore J. Forstmann, "Violating Our Rules of Prudence," *Wall Street Journal*, October 25, 1988.

13. Marshall E. Blume and Donald B. Keim, "The Risk and Return of Low-Grade Bonds: An Update," *Financial Analysts Journal*, September/October 1991, pp. 85–89.

14. W. B. Hickman, *Corporate Bond Quality and Investor Experience* (New York: National Bureau of Economic Research, 1958).

15. G. Pye, "Gauging the Default Premium," *Financial Analysts Journal*, January/February 1974, pp. 49–52.

16. Edward Altman and Scott Nammacher, "The Default Experience on High Yield Corporate Debt," *Financial Analysts Journal*, July/August 1985, pp. 25–41.

17. Harold G. Fraine and Robert H. Mills, "The Effect of Defaults and Credit Deterioriation on Yields of Corporate Bonds," *Journal of Finance*, September 1961, p. 433.

18. Charles D. Ellis, quoted in Tom Herman, "A Primer on the Treasury Market: How the Government Sells its Debt," *Wall Street Journal*, August 19, 1991.

19. Gerald Krefetz, *How to Read and Profit from Financial News* (New York: Ticknor & Fields, 1984), p. 43.

20. Ann-Marie Meulendyke, *U.S. Monetary Policy and Financial Markets* (New York: Federal Reserve Bank of New York, 1990), p. 87.

21. Charles R. Morris, "The Treasury Bond Scandal—Was Anyone Shocked?" *Los Angeles Times*, September 1, 1991.

22. Geoffrey Bell, quoted in Tom Herman, "A Primer on the Treasury Market: How the Government Sells its Debt," *Wall Street Journal*, August 19, 1991.

23. Quoted in Milton Friedman, "How to Sell Government Securities," *Wall Street Journal*, August 28, 1991.

24. Milton Friedman, "How to Sell Government Securities," *Wall Street Journal*, August 28, 1991.

25. James Flanigan, "Tax Reform: Time for Logical Deductions," *Los Angeles Times*, March 15, 1987.

26. Karen Slater, Premium Municipal Bonds Touted for Overall Return," *Wall Street Journal*, June 3, 1988.

27. Andrew Tobias, *The Only Investment Guide You'll Ever Need* (New York: Harcourt Brace Jovanovich,

1978), p. 3.

28. Standard & Poor's, *Debt Ratings Criteria: Municipal Overview*, 1986, p. 23.

29. Standard & Poor's, *Debt Ratings Criteria: Industrial Overview*, 1986. p. iii.

30. John Kenneth Galbraith, "A Classic Case of 'Euphoric Insanity,' " *New York Times*, November 23, 1986.

# CHAPTER 8

1. "Housing Squeeze Tightens More Here," *Houston Chronicle*, April 3, 1980.

2. Don G. Campbell, "S&Ls Turn to Mortgage Acceleration to Help Bail Themselves Out," *Los Angeles Times*, September 12, 1982.

3. Andrew Carron, of the Brookings Institution, quoted in "While Congress Fiddles, More Thrifts Burn," *The Economist*, February 27, 1982, p. 73.

4. Dennis Jacobe, director of research at the U.S. League of Savings Associations, quoted in Eric N. Berg, "Fixed-Rate Mortgages Held Threat to Lenders," *New York Times*, March 10, 1986.

5. Franco Modigliani, "Comment," in James Tobin, ed., *Macroeconomics: Prices and Quantities* (Washington, D.C.: Brookings Institution, 1983), p. 243. One example is an April 11, 1987 *Wall Street Journal* column (David B. Hilder, "ARMs Race On, But Borrowers Face Choices") in which negative amortization is said to be a "drawback."

6. "Nibbling Down Affordable Mortgages," *Business Week*, March 14, 1983, p. 153.

7. R. J. Turner, *The Mortgage Maze* (Arlington, Va.: Alexandria House Books, 1982), p. 64.

8. *Ibid.*, p. 97.

9. Les Gapay, "Don't Bank on It: Thinking of Refinancing? Read This First," *Barron's*, June 30, 1986.

10. Turner, *op. cit.*, pp. 242–243.

11. Gordon Bjork, *Wall Street Journal*, March 29, 1989.

12. Don G. Campbell, "Early Loan Payoff Gains Popularity," *Los Angeles Times*, October 20, 1985.

13. "Hot Tips," *Sylvia Porter's Personal Finance*, February 1986, p. 18.

14. Turner, *op. cit.*, p. 228.

15. Don G. Campbell, "Biweekly 'Yuppie Mortgages' Interest State Lenders," *Los Angeles Times*, April 26, 1987.

16. Don G. Campbell, "Creating a Market for Biweeklies," *Los Angeles Times*, April 26, 1987.

17. First Federal Savings of the Palm Beaches, letter dated July 11, 1986.

18. "A Guide to the Federal Home Loan Bank System," FHLB System Publication Corporation, March 1987, p. 59.

# CHAPTER 12

1. Ann-Marie Meulendyke, *U.S. Monetary Policy and Financial Markets*, Federal Reserve Bank of New York, 1989, p. 85.

# CHAPTER 13

1. Charles Mackay, *Memoirs of Extraordinary Popular Delusions and the Madness of Crowds* (London: Richard Bentley, 1841; reprinted Boston: L. C. Page, 1932), p. 37.
2. John Kenneth Galbraith, *Money* (Boston: Houghton Mifflin, 1975), pp. 73–74.
3. A. B. Hepburn, *A History of Currency in the United States* (New York: Macmillan, 1915), p. 102.
4. Quoted in Herman E. Krooss and Martin R. Blyn, *A History of Financial Intermediaries* (New York: Random House, 1971).
5. William M. Gouge, *A Short History of Paper Money and Banking in the United States* (1835; reprinted New York: Augustus M. Kelly, 1968).
6. H. Parker Willis and George W. Edwards, *Banking and Business* (New York: Harper and Brothers, 1925), pp. 96–97; *New York Times*, March 22, 1931, Section IV, p. 10.
7. John Maynard Keynes, *A Treatise on Money*, Vol. 1 (London: Macmillan, 1930), pp. 41–43.
8. See, for example, John Wenninger and Charles M. Sivesind, "Defining Money for a Changing Financial System," *Federal Reserve Bank of New York Quarterly Review*, Spring 1979, pp. 1–8.
9. Elizabeth Lederman, "Progress in Retail Payments," *Federal Reserve Bank of San Francisco Weekly*, February 7, 1992, p. 1.
10. David B. Humphrey and Allen N. Berger, "Market Failure and Resource Use: Economic Incentives to Use Different Payment Instruments," in David B. Humphrey, ed., *The U.S. Payment System: Efficiency, Risk, and the Role of the Federal Reserve* (Boston: Kluwer Academic Publishers, 1990).
11. *Wall Street Journal*, December 29, 1979.

# CHAPTER 14

1. See Herman E. Krooss and Martin R. Blyn, *A History of Financial Intermediaries* (New York: Random House, 1971), pp. 134–136.

2. Condy Raguet, *A Treatise on Currency and Banking* (1839; reprinted New York: Augustus M. Kelley, 1967), p. 92.
3. Herman E. Krooss and Martin R. Blyn, *A History of Financial Intermediaries* (New York: Random House, 1971), p. 134.
4. Both quoted in Krooss and Blyn, *ibid.*, p. 119.
5. Milton Friedman and Anna Jacobsen Schwartz, *A Monetary History of the United States, 1867–1960* (Princeton, N.J.: Princeton University Press, 1963), pp. 269–270.
6. John Kenneth Galbraith, *Money* (Boston: Houghton-Mifflin, 1975), pp. 131, 175–180.
7. For example, Krooss and Blyn, *op. cit.*, p. 170
8. Galbraith, *op. cit.*, p. 194.
9. *Ibid.*, pp. 186–187.
10. Krooss and Blyn, *op. cit.*, p. 13.
11. Arthur Okun, "Rules and Roles for Fiscal and Monetary Policy" in J. J. Diamond, ed., *Fiscal and Monetary Policy: The Eclectic Economist Views the Controversy* (Chicago: De Paul University, 1971), p. 59.
12. R. Alton Gilbert and Geoffrey E. Wood, "Coping with Bank Failures: Some Lessons from the United States and the United Kingdom," *Federal Reserve Bank of St. Louis Economic Review*, December 1986, pp. 5–14.
13. Fred Schwed, Jr., *Where Are the Customers' Yachts?* (New York: Simon & Schuster, 1940), p. 91.
14. *Time*, November 18, 1929, p. 45.

# CHAPTER 15

1. *New York Times*, May 25, 1980.
2. "Concerns Mount Over Banks' Liabilities, *New York Times*, June 25, 1985.
3. David B. Hilder, "More Thrifts Grow Big by Investing in Areas Other Than Mortgages," *Wall Street Journal*, May 6, 1987.
4. Don G. Campbell, "S&Ls Turn to Mortgage Acceleration to Help Bail Themselves Out," *Los Angeles Times*, September 12, 1982.
5. *Ibid.*
6. "While Congress Fiddles, More Thrifts Burn," *The Economist*, February 27, 1982.
7. Richard F. Janssen and Edward P. Foldessy, "After a Near-Disaster, Savings Banks Vow to Take Tougher Stance in Making Loans," *Wall Street Journal*, May 20, 1980.
8. Karlyn Mitchell, "Interest Rate Risk Management at Tenth District Banks," *Federal Reserve Bank of Kansas City Economic Review*, May 1985, pp. 3–19.
9. The data in this exercise are from CalFed's 1985 *Annual Report*, pp. 7, 28–29.
10. Mitchell, *op. cit.*

# CHAPTER 16

1. "A Guide to the Federal Home Loan Bank System," FHLB System Publication Corporation, March 1987, p. 18.
2. *Wall Street Journal*, July 18, 1980.
3. Quoted in Paulette Thomas and Thomas E. Ricks, "Just What Happened to All That Money Savings & Loans Lost?" *Wall Street Journal*, December 5, 1990.
4. "A Guide to the Federal Home Loan Bank System," FHLB System Publication Corporation, March 1987.
5. "Who's Killing the Thrifts?" *Newsweek*, November 10, 1986.
6. James Ring Adams, The Big Fix," *The American Spectator*, March 1989, pp. 21–24.
7. Charles McCoy and Paulette Thomas, "Hundreds of S&Ls Fall Hopelessly Short of New Capital Rules," *Wall Street Journal*, December 7, 1989.
8. Paulette Thomas, "As S&L Bailout Plan Draws Nearer Passage, Flaws Become Clearer," *Wall Street Journal*, July 21, 1989.
9. Russ Wiles, "Mutual Funds," *Los Angeles Times*, September 22, 1991.
10. James Tobin, "Deposit Interest Ceilings as a Monetary Control," *Journal of Money, Credit, and Banking*, February 1970, pp. 4–14.
11. "A Guide to the Federal Home Loan Bank System," FHLB System Publication Corporation, March 1987, p. 59.
12. The Benham Group, advertising supplement, *Wall Street Journal*, December 12, 1991.
13. Pomona First Federal Savings, *Interest*, Fall 1989, p. 3.
14. Christian Hill and Michael Allen, "High Yields for Deposits Fall, Thanks to Thrift Rescue," *Wall Street Journal*, August 24, 1989.

# CHAPTER 17

1. Robert B. Avery et al., "Survey of Consumer Finances, 1983: A Second Report," *Federal Reserve Bulletin*, December 1984, pp. 866–867.
2. Thomas A. Durkin, "Finance Companies 1977–1985," *Finance Facts*, May/June 1986.
3. *Federal Reserve Bulletin*, December 1991, p. A38.
4. *Federal Reserve Bulletin*, December 1991, pp. A35 and A38.
5. Robert B. Avery et al., "Survey of Consumer Finances, 1983: A Second Report," *Federal Reserve Bulletin*, December 1984, pp. 866–867.
6. Robin Gross and Jean V. Cullen, *Help! The Basics of Borrowing Money* (New York: Times Books, 1980), p. 45.

7. "How to Save on a Car Loan," *Consumer Reports*, April 1978, pp. 201–202.
8. John R. Emshwiller, "Running on Empty: Car Pawning Grows as Cash-Strapped Owners Hock the Rolls," *Wall Street Journal*, December 11, 1991.
9. *Ibid.*
10. David Henry, "Lender of Last Resort," *Forbes*, May 18, 1987, pp. 73–75.
11. David Pauly, "Bracing for the Great Car Glut," *Newsweek*, September 15, 1986, p. 59.
12. Douglas R. Sease, "Buying a Car? Here's How to Figure Savings in Latest Offers from GM, Ford, and Chrysler," *Wall Street Journal*, May 3, 1982.
13. S. J. Diamond, "Credit or Cash? The Difference Can Add Up," *Los Angeles Times*, September 23, 1985; also see S. J. Diamond, "Credit Doesn't Always Rate Better than Cash," *Los Angeles Times*, September 30, 1985.

# CHAPTER 18

1. Kevin Pritchett, "Hertz Slaps Some New Yorkers with a Stiff Surcharge," *Wall Street Journal*, January 3, 1992.
2. *Statistisk arsbok for Sverige, 1986* (Stockholm: Statistiska Central Byran, 1986), pp. 55–56.
3. Paul Kagan Associates, reported in Laura Landro, "Summer Movies Off to Bruising Start," *Wall Street Journal*, June 7, 1990.
4. Mona J. Gardner and Dixie L. Mills, *Managing Financial Institutions* (Chicago: Dryden, 1988), p. 643.
5. Irwin T. Vanderhoof, "The Use of Duration in the Dynamic Programming of Investments," in George G. Kaufman, G. O. Bierwag, and Alden Toevs, *Innovations in Bond Portfolio Management: Duration Analysis and Immunization*, Greenwich, Conn.: JAI Press, 1983, p. 46.
6. Jeffrey O'Connell, "Living with Life Insurance," *New York Times Magazine*, May 19, 1974, pp. 34, 98–102.
7. Burton G. Malkiel, *A Random Walk Down Wall Street*, 4th ed. (New York, W. W. Norton, 1985), p. 242.
8. Richard W. McEnally, "Rethinking Our Thinking About Interest Rates," *Financial Analysts Journal*, March/April 1986, p. 64.
9. Bob Edwards, "Bond Analysis: The Concept of Duration," *American Association of Individual Investors Journal*, March 1984, p. 34.

# CHAPTER 19

1. EBRI, *Quarterly Pension Investment Report*, 4th quarter 1990.
2. Diane Hal Gropper, "Propping Up the PBGC," *Institutional Investor*, September 1986, pp. 157–170

3. Ralph Nader and Kate Blackwell, *You and Your Pension* (New York: Grossman, 1973), pp. 70–71.

4. U.S. Senate Committee on Labor and Public Welfare, *Interim Report of Activities of the Private Welfare and Pension Plan Study, 1971* (Washington, D.C.: U.S. Government Printing Office, 1972), p. 85.

5. Zvi Bodie and L. E. Papke, "Pension Fund Finance," in Zvi Bodie and A. Munnell, eds., *Pensions and the Economy: Sources, Uses and Limitations of Data* (Philadelphia: University of Pennsylvania, 1991); for some Canadian data, see D. Don Ezra and Keith P. Ambachtsheer, "Pension Funds: Rich or Poor," *Financial Analysts Journal*, March/April 1985, pp. 43–56.

6. Jeremy Bulow and Myron Scholes, "Who Owns the Assets in a Defined-Benefit Pension Plan?" in Zvi Bodie and John Shoven, eds., *Financial Aspects of the U.S. Pension System* (Chicago: University of Chicago Press, 1983).

7. For a more detailed analysis, see Richard J. Kientz and Clyde P. Stickney, "Immunization of Pension Funds and Sensitivity to Actuarial Assumptions," *Journal of Risk and Insurance*, June 1980, pp. 223–239.

8. "The Abiding Faith in Active Management," *Institutional Investor*, May 1986, pp. 97, 100.

9. See, for example, Gary P. Brinson, Brian D. Singer, and Gilbert L. Beebower, "Determinants of Portfolio Performance II: An Update," *Financial Analysts Journal*, May/June 1991, pp. 40–48.

10. Pomona First Federal Savings, *Interest*, Summer 1983.

11. Robert L. Rose, "Retirement Planning Should Begin with Early Look at Social Security," *Wall Street Journal*, April 30, 1985.

12. "The Best Places for Your Cash in 1986," *Money*, January 1986.

13. Andrea Rock, "Profiting from the IRA Revolution," *Money Guide/IRA 1986*, published by *Money* magazine.

14. Richard W. McEnally, "Rethinking Our Thinking About Interest Rates," *Financial Analysts Journal*, March/April 1986, p. 65.

# CHAPTER 20

1. Robert M. Bleiberg, "What Price Stewardship?—Management Keeps Putting Its Interest Ahead of Shareholders," *Barron's*, February 15, 1982, p. 11.

2. *Barron's* has exposed and opposed such actions time and again; for example, "Private Fiefdom?—McGraw-Hill Stockholders Are Getting a Raw Deal," February 5, 1979; "More 'Scorched Earth,'—Who is Standing Up for Shareholder Rights?" May 5, 1980; "Corporation or Fiefdom?—Conflicts Between Shareholders, Management Mount," July 7, 1980; "One Shareholder, One Vote?—Scholars Challenge Some Widespread Myths About Corporations," August 24, 1981; and "What Price Stewardship?—Management Keeps Putting Its Interest Ahead of Shareholders," February 15, 1982.

3. Quoted in Michael A. Hiltzik, "Investors Relenquish Key Rights," *Los Angeles Times*, May 18, 1986.

4. *Ibid.*

5. See, for example, Michael C. Jensen, "Takeovers: Folklore and Science," *Harvard Business Review*, November/December 1984, pp. 109–121.

6. "The Story Behind the Deal," *Investment Dealer Digest*, April 12, 1983.

7. Quoted in Robert E. Dallos, "Companies Get Bullish on Security," *Los Angeles Times*, February 28, 1983.

8. Securities Industry Association, *Securities Industry Trends*, May 1991.

9. John F. Lawrence, "Let's Outlaw Abuses Behind Takeover Bids," *Los Angeles Times*, March 15, 1987.

10. David J. Skinner, "Common Stocks," in Jack P. Friedman, ed., *Encyclopedia of Investments*, 2nd ed. (Boston: Warren, Gorham & Lamont, 1990), p. 143.

11. Andrew Tobias, *The Only Investment Guide You'll Ever Need* (New York: Harcourt Brace Jovanovich, 1978), p. 118.

12. Louis Rukeyser, *How to Make Money in Wall Street* (Garden City, N.J.: Doubleday, 1974), p. 129.

# CHAPTER 21

1. Investment Company Institute, *1987 Mutual Fund Fact Book* (Washington, D.C.: Investment Company Institute, 1987).

2. Kathryn McGrath, quoted in *Money*, September 1986, p. 13.

3. Irwin Friend, Marshall Blume, and Jean Crockett, *Mutual Funds and Other Institutional Investors: A New Perspective*, Twentieth Century Fund Study (New York: McGraw-Hill, 1971), also found that mutual funds as a whole underperformed the market and that investors in load funds did worse than those in no-loads.

4. An early proponent of this view is Eugene F. Pratt, "Myths Associated with Closed-End Investment Companies," *Financial Analysts Journal*, July/August 1966, pp. 79–82. Some empirical evidence is given by Burton G. Malkiel, "The Valuation of Closed-End Investment-Company Shares," *Journal of Finance*, June 1977, pp. 847–859.

5. Quoted in Gilbert Kaplan and Chris Welles, *The Money Managers* (New York: Random House, 1969).

6. Pamela Sebastian and Jan Wong, "Fidelity Is Scrambling to Keep High Flying as Magellan Slows Up," *Wall Street Journal*, August 15, 1986; Randall Smith, "Some Mutual Funds' Hot Records May Hide Companies' Cool Moves," *Wall Street Journal*, March 14, 1985.

7. Quoted in Andrew Tobias, *The Only Investment Guide You'll Ever Need* (New York: Harcourt Brace Jovanovich, 1978), p. 133.

8. Fred Schwed, Jr., *Where Are the Customers' Yachts?* (New York: Simon & Schuster, 1940), p. 87.

9. The seminal study is William F. Sharpe, "Mutual Fund Performance," *Journal of Business*, January, 1966, pp. 119–138.

10. Michael C. Jensen, "The Performance of Mutual Funds in the Period 1945–64," *Journal of Finance*, May 1968, pp. 389–416.

11. A. W. Bigus, "Whatever Happened to Mutual Funds?" *Esquire*, December 1973, pp. 48–54.

12. Fidelity Investments, *Investment Vision*, November/December 1987, p. 9.

13. Michael Laurence, "Playboy's Guide to Mutual Funds," *Playboy*, June 1969, p. 196.

14. *Ibid.*, p. 186.

15. L. J. Davis, "The Next Panic," *Harper's Magazine*, May 1987, p. 38.

16. Wiesenberger Investment Companies Service, *Investment Companies 1992* (New York: Warren, Gorham & Lamont).

17. Michael Laurence, *op. cit.*, p. 197.

18. Dean LeBaron, President of Batterymarch Financial Management, in a February 1986 speech to fellow money managers and corporate financial executives, quoted in "LeBaron: Institutions Are Losing Their Grip," *Investment Management World*, March/April 1986, p. 5.

19. C. C. Hazard, *Confessions of a Wall Street Insider* (Chicago: Playboy Paperback, 1972), p. 25.

20. Michael Laurence, *op. cit.*, p. 152.

21. Wiesenberger Investment Companies Service, *Investment Companies 1992* (New York: Warren, Gorham & Lamont).

22. Michael Siconolfi, "Closed-End Funds Open to Gimmicks That Lift Prices," *Wall Street Journal*, April 13, 1989.

23. Thomas C. Noddings, *Advanced Investment Strategies* (Homewood, Ill.: Dow Jones–Irwin, 1978), p. 127.

# CHAPTER 22

1. Arthur F. Burns, "Maintaining the Soundness of Our Banking System," Speech to American Bankers Association Convention, Honolulu, Hawaii, October 21, 1974, pp. 18–19.

2. Frank Wille, "Dissenting Statement, FDIC Approves Merger in Alice, Texas," News Release, FDIC, August 18, 1975.

3. Editorial, "The Centralizing of the System," *Financier*, April 1980, pp. 5–6.

4. Thomas Havrilesky and John Gildea, "Packing the Board of Governors," *Challenge*, March/April 1990, pp. 52–55.

5. Economic Policy Commission, American Bankers Association, *The Guaranty of Bank Deposits* (New York: ABA, 1933), p. 43.

6. Quoted in Arthur M. Schlesinger, Jr., *The Coming of the New Deal* (Boston: Houghton Mifflin, 1958), p. 443.

7. For example, R. Alton Gilbert, "Bank Failures and Public Policy," *Federal Reserve Bank of St. Louis Economic Review*, November 1975, p. 12; see also K. E. Scott and T. Mayer, "Risk and Regulation in Banking: Some Proposals for Federal Deposit Insurance Reform," *Stanford Law Review*, May 1971, pp. 857–902.

8. Katrina Simons and Stephen Cross, "Do Capital Markets Predict Problems in Large Commercial Banks?" *New England Economic Review*, Federal Reserve Bank of Boston, May/June 1991, pp. 51–56.

9. Stephen Labaton, "Bank Reports on Assets Are Doubted," *New York Times*, June 25, 1991.

10. Federal Deposit Insurance Corporation, *The First Fifty Years: A History of the FDIC, 1933–1983* (Washington, D.C.: FDIC, 1984), pp. 97–98.

11. See "The Examiners: Now the Customers Check Out the Banks; So Do Other Banks," *Wall Street Journal*, September 9, 1976.

12. Gary Smith, *Investments* (Boston: Little, Brown/Scott, Foresman, 1990), pp. 190–195.

13. For example, Edward J. Kane, National Bureau of Economic Research, Working Paper No. 2317, 1987.

14. Richard F. Janssen and Edward P. Foldessy, "After a Near-Disaster, Savings Banks Vow to Take Tougher Stance in Making Loans," *Wall Street Journal*, May 20, 1980.

15. H. Parker Willis, John M. Chapman, and Ralph W. Robey, *Contemporary Banking* (New York: Harper, 1933), p. 560.

16. Federal Reserve Board of Governors, *Annual Report*, 1956, pp. 52–55.

17. Dan Dorfman, "Fed Banking on Housing Slump to Nail Down Inflation," *Chicago Tribune*, April 20, 1980.

18. James Tobin, "Deposit Interest Ceilings as a Monetary Control," *Journal of Money, Credit and Banking*, February 1970, pp. 4–14.

19. Michael Weinstein, "ATM Makers Perceive Opportunities Despite Signs of Saturation," *American Banker*, December 19, 1984, p. 14.

20. John Duffy, executive vice president of Security Pacific Corporation, *Wall Street Journal*, September 3, 1980.

21. Richard Flamson, chief executive officer of Security Pacific Corporation, *Wall Street Journal*, September 3, 1980.

22. Herbert Stein, "Backstage at the Fed," *Wall Street Journal*, April 4, 1986.

23. *Wall Street Journal*, June 12, 1980.
24. Tobin, *op. cit.*, p. 10.
25. Quoted in Jonathan D. Aronson, *Money and Power: Banks and the World Monetary System* (Beverly Hills, Calif.: Sage Publications, 1977).
26. "Banking Deregulation Benefits Many People But Stirs Some Worry," *Wall Street Journal*, September 30, 1985.
27. Bruce Horovitz, "Behind the Scenes of a Bank Take-over by FDIC," *Los Angeles Times*, January 5, 1986.
28. James Bates and Daniel Akst, "Regulators Close Center National Bank," *Los Angeles Times*, April 12, 1986.
29. Michael Quint, "Accounting Proposal Irks Bankers," *New York Times*, November 21, 1989.
30. Eric N. Compton, *The New World of Commercial Banking* (Lexington, Mass.: D. C. Heath, 1987), p. 105.
31. James McMahon, vice president of the Western Independent Bankers group. *New York Times*, October 19, 1980.

# CHAPTER 23

1. Kenneth Bacon, staff reporter, *Wall Street Journal*, August 4, 1980, p. 1.
2. John Wood, "A Model of Federal Reserve Behavior," in George Horwich, ed., *Monetary Process and Policy* (Homewood, Ill.: Irwin, 1967).
3. Peter S. Rose, "Banker Attitudes Toward the Federal Reserve System: Survey Results," *Journal of Bank Research*, Summer 1977, pp. 77–84.
4. Marvin Goodfriend and William Whelpley, "Federal Funds," in Timothy Q. Cook and Timothy D. Rowe, eds., *Instruments of the Money Market*, 6th ed. (Richmond, Va.: Federal Reserve Bank of Richmond, 1986), p. 18.
5. G. J. Santoni, "The Monetary Control Act, Reserve Taxes and the Stock Prices of Commercial Banks," *Federal Reserve Bank of St. Louis Economic Review*, June/July 1985, pp. 12–20.
6. Alexandra Peers, "How Discount-Rate Rise Will Affect Consumer Fees—and When," *Wall Street Journal*, February 27, 1989.
7. *Houston Chronicle*, February 15, 1980.
8. *Report of the Committees on Finance and Industry* (London: His Majesty's Stationery Office, 1931), p. 97.
9. Federal Reserve Bank of St. Louis, *U.S. Financial Data*, December 10, 1982, p. 1.
10. Investment newsletter, "Capital Gains," 1986.
11. J. Anthony Boeckh and Richard Coghlan, "The Inflation Risk and Prospective Returns for the 1980s," in J. Anthony Boeckh and Richard T. Coghlan, eds., *The Stock Market and Inflation* (Homewood, Ill.: Dow Jones–Irwin, 1982), pp. 146–147.

12. Robert J. Samuelson, "Interest Rates are Lower—Does That Equal Right?" *Los Angeles Times*, March 13, 1986.
13. Edward P. Foldessy, "Fed Reprimands Some New York Banks for Abusing Their Borrowing Privileges," *Wall Street Journal*, October 25, 1977.

# CHAPTER 24

1. Paul Samuelson, "Money, Interest Rates and Economic Activity: Their Interrelationships in a Market Economy," in American Bankers Association, *Proceedings of a Symposium on Money, Interest Rates, and Economic Activity* (New York: ABA, 1967), p. 44.
2. Thomas Havrilesky, "Monetary Policy Signaling from the Administration to the Federal Reserve," *Journal of Money, Credit, and Banking*, February 1988, pp. 83–101.
3. Sherman Maisel, *Managing the Dollar* (New York: Norton, 1975), p. 278.
4. Havrilesky has found some empirical evidence that the Federal Reserve's monetary policy is influenced by bankers: Thomas Havrilesky, "The Influence of the Federal Advisory Council on Monetary Policy," *Journal of Money, Credit, and Banking*, February 1990, pp. 37–50.
5. A. M. Schlesinger, Jr., *The Crisis of the Old Order* (Boston: Houghton Mifflin, 1957), p. 231.
6. John Maynard Keynes, *The General Theory of Employment, Interest, and Money* (London: Macmillan, 1936).
7. *New York World*, October 15, 1930.
8. John Kareken and Robert Solow, "Lags in Monetary Policy," in Commission on Money and Credit, *Stabilization Policies* (Englewood Cliffs, N.J.: Prentice-Hall, 1963).
9. Gary Fromm and Lawrence Klein, "A Comparison of Eleven Econometric Models on the United States," *American Economic Review*, May 1973.
10. Kareken and Solow, *op. cit.*, p. 2.
11. Milton Friedman, "The Lag in the Effect of Monetary Policy," *Journal of Political Economy*, October, 1961, pp. 447–466.
12. Keynes, *op. cit.*, p. 33.
13. For a formal analysis see Gary Smith, "Monetarism, Bondism, and Inflation," *Journal of Money, Credit, and Banking*, May 1982.
14. Henry C. Simons, "Rules vs. Authorities in Monetary Policy," *Journal of Political Economy*, February 1936, pp. 13–14, 29–30.
15. *Ibid.*, p. 16.
16. *Ibid.*, p. 30.
17. Henry Simons, *Economic Policy for a Free Society* (Chicago: University of Chicago Press, 1948).

18. Edward S. Shaw, "Money Supply and Stable Economic Growth," in H. H. Jacoby, ed., *United States Monetary Policy* (New York: Praeger, 1964), p. 89.

19. Robert E. Lucas, Jr., "Unemployment Policy," *American Economic Review*, 68, May 1978, p. 357.

20. Robert E. Lucas, Jr., "Tobin and Monetarism: A Review Article," *Journal of Economic Literature*, June 1981, pp. 562–563.

21. Paul Samuelson, "Reflections on Central Banking," reprinted in *The Collected Scientific Papers of Paul Samuelson*, Vol. 2, Joseph Stiglitz, ed. (Boston: M.I.T. Press, 1966), p. 1362.

22. Laurie McGinley, "The Fed Is Bracing for Political Criticism as Campaign Goes On," *Wall Street Journal*, February 1, 1984.

23. *Los Angeles Times*, November 22, 1981.

24. Leonall C. Anderson, "The State of the Monetarist Debate," *Federal Reserve Bank of St. Louis Economic Review*, September 1973, p. 4.

25. Milton Friedman, "Lessons from the 1979–1982 Monetary Policy Experiment," *American Economic Review*, Papers and Proceedings, May 1984, pp. 397–400.

26. Charles P. Kindleberger, *Manias, Panics, and Crashes* (New York: Basic Books, 1978), p. 73.

27. Herbert Stein, *Presidential Economics* (New York: Simon & Schuster, 1984), p. 250.

28. Lyle Gramley, "Financial Innovation and Monetary Policy," *Federal Reserve Bulletin*, July 1982, p. 396.

29. Victor A. Canto and Arthur B. Laffer, "Monetary Policy Caused the Crash: Not Tight Enough," *Wall Street Journal*, October 22, 1987.

30. Herbert Stein, *op. cit.*, p. 222.

# CHAPTER 25

1. For example, see Irving Fisher, *The Purchasing Power of Money* (New York: Macmillan, 1911).

2. John Burr Williams, *The Theory of Investment Value* (Cambridge, Mass.: Harvard University Press, 1938), p. 52.

3. Milton Friedman, "The Quantity Theory of Money: A Restatement," in *Studies in the Quantity Theory of Money* (Chicago: University of Chicago Press, 1956), pp. 3–21.

4. For example, see Thomas Mayer, *The Structure of Monetarism* (New York: W. W. Norton, 1978).

5. A frequently cited survey is David Laidler, *The Demand for Money: Theories and Evidence*, 3rd ed. (New York: Dun-Donnelly, 1985).

6. See Friedman's comments in *Milton Friedman's Monetary Framework*, Robert J. Gordon, ed. (Chicago: University of Chicago Press, 1974).

7. Lyle Gramley, "Financial Innovation and Monetary Policy," *Federal Reserve Bulletin*, July 1982, p. 396.

8. In a number of empirical macro models, attempts to peg monetary aggregates lead to unstable policies. See John H. Ciccolo, "Is Short-Run Monetary Control Feasible?" Federal Reserve Bank of New York, 1974; and Lawrence Radecki, "Short-Run Monetary Control: An Analysis of Some Possible Dangers," *Federal Reserve Bank of New York Quarterly Review*, Spring 1982, pp. 1–10. Also see Henry C. Wallich and Peter M. Keir, "The Role of Operating Guides in U.S. Monetary Policy: An Historical Review," *Federal Reserve Bulletin*, September 1979, esp. p. 688.

9. "Solomon Sees Fed Policy Changes," *Los Angeles Times*, December 29, 1981.

10. Edward S. Shaw, "Money Supply and Stable Economic Growth," in H. H. Jacoby, ed., *United States Monetary Policy* (New York: Praeger, 1964), pp. 74–76.

11. Karl Brunner, Alan Meltzer, the St. Louis Fed, and even Milton Friedman have all expressed support for targeting the monetary base; see, for example, Milton Friedman, "Monetary Policy for the 1980s," in John H. Moore, ed., *To Promote Prosperity: U.S. Domestic Policy in the Mid-1980s* (Stanford, Calif.: Hoover Institution Press, 1984), pp. 23–60.

12. Anthony Harris, "Competition vs. Monetarism, Study in Policy Schizophrenia," *Financier*, October 1981, p. 48.

13. Herbert Stein, "Verbal Windfall," *New York Times Magazine*, September 9, 1979, p. 14.

14. Paul Volcker, "A Broader Role for Monetary Targets," *Federal Reserve Bank of New York Quarterly Review*, Spring 1977, p. 27.

15. Federal Reserve Bank of Cleveland, *Economic Trends*, November 1989, p. 2.

16. William T. Gavin, "The $M1$ Target and Disinflation Policy," *Economic Commentary*, Federal Reserve Bank of Cleveland, October 1, 1985, p. 1.

17. Edward Yardeni, *Money & Business Alert*, Prudential-Bache Securities, January 15, 1986.

18. Franco Modigliani, *New York Times*, November 6, 1977.

19. Associated Press, "NOW Account Funds Cause $M1B$ to Surge $11.6 Billion." *Houston Chronicle*, January 17, 1981.

20. James Tobin, "The Monetary Interpretation of History, A Review Article," *American Economic Review*, June 1965, pp. 464–485.

21. Lindley H. Clark, Jr., *Wall Street Journal*, September 30, 1980.

22. Paul A. Volcker, statement before the Subcommittee on Monopolies and Commercial Law of the Committee on the Judiciary, U.S. House of Representatives, May 5, 1982; printed in the *Federal Reserve Bulletin*, May 1982, pp. 298–301.

23. Federal Reserve Bank of Cleveland, *Economic Trends*, January 1990, p. 2.
24. William T. Gavin, "The *M*1 Target and Disinflation Policy," *Economic Commentary*, Federal Reserve Bank of Cleveland, October 1, 1985.
25. Wallich and Keir, *op. cit.*, p. 688.

# CHAPTER 26

1. Lindley H. Clark, Jr., "Speaking of Business: The Elderly Economist," *Wall Street Journal*, February 12, 1980.
2. *Federal Reserve Bulletin*, October 1979, p. 830.
3. "Record of Policy Actions of the Federal Open Market Committee," *Federal Reserve Bulletin*, December 1979, p. 974.
4. *Wall Street Journal*, October 30, 1980.
5. *Wall Street Journal*, October 14, 1980.
6. Quoted in Kenneth Bacon, "Better Economic News Helps Smother Flames of Fed-Carter Dispute," *Wall Street Journal*, October 6, 1980.
7. John T. Wooley, *Monetary Politics* (London: Cambridge University Press, 1984), p. 105.
8. *Wall Street Journal*, August 26, 1981.
9. Paul Volcker, July 1985, quoted in Edward Yardeni, *Money & Business Alert*, Prudential-Bache Securities, January 27, 1988.
10. Michael C. Keeley and Gary C. Zimmerman, "Interest Checking and *M*1," *Federal Reserve Bank of San Francisco Weekly Letter*, November 21, 1986.
11. Alan Walters, "The Right Stuff," *The Economist*, May 4, 1985, pp. 23–25.
12. Preston Martin, speech to an Agricultural Outlook Conference, quoted in Prudential-Bache Securities, *Money & Business Alert*, December 4, 1985.
13. Lucien O. Hooper, "Coping with Indefiniteness," *Financial World*, April 18–May 1, 1984, p. 4.
14. *Wall Street Journal*, September 15, 1980.
15. Associated Press, "Money Supply Climbs $4.2 Billion," *Los Angeles Times*, May 2, 1986.
16. W. Lee Hoskins, "Breaking the Inflation-Recession Cycle," *Economic Commentary*, Federal Reserve Bank of Cleveland, October 15, 1989, p. 1.
17. *Wall Street Journal*, October 29, 1980.
18. Robert J. Gordon, *Economist*, November 15, 1982.
19. Congressional Budget Office, "The Economic and Budget Outlook: An Update," August 1985, pp. 40–41.
20. Edward Yardeni, *Money & Business Alert*, Prudential-Bache Securities, January 8, 1986, p. 1; the quotations from the Volcker letter are also from Yardeni.
21. "Record of Policy Actions of the Federal Open Market Committee," *Federal Reserve Bulletin*, August 1988, p. 540.
22. Edward Yardeni, *Money & Business Alert*, Prudential-Bache Securities, February 16, 1986.
23. Jude L. Naes, Jr., *U.S. Financial Data*, Federal Reserve Bank of St. Louis, October 29, 1982, p. 1.
24. Bharat Trehan and Carl Walsh, "Examining the Recent Surge in *M*1," *Federal Reserve Bank of San Francisco Weekly Letter*, November 15, 1985, pp. 1–3.
25. James D. Bowyer, "Money," *United*, April 1986, p. 16.

# Answers to Selected Exercises

## CHAPTER 1

1. Financial assets are paper claims; real assets are tangible, physical assets.

   a. financial
   b. financial
   c. financial
   d. real

3. Income is the flow of cash or services from an asset; a capital gain (or loss) occurs when the asset is sold for more (or less) than the purchase price. An unrealized capital gain represents the difference between an asset's purchase price and the price that could be received by selling it; the gain is not actually realized until the asset is in fact sold.

   a. (unrealized) capital gain
   b. (cash) income
   c. (service) income
   d. (unrealized) capital loss

5. The young typically spend more than they earn by borrowing money in order to pay for cars, houses, and their education. They expect their income to rise over time and intend to repay their loans with this income. The elderly typically spend more than they earn because they are no longer working full time. Their retirement spending is financed by the money they saved during their working years.

9. The respective answers are c, a, and b. The most appropriate choices are an investment bank to help you incorporate, a commercial bank for a checking account, and a mutual fund for a stock portfolio.

## CHAPTER 2

1. A commodity money is useful; fiat money has little or no value as a commodity.

   a. commodity
   b. fiat
   c. commodity
   d. fiat
   e. fiat

7. Yap stones are a medium of exchange, not barter — these stones are accepted not because they will be used,

but because they can be traded to other people.

9. Bad money drives out good in that these rare coins (good money) have more value to collectors than as a medium of exchange. The bad money that circulates is of no interest to collectors.

11. Gresham's Law predicts that silver dollars will be withdrawn from circulation when their silver content is worth more than a dollar.

13. If the price of gold (dollars/ounce) is fixed, then a deflation (a decline in dollars/commodities) implies a decrease in the amount of gold needed to buy commodities (ounces/commodities).

21. An increase in the price of gold relative to other things implies a decline in the price of other things relative to gold (deflation).

23. An enlarged supply of a commodity reduces its price (dollars/commodity), implying that it takes fewer dollars and fewer other commodities to buy this particular commodity. An increase in the supply of money also reduces its price (commodities/dollar), implying that it takes fewer commodities to buy a dollar. A decline in commodities/dollar is an increase in dollars/commodity; that is, inflation.

29. If the statisticians underestimate quality improvements, they will overestimate price increases — thus leading them to overestimate inflation and underestimate real income.

## CHAPTER 3

1. These exchange rates can be determined by taking the ratio of the two currencies' exchange rates relative to the dollar. The appropriate ratio can be confirmed by keeping track of the units; for example, (dollars/mark) divided by (dollars/yen) gives yen/mark.

   a. $\dfrac{0.6109 \text{ dollars/mark}}{0.007692 \text{ dollars/yen}} = 79.4202 \dfrac{\text{yen}}{\text{mark}}$

   b. $\dfrac{1.7725 \text{ dollars/pound}}{0.17835 \text{ dollars/franc}} = 9.9383 \dfrac{\text{francs}}{\text{pound}}$

   c. $\dfrac{1}{9.9383 \text{ francs/pound}} = 0.10062 \dfrac{\text{pounds}}{\text{franc}}$

7. An increase in the dollar price of U.S. goods and services makes these uncompetitive on world markets, unless the value of the dollar declines.

13. Purchasing power parity implies that a currency will depreciate if the country experiences relatively rapid

inflation. During the period 1974–1988, there was a large increase in the exchange rates of Icelandic krona/U.S. dollar and Turkish lira/U.S. dollar, showing that these currencies depreciated relative to the U.S. dollar. The purchasing-power-parity explanation is that these two nations experienced more rapid inflation than the United States (and they did). The appreciation in the Taiwan dollar relative to the U.S. dollar, in contrast, is explained by its less rapid rate of inflation.

15. Speculators who buy dollars and sell yen are betting on an appreciation in the value of the dollar — here that the exchange rate will rise above 130 yen/dollar. If they are right, then (neglecting interest) they can use each dollar to buy more than the 130 yen needed to repay their loan.

17. Because the United Kingdom experienced a faster rate of inflation than the United States between 1976 and 1988, the pound should have depreciated relative to the dollar. (Equivalently, the dollar should have strengthened relative to the pound.) The fact that the exchange rate was virtually the same in 1988 and 1976 suggests that the dollar was undervalued in 1988 (or overvalued in 1976). A scrutiny of balance-of-payments data might suggest which was the case.

19. When a nation's currency appreciates, its products become more expensive to foreigners and foreign products become less expensive — which can reduce domestic sales, production, and employment. The nation benefits from a currency appreciation because it can acquire more foreign products for less of its own products.

27. If a change in exchange rates made British products more competitive, then the British pound must have depreciated, making British products less expensive to foreigners.

# CHAPTER 4

1. A 10 percent return each year gives a larger future value than a 5 percent return one year and a 15 percent return the next. (This example illustrates the difference between geometric and arithmetic means and also, comparing (b) with (c), that it doesn't matter the order in which the returns are earned.)

   a. $\$1000(1.10)(1.10) = \$1210$
   b. $\$1000(1.05)(1.15) = \$1207.50$
   c. $\$1000(1.15)(1.05) = \$1207.50$

3. The future value is $\$4000(1.10)^{20} = \$26,910.00$

9. Other things being equal, it is better to borrow at 10 percent than to use funds earning 12 percent. However, the college's required return should depend on the riskiness of the publishing house (and any other relevant characteristics).

11. Using Equation 4.6 and recognizing that the first payment is immediate, the present value is

$$P = \$25,000 + \frac{\$25,000}{(1+\$.10)} + \frac{\$25,000}{(1+\$.10)^2} + \cdots + \frac{\$25,000}{(1+\$.10)^{39}}$$

$$= \$25,000 + \frac{\$25,000}{\$.10}\left[1 - \frac{1}{(1+\$.10)^{39}}\right]$$

$$= \$268,923.90$$

13. The implicit rate of return $R$ is given by the equation $\$14,570(1 + R)^{13} = \$28,580$; the solution is $R = 5.32$ percent. The assumed tuition growth rate $g$ is determined by $\$11,500(1 + g)^{13} = \$28,580$; the solution is $g = 7.25$ percent.

19. The implicit annual return $R$ is 6.66 percent:

$$\$55(1 + R)^{45} = \$1000$$

$$1 + R = \left(\frac{\$1000}{\$55}\right)^{1/45} = 1.0666$$

27. Using the future-value formula,

$(1 + .025/30)^{360} =$
   1.3497, an effective annual rate of 34.97 percent.
$(1 + .020/30)^{360} =$
   1.2711, an effective annual rate of 27.11 percent.

29. During deflations, nominal interest rates are likely to be low, but never negative (because investors can earn a 0 percent return simply by holding on to their money). Real interest rates are unusually high during deflations, because during an $x$ percent deflation, the real rate of interest,

$$r = R - \pi = R - (-x) = R + x$$

must be at least $x$ percent. For instance, with a 10 percent deflation, the real interest rate must be at least 10 percent.

# CHAPTER 5

1. The Hicks Equation is based on the assumption that bonds are priced so that all such strategies do equally well.

3. The expected return on a 1-year zero issued a year from now is 12.04 percent:

$$(1 + R_2)^2 = (1 + R_1)(1 + R_1^{+1})$$
$$(1 + .10)^2 = (1 + .08)(1 + R_1^{+1})$$
$$1 + R_1^{+1} = \frac{(1 + .10)^2}{1 + .08}$$
$$1 + R_1^{+1} = 1.1204$$

Using this answer, the expected return on a 1-year zero issued 2 years from now is 16.11 percent:

$$(1 + R_3)^3 = (1 + R_1)(1 + R_1^{+1})(1 + R_1^{+2})$$
$$(1 + .12)^3 = (1 + .08)(1 + .1204)(1 + R_1^{+2})$$
$$1 + R_1^{+2} = \frac{(1 + .12)^3}{(1 + .08)(1 + .1204)}$$
$$1 + R_1^{+2} = 1.1611$$

7. a. Bond prices are inversely related to interest rates.
   b. After interest rates have risen, it is too late to switch to short-term securities because, according to the expectations hypothesis, all bonds are priced to do equally well.
   c. Short-term securities have less capital risk than do long-term securities, though the amount of risk doesn't necessarily rise with interest rates; again, it pays to switch before interest rates rise, not after.

11. A general expectation of lower interest rates would already be reflected in the term structure. To bet against the term structure, he needs to disagree with the interest-rate predictions embedded in it.

    a. Buy long-term bonds and hope for capital gains.
    b. Borrow at a variable rate and hope to roll it over at a lower rate.
    c. Sell 15-year bonds and hope their prices will increase less than the prices of 30-year bonds.

13. The duration of an asset is a present-value weighted measure of the average wait until receiving the asset's cash flow; if there is any cash flow before maturity, the average wait must be less than the maturity. For zeros, with no cash flow before maturity, the duration is, contrary to the quotation, equal to the zero's maturity. As the size of the coupons increase relative to the maturation value, the average wait (and the duration) decline.

17. It has less capital risk and more nearly (though certainly not perfectly) matches the duration of their liabilities.

19. There is still the worry that interest rates will decline, forcing Eckstein's clients to roll over their investments at disappointingly low interest rates.

23. Inflation does reduce the real value of fixed-income securities. But if inflation is the order of the day, such inflation expectations will presumably already be reflected in low prices and high yields for fixed-income securities. Inflation risk refers to the possibility of unanticipated inflation.

# CHAPTER 6

1. Rearranging Equation 6.2,

$$P = \frac{\$10,000}{1 + R\frac{n}{365}}$$
$$= \frac{\$10,000}{1 + .10\frac{n}{365}}$$

Using the indicated values of $n$,

a. $n = 365$ implies $P = \$9090.91$
b. $n = 30$ implies $P = \$9918.48$
c. $n = 1$ implies $P = \$9999.26$

3. We can use Equation 6.4 where $R$ is the correct yield, $d = .10$ is the reported interest rate, and $n$ is the number of days until maturity:

$$R = \frac{365(.10)}{360 - n(.10)}$$
$$= \frac{365d}{360 - nd}$$

The answers work out to be

a. 11.27 percent
b. 10.22 percent
c. 10.14 percent

7. The daily rate is obtained by dividing the annual rate by 365:

$$(.10/365)\$10,000 = \$2.74.$$

9. Using Equation 6.5, the taxable equivalent yield is

$$\frac{R_M}{1 - t} = \frac{8\%}{1 - .15} = 9.41\% \text{ for } t = .15$$
$$= \frac{8\%}{1 - .33} = 11.94\% \text{ for } t = .33$$

11. Equation 6.6 shows that the break-even tax rate is

$$t^* = \frac{R_C - R_M}{R_C} = \frac{8\% - 6\%}{8\%} = .25$$

Therefore, investors with a tax rate above 25 percent receive the higher after-tax return from the municipal bond.

13. A decision to roll over a series of short-term loans with fluctuating interest rates, instead of locking in a fixed rate by issuing a long-term bond, is implicitly a wager that future interest rates will be lower than the forward rates embedded in the term structure.

17. If there is more default risk at small banks, then risk-averse investors will require higher interest rates on CDs from small banks. Thus CD rates will be lower at banks that are too big to fail.

27. If the U.S. dollar is expected to depreciate relative to the yen, U.S. interest rates must be above Japanese interest rates for dollar-denominated securities to be as attractive as yen-denominated securities. These higher U.S. interest rates will offset the depreciation of the dollar.

# CHAPTER 7

1. U.S. Treasury securities are free of default risk. They do have interest-rate risk and inflation risk.

5. The reported 45:15 price means $45 15/32 per $100 of face value — or $454,687.50 for $1 million face value. If we assume that there are exactly ten years until maturity, the future value formula

$$\$454{,}687.50(1 + y)^{10} = \$1{,}000{,}000$$

or, equivalently, the present-value formula

$$\$454{,}687.50 = \frac{\$1{,}000{,}000}{(1 + y)^{10}}$$

implies a yield to maturity of $y = 0.0820$ (8.20 percent). If we assume $10\frac{1}{2}$ years until maturity, the present-value formula

$$\$454{,}687.50 = \frac{\$1{,}000{,}000}{(1 + y)^{10\,1/12}}$$

implies a yield to maturity of $y = 0.0813$ (8.13 percent).

7. Using Equation 7.1,

$$P = \frac{C}{(1 + y)} + \cdots + \frac{C}{(1 + y)^n} + \frac{M}{(1 + y)^n}$$
$$= \frac{\$600}{(1 + .10)} + \cdots + \frac{\$600}{(1 + .10)^{10}} + \frac{\$5000}{(1 + .10)^{10}}$$
$$= \$5614.46$$

13. In order to corner the market, Salomon Brothers paid relatively high prices, reducing the interest rates that the Treasury paid on these two-year notes.

17. Such a bond could be attractively priced if the bond's coupon rate was sufficiently larger than current interest rates. For example, a 20-year bond with 10 percent coupons (5 percent semiannually) has a $1200 market value at a 7.98 percent yield to maturity.

19. The tax change now puts banks in the same position as individuals, who are not allowed to deduct interest when they borrow money to buy municipal bonds. Otherwise, it is profitable to borrow at 10 percent before taxes, which is $(1 - t)10\%$ after-taxes, to buy municipal bonds paying 10 percent. This tax change reduced bank demand for municipal bonds.

23. The yield to maturity on these 17-year bonds is given by Equation 7.2,

$$P = \frac{C/2}{(1 + y/2)} + \cdots + \frac{C/2}{(1 + y/2)^{2n}} + \frac{M}{(1 + y/2)^{2n}}$$

$$107\ 10/32 = \frac{\$8.75/2}{(1 + y/2)} + \cdots$$

$$+ \frac{\$8.75/2}{(1 + y/2)^{2(17)}} + \frac{\$100}{(1 + y/2)^{2(17)}}$$

The yield to call is obtained by replacing the 17-year maturity date with the 12-year call date:

$$107\ 10/32 = \frac{\$8.75/2}{(1 + y/2)} + \cdots$$

$$+ \frac{\$8.75/2}{(1 + y/2)^{2(17)}} + \frac{\$100}{(1 + y/2)^{2(17)}}$$

The yield to maturity is larger than the yield to call because the investor will not be able to earn these relatively high coupons (higher than the yield to maturity, because the bond is selling for a premium) if the bond is called before maturity. Stated somewhat differently, the yield to maturity is larger than the yield to call, because calling a bond that is selling for a premium over its face value reduces the yield. (The yield to maturity works out to be 7.97 percent, and the yield to call is 7.81 percent.)

29. You pay $1000 now in order to receive $1050 after $t$ years. The rate of return $R$ is given by

$$\$1000 = \frac{\$1050}{(1 + R)^t}$$

or

$$(1 + R)^t = \frac{\$1050}{\$1000} = 1.05$$

Solving for $t = 0.5$, 1, and 4.5 gives

a. $R = 10.25$ percent
b. $R = 5$ percent
c. $R = 1.09$ percent

# CHAPTER 8

1. Because the money is borrowed at 10 percent, if the investment earns 10 percent, the investor's return is also 10 percent. With $80,000 invested and the investor putting up $20,000, leverage is 4:1. Therefore, if the investment return turns out to be 50 percent, this 40 percent excess over 10 percent is multiplied by 4 to give a $10\% + 4(50\% - 10\%) = 170\%$ return on the

investor's own money. If the overall return is $-10$ percent, the investor's return is $10\% + 4(-10\% - 10\%) = -70\%$. Here are the details:

| Return on $80,000 | | Loan Interest | Return on $20,000 | |
|---|---|---|---|---|
| Percent | Dollar | | Dollar | Percent |
| 10% | $8,000 | $6,000 | $ 2,000 | 10% |
| 50% | 40,000 | 6,000 | 34,000 | 170% |
| −10% | −8,000 | 6,000 | −14,000 | −70% |

3. The bank's leverage is 20:1. If it borrows at 7 percent and invests at 7 percent, its return will be 7 percent. If it borrows at 7 percent and invests at 9 percent, its return will be $7\% + 20(9\% - 7\%) = 47\%$. If it borrows at 7 percent, it will have a $-100$ percent return if the rate of return $R$ on its investments satisfies this equation:

$$-100\% = 7\% + 20(R - 7\%)$$

Solving,

$$R = 7\% - (100\% + 7\%)/20$$
$$R = 1.65\%$$

5. The application of Equation 8.2 gives monthly payments of $132.15:

$$X = \frac{(APR/12)P}{\left[1 - \dfrac{1}{(1 + APR/12)^n}\right]}$$
$$= \frac{(.10/12)\$10,000}{\left[1 - \dfrac{1}{(1 + .10/12)^{120}}\right]}$$
$$= \$132.15$$

versus annual payments of $1627.45:

$$X = \frac{(APR)P}{\left[1 - \dfrac{1}{(1 + APR)^n}\right]}$$
$$= \frac{(.10)\$10,000}{\left[1 - \dfrac{1}{(1 + .10)^{10}}\right]}$$
$$= \$1627.45$$

Twelve monthly payments come to $12(\$132.15) = \$1585.80$. The twelve monthly payments are less than the annual payment because the monthly payments begin paying off the principal earlier — after the first month, instead of waiting until a full year has passed. The payments with each loan reflect 10 percent interest

on the unpaid balance. Because the unpaid balance declines faster with the monthly loan, less total interest and, hence, fewer total payments are due.

9. Using a computer program or Equation 8.2, the monthly payments on the assumable $60,000 mortgage are $428.77:

$$X = \frac{(APR/12)P}{\left[1 - \dfrac{1}{(1 + APR/12)^n}\right]}$$
$$= \frac{(.09/12)\$60,000}{\left[1 - \dfrac{1}{(1 + .09/12)^{360}}\right]}$$
$$= \$428.77$$

The unpaid balance $B$ can be determined by a computer program or by equating the amount borrowed to the present value of five years of monthly payments and the unpaid balance if the loan is paid off after five years:

$$\$60,000 = \frac{\$428.77}{(1 + .09/12)} + \frac{\$428.77}{(1 + .09/12)^2} + \cdots$$
$$+ \frac{\$428.77}{(1 + .09/12)^{60}} + \frac{B}{(1 + .09/12)^{60}}$$
$$= \frac{\$428.77}{.09/12}\left[1 - \frac{1}{(1 + .09/12)^{60}}\right]$$
$$+ \frac{B}{(1 + .09/12)^{60}}$$

The solution works out to be $B = \$57,528.10$.

The monthly payments on the $20,000 25-year loan at 20 percent are $335.69:

$$X = \frac{(APR/12)P}{\left[1 - \dfrac{1}{(1 + APR/12)^n}\right]}$$
$$= \frac{(.20/12)\$20,000}{\left[1 - \dfrac{1}{(1 + .20/12)^{300}}\right]}$$
$$= \$335.69$$

Because the home buyer will have a total loan of $\$57,528.10 + \$20,000 = \$77,528.10$ and makes monthly payments of $\$428.77 + \$335.69 = \$818.46$, the implicit annual percentage rate $(APR)$ is given by

$$\$77,528.10 = \frac{\$818.46}{(1 + APR/12)} + \frac{\$818.46}{(1 + APR/12)^2} + \cdots$$
$$+ \frac{\$818.46}{(1 + APR/12)^{300}}$$
$$= \frac{\$818.46}{APR/12}\left[1 - \frac{1}{(1 + APR/12)^{300}}\right]$$

Trial and error or a computer program gives an annual percentage rate of $APR = 0.1203$ (12.03 percent).

15. The requisite monthly payments $X$ are given by

$$\$100{,}000 = \frac{X}{(1 + .10/12)} + \frac{X}{(1 + .10/12)^2} + \cdots$$

$$+ \frac{X}{(1 + .10/12)^{360}}$$

$$= \frac{X}{.10/12}\left[1 - \frac{1}{(1 + .10/12)^{360}}\right]$$

which implies

$$X = \frac{(.10/12)\$100{,}000}{\left[1 - \frac{1}{(1 + .10/12)^{360}}\right]}$$

$$= \$877.57$$

The unpaid balance $B$ after 60 months can be determined by a computer program or by

$$\$100{,}000 = \frac{\$877.57}{(1 + .10/12)} + \frac{\$877.57}{(1 + .10/12)^2} + \cdots$$

$$+ \frac{\$877.57}{(1 + .10/12)^{60}} + \frac{B}{(1 + .10/12)^{60}}$$

$$= \frac{\$877.57}{.10/12}\left[1 - \frac{1}{(1 + .10/12)^{60}}\right] + \frac{B}{(1 + .10/12)^{60}}$$

The solution is $B = \$96{,}574.32$. If the borrower pays 5 points (and consequently receives $\$100{,}000 - (5\%)(\$100{,}000) = \$95{,}000$) and must pay a \$5000 prepayment penalty in addition to the \$96,574.32 unpaid balance, the effective annual interest rate $R$ is given by

$$\$95{,}000 = \frac{\$877.57}{(1 + R/12)} + \frac{\$877.57}{(1 + R/12)^2} + \cdots$$

$$+ \frac{\$877.57}{(1 + R/12)^{60}} + \frac{\$96{,}574.32 + \$5000}{(1 + R/12)^{60}}$$

$$= \frac{\$877.57}{R/12}\left[1 - \frac{1}{(1 + R/12)^{60}}\right] + \frac{\$101{,}574.32}{(1 + R/12)^{60}}$$

Trial and error (or a computer program) gives a solution of $R = 0.1210$ (12.10 percent).

17. All of his calculations involve total payments and ignore the time value of money. He might consider whether he could refinance for $22\frac{1}{2}$ years at 9 percent to 10 percent, choosing to borrow that amount that would give him the same monthly payments he has now, and see if this new loan covers his unpaid balance plus the \$3500 to \$4000 in closing costs.

    In fact, it would. His current monthly payments are \$630.69 (using Equation 8.2). He could borrow \$67,631.09 at 10 percent (the high end of the stated range) for $22\frac{1}{2}$ years, with monthly payments of \$630.69. The unpaid balance on the current loan is \$54,173.34

(using a computer program). The \$13,457.75 difference between the new loan and the unpaid balance would allow him to pay \$3000 to \$4000 in closing costs and pocket nearly \$10,000.

21. Consider a \$100,000 30-year mortgage repaid monthly at a 4 percent annual interest rate. The monthly payments are \$477.42:

$$\$100{,}000 = \frac{X}{(1 + .04/12)} + \frac{X}{(1 + .04/12)^2} + \cdots$$

$$+ \frac{X}{(1 + .04/12)^{360}}$$

$$= \frac{X}{.04/12}\left[1 - \frac{1}{(1 + .04/12)^{360}}\right]$$

$$X = \frac{(.04/12)\$100{,}000}{\left[1 - \frac{1}{(1 + .04/12)^{360}}\right]}$$

$$= \$477.42$$

At an 8 percent interest rate, the monthly payments are \$733.76:

$$\$100{,}000 = \frac{X}{(1 + .08/12)} + \frac{X}{(1 + .08/12)^2} + \cdots$$

$$+ \frac{X}{(1 + .08/12)^{360}}$$

$$= \frac{X}{.08/12}\left[1 - \frac{1}{(1 + .08/12)^{360}}\right]$$

$$X = \frac{(.08/12)\$100{,}000}{\left[1 - \frac{1}{(1 + .08/12)^{360}}\right]}$$

$$= \$733.76$$

The ratio $\$733.76/\$477.42 = 1.5369$ shows that the monthly payments are consistent with the quotation in the exercise, 53.69 percent larger with an interest rate of 8 percent instead of 4 percent.

    With a graduated payment mortgage, the monthly payments could start out low (at \$477.42, as it turns out) and then increase by 4 percent annually along with consumer prices and, it is hoped, household income and the value of the house.

23. The comparisons in this quotation are useless because they neglect the time value of money. In present-value terms, using your personal required return, the amount that you save will be far smaller than they report and might actually be a loss rather than a saving. If the loan rate is lower than your required rate of return, perhaps because it is a sweetheart loan from an employer or the government, you want to borrow as much as you can for as long as you can.

# CHAPTER 9

1. The total tax on a dollar of profits is the corporate 46 percent tax plus a 50 percent tax on the $(1 - .46)$ that the company pays out as dividends: $.46 + .50(1 - .46) = .73$, a 73 percent tax rate. Equivalently, the shareholder receives $(1 - .46)(1 - .50) = .27$ (27 percent after taxes).

3. Those persons who bought stock at 56½ gained. The partners who owned Morgan Stanley before it went public and were given shares of stock as compensation lost because the new corporation could have had an additional $(\$71.25 - \$56.50)(4,500,000) = \$66,375,000$ in cash.

7. The percentage change in the Dow Jones Industrial Average is given by $(1546.67 - 144.13)/144.13 = 10.73$ (that is, 1,073 percent). The percentage change in the S&P 500 was $(211.28 - 10.60)/10.60 = 18.93$ (that is, 1,893 percent). The S&P 500, the broader index, increased more than the blue-chip dominated Dow, showing that the blue chips did not increase as much as other, less prominent, companies.

9. To provide \$100,000 a year forever, we use the consol formula (or Equation 9.2, with $g = 0$):

$$\frac{\$100,000}{.10} = \$1,000,000$$

For a constantly growing salary, we use Equation 9.2 and find that 5 percent growth doubles the necessary endowment:

$$\frac{\$100,000}{.10 - .05} = \$2,000,000$$

11. Present-value analysis tells us that an increase in interest rates raises shareholder required returns, reducing the present value of a given cash flow. Rather than a drop in stock prices causing interest rates to increase, it is more plausible that an increase in interest rates causes stock prices to decline.

13. The author is using the constant-growth dividend-discount model formula

$$P = \frac{D}{R - g}$$
$$= \frac{\$50,000}{.25 - .05}$$
$$= 5(\$50,000) = \$250,000$$

The value of 5 for the capitalization rate comes from $1/(R - g)$. Broad industry norms may be useful in estimating risk premiums (for the required return) and growth rates, but should be used with caution because individual companies may deserve risk premiums or growth rates that differ considerably from industry averages.

19. The memo suggests a Ponzi scheme in which the money of new investors is used to pay off old investors. A legitimate business might have a temporary cash-flow problem and be unable to raise sufficient funds quickly because its assets are illiquid. If I were a bank officer trying to distinguish a legitimate business from a fraud, I would look for evidence that the company had used investor funds to acquire income-producing assets.

29. People will buy stock even if they know that they possess no inside information (just as they now buy Treasury bills and deposit money in savings accounts), because stocks do yield a cash flow.

# CHAPTER 10

1. The pension fund's subjective probability that the rate of inflation will be below 5 percent is 2/3. If $P_a$ is the probability that the rate of inflation will be 5 percent or higher and $P_b$ is the probability that the rate of inflation will be below 5 percent, then $P_b = 2P_a$ and $P_a + P_b = 1$ implies that $P_a = 1/3$ and $P_b = 2/3$.

3. The expected value of the percentage of the loans that will default is a probability-weighted average of the three possible default rates:

$$\mu = 1\%(.30) + 3\%(.40) + 8\%(.30) = 3.9\%$$

Similarly, the expected value of the portfolio return is a probability-weighted average of the three possible returns:

$$\mu = 12\%(.30) + 10\%(.40) + 5\%(.30) = 9.1\%$$

9. The expected value of this policy for the insurance company is

$$\mu = (\$2000 - \$0).999 + (\$2000 - \$1,000,000).001$$
$$= \$2000 - (\$1,000,000).001$$
$$= \$1000$$

This is a zero-sum game, and the expected value to Howard is $-\$1,000$. Even though the expected value is negative, Howard might buy the policy if he is sufficiently risk-averse.

15. a. $\mu = \$40(.5) + \$20(.5) = \$30$
   b. If she accepts \$27, she is acting risk averse.
   c. Someone who is risk-seeking or has a different assessment of the payoffs or probabilities might be willing to pay more than \$30.

17. The expected value is

$$\mu = (+40\%)(.10) + (20\%)(.20) + (0\%)(.40)$$
$$+ (-20\%)(.20) + (-40\%)(.10)$$
$$= 0\%$$

The variance is

$$\sigma^2 = (40\% - 0\%)^2(.10) + (20\% - 0\%)^2(.20) + \ldots$$
$$+ (-40\% - 0\%)^2(.10)$$
$$= 480$$

and the standard deviation is

$$\sigma = \sqrt{480}$$
$$= 21.91\%$$

23. There is a .95 probability that the value of a normally distributed random variable will be within two standard deviations of its expected value. Applying this two-standard-deviations rule here, approximately 95% of the IBM returns should be between $0.12\% - 1.28\% = -1.16\%$ and $0.12\% + 1.28\% = 1.40\%$.

27. The CAPM model gives the expected return on a stock or portfolio as

$$E_i = R_0 + \beta_i(E_m - R_0)$$

If $R_0 = 11$ percent and $E_M = 15$ percent, then

$$E_i = 11\% + \beta_i(15\% - 11\%)$$
$$= 11\% + 1.0(15\% - 11\%) = 15\% \text{ for } \beta_i = 1.0$$
$$= 11\% + 0.5(15\% - 11\%) = 13\% \text{ for } \beta_i = 0.5$$

31. The safety ratings are probably approximations of the standard deviation of each individual stock's return — which includes both systematic and unsystematic risk. In a large diversified portfolio (Value Line uses 15 stocks for a standard rule of thumb), the unsystematic risk will be diversified away and the stock's beta coefficients will be the most important determinant of the riskiness of the portfolio.

# CHAPTER 11

1. a. $98\frac{1}{32}$ of 100; that is $98,031.25 for a bond with $100,000 face value.
   b. 6,025.
   c. $98\frac{1}{32}$ of 100 implies a price of $98,031.25 for a $100,000 bond. The price for 1000 such bonds is $98,031,250.
   d. $97\frac{22}{32} - 98\frac{1}{32} = -\frac{11}{32}$ of 100, or $-$343.75 for a $100,000 bond.

   e. From the Change column, $-\frac{11}{32}$ of 100, or $-$343.75 for a $100,000 bond.

5. This wheat farmer might be speculating on an increase in wheat prices.

9. The three-month, six-month, and nine-month futures prices should increase progressively by the three-month cost of carry: $6 per 50 troy ounces plus $(6\%)/4 = 1.5\%$ interest on the price of platinum.

15. Savings and loans will experience a loss if interest rates go up; in order to offset these potential losses, they need to take actions that will be profitable if interest rates go up.

   a. No, their mortgage assets are already too long-term.
   b. Yes, this makes them short-term assets.
   c. No, this gives them even longer-term assets.
   d. No, these will lose money if interest rates go up. They should sell bond futures.
   e. No, these will lose money if bond prices go down (interest rates go up). They should sell bond calls.
   f. Yes, these will make money if bond prices fall (interest rates go up).

19. You want the price of T-bill futures to rise relative to the price of Eurodollar futures and, hence, T-bill interest rates to fall relative to Eurodollar rates, *widening* the interest rate differential.

21. They were selling puts; put prices increase rapidly when stock prices fall.

25. a. Call prices on any asset decline as the exercise price increases, because the exercise value of the call is diminished by the higher exercise price. Similarly, the exercise value of a put option increases as the exercise price increases.
   b. The March 1990 calls are worth more than the December 1989 calls because there is more time until expiration and, hence, more opportunity for the asset's price to rise above the exercise price. Similarly, the March 1990 puts are worth more than the December 1989 puts because there is more time until expiration and, hence, more opportunity for the asset's price to fall below the exercise price.

29. As part of a hedge strategy, an option might lose money while other components of the strategy are making money. Suppose, for example, that an investor buys stock and buys a put. If the price of the stock soars, the put will lose money, even though there is an overall profit. Of course, if the investor knew that the price was going to soar, there would have been no need to buy the put; but in the absence of inside information, the put was purchased as insurance against a price collapse. When the price does rise, the investor loses money on the put profitably.

# CHAPTER 12

1. The U.S. bank got back more dollars than it paid: the bank bought 10 million deutschemarks for 0.50 dollars/mark ($5 million) and sold them back for 0.51 dollars/mark ($5.1 million), a $100,000 profit. The German bank paid more dollars than it received: it sold 10 million deutschemarks for 0.50 dollars/mark ($5 million) and repurchased them for 0.51 dollars/mark ($5.1 million), a $100,000 loss. The German bank might have agreed to this swap because it could earn at least a 2 percent higher interest rate on dollars than on deutschemarks.

3. This German firm will profit from an appreciation of the mark relative to the dollar because it can then use fewer marks to repay the bond coupons and principal.

5. Because it has mark-denominated liabilities and yen-denominated assets, it should swap mark-denominated liabilities for yen-denominated liabilities in order to protect itself from changes in the value of the mark relative to the yen.

9. This firm is betting that interest rates will decline so that the interest payments on its floating-rate loan will decline.

13. Swapping fixed-rate debts for variable-rate debts would shorten the duration of their liabilities, exacerbating the mismatch between their long-duration assets and short-duration liabilities — borrowing short to lend long.

17. The prime rate is higher than the Treasury-bill rate because private businesses have more default risk than the U.S. Treasury. (Also, the interest on Treasury-bills is exempt from state and local income taxes.) Swapping a loan indexed to the prime rate for a loan indexed to the Treasury-bill rate is an implicit wager that the spread between prime rate and the Treasury-bill rate will widen, so that this firm's interest payments will be lower than if the firm's loan were indexed to the prime rate.

19. Renault's floating-rate payments declined while Beverly Hills' interest payments were fixed, making the swap more profitable for Renault.

# CHAPTER 13

1. The level of deposits is given by the simple deposit multiplier model, either Equation 13.2 or else Equation 13.6 with $c = 0$. If a fraction $k$ of deposits is kept on reserve, then a fraction $1 - k$ is lent. With a $100 million monetary base,

deposits: $D = \dfrac{B}{k} = \dfrac{\$100 \text{ million}}{.25} = \$400 \text{ million}$

loans: $(1 - k)D = .75(\$400 \text{ million}) = \$300 \text{ million}$

With a $150 million monetary base,

deposits: $D = \dfrac{B}{k} = \dfrac{\$150 \text{ million}}{.25} = \$600 \text{ million}$

loans: $(1 - k)D = .75(\$600 \text{ million}) = \$450 \text{ million}$

3. Deposits are given by the deposit-multiplier-model's Equation 13.6:

$$D = \frac{B}{k + c}$$

If a fraction $k$ of deposits are kept on reserve, then a fraction $1 - k$ is lent and loans are equal to

$$(1 - k)D = \frac{1 - k}{k + c}B$$

With $k = .10$ and $c = .15$,

deposits: $D = \dfrac{B}{k + c} = \dfrac{\$60 \text{ billion}}{.10 + .15} = \$240 \text{ billion}$

loans: $(1 - k)D = .90(\$240 \text{ billion}) = \$216 \text{ billion}$

If $c$ increases from .15 to .20, then

deposits: $D = \dfrac{B}{k + c} = \dfrac{\$60 \text{ billion}}{.10 + .20} = \$200 \text{ billion}$

loans: $(1 - k)D = .90(\$200 \text{ billion}) = \$180 \text{ billion}$

Deposits and loans contract because the public deposits less money in banks to be lent and redeposited.

9. People simply use checks more frequently than cash, giving a faster turnover of checking-account deposits than of currency outside banks. The important point is to distinguish between the size of currency holdings or checking-account balances (a stock, measuring the level at a point in time) and the volume of payments during some period of time (a flow).

   Suppose that there is a constant $100 in currency outside banks and $300 in checking-account balances; cash is never deposited or withdrawn during the year. Now suppose that there are $50,000 in transactions during the year, of which $5000 are cash transactions and $45,000 use checks. For $100 in currency to make $5000 in transactions, each dollar must, on average, be used $5000/$100 = 50 times during the year. For $300 in checking-account balances to make $45,000 in transactions, each checking-account dollar must, on average, be used $45,000/$300 = 150 times during the year. Check transactions are nine times the size of cash transactions, even though checking-account balances are only three times the size of cash holdings, because checking-account money turns over three times as fast as cash.

11. A reduction in reserve requirements reduces bank reserves relative to deposits, allowing banks to lend more, some of which will be redeposited and re-lent — increasing monetary aggregates, bank loans, and bank profits. More formally, inspection of Equation 13.9 shows that a reduction in $k$ (the ratio of bank reserves relative to deposits) increases $M1$:

$$M1 = C + D_1 = cD + (D_1/D)D$$
$$= (c + D_1/D)D = \left(\frac{c + D_1/D}{k(D_1/D) + c}\right)B$$

Bank profits expand because banks are not compelled to hold as much idle reserves.

13. The key mathematical fact is that, if two quantities $X$ and $Y$ are both positive, then whether a ratio $X/Y$ increases or decreases depends on whether the percentage increase in $X$ is larger or smaller than the percentage increase in $Y$. This can be shown by using 1 and 0 subscripts to denote the new and old values, and letting $\%\Delta X$ be the percentage increase in $X$:

$$\frac{X_1/Y_1}{X_0/Y_0} = \frac{X_1/X_0}{Y_1/Y_0} = \frac{1 + \%\Delta X_1}{1 + \%\Delta Y_1}$$

This shows that, for positive values of $X$ and $Y$, the ratio $X/Y$ increases if $\%\Delta X$ is larger than $\%\Delta Y$. Applying this rule to the questions asked:

  a. In 1984, $M1$ increased by a smaller percentage than $B$, and the money multiplier $M1/B$ consequently declined; $M2$, in contrast, increased by a larger percentage than $B$, so that $M2/B$ increased. In 1985 the reverse was true: $M1/B$ increased while $M2/B$ declined.
  b. $GNP$ increased by more than $M1$ or $M2$ in 1984, so that $GNP/M1$ and $GNP/M2$ increased; in 1985 $GNP$ increased by less than $M1$ or $M2$, and both $GNP/M1$ and $GNP/M2$ decreased.
  c. The data show that $M1$ s rate of increase rose in 1985, while $M2$'s rate of increase declined. Most likely, the public shifted funds into transaction accounts from the nontransaction accounts that are excluded from $M1$.

15. If there were no reserve requirements, banks would still keep some reserves to meet fluctuations in daily deposits and withdrawals. With no reserve requirements, there would not be a theoretical upper limit on the possible level of deposits: as the ratios of reserves and currency outside banks to deposits approach zero, deposits become infinitely large.

21. The funds placed in Individual Retirement Accounts (IRAs) are not readily available for bill-paying because there is a substantial withdrawal penalty.

23. Those who use their credit cards to borrow money pay high interest rates and provide banks with substantial profits. Those who use their credit cards to make purchases and pay their monthly credit card bills in full do not borrow money; instead of paying interest, these card users get interest-free loans from banks (during the time between the use of the card and the payment of the monthly bill). Banks would prefer that these on-timers use debit cards so that they pay for purchases immediately, rather than at the end of the month.

# CHAPTER 14

1. Banks have not lost $30 million in deposits. They have usefully lent this money. They do have illiquid assets and liquid liabilities.
3. As explained in the text, large banks benefit from various economies of scale involving risk-pooling and specialization.
5. Many of those who invest in physical capital want to finance these investments by borrowing, rather than out of their own savings. Many of those who save do not want to invest in physical capital. Financial intermediaries bring these investors and savers together.
9. Investors can diversify away micro, idiosyncratic risks. The test of whether a risk is idiosyncratic or macro depends on whether it can be diversified away — whether there is safety in numbers.

  a. idiosyncratic
  b. macro
  c. idiosyncratic
  d. macro
  e. macro

11. There are many plausible answers. Among the macro events are the following: wars or natural disasters occur (ruled out by most insurance policies); life expectancies change for the better because of new drugs, cleaner air and water, or reduced tobacco consumption; life expectancies change for the worse because of deteriorating diet, diminished exercise, or the spread of a serious contagious disease. Some micro events are these: someone is killed in a car accident or dies of a heart attack. A large insurance company can diversify away micro, idiosyncratic risk by having a large number of policyholders.
15. To the extent a higher discount rate reduced the money supply, it enhanced the convertibility of the currency that remained in circulation. An increase in the discount rate tightens money and credit, weakening the economy.
19. The decline in bank borrowing from the Fed reduced the money supply. The Fed could have offset this decline by making open market purchases.

# CHAPTER 15

1. The data in Table 15.7 show that aggregate net worth divided by total assets is equal to \$99.9 billion/\$2801.0 billion = .0357. Aggregate commercial bank leverage is the inverse of this: 1/.0357 = 28.04.

3. Its leverage is equal to asset/net worth = 1/.02 = 50. Equation 15.2 gives its return on net worth as

gross return = 10 percent: $10\% + 50(10\% - 10\%) = 10\%$
gross return = 8 percent: $10\% + 50(8\% - 10\%) = -90\%$

5. a. Its leverage is 100/10 = 10.
   b. The average interest rate on its deposits and bonds is

$$\frac{70}{90}10\% + \frac{20}{90}10\% = 10\%$$

   c. The average gross rate of return on its assets is

$$\frac{5}{100}0\% + \frac{60}{100}12\% + \frac{35}{100}10\% = 10.7\%$$

   d. Its net return on net worth is

$$10\% + 10(10.7\% - 10\%) = 17\%$$

7. The average interest rate is a weighted average:

$.01(5\%) + .03(6\%) + .08(7\%) + .20(8\%)$
$+ .30(9\%) + .24(10\%) + .10(11\%) + .04(12\%) = 9.07\%$

about 2 percentage points lower than the 11 percent average cost of funds.

13. They will lose. If the dollar appreciates relative to the franc while this company is holding francs, this appreciation of the dollar reduces the value of its francs and reduces the amount of dollars that it can purchase with its francs.

15. The increase in bank reserves mandated by increased reserve requirements reduces the deposit multiplier and tightens credit conditions.

19. The gap is defined as

(rate-sensitive assets) − (rate-sensitive liabilities)

This bank has a positive gap of $500,000,000 - \$200,000,000 = \$300,000,000$, which implicitly is a bet that interest rates will increase — causing the bank's income to increase more than its expenses. If interest rates increase by 4 percentage points, the bank's net income should increase by 4 percent ($300,000,000) = $12,000,000.

27. The duration of this bank's 1-year Treasury bills is one year, and its asset duration is consequently 0(80/100) + 1(20/100) = 0.2 years. The duration of its five-year

zeros is 5 years, and its liability duration is consequently 0(50/90) + 5(40/90) = 2.222 years. Its duration gap is given by Equation 15.3: 0.2 − 2.222(90/100) = −1.8 years. Because it has a negative duration gap, this bank's net worth will increase if market interest rates increase.

# CHAPTER 16

1. There were more checking accounts at commercial banks in the 1950s because thrift institutions were not authorized to offer checking accounts until the 1980s.

3. In the 1960s, the ratio of short-term consumer loans to mortgages was higher at credit unions than at S&Ls because of restrictions on these institutions.

5. A 15-year mortgage has a much shorter duration than does a 30-year mortgage, allowing the thrift to reduce the duration of its assets so that it better matches the duration of its liabilities.

9. A decline in interest rates increases the market value of fixed-rate mortgages and reduces the income from adjustable-rate mortgages. This decline was more profitable for thrifts that had mostly fixed-rate mortgages.

11. This was a low-interest mortgage, and the savings bank wanted to get its money back as soon as possible so that it could relend the money at current high interest rates.

13. Its leverage is

$$\text{leverage} = \frac{\text{total assets}}{\text{net worth}} = \frac{1}{0.03} = 33.3$$

If the thrift borrows at 8 percent to invest at 8 percent, its return on net worth is also 8 percent. If it borrows at 8 percent to invest at 5 percent, we can use Equation 15.2:

$$\binom{\text{return on}}{\text{net worth}} = \binom{\text{interest}}{\text{rate}}_{\text{on debt}}$$

$$+ (\text{leverage})\left[\binom{\text{gross return}}{\text{on total}}_{\text{assets}} - \binom{\text{interest}}{\text{rate}}_{\text{on debt}}\right]$$

$$= 8\% + 33.3(5\% - 8\%)$$
$$= -92\%$$

15. A thrift institution with long-term fixed-rate assets and short-term variable-rate liabilities will suffer losses if interest rates increase unexpectedly, increasing the interest it pays on its liabilities without a corresponding increase in its interest income. Alternatively, an unexpected increase in interest rates will reduce the market value of its assets by more than it reduces the market value of the thrift's liabilities. To hedge this interest-rate risk, the thrift could sell bond futures. An unexpected increase in interest rates will cause the price of

bond futures to decline, giving profits to those who have sold bond futures. These bond-futures profits will offset the losses that the thrift experiences on the rest of its portfolio.

Another way that the thrift could hedge its interest-rate risk is to swap its short-term variable-rate liabilities for long-term fixed-rate liabilities, to match its long-term fixed-rate assets.

17. Many insolvent, zombie savings and loan associations paid high interest rates in order to attract depositors, forcing healthy S&Ls to pay high deposit rates too.

19. The closing of thrifts that did not meet FIRREA's strict requirements reduced the amount of funds flowing through savings and loan associations into mortgages. In addition, FIRREA's risk-based capital requirements penalize nonsecuritized mortgages and Fannie Mae and Freddie Mac securities.

# CHAPTER 17

1. The piano manufacturer wants to encourage piano sales; also, if the piano is repossessed, it is of more use to a piano manufacturer than to a bank.

3. Finance company customers are often individuals who are judged less creditworthy by banks; higher interest rates are consequently required to cover the greater risk of default. If finance companies cannot charge more than 10 percent interest, they won't be much interested in making loans to their traditional clientele.

5. People who live in mobile homes may be less creditworthy because they have lower incomes and are more transient. With a mobile home, they can literally pick up and move their collateral.

9. A homeowner is less likely to leave town suddenly, abandoning the house. The length of time lived at the current address is a measure of whether the applicant moves frequently.

13. To bet on a rise in interest rates, finance companies (as with other investors) should borrow long-term; a rise in interest rates will then reduce the present value of their liabilities without much affecting the present value of their assets (and raise their interest income without affecting their interest expenses). To minimize interest-rate risk, they should borrow short-term in order to match their asset and liability durations.

15. A disadvantage of increased leverage is that the company's profits net of interest payments would become more volatile and the company consequently might have its bond rating reduced and have to pay higher interest rates on its borrowing.

19. The appropriate present-value equation is

$$\$1000 = \frac{\$91.67}{(1 + APR/12)} + \frac{\$91.67}{(1 + APR/12)^2} + \cdots$$
$$+ \frac{\$91.67}{(1 + APR/12)^{12}}$$
$$= \frac{\$91.67}{APR/12}\left(1 - \frac{1}{(1 + APR/12)^{12}}\right)$$

Trial and error (perhaps using a computer program) gives an annual percentage rate of $APR = 0.1798$ (17.98 percent).

23. With monthly compounding, the effective annual interest rate $R$ is given by this calculation:

$$1 + R = (1 + .10)^{12} \text{ implies } R = 213.84 \text{ percent}$$

27. Reducing the interest rate from 10 percent to 2.9 percent is equivalent to reducing the price by $1000, since the monthly payments are $290.38 for a 36-month $10,000 loan at 2.9 percent, and are a nearly identical $290.41 for a 36-month $9000 loan at 10 percent:

*Borrow $10,000 at 2.9 percent:*

$$\$10,000 = \frac{X}{(1 - .029/12)} + \frac{X}{(1 - .029/12)^2} + \cdots$$
$$+ \frac{X}{(1 - .029/12)^{36}}$$
$$= \frac{X}{0.029/12}\left[1 - \frac{1}{(1 - .029/12)^{36}}\right]$$
$$X = \frac{(0.029/12)\$10,000}{\left[1 - \frac{1}{(1 - .029/12)^{36}}\right]}$$
$$= \$290.38$$

*Borrow $9000 at 10 percent:*

$$\$9000 = \frac{X}{(1 - .10/12)} + \frac{X}{(1 - .10/12)^2} + \cdots$$
$$+ \frac{X}{(1 - .10/12)^{36}}$$
$$= \frac{X}{0.10/12}\left[1 - \frac{1}{(1 - 0.10/12)^{36}}\right]$$
$$X = \frac{(0.10/12)\$9000}{\left[1 - \frac{1}{(1 - .10/12)^{36}}\right]}$$
$$= \$290.41$$

# CHAPTER 18

1. Table 18.1 shows the cost of a one-year $100,000 life insurance policy for a 55-year-old woman to be $205.

For the expected value to equal half of this $205, the probability $P$ of death is given by

$$\$102.50 = \$100,000(P) + \$0(1 - P)$$

which implies $P = \$102.50/\$100,000 = 0.001025$.

5. The expected value of the 25 percent stake is $.10(\$3,000,000/4) + .90(\$0/4) = \$75,000$. Because this expected value is less than the $80,000 cost, a risk-neutral insurance company should sell its stake.

9. The expected value of the policy is

$$\mu = \$2,000,000(.2) + \$0(.8) = \$400,000$$

For the cost of the policy to be twice its expected value, the insurance company must charge $800,000. A rational homeowner might pay $800,000 for such a policy if he or she is risk averse or else believes that the probability that the property will be washed away is larger than 0.4.

15. Life insurance is intended to avoid financial hardship for the beneficiaries if the policyholder dies. If the policyholder's beneficiaries are a spouse or children and their assets accumulate over time, there is less need for life insurance.

17. According to the law of large numbers, one cannot determine *which* particular individuals will die; but you must know the *probability* of death in order to predict the fraction of a large group that will die.

21. The policies are worth more than the company's current assets (which come from shareholder premiums) because the policies will not pay off for some time and the premiums will be invested to earn interest.

27. The expected value of wealth from the house is equal to the expected value of the policy minus the cost of the policy:

$$E[W] = \langle kH(P) + H(1 - P) \rangle - kC$$
$$= k(HP - C) + H(1 - P)$$

This equation shows an increase in $k$ increases the expected value of wealth if and only if $C < HP$; that is, if the cost of insurance is less than the expected damage. If $C < HP$, then $k$ will be set as high as possible. If $C > HP$, then $k$ will be set equal to zero.

35. A bond's price risk is highest when the bond is held only a short while, and this risk declines to a minimum when the holding period is equal to the bond's *maturity*. Reinvestment risk is highest when the bond is held until maturity and declines to a minimum when the holding period is *a short while*. The total risk, price risk plus reinvestment risk, is highest when the bond is held a short while or until maturity and is at a minimum when the holding period is equal to the bond's duration.

# CHAPTER 19

1. TIAA–CREF is a defined-contribution plan, because the pension benefit depends on the professor's pension contributions and TIAA–CREF's success in investing these funds, not on a formula related to wages, years of employment, and so on.

3. This company's vesting formula discourages the hiring of older workers because they vest sooner. For example, a person hired at age 58 would have to work only 1 year to become vested; someone hired at age 20 would have to work for 20 years.

5. The one-year delay causes $2000 not to be invested in the IRA at age 25. Thus, the reported calculation is $\$2000(1.10)^{40} = \$90,518.51$. This calculation is misleading because delaying a year does not reduce your wealth by $90,518.51. You must pay taxes when the money is withdrawn from the IRA, and, in addition, the $2000 not invested in the IRA can be invested elsewhere. If you are in a 28 percent tax bracket and invest the $2000 outside the IRA at 10 percent, then

$2000 inside the IRA yields
$$(1 - .28)\$90,518.51 = \$65,173.33$$
$2000 outside the IRA yields
$$\$2000(1 + (1 - .28).10)^{40} = \underline{\$32,271.67}$$
$$\text{difference} = \$32,901.66$$

7. An increase in the level of prices from $1.00 in 1985 to $4.40 in 2023 will reduce the purchasing power of $27,500 in 2023 to $\$27,500/\$4.40 = \$6250$ in 1985 dollars.

9. In private pension funds, contributions are invested and accumulate to provide retirement benefits. This system protects employee pensions if a company should go bankrupt.

15. If $R$ is the before-tax return on money invested outside the retirement plan, the after-tax rate of return is $(1 - .40)R$. As explained in the text, the effective after-tax interest rate on the retirement money is equal to its before-tax interest rate, here 9 percent. For these two returns to be equal, $(1 - .40)R = 9\%$, $R$ must equal $9\%/(1 - .40) = 15\%$.

17. An increase in the rate of inflation will increase wages shortly before retirement relative to average wages over the entire career and therefore have more effect on the retirement benefits of a worker who is in a final-pay defined-benefit plan.

19. The future-value calculation

$$X(1 + .10)^{40} = \$1,000,000$$

implies

$$X = \frac{\$1,000,000}{(1 + .10)^{40}} = \$22,095$$

There is considerable risk in rolling over a series of one-year Treasury bills because interest rates may fall. The pension fund could guarantee its rate of return by purchasing a 40-year Treasury zero.

# CHAPTER 20

1. An initial public offering is generally more difficult to value because, unlike the issuance of additional shares, there is no existing market for the shares and no direct evidence of the price that investors are willing to pay for them.
3. There is a risk in underwriting a new issue because the underwriters may not be able to sell all of the securities for more than they paid for them; a syndicate spreads this risk among several investment banks. In addition, a syndicate increases the pool of potential customers for the securities (and also information about investor reaction to the proposed pricing of the new issue).
5. A corporation's board of directors might enthusiastically recommend shareholder approval of a takeover offer because the offer is substantially above the current market price of the stock and, therefore, is financially advantageous to shareholders.
9. The bid price was $750,000; the ask price $1,500,000. This is a very wide spread: you lose $750,000 (half of the ask price) on a round-trip transaction, buying for $1,500,000 and immediately selling for $750,000.
11. When an investment bank brokerages a shopping center, it does not invest its own money; its income comes from the brokerage commission it receives for bringing together the buyer and seller. Brokeraging transactions is less risky than investing in shopping centers. Also, the investment bank may not think the shopping center is worth as much as the buyer is willing to pay.
17. If the price increases from $25 to $30, that is a 20 percent profit. With 2:1 leverage, the return is doubled to 50 percent. (Since no time has passed, no interest is due on the loan; the interest rate on the loan is consequently irrelevant.) If the price instead drops 25 percent, from $25 to $20, leverage doubles your loss to −50 percent.
21. It is implicitly betting on a decline in interest rates, so that the interest rates on its overnight repos will decline, while it experiences capital gains on its long-term Treasury bonds.
23. Because they are riskier, double-A rates are above triple-A rates. If the spread is unusually large, this means that double-A interest rates are unusually high relative

to triple-A rates, and double-A prices are therefore unusually low. By purchasing double-A bonds and selling triple-A bonds, the security dealer can bet on the spread narrowing and still be protected from a general movement in interest rates.

# CHAPTER 21

3. To purchase one share, worth $69.29, you have to pay $71.43, which represents a 3.1 percent load:

$$\frac{\$71.43 - \$69.29}{\$69.29} = 0.0309 \text{ (that is, 3.09 percent)}$$

(The fund figures the load as ($71.43 − $69.29)/$71.43 = 3.00 percent.)
7. The mutual funds grew to $113,500 (11.14 percent a year); the NYSE composite grew to $151,377 (12.54 percent a year):

$$\$10,000(1 + R)^{23} = \$113,500 \text{ implies}$$
$$R = .1114 \text{ (11.14 percent)}$$
$$\$10,000(1 + .1254)^{23} = \$151,377$$

9. Mutual funds strongly encourage their shareholders to reinvest their dividends and capital gains because the fund's management fees depend on the size of the fund's assets.
11. As is explained in the text, even if the discount persists, it gives investors an advantage in that the purchaser of closed-end shares invests $20 and gets the dividends and capital gains on $25 in assets, less the fund's expenses.
19. It is not worth paying for this advice, because there is little or no consistency in mutual fund performance.
21. They had to use the proceeds from the RJR buyout to buy shares of the replacement company and the other 499 companies in proportion to their respective market values.
23. Mutual funds do not invariably lose money; but they don't, on average, do better than a monkey throwing darts.
27. Five of the ten best funds in 1990 were above average (ranks 1 to 45) in 1991, and five were below average (ranks 46 to 90). This evidence is consistent with the hypothesis that there is no consistency in mutual fund performance — that funds that have done well in the past are no more likely to do well in the future than they are to do poorly.

# CHAPTER 22

1. Reserve requirements are expensive for banks that are compelled to hold idle reserves, funds that could be lent and earn interest. This expense increases when loan demand is strong and interest rates are high.

3. There might be runs on low-rated banks if this were public knowledge.

7. As predicted by the quotation, deposit-rate ceilings did encourage new ways of bringing together small lenders (depositors) and large borrowers — most notably, money-market mutual funds.

9. These unannounced visits are intended to ensure that the bank is keeping accurate up-to-date records.

13. The automobile owner who buys theft insurance may be less careful about locking the car, parking the car in safe locations, and taking other precautions to minimize the chance of theft. A deductible clause is intended to alleviate this moral-hazard problem by making the car owner bear some of the expense if there is a theft.

17. Independence Bank agreed to sell $18.7 million in assets for $16.9 million because these assets — though carried on its books at $18.7 million — were worth considerably less, either because these were problem loans in danger of default or else fixed-rate low-interest loans. Independence apparently got $36.7 million in deposit liabilities and $19.7 million in assets plus $16.9 million in cash — a total of $36.7 million after rounding. Independence must have paid the additional $322,000 for this deal because some of these liabilities were fixed-rate low-interest deposits or because some of the bank's assets — perhaps its buildings and structures — were worth more than the amount shown on the bank's books.

19. If financial institutions report the value of their bonds at market value or cost, whichever is lower, they won't show the capital gains on bonds that have appreciated in value. This might encourage them to realize these profits by selling bonds that have appreciated, which will force them to pay taxes on these realized capital gains. The qualification "unless they have the ability and intention to hold the securities until maturity" allows financial institutions to avoid reporting capital losses on their bond portfolio merely by stating that they do not intend to sell these bonds; this is like the investor who buys a stock or bond that goes down in price and pretends that "I haven't lost anything as long as I don't sell." The individual or bank holding low-interest assets in a high-interest economy has lost something.

23. ATMs are automated teller machines. Texas state law was paradoxical because ATMs can be considered (limited) bank branches that allow deposits, withdrawals, and account information.

# CHAPTER 23

1. a. Tax payments to the Treasury reduce the monetary base (until the Treasury spends the money).
   b. Shopping has no effect on the monetary base.
   c. A snowstorm will increase the monetary base if it creates Federal Reserve float, the simultaneous crediting of reserves to two banks.

3. Fedwire float creates profit for Fedwire users: both senders and recipients are credited with interest-earning funds until the end of the day.

7. Equation 23.5 gives

   a. effective cost of funds =
   $$\frac{R}{1-k} = \frac{.06}{1-.10} = .0667 \text{ (6.67 percent)}$$

   b. effective cost of funds =
   $$\frac{R}{1-k} = \frac{.05}{1-.20} = .0625 \text{ (6.25 percent)}$$

9. The average reserve requirement can be determined by calculating the bank's total required reserves and then dividing by total deposits:

   $$\frac{\text{average reserve}}{\text{requirement}} = \frac{\text{reserves}}{\text{deposits}}$$
   $$= \frac{.10(\$500) + .00\,(\$500)}{\$1000} = \frac{\$50}{\$1000} = .05$$

   Alternatively, this equation can be rearranged as a weighted average of its reserve requirements, using as weights the fractions of total deposits subject to each reserve requirement:

   $$\frac{\text{average reserve}}{\text{requirement}} = \frac{.10(\$500) + .00(\$500)}{\$1000}$$
   $$= .10\left(\frac{\$500}{\$1000}\right) + .00\left(\frac{\$500}{\$1000}\right)$$
   $$= .10(.5) + .00(.5) = .05$$

13. The bank's required reserves were reduced by $(.1625 - .12)(\$1 \text{ billion}) = \$42.5$ million, on which the bank can earn $(10\%)(\$42.5 \text{ million}) = \$4.25$ million. Checking, if it invested $(1 - .1625)(\$1 \text{ billion})$ at 10 percent, the bank would earn $83.75 million annually; investing $(1 - .12)(\$1 \text{ billion})$, it earns $88 million annually; the additional $4.25 million represents about a 5 percent increase in annual income.

17. By avoiding reserve requirements, the brokerage firm is able to invest all of the customer's money and pay the customer more interest. Banks hold cash to satisfy daily withdrawals, but people don't show up at brokerage

firms asking for cash. The brokerage firm keeps the customer's money in an easily liquidated money-market fund (not illiquid business loans or home mortgages); if there are net withdrawals for the day, it sells some of the Treasury bills and other liquid assets held by the money-market fund.

23. An increase in the discount rate tightens financial markets by making discount-window borrowing more expensive for banks and, perhaps more importantly, signals the Fed's intentions to maintain higher interest rates. An increase in interest rates reduces the present value of cash flows, including the market value of bonds.

   An increase in the discount rate might have little or no effect on bond prices if it did not signal a change in Fed policy but was instead a defensive reaction to financial market conditions — a reaction that was well anticipated by market participants.

33. Concerned about inflation, the Federal Reserve increased reserve requirements (evaporating bank-created money) and made open-market sales (trading securities for gold). (After a sharp business contraction in 1938, the Fed was forced to retreat somewhat from this ill-timed fight against inflation.)

# CHAPTER 24

1. Monetary policies directly alter the monetary base and monetary aggregates; fiscal policies involve government spending and taxation.

   a. monetary
   b. fiscal
   c. fiscal
   d. monetary
   e. monetary

3. Reagan's strategist was concerned that Volcker's Fed would engineer a recession to combat inflation and that the timing would happen to coincide with the election.

7. Friedman's graph suggests a short, predictable lag between money and nominal GNP, but his recommendation that the Fed not use monetary policy to stabilize the economy is based on his assertion that the lags are long and variable.

9. This is the new classical argument that employment increases (and unemployment declines) when an unexpected inflation causes workers to overestimate their real wages.

13. The key issue in new classical models is whether prices increase by more or less than anticipated. An increase in the money supply could be larger or smaller than antici-

pated, causing more or less inflation than expected — causing real wages to be smaller or larger than workers believe to be the case and causing employment to expand or contract. If increases in the money supply and in prices are as likely to be larger than anticipated as they are to be smaller than anticipated, then an increase in the money supply is as likely to increase employment as to reduce it.

# CHAPTER 25

1. The value of velocity is

$$V = \frac{PT}{M} = \frac{\$120(100 \text{ billion})}{\$1000 \text{ billion}} = \frac{\$12,000 \text{ billion}}{\$1000 \text{ billion}} = 12$$

Twelve transactions a year implies, on average, about one month (or 30 days) between transactions.

3. The quantity theory equation $MV = Py$ implies that (approximately)

$$\%\Delta P = \%\Delta M + \%\Delta V - \%\Delta y$$

Here,

$$\%\Delta P = 4\% + 2\% - 2\% = 4\%$$

The exact value for the inflation rate can be determined by letting 0 and 1 subscripts denote the past and present values, respectively:

$$1 + \%\Delta P = \frac{P_1}{P_0} = \frac{M_1 V_1 / y_1}{M_0 V_0 / y_0}$$
$$= \frac{M_1}{M_0} \frac{V_1}{V_0} \frac{y_0}{y_1} = \frac{(1 + \%\Delta M)(1 + \%\Delta V)}{(1 + \%\Delta y)}$$

Here, the exact value of the inflation rate is 4 percent:

$$1 + \%\Delta P = \frac{(1 + .04)(1 + .02)}{(1 + .02)} = 1.04$$

5. The value of velocity is

$$V = \frac{Py}{M} = \frac{\$5000 \text{ billion}}{\$1000 \text{ billion}} = 5$$

If velocity is constant and the money supply falls by 10 percent, to \$900 billion, then nominal gross domestic product will fall by 10 percent, too, to \$4500 billion:

$$Py = MV = (\$900 \text{ billion})(5) = \$4500 \text{ billion}$$

If both velocity and real gross domestic product are constant, then a 10 percent decline in the money supply will reduce the price level by 10 percent.

9. If prices increase by 100 percent, then something that costs $1 will cost $2; if prices increase by 19,800 percent, then something that costs $1 will cost $199. Applying the compounding formula (Equation 4.1), the daily rate of inflation $\pi$ is 19.3 percent:

$$\$1(1 + \pi)^{30} = \$199$$
$$\pi = 199^{1/30} - 1$$
$$= .193 \ (19.3 \ \text{percent})$$

13. An increase in the demand for monetary base relative to nominal income means a decline in velocity.

   a. increased money demand by banks, reduced velocity
   b. reduced money demand by the public, increased velocity
   c. diminished money demand, increased velocity

17. The quantity theory equation $MV = Py$ implies that if the money supply $M$ is steady while velocity $V$ declines, then nominal gross domestic product $Py$ will decline.

21. The shift of funds out of checking accounting included in $M1$ reduced $M1$ relative to nominal gross domestic product, increasing $M1$ velocity.

23. Velocity is given by $V = Py/M$. If the money supply $M$ explodes, with relatively little change in nominal gross domestic product, then velocity declines. Therefore an explosion of $M1$ will reduce $M1$ velocity. A transfer of funds from time and savings accounts to Super NOW accounts wouldn't seem to have any direct effect on GDP; people would simply be keeping their savings in a different type of account. To the extent that Super NOW accounts are subject to higher reserve requirements than time and savings accounts, I expect such a shift of funds to be contractionary, as it reduces the amount of funds available to banks for lending.

29. The quantity theory equation $MV = Py$ implies $\%\Delta M = \%\Delta(Py) - \%\Delta V$, showing that the Fed's target rate of growth of money can be based on a desired rate of growth of nominal GDP and an assumed rate of growth of velocity. Unpredictable fluctuations in velocity make it more difficult to determine appropriate monetary growth targets.

# CHAPTER 26

1. During an inflationary period, there will be upward pressure on nominal interest rates because investors won't settle for low returns on financial assets when they can get high returns by investing in real assets. Similarly, borrowers will be willing to pay high nominal interest rates to obtain the funds to buy real assets that are rapidly appreciating in value. If the Fed attempts to maintain low interest rates by making open-market purchases, it will increase the money supply and stimulate the economy and inflation even more.

3. Net-free reserves could increase during an economic boom if the Fed pursued an aggressively expansionary monetary policy, making open-market purchases and cutting reserve requirements to stimulate the economy. Net-free reserves could increase during a recession if, instead of lending money, banks accumulate reserves.

5. Some monetarists, such as Milton Friedman, argue that a central bank should choose a monetary target not for its logical coherence, but for its suitability as a target — how well this particular monetary aggregate can be controlled and how closely it is correlated with the central bank's ultimate targets, such as nominal gross domestic product. Other monetarists argue that some financial assets that are not a medium of exchange are nonetheless so easily converted into a medium of exchange that these near-moneys ought logically to be counted as money.

7. Because time deposits have lower reserve requirements than do transaction accounts, a shift from transaction accounts to time deposits reduces average reserve requirements, allowing banks to lend a larger fraction of their deposits, increasing bank lending and deposits, reducing interest rates, and easing credit conditions — despite the decline in $M1$.

9. Preston Martin was referring to $M1$'s reliability as a monetary target. If $M1$ velocity $V1 = Py/M1$ is predictable, then a target for nominal gross domestic product $Py$ can be achieved by hitting a target for $M1$. If there is an unexpected decline in $M1$ velocity, then nominal GDP will be lower than intended if the Fed hits its $M1$ target.

11. The law of one price and purchasing power parity imply that a nation with relatively rapid inflation will experience a depreciation in the value of its currency. If U.S. prices rose without a depreciation of the dollar, U.S. products would be uncompetitive on world markets.

17. If the same amount of transactions balances are used to produce fewer U.S. goods, then velocity (the ratio of gross domestic product to $M1$) will decline.

21. It is plausible that, when market interest rates increase, banks will raise interest rates on deposits that are not subject to rate ceilings in order to hold on to their depositors, and that households and businesses will shift funds out of deposits subject to rate ceilings into deposits whose interest rates are rising. A shift from checkable deposits (with substantial reserve requirements) to time deposits (with little or no reserve requirements) will raise average reserve requirements and tighten financial markets.

# Glossary

**actuary**  One who uses statistical data to estimate the probability of losses of various sizes for insurance policyholders with various characteristics (for example, their age or smoking habits, the proximity of a house to the fire department) and calculates the corresponding insurance premiums required for the insurance company to be profitable.

**adjustable-rate loan**  Loan on which the interest rate rises and falls with market interest rates, protecting lending institutions whose deposit rates move with market interest rates. These flexible-rate loans are also known as variable-rate, renegotiable-rate, rollover loans, and so on, and have a variety of terms and conditions. If the monthly payments are fixed while the loan rate fluctuates, there may be negative amortization.

**adverse selection**  Self-selection that is disadvantageous for the less informed parties to a contract. For example, insurance companies cannot perfectly identify high-risk and low-risk people and consequently offer the same premiums to people with differing degrees of risk. Adverse selection occurs when people who are above-average risks buy lots of insurance and low-risk people buy little or no insurance, thereby invalidating the probabilities on which the insurance premiums are based.

**amortized loan**  Loan that is paid off gradually rather than with a single balloon payment at the end. The periodic payments include principal as well as interest. The most common amortized loan involves constant monthly payments over the life of the loan, with $n$ monthly payments $X$ set so that their present value at the stated annual percentage rate $APR$ is equal to the amount borrowed $P$: $X = (APR/12)P/\{1 - 1/(1 + APR/12)^n\}$.

**announcement effect**  Situation that occurs when the announcement of a policy change, unimportant by itself, signals intentions that are likely to be carried out in other ways. In recent years, discount-rate changes have been more signal than substance. Changes in discount rates are seldom large enough to affect financial markets very much, but because the announcement of a change in the discount rate conveys information about Federal Reserve objectives, an unexpected change in the discount rate (or the absence of a change) sometimes sends tremors through financial markets.

**annual percentage rate (APR)**  Usual form in which a loan rate is quoted. The annual percentage rate is divided by the number of payments per year to determine the periodic loan rate. For example, a loan with monthly payments and a 15 percent $APR$ has a monthly loan rate that is equal to $APR/12 = 15\%/12 = 1.25\%$.

**arbitrage**  Virtually risk-free exploitation of price discrepancies; for example, simultaneously buying a stock on one exchange for $20 a share and selling it on another for $22. (*See also* **risk arbitrage**.)

**arbitrage pricing theory (APT)**  Asset pricing theory that takes into account the fact that asset returns are affected by a variety of diverse factors. Assuming that asset returns can be modeled as dependent on various factors and on an idiosyncratic error term that is independent of the factors and of the idiosyncratic influences on other asset returns, assets will be priced in a manner analogous to CAPM, with risk premiums for macro factor risks that cannot be diversified away.

**ask price**  Price at which a dealer is willing to sell a security; the bid price is the price at which a dealer is willing to buy a security.

**automated teller machines (ATMs)**  Machines that allow customers to make deposits and withdrawals and obtain account information without actually entering the deposit institution. The first ATMs were installed in the outside walls of banks to allow for after-hours transactions; much of the subsequent growth in ATMs has occurred off bank premises.

**back-end load** Redemption fee imposed by some mutual funds when an investor withdraws money from the fund.

**balloon loan** A loan on which the periodic payments include little or no repayment of the principal; thus the last payment (the balloon payment) must be relatively large. Before the Great Depression, most home mortgages were three- to five-year balloon loans on which only interest was paid until maturity, at which time a balloon payment equal to the size of the loan was due. Now, conventional mortgages are amortized, so that the principal is paid off during the term of the loan.

**Bank Holding Company Act** Act of 1956, amended in 1970, that defines a bank as an institution that both accepts deposits that can be withdrawn on demand and makes commercial loans. A financial institution that did one of these activities, but not both, technically was not a bank but was what some call a nonbank bank, and hence was not regulated by the Federal Reserve. The Competitive Banking Equality Act of 1987 closed the nonbank bank loophole by defining a bank as any FDIC-insured institution, but the act exempted nonbank banks established before March 5, 1986.

**banker's acceptance** Promissory note issued by a firm that a bank stamps "accepted" to guarantee that the bank will repay the note if the firm does not. Banker's acceptances are widely used in international trade and are often resold in secondary markets.

**barter** Trading of goods and services for other goods and services; for example, corn traded for potatoes or wood for leather.

**basis** Difference between the futures price and the spot price of an item. For precious metals, financial assets, and other things that can be stored and sold short, the basis is determined by the cost of carry — the cost, including foregone interest, of buying the item now and holding it until the delivery date. Because the cost of carry is usually positive, futures prices are generally above spot prices and increase with the amount of time until delivery.

**basis point** Term used by financial market participants to describe a hundredth of a percentage point, because interest rates generally change by only a fraction of a percent each day; for example, an increase from 8.50 percent to 8.58 percent is 8 basis points.

**bearer bond** Bond for which proof of ownership is demonstrated by possession of the security, in contrast to a registered bond for which the name of the owner is registered with the trustee and payments can be mailed directly to the owner without the physical presentation of the bond certificate.

**beta coefficient** Parameter in the single-index model and the capital asset pricing model that measures the extent to which the return on a particular asset moves with the overall market return on all assets. An asset's beta coefficient is estimated from the slope of a line fit to a scatter diagram of returns on the asset and on a market index.

**bid price** The price at which a dealer is willing to buy a security; the ask price is the price at which a dealer is willing to sell a security.

**big board** New York Stock Exchange, on which the stocks of many prominent U.S. corporations are traded.

**bills-only policy** Policy that the Fed followed during much of the 1950s of restricting its open market operations to Treasury bills.

**bimetallic standard** Monetary standard under which a nation uses two metals with fixed prices as money. For instance, in the Mint Act of 1792, the U.S. Congress established a bimetallic standard with the price of gold fixed at $19.39 per troy ounce and the price of silver at $1.292 an ounce.

**book value** Net worth (assets minus liabilities) of a company, often calculated on a per share basis, that is shown on the firm's balance sheets. The market price of the company's stock may be above or below book value, because investors value a firm for the profitability of its assets, whereas accountants look at depreciated cost.

**Bretton Woods agreement** Agreement in 1944 that established fixed exchange rates, with the participating nations agreeing to make whatever currency transactions were required to maintain these exchange rates. This system worked tolerably well through the 1950s but came apart in the 1960s. Since 1973, the major exchange rates have been allowed to fluctuate.

**broker** Agent that arranges trades between buyers and sellers without risking any of its own capital, in contrast to a dealer that participates in trades, buying and selling for its own account.

**buying on margin** Buying stock with borrowed money, thus creating leverage that multiplies the gains or losses when the return on the stock is not equal to the interest rate on the loan. The Federal Reserve sets margin requirements (currently 50 percent), the minimum margin that brokerage firms must require of their customers. With an $x$ percent margin requirement, a stock buyer must pay at least $x$ percent of the cost of the stock, borrowing the rest from the brokerage firm.

**call option** Option that gives its holder the right, but not the obligation, to buy an asset at a fixed price on or before a specified date. For instance, a call option could give the owner the right to buy a share of ABC stock for $100 at any time within the next six months.

**call provision** Provision in some Treasury bonds and many corporate and municipal bonds that allows the issuer to redeem the bond before maturity at a specified price. Purchasers of callable bonds typically have some call protection, specifying that the bond cannot be called in the first few years after issuance and that the issuer must pay a premium over face value (like a mortgage's prepayment penalty) if the bond is called.

**capital account** Tabulation of a nation's international purchases and sales of assets. A capital *outflow* for the United States is a U.S. purchase of foreign assets; for example, an exchange of U.S. dollars for German bonds and Japanese

stock. A U.S. capital *inflow* is a foreign purchase of U.S. assets; for example, Germans buying Treasury bills and Japanese buying IBM stock. A capital account *surplus* finances a current account deficit, and a capital account *deficit* accompanies a current account surplus.

**capital asset pricing model (CAPM)** Model of asset prices in which an asset's beta coefficient gauges the macro, systematic risk that cannot be diversified away. According to CAPM, risk-averse investors will not hold assets with high beta coefficients unless they are compensated with large risk premiums: $E_i - R_0 = \beta_i(E_M - R_0)$.

**capital gain** Profit made when an asset is sold for more than its purchase price. A *capital loss* occurs if the sale price is less than the purchase price.

**capital market** Market in which securities with more than one year until maturity are bought and sold. (*See also* **money market**.)

**capital risk** Unexpected change in an asset's price caused by an unexpected change in interest rates. The longer an asset's duration, the more sensitive is its price to interest rate fluctuations, and the larger the capital risk.

**cash flow** Coupons, dividends, rent, or other payments from an asset. The present value of a cash flow is equal to the sum of the present values of the individual payments.

**central bank** Institution responsible for managing a nation's money supply; the U.S. central bank is the Federal Reserve.

**certificate of deposit (CD)** Bank-issued deposit certificate that cannot be redeemed before a fixed expiration date. Large negotiable CDs are issued by banks in denominations of $100,000 or more and can be sold in the secondary market.

**closed-end fund** Investment company that has a fixed number of shares outstanding. The shares of closed-end funds are traded on the stock exchanges or over the counter, at a market price that need not equal the fund's net asset value.

**collateral** Real estate, automobiles, stocks, bonds, and other assets put up by a borrower as security for a loan. These assets become the property of the lender if the borrower defaults.

**collateralized mortgage obligation (CMO)** Bondlike instrument that is issued by some mortgage pools. CMOs have fixed interest rates and are divided into several classes. The last class of securities, called the accrual class or Z class, is like zero-coupon bonds in that the payment of interest and principal does not begin until the prior classes have been repaid.

**commercial bank** Deposit intermediary that accepts deposits and makes loans.

**commercial loan theory of banking** *See* **Real Bills doctrine**.

**commercial paper** Short-term bonds issued by low-risk companies.

**commodity money** Commodity that is used as a medium of exchange — for example, tobacco in colonial Virginia.

**common stock** Corporate stock, the holders of which are the legal owners of the firm. The name indicates that the shareholders own the firm "in common." Stockholders elect (normally with one vote per share) a board of directors that hires the top executives, supervises the management of the firm, and decides the dividends to be paid to shareholders.

**compensating balance** Balance, usually equal to 10 or 20 percent of the size of a loan, that a bank may require a firm to deposit in a low-interest or no-interest checking account in order to obtain a line of credit, allowing it to borrow funds as needed.

**compound interest** Interest earned on interest, a powerful arithmetic that causes seemingly slight differences in annual returns to grow to large differences in wealth after many years. Over short horizons, the monthly, daily, or even continuously crediting of interest increases the effective return on a bank deposit or other investment, by accumulating interest on interest. An amount $P$ invested at an annual rate of return $R$, compounded $m$ times a year, grows to $P(1 + R/m)^m$ after 1 year and to $P(1 + R/m)^{mn}$ after $n$ years.

**consol** Also called a *perpetuity*, bond paying a perpetual cash flow that continues period after period, forever. For a required rate of return $R$, the present value of a consol paying $X$ each period is $P = X/R$.

**constant-dividend-growth model** Stock pricing model in which a stock's dividend $D_1$ grows at a constant rate $g$ and the investor's required return is $R > g$; the present value of this stock simplifies to the central equation of fundamental analysis, $P = D_1/(R - g)$.

**consumer price index (CPI)** Widely followed price index that attempts to measure changes in the cost of living for typical U.S. households.

**consumption goods** Goods that last only a short while, such as ice cream and strawberries. Gross domestic product can be divided into consumption and investment goods. (*See* **investment goods**.)

**continuous compounding** Interest calculations that assume that the frequency of compounding is infinitely large (and the time between compounding infinitesimally small), giving

$$\text{limit } (1 + R/m)^m$$
$$(m \to \infty)$$

where $e = 2.718 \ldots$ is the base of natural logarithms.

**convertible bond** Bond that the owner can convert into another security, usually common stock, at a specified conversion ratio — for example, 20 shares for each bond.

**corporate bond** Fixed-income security issued by corporations to purchase new plants and equipment, pay current bills, and finance the takeover of other companies.

**cost of carry** Cost of buying a commodity now and then holding it until the delivery date of a futures' contract. This cost includes storage, spoilage, insurance, and foregone interest, less any cash flow from the commodity while it is being held.

**coupon** Periodic (usually semiannual) interest payment on a bond, made in addition to a final payment when the bond matures. These payments are called *coupons* because, traditionally, they were cut from the bond certificate and redeemed through a local bank or security dealer.

**coupon rate**  Annual coupon as a percentage of a bond's face value; for example, a bond that pays $1000 at maturity and $45.00 every 6 months has a 9 percent coupon rate.

**covering**  Situation that occurs when, instead of taking delivery, the buyer of a futures contract reverses the position by selling the contract before the delivery date; a contract writer can reverse this short position by purchasing the contract.

**crawling peg**  Float in which the central bank pegs an exchange rate, but periodically adjusts the peg to correct substantial demand-supply imbalances. (*See also* **managed float** and **dirty float**.)

**creative financing**  Novel ways of financing real estate transactions, usually involving a loan from the seller. Buyers and sellers turn to creative financing when money is tight and it is therefore difficult to borrow money from financial institutions.

**credit union**  Nonprofit, tax exempt (generally very small) deposit intermediary for members who share a common bond — for example, a firm's employees or the members of a trade union. Credit unions use member deposits to lend money to other members; in contrast to S&Ls and savings banks, credit union assets are predominantly consumer loans rather than mortgages.

**credit-scoring model**  System used by some banks to quantify an individual's credit-worthiness based on the economic and demographic characteristics and default frequencies of past borrowers.

**currency appreciation**  Situation in which a nation's currency becomes more expensive relative to currencies of other nations. Before World War I, a British pound cost $4.76; in 1989, it cost $1.50. Over this period, dollars appreciated relative to the pound, and the pound depreciated relative to the dollar.

**currency depreciation**  Situation in which a nation's currency becomes less expensive relative to currencies of other nations.

**currency outstanding**  *See* **U.S. currency outstanding**.

**currency swap**  In effect, an exchange of assets or liabilities denominated in different currencies; for example, two parties might issue bonds denominated in different currencies and then agree to swap the proceeds and repay each other's debts — effectively transforming each debt into the other currency.

**current account**  Nation's net international purchases of currently produced goods and services plus its net international transfer payments. The current-account balance must be financed by the sale or acquisition of financial assets — an increase or decrease in foreign claims against the nation. Thus a current account deficit must be financed by a capital account surplus (and vice versa).

**daily limit**  Specified limit, set by exchanges, on the daily change in the settlement prices of some futures contracts.

**daily settlement**  Daily transfer of funds from winners to losers required by futures exchanges, using end-of-day settlement prices. Also called *marking to market*.

**dealer**  Individual or firm that participates in trades, buying, and selling for its own account, in contrast to a broker that arranges trades between buyers and sellers without risking any of its own capital.

**debasement**  Degrading coins by mixing in less expensive metals; for example, making gold coins that are only 80 percent gold and 20 percent base metal.

**debit card**  Similar in appearance to a credit card and used in stores like a credit card, but actually representing an electronic checking account in that funds are automatically transferred from the customer's bank account to the merchant's account.

**debt**  In contrast to equity, legally binding contract to pay a specified amount of money.

**default**  Situation that occurs when a borrower violates the terms of the debt contract; for example, by not making a scheduled coupon payment on time. A default is not necessarily a complete loss, in that it may be a temporary suspension of coupon payments or a prelude to a partial payment; in the first month after default, a bond typically trades at about 40 percent of its face value.

**defined-benefit plan**  Retirement plan in which the employee's retirement benefits are specified — often by a formula that takes into account salary and years of employment — and the plan's sponsor adjusts the contributions, as needed, to meet these promised benefits.

**defined-contribution plan**  Retirement plan in which contributions are credited to each employee's personal account, and the retirement benefits depend on the size of these contributions and the rate of return the pension fund earns on them.

**deposit multiplier**  Ratio of deposits to the monetary base. Fractional reserve banking multiplies the monetary base into a much larger amount of deposits. The ratio of the change in deposits to a change in the monetary base will not equal the deposit multiplier unless the deposit multiplier is constant.

**dirty float**  Policy under which the central bank allows the exchange rate to fluctuate with demand and supply, but occasionally enters the market, often surreptitiously. (*See also* **crawling peg** and **managed float**.)

**discount basis**  Calculation of interest rates relative to the amount paid back rather than the amount loaned: for example, the calculation of Treasury-bill rates relative to face value rather than purchase price. Banks are no longer allowed to calculate consumer-loan rates on a discount basis.

**discount broker**  Security broker that just executes trades, in contrast to a full-service broker who also advises investors.

**discount rate**  Interest rate that Federal Reserve banks charge on loans made to deposit institutions.

**discount window**  Window through which deposit institutions can borrow money from the Federal Reserve. The discount window was intended to defuse bank runs by making Federal Reserve banks reliable lenders of last resort, a source of emergency cash for banks.

**disintermediation**  Movement of funds that occurred when interest rates rose above deposit rate ceilings; instead of depositing money in financial intermediaries, savers withdrew money and purchased Treasury bills and other money-market securities. During periods of disintermediation, when deposits shrink, intermediaries must look elsewhere for funds or cut back on their lending.

**diversified portfolio**  Strategy of investing in several imperfectly correlated (or, better, negatively correlated) assets to reduce risk. Diversification, counting on asset gains and losses to offset each other, is of no interest to those who are risk neutral or risk seeking, but is very attractive to risk-averse investors.

**divisibility**  Extent to which a fraction of an asset can be purchased or sold for a like fraction of the price of the whole asset.

**Dow Jones Industrial Average**  Widely followed average of stock prices of thirty prominent blue-chip companies, using a divisor that changes occasionally to offset substitutions and stock splits, thereby maintaining a logically consistent daily index of stock prices. In contrast are market value indexes, such as the S&P 500 and the NYSE indexes, which weight each stock's price by the number of shares outstanding.

**dual banking system**  System in the United States in which banks can be chartered (and supervised) by either the federal or state government. Presently, about one-third of all banks are federally chartered.

**dual-purpose fund**  Investment company with two classes of shareholders — income and capital. The income shareholders receive all the dividends from the stock in the fund's portfolio and, on the termination date, a specified redemption price (if the fund has sufficient assets); the capital shareholders receive any excess of the value of the fund's portfolio over this redemption price.

**duration**   Present-value weighted average number of years until an asset's cash flow is received, approximately equal to the percentage change in the asset's present value resulting from a one-percentage-point change in the required return. The duration of a bond with coupons is less than its maturity and decreases as the coupons increase.

**duration gap**   Comparison of a bank's asset and liability duration, taking into account that assets are somewhat larger than liabilities other than net worth.

$$\text{duration gap} = \begin{pmatrix}\text{duration} \\ \text{of assets}\end{pmatrix} - \begin{pmatrix}\text{duration} \\ \text{of liabilities}\end{pmatrix}\begin{pmatrix}\dfrac{\text{liabilities}}{\text{assets}}\end{pmatrix}$$

The size of the duration gap is an estimate of the change in net worth, as a percentage of total assets, resulting from a one-percentage-point increase in interest rates.

**Edge Act**   Act of 1919 that allows bank holding companies to establish interstate subsidiaries (Edge Act corporations) for accepting deposits and making loans related to international business transactions.

**efficient market**   Market in which there are no obviously mispriced securities and, therefore, no transactions that can be counted on to make abnormally large profits. The efficient market hypothesis does not assume that a stock's price is equal to some objective measure of its intrinsic value, or even that all investors agree on that value — only that investors cannot consistently make unusually large profits trading on information. The weak, semistrong, and strong forms of the efficient market hypothesis say that abnormal profits cannot be made using information about past stock prices, all public information, and all information, respectively.

**electronic funds transfer system**   Computerized network in which transactions are electronically recorded and funds instantly transferred from the buyer's account to the seller's account.

**Employment Retirement Income Security Act (ERISA)**   Federal legislation, passed in 1974, which mandates reasonable vesting and portability and protects pensions from mismanagement or underfunding. ERISA also broadens the opportunities for persons who are self-employed or who work for companies that do not have retirement plans to make tax-deferred retirement contributions. ERISA does not apply to government retirement plans.

**equation of exchange**   Equation $MV_T = P_T T$, where $M$ is the money supply, $T$ is the number of transactions, $P_T$ is the average price of these transactions, and $V_T$ is velocity, the average number of times that money is exchanged during a given accounting period. The equation of exchange is an accounting identity based on the observation that in every transaction, the buyer exchanges a quantity of money equal to the price of the purchased item.

**equity**   In contrast to corporate debt and other fixed-income securities, a claim on the company's profits after interest and other expenses have been paid; and, in the event of liquidation, a claim on the company's assets after its debts have been settled.

**Eurodollars**   U.S. dollar deposits in foreign banks or foreign branches of U.S. banks.

**excess reserves**   Reserves held by depository institutions beyond those required by the Federal Reserve.

**exchange rate**   Price of one currency in terms of another; for example, the U.S. dollar price of German marks.

**exchange-rate risk**   Uncertainty about future exchange rates and consequently about the rate of return on an investment denominated in one currency (such as francs) in terms of another (such as dollars). The rate of return, measured in domestic currency, on an investment denominated in foreign currency is equal to the foreign rate of return plus the rate of appreciation of the foreign currency relative to the domestic currency.

**exercise date**   Date on which an option contract expires.

**exercise price**   Price at which an option contract can be exercised (also called the striking price).

**exercise value**   The minimum value of an option — the amount an option holder could save by exercising the option instead of buying or selling the asset at its market price. The exercise value of a call option is equal to the difference $P - E$ between the value of the asset $P$ and the option's exercise price $E$ if $P > E$ (and zero otherwise). The exercise value of a put is equal to $E - P$ if $P < E$ (and zero otherwise).

**expectations hypothesis**   Theory that explains the term structure of interest rates by interest-rate expectations — specifically, the Hicks Equation. If securities are priced so that a strategy of rolling over short-term bonds is expected to do as well as a strategy of holding long-term bonds, then when no change in one-year rates is anticipated, comparable assets of differing maturities will all be priced to have the same yield. Longer-term rates will be above the current one-year rate if rates are expected to rise in the future and will be below if rates are expected to decline.

**expected value**   Usually denoted by the Greek symbol $\mu$, a weighted average of the possible returns, using probabilities as weights to reflect the likelihood of each outcome: $\mu = x_1 P[x_1] + x_2 P[x_2] + \ldots + x_n P[x_n]$. The expected value is the long-run average if the frequency with which each outcome occurs corresponds to its probability.

**Fannie Mae**   *See* **Federal National Mortgage Association**.

**Federal Deposit Insurance Corporation (FDIC)**   Agency established in the 1930s to insure deposits against bank failure, which has eliminated the panicky bank runs that plagued banks in the past.

**federal funds**   Large, overnight loans of reserves deposited at the Federal Reserve Banks. Although these are loans among banks, they are called federal funds because it is the Federal Reserve that electronically credits one bank and debits another.

**federal funds rate**   The interest rate on interbank loans through the federal funds market.

**Federal Home Loan Bank (FHLB) system**   System created in the 1930s to supervise and assist savings and loan associations and other residential mortgage lenders. The Federal Home Loan Bank Board supervised the FHLB system until 1989, when it was replaced by two new organizations: the Office of Thrift Supervision, which now charters, regulates, and supervises S&Ls, and the Federal Housing Finance Board, which now oversees the twelve Federal Home Loan Banks.

**Federal Home Loan Mortgage Corporation (FHLMC, or Freddie Mac)**   Agency established in 1970 by the Federal Home Loan Board. It resembles both Fannie Mae and Ginnie Mae in that it puts together pools of mortgages, financing its purchases by instruments called Guaranteed Mortgage Certificates (GMCs) and Collateralized Mortgage Obligations (CMOs).

**Federal National Mortgage Association (FNMA, or Fannie Mae)**   Agency established in 1938 to funnel funds to mortgage borrowers. In 1968, it was split into two separate organizations: a private corporation that retained the name Fannie Mae, and a government corporation, the Government National Mortgage Association (Ginnie Mae). Fannie Mae sells short- and medium-term bonds, using the proceeds to buy mortgages from mortgage bankers and other mortgage originators. Although privately owned, Fannie Mae is subject to government supervision; in return, Fannie Mae borrows some money directly from the federal government and is able to borrow privately at relatively low rates because it is a quasi-governmental agency.

**Federal Open Market Committee (FOMC)**   Committee consisting of the seven Fed Governors and five of the twelve Federal Reserve Bank presidents. Most monetary policy decisions are made at its periodic meetings.

**Federal Reserve Board (Fed)**   Primary monetary authority of the United States, composed of seven governors, appointed by the president to overlapping fourteen-year terms.

**Federal Savings and Loan Insurance Corporation (FSLIC)**  Agency established by Congress in 1933 to insure deposits in savings and loan associations. In 1989 the insolvent FSLIC was replaced with a new deposit insurance fund for thrifts, the Savings Association Insurance Fund (SAIF), administered by the Federal Deposit Insurance Corporation (FDIC).

**fiat money**  Something that has little value as a commodity but, because of law or tradition, is accepted as a medium of exchange; for example, Yap stones and U.S. Federal Reserve notes.

**finance company**  Company (other than a deposit intermediary) whose primary assets are loans to households and businesses. Finance companies are financial intermediaries that borrow funds (but not through deposits) for relending, making a profit on the difference between the interest rates they pay to borrow money and the interest rates they charge for lending it.

**financial asset**  Paper claim, such as a bank deposit, bond, or stock. In the United States and other countries with well-developed financial markets, many savers invest in financial assets that are issued by borrowers to raise funds to lend to others or to acquire physical assets.

**Financial Institutions Reform, Recovery, and Enforcement Act (FIRREA)**  Act of 1989 that imposes higher, asset-based capital requirements on deposit institutions, which are to be strictly enforced by the prompt closure of insolvent institutions. An insured deposit intermediary must either be chartered as a bank or be a Qualified Thrift Lender with most of its assets in residential mortgage-related assets. The insolvent FSLIC was replaced by a new deposit insurance fund for thrifts, the Savings Association Insurance Fund (SAIF), administered by the FDIC. The Office of Thrift Supervision (OTS) was established, with the power to charter, regulate, and supervise all thrifts, whether state or federally chartered.

**financial intermediary**  Commercial bank, credit union, insurance company, or mutual fund that borrows from some economic agents and lends to others.

**financial market**  Established market for trading bonds, stocks, and other financial assets. These markets come in many different forms (such as the New York Stock Exchange and the over-the-counter market) and involve a variety of agents (including brokers and dealers).

**fiscal policy**  Expenditures and tax rates of the federal government, which are determined by Congress and the president. Any deficit between federal outlays and revenue is financed by the sale of Treasury debt; the Federal Reserve can use open market operations to monetize as much or as little of this debt as it wishes. (*See also* **monetary policy**.)

**fixed-income security**  Financial asset for which the amount of money to be repaid is specified in the promissory note.

**float**  Situation created by discrepancies in the dates on which payments and receipts are recorded. The Federal Reserve's check-clearing procedures create float for banks when one bank is credited with reserves from a cashed check before another bank's reserves are debited. Federal Reserve float is an interest-free loan to banks from the Federal Reserve.

**flow**  Measurement of the volume of transactions during a specified period of time; for example, gross domestic product, capital gains, and the federal deficit during the year 1992. (*See also* **stock**.)

**forward contract**  Private agreement to deliver a certain item on a specified date at a price agreed to today, but not paid until delivery. A futures contract is similar, but standardized and traded on organized exchanges.

**forward price**  Price agreed to today but not paid until the specified future delivery date. A U.S. importer who has agreed to pay a certain amount of yen for a product six months from now and wants to guarantee the dollar cost of the product can pay dollars now for a six-month forward contract for yen.

**forward rate**  The implicit future rate of return embedded in the term structure of interest rates, in the sense that these rates are the future interest-rate values for which the strategies of buying long-term securities and rolling over short-term securities do equally well. An investor whose interest-rate expectations are not equal to these implicit forward rates has reason for preferring shorts to longs, or vice versa.

**fractional reserve banking** Situation in which depository institutions keep only a fraction of their deposits as reserves. If these deposits are a medium of exchange, then the depository institutions multiply the money supply.

**Freddie Mac** *See* **Federal Home Loan Mortgage Corporation**.

**full-service broker** Security broker that advises investors and handles trades, in contrast to a discount broker that just executes trades.

**fundamental analysis** Analysis used by investors to compare the price of a security to the present value of the anticipated cash flow. This approach leads to a study of a firm's dividends, earnings, and assets.

**future value** Value of an investment after it has earned a specified rate of return for a given number of years. If an amount $P$ earns an annual rate of return $R$ for $n$ years, the investment grows to a future value $F = P(1 + R)^n$.

**futures contract** Agreement to deliver a certain item on a specified date at a price that is agreed to today, but not paid until delivery; for example, a mill might agree to pay a farmer $3 a bushel for 100,000 bushels of wheat delivered six months from now — thus eliminating the mill's uncertainty about the cost of wheat and the farmer's uncertainty about revenue. Unlike forward contracts, futures contracts are standardized and traded on organized exchanges. Futures can be used for hedging a position (for example, a farmer can sell wheat futures), for speculation (for example, a wager on the price of silver); or for arbitrage (for example, stock index arbitrage).

**gap** Measurement of the sensitivity of a bank's net income to interest rates:

$$\text{gap} = \begin{pmatrix} \text{rate sensitive} \\ \text{assets} \end{pmatrix} - \begin{pmatrix} \text{rate sensitive} \\ \text{liabilities} \end{pmatrix}$$

If there is a change in the interest rates on a bank's rate-sensitive assets and liabilities, its annual income will change by the size of its gap multiplied by the size of the change in interest rates.

**gap analysis** Techniques by which banks gauge their exposure to interest-rate risk. Gap analysis focuses on how interest rates affect income; in contrast, *duration analysis* considers the effect of interest rates on net worth. Gap analysis measures the effect of interest rates on income by estimating the fraction of assets and liabilities that are adjustable-rate, with interest rates that move up and down with market interest rates during some target horizon, perhaps one year.

**Garn–St Germain Depository Institutions Act** Established in 1982 in response to the S&L crisis, this act hastened the deregulation of banking. Banks and thrifts were authorized to offer money market deposit accounts, with no interest-rate ceiling and no reserve requirement, so that they could compete with money-market funds. Federal thrifts were allowed to diversify their assets away from home mortgages by making business loans and by increasing their consumer loans and loans secured by nonresidential real estate. The Act affirmed the power of the FDIC and FSLIC to arrange interstate mergers if necessary and to allow banks to make interstate acquisitions of closed banks or thrifts with assets of at least $500 million.

**generally accepted accounting principles (GAAP)** Principles adopted by the Financial Accounting Standards Board (FASB), an independent group, financially supported by the accounting industry, which from time to time publishes its opinions on accounting practices that it considers acceptable. The Securities and Exchange Commission (SEC) requires that financial statements conform to generally accepted accounting principles.

**Ginnie Mae** *See* **Government National Mortgage Association**.

**Glass–Steagall Act** Act of 1933 that prohibits U.S. commercial banks from engaging in investment banking activities, that is, helping state and local governments and businesses raise money through the sale of securities. To comply with the law, banks were forced to specialize in either commercial or investment banking. Foreign banks can operate both as commercial and investment banks in the United States, unconstrained by Glass–Steagall.

**gold standard**  Monetary standard under which a nation's money is either gold or convertible into gold at a fixed price. Between 1834 and 1933, with the exception of the Civil War period and an occasional financial panic, the United States was effectively on a gold standard under which the government bought and sold gold at the fixed price of $20.67 per ounce. Consistent with this commitment, the U.S. twenty-dollar gold piece contained a little less than an ounce of gold.

**goods-and-services balance**  Nation's foreign balance, encompassing both goods and services, including interest and dividend payments, tourist expenditures, purchases and sales of military equipment, and foreign expenses of operating military bases abroad. (*See also* **trade balance**.)

**Government National Mortgage Association (GNMA, or Ginnie Mae)**  Agency established in 1968 when the Federal National Mortgage Association (FNMA, or Fannie Mae) was split into two separate organizations: a private corporation that retained the name Fannie Mae and a government corporation, the Government National Mortgage Association (GNMA, or Ginnie Mae). The GNMA is part of the Department of Housing and Urban Development and administers government mortgage subsidy programs that had previously been handled by Fannie Mae — for example, using Treasury money to make HUD-subsidized mortgages. In 1970, Ginnie Mae created the revolutionary idea of selling pass-through GNMA certificates to finance the purchase of mortgages from private institutions.

**graduated-payment mortgage (GPM)**  Mortgage for which the monthly payments are initially low and then increase over time to ease the financial burden on young homeowners who expect nominal income to grow steadily. Ideally, the mortgage payments will be a constant fraction of income, rather than a constant dollar amount.

**Gresham's Law**  Axiom that bad money drives out good; that is, a medium of exchange that is more valuable in some nonmonetary use will be withdrawn from circulation — for example, silver dollars containing more than a dollar's worth of silver, or a rare quarter worth more than 25 cents to a collector.

**gross domestic product (GDP)**  Market value of output within a country, regardless of the citizenship of the workers and the ownership of the firms. The value of goods produced in Germany by U.S. citizens and U.S. firms is included in German GDP, but not U.S. GDP.

**gross national product (GNP)**  Market value of the aggregate production of new goods and services — houses, automobiles, haircuts, financial advice — by a nation's citizens and firms, regardless of their location, during a specified period of time, usually a year or a quarter of a year. GNP excludes the purchase and sale of items that were produced in earlier periods, such as the purchase of a used car, an old house, or a painting by Andy Warhol. Gross national product is not a comprehensive measure of production because it excludes most activities that do not involve a financial transaction; for example, do-it-yourself projects and voluntary activities. (*See also* **gross domestic product**.)

**Hicks equation**  Equation showing how, in accordance with the Expectations Hypothesis, the term structure of interest rates is such that long-term rates are the product of the current and anticipated future short-term rates:

$$(1 + R_n)^n = (1 + R_1)(1 + R_1^{+1})\ldots(1 + R_1^{n-1})$$

**high-powered money**  Label sometimes applied to the monetary base because, with fractional reserve banking, government money can support a much larger quantity of deposit money.

**holding company**  Legal structure used by some banks to evade restrictions on branching and other activities. Holding companies can control a variety of banking and nonbanking subsidiaries. Some holding companies are established to administer several banks; others are conglomerates that control a variety of nonfinancial businesses as well as banks.

**hyperinflation** Extremely rapid rate of inflation. In Germany from 1922–1923, prices increased at a rate of 322 percent a month; in Hungary from 1945–1946, prices increased by 19,800 percent a month.

**idiosyncratic risk** Also called *micro risk, unsystematic risk,* or *diversifiable risk,* it arises from events specific to individual companies and can be diversified away.

**immunized** Situation in which the realized rate of return on an investment over a specified horizon is not affected by (small) changes in interest rates, occurring when the investment's duration is equal to the horizon.

**income** Benefits received while owning an asset. Income includes the cash flow generated by the investment — the interest from a bond, dividends from a stock, rent from an apartment building — as well as the services provided by an asset — transportation from a car, shelter from a house, and pleasure from fine art.

**income risk** Uncertainty about the rates of return that the cash flow from an investment will earn when it is reinvested. The purchase of long-term assets is profitable if interest rates fall unexpectedly; rolling over short-term assets does well if interest rates rise unexpectedly.

**index arbitrage** Attempt to earn risk-free profits whenever the basis, or spread between the price of a stock index futures contract and the index itself, differs from the cost of carry (the Treasury-bill rate minus dividend yield on the stocks in the index) by more than the transactions costs that arbitrage entails. Arbitragers buy stocks and sell futures if the futures price is too high and do the reverse if it is too low.

**index fund** Investment company that tries to replicate the performance of a designated market index by buying the securities in this index in proportion to their index weights.

**individual retirement account (IRA)** Individually directed defined-contribution retirement plan, which was originally intended for employees who are not covered by a pension plan. Anyone, self-employed or not, may put up to $2,000 of earned income (some of which may be tax deductible) into an IRA account annually.

**inflation** Persistent, continuing increase in the prices of goods and services. Inflation is often measured by the change in the consumer price index (CPI), which monitors the cost of a standard basket of goods and services.

**inflation risk** Risk created by uncertainty about future prices, because the purchasing power of the proceeds from an investment depends on the future course of prices. An unexpected increase or decrease in the rate of inflation erodes or swells, respectively, the purchasing power of fixed nominal cash flows. Although inflation and interest rates do not move in locked step, a strategy of rolling over short-term assets at least offers the likelihood that nominal interest rates will increase if inflation does.

**initial public offering (IPO)** Corporation's initial sale of shares to the public.

**insured pension plans** Private pension plans that are managed by life insurance companies.

**interest-rate parity equation** Equation stating that, for the basis to equal the cost of carry, the difference between the dollar futures and spot prices of a foreign currency should approximately equal the difference between U.S. and foreign interest rates.

**interest-rate swap** In effect, an exchange of interest rate obligations, allowing a floating-rate debt to be converted into a fixed-rate debt (and vice versa) or into a floating-rate debt linked to a different interest-rate index; for example, a firm that has borrowed money with a floating interest rate might swap interest payments with a firm that has borrowed money at a fixed interest rate, thereby effectively converting the first firm's liability from floating-rate to fixed-rate debt and transforming the second firm's liability from fixed-rate to floating-rate.

**intermediate targets**  Targets often used by the Fed to help achieve its ultimate objectives. For example, the Fed might use $M1$ as an intermediate target, aiming for a 5 percent increase in $M1$ during the next 12 months, not because it particularly cares about the rate of growth of $M1$, but because it believes that by hitting its 5 percent target for $M1$, it will be able to accomplish its objectives regarding unemployment, inflation, and other variables of real economic consequence.

**International Monetary Fund (IMF)**  Organization established at Bretton Woods to lend foreign exchange to nations that need to buy their currency in order to stabilize exchange rates. The IMF now lends foreign exchange to nations that need help paying for imports.

**international reserves**  Gold and foreign assets held by central banks that can be used, if needed, to make international transactions. Roughly two-thirds of the aggregate foreign assets held by central banks worldwide are denominated in U.S. dollars.

**intrinsic value**  Present value of an asset's prospective cash flow, discounted by the investor's required return, taking into account the returns available on alternative investments, its risk, and other salient considerations. An asset is worth buying if its intrinsic value is larger than its price, but not otherwise.

**investment bank**  Firm that helps businesses and government agencies issue new securities in the primary market.

**investment company**  Company that pools investor funds and buys a portfolio of securities, providing diversification and, it is hoped, superior management. These may be either open-end or closed-end.

**investment goods**  Those components of gross domestic product that last for a considerable period of time, such as factories and apartment buildings. *See also* **consumption goods**.

**junk bond**  The generic label for low-quality debt. Junk bonds are unrated bonds or low-rated bonds issued by companies that are either not well known or else known to be risky. Some of these bonds are *new junk*, which are sold to finance risky ventures; and some of them are *fallen angels*, which are bonds issued by companies that were once financially secure and now are not.

**L (liquidity)**  Broad monetary aggregate that includes $M3$, savings bonds, short-term liquid Treasury securities, commercial paper, and banker's acceptances.

**law of large numbers**  Statistical principle that if an event has a probability $P$ of occurring in a single trial, then in a large number of independent trials, the fraction of these trials in which the event occurs will almost certainly be close to $P$; for example, in 1 million flips of a fair coin, the fraction of the flips that are heads will almost certainly be close to .5.

**law of one price**  Axiom that the domestic price of a foreign item will equal the domestic price of a comparable domestic item. Otherwise, no one will buy the more expensive item.

**leverage**  Situation that occurs when a relatively small investment reaps the benefits or losses from a much larger investment; for example, the use of borrowed money to finance an investment. Leverage is said to be a two-edged sword because it multiplies both gains and losses. If a fraction $x$ of an investment is your own money, then your degree of leverage is $1/x$. If you pay an interest rate $B$ on the borrowed money and earn a rate of return $R$ on the total investment, then the rate of return on your own money is $B + (1/x)(R - B)$.

**liability managment**  Aggressive search by banks for attractive sources of funds. Since the early 1960s, banks have increasingly come to view the garnering of funds as important as their allocation.

**life annuity**  Contract that pays a person (the "annuitant") a periodic income as long as one or more specified persons are still alive. The purpose of life annuities is to protect the beneficiaries if they live unusually long lives.

**limited liability**   Legal principle that although stockholders are the legal owners of a corporation, they are not personally responsible for its debts; their potential loss is limited to the amount of money they have invested in the firm's stock.

**liquid asset**   Cash or other asset that can readily be converted into cash. In order to accommodate withdrawal risks, both through deposits and loans, banks must maintain an effective balance between liquid assets and illiquid assets.

**liquidity**   Gauge of the ease with which an asset can be converted into a medium of exchange. Liquidity can be measured by how far ahead one has to look for a buyer in order to obtain a competitive price.

**liquidity constrained**   Households or businesses that have a limited ability to borrow against future income.

**liquidity preference**   Preference to keep wealth in the form of ready cash. Money is a store of value, one of many possible ways of providing for future consumption. The opportunity cost of holding money is the higher rate of return that can be earned on other assets, including interest on bonds. Therefore, interest rates have a decisive influence on the decision to hold cash rather than bonds.

**liquidity-premium hypothesis**   The hypothesis that, because investors are more concerned with capital risk than income risk, they have a natural preference for short-term assets and require relatively high returns on long-term bonds — higher than predicted by the simple expectations hypothesis. According to this theory, the term structure is normally upward sloping.

**load fee**   Sales charge that some mutual funds levy on investors when they buy shares in the fund; the load fee may be split between the fund and the salesperson who persuades the investor to buy shares.

**London Interbank Offered Rate (LIBOR)**   Interest rate that international banks charge each other for large Eurodollar loans — loans denominated in U.S. dollars. LIBOR is commonly used as an international benchmark to fix the minimum interest rate that bank syndicates charge on Eurodollar loans.

**M1**   Narrow monetary aggregate that includes currency outside banks, traveler's checks, commercial bank checking accounts, and other transaction accounts.

**M2**   Monetary aggregate that includes M1, overnight Eurodollars and repurchase agreements, money-market deposit accounts, money-market mutual fund shares, savings deposits, and small (less than $100,000) time deposits.

**M3**   Monetary aggregate that includes M2, large time deposits ($100,000 plus), term Eurodollars, term repurchase agreements, and institutional money-market fund shares.

**McFadden Act**   Largely motivated by a fear that Bank of America would span the nation, this 1927 act prohibits interstate branching and allows each state to regulate branching within its borders.

**macro risk**   *See* **systematic risk**.

**managed float**   Policy under which the central bank intervenes in foreign exchange markets to manipulate exchange rates. (*See also* **crawling peg** and **dirty float**.)

**margin**   Initial amount that must be put up by an investor who borrows money from a broker to buy stock. The investor must also keep the account's equity (market value minus loan) above the broker's maintenance margin requirement. (*See also* **buying on margin**.)

**market segmentation hypothesis**   Hypothesis that investors have diverse preferences and specialize in different bond maturities. Some investors, such as life insurance companies and pension funds, have long horizons and prefer long-term bonds to minimize income risk, while other investors, particularly those most concerned with real rates of return, prefer to roll over short-term assets. If the market is sharply segmented, then the interest rates on different maturities might depend solely on demand and supply within that segment of the market — allowing very different interest rates on bonds that have only slightly different maturities.

**marking to market**   Daily transfer of funds from winners to losers required by futures exchanges, using end-of-day settlement prices. Also called the *daily settlement*.

**mean**   Expected value μ of a probability distribution: the probability-weighted average of the possible outcomes. The mean of a set of data is the average value of the observations.

**medium of exchange**   Commonly exchanged items that the recipients intend to trade for other items; for example, gold in nineteenth-century America and Federal Reserve notes today.

**merchandise trade balance**   Nation's exports of commodities minus its imports.

**merchant banking**   Situation in which a securities firm invests its own money in real estate, new security issues, mergers and acquisitions, and other ventures. Traditionally, U.S. investment banks have been reluctant to invest their own money in their customers' businesses or securities, because of the possibility of conflicts of interest.

**micro risk**   *See* **unsystematic risk**.

**modified duration**   A measure obtained by dividing the conventional duration $D$ by $1 + R$ to provide a more accurate estimate of the percentage change in an asset's present value $P$ resulting from a one-percentage-point change in the required return $R$: modified duration = $D/(1 + R)$.

**monetarism**   View that monetary disturbances are the principal cause of economic fluctuations. Although often identified with Milton Friedman and the quantity theory, monetarists are a diverse group with varying adherences to the classical beliefs that, in the short-run or the long-run, the quantity theory holds and the economy is always at full employment.

**monetary aggregates**   Aggregates, including $M1$, $M2$, $M3$, and $L$, through which the Fed monitors the nation's monetary assets.

**monetary base**   Outstanding amount of government money, which is held either as bank reserves or as currency outside of banks.

**monetary policy**   Use of open market operations, reserves requirements, and discount rates by a nation's central bank (in the United States, the Federal Reserve) in order to alter the monetary base and monetary aggregates (*See also* **fiscal policy**.)

**monetized**   Extent to which the federal deficit is financed by an increase in the monetary base (what is loosely called "printing money"). A federal deficit must implicitly be financed either by an increase in publicly held Treasury bonds or in the monetary base.

**money illusion**   Focusing on nominal rather than real data; for example, using nominal wages to choose between work and leisure.

**money market**   Market in which securities with less than one year until maturity are bought and sold. (*See also* **capital market**.)

**money market deposit account (MMDAs)**   Bank account that was authorized in 1982 to allow deposit institutions to compete with money-market funds. Depositors can make an unlimited number of withdrawals either in person or by mail and are allowed a maximum of three checks a month or a total of six monthly withdrawals by check, telephone, or automatic bill paying. These accounts have no reserve requirements and, unlike money-market funds, are federally insured.

**money-market fund**   Mutual fund that purchases short-term securities such as bank CDs and Treasury bills, thereby providing a very liquid investment for small investors. Shareholders can quickly and easily withdraw their money by giving either written or telephoned instructions. Most funds allow their shareholders to write checks payable to a third party, typically with a $500 minimum.

**moral hazard**   Problem that occurs when one of the parties to a contract alters his or her behavior so as to profit from the contract at the expense of the other party. For example, a homeowner who has fire insurance may become less careful about avoiding a fire; or a person with medical insurance may be less frugal about medical expenses. One common criticism of deposit insurance is that there is a moral-hazard problem in that it encourages reckless banking practices.

**mortgage-backed security**   Security issued by the Government National Mortgage Association (Ginnie Mae) and others that is collateralized by mortgages purchased from banks, S&Ls, mortgage bankers, and other financial institutions.

**municipal security (muni)**   Security issued by state and local governments and related agencies, of which the interest income is generally exempt from federal income taxes.

**mutual fund**   *See* **open-end investment company**.

**mutual savings bank**   Deposit intermediary that is legally owned by its depositors but, in practice, is very similar to a savings and loan association.

**National Association of Security Dealers Automated Quotation (NASDAQ)**   Nationwide computerized price quotation network for many over-the-counter securities.

**National Credit Union Administration**   Federal agency that initiated nationwide credit union deposit insurance in 1970.

**negative amortization**   Increase in the unpaid balance when the monthly loan payment is insufficient to cover the interest charge. This can occur in many business and personal loans (such as a line of credit from a bank, loans from a stock broker, or credit card balances) where there is no set repayment schedule. It can also occur with adjustable-rate loans if the monthly payment does not increase when interest charges do.

**negotiable certificate of deposit (CD)**   Zero-coupon security issued by a bank in denominations of at least $100,000 — usually more than $1 million. Often described as "large CDs" or "negotiable CDs," they generally mature in one to six months, and although they cannot be redeemed at the issuing bank until maturity, there is an active secondary market.

**negotiable order of withdrawal (NOW) account**   Established by a favorable court decision in 1972 in Massachusetts that allowed what

is, in essence, a checking account paying 5¼ percent interest — at a time when interest-paying checking accounts were illegal. NOW accounts were explicitly authorized by the 1980 Depository Institutions Deregulation and Monetary Control Act.

**net asset value (NAV)**   Total market value of an investment company's portfolio divided by the number of outstanding shares; an open-end company will redeem shares or issue new ones at a price equal to its current net asset value.

**new classical economists**   Robert Lucas and other economists who extended classical economic models, in which the economy is always at full-employment, to allow for voluntary fluctuations in employment and output caused by worker misperceptions of real wages.

**1951 Accord**   Accord between the Fed and the Treasury that established the important principle that the Federal Reserve is an independent branch of government and free to follow monetary policies that it deems appropriate.

**no-load fund (or no-load)**   Mutual fund offered by an investment company that does not charge load fees. All closed-end funds are no-load.

**nominal**   Relating to economic data such as wage rates, income, or wealth, that are recorded in dollars (or marks in Germany, yen in Japan), as opposed to *real data* that measure purchasing power.

**nominal rate of return**   Rate of return that compares the dollars received from an investment with the dollars invested, without adjusting for the purchasing power of these dollars. The *real rate of return* measures the percentage increase in purchasing power and is approximately equal to the nominal rate of return minus the rate of inflation.

**nonbank bank**   As defined by the Bank Holding Company Act of 1956, amended in 1970, a financial institution that either accepts deposits that can be withdrawn on demand or that makes commercial loans, but not both. Nonbank banks were not regulated by the Federal Reserve until 1987, when the Competitive Banking Equality Act closed the nonbank bank loophole by defining a bank as any FDIC-insured institution; however, it exempted nonbank banks established before March 5, 1986.

**noninsured pension plan**   Private pension plan that is managed by a trustee, such as the trust department of a commercial bank.

**nontraded goods**   Goods and services that are not governed by the law of one price because of prohibitive import and export expenses; for example, it can cost much more for a haircut and a round of golf in Japan than in the United States because it is impractical for the Japanese to have their hair cut in Iowa and play golf in Georgia.

**normal distribution**   Widely used bell-shaped Gaussian probability distribution. For many assets, this is a reasonable, useful approximation for describing investor uncertainty about the asset's return. A normal distribution is symmetrical about its mean with about a two-thirds probability of being within one standard deviation of its mean and about a 95 percent probability of being within two standard deviations.

**open interest**   Total daily amount of outstanding option or futures contracts. Those who own contracts are said to be "long," while those who have written these contracts are "short."

**open market operation**   Central bank's purchases and sales of securities. These transactions expand or contract the nation's monetary base and are, in practice, the predominant instrument of Federal Reserve monetary policy in the United States.

**open-end investment company**   Investment company whose shares increase as more money is invested in the fund and decline as money is withdrawn. Each day, or several times a day, the fund calculates its net asset value (NAV) and stands ready to issue or redeem shares at this price.

**operating target**   Target used by the Fed to help achieve its intermediate target. For instance, the Fed may want to reduce the rate of inflation and decide to use a 5 percent rate of growth of $M1$ as intermediate target. Because $M1$ contains checkable deposits subject to reserve requirements, there may be a close rela-

tionship between bank reserves and $M1$. If so, the Fed might set an operating target of, say, 5 percent annual growth in bank reserves, hoping that this will ensure a 5 percent annual growth of $M1$ and that this growth rate for $M1$ will reduce inflation as desired.

**Operation Twist**   Policy that the Fed followed (halfheartedly) during the 1960s to twist the term structure of interest rates by buying long-term and selling short-term securities. The Fed hoped that low long-term interest rates would encourage households and businesses to borrow and spend and that high short-term interest rates would encourage investors to buy U.S. securities.

**option contract**   Contract that gives one of the parties the right, but not the obligation, to buy or sell an item in the future at a price that is specified now. A mill might pay a farmer $20,000 for an option giving it the right to buy 100,000 bushels of wheat six months from now at $3 a bushel. If the market price of wheat drops below $3, then the mill will not exercise its option. Because options do not have to be exercised, but merely valued on the expiration date, contracts can be written on intangible things such as the S&P 500 stock index. (*See also* **call option** and **put option**.)

**over the counter (OTC)**   Trading of securities that are not listed on organized exchanges, using dealers who make a market by quoting prices at which they are willing to buy and sell a security. The prices of many OTC securities are reported on the National Association of Securities Dealers Automatic Quotations system (NASDAQ).

**pass-through security**   One type of security created when banks and other institutions that originate mortgage loans sell these mortgages to GNMA and other agencies that form mortgage pools. The originating institution sends the mortgage interest and principal payments to GNMA, which passes them through to those who own GNMA certificates. GNMA guarantees the payment of interest and principal and, in return, levies a fee on each mortgage pool it creates.

**pay-as-you-go plan**   Retirement plan, such as the Social Security system and pension plans for federal employees, in which retirement benefits are paid out of current tax revenue, rather than out of contributions that are invested on behalf of employees.

**pension fund**   Organization that administers a pension plan by collecting and disbursing funds as well as managing the plan's investment portfolio.

**pension plan**   Program that provides income for workers who retire or become disabled, usually in the form of an annuity that makes constant monthly payments until the employee dies or the employee's dependents exhaust their legal claims.

**perfect substitutes**   Securities that (neglecting yields) are equally attractive, taking into account such factors as liquidity, transaction costs, and risk. Such securities should be priced to give the same anticipated yield. The more that securities are close substitutes for each other, the more their yields will move in unison.

**points**   Loan fee equal to a specified percentage of the loan paid at the time the loan is made. For example, for a $100,000 loan at "12 percent plus 5 points," the borrower receives $95,000 ($100,000 less the 5 percent points charge) but pays 12 percent interest on the full $100,000 loan. Points were originally devised to circumvent usury ceilings, which restrict stated rather than effective interest rates on loans.

**political business cycle**   Preelection stimulus and postelection restraint of the economy by an incumbent party.

**Ponzi scheme**   Investment swindle in which money from new investors is used to pay off earlier ones. Such schemes require an ever-expanding group of participants and collapse when new players cannot be found.

**portfolio insurance**   Flexible procedure for limiting losses by selling securities continuously as prices drop (buying as prices rise). Enough investors following these mechanical rules could destabilize financial markets.

**preferred stock**   Stock that pays specified, guaranteed dividends, like a bond's coupons, and generally has no voting privileges. Such stock is "preferred" because its promised dividends must be paid before dividends can be paid on common stock. *Cumulative preferred stock* specifies that all current and past obligated dividends must be paid before common stockholders can receive a dividend.

**prepayment penalty**   Money that the borrower must pay the lender if the loan is repaid early. This protects lenders if interest rates fall and the borrower refinances the loan.

**present value**   Amount that an investor is willing to pay for a cash flow, determined by discounting the cash flow by the investor's required rate of return; for a single payment $F$ after $n$ years and a required rate of return $R$, the present value is given by $P = F/(1 + R)^n$.

**primary dealer**   Some forty securities dealers who are allowed to trade directly with the Federal Reserve and to submit competitive bids at auctions of Treasury securities. About one third of the primary dealers are departments of commercial banks; the remaining two thirds are nonbank securities dealers such as Salomon Brothers and Goldman Sachs.

**primary market**   Market in which the initial issuance of a security is said to occur; for example, a household deposits money in a savings account, the U.S. Treasury raises money by selling bonds, and a business incorporates by issuing stock. In each case, a financial record of the transaction is created, showing the existence of a debt or of equity. Later trades of these certificates occur in the **secondary market**.

**primary reserves**   Cash, deposits with the Fed, and deposits in other banks with which a bank can maintain its liquidity. (*See also* **secondary reserves**.)

**prime rate**   Traditionally, the interest rate charged on six-month commercial loans to customers (usually businesses) that are deemed to have the lowest risk of default. Large businesses are generally reluctant to tie their lending rate to the prime rate, which is set unilaterally by banks, and instead, insist on a benchmark rate, such as LIBOR, that is determined in competitive financial markets.

**private placement**   Security issue in which the investment banker arranges for a small number of investors (typically pension funds and life insurance companies) to purchase all of the securities at a negotiated price. Privately placed securities are exempt from SEC registration requirements and have lower underwriting and administrative expenses than public offerings, particularly for small issues.

**probabilities**   Information used to quantify uncertainty by describing which outcomes are likely and which are unlikely. Probabilities cannot be negative and must add to one. With coins, dice, and cards we may be able to reason the probabilities from the physical characteristics of the experiment; investment probabilities are inherently subjective.

**probability distribution**   Distribution used to specify probabilities for ranges of outcomes; for example, a 10 percent chance that the return will be between $200 and $300, a 30 percent chance that it will be between $100 and $200, and so on. In a graphical representation of a probability distribution, the area under the curve shows the probability for that range of outcomes.

**program trading**   Originally, the buying or selling of a diversified portfolio of stocks; now associated with index futures because these are the easiest way to trade baskets of stocks. (*See also* **index arbitrage** and **portfolio insurance**.)

**prudent man rule**   Traditional legal precept that an investment manager should use the same care and judgment that a prudent person would use with his or her own personal investments.

**purchasing power parity**   Based on the law of one price, principle holds that the percentage change in an exchange rate is approximately equal to the difference in the two nations' rates of inflation. If, for example, the United States has a 5 percent inflation and Germany has a 2 percent inflation, the dollar should depreciate by 3 percent relative to the mark.

**pure arbitrage**   Riskless transaction in which an identical security is simultaneously purchased and sold for different prices in two different markets; for example, buying a stock on the New York Stock Exchange and simultaneously selling the stock for a higher price on the London Stock Exchange.

**put option**   Option that gives the owner the right to sell an asset at a fixed price on or before a specified date. A put option becomes increasingly valuable if the price of the underlying asset declines.

**quantity theory**   Assumption that velocity, the ratio of nominal gross domestic product to some measure of the money supply, is constant — implying that nominal gross domestic product moves proportionately with the money supply. Because the opportunity cost of holding money is the interest that can be earned on other assets, velocity is in fact positively related to interest rates.

**random walk hypothesis**   Weak form of the efficient market hypothesis, which states that each change in a stock's price is unrelated to previous changes — much as each flip of a coin is unrelated to previous tosses or each step by a drunkard is unrelated to previous steps.

**rate of return**   Income (the benefits you receive while owning the asset) plus capital gains (the profits made when the asset is sold).

**rational expectations**   Expectations based on the efficient utilization of available information. If, as in the new classical models, all unemployment is voluntary with economic fluctuations due to errors in assessing prices, then rational expectations imply that well-anticipated changes in the money supply do not cause mistakes in gauging the price level and consequently have no effect on employment or output.

**real**   Relating to economic data such as wage rates, income, or wealth that are recorded in terms of purchasing power. Real data are constructed by deflating nominal data by a price index. A **real interest rate** is a nominal interest rate minus the rate of change of a price index.

**real asset**   Tangible physical asset, such as land, houses, livestock, and precious metals, in contrast to a **financial asset**.

**Real Bills doctrine**   Also known as the commercial loan theory, this principle states that bank loans should be short-term, self-liquidating, and productive. This doctrine was intended to assure bank liquidity and also appropriately regulate the money supply. In practice, this strategy helps liquidity but does not guarantee it, and causes the money supply to move with the business cycle.

**real rate of return**   Measurement of the percentage increase in purchasing power provided by an investment; approximately equal to the nominal (dollar) percentage return minus the percentage rate of inflation.

**realized rate of return**   Calculated rate of return on an investment, taking into account the proceeds from the reinvestment of the cash flow, if any.

**registered bond**   Bond for which the owner registers with the bond's trustee and receives coupon payments without the physical presentation of the bond certificate. Since 1983, all U.S. Treasury securities have been in registered form. (*See also* **bearer bond**.)

**regulated investment company**   Company that satisfies the criteria established by the Investment Company Act of 1940 — a designation that exempts such a company from corporate taxes. Among these criteria, the company must register with the SEC and comply with its disclosure requirements, own a diversified portfolio, and distribute at least 90 percent of its interest and dividend income as it is received.

**Regulation Q**   Regulation that limited interest rates on some types of deposits. Persuaded that competitive pressures to pay high interest rates on deposits had led banks to make high-interest, high-risk loans, the Banking Acts of 1933 and 1935 prohibited institutions other than commercial banks from offering checking accounts, prohibited the payment of interest on checking accounts, and, under Regulation Q, gave the Federal Reserve the power to set the maximum interest rates that banks could pay on other types of deposits. These deposit-rate ceilings were phased out by the 1980 Depository Institutions Deregulation and Monetary Control Act.

**repurchase agreement (RP** or **repo)**   Agreement in which a borrower sells securities to a lender and agrees to repurchase the securities at a higher price on a given date — often the next day. In this way, money is lent, using securities as collateral.

**required rate of return**   Rate used to determine the present value of a cash flow; the rate depends on the returns available on alternative investments and other characteristics (such as the riskiness of the cash flow) that make this investment relatively attractive or unattractive.

**reserve requirements**   Government requirements compelling banks to hold some fraction of their deposits as reserves, either as cash in their vaults or as deposits with the Federal Reserve that earn no interest.

**reversing**   Action in which the buyer of a futures contract, rather than taking delivery, covers the position by selling the contract before the delivery date; a contract writer can reverse this position by repurchasing the contract.

**risk**   Uncertain situation. The risk of a promised cash flow or anticipated asset return is often gauged by the standard deviation. Risk-averse investors require high expected returns from risky investments.

**risk arbitrage**   Arbitrage transaction that will be profitable if a proposed corporate merger, acquisition, or restructuring takes place; for example, buying a company's stock for $38 after a corporate raider has announced an offer to buy the company's stock for $40.

**risk averse**   Term that describes a person who sacrifices expected return to reduce risk and prefers a diversified portfolio containing dissimilar assets. Diversification reduces risk most effectively if the asset returns are uncorrelated or, even better, if they are negatively correlated. A risk-averse person would certainly buy insurance if the expected return were zero, and may purchase insurance with a negative expected return.

**risk neutral**   Term that describes a person who chooses the alternative with the highest expected return, placing all eggs in one basket. A risk-neutral person does not like insurance or lottery tickets because both have negative expected returns.

**risk seeking**    Term that describes a person who accepts fair bets and will even sacrifice expected return to increase risk; for example, one who buys a lottery ticket if the expected value is zero and maybe buys one with a negative expected return. Like the risk-neutral person, the risk seeker shuns diversification.

**Sallie Mae**    *See* **Student Loan Marketing Association**.

**savings and loan associations (S&Ls)**    Until the 1980s, very specialized deposit intermediaries — either state or federally chartered — that used funds obtained from their depositors' time and savings accounts to make long-term, fixed-rate mortgages.

**secondary market**    Market in which assets are traded after their initial issuance in the primary market. After a company issues bonds or stock in the primary market, using the services of an investment banker, these notes and shares may pass from hand to hand in the secondary market, either on an exchange or over the counter.

**secondary reserves**    Treasury bills and other very safe, short-term assets that can be converted into cash almost immediately, which are held in addition to a bank's primary reserves to maintain liquidity. (*See also* **primary reserves**.)

**Securities and Exchange Commission (SEC)**    Federal agency established by Congress to enforce the provisions of the Securities Act of 1933 and the Securities Exchange Act of 1934, which were passed in the aftermath of the stock market crash and subsequent economic depression. The SEC oversees the public sale of securities in the primary market and trading in the secondary market, with a wide range of powers designed to ensure the fairness and integrity of these markets, including prohibiting fraud and compelling the disclosure of pertinent information.

**securitization**    Conversion of illiquid loans into marketable loan-backed securities. For example, more than half of all residential mortgages are now resold in the secondary mortgage market, and these mortgages are securitized in that investors no longer have to be mortgage bankers or savings and loan associations to invest in mortgages.

**securitization of borrowing**    Sale of securities directly to investors, instead of relying on financial intermediaries to channel funds from investors to business borrowers.

**security brokerage**    Agent that executes security trades for investors in the secondary market.

**seigniorage**    Profits made from issuing money, including the difference between a money's value in exchange and its value as a commodity.

**semi-strong form**    Form of the efficient market hypothesis stating that abnormal returns cannot be consistently earned using any publicly available information, including past prices and such data as interest rates, inflation, and corporate earnings. Therefore, fundamental analysis cannot beat the market.

**settlement price**    Price, equal to the closing price for actively traded contracts, set by futures exchanges at the end of each trading day, to determine each trader's profit or loss that day. Those having losses must make cash payments (daily settlements) to the brokerage accounts of those having profits before the beginning of the next trading day.

**sinking fund**    Bond provision stating that the issuer will put a certain amount of money into a fund each year to redeem some of its bonds, thereby reducing its indebtedness. These bonds can be called by lottery at a specified premium over face value or repurchased in the secondary market if the market price is lower than the call price.

**smart card**    Card that is used like a debit card to make immediate payment for goods and services but that has an embedded microprocessor that records the user's transactions and financial situation.

**Special Drawing Rights (SDRs)**    "Paper gold" used within the IMF to allow balance-of-payments deficit nations to purchase foreign exchange from surplus nations.

**specialist** Designated person at the NYSE who collects orders and acts as both a broker (trading for others) and a dealer (trading for oneself). As a broker, the specialist executes a transaction when someone is willing to buy at a price at which another is willing to sell. Specialists also act as dealers in order to maintain a "fair and orderly" market by buying or selling, as needed, for their own accounts.

**speculative bubble** Situation that occurs when asset prices lose touch with intrinsic values, when people hope to profit not from the asset's cash flow but from selling the asset at ever-higher prices. During these speculative bubbles, it seems foolish to sit on the sidelines while others become rich; in retrospect, it looks like mass hysteria. When the bubble bursts, buyers cannot be found and prices fall precipitously.

**speculator** Someone who buys an asset not to gain the long-run cash flow but to sell a short while later at a higher price, in contrast to an investor who is willing to hold an asset forever.

**spot price** Current market price of an item for immediate delivery.

**standard deviation** Square root of the variance, which gauges the spread of a distribution and thus gauges risk by measuring how certain we are that the return will be close to its expected value. The standard deviation has the same units (percent or dollars) as the data, while the units for the variance are dollars-squared or percent-squared.

**sterilized intervention** Situation that occurs when a central bank uses open market purchases or sales to offset the effects of its foreign exchange transactions on the monetary base. For instance, if the value of the dollar is falling relative to the Japanese yen, the Fed might support the dollar by buying dollars with yen. This purchase of dollars reduces the monetary base, but the Fed can put these dollars back into circulation by using them to purchase Treasury bills. Because there is no change in the monetary base, this is a sterilized intervention.

**stock** When referring to economic data, the measurement of the level of an economic variable at a specific time; for example, the monetary base, $M1$, and the federal debt on December 31, 1992. (*See also* **flow**.)

**striking price** Price at which an option contract can be exercised; also called the *exercise price*.

**strong form** Form of the efficient-market hypothesis that holds that there is no information, public or private, that allows some investors to beat the market consistently. This hypothesis is contradicted by evidence that a few do profit by using information not available to other investors, often in violation of federal laws.

**Student Loan Marketing Association (Sallie Mae)** Agency created in 1972 to provide a secondary market for federally guaranteed student loans. Sallie Mae issues unsecured short-term and long-term debts, using the proceeds to purchase student loans from banks, educational institutions, and government agencies.

**swap** Term used in financial markets to describe contracts in which two parties agree to make one or more exchanges of specified assets; for example, *see* **currency swap** and **interest-rate swap**.

**systematic risk** Also called macro risk, market risk, or nondiversifiable risk, this risk concerns macroeconomic events such as unanticipated changes in interest rates, inflation, and the unemployment rate that affect all securities. With macro risk, there is no safety in numbers — mere diversification cannot protect investors from recession or high interest rates.

**T-account** Account that shows the changes on a balance sheet caused by some financial event.

**taxable equivalent yield** Interest rate that would have to be earned on a taxable corporate security for it to have the same after-tax return as a tax-exempt municipal bond. For an investor with a tax rate $t$, the taxable equivalent yield on a municipal security with a tax-exempt interest rate $R_M$ is $R_M/(1 - t)$.

**tax-exempt bond** Bond on which the interest is free of income taxes. The term usually refers to state and local bonds, also called *municipals* or *munis*, that are exempt from federal income taxes. A bond that is exempt from both state and federal taxes (for example, a California bond held by a Californian) is said to be double tax-exempt. Bonds that are exempt from federal, state, and city income taxes are called triple tax-exempt.

**term life insurance**   Temporary insurance, usually for one to five years, that provides a death benefit (called the face value) while the insurance is in effect but generally has no value unless the insured person dies. Term life insurance is pure insurance, without contractual saving.

**term structure of interest rates**   Description of the yields to maturity on zero-coupon bonds that have different maturities but are otherwise identical; a yield curve compares the yields to maturity on coupon bonds of various maturities. The expectations hypothesis states that the relationship between short-term and long-term interest rates reflects the anticipated future course of interest rates.

**Tobin's q**   The ratio of market value of a firm to the replacement cost of its assets. A $q$ value larger than one indicates that the firm's profit rate exceeds the shareholders' required return on their stock and that the firm will benefit shareholders if it retains additional earnings for expansion. A firm with a $q$ less than one is worth more dead than alive.

**trade balance**   A nation's exports of commodities minus its imports, often interpreted as a rough barometer of the competitiveness of its industries.

**Treasury bill (T-bill)**   Federal government security with a maturity of less than one year, which is sold to raise money for government expenditures. There are no periodic interest payments; the investor's return is equal to the difference between the bill's purchase price and its face value, which is received when the bill matures. Unlike virtually all other securities, the financial press traditionally calculates T-bill returns on a discount basis, relative to the bill's face value rather than the purchase price, and thereby understates the investor's actual rate of return.

**Treasury bond**   Treasury security that is issued with a maturity longer than 10 years.

**Treasury note**   Treasury security that is issued with a maturity of 2 to 10 years.

**turnover**   Gauge of an investment company's annual trading of securities, using the ratio of the dollar value of the company's annual sales (or purchases) of securities to its total assets. A fund with a $100 million portfolio that buys and sells $50 million in securities in a year has a turnover of 50 percent.

**underwriting**   An agreement, in advance of the issuing date, to purchase the securities issued by a business or government agency and to market these to the public.

**unit banking**   Laws permitting a bank to have only one geographic location. In 1975, there were still 15 states (mostly in the Midwest) that completely prohibited bank branches. In 1991, only one state (Colorado) still had a unit banking law.

**unsystematic risk**   Micro risk, or idiosyncratic risk, that arises from events specific to individual assets and can be diversified away — for example, the health of a key executive.

**U.S. currency outstanding**   Currency held by the private sector. U.S. currency outstanding is equal to Federal Reserve notes plus Treasury notes and coin minus Fed holdings of Treasury currency and Treasury holdings of Fed currency. Because some of this outstanding currency is inside bank vaults and some is in private hands outside banks, U.S. currency outstanding is also equal to vault cash plus currency outside banks.

**variance**   Average squared deviation of the outcomes about their mean — thus a measure of whether the possible (or actual) values are close to the mean or scattered widely. For a probability distribution, the probabilities are used as weights in calculating this average; for empirical data, the observed frequencies are used. (If the data are a small sample, statisticians usually divide by $n - 1$ rather than $n$.)

**velocity** The ratio of the nominal value of some measure of transactions to some measure of the money supply. Velocity is the average number of times that this money is exchanged for these transactions during a given accounting period. $M1$ velocity, for example, is the ratio of nominal gross domestic product to $M1$.

**vested benefits** Benefits based on pension contributions that are made while an employee works for a firm. In a vested plan, an employee who leaves a firm before retirement is entitled to retirement benefits. In a nonvested plan, an employee who leaves the firm — voluntarily or involuntarily — loses all retirement benefits.

**weak form** Form of the efficient market hypothesis that holds that past data on stock prices are of no use in predicting future price changes.

**yield curve** Similar to the term structure, graph that compares the yields to maturity on coupon-paying bonds with different maturities.

**yield to call** Yield that is calculated like the yield to maturity but assumes that the bond will be called at the first opportunity.

**yield to maturity** The discount rate at which the present value of the bond's coupons and principal is equal to its price. A bond's price is higher than its face value when its yield to maturity is below the coupon rate and is less than its face value when its yield is above the coupon rate.

**zero-coupon bond (zero)** Bond that pays no coupons; as with T-bills, the buyer receives a single, lump-sum payment at maturity. A series of zeros maturing at 6-month intervals can be created by stripping away the coupons from conventional bonds. The implicit annual rate of return $R$ on a zero costing $P$ that pays an amount $F$ in $n$ years is given by the compound interest formula $P(1 + R)^n = F$.

# Index

## Historical Annual Data, 1959–1991

| Year | United States Population | Real Gross Domestic Product (1987$) | Unemployment Rate | Consumer Price Index | Annual Rate of Inflation | Interest Rate on One-Year Treasury Bills |
|------|------|------|------|------|------|------|
| 1959 | 177.830 | 1928.8 | 5.5 | 29.1 | 1.7 | 4.05 |
| 1960 | 180.671 | 1970.8 | 5.5 | 29.6 | 1.4 | 3.44 |
| 1961 | 183.691 | 2023.8 | 6.7 | 29.9 | 0.7 | 2.83 |
| 1962 | 186.538 | 2128.1 | 5.5 | 30.2 | 1.3 | 3.03 |
| 1963 | 189.242 | 2215.6 | 5.7 | 30.6 | 1.6 | 3.33 |
| 1964 | 191.889 | 2340.6 | 5.2 | 31.0 | 1.0 | 3.77 |
| 1965 | 194.303 | 2470.5 | 4.5 | 31.5 | 1.9 | 4.10 |
| 1966 | 196.560 | 2616.2 | 3.8 | 32.4 | 3.5 | 5.13 |
| 1967 | 198.712 | 2685.2 | 3.8 | 33.4 | 3.0 | 4.77 |
| 1968 | 200.706 | 2796.9 | 3.6 | 34.8 | 4.7 | 5.53 |
| 1969 | 202.677 | 2873.0 | 3.5 | 36.7 | 6.2 | 6.91 |
| 1970 | 205.052 | 2873.9 | 4.9 | 38.8 | 5.6 | 6.60 |
| 1971 | 207.661 | 2955.9 | 5.9 | 40.5 | 3.3 | 4.72 |
| 1972 | 209.896 | 3107.1 | 5.6 | 41.8 | 3.4 | 4.83 |
| 1973 | 211.909 | 3268.6 | 4.9 | 44.4 | 8.7 | 7.13 |
| 1974 | 213.854 | 3248.1 | 5.6 | 49.3 | 12.9 | 7.86 |
| 1975 | 215.973 | 3221.7 | 8.5 | 53.8 | 6.9 | 6.40 |
| 1976 | 218.035 | 3380.8 | 7.7 | 56.9 | 4.9 | 5.60 |
| 1977 | 220.239 | 3533.2 | 7.1 | 60.6 | 6.7 | 5.79 |
| 1978 | 222.585 | 3703.5 | 6.1 | 65.2 | 9.0 | 7.89 |
| 1979 | 222.055 | 3796.8 | 5.8 | 72.6 | 13.3 | 9.99 |
| 1980 | 227.722 | 3776.3 | 7.1 | 82.4 | 12.5 | 11.19 |
| 1981 | 229.958 | 3843.1 | 7.6 | 90.9 | 8.9 | 13.57 |
| 1982 | 232.192 | 3760.3 | 9.7 | 96.5 | 3.8 | 11.38 |
| 1983 | 234.321 | 3906.6 | 9.6 | 99.6 | 3.8 | 8.99 |
| 1984 | 236.370 | 4148.5 | 7.5 | 103.9 | 3.9 | 10.17 |
| 1985 | 238.492 | 4279.8 | 7.2 | 107.6 | 3.8 | 7.96 |
| 1986 | 240.860 | 4404.5 | 7.0 | 109.6 | 1.1 | 6.16 |
| 1987 | 242.836 | 4540.0 | 6.2 | 113.6 | 4.4 | 6.43 |
| 1988 | 245.057 | 4718.6 | 5.5 | 118.3 | 4.4 | 7.26 |
| 1989 | 247.343 | 4836.9 | 5.3 | 124.0 | 4.6 | 8.08 |
| 1990 | 249.975 | 4884.9 | 5.5 | 130.7 | 6.1 | 7.49 |
| 1991 | 252.626 | 4848.4 | 6.7 | 136.2 | 3.1 | 5.60 |